# Places
# Rated
# Almanac

### Note to the Reader

Subsequent to the first printing of *Places Rated Almanac*, errors were discovered which, when corrected for this printing, have raised the overall rankings of Rochester, New York (from 32nd to ninth place); Waterbury, Connecticut (from 300 to 245); and Davenport-Moline, Iowa–Illinois (from 220 to 183). Minor corrections have also been made throughout the book, so the ranks of a number of metro areas will differ slightly from those in earlier printings. The difference in point scores that separate rankings is often very small; therefore, it may take a change in rank of 25 places or more to indicate a significant difference in quality between two metro areas.

# Places Rated Almanac

## Your guide to finding the best places to live in America

Richard Boyer & David Savageau

**Rand McNally & Company**

Chicago · New York · San Francisco

## Acknowledgments

Each time we produce a volume in the *Places Rated* series, we realize that the book could not have been written but for the help we've gotten from so many sources.

We are indebted to scores of people in government and with private organizations, many of whom we have come to know personally over the years. They have not only kept our research pointed in proper directions, but more than a few times have blocked our turns into blind alleys. Many of the improvements in this edition of *Places Rated Almanac* were originally suggested by them. Thanks to their generosity, pertinent data that would not otherwise have seen daylight are published here for the first time. These sources, along with other of their publications, are cited throughout.

We would like to thank our editors at Rand McNally for their many contributions at every step of the way. Special mention should also be made of Karyl Savageau and Donna Seymour for their valuable assistance in preparing the manuscript.

## Publisher's Note

This book contains information provided by many sources. It is published for general reference and not as a substitute for independent verification by users when circumstances warrant. Although care and diligence have been used in its preparation, the publisher does not guarantee the accuracy of the information. The interpretation of the data and the views expressed are the authors' and not necessarily those of Rand McNally & Company.

Printed in the United States of America
Library of Congress Catalog Card No.: 84–43149

First printing, February 1985
Second printing, March 1985
Third printing, April 1985
Fourth printing, May 1985
Fifth printing, October 1985
Sixth printing, October 1986

# Contents

# Introduction

Why do you live where you do? Are you there because of family ties? A job commitment? A sentimental attachment to hometown turf? Will you spend the rest of your life there?

Much has been made of Americans moving. From time to time a majority of those polled by the Gallup Organization say they would prefer to live somewhere else. Most of us will change our address several times during our lives, but we will do it simply by moving from one neighborhood to another nearby. Each year, however, six million Americans move to another state. They may count six million different reasons among them for relocating a long distance, but they do have one thing in common—the need for information.

The response to the first edition of *Places Rated Almanac*, published in 1981, confirmed that people are indeed eager for a reliable, practical source of information about places. This new edition takes the same general approach as its predecessor but has been thoroughly updated, revised, and expanded. In 1977, when we began research for the first edition, there were 277 federally defined metropolitan areas in the United States. Now, as a result of population growth revealed by the 1980 census, our *Places Rated* universe has grown to 329. Besides the greatly expanded list of places, this edition introduces a number of new features and improvements, many based on the suggestions of experts in government, academia, and private organizations.

Like its predecessor, this edition of *Places Rated Almanac* is meant for people who are thinking of moving as well as for armchair travelers who enjoy finding out about American cities and towns and what they have to offer. As an almanac, it provides thousands of facts about 329 U.S. metropolitan areas, where 75 percent of Americans live. You won't find this information in standard guidebooks or blandishments from the chamber of commerce. In what other single source, for instance, can you find out which place has the best public transit, the least earthquake risk, and the most good restaurants per capita? But *Places Rated Almanac* is more than a collection of interesting, odd, and useful information about metro areas, for it also rates and ranks them on nine factors that greatly influence the quality of life: climate, housing, health care, crime, transportation, education, the arts, recreation, and economics.

*Places Rated Almanac* might be considered a self-help book with a difference: Instead of pointing the way toward upward mobility, as most such books do, it helps you determine whether geographical mobility might be the route to a more satisfying life. Where you live can significantly affect your happiness and personal success; it just may be that your current location doesn't match your needs and preferences. After all, given the incredible variety offered throughout the country, what are the odds that the place where you happen to live is the right one for you?

After using *Places Rated Almanac,* your hunch that you've never had it so good might well be confirmed. On the other hand, you may be in for a surprise. And if you're part of the discontented majority identified by pollsters, you may find yourself asking: What am I waiting for?

## RATING PLACES—AN AMERICAN TRADITION

"The tradition of hating New York started long before it began asking the rest of us to pay its bills while condescendingly viewing us as amusing rustics," Mike Royko wrote in a Chicago *Sun-Times* column back in 1978. "Actually, I like New York," he continued. "There are better reasons to hate cities like Cleveland or Indianapolis or Detroit or Dallas. But I do dislike New Yorkers. . . ."

It may seem the height of effrontery, this business of judging American places. Yet we all do it, privately. Some lump Baltimore, Buffalo, Cleveland, Pittsburgh, and all of New Jersey together as object lessons in where the sins of free enterprise ultimately get you. Others suspect that living in Des Moines or Omaha couldn't be duller, that life in Chicago is spent avoiding shoot-outs, that Seattle is fog-bound and rainsoaked, and that residents of Los Angeles spend most of their time behind a steering wheel.

Passing judgment on different locales isn't just a current pastime; Americans have been at it for quite a while. To entice seventeenth-century colonists to pick Maryland over Virginia, promoters assembled figures showing heavier turkeys, more plentiful deer, and fewer deaths from foul summer diseases and Indian massacres, all yours if you settled in the northern reaches of Chesapeake Bay. In the nineteenth century, many northern observers connected the South's slaveholding and rebellious ways with the region's broilingly hot climate and an overabundance of lunatics, drunkards, and wastrels per capita.

In our own century, the process of comparing places has borrowed a great deal from statistical methods. One of America's education pioneers, E. L. Thorndike, in the late 1930s devised a "goodness index" drawn from 39 indicators for measuring a city's day-to-day living. Since then, others have jumped into the rating game. In 1983, Prof. Murray Straus, a sociologist at the University of New Hampshire, selected factors such as divorce, mortgage foreclosures, high school dropouts, personal bankruptcies, abortions, and new welfare cases to determine the most "stressful" states. Nevada and Alaska were numbers one and two on the stress list. And the most laid-back state, according to the indicators? Nebraska.

### The Ways Places Are Rated

*Places Rated Almanac,* we believe, is more useful than any system that limits its evaluations to the 50 states because statewide averages can hide local realities. For mobile people, there may be more differences between the Texas metro areas of San Antonio and San Angelo than there are between the Lone Star State and Florida. This guide is also more objective than the opinions travelers may exchange in an airport bar or at a rest stop on the Interstate highway. Each of the 329 metro areas is rated by criteria that most people thinking of moving would deem important.

- Climate is rated on mildness; that is, how close temperatures remain to 65 degrees Fahrenheit throughout the year.
- Housing is compared in terms of dollar costs. We look at prices for single homes, plus the taxes and utilities a would-be homeowner can expect to pay. We also note the supply of apartments, mobile homes, and condominiums, as well as rental costs.
- Health care is evaluated on the basis of the supply of general health care facilities and special options available.
- Crime is measured by the annual number of violent and property crimes per 100,000 population.
- Transportation measures both assets and performance, including local commuting time, public transit, and the supply of intercity travel options by way of air, rail, and Interstate highway.
- Education ratings are based on each metro area's elementary and secondary school systems as well as options in higher education.
- The chapter on the arts compares cultural assets, among them museums and libraries, opera companies and symphony orchestras.
- Recreation also rates assets, from good restaurants to public golf courses, zoos, professional sports teams, inland lakes, and national parks acreage.
- Economics looks at local living costs, household income, tax bites, and the metro area's recent track record for job and income growth.

Some readers may fault *Places Rated*'s criteria. Some of the standards for rating health care, recreational and cultural life, and education, for example, tend to favor big metro areas. On the other hand, the methods for scoring climate, safety from crime, economic health, and affordable housing have nothing to do with population size; in fact, many smaller metro areas lead in these categories.

You may not agree with our rating system. If you like, you can devise your own method using the vast array of data presented. You may rule out metro areas with more than one million people. As long as summers aren't hot, you may not care a hoot for relative humidity, wind speed, and rainfall. You may have little interest in wildlife refuges or ocean shorelines but place a premium on good public schools. For you, a medium-sized metro area with good public transit and a record of job expansion may be more desirable than one with an abundant supply of performing arts and professional sports attractions.

We have tried to put together the most up-to-date facts for all 329 metro areas. In most instances, our information is as fresh as 1984; in a few isolated cases, the most recent statistics predate 1980. Our sources, which we document throughout the book, are principally different agencies of the federal government, but pertinent private sources have also been tapped.

*Places Rated Almanac* is like a snapshot of a moving target; metro areas are dynamic and won't always sit still for their statistical portraits. A continued turn-around in the automobile industry can improve the job and income prospects of more than a few Great Lakes metro areas, just as a prolonged cold snap and a natural gas shortage can markedly increase the costs of owning a Maryland home. With so much in life that can't be predicted, it's necessary to supplement *Places Rated Almanac* with your own independent verification.

But for now you can be sure that you'll find more affordable homes in Joplin, Missouri, than in Joliet, Illinois; public golf courses in greater supply in Akron than in Atlanta; more flights out of Denver's airport than Detroit's; and more acres of national public parkland in Fort Collins–Loveland, Colorado, than in Fort Pierce, Florida.

## Why Have the Rankings Changed?

If you compare a metro area's ranks in this edition with its ranks in the previous one, you'll find that many have improved while others have slipped. There are several reasons.

First, of course, is simply that more places—329 instead of 277—are being rated; thus, a metro area might receive a lower absolute rank and still maintain the same *relative* position in the ratings. Besides there being a greater number of places, their geographic definitions, as established by the U.S. Office of Management and Budget, or OMB (more on this below), have changed. Only 166 of the 329 metro areas are exactly the same geographic entities they were in *Places Rated*'s 1981 edition (and 21 of these now have different names). For the rest, many have either gained or lost component counties, others were created by the merger of previously separate metro areas or by the partition of large ones, and 44 are entirely new areas that have qualified for metropolitan status because of their recent population growth.

Statistics have changed over the past few years, too. Figures for average household income, violent and property crimes, tax rates, golf courses, and airline departures are just a few of many that have been brought up to date for this edition. The upgrading of a symphony orchestra or the departure of a pro sports team could also cause a change in a metro area's ranking.

In many chapters, the criteria for rating the metro areas have undergone modification. Some of the factors have been weighted differently: The number of days when the outdoor thermometer hits 90 degrees Fahrenheit, for example, counts as a greater penalty against a metro area in this edition of *Places Rated* than it did in its predecessor. New scoring factors have been added in several chapters, such as a hospitalization/

---

### Finding Your Way in the Chapters

*Places Rated Almanac* contains thousands of useful facts and many descriptive sections, and it is organized so that readers can find specific items that interest them. Each of its nine chapters has four parts:

- The **introductory section** gives basic information on the chapter's topic, interspersed with facts and figures to help you evaluate metro areas. We also describe the system used to rate and rank the 329 metro areas for that particular topic. At the end of this section, two metro areas are selected for a sample comparison to show why one place performs better than another in the ratings.
- **Places Rated:** This part ranks the 329 metro areas. They are listed first in their rank order, from best to worst, along with their score. (Metro areas that receive the same score are assigned the same rank and are listed in alphabetical order.) An alphabetical list with individual rankings follows so that you can quickly find the ranks of specific places.
- **Place Profiles:** Arranged alphabetically by metro area, these capsule comparisons cover all the elements used to rate the metro areas and usually give additional data. The Place Profiles can be columns of information (like the recreation profiles) or page-wide charts (like the economics profiles); the climate profiles have their own special format. All are designed to help you see differences among metro areas at a glance.
- **Et Cetera:** This section expands on the quality-of-life features mentioned in the introductory section. It contains information on other topics as well. These can range all the way from lists of metro area professional sports championships, state-by-state high school graduation requirements, and metro area Fortune 500 headquarters, to essays on water shortages and contradictory traffic laws.

The final chapter, "Putting It All Together," adds up the ranks to identify America's best all-around metro areas and discusses the good and bad points of the top 20. Here we also weigh the pros and cons of living in big and small metro areas, and give examples of how using personal preferences to devise your own scoring system can lead to different rankings.

insurance costs index in the Health Care chapter and a whole new category called Outdoor Recreation Assets in the Recreation chapter. And other scoring factors have been dropped, such as data for hospital beds, which were excluded from a metro area's health care rating because they are no longer regarded as the critical measurement for health care supply they once were. As much as is practical, we have tried to point out such scoring changes in each chapter.

Finally, a major scoring innovation has been made to reflect the fact that certain major assets—such as theme parks, pro sports arenas, large symphony orchestras, airports, and major medical centers—are frequently enjoyed or used in one metro area by residents of another. The federal government, in its classification of metropolitan areas for statistical purposes, has given some expression to this reality by grouping certain closely related metro areas into Consolidated Metropolitan Statistical Areas (CMSAs). Seventy-six of the 329 metro areas in *Places Rated Almanac* are included in 22 CMSA complexes. The Los Angeles–Anaheim–Riverside CMSA, for example, includes four metropolitan areas: Anaheim–Santa Ana, Los Angeles–Long Beach, Oxnard–Ventura, and Riverside–San Bernardino. (A complete list of CMSAs and their component metro areas is in the Appendix).

In its chapters rating health care, transportation, cultural assets, and recreational opportunities, *Places Rated* now recognizes the importance of shared assets by awarding bonus points to metro areas that are members of CMSAs. The way these CMSA Access points are calculated is explained in detail in each of the affected chapters. The impact of the CMSA Access factor on the rankings of some member metro areas is pronounced.

## METROPOLITAN AREAS

Certainly this second edition of *Places Rated Almanac* offers readers a wide range of places for research and consideration. Whether your motivation is personal relocation, plant expansion, personnel placement, or mere curiosity, the 329 metro areas presented here— from Abilene, Texas, to Yuba City, California; from huge New York (pop. 8,274,961) to tiny Enid, Oklahoma (pop. 62,820); from Anchorage to Miami–Hialeah— cover the entire spectrum of American cities. There are agricultural centers and fashion markets; mill towns and bedroom communities; financial centers and small college towns. You'll find resort communities, entertainment meccas, and cultural havens right next to ports of entry, rail centers, and industrial giants.

What is a metropolitan area? Standard metropolitan area definitions were first developed and issued about 35 years ago by the OMB for use by all federal agencies compiling general statistical data, including census statistics on population, housing, industry trade, current employment and payroll data, and local

housing market and labor market analyses. In 1981, when the first edition of *Places Rated Almanac* was published, the OMB nomenclature for these statistical entities was Standard Metropolitan Statistical Areas (SMSAs), and these were the basic entities we compared throughout the book.

On June 30, 1983, as a result of periodic government review of metropolitan area definitions, a new three-tiered system of designations went into effect: Metropolitan Statistical Areas (MSAs), Primary Metropolitan Statistical Areas (PMSAs), and Consolidated Metropolitan Statistical Areas (CMSAs). For all practical purposes, the units now referred to as MSAs and PMSAs are the equivalent of the former SMSAs, and it is these units that are compared in this book and referred to as metro areas. Of the 329 metro areas, 253 are MSAs and 76 are PMSAs. The main difference between MSAs and PMSAs is that MSAs are "standalone" metro areas, whereas PMSAs are metropolitan entities that are also joined with other PMSAs in the megalopolitan complexes designated CMSAs.

Metropolitan statistical areas are defined according to detailed federal standards. The general concept underlying these definitions is that of a geographic area consisting of a large population nucleus together with adjacent communities that have a high degree of economic and social integration with that nucleus. Broadly speaking, an area qualifies as a metropolitan area in one of two ways: if there is a city with a population of at least 50,000, or an urbanized area (embracing one or more towns) of at least 50,000 located in a county or counties with a total population of at least 100,000 (75,000 in New England). In either case, for statistical purposes the metropolitan area's boundaries coincide with the boundaries of the surrounding county or counties (except in New England, where towns and cities are the basis of OMB designations). Most metro areas are within single states; 34 of them, however, cross state boundaries. Metropolitan Cincinnati, for example, includes three counties in Ohio, three in Kentucky, and one in Indiana; Memphis takes in two counties in Tennessee, plus one in Arkansas and one in Mississippi. (Puerto Rico has six metro areas, but *Places Rated* confines its comparisons to places within the United States.)

There is a good reason for focusing on these entities rather than on cities, counties, or states. Thanks to the automobile, cities, counties, and states have become less relevant to an individual's daily personal geography. Commonly, we live in one community, such as the suburb of a large city; commute to a job in another; patronize the restaurants, shopping centers, and recreation assets of all the towns around; and every two years approve or disapprove of our district's congressional representative. We pay taxes or fees to water, sewer, park, and school districts that often cross city lines. The perimeters of metro areas supersede the anachronistic political boundaries of incorporated areas and include not only the frequently troubled and depressed older city cores but also the newer suburbs with their sleek new malls, office parks, factories, and choice residential districts. For example, metropolitan Newark includes affluent Morris County; the Cleveland metro area includes Shaker Heights; and the Boston area, with its 106 cities and towns, takes in a wealthy fringe of high-tech industries.

The list below provides the county definitions of the metropolitan areas rated in this edition of *Places Rated Almanac* (metro areas classified as PMSAs are identified by an asterisk). The number of metro areas is constantly on the rise. Recently, two additional areas —Naples, Florida, and Santa Fe, New Mexico—were designated MSAs. Whatever their number, the chances are good that you, like three of every four Americans, live in one of the official metropolitan areas surveyed here.

## The Places We Rate:
## 329 Metropolitan Areas

| Metro Areas and Component Counties | Population 1980 | Population 1970 | Population Change, 1970–1980 | Metro Areas and Component Counties | Population 1980 | Population 1970 | Population Change, 1970–1980 |
|---|---|---|---|---|---|---|---|
| **Abilene, TX** Taylor County | 110,932 | 97,853 | +13.4% | **Atlanta, GA** Barrow, Butts, Cherokee, Clayton, Cobb, Coweta, De Kalb, Douglas, Fayette, Forsyth, Fulton, Gwinnett, Henry, Newton, Paulding, Rockdale, Spalding, and Walton counties | 2,138,231 | 1,684,200 | +27.0% |
| **Akron, OH**\* Portage and Summit counties | 660,328 | 679,239 | − 2.8 | | | | |
| **Albany, GA** Dougherty and Lee counties | 112,402 | 96,683 | +16.3 | | | | |
| **Albany–Schenectady–Troy, NY** Albany, Greene, Montgomery, Rensselaer, Saratoga, and Schenectady counties | 835,880 | 811,113 | + 3.1 | **Atlantic City, NJ** Atlantic and Cape May counties | 276,385 | 234,597 | +17.8 |
| | | | | **Augusta, GA–SC** Columbia, McDuffie, and Richmond counties, GA; Aiken County, SC | 345,918 | 291,063 | +18.8 |
| **Albuquerque, NM** Bernalillo County | 419,700 | 315,774 | +32.9 | | | | |
| **Alexandria, LA** Rapides Parish | 135,282 | 118,078 | +14.6 | **Aurora–Elgin, IL**\* Kane and Kendall counties | 315,607 | 277,379 | +13.8 |
| **Allentown–Bethlehem, PA–NJ** Carbon, Lehigh, and Northampton counties, PA; Warren County, NJ | 635,481 | 594,382 | + 6.9 | **Austin, TX** Hays, Travis, and Williamson counties | 536,688 | 360,463 | +48.9 |
| **Alton–Granite City, IL**\* Jersey and Madison counties | 268,229 | 269,403 | − 0.4 | **Bakersfield, CA** Kern County | 403,089 | 330,234 | +22.1 |
| **Altoona, PA** Blair County | 136,621 | 135,356 | + 0.9 | **Baltimore, MD** Baltimore city; Anne Arundel, Baltimore, Carroll, Harford, Howard, and Queen Annes counties | 2,199,531 | 2,089,438 | + 5.3 |
| **Amarillo, TX** Potter and Randall counties | 173,699 | 144,396 | +20.2 | | | | |
| | | | | **Bangor, ME** Parts of Penobscot and Waldo counties | 83,919 | 79,933 | + 5.0 |
| **Anaheim–Santa Ana, CA**\* Orange County | 1,932,709 | 1,421,233 | +36.0 | **Baton Rouge, LA** Ascension, East Baton Rouge, Livingston, and West Baton Rouge parishes | 494,151 | 375,628 | +31.6 |
| **Anchorage, AK** Anchorage Borough | 174,431 | 126,385 | +38.0 | | | | |
| **Anderson, IN** Madison County | 139,336 | 138,522 | + 0.6 | | | | |
| **Anderson, SC** Anderson County | 133,235 | 105,474 | +26.3 | **Battle Creek, MI** Calhoun County | 141,557 | 141,963 | − 0.3 |
| **Ann Arbor, MI**\* Washtenaw County | 264,748 | 234,103 | +13.1 | **Beaumont–Port Arthur, TX** Hardin, Jefferson, and Orange counties | 375,497 | 347,568 | + 8.0 |
| **Anniston, AL** Calhoun County | 119,761 | 103,092 | +16.2 | | | | |
| **Appleton–Oshkosh–Neenah, WI** Calumet, Outagamie, and Winnebago counties | 291,369 | 276,948 | + 5.2 | **Beaver County, PA**\* Beaver County | 204,441 | 208,418 | − 1.9 |
| | | | | **Bellingham, WA** Whatcom County | 106,701 | 81,983 | +30.2 |
| **Asheville, NC** Buncombe County | 160,934 | 145,056 | +10.9 | **Benton Harbor, MI** Berrien County | 171,276 | 163,940 | + 4.5 |
| **Athens, GA** Clarke, Jackson, Madison, and Oconee counties | 130,015 | 107,702 | +20.7 | **Bergen–Passaic, NJ**\* Bergen and Passaic counties | 1,292,970 | 1,357,930 | − 4.8 |

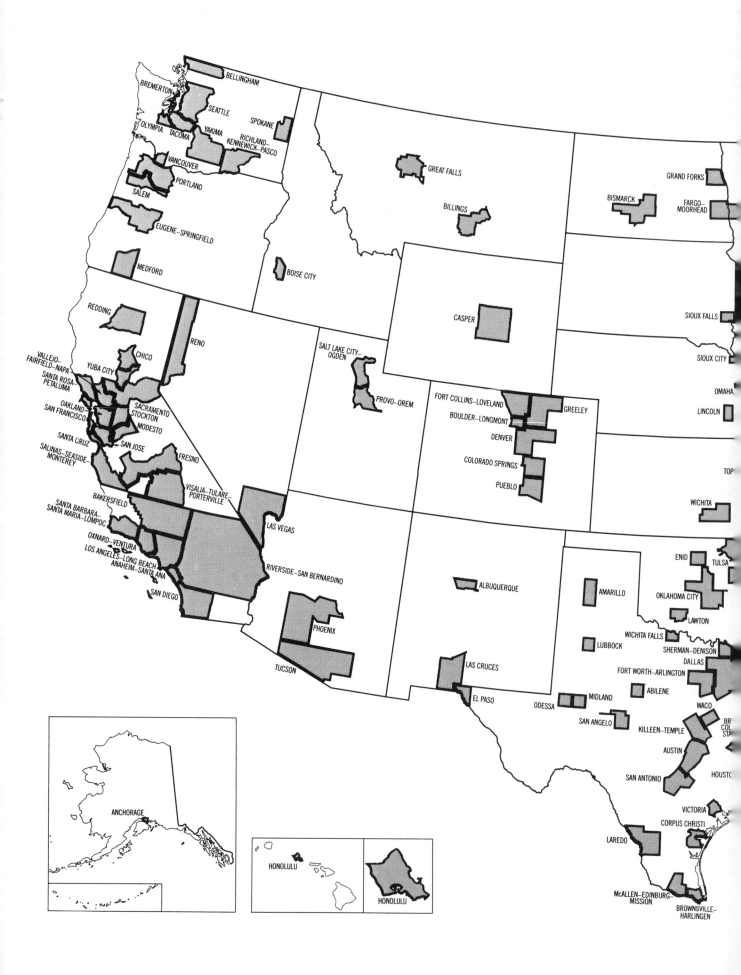

# Places Rated Almanac
## 329 Metropolitan Areas

| Metro Areas and Component Counties | Population 1980 | Population 1970 | Population Change, 1970–1980 |
|---|---|---|---|
| **Billings, MT**<br>Yellowstone County | 108,035 | 87,367 | +23.7% |
| **Biloxi–Gulfport, MS**<br>Hancock and Harrison counties | 182,202 | 151,969 | +19.9 |
| **Binghamton, NY**<br>Broome and Tioga counties | 263,460 | 268,328 | − 1.8 |
| **Birmingham, AL**<br>Blount, Jefferson, St. Clair, Shelby, and Walker counties | 883,946 | 794,083 | +11.3 |
| **Bismarck, ND**<br>Burleigh and Morton counties | 79,988 | 61,024 | +31.1 |
| **Bloomington, IN**<br>Monroe County | 98,785 | 85,221 | +15.9 |
| **Bloomington–Normal, IL**<br>McLean County | 119,149 | 104,389 | +14.1 |
| **Boise City, ID**<br>Ada County | 173,036 | 112,230 | +54.2 |
| **Boston, MA***<br>Parts of Bristol, Essex, Middlesex, Norfolk, Plymouth, and Worcester counties; Suffolk County | 2,805,911 | 2,887,191 | − 2.8 |
| **Boulder–Longmont, CO***<br>Boulder County | 189,625 | 131,889 | +43.8 |
| **Bradenton, FL**<br>Manatee County | 148,442 | 97,115 | +52.9 |
| **Brazoria, TX***<br>Brazoria County | 169,587 | 108,312 | +56.6 |
| **Bremerton, WA**<br>Kitsap County | 147,152 | 101,732 | +44.6 |
| **Bridgeport–Milford, CT***<br>Parts of Fairfield and New Haven counties | 438,557 | 443,714 | − 1.2 |
| **Bristol, CT***<br>Parts of Hartford and Litchfield counties | 73,762 | 69,878 | + 5.6 |
| **Brockton, MA***<br>Parts of Bristol, Norfolk, and Plymouth counties | 182,891 | 162,750 | +12.4 |
| **Brownsville–Harlingen, TX**<br>Cameron County | 209,727 | 140,368 | +49.4 |
| **Bryan–College Station, TX**<br>Brazos County | 93,588 | 57,978 | +61.4 |
| **Buffalo, NY***<br>Erie County | 1,015,472 | 1,113,491 | − 8.8 |
| **Burlington, NC**<br>Alamance County | 99,319 | 96,502 | + 2.9 |
| **Burlington, VT**<br>Parts of Chittenden, Franklin, and Grand Isle counties | 115,308 | 99,145 | +16.3 |
| **Canton, OH**<br>Carroll and Stark counties | 404,421 | 393,789 | + 2.7 |
| **Casper, WY**<br>Natrona County | 71,856 | 51,264 | +40.2 |
| **Cedar Rapids, IA**<br>Linn County | 169,775 | 163,213 | + 4.0 |
| **Champaign–Urbana–Rantoul, IL**<br>Champaign County | 168,392 | 163,281 | + 3.1 |
| **Charleston, SC**<br>Berkeley, Charleston, and Dorchester counties | 430,462 | 336,036 | +28.1% |
| **Charleston, WV**<br>Kanawha and Putnam counties | 269,595 | 257,140 | + 4.4 |
| **Charlotte–Gastonia–Rock Hill, NC–SC**<br>Cabarrus, Gaston, Lincoln, Mecklenburg, Rowan, and Union counties, NC; York County, SC | 971,391 | 840,347 | +15.6 |
| **Charlottesville, VA**<br>Charlottesville city; Albemarle, Fluvanna, and Greene counties | 113,568 | 89,529 | +26.9 |
| **Chattanooga, TN–GA**<br>Hamilton, Marion, and Sequatchie counties, TN; Catoosa, Dade, and Walker counties, GA | 426,540 | 370,857 | +19.0 |
| **Chicago, IL***<br>Cook, Du Page, and McHenry counties | 6,060,387 | 6,093,287 | − 0.5 |
| **Chico, CA**<br>Butte County | 143,851 | 101,969 | +41.1 |
| **Cincinnati, OH–KY–IN***<br>Clermont, Hamilton, and Warren counties, OH; Boone, Campbell, and Kenton counties, KY; Dearborn County, IN | 1,401,491 | 1,387,207 | + 1.3 |
| **Clarksville–Hopkinsville, TN–KY**<br>Montgomery County, TN; Christian County, KY | 150,220 | 118,945 | +33.4 |
| **Cleveland, OH***<br>Cuyahoga, Geauga, Lake, and Medina counties | 1,898,825 | 2,063,729 | − 8.0 |
| **Colorado Springs, CO**<br>El Paso County | 309,424 | 235,972 | +39.5 |
| **Columbia, MO**<br>Boone County | 100,376 | 80,935 | +24.0 |
| **Columbia, SC**<br>Lexington and Richland counties | 410,088 | 322,880 | +27.0 |
| **Columbus, GA–AL**<br>Chattahoochee and Muscogee counties, GA; Russell County, AL | 239,196 | 238,584 | + 0.3 |
| **Columbus, OH**<br>Delaware, Fairfield, Franklin, Licking, Madison, Pickaway, and Union counties | 1,243,833 | 1,149,432 | + 8.2 |
| **Corpus Christi, TX**<br>Nueces and San Patricio counties | 326,228 | 284,832 | +14.5 |
| **Cumberland, MD–WV**<br>Allegany County, MD; Mineral County, WV | 107,782 | 107,153 | + 0.6 |
| **Dallas, TX***<br>Collin, Dallas, Denton, Ellis, Kaufman, and Rockwall counties | 1,957,378 | 1,556,324 | +25.8 |
| **Danbury, CT***<br>Parts of Fairfield and Litchfield counties | 170,369 | 136,462 | +24.9 |

| Metro Areas and Component Counties | Population 1980 | Population 1970 | Population Change, 1970–1980 | Metro Areas and Component Counties | Population 1980 | Population 1970 | Population Change, 1970–1980 |
|---|---|---|---|---|---|---|---|
| **Danville, VA** Danville city and Pittsylvania County | 111,789 | 105,180 | + 6.3% | **Fayetteville–Springdale, AR** Washington County | 100,494 | 77,370 | +29.9% |
| **Davenport–Rock Island–Moline, IA–IL** Scott County, IA; Henry and Rock Island counties, IL | 383,958 | 362,638 | + 5.9 | **Fitchburg–Leominster, MA** Parts of Middlesex and Worcester counties | 94,018 | 93,732 | + 0.3 |
| **Dayton–Springfield, OH** Clark, Greene, Miami, and Montgomery counties | 942,083 | 974,927 | − 3.4 | **Flint, MI** Genesee County | 450,449 | 445,589 | + 1.1 |
| **Daytona Beach, FL** Volusia County | 258,762 | 169,487 | +52.7 | **Florence, AL** Colbert and Lauderdale counties | 135,065 | 117,743 | +14.7 |
| **Decatur, IL** Macon County | 131,375 | 125,010 | + 5.1 | **Florence, SC** Florence County | 110,163 | 89,636 | +22.9 |
| **Denver, CO**\* Adams, Arapahoe, Denver, Douglas, and Jefferson counties | 1,428,836 | 1,106,384 | +29.2 | **Fort Collins–Loveland, CO** Larimer County | 149,184 | 89,900 | +65.9 |
| **Des Moines, IA** Dallas, Polk, and Warren counties | 367,561 | 339,647 | + 8.2 | **Fort Lauderdale–Hollywood–Pompano Beach, FL**\* Broward County | 1,018,200 | 620,100 | +64.2 |
| **Detroit, MI**\* Lapeer, Livingston, Macomb, Monroe, Oakland, St. Clair, and Wayne counties | 4,488,072 | 4,554,266 | − 1.5 | **Fort Myers, FL** Lee County | 205,266 | 105,216 | +95.1 |
| **Dothan, AL** Dale and Houston counties | 122,453 | 109,569 | +11.8 | **Fort Pierce, FL** Martin and St. Lucie counties | 151,196 | 78,871 | +91.7 |
| **Dubuque, IA** Dubuque County | 93,745 | 90,609 | + 3.5 | **Fort Smith, AR–OK** Crawford and Sebastian counties, AR; Sequoyah County, OK | 162,813 | 128,284 | +26.9 |
| **Duluth, MN–WI** St. Louis County, MN; Douglas County, WI | 266,650 | 265,350 | + 0.5 | **Fort Walton Beach, FL** Okaloosa County | 109,920 | 88,187 | +24.6 |
| **East St. Louis–Belleville, IL**\* Clinton and St. Clair counties | 300,148 | 313,906 | − 4.4 | **Fort Wayne, IN** Allen, De Kalb, and Whitley counties | 354,156 | 334,687 | + 5.8 |
| **Eau Claire, WI** Chippewa and Eau Claire counties | 130,932 | 114,936 | +13.9 | **Fort Worth–Arlington, TX**\* Johnson, Parker, and Tarrant counties | 973,138 | 795,244 | +22.4 |
| **El Paso, TX** El Paso County | 479,899 | 359,291 | +33.6 | **Fresno, CA** Fresno County | 514,621 | 413,329 | +24.5 |
| **Elkhart–Goshen, IN** Elkhart County | 137,330 | 126,529 | + 8.5 | **Gadsden, AL** Etowah County | 103,057 | 94,144 | + 9.5 |
| **Elmira, NY** Chemung County | 97,656 | 101,537 | − 3.8 | **Gainesville, FL** Alachua and Bradford counties | 171,371 | 119,389 | +43.5 |
| **Enid, OK** Garfield County | 62,820 | 56,343 | +11.5 | **Galveston–Texas City, TX**\* Galveston County | 195,940 | 169,812 | +15.4 |
| **Erie, PA** Erie County | 279,780 | 263,654 | + 6.1 | **Gary–Hammond, IN**\* Lake and Porter counties | 642,781 | 633,367 | + 1.5 |
| **Eugene–Springfield, OR** Lane County | 275,226 | 215,401 | +27.8 | **Glens Falls, NY** Warren and Washington counties | 109,649 | 102,127 | + 7.4 |
| **Evansville, IN–KY** Posey, Vanderburgh, and Warrick counties, IN; Henderson County, KY | 276,252 | 254,515 | + 8.5 | **Grand Forks, ND** Grand Forks County | 66,100 | 61,102 | + 8.2 |
| **Fall River, MA–RI**\* Parts of Bristol County, MA; parts of Newport County, RI | 157,222 | 152,361 | + 3.2 | **Grand Rapids, MI** Kent and Ottawa counties | 601,680 | 539,225 | +11.6 |
| **Fargo–Moorhead, ND–MN** Cass County, ND; Clay County, MN | 137,574 | 120,261 | +14.4 | **Great Falls, MT** Cascade County | 80,696 | 81,804 | − 1.4 |
| **Fayetteville, NC** Cumberland County | 247,160 | 212,042 | +16.6 | **Greeley, CO** Weld County | 123,438 | 89,297 | +38.2 |
| | | | | **Green Bay, WI** Brown County | 175,280 | 158,244 | +10.8 |

| Metro Areas and Component Counties | Population 1980 | Population 1970 | Population Change, 1970–1980 | Metro Areas and Component Counties | Population 1980 | Population 1970 | Population Change, 1970–1980 |
|---|---|---|---|---|---|---|---|
| **Greensboro– Winston-Salem–High Point, NC** Davidson, Davie, Forsyth, Guilford, Randolph, Stokes, and Yadkin counties | 851,851 | 742,984 | +14.7% | **Johnson City–Kingsport– Bristol, TN–VA** Carter, Hawkins, Sullivan, Unicoi, and Washington counties, TN; Bristol city and Scott and Washington counties, VA | 433,638 | 373,591 | +16.1% |
| **Greenville–Spartanburg, SC** Greenville, Pickens, and Spartanburg counties | 569,066 | 473,454 | +20.2 | **Johnstown, PA** Cambria and Somerset counties | 264,506 | 262,822 | + 0.6 |
| **Hagerstown, MD** Washington County | 113,086 | 103,829 | + 8.9 | **Joliet, IL***  Grundy and Will counties | 355,042 | 274,360 | +29.4 |
| **Hamilton–Middletown, OH***  Butler County | 258,787 | 226,207 | +14.4 | **Joplin, MO** Jasper and Newton counties | 127,513 | 112,833 | +13.0 |
| **Harrisburg–Lebanon– Carlisle, PA** Cumberland, Dauphin, Lebanon, and Perry counties | 555,158 | 510,170 | + 8.8 | **Kalamazoo, MI** Kalamazoo County | 212,378 | 201,550 | + 5.4 |
| **Hartford, CT***  Parts of Hartford, Litchfield, Middlesex, New London, and Tolland counties | 715,923 | 710,926 | + 0.7 | **Kankakee, IL** Kankakee County | 102,926 | 97,250 | + 5.8 |
| **Hickory, NC** Alexander, Burke, and Catawba counties | 202,711 | 170,703 | +18.8 | **Kansas City, KS***  Johnson, Leavenworth, Miami, and Wyandotte counties | 519,031 | 479,512 | + 8.3 |
| **Honolulu, HI** Honolulu County | 762,565 | 630,528 | +20.9 | **Kansas City, MO***  Cass, Clay, Jackson, Lafayette, Platte, and Ray counties | 914,427 | 893,634 | + 2.3 |
| **Houma–Thibodaux, LA** Lafourche and Terrebonne parishes | 176,876 | 144,990 | +22.0 | **Kenosha, WI***  Kenosha County | 123,137 | 117,917 | + 4.4 |
| **Houston, TX***  Fort Bend, Harris, Liberty, Montgomery, and Waller counties | 2,735,766 | 1,891,004 | +44.6 | **Killeen–Temple, TX** Bell and Coryell counties | 214,656 | 159,794 | +34.3 |
| **Huntington–Ashland, WV–KY–OH** Cabell and Wayne counties, WV; Boyd, Carter, and Greenup counties, KY; Lawrence County, OH | 336,410 | 306,785 | + 9.7 | **Knoxville, TN** Anderson, Blount, Grainger, Jefferson, Knox, Sevier, and Union counties | 565,970 | 476,538 | +18.8 |
| **Huntsville, AL** Madison County | 196,966 | 186,540 | + 5.6 | **Kokomo, IN** Howard and Tipton counties | 103,715 | 99,848 | + 3.9 |
| **Indianapolis, IN** Boone, Hamilton, Hancock, Hendricks, Johnson, Marion, Morgan, and Shelby counties | 1,166,575 | 1,111,352 | + 5.0 | **La Crosse, WI** La Crosse County | 91,056 | 80,468 | +13.2 |
| **Iowa City, IA** Johnson County | 81,717 | 72,127 | +13.3 | **Lafayette, IN** Tippecanoe County | 121,702 | 109,378 | +11.3 |
| **Jackson, MI** Jackson County | 151,495 | 143,274 | + 5.7 | **Lafayette, LA** Lafayette and St. Martin parishes | 190,231 | 144,096 | +32.0 |
| **Jackson, MS** Hinds, Madison, and Rankin counties | 362,038 | 288,643 | +25.4 | **Lake Charles, LA** Calcasieu Parish | 167,223 | 145,415 | +15.0 |
| **Jacksonville, FL** Clay, Duval, Nassau, and St. Johns counties | 722,252 | 612,585 | +17.9 | **Lake County, IL***  Lake County | 440,372 | 382,638 | +15.0 |
| **Jacksonville, NC** Onslow County | 112,784 | 103,126 | + 9.4 | **Lakeland–Winter Haven, FL** Polk County | 321,652 | 228,515 | +40.8 |
| **Janesville–Beloit, WI** Rock County | 139,420 | 131,970 | + 5.6 | **Lancaster, PA** Lancaster County | 362,346 | 320,079 | +13.2 |
| **Jersey City, NJ***  Hudson County | 556,972 | 607,839 | − 8.4 | **Lansing–East Lansing, MI** Clinton, Eaton, and Ingham counties | 419,750 | 378,423 | +10.9 |
| | | | | **Laredo, TX** Webb County | 99,258 | 72,859 | +36.2 |
| | | | | **Las Cruces, NM** Dona Ana County | 96,340 | 69,773 | +38.1 |
| | | | | **Las Vegas, NV** Clark County | 463,087 | 273,288 | +69.5 |

| Metro Areas and Component Counties | Population 1980 | Population 1970 | Population Change, 1970–1980 | Metro Areas and Component Counties | Population 1980 | Population 1970 | Population Change, 1970–1980 |
|---|---|---|---|---|---|---|---|
| Lawrence, KS<br>Douglas County | 67,640 | 57,932 | +16.8% | Memphis, TN–AR–MS<br>Shelby and Tipton counties, TN; Crittenden County, AR; De Soto County, MS | 913,472 | 834,103 | + 9.5% |
| Lawrence–Haverhill, MA–NH*<br>Parts of Essex County, MA; parts of Rockingham County, NH | 339,090 | 300,943 | +12.7 | Miami–Hialeah, FL*<br>Dade County | 1,625,781 | 1,267,792 | +28.2 |
| Lawton, OK<br>Comanche County | 112,456 | 108,144 | + 4.0 | Middlesex–Somerset–Hunterdon, NJ*<br>Hunterdon, Middlesex, and Somerset counties | 886,383 | 851,903 | + 4.1 |
| Lewiston–Auburn, ME<br>Parts of Androscoggin County | 84,690 | 80,135 | + 5.7 | Middletown, CT*<br>Parts of Middlesex County | 81,582 | 73,769 | +10.6 |
| Lexington–Fayette, KY<br>Bourbon, Clark, Fayette, Jessamine, Scott, and Woodford counties | 317,629 | 266,701 | +19.1 | Midland, TX<br>Midland County | 82,636 | 65,433 | +26.3 |
| Lima, OH<br>Allen and Auglaize counties | 154,795 | 149,746 | + 3.4 | Milwaukee, WI*<br>Milwaukee, Ozaukee, Washington, and Waukesha counties | 1,397,143 | 1,403,884 | − 0.5 |
| Lincoln, NE<br>Lancaster County | 192,884 | 167,972 | +14.8 | Minneapolis–St. Paul, MN–WI<br>Anoka, Carver, Chisago, Dakota, Hennepin, Isanti, Ramsey, Scott, Washington, and Wright counties, MN; St. Croix County, WI | 2,137,133 | 1,981,951 | + 7.8 |
| Little Rock–North Little Rock, AR<br>Faulkner, Lonoke, Pulaski, and Saline counties | 474,484 | 381,123 | +24.5 | | | | |
| Longview–Marshall, TX<br>Gregg and Harrison counties | 151,752 | 120,770 | +25.7 | Mobile, AL<br>Baldwin and Mobile counties | 443,536 | 376,690 | +17.8 |
| Lorain–Elyria, OH*<br>Lorain County | 274,909 | 256,843 | + 7.0 | Modesto, CA<br>Stanislaus County | 265,900 | 194,506 | +36.7 |
| Los Angeles–Long Beach, CA*<br>Los Angeles County | 7,477,503 | 7,041,980 | + 6.2 | Monmouth–Ocean, NJ*<br>Monmouth and Ocean counties | 849,211 | 670,319 | +26.7 |
| Louisville, KY–IN<br>Bullitt, Jefferson, Oldham, and Shelby counties, KY; Clark, Floyd, and Harrison counties, IN | 956,756 | 906,752 | + 5.5 | Monroe, LA<br>Ouachita Parish | 139,241 | 115,387 | +20.7 |
| | | | | Montgomery, AL<br>Autauga, Elmore, and Montgomery counties | 272,687 | 225,911 | +20.7 |
| Lowell, MA–NH*<br>Parts of Middlesex County, MA; parts of Hillsborough County, NH | 243,142 | 225,447 | + 7.8 | Muncie, IN<br>Delaware County | 128,587 | 129,219 | − 0.5 |
| Lubbock, TX<br>Lubbock County | 211,651 | 179,295 | +18.1 | Muskegon, MI<br>Muskegon County | 157,589 | 157,426 | + 0.1 |
| Lynchburg, VA<br>Lynchburg city; Amherst and Campbell counties | 141,289 | 124,960 | +13.1 | Nashua, NH*<br>Parts of Hillsborough and Rockingham counties | 142,527 | 100,011 | +42.1 |
| Macon–Warner Robins, GA<br>Bibb, Houston, Jones, and Peach counties | 263,591 | 234,550 | +12.4 | Nashville, TN<br>Cheatham, Davidson, Dickson, Robertson, Rutherford, Sumner, Williamson, and Wilson counties | 850,505 | 699,271 | +21.4 |
| Madison, WI<br>Dane County | 323,545 | 290,272 | +11.5 | Nassau–Suffolk, NY*<br>Nassau and Suffolk counties | 2,605,813 | 2,555,868 | + 1.9 |
| Manchester, NH<br>Parts of Hillsborough, Merrimack, and Rockingham counties | 129,305 | 115,225 | +12.2 | New Bedford, MA<br>Parts of Bristol and Plymouth counties | 166,699 | 158,682 | + 5.0 |
| Mansfield, OH<br>Richland County | 131,205 | 129,997 | + 0.9 | New Britain, CT*<br>Parts of Hartford County | 142,241 | 145,269 | − 2.1 |
| McAllen–Edinburg–Mission, TX<br>Hidalgo County | 283,229 | 181,535 | +56.1 | New Haven–Meriden, CT<br>Parts of Middlesex and New Haven counties | 500,474 | 488,732 | + 2.4 |
| Medford, OR<br>Jackson County | 132,456 | 94,533 | +40.1 | New London–Norwich, CT–RI<br>Parts of New London and Windham counties, CT; parts of Washington County, RI | 250,839 | 242,624 | + 3.4 |
| Melbourne–Titusville–Palm Bay, FL<br>Brevard County | 272,959 | 230,006 | +18.7 | | | | |

| Metro Areas and Component Counties | Population 1980 | Population 1970 | Population Change, 1970–1980 | Metro Areas and Component Counties | Population 1980 | Population 1970 | Population Change, 1970–1980 |
|---|---|---|---|---|---|---|---|
| **New Orleans, LA** Jefferson, Orleans, St. Bernard, St. Charles, St. John The Baptist, and St. Tammany parishes | 1,256,256 | 1,099,833 | +14.0% | **Pensacola, FL** Escambia and Santa Rosa counties | 289,782 | 243,075 | +19.0% |
| **New York, NY***  Bronx, Kings, New York, Putnam, Queens, Richmond, Rockland, and Westchester counties | 8,274,961 | 9,076,568 | − 8.8 | **Peoria, IL** Peoria, Tazewell, and Woodford counties | 365,864 | 341,979 | + 6.9 |
| **Newark, NJ***  Essex, Morris, Sussex, and Union counties | 1,878,959 | 1,936,624 | − 3.0 | **Philadelphia, PA–NJ***  Bucks, Chester, Delaware, Montgomery, and Philadelphia counties, PA; Burlington, Camden, and Gloucester counties, NJ | 4,716,818 | 4,824,110 | − 2.2 |
| **Niagara Falls, NY***  Niagara County | 227,354 | 235,720 | − 3.5 | **Phoenix, AZ** Maricopa County | 1,509,052 | 971,228 | +55.4 |
| **Norfolk–Virginia Beach– Newport News, VA** Chesapeake, Hampton, Newport News, Norfolk, Poquoson, Portsmouth, Suffolk, Virginia Beach, and Williamsburg cities; Gloucester, James City, and York counties | 1,160,311 | 1,058,764 | + 9.5 | **Pine Bluff, AR** Jefferson County | 90,718 | 85,329 | + 6.3 |
| **Norwalk, CT***  Parts of Fairfield County | 126,692 | 127,595 | − 0.7 | **Pittsburgh, PA***  Allegheny, Fayette, Washington, and Westmoreland counties | 2,218,870 | 2,347,611 | − 5.5 |
| **Oakland, CA***  Alameda and Contra Costa counties | 1,761,759 | 1,627,562 | + 8.2 | **Pittsfield, MA** Parts of Berkshire County | 83,490 | 88,094 | − 5.2 |
| **Ocala, FL** Marion County | 122,488 | 69,030 | +77.4 | **Portland, ME** Parts of Cumberland and York counties | 193,831 | 171,870 | +12.7 |
| **Odessa, TX** Ector County | 115,374 | 92,660 | +24.3 | **Portland, OR***  Clackamas, Multnomah, Washington, and Yamhill counties | 1,105,699 | 918,889 | +20.3 |
| **Oklahoma City, OK** Canadian, Cleveland, Logan, McClain, Oklahoma, and Pottawatomie counties | 860,969 | 718,737 | +19.6 | **Portsmouth–Dover– Rochester, NH–ME** Parts of Rockingham and Strafford counties, NH; part of York County, ME | 190,938 | 161,199 | +18.4 |
| **Olympia, WA** Thurston County | 124,264 | 76,894 | +61.6 | **Poughkeepsie, NY** Dutchess County | 245,055 | 222,295 | +10.1 |
| **Omaha, NE–IA** Douglas, Sarpy, and Washington counties, NE; Pottawattamie County, IA | 585,122 | 555,956 | + 5.2 | **Providence, RI***  Parts of Bristol, Kent, Newport, Providence, and Washington counties | 618,514 | 612,362 | + 1.0 |
| **Orange County, NY***  Orange County | 259,603 | 221,657 | +17.0 | **Provo–Orem, UT** Utah County | 218,106 | 137,776 | +58.3 |
| **Orlando, FL** Orange, Osceola, and Seminole counties | 700,055 | 453,270 | +54.4 | **Pueblo, CO** Pueblo County | 125,972 | 118,238 | + 6.5 |
| **Owensboro, KY** Daviess County | 85,949 | 79,486 | + 8.1 | **Racine, WI***  Racine County | 173,132 | 170,838 | + 1.0 |
| **Oxnard–Ventura, CA***  Ventura County | 529,174 | 378,497 | +39.8 | **Raleigh–Durham, NC** Durham, Franklin, Orange, and Wake counties | 561,222 | 446,074 | +25.6 |
| **Panama City, FL** Bay County | 97,740 | 75,283 | +29.5 | **Reading, PA** Berks County | 312,509 | 296,382 | + 5.4 |
| **Parkersburg–Marietta, WV–OH** Wood County, WV; Washington County, OH | 157,914 | 143,978 | + 9.6 | **Redding, CA** Shasta County | 115,715 | 77,640 | +49.0 |
| **Pascagoula, MS** Jackson County | 118,015 | 87,975 | +34.1 | **Reno, NV** Washoe County | 193,623 | 121,068 | +59.9 |
| **Pawtucket–Woonsocket– Attleboro, RI–MA***  Parts of Providence County, RI; parts of Bristol, Norfolk, and Worcester counties, MA | 307,403 | 300,694 | + 2.2 | **Richland–Kennewick– Pasco, WA** Benton and Franklin counties | 144,469 | 93,356 | +54.8 |
| | | | | **Richmond–Petersburg, VA** Colonial Heights, Hopewell, Petersburg, and Richmond cities; Charles City, Chesterfield, Dinwiddie, Goochland, Hanover, Henrico, New Kent, Powhatan, and Prince George counties | 761,311 | 676,351 | +12.6 |

| Metro Areas and Component Counties | Population 1980 | Population 1970 | Population Change, 1970–1980 |
|---|---|---|---|
| **Riverside–San Bernardino, CA**\* Riverside and San Bernardino counties | 1,558,182 | 1,139,149 | +36.8% |
| **Roanoke, VA** Roanoke and Salem cities; Botetourt and Roanoke counties | 220,393 | 199,629 | +10.4 |
| **Rochester, MN** Olmsted County | 92,006 | 84,104 | + 9.3 |
| **Rochester, NY** Livingston, Monroe, Ontario, Orleans, and Wayne counties | 971,230 | 961,516 | + 1.0 |
| **Rockford, IL** Boone and Winnebago counties | 279,514 | 272,063 | + 2.7 |
| **Sacramento, CA** El Dorado, Placer, Sacramento, and Yolo counties | 1,099,814 | 847,626 | +29.5 |
| **Saginaw–Bay City–Midland, MI** Bay, Midland, and Saginaw counties | 421,518 | 400,851 | + 5.1 |
| **St. Cloud, MN** Benton, Sherburne, and Stearns counties | 163,256 | 134,585 | +21.4 |
| **St. Joseph, MO** Buchanan County | 87,888 | 86,915 | + 1.1 |
| **St. Louis, MO–IL**\* St. Louis city and Franklin, Jefferson, St. Charles, and St. Louis counties, MO; Monroe County, IL | 1,808,621 | 1,846,067 | − 2.0 |
| **Salem, OR** Marion and Polk counties | 249,895 | 186,658 | +33.9 |
| **Salem–Gloucester, MA**\* Parts of Essex County | 258,175 | 262,687 | − 1.7 |
| **Salinas–Seaside–Monterey, CA** Monterey County | 290,444 | 247,450 | +17.2 |
| **Salt Lake City–Ogden, UT** Davis, Salt Lake, and Weber counties | 910,222 | 683,913 | +32.8 |
| **San Angelo, TX** Tom Green County | 84,784 | 71,047 | +19.1 |
| **San Antonio, TX** Bexar, Comal, and Guadalupe counties | 1,071,954 | 888,179 | +20.5 |
| **San Diego, CA** San Diego County | 1,861,846 | 1,357,854 | +37.1 |
| **San Francisco, CA**\* Marin, San Francisco, and San Mateo counties | 1,488,871 | 1,481,687 | + 0.5 |
| **San Jose, CA**\* Santa Clara County | 1,295,071 | 1,065,313 | +21.4 |
| **Santa Barbara–Santa Maria–Lompoc, CA** Santa Barbara County | 298,694 | 264,324 | +12.9 |
| **Santa Cruz, CA**\* Santa Cruz County | 188,141 | 123,790 | +51.5 |
| **Santa Rosa–Petaluma, CA**\* Sonoma County | 299,681 | 204,885 | +46.3 |
| **Sarasota, FL** Sarasota County | 202,251 | 120,413 | +68.5 |
| **Savannah, GA** Chatham and Effingham counties | 220,553 | 201,448 | + 9.5% |
| **Scranton–Wilkes-Barre, PA** Columbia, Lackawanna, Luzerne, Monroe, and Wyoming counties | 728,796 | 696,078 | + 4.7 |
| **Seattle, WA**\* King and Snohomish counties | 1,607,469 | 1,424,605 | +12.7 |
| **Sharon, PA** Mercer County | 128,299 | 127,225 | + 0.8 |
| **Sheboygan, WI** Sheboygan County | 100,935 | 96,660 | + 4.4 |
| **Sherman–Denison, TX** Grayson County | 89,796 | 83,225 | + 7.9 |
| **Shreveport, LA** Bossier and Caddo parishes | 333,079 | 296,061 | +12.5 |
| **Sioux City, IA–NE** Woodbury County, IA; Dakota County, NE | 117,457 | 116,189 | + 1.1 |
| **Sioux Falls, SD** Minnehaha County | 109,435 | 95,209 | +14.9 |
| **South Bend–Mishawaka, IN** St. Joseph County | 241,617 | 244,827 | − 1.3 |
| **Spokane, WA** Spokane County | 341,835 | 287,487 | +18.9 |
| **Springfield, IL** Menard and Sangamon counties | 187,789 | 171,020 | + 9.8 |
| **Springfield, MA** Parts of Hampden and Hampshire counties | 515,259 | 528,072 | − 2.4 |
| **Springfield, MO** Christian and Greene counties | 207,704 | 168,053 | +23.6 |
| **Stamford, CT**\* Parts of Fairfield County | 198,854 | 206,340 | − 3.6 |
| **State College, PA** Centre County | 112,760 | 99,267 | +13.6 |
| **Steubenville–Weirton, OH–WV** Jefferson County, OH; Brooke and Hancock counties, WV | 163,099 | 166,385 | − 1.6 |
| **Stockton, CA** San Joaquin County | 347,342 | 291,073 | +19.3 |
| **Syracuse, NY** Madison, Onondaga, and Oswego counties | 642,971 | 636,596 | + 1.0 |
| **Tacoma, WA**\* Pierce County | 485,643 | 412,344 | +17.8 |
| **Tallahassee, FL** Gadsden and Leon counties | 190,220 | 142,231 | +33.7 |
| **Tampa–St. Petersburg–Clearwater, FL** Hernando, Hillsborough, Pasco, and Pinellas counties | 1,613,603 | 1,105,553 | +44.2 |
| **Terre Haute, IN** Clay and Vigo counties | 137,247 | 138,461 | − 0.9 |

| Metro Areas and Component Counties | Population 1980 | Population 1970 | Population Change, 1970–1980 | Metro Areas and Component Counties | Population 1980 | Population 1970 | Population Change, 1970–1980 |
|---|---|---|---|---|---|---|---|
| **Texarkana, TX–Texarkana, AR** Bowie County, TX; Miller County, AR | 113,067 | 102,294 | +10.5% | Manassas Park cities, VA; Arlington, Fairfax, Loudoun, Prince William, and Stafford counties, VA | | | |
| **Toledo, OH** Fulton, Lucas, and Wood counties | 616,864 | 606,344 | + 1.7 | **Waterbury, CT** Parts of Litchfield and New Haven counties | 204,968 | 196,134 | + 4.5% |
| **Topeka, KS** Shawnee County | 154,916 | 155,322 | − 0.3 | **Waterloo–Cedar Falls, IA** Black Hawk and Bremer counties | 162,781 | 155,653 | + 4.6 |
| **Trenton, NJ*** Mercer County | 307,863 | 304,116 | + 1.2 | **Wausau, WI** Marathon County | 111,270 | 97,457 | +14.1 |
| **Tucson, AZ** Pima County | 531,443 | 351,667 | +51.1 | **West Palm Beach–Boca Raton–Delray Beach, FL** Palm Beach County | 576,863 | 348,993 | +65.3 |
| **Tulsa, OK** Creek, Osage, Rogers, Tulsa, and Wagoner counties | 657,173 | 525,852 | +25.0 | **Wheeling, WV–OH** Marshall and Ohio counties, WV; Belmont County, OH | 185,566 | 181,954 | + 2.0 |
| **Tuscaloosa, AL** Tuscaloosa County | 137,541 | 116,029 | +18.5 | **Wichita, KS** Butler and Sedgwick counties | 411,313 | 389,352 | + 5.6 |
| **Tyler, TX** Smith County | 128,366 | 97,096 | +33.2 | **Wichita Falls, TX** Wichita County | 121,082 | 120,563 | + 0.4 |
| **Utica–Rome, NY** Herkimer and Oneida counties | 320,180 | 340,477 | − 6.0 | **Williamsport, PA** Lycoming County | 118,416 | 113,296 | + 4.5 |
| **Vallejo–Fairfield–Napa, CA*** Napa and Solano counties | 334,402 | 251,129 | +33.2 | **Wilmington, DE–NJ–MD*** New Castle County, DE; Salem County, NJ; Cecil County, MD | 523,221 | 499,493 | + 4.8 |
| **Vancouver, WA*** Clark County | 192,227 | 128,454 | +49.6 | **Wilmington, NC** New Hanover County | 103,471 | 82,996 | +24.7 |
| **Victoria, TX** Victoria County | 68,807 | 53,766 | +28.0 | **Worcester, MA** Parts of Worcester County | 402,918 | 399,682 | + 0.8 |
| **Vineland–Millville–Bridgeton, NJ*** Cumberland County | 132,866 | 121,374 | + 9.5 | **Yakima, WA** Yakima County | 172,508 | 145,212 | +18.8 |
| **Visalia–Tulare–Porterville, CA** Tulare County | 245,738 | 188,322 | +30.5 | **York, PA** Adams and York counties | 381,255 | 329,540 | +15.7 |
| **Waco, TX** McLennan County | 170,755 | 147,553 | +15.7 | **Youngstown–Warren, OH** Mahoning and Trumbull counties | 531,350 | 537,124 | − 1.1 |
| **Washington, DC–MD–VA** District of Columbia; Calvert, Charles, Frederick, Montgomery, and Prince Georges counties, MD; Alexandria, Fairfax, Falls Church, Manassas, and | 3,250,822 | 3,040,307 | + 6.9 | **Yuba City, CA** Sutter and Yuba counties | 101,979 | 86,671 | +17.7 |

*Source:* U.S. Office of Management and Budget, 1983.

*An asterisk identifies a Primary Metropolitan Statistical Area.

The list above includes Metropolitan Statistical Areas and Primary Metropolitan Statistical Areas as defined by the Office of Management and Budget as of June 30, 1983.

# Places
# Rated
# Almanac

# Climate & Terrain:

## Fundamental Considerations

Have you given much thought to what kind of climate you'd like to live in? Most Americans prefer (or say they prefer) mild, sunny climates. Yet when asked where the mild climates are, they are likely to answer that the "good, warm" weather is in the South. In fact, many of America's best climates are located north of the Mason-Dixon line, some in places that might surprise you.

Americans have an enormous variety of climates to choose from. There are northern maritime climates, extremely mild Mediterranean climates, southerly mountain climates, lowland desert climates, tropical "paradise" climates, desert highland climates, rugged northern continental climates, windward slope climates, leeward slope climates, humid subtropical climates—in fact, just about every kind of climate on the face of the earth. You name it, you can probably find it somewhere in the United States.

The weather events that make up a place's climate —rain, snow, heat, cold, drought, wind—can vary, sometimes dramatically, from year to year. But climate cannot be bought, built, remodeled, or relocated. A place's climate is there for keeps, and patterns of weather and climate have a profound effect on our lives. The economic impact of climate, for example, seems greater each year as heating and cooling costs continue to rise. Air-conditioning is almost always more expensive than home heating. Thus, people who

assumed they'd save on utility bills by moving to the Sun Belt might well be mistaken. A better bet for these people could be a milder climate in such middle-latitude states as Arkansas or North Carolina. The financial considerations for companies putting up large office buildings or warehouses, which are extremely expensive to heat and cool, are even more compelling. In fact, the site for a corporate building or relocation may hinge more on climate than on proximity to major transportation facilities.

Most of us have found that weather profoundly affects our moods and emotions. Long, snowy winters that confine people indoors can have adverse emotional effects; many people become irritable when the weather gets so hot they cannot sleep. We are cheered by brisk, sunny weather but sobered by cloudy, rainy days or very cold temperatures.

Relative humidity, barometric pressure, and altitude are just a few factors related to climate or terrain that can influence your physical well-being. There is no proven link between longevity and climate, although the three places on the globe whose populations have the highest percentage of centenarians—the Caucasus Mountains of the Soviet Union, the mountains of Bolivia, and northwestern India—are all in southerly latitudes at high elevations. But in America, where careful records have been kept for generations, a similar situation does not exist. In fact, most of the

1

highest average life spans occur in states with severe climates—Minnesota, North Dakota, and Iowa, for example.

It has been shown, however, that people with certain chronic diseases or disorders are far more comfortable in some climates than others. Asthmatics generally do best in warm, dry places that have a minimum of airborne allergens and no molds. People with rheumatism or arthritis find comfort in warm, moist, southerly climates where the weather is fairly constant and the atmospheric pressure undergoes the least daily change. Those who suffer from lung disorders such as tuberculosis or emphysema seem to do best in mountainous locales with lots of clear air and sunshine.

## FACTORS THAT DETERMINE CLIMATE

Five factors have a major influence on the climate of a particular area: water, latitude, elevation, prevailing winds, and mountain ranges.

Water, especially in large bodies like oceans, has a moderating effect on temperatures. Water warms up slowly, holds much more heat than does land, and cools more slowly. Therefore, places near or surrounded by large bodies of water tend to be cooler in summer and warmer in winter than others far from water. Marine climates are thus by definition relatively mild. San Francisco, with water on three sides, has one of the most even climates on the continent.

On the other hand, places located in the middle of large land masses, away from the moderating effects of water, experience large swings of temperature. The tendency is for this kind of climate—called continental —to be more rigorous in the higher latitudes. The closer to the poles one moves, the more exaggerated are the seasonal shifts, because polar (and very northerly) locations undergo the greatest seasonal variation in the amount and intensity of sunlight. In Fairbanks, Alaska, for example, the average "day" (the period between the sun's rising and setting) in December is only four hours long. But in late June, each day receives more than 18 hours of sun, and the heat is intense. Places in the North and Far North, then, can experience not only bitterly cold winters but broiling summers as well!

Elevation, or height above sea level, has the same general effect as a higher latitude. Each 1,000 feet of elevation lowers the average temperature by 3.3 degrees Fahrenheit. Places that combine high altitudes with southerly latitudes seem to get the best of both North and South, enjoying the mild, short winters of

**Climatic Regions of the United States**

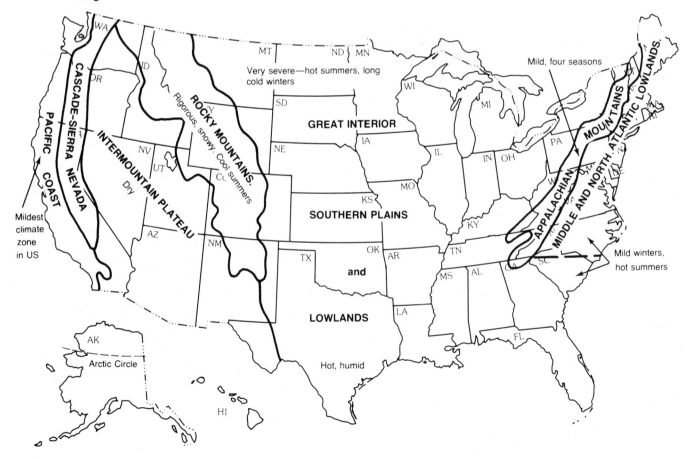

the South and the cooler nights and crisp falls of the North. Locations in the southern Appalachian Mountains and in the mountains of the Southwest have long been known for their mild, four-season climates.

To understand how prevailing winds influence climate, we have only to look at a pair of metro areas: Portland, Oregon, and Portland, Maine. Each is located at a rather northerly latitude. Both are also situated on ocean coasts. Thus one would naturally suppose that the two Portlands would have roughly the same type of climate. Why, then, is Portland, Oregon, so much milder? The answer lies in the prevailing winds that sweep across our continent. America's prevailing winds blow from west to east. Places along the West Coast receive the full impact of winds that have moved thousands of miles over water; cities even hundreds of miles inland still feel some of the beneficial effects of the Pacific winds. But inland cities in the East feel few consequences of the Atlantic save on those rare occasions when the prevailing wind direction *doesn't* prevail. And, sad to say, this reversal of wind direction often means a storm.

Mountain ranges help determine climate and weather because they act as giant barriers that deflect and channel winds and weather. The weather—and also climate—on one side of a mountain range is often radically different from that on the other. Because of this, mountain ranges are natural dividing points between climate zones.

## AMERICA'S MAJOR CLIMATIC REGIONS

Mountain ranges delineate the seven major climatic regions of the continental United States. The Pacific Coast is the mildest of these regions, and the northern portion of the Great Interior is the most rigorous. The Intermountain Plateau (which is also called the Great Basin), lying between the Sierra Nevada to the west and the Rocky Mountains to the east, is noted primarily for its dryness. Some of the best climates for variety and mildness are found in the southern portion of this area. The southern half of the Appalachian Mountains region also offers climates that are both mild and variable.

Most Americans live in the large climatic zone that includes the Great Interior, Southern Plains, and Lowlands regions. This zone, ironically, also happens to be the least desirable as far as mildness and human comfort are concerned. Those who live in its northern part are plagued by severe winters and hot, humid summers with very short springs and autumns. In the southern portion, winters are mild while springs and autumns are longer, but the steam-bath summers are very uncomfortable and debilitating. The climate of the East Coast, called the Middle and North Atlantic Lowlands, is similar to that of the Great Interior, but milder and somewhat damper. Right on the coast, winters are milder and summers are noticeably cooler.

### The 8 Coldest Metro Areas

| | Zero-Degree Days per Year | Freezing Days per Year |
|---|---|---|
| Fargo–Moorhead, ND–MN | 54 | 181 |
| Duluth, MN–WI | 51 | 187 |
| Bismarck, ND | 51 | 186 |
| Anchorage, AK | 41 | 192 |
| Rochester, MN | 35 | 165 |
| Minneapolis–St. Paul, MN–WI | 34 | 158 |
| Sioux Falls, SD | 33 | 171 |
| Waterloo–Cedar Falls, IA | 31 | 159 |

Listed above are those metro areas described in the Place Profiles that combine more than 30 zero-degree days per year with more than 150 freezing days.

### The 12 Hottest Metro Areas

| | 90-Degree Days per Year | July Noon Relative Humidity |
|---|---|---|
| San Antonio, TX | 111 | 55% |
| Fort Myers, FL | 106 | 65 |
| Orlando, FL | 104 | 65 |
| Brownsville–Harlingen, TX | 102 | 55 |
| Austin, TX | 101 | 55 |
| Corpus Christi, TX | 96 | 65 |
| Tallahassee, FL | 87 | 65 |
| Shreveport, LA | 87 | 55 |
| Jacksonville, FL | 82 | 65 |
| Mobile, AL | 81 | 65 |
| Tampa–St. Petersburg–Clearwater, FL | 81 | 65 |
| Houston, TX | 81 | 60 |

Listed above are those metro areas described in the Place Profiles that combine 80 or more 90-degree days with a July noon relative humidity of 55 percent or higher. Three metro areas have more than 130 ninety-degree days per year—Phoenix, AZ (164); Tucson, AZ (139); and Las Vegas, NV (131)—but all of them have a July relative humidity of less than 30 percent.

### The 10 Sunniest Metro Areas / ...and the 11 Drizzliest

| | Clear Days per Year | | Precipitation Days per Year |
|---|---|---|---|
| Chico, CA | 219 | Saginaw–Bay City–Midland, MI | 181 |
| Las Vegas, NV | 216 | Buffalo, NY | 168 |
| Phoenix, AZ | 214 | Syracuse, NY | 168 |
| Bakersfield, CA | 202 | Binghamton, NY | 163 |
| Fresno, CA | 200 | Olympia, WA | 163 |
| Tucson, AZ | 198 | Seattle, WA | 160 |
| El Paso, TX | 194 | Cleveland, OH | 156 |
| Sacramento, CA | 193 | Akron, OH | 153 |
| Santa Barbara–Santa Maria–Lompoc, CA | 177 | Burlington, VT | 153 |
| Santa Rosa–Petaluma, CA | 176 | Pittsburgh, PA | 152 |
| | | Portland, OR | 152 |

Listed above are those metro areas described in the Place Profiles that have more than 175 clear days per year or more than 150 precipitation days per year. A precipitation day is one on which at least .01 inch of precipitation falls.

There are some excellent climates to be found in this region, especially in coastal locations.

The high-altitude regions that include the Rocky Mountains, the Cascades and Sierra Nevada, and the northern half of the Appalachian Mountains are resort areas because they all have cool, crisp, sunny summers with cold nights, and winters that provide plenty of snow for outdoor sports. These places are popular with people who enjoy a stimulating yet not too mild climate.

The Alaskan climate varies from bitterly cold in the northern tundra area—about one fifth of the state lies north of the Arctic Circle—to relatively mild temperatures in the interior and southern regions. The southern area experiences abundant rainfall, the Aleutian Islands chain being one of the stormiest regions in the world.

Hawaii is the only state situated in the tropical zone. The islands undergo relatively small temperature changes, with summer temperatures averaging only 4 degrees to 8 degrees higher than those in winter. Moisture-bearing trade winds from over the Pacific have a moderating effect on the heat associated with a tropical climate.

## JUDGING CLIMATE MILDNESS

Temperature affects human comfort and our daily range of activities more than any other climate-related variable. Bioclimatologists—scientists who study the connection between weather and health—generally agree that an average temperature of 65 degrees Fahrenheit with 65 percent humidity is ideal for work, play, and general well-being. *Places Rated* uses 65 degrees Fahrenheit as a standard for mildness in the discussions that follow.

Because most people tend to favor mild, sunny climates, *Places Rated* compares the 329 metro areas on the basis of climate mildness, using a combination of temperature and humidity factors. "Mild," as we use the term, does not necessarily mean warm but simply refers to the absence of great variations or extremes of temperature. A mild climate is characterized by cool summers and warm winters, with long falls and springs. *Places Rated* defines the mildest climates as those whose mean temperatures remain closest to 65 degrees Fahrenheit for the greatest percentage of time. Any deviations from this mean are labeled negative indicators, and are scored as such. Each place's final score indicates its climate mildness.

Nearly all climate and weather data presented in this chapter are from the National Oceanic and Atmospheric Administration (NOAA), the National Climatic Center, Asheville, North Carolina, and its two-volume publication *Local Climatological Data*. The National Climatic Center houses the world's largest climate data bank, with the equivalent of 25 miles of shelf space devoted solely to worldwide climate and weather data and research.

Some of the figures we present are referred to by the NOAA as 30-year normals—mean averages collected over three decades. Each ten years, the data for the new decade are added into the normal, and the data for the earliest ten years are dropped. Data are collected and averaged over this rather long period to flatten out irregularities and weather extremes. Atypical events such as blizzards and heat waves have little overall effect on a 30-year normal. Other figures are the means of annual records kept for periods ranging from a few years to more than 100 years. Mean temperatures are the average of the highest and lowest readings during a given period. For example, to determine the mean temperature for a particular month, the mean maximum temperature (the average of the highest daily readings during the month) and the mean minimum temperature (the average of the lowest) are averaged.

Each metro area is given a base number of 1,000 points, from which points are subtracted according to the following indicators, based on yearly averages:

1. *Very hot and very cold months.* Ten points are subtracted for each month in which the mean temperature is above 70 degrees or below 32. An additional 10 points are subtracted, for a total of 20 points, if the mean temperature is above 80 degrees or below 20.
2. *Seasonal temperature variation.* The difference in degrees Fahrenheit between the summer mean maximum temperature and the winter mean minimum is subtracted from the base score.
3. *Heating- and cooling-degree days.* The total number of these days per year is divided by 50, and the result is subtracted from the score. The base temperature for arriving at heating- and cooling-degree days is 65 degrees, the standard established by the American gas industry. If, for example, the average temperature on a summer day is 66 degrees, 1 degree of cooling is necessary, which counts as 1 cooling-degree day. Similarly, if the average temperature on a particular winter day is 55 degrees, 10 degrees of heating are needed, yielding 10 heating-degree days.
4. *Freezing days.* One point is subtracted for each day on which the average temperature is 32 degrees or below.
5. *Zero-degree days.* Five additional points are subtracted for each day the temperature drops to zero or below.
6. *Ninety-degree days.* Since relative humidity has a profound effect on felt heat and daily temperature range, points are subtracted in accordance with each location's mean relative humidity at noon in July, when high temperatures are most likely to occur (see the map on page 59). For each day with a high of at least 90 degrees, 4 points are subtracted if the metro area's July relative humidity is more than 60 percent, 3 points if relative humidity is 51 percent to 60 percent, 2 points if relative

### *Places Rated*'s Mildest and Wildest Metro Areas

● Mildest Climates
▲ Most Rigorous Climates

## Mild and Wild

With such a large variety of climates in the United States, a mix of places around the country qualify for the descriptions "mild" and "wild."

The area of greatest mildness is the Pacific Coast, as the map "*Places Rated*'s Mildest and Wildest Metro Areas" illustrates. This region contains 23 of the 35 top-ranked climates. The California metro areas owe their high ratings in part to their southerly locations, but all 23 (as well as the Honolulu metro area) are indebted to the moderating influence of the Pacific, which reduces their seasonal shifts to a minimum and practically rules out any zero-degree or 90-degree days.

The second mildest region in America is located in the southern Appalachian Mountains, in sections of Georgia, North and South Carolina, Tennessee, and Virginia. Here, southerly latitudes provide mild winters and long springs and falls, while high elevations offer relief from the hot, muggy summers that plague most other southern locations.

Other mild areas are to be found along the Atlantic coast in New York and Connecticut, and in the southern tip of the Rocky Mountains, near Albuquerque. This mountain region resembles the southern Appalachians, except that it is noticeably drier.

The climates of America's most rigorous metro areas are characterized by great swings in tempera-ture from season to season and from day to day. They have either a winter that is cold and long, a summer that is long, hot, and humid, or both. Most of these rigorous places are located inside the wide band stretching up the center of the continent that is known as the Great Interior.

Besides the northern and southern extremes of the Great Interior, rigorous climates are found in Alaska, northern New England, the northern Rockies, and the Florida peninsula. A characteristic of all these places is an excessive number of 90-degree days and/or zero-degree days.

In a few areas, good and bad weather bump up against each other. Metro areas located in northern New England experience long, cold, snowy winters and a lot of cloudiness, and thus we find Burlington, Vermont, and Manchester, New Hampshire, near the bottom of the *Places Rated* climate list. However, not far from up-country New Hampshire are the coastal waters of Cape Ann, Massachusetts, and the mild climate of Salem–Gloucester.

Similarly, although the neighboring Texas metro areas of Victoria and McAllen–Edinburg–Mission have rigorous climates because of the excessive heat and humidity during the summer, nearby Galveston–Texas City, with its coastal location and sea breezes, ranks as one of America's mildest metro areas.

humidity is 41 percent to 50 percent, and 1 point if relative humidity is 40 percent or lower.

(The alert reader will note two changes from the formula used in the earlier edition of *Places Rated Almanac* to determine climate mildness. Adjustments in the deductions for zero-degree days and for 90-degree days result in a slightly greater penalty for very cold days and for hot, humid weather.)

### Sample Comparison: Santa Rosa, California, and Waterloo–Cedar Falls, Iowa

The contrasts between Santa Rosa's Mediterranean-style maritime climate and the rugged continental climate of Waterloo–Cedar Falls are illustrated below using the *Places Rated* formula.

In the first scoring category—very hot and very cold months—Santa Rosa, nestled in the golden-brown hills of California wine country, has no months with average mean temperatures below 32 or above 70 degrees Fahrenheit (and thus, obviously, no months below 20 or above 80). Therefore, Santa Rosa loses no points for this criterion. Waterloo–Cedar Falls, on the other hand, has three months in which the mean temperature is below 32 (minus 10 points each) and one month with a mean temperature below 20 (minus 20 points). Furthermore, this metro area on Iowa's northern plains has warm summers, with two months whose average mean temperatures top 70 degrees (minus 20 points). Waterloo–Cedar Falls is penalized a total of 70 points in this category.

The average maximum summer temperature in Waterloo–Cedar Falls is 84, and its minimum winter temperature is 7, amounting to a seasonal temperature variation of 77 degrees and lowering its mildness score by a further 77 points. Santa Rosa's summer maximum and winter minimum readings, only 48 degrees apart, result in 48 penalty points.

Waterloo–Cedar Falls has 8,090 heating- and cooling-degree days. This number divided by 50 yields 162 points to be subtracted. Santa Rosa's 3,900 heating- and cooling-degree days give it a minus score of 78.

There are 159 freezing days each year in Waterloo–Cedar Falls (minus 159 points), and 31 days at zero or below, which reduce its score by another 155 points, or 5 points for each zero-degree day. (Any place with ten or more zero-degree days per year can be considered to have a rigorous winter.) And if that isn't bad enough, in summer Waterloo–Cedar Falls also has 15 ninety-degree days; a July noon relative humidity of about 47 percent means a penalty of 2 points for each of these days. These penalties for freezing days, zero-degree days, and 90-degree days amount to a substantial 344 points, and when added to its other deductions leave Waterloo–Cedar Falls with a final score of 347, only 18 places short of the bottom of the ranking list.

The California metro area, in contrast, has only 43 freezing days (for minus 43 points) and no zero-degree days. However, it does have 33 ninety-degree days, losing 3 points for each one due to a summer humidity of 55 percent. When all its deductions are totaled, Santa Rosa finishes with a mildness score of 732, or 19th out of the 329 metro areas.

## Places Rated: Metro Areas Ranked for Climate Mildness

Six criteria are used to determine a score for climate mildness: (1) very hot and very cold months, (2) seasonal temperature variation, (3) heating- and cooling-degree days, (4) freezing days, (5) zero-degree days, and (6) ninety-degree days.

Because the NOAA publication *Local Climatological Data* does not provide specific data for all metro areas, the scores for some places are calculated from data for the nearest substation (this information appears in the *NOAA Series 20*). Scores arrived at in this way are enclosed in parentheses. Metro areas that receive tie scores are given the same rank and are listed in alphabetical order.

Those metro areas described in the Place Profiles later on in this chapter are shown in boldface type in the lists below.

### Metro Areas from Best to Worst

| Places Rated Rank | Places Rated Score | Places Rated Rank | Places Rated Score | Places Rated Rank | Places Rated Score |
|---|---|---|---|---|---|
| 1. Oakland, CA | (910) | 5. **Los Angeles–Long Beach, CA** | 885 | 9. Salinas–Seaside–Monterey, CA | (843) |
| 1. **San Francisco, CA** | 910 | | | 9. Santa Cruz, CA | (843) |
| 3. **San Diego, CA** | 903 | 7. **Santa Barbara–Santa Maria–Lompoc, CA** | 855 | | |
| 4. Oxnard–Ventura, CA | (890) | | | 11. Vallejo–Fairfield–Napa, CA | (821) |
| 5. Anaheim–Santa Ana, CA | 885 | 8. San Jose, CA | (850) | 12. Bremerton, WA | (808) |

| Places Rated Rank | Places Rated Score |
|---|---|
| 12. **Seattle, WA** | 808 |
| 12. Tacoma, WA | (808) |
| 15. Bellingham, WA | (772) |
| | |
| 16. **Portland, OR** | 768 |
| 16. Vancouver, WA | (768) |
| 18. **Eugene–Springfield, OR** | 741 |
| 19. **Santa Rosa–Petaluma, CA** | (732) |
| 20. Galveston–Texas City, TX | (727) |
| | |
| 21. **Olympia, WA** | 726 |
| 22. **Honolulu, HI** | 717 |
| 23. Salem, OR | 716 |
| 24. **Atlanta, GA** | 696 |
| 25. Asheville, NC | 694 |
| | |
| 26. **Knoxville, TN** | 670 |
| 27. Redding, CA | (664) |
| 27. Richland–Kennewick–Pasco, WA | (664) |
| 29. **Johnson City–Kingsport–Bristol, TN–VA** | 663 |
| 30. **Albuquerque, NM** | 659 |
| | |
| 31. Nassau–Suffolk, NY | (656) |
| 32. **Greenville–Spartanburg, SC** | 655 |
| 33. **Roanoke, VA** | 652 |
| 34. Bridgeport–Milford, CT | 648 |
| 34. Norwalk, CT | (648) |
| | |
| 34. Stamford, CT | (648) |
| 37. **Raleigh–Durham, NC** | 647 |
| 38. **Charlotte–Gastonia–Rock Hill, NC–SC** | 644 |
| 38. Salem–Gloucester, MA | (644) |
| 40. Fall River, MA–RI | (643) |
| | |
| 40. **New Bedford, MA** | (643) |
| 42. Lynchburg, VA | 642 |
| 43. Modesto, CA | (639) |
| 44. **New York, NY** | 638 |
| 45. Burlington, NC | (637) |
| | |
| 46. Huntington–Ashland, WV–KY–OH | 636 |
| 46. Trenton, NJ | (636) |
| 48. **Lexington–Fayette, KY** | 635 |
| 49. **Miami–Hialeah, FL** | 634 |
| 50. **Norfolk–Virginia Beach–Newport News, VA** | 632 |
| | |
| 51. **Washington, DC–MD–VA** | 631 |
| 52. **Philadelphia, PA–NJ** | 630 |
| 53. **Charleston, WV** | 627 |
| 54. Greensboro–Winston-Salem–High Point, NC | 626 |
| 55. Stockton, CA | 625 |
| | |
| 56. **Boston, MA** | 623 |
| 56. Hickory, NC | (623) |
| 58. Charlottesville, VA | (618) |
| 59. Parkersburg–Marietta, WV–OH | 617 |
| 60. **Louisville, KY–IN** | 616 |
| | |
| 61. **Atlantic City, NJ** | 615 |
| 61. Monmouth–Ocean, NJ | (615) |
| 61. Riverside–San Bernardino, CA | (615) |
| 61. Vineland–Millville–Bridgeton, NJ | (615) |
| 65. Reading, PA | (614) |
| | |
| 66. **Birmingham, AL** | 612 |
| 67. **Medford, OR** | 611 |
| 68. **Amarillo, TX** | 609 |

| Places Rated Rank | Places Rated Score |
|---|---|
| 69. Yuba City, CA | (608) |
| 70. Erie, PA | 605 |
| | |
| 71. **Lubbock, TX** | 604 |
| 72. **Chico, CA** | (603) |
| 72. **Midland, TX** | 603 |
| 72. Odessa, TX | (603) |
| 75. Fort Pierce, FL | (602) |
| | |
| 76. Athens, GA | 601 |
| 76. Jersey City, NJ | (601) |
| 76. Newark, NJ | 601 |
| 79. **Huntsville, AL** | 600 |
| 79. **Nashville, TN** | 600 |
| | |
| 81. Wilmington, DE–NJ–MD | 597 |
| 82. Middletown, CT | (593) |
| 83. **Boise City, ID** | 592 |
| 83. **El Paso, TX** | 592 |
| 85. Anderson, SC | (591) |
| | |
| 85. **Cumberland, MD–WV** | (591) |
| 87. **Tucson, AZ** | 589 |
| 88. Beaver County, PA | (586) |
| 88. Pawtucket–Woonsocket–Attleboro, RI–MA | (586) |
| 88. **Pittsburgh, PA** | 586 |
| | |
| 88. Providence, RI | 586 |
| 92. **Richmond–Petersburg, VA** | 585 |
| 93. **Biloxi–Gulfport, MS** | (584) |
| 93. **Cincinnati, OH–KY–IN** | 584 |
| 93. Pascagoula, MS | (584) |
| | |
| 96. New Haven–Meriden, CT | (583) |
| 96. New London–Norwich, CT–RI | (583) |
| 98. Melbourne–Titusville–Palm Bay, FL | (582) |
| 99. Joplin, MO | (580) |
| 99. Muskegon, MI | 580 |
| | |
| 101. **Cleveland, OH** | 579 |
| 101. Lorain–Elyria, OH | (579) |
| 103. **Chattanooga, TN–GA** | 576 |
| 103. **Sacramento, CA** | 576 |
| 105. **Akron, OH** | 575 |
| | |
| 105. Brockton, MA | (575) |
| 105. Canton, OH | (575) |
| 105. Scranton–Wilkes-Barre, PA | 575 |
| 105. **State College, PA** | (575) |
| 110. **Spokane, WA** | 574 |
| | |
| 111. Fort Lauderdale–Hollywood–Pompano Beach, FL | (572) |
| 112. **Buffalo, NY** | 571 |
| 113. Sharon, PA | (570) |
| 113. Youngstown–Warren, OH | 570 |
| 115. **Charleston, SC** | 569 |
| | |
| 115. Danbury, CT | (569) |
| 115. Waterbury, CT | (569) |
| 118. Hagerstown, MD | (568) |
| 119. **Baltimore, MD** | 567 |
| 120. Benton Harbor, MI | (566) |
| | |
| 121. Jacksonville, NC | (564) |
| 121. **Wilmington, NC** | 564 |
| 123. Worcester, MA | 562 |
| 124. Altoona, PA | (561) |
| 124. Daytona Beach, FL | 561 |
| | |
| 124. Fayetteville, NC | (561) |
| 127. Anniston, AL | (560) |

| Places Rated Rank | Places Rated Score |
|---|---|
| 127. **Bakersfield, CA** | 560 |
| 129. Allentown–Bethlehem, PA–NJ | 559 |
| 129. Bergen–Passaic, NJ | (559) |
| | |
| 129. **Fresno, CA** | 559 |
| 129. Lancaster, PA | 559 |
| 129. Middlesex–Somerset–Hunterdon, NJ | (559) |
| 134. Bloomington, IN | (558) |
| 134. **Columbus, OH** | 558 |
| | |
| 134. Mansfield, OH | 558 |
| 134. Williamsport, PA | 558 |
| 138. **Indianapolis, IN** | 557 |
| 138. Terre Haute, IN | (557) |
| 140. **Harrisburg–Lebanon–Carlisle, PA** | (556) |
| | |
| 140. **Las Vegas, NV** | 556 |
| 142. Niagara Falls, NY | (554) |
| 142. **Oklahoma City, OK** | 554 |
| 144. Florence, SC | (552) |
| 144. Las Cruces, NM | (552) |
| | |
| 146. **Binghamton, NY** | 550 |
| 146. **Evansville, IN–KY** | 550 |
| 148. Fayetteville–Springdale, AR | (549) |
| 148. **Kansas City, KS** | 549 |
| 148. Kansas City, MO | 549 |
| | |
| 151. Lawrence–Haverhill, MA–NH | (548) |
| 151. **Syracuse, NY** | 548 |
| 151. Utica–Rome, NY | (548) |
| 154. Johnstown, PA | (547) |
| 155. Ann Arbor, MI | (546) |
| | |
| 155. Florence, AL | (546) |
| 157. Danville, VA | (545) |
| 157. South Bend–Mishawaka, IN | (545) |
| 159. Clarksville–Hopkinsville, TN–KY | (544) |
| 159. **Dallas, TX** | 544 |
| | |
| 159. Dayton–Springfield, OH | 544 |
| 159. **Springfield, MO** | 544 |
| 163. Visalia–Tulare–Porterville, CA | (543) |
| 164. Hamilton–Middletown, OH | (542) |
| 164. **Savannah, GA** | 542 |
| | |
| 164. Steubenville–Weirton, OH–WV | (542) |
| 164. Wheeling, WV–OH | (542) |
| 168. **Columbia, MO** | (541) |
| 168. **Salt Lake City–Ogden, UT** | 541 |
| 170. Flint, MI | 540 |
| | |
| 170. York, PA | (540) |
| 172. Nashua, NH | (538) |
| 173. Alton–Granite City, IL | (537) |
| 173. East St. Louis–Belleville, IL | 537 |
| 173. **St. Louis, MO–IL** | 537 |
| | |
| 176. **Detroit, MI** | 536 |
| 176. Fort Walton Beach, FL | (536) |
| 176. Panama City, FL | 536 |
| 176. Pensacola, FL | 536 |
| 176. **Phoenix, AZ** | 536 |
| | |
| 176. Rochester, NY | 536 |
| 182. **Reno, NV** | 535 |
| 182. **Yakima, WA** | 535 |
| 184. **Augusta, GA–SC** | 534 |
| 185. Anderson, IN | (530) |

| Places Rated Rank | Places Rated Score | Places Rated Rank | Places Rated Score | Places Rated Rank | Places Rated Score |
|---|---|---|---|---|---|
| 185. Muncie, IN | (530) | 234. Fort Collins–Loveland, CO | (490) | 277. Tampa–St. Petersburg–Clearwater, FL | 440 |
| 185. Tulsa, OK | 530 | 234. Greeley, CO | (490) | 282. Austin, TX | 435 |
| 188. Fort Worth–Arlington, TX | (528) | | | 283. Cedar Rapids, IA | (434) |
| 189. Battle Creek, MI | (527) | 234. Lewiston–Auburn, ME | (490) | 283. Iowa City, IA | (434) |
| 189. Kalamazoo, MI | (527) | 237. Poughkeepsie, NY | (488) | 285. Lafayette, LA | (429) |
| | | 237. San Angelo, TX | 488 | | |
| 191. Colorado Springs, CO | 526 | 239. Bloomington–Normal, IL | (487) | 286. Baton Rouge, LA | 427 |
| 191. Columbia, SC | 526 | 240. Gary–Hammond, IN | (483) | 286. Houma–Thibodaux, LA | (427) |
| 191. Gadsden, AL | (526) | | | 288. Houston, TX | 424 |
| 191. Lowell, MA–NH | 526 | 240. Kankakee, IL | (483) | 288. Laredo, TX | (424) |
| 195. Champaign–Urbana–Rantoul, IL | (525) | 240. Montgomery, AL | 483 | 290. Beaumont–Port Arthur, TX | 423 |
| | | 240. Portland, ME | 483 | | |
| 196. Owensboro, KY | (524) | 244. Fort Smith, AR–OK | 482 | 290. Brazoria, TX | (423) |
| 196. Sherman–Denison, TX | (524) | 244. Pittsfield, MA | (482) | 292. Dubuque, IA | 419 |
| 196. Springfield, IL | 524 | | | 293. Jackson, MS | 412 |
| 199. Lima, OH | (522) | 246. Decatur, IL | (480) | 293. Waco, TX | 412 |
| 200. Abilene, TX | 521 | 246. Lansing–East Lansing, MI | 480 | 295. Great Falls, MT | 410 |
| | | 248. Joliet, IL | (479) | | |
| 200. Denver, CO | 521 | 248. Lawton, OK | (479) | 296. Manchester, NH | (404) |
| 200. Elkhart–Goshen, IN | (521) | 250. Albany–Schenectady–Troy, NY | 476 | 296. Tallahassee, FL | 404 |
| 203. Alexandria, LA | 520 | | | 298. Gainesville, FL | (402) |
| 204. Jackson, MI | (518) | | | 299. Casper, WY | 401 |
| 204. Toledo, OH | 518 | 250. Glens Falls, NY | (476) | 300. Lincoln, NE | 398 |
| | | 252. St. Joseph, MO | (475) | | |
| 206. Columbus, GA–AL | (517) | 253. Aurora–Elgin, IL | (474) | 300. San Antonio, TX | 398 |
| 207. Bristol, CT | (516) | 254. Tuscaloosa, AL | (470) | 302. Appleton–Oshkosh–Neenah, WI | (396) |
| 207. Hartford, CT | 516 | 255. Lake Charles, LA | 469 | 303. Sarasota, FL | (391) |
| 207. New Britain, CT | (516) | | | 304. Sioux City, IA–NE | 385 |
| 210. Saginaw–Bay City–Midland, MI | (515) | 255. Portsmouth–Dover–Rochester, NH–ME | (469) | 305. Bryan–College Station, TX | (383) |
| | | 257. Albany, GA | (468) | | |
| 211. Chicago, IL | 514 | 258. Elmira, NY | (467) | 305. Burlington, VT | 383 |
| 211. Lake County, IL | 514 | 258. Texarkana, TX–Texarkana, AR | (467) | 307. Madison, WI | 378 |
| 211. Memphis, TN–AR–MS | 514 | | | 308. Green Bay, WI | 367 |
| 214. Grand Rapids, MI | 513 | 260. Janesville–Beloit, WI | (466) | 309. Killeen–Temple, TX | (365) |
| 214. Lawrence, KS | (513) | | | 310. Corpus Christi, TX | 362 |
| | | 260. Rockford, IL | 466 | | |
| 216. Kokomo, IN | (512) | 262. Pine Bluff, AR | (463) | 311. La Crosse, WI | 352 |
| 217. Fort Wayne, IN | 509 | 263. Enid, OK | (461) | 312. Waterloo–Cedar Falls, IA | (347) |
| 217. Orange County, NY | (509) | 264. Milwaukee, WI | 460 | 313. Fort Myers, FL | (342) |
| 217. West Palm Beach–Boca Raton–Delray Beach, FL | 509 | 265. Boulder–Longmont, CO | (459) | 314. Dothan, AL | (336) |
| | | | | 314. Victoria, TX | 336 |
| 220. Shreveport, LA | 508 | 266. Jacksonville, FL | 457 | | |
| | | 266. Orlando, FL | 457 | 316. Ocala, FL | (333) |
| 221. Fitchburg–Leominster, MA | (507) | 268. Wichita Falls, TX | 456 | 317. Rochester, MN | 308 |
| 222. Topeka, KS | 501 | 269. Monroe, LA | (455) | 317. Wausau, WI | (308) |
| 223. Longview–Marshall, TX | (500) | 270. Springfield, MA | (453) | 319. Lakeland–Winter Haven, FL | (307) |
| 223. Provo–Orem, UT | (500) | | | 320. Minneapolis–St. Paul, MN–WI | 293 |
| 223. Tyler, TX | (500) | 271. Billings, MT | 452 | | |
| | | 272. Bangor, ME | (451) | | |
| 226. New Orleans, LA | 498 | 273. Macon–Warner Robins, GA | (447) | 321. Sioux Falls, SD | 276 |
| 227. Little Rock–North Little Rock, AR | 497 | 274. Des Moines, IA | 444 | 322. Eau Claire, WI | 257 |
| 227. Pueblo, CO | 497 | 275. Mobile, AL | 442 | 323. McAllen–Edinburg–Mission, TX | (238) |
| 229. Kenosha, WI | (496) | | | 324. Anchorage, AK | 195 |
| 229. Racine, WI | (496) | 275. Sheboygan, WI | (442) | 324. St. Cloud, MN | (195) |
| | | 277. Bradenton, FL | (440) | | |
| 231. Lafayette, IN | (494) | 277. Brownsville–Harlingen, TX | 440 | 326. Duluth, MN–WI | 193 |
| 231. Wichita, KS | 494 | 277. Davenport–Rock Island–Moline, IA–IL | 440 | 327. Bismarck, ND | 149 |
| 233. Peoria, IL | 491 | 277. Omaha, NE–IA | 440 | 328. Fargo–Moorhead, ND–MN | 148 |
| | | | | 329. Grand Forks, ND | (105) |

## Metro Areas Listed Alphabetically

| Metro Area | Places Rated Rank | Metro Area | Places Rated Rank | Metro Area | Places Rated Rank |
|---|---|---|---|---|---|
| **Abilene, TX** | 200 | **Charleston, WV** | 53 | **Galveston–Texas City, TX** | 20 |
| **Akron, OH** | 105 | **Charlotte–Gastonia–Rock Hill,** | | Gary–Hammond, IN | 240 |
| Albany, GA | 257 | **NC–SC** | 38 | Glens Falls, NY | 250 |
| Albany–Schenectady–Troy, NY | 250 | Charlottesville, VA | 58 | | |
| **Albuquerque, NM** | 30 | **Chattanooga, TN–GA** | 103 | Grand Forks, ND | 329 |
| | | **Chicago, IL** | 211 | **Grand Rapids, MI** | 214 |
| Alexandria, LA | 203 | | | **Great Falls, MT** | 295 |
| Allentown–Bethlehem, PA–NJ | 129 | **Chico, CA** | 72 | Greeley, CO | 234 |
| Alton–Granite City, IL | 173 | **Cincinnati, OH–KY–IN** | 93 | **Green Bay, WI** | 308 |
| Altoona, PA | 124 | Clarksville–Hopkinsville, TN–KY | 159 | | |
| **Amarillo, TX** | 68 | Cleveland, OH | 101 | Greensboro–Winston-Salem– | |
| | | Colorado Springs, CO | 191 | High Point, NC | 54 |
| Anaheim–Santa Ana, CA | 5 | | | **Greenville–Spartanburg, SC** | 32 |
| **Anchorage, AK** | 324 | Columbia, MO | 168 | Hagerstown, MD | 118 |
| Anderson, IN | 185 | **Columbia, SC** | 191 | Hamilton–Middletown, OH | 164 |
| Anderson, SC | 85 | **Columbus, GA–AL** | 206 | **Harrisburg–Lebanon–Carlisle, PA** | 140 |
| Ann Arbor, MI | 155 | **Columbus, OH** | 134 | | |
| | | Corpus Christi, TX | 310 | **Hartford, CT** | 207 |
| Anniston, AL | 127 | | | Hickory, NC | 56 |
| Appleton–Oshkosh–Neenah, WI | 302 | **Cumberland, MD–WV** | 85 | **Honolulu, HI** | 22 |
| **Asheville, NC** | 25 | **Dallas, TX** | 159 | Houma–Thibodaux, LA | 286 |
| Athens, GA | 76 | Danbury, CT | 115 | **Houston, TX** | 288 |
| **Atlanta, GA** | 24 | Danville, VA | 157 | | |
| | | **Davenport–Rock Island–Moline,** | | Huntington–Ashland, WV–KY–OH | 46 |
| **Atlantic City, NJ** | 61 | **IA–IL** | 277 | **Huntsville, AL** | 79 |
| **Augusta, GA–SC** | 184 | | | **Indianapolis, IN** | 138 |
| Aurora–Elgin, IL | 253 | Dayton–Springfield, OH | 159 | Iowa City, IA | 283 |
| **Austin, TX** | 282 | Daytona Beach, FL | 124 | Jackson, MI | 204 |
| **Bakersfield, CA** | 127 | Decatur, IL | 246 | | |
| | | **Denver, CO** | 200 | **Jackson, MS** | 293 |
| **Baltimore, MD** | 119 | **Des Moines, IA** | 274 | **Jacksonville, FL** | 266 |
| **Bangor, ME** | 272 | | | Jacksonville, NC | 121 |
| Baton Rouge, LA | 286 | **Detroit, MI** | 176 | Janesville–Beloit, WI | 260 |
| Battle Creek, MI | 189 | Dothan, AL | 314 | Jersey City, NJ | 76 |
| Beaumont–Port Arthur, TX | 290 | Dubuque, IA | 292 | | |
| | | **Duluth, MN–WI** | 326 | **Johnson City–Kingsport–** | |
| Beaver County, PA | 88 | East St. Louis–Belleville, IL | 173 | **Bristol, TN–VA** | 29 |
| Bellingham, WA | 15 | | | Johnstown, PA | 154 |
| Benton Harbor, MI | 120 | Eau Claire, WI | 322 | Joliet, IL | 248 |
| Bergen–Passaic, NJ | 129 | **El Paso, TX** | 83 | Joplin, MO | 99 |
| **Billings, MT** | 271 | Elkhart–Goshen, IN | 200 | Kalamazoo, MI | 189 |
| | | Elmira, NY | 258 | | |
| **Biloxi–Gulfport, MS** | 93 | Enid, OK | 263 | Kankakee, IL | 240 |
| **Binghamton, NY** | 146 | | | **Kansas City, KS** | 148 |
| **Birmingham, AL** | 66 | Erie, PA | 70 | Kansas City, MO | 148 |
| **Bismarck, ND** | 327 | **Eugene–Springfield, OR** | 18 | Kenosha, WI | 229 |
| Bloomington, IN | 134 | **Evansville, IN–KY** | 146 | Killeen–Temple, TX | 309 |
| | | Fall River, MA–RI | 40 | | |
| Bloomington–Normal, IL | 239 | **Fargo–Moorhead, ND–MN** | 328 | **Knoxville, TN** | 26 |
| **Boise City, ID** | 83 | | | Kokomo, IN | 216 |
| **Boston, MA** | 56 | Fayetteville, NC | 124 | **La Crosse, WI** | 311 |
| Boulder–Longmont, CO | 265 | Fayetteville–Springdale, AR | 148 | Lafayette, IN | 231 |
| Bradenton, FL | 277 | Fitchburg–Leominster, MA | 221 | Lafayette, LA | 285 |
| | | Flint, MI | 170 | | |
| Brazoria, TX | 290 | Florence, AL | 155 | Lake Charles, LA | 255 |
| Bremerton, WA | 12 | | | Lake County, IL | 211 |
| Bridgeport–Milford, CT | 34 | Florence, SC | 144 | Lakeland–Winter Haven, FL | 319 |
| Bristol, CT | 207 | Fort Collins–Loveland, CO | 234 | Lancaster, PA | 129 |
| Brockton, MA | 105 | Fort Lauderdale–Hollywood– | | Lansing–East Lansing, MI | 246 |
| | | Pompano Beach, FL | 111 | | |
| **Brownsville–Harlingen, TX** | 277 | **Fort Myers, FL** | 313 | Laredo, TX | 288 |
| Bryan–College Station, TX | 305 | Fort Pierce, FL | 75 | Las Cruces, NM | 144 |
| **Buffalo, NY** | 112 | | | **Las Vegas, NV** | 140 |
| Burlington, NC | 45 | **Fort Smith, AR–OK** | 244 | Lawrence, KS | 214 |
| **Burlington, VT** | 305 | Fort Walton Beach, FL | 176 | Lawrence–Haverhill, MA–NH | 151 |
| | | **Fort Wayne, IN** | 217 | | |
| Canton, OH | 105 | Fort Worth–Arlington, TX | 188 | Lawton, OK | 248 |
| **Casper, WY** | 299 | **Fresno, CA** | 129 | Lewiston–Auburn, ME | 234 |
| Cedar Rapids, IA | 283 | | | **Lexington–Fayette, KY** | 48 |
| Champaign–Urbana–Rantoul, IL | 195 | Gadsden, AL | 191 | Lima, OH | 199 |
| **Charleston, SC** | 115 | Gainesville, FL | 298 | **Lincoln, NE** | 300 |

| Metro Area | Places Rated Rank | Metro Area | Places Rated Rank | Metro Area | Places Rated Rank |
|---|---|---|---|---|---|
| **Little Rock–North Little Rock, AR** | 227 | Panama City, FL | 176 | Sharon, PA | 113 |
| Longview–Marshall, TX | 223 | Parkersburg–Marietta, WV–OH | 59 | Sheboygan, WI | 275 |
| Lorain–Elyria, OH | 101 | Pascagoula, MS | 93 | | |
| **Los Angeles–Long Beach, CA** | 5 | | | Sherman–Denison, TX | 196 |
| **Louisville, KY–IN** | 60 | Pawtucket–Woonsocket–Attleboro, RI–MA | 88 | **Shreveport, LA** | 220 |
| | | Pensacola, FL | 176 | **Sioux City, IA–NE** | 304 |
| Lowell, MA–NH | 191 | **Peoria, IL** | 233 | **Sioux Falls, SD** | 321 |
| **Lubbock, TX** | 71 | **Philadelphia, PA–NJ** | 52 | South Bend–Mishawaka, IN | 157 |
| Lynchburg, VA | 42 | **Phoenix, AZ** | 176 | | |
| Macon–Warner Robins, GA | 273 | | | **Spokane, WA** | 110 |
| **Madison, WI** | 307 | Pine Bluff, AR | 262 | **Springfield, IL** | 196 |
| | | **Pittsburgh, PA** | 88 | Springfield, MA | 270 |
| **Manchester, NH** | 296 | Pittsfield, MA | 244 | **Springfield, MO** | 159 |
| Mansfield, OH | 134 | **Portland, ME** | 240 | Stamford, CT | 34 |
| McAllen–Edinburg–Mission, TX | 323 | **Portland, OR** | 16 | | |
| **Medford, OR** | 67 | | | **State College, PA** | 105 |
| Melbourne–Titusville–Palm Bay, FL | 98 | Portsmouth–Dover–Rochester, NH–ME | 255 | Steubenville–Weirton, OH–WV | 164 |
| | | Poughkeepsie, NY | 237 | Stockton, CA | 55 |
| **Memphis, TN–AR–MS** | 211 | Providence, RI | 88 | **Syracuse, NY** | 151 |
| Miami–Hialeah, FL | 49 | Provo–Orem, UT | 223 | Tacoma, WA | 12 |
| Middlesex–Somerset–Hunterdon, NJ | 129 | Pueblo, CO | 227 | | |
| Middletown, CT | 82 | | | **Tallahassee, FL** | 296 |
| **Midland, TX** | 72 | Racine, WI | 229 | **Tampa–St. Petersburg–Clearwater, FL** | 277 |
| | | **Raleigh–Durham, NC** | 37 | Terre Haute, IN | 138 |
| **Milwaukee, WI** | 264 | Reading, PA | 65 | Texarkana, TX–Texarkana, AR | 258 |
| **Minneapolis–St. Paul, MN–WI** | 320 | Redding, CA | 27 | **Toledo, OH** | 204 |
| **Mobile, AL** | 275 | **Reno, NV** | 182 | | |
| Modesto, CA | 43 | | | Topeka, KS | 222 |
| Monmouth–Ocean, NJ | 61 | Richland–Kennewick–Pasco, WA | 27 | Trenton, NJ | 46 |
| | | **Richmond–Petersburg, VA** | 92 | **Tucson, AZ** | 87 |
| Monroe, LA | 269 | Riverside–San Bernardino, CA | 61 | **Tulsa, OK** | 185 |
| **Montgomery, AL** | 240 | **Roanoke, VA** | 33 | Tuscaloosa, AL | 254 |
| Muncie, IN | 185 | **Rochester, MN** | 317 | | |
| Muskegon, MI | 99 | | | Tyler, TX | 223 |
| Nashua, NH | 172 | Rochester, NY | 176 | Utica–Rome, NY | 151 |
| | | **Rockford, IL** | 260 | Vallejo–Fairfield–Napa, CA | 11 |
| **Nashville, TN** | 79 | **Sacramento, CA** | 103 | Vancouver, WA | 16 |
| Nassau–Suffolk, NY | 31 | **Saginaw–Bay City–Midland, MI** | 210 | Victoria, TX | 314 |
| **New Bedford, MA** | 40 | St. Cloud, MN | 324 | | |
| New Britain, CT | 207 | | | Vineland–Millville–Bridgeton, NJ | 61 |
| New Haven–Meriden, CT | 96 | St. Joseph, MO | 252 | Visalia–Tulare–Porterville, CA | 163 |
| | | **St. Louis, MO–IL** | 173 | Waco, TX | 293 |
| New London–Norwich, CT–RI | 96 | Salem, OR | 23 | **Washington, DC–MD–VA** | 51 |
| **New Orleans, LA** | 226 | Salem–Gloucester, MA | 38 | Waterbury, CT | 115 |
| **New York, NY** | 44 | Salinas–Seaside–Monterey, CA | 9 | | |
| Newark, NJ | 76 | | | **Waterloo–Cedar Falls, IA** | 312 |
| Niagara Falls, NY | 142 | **Salt Lake City–Ogden, UT** | 168 | Wausau, WI | 317 |
| | | **San Angelo, TX** | 237 | West Palm Beach–Boca Raton–Delray Beach, FL | 217 |
| **Norfolk–Virginia Beach–Newport News, VA** | 50 | **San Antonio, TX** | 300 | Wheeling, WV–OH | 164 |
| Norwalk, CT | 34 | **San Diego, CA** | 3 | **Wichita, KS** | 231 |
| Oakland, CA | 1 | **San Francisco, CA** | 1 | | |
| Ocala, FL | 316 | | | Wichita Falls, TX | 268 |
| Odessa, TX | 72 | San Jose, CA | 8 | Williamsport, PA | 134 |
| | | **Santa Barbara–Santa Maria–Lompoc, CA** | 7 | Wilmington, DE–NJ–MD | 81 |
| **Oklahoma City, OK** | 142 | Santa Cruz, CA | 9 | **Wilmington, NC** | 121 |
| **Olympia, WA** | 21 | **Santa Rosa–Petaluma, CA** | 19 | Worcester, MA | 123 |
| **Omaha, NE–IA** | 277 | Sarasota, FL | 303 | | |
| Orange County, NY | 217 | | | **Yakima, WA** | 182 |
| **Orlando, FL** | 266 | Savannah, GA | 164 | York, PA | 170 |
| | | Scranton–Wilkes-Barre, PA | 105 | Youngstown–Warren, OH | 113 |
| Owensboro, KY | 196 | **Seattle, WA** | 12 | Yuba City, CA | 69 |
| Oxnard–Ventura, CA | 4 | | | | |

# Place Profiles: Climate and Terrain of 140 Selected Weather Stations

The pages that follow are brief profiles of 140 weather stations, which were carefully selected to present a sampling of reports from weather stations all over the country. The figures given in each profile are taken from extensive government data tables. The narrative summaries, describing climate and terrain, are condensations of those that appear in the NOAA publication *Local Climatological Data*.

These summaries provide brief descriptions of each location and point out important or distinctive features of the climate and the local terrain. When terrain is described in the profiles, it is usually in connection with the effect—if any—it has on the climate in the immediate area. But few people would deny that terrain is an important element in its own right; to many it's as important as climate. Some people prefer mountains or seacoast, others rolling plains or forest. Rather than attempt to judge, rate, or score terrain, *Places Rated* simply describes it briefly and lets you decide.

The table of average temperatures on the right-hand side of each profile is a detailed and extremely useful set of data, from which you can get a clear idea of the temperature ranges, averages, and extremes of each place. For example, if you want to know how hot it gets in Albuquerque in July, simply look at the table in Albuquerque's profile. There you'll see that in July the daily high temperatures (which usually occur in midafternoon) average 92.2 degrees Fahrenheit. That sounds hot, and it is. But note that the average low, or minimum, temperature for the same month is only 65.2 degrees. The minimum temperature generally occurs in the early hours of the morning. Therefore,

even a quick glance at these temperatures tells us that Albuquerque in the summer has hot days and cool nights, with a mean temperature of less than 80 degrees (78.7). This is in keeping with Albuquerque's dry, desert location and altitude of about 5,000 feet.

Rounding out the weather picture of each locale are data such as wind speed, amount of snow and rain, number of heating- and cooling-degree days, clear and cloudy days, storms, very hot and cold days, and precipitation days (days on which there is at least .01 inch of precipitation). To derive the greatest benefit from these assorted indicators, compare two or more metro areas. Which has more snow? More rain? More 90-degree days? Comparing two places you're interested in may lead to your deciding which to visit first.

A unique visual device in each profile is the circular graph showing the length of each season. These graphs are prepared from a formula developed by *Places Rated* and reflect the theory that seasonal change should be defined and measured by weather conditions, human activities, and growth or dormancy of plant life rather than by the calendar. In *Places Rated Almanac*, the seasons are defined as follows: Summer begins when the mean monthly temperature rises above 60 degrees Fahrenheit; summer ends when it falls below 60. Winter begins when the average daily low falls below 32 degrees and ends when it rises above that mark. The remaining portions of the year constitute fall and spring. (In the seasonal graphs, winter is shown by the black segments, spring and fall appear as gray, and summer is white.)

A star preceding a metro area's name highlights it as one of the top 25 places for climate mildness.

---

## Abilene, TX

**Terrain:** Rolling plains, treeless except for mesquite, broken by low hills to the south and west. Land rises gently to the south and east. Primarily cattle-grazing terrain, with some dry-land cotton and feed.
**Climate:** Lies roughly midway between the humid climate of East Texas and the semiarid climate to the west and north. Most rain occurs in thunderstorms during April, May, June, September, and October. Severe storms or tornadoes are rare. Summer brings hot days and cool nights, with temperatures dropping to the 60s or 70s most nights. High summer temperatures are usually associated with clear skies, southwesterly winds, and dry air. Low relative humidity, however, makes the climate comfortable. The region receives almost 70% of possible sunshine over the year. Rapid temperature changes occur in winter, as polar air replaces warm, moist tropical air. Temperatures may fall 30 degrees in one hour. Strongest winds come from the north and often bring cold and severe weather.

**Pluses:** Warm, sunny, and dry.     **Minuses:** Hot summer days; can be dusty.

**Places Rated Score: 521**     **Places Rated Rank: 200**

**Elevation: 1,790 feet**

Relative Humidity: 59%
Wind Speed: 12.2 mph

Seasonal Change

Annual Rainfall 24 in

Annual Snowfall 5 in

Clear 148 days     Partly Cloudy 98 days     Cloudy 119 days

Precipitation Days: 65     Storm Days: 42

| Average Temperatures | | | |
|---|---|---|---|
| | Daily High | Daily Low | Monthly Mean |
| January | 55.7 | 31.7 | 43.7 |
| February | 59.9 | 35.9 | 47.9 |
| March | 67.3 | 41.7 | 54.5 |
| April | 77.7 | 52.7 | 65.2 |
| May | 83.9 | 60.8 | 72.4 |
| June | 91.6 | 69.0 | 80.3 |
| July | 95.3 | 72.4 | 83.9 |
| August | 95.3 | 71.9 | 83.6 |
| September | 87.5 | 64.6 | 76.1 |
| October | 78.0 | 54.2 | 66.1 |
| November | 66.2 | 42.0 | 54.1 |
| December | 58.2 | 34.5 | 46.4 |

Zero-Degree Days: 0
Freezing Days: 56
90-Degree Days: 89
Heating- and Cooling-Degree Days: 5,076

## Akron, OH

**Terrain:** Rolling, with highest elevations almost 1,300 feet above sea level. Many small lakes provide water for local industry as well as recreation for the densely populated region. The area is mainly industrial; the number of agricultural operations has diminished rapidly in recent years.

**Climate:** Lake Erie has a considerable effect on area weather, tempering cold air masses during the winter and contributing to brief but heavy snow squalls until the lake freezes over. Snowfall is much heavier north of the weather station near the lake, in the area commonly referred to as the Snow Belt. Spring comes late here. Summers are moderately warm, though humid. September, October, and November are pleasant, but there is considerable morning fog. Average date of last freeze: April 30. First freeze: October 22.

**Pluses:** Pleasant falls.

**Minuses:** Cold, wet winters with heavy snowfalls; damp and cloudy.

**Places Rated Score: 575**

**Places Rated Rank: 105**

**Elevation: 1,027 feet**

Relative Humidity: 71%
Wind Speed: 9.9 mph

Seasonal Change

Annual Rainfall 35 in

Annual Snowfall 48 in

Clear 70 days | Partly Cloudy 101 days | Cloudy 194 days

Precipitation Days: 153  Storm Days: 40

| Average Temperatures | | | |
|---|---|---|---|
| | Daily High | Daily Low | Monthly Mean |
| January | 33.9 | 18.6 | 26.3 |
| February | 36.0 | 19.4 | 27.7 |
| March | 45.4 | 26.9 | 36.2 |
| April | 59.3 | 37.7 | 48.5 |
| May | 69.8 | 47.5 | 58.7 |
| June | 79.4 | 57.1 | 68.3 |
| July | 82.6 | 60.8 | 71.7 |
| August | 81.3 | 59.3 | 70.3 |
| September | 74.7 | 52.7 | 63.7 |
| October | 63.7 | 42.8 | 53.3 |
| November | 48.6 | 32.7 | 40.7 |
| December | 36.5 | 22.2 | 29.4 |

Zero-Degree Days: 5
Freezing Days: 128
90-Degree Days: 7
Heating- and Cooling-Degree Days: 6,858

## Albany–Schenectady–Troy, NY

**Terrain:** On the west bank of the Hudson River 150 miles north of New York City and 8 miles south of the confluence of the Hudson and Mohawk rivers. The point at which the city meets the river is only a few feet above sea level. Eleven miles west, the Helderberg escarpment rises to between 1,400 and 1,800 feet. To the east is a rugged valley floor rising to hills 1,600 to 2,000 feet high. The valley floor on which the city is located is gently rolling.

**Climate:** Harsh continental but subject to some moderating influences from the Atlantic, to the south. Winters are cold and occasionally severe. Maximum temperatures during cold months often do not rise above 32° F. In the warmer months, temperatures rise quickly during the day to moderate levels, then fall rapidly at night to moderate to cool. Occasional hot spells of a week or so occur during the summer. The growing season is about 160 days, long for a city in this latitude. Average date of last freeze: April 27. First freeze: October 13.

**Pluses:** Cool summer nights.

**Minuses:** Cold, snowy winters.

**Places Rated Score: 476**

**Places Rated Rank: 250**

**Elevation: 292 feet**

Relative Humidity: 71%
Wind Speed: 8.9 mph

Seasonal Change

Annual Rainfall 33 in

Annual Snowfall 71 in

Clear 71 days | Partly Cloudy 111 days | Cloudy 183 days

Precipitation Days: 135  Storm Days: 28

| Average Temperatures | | | |
|---|---|---|---|
| | Daily High | Daily Low | Monthly Mean |
| January | 30.4 | 12.5 | 21.5 |
| February | 32.7 | 14.3 | 23.5 |
| March | 42.6 | 24.2 | 33.4 |
| April | 58.0 | 35.7 | 46.9 |
| May | 69.7 | 45.7 | 57.7 |
| June | 79.4 | 55.6 | 67.5 |
| July | 83.9 | 60.1 | 72.0 |
| August | 81.4 | 57.8 | 69.6 |
| September | 73.7 | 50.1 | 61.9 |
| October | 62.8 | 40.0 | 51.4 |
| November | 48.1 | 31.1 | 39.6 |
| December | 34.1 | 17.7 | 25.9 |

Zero-Degree Days: 17
Freezing Days: 155
90-Degree Days: 8
Heating- and Cooling-Degree Days: 7,462

## Albuquerque, NM

**Terrain:** Rests in the Rio Grande Valley 55 miles southwest of Santa Fe, and is surrounded by mountains, most of them to the east. These mountainous areas receive more precipitation than does the city proper. With an annual rainfall of 8 inches, only the most hardy desert flora can grow. However, successful farming—primarily fruit and produce—is carried out in the valley by irrigation.

**Climate:** Arid continental. No muggy days. Half the moisture falls between July and September in the form of brief but severe thunderstorms. Long drizzles are unknown. These storms do not greatly interfere with outdoor activities, and they have a moderating effect on the heat. The hottest month is July, with temperatures reaching 90° F almost constantly. However, the low humidity and cool nights make the heat much less felt.

**Pluses:** Sunny and dry, with mild winters.

**Minuses:** Dust storms.

**Places Rated Score: 659**

**Places Rated Rank: 30**

**Elevation: 5,314 feet**

Relative Humidity: 43%
Wind Speed: 9 mph

Seasonal Change

Annual Rainfall 7.7 in

Annual Snowfall 11 in

Clear 172 days | Partly Cloudy 111 days | Cloudy 82 days

Precipitation Days: 59    Storm Days: 43

| Average Temperatures | | | |
|---|---|---|---|
| | Daily High | Daily Low | Monthly Mean |
| January | 46.9 | 23.5 | 35.2 |
| February | 52.6 | 27.4 | 40.0 |
| March | 59.2 | 32.3 | 45.8 |
| April | 70.1 | 41.4 | 55.8 |
| May | 79.9 | 50.7 | 65.3 |
| June | 89.5 | 59.7 | 74.6 |
| July | 92.2 | 65.2 | 78.7 |
| August | 89.7 | 63.4 | 76.6 |
| September | 83.4 | 56.7 | 70.1 |
| October | 71.7 | 44.7 | 58.2 |
| November | 57.1 | 31.8 | 44.5 |
| December | 47.5 | 24.9 | 36.2 |

Zero-Degree Days: 1
Freezing Days: 123
90-Degree Days: 61
Heating- and Cooling-Degree Days: 5,608

## Alexandria, LA

**Terrain:** Located along the Red River in the geographic center of the state. The area is heavily wooded and is the site of the Kisatchie National Forest. The river is lined by high levees, which protect the surrounding land and cities from floods. The terrain is mostly flat.
**Climate:** Generally subtropical and humid. The winter months are mild, with short cold spells that occur when severely cold air moving across the Plains and the Mississippi Valley invades the city. Snowfall here is negligible, averaging less than an inch a year. Rainfall is heavy in all seasons. Summers are hot, humid, and uncomfortable, but temperatures in April, May, and especially late September through November are pleasant. Severe storms, including hailstorms and tornadoes, occur in all seasons.

**Pluses:** Mild winters.

**Minuses:** Hot and humid; stormy.

**Places Rated Score: 520**

**Places Rated Rank: 203**

**Elevation: 118 feet**

Relative Humidity: 77%
Wind Speed: 6.2 mph

Seasonal Change

Annual
Rainfall 54 in

Annual
Snowfall .7 in

Clear
110 days

Partly Cloudy
109 days

Cloudy
146 days

Precipitation Days: 106   Storm Days: 69

| Average Temperatures | | | |
| --- | --- | --- | --- |
| | Daily High | Daily Low | Monthly Mean |
| January | 58.6 | 36.7 | 47.7 |
| February | 61.8 | 39.2 | 50.5 |
| March | 68.3 | 44.3 | 56.3 |
| April | 76.9 | 54.1 | 65.5 |
| May | 83.7 | 60.8 | 72.3 |
| June | 89.6 | 67.5 | 78.6 |
| July | 91.4 | 70.4 | 80.9 |
| August | 91.8 | 69.6 | 80.7 |
| September | 87.0 | 64.0 | 75.5 |
| October | 79.6 | 51.9 | 65.8 |
| November | 68.6 | 42.5 | 55.6 |
| December | 61.0 | 37.8 | 49.4 |

Zero-Degree Days: 0
Freezing Days: 43
90-Degree Days: 75
Heating- and Cooling-Degree Days: 4,393

## Amarillo, TX

**Terrain:** Located in the heart of the Panhandle, Amarillo sits on the cap rock, or High Plains, of the Southwest. The area, which includes part of Oklahoma and northern Mexico, has often been called the Dust Bowl. It is a plateau with scrubby growth; cotton and sorghum are the primary crops. Amarillo lies between the Canadian and Red rivers.
**Climate:** The area is generally dry, but thunderstorms occur between April and September. This, however, can vary greatly from year to year, and droughts are fairly frequent. The area is subject to rapid and great temperature changes, especially in winter, when cold air comes down from the Plains and the Rocky Mountains at high speed. Nearness to paths of moving pressure systems causes strong winds, especially in March and April. Though summer days are hot, the low humidity lessens the felt heat and makes for pleasant mornings and nights.

**Pluses:** Sunny, dry, and mild, with distinct seasons.

**Minuses:** Hot; can be dusty.

**Places Rated Score: 609**

**Places Rated Rank: 68**

**Elevation: 3,604 feet**

Relative Humidity: 55%
Wind Speed: 13.7 mph

Seasonal Change

Annual
Rainfall 20 in

Annual
Snowfall 14.4 in

Clear
163 days

Partly Cloudy
102 days

Cloudy
100 days

Precipitation Days: 67   Storm Days: 48

| Average Temperatures | | | |
| --- | --- | --- | --- |
| | Daily High | Daily Low | Monthly Mean |
| January | 49.4 | 22.5 | 36.0 |
| February | 53.0 | 26.4 | 39.7 |
| March | 60.0 | 31.2 | 45.6 |
| April | 70.9 | 42.1 | 56.5 |
| May | 79.2 | 51.9 | 65.6 |
| June | 88.0 | 61.2 | 74.6 |
| July | 91.4 | 65.9 | 78.7 |
| August | 90.4 | 64.7 | 77.6 |
| September | 82.9 | 56.7 | 69.8 |
| October | 72.9 | 46.1 | 59.5 |
| November | 60.0 | 32.5 | 46.3 |
| December | 51.5 | 25.5 | 38.5 |

Zero-Degree Days: 2
Freezing Days: 108
90-Degree Days: 63
Heating- and Cooling-Degree Days: 5,616

## Anchorage, AK

**Terrain:** Situated in a broad valley with adjacent narrow bodies of water. Terrain rises gradually to the east with marshes interspersed with glacial moraines, depressions, streams, and knolls. Beyond this area, the Chugach Mountains rise sharply to between 4,000 feet and 5,000 feet, with some peaks 8,000 feet to 10,000 feet high. These mountains block the warm air and the moisture from the Gulf of Alaska. Approximately 100 miles north lies the Alaska Range, which keeps much of the very cold air from the interior. Consequently, when temperatures in the interior are −50° F or −60° F, they will be −15° F to −30° F in Anchorage. The two ranges can also act as a trap, stalling very cold air when winds are light.
**Climate:** The four seasons are well marked in Anchorage, though in length and other characteristics they differ considerably from the standards of the middle latitudes. The rivers and lakes thaw in mid-April to early May. Snow arrives in October, leaves in mid-April.

**Pluses:** Well-defined, four-season climate.

**Minuses:** Rigorous.

**Places Rated Score: 195**

**Places Rated Rank: 324**

**Elevation: 132 feet**

Relative Humidity: 71%
Wind Speed: 6.7 mph

Seasonal Change

Annual
Rainfall 14 in

Annual
Snowfall 70 in

Clear
64 days

Partly Cloudy
67 days

Cloudy
234 days

Precipitation Days: 113   Storm Days: 1

| Average Temperatures | | | |
| --- | --- | --- | --- |
| | Daily High | Daily Low | Monthly Mean |
| January | 20.0 | 3.5 | 11.8 |
| February | 26.6 | 8.9 | 17.8 |
| March | 32.8 | 14.6 | 23.7 |
| April | 43.8 | 26.8 | 35.3 |
| May | 55.2 | 37.2 | 46.2 |
| June | 62.9 | 46.2 | 54.6 |
| July | 65.6 | 50.1 | 57.9 |
| August | 63.8 | 48.0 | 55.9 |
| September | 55.7 | 40.4 | 48.1 |
| October | 41.8 | 27.8 | 34.8 |
| November | 28.3 | 13.9 | 21.1 |
| December | 20.6 | 5.3 | 13.0 |

Zero-Degree Days: 41
Freezing Days: 192
90-Degree Days: 12
Heating- and Cooling-Degree Days: 10,911

## ★ Asheville, NC

**Terrain:** Located on both banks of the French Broad River, near the center of the basin of the same name. Two miles upstream from Asheville, the Swannanoa River joins the French Broad River from the east. The entire valley is called the Asheville Plateau and is flanked on the east and west by mountain ranges. Thirty miles south, the Blue Ridge Mountains form an escarpment, with an average elevation of 2,700 feet. Tallest peaks near Asheville are Mount Mitchell (6,684 feet), 20 miles northeast, and Big Pisgah (5,721 feet), 16 miles southwest.

**Climate:** Temperate but invigorating. Considerable variation in temperature occurs from day to day throughout the year. The valley has a pronounced effect on wind direction, which is mostly from the northwest. Destructive weather events are rare. However, the French Broad Valley is subject to flooding, with especially high flooding occurring in 12-year cycles.

**Pluses:** Long spring, beginning early.

**Minuses:** Drizzly, flood-prone.

**Places Rated Score: 694**

**Places Rated Rank: 25**

**Elevation: 2,207 feet**

Relative Humidity: 77%
Wind Speed: 7.8 mph

Seasonal Change

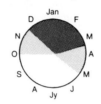

Annual Rainfall 45 in

Annual Snowfall 18 in

Clear 102 days
Partly Cloudy 107 days
Cloudy 156 days

Precipitation Days: 128   Storm Days: 49

| Average Temperatures | | | |
|---|---|---|---|
| | Daily High | Daily Low | Monthly Mean |
| January | 48.4 | 27.3 | 37.9 |
| February | 50.6 | 28.2 | 39.4 |
| March | 58.3 | 33.5 | 45.9 |
| April | 69.4 | 42.4 | 55.9 |
| May | 76.8 | 50.6 | 63.7 |
| June | 82.5 | 58.7 | 70.6 |
| July | 84.3 | 62.6 | 73.5 |
| August | 83.8 | 61.8 | 72.8 |
| September | 78.0 | 55.4 | 66.7 |
| October | 69.1 | 44.5 | 56.8 |
| November | 58.2 | 34.3 | 46.3 |
| December | 49.3 | 28.1 | 38.7 |

Zero-Degree Days: 1
Freezing Days: 106
90-Degree Days: 5
Heating- and Cooling-Degree Days: 5,109

## ★ Atlanta, GA

**Terrain:** Located in the foothills of the southern Appalachians in north central Georgia. Terrain is rolling to hilly and slopes downward toward the east, west, and south. With a mean elevation of 1,000 feet and a location on a plateau with mountains to the north, Atlanta's exposure to the cold north air is blocked, and its elevation retards the moist hot air from the Gulf of Mexico.

**Climate:** Abundant rainfall fosters natural vegetation and growth of crops. In summer, afternoon high temperatures equal or exceed 90° F one day in five, but a temperature of 100° F is rare. Atlanta's winters are mild: Cold spells are not unusual, but they rarely disrupt outdoor activities for extended periods. Snow is very light and usually does not stay on the ground long. Ice storms, however, occur about one year in ten and cause heavy damage. Atlanta averages 50 thunderstorms a year, which occur mostly in the spring, sometimes spinning off destructive tornadoes. Average date of last freeze: March 24. First freeze: November 12. Average growing period: 233 days.

**Pluses:** Mild, sunny, pleasant.

**Minuses:** Hot summers, stormy.

**Places Rated Score: 696**

**Places Rated Rank: 24**

**Elevation: 1,034 feet**

Relative Humidity: 70%
Wind Speed: 9.1 mph

Seasonal Change

Annual Rainfall 48 in

Annual Snowfall 2 in

Clear 108 days
Partly Cloudy 111 days
Cloudy 146 days

Precipitation Days: 116   Storm Days: 50

| Average Temperatures | | | |
|---|---|---|---|
| | Daily High | Daily Low | Monthly Mean |
| January | 51.4 | 33.4 | 42.4 |
| February | 54.5 | 35.5 | 45.0 |
| March | 61.1 | 41.1 | 51.1 |
| April | 71.4 | 50.7 | 61.1 |
| May | 79.0 | 59.2 | 69.1 |
| June | 84.6 | 66.6 | 75.6 |
| July | 86.5 | 69.4 | 78.0 |
| August | 86.4 | 68.6 | 77.5 |
| September | 81.2 | 63.4 | 72.3 |
| October | 72.5 | 52.3 | 62.4 |
| November | 61.9 | 40.8 | 51.4 |
| December | 52.7 | 34.3 | 43.5 |

Zero-Degree Days: 0
Freezing Days: 59
90-Degree Days: 19
Heating- and Cooling-Degree Days: 4,684

## Atlantic City, NJ

**Terrain:** Located on a sand island south of Absecon Inlet on the southeast coast of New Jersey. Surrounding terrain, composed of tidal marshes and beach sand, is flat and lies slightly above sea level.

**Climate:** Continental, but the moderating influence of the Atlantic Ocean is apparent throughout the year. Summers are relatively cooler, winters warmer than those of other places at the same latitude. During the warm season, sea breezes in the late morning and afternoon prevent excessive heat. On occasion, sea breezes may lower the temperature between 15 degrees and 20 degrees within a half hour. Temperatures of 90° F or higher are recorded only about three times a year here. Fall is long, lasting until almost mid-November. On the other hand, warming is somewhat delayed in the spring. Ocean temperatures range from an average near 37° F in winter to 72° F in August. Precipitation is moderate and well distributed throughout the year, but great variation is seen from year to year in precipitation during the late summer and early fall (August, September, and October).

**Pluses:** Moderate temperatures.

**Minuses:** Late springs.

**Places Rated Score: 615**

**Places Rated Rank: 61**

**Elevation: 10 feet**

Relative Humidity: 73%
Wind Speed: 10.7 mph

Seasonal Change

Annual Rainfall 46 in

Annual Snowfall 16 in

Clear 96 days
Partly Cloudy 108 days
Cloudy 161 days

Precipitation Days: 112   Storm Days: 25

| Average Temperatures | | | |
|---|---|---|---|
| | Daily High | Daily Low | Monthly Mean |
| January | 41.4 | 24.0 | 32.7 |
| February | 42.9 | 24.9 | 33.9 |
| March | 50.7 | 31.5 | 41.1 |
| April | 62.3 | 41.0 | 51.7 |
| May | 72.4 | 50.7 | 61.6 |
| June | 80.8 | 59.7 | 70.3 |
| July | 84.7 | 65.4 | 75.1 |
| August | 83.0 | 63.8 | 73.4 |
| September | 77.3 | 56.8 | 67.1 |
| October | 67.5 | 45.9 | 56.7 |
| November | 55.9 | 36.1 | 46.0 |
| December | 44.2 | 26.0 | 35.1 |

Zero-Degree Days: 1
Freezing Days: 15
90-Degree Days: 16
Heating- and Cooling-Degree Days: 5,810

## Augusta, GA–SC

**Terrain:** Located in eastern Georgia on the Savannah River, which forms part of the boundary between Georgia and South Carolina. The dividing line between the Piedmont Plateau and the Coastal Plain, which is known as the fall line, passes through the Savannah River basin in a northeast-southwest direction near Augusta. The terrain consists of low hills to the western half of the city and swampland immediately to the north and east.
**Climate:** Warm and mild, with occasional hot spells. In the winter, measurable snow is a rarity and remains on the ground only a short time. In 100 years of weather records, a temperature of zero or colder has never been reached. The growing season averages 241 days, from March 16 to November 16, although frosts have been reported as late as April 21 and as early as October 17. Although Augusta is protected from flooding of the Savannah River by two multipurpose dams, the potential for flooding still exists in some low-lying areas.

**Pluses:** Very brief winters.

**Minuses:** Can be hot, flood-prone.

**Places Rated Score: 534**     **Places Rated Rank: 184**

**Elevation: 136 feet**

Relative Humidity: 72%
Wind Speed: 6.6 mph

Seasonal Change

 Annual Rainfall 43 in

Annual Snowfall 1.3 in

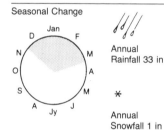

Clear 110 days   Partly Cloudy 107 days   Cloudy 148 days

Precipitation Days: 107  Storm Days: 55

| Average Temperatures | Daily High | Daily Low | Monthly Mean |
|---|---|---|---|
| January | 56.7 | 34.0 | 45.8 |
| February | 60.5 | 36.1 | 48.3 |
| March | 67.1 | 42.0 | 54.6 |
| April | 76.9 | 50.7 | 63.8 |
| May | 84.2 | 59.1 | 71.7 |
| June | 89.6 | 66.7 | 78.2 |
| July | 90.8 | 69.9 | 80.4 |
| August | 90.2 | 69.0 | 79.6 |
| September | 85.2 | 63.2 | 74.2 |
| October | 77.0 | 51.2 | 64.1 |
| November | 67.1 | 40.2 | 53.7 |
| December | 58.7 | 34.1 | 46.4 |

Zero-Degree Days: 0
Freezing Days: 59
90-Degree Days: 63
Heating- and Cooling-Degree Days: 4,542

## Austin, TX

**Terrain:** Located on the Colorado River where it crosses the Balcones escarpment, which separates the Texas hill country from the blackland prairies of East Texas. Elevations within the city limits vary from 400 feet to 900 feet above sea level. Native trees include cedar, oak, walnut, mesquite, and pecan.
**Climate:** Subtropical. Although summers are hot, the nights are a bit cooler, with temperatures usually dropping into the 70s. Winters are mild, with below-freezing temperatures on fewer than 25 days; strong northers may bring cold spells, but these rarely last more than a few days. Precipitation is well distributed but heaviest in late spring, with a secondary rainfall peak in September. With summer come heavy thunderstorms; in winter, the rain tends to be slow and steady. Snowfall (1 inch per year) is inconsequential. Prevailing winds are southerly. Destructive weather is infrequent. Freeze-free season: 270 days. Average date of last freeze: March 3. First freeze: November 28.

**Pluses:** Mild winters.

**Minuses:** Hot.

**Places Rated Score: 435**     **Places Rated Rank: 282**

**Elevation: 570 feet**

Relative Humidity: 67%
Wind Speed: 9.4 mph

Seasonal Change

Annual Rainfall 33 in

Annual Snowfall 1 in

Clear 115 days   Partly Cloudy 116 days   Cloudy 134 days

Precipitation Days: 82   Storm Days: 41

| Average Temperatures | Daily High | Daily Low | Monthly Mean |
|---|---|---|---|
| January | 60.0 | 39.3 | 49.7 |
| February | 63.8 | 42.8 | 53.3 |
| March | 70.7 | 48.2 | 59.5 |
| April | 79.0 | 58.2 | 68.6 |
| May | 85.2 | 65.1 | 75.2 |
| June | 91.7 | 71.4 | 81.6 |
| July | 95.4 | 73.7 | 84.6 |
| August | 95.9 | 73.5 | 84.7 |
| September | 89.4 | 68.4 | 78.9 |
| October | 81.3 | 58.9 | 70.1 |
| November | 70.2 | 48.0 | 59.1 |
| December | 63.0 | 41.6 | 52.3 |

Zero-Degree Days: 0
Freezing Days: 23
90-Degree Days: 101
Heating- and Cooling-Degree Days: 4,645

## Bakersfield, CA

**Terrain:** Situated in the extreme southern end of the great San Joaquin Valley, the city is partially surrounded by a horseshoe-shaped rim of mountains with an opening at the northwest. The Sierra Nevada to the northeast block much of the cold air that flows southward over the country in the winter. This range also catches and stores snow, which is used for irrigation in the valley below. The valley is suited for Mediterranean and specialized forms of agriculture.
**Climate:** Because of the surrounding topography, there are three different climates within short distances of each other: valley, mountain, and desert. The overall climate, however, is warm and semiarid. Ninety percent of the precipitation falls between October and April, typical of the southern half of California. Thunderstorms and snow are rare in the valley. Summers are hot, cloudless, and dry but occasionally relieved by ocean breezes from the west. Winters are mild. Average growing season: 265 days.

**Pluses:** Dry; mild winters.

**Minuses:** Hot summers.

**Places Rated Score: 560**     **Places Rated Rank: 127**

**Elevation: 492 feet**

Relative Humidity: 52%
Wind Speed: 6.4 mph

Seasonal Change

Annual Rainfall 6 in

Annual Snowfall 0 in

Clear 202 days   Partly Cloudy 79 days   Cloudy 84 days

Precipitation Days: 36   Storm Days: 3

| Average Temperatures | Daily High | Daily Low | Monthly Mean |
|---|---|---|---|
| January | 57.5 | 37.4 | 47.5 |
| February | 63.3 | 41.4 | 52.4 |
| March | 68.6 | 44.5 | 56.6 |
| April | 75.5 | 49.9 | 62.7 |
| May | 83.6 | 56.0 | 69.8 |
| June | 91.5 | 62.3 | 76.9 |
| July | 99.1 | 68.7 | 83.9 |
| August | 96.5 | 66.6 | 81.6 |
| September | 91.1 | 62.1 | 76.6 |
| October | 80.5 | 53.3 | 66.9 |
| November | 67.8 | 44.2 | 56.0 |
| December | 57.4 | 38.4 | 47.9 |

Zero-Degree Days: 0
Freezing Days: 11
90-Degree Days: 110
Heating- and Cooling-Degree Days: 4,364

## Baltimore, MD

**Terrain:** Baltimore lies in a region about midway between the rigorous climates of the North and the mild ones of the South. It is also adjacent to the modifying influences of Chesapeake Bay and the Atlantic Ocean. Since this region is near the usual path of the low-pressure systems that move across the country, shifts in wind direction are frequent and contribute to the changeable character of the weather. The net effect of the Appalachian Mountains to the west and the ocean to the east is to produce an equable climate compared with other locations farther inland at the same latitude.

**Climate:** Rainfall is fairly uniform throughout the year but is greatest in late summer and early fall. This is also the time of hurricanes and severe thunderstorms. In summer, Baltimore is influenced by the great high-pressure system known as the Bermuda High. This high brings a constant flow of warm, humid air masses from the Deep South. These air masses, as well as the proximity of water, account for the high humidity here.

**Pluses:** Mild for its latitude.          **Minuses:** Humid, stormy.

**Places Rated Score: 567**          **Places Rated Rank: 119**

**Elevation: 155 feet**

Relative Humidity: 67%
Wind Speed: 9.5 mph

Seasonal Change

Annual
Rainfall 40 in

Clear
106 days

Partly Cloudy
109 days

Cloudy
150 days

Precipitation Days: 112  Storm Days: 26

| Average Temperatures | | | |
|---|---|---|---|
| | Daily High | Daily Low | Monthly Mean |
| January | 41.9 | 24.9 | 33.4 |
| February | 43.9 | 25.7 | 34.8 |
| March | 53.0 | 32.5 | 42.8 |
| April | 65.2 | 42.4 | 53.8 |
| May | 74.8 | 52.5 | 63.7 |
| June | 83.2 | 61.6 | 72.4 |
| July | 86.7 | 66.5 | 76.6 |
| August | 85.1 | 64.7 | 74.9 |
| September | 79.0 | 57.9 | 68.5 |
| October | 68.3 | 46.4 | 57.4 |
| November | 56.1 | 36.0 | 46.1 |
| December | 43.9 | 26.6 | 35.3 |

Zero-Degree Days: 0
Freezing Days: 100
90-Degree Days: 31
Heating- and Cooling-Degree Days: 5,837

## Bangor, ME

**Terrain:** Located in east-central Maine at the navigable head of the Penobscot River, about 80 miles northeast of the state capital, Augusta. By means of the Penobscot River, Bangor links the vast timber forests of Maine's northern interior with Penobscot Bay, to the south. It has always been an important trading and commercial center, especially for the lumber industry.

**Climate:** Decidedly continental in character; summers are pleasant, with cool nights, and winters are moderately severe and fairly long. The extremes of weather caused by this northerly location are somewhat modified by Bangor's setting less than 50 miles from the Atlantic Ocean. The tempering effect of the Atlantic is felt most during the summer, when southerly winds bring ocean-cooled air northward. In the winter, westerly and northerly winds predominate, enhancing the cold. Precipitation is dependable and abundant, with an average of 43 inches of rain and almost 100 inches of snow each year.

**Pluses:** Comfortable summers.          **Minuses:** Long, cold winters.

**Places Rated Score: 451**          **Places Rated Rank: 272**

**Elevation: 202 feet**

Relative Humidity: 74%
Wind Speed: 8.8 mph

Seasonal Change

Annual
Rainfall 43 in

Annual
Snowfall 97 in

Clear
107 days

Partly Cloudy
98 days

Cloudy
160 days

Precipitation Days: 136  Storm Days: 17

| Average Temperatures | | | |
|---|---|---|---|
| | Daily High | Daily Low | Monthly Mean |
| January | 26.9 | 9.8 | 18.4 |
| February | 29.5 | 10.4 | 20.0 |
| March | 38.0 | 21.3 | 29.7 |
| April | 50.8 | 32.5 | 41.7 |
| May | 63.4 | 42.3 | 52.9 |
| June | 73.3 | 52.3 | 62.8 |
| July | 77.7 | 57.6 | 67.7 |
| August | 76.0 | 55.8 | 65.9 |
| September | 67.9 | 47.9 | 57.9 |
| October | 57.3 | 39.0 | 48.2 |
| November | 44.6 | 30.2 | 37.4 |
| December | 31.3 | 15.8 | 23.6 |

Zero-Degree Days: 18
Freezing Days: 157
90-Degree Days: 3
Heating- and Cooling-Degree Days: 8,113

## Billings, MT

**Terrain:** Situated on the border between the Great Plains and the Rocky Mountains, and located on the west bank of the Yellowstone River. Billings is the center of a vast, rich agricultural belt; irrigation and sufficient rain during early spring and fall make it possible to raise a variety of crops here.

**Climate:** Takes on the character of both the Plains and the Rockies but is classified as semiarid. About a third of the yearly total of 14 inches of rain falls during May and June. The winter is usually dry and cold, although heavy snows can occur anytime during the winter months. The heaviest snows come either in spring or fall, when the temperature may take an unexpected drop. Blizzard conditions are expected. Severe cold spells are sometimes relieved by the Chinook, or "drainage," winds moving down Yellowstone Valley and bringing warm Pacific air. Springs: changeable, cloudy, cool. Summers: mild, dry, sunny, with cool to cold nights.

**Pluses:** Cool summers.          **Minuses:** Fairly rugged.

**Places Rated Score: 452**          **Places Rated Rank: 271**

**Elevation: 3,570 feet**

Relative Humidity: 55%
Wind Speed: 11.5 mph

**Seasonal Change**

Annual
Rainfall 14 in

Annual
Snowfall 56 in

Clear
90 days

Partly Cloudy
116 days

Cloudy
159 days

Precipitation Days: 95  Storm Days: 29

| Average Temperatures | | | |
|---|---|---|---|
| | Daily High | Daily Low | Monthly Mean |
| January | 31.2 | 12.5 | 21.9 |
| February | 37.1 | 17.7 | 27.4 |
| March | 42.1 | 23.1 | 32.6 |
| April | 55.8 | 33.4 | 44.6 |
| May | 65.7 | 43.3 | 54.5 |
| June | 73.7 | 51.5 | 62.6 |
| July | 85.6 | 58.0 | 71.8 |
| August | 83.8 | 56.3 | 70.1 |
| September | 71.3 | 46.5 | 58.9 |
| October | 61.0 | 37.5 | 49.3 |
| November | 45.0 | 26.4 | 35.7 |
| December | 35.8 | 17.7 | 26.8 |

Zero-Degree Days: 18
Freezing Days: 152
90-Degree Days: 28
Heating- and Cooling-Degree Days: 7,763

## Biloxi–Gulfport, MS

**Terrain:** In speaking of the Mississippi Gulf Coast, one usually thinks of the thickly settled area stretching from St. Louis Bay at Pass Christian to Biloxi Bay and Ocean Springs. This area is climatologically homogeneous, and a summary of any town (in this case, Biloxi–Gulfport) is applicable to the others. The terrain is flat, consisting of low-lying delta floodplains sloping down to sand beaches and rather shallow harbors and bays.

**Climate:** The Gulf waters have a modifying effect on the local climate that is not felt farther inland. Temperatures of 90° F or higher occur only half as often here as they do in Hattiesburg, 60 miles north. However, there is no such reverse effect on cold air moving down from the north in winter. Rainfall is plentiful and is heaviest in July, with totals in March and September following close behind. Damage from hurricanes and tropical storms can occur six to seven times a year.

**Pluses:** Warm, mild beach climate.

**Minuses:** Winters relatively chilly; hurricane-prone.

**Places Rated Score: 584**        **Places Rated Rank: 93**

**Elevation: 15 feet**

Relative Humidity: 77%
Wind Speed: 9.1 mph

Seasonal Change

Annual Rainfall 59 in

Annual Snowfall 0 in

Clear 100 days    Partly Cloudy 119 days    Cloudy 146 days

Precipitation Days: 75    Storm Days: 94

| Average Temperatures | | | |
|---|---|---|---|
| | Daily High | Daily Low | Monthly Mean |
| January | 61.7 | 45.5 | 53.6 |
| February | 63.6 | 47.2 | 55.4 |
| March | 68.2 | 52.0 | 60.1 |
| April | 75.0 | 59.6 | 67.3 |
| May | 82.4 | 67.2 | 74.8 |
| June | 87.9 | 73.2 | 80.6 |
| July | 89.3 | 74.5 | 81.9 |
| August | 89.6 | 74.2 | 81.9 |
| September | 85.9 | 70.3 | 78.1 |
| October | 79.1 | 60.7 | 69.9 |
| November | 68.8 | 50.4 | 59.6 |
| December | 62.6 | 46.2 | 54.4 |

Zero-Degree Days: 0
Freezing Days: 11
90-Degree Days: 52
Heating- and Cooling-Degree Days: 3,652

## Binghamton, NY

**Terrain:** Binghamton, in south-central New York State, lies in a narrow valley at the confluence of the Susquehanna and Chenango rivers. Within a radius of approximately 5 miles around the city, hills rise to some 1,400 feet to 1,600 feet. In the spring, melting snow and rains sometimes cause flooding along the riverbanks.

**Climate:** Representative of the humid area of the northeastern United States and decidedly continental in character. Since the area is adjacent to the so-called St. Lawrence Valley storm track and is also subject to intruding Arctic air masses that approach from the west and north, the local weather undergoes frequent and rapid changes. Winters are cold but usually not severe. However, moisture-laden winds from the Great Lakes bring much snow. Summers are pleasantly cool and invigorating.

**Pluses:** Nice summers.

**Minuses:** Cloudy, snowy.

**Places Rated Score: 550**        **Places Rated Rank: 146**

**Elevation: 1,590 feet**

Relative Humidity: 74%
Wind Speed: 10.3 mph

Seasonal Change

Annual Rainfall 37 in

Annual Snowfall 86 in

Clear 49 days    Partly Cloudy 102 days    Cloudy 214 days

Precipitation Days: 163    Storm Days: 31

| Average Temperatures | | | |
|---|---|---|---|
| | Daily High | Daily Low | Monthly Mean |
| January | 28.7 | 15.2 | 22.0 |
| February | 30.1 | 15.4 | 22.8 |
| March | 38.9 | 23.7 | 31.3 |
| April | 54.0 | 35.3 | 44.7 |
| May | 65.0 | 45.2 | 55.1 |
| June | 74.5 | 55.1 | 64.8 |
| July | 78.5 | 59.6 | 69.1 |
| August | 76.8 | 57.8 | 67.3 |
| September | 69.4 | 50.9 | 60.2 |
| October | 59.2 | 41.4 | 50.3 |
| November | 44.5 | 31.8 | 38.2 |
| December | 31.3 | 19.4 | 25.4 |

Zero-Degree Days: 8
Freezing Days: 147
90-Degree Days: 2
Heating- and Cooling-Degree Days: 7,654

## Birmingham, AL

**Terrain:** Hilly and located in a valley between a ridge of hills, extending from the northeast to the west, and the Red Mountain ridge, covering the east to the southwest. This valley is 8 miles long and 2 miles to 4 miles wide. The Red Mountain ridge approaches a height of 600 feet above the valley floor. Rolling terrain extends to the southwest and west. The hills in the Birmingham area, which extend to the northeast and north, are the foothills of the Appalachians and the Cumberland Plateau.

**Climate:** Ideal solar radiation and cold-air drainage produce extreme temperature inversions and low minimum temperatures. Located 300 miles from the Gulf of Mexico, Birmingham is safe from the direct effects of tropical hurricanes, although it does receive heavy rains from these storms. Birmingham occasionally receives very low temperatures. Average growing season: 239 days.

**Pluses:** Mild winters.

**Minuses:** Humid, rainy.

**Places Rated Score: 612**        **Places Rated Rank: 66**

**Elevation: 630 feet**

Relative Humidity: 72%
Wind Speed: 7.4 mph

Seasonal Change

Annual Rainfall 53 in

Annual Snowfall 1 in

Clear 99 days    Partly Cloudy 111 days    Cloudy 155 days

Precipitation Days: 118    Storm Days: 58

| Average Temperatures | | | |
|---|---|---|---|
| | Daily High | Daily Low | Monthly Mean |
| January | 54.3 | 34.1 | 44.2 |
| February | 57.7 | 36.1 | 46.9 |
| March | 64.8 | 41.8 | 53.3 |
| April | 75.3 | 51.0 | 63.2 |
| May | 82.5 | 58.4 | 70.5 |
| June | 88.4 | 66.4 | 77.4 |
| July | 90.3 | 69.5 | 79.9 |
| August | 89.7 | 68.7 | 79.2 |
| September | 84.7 | 63.0 | 73.9 |
| October | 75.8 | 50.8 | 63.3 |
| November | 64.0 | 40.1 | 52.1 |
| December | 55.5 | 34.9 | 45.2 |

Zero-Degree Days: 0
Freezing Days: 60
90-Degree Days: 39
Heating- and Cooling-Degree Days: 4,772

## Bismarck, ND

**Terrain:** Located in south central North Dakota, near the center of the North American land mass, on the east bank of the Missouri River in a shallow basin 7 miles wide and 11 miles long. The closest hills, about 3 miles away, are 200 feet or 300 feet high. West, across the river, the land is hilly and considerably higher.

**Climate:** Semiarid, typically continental in character, and invigorating. The normal average temperature range from summer to winter is 135 degrees, typical of the northern Great Plains. In summer, readings of 100° F or more may be expected six years out of ten. Readings of –30° F in winter are experienced seven years out of ten. On seven days of the year, the temperature does not rise above zero.

**Pluses:** Invigorating, variable.

**Minuses:** Rugged, rigorous; Bismarck has one of the most extreme climates in America—definitely *not* for the faint of heart.

**Places Rated Score: 149**

**Places Rated Rank: 327**

**Elevation: 1,660 feet**

Relative Humidity: 66%
Wind Speed: 10.6 mph

Seasonal Change

Annual Rainfall 16 in

Annual Snowfall 38 in

Clear 94 days    Partly Cloudy 105 days    Cloudy 166 days

Precipitation Days: 96    Storm Days: 34

| Average Temperatures | | | |
| --- | --- | --- | --- |
| | Daily High | Daily Low | Monthly Mean |
| January | 19.1 | –2.8 | 8.2 |
| February | 24.5 | 2.4 | 13.5 |
| March | 35.4 | 14.7 | 25.1 |
| April | 54.8 | 31.1 | 43.0 |
| May | 67.1 | 41.7 | 54.4 |
| June | 75.8 | 51.8 | 63.8 |
| July | 84.3 | 57.3 | 70.8 |
| August | 83.5 | 54.9 | 69.2 |
| September | 71.3 | 43.7 | 57.5 |
| October | 60.3 | 33.2 | 46.8 |
| November | 39.4 | 18.3 | 28.9 |
| December | 26.0 | 5.2 | 15.6 |

Zero-Degree Days: 51
Freezing Days: 186
90-Degree Days: 22
Heating- and Cooling-Degree Days: 9,531

## Boise City, ID

**Terrain:** Cradled in the valley of the Boise River about 8 miles below the mouth of a mountain canyon, where this valley widens. The Boise Mountains rise to a height of 5,000 feet to 6,000 feet within 8 miles. Their slopes are partially mantled with sagebrush and chaparral, changing to stands of fir, spruce, and pine trees higher up.

**Climate:** Almost a typical upland continental climate in summer but one tempered by periods of cloudy or stormy and mild weather during almost every winter. The cause of this modification in the winter months is the flow of warm, moist Pacific air, called Chinook winds. While this air is considerably moderated by the time it reaches Boise, its effect is nonetheless felt. Summer hot spells rarely last longer than a few days, but temperatures may reach 100° F each year. However, due to the low humidity, the average 5:00 PM July temperature of 62° F is comfortable. In general, the climate is dry and temperate, with enough variation to be stimulating.

**Pluses:** Mild; low humidity.

**Minuses:** Stormy winters.

**Places Rated Score: 592**

**Places Rated Rank: 83**

**Elevation: 2,868 feet**

Relative Humidity: 57%
Wind Speed: 9 mph

Seasonal Change

Annual Rainfall 12 in

Annual Snowfall 21 in

Clear 124 days    Partly Cloudy 90 days    Cloudy 151 days

Precipitation Days: 91    Storm Days: 15

| Average Temperatures | | | |
| --- | --- | --- | --- |
| | Daily High | Daily Low | Monthly Mean |
| January | 36.5 | 21.4 | 29.0 |
| February | 43.8 | 27.2 | 35.5 |
| March | 51.6 | 30.5 | 41.1 |
| April | 61.4 | 36.5 | 49.0 |
| May | 70.6 | 44.1 | 57.4 |
| June | 78.3 | 51.2 | 64.8 |
| July | 90.5 | 58.5 | 74.5 |
| August | 87.6 | 56.7 | 72.2 |
| September | 77.6 | 48.5 | 63.1 |
| October | 64.7 | 39.4 | 52.1 |
| November | 48.9 | 30.7 | 39.8 |
| December | 39.1 | 25.0 | 32.1 |

Zero-Degree Days: 2
Freezing Days: 124
90-Degree Days: 43
Heating- and Cooling-Degree Days: 6,547

## Boston, MA

**Terrain:** Located in Massachusetts Bay at the mouths of the Mystic and Charles rivers. The western section of Massachusetts Bay is called Boston Bay, and its innermost part is called Boston Harbor, a large, sheltered body of water studded with many small islands, known as the Harbor Islands. Sections of Boston are rolling; two of the more famous hills are Beacon Hill in Boston and Bunker Hill in Charlestown.

**Climate:** Boston's proximity to the ocean greatly influences its climate —roughly described as damp, changeable, and relatively mild, considering its northern location. Sea breezes from the Atlantic do a great deal to moderate the temperature in both summer and winter. Hot summer afternoons as well as winter cold snaps (which may be severe and aggravated by high winds) are frequently relieved by these breezes. Rain is plentiful and well distributed throughout the year. Boston receives a great amount of snow, although in the city proper and to the south it often falls as sleet with no accumulation.

**Pluses:** Great variety, frequent changes.

**Minuses:** Rainy, snowy.

**Places Rated Score: 623**

**Places Rated Rank: 56**

**Elevation: 29 feet**

Relative Humidity: 67%
Wind Speed: 12.6 mph

Seasonal Change

Annual Rainfall 43 in

Annual Snowfall 42 in

Clear 99 days    Partly Cloudy 106 days    Cloudy 160 days

Precipitation Days: 128    Storm Days: 19

| Average Temperatures | | | |
| --- | --- | --- | --- |
| | Daily High | Daily Low | Monthly Mean |
| January | 35.9 | 22.5 | 29.2 |
| February | 37.5 | 23.3 | 30.4 |
| March | 44.6 | 31.5 | 38.1 |
| April | 56.3 | 40.8 | 48.6 |
| May | 67.1 | 50.1 | 58.6 |
| June | 76.6 | 59.3 | 68.0 |
| July | 81.4 | 65.1 | 73.3 |
| August | 79.3 | 63.3 | 71.3 |
| September | 72.2 | 56.7 | 64.5 |
| October | 63.2 | 47.5 | 55.4 |
| November | 51.7 | 38.7 | 45.2 |
| December | 39.3 | 26.6 | 33.0 |

Zero-Degree Days: 1
Freezing Days: 99
90-Degree Days: 12
Heating- and Cooling-Degree Days: 6,282

## Brownsville–Harlingen, TX

**Terrain:** Situated at the extreme southern tip of Texas, on the Mexican border, and on the alluvial soils of the Rio Grande. The only more southerly city in America is Key West, Florida. The Gulf of Mexico is 18 miles to the east, and more than half the land toward the coast consists of tidal marshlands, which have the net effect of "moving" the coast 10 miles nearer to the city.

**Climate:** Humid subtropical. It's always summer here, accounting for the area's agricultural importance in growing citrus fruits, cotton, and warm-weather vegetables. Part of the climate is man-made: Irrigation, used for all the crops, adds considerably to the humidity. Summer temperatures follow a predictable pattern of lower 90s in the day and middle 70s at night. Gulf breezes help temper the summer heat. This is a popular tourist spot in the winter months. The normal daily January minimum temperature is 51° F.

**Pluses:** Long growing season.     **Minuses:** Hot.

**Places Rated Score: 440**     **Places Rated Rank: 277**

**Elevation: 20 feet**

Relative Humidity: 76%
Wind Speed: 11.8 mph

Seasonal Change

Annual Rainfall 25 in

Annual Snowfall 0 in

Clear 96 days     Partly Cloudy 138 days     Cloudy 131 days

Precipitation Days: 73     Storm Days: 24

| | Average Temperatures | | |
| --- | --- | --- | --- |
| | Daily High | Daily Low | Monthly Mean |
| January | 69.5 | 51.0 | 60.3 |
| February | 72.7 | 54.1 | 63.4 |
| March | 76.6 | 58.8 | 67.7 |
| April | 83.1 | 66.7 | 74.9 |
| May | 87.1 | 71.4 | 79.3 |
| June | 90.6 | 75.0 | 82.8 |
| July | 92.8 | 75.9 | 84.4 |
| August | 93.0 | 75.7 | 84.4 |
| September | 89.9 | 73.2 | 81.6 |
| October | 84.7 | 66.6 | 75.7 |
| November | 77.5 | 58.7 | 68.1 |
| December | 72.3 | 53.3 | 62.8 |

Zero-Degree Days: 0
Freezing Days: 2
90-Degree Days: 102
Heating- and Cooling-Degree Days: 4,524

## Buffalo, NY

**Terrain:** The surrounding country is comparatively low and level to the west, and gently rolling to the east and south, rising to pronounced hills within 12 miles to 18 miles, and to 1,000 feet above Lake Erie at a point 35 miles south-southeast of the city. The eastern end of Lake Erie is 9 miles to the west-southwest, and Lake Ontario is 25 miles to the north. The two lakes are connected by the Niagara River and the famous falls of the same name.

**Climate:** The weather here is varied and changeable. Wide seasonal swings of temperature are tempered somewhat by the surrounding lakes. Spring comes late, primarily because of the ice buildup and cold water on Lake Erie. Summers are mild, with more sun here than anywhere else in the state. Thunderstorms are infrequent. Autumn has long, dry periods and is frost-free until mid-October. Winters are famous for snow: 90 inches are expected each year.

**Pluses:** Pleasant summers.     **Minuses:** Snowy, cloudy.

**Places Rated Score: 571**     **Places Rated Rank: 112**

**Elevation: 706 feet**

Relative Humidity: 73%
Wind Speed: 12.3 mph

Seasonal Change

Annual Rainfall 36 in

Annual Snowfall 90 in

Clear 55 days     Partly Cloudy 104 days     Cloudy 206 days

Precipitation Days: 168   Storm Days: 31

| | Average Temperatures | | |
| --- | --- | --- | --- |
| | Daily High | Daily Low | Monthly Mean |
| January | 29.8 | 17.6 | 23.7 |
| February | 31.0 | 17.7 | 24.4 |
| March | 39.0 | 25.2 | 32.1 |
| April | 53.3 | 36.4 | 44.9 |
| May | 64.3 | 45.9 | 55.1 |
| June | 75.1 | 56.3 | 65.7 |
| July | 79.5 | 60.7 | 70.1 |
| August | 77.6 | 59.1 | 68.4 |
| September | 70.8 | 52.3 | 61.6 |
| October | 60.2 | 42.7 | 51.5 |
| November | 46.1 | 33.5 | 39.8 |
| December | 33.6 | 22.2 | 27.9 |

Zero-Degree Days: 5
Freezing Days: 137
90-Degree Days: 2
Heating- and Cooling-Degree Days: 7,364

## Burlington, VT

**Terrain:** Located on the eastern shore of Lake Champlain at the widest part of that lake. About 35 miles to the west lie the highest peaks of the Adirondacks; the foothills of the Green Mountains begin 10 miles to the east and southeast.

**Climate:** Burlington's northerly latitude assures the variety and vigor of a true New England climate. Lake Champlain, however, has a tempering effect; during the winter months, temperatures along the lakeshore often run from 5 degrees to 10 degrees warmer than those at the airport 3.5 miles away. The summer, while not long compared with most, is quite pleasant, with only four 90-degree days per year on the average. Fall is cool, extending through October. Winters are cold, with intense cold snaps (usually not lasting long) formed by high-pressure systems moving down from central Canada and Hudson Bay. Because of its location in the path of the St. Lawrence Valley storm track and the effects of the lake, Burlington is one of the cloudiest cities in the United States.

**Pluses:** Cool summers.     **Minuses:** Long, cold winters.

**Places Rated Score: 383**     **Places Rated Rank: 305**

**Elevation: 340 feet**

Relative Humidity: 71%
Wind Speed: 8.8 mph

Seasonal Change

Annual Rainfall 33 in

Annual Snowfall 79 in

Clear 58 days     Partly Cloudy 103 days     Cloudy 204 days

Precipitation Days: 153   Storm Days: 25

| | Average Temperatures | | |
| --- | --- | --- | --- |
| | Daily High | Daily Low | Monthly Mean |
| January | 25.9 | 7.6 | 16.8 |
| February | 28.2 | 8.9 | 18.6 |
| March | 38.0 | 20.1 | 29.1 |
| April | 53.3 | 32.6 | 43.0 |
| May | 66.1 | 43.5 | 54.8 |
| June | 76.5 | 53.9 | 65.2 |
| July | 81.0 | 58.5 | 69.8 |
| August | 78.3 | 56.4 | 67.4 |
| September | 70.0 | 48.6 | 59.3 |
| October | 58.7 | 38.8 | 48.8 |
| November | 44.3 | 29.7 | 37.0 |
| December | 30.3 | 14.8 | 22.6 |

Zero-Degree Days: 28
Freezing Days: 163
90-Degree Days: 5
Heating- and Cooling-Degree Days: 8,272

## Casper, WY

**Terrain:** Located in the central part of the state in the North Platte River valley. The nearby countryside is rolling and hilly with considerable flat prairie land in all directions except south, where Casper Mountain rises 3,500 feet above the valley floor. The prairie land is used mostly for grazing.

**Climate:** Rather dry due to the effective moisture barrier of the Cascades, the Sierra Nevada, and the Rocky Mountains, which block most of the moist Pacific winds. Summertime precipitation is almost all in the form of thunderstorms, which generally provide ample moisture for grasslands. Annual snowfall averages 77 inches, but the winter season is not severe, contrary to common belief. The dryness of the air prevents discomfort during both the warm summer months and winter cold snaps. Summer highs average 84° F, winter lows 15° F.

**Pluses:** Invigorating.

**Minuses:** Short summers, long winters.

**Places Rated Score: 401**

**Places Rated Rank: 299**

**Elevation: 5,338 feet**

Relative Humidity: 56%
Wind Speed: 13 mph

Seasonal Change

Annual Rainfall 11 in

Annual Snowfall 77 in

Clear 109 days  Partly Cloudy 110 days  Cloudy 146 days

Precipitation Days: 93  Storm Days: 34

| Average Temperatures | | | |
|---|---|---|---|
| | Daily High | Daily Low | Monthly Mean |
| January | 33.6 | 12.7 | 23.2 |
| February | 37.7 | 15.9 | 26.8 |
| March | 42.6 | 19.4 | 31.0 |
| April | 55.5 | 29.9 | 42.7 |
| May | 66.1 | 39.3 | 52.7 |
| June | 76.3 | 47.4 | 61.9 |
| July | 87.1 | 54.9 | 71.0 |
| August | 85.6 | 53.5 | 69.6 |
| September | 74.1 | 43.3 | 58.7 |
| October | 61.4 | 33.9 | 47.7 |
| November | 44.8 | 22.9 | 33.9 |
| December | 36.2 | 16.2 | 26.2 |

Zero-Degree Days: 21
Freezing Days: 185
90-Degree Days: 25
Heating- and Cooling-Degree Days: 8,013

## Charleston, SC

**Terrain:** Before the expansion begun in 1960, Charleston was limited to the peninsula bounded on the west and south by the Ashley River, on the east by the Cooper River, and on the southeast by a spacious harbor that contains historic Fort Sumter. The terrain is generally level and the soil sandy to sandy loam. Because of the low elevation, a portion of the city and nearby coastal islands are vulnerable to tidal flooding.

**Climate:** Generally temperate, modified considerably by the ocean. Summer is warm and humid, but temperatures over 100° F are infrequent. Most rain—41% of the annual total—occurs then. The fall passes from an Indian summer to the prewinter cold spells that begin in November. From late September to early November, the weather is very pleasant, being cool and sunny. Winters are mild; temperatures of 20° F or less are very unusual. Spring is warm, windy, and changeable. Most storms occur then.

**Pluses:** Pleasant falls, mild winters.

**Minuses:** Hot, humid, stormy.

**Places Rated Score: 569**

**Places Rated Rank: 115**

**Elevation: 48 feet**

Relative Humidity: 76%
Wind Speed: 8.8 mph

Seasonal Change

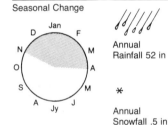

Annual Rainfall 52 in

Annual Snowfall .5 in

Clear 101 days  Partly Cloudy 113 days  Cloudy 151 days

Precipitation Days: 115  Storm Days: 56

| Average Temperatures | | | |
|---|---|---|---|
| | Daily High | Daily Low | Monthly Mean |
| January | 59.8 | 37.3 | 48.6 |
| February | 61.9 | 39.0 | 50.5 |
| March | 67.8 | 45.1 | 56.5 |
| April | 76.2 | 53.0 | 64.6 |
| May | 83.1 | 61.1 | 72.1 |
| June | 87.7 | 68.1 | 77.9 |
| July | 89.1 | 71.2 | 80.2 |
| August | 88.6 | 70.6 | 79.6 |
| September | 84.5 | 65.9 | 75.2 |
| October | 77.1 | 55.1 | 66.1 |
| November | 68.4 | 44.1 | 56.3 |
| December | 60.8 | 37.7 | 49.3 |

Zero-Degree Days: 0
Freezing Days: 36
90-Degree Days: 47
Heating- and Cooling-Degree Days: 4,224

## Charleston, WV

**Terrain:** Situated in the western foothills of the Appalachians at the junction of the Kanawha and Elk rivers.

**Climate:** Characterized by sharp temperature contrasts, both seasonal and day-to-day. May through September is generally warm; November through March moderately cold. April and October are months of rapid transition. Cold spells occur on the average of two or three times each winter, but they seldom last longer than several days. Ample precipitation is well distributed throughout the year, with a maximum in July and a minimum in October. Because of the conditions of terrain and air flow, Charleston experiences 111 fog days per year, more than any other major city in the United States.

**Pluses:** Changeable climate.

**Minuses:** Foggy, rainy.

**Places Rated Score: 627**

**Places Rated Rank: 53**

**Elevation: 951 feet**

Relative Humidity: 70%
Wind Speed: 6.5 mph

Seasonal Change

Annual Rainfall 41 in

Annual Snowfall 32 in

Clear 59 days  Partly Cloudy 116 days  Cloudy 190 days

Precipitation Days: 149  Storm Days: 43

| Average Temperatures | | | |
|---|---|---|---|
| | Daily High | Daily Low | Monthly Mean |
| January | 43.6 | 25.3 | 34.5 |
| February | 46.2 | 26.8 | 36.5 |
| March | 55.2 | 33.8 | 44.5 |
| April | 67.9 | 43.8 | 55.9 |
| May | 76.6 | 52.3 | 64.5 |
| June | 83.4 | 60.6 | 72.0 |
| July | 85.6 | 64.3 | 75.0 |
| August | 84.4 | 62.8 | 73.6 |
| September | 79.0 | 55.9 | 67.5 |
| October | 69.1 | 44.8 | 57.0 |
| November | 55.8 | 35.0 | 45.4 |
| December | 45.2 | 27.2 | 36.2 |

Zero-Degree Days: 1
Freezing Days: 101
90-Degree Days: 21
Heating- and Cooling-Degree Days: 5,645

## Charlotte–Gastonia–Rock Hill, NC–SC

**Terrain:** Charlotte is located in the southern Piedmont, an area of rolling country between the mountains to the west and the Coastal Plain to the east. The mountains extend from southwest to northeast, being about 80 miles to 90 miles from the city to the west and north. The ocean is approximately 160 miles to the southeast. The mountains have a moderating effect on winter temperatures, causing appreciable warming of cold air coming from the west and northwest. The ocean is too distant to affect summer weather, but it moderates winter weather.

**Climate:** Moderate, characterized by cool winters and summers that are quite warm. Winter weather is changeable, alternating between mild and cool spells, with occasional cold periods. Extreme cold is rare. Snow is infrequent, occurring, on the average, once a month from December through March. Summers are long and warm, with afternoon temperatures frequently in the 90s. Nights are cooler, with temperatures dropping into the low 70s even in the warmest months.

**Pluses:** Moderate, mild winters.    **Minuses:** Long summers.

**Places Rated Score: 644**    **Places Rated Rank: 38**

**Elevation: 769 feet**

Relative Humidity: 69%
Wind Speed: 7.6 mph

Seasonal Change

Annual Rainfall 43 in

Annual Snowfall 6 in

Clear 111 days    Partly Cloudy 103 days    Cloudy 151 days

Precipitation Days: 111    Storm Days: 42

| Average Temperatures | | | |
| --- | --- | --- | --- |
| | Daily High | Daily Low | Monthly Mean |
| January | 52.1 | 32.1 | 42.1 |
| February | 54.9 | 33.1 | 44.0 |
| March | 62.2 | 39.0 | 50.6 |
| April | 72.7 | 48.9 | 60.8 |
| May | 80.2 | 57.4 | 68.8 |
| June | 86.4 | 65.3 | 75.9 |
| July | 88.3 | 68.7 | 78.5 |
| August | 87.4 | 67.9 | 77.7 |
| September | 82.0 | 61.9 | 72.0 |
| October | 73.1 | 50.3 | 61.7 |
| November | 62.4 | 39.6 | 51.0 |
| December | 52.5 | 32.4 | 42.5 |

Zero-Degree Days: 0
Freezing Days: 71
90-Degree Days: 31
Heating- and Cooling-Degree Days: 4,814

## Chattanooga, TN–GA

**Terrain:** Local topography is complex, with the difference in elevation between minor valleys and ridges being as much as 500 feet. The city is located in the southern portion of the Great Valley of the Tennessee, an area of the Tennessee River between the Cumberland Mountains to the west and the Appalachian Mountains to the east. Most of the city lies south of the river. In winter the Cumberlands have a moderating influence on the local climate, retarding the flow of cold air from the north and west.

**Climate:** Moderate, characterized by cool winters and summers that are quite warm. Winter weather is changeable and alternates between cool spells and an occasional cold period. Extreme or prolonged cold is rare. Summer temperatures average in the high 80s or low 90s. Most afternoon summer temperatures are modified by brief thundershowers, which cause the mercury to drop 10 degrees to 15 degrees.

**Pluses:** Mild winters.    **Minuses:** Can be hot and muggy.

**Places Rated Score: 576**    **Places Rated Rank: 103**

**Elevation: 665 feet**

Relative Humidity: 72%
Wind Speed: 6.2 mph

Seasonal Change

Annual Rainfall 52 in

Annual Snowfall 4.2 in

Clear 107 days    Partly Cloudy 106 days    Cloudy 152 days

Precipitation Days: 121    Storm Days: 56

| Average Temperatures | | | |
| --- | --- | --- | --- |
| | Daily High | Daily Low | Monthly Mean |
| January | 49.9 | 30.5 | 40.2 |
| February | 53.4 | 32.3 | 42.9 |
| March | 61.2 | 38.4 | 49.8 |
| April | 72.9 | 48.1 | 60.5 |
| May | 81.0 | 56.0 | 68.5 |
| June | 87.5 | 64.5 | 76.0 |
| July | 89.5 | 68.1 | 78.8 |
| August | 89.0 | 67.0 | 78.0 |
| September | 83.4 | 60.4 | 71.9 |
| October | 73.5 | 48.1 | 60.8 |
| November | 60.7 | 37.1 | 48.9 |
| December | 50.9 | 31.4 | 41.2 |

Zero-Degree Days: 0
Freezing Days: 75
90-Degree Days: 49
Heating- and Cooling-Degree Days: 5,141

## Chicago, IL

**Terrain:** Sprawls along the southwest shore of Lake Michigan on a plain that, for the most part, is only some tens of feet above the lake. Topography does not significantly affect air flow in or near the city, except that lower frictional drag over Lake Michigan permits winds to be frequently stronger along the lakeshore. Terrain is basically flat.

**Climate:** Predominantly continental, with warm to hot summers and cold winters. The climate of the city proper is modified by the lake, with summer temperatures near the shore often 10 degrees cooler than elsewhere. Summer hot spells—an uncomfortable combination of high temperature and high humidity—may last for several days, then end abruptly with a shift of winds to the north or northwest. They are often accompanied by thunderstorms. The normal heating season lasts from mid-September to early June. The air-conditioning season lasts from mid-June to early September.

**Pluses:** Changeable; pleasant falls.    **Minuses:** Hot summers, cold winters, cloudy.

**Places Rated Score: 514**    **Places Rated Rank: 211**

**Elevation: 623 feet**

Relative Humidity: 67%
Wind Speed: 10.4 mph

Seasonal Change

Annual Rainfall 34 in

Annual Snowfall 40 in

Clear 94 days    Partly Cloudy 103 days    Cloudy 168 days

Precipitation Days: 123    Storm Days: 40

| Average Temperatures | | | |
| --- | --- | --- | --- |
| | Daily High | Daily Low | Monthly Mean |
| January | 31.5 | 17.0 | 24.3 |
| February | 34.6 | 20.2 | 27.4 |
| March | 44.6 | 29.0 | 36.8 |
| April | 59.3 | 40.4 | 49.9 |
| May | 70.3 | 49.7 | 60.0 |
| June | 80.5 | 60.3 | 70.5 |
| July | 84.4 | 65.0 | 74.7 |
| August | 83.3 | 64.1 | 73.7 |
| September | 75.8 | 56.0 | 65.9 |
| October | 65.1 | 45.6 | 55.4 |
| November | 48.1 | 32.6 | 40.4 |
| December | 35.3 | 21.6 | 28.5 |

Zero-Degree Days: 7
Freezing Days: 119
90-Degree Days: 21
Heating- and Cooling-Degree Days: 7,052

## Chico, CA

**Terrain:** Lies in the northern third of the Sacramento River valley in the foothills of the Sierra Nevada. The city itself is about 6 miles east of the Sacramento River. The lower slopes of the nearby Sierra foothills are cut by well-defined canyons draining from northeast to southwest. To the west the Coast Ranges rise up to 7,000 feet; to the east, the peaks of the Sierra Nevada reach as high as 9,000 feet. Thus Chico and the other towns of the upper valley are sheltered from ocean breezes and the extreme dryness of the Great Basin.

**Climate:** As a result of its inland location, Chico experiences a considerable range of temperature. However, even in winter the average low temperature is not below freezing, which enhances the region's agricultural productivity, particularly in fruit- and nut-growing. Chico receives 26 inches of rain per year, most of it in the cooler winter months.

**Pluses:** Mild, sunny, variable.    **Minuses:** Hot summer days.

**Places Rated Score: 603**    **Places Rated Rank: 72**

**Elevation: 230 feet**

Relative Humidity: 68%
Wind Speed: 8 mph

Seasonal Change

Annual Rainfall 26 in

Annual Snowfall .6 in

Clear 219 days    Partly Cloudy 57 days    Cloudy 89 days

Precipitation Days: 62    Storm Days: 7

| Average Temperatures | | | |
|---|---|---|---|
| | Daily High | Daily Low | Monthly Mean |
| January | 53.3 | 35.7 | 44.6 |
| February | 59.1 | 38.4 | 48.8 |
| March | 65.2 | 40.9 | 53.1 |
| April | 72.8 | 45.3 | 59.1 |
| May | 80.6 | 50.9 | 65.8 |
| June | 89.0 | 56.4 | 72.7 |
| July | 96.5 | 60.7 | 78.6 |
| August | 94.5 | 58.2 | 76.4 |
| September | 89.8 | 54.8 | 72.3 |
| October | 78.3 | 48.1 | 63.2 |
| November | 65.6 | 39.9 | 52.8 |
| December | 55.0 | 36.7 | 45.9 |

Zero-Degree Days: 0
Freezing Days: 36
90-Degree Days: 92
Heating- and Cooling-Degree Days: 3,816

## Cincinnati, OH–KY–IN

**Terrain:** Located on the bank of the Ohio River in extreme southwestern Ohio. It extends over two ranges of hills bisected by the Mill Creek Valley, with hills extending some 400 feet above the valley floor. The city incorporates the lower portion of the Little Miami Valley to the east and extends to within 5 or 6 miles of the Great Miami Valley to the west.

**Climate:** Basically continental, with a wide range in temperature. Subject to frequent changes in weather due to the passage of numerous cyclonic storms in winter and spring, and thunderstorms during the summer. Fall is very pleasant, with the least rainfall of any season, an abundance of sunshine, and comfortable temperatures. Average freeze-free period: 198 days. Average date of last freeze: April 10. First freeze: October 25.

**Pluses:** Milder version of continental climate.    **Minuses:** Summers can be hot; flooding approximately every three years.

**Places Rated Score: 584**    **Places Rated Rank: 93**

**Elevation: 869 feet**

Relative Humidity: 70%
Wind Speed: 7.1 mph

Seasonal Change

Annual Rainfall 40 in

Annual Snowfall 19 in

Clear 80 days    Partly Cloudy 97 days    Cloudy 188 days

Precipitation Days: 131  Storm Days: 50

| Average Temperatures | | | |
|---|---|---|---|
| | Daily High | Daily Low | Monthly Mean |
| January | 39.8 | 24.3 | 32.1 |
| February | 42.9 | 25.8 | 34.4 |
| March | 52.2 | 33.5 | 42.9 |
| April | 65.5 | 44.6 | 55.1 |
| May | 75.2 | 53.6 | 64.4 |
| June | 83.6 | 62.5 | 73.1 |
| July | 86.6 | 65.8 | 76.2 |
| August | 86.0 | 64.1 | 75.1 |
| September | 79.8 | 57.0 | 68.4 |
| October | 68.8 | 46.7 | 57.8 |
| November | 53.0 | 36.2 | 44.6 |
| December | 41.8 | 27.1 | 34.4 |

Zero-Degree Days: 2
Freezing Days: 98
90-Degree Days: 28
Heating- and Cooling-Degree Days: 6,032

## Cleveland, OH

**Terrain:** Situated on the south shore of Lake Erie, with a lake frontage of 31 miles. The surrounding terrain is mostly level, except for a ridge of the southeastern edge of the city rising some 500 feet above shore level. A rather deep north-south valley, in which flows the Cuyahoga River, approximately bisects the city. Local topography is of minor importance to the climate.

**Climate:** In the winter, Cleveland lies in the path of many cold air masses advancing south and east out of Canada, but the low temperatures are somewhat modified by the air having passed over the comparatively warm water of the lake. But this also means considerable winter cloudiness and frequent snows. Spring is generally a brief transition period. Summer heat is moderated somewhat by the lake, since breezes are felt a considerable distance inland. Fall is the most pleasant season, with mild, sunny weather often extending into November or even early December. Average growing season: 195 days.

**Pluses:** Long, sunny falls.    **Minuses:** Cloudy, snowy.

**Places Rated Score: 579**    **Places Rated Rank: 101**

**Elevation: 805 feet**

Relative Humidity: 72%
Wind Speed: 10.8 mph

Seasonal Change

Annual Rainfall 35 in

Annual Snowfall 52 in

Clear 70 days    Partly Cloudy 98 days    Cloudy 197 days

Precipitation Days: 156  Storm Days: 36

| Average Temperatures | | | |
|---|---|---|---|
| | Daily High | Daily Low | Monthly Mean |
| January | 33.4 | 20.3 | 26.9 |
| February | 35.0 | 20.8 | 27.9 |
| March | 44.1 | 28.1 | 36.1 |
| April | 58.0 | 38.5 | 48.3 |
| May | 68.4 | 48.1 | 58.3 |
| June | 78.2 | 57.5 | 67.9 |
| July | 81.6 | 61.2 | 71.4 |
| August | 80.4 | 59.6 | 70.0 |
| September | 74.2 | 53.5 | 63.9 |
| October | 63.6 | 43.9 | 53.8 |
| November | 48.8 | 34.4 | 41.6 |
| December | 36.4 | 24.1 | 30.3 |

Zero-Degree Days: 5
Freezing Days: 125
90-Degree Days: 8
Heating- and Cooling-Degree Days: 6,767

## Colorado Springs, CO

**Terrain:** At an elevation of more than 6,000 feet, Colorado Springs is located in relatively flat semiarid country on the eastern slope of the Rocky Mountains. Immediately to the west, the mountains rise abruptly to heights ranging from 10,000 feet to 14,000 feet. To the east lies the gently undulating prairie land of eastern Colorado. The land slopes upward to the north, reaching an average height of 8,000 feet within 20 miles, at the top of Palmer Lake Divide.

**Climate:** The terrain of the area, particularly its wide range of elevations, helps to give Colorado Springs the pleasant plains-and-mountain mixture of climate that has established it as a desirable place to live. Precipitation is generally light, with 80% of it falling between April 1 and September 30. Heavy downpours accompany summer thunderstorms. Temperatures are on the mild side for a city in this latitude and at this elevation.

**Pluses:** Dry, sunny, variable.    **Minuses:** Long winters.

**Places Rated Score: 526**        **Places Rated Rank: 191**

**Elevation: 6,170 feet**

Relative Humidity: 49%
Wind Speed: 10.4 mph

Seasonal Change

Annual Rainfall 16 in

Annual Snowfall 40 in

Clear 130 days    Partly Cloudy 119 days    Cloudy 116 days

Precipitation Days: 87    Storm Days: 59

| Average Temperatures | | | |
|---|---|---|---|
| | Daily High | Daily Low | Monthly Mean |
| January | 41.0 | 16.1 | 28.6 |
| February | 43.6 | 18.9 | 31.3 |
| March | 47.7 | 22.8 | 35.3 |
| April | 59.2 | 33.1 | 46.2 |
| May | 68.4 | 42.6 | 55.5 |
| June | 78.1 | 51.1 | 64.6 |
| July | 84.4 | 57.0 | 70.7 |
| August | 82.4 | 55.8 | 69.1 |
| September | 74.9 | 46.9 | 60.9 |
| October | 64.2 | 36.8 | 50.5 |
| November | 49.8 | 25.1 | 37.5 |
| December | 43.1 | 18.9 | 31.0 |

Zero-Degree Days: 7
Freezing Days: 162
90-Degree Days: 15
Heating- and Cooling-Degree Days: 6,934

## Columbia, MO

**Terrain:** Columbia is located on the broad, gently rolling plains of northern Missouri in the valley of the Missouri River. Its elevation is almost 900 feet, and its location dictates a continental climate.

**Climate:** With its interior location, Columbia experiences moderately cold winters and warm, often humid summers. Each summer brings some temperatures over 100° F, and winter lows reach zero an average of eight times annually. Yet summer hot spells are relieved by thunderstorms, and winter cold snaps are often interrupted by days that are almost balmy, with temperatures as high as the 50s and 60s. The late spring and early summer months are the rainiest, but by late summer the rain diminishes so that by middle or late August, the moisture in the top two feet of soil is often depleted. The last spring freeze is usually on April 9; first autumn frost is October 24.

**Pluses:** Variable, sunny.    **Minuses:** Tornado-prone.

**Places Rated Score: 541**        **Places Rated Rank: 168**

**Elevation: 887 feet**

Relative Humidity: 69%
Wind Speed: 9.8 mph

Seasonal Change

Annual Rainfall 37 in

Annual Snowfall 24 in

Clear 100 days    Partly Cloudy 91 days    Cloudy 174 days

Precipitation Days: 109  Storm Days: 51

| Average Temperatures | | | |
|---|---|---|---|
| | Daily High | Daily Low | Monthly Mean |
| January | 38.0 | 20.6 | 29.3 |
| February | 42.7 | 24.5 | 33.6 |
| March | 51.3 | 32.0 | 41.7 |
| April | 65.3 | 44.6 | 55.0 |
| May | 74.5 | 54.3 | 64.4 |
| June | 82.7 | 63.3 | 73.0 |
| July | 87.4 | 67.1 | 77.3 |
| August | 86.4 | 65.5 | 76.0 |
| September | 79.4 | 57.2 | 68.3 |
| October | 69.2 | 46.7 | 58.0 |
| November | 53.6 | 34.2 | 43.9 |
| December | 41.1 | 24.5 | 32.8 |

Zero-Degree Days: 8
Freezing Days: 108
90-Degree Days: 39
Heating- and Cooling-Degree Days: 6,352

## Columbia, SC

**Terrain:** Located on the Congaree River in the center of the state, near the confluence of the Broad and Saluda rivers. The fall line, or division between the Piedmont and the Coastal Plain, is near Columbia. The soil ranges from sand to clay loam. Terrain is rolling, sloping from about 350 feet above sea level in the northern part of the city to about 200 feet at the city's southeastern edge.

**Climate:** Although the Appalachian chain to the north shields the city from northern cold fronts in the winter, the surrounding gently rolling terrain offers little moderating effect on summer heat. Summers are long and hot, with high temperatures from May to September. Temperatures will surpass 100° F an average of six times a year. Winters are mild: Only about a third of the days have freezing temperatures. Snow accumulation is very rare. Spring is changeable and may bring some violent weather. Fall is cool, pleasant, and very sunny. Some grazing crops are grown year-round. Average growing period: 217 days.

**Pluses:** Cool, sunny falls.    **Minuses:** Long, hot summers.

**Places Rated Score: 526**        **Places Rated Rank: 191**

**Elevation: 225 feet**

Relative Humidity: 73%
Wind Speed: 6.9 mph

Seasonal Change

Annual Rainfall 46 in

Annual Snowfall 2 in

Clear 120 days    Partly Cloudy 103 days    Cloudy 142 days

Precipitation Days: 111  Storm Days: 54

| Average Temperatures | | | |
|---|---|---|---|
| | Daily High | Daily Low | Monthly Mean |
| January | 56.9 | 33.9 | 45.4 |
| February | 59.7 | 35.5 | 47.6 |
| March | 66.5 | 41.9 | 54.2 |
| April | 76.9 | 51.3 | 64.1 |
| May | 84.5 | 59.6 | 72.1 |
| June | 90.3 | 67.2 | 78.8 |
| July | 92.0 | 70.3 | 81.2 |
| August | 91.0 | 69.4 | 80.2 |
| September | 85.4 | 63.5 | 74.5 |
| October | 77.1 | 51.3 | 64.2 |
| November | 66.9 | 40.6 | 53.8 |
| December | 57.9 | 34.1 | 46.0 |

Zero-Degree Days: 0
Freezing Days: 60
90-Degree Days: 64
Heating- and Cooling-Degree Days: 4,685

## Columbus, GA–AL

**Terrain:** Located on the Chattahoochee River at the western boundary of Georgia, about 225 miles west of the Atlantic and 170 miles north of the Gulf of Mexico. Elevation ranges from between 200 feet to 500 feet. The terrain is basically level, and effects of terrain on climate are therefore negligible.

**Climate:** Humid and warm, with pronounced maritime effects at some periods and equally pronounced continental effects at others. Rainfall averages an abundant 51 inches a year; the wettest months are March and July, the driest October. Snow is rare but by no means unknown, with each winter usually bringing at least a few flakes. Most days in June, July, and August will see a high of 90° F or higher, with accompanying high humidity. The unpleasant effects of this heat are perhaps balanced by the mild winters, during which temperatures seldom drop below 20° F.

**Pluses:** Very mild winters.    **Minuses:** Hot summers; humid.

**Places Rated Score: 517**    **Places Rated Rank: 206**

**Elevation: 445 feet**

Relative Humidity: 73%
Wind Speed: 6.8 mph

Seasonal Change

Annual
Rainfall 51 in

Annual
Snowfall .5 in

Clear
113 days

Partly Cloudy
103 days

Cloudy
149 days

Precipitation Days: 111   Storm Days: 58

| Average Temperatures | | | |
| --- | --- | --- | --- |
| | Daily High | Daily Low | Monthly Mean |
| January | 57.8 | 35.9 | 46.9 |
| February | 60.9 | 37.8 | 49.4 |
| March | 67.4 | 43.3 | 55.4 |
| April | 77.3 | 51.8 | 64.4 |
| May | 84.7 | 60.0 | 72.4 |
| June | 89.9 | 67.5 | 78.7 |
| July | 90.8 | 70.4 | 80.6 |
| August | 90.8 | 69.8 | 80.3 |
| September | 85.8 | 65.1 | 75.5 |
| October | 77.4 | 53.4 | 65.4 |
| November | 66.8 | 41.9 | 54.4 |
| December | 59.0 | 36.3 | 47.7 |

Zero-Degree Days: 0
Freezing Days: 46
90-Degree Days: 74
Heating- and Cooling-Degree Days: 4,521

## Columbus, OH

**Terrain:** Situated in the center of the state and in the drainage area of the Ohio River. Four small rivers—the Scioto, Alum, Big Walnut, and Olentangy—flow through and near the city.

**Climate:** The city is located in an area of changeable weather. Cold air masses from central and northwest Canada frequently invade the region. Tropical Gulf masses often reach central Ohio during the summer but to a much lesser extent in fall and winter. Columbus's four rivers provide variations in the microclimate of the area, contributing to the formation of shallow ground fog at daybreak in the summer and fall.

**Pluses:** Changeable climate.    **Minuses:** Cold spells.

**Places Rated Score: 558**    **Places Rated Rank: 134**

**Elevation: 833 feet**

Relative Humidity: 70%
Wind Speed: 8.7 mph

Seasonal Change

Annual
Rainfall 37 in

Annual
Snowfall 28 in

Clear
75 days

Partly Cloudy
106 days

Cloudy
184 days

Precipitation Days: 136   Storm Days: 42

| Average Temperatures | | | |
| --- | --- | --- | --- |
| | Daily High | Daily Low | Monthly Mean |
| January | 36.4 | 20.4 | 28.4 |
| February | 39.2 | 21.4 | 30.3 |
| March | 49.3 | 29.1 | 39.2 |
| April | 62.8 | 39.5 | 51.2 |
| May | 72.9 | 49.3 | 61.1 |
| June | 81.9 | 58.9 | 70.4 |
| July | 84.8 | 62.4 | 73.6 |
| August | 83.7 | 60.1 | 71.9 |
| September | 77.6 | 52.7 | 65.2 |
| October | 66.4 | 42.0 | 54.2 |
| November | 50.9 | 32.4 | 41.7 |
| December | 38.7 | 22.7 | 30.7 |

Zero-Degree Days: 4
Freezing Days: 122
90-Degree Days: 15
Heating- and Cooling-Degree Days: 6,511

## Corpus Christi, TX

**Terrain:** Located on Corpus Christi Bay, an inlet in the Gulf of Mexico. It is in the southern part of the Texas Gulf coastline, roughly halfway between Galveston to the north and Brownsville to the south. Padre Island National Seashore adjoins the city. Climate and abundant beaches make the area a major resort center.

**Climate:** Although located on the Gulf, Corpus Christi has a climate midway between humid subtropical conditions to the northeast along the Gulf Coast and the semiarid ones to the west and southwest. Peak rainfall months are May and September, with the winter months being the driest. Tropical storms, which may occur from June through November, add a large portion to the total rainfall. There is little variation in the summer temperature from day to day, which averages in the high 80s or low 90s. But nights are cooler, even pleasant, with temperatures dropping into the low 70s because of sea breezes.

**Pluses:** Winter vacation spot.    **Minuses:** Storms.

**Places Rated Score: 362**    **Places Rated Rank: 310**

**Elevation: 44 feet**

Relative Humidity: 77%
Wind Speed: 12 mph

Seasonal Change

Annual
Rainfall 29 in

Annual
Snowfall 0 in

Clear
104 days

Partly Cloudy
118 days

Cloudy
143 days

Precipitation Days: 77   Storm Days: 31

| Average Temperatures | | | |
| --- | --- | --- | --- |
| | Daily High | Daily Low | Monthly Mean |
| January | 66.5 | 46.1 | 56.3 |
| February | 69.8 | 49.3 | 59.6 |
| March | 75.5 | 54.2 | 64.9 |
| April | 82.1 | 63.4 | 72.8 |
| May | 86.6 | 69.1 | 77.9 |
| June | 91.2 | 73.6 | 82.4 |
| July | 94.4 | 75.2 | 84.8 |
| August | 94.8 | 75.4 | 85.1 |
| September | 90.0 | 72.0 | 81.0 |
| October | 84.1 | 63.7 | 73.9 |
| November | 75.2 | 54.6 | 64.9 |
| December | 69.3 | 48.9 | 59.1 |

Zero-Degree Days: 0
Freezing Days: 7
90-Degree Days: 96
Heating- and Cooling-Degree Days: 4,404

## Cumberland, MD–WV

**Terrain:** Cumberland, the seat of Allegany County and Maryland's third largest city, is located in what is called the Ridge and Valley Physiographic Province, with the valleys and ridges running from northeast to southwest. The valleys drain southward into the Potomac Basin and vary from narrow, steep-sided trenches to broad, gently sloping valleys. Most of Cumberland lies on the valley floor, but nearby elevations range from 600 feet to 900 feet. The surrounding terrain is fairly rugged.

**Climate:** A variable continental-type climate on the mild side. The ridge-and-valley terrain exerts strong influences on local weather, with considerable variation observed over short distances. The annual rainfall of 37 inches is evenly distributed throughout the year. June is usually the wettest month and November the driest. Prevailing winds are from the northwest. There are about 35 thunderstorms a year on the average.

**Pluses:** Mild and variable.          **Minuses:** Cloudy.

**Places Rated Score: 591**          **Places Rated Rank: 85**

**Elevation: 945 feet**

Relative Humidity: 70%
Wind Speed: 8 mph

Seasonal Change

Annual
Rainfall 37 in

Annual
Snowfall 33 in

Clear
102 days

Partly Cloudy
114 days

Cloudy
149 days

Precipitation Days: 122   Storm Days: 35

| | Average Temperatures | | |
| --- | --- | --- | --- |
| | Daily High | Daily Low | Monthly Mean |
| January | 40.8 | 23.6 | 32.2 |
| February | 43.8 | 25.3 | 34.6 |
| March | 51.2 | 30.8 | 41.0 |
| April | 64.8 | 41.3 | 53.1 |
| May | 75.7 | 50.0 | 62.9 |
| June | 82.7 | 57.5 | 70.1 |
| July | 86.5 | 61.3 | 73.9 |
| August | 84.8 | 60.3 | 72.6 |
| September | 78.4 | 53.3 | 65.9 |
| October | 68.6 | 43.4 | 56.0 |
| November | 53.2 | 34.3 | 43.8 |
| December | 41.2 | 25.0 | 33.1 |

Zero-Degree Days: 1
Freezing Days: 114
90-Degree Days: 27
Heating- and Cooling-Degree Days: 5,788

## Dallas, TX

**Terrain:** Located in north central Texas, about 250 miles north of the Gulf of Mexico, near the headwaters of the Trinity River. This hilly area marks the upper boundary of the Coastal Plain. Grasses, live oaks, and coniferous trees compose most of the local vegetation.

**Climate:** Humid, subtropical, with hot summers. It is also continental, characterized by a wide range in annual temperature. Winters tend to be mild, but "northers" occur, bringing cold air masses down from the Great Plains and the Rocky Mountains. These cold snaps are not prolonged, however. Much of the rain falls at night; downpours may accompany thunderstorms during April and May. July and August are relatively dry. Hail falls about two or three times a year. Snowfall is slight and doesn't accumulate. Average freeze-free growing period: 249 days.

**Pluses:** Wide range of weather.          **Minuses:** Hot summers.

**Places Rated Score: 544**          **Places Rated Rank: 159**

**Elevation: 596 feet**

Relative Humidity: 67%
Wind Speed: 11 mph

Seasonal Change

Annual
Rainfall 32 in

Annual
Snowfall 3 in

Clear
138 days

Partly Cloudy
95 days

Cloudy
132 days

Precipitation Days: 79   Storm Days: 46

| | Average Temperatures | | |
| --- | --- | --- | --- |
| | Daily High | Daily Low | Monthly Mean |
| January | 55.7 | 33.9 | 44.8 |
| February | 59.8 | 37.6 | 48.7 |
| March | 66.6 | 43.3 | 55.0 |
| April | 76.3 | 54.1 | 65.2 |
| May | 82.8 | 62.1 | 72.5 |
| June | 90.8 | 70.3 | 80.6 |
| July | 95.5 | 74.0 | 84.8 |
| August | 96.1 | 73.7 | 84.9 |
| September | 88.5 | 66.8 | 77.7 |
| October | 79.2 | 56.0 | 67.6 |
| November | 67.5 | 44.1 | 55.8 |
| December | 58.7 | 37.0 | 47.9 |

Zero-Degree Days: 0
Freezing Days: 39
90-Degree Days: 88
Heating- and Cooling-Degree Days: 4,969

## Davenport–Rock Island–Moline, IA–IL

**Terrain:** Located on the banks of the Mississippi River. Topography characterized by rolling agricultural prairie. Close to the river there is considerable truck gardening and dairying. Field production of grains and livestock is greater in rolling prairie, away from the large streams.

**Climate:** Temperate continental, with a wide temperature range throughout the year. Some intensely hot, usually humid periods in summer and severely cold periods in winter. Proximity to major storm tracks brings substantial weather changes, frequently occurring at three- or four-day intervals. Maxima of 90° F or higher have occurred as frequently as 55 days a year (1936), but in 1882 there were none. Readings of zero or below have been made during every winter, ranging from 37 times in 1874–75 to one time during four other winters.

**Pluses:** Variable climate with average growing season and even precipitation.          **Minuses:** Unpredictable climate, long winters, hot summer stretches.

**Places Rated Score: 440**          **Places Rated Rank: 277**

**Elevation: 594 feet**

Relative Humidity: 70%
Wind Speed: 9.9 mph

Seasonal Change

Annual
Rainfall 36 in

Annual
Snowfall 30 in

Clear
101 days

Partly Cloudy
101 days

Cloudy
163 days

Precipitation Days: 112   Storm Days: 47

| | Average Temperatures | | |
| --- | --- | --- | --- |
| | Daily High | Daily Low | Monthly Mean |
| January | 30.0 | 13.0 | 21.5 |
| February | 34.3 | 17.0 | 25.7 |
| March | 45.0 | 26.4 | 35.7 |
| April | 61.3 | 39.8 | 50.6 |
| May | 72.0 | 50.2 | 61.1 |
| June | 81.4 | 60.2 | 70.8 |
| July | 85.2 | 63.8 | 74.5 |
| August | 83.8 | 62.0 | 72.9 |
| September | 76.0 | 53.2 | 64.6 |
| October | 66.0 | 42.8 | 54.4 |
| November | 48.1 | 30.2 | 39.2 |
| December | 34.6 | 18.5 | 26.6 |

Zero-Degree Days: 16
Freezing Days: 136
90-Degree Days: 22
Heating- and Cooling-Degree Days: 7,288

## Denver, CO

**Terrain:** The Mile-High City rests on the eastern slope of the Rocky Mountains. It is far from any source of moisture and is isolated from the Pacific Ocean by three mountain ranges: the Coastal Ranges, the Sierra Nevada, and the Rockies.

**Climate:** A mild, sunny, semiarid climate, reaching over much of the central Rocky Mountain region. This tempered climate lacks the extremely cold winter mornings of the high elevations and remote mountain valleys, as well as the hot summer afternoons of lower altitudes. There is little humidity or precipitation, and lots of sunshine. During the cold months, invasion of cold air from the north can be abrupt and severe. Yet many of these air masses from Canada are too low to reach Denver and so are deflected off to the east by the mountains. For this reason, Denver often has milder winters than cities of comparable latitude on the Great Plains. Spring is wet, cloudy, and windy. Summers are cool. Fall is the most pleasant season.

**Pluses:** Sunny; dry; comparatively mild winters.

**Minuses:** Cold snaps in winter, stormy springs.

**Places Rated Score: 521**

**Places Rated Rank: 200**

**Elevation: 5,332 feet**

Relative Humidity: 53%
Wind Speed: 9.1 mph

Seasonal Change

Annual Rainfall 16 in

Annual Snowfall 60 in

| Clear 115 days | Partly Cloudy 131 days | Cloudy 119 days |

Precipitation Days: 88    Storm Days: 41

| Average Temperatures | | | |
|---|---|---|---|
| | Daily High | Daily Low | Monthly Mean |
| January | 43.5 | 16.2 | 29.9 |
| February | 46.2 | 19.4 | 32.8 |
| March | 50.1 | 23.8 | 37.0 |
| April | 61.0 | 33.9 | 47.5 |
| May | 70.3 | 43.6 | 57.0 |
| June | 80.1 | 51.9 | 66.0 |
| July | 87.4 | 58.6 | 73.0 |
| August | 85.8 | 57.4 | 71.6 |
| September | 77.7 | 47.8 | 62.8 |
| October | 66.8 | 37.2 | 52.0 |
| November | 53.3 | 25.4 | 39.4 |
| December | 46.2 | 18.9 | 32.6 |

Zero-Degree Days: 10
Freezing Days: 163
90-Degree Days: 32
Heating- and Cooling-Degree Days: 6,641

## Des Moines, IA

**Terrain:** Located close to the center of Iowa, and roughly in the geographic center of the continental United States. The terrain is flat to gently rolling prairie, ideally suited to agriculture. Most of the soil in Iowa is dark, rich, sandy loam with good drainage. The state has the highest rate of agricultural production per acre in the nation.

**Climate:** Situated in the center of the country far from any large body of water, Des Moines, not surprisingly, has a continental climate, characterized by rather long, cold winters, hot summers, and short springs and falls. Winter cold is often intensified by the winds that sweep over the flat land.

**Pluses:** Sunny falls.

**Minuses:** Climate tending toward rigorous.

**Elevation: 963 feet**

Relative Humidity: 69%
Wind Speed: 11.1 mph

Seasonal Change

Annual Rainfall 31 in

Annual Snowfall 33 in

| Clear 103 days | Partly Cloudy 96 days | Cloudy 166 days |

Precipitation Days: 106  Storm Days: 50

| Average Temperatures | | | |
|---|---|---|---|
| | Daily High | Daily Low | Monthly Mean |
| January | 27.5 | 11.3 | 19.4 |
| February | 32.5 | 15.8 | 24.2 |
| March | 42.5 | 25.2 | 33.9 |
| April | 59.7 | 39.2 | 49.5 |
| May | 70.9 | 50.9 | 60.9 |
| June | 79.8 | 61.1 | 70.5 |
| July | 84.9 | 65.3 | 75.1 |
| August | 83.2 | 63.4 | 73.3 |
| September | 74.6 | 54.0 | 64.3 |
| October | 64.9 | 43.6 | 54.3 |
| November | 46.4 | 29.2 | 37.8 |
| December | 32.8 | 17.2 | 25.0 |

Zero-Degree Days: 16
Freezing Days: 137
90-Degree Days: 21
Heating- and Cooling-Degree Days: 7,638

**Places Rated Score: 444**

**Places Rated Rank: 274**

## Detroit, MI

**Terrain:** Detroit is located in the southeastern corner of the state, across the St. Clair River from Windsor, Ontario. Consequently, it is one of the few metro areas that cross international boundaries. Detroit lies on an important waterway that connects Lake Huron to Lake Erie. Nearly flat land slopes up gently from the water's edge northwestward for about 10 miles, then gives way to increasingly rolling terrain. The Irish Hills, about 40 miles northwest, are more than 1,000 feet high.

**Climate:** The winters, while cold, are modified by the Great Lakes, which warm and moisten the cold Arctic air that passes over the northern Plains. As a result, however, the area is quite cloudy, especially in the winter. Summers in the city are warm and sunny. Brief showers usually occur every few days but often fall on only part of the city. Winter storms may bring rain, snow, or both. Freezing rain and sleet are common. Though cloudy, Detroit's proximity to the Great Lakes helps give it a milder climate than one would expect in a place so far north.

**Pluses:** Mild for its latitude.

**Minuses:** Cold winters, cloudy.

**Elevation: 664 feet**

Relative Humidity: 72%
Wind Speed: 10.4 mph

Seasonal Change

Annual Rainfall 32 in

Annual Snowfall 39 in

| Clear 75 days | Partly Cloudy 110 days | Cloudy 180 days |

Precipitation Days: 133  Storm Days: 33

| Average Temperatures | | | |
|---|---|---|---|
| | Daily High | Daily Low | Monthly Mean |
| January | 31.9 | 17.3 | 24.6 |
| February | 34.3 | 18.8 | 26.6 |
| March | 43.8 | 26.7 | 35.3 |
| April | 58.1 | 37.3 | 47.7 |
| May | 69.1 | 47.0 | 58.1 |
| June | 79.4 | 57.2 | 68.3 |
| July | 83.4 | 61.1 | 72.3 |
| August | 82.0 | 59.5 | 70.8 |
| September | 74.8 | 52.3 | 63.6 |
| October | 64.1 | 42.1 | 53.1 |
| November | 47.8 | 32.3 | 40.1 |
| December | 35.4 | 21.5 | 28.5 |

Zero-Degree Days: 7
Freezing Days: 139
90-Degree Days: 11
Heating- and Cooling-Degree Days: 7,073

**Places Rated Score: 536**

**Places Rated Rank: 176**

## Duluth, MN–WI

**Terrain:** Located at Lake Superior's western tip, Duluth lies at the base of a range of hills that rise abruptly to between 600 feet and 800 feet above the lake level. Two or 3 miles back from the waterfront, however, the country assumes the character of a slightly rolling plateau. Directly opposite, on the flats occupying the east banks of St. Louis Bay, lies the city of Superior, Wisconsin. These two cities are referred to as the Twin Ports.

**Climate:** Rugged continental in character. Winters are long and quite cold. Snow comes early and remains on the ground until springtime. While the airport area receives more than 75 inches of snow a year, the city proper receives only about 55 inches. Summers are seldom hot, due to the northerly latitude and proximity of Lake Superior.

**Pluses:** Cool summers, rugged four-season climate.

**Minuses:** Cold.

**Elevation: 1,417 feet**

Relative Humidity: 71%
Wind Speed: 11.4 mph

Seasonal Change

Annual Rainfall 30 in

Annual Snowfall 78 in

Clear 77 days | Partly Cloudy 103 days | Cloudy 185 days

Precipitation Days: 135   Storm Days: 35

### Average Temperatures

| | Daily High | Daily Low | Monthly Mean |
|---|---|---|---|
| January | 17.6 | −.6 | 8.5 |
| February | 22.1 | 2.0 | 12.1 |
| March | 32.6 | 14.4 | 23.5 |
| April | 47.8 | 29.3 | 38.6 |
| May | 60.0 | 38.8 | 49.4 |
| June | 69.7 | 48.3 | 59.0 |
| July | 76.4 | 54.7 | 65.6 |
| August | 74.4 | 53.7 | 64.1 |
| September | 64.0 | 44.8 | 54.4 |
| October | 54.3 | 36.2 | 45.3 |
| November | 35.3 | 21.4 | 28.4 |
| December | 22.5 | 6.3 | 14.4 |

Zero-Degree Days: 51
Freezing Days: 187
90-Degree Days: 2
Heating- and Cooling-Degree Days: 9,932

**Places Rated Score: 193**          **Places Rated Rank: 326**

---

## El Paso, TX

**Terrain:** Located at the extreme western tip of Texas at an elevation of 3,700 feet. Across the Rio Grande to the south lies Ciudad Juárez, Mexico. The Franklin Mountains begin within the city limits and extend northward for about 16 miles. Some of these peaks reach as high as 4,500 feet to 5,000 feet above sea level. The general terrain is composed of mountains and mesas characteristic of western Texas and New Mexico.

**Climate:** Dry and sunny. Summer temperatures are high but not extreme. The very low relative humidity (39%) lessens the felt heat. The winter is mild, typical of arid areas at low altitudes. Rainfall is scarce year-round and fosters only scrublike desert vegetation. Irrigation is necessary for crops, gardens, and lawns. Winter nights can be cold, but the days are warm, averaging in the 50s. Similarly, summer days are hot but the nights cool, averaging in the 60s.

**Pluses:** Mild winters, low humidity.

**Minuses:** Dust storms and sandstorms.

**Elevation: 3,700 feet**

Relative Humidity: 39%
Wind Speed: 9.6 mph

Seasonal Change

Annual Rainfall 8 in

Annual Snowfall 5 in

Clear 194 days | Partly Cloudy 100 days | Cloudy 71 days

Precipitation Days: 45   Storm Days: 36

### Average Temperatures

| | Daily High | Daily Low | Monthly Mean |
|---|---|---|---|
| January | 57.0 | 30.2 | 43.6 |
| February | 62.5 | 34.3 | 48.4 |
| March | 68.9 | 40.3 | 54.6 |
| April | 78.5 | 49.3 | 63.9 |
| May | 87.2 | 57.2 | 72.2 |
| June | 94.9 | 65.7 | 80.3 |
| July | 94.6 | 69.9 | 82.3 |
| August | 92.8 | 68.2 | 80.5 |
| September | 87.4 | 61.0 | 74.2 |
| October | 78.5 | 49.5 | 64.0 |
| November | 66.1 | 37.0 | 51.6 |
| December | 57.8 | 30.9 | 44.4 |

Zero-Degree Days: 0
Freezing Days: 64
90-Degree Days: 103
Heating- and Cooling-Degree Days: 4,776

**Places Rated Score: 592**          **Places Rated Rank: 83**

---

## ★ Eugene–Springfield, OR

**Terrain:** Situated at the southern end of the fertile Willamette Valley. This valley is bounded on both sides by mountain ranges: the Cascades to the east and the Coast Ranges to the west. To the north, the valley widens and levels out. Hills of the rolling, wooded Coast Ranges begin about 5 miles west of the airport and rise to between 1,500 feet and 2,000 feet midway between the city and the Pacific, 50 miles to the west. The Cascades, 75 miles east, reach heights of 10,000 feet. These sheltering ranges and the proximity of the ocean contribute heavily to Eugene's extremely mild climate. This is one of the nation's most important agricultural and lumbering areas.

**Climate:** Very mild maritime climate. Temperature minima below 20° F occur only five times a year. The temperature rarely reaches the mid-90s. Seasonal change is gradual, with intermediate seasons being as long as summer and winter.

**Pluses:** Mild; gradual change of seasons.

**Minuses:** Cloudy, damp.

**Elevation: 373 feet**

Relative Humidity: 77%
Wind Speed: 7.6 mph

Seasonal Change

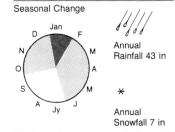

Annual Rainfall 43 in

Annual Snowfall 7 in

Clear 77 days | Partly Cloudy 81 days | Cloudy 207 days

Precipitation Days: 137   Storm Days: 5

### Average Temperatures

| | Daily High | Daily Low | Monthly Mean |
|---|---|---|---|
| January | 45.6 | 33.1 | 39.4 |
| February | 51.7 | 35.2 | 43.5 |
| March | 55.2 | 36.5 | 45.9 |
| April | 61.2 | 39.4 | 50.3 |
| May | 67.8 | 43.7 | 55.8 |
| June | 74.1 | 48.7 | 61.4 |
| July | 82.6 | 51.1 | 66.9 |
| August | 81.3 | 50.9 | 66.1 |
| September | 76.5 | 47.4 | 62.0 |
| October | 64.0 | 42.3 | 53.2 |
| November | 53.1 | 38.1 | 45.6 |
| December | 47.4 | 35.6 | 41.5 |

Zero-Degree Days: 0
Freezing Days: 54
90-Degree Days: 15
Heating- and Cooling-Degree Days: 4,739

**Places Rated Score: 741**          **Places Rated Rank: 18**

## Evansville, IN–KY

**Terrain:** Located on the Ohio River near the juncture of Indiana, Illinois, and Kentucky. The country around Evansville ranges from level to rolling. Dress Regional Airport, where weather observations have been made since 1940, is in a shallow valley with low hills to the east and west that run parallel to the valley but slope downward to the south. The open end of this valley slopes down to the south-southwest toward Evansville and the Ohio River.

**Climate:** Prevailing wind here is from the south, and, although Evansville is 550 miles from the Gulf of Mexico, its weather generally resembles that of its neighbors to the south. Strong cold winds sometimes blow from the north and northwest following cold fronts. As soon as the high-pressure ridge moves by, the wind backs around again from the south. Snowfall varies a great deal from year to year; accumulation is rare. Average growing season: 199 days. Average date of last freeze: April 7. First freeze: October 23.

**Pluses:** Influenced by Gulf winds.

**Minuses:** Summers can be hot and humid.

**Places Rated Score: 550**

**Places Rated Rank: 146**

**Elevation: 388 feet**

Relative Humidity: 70%
Wind Speed: 8.3 mph

Seasonal Change

Annual Rainfall 42 in

Annual Snowfall 13 in

Clear 103 days   Partly Cloudy 100 days   Cloudy 162 days

Precipitation Days: 114   Storm Days: 45

| Average Temperatures | | | |
| --- | --- | --- | --- |
| | Daily High | Daily Low | Monthly Mean |
| January | 41.5 | 23.7 | 32.6 |
| February | 45.4 | 26.4 | 35.9 |
| March | 54.6 | 34.0 | 44.3 |
| April | 67.9 | 45.5 | 56.7 |
| May | 77.0 | 54.4 | 65.7 |
| June | 86.0 | 63.4 | 74.7 |
| July | 88.9 | 66.7 | 77.8 |
| August | 88.0 | 64.4 | 76.2 |
| September | 81.4 | 56.7 | 69.1 |
| October | 71.2 | 45.2 | 58.2 |
| November | 55.2 | 34.5 | 44.9 |
| December | 44.0 | 26.5 | 35.3 |

Zero-Degree Days: 3
Freezing Days: 103
90-Degree Days: 39
Heating- and Cooling-Degree Days: 5,993

## Fargo–Moorhead, ND–MN

**Terrain:** Moorhead, Minnesota, and Fargo, North Dakota, are twin cities in the Red River valley of the north. This river flows between the two cities and is part of the Hudson Bay drainage area. The river has no effect on the climate but does cause occasional severe spring flooding. Surrounding terrain is flat and open.

**Climate:** Summers are generally comfortable, with a few days of hot and humid weather; nights are cool. Winter months are cold and dry, with maximum temperatures rising above freezing only six times per month. At night, the temperature drops below zero half the time. With the flat terrain, surface friction has little slowing effect on the wind, contributing to the legendary Dakota blizzards. Strong winds with even light snowfall cause heavy snowdrifts. Surprisingly, the area averages only 35 inches of snow per year.

**Pluses:** Pleasant, dry summers.

**Minuses:** Extremely rigorous; ranks next to last in mildness of the 329 metro areas.

**Places Rated Score: 148**

**Places Rated Rank: 328**

**Elevation: 899 feet**

Relative Humidity: 71%
Wind Speed: 12.7 mph

Seasonal Change

Annual Rainfall 20 in

Annual Snowfall 35 in

Clear 87 days   Partly Cloudy 112 days   Cloudy 166 days

Precipitation Days: 102   Storm Days: 33

| Average Temperatures | | | |
| --- | --- | --- | --- |
| | Daily High | Daily Low | Monthly Mean |
| January | 15.4 | –3.6 | 5.9 |
| February | 20.6 | .8 | 10.7 |
| March | 33.5 | 14.9 | 24.2 |
| April | 52.6 | 31.9 | 42.3 |
| May | 66.8 | 42.3 | 54.6 |
| June | 75.9 | 53.4 | 64.7 |
| July | 82.8 | 58.6 | 70.7 |
| August | 81.6 | 56.8 | 69.2 |
| September | 69.6 | 46.2 | 57.9 |
| October | 58.4 | 35.5 | 47.0 |
| November | 37.2 | 20.0 | 28.6 |
| December | 21.9 | 4.1 | 13.0 |

Zero-Degree Days: 54
Freezing Days: 181
90-Degree Days: 15
Heating- and Cooling-Degree Days: 9,744

## Fort Myers, FL

**Terrain:** Located on the south bank of the Caloosahatchee River, about 15 miles from the Gulf of Mexico, Fort Myers sits on land that is level and low, with lush greenery.

**Climate:** Subtropical, with temperature extremes of both summer and winter checked by the influence of the Gulf. The average annual mean temperature is a warm 74° F, with averages ranging from the low 60s in January to the low 80s in the summer months. Winters are mild, with many bright, warm days and moderately cool nights. Maximum temperatures average in the low 90s from June through the first part of September, with daily highs of 90° F or greater on 80% of the days. Rainfall averages more than 50 inches annually, with two thirds of this total coming between June and September. Most rain falls as late afternoon or early evening thunderstorms, which in the summer bring welcome relief from the heat and occur almost every day.

**Pluses:** Mild, sunny winters.

**Minuses:** Hot, humid, stormy.

**Places Rated Score: 342**

**Places Rated Rank: 313**

**Elevation: 15 feet**

Relative Humidity: 76%
Wind Speed: 8.2 mph

Seasonal Change

Annual Rainfall 54 in

Annual Snowfall 0 in

Clear 103 days   Partly Cloudy 161 days   Cloudy 101 days

Precipitation Days: 112   Storm Days: 93

| Average Temperatures | | | |
| --- | --- | --- | --- |
| | Daily High | Daily Low | Monthly Mean |
| January | 74.7 | 52.3 | 63.5 |
| February | 76.0 | 53.3 | 64.7 |
| March | 79.7 | 57.3 | 68.5 |
| April | 84.8 | 61.8 | 73.3 |
| May | 89.0 | 66.4 | 77.7 |
| June | 90.5 | 71.7 | 81.1 |
| July | 91.1 | 73.8 | 82.5 |
| August | 91.5 | 74.1 | 82.8 |
| September | 89.8 | 73.4 | 81.6 |
| October | 85.3 | 67.5 | 76.4 |
| November | 79.9 | 58.8 | 69.4 |
| December | 75.9 | 53.6 | 64.8 |

Zero-Degree Days: 0
Freezing Days: 1
90-Degree Days: 106
Heating- and Cooling-Degree Days: 4,168

## Fort Smith, AR–OK

**Terrain:** Located at the confluence of the Poteau and Arkansas rivers. About 20 miles to the northwest are the Cookson Hills, which have an elevation of 1,500 feet. To the northeast are the Boston Mountains (in the Ozark region of Arkansas), 2,700 feet high. To the west, south, and east, the terrain is broken hills separated by creek- and river-bottom land. The bottomlands are very fertile and produce large yields of hay, beans, and spinach. Small wild game is plentiful; lakes and streams have an abundance of game fish.
**Climate:** Well suited to raising fruits and berries. The climate is generally mild, except during the summer, which can be hot.

**Pluses:** Mild.

**Minuses:** Hot summers.

**Elevation: 463 feet**

Relative Humidity: 68%
Wind Speed: 7.6 mph

Seasonal Change

Annual
Rainfall 42 in

Annual
Snowfall 6 in

Clear
124 days

Partly Cloudy
96 days

Cloudy
145 days

Precipitation Days: 96    Storm Days: 57

| Average Temperatures | | | |
| --- | --- | --- | --- |
| | Daily High | Daily Low | Monthly Mean |
| January | 49.9 | 28.0 | 39.0 |
| February | 54.6 | 32.0 | 43.3 |
| March | 62.1 | 38.5 | 50.3 |
| April | 74.2 | 50.2 | 62.2 |
| May | 81.3 | 58.8 | 70.1 |
| June | 89.0 | 67.0 | 78.0 |
| July | 93.8 | 70.5 | 82.2 |
| August | 93.5 | 69.3 | 81.4 |
| September | 86.3 | 61.7 | 74.0 |
| October | 76.5 | 49.9 | 63.2 |
| November | 62.7 | 38.0 | 50.4 |
| December | 52.2 | 30.8 | 41.5 |

Zero-Degree Days: 0
Freezing Days: 80
90-Degree Days: 65
Heating- and Cooling-Degree Days: 5,358

**Places Rated Score: 482**        **Places Rated Rank: 244**

---

## Fort Wayne, IN

**Terrain:** Located at the junction of the St. Mary's, St. Joseph, and Maumee rivers in northeastern Indiana. Terrain is generally level south and east of the city. Southwest and west, the land is somewhat rolling, while to the northwest and north it becomes slightly hilly. The highest point in the area is 40 miles north, near the town of Angola, where the elevation is 1,060 feet above sea level.
**Climate:** Similar to that of other midwestern cities at the same latitude. Precipitation is well distributed throughout the year, varying from a monthly rate of 2 inches in February to 4 inches in May. Damaging hailstorms may be expected twice a year. Snow usually covers the ground for 30 days each winter, but heavy snowstorms are rare. Average date of last freeze: April 26. First freeze: October 17.

**Pluses:** Milder version of Great Interior climate.

**Minuses:** Cold winters, hot summers.

**Elevation: 828 feet**

Relative Humidity: 72%
Wind Speed: 10.3 mph

Seasonal Change

Annual
Rainfall 36 in

Annual
Snowfall 31 in

Clear
77 days

Partly Cloudy
105 days

Cloudy
183 days

Precipitation Days: 131   Storm Days: 41

| Average Temperatures | | | |
| --- | --- | --- | --- |
| | Daily High | Daily Low | Monthly Mean |
| January | 32.6 | 17.9 | 25.3 |
| February | 35.5 | 19.7 | 27.6 |
| March | 45.1 | 27.9 | 36.5 |
| April | 59.5 | 39.0 | 49.3 |
| May | 70.2 | 48.9 | 59.6 |
| June | 80.1 | 58.8 | 69.5 |
| July | 83.6 | 62.4 | 73.0 |
| August | 82.2 | 60.4 | 71.3 |
| September | 75.9 | 53.0 | 64.5 |
| October | 64.6 | 42.5 | 53.6 |
| November | 48.3 | 32.0 | 40.2 |
| December | 35.7 | 21.4 | 28.6 |

Zero-Degree Days: 10
Freezing Days: 134
90-Degree Days: 14
Heating- and Cooling-Degree Days: 6,957

**Places Rated Score: 509**        **Places Rated Rank: 217**

---

## Fresno, CA

**Terrain:** Rests in the middle of the San Joaquin Valley, near its eastern edge. The valley runs northwest to southeast and is about 225 miles long, with an average width of about 50 miles. The terrain around Fresno is generally level, with an abrupt upward slope 15 miles eastward to the foothills of the Sierra Nevada. This mountain range lies 50 miles to the east and has elevations from 12,000 feet to 14,000 feet. Forty-five miles to the west lie the foothills of the Coast Ranges.
**Climate:** Dry and sunny. Winters are mild, summers are hot. Ninety percent of the city's precipitation falls between November and April. Summers are virtually rainless. Because of the great amount of sunshine the valley receives, and the blockage of cooler moist air from the Pacific, daily maximum temperatures in July climb to the upper 90s. But on summer afternoons, the relative humidity is only 5% to 8%; on winter mornings, it is 90%.

**Pluses:** Sunny; nice springs and falls.

**Minuses:** Hot summers.

**Elevation: 327 feet**

Relative Humidity: 61%
Wind Speed: 6.3 mph

Seasonal Change

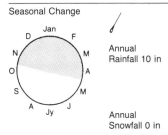

Annual
Rainfall 10 in

Annual
Snowfall 0 in

Clear
200 days

Partly Cloudy
71 days

Cloudy
94 days

Precipitation Days: 44    Storm Days: 6

| Average Temperatures | | | |
| --- | --- | --- | --- |
| | Daily High | Daily Low | Monthly Mean |
| January | 54.8 | 35.8 | 45.3 |
| February | 60.8 | 39.0 | 49.9 |
| March | 66.6 | 41.2 | 53.9 |
| April | 74.3 | 46.2 | 60.3 |
| May | 82.9 | 51.9 | 67.4 |
| June | 90.3 | 57.5 | 73.9 |
| July | 98.2 | 62.9 | 80.6 |
| August | 96.0 | 60.6 | 78.3 |
| September | 91.0 | 56.5 | 73.8 |
| October | 79.8 | 48.6 | 64.2 |
| November | 66.1 | 40.8 | 53.5 |
| December | 54.6 | 36.9 | 45.8 |

Zero-Degree Days: 0
Freezing Days: 29
90-Degree Days: 107
Heating- and Cooling-Degree Days: 4,321

**Places Rated Score: 559**        **Places Rated Rank: 129**

## ★ Galveston–Texas City, TX

**Terrain:** Located on Galveston Island, off the southeast coast of Texas. The island is nearly 3 miles across at its widest point and 29 miles long. It is bounded on the southeast by the Gulf of Mexico and on the northwest by Galveston Bay, which is about 3 miles wide at this point. The island's low-lying terrain makes it especially vulnerable to tidal surges.

**Climate:** Predominantly marine, with periods of modified continental influence during the colder months, when cold fronts from the Northwest sometimes reach the coast. Winters are very mild, with temperatures below 34° F recorded only about four times each winter. Normal daily maximum temperatures range from 60° F in January to 88° F in August, while minima range from 48° F in January to the upper 70s in the summer. The Great Hurricane of 1900, which swept over the island and killed approximately 6,000 people, was the worst natural disaster in American history. It also made inland Houston the major regional city, relegating Galveston to a resort community.

**Pluses:** Mild maritime climate.    **Minuses:** Hot summer spells.

**Places Rated Score: 727**    **Places Rated Rank: 20**

**Elevation: 7 feet**

Relative Humidity: 78%
Wind Speed: 11 mph

Seasonal Change

Annual Rainfall 42 in

Annual Snowfall 0 in

Clear 94 days    Partly Cloudy 109 days    Cloudy 162 days

Precipitation Days: 96    Storm Days: 70

| Average Temperatures | | | |
| --- | --- | --- | --- |
| | Daily High | Daily Low | Monthly Mean |
| January | 59.4 | 48.3 | 53.9 |
| February | 61.5 | 50.9 | 56.2 |
| March | 66.0 | 55.9 | 61.0 |
| April | 73.3 | 65.0 | 69.2 |
| May | 80.0 | 71.8 | 75.9 |
| June | 85.2 | 77.4 | 81.3 |
| July | 87.4 | 79.0 | 83.2 |
| August | 87.6 | 78.9 | 83.3 |
| September | 84.6 | 75.3 | 80.0 |
| October | 78.0 | 68.1 | 73.1 |
| November | 68.8 | 58.2 | 63.5 |
| December | 62.7 | 51.5 | 57.1 |

Zero-Degree Days: 0
Freezing Days: 4
90-Degree Days: 11
Heating- and Cooling-Degree Days: 4,228

## Grand Rapids, MI

**Terrain:** Located in the Grand River valley 30 miles east of Lake Michigan. The Grand River, Michigan's largest stream, bisects the city. The valley has tall hills and bluffs rising on all sides, ranging in elevation from 600 feet to 1,000 feet. The area is known for fruit growing, especially peaches and cherries.

**Climate:** Largely determined by the proximity of Lake Michigan. In spring, the cooling effect of the lake retards the growth of vegetation until the danger of frost is past. In the fall, the warming effect holds off frost until the crops have matured. Summer days are warm and pleasant, with cooler nights. Winters are snowy and cold, but extremely cold temperatures or prolonged cold spells are rare because of the warm lake breeze. Average growing season: 170 days. Average date of last freeze: April 25. First freeze: October 12.

**Pluses:** Pleasant summers, temperatures moderated by Lake Michigan.    **Minuses:** Very cloudy, lots of snow.

**Places Rated Score: 513**    **Places Rated Rank: 214**

**Elevation: 803 feet**

Relative Humidity: 73%
Wind Speed: 9.9 mph

Seasonal Change

Annual Rainfall 32 in

Annual Snowfall 77 in

Clear 67 days    Partly Cloudy 96 days    Cloudy 202 days

Precipitation Days: 144    Storm Days: 37

| Average Temperatures | | | |
| --- | --- | --- | --- |
| | Daily High | Daily Low | Monthly Mean |
| January | 30.3 | 16.0 | 23.2 |
| February | 32.6 | 16.4 | 24.5 |
| March | 42.0 | 24.2 | 33.1 |
| April | 57.3 | 35.6 | 46.5 |
| May | 68.8 | 45.4 | 57.1 |
| June | 79.1 | 55.6 | 67.4 |
| July | 83.3 | 59.6 | 71.5 |
| August | 81.9 | 58.1 | 70.0 |
| September | 73.9 | 50.8 | 62.4 |
| October | 63.1 | 40.8 | 52.0 |
| November | 46.2 | 31.1 | 38.7 |
| December | 33.9 | 20.8 | 27.4 |

Zero-Degree Days: 8
Freezing Days: 149
90-Degree Days: 11
Heating- and Cooling-Degree Days: 7,376

## Great Falls, MT

**Terrain:** Located astride the main stem of the Missouri River at its confluence with the Sun River. Except to the north and northeast, the valley is bordered by mountain ranges, which lie about 30 miles away from east to south, 40 miles to the southwest, and 60 miles to 100 miles from west to northwest. Terrain plays an important part in the climate here: The Continental Divide to the west and the Big Belt and Little Belt mountains to the south are major factors in producing the frequent wintertime Chinook winds blowing through this part of the state.

**Climate:** Semiarid. Summers are cool, sunny, and pleasant. Seventy percent of the annual rainfall occurs between April and September, the growing season. Winters are cold but continually modified by Chinook winds, which bear warm air from the Pacific, causing rapid warming and preventing accumulation of snow.

**Pluses:** Good, rigorous climate.    **Minuses:** Long winters.

**Places Rated Score: 410**    **Places Rated Rank: 295**

**Elevation: 702 feet**

Relative Humidity: 55%
Wind Speed: 13.1 mph

Seasonal Change

Annual Rainfall 15 in

Annual Snowfall 57 in

Clear 81 days    Partly Cloudy 106 days    Cloudy 178 days

Precipitation Days: 100    Storm Days: 26

| Average Temperatures | | | |
| --- | --- | --- | --- |
| | Daily High | Daily Low | Monthly Mean |
| January | 29.3 | 11.6 | 20.5 |
| February | 35.9 | 17.2 | 26.6 |
| March | 40.4 | 20.6 | 30.5 |
| April | 54.5 | 32.3 | 43.4 |
| May | 65.0 | 41.5 | 53.3 |
| June | 72.1 | 49.5 | 60.8 |
| July | 83.7 | 54.9 | 69.3 |
| August | 81.8 | 53.0 | 67.4 |
| September | 70.0 | 44.6 | 57.3 |
| October | 59.4 | 37.1 | 48.3 |
| November | 43.4 | 25.7 | 34.6 |
| December | 34.7 | 18.2 | 36.5 |

Zero-Degree Days: 28
Freezing Days: 156
90-Degree Days: 22
Heating- and Cooling-Degree Days: 7,991

## Green Bay, WI

**Terrain:** Located at the mouth of the Fox River, which empties into the southernmost end of Green Bay, a long and narrow bay off Lake Michigan in northeastern Wisconsin. The comparatively small temperature variation and the fact that the majority of precipitation falls during the growing periods contribute to successful dairy farming, as well as large acreages of vegetables, grown mostly for canning. Apple and cherry orchards predominate locally, with potatoes grown widely farther west.

**Climate:** Continental, modified somewhat by the proximity of Lake Superior to the northwest and Lake Michigan and Green Bay to the east. Summers are pleasant, with cool evenings and nights. Winters tend to be long and cold. Has a moderate amount of snow for a city in this region and latitude.

**Pluses:** Cool summers.          **Minuses:** Long winters.

**Places Rated Score: 367**          **Places Rated Rank: 308**

**Elevation: 702 feet**

Relative Humidity: 73%
Wind Speed: 10.2 mph

Seasonal Change

Annual Rainfall 27 in

Annual Snowfall 43 in

Clear 90 days     Partly Cloudy 102 days     Cloudy 173 days

Precipitation Days: 120   Storm Days: 35

| Average Temperatures | | | |
| --- | --- | --- | --- |
| | Daily High | Daily Low | Monthly Mean |
| January | 23.9 | 6.9 | 15.4 |
| February | 27.2 | 8.8 | 18.0 |
| March | 37.1 | 20.1 | 28.6 |
| April | 54.1 | 33.5 | 43.8 |
| May | 65.8 | 43.1 | 54.5 |
| June | 75.8 | 53.2 | 64.5 |
| July | 80.7 | 57.7 | 69.2 |
| August | 79.1 | 56.3 | 67.7 |
| September | 69.8 | 48.0 | 58.9 |
| October | 59.6 | 38.7 | 49.2 |
| November | 41.8 | 26.4 | 34.1 |
| December | 28.6 | 13.2 | 20.9 |

Zero-Degree Days: 29
Freezing Days: 163
90-Degree Days: 7
Heating- and Cooling-Degree Days: 8,484

## Greenville–Spartanburg, SC

**Terrain:** Located on the Piedmont Plateau, on the eastern slope of the southern Appalachian Mountains. It is rolling country with the first ridge of mountains about 20 miles to the northwest. These mountains usually protect the area from the full force of the cold air masses that move southeastward from central Canada during the winter.

**Climate:** The area's elevation is conducive to cool nights, even during the summer months. The temperature rises to 90° F or above on almost half of the days during the summer but usually falls to 70° F or lower at night. Winters are mild and pleasant, with the temperature falling below freezing during daylight hours only several times annually, though the nights are colder. There are usually two freezing rainstorms and two or three small snowstorms each winter. Rainfall is abundant and well distributed throughout the year. The region is fairly stormy, but tornadoes are infrequent. Average growing season: 225 days.

**Pluses:** Mildness coupled with          **Minuses:** Hot summers.
variety.

**Places Rated Score: 655**          **Places Rated Rank: 32**

**Elevation: 971 feet**

Relative Humidity: 70%
Wind Speed: 6.8 mph

Seasonal Change

Annual Rainfall 48 in

Annual Snowfall 6 in

Clear 117 days     Partly Cloudy 104 days     Cloudy 144 days

Precipitation Days: 119   Storm Days: 44

| Average Temperatures | | | |
| --- | --- | --- | --- |
| | Daily High | Daily Low | Monthly Mean |
| January | 51.6 | 33.0 | 42.3 |
| February | 54.1 | 34.7 | 44.4 |
| March | 61.6 | 40.2 | 50.9 |
| April | 72.0 | 49.9 | 61.0 |
| May | 79.9 | 58.3 | 69.1 |
| June | 85.9 | 65.9 | 75.9 |
| July | 87.6 | 69.0 | 78.3 |
| August | 86.8 | 68.1 | 77.5 |
| September | 81.0 | 62.3 | 71.7 |
| October | 72.4 | 50.9 | 61.7 |
| November | 61.8 | 40.1 | 51.0 |
| December | 52.4 | 33.3 | 42.9 |

Zero-Degree Days: 0
Freezing Days: 68
90-Degree Days: 29
Heating- and Cooling-Degree Days: 4,736

## Harrisburg–Lebanon–Carlisle, PA

**Terrain:** Situated on the east bank of the Susquehanna River in the Great Valley formed by the eastern foothills of the Appalachian chain and about 60 miles southeast of the state's geographic center. It is nestled in a saucerlike depression 8 miles to 10 miles south of the Blue Mountains. This serves as a barrier to severe winter weather experienced 50 miles to 100 miles to the north and west. Although Harrisburg is too far inland (150 miles) to derive full benefits of the coastal climate, it does receive precipitation produced when warm, maritime air from the Atlantic is forced upslope to cross the Blue Ridge Mountains.

**Climate:** Although the saucer-shaped valley protects the area from generally severe winter weather, it often traps cool air, which causes the accumulation of heavy fog and industrial smoke. Fortunately, the weather is changeable enough so that this trapped air does not remain for long. Average growing season: 201 days.

**Pluses:** Relatively mild winters,          **Minuses:** Damp, foggy.
changeable weather.

**Places Rated Score: 556**          **Places Rated Rank: 140**

**Elevation: 351 feet**

Relative Humidity: 67%
Wind Speed: 7.7 mph

Seasonal Change

Annual Rainfall 36 in

Annual Snowfall 35 in

Clear 86 days     Partly Cloudy 107 days     Cloudy 172 days

Precipitation Days: 125   Storm Days: 33

| Average Temperatures | | | |
| --- | --- | --- | --- |
| | Daily High | Daily Low | Monthly Mean |
| January | 37.7 | 22.5 | 30.1 |
| February | 40.5 | 24.0 | 32.3 |
| March | 50.7 | 31.2 | 41.0 |
| April | 64.1 | 41.5 | 52.8 |
| May | 74.5 | 51.6 | 63.1 |
| June | 83.0 | 61.0 | 72.0 |
| July | 86.8 | 65.4 | 76.1 |
| August | 84.6 | 63.2 | 73.9 |
| September | 78.0 | 56.0 | 67.0 |
| October | 66.9 | 44.6 | 55.8 |
| November | 52.9 | 34.7 | 43.8 |
| December | 40.1 | 25.0 | 32.6 |

Zero-Degree Days: 1
Freezing Days: 107
90-Degree Days: 24
Heating- and Cooling-Degree Days: 6,249

# Hartford, CT

**Terrain:** Located on the Connecticut River on a slight rise of ground between north-south mountain ranges whose heights do not exceed 1,200 feet. It is near the state's geographic center, about 30 miles due north of Long Island Sound.

**Climate:** Varies from the cold continental climate in winter to the warm maritime air of summer. Hartford's latitude places it well within the northern temperate climate zone, with westerly winds bearing the majority of weather systems. The average wintertime polar front, which is the boundary between masses of cold, dry polar air and the warm, moist air of the tropics, is just south of New England. This helps explain the great changeability of the weather in New England, characterized by rapidly shifting winds and temperatures, and frequent storms. Hartford's proximity to the ocean is also significant, since many storms move upward along the Atlantic Coast, frequently producing strong and persistent northeast winds.

**Pluses:** Changeable, varied, yet relatively mild.

**Minuses:** Stormy.

**Places Rated Score: 516**　　**Places Rated Rank: 207**

**Elevation: 179 feet**

Relative Humidity: 68%
Wind Speed: 9 mph

Seasonal Change

Annual Rainfall 43 in

Annual Snowfall 53 in

Clear 78 days　Partly Cloudy 110 days　Cloudy 177 days

Precipitation Days: 128　Storm Days: 22

| Average Temperatures | | | |
|---|---|---|---|
| | Daily High | Daily Low | Monthly Mean |
| January | 33.4 | 16.1 | 24.8 |
| February | 35.7 | 17.9 | 26.8 |
| March | 44.6 | 26.6 | 35.6 |
| April | 58.9 | 36.5 | 47.7 |
| May | 70.3 | 46.2 | 58.3 |
| June | 79.5 | 56.0 | 67.8 |
| July | 84.1 | 61.2 | 72.7 |
| August | 81.9 | 58.9 | 70.4 |
| September | 74.5 | 51.0 | 62.8 |
| October | 64.3 | 40.8 | 52.6 |
| November | 50.6 | 31.9 | 41.3 |
| December | 36.8 | 19.6 | 28.2 |

Zero-Degree Days: 6
Freezing Days: 36
90-Degree Days: 20
Heating- and Cooling-Degree Days: 6,934

# ★ Honolulu, HI

**Terrain:** Oahu, the island on which Honolulu is located, is the third largest of the Hawaiian Islands. The Koolau Range, at an average height of 2,000 feet, parallels the northeast coast. The Waianae Mountains, somewhat higher in elevation, parallel the west coast. Much of the city lies along the coastal plain, leeward (relative to the trade winds) of the Koolaus.

**Climate:** Mild marine tropical. Honolulu shows the least seasonal temperature change of any American city: The difference between the mean January minimum temperature and the August maximum mean temperature is only about 22 degrees. Honolulu's location just south of the Tropic of Cancer in the Pacific Ocean assures this mildness. It has no snow, fog, or freezing weather, and an average of only nine 90-degree days and seven thunderstorms a year. There are no heating-degree days here. Although it can be uncomfortably warm occasionally, the persistent trade winds give relief.

**Pluses:** Extremely mild.

**Minuses:** A bit monotonous.

**Places Rated Score: 717**　　**Places Rated Rank: 22**

**Elevation: 15 feet**

Relative Humidity: 67%
Wind Speed: 11.8 mph

Seasonal Change

Annual Rainfall 23 in

Annual Snowfall 0 in

Clear 90 days　Partly Cloudy 174 days　Cloudy 101 days

Precipitation Days: 102　Storm Days: 7

| Average Temperatures | | | |
|---|---|---|---|
| | Daily High | Daily Low | Monthly Mean |
| January | 79.3 | 65.3 | 72.3 |
| February | 79.2 | 65.3 | 72.3 |
| March | 79.7 | 66.3 | 73.0 |
| April | 81.4 | 68.1 | 74.8 |
| May | 83.6 | 70.2 | 76.9 |
| June | 85.6 | 72.2 | 78.9 |
| July | 86.8 | 73.4 | 80.1 |
| August | 87.4 | 74.0 | 80.7 |
| September | 87.4 | 73.4 | 80.4 |
| October | 85.8 | 72.0 | 78.9 |
| November | 83.2 | 69.8 | 76.5 |
| December | 80.3 | 67.1 | 73.7 |

Zero-Degree Days: 0
Freezing Days: 0
90-Degree Days: 9
Heating- and Cooling-Degree Days: 4,221

# Houston, TX

**Terrain:** Located in the flat Coastal Plain of the state, about 50 miles inland from the Gulf of Mexico and 25 miles from Galveston Bay. The surrounding numerous small streams and bayous, together with the bay, favor the development of both ground and advective fogs. The land is low and flat and, since it receives almost 50 inches of rain a year, is ideal for agriculture—especially fruit farming—and livestock raising.

**Climate:** Predominantly marine. Temperatures are modified by winds from the Gulf. Winters are mild. Summer days are hot and humid, though the evenings are relatively cool. Polar air penetrates the area frequently enough to provide some stimulating variety. Although temperatures dip below freezing occasionally, they never remain there long, accounting for a year-round growing season. Destructive windstorms are fairly infrequent, but thunderstorms and hurricanes occur occasionally.

**Pluses:** Mild winters.

**Minuses:** Hot and humid.

**Places Rated Score: 424**　　**Places Rated Rank: 288**

**Elevation: 108 feet**

Relative Humidity: 77%
Wind Speed: 6.1 mph

Seasonal Change

Annual Rainfall 48 in

Annual Snowfall 0 in

Clear 94 days　Partly Cloudy 109 days　Cloudy 162 days

Precipitation Days: 107　Storm Days: 69

| Average Temperatures | | | |
|---|---|---|---|
| | Daily High | Daily Low | Monthly Mean |
| January | 62.6 | 41.5 | 52.1 |
| February | 66.0 | 44.6 | 55.3 |
| March | 71.8 | 49.8 | 60.8 |
| April | 79.4 | 59.3 | 69.4 |
| May | 85.9 | 65.6 | 75.8 |
| June | 91.3 | 70.9 | 81.1 |
| July | 93.8 | 72.8 | 83.3 |
| August | 94.3 | 72.4 | 83.4 |
| September | 90.1 | 68.2 | 79.2 |
| October | 83.5 | 58.3 | 70.9 |
| November | 73.0 | 49.1 | 61.1 |
| December | 65.8 | 43.4 | 54.6 |

Zero-Degree Days: 0
Freezing Days: 24
90-Degree Days: 81
Heating- and Cooling-Degree Days: 4,323

## Huntsville, AL

**Terrain:** The city is almost surrounded by the foothills of the Appalachian Mountains. The Tennessee River winds its way westward about 7 miles south of the city, and the broad and fertile Tennessee Valley, with flat to gently rolling terrain, extends to the west.

**Climate:** Cold air masses from the north predominate during the winter, but at times mild air from the Gulf of Mexico, spreading northward to Huntsville and beyond, may persist for several days. There are very few severely cold days. Temperatures drop below zero on an average of once a year. Springs are variable and can be stormy as cold polar air and warm Gulf air meet. Summers are hot and humid, relieved only by the showers that come about every three days. Falls are dry, cooler, and pleasant. The length of the growing season, 241 days, and high rainfall make the area suitable for truck farming.

**Pluses:** Mild yet variable winter through spring.

**Minuses:** Hot, humid summers.

**Places Rated Score: 600**

**Places Rated Rank: 79**

**Elevation: 644 feet**

Relative Humidity: 73%
Wind Speed: 8 mph

Seasonal Change

Annual
Rainfall 52 in

Annual
Snowfall 3 in

Clear
106 days

Partly Cloudy
101 days

Cloudy
158 days

Precipitation Days: 121   Storm Days: 58

| Average Temperatures | | | |
| --- | --- | --- | --- |
| | Daily High | Daily Low | Monthly Mean |
| January | 50.5 | 31.3 | 40.9 |
| February | 54.0 | 33.2 | 43.6 |
| March | 61.7 | 39.8 | 50.8 |
| April | 73.1 | 50.2 | 61.7 |
| May | 80.9 | 58.3 | 69.6 |
| June | 87.9 | 65.9 | 76.9 |
| July | 90.2 | 68.8 | 79.5 |
| August | 90.2 | 67.7 | 79.0 |
| September | 84.2 | 61.6 | 72.9 |
| October | 74.5 | 49.8 | 62.2 |
| November | 61.6 | 38.9 | 50.3 |
| December | 52.1 | 32.7 | 42.4 |

Zero-Degree Days: 0
Freezing Days: 65
90-Degree Days: 38
Heating- and Cooling-Degree Days: 5,110

## Indianapolis, IN

**Terrain:** Located in the central part of the state on mostly level or slightly rolling terrain. The greater part of the city lies east of the White River, which flows approximately from north to south. From Weir Cook Airport, 7 miles southwest of the city, the terrain slopes gradually downward to the city, then upward again past the city to the east.

**Climate:** Continental. Rather warm summers, moderately cold winters, and occasional wide variations in temperatures, especially during the cold season. Snowfalls of 3 inches or more occur about three times annually. Periods of muggy weather can occur in summer, although usually air masses from the Gulf of Mexico are soon replaced by cooler air from the northern Plains and Great Lakes. Occasionally, hot dry winds from the Southwest prevail. Late spring and fall are the most pleasant seasons. Precipitation, well distributed throughout the year, is normally adequate for good crops. Several flood-control reservoirs protect most formerly flood-prone areas.

**Pluses:** Pleasant springs and falls.

**Minuses:** Humid spells in summer, cold winters.

**Places Rated Score: 557**

**Places Rated Rank: 138**

**Elevation: 808 feet**

Relative Humidity: 73%
Wind Speed: 9.7 mph

Seasonal Change

Annual
Rainfall 39 in

Annual
Snowfall 21 in

Clear
90 days

Partly Cloudy
101 days

Cloudy
174 days

Precipitation Days: 122   Storm Days: 45

| Average Temperatures | | | |
| --- | --- | --- | --- |
| | Daily High | Daily Low | Monthly Mean |
| January | 36.0 | 19.7 | 27.9 |
| February | 39.3 | 22.1 | 30.7 |
| March | 49.0 | 30.3 | 39.7 |
| April | 62.8 | 41.8 | 52.3 |
| May | 72.9 | 51.5 | 62.2 |
| June | 82.3 | 61.1 | 71.7 |
| July | 85.4 | 64.6 | 75.0 |
| August | 84.0 | 62.4 | 73.2 |
| September | 77.7 | 54.9 | 66.3 |
| October | 67.0 | 44.3 | 55.7 |
| November | 50.5 | 32.8 | 41.7 |
| December | 38.7 | 23.1 | 30.9 |

Zero-Degree Days: 7
Freezing Days: 122
90-Degree Days: 15
Heating- and Cooling-Degree Days: 6,551

## Jackson, MS

**Terrain:** Jackson is about 45 miles east of the Mississippi River on the west bank of the Pearl River and about 150 miles north of the Gulf of Mexico. The terrain is gently rolling, with no local topographic features that appreciably influence the weather. Alluvial plains up to 3 miles wide extend along the river near Jackson. Some levees have been built on both sides of the river.

**Climate:** Significantly humid during most of the year, with one short cold season and one long warm one. In summer, the southerly winds and accompanying warm Gulf air masses predominate, resulting in a warm, humid maritime climate. Summer days are hot and humid, and often so are the nights. In winter, colder northern air occasionally invades the area, causing rapid and sometimes dramatic temperature shifts. Average freeze-free period: 235 days.

**Pluses:** Long summers.

**Minuses:** Hot, humid, stormy.

**Places Rated Score: 412**

**Places Rated Rank: 293**

**Elevation: 331 feet**

Relative Humidity: 75%
Wind Speed: 7.6 mph

Seasonal Change

Annual
Rainfall 49 in

Annual
Snowfall 1 in

Clear
109 days

Partly Cloudy
108 days

Cloudy
148 days

Precipitation Days: 112   Storm Days: 65

| Average Temperatures | | | |
| --- | --- | --- | --- |
| | Daily High | Daily Low | Monthly Mean |
| January | 58.4 | 35.8 | 47.1 |
| February | 61.7 | 37.8 | 49.8 |
| March | 68.7 | 43.4 | 56.1 |
| April | 78.2 | 53.1 | 65.7 |
| May | 85.0 | 60.4 | 72.7 |
| June | 91.0 | 67.7 | 79.4 |
| July | 92.7 | 70.6 | 81.7 |
| August | 92.6 | 69.8 | 81.2 |
| September | 88.0 | 64.0 | 76.0 |
| October | 80.1 | 51.5 | 65.8 |
| November | 68.5 | 42.0 | 55.3 |
| December | 60.5 | 37.3 | 48.9 |

Zero-Degree Days: 0
Freezing Days: 47
90-Degree Days: 78
Heating- and Cooling-Degree Days: 4,621

## Jacksonville, FL

**Terrain:** Jacksonville, located on the St. Johns River about 16 miles inland from the Atlantic Ocean, is near the northern boundary of the trade winds. The surrounding terrain is level.

**Climate:** Humid subtropical. The atmosphere is moist, with an average relative humidity of about 75%, ranging from a high of 90% in early morning to about 55% in late afternoon. The average daily sunshine ranges from five and one-half hours in December to nine hours in May. The greatest amount of rain, mostly in the form of local thundershowers, falls during the last summer months, when a measurable amount can be expected every other day.

**Pluses:** Pleasant winters.

**Minuses:** Hot, stormy summers.

**Places Rated Score: 457**          **Places Rated Rank: 266**

**Elevation: 31 feet**

Relative Humidity: 75%
Wind Speed: 8.5 mph

Seasonal Change

Annual Rainfall 54 in

Annual Snowfall 0 in

Clear 98 days    Partly Cloudy 128 days    Cloudy 139 days

Precipitation Days: 116  Storm Days: 64

| Average Temperatures | | | |
|---|---|---|---|
| | Daily High | Daily Low | Monthly Mean |
| January | 64.6 | 44.5 | 54.6 |
| February | 66.9 | 45.7 | 56.3 |
| March | 72.2 | 50.1 | 61.2 |
| April | 79.0 | 57.1 | 68.1 |
| May | 84.6 | 63.9 | 74.3 |
| June | 88.3 | 70.0 | 79.2 |
| July | 90.0 | 72.0 | 81.0 |
| August | 89.7 | 72.3 | 81.0 |
| September | 86.0 | 70.4 | 78.2 |
| October | 79.2 | 61.7 | 70.5 |
| November | 71.4 | 51.0 | 61.2 |
| December | 65.6 | 45.1 | 55.4 |

Zero-Degree Days: 0
Freezing Days: 12
90-Degree Days: 82
Heating- and Cooling-Degree Days: 3,923

## Johnson City–Kingsport–Bristol, TN–VA

**Terrain:** This tri-city area is located in the extreme upper east Tennessee Valley. Mountain ranges begin about 10 miles to the southeast and 15 miles to the west and north, with many peaks and ridges rising to 4,000 feet, and some to 6,000 feet in the southeast.

**Climate:** The topography has considerable influence on the weather changes peculiar to this area. Moist easterly air flow in the lower levels of the atmosphere is more or less blocked on the eastern slopes of the mountains, thus producing an abundance of precipitation in these higher ridges and reaching the tri-city area drier and slightly warmer. Although average annual rainfall is 41 inches in the vicinity, annual amounts of 80 inches have been recorded in mountainous sections to the east and south. Snowfall seldom begins before November and rarely remains on the ground more than a few days. Mountainous regions to the southeast, however, are frequently blanketed for long periods.

**Pluses:** Mild winters.

**Minuses:** Can be drizzly.

**Places Rated Score: 663**          **Places Rated Rank: 29**

**Elevation: 1,525 feet**

Relative Humidity: 72%
Wind Speed: 5.6 mph

Seasonal Change

Annual Rainfall 41 in

Annual Snowfall 16 in

Clear 90 days    Partly Cloudy 112 days    Cloudy 163 days

Precipitation Days: 134  Storm Days: 45

| Average Temperatures | | | |
|---|---|---|---|
| | Daily High | Daily Low | Monthly Mean |
| January | 46.0 | 26.7 | 36.4 |
| February | 48.9 | 28.4 | 38.7 |
| March | 57.1 | 34.5 | 45.8 |
| April | 68.3 | 44.2 | 56.3 |
| May | 77.1 | 52.6 | 64.9 |
| June | 84.0 | 60.7 | 72.4 |
| July | 85.9 | 64.4 | 75.2 |
| August | 85.3 | 63.1 | 74.2 |
| September | 80.4 | 56.6 | 68.5 |
| October | 70.4 | 45.3 | 57.9 |
| November | 56.9 | 34.5 | 45.7 |
| December | 47.3 | 28.0 | 37.7 |

Zero-Degree Days: 1
Freezing Days: 96
90-Degree Days: 13
Heating- and Cooling-Degree Days: 5,413

## Kansas City, KS

**Terrain:** Kansas City is very near the geographic center of the United States. The surrounding terrain is gently rolling. Its continental climate is modified by a lack of natural obstructions to the free sweep of air currents from all directions.

**Climate:** Early spring brings a period of frequent and rapid fluctuations of weather, tapering off as spring progresses. Summer days are warm, sometimes hot, but nights are mild with moderate humidity. As with so many locations in America's heartland, fall is the most pleasant season, characterized by many mild sunny days and cool nights. Average date of last freeze: April 7. First freeze: October 26.

**Pluses:** Sunny; good four-season climate.

**Minuses:** Variable weather in early spring; winters can be cold, summers hot.

**Places Rated Score: 549**          **Places Rated Rank: 148**

**Elevation: 1,025 feet**

Relative Humidity: 68%
Wind Speed: 10.3 mph

Seasonal Change

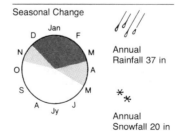

Annual Rainfall 37 in

Annual Snowfall 20 in

Clear 132 days    Partly Cloudy 85 days    Cloudy 148 days

Precipitation Days: 97   Storm Days: 47

| Average Temperatures | | | |
|---|---|---|---|
| | Daily High | Daily Low | Monthly Mean |
| January | 36.2 | 19.3 | 27.8 |
| February | 41.9 | 24.2 | 33.1 |
| March | 50.5 | 31.8 | 41.2 |
| April | 64.8 | 45.1 | 55.0 |
| May | 74.3 | 55.7 | 65.0 |
| June | 82.6 | 65.2 | 73.9 |
| July | 88.0 | 69.6 | 78.8 |
| August | 86.7 | 68.1 | 77.4 |
| September | 78.8 | 58.8 | 68.8 |
| October | 68.9 | 48.3 | 58.6 |
| November | 52.7 | 34.5 | 43.6 |
| December | 40.4 | 24.1 | 32.3 |

Zero-Degree Days: 5
Freezing Days: 105
90-Degree Days: 40
Heating- and Cooling-Degree Days: 6,581

## Knoxville, TN

**Terrain:** Located in a broad valley between the Cumberland Mountains to the northwest and the Great Smoky Mountains to the southeast. The Cumberland Mountains serve to retard and weaken the force of the cold winter air moving down from the northern Plains during the colder months, and the Smoky Mountains shelter Knoxville from much of the hot, humid tropical air that moves northward during the summertime.

**Climate:** Moderate, thanks to the sheltering effects of the two mountain ranges. Though summers are long, the nights are almost always cool, with the average diurnal variation being about 20 degrees. The mean daytime temperature for July is 81° F, but nighttime temperatures are in the mid-70s.

**Pluses:** Mild mountain climate.

**Minuses:** Somewhat stormy in summer.

**Places Rated Score: 670**

**Places Rated Rank: 26**

**Elevation: 980 feet**

Relative Humidity: 71%
Wind Speed: 7.3 mph

Seasonal Change

Annual Rainfall 46 in

Annual Snowfall 12 in

Clear 95 days
Partly Cloudy 107 days
Cloudy 163 days

Precipitation Days: 128   Storm Days: 47

| Average Temperatures | | | |
|---|---|---|---|
| | Daily High | Daily Low | Monthly Mean |
| January | 48.9 | 32.2 | 40.6 |
| February | 52.0 | 33.5 | 42.8 |
| March | 60.4 | 39.4 | 49.9 |
| April | 72.0 | 48.6 | 60.3 |
| May | 79.8 | 56.9 | 68.4 |
| June | 86.1 | 64.8 | 75.5 |
| July | 88.0 | 68.3 | 78.2 |
| August | 87.3 | 67.2 | 77.3 |
| September | 82.0 | 61.2 | 71.6 |
| October | 71.8 | 50.0 | 60.9 |
| November | 58.9 | 39.4 | 49.2 |
| December | 49.8 | 33.1 | 41.5 |

Zero-Degree Days: 1
Freezing Days: 71
90-Degree Days: 19
Heating- and Cooling-Degree Days: 5,047

## La Crosse, WI

**Terrain:** Situated on the east bank of the Mississippi River at the confluence of the Mississippi, Black, and La Crosse rivers. The town is on a level, sandy plain, but steep-sided hills with narrow valleys are characteristic of most of the surrounding area. The leading field crops are corn, hay, and oats. Dairying is the principal farm activity.

**Climate:** The location of the city in a natural bowl between the hills results in colder temperatures at night due to air drainage and in valley fogs that often persist through forenoon. The continental climate means frequent variations in temperature. Winters are cold and humid; snows are frequent. Summers are warm and moderately humid. Most of the annual precipitation falls during the main growing season extending from May to September.

**Pluses:** Five-month growing season with above-average rainfall.

**Minuses:** Long, cold winters with frequent snow.

**Places Rated Score: 352**

**Places Rated Rank: 311**

**Elevation: 672 feet**

Relative Humidity: 72%
Wind Speed: 8.9 mph

Seasonal Change

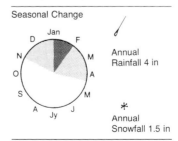

Annual Rainfall 29 in

Annual Snowfall 43 in

Clear 95 days
Partly Cloudy 97 days
Cloudy 173 days

Precipitation Days: 109   Storm Days: 40

| Average Temperatures | | | |
|---|---|---|---|
| | Daily High | Daily Low | Monthly Mean |
| January | 25.0 | 7.1 | 16.1 |
| February | 29.7 | 10.3 | 20.0 |
| March | 40.0 | 22.1 | 31.1 |
| April | 57.8 | 37.4 | 47.6 |
| May | 69.3 | 48.7 | 59.0 |
| June | 78.4 | 58.5 | 68.5 |
| July | 83.0 | 62.5 | 72.8 |
| August | 81.7 | 61.0 | 71.4 |
| September | 71.8 | 51.8 | 61.8 |
| October | 61.8 | 41.7 | 51.8 |
| November | 43.0 | 27.8 | 35.4 |
| December | 29.6 | 14.0 | 21.8 |

Zero-Degree Days: 26
Freezing Days: 152
90-Degree Days: 16
Heating- and Cooling-Degree Days: 8,112

## Las Vegas, NV

**Terrain:** Situated near the center of a broad desert valley surrounded by mountains ranging from 2,000 feet to 10,000 feet higher than the valley's floor. These mountains act as effective barriers to moisture-laden storms moving eastward from the Pacific Ocean, so that Las Vegas sees very few overcast or rainy days.

**Climate:** Summers are typical of a desert climate—low humidity with maximum temperatures in the 100-degree levels. Nearby mountains contribute to relatively cool nights, with minimums between 70° F and 75° F. Springs and falls are ideal: Outdoor activities are rarely interrupted by adverse weather conditions. Winters, too, are mild, with daytime averages of 60° F, clear skies, and warm sunshine.

**Pluses:** Mild year-round climate with especially pleasant springs and falls.

**Minuses:** High winds, though infrequent, bring dust and sand.

**Places Rated Score: 556**

**Places Rated Rank: 140**

**Elevation: 2,180 feet**

Relative Humidity: 29%
Wind Speed: 9 mph

Seasonal Change

Annual Rainfall 4 in

Annual Snowfall 1.5 in

Clear 216 days
Partly Cloudy 84 days
Cloudy 65 days

Precipitation Days: 24   Storm Days: 15

| Average Temperatures | | | |
|---|---|---|---|
| | Daily High | Daily Low | Monthly Mean |
| January | 55.7 | 32.6 | 44.2 |
| February | 61.3 | 36.9 | 49.1 |
| March | 67.8 | 41.7 | 54.8 |
| April | 77.5 | 50.0 | 63.8 |
| May | 87.5 | 59.0 | 73.3 |
| June | 97.2 | 67.4 | 82.3 |
| July | 103.9 | 75.3 | 89.6 |
| August | 101.5 | 73.3 | 87.4 |
| September | 94.8 | 65.4 | 80.1 |
| October | 81.0 | 53.1 | 67.1 |
| November | 65.7 | 40.8 | 53.3 |
| December | 56.7 | 33.7 | 45.2 |

Zero-Degree Days: 0
Freezing Days: 41
90-Degree Days: 131
Heating- and Cooling-Degree Days: 5,547

## Lexington–Fayette, KY

**Terrain:** Located in the heart of the Kentucky Bluegrass region on a gently rolling plateau with varying elevations of 900 feet to 1,050 feet. The surrounding country is noted for its beauty, fertile soil, excellent grass, stock farms, and burley tobacco. There are no bodies of water nearby that are large enough to have an effect on climate.

**Climate:** Decidedly continental, temperate, yet subject to sudden large but brief changes in temperature. Precipitation is evenly distributed throughout the winter, spring, and summer, with an average of 12 inches falling in each of these seasons. Snowfall is variable, but the ground does not retain snow for more than a few days at a time. The months of September and October are the most pleasant of the year; they have the least precipitation, the most clear days, and generally comfortable temperatures.

**Pluses:** Temperate, four-season climate with pleasant falls.

**Minuses:** Large diurnal temperature range.

**Places Rated Score: 635**

**Places Rated Rank: 48**

**Elevation: 989 feet**

Relative Humidity: 70%
Wind Speed: 9.7 mph

Seasonal Change

Annual Rainfall 50 in

Annual Snowfall 16 in

Clear 95 days   Partly Cloudy 102 days   Cloudy 168 days

Precipitation Days: 130   Storm Days: 47

| Average Temperatures | | | |
| --- | --- | --- | --- |
| | Daily High | Daily Low | Monthly Mean |
| January | 41.3 | 24.5 | 32.9 |
| February | 44.3 | 26.2 | 35.3 |
| March | 53.4 | 33.7 | 43.6 |
| April | 66.0 | 44.6 | 55.3 |
| May | 75.5 | 53.8 | 64.7 |
| June | 83.5 | 62.5 | 73.0 |
| July | 86.4 | 65.9 | 76.2 |
| August | 85.5 | 64.4 | 75.0 |
| September | 79.6 | 57.6 | 68.6 |
| October | 68.8 | 46.8 | 57.8 |
| November | 53.9 | 35.3 | 44.6 |
| December | 43.7 | 27.2 | 35.5 |

Zero-Degree Days: 2
Freezing Days: 97
90-Degree Days: 16
Heating- and Cooling-Degree Days: 5,926

## Lincoln, NE

**Terrain:** Lies on rolling prairie in southeastern Nebraska beyond the edge of the tornado and hail belt.

**Climate:** The majority of winter outbreaks of severely cold air from Canada move over the Lincoln area. However, the centers of some cold air masses move so far to the east that their full effect is not felt here. The Chinook effect often produces rapid rises in temperature during the winter, with a shift of the wind to westerly. An average winter brings 26 inches of snow, most of which doesn't melt until spring. The crop season, April through September, receives three fourths of the yearly precipitation. Nighttime showers occur mostly in the summer. There is much sunshine—Lincoln receives an average of 64% of possible sunlight—with humidity at a comfortable level, except for short periods during the summer.

**Pluses:** Varied but not too rigorous continental climate.

**Minuses:** Occasional high winds and high temperature combinations; long winters.

**Places Rated Score: 398**

**Places Rated Rank: 300**

**Elevation: 1,189 feet**

Relative Humidity: 68%
Wind Speed: 10.5 mph

Seasonal Change

Annual Rainfall 29 in

Annual Snowfall 26 in

Clear 115 days   Partly Cloudy 97 days   Cloudy 153 days

Precipitation Days: 88   Storm Days: 48

| Average Temperatures | | | |
| --- | --- | --- | --- |
| | Daily High | Daily Low | Monthly Mean |
| January | 32.8 | 11.7 | 22.2 |
| February | 38.3 | 17.4 | 27.9 |
| March | 47.0 | 26.0 | 36.5 |
| April | 63.4 | 39.2 | 51.3 |
| May | 73.4 | 50.6 | 62.0 |
| June | 83.1 | 60.9 | 72.0 |
| July | 88.9 | 65.7 | 77.3 |
| August | 87.0 | 64.2 | 75.6 |
| September | 77.5 | 53.6 | 65.6 |
| October | 67.6 | 44.2 | 54.9 |
| November | 50.3 | 27.8 | 39.0 |
| December | 37.7 | 16.9 | 27.3 |

Zero-Degree Days: 17
Freezing Days: 146
90-Degree Days: 43
Heating- and Cooling-Degree Days: 7,366

## Little Rock–North Little Rock, AR

**Terrain:** Located on the Arkansas River near the geographic center of the state. To the west lie the Ouachita Mountains and to the east the flat lowlands of the Mississippi River valley.

**Climate:** Modified four-season continental climate. The area is exposed to all North American air-mass types, but the Gulf of Mexico gives the summer season prolonged periods of warm and humid weather. Sixty-two percent of the normal annual precipitation occurs during the growing season, averaging 233 days. Winters are mild, but polar and Arctic outbreaks are not uncommon. Glaze and ice storms, though infrequent, can be severe.

**Pluses:** Negligible snow, long growing season, sufficient precipitation.

**Minuses:** Long periods of warm, humid days in summer.

**aces Rated Score: 497**

**Places Rated Rank: 227**

**Elevation: 265 feet**

Relative Humidity: 70%
Wind Speed: 8.2 mph

Seasonal Change

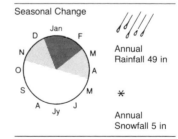

Annual Rainfall 49 in

Annual Snowfall 5 in

| Average Temperatures | | | |
| --- | --- | --- | --- |
| | Daily High | Daily Low | Monthly Mean |
| January | 50.1 | 28.9 | 39.5 |
| February | 53.8 | 31.9 | 42.9 |
| March | 61.8 | 38.7 | 50.3 |
| April | 73.5 | 49.9 | 61.7 |
| May | 81.4 | 58.1 | 69.8 |
| June | 89.3 | 66.8 | 78.1 |
| July | 92.6 | 70.1 | 81.4 |
| August | 92.6 | 68.6 | 80.6 |
| September | 85.8 | 60.8 | 73.3 |
| October | 76.0 | 48.7 | 62.4 |
| November | 62.4 | 38.1 | 50.3 |
| December | 52.1 | 31.1 | 41.6 |

Zero-Degree Days: 0
Freezing Days: 63
90-Degree Days: 70
eating- and Cooling-Degree Days: 5,279

# ★ Los Angeles–Long Beach, CA

**Terrain:** Predominating influences on the climate of Los Angeles are the Pacific Ocean, 3 miles to the west, and the southern California coastal mountain ranges, which line the inland side of the coastal plain of the city and act as buffers to the more extreme conditions of the interior.

**Climate:** The most characteristic features of this mild, two-season climate are low clouds at night and morning, and sunny afternoons that prevail during the spring and summer and occur often during the remainder of the year. Combined with a sea breeze, the coastal cloudiness is associated with mild temperatures throughout the year. Pronounced differences in temperature, humidity, fog, sunshine, and rain occur over fairly short distances on the coastal plains and adjoining foothills. Temperature ranges are least and humidity higher close to the coast; precipitation increases with elevation.

**Pluses:** Positive benefits from Pacific Ocean and surrounding foothills.

**Minuses:** Frequent haze, fog, and smoke; dry Santa Ana winds.

**Places Rated Score: 885**

**Places Rated Rank: 5**

**Elevation: 104 feet**

Relative Humidity: 71%
Wind Speed: 7.4 mph

Seasonal Change

Annual Rainfall 12 in

Annual Snowfall 0 in

Clear 143 days
Partly Cloudy 115 days
Cloudy 107 days

Precipitation Days: 35     Storm Days: 3

| Average Temperatures | | | |
|---|---|---|---|
| | Daily High | Daily Low | Monthly Mean |
| January | 63.5 | 45.4 | 54.5 |
| February | 64.1 | 47.0 | 55.6 |
| March | 64.3 | 48.6 | 56.5 |
| April | 65.9 | 51.7 | 58.8 |
| May | 68.4 | 55.3 | 61.9 |
| June | 70.3 | 58.6 | 64.5 |
| July | 74.8 | 62.1 | 68.5 |
| August | 75.8 | 63.2 | 69.5 |
| September | 75.7 | 61.6 | 68.7 |
| October | 72.9 | 57.5 | 65.2 |
| November | 69.6 | 51.3 | 60.5 |
| December | 66.5 | 47.3 | 56.9 |

Zero-Degree Days: 0
Freezing Days: 0
90-Degree Days: 5
Heating- and Cooling-Degree Days: 2,437

# Louisville, KY–IN

**Terrain:** Located on the south bank of the Ohio River, about 400 miles southwest of Pittsburgh. The eastern part of the city is residential and consists of rolling hills and plateaus. The western, industrial part lies on the river's floodplain. A low range of hills on the Indiana bank provides a partial barrier to icy blasts of winter.

**Climate:** Continental, but more variable because of its position in midlatitudes, in the belt of westerly winds, not completely shut off from the Gulf of Mexico. Winters are moderately cold. Snows, although seldom heavy, are a usual occurrence from November through March. Summers are quite warm, with high relative humidity and rainstorms of high intensity common during both springs and summers.

**Pluses:** Well-defined seasons with good precipitation.

**Minuses:** Humid summers, intense rainfalls.

**Places Rated Score: 616**

**Places Rated Rank: 60**

**Elevation: 488 feet**

Relative Humidity: 69%
Wind Speed: 8.4 mph

Seasonal Change

Annual Rainfall 43 in

Annual Snowfall 17 in

Clear 94 days
Partly Cloudy 103 days
Cloudy 168 days

Precipitation Days: 124   Storm Days: 45

| Average Temperatures | | | |
|---|---|---|---|
| | Daily High | Daily Low | Monthly Mean |
| January | 42.0 | 24.5 | 33.3 |
| February | 45.0 | 26.5 | 35.8 |
| March | 54.0 | 34.0 | 44.0 |
| April | 66.9 | 44.8 | 55.9 |
| May | 75.6 | 53.9 | 64.8 |
| June | 83.7 | 62.9 | 73.3 |
| July | 87.3 | 66.4 | 76.9 |
| August | 86.8 | 64.9 | 75.9 |
| September | 80.5 | 57.7 | 69.1 |
| October | 70.3 | 45.9 | 58.1 |
| November | 54.9 | 35.1 | 45.0 |
| December | 44.1 | 27.1 | 35.6 |

Zero-Degree Days: 2
Freezing Days: 92
90-Degree Days: 24
Heating- and Cooling-Degree Days: 5,908

# Lubbock, TX

**Terrain:** Located in a plateau area of northwestern Texas that is often referred to as the South Plains region. It is an essentially level area with numerous small playas, small stream valleys, and low hummocks. There are no appreciable terrain features that affect wind flow across the plateau.

**Climate:** Semiarid, transitional between desert conditions to the west and humid climates to the east. Normal precipitation is 18 inches per year, with maximum precipitation occurring during May, June, and July, when warm tropical air is carried inland from the Gulf of Mexico. This air mass produces moderate to heavy afternoon and evening convective thunderstorms, sometimes with hail. Dry daytime winds help alleviate summer heat.

**Pluses:** Generally pleasant climate year-round.

**Minuses:** During dry spells, high winds cause dusty conditions.

**Places Rated Score: 604**

**Places Rated Rank: 71**

**Elevation: 3,241 feet**

Relative Humidity: 56%
Wind Speed: 10.8 mph

Seasonal Change

Annual Rainfall 18 in

Annual Snowfall 9.6 in

Clear 164 days
Partly Cloudy 103 days
Cloudy 98 days

Precipitation Days: 60   Storm Days: 45

| Average Temperatures | | | |
|---|---|---|---|
| | Daily High | Daily Low | Monthly Mean |
| January | 53.4 | 24.8 | 39.1 |
| February | 57.0 | 28.3 | 42.7 |
| March | 63.8 | 34.0 | 48.9 |
| April | 74.8 | 45.1 | 60.0 |
| May | 82.5 | 54.5 | 68.5 |
| June | 90.6 | 63.6 | 77.1 |
| July | 92.4 | 66.9 | 79.7 |
| August | 91.3 | 65.5 | 78.4 |
| September | 83.8 | 58.2 | 71.0 |
| October | 74.7 | 47.3 | 61.0 |
| November | 63.1 | 34.4 | 48.8 |
| December | 55.2 | 27.4 | 41.3 |

Zero-Degree Days: 0
Freezing Days: 98
90-Degree Days: 77
Heating- and Cooling-Degree Days: 5,192

# Madison, WI

**Terrain:** Madison sits on a narrow isthmus of land between Lakes Mendota (15 square miles) and Monona (5 square miles). Normally these lakes are frozen from December 17 to April 5. Most farming is dairying, with field crops mainly of corn, oats, and alfalfa. The majority of fruits grown are apples, strawberries, and raspberries.

**Climate:** Continental, typical of interior North America, with a large annual temperature range and frequent short periods of temperature changes. The absolute temperature range is from 107° F to −37° F. Winter temperatures average 20° F and summer ones 68° F. The most common air masses are of polar origin, with occasional outbreaks of Arctic air during the winter. Much of the precipitation falls between May and September. Lighter winter precipitation falls over a longer period of time. Average growing season: 175 days.

**Pluses:** Pleasant summers with moderate growing season; even precipitation.

**Minuses:** Long, severe winters.

**Places Rated Score: 378**

**Places Rated Rank: 307**

**Elevation: 866 feet**

Relative Humidity: 73%
Wind Speed: 9.9 mph

Seasonal Change

Annual Rainfall 30 in

Annual Snowfall 39 in

Clear 94 days | Partly Cloudy 96 days | Cloudy 175 days

Precipitation Days: 117  Storm Days: 40

| Average Temperatures | | | |
|---|---|---|---|
| | Daily High | Daily Low | Monthly Mean |
| January | 25.4 | 8.2 | 16.8 |
| February | 29.5 | 11.1 | 20.3 |
| March | 39.2 | 21.2 | 30.2 |
| April | 56.0 | 34.6 | 45.3 |
| May | 67.3 | 44.6 | 56.0 |
| June | 76.9 | 54.6 | 65.8 |
| July | 81.4 | 58.8 | 70.1 |
| August | 80.0 | 57.3 | 68.7 |
| September | 70.9 | 48.5 | 59.7 |
| October | 60.9 | 38.9 | 49.9 |
| November | 43.0 | 26.4 | 34.7 |
| December | 29.8 | 14.0 | 21.9 |

Zero-Degree Days: 25
Freezing Days: 164
90-Degree Days: 12
Heating- and Cooling-Degree Days: 8,190

# Manchester, NH

**Terrain:** Surrounded by hills, with many lakes and ponds. Manchester is situated on the Merrimack River near the geographic center of the New England region. The countryside is generously wooded, most of it land that was formerly used for farming. Mount Washington, the highest peak in the Presidential Chain of the White Mountains (and the site of perhaps the most violent weather in the continental United States), is 75 miles north.

**Climate:** Northwesterly winds prevail here, bringing cold, dry air during the winter and pleasantly cool, dry air in the summer. Although the winters here are long, cold, and snowy, the summers are ideal, with warm sunny days and cool nights. Thus the Manchester area and New Hampshire in general offer year-round recreation: Ski areas and other resorts dot the countryside. Agriculture is limited to freeze-resistant crops, such as potatoes and apples, and to forage crops for the dairy industry.

**Pluses:** Good rugged climate, pleasant summers.

**Minuses:** Long, cold, snowy winters.

**Places Rated Score: 404**

**Places Rated Rank: 296**

**Elevation: 346 feet**

Relative Humidity: 73%
Wind Speed: 6.7 mph

Seasonal Change

Annual Rainfall 36 in

Annual Snowfall 64 in

Clear 92 days | Partly Cloudy 113 days | Cloudy 160 days

Precipitation Days: 125  Storm Days: 21

| Average Temperatures | | | |
|---|---|---|---|
| | Daily High | Daily Low | Monthly Mean |
| January | 31.3 | 9.9 | 20.6 |
| February | 33.8 | 11.3 | 22.6 |
| March | 42.4 | 22.1 | 32.3 |
| April | 56.7 | 31.7 | 44.2 |
| May | 68.6 | 41.5 | 55.1 |
| June | 77.7 | 51.6 | 64.7 |
| July | 82.6 | 56.7 | 69.7 |
| August | 80.1 | 54.2 | 67.2 |
| September | 72.4 | 46.5 | 59.5 |
| October | 62.3 | 36.3 | 49.3 |
| November | 47.9 | 28.1 | 38.0 |
| December | 34.6 | 14.9 | 24.8 |

Zero-Degree Days: 26
Freezing Days: 176
90-Degree Days: 11
Heating- and Cooling-Degree Days: 7,709

# Medford, OR

**Terrain:** Located in a mountain valley formed by the famous Rogue River and one of its tributaries, Bear Creek. Most of the valley ranges in elevation from 1,300 feet to 1,400 feet above sea level. The valley's outlet to the ocean 80 miles west is the narrow canyon of the Rogue.

**Climate:** Moderate, with marked seasonal characteristics. Late fall, winter, and early spring are cloudy, damp, and cool. The remainder of the year is warm, dry, and sunny. The rain shadow afforded by the Siskiyous and the Coast Ranges results in relatively light rainfall, most of which falls in the wintertime. Snowfalls are very light and seldom remain on the ground more than 24 hours. Winters are mild, with the temperatures just dipping below freezing during December and January. Summer days can reach 90° F, but nights are cool. The climate is ideal for truck and fruit farming, and the area is dotted with orchards.

**Pluses:** Very mild four-season climate; sunny summers.

**Minuses:** Half the year is damp and cloudy.

**Places Rated Score: 611**

**Places Rated Rank: 67**

**Elevation: 1,298 feet**

Relative Humidity: 67%
Wind Speed: 4.8 mph

Seasonal Change

Annual Rainfall 21 in

Annual Snowfall 8 in

Clear 117 days | Partly Cloudy 79 days | Cloudy 169 days

Precipitation Days: 101  Storm Days: 9

| Average Temperatures | | | |
|---|---|---|---|
| | Daily High | Daily Low | Monthly Mean |
| January | 44.2 | 29.0 | 36.6 |
| February | 51.8 | 30.7 | 41.3 |
| March | 56.7 | 32.8 | 44.8 |
| April | 63.8 | 36.6 | 50.2 |
| May | 71.7 | 42.8 | 57.3 |
| June | 79.4 | 49.1 | 64.3 |
| July | 89.5 | 53.8 | 71.7 |
| August | 87.8 | 52.9 | 70.4 |
| September | 82.1 | 46.7 | 64.4 |
| October | 67.4 | 39.1 | 53.4 |
| November | 52.7 | 34.2 | 43.5 |
| December | 44.2 | 31.1 | 37.7 |

Zero-Degree Days: 0
Freezing Days: 90
90-Degree Days: 54
Heating- and Cooling-Degree Days: 5,492

## Memphis, TN–AR–MS

**Terrain:** Located on the east bank of the Mississippi River in slightly rolling topography, across from the level alluvial area on the Arkansas side. Major crops are cotton, corn, peaches, apples, and vegetables. The climate is favorable for dairying and for raising cattle and hogs.
**Climate:** Though not in the normal paths of storms coming from the Gulf of Mexico or from Canada, Memphis is affected by both and therefore has comparatively frequent changes in weather. Extremes in highs and lows are relatively rare; the average annual temperature is in the low 60s and varies from the low 40s in January to the low 80s in July. Average growing season: 230 days.

**Pluses:** Short winters, long summers, moderate temperature variation.

**Minuses:** Frequent weather changes, occasional humid periods in summer.

**Places Rated Score: 514**

**Places Rated Rank: 211**

**Elevation: 284 feet**

Relative Humidity: 69%
Wind Speed: 9.2 mph

Seasonal Change

Annual Rainfall 49 in

Annual Snowfall 6 in

Clear 118 days  Partly Cloudy 99 days  Cloudy 148 days

Precipitation Days: 106  Storm Days: 53

| Average Temperatures | | | |
|---|---|---|---|
| | Daily High | Daily Low | Monthly Mean |
| January | 49.4 | 31.6 | 40.5 |
| February | 53.1 | 34.4 | 43.8 |
| March | 60.8 | 41.1 | 51.0 |
| April | 72.7 | 52.3 | 62.5 |
| May | 81.2 | 60.6 | 70.9 |
| June | 88.7 | 68.5 | 78.6 |
| July | 91.6 | 71.5 | 81.6 |
| August | 90.6 | 70.1 | 80.4 |
| September | 84.3 | 62.8 | 73.6 |
| October | 74.9 | 51.1 | 63.0 |
| November | 61.5 | 40.3 | 50.9 |
| December | 51.7 | 33.7 | 42.7 |

Zero-Degree Days: 0
Freezing Days: 59
90-Degree Days: 64
Heating- and Cooling-Degree Days: 5,256

## Miami–Hialeah, FL

**Terrain:** Located on the lower east coast of Florida. To the east lies Biscayne Bay, and east of it Miami Beach. The surrounding country-side is level and sparsely wooded.
**Climate:** Essentially subtropical marine, characterized by a long, warm summer with abundant rainfall and a mild, dry winter. The Atlantic Ocean greatly influences the city's small range of daily temperature and aids the rapid warming of colder air masses that pass to the east of the state. During the early morning hours, more rainfall occurs at Miami Beach than at the airport (9 miles inland), while during the afternoon the reverse is true. Even more striking is the difference in the annual number of days over 90° F: at Miami Beach, 15 days; at the airport, 60. Freezing temperatures occur occasionally in surrounding farming districts but almost never near the ocean. In 1977, for the first time in Miami's history, traces of snow were reported. Tropical hurricanes affect the area and are most frequent in early fall.

**Pluses:** Single-season, sub-tropical climate.

**Minuses:** Hurricanes, frequent thunderstorms.

**Places Rated Score: 634**

**Places Rated Rank: 49**

**Elevation: 12 feet**

Relative Humidity: 75%
Wind Speed: 9.1 mph

Seasonal Change

Annual Rainfall 60 in

Annual Snowfall 0 in

Clear 76 days  Partly Cloudy 172 days  Cloudy 117 days

Precipitation Days: 129  Storm Days: 75

| Average Temperatures | | | |
|---|---|---|---|
| | Daily High | Daily Low | Monthly Mean |
| January | 75.6 | 58.7 | 67.2 |
| February | 76.6 | 59.0 | 67.8 |
| March | 79.5 | 63.0 | 71.3 |
| April | 82.7 | 67.3 | 75.0 |
| May | 85.3 | 70.7 | 78.0 |
| June | 88.0 | 73.9 | 81.0 |
| July | 89.1 | 75.5 | 82.3 |
| August | 89.9 | 75.8 | 82.9 |
| September | 88.3 | 75.0 | 81.7 |
| October | 84.6 | 71.0 | 77.8 |
| November | 79.9 | 64.5 | 72.2 |
| December | 76.6 | 60.0 | 68.3 |

Zero-Degree Days: 0
Freezing Days: 0
90-Degree Days: 30
Heating- and Cooling-Degree Days: 4,244

## Midland, TX

**Terrain:** Located on the southern extension of the South Plains region of Texas. Topography is level, with only slight and infrequent undulations. Vegetation consists mainly of grasses, and there are very few trees in the area, most of them mesquite.
**Climate:** Semiarid. Droughts occur with monotonous frequency, resulting in dust storms so severe that suspended dust remains in the air several days after the storm has passed. Though summer afternoon temperatures are frequently above 90° F, low humidity and rapid evaporation have a cooling effect. The climate is generally pleasant, with the most disagreeable weather concentrated in late winter and spring.

**Pluses:** Short winters; long, pleasant summers and falls.

**Minuses:** Severe drought conditions, frequent dust storms.

**Places Rated Score: 603**

**Places Rated Rank: 72**

**Elevation: 2,862 feet**

Relative Humidity: 53%
Wind Speed: 10.8 mph

Seasonal Change

Annual Rainfall 14 in

Annual Snowfall 3.5 in

Clear 167 days  Partly Cloudy 97 days  Cloudy 101 days

Precipitation Days: 51  Storm Days: 36

| Average Temperatures | | | |
|---|---|---|---|
| | Daily High | Daily Low | Monthly Mean |
| January | 57.8 | 29.4 | 43.6 |
| February | 62.1 | 33.5 | 47.8 |
| March | 69.4 | 39.2 | 54.3 |
| April | 79.1 | 49.4 | 64.3 |
| May | 86.5 | 58.1 | 72.3 |
| June | 92.8 | 66.9 | 79.9 |
| July | 95.0 | 69.5 | 82.3 |
| August | 94.4 | 69.1 | 81.8 |
| September | 87.9 | 62.8 | 75.4 |
| October | 79.2 | 52.4 | 65.8 |
| November | 67.5 | 39.1 | 53.3 |
| December | 60.1 | 31.6 | 45.9 |

Zero-Degree Days: 0
Freezing Days: 65
90-Degree Days: 89
Heating- and Cooling-Degree Days: 4,871

## Milwaukee, WI

**Terrain:** Milwaukee is situated on the west shore of Lake Michigan, 50 miles north of Chicago.

**Climate:** Influenced by storms that move eastward across the upper Ohio River valley and the Great Lakes region. Large high-pressure systems moving southeastward out of Canada also have an effect, and it is seldom that two or three days will pass without a distinct change in the weather, particularly during winter and spring. The major influence on the climate is Lake Michigan, which has a particularly marked effect when the temperature of the water differs considerably from that of the air. Generally, the lake cools the shoreline in summer and warms it in winter. Thunderstorms occur less frequently in Milwaukee than in areas to the south and west. Winters are cloudy. Summers are usually clear, receiving an average of 70% of possible sunshine.

**Pluses:** Lake Michigan has a moderating effect on temperature extremes.

**Minuses:** Subject to severe winter storm systems.

**Places Rated Score: 460**

**Places Rated Rank: 264**

**Elevation: 693 feet**

Relative Humidity: 73%
Wind Speed: 11.8 mph

Seasonal Change

Annual Rainfall 29 in

Annual Snowfall 45 in

Clear
96 days

Partly Cloudy
99 days

Cloudy
170 days

Precipitation Days: 122　Storm Days: 36

| Average Temperatures | | | |
|---|---|---|---|
| | Daily High | Daily Low | Monthly Mean |
| January | 27.3 | 11.4 | 19.4 |
| February | 30.3 | 14.6 | 22.5 |
| March | 39.4 | 23.4 | 31.4 |
| April | 54.6 | 34.7 | 44.7 |
| May | 65.0 | 43.3 | 54.2 |
| June | 75.3 | 53.6 | 64.5 |
| July | 80.4 | 59.3 | 69.9 |
| August | 79.7 | 58.7 | 69.2 |
| September | 71.5 | 50.7 | 61.1 |
| October | 61.4 | 40.6 | 51.0 |
| November | 44.4 | 28.5 | 36.5 |
| December | 31.5 | 16.8 | 24.2 |

Zero-Degree Days: 16
Freezing Days: 146
90-Degree Days: 9
Heating- and Cooling-Degree Days: 7,894

## Minneapolis–St. Paul, MN–WI

**Terrain:** The Twin Cities are located at the confluence of the Mississippi and Minnesota rivers over the heart of an artesian water basin. The topography is flat or gently rolling with numerous lakes that are small, shallow, and ice-covered in winter.

**Climate:** Predominantly continental (the two cities are near the geographic center of North America). There are wide variations in temperature, ample summer rainfall, and scanty winter precipitation. In general, there exists a tendency toward extremes in almost all climatic features.

**Pluses:** Changeable weather that many find stimulating and invigorating.

**Minuses:** Extreme weather features; severe, long winters.

**Places Rated Score: 283**

**Places Rated Rank: 320**

**Elevation: 838 feet**

Relative Humidity: 69%
Wind Speed: 10.5 mph

Seasonal Change

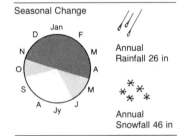

Annual Rainfall 26 in

Annual Snowfall 46 in

Clear
100 days

Partly Cloudy
100 days

Cloudy
165 days

Precipitation Days: 113　Storm Days: 36

| Average Temperatures | | | |
|---|---|---|---|
| | Daily High | Daily Low | Monthly Mean |
| January | 21.2 | 3.2 | 12.2 |
| February | 25.9 | 7.1 | 16.5 |
| March | 36.9 | 19.6 | 28.3 |
| April | 55.5 | 34.7 | 45.1 |
| May | 67.9 | 46.3 | 57.1 |
| June | 77.1 | 56.7 | 66.9 |
| July | 82.4 | 61.4 | 71.9 |
| August | 80.8 | 59.6 | 70.2 |
| September | 70.7 | 49.3 | 60.0 |
| October | 60.7 | 39.2 | 50.0 |
| November | 40.6 | 24.2 | 32.4 |
| December | 26.6 | 10.6 | 18.6 |

Zero-Degree Days: 34
Freezing Days: 158
90-Degree Days: 15
Heating- and Cooling-Degree Days: 8,744

## Mobile, AL

**Terrain:** Located at the head of Mobile Bay, approximately 30 miles from the Gulf of Mexico.

**Climate:** Although Mobile has not had a destructive hurricane since 1926, this seems to be due more to chance than to location. The area is subject to hurricanes from the West Indies and the Gulf of Mexico. The normal annual rainfall is among the highest in the United States. It is evenly distributed throughout the year, with a slight maximum at the height of the summer thunderstorm season (there are thunderstorms every other day during July and August). Most of these storms are showers; long periods of continuous rain are rare. The growing season averages 274 days, enough for citrus fruit to be grown in the area.

**Pluses:** Mild winters, ample and even precipitation.

**Minuses:** Summers are hot and muggy with frequent thunderstorms, area prone to hurricanes.

**Places Rated Score: 442**

**Places Rated Rank: 275**

**Elevation: 221 feet**

Relative Humidity: 73%
Wind Speed: 9.2 mph

Seasonal Change

Annual Rainfall 67 in

Clear
100 days

Partly Cloudy
117 days

Cloudy
148 days

Precipitation Days: 124　Storm Days: 80

| Average Temperatures | | | |
|---|---|---|---|
| | Daily High | Daily Low | Monthly Mean |
| January | 61.1 | 41.3 | 51.2 |
| February | 64.1 | 43.9 | 54.0 |
| March | 69.5 | 49.2 | 59.4 |
| April | 78.0 | 57.7 | 67.9 |
| May | 85.0 | 64.5 | 74.8 |
| June | 89.8 | 70.7 | 80.3 |
| July | 90.5 | 72.6 | 81.6 |
| August | 90.6 | 72.3 | 81.5 |
| September | 86.5 | 68.4 | 77.5 |
| October | 79.7 | 58.0 | 68.9 |
| November | 69.5 | 47.5 | 58.5 |
| December | 63.0 | 42.8 | 52.9 |

Zero-Degree Days: 0
Freezing Days: 19
90-Degree Days: 81
Heating- and Cooling-Degree Days: 4,261

## Montgomery, AL

**Terrain:** Located in a gently rolling area of southern Alabama. No local topographic features appreciably influence climate.

**Climate:** From June through September, humidity and temperature conditions show little daily change. During summer, 100-degree readings are infrequent. From April through September, all precipitation is from local heat thundershowers in the afternoon. Rain is abundant and includes all types and intensities from December through March. During the coldest months (December, January, and February), there are frequent shifts between mild, moist air from the Gulf of Mexico and dry, cool continental air. Hard freezes are infrequent during winter; snow is rare enough to be a curiosity.

**Pluses:** Mild, two-season climate with abundant rainfall.

**Minuses:** Humid summers and falls, lots of cloudy days.

**Places Rated Score: 483**

**Places Rated Rank: 240**

**Elevation: 202 feet**

Relative Humidity: 73%
Wind Speed: 6.8 mph

Seasonal Change

Annual Rainfall 50 in

Annual Snowfall .2 in

Clear 107 days
Partly Cloudy 109 days
Cloudy 149 days

Precipitation Days: 109   Storm Days: 62

| Average Temperatures | | | |
|---|---|---|---|
| | Daily High | Daily Low | Monthly Mean |
| January | 57.9 | 37.1 | 47.5 |
| February | 61.4 | 39.7 | 50.6 |
| March | 67.7 | 45.2 | 56.5 |
| April | 76.8 | 53.6 | 65.2 |
| May | 83.6 | 61.2 | 72.4 |
| June | 89.2 | 68.6 | 78.9 |
| July | 90.5 | 71.5 | 81.0 |
| August | 90.7 | 70.7 | 80.7 |
| September | 86.5 | 65.5 | 76.0 |
| October | 78.0 | 53.5 | 65.8 |
| November | 67.2 | 42.7 | 55.0 |
| December | 59.3 | 37.7 | 48.5 |

Zero-Degree Days: 0
Freezing Days: 39
90-Degree Days: 66
Heating- and Cooling-Degree Days: 4,507

## Nashville, TN

**Terrain:** Located on the Cumberland River in the northwestern corner of the Nashville Basin, near the escarpment of the Highland Rim. The rim rises 400 feet above the mean elevation of the basin, forming an amphitheater around the city from the southwest to the southeast.

**Climate:** Moderate temperatures. Extremes of heat or cold are rare, yet fairly frequent changes give variety. The humidity is moderate compared with other locations east of the Mississippi River and south of the Ohio River. The city is not in the most highly traveled path of general storm systems that cross the country; however, it is in a zone that experiences thunderstorms moderately often. Average growing season: 211 days.

**Pluses:** Fairly mild four-season climate, long summers.

**Minuses:** Relatively few clear days.

**Places Rated Score: 600**

**Places Rated Rank: 79**

**Elevation: 605 feet**

Relative Humidity: 71%
Wind Speed: 7.9 mph

Seasonal Change

Annual Rainfall 46 in

Annual Snowfall 10.7 in

Clear 103 days
Partly Cloudy 107 days
Cloudy 155 days

Precipitation Days: 119   Storm Days: 55

| Average Temperatures | | | |
|---|---|---|---|
| | Daily High | Daily Low | Monthly Mean |
| January | 47.6 | 29.0 | 38.3 |
| February | 50.9 | 31.0 | 41.0 |
| March | 59.2 | 38.1 | 48.7 |
| April | 71.3 | 48.8 | 60.1 |
| May | 79.8 | 57.3 | 68.5 |
| June | 87.5 | 65.7 | 76.6 |
| July | 90.2 | 69.0 | 79.6 |
| August | 89.2 | 67.7 | 78.5 |
| September | 83.5 | 60.5 | 72.0 |
| October | 73.2 | 48.6 | 60.9 |
| November | 59.0 | 37.7 | 48.4 |
| December | 49.6 | 31.1 | 40.4 |

Zero-Degree Days: 1
Freezing Days: 75
90-Degree Days: 37
Heating- and Cooling-Degree Days: 5,390

## New Bedford, MA

**Terrain:** New Bedford, one of America's most famous whaling ports, lies at the mouth of the Acushnet River in Buzzards Bay. The terrain is relatively flat and low-lying, which makes New Bedford especially vulnerable to tidal hurricane surges. Because of severe hurricanes that have struck the area over the last 50 years, huge floodgates have been installed around the city and remain an interesting sight.

**Climate:** Although this fishing port and manufacturing center is only an hour and a half south of Boston, there's a great difference between the climates of the two cities. New Bedford, located on the northern portion of Rhode Island Sound in a large bay, is almost surrounded by ocean. Thus, it enjoys a modified maritime climate characterized by cool summer ocean breezes and warm ocean air in the wintertime. When Boston is in the midst of a blizzard, New Bedford is usually experiencing rain or sleet that melts away in a few days. Similarly, when Boston and points north simmer in a summer heat wave, New Bedford is usually cooler.

**Pluses:** Mild maritime climate.

**Minuses:** Ice storms.

**Places Rated Score: 643**

**Places Rated Rank: 40**

**Elevation: 60 feet**

Relative Humidity: 76%
Wind Speed: 10 mph

Seasonal Change

Annual Rainfall 45 in

Annual Snowfall 36 in

Clear 97 days
Partly Cloudy 114 days
Cloudy 154 days

Precipitation Days: 79   Storm Days: 14

| Average Temperatures | | | |
|---|---|---|---|
| | Daily High | Daily Low | Monthly Mean |
| January | 36.3 | 21.6 | 29.0 |
| February | 38.4 | 22.7 | 30.6 |
| March | 45.2 | 29.6 | 37.4 |
| April | 56.8 | 38.5 | 47.7 |
| May | 67.3 | 47.6 | 57.5 |
| June | 76.6 | 57.6 | 67.1 |
| July | 81.7 | 63.8 | 72.8 |
| August | 80.3 | 62.4 | 71.3 |
| September | 73.4 | 55.2 | 64.3 |
| October | 63.3 | 45.7 | 54.5 |
| November | 51.0 | 36.3 | 43.7 |
| December | 40.2 | 25.8 | 33.1 |

Zero-Degree Days: 0
Freezing Days: 110
90-Degree Days: 5
Heating- and Cooling-Degree Days: 6,373

# New Orleans, LA

**Terrain:** The metropolitan area is surrounded by water: Lake Pontchartrain (610 square miles) to the north; the Mississippi River to the east and south; bayous, lakes, and marshy delta land to the west and south. Elevations in the city vary from a few feet above mean sea level to a few feet below. A massive levee system offers protection from river flooding and tidal surges.

**Climate:** Best described as humid with surrounding water modifying the temperature and decreasing the range of temperatures. Heavy and frequent rains are typical, and there are daily afternoon thunderstorms from mid-June through September. From December to March, precipitation is likely to be steady rain of two or three days' duration, instead of showers. During winter and spring, cold rain forms fogs that inhibit air and river transportation. The city has been hard hit by three hurricanes since 1900.

**Pluses:** Tropical climate moderated by water.

**Minuses:** Hot and humid, heavy rains and fogs, hurricanes.

**Places Rated Score: 498**　　　　**Places Rated Rank: 226**

**Elevation: 30 feet**

Relative Humidity: 77%
Wind Speed: 8.4 mph

Seasonal Change

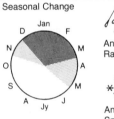

Annual Rainfall 57 in

Annual Snowfall .2 in

Clear 109 days　Partly Cloudy 120 days　Cloudy 136 days

Precipitation Days: 113　Storm Days: 68

| Average Temperatures | | | |
| --- | --- | --- | --- |
| | Daily High | Daily Low | Monthly Mean |
| January | 62.3 | 43.5 | 52.9 |
| February | 65.1 | 46.0 | 55.6 |
| March | 70.4 | 50.9 | 60.7 |
| April | 78.4 | 58.8 | 68.6 |
| May | 84.9 | 65.3 | 75.1 |
| June | 89.6 | 71.2 | 80.4 |
| July | 90.4 | 73.3 | 81.9 |
| August | 90.6 | 73.1 | 81.9 |
| September | 86.6 | 69.7 | 78.2 |
| October | 79.9 | 59.6 | 69.8 |
| November | 70.3 | 49.8 | 60.1 |
| December | 64.2 | 45.3 | 54.8 |

Zero-Degree Days: 0
Freezing Days: 13
90-Degree Days: 67
Heating- and Cooling-Degree Days: 4,171

# New York, NY

**Terrain:** Located on the Atlantic Coastal Plain at the mouth of the Hudson River. Topography is diversified by numerous waterways: All but one of the city's five boroughs are situated on islands.

**Climate:** Close to the path of most storm and frontal systems that move across the continent. Therefore, weather conditions affecting the city approach from a westerly direction. New York City can thus experience higher temperatures in summer and lower ones in winter than would otherwise be expected in a coastal area. However, the frequent passage of weather systems often helps reduce the length of warm and cold spells and also keeps periods of air stagnation brief. Although continental influence is dominant, ocean influence is by no means absent. Sea breezes moderate the afternoon heat of summer and delay the advent of winter snows. The Atlantic's influence is also measured in the length of the frost-free season—more than 200 days.

**Pluses:** Moderating ocean influence, mild summers and falls.

**Minuses:** Coastal storms bring record snow and rain.

**Places Rated Score: 638**　　　　**Places Rated Rank: 44**

**Elevation: 87 feet**

Relative Humidity: 65%
Wind Speed: 9.4 mph

Seasonal Change

Annual Rainfall 40 in

Annual Snowfall 29 in

Clear 107 days　Partly Cloudy 125 days　Cloudy 133 days

Precipitation Days: 121　Storm Days: 20

| Average Temperatures | | | |
| --- | --- | --- | --- |
| | Daily High | Daily Low | Monthly Mean |
| January | 38.5 | 25.9 | 32.2 |
| February | 40.2 | 26.5 | 33.4 |
| March | 48.4 | 33.7 | 41.1 |
| April | 60.7 | 43.5 | 52.1 |
| May | 71.4 | 53.1 | 62.3 |
| June | 80.5 | 62.6 | 71.6 |
| July | 85.2 | 68.0 | 76.6 |
| August | 83.4 | 66.4 | 74.9 |
| September | 76.8 | 59.9 | 68.4 |
| October | 66.8 | 50.6 | 58.7 |
| November | 54.0 | 40.8 | 47.4 |
| December | 41.4 | 29.5 | 35.5 |

Zero-Degree Days: 0
Freezing Days: 81
90-Degree Days: 16
Heating- and Cooling-Degree Days: 5,916

# Norfolk–Virginia Beach–Newport News, VA

**Terrain:** Located on low level land, with Chesapeake Bay immediately to the north, Hampton Roads to the west, and the Atlantic Ocean to the east.

**Climate:** The metro area is in a favorable geographic position, being north of the track of hurricanes and tropical storms and south of high-latitude storm systems. Winters are mild. Springs and falls are especially pleasant. Summers, though, are warm, humid, and long. A temperature of zero has never been recorded here, although there is occasional snow.

**Pluses:** Four-season climate suited for year-round outdoor activities.

**Minuses:** Long, humid summers.

**Places Rated Score: 632**　　　　**Places Rated Rank: 50**

**Elevation: 30 feet**

Relative Humidity: 71%
Wind Speed: 10.6 mph

Seasonal Change

Annual Rainfall 45 in

Annual Snowfall 7 in

Clear 110 days　Partly Cloudy 102 days　Cloudy 153 days

Precipitation Days: 115　Storm Days: 37

| Average Temperatures | | | |
| --- | --- | --- | --- |
| | Daily High | Daily Low | Monthly Mean |
| January | 48.8 | 32.2 | 40.5 |
| February | 50.0 | 32.7 | 41.4 |
| March | 57.3 | 38.9 | 48.1 |
| April | 67.7 | 47.9 | 57.8 |
| May | 76.2 | 57.2 | 66.7 |
| June | 83.5 | 65.5 | 74.5 |
| July | 86.6 | 69.9 | 78.3 |
| August | 84.9 | 68.9 | 76.9 |
| September | 79.6 | 63.9 | 71.8 |
| October | 70.1 | 53.3 | 61.7 |
| November | 60.5 | 42.6 | 51.6 |
| December | 50.6 | 34.0 | 42.3 |

Zero-Degree Days: 0
Freezing Days: 54
90-Degree Days: 30
Heating- and Cooling-Degree Days: 4,929

## Oklahoma City, OK

**Terrain:** Situated along the North Canadian River at the geographic center of the state. The countryside is rolling, with the nearest hills, the Arbuckles, 80 miles south.

**Climate:** Although some influence is exerted at times by warm, moist air from the Gulf of Mexico, the climate of the city falls mainly under continental controls characteristic of the Great Plains. The continental effect produces pronounced daily and seasonal temperature changes and considerable variation in seasonal and annual precipitation. Summers are long and usually hot. Winters are comparatively mild and short.

**Pluses:** Clear days, mild winters.

**Minuses:** Long, hot summers; tornadoes.

**Places Rated Score: 554**

**Places Rated Rank: 142**

**Elevation: 1,304 feet**

Relative Humidity: 65%
Wind Speed: 12.8 mph

Seasonal Change

Annual Rainfall 31 in

Annual Snowfall 9 in

Clear 141 days
Partly Cloudy 96 days
Cloudy 128 days

Precipitation Days: 81     Storm Days: 51

| Average Temperatures | | | |
|---|---|---|---|
| | Daily High | Daily Low | Monthly Mean |
| January | 47.6 | 26.0 | 36.8 |
| February | 52.6 | 30.0 | 41.3 |
| March | 59.8 | 36.5 | 48.2 |
| April | 71.6 | 49.1 | 60.4 |
| May | 78.7 | 57.9 | 68.3 |
| June | 87.0 | 66.6 | 76.8 |
| July | 92.6 | 70.4 | 81.5 |
| August | 92.5 | 69.6 | 81.1 |
| September | 84.7 | 61.3 | 73.0 |
| October | 74.2 | 50.6 | 62.4 |
| November | 60.9 | 37.4 | 49.2 |
| December | 50.7 | 29.2 | 40.0 |

Zero-Degree Days: 0
Freezing Days: 80
90-Degree Days: 64
Heating- and Cooling-Degree Days: 5,571

## ★ Olympia, WA

**Terrain:** The capital of the state of Washington, Olympia lies at the southernmost end of Puget Sound, some 60 miles south-southwest of Seattle. The Olympic Peninsula, with its fine remnants of the Pacific Northwest rain forests, active glaciers, and alpine meadows, lies to the northwest. The city and vicinity are well protected by the Coast Ranges from the strong south and southwest winds accompanying many Pacific storms during the fall and winter.

**Climate:** Characterized by warm, generally dry summers and wet, mild winters. Fall rains begin in October and continue with few interruptions until spring. During the rainy season there is little variation in temperature, with days in the 40s and 50s and nights in the 30s, and constant cloud cover. The summer highs are between 60° F and 80° F, with up to 20 days without rain. The summer is marked by clear skies at night and frequent morning fog.

**Pluses:** Mild winters, dry summers.

**Minuses:** Cloudy, damp, rainy.

**Places Rated Score: 726**

**Places Rated Rank: 21**

**Elevation: 195 feet**

Relative Humidity: 71%
Wind Speed: 6.7 mph

Seasonal Change

Annual Rainfall 51 in

Annual Snowfall 19 in

Clear 49 days
Partly Cloudy 88 days
Cloudy 228 days

Precipitation Days: 163     Storm Days: 5

| Average Temperatures | | | |
|---|---|---|---|
| | Daily High | Daily Low | Monthly Mean |
| January | 44.0 | 30.4 | 37.2 |
| February | 49.0 | 32.4 | 41.0 |
| March | 53.6 | 32.8 | 43.2 |
| April | 59.9 | 36.5 | 48.2 |
| May | 67.2 | 40.8 | 54.0 |
| June | 71.9 | 45.9 | 58.9 |
| July | 78.4 | 48.7 | 63.6 |
| August | 77.2 | 48.4 | 62.8 |
| September | 72.1 | 45.0 | 58.6 |
| October | 61.2 | 40.0 | 50.6 |
| November | 51.3 | 35.2 | 43.3 |
| December | 45.8 | 33.1 | 39.5 |

Zero-Degree Days: 0
Freezing Days: 89
90-Degree Days: 6
Heating- and Cooling-Degree Days: 5,631

## Omaha, NE–IA

**Terrain:** Situated on the west bank of the Missouri River among rolling hills that rise 300 feet above the riverbank.

**Climate:** Typically continental, with relatively warm summers and cold, dry winters. It is situated midway between two climates, those of the humid East and the dry West, and receives weather conditions characteristic of both. Omaha is also affected by most storms, or "lows," that cross the country. This causes periodic and rapid changes in weather, especially during the winter.

**Pluses:** Moderate growing season with adequate rainfall.

**Minuses:** Long, cold winters.

**Places Rated Score: 440**

**Places Rated Rank: 277**

**Elevation: 982 feet**

Relative Humidity: 68%
Wind Speed: 10.9 mph

Seasonal Change

Annual Rainfall 30 in

Annual Snowfall 32 in

Clear 113 days
Partly Cloudy 107 days
Cloudy 145 days

Precipitation Days: 99     Storm Days: 48

| Average Temperatures | | | |
|---|---|---|---|
| | Daily High | Daily Low | Monthly Mean |
| January | 32.7 | 12.4 | 22.6 |
| February | 38.5 | 17.4 | 28.0 |
| March | 47.7 | 26.4 | 37.1 |
| April | 64.4 | 40.1 | 52.3 |
| May | 74.4 | 51.5 | 63.0 |
| June | 83.1 | 61.3 | 72.2 |
| July | 88.6 | 65.8 | 77.2 |
| August | 87.2 | 64.0 | 75.6 |
| September | 78.6 | 54.0 | 66.3 |
| October | 69.1 | 42.6 | 55.9 |
| November | 50.9 | 29.1 | 40.0 |
| December | 37.8 | 18.1 | 28.0 |

Zero-Degree Days: 13
Freezing Days: 138
90-Degree Days: 38
Heating- and Cooling-Degree Days: 7,222

## Orlando, FL

**Terrain:** Located in the central section of the Florida peninsula, almost surrounded by lakes. The countryside is flat, with no natural barriers to exterior weather systems.

**Climate:** Because of the surrounding water, relative humidity remains high year-round, hovering near 90% at night and dipping to 50% in the afternoon. The rainy season extends from June through September; afternoon thundershowers occur daily. Rain is light during the winter, and snow and sleet are rare. Winter temperatures may drop to freezing at night, but days are usually pleasant, with brilliant sunshine.

**Pluses:** Mild.

**Minuses:** Humid year-round; hot summers with daily thundershowers.

**Elevation: 106 feet**

Relative Humidity: 74%
Wind Speed: 8.7 mph

Seasonal Change

Annual Rainfall 51 in

Annual Snowfall 0 in

| Average Temperatures | | | |
|---|---|---|---|
| | Daily High | Daily Low | Monthly Mean |
| January | 70.5 | 50.0 | 60.3 |
| February | 71.8 | 51.2 | 61.5 |
| March | 76.0 | 55.7 | 65.9 |
| April | 81.5 | 61.1 | 71.3 |
| May | 86.7 | 66.1 | 76.4 |
| June | 89.3 | 71.1 | 80.2 |
| July | 89.8 | 72.9 | 81.4 |
| August | 90.0 | 73.5 | 81.8 |
| September | 87.9 | 72.3 | 80.1 |
| October | 82.5 | 66.0 | 74.3 |
| November | 76.2 | 56.9 | 66.6 |
| December | 71.5 | 51.5 | 61.5 |

Clear 94 days  Partly Cloudy 148 days  Cloudy 123 days

Zero-Degree Days: 0
Freezing Days: 2
90-Degree Days: 104
Heating- and Cooling-Degree Days: 3,959

**Places Rated Score: 457**   **Places Rated Rank: 266**

Precipitation Days: 116  Storm Days: 81

## Peoria, IL

**Terrain:** Located on the Illinois River, with gently rising topography extending to level tableland.

**Climate:** Typically continental, characterized by changeable weather and a wide range of temperatures. For example, 1936 had 17 days with temperatures of 100° F or higher in July, while the early part of that same year had 26 days within a 31-day period when the temperature was zero. The same year had the absolute maximum record of 113° F, set on July 15. June and September are usually the most pleasant months of the year. During October and early November, residents enjoy Indian summer, with its extended period of warm, dry weather.

**Pluses:** Invigorating continental climate, with especially pleasant falls.

**Minuses:** Periods of extreme cold and extreme heat.

**Elevation: 662 feet**

Relative Humidity: 72%
Wind Speed: 10.3 mph

Seasonal Change

Annual Rainfall 35 in

Annual Snowfall 23 in

| Average Temperatures | | | |
|---|---|---|---|
| | Daily High | Daily Low | Monthly Mean |
| January | 31.9 | 15.7 | 23.8 |
| February | 36.0 | 19.3 | 27.7 |
| March | 46.5 | 28.1 | 37.3 |
| April | 61.7 | 40.8 | 51.3 |
| May | 72.3 | 50.7 | 61.5 |
| June | 81.7 | 60.9 | 71.3 |
| July | 85.5 | 64.6 | 75.1 |
| August | 84.0 | 62.9 | 73.5 |
| September | 76.4 | 54.6 | 65.5 |
| October | 65.9 | 44.0 | 55.0 |
| November | 48.7 | 31.1 | 39.9 |
| December | 35.7 | 20.3 | 28.0 |

Clear 97 days  Partly Cloudy 100 days  Cloudy 168 days

Zero-Degree Days: 11
Freezing Days: 132
90-Degree Days: 17
Heating- and Cooling-Degree Days: 7,066

**Places Rated Score: 491**   **Places Rated Rank: 233**

Precipitation Days: 111  Storm Days: 49

## Philadelphia, PA–NJ

**Terrain:** Situated on the Schuylkill and Delaware rivers on the eastern border of Pennsylvania. The Appalachian Mountains to the west and the Atlantic Ocean to the east have a moderating effect on the city's climate.

**Climate:** Sustained periods of very high or very low temperatures seldom last for more than three or four days. Occasionally during the summer, the area becomes engulfed in marine air, so that high humidity adds to the discomfort of warm temperatures. Precipitation is evenly distributed throughout the year, with maximum amounts during late summer. Snowfall often is considerably higher in the northern suburbs than in the city, where sometimes rain will fall instead. Winters often bring high winds, accompanying cold air after the passage of a deep low-pressure system.

**Pluses:** Four-season climate moderated by the proximity of the Atlantic Ocean.

**Minuses:** Humid summer periods; high winter winds accentuate the cold.

**Elevation: 28 feet**

Relative Humidity: 67%
Wind Speed: 9.6 mph

Seasonal Change

Annual Rainfall 40 in

Annual Snowfall 20 in

| Average Temperatures | | | |
|---|---|---|---|
| | Daily High | Daily Low | Monthly Mean |
| January | 40.1 | 24.4 | 32.3 |
| February | 42.2 | 25.5 | 33.9 |
| March | 51.2 | 32.5 | 41.9 |
| April | 63.5 | 42.3 | 52.9 |
| May | 74.1 | 52.3 | 63.2 |
| June | 83.0 | 61.6 | 72.3 |
| July | 86.8 | 66.7 | 76.8 |
| August | 84.8 | 64.7 | 74.8 |
| September | 78.4 | 57.8 | 68.1 |
| October | 67.9 | 46.9 | 57.4 |
| November | 55.5 | 36.9 | 46.2 |
| December | 43.2 | 27.2 | 35.2 |

Clear 92 days  Partly Cloudy 113 days  Cloudy 160 days

Zero-Degree Days: 0
Freezing Days: 101
90-Degree Days: 19
Heating- and Cooling-Degree Days: 5,969

**Places Rated Score: 630**   **Places Rated Rank: 52**

Precipitation Days: 116  Storm Days: 27

## Phoenix, AZ

**Terrain:** Located in the center of the Salt River valley, on a broad, oval, nearly flat plain. To the south, west, and north are nearby mountain ranges, and 35 miles to the east are the famous Superstition Mountains, which rise to 5,000 feet.

**Climate:** Typical desert; with low annual rainfall and low humidity. Daytime temperatures are high throughout the summer. Winters are mild, but nighttime temperatures frequently drop below freezing during December, January, and February. The valley floor is generally free of wind except during the thunderstorm season, in July and August, when local gusts flow from the east. The majority of days are clear and sunny, except for July and August; then, considerable afternoon cloudiness builds up over nearby mountains.

**Pluses:** Dry, two-season desert climate.

**Minuses:** Hot summers.

**Places Rated Score: 536**          **Places Rated Rank: 176**

**Elevation: 1,107 feet**

Relative Humidity: 36%
Wind Speed: 6.2 mph

Seasonal Change

Annual Rainfall 7 in

Annual Snowfall 0 in

Clear 214 days    Partly Cloudy 81 days    Cloudy 70 days

Precipitation Days: 34    Storm Days: 23

| Average Temperatures | | | |
|---|---|---|---|
| | Daily High | Daily Low | Monthly Mean |
| January | 64.8 | 37.6 | 51.2 |
| February | 69.3 | 40.8 | 55.1 |
| March | 74.5 | 44.8 | 59.7 |
| April | 83.6 | 51.8 | 67.7 |
| May | 92.9 | 59.6 | 76.3 |
| June | 101.5 | 67.7 | 84.6 |
| July | 104.8 | 77.5 | 91.2 |
| August | 102.2 | 76.0 | 89.1 |
| September | 98.4 | 69.1 | 83.8 |
| October | 87.6 | 56.8 | 72.2 |
| November | 74.7 | 44.8 | 59.8 |
| December | 66.4 | 38.5 | 52.5 |

Zero-Degree Days: 0
Freezing Days: 32
90-Degree Days: 164
Heating- and Cooling-Degree Days: 5,060

## Pittsburgh, PA

**Terrain:** Lies at the foothills of the Allegheny Mountains at the confluence of the Allegheny and Monongahela rivers, forming the Ohio. The city is approximately 100 miles south of Lake Erie.

**Climate:** Humid, continental type, modified only slightly by its nearness to the Atlantic Seaboard and the Great Lakes. The predominant air is of polar origin from Canada and moves in by way of storm tracks, which vary in origin from Hudson Bay to the Rockies. There are frequent inversions of air from the Gulf of Mexico during the summer, resulting in spells of warm, humid weather. Precipitation is well distributed; during the winter, one fourth of it is snow, and there is a 50% chance of measurable precipitation on any given day.

**Pluses:** Variable continental climate.

**Minuses:** Cloudy, wet, cold winters; occasional humid summer days.

**Places Rated Score: 586**          **Places Rated Rank: 88**

**Elevation: 1,223 feet**

Relative Humidity: 68%
Wind Speed: 9.4 mph

Seasonal Change

Annual Rainfall 36 in

Annual Snowfall 45 in

Clear 59 days    Partly Cloudy 102 days    Cloudy 204 days

Precipitation Days: 152    Storm Days: 36

| Average Temperatures | | | |
|---|---|---|---|
| | Daily High | Daily Low | Monthly Mean |
| January | 35.3 | 20.8 | 28.1 |
| February | 37.3 | 21.3 | 29.3 |
| March | 47.2 | 29.0 | 38.1 |
| April | 60.9 | 39.4 | 50.2 |
| May | 70.8 | 48.7 | 59.8 |
| June | 79.5 | 57.7 | 68.6 |
| July | 82.5 | 61.3 | 71.9 |
| August | 80.9 | 59.4 | 70.2 |
| September | 74.9 | 52.7 | 63.8 |
| October | 63.9 | 42.4 | 53.2 |
| November | 49.3 | 33.3 | 41.3 |
| December | 37.3 | 23.6 | 30.5 |

Zero-Degree Days: 5
Freezing Days: 124
90-Degree Days: 7
Heating- and Cooling-Degree Days: 6,577

## Portland, ME

**Terrain:** Located on a hilly section of the southern coast of Maine, some 45 miles southeast of the White Mountains.

**Climate:** As a rule, the city has very pleasant summers and falls, cold winters with frequent thaws, and disagreeable springs. Autumn has the greatest number of sunny days. Winters are severe: They begin late but extend deep into what is normally considered springtime, and temperatures well below zero are recorded frequently. Normal monthly precipitation is uniform throughout the year, but heavy snowfalls, sometimes totaling more than 100 inches per year, do occur.

**Pluses:** Northern marine setting with extremely pleasant summers and falls.

**Minuses:** Severe winters, with heavy snows, extending well into normal springtime.

**Places Rated Score: 483**          **Places Rated Rank: 240**

**Elevation: 63 feet**

Relative Humidity: 74%
Wind Speed: 8.8 mph

Seasonal Change

Annual Rainfall 41 in

Annual Snowfall 74 in

Clear 107 days    Partly Cloudy 98 days    Cloudy 160 days

Precipitation Days: 127    Storm Days: 18

| Average Temperatures | | | |
|---|---|---|---|
| | Daily High | Daily Low | Monthly Mean |
| January | 31.2 | 11.7 | 21.5 |
| February | 33.3 | 12.5 | 22.9 |
| March | 40.8 | 22.8 | 31.8 |
| April | 52.8 | 32.5 | 42.7 |
| May | 63.6 | 41.7 | 52.7 |
| June | 73.2 | 51.1 | 62.2 |
| July | 79.1 | 56.9 | 68.0 |
| August | 77.6 | 55.2 | 66.4 |
| September | 69.9 | 47.4 | 58.7 |
| October | 60.2 | 38.0 | 49.1 |
| November | 47.5 | 29.7 | 38.6 |
| December | 34.9 | 16.4 | 25.7 |

Zero-Degree Days: 15
Freezing Days: 160
90-Degree Days: 5
Heating- and Cooling-Degree Days: 7,750

## ★ Portland, OR

**Terrain:** Situated 65 miles inland from the Pacific Ocean and midway between the northerly oriented low Coast Ranges on the west and the higher Cascade Range on the east, each 30 miles distant. The long growing season, with its mild temperatures and ample moisture, favors local nursery and seed industries.

**Climate:** A rain climate in winter, marked by relatively mild temperatures and cloudy skies. Summers are pleasantly mild with northwesterly winds and very little precipitation. Fall and spring are transitional in nature. Fog occurs frequently in fall and winter. At all times, incursions of marine air are a moderating influence. Extremes in winter and summer come from the continental interior. Destructive winds are infrequent.

**Pluses:** Short winters; long, pleasant summers; ample precipitation.

**Minuses:** Daily rains during winter and part of spring; often cloudy.

**Places Rated Score: 768**  **Places Rated Rank: 16**

**Elevation: 39 feet**

Relative Humidity: 74%
Wind Speed: 7.8 mph

Seasonal Change

Annual Rainfall 38 in

Annual Snowfall 7 in

Clear 69 days  Partly Cloudy 68 days  Cloudy 228 days

Precipitation Days: 152    Storm Days: 7

| Average Temperatures | | | |
| --- | --- | --- | --- |
| | Daily High | Daily Low | Monthly Mean |
| January | 43.6 | 32.5 | 38.1 |
| February | 50.1 | 35.5 | 42.8 |
| March | 54.3 | 37.0 | 45.7 |
| April | 60.3 | 40.8 | 50.6 |
| May | 67.0 | 46.3 | 56.7 |
| June | 72.1 | 51.8 | 62.0 |
| July | 79.0 | 55.2 | 67.1 |
| August | 78.1 | 55.0 | 66.6 |
| September | 73.9 | 50.5 | 62.2 |
| October | 62.9 | 44.7 | 53.8 |
| November | 52.1 | 38.5 | 45.3 |
| December | 46.0 | 35.3 | 40.7 |

Zero-Degree Days: 0
Freezing Days: 44
90-Degree Days: 10
Heating- and Cooling-Degree Days: 5,092

## Raleigh–Durham, NC

**Terrain:** Situated in the transition zone between the Coastal Plain and the Piedmont Plateau of North Carolina. The surrounding topography is rolling, with elevations from 200 feet to 500 feet within a 10-mile radius.

**Climate:** Because it is located between mountains to the west and the Atlantic Coast to the east and south, the metro area enjoys a favorable climate. The mountains form a partial barrier to cold air masses moving eastward from the nation's interior, so that there are very few days in the heart of the winter when the temperature falls below 20° F. Tropical air is present over the eastern and central sections of North Carolina during much of the summer, bringing warm temperatures and high humidity. In midsummer, afternoon temperatures reach 90° F or higher on an average of every fourth day. Rainfall is well distributed throughout the year. July has, on the average, the greatest amount of rainfall, and November the least.

**Pluses:** Mild four-season climate.

**Minuses:** Long, humid summers.

**Places Rated Score: 647**  **Places Rated Rank: 37**

**Elevation: 441 feet**

Relative Humidity: 71%
Wind Speed: 7.9 mph

Seasonal Change

Annual Rainfall 43 in

Annual Snowfall 7 in

Clear 113 days  Partly Cloudy 107 days  Cloudy 145 days

Precipitation Days: 112   Storm Days: 46

| Average Temperatures | | | |
| --- | --- | --- | --- |
| | Daily High | Daily Low | Monthly Mean |
| January | 51.0 | 30.0 | 40.5 |
| February | 53.2 | 31.1 | 42.2 |
| March | 61.0 | 37.4 | 49.2 |
| April | 72.2 | 46.7 | 59.5 |
| May | 79.4 | 55.4 | 67.4 |
| June | 85.6 | 63.1 | 74.4 |
| July | 87.7 | 67.2 | 77.5 |
| August | 86.8 | 66.2 | 76.5 |
| September | 81.5 | 59.7 | 70.6 |
| October | 72.4 | 48.0 | 60.2 |
| November | 62.1 | 37.8 | 50.0 |
| December | 51.9 | 30.5 | 41.2 |

Zero-Degree Days: 0
Freezing Days: 82
90-Degree Days: 25
Heating- and Cooling-Degree Days: 4,908

## Reno, NV

**Terrain:** Located at the west edge of Truckee Meadows in a semiarid plateau lying in the lee of the Sierra Nevada. To the west, this range rises to elevations of 9,000 feet to 10,000 feet, and hills to the east reach 6,000 feet to 7,000 feet. The Truckee River, flowing from the Sierra Nevada eastward through Reno, drains into Pyramid Lake to the northeast.

**Climate:** Sunshine is abundant throughout the year. Temperatures are mild, but the daily range may exceed 45 degrees. Even when afternoons reach the upper 90s, a light jacket is needed shortly after sunset. Nights with a minimum temperature over 60° F are rare. Afternoon temperatures are moderate, and only about ten days a year fail to reach a level above freezing. Humidity is very low during the summer months and moderately low during winter.

**Pluses:** Mild, sunny climate in alpine setting.

**Minuses:** Considerable daily temperature variation, little precipitation.

**Places Rated Score: 535**  **Places Rated Rank: 182**

**Elevation: 4,400 feet**

Relative Humidity: 50%
Wind Speed: 6.3 mph

Seasonal Change

Annual Rainfall 7 in

Annual Snowfall 27 in

Clear 165 days  Partly Cloudy 90 days  Cloudy 110 days

Precipitation Days: 49    Storm Days: 13

| Average Temperatures | | | |
| --- | --- | --- | --- |
| | Daily High | Daily Low | Monthly Mean |
| January | 45.4 | 18.3 | 31.9 |
| February | 51.1 | 23.0 | 37.1 |
| March | 56.0 | 24.6 | 40.3 |
| April | 64.0 | 29.6 | 46.8 |
| May | 72.2 | 37.0 | 54.6 |
| June | 80.4 | 42.5 | 61.5 |
| July | 91.1 | 47.4 | 69.3 |
| August | 89.0 | 44.8 | 66.9 |
| September | 81.8 | 38.6 | 60.2 |
| October | 70.0 | 30.5 | 50.3 |
| November | 56.3 | 23.9 | 40.1 |
| December | 46.4 | 19.6 | 33.0 |

Zero-Degree Days: 3
Freezing Days: 189
90-Degree Days: 52
Heating- and Cooling-Degree Days: 6,351

## Richmond–Petersburg, VA

**Terrain:** Located in east-central Virginia at the head of navigation on the James River between Tidewater Virginia and the Piedmont. The Blue Ridge Mountains lie about 90 miles to the west and the Chesapeake Bay 60 miles to the east.

**Climate:** Water- and mountain-modified continental, with warm, humid summers and generally mild winters. The mountains to the west act as a barrier to outbreaks of cold, continental air in winter; the open waters of the Chesapeake Bay and the Atlantic also contribute to mild winters and to humid summers. Coldest weather usually occurs in late December and in January, with a normal temperature range from 20° F to 50° F. Precipitation is uniformly distributed throughout the year, though dry periods do occur in the autumn, when long periods of pleasant, mild weather are most common.

**Pluses:** Modified continental climate with long growing season.

**Minuses:** Humid summers, severe thunderstorms, hurricanes.

**Places Rated Score: 585**

**Places Rated Rank: 92**

**Elevation: 177 feet**

Relative Humidity: 72%
Wind Speed: 7.5 mph

Seasonal Change

Annual Rainfall 43 in

Annual Snowfall 14 in

Clear 103 days
Partly Cloudy 107 days
Cloudy 155 days

Precipitation Days: 113  Storm Days: 37

| Average Temperatures | | | |
|---|---|---|---|
| | Daily High | Daily Low | Monthly Mean |
| January | 47.4 | 27.6 | 37.5 |
| February | 49.9 | 28.8 | 39.4 |
| March | 58.2 | 35.5 | 46.9 |
| April | 70.3 | 45.2 | 57.8 |
| May | 78.4 | 54.5 | 66.5 |
| June | 85.4 | 62.9 | 74.2 |
| July | 88.2 | 67.5 | 77.9 |
| August | 86.6 | 65.9 | 76.3 |
| September | 80.9 | 59.0 | 70.0 |
| October | 71.2 | 47.4 | 59.3 |
| November | 60.6 | 37.3 | 49.0 |
| December | 49.1 | 28.8 | 39.0 |

Zero-Degree Days: 0
Freezing Days: 85
90-Degree Days: 41
Heating- and Cooling-Degree Days: 5,292

## Roanoke, VA

**Terrain:** Located in the part of the Great Valley that runs from the northernmost part of Virginia southwest to Scott County. The Blue Ridge Mountains are to the west, the Allegheny Mountains to the north.

**Climate:** Mild. The mountain barrier moderates cold air from the north before it reaches the area. The elevation of the city usually produces cool summer nights. Rainfall is well distributed throughout the year, with an average of 23 inches in the warm season. Snow usually falls each winter, with extremes ranging from a trace to 60 inches.

**Pluses:** Invigorating, but rare extremes of temperature do occur.

**Minuses:** Roanoke River liable to flood.

**Places Rated Score: 652**

**Places Rated Rank: 33**

**Elevation: 1,176 feet**

Relative Humidity: 65%
Wind Speed: 8.3 mph

Seasonal Change

Annual Rainfall 39 in

Annual Snowfall 25 in

Clear 103 days
Partly Cloudy 114 days
Cloudy 148 days

Precipitation Days: 121  Storm Days: 38

| Average Temperatures | | | |
|---|---|---|---|
| | Daily High | Daily Low | Monthly Mean |
| January | 45.6 | 27.2 | 36.4 |
| February | 47.9 | 28.3 | 38.1 |
| March | 56.3 | 34.3 | 45.3 |
| April | 67.9 | 43.9 | 55.9 |
| May | 76.1 | 52.7 | 64.4 |
| June | 83.0 | 60.4 | 71.7 |
| July | 85.9 | 64.4 | 75.2 |
| August | 84.9 | 63.3 | 74.1 |
| September | 79.5 | 56.5 | 68.0 |
| October | 69.9 | 45.6 | 57.8 |
| November | 57.6 | 35.8 | 46.7 |
| December | 46.6 | 28.1 | 37.4 |

Zero-Degree Days: 0
Freezing Days: 92
90-Degree Days: 20
Heating- and Cooling-Degree Days: 5,337

## Rochester, MN

**Terrain:** Located in the Zumbro River valley in southeastern Minnesota amid rolling farmland.

**Climate:** Continental weather pattern with four definite seasons. Winters are cold, but summers are pleasant, with temperatures reaching as high as 90° F on only seven days in an average summer. Thunderstorms (sometimes heavy downpours) occur about once every three days, on the average, during the growing season. These storms often cause high winds. About four times each year, hail will fall. Tornadoes are rare but do occur. Heavy fog occurs 35 times a year on the average.

**Pluses:** Invigorating four seasons with especially pleasant summers.

**Minuses:** Cold winters lasting at least five months.

**Places Rated Score: 308**

**Places Rated Rank: 317**

**Elevation: 1,320 feet**

Relative Humidity: 74%
Wind Speed: 12.7 mph

Seasonal Change

Annual Rainfall 27 in

Annual Snowfall 44 in

Clear 91 days
Partly Cloudy 96 days
Cloudy 178 days

Precipitation Days: 115  Storm Days: 41

| Average Temperatures | | | |
|---|---|---|---|
| | Daily High | Daily Low | Monthly Mean |
| January | 21.9 | 3.9 | 12.9 |
| February | 26.4 | 7.4 | 16.9 |
| March | 36.5 | 19.1 | 27.8 |
| April | 54.9 | 34.1 | 44.5 |
| May | 67.1 | 45.3 | 56.2 |
| June | 76.4 | 55.5 | 66.0 |
| July | 80.7 | 59.5 | 70.1 |
| August | 79.4 | 57.7 | 68.6 |
| September | 70.2 | 48.3 | 59.3 |
| October | 60.4 | 38.7 | 49.6 |
| November | 40.9 | 24.2 | 32.6 |
| December | 26.9 | 10.9 | 18.9 |

Zero-Degree Days: 35
Freezing Days: 165
90-Degree Days: 7
Heating- and Cooling-Degree Days: 8,701

## Rockford, IL

**Terrain:** Located northwest of the Chicago area in rolling prairie.
**Climate:** When winter winds blow from Lake Michigan, cloudiness is often increased, and temperatures are somewhat higher than those to the west around the Mississippi. The lake can also be a moderating influence in summer, sometimes lowering temperatures. Summers are usually hot, however, but oppressive heat seldom prevails for extended periods. Winters are cold, and snow cover is continuous from late December through February.

**Pluses:** Adequate snow cover for diversified winter sports.

**Minuses:** Long, cold winters; hot summers.

**Elevation: 743 feet**

Relative Humidity: 72%
Wind Speed: 9.9 mph

Seasonal Change

Annual Rainfall 37 in

Annual Snowfall 33 in

Clear 96 days    Partly Cloudy 100 days    Cloudy 169 days

| | Daily High | Daily Low | Monthly Mean |
|---|---|---|---|
| January | 28.9 | 11.5 | 20.2 |
| February | 32.6 | 15.3 | 24.0 |
| March | 43.1 | 25.0 | 34.1 |
| April | 59.1 | 37.3 | 48.2 |
| May | 70.3 | 47.2 | 58.8 |
| June | 79.9 | 57.7 | 68.8 |
| July | 84.2 | 61.4 | 72.8 |
| August | 82.8 | 60.1 | 71.5 |
| September | 74.7 | 51.8 | 63.3 |
| October | 64.3 | 41.1 | 52.7 |
| November | 46.5 | 28.7 | 37.6 |
| December | 33.1 | 16.7 | 24.9 |

Average Temperatures

Zero-Degree Days: 16
Freezing Days: 142
90-Degree Days: 13
Heating- and Cooling-Degree Days: 7,559

**Places Rated Score: 466**        **Places Rated Rank: 260**        Precipitation Days: 114   Storm Days: 42

## Sacramento, CA

**Terrain:** Located in the heart of a broad, flat valley between California's Coast Ranges and the Sierra Nevada. The land is tabletop-flat and, when irrigated, perfect for growing fruits and vegetables.
**Climate:** The two mountain ranges shelter the area from many storms and violent weather, thus adding to the mildness of the climate. Occasionally, however, northerly winds, called northers, reach the valley over the Siskiyou Mountains, causing heat waves. Summers are sunny and hot, but low humidity lessens the felt heat. Winters are mild, and snow is rare enough to not be regarded a climatic feature.

**Pluses:** Sunny, mild.

**Minuses:** Hot winds from the north on occasion, hot summers.

**Elevation: 25 feet**

Relative Humidity: 66%
Wind Speed: 8.3 mph

Seasonal Change

Annual Rainfall 17 in

Annual Snowfall .1 in

Clear 193 days    Partly Cloudy 72 days    Cloudy 100 days

| | Daily High | Daily Low | Monthly Mean |
|---|---|---|---|
| January | 53.0 | 37.1 | 45.1 |
| February | 59.1 | 40.4 | 49.8 |
| March | 64.1 | 41.9 | 53.0 |
| April | 71.3 | 45.3 | 58.3 |
| May | 78.8 | 49.8 | 64.3 |
| June | 86.4 | 54.6 | 70.5 |
| July | 92.9 | 57.5 | 75.2 |
| August | 91.3 | 56.9 | 74.1 |
| September | 87.7 | 55.3 | 71.5 |
| October | 77.1 | 49.5 | 63.3 |
| November | 63.6 | 42.4 | 53.0 |
| December | 53.3 | 38.3 | 45.8 |

Average Temperatures

Zero-Degree Days: 0
Freezing Days: 17
90-Degree Days: 77
Heating- and Cooling-Degree Days: 4,002

**Places Rated Score: 576**        **Places Rated Rank: 103**        Precipitation Days: 57        Storm Days: 5

## Saginaw–Bay City–Midland, MI

**Terrain:** Located south of the tip of Saginaw Bay on the Saginaw River, which flows into the bay. To the west, the land is level and sandy; to the east, it is heavy and fertile lake-bed clay. The metro area is far enough from the bay (and Lake Huron) to be considered an inland location. However, these bodies of water do moderate the climate somewhat.
**Climate:** The highest temperature ever recorded here was 111° F on July 13, 1936. The coldest was –18° F on February 9, 1934. However, the area averages only five zero-degree days per year, which is low for a location this far north away from an ocean. On the other hand, there are 16 ninety-degree days each summer, on average. Heaviest rainfall is in May. Cloud cover is most frequent in November but is generally less so than that in other places in the state nearer Lake Michigan. The driest month is usually January.

**Pluses:** Pleasant summers with cool nights.

**Minuses:** Long winters, cloudy.

**Elevation: 662 feet**

Relative Humidity: 76%
Wind Speed: 10 mph

Seasonal Change

Annual Rainfall 29 in

Annual Snowfall 47 in

Clear 67 days    Partly Cloudy 96 days    Cloudy 202 days

| | Daily High | Daily Low | Monthly Mean |
|---|---|---|---|
| January | 30.4 | 16.5 | 23.5 |
| February | 31.3 | 16.1 | 23.7 |
| March | 40.1 | 24.4 | 32.3 |
| April | 54.9 | 34.6 | 44.8 |
| May | 67.5 | 45.1 | 56.3 |
| June | 78.1 | 55.6 | 66.9 |
| July | 83.8 | 59.8 | 71.8 |
| August | 81.2 | 57.9 | 69.6 |
| September | 72.7 | 50.7 | 61.7 |
| October | 61.4 | 40.8 | 51.1 |
| November | 45.1 | 30.7 | 37.9 |
| December | 33.5 | 20.9 | 27.2 |

Average Temperatures

Zero-Degree Days: 5
Freezing Days: 147
90-Degree Days: 16
Heating- and Cooling-Degree Days: 7,362

**Places Rated Score: 515**        **Places Rated Rank: 210**        Precipitation Days: 181   Storm Days: 38

## St. Louis, MO–IL

**Terrain:** Located at the confluence of the Missouri and Mississippi rivers and slightly east of the geographic center of the United States. The surrounding terrain is gently rolling, with occasional high bluffs characteristic of parts of the Mississippi Valley.

**Climate:** Modified continental. St. Louis is in the enviable position of having a changeable, four-season climate without prolonged periods of extreme cold, heat, or humidity. To the south is the warm, moist air of the Gulf of Mexico and to the north the region of cold polar air masses. Alternating invasions by these influences, and the conflict along the frontal zones where they meet, produce a great variety of weather conditions, but none lasting long enough to become monotonous. Winters are brisk but seldom severe. Snowfall averages less than 20 inches per season. Summers are quite warm, often uncomfortably so when coupled with high humidity. These oppressive spells usually are relieved by storms.

**Pluses:** Changeable weather, relatively mild winters.

**Minuses:** Hot, humid summers.

**Places Rated Score: 537**

**Places Rated Rank: 173**

**Elevation: 564 feet**

Relative Humidity: 70%
Wind Speed: 9.5 mph

Seasonal Change

Annual Rainfall 36 in

Annual Snowfall 18 in

Clear 105 days
Partly Cloudy 101 days
Cloudy 159 days

Precipitation Days: 108  Storm Days: 45

| Average Temperatures | | | |
|---|---|---|---|
| | Daily High | Daily Low | Monthly Mean |
| January | 39.9 | 22.6 | 31.3 |
| February | 44.2 | 26.0 | 35.1 |
| March | 53.0 | 33.5 | 43.3 |
| April | 67.0 | 46.0 | 56.5 |
| May | 76.0 | 55.5 | 65.8 |
| June | 84.9 | 64.8 | 74.9 |
| July | 88.4 | 68.8 | 78.6 |
| August | 87.2 | 67.1 | 77.2 |
| September | 80.1 | 59.1 | 69.6 |
| October | 69.8 | 48.4 | 59.1 |
| November | 54.1 | 35.9 | 45.0 |
| December | 42.7 | 26.5 | 34.6 |

Zero-Degree Days: 3
Freezing Days: 107
90-Degree Days: 37
Heating- and Cooling-Degree Days: 6,225

## Salt Lake City–Ogden, UT

**Terrain:** Spectacular setting. To the east, the Wasatch Mountains rise from heights of 8,000 feet to 12,000 feet; to the southwest, the Oguirrh Mountains climb to 10,000 feet.

**Climate:** Though by no means mild, it is modified by the surrounding mountains, which deflect stormy weather elsewhere. There are four well-defined seasons, including a long winter. Summers are hot, but the dry air lessens felt heat, and nights are cool. Winters are cold but not severe. Most of the precipitation is snow, with accumulations staying on the ground for most of the winter. Fall is short, with spring longer and sometimes stormy. Nearby Great Salt Lake also helps modify the climate.

**Pluses:** Scenic setting, good rigorous climate.

**Minuses:** Cold, snowy winters.

**Places Rated Score: 541**

**Places Rated Rank: 168**

**Elevation: 4,227 feet**

Relative Humidity: 54%
Wind Speed: 8.7 mph

Seasonal Change

Annual Rainfall 15 in

Annual Snowfall 58 in

Clear 129 days
Partly Cloudy 103 days
Cloudy 133 days

Precipitation Days: 88  Storm Days: 35

| Average Temperatures | | | |
|---|---|---|---|
| | Daily High | Daily Low | Monthly Mean |
| January | 37.4 | 18.5 | 28.0 |
| February | 43.4 | 23.3 | 33.4 |
| March | 50.8 | 28.3 | 39.6 |
| April | 61.8 | 36.6 | 49.2 |
| May | 72.4 | 44.2 | 58.3 |
| June | 81.3 | 51.1 | 66.2 |
| July | 92.8 | 60.5 | 76.7 |
| August | 90.2 | 58.7 | 74.5 |
| September | 80.3 | 43.3 | 64.8 |
| October | 66.4 | 38.4 | 52.4 |
| November | 50.0 | 28.1 | 39.1 |
| December | 39.0 | 21.5 | 30.3 |

Zero-Degree Days: 3
Freezing Days: 134
90-Degree Days: 58
Heating- and Cooling-Degree Days: 6,910

## San Angelo, TX

**Terrain:** Lies on the northern edge of the Edwards Plateau. The land is flat, sometimes slightly rolling, and is classified as semiarid, or steppe, covered with grass, thorny bush, and cacti.

**Climate:** San Angelo is situated between the humid climate of eastern Texas and the dry High Plains and the Basin and Range region of western Texas. It is hot, though usually dry. However, uncomfortable hot spells with humid air permeate the area occasionally. The wind is brisk, modifying summer heat. Summers are long, winters short and mild.

**Pluses:** Dry sunny climate, long summers, short winters.

**Minuses:** Can be dusty; humid hot spells.

**Places Rated Score: 488**

**Places Rated Rank: 237**

**Elevation: 1,908 feet**

Relative Humidity: 59%
Wind Speed: 10.5 mph

Seasonal Change

Annual Rainfall 18 in

Annual Snowfall 3 in

Clear 157 days
Partly Cloudy 97 days
Cloudy 111 days

Precipitation Days: 57  Storm Days: 37

| Average Temperatures | | | |
|---|---|---|---|
| | Daily High | Daily Low | Monthly Mean |
| January | 59.1 | 33.6 | 46.4 |
| February | 63.2 | 37.5 | 50.4 |
| March | 70.7 | 43.5 | 57.1 |
| April | 80.4 | 54.0 | 67.2 |
| May | 86.5 | 62.4 | 74.5 |
| June | 93.4 | 69.8 | 81.6 |
| July | 96.9 | 72.4 | 84.7 |
| August | 96.9 | 72.0 | 84.5 |
| September | 88.4 | 65.1 | 76.8 |
| October | 79.6 | 54.7 | 67.2 |
| November | 68.5 | 42.5 | 55.5 |
| December | 61.4 | 35.2 | 48.3 |

Zero-Degree Days: 0
Freezing Days: 52
90-Degree Days: 109
Heating- and Cooling-Degree Days: 4,942

# San Antonio, TX

**Terrain:** Located between the Edwards Plateau and the Gulf Coastal Plain of south central Texas. Terrain is rolling. Vegetation consists of grasses and live oak trees, along with mesquite and cacti. Soils are blackland clay and silty loam.

**Climate:** Two-season, with mild weather during normal winter months and a long, hot summer. Though 140 miles from the Gulf of Mexico, the city feels the influence of its hot moist air. Thunderstorms and rains have occurred in every month of the year, but they are most common during the summer, with most rain falling in May and September. The winds during the winter are from the north, and from the south in the summer. Skies are clear more than 30% of the time, and cloudy about 30%.

**Pluses:** No winter, attractive terrain.

**Minuses:** Hot, muggy summers.

**Places Rated Score: 398**

**Places Rated Rank: 300**

**Elevation: 794 feet**

Relative Humidity: 67%
Wind Speed: 9.3 mph

Seasonal Change

Annual Rainfall 28 in

Annual Snowfall .5 in

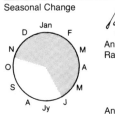

Clear 110 days · Partly Cloudy 117 days · Cloudy 138 days

Precipitation Days: 81 · Storm Days: 36

| Average Temperatures | | | |
|---|---|---|---|
| | Daily High | Daily Low | Monthly Mean |
| January | 61.6 | 39.8 | 50.7 |
| February | 65.6 | 43.4 | 54.5 |
| March | 72.5 | 49.1 | 60.8 |
| April | 80.3 | 58.8 | 69.6 |
| May | 86.2 | 65.7 | 76.0 |
| June | 92.4 | 72.0 | 82.2 |
| July | 95.6 | 73.8 | 84.7 |
| August | 95.9 | 73.4 | 84.7 |
| September | 89.8 | 68.8 | 79.3 |
| October | 81.8 | 59.2 | 70.5 |
| November | 71.1 | 48.2 | 59.7 |
| December | 64.4 | 41.8 | 53.2 |

Zero-Degree Days: 0
Freezing Days: 22
90-Degree Days: 111
Heating- and Cooling-Degree Days: 4,564

# ★ San Diego, CA

**Terrain:** Located on San Diego Bay in the southwest corner of California near the Mexican border. Its coastal location is backed by coastal foothills and mountains to the east.

**Climate:** One of the mildest in North America: typically marine, sometimes called Mediterranean. There are no freezing days and an average of only three 90-degree days each year. San Diego has abundant sunshine and mild sea breezes. Only two seasons occur here: a dry, mild summer and a spring that is cooler, with some rain. Storms are practically unknown, though there is considerable fog along the coast, and many low clouds in early morning and evening during the summer.

**Pluses:** One of the best climates for sun and mildness.

**Minuses:** Paradise climate lacking variety and seasonal contrasts.

**Places Rated Score: 903**

**Places Rated Rank: 3**

**Elevation: 28 feet**

Relative Humidity: 68%
Wind Speed: 6.7 mph

Seasonal Change

Annual Rainfall 9 in

Annual Snowfall 0 in

Clear 150 days · Partly Cloudy 117 days · Cloudy 98 days

Precipitation Days: 41 · Storm Days: 3

| Average Temperatures | | | |
|---|---|---|---|
| | Daily High | Daily Low | Monthly Mean |
| January | 64.6 | 45.8 | 55.2 |
| February | 65.6 | 47.8 | 56.7 |
| March | 66.0 | 50.1 | 58.1 |
| April | 67.6 | 53.8 | 60.7 |
| May | 69.4 | 57.2 | 63.3 |
| June | 71.1 | 59.9 | 65.5 |
| July | 75.3 | 63.9 | 69.6 |
| August | 77.3 | 65.4 | 71.4 |
| September | 76.5 | 63.2 | 69.9 |
| October | 73.8 | 58.4 | 66.1 |
| November | 70.1 | 51.5 | 60.8 |
| December | 66.1 | 55.4 | 62.9 |

Zero-Degree Days: 0
Freezing Days: 0
90-Degree Days: 3
Heating- and Cooling-Degree Days: 2,229

# ★ San Francisco, CA

**Terrain:** Unique location—at the northern end of a narrow peninsula that separates San Francisco Bay from the Pacific Ocean and forms the southern shore of the Golden Gate Bridge—causes San Francisco to be known as the Air-Conditioned City.

**Climate:** Two-season climate: a cool, pleasant summer and a mild spring. Flowers bloom throughout the year, and warm clothing is needed every month. Sea fogs and associated low stratus clouds are a striking characteristic of the city's climate. On the average, though, the sun shines during 66% of the daylight hours. There are wide contrasts in climate within short distances of the bay; nearby communities of Marin County, to the north across the Golden Gate and sheltered from the prevailing winds by high peaks and ridges of the Coast Ranges, enjoy warmer and sunnier weather than the city.

**Pluses:** Mild, springlike weather ten months of the year; ranks first among the 329 metro areas.

**Minuses:** Invariable climate patterns; fogs and cloudy days.

**Places Rated Score: 910**

**Places Rated Rank: 1**

**Elevation: 155 feet**

Relative Humidity: 75%
Wind Speed: 8.7 mph

Seasonal Change

Annual Rainfall 21 in

Annual Snowfall 0 in

Clear 162 days · Partly Cloudy 103 days · Cloudy 100 days

Precipitation Days: 67 · Storm Days: 2

| Average Temperatures | | | |
|---|---|---|---|
| | Daily High | Daily Low | Monthly Mean |
| January | 55.3 | 41.2 | 48.3 |
| February | 58.6 | 43.8 | 51.2 |
| March | 61.0 | 44.9 | 53.0 |
| April | 63.5 | 47.0 | 55.3 |
| May | 66.6 | 49.9 | 58.3 |
| June | 70.2 | 53.0 | 61.6 |
| July | 70.9 | 54.0 | 62.5 |
| August | 71.6 | 54.3 | 63.0 |
| September | 73.6 | 54.5 | 64.1 |
| October | 70.3 | 51.6 | 61.0 |
| November | 63.3 | 47.2 | 55.3 |
| December | 56.5 | 42.9 | 49.7 |

Zero-Degree Days: 0
Freezing Days: 0
90-Degree Days: 1
Heating- and Cooling-Degree Days: 3,119

## ★ Santa Barbara–Santa Maria–Lompoc, CA

**Terrain:** Located in the Santa Maria Valley 150 miles north of Los Angeles and 250 miles south of San Francisco. The valley is flat and fertile, opening onto the Pacific Ocean at its widest point and tapering inland at a distance of 30 miles from the coast. It is bounded by the foothills of the San Rafael Mountains, the Solomon Hills, and the Casmalia Hills.

**Climate:** Rainfall season, typical of the California coast, is winter. During the rest of the year, particularly from June to October, there is little or no precipitation. Clear, sunshiny afternoons prevail on most days. At night and in the morning, however, the California stratus and fog appear.

**Pluses:** Year-round mildness moving through gradual transitions.

**Minuses:** No distinct seasonal changes, night and morning fogs.

**Places Rated Score: 855**

**Places Rated Rank: 7**

**Elevation: 238 feet**

Relative Humidity: 74%
Wind Speed: 7 mph

Seasonal Change

Annual Rainfall 12 in

Annual Snowfall 0 in

Clear 177 days  Partly Cloudy 108 days  Cloudy 80 days

Precipitation Days: 45    Storm Days: 2

| Average Temperatures | | | |
|---|---|---|---|
| | Daily High | Daily Low | Monthly Mean |
| January | 62.7 | 38.3 | 50.5 |
| February | 63.6 | 40.3 | 52.0 |
| March | 64.3 | 41.3 | 52.8 |
| April | 66.0 | 43.7 | 54.9 |
| May | 67.4 | 46.7 | 57.1 |
| June | 69.7 | 49.5 | 59.6 |
| July | 71.8 | 52.4 | 62.1 |
| August | 72.1 | 52.5 | 62.3 |
| September | 73.9 | 51.2 | 62.6 |
| October | 73.3 | 47.5 | 60.4 |
| November | 69.2 | 42.9 | 56.1 |
| December | 64.2 | 39.3 | 51.8 |

Zero-Degree Days: 0
Freezing Days: 24
90-Degree Days: 6
Heating- and Cooling-Degree Days: 3,137

## ★ Santa Rosa–Petaluma, CA

**Terrain:** Located in the east-central portion of the Petaluma–Santa Rosa–Russian River valley, which extends northwestward from San Pablo Bay, about 45 miles from the Golden Gate Bridge. This valley runs parallel to the Pacific Coast, with only low hills (300 feet to 500 feet) between it and the ocean 25 miles southwest. Higher hills rise to the east of the metro area, with greater elevations about 10 miles farther east, in the foothills of the Coast Ranges.

**Climate:** The nearness of the ocean and the surrounding topography join with the prevailing westerly circulation to produce a predominantly southerly air flow year-round. However, the area is sufficiently far inland to assure it a more varied climate than San Francisco's. Summers are warmer, winters cooler, and there is more daily temperature shift, as well as less fog and drizzle.

**Pluses:** Mild, yet sunnier and warmer than coastal locations; ideal retirement climate.

**Minuses:** Some hot weather.

**Places Rated Score: 732**

**Places Rated Rank: 19**

**Elevation: 167 feet**

Relative Humidity: 70%
Wind Speed: 7 mph

Seasonal Change

Annual Rainfall 30 in

Annual Snowfall 0 in

Clear 176 days  Partly Cloudy 109 days  Cloudy 80 days

Precipitation Days: 47    Storm Days: 4

| Average Temperatures | | | |
|---|---|---|---|
| | Daily High | Daily Low | Monthly Mean |
| January | 57.1 | 35.7 | 46.4 |
| February | 62.3 | 37.9 | 50.1 |
| March | 66.6 | 39.5 | 53.1 |
| April | 70.1 | 40.1 | 55.1 |
| May | 75.0 | 44.6 | 59.8 |
| June | 80.2 | 49.2 | 64.1 |
| July | 83.6 | 48.8 | 66.4 |
| August | 83.4 | 48.8 | 66.1 |
| September | 83.3 | 47.7 | 65.5 |
| October | 77.7 | 44.3 | 61.0 |
| November | 67.7 | 39.2 | 53.5 |
| December | 58.4 | 37.0 | 47.7 |

Zero-Degree Days: 0
Freezing Days: 43
90-Degree Days: 33
Heating- and Cooling-Degree Days: 3,900

## Savannah, GA

**Terrain:** Surrounded by flat land, low and marshy to the north and east, rising to several feet above sea level to the west and south. About half the land to the west and south is clear of trees; the other half is woods, much of which lie in swamp.

**Climate:** Temperate with a seasonal mean temperature of 51° F in winter, 64° F in spring, 80° F in summer, and 66° F in autumn. Summer temperatures are moderated by thundershowers almost every afternoon. Sunshine is adequate in all seasons; seldom are there more than two or three days in succession without it. The long growing season is accompanied by abundant rain.

**Pluses:** Mild winters, pleasant autumns.

**Minuses:** Low, marshy terrain; humid summers.

**Places Rated Score: 542**

**Places Rated Rank: 164**

**Elevation: 51 feet**

Relative Humidity: 74%
Wind Speed: 8.1 mph

Seasonal Change

Annual Rainfall 51 in

Annual Snowfall .3 in

Clear 104 days  Partly Cloudy 113 days  Cloudy 148 days

Precipitation Days: 112  Storm Days: 64

| Average Temperatures | | | |
|---|---|---|---|
| | Daily High | Daily Low | Monthly Mean |
| January | 61.1 | 38.7 | 49.9 |
| February | 63.6 | 40.5 | 52.1 |
| March | 69.5 | 46.4 | 58.0 |
| April | 77.8 | 54.3 | 66.1 |
| May | 84.8 | 61.8 | 73.3 |
| June | 89.3 | 68.8 | 79.1 |
| July | 90.8 | 71.3 | 81.1 |
| August | 90.3 | 70.9 | 80.6 |
| September | 85.4 | 66.9 | 76.2 |
| October | 78.2 | 55.9 | 67.1 |
| November | 69.3 | 44.9 | 57.1 |
| December | 62.1 | 38.7 | 50.4 |

Zero-Degree Days: 0
Freezing Days: 35
90-Degree Days: 54
Heating- and Cooling-Degree Days: 4,269

## ★ Seattle, WA

**Terrain:** Located on Puget Sound on the northwest Pacific coast of Washington. The Cascade Range and the Olympic Mountains serve as barriers to easterly and northerly weather systems.

**Climate:** Midlatitude coast climate, characterized by moderate temperatures, a pronounced though not sharply defined rainy season, and considerable cloudiness, particularly during the winter. Occasionally, severe winter storms come in from the north. Summers are very pleasant, and winters are relatively mild, with prevailing temperatures in the 40s. Summer heat and winter cold are modified by the nearness of the ocean.

**Pluses:** Mild temperatures, especially pleasant summers and autumns.

**Minuses:** Wet winters, ground fogs, lots of drizzle.

**Places Rated Score: 808**          **Places Rated Rank: 12**

**Elevation: 450 feet**

Relative Humidity: 74%
Wind Speed: 9.3 mph

Seasonal Change

Annual Rainfall 39 in

Annual Snowfall 15 in

Clear 57 days   Partly Cloudy 79 days   Cloudy 229 days

Precipitation Days: 160   Storm Days: 7

| Average Temperatures | | | |
|---|---|---|---|
| | Daily High | Daily Low | Monthly Mean |
| January | 43.4 | 33.0 | 38.2 |
| February | 48.5 | 36.0 | 42.3 |
| March | 51.5 | 36.6 | 44.1 |
| April | 57.0 | 40.3 | 48.7 |
| May | 64.1 | 45.6 | 54.9 |
| June | 69.0 | 50.6 | 59.8 |
| July | 75.1 | 53.8 | 64.5 |
| August | 73.8 | 53.7 | 63.8 |
| September | 68.7 | 50.4 | 59.6 |
| October | 59.4 | 44.9 | 52.2 |
| November | 50.4 | 38.8 | 44.6 |
| December | 45.4 | 35.5 | 40.5 |

Zero-Degree Days: 0
Freezing Days: 32
90-Degree Days: 3
Heating- and Cooling-Degree Days: 5,314

## Shreveport, LA

**Terrain:** Located on the west bank of the Red River opposite Bossier City, in the northwestern section of the state, some 30 miles south of Arkansas and 15 miles east of the Texas state line. Part of the city is situated in the Red River bottomlands and the remainder in the gently rolling hills that begin a mile west of the river.

**Climate:** Transitional between the humid subtropical climate prevalent to the south and the continental climates of the Great Plains and Middle West to the north. Winter months are normally mild, with cold spells generally of short duration. The typical pattern is a drop in temperature the first day, minimum temperatures the second day, and gradual warming on the third. Summers are hot and humid, relieved only by the thunderstorms that come about eight times per month during that season. April and May are pleasant. Fall, which lasts from late September until December, is delightful for outdoor activities.

**Pluses:** Mild winters, long falls.

**Minuses:** Hot, steamy summers; occasional flooding.

**Places Rated Score: 508**          **Places Rated Rank: 220**

**Elevation: 259 feet**

Relative Humidity: 71%
Wind Speed: 8.8 mph

Seasonal Change

Annual Rainfall 45 in

Annual Snowfall 1 in

Clear 118 days   Partly-Cloudy 99 days   Cloudy 148 days

Precipitation Days: 97   Storm Days: 54

| Average Temperatures | | | |
|---|---|---|---|
| | Daily High | Daily Low | Monthly Mean |
| January | 56.6 | 37.8 | 47.2 |
| February | 60.4 | 40.6 | 50.5 |
| March | 67.3 | 46.2 | 56.8 |
| April | 76.9 | 55.9 | 66.4 |
| May | 83.6 | 63.1 | 73.4 |
| June | 90.1 | 70.2 | 80.2 |
| July | 93.5 | 72.8 | 83.2 |
| August | 93.8 | 72.5 | 83.2 |
| September | 87.9 | 66.8 | 77.4 |
| October | 79.3 | 55.7 | 67.5 |
| November | 67.2 | 45.2 | 56.2 |
| December | 58.9 | 39.4 | 49.2 |

Zero-Degree Days: 0
Freezing Days: 1
90-Degree Days: 87
Heating- and Cooling-Degree Days: 4,705

## Sioux City, IA–NE

**Terrain:** Sioux City is located along the Missouri River at a point where Iowa touches both Nebraska and South Dakota. The terrain is rolling, except for the river valleys and bottomlands. The Sioux City business district lies in the river valley, and the residential sections, for the most part, are spread over the hills, which range from 100 feet to 200 feet higher. Corn, small grains, and grazing grasses are products of abundant rainfall here.

**Climate:** Typically continental and largely determined by the movement and interaction of the large-scale weather systems. Under normal conditions, winters are cold and summers warm, with most rain falling between April and September. Except for an occasional dry year, rain is plentiful. There is considerable fluctuation in temperature and precipitation from season to season and year to year, as elsewhere in the northern Plains. Average growing season: 160 days. The first freeze is in early October and the last in late April.

**Pluses:** Variable.

**Minuses:** Rugged continental.

**Places Rated Score: 385**          **Places Rated Rank: 304**

**Elevation: 1,103 feet**

Relative Humidity: 69%
Wind Speed: 10.9 mph

Seasonal Change

Annual Rainfall 26 in

Annual Snowfall 31 in

Clear 107 days   Partly Cloudy 103 days   Cloudy 155 days

Precipitation Days: 98   Storm Days: 45

| Average Temperatures | | | |
|---|---|---|---|
| | Daily High | Daily Low | Monthly Mean |
| January | 28.2 | 7.7 | 18.0 |
| February | 33.3 | 13.4 | 23.4 |
| March | 42.9 | 23.4 | 33.2 |
| April | 61.3 | 37.4 | 49.4 |
| May | 72.5 | 49.3 | 60.9 |
| June | 81.3 | 59.3 | 70.3 |
| July | 86.7 | 63.9 | 75.3 |
| August | 84.8 | 62.1 | 73.5 |
| September | 75.3 | 51.4 | 63.4 |
| October | 65.8 | 40.4 | 53.1 |
| November | 47.0 | 25.6 | 36.3 |
| December | 33.3 | 13.6 | 23.5 |

Zero-Degree Days: 22
Freezing Days: 150
90-Degree Days: 24
Heating- and Cooling-Degree Days: 7,885

## Sioux Falls, SD

**Terrain:** Located in the Big Sioux River valley in the southeastern portion of South Dakota. Surrounding terrain is gently rolling. Within a 100-mile radius of the city, the land slopes upward 300 feet to 400 feet in the north and northwest and downward in the southeast. There is little change in elevation in the other directions.

**Climate:** Invigorating continental. Cold air masses from the north often move in very rapidly, causing strong, gusty winds for several hours. During late fall and winter, these cold fronts sometimes bring temperature drops of 20 degrees to 30 degrees in a day. Severe cold spells rarely last more than a few days. During a cold winter, frost may penetrate the ground to a depth of 3 feet to 4 feet unless there is heavy snow cover to protect the ground. There are usually one to two very heavy snowstorms each winter. Summer temperatures may climb over 100° F once or twice a year. Thunderstorms are frequent, especially during June and July. Occasional tornadoes and floods.

**Pluses:** Vigorous four-season climate.

**Minuses:** Extremes in temperature, snowy winters.

**Places Rated Score: 276**

**Places Rated Rank: 321**

**Elevation: 1,427 feet**

Relative Humidity: 69%
Wind Speed: 11.2 mph

Seasonal Change

Annual Rainfall 25 in

Annual Snowfall 39 in

Clear 105 days  Partly Cloudy 105 days  Cloudy 155 days

Precipitation Days: 93  Storm Days: 43

| Average Temperatures | | | |
|---|---|---|---|
| | Daily High | Daily Low | Monthly Mean |
| January | 24.6 | 3.7 | 14.2 |
| February | 29.7 | 9.0 | 19.4 |
| March | 39.7 | 20.2 | 30.0 |
| April | 57.8 | 34.4 | 46.1 |
| May | 69.7 | 45.7 | 57.7 |
| June | 78.9 | 56.3 | 67.6 |
| July | 85.1 | 61.5 | 73.3 |
| August | 83.8 | 59.8 | 71.8 |
| September | 73.0 | 48.7 | 60.9 |
| October | 62.7 | 37.6 | 50.2 |
| November | 43.5 | 22.7 | 33.1 |
| December | 29.6 | 10.4 | 20.0 |

Zero-Degree Days: 33
Freezing Days: 171
90-Degree Days: 28
Heating- and Cooling-Degree Days: 8,557

## Spokane, WA

**Terrain:** Spokane lies on the eastern edge of the broad Columbia Basin area of Washington, which is bounded by the Cascade Range on the west and the Rocky Mountains to the east. The elevations in eastern Washington vary from less than 400 feet above sea level near Pasco to 5,000 feet in the extreme eastern edge of the state. Spokane is in the upper plateau area, where the long, gradual slope from the Columbia River meets the sharp rise of the Rockies.

**Climate:** Combines some of the characteristics of the damp coastal climate with the arid interior climate. Most air masses are brought from the west or southwest and lose most of their moisture passing over the Coast and Cascade ranges. Sometimes dry, continental air masses from the east invade the area, bringing high temperatures with low humidity in the summer and subzero temperatures in the winter. Generally, Spokane has a mild, arid climate during summer and a cold, coastal climate during winter.

**Pluses:** Mild, dry summers.

**Minuses:** Damp winters.

**Places Rated Score: 574**

**Places Rated Rank: 110**

**Elevation: 2,365 feet**

Relative Humidity: 63%
Wind Speed: 8.7 mph

Seasonal Change

Annual Rainfall 17 in

Annual Snowfall 53 in

Clear 89 days  Partly Cloudy 87 days  Cloudy 189 days

Precipitation Days: 114  Storm Days: 11

| Average Temperatures | | | |
|---|---|---|---|
| | Daily High | Daily Low | Monthly Mean |
| January | 31.9 | 19.6 | 25.4 |
| February | 39.0 | 25.3 | 32.2 |
| March | 46.2 | 28.8 | 37.5 |
| April | 57.0 | 35.2 | 46.1 |
| May | 66.5 | 42.8 | 54.7 |
| June | 73.6 | 49.4 | 61.5 |
| July | 84.3 | 55.1 | 69.7 |
| August | 81.9 | 54.0 | 68.0 |
| September | 72.5 | 46.7 | 59.6 |
| October | 58.1 | 37.5 | 47.8 |
| November | 41.8 | 29.2 | 35.5 |
| December | 33.9 | 24.0 | 29.0 |

Zero-Degree Days: 5
Freezing Days: 141
90-Degree Days: 21
Heating- and Cooling-Degree Days: 7,225

## Springfield, IL

**Terrain:** Surrounding country is nearly level. There are no large hills in the area, but rolling terrain is found near the Sangamon River and Spring Creek.

**Climate:** Typically continental in character, with warm to hot summers and cold winters. Monthly average temperatures range from the upper 20s in January to the upper 70s in July. Considerable variation takes place frequently within each season. Although summer weather is often uncomfortably warm and humid, winters are less severe than those farther to the north, although prairie winds may accentuate the cold. Summers are sunny.

**Pluses:** Changeable climate.

**Minuses:** Hot summers, rather cold winters.

**Places Rated Score: 524**

**Places Rated Rank: 196**

**Elevation: 613 feet**

Relative Humidity: 71%
Wind Speed: 11.4 mph

Seasonal Change

Annual Rainfall 35 in

Annual Snowfall 22 in

Clear 108 days  Partly Cloudy 92 days  Cloudy 165 days

Precipitation Days: 112  Storm Days: 50

| Average Temperatures | | | |
|---|---|---|---|
| | Daily High | Daily Low | Monthly Mean |
| January | 34.8 | 18.6 | 26.7 |
| February | 38.9 | 21.8 | 30.4 |
| March | 48.7 | 30.1 | 39.4 |
| April | 63.6 | 42.6 | 53.1 |
| May | 74.1 | 52.6 | 63.4 |
| June | 83.3 | 62.5 | 72.9 |
| July | 86.6 | 65.6 | 76.1 |
| August | 85.0 | 63.7 | 74.4 |
| September | 78.7 | 55.6 | 67.2 |
| October | 68.1 | 45.0 | 56.6 |
| November | 51.0 | 32.7 | 41.9 |
| December | 38.2 | 22.7 | 30.5 |

Zero-Degree Days: 8
Freezing Days: 119
90-Degree Days: 28
Heating- and Cooling-Degree Days: 6,674

# Springfield, MO

**Terrain:** Located on very gently rolling tableland, almost atop the crest of the Missouri Ozark Plateau. The average elevation of the city proper is just over 1,300 feet above sea level.

**Climate:** As a result of this advantageous position, the city and surrounding countryside enjoy what is described as a plateau climate. The area possesses the mild and changeable climate often associated with high places in southerly latitudes, with warmer winters and cooler summers than other parts of the state at lower elevations. The city sits astride two major drainage systems: the Missouri River system to the north and the White-Mississippi system to the south.

**Pluses:** Mild, changeable.

**Minuses:** Short springs and falls.

**Elevation: 1,270 feet**

Relative Humidity: 70%
Wind Speed: 11.2 mph

Seasonal Change

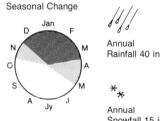

Annual Rainfall 40 in

Annual Snowfall 15 in

Clear 117 days    Partly Cloudy 99 days    Cloudy 149 days

Precipitation Days: 107  Storm Days: 58

| Average Temperatures | | | |
| --- | --- | --- | --- |
| | Daily High | Daily Low | Monthly Mean |
| January | 43.2 | 22.6 | 32.9 |
| February | 47.5 | 26.5 | 37.0 |
| March | 55.1 | 32.8 | 44.0 |
| April | 68.0 | 45.0 | 56.5 |
| May | 76.1 | 54.0 | 65.1 |
| June | 84.2 | 62.9 | 73.6 |
| July | 89.0 | 66.5 | 77.8 |
| August | 88.9 | 65.2 | 77.1 |
| September | 81.2 | 57.3 | 69.3 |
| October | 71.1 | 46.8 | 59.0 |
| November | 56.4 | 34.5 | 45.5 |
| December | 45.7 | 26.3 | 36.0 |

Zero-Degree Days: 3
Freezing Days: 105
90-Degree Days: 40
Heating- and Cooling-Degree Days: 5,952

**Places Rated Score: 544**          **Places Rated Rank: 159**

# State College, PA

**Terrain:** Located in Centre County, the geographic center of Pennsylvania. The orientation of the ridges and valleys of the Appalachian Mountains is northeast to southwest. Elevations within Centre County vary from 977 feet to 2,400 feet. The largest valley in the area is Nittany Valley, much of which is under cultivation. The surrounding higher elevations are covered with second-growth forests.

**Climate:** A composite of the relatively dry midwestern continental climate and the more humid climate characteristic of the eastern seaboard. Prevailing westerly winds carry weather disturbances from the interior of the country into the area. Coastal storms occasionally affect the local weather as they move toward the northeast, but generally the Atlantic is too distant to have a noticeable effect on the climate. Winters are cold and relatively dry, with thick cloud cover. Summer and fall are the most pleasant seasons of the year.

**Pluses:** Nice falls and summers.

**Minuses:** Humid, lots of cloudy days.

**Elevation: 1,200 feet**

Relative Humidity: 67%
Wind Speed: 7.8 mph

Seasonal Change

Annual Rainfall 37 in

Annual Snowfall 48 in

Clear 66 days    Partly Cloudy 114 days    Cloudy 185 days

Precipitation Days: 122  Storm Days: 35

| Average Temperatures | | | |
| --- | --- | --- | --- |
| | Daily High | Daily Low | Monthly Mean |
| January | 34.2 | 19.8 | 27.0 |
| February | 36.1 | 20.2 | 28.2 |
| March | 45.4 | 27.7 | 36.5 |
| April | 59.2 | 38.9 | 49.1 |
| May | 70.2 | 48.8 | 59.3 |
| June | 78.7 | 57.3 | 68.0 |
| July | 82.6 | 61.1 | 71.9 |
| August | 80.7 | 59.1 | 69.9 |
| September | 73.5 | 52.0 | 62.8 |
| October | 62.9 | 42.5 | 52.7 |
| November | 48.7 | 33.2 | 41.0 |
| December | 36.3 | 22.9 | 29.6 |

Zero-Degree Days: 4
Freezing Days: 132
90-Degree Days: 8
Heating- and Cooling-Degree Days: 6,797

**Places Rated Score: 575**          **Places Rated Rank: 105**

# Syracuse, NY

**Terrain:** Located at approximately the geographic center of New York State. Gently rolling terrain stretches northward for about 30 miles to the eastern end of Lake Ontario. Oneida Lake lies about 8 miles northeast of the city. Five miles to the south, hills rise to about 1,500 feet. Immediately to the west, terrain is gently rolling, with elevations 500 feet to 800 feet above sea level.

**Climate:** Continental and comparatively humid. Nearly all cyclonic systems moving from the interior of the country and passing through the St. Lawrence Valley will affect Syracuse. Seasonal and daily changes are marked and produce an invigorating climate. Winters can be cold and severe; daytime temperatures average 35° F, nighttime lows around 18° F. Autumn, winter, and spring show great changeability. Summer nights generally are cool, but days can be uncomfortable because of the humidity. The area is overcast, and the cloudiest months are December, January, and February.

**Pluses:** Changeable weather.

**Minuses:** Snowy, cloudy, rigorous in general.

**Elevation: 408 feet**

Relative Humidity: 73%
Wind Speed: 9.8 mph

Seasonal Change

Annual Rainfall 36 in

Annual Snowfall 109 in

Clear 64 days    Partly Cloudy 100 days    Cloudy 201 days

Precipitation Days: 168  Storm Days: 29

| Average Temperatures | | | |
| --- | --- | --- | --- |
| | Daily High | Daily Low | Monthly Mean |
| January | 31.4 | 15.8 | 23.6 |
| February | 32.7 | 16.5 | 24.6 |
| March | 41.5 | 24.8 | 33.2 |
| April | 56.5 | 36.4 | 46.5 |
| May | 67.6 | 46.0 | 56.8 |
| June | 77.7 | 56.1 | 66.9 |
| July | 82.0 | 61.0 | 71.5 |
| August | 80.2 | 59.2 | 69.7 |
| September | 73.3 | 52.3 | 62.8 |
| October | 62.4 | 42.5 | 52.5 |
| November | 48.3 | 33.6 | 41.0 |
| December | 35.0 | 21.2 | 28.1 |

Zero-Degree Days: 9
Freezing Days: 138
90-Degree Days: 6
Heating- and Cooling-Degree Days: 7,229

**Places Rated Score: 548**          **Places Rated Rank: 151**

## Tallahassee, FL

**Terrain:** Located in flat topography in northwest Florida about 20 miles from the Gulf of Mexico.

**Climate:** Average year-round temperatures compare with those of southern portions of California, Brazil, China, and Australia. The yearly average of 68° F has varied from 64° F to 71° F. In contrast to the southern part of Florida, there is a more definite march of the four seasons here, with considerable winter rainfall and much less winter sunshine. Summer is the least pleasant time of the year; thunderstorms occur on the average of every other day. High humidities and high temperatures cause discomfort. Maxima of 90° F or higher occur on an average of almost 90 days per year, with readings as high as 95° F on 22 of those days.

**Pluses:** Warm winters, sufficient rainfall.

**Minuses:** Long, humid summers; few clear days relative to the rest of the state.

**Places Rated Score: 404**　　　**Places Rated Rank: 296**

**Elevation: 68 feet**

Relative Humidity: 76%
Wind Speed: 7.0 mph

Seasonal Change

Annual Rainfall 62 in

Annual Snowfall 0 in

Clear 95 days　　Partly Cloudy 138 days　　Cloudy 132 days

Precipitation Days: 119　Storm Days: 86

| Average Temperatures | | | |
| --- | --- | --- | --- |
| | Daily High | Daily Low | Monthly Mean |
| January | 64.2 | 41.0 | 52.6 |
| February | 66.5 | 43.0 | 54.8 |
| March | 72.1 | 48.4 | 60.3 |
| April | 80.1 | 55.7 | 67.9 |
| May | 86.7 | 62.8 | 74.8 |
| June | 90.4 | 69.6 | 80.0 |
| July | 90.6 | 71.6 | 81.1 |
| August | 90.5 | 71.7 | 81.1 |
| September | 87.4 | 68.7 | 78.1 |
| October | 80.6 | 57.9 | 69.3 |
| November | 71.4 | 46.4 | 58.9 |
| December | 65.1 | 41.3 | 53.2 |

Zero-Degree Days: 0
Freezing Days: 36
90-Degree Days: 87
Heating- and Cooling-Degree Days: 4,126

## Tampa–St. Petersburg–Clearwater, FL

**Terrain:** Located in flat topography on the Gulf coast of Florida.

**Climate:** An outstanding feature is the summer thunderstorm season. On the average, there are 88 days of thundershowers per year, occurring mostly in the afternoons in July, August, and September. The resulting temperature drop from 90° F to 70° F produces an agreeable physiologic reaction. Temperature throughout the year is modified by the waters of the Gulf of Mexico and surrounding bays. Snowfall is negligible, and freezing temperatures are rare; during the cooling season, however, night ground fogs occur frequently because of the flat terrain.

**Pluses:** Mild Gulf climate.

**Minuses:** Gulf hurricanes, regular summer thundershowers.

**Places Rated Score: 440**　　　**Places Rated Rank: 277**

**Elevation: 11 feet**

Relative Humidity: 74%
Wind Speed: 8.8 mph

Seasonal Change

Annual Rainfall 49 in

Annual Snowfall 0 in

Clear 98 days　　Partly Cloudy 140 days　　Cloudy 127 days

Precipitation Days: 107　Storm Days: 88

| Average Temperatures | | | |
| --- | --- | --- | --- |
| | Daily High | Daily Low | Monthly Mean |
| January | 70.6 | 50.1 | 60.4 |
| February | 71.9 | 51.7 | 61.8 |
| March | 76.1 | 55.9 | 66.0 |
| April | 82.4 | 61.6 | 72.0 |
| May | 87.5 | 66.9 | 77.2 |
| June | 89.9 | 72.0 | 81.0 |
| July | 90.1 | 73.7 | 81.9 |
| August | 90.4 | 74.0 | 82.2 |
| September | 89.0 | 72.6 | 80.8 |
| October | 83.9 | 65.5 | 74.7 |
| November | 77.1 | 56.4 | 66.8 |
| December | 72.0 | 51.2 | 61.6 |

Zero-Degree Days: 0
Freezing Days: 4
90-Degree Days: 81
Heating- and Cooling-Degree Days: 4,084

## Toledo, OH

**Terrain:** Located on the western end of Lake Erie at the mouth of the Maumee River, on flat ground. The city has excellent harbor facilities, making it a large transportation center for rail, water, and motor freight. Generally rich agricultural land is found in the surrounding area, especially up the Maumee River toward the Indiana state line.

**Climate:** Nearness to Lake Erie has a moderating effect on temperature, and extremes are seldom recorded. Humidity is high, and there is an excessive amount of cloudiness. In the winter months, the sun shines during only 30% of the daylight hours; December and January, the cloudiest months, sometimes receive as little as 16% of the possible amount of sunshine.

**Pluses:** Lakefront location moderates extreme temperatures.

**Minuses:** Humid, cloudy.

**Places Rated Score: 518**　　　**Places Rated Rank: 204**

**Elevation: 692 feet**

Relative Humidity: 72%
Wind Speed: 9.5 mph

Seasonal Change

Annual Rainfall 32 in

Annual Snowfall 37 in

Clear 71 days　　Partly Cloudy 110 days　　Cloudy 184 days

Precipitation Days: 136　Storm Days: 40

| Average Temperatures | | | |
| --- | --- | --- | --- |
| | Daily High | Daily Low | Monthly Mean |
| January | 32.4 | 17.2 | 24.8 |
| February | 35.2 | 18.9 | 27.1 |
| March | 45.0 | 26.6 | 35.8 |
| April | 59.5 | 37.2 | 48.4 |
| May | 70.5 | 47.1 | 58.8 |
| June | 80.5 | 57.2 | 68.9 |
| July | 83.8 | 60.8 | 72.3 |
| August | 82.4 | 59.1 | 70.8 |
| September | 75.7 | 51.8 | 63.8 |
| October | 64.8 | 41.2 | 53.0 |
| November | 48.0 | 31.1 | 39.6 |
| December | 35.4 | 20.5 | 28.0 |

Zero-Degree Days: 8
Freezing Days: 145
90-Degree Days: 13
Heating- and Cooling-Degree Days: 7,066

## Tucson, AZ

**Terrain:** Lies at the foot of the Catalina Mountains in a flat to gently rolling valley floor in southern Arizona.
**Climate:** Desert, characterized by a long, hot season beginning in April and ending in October. Temperature maxima above 90° F are the rule during this period; on 41 days each year, on the average, the temperature reaches 100° F. These high temperatures are modified by low humidity, reducing discomfort. Tucson lies in the zone receiving more sunshine than any other in the United States. Clear skies or very thin, high clouds permit intense surface heating during the day and active radiational cooling at night, a process enhanced by the characteristic atmospheric dryness.

**Pluses:** Clear, warm, dry.          **Minuses:** Intense summer
                                                 heat.

**Places Rated Score: 589**          **Places Rated Rank: 87**

**Elevation: 2,555 feet**

Relative Humidity: 38%
Wind Speed: 8.2 mph

Seasonal Change

Annual
Rainfall 11 in

Annual
Snowfall 2 in

| | Average Temperatures | | |
|---|---|---|---|
| | Daily High | Daily Low | Monthly Mean |
| January | 63.5 | 38.2 | 50.9 |
| February | 67.0 | 39.9 | 53.5 |
| March | 71.5 | 43.6 | 57.6 |
| April | 80.7 | 50.3 | 65.5 |
| May | 89.6 | 57.5 | 73.6 |
| June | 97.9 | 66.2 | 82.1 |
| July | 98.3 | 74.2 | 86.3 |
| August | 95.3 | 72.3 | 83.8 |
| September | 93.1 | 67.1 | 80.1 |
| October | 83.8 | 56.4 | 70.1 |
| November | 72.2 | 44.8 | 58.5 |
| December | 64.8 | 39.1 | 52.0 |

Clear
198 days

Partly Cloudy
89 days

Cloudy
78 days

Precipitation Days: 50    Storm Days: 40

Zero-Degree Days: 0
Freezing Days: 21
90-Degree Days: 139
Heating- and Cooling-Degree Days: 4,566

## Tulsa, OK

**Terrain:** Lies along the Arkansas River at an elevation of almost 700 feet above sea level. The surrounding terrain is gently rolling. There are no natural formations—such as mountains or large water surfaces —that influence its climate.
**Climate:** At a latitude of 30 degrees north, Tulsa is far enough north to escape long periods of heat in summer, yet far enough south to miss the extreme cold of winter. The influence of warm moist air from the Gulf of Mexico is often felt in the high humidity, but the climate is essentially continental, characterized by rapid temperature changes. Generally, the winter months are mild. Temperatures of 100° F or higher are frequently experienced from the latter part of July to early September but are usually accompanied by low humidity and a good southerly breeze. Fall is long, with a great number of pleasant, sunny days and cool, bracing nights.

**Pluses:** Four-season climate      **Minuses:** Hot periods during
with long summers                          summer months, tor-
and pleasant falls.                          nadoes.

**Places Rated Score: 530**          **Places Rated Rank: 185**

**Elevation: 676 feet**

Relative Humidity: 67%
Wind Speed: 10.6 mph

Seasonal Change

Annual
Rainfall 37 in

Annual
Snowfall 9 in

| | Average Temperatures | | |
|---|---|---|---|
| | Daily High | Daily Low | Monthly Mean |
| January | 47.0 | 26.1 | 36.6 |
| February | 52.2 | 30.2 | 41.2 |
| March | 59.7 | 36.9 | 48.3 |
| April | 71.8 | 49.7 | 60.8 |
| May | 79.2 | 58.4 | 68.8 |
| June | 87.3 | 67.3 | 77.3 |
| July | 92.8 | 71.4 | 82.1 |
| August | 92.7 | 70.0 | 81.4 |
| September | 84.8 | 61.7 | 73.3 |
| October | 75.0 | 50.8 | 62.9 |
| November | 60.8 | 38.0 | 49.4 |
| December | 50.1 | 29.5 | 39.8 |

Clear
127 days

Partly Cloudy
101 days

Cloudy
137 days

Precipitation Days: 90    Storm Days: 52

Zero-Degree Days: 1
Freezing Days: 85
90-Degree Days: 70
Heating- and Cooling-Degree Days: 5,629

## Washington, DC–MD–VA

**Terrain:** Situated at the western edge of the Middle Atlantic Coastal Plain, 50 miles east of the Blue Ridge Mountains and 35 miles west of Chesapeake Bay at the junction of the Potomac and Anacostia rivers.
**Climate:** Summers are warm and humid, winters mild; generally pleasant weather prevails in the spring and autumn. The coldest weather occurs in late January and early February, and the warmest month is July. There are no pronounced wet and dry seasons. Thunderstorms, during the summer, often bring sudden and heavy showers and damaging winds, hail, or lightning. In winter, snow accumulations of more than 10 inches are rare.

**Pluses:** Pleasant springs and      **Minuses:** Humid summers,
autumns, relatively                          heavy thunder-
mild winters.                                  storms.

**Places Rated Score: 631**          **Places Rated Rank: 51**

**Elevation: 65 feet**

Relative Humidity: 64%
Wind Speed: 9.3 mph

Seasonal Change

Annual
Rainfall 39 in

Annual
Snowfall 16 in

| | Average Temperatures | | |
|---|---|---|---|
| | Daily High | Daily Low | Monthly Mean |
| January | 43.5 | 27.7 | 35.6 |
| February | 46.0 | 28.6 | 37.3 |
| March | 55.0 | 35.2 | 45.1 |
| April | 67.1 | 45.7 | 56.4 |
| May | 76.6 | 55.7 | 66.2 |
| June | 84.6 | 64.6 | 74.6 |
| July | 88.2 | 69.1 | 78.7 |
| August | 86.6 | 67.6 | 77.1 |
| September | 80.2 | 61.0 | 70.6 |
| October | 69.8 | 49.7 | 59.8 |
| November | 57.2 | 38.8 | 48.0 |
| December | 45.2 | 29.5 | 37.4 |

Clear
101 days

Partly Cloudy
106 days

Cloudy
158 days

Precipitation Days: 111    Storm Days: 29

Zero-Degree Days: 0
Freezing Days: 75
90-Degree Days: 37
Heating- and Cooling-Degree Days: 5,626

## Waterloo–Cedar Falls, IA

**Terrain:** Situated on the banks of the Cedar River in northeast Iowa, this area is far removed from the moderating influences of any large body of water. The terrain is level to very gently rolling and is ideally suited to agriculture. The flat, open topography has no influence on climate other than the fact that it offers little resistance to winds, which in the winter can greatly enhance the windchill factor.

**Climate:** Definitely continental in character, with hot summers, cold winters, and short springs and falls. The average annual rainfall is 34 inches, with 71% of this total falling in the April-to-September crop season. As befits its landlocked, northerly location, the temperature range in Waterloo–Cedar Falls is large: January's mean temperature is 16° F, July's 73° F. The lowest and highest temperatures ever recorded here are –34° F and 112° F. Bitterly cold days of zero or below average 31 in number. The mercury hits 90° F or above on an average of 15 days a year, including two 100-degree days.

**Pluses:** Sunny falls.

**Minuses:** Hot summers, cold winters.

**Places Rated Score: 347**   **Places Rated Rank: 312**

**Elevation: 868 feet**

Relative Humidity: 72%
Wind Speed: 10.7 mph

Seasonal Change

Annual Rainfall 34 in

Annual Snowfall 31 in

Clear 92 days | Partly Cloudy 102 days | Cloudy 171 days

Precipitation Days: 99    Storm Days: 43

| Average Temperatures | | | |
| --- | --- | --- | --- |
| | Daily High | Daily Low | Monthly Mean |
| January | 25.7 | 6.9 | 16.3 |
| February | 30.2 | 11.3 | 20.8 |
| March | 40.6 | 22.3 | 31.5 |
| April | 58.5 | 36.3 | 47.4 |
| May | 70.0 | 47.5 | 58.8 |
| June | 79.4 | 57.6 | 68.5 |
| July | 83.6 | 61.5 | 72.6 |
| August | 82.1 | 59.5 | 70.8 |
| September | 73.3 | 49.8 | 61.6 |
| October | 63.5 | 39.7 | 51.6 |
| November | 44.6 | 25.6 | 35.1 |
| December | 30.6 | 12.9 | 21.8 |

Zero-Degree Days: 31
Freezing Days: 159
90-Degree Days: 15
Heating- and Cooling-Degree Days: 8,090

## Wichita, KS

**Terrain:** Located in gentle sloping topography. There are no large bodies of water nearby to affect the city's climate.

**Climate:** Because it lies in the path of alternate masses of warm, moist air moving northward from the Gulf of Mexico and cold, dry air from the polar regions, the city is subject to frequent and often abrupt weather changes. Summers are usually warm and occasionally hot (there are more than 60 days over 90° F during that time). Winters are mild, and snowfalls are light, averaging 16 inches a year.

**Pluses:** Four-season Great Plains climate with mild winters.

**Minuses:** Tornadoes, long summers that can be hot.

**Places Rated Score: 494**   **Places Rated Rank: 268**

**Elevation: 1,340 feet**

Relative Humidity: 66%
Wind Speed: 12.6 mph

Seasonal Change

Annual Rainfall 31 in

Annual Snowfall 16 in

Clear 127 days | Partly Cloudy 97 days | Cloudy 141 days

Precipitation Days: 84    Storm Days: 55

| Average Temperatures | | | |
| --- | --- | --- | --- |
| | Daily High | Daily Low | Monthly Mean |
| January | 41.4 | 21.2 | 31.3 |
| February | 47.1 | 25.4 | 36.3 |
| March | 55.0 | 32.1 | 43.6 |
| April | 68.1 | 45.1 | 56.6 |
| May | 77.1 | 55.0 | 66.1 |
| June | 86.5 | 65.0 | 75.8 |
| July | 91.7 | 69.6 | 80.7 |
| August | 91.0 | 68.3 | 79.7 |
| September | 81.9 | 59.2 | 70.6 |
| October | 71.3 | 47.9 | 59.6 |
| November | 55.8 | 33.8 | 44.8 |
| December | 44.3 | 24.6 | 34.5 |

Zero-Degree Days: 2
Freezing Days: 114
90-Degree Days: 62
Heating- and Cooling-Degree Days: 6,360

## Wilmington, NC

**Terrain:** Located in the Tidewater section of southeastern North Carolina, near the Atlantic Ocean. The city proper is built adjacent to the east bank of the Cape Fear River. The surrounding terrain, typical of the state's Coastal Plain, is low-lying (the average elevation is less than 40 feet) and level. There are many rivers, creeks, and lakes nearby, most with considerable swampy growth surrounding them. Large tracts of woods alternate with cultivated fields.

**Climate:** Wilmington's climate shows a strong maritime influence. Summers are quite warm and humid, but excessive heat is rare. During the colder part of the year, polar air masses reach the coastal areas, causing sharp drops in temperature. However, much of the coldness of these air masses has diminished by the time they reach the Wilmington area. Rainfall is ample and well distributed, with most occurring in summer in the form of thundershowers. In winter, rain may fall steadily for several days. Snowfall is very slight.

**Pluses:** Warm, moist, mild.

**Minuses:** Hot and muggy in summertime.

**Places Rated Score: 564**   **Places Rated Rank: 121**

**Elevation: 30 feet**

Relative Humidity: 75%
Wind Speed: 8.9 mph

Seasonal Change

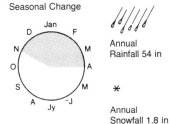

Annual Rainfall 54 in

Annual Snowfall 1.8 in

Clear 113 days | Partly Cloudy 106 days | Cloudy 146 days

Precipitation Days: 117    Storm Days: 46

| Average Temperatures | | | |
| --- | --- | --- | --- |
| | Daily High | Daily Low | Monthly Mean |
| January | 56.6 | 36.2 | 46.4 |
| February | 58.7 | 37.5 | 48.1 |
| March | 64.9 | 43.7 | 54.3 |
| April | 74.3 | 52.2 | 63.3 |
| May | 81.4 | 60.9 | 71.2 |
| June | 86.8 | 68.2 | 77.5 |
| July | 88.8 | 72.0 | 80.4 |
| August | 88.0 | 71.0 | 79.5 |
| September | 83.5 | 65.9 | 74.7 |
| October | 75.4 | 55.1 | 65.3 |
| November | 66.8 | 44.3 | 55.6 |
| December | 58.2 | 36.7 | 47.5 |

Zero-Degree Days: 0
Freezing Days: 45
90-Degree Days: 45
Heating- and Cooling-Degree Days: 4,397

## Yakima, WA

**Terrain:** Located in a small east-west valley in the upper part of the irrigated Yakima Valley in Washington. The local topography is complex, with a number of minor valleys and ridges giving a local elevation as high as 500 feet.

**Climate:** Relatively mild and dry, with characteristics of both maritime and continental climates, modified by the Cascade and the Rocky Mountain ranges. Summers are dry and hot. Winters are cool with only light snowfall, usually 20 inches to 25 inches per year.

**Pluses:** Combination of marine and continental climatic features.

**Minuses:** Cloudy winters, hot summers.

**Elevation: 1,066 feet**

Relative Humidity: 60%
Wind Speed: 7.2 mph

Seasonal Change

Annual Rainfall 8 in

Annual Snowfall 25 in

Clear 112 days

Partly Cloudy 90 days

Cloudy 163 days

| Average Temperatures | | | |
|---|---|---|---|
| | Daily High | Daily Low | Monthly Mean |
| January | 36.4 | 18.6 | 27.5 |
| February | 46.1 | 25.2 | 35.7 |
| March | 54.8 | 28.8 | 41.8 |
| April | 64.1 | 34.8 | 49.5 |
| May | 73.1 | 42.6 | 57.9 |
| June | 79.7 | 49.3 | 64.5 |
| July | 88.1 | 53.3 | 70.7 |
| August | 85.9 | 51.2 | 68.6 |
| September | 78.3 | 44.3 | 61.3 |
| October | 64.7 | 35.4 | 50.1 |
| November | 48.5 | 28.3 | 36.4 |
| December | 39.1 | 23.5 | 31.3 |

Zero-Degree Days: 4
Freezing Days: 150
90-Degree Days: 33
Heating- and Cooling-Degree Days: 6,488

**Places Rated Score: 535**

**Places Rated Rank: 182**

Precipitation Days: 67    Storm Days: 7

# Et Cetera

## IT'S NOT THE HEAT, IT'S THE HUMIDITY

Humidity, or the amount of moisture in the air, is an extremely important factor in climatic comfort. As anyone who has experienced a hot, humid summer knows, humidity intensifies heat. A hot day that is also humid is uncomfortable because the body's natural cooling process of evaporation is retarded.

But there is another reason damp air increases felt heat in the summertime. Just as warm air is able to hold more moisture, so damp air is able to hold heat better, and longer. Therefore, in hot, humid climates, heat is retained in the damp air even after the sun goes down, resulting in nights that are almost as hot as the days. In contrast, dry climates offer greater comfort not only during hot summer days but also during the nights, which can be cool and sometimes even chilly.

Excessive humidity can aggravate certain types of arthritis and rheumatism and, combined with low temperatures, can have a harmful effect on those suffering from pulmonary diseases. Very moist air also encourages the growth of a wide variety of bacteria and molds, thus increasing the chances of infection.

Low humidity can also have undesirable consequences. When the humidity falls below 50 percent, most of us experience dry nasal passages and perhaps a dry, tickling throat. In some areas of the Southwest where the relative humidity can drop to 20 percent or below, many people suffer from nosebleeds, flaking skin, and a constant sore throat.

The table "Temperature, Humidity, and Apparent Temperature" examines the relationship between rela-

## Temperature, Humidity, and Apparent Temperature

**Apparent Temperature**

| Air Temperature (°F) | 0 | 5 | 10 | 15 | 20 | 25 | 30 | 35 | 40 | 45 | 50 | 55 | 60 | 65 | 70 | 75 | 80 | 85 | 90 | 95 | 100 |
|---|---|---|---|---|---|---|---|---|---|---|---|---|---|---|---|---|---|---|---|---|---|
| 110 | 99 | 102 | 105 | 108 | 112 | 117 | 123 | 130 | 137 | 143 | 150 | | | | | | | | | | |
| 105 | 95 | 97 | 100 | 102 | 105 | 109 | 113 | 118 | 123 | 129 | 135 | 142 | 149 | | | | | | | | |
| 100 | 91 | 93 | 95 | 97 | 99 | 101 | 104 | 107 | 110 | 115 | 120 | 126 | 132 | 138 | 144 | | | | | | |
| 95 | 87 | 88 | 90 | 91 | 93 | 94 | 96 | 98 | 101 | 104 | 107 | 110 | 114 | 119 | 124 | 130 | 136 | | | | |
| 90 | 83 | 84 | 85 | 86 | 87 | 88 | 90 | 91 | 93 | 95 | 96 | 98 | 100 | 102 | 106 | 109 | 113 | 117 | 122 | | |
| 85 | 78 | 79 | 80 | 81 | 82 | 83 | 84 | 85 | 86 | 87 | 88 | 89 | 90 | 91 | 93 | 95 | 97 | 99 | 102 | 105 | 108 |
| 80 | 73 | 74 | 75 | 76 | 77 | 77 | 78 | 79 | 79 | 80 | 81 | 81 | 82 | 83 | 85 | 86 | 86 | 87 | 88 | 89 | 91 |
| 75 | 69 | 69 | 70 | 71 | 72 | 72 | 73 | 73 | 74 | 74 | 75 | 75 | 76 | 76 | 77 | 77 | 78 | 78 | 79 | 79 | 80 |
| 70 | 64 | 64 | 65 | 65 | 66 | 66 | 67 | 67 | 68 | 68 | 69 | 69 | 70 | 70 | 70 | 70 | 71 | 71 | 71 | 71 | 72 |

**Relative Humidity (%)**

**July Noon Average Relative Humidity**

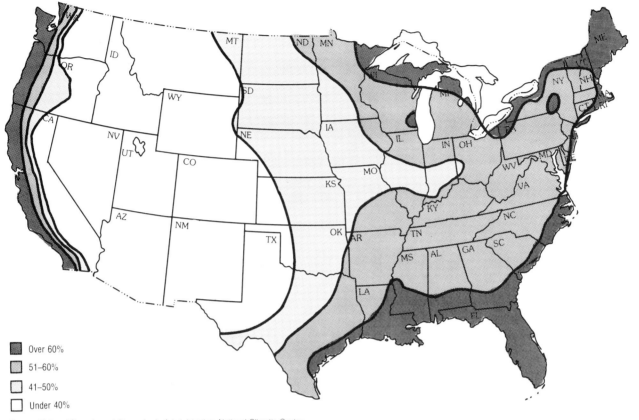

Over 60%

51–60%

41–50%

Under 40%

*Source:* National Oceanic and Atmospheric Administration, National Climatic Center

tive humidity and temperature. Relative humidity is the ratio of the amount of water vapor present in the air to the greatest possible amount of water vapor air can hold at that temperature. To find the apparent temperature, locate the air temperature at the left and the relative humidity along the bottom. The intersection of the horizontal row of figures opposite the temperature with the vertical row above the relative humidity is the apparent temperature. For example, an air temperature of 85 degrees Fahrenheit feels like 89 degrees at 55 percent relative humidity but like 102 when the humidity is 90 percent.

## GOING TO EXTREMES

Many people gripe about the weather in the places they live. True, extreme weather does occur routinely in some of the rugged climates of North America. But how bad is your local climate compared with some really nasty places? Below are some ridiculous extremes.

*Mount Washington, New Hampshire.* New England's highest peak, Mount Washington claims justifiably to have the world's worst weather. Here, even in midsummer, the temperature may drop 50 or 60 de-

grees Fahrenheit in a matter of minutes. People visiting the summit are warned to bring parkas with them, even in July. Despite these warnings, deaths occur every year on Mount Washington. The weather station on the summit (which provides data for the NOAA's *Local Climatological Data*) reports winds in excess of 100 miles per hour with dismal regularity. On April 12, 1934, a gust traveling at 231 miles per hour was recorded here. This is the greatest wind speed— excluding those of tornado funnel clouds—ever measured on the earth's surface. In fact, the winds are so severe on Mount Washington's summit that a standard anemometer, which consists of three rotating metal cups, cannot survive. Instead, the station must employ a pitot tube, a wind-measuring device used on aircraft. Fingers of ice, called rime ice, form very rapidly here on buildings and vehicles during icy weather and often measure up to two or three feet in length.

Meteorologically speaking, the summit of Mount Washington is an arctic island in an otherwise temperate zone. It is surrounded by clouds or fog on at least 300 days each year, the average annual snowfall is 242 inches, and the average year-round temperature is 27 degrees.

### The 10 Snowiest Metro Areas

| | Inches per Year |
|---|---|
| Syracuse, NY | 109 |
| Bangor, ME | 97 |
| Buffalo, NY | 90 |
| Binghamton, NY | 86 |
| Burlington, VT | 79 |
| Duluth, MN–WI | 78 |
| Casper, WY | 77 |
| Grand Rapids, MI | 77 |
| Portland, ME | 74 |
| Albany–Schenectady–Troy, NY | 71 |

### . . . and the 11 Stormiest

| | Storm Days per Year |
|---|---|
| Biloxi–Gulfport, MS | 94 |
| Fort Myers, FL | 93 |
| Tampa–St. Petersburg–Clearwater, FL | 88 |
| Tallahassee, FL | 86 |
| Orlando, FL | 81 |
| Mobile, AL | 80 |
| Miami–Hialeah, FL | 75 |
| Galveston–Texas City, TX | 70 |
| Alexandria, LA | 69 |
| Houston, TX | 69 |
| New Orleans, LA | 68 |

Listed above are those metro areas described in the Place Profiles that have more than 70 inches of snow per year or more than 65 storm days per year.

### The 8 Dampest Metro Areas

| | Relative Humidity |
|---|---|
| Galveston–Texas City, TX | 78% |
| Alexandria, LA | 77 |
| Asheville, NC | 77 |
| Biloxi–Gulfport, MS | 77 |
| Corpus Christi, TX | 77 |
| Eugene–Springfield, OR | 77 |
| Houston, TX | 77 |
| New Orleans, LA | 77 |

### . . . and the 7 Driest

| | Relative Humidity |
|---|---|
| Las Vegas, NV | 29% |
| Phoenix, AZ | 36 |
| Tucson, AZ | 38 |
| El Paso, TX | 39 |
| Albuquerque, NM | 43 |
| Colorado Springs, CO | 49 |
| Reno, NV | 50 |

Listed above are those metro areas described in the Place Profiles with an average relative humidity greater than 76 percent or lower than 51 percent.

How would Mount Washington score according to the *Places Rated* formula? With, among other things, 66 zero-degree days, 243 freezing days, 13,878 heating-degree days, and many months during which the mean temperature is below 20 degrees, Mount Washington receives a climate mildness score of minus 19.

*Greenland Ranch, Death Valley, California.* So you think it gets hot where you live? Try Greenland Ranch, in California's Death Valley. They didn't name it Death Valley just for effect, you know. There is no weather station here recording data for the NOAA's *Local Climatological Data*, so the best we can do is roughly estimate the climate score. Suffice it to say that America's all-time heat record of 134 degrees Fahrenheit was set in Greenland Ranch. This is only 2 degrees lower than the highest temperature ever recorded on the face of the earth, at Al Aziziyah, Libya, in 1922. The exact number of 90-degree days in Greenland Ranch is not recorded, but data show that during five months the mean daily temperature exceeds 80 degrees. In July, the mean daily temperature is above 100. The mean maximum temperature for the months of May through September are as follows: 99.2, 109.2, 116.1, 113.6, and

105.5. Think about it the next time you complain about summer heat.

*Barrow, Alaska.* The settlement of Barrow is located on the northern coastline of Alaska, well above the Arctic Circle. The monthly mean temperatures are below zero during six months of the year. The average daily maximum temperature in the hottest month, July, is only 44 degrees. Yet Barrow does record three 90-degree days thanks to its very long "summer" days. It has an average of 323 freezing days a year and 170 zero-degree days. It also has more than 20,000 heating-degree days. Barrow's *Places Rated* climate score? Minus 829!

## ARE WE RUNNING OUT OF WATER?

Climate and terrain have an importance far more profound than simple considerations of pleasant weather and attractive surroundings. They also determine an area's access to one of America's most precious natural resources: the abundance of fresh water found in lakes, rivers, and streams, and in the underground aquifers that feed our wells. The Great Lakes, which the United States shares with Canada, contain more than one fifth of the world's supply of surface fresh water. By any reckoning, these giant inland seas of usable, drinkable water are among the most valuable resources on the planet.

And yet we hear increasing cries of alarm concerning our supplies of fresh water. Some areas of the nation appear to be rapidly depleting both surface water and groundwater. In other areas, serious pollution threatens. Even in regions like New England, where water is plentiful, growing numbers of metro areas are faced with shortages due to antiquated water delivery systems and purification plants. The situation is further complicated by growing competition for water between farmers on the one hand and urban residents and industry on the other, and by the efforts of American Indians to recapture water rights taken from them more than a hundred years ago.

So is America really faced with a water shortage? No and yes.

*No.* America has plenty of water. The national supply of renewable fresh water is about 1,400 billion gallons of water per day. Of this total, about 380 billion gallons per day is withdrawn for use by the nation's homes, farms, and industry. Of the 380 billion gallons withdrawn, about 280 billion gallons per day is returned to lakes and streams. Although a large percentage of the country's waste is carried by this return flow, much of the returned water is usable. Withdrawn water that is not returned to lakes or streams (either due to evaporation or ingestion by humans and livestock) is termed consumed water. On any given day, then, some 100 billion gallons of water is consumed, or only about one fourteenth of the total amount of water available.

*Yes.* Although the total average supply is more than plentiful, the problem arises from the uneven distribution of that supply. Most places in America have adequate water supplies. Some have much more than they can ever use. And a few are already facing a water crisis. Predictably, the majority of areas that suffer most from lack of water are those that receive scant rainfall. The Great Basin area receives the least precipitation since it is located between two high mountain ranges, which block moisture-laden air. In Nevada, Arizona, and New Mexico, the southern part of this region, the water problem is greatest. Several other parts of the West and Southwest are also troubled by shortages.

## Where Our Water Comes From

There are two main sources of water, those on the surface of the earth (rivers, lakes, and streams) and those below the surface. We're all familiar with the aboveground sources, and many people assume they represent all our water resources. Actually, 80 percent of U.S. water reserves are located below ground in aquifers. Aquifers are composed of water-permeable rock or gravel through which groundwater percolates from the earth's surface. Since the water flows through many layers of sand, gravel, and rock, it is usually cleaned by this natural filter as it flows. Therefore wells, which often tap aquifers, are known for the purity and high mineral content of their water. Unless otherwise polluted, well water is good water.

But as water is pumped out, the aquifer becomes depleted. It will refill with water if left alone for a while; its water level, or table, will rise again. The time required for the aquifer's water table to return to its normal level is called the recharge rate. If the rate of depletion exceeds the recharge rate, the aquifer will continue to be depleted, and its water table will continue to fall. This process is called groundwater mining.

Many aquifers are located directly below, or nearby, big lakes or rivers that feed them. However, many of our biggest aquifers fortunately lie under dry ground, so they can supply water to what would otherwise be water-starved places.

One such formation is the huge High Plains aquifer, which lies deep below Texas, Oklahoma, New Mexico, Kansas, Colorado, Nebraska, South Dakota, and Wyoming, and covers 177,000 square miles. If it were on the surface instead of below ground, it would be the largest lake in the world (the largest is the Caspian Sea, at 152,084 square miles). For decades, this giant underground cistern has provided irrigation and drinking water for the eight states mentioned above. There are about 170,000 wells tapping the High Plains aquifer, watering 14.3 million acres of farmland that produce 15 percent of America's corn, wheat,

sorghum, and cotton, and nourish 38 percent of its livestock. But the aquifer's water table is falling rapidly. Water is being pumped out of it eight times faster than it can recharge itself. If groundwater mining continues at the present rate, experts predict, the aquifer (which took at least 10,000 years to form) could begin to dry up around the year 2000.

## Water-Resource Regions

The U.S. Geological Survey has divided the nation into 20 water-resource regions, based on their water systems and named accordingly. Thus there are the Great Lakes, the Missouri, and the Arkansas-Red-White regions, the last named for the system of rivers that feeds Oklahoma, northern Texas, and parts of New Mexico and Colorado.

The map "Water-Resource Regions" presents a vivid summary of water availability and rates of groundwater mining in America. The unshaded regions are in no danger of depleting their renewable supplies of water. The lightly shaded areas are at some risk of running short, but this probably will not happen in the immediate future unless there are several severe drought years in a row. The darker areas represent water-resource regions that are consuming more than 40 percent of their renewable water supplies. The region with the darkest shading, the Lower Colorado (so named for the Colorado River, whose lower section flows through Arizona and forms the boundary between Arizona and California), is using more than 100 percent of its supplies and is mining its groundwater reserves.

## Metro Areas with Water Problems

Not only do areas of the country differ in the amount of water readily available to them; they also differ in the quality and purity of their water. The list below pinpoints the major water problems in 269 metro areas. Data are from the 1984 report from the U.S. Geological Survey entitled *Water-Supply Paper 2250*. Metro areas that do not appear on the list—a total of 60—have no significant water troubles.

The major problems delineated are: groundwater mining; insufficient surface water; decreased streamflow, or water in the stream channel, which reduces the water supply; hazardous wastes in groundwater; radioactive wastes in groundwater; pollution of groundwater and/or surface water; flooding; saline-water intrusion in aquifers; sedimentation, which can restrict shipping, increase the potential for flooding, and reduce the capacities of reservoirs; chemical-industrial wastes; wetlands depletion; rising groundwater tables; eutrophication of lakes (the process by which waters become enriched with plant nutrients from the addition of sewage, fertilizers, or wastes, thus upsetting the ecological balance, destroying plant and animal life, and rendering the water unusable for

**Water-Resource Regions, Showing Average Consumptive
Use As a Percentage of Renewable Water Supply**

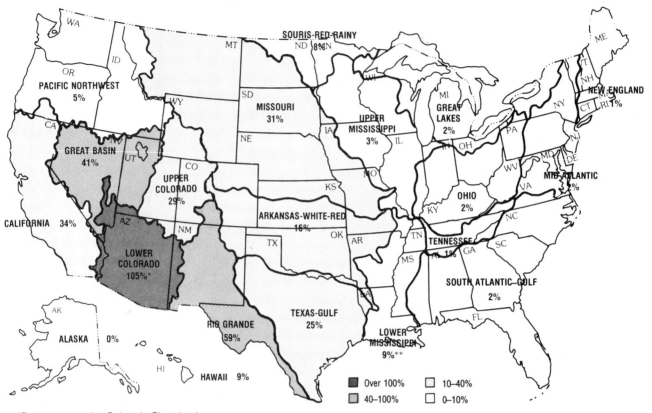

*Represents entire Colorado River basin
**Represents entire Mississippi River basin

Source: U.S. Geological Survey, *Water-Supply Paper 2250*, "National Water Summary 1983—Hydrologic Events and Issues."

public consumption or recreation); and acid rain (a more detailed discussion of acid rain is found in the chapter "Health Care & Environment").

In some instances, problems arising from management of water resources are mentioned. For example, resource development, or the extracting of minerals from the earth, is considered hazardous by the U.S. Geological Survey because the water needed to mine and process minerals may reduce water supplies and because wastes that result from such mining can contaminate surface water and groundwater. In those metro areas where resource development is taking place, the kinds of mining under way are listed.

Metro areas that *Places Rated* deems especially prone to water problems, based on the U.S. Geological Survey paper, are preceded by one, two, or three

triangles (▲), depending on the severity of the situation, with three triangles indicating the worst problems. Of the 269 metro areas described, 41 receive one triangle, 21 two triangles, and only 9 three triangles: Bakersfield, California; Fresno, California; Las Vegas, Nevada; Modesto, California; Norfolk–Virginia Beach–Newport News, Virginia; Phoenix, Arizona; Sacramento, California; Tucson, Arizona; and Visalia–Tulare–Porterville, California.

It should be noted that *Water-Supply Paper 2250* points out situations that may not now be causing damage but that will probably do so in the next few years. These problems should not discourage you from considering a move to a certain metro area. You should, however, make inquiries about the local water situation before reaching a final decision.

## Metro Areas with Water Problems, by State

### ALABAMA
Dothan: Groundwater mining.
Florence: Sinkholes.
Huntsville: Sinkholes.
Mobile: Pollution and increased sedimentation of Mobile River and Mobile Bay.
(See also Georgia, Columbus)

### ALASKA
Anchorage: Current systems cannot meet projected demands, some septic pollution.

### ARIZONA
▲▲▲ Phoenix: Groundwater pollution, hazardous wastes, severe groundwater mining.
▲▲▲ Tucson: Groundwater mining, hazardous wastes.

### ARKANSAS
Fayetteville–Springdale: Surface-water pollution.
Fort Smith (AR–OK): Surface-water pollution.
Little Rock–North Little Rock: Surface-water pollution.
Pine Bluff: Groundwater mining.
(See also Tennessee, Memphis; Texas, Texarkana)

### CALIFORNIA
▲ Anaheim–Santa Ana: Groundwater mining, saline-water intrusion.
▲▲▲ Bakersfield: Groundwater mining.
▲▲▲ Fresno: Groundwater mining, land subsidence.
▲ Los Angeles–Long Beach: Groundwater mining, saline-water intrusion.
▲▲▲ Modesto: Groundwater mining.
▲ Oakland: Decreased streamflow, some heavy-metal pollution.
▲ Oxnard–Ventura: Groundwater mining, saline-water intrusion.
Redding: Hazardous wastes.
Riverside–San Bernardino: Hazardous wastes.*
▲▲▲ Sacramento: Groundwater mining, hazardous wastes.
▲ Salinas–Seaside–Monterey: Groundwater mining, saline-water intrusion.
▲ San Diego: Groundwater mining.
▲ San Francisco: Decreased streamflow, some heavy-metal pollution.
▲▲ San Jose: Groundwater mining, saline-water intrusion.
▲ Santa Cruz: Groundwater mining, saline-water intrusion.
Santa Rosa–Petaluma: Hazardous wastes.
▲▲ Stockton: Groundwater mining, decreased streamflow.

Vallejo–Fairfield–Napa: Decreased streamflow, hazardous wastes.
▲▲▲ Visalia–Tulare–Porterville: Groundwater mining, land subsidence.
Yuba City: Some groundwater mining.

### COLORADO
Boulder–Longmont: Hazardous wastes.
▲ Denver: Hazardous wastes, eutrophication, pollution.

### CONNECTICUT
Bridgeport–Milford: Groundwater mining.
Danbury: Groundwater mining.
Hartford: Surface-water pollution.
Middletown: Surface-water pollution.
New Haven–Meriden: Groundwater mining, surface-water pollution.
New London–Norwich (CT–RI): Groundwater mining, surface-water pollution.
Norwalk: Groundwater mining.
Stamford: Groundwater mining.

### DELAWARE
▲ Wilmington (DE–NJ–MD): Groundwater mining, flooding, hazardous wastes.

### FLORIDA
▲ Bradenton: Groundwater mining, saline-water intrusion.
Daytona Beach: Groundwater mining.
▲ Fort Lauderdale–Hollywood–Pompano Beach: Groundwater mining, hazardous wastes, saline-water intrusion.
Fort Myers: Groundwater mining.
Fort Pierce: Groundwater mining.
Fort Walton Beach: Groundwater mining.
▲ Jacksonville: Groundwater mining, hazardous wastes.
▲▲ Lakeland–Winter Haven: Groundwater mining, hazardous wastes, phosphate mining.
Melbourne–Titusville–Palm Bay: Groundwater mining.
▲▲ Miami–Hialeah: Groundwater mining, surface-water pollution, saline-water intrusion, hazardous wastes.
Ocala: Sinkholes.
Orlando: Groundwater mining.
▲ Pensacola: Groundwater mining, hazardous wastes.
Sarasota: Groundwater mining, saline-water intrusion.
Tallahassee: Some groundwater mining, sinkholes.
▲▲ Tampa–St. Petersburg–Clearwater: Groundwater mining, saline-water intrusion, hazardous wastes.
▲ West Palm Beach–Boca Raton–Delray Beach: Groundwater mining, saline-water intrusion, surface-water pollution.

### GEORGIA
▲ Albany: Groundwater mining, pesticide pollution, sinkholes.
Athens: Surface-water shortages.
Atlanta: Surface-water pollution, some surface-water shortages.
Columbus (GA–AL): Groundwater mining.

Macon–Warner Robins: Surface-water pollution.
▲ Savannah: Groundwater mining, saline-water intrusion.
(See also Tennessee, Chattanooga)

### HAWAII
▲▲ Honolulu: Groundwater mining, surface-water pollution, saline-water intrusion.

### IDAHO
Boise City: Groundwater pollution, hazardous wastes.

### ILLINOIS
Alton–Granite City: Rising groundwater tables.
Aurora–Elgin: Groundwater mining, flooding.
Champaign–Urbana–Rantoul: Surface-water pollution.
Chicago: Groundwater mining, flooding.
Decatur: Surface-water pollution.
East St. Louis–Belleville: Rising groundwater tables.
Joliet: Groundwater mining, flooding.
Kankakee: Surface-water pollution, hazardous wastes.
▲ Lake County: Groundwater mining, flooding, hazardous wastes.
Peoria: Surface-water pollution.
▲ Rockford: Surface-water pollution, hazardous wastes.
Springfield: Surface-water pollution.
(See also Iowa, Davenport–Rock Island–Moline; Missouri, St. Louis)

### INDIANA
Anderson: Surface-water pollution.
Bloomington: Surface-water pollution, hazardous wastes in groundwater.
Elkhart–Goshen: Flooding, groundwater and surface-water pollution.
Fort Wayne: Hazardous wastes in groundwater.
▲▲ Gary–Hammond: Surface-water and groundwater pollution, hazardous wastes.
▲ Indianapolis: Extensive surface-water pollution.
Kokomo: Surface-water pollution.
Lafayette: Groundwater mining.
Muncie: Surface-water pollution.
▲ South Bend–Mishawaka: Flooding, surface-water and groundwater pollution, hazardous wastes.
Terre Haute: Surface-water pollution.
(See also Ohio, Cincinnati)

### IOWA
Davenport–Rock Island–Moline (IA–IL): Surface-water pollution.
Des Moines: Surface-water and groundwater pollution, hazardous wastes.
Dubuque: Pollution in groundwater.
Sioux City (IA–NE): Surface-water scarcity.

### KANSAS
Kansas City: Hazardous wastes in surface water and groundwater.

---

*According to a University of California study released in August 1984, seepage from a toxic waste pit near Riverside threatens major contamination of the Chino Basin aquifer, which supplies drinking water to half a million people in this region. The extent of contamination and the effectiveness of preventive action will not be known for many months.

Topeka: Surface-water pollution.
▲ Wichita: Saline-water intrusion in surface water and groundwater, hazardous wastes.

## KENTUCKY
Lexington–Fayette: Surface-water scarcity.
(See also Ohio, Cincinnati; Tennessee, Clarksville–Hopkinsville; West Virginia, Huntington–Ashland)

## LOUISIANA
Alexandria: Hazardous wastes in groundwater.
Baton Rouge: Groundwater mining.
Houma–Thibodaux: Wetlands and estuaries threatened.
Lafayette: Groundwater mining.
Lake Charles: Groundwater mining.
Monroe: Groundwater mining.
▲ New Orleans: Wetlands and estuaries threatened, potential for radioactive wastes in groundwater.

## MAINE
Lewiston–Auburn: Groundwater and surface-water shortages.
Portland: Hazardous wastes in surface water and groundwater.
(See also New Hampshire, Portsmouth–Dover–Rochester)

## MARYLAND
▲▲ Baltimore: Hazardous wastes in groundwater, acid rain, Chesapeake Bay threatened by nutrient enrichment (the first step in eutrophication), hazardous wastes, and a decrease in important submerged aquatic vegetation.
Cumberland (MD–WV): Pollution from coal mining.
Hagerstown: Acid rain, hazardous wastes in groundwater.
(See also Delaware, Wilmington)

## MASSACHUSETTS
Boston: Not enough fresh water for peak demand.
Fall River (MA–RI): Hazardous wastes in groundwater.
Fitchburg–Leominster: Hazardous wastes in surface water and groundwater.
Lawrence–Haverhill (MA–NH): Hazardous wastes in surface water and groundwater.
Lowell (MA–NH): Hazardous wastes and highway deicing salts in groundwater.
Worcester: Highway deicing salts in surface water and groundwater.
(See also Rhode Island, Pawtucket–Woonsocket–Attleboro)

## MICHIGAN
Benton Harbor: Hazardous wastes in surface water.
Detroit: Hazardous wastes in surface water.
Flint: Hazardous wastes in surface water.
Kalamazoo: Hazardous wastes in surface water.
Lansing–East Lansing: Hazardous wastes in surface water.

Muskegon: Hazardous wastes in surface water (Lake Michigan).
Saginaw–Bay City–Midland: Hazardous wastes in surface water (Saginaw River and Saginaw Bay).

## MINNESOTA
▲ Duluth (MN–WI): Natural salinity of groundwater, waste sites or landfills that contain hazardous materials, acid rain, erosion and sedimentation.
▲ Minneapolis–St. Paul (MN–WI): Groundwater mining, eutrophication, hazardous wastes.
Rochester: Nitrates in groundwater.
St. Cloud: Acid rain.
(See also North Dakota, Fargo–Moorhead)

## MISSISSIPPI
Biloxi–Gulfport: Groundwater mining and surface-water depletion.
Jackson: Groundwater mining and surface-water depletion, flooding, saline-water intrusion.
Pascagoula: Groundwater mining and surface-water depletion.
(See also Tennessee, Memphis)

## MISSOURI
Columbia: Some saline-water intrusion.
▲ Joplin: Dioxin in surface water and groundwater, resource development (lead and zinc mining).
Kansas City: Resource development (coal mining).
St. Joseph: Erosion and sedimentation, saline-water intrusion.
St. Louis (MO–IL): Dioxin in surface water and groundwater, possible depletion of river surface water.
▲ Springfield: Dioxin in surface water and groundwater, sinkholes, groundwater mining.

## MONTANA
Great Falls: Erosion and sedimentation of surface water.

## NEBRASKA
(See Iowa, Sioux City)

## NEVADA
▲▲▲ Las Vegas: Surface-water depletion and groundwater mining, land subsidence, surface-water pollution, radioactive wastes and chemicals in groundwater.
Reno: Surface-water depletion and pollution, some groundwater mining.

## NEW HAMPSHIRE
Manchester: Surface-water and stream pollution.
Nashua: Hazardous wastes in surface water and groundwater.
Portsmouth–Dover–Rochester (NH–ME): Hazardous wastes in surface water and groundwater.
(See also Massachusetts, Lawrence–Haverhill and Lowell)

## NEW JERSEY
▲ Atlantic City: Pollution of estuaries, flooding, saline-water intrusion, acid rain.

▲ Bergen–Passaic: Surface-water scarcity, surface-water pollution, flooding.
▲ Jersey City: Surface-water pollution and scarcity, pollution of estuaries, flooding.
▲ Middlesex–Somerset–Hunterdon: Surface-water pollution and scarcity, acid rain.
▲▲ Monmouth–Ocean: Surface-water scarcity, saline-water intrusion, pollution of estuaries, acid rain.
▲ Newark: Surface-water pollution and scarcity, flooding.
▲▲ Trenton: Surface-water pollution and scarcity, pollution of estuaries, flooding, acid rain.
▲ Vineland–Millville–Bridgeton: Saline-water intrusion, acid rain.
(See also Delaware, Wilmington; Pennsylvania, Allentown–Bethlehem and Philadelphia)

## NEW MEXICO
▲▲ Albuquerque: Groundwater mining, nitrates and hazardous wastes in groundwater.

## NEW YORK
Albany–Schenectady–Troy: Acid rain.
Glens Falls: Acid rain.
▲▲ Nassau–Suffolk: Bacteria in surface water, groundwater mining, saline-water intrusion, radioactive wastes in groundwater.
New York: Rising groundwater, some saline-water intrusion.
Niagara Falls: Rising groundwater levels.
Orange County: Some groundwater mining.
Rochester: Eutrophication.

## NORTH CAROLINA
Asheville: Surface-water scarcity and pollution.
Burlington: Surface-water pollution.
Charlotte–Gastonia–Rock Hill (NC–SC): Surface-water pollution.
Greensboro–Winston-Salem–High Point: Surface-water pollution.
Hickory: Surface-water pollution.
Jacksonville: Groundwater mining.
Raleigh–Durham: Surface-water scarcity, surface-water pollution.

## NORTH DAKOTA
▲ Bismarck: Resource development (lignite mining), wetlands drainage, eutrophication.
Fargo–Moorhead (ND–MN): Flooding, surface-water scarcity and pollution.
Grand Forks: Flooding, surface-water pollution.

## OHIO
Akron: Resource development (coal mining and oil and gas production), erosion and sedimentation.
Canton: Resource development (coal mining and oil and gas production), erosion and sedimentation.
Cincinnati (OH–KY–IN): Erosion and sedimentation, hazardous wastes in groundwater.
Cleveland: Erosion and sedimentation, resource development (oil and gas production).

## Water Wars

Although many small conflicts arising from water usage, pollution, and diversion exist throughout the nation, the biggest battles for water are being fought in the Southwest.

*Arizona.* Of all the states in the nation, this one is in the most danger of facing a water crisis. Arizonans now pump twice as much groundwater from their aquifers as is being replaced by natural recharge. Large, fast-growing metro areas like Phoenix and Tucson are headed for trouble. However, a recent U.S. Supreme Court decision has granted Arizona the right to tap the lower Colorado River, which it shares with California as a common boundary. By 1985, Phoenix will receive this river water through a series of aqueducts and canals, thus easing the strain on the underground aquifers; Tucson is slated to do the same as of 1989. But this is not a total solution, since the water Arizona will get is now going to Southern California.

*California.* This state is hurting for water in two areas: the 20,000-square-mile Central Valley and the metro areas of Southern California. In the Central Valley, where almost half of America's fruits and vegetables are grown on land that is fertile, flat, and totally irrigated for year-round productivity, the groundwater supplies are being pumped dry at an alarming rate. According to the U.S. Geological Survey's *Water-Supply Paper 2250,* "National Water Summary 1983—Hydrologic Events and Issues," this valley is probably the most heavily pumped area in the nation. The report warns that not only groundwater mining but land subsidence, or sinking, is a direct result of this heavy pumping. In the future, if alternative supplies are not developed, the amount of farming in the Central Valley will be drastically reduced. This could have serious implications for California's economy.

The giant metro areas of Los Angeles–Long Beach and San Diego have always had water scarcities. As they have grown explosively over the last 30 years,

the problem has increased. Southern California has depended on diverted water from the lower Colorado for half its water needs. Soon the Colorado water will also go to Phoenix and Tucson, thus aggravating the problem. The only viable solution is to pipe water from moisture-rich Northern California, which receives about 60 percent of the state's rainfall and has only 40 percent of the population. Plans for this massive undertaking are still in the preliminary stage.

*The Southwest and High Plains.* Eastern New Mexico, northwestern Texas, Oklahoma, and the states to the north of these make up the area known as the High Plains. This huge region is rife with dissent over water. New Mexico is bitter about the "piracy" of water by El Paso, Texas, from New Mexico's Elephant Butte Reservoir. The Land of Enchantment has also locked horns with Colorado over use of the Vermejo River, which rises in Colorado and flows through New Mexico.

Texas, a huge state growing like Topsy, has water woes that are becoming grave. Even in the Texas Gulf region, which receives plenty of rain, extensive groundwater mining has led to the intrusion of salt water in freshwater aquifers and to land subsidence. Those "mysterious" sinkholes you see on the evening news are actually easily explained: They're the result of water being sucked out of underlying rock strata. West Texas and North Texas continually face drought. When the High Plains aquifer begins to go dry, an alternative source will be as far away as the Mississippi River or the Great Lakes—and extremely costly.

The High Plains region, which has increased its agricultural yields dramatically in the past 20 years as a direct result of irrigation, faces long-term groundwater mining. The importance of the High Plains aquifer cannot be overemphasized. When that gigantic underground sea is drained, the entire region will be in considerable trouble.

---

**Columbus:** Erosion and sedimentation, resource development (oil and gas production).
**Dayton–Springfield:** Erosion and sedimentation.
**Hamilton–Middletown:** Erosion and sedimentation, hazardous wastes in groundwater.
**Lima:** Erosion and sedimentation.
**Lorain–Elyria:** Erosion and sedimentation.
**Mansfield:** Erosion and sedimentation, resource development (oil and gas production).
**Steubenville–Weirton (OH–WV):** Resource development (coal mining and oil and gas production).
**Toledo:** Erosion and sedimentation.
▲ **Youngstown–Warren:** Hazardous wastes in groundwater, resource development (coal mining and oil and gas production).

(*See also* West Virginia, Huntington–Ashland, Parkersburg–Marietta, and Wheeling)

### OKLAHOMA
**Oklahoma City:** Surface-water pollution, hazardous wastes in groundwater.
**Tulsa:** Natural salinity of surface water.
(*See also* Arkansas, Fort Smith)

### OREGON
**Eugene–Springfield:** Acid rain.
**Medford:** Acid rain, degradation of aquatic habitats in surface water.
**Portland:** Groundwater mining, hazardous wastes in groundwater.
**Salem:** Hazardous wastes in groundwater.

### PENNSYLVANIA
**Allentown–Bethlehem (PA–NJ):** Hazardous wastes in groundwater, sinkholes, landslide-prone areas.

**Erie:** Hazardous wastes in groundwater.
**Harrisburg–Lebanon–Carlisle:** Sinkholes.
**Lancaster:** Agricultural runoff (fertilizers and organic or chemical wastes) in surface water and groundwater, sinkholes.
▲▲ **Philadelphia (PA–NJ):** Sinkholes, erosion and sedimentation, hazardous wastes and industrial wastes in groundwater.
▲ **Pittsburgh:** Hazardous wastes in groundwater, landslide-prone areas, inadequate river water.
**Scranton–Wilkes-Barre:** Hazardous wastes in groundwater.
**State College:** Sinkholes, hazardous wastes in groundwater.
**York:** Hazardous wastes in groundwater.

## RHODE ISLAND
**Pawtucket–Woonsocket–Attleboro (RI–MA):** Groundwater insufficiency, hazardous wastes in groundwater.
**Providence:** Groundwater insufficiency, hazardous wastes in groundwater.
(*See also* Connecticut, New London–Norwich; Massachusetts, Fall River)

## SOUTH CAROLINA
**Anderson:** Hazardous wastes in river water.
**Charleston:** Surface-water scarcity, excess fluoride and chloride in groundwater.
**Columbia:** Saline-water intrusion, excess fluoride and chloride in groundwater.
**Florence:** Excess fluoride and chloride in groundwater, saline-water intrusion.
**Greenville–Spartanburg:** Surface-water scarcity.
(*See also* North Carolina, Charlotte–Gastonia–Rock Hill)

## SOUTH DAKOTA
**Sioux Falls:** Eutrophication, groundwater mining.

## TENNESSEE
**Chattanooga (TN–GA):** Resource development (coal mining), sinkholes, surface-water pollution, hazardous wastes in groundwater.
**Clarksville–Hopkinsville (TN–KY):** Surface-water pollution, sinkholes.
**Johnson City–Kingsport–Bristol (TN–VA):** Sinkholes, surface-water pollution.
**Knoxville:** Sinkholes, radioactive wastes in groundwater.
**Memphis (TN–AR–MS):** Surface-water pollution, hazardous wastes in groundwater.
▲ **Nashville:** Surface-water scarcity, sinkholes, surface-water pollution.

## TEXAS
**Abilene:** Groundwater pollution.
▲▲ **Amarillo:** Groundwater mining and pollution, eutrophication, natural salinity of surface water.
**Austin:** Groundwater and surface-water pollution.
▲ **Beaumont–Port Arthur:** Groundwater mining, surface-water pollution, hazardous wastes in groundwater.
▲▲ **Brazoria:** Groundwater mining, land subsidence, hazardous wastes in groundwater, surface-water pollution.
**Brownsville–Harlingen:** Pollution of groundwater and surface water.
**Bryan–College Station:** Pollution of groundwater, resource development (lignite mining).
**Corpus Christi:** Groundwater mining and pollution.
▲ **Dallas:** Groundwater mining, hazardous wastes in groundwater, groundwater pollution, eutrophication.
**El Paso:** Groundwater mining, surface-water pollution, water disputes with New Mexico and Mexico.
▲▲ **Fort Worth–Arlington:** Groundwater mining and pollution, hazardous wastes

and eutrophication in groundwater, surface-water pollution.
▲▲ **Galveston–Texas City:** Groundwater mining, saline-water intrusion, land subsidence, hazardous wastes in groundwater, surface-water pollution.
▲▲ **Houston:** Groundwater mining, saline-water intrusion, land subsidence, hazardous wastes in groundwater, surface-water pollution.
**Killeen–Temple:** Groundwater mining, surface-water pollution.
**Longview–Marshall:** Groundwater pollution, resource development (lignite mining).
**Lubbock:** Groundwater mining.
**McAllen–Edinburg–Mission:** Surface-water and groundwater pollution.
**Midland:** Groundwater mining and pollution.
**Odessa:** Groundwater mining and pollution.
**San Angelo:** Groundwater pollution.
▲ **San Antonio:** Groundwater mining and pollution, surface-water pollution.
**Sherman–Denison:** Groundwater mining, eutrophication.
**Texarkana, TX–Texarkana, AR:** Resource development (lignite mining).
**Tyler:** Groundwater pollution, resource development (lignite mining).
**Waco:** Groundwater mining, eutrophication.
**Wichita Falls:** Groundwater pollution, natural salinity of surface water.

## UTAH
▲▲ **Provo–Orem:** Surface-water and groundwater shortages, landslides, flooding.
▲▲ **Salt Lake City–Ogden:** Groundwater depletion, acid rain, surface-water pollution, flooding.

## VERMONT
▲ **Burlington:** Flooding, eutrophication, hazardous wastes in surface water and groundwater.

## VIRGINIA
**Charlottesville:** Radioactivity in groundwater, flooding.
**Danville:** Radioactivity in groundwater.
**Lynchburg:** Radioactivity in groundwater.
▲▲▲ **Norfolk–Virginia Beach–Newport News:** Eutrophication, surface-water depletion, groundwater mining, pollution of surface water and bottom sediments, hazardous wastes in surface water and groundwater, bacteria and chemical elements in groundwater.
**Richmond–Petersburg:** Bacteria and chemical elements in groundwater, radioactivity in groundwater.
**Roanoke:** Flooding, hazardous wastes in surface water and groundwater.
(*See also* Tennessee, Johnson City–Kingsport–Bristol)

## WASHINGTON
**Bellingham:** Groundwater mining, saline-water intrusion, volcanic danger.*

**Bremerton:** Saline-water intrusion, groundwater mining.
**Olympia:** Pollution of bottom sediments.
**Richland–Kennewick–Pasco:** Natural salinity of groundwater.
**Seattle:** Hazardous wastes in groundwater, volcanic danger.*
**Spokane:** Nitrates in, and natural salinity of, groundwater.
**Tacoma:** Pollution of bottom sediments, volcanic danger.*
**Vancouver:** Hazardous wastes in groundwater.
**Yakima:** Hazardous wastes in, and natural salinity of, groundwater.

## WEST VIRGINIA
▲▲ **Charleston:** Resource development (coal mining), surface-water pollution, surface-water scarcity, possibility of unsafe dams.
**Huntington–Ashland (WV–KY–OH):** Resource development (coal mining), hazardous wastes in surface water and groundwater, surface-water scarcity.
**Parkersburg–Marietta (WV–OH):** Hazardous wastes in surface water and groundwater, surface-water scarcity.
**Wheeling (WV–OH):** Resource development (coal mining), surface-water scarcity, possibility of unsafe dams.
(*See also* Maryland, Cumberland; Ohio, Steubenville–Weirton)

## WISCONSIN
**Appleton–Oshkosh–Neenah:** Groundwater mining, surface-water pollution.
**Eau Claire:** Acid rain.
**Green Bay:** Groundwater mining, surface-water pollution.
**Janesville–Beloit:** Surface-water pollution.
**Kenosha:** Groundwater mining, surface-water pollution.
**La Crosse:** Surface-water pollution.
**Madison:** Surface-water and groundwater pollution.
**Milwaukee:** Groundwater mining, surface-water pollution.
**Racine:** Groundwater mining, surface-water pollution.
**Sheboygan:** Groundwater mining, surface-water pollution.
**Wausau:** Acid rain, surface-water pollution.
(*See also* Minnesota, Duluth and Minneapolis–St. Paul)

## WYOMING
**Casper:** Resource development (mining of coal, oil shale, and uranium, and oil and gas production), eutrophication, insufficient drainage.

---

*According to the U.S. Geological Survey paper, a large eruption of any of the five active volcanoes in Washington—Glacier Peak, Mount Adams, Mount Baker (near Bellingham), Mount Rainier (near Seattle and Tacoma), and Mount St. Helens—could have "devastating consequences." The intrusion of fresh and salt water in molten magma could cause massive flooding from mudflows as well as huge steam explosions.

# NATURAL HAZARDS

We're all familiar—even if only through television or newspapers—with the awesome destruction that nature can unleash. Perhaps no sight in recent memory was more dramatic than the eruption of Mount St. Helens in 1980, an initial blast equivalent to 10 million tons of TNT, which blew off the topmost 1,300 feet of the mountain. Volcanic eruptions can wipe out lives and property in an instant. Fortunately, however, volcanoes usually give warning of impending activity, as did Mount St. Helens. Even more fortunately, the places where volcanic activity is a potential hazard are very few. A number of violent natural events are much more common and widespread, and although they may be less cataclysmic than a full-blown volcanic eruption, they can cause great damage and threaten lives. Many of these natural hazards follow definite geographic patterns within the United States, and some metro areas are at much greater risk than others.

## The Sun Belt Is Also a Storm Belt

Many if not most severe storms occur in the southern half of the nation. For this reason, you might say that the Sun Belt is also a storm belt.

*Thunderstorms and Lightning.* Thunderstorms are common and don't usually cause death. But lightning kills 200 Americans a year. It remains the most common and frequent natural danger. At any given moment there are about 2,000 thunderstorms in progress around the globe; in the time it takes you to read this paragraph, lightning will have struck the earth 700 times.

Florida, the Sunshine State, is actually the country's stormiest state, with three times as much thunder and lightning as any other. California, on the other hand, is one of the most storm-free states along with Oregon and Washington. In a typical year, coastal California towns will average between two and five thunderstorm episodes. Most American towns average between 35 and 50. Fort Myers, Florida, averages 128. (A thunderstorm episode represents the presence of a single storm cell; a place like Fort Myers can register four or five episodes in a single day.)

The Place Profiles earlier in this chapter tell how many thunderstorm days each place can expect in an average year. The southeastern quadrant of our country generally receives more rain and thunderstorms than the rest, although the thunderstorms of the Great Plains are awesome spectacles.

*Tornadoes.* While they are not nearly as large or long-lived as hurricanes and release much less total force, tornadoes have more destructive and killing power concentrated in a small area than any other storm known. For absolute ferocity and wind speed, a tornado has no rival.

The hallmark of this vicious inland storm is the huge, snakelike funnel cloud that sweeps and bounces along the ground, destroying buildings, sweeping up cars, trains, livestock, and trees, and sucking them up hundreds of feet into the whirling vortex. Wind speeds close to 300 miles per hour have been recorded.

Although no one can tell for certain just where a particular tornado might touch down, their season, origin, and direction of travel are fairly predictable. Tornado season reaches its peak in late spring and early summer, and most storms originate in the central and southern Great Plains, in the states of Oklahoma, Texas, Arkansas, Kansas, and Missouri. After forming in the intense heat and rising air of the Plains, these storms proceed toward the northeast at speeds averaging 25 to 40 miles per hour. Most tornadoes do not last very long or travel very far. Half of all tornadoes reported travel less than five miles on the ground; a few have been tracked for more than 200 miles.

Metro areas in Oklahoma, eastern Texas, Arkansas, northern Louisiana and Mississippi, eastern Tennessee, Kansas, Missouri, and parts of Nebraska, Iowa, and Illinois have a high potential for tornado damage and danger. Nearly one third of all tornadoes ever reported in the United States have occurred within the boundaries of Kansas, Oklahoma, and Texas.

*Hurricanes.* Giant tropical cyclonic storms that originate at sea, hurricanes are unmatched for sheer power over a very large area. Hurricanes last for days, measure hundreds of miles across, and release tremendous energy in the form of high winds, torrential rains, lightning, and tidal surges. They usually occur from June through November and strike the Gulf states and southern segments of the Atlantic Coast primarily, though they will also strike locations farther north. Like thunderstorms, hurricanes are much less frequent and less severe on the Pacific Coast.

Hurricanes usually originate in the tropical waters of the Atlantic Ocean. Most of them occur toward summer's end because it takes that long for the water temperature and evaporation rate to rise sufficiently to begin the cyclonic, counterclockwise rotation of a wind system around a low-pressure system. When the wind velocities are less than 39 miles per hour, this cyclone is called a tropical depression; when wind velocities are between 39 and 74 miles per hour, the cyclone is called a tropical storm. And when the winds reach 74 miles per hour, the storm becomes a hurricane.

Often the greatest danger and destruction from hurricanes are due not to the winds but to the tidal surges that can sweep ashore with seas 15 or more feet higher than normal high tides. Although Florida and the southern coasts are most vulnerable to hurricanes, locations as far north as Cape Cod and the coast of Maine are by no means immune.

## Earthquake Risks

The cause of an earthquake is the pressure building between two contiguous masses of rock—called plates —that are moving slowly but inexorably toward each

## Tornado and Hurricane Risk Areas

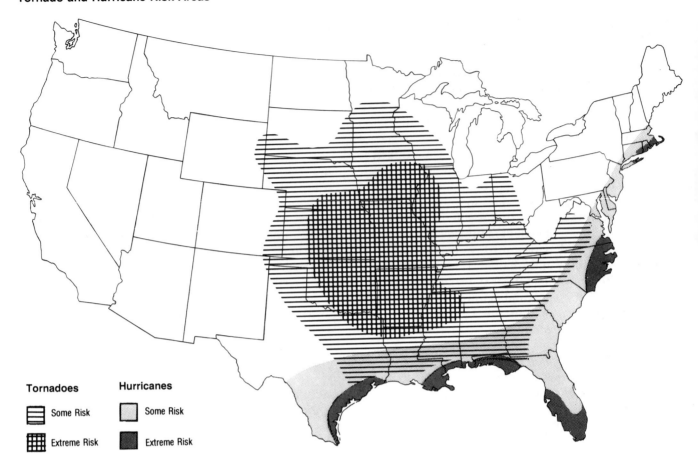

**Tornadoes**

Some Risk

Extreme Risk

**Hurricanes**

Some Risk

Extreme Risk

## Earthquake Hazard Zones

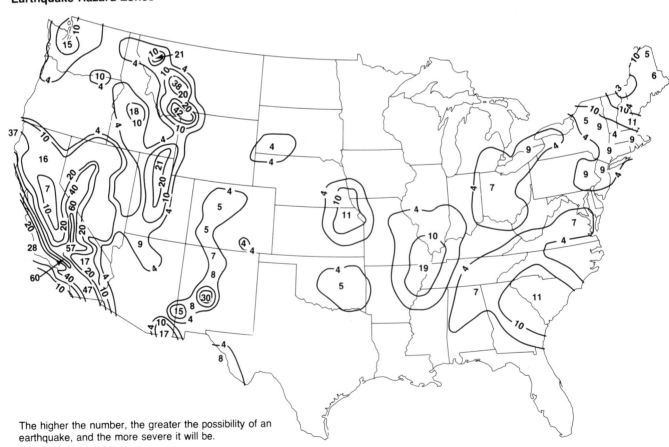

The higher the number, the greater the possibility of an earthquake, and the more severe it will be.

*Source:* U.S. Geological Survey Open-File Report 76-416, 1976.

other in slightly different directions. When the pressure becomes too great for the rock substance to hold, it shears suddenly. This shearing, along with the consequent shuddering, swaying, and even shifting of immense masses of underground rock, is experienced on the earth's surface as an earthquake.

Those conditions necessary to cause an earthquake exist only in certain areas. The entire area ringing the Pacific Ocean is earthquake-prone, from western South America to Central America, North America's Pacific states, and Alaska, through the Aleutian chain across to Japan, down through China, and ending in New Zealand (which has more earthquakes than any other place in the world).

According to the map "Earthquake Hazard Zones," although huge stretches of America are free from the threat of earthquakes, some areas appear to be resting on powder kegs. (U.S. Geological Survey seismologists warn that the map is still experimental and that its predictions cannot be guaranteed.)

*Northeast.* There is a good deal of disagreement among geologists concerning earthquake risk in the Northeast. A number of theories about seismic trends have been advanced, and attempts have been made to relate these trends to various fault systems. The best known of these systems is the Boston-Ottawa trend, shown on the map as a continuous area from the Atlantic coast of Massachusetts to the St. Lawrence River valley, encompassing the two cities for which it is named. Most people are unaware that Boston suffered a severe earthquake in the 1700s and that it remains earthquake-prone today.

*Southeast.* One theory about earthquake risk is that possible earthquake epicenters (the points of origin of ground tremors) are not randomly distributed but occur in zones. In the Southeast, these zones run both parallel to and across the Appalachian Mountains. The greatest shock recorded east of the Mississippi occurred in Charleston, South Carolina, in 1886. The present hazard in South Carolina and eastern Georgia is as high as in the Boston-Ottawa trend.

*Midwest and Rocky Mountains Regions.* The zone of greatest hazard in the Mississippi Valley lies around the side of the cataclysmic series of quakes that occurred near New Madrid, Missouri. The biggest city in this zone is Memphis. The risk of seismic activity is greater in the Rocky Mountains region. The three biggest mountain cities—Denver, Albuquerque, and Salt Lake City—all lie within risk zones.

*Pacific Northwest.* The Puget Sound area near Seattle has experienced two major shocks within the past 30 years, both causing considerable damage. And in 1964, an earthquake in Anchorage registered 8.4 on

## America's Other Earthquake Hazard

Most people know that California is the most earthquake-ridden state in America. Three major faults, or unstable cracks in the earth's surface, contribute to continual and severe seismic activity there. The most destructive earthquake in U.S. history in terms of property and casualties occurred in San Francisco in 1906, killing 452 people and destroying 28,000 buildings through tremors and resulting fire.

But what was probably the most powerful earthquake ever to strike in America took place in another danger zone, one less well known than the quake-prone Golden State—the Mississippi Valley. This earthquake hit on February 7, 1812, in New Madrid, Missouri, and its tremors cracked pavement and rang church bells as far away as Washington, D.C., about 700 miles distant. Its force has been estimated at 8.6 on the Richter scale (the San Francisco earthquake has been estimated at 8.3). This was one of a series of severe quakes over the winter of 1811–12 that changed the course of the Mississippi River and created nearby Reelfoot Lake. Yet another major earthquake followed in 1895, striking the area with a Richter force of 6.5.

All these quakes have been attributed to the New Madrid Fault, which runs along the western border of Tennessee. According to a statement made by the Federal Emergency Management Agency in early 1984, scientists believe it is likely that increasing pressure on the fault will lead to a recurrence before the year 2000, one that could cause thousands of deaths and up to $60 billion in damage. Such a quake could register as high as 7.5, experts say, and affect 21 states, from Kansas east to Pennsylvania and from Illinois south to Louisiana.

the Richter scale (a nine-point span on a seismograph used to express the relative magnitude of an earthquake).

*California and Nevada.* Much more seismic activity (and, therefore, more research and data) is present in California and Nevada than anywhere else in America. The greatest hazards in the United States are found in the San Andreas, Owens Valley, and Garlock fault systems, which are shown on the map as zones numbered as high as 60. All the metro areas in California are affected by these faults, particularly (in alphabetical order) Bakersfield, Los Angeles–Long Beach, Oakland, San Francisco, and San Jose. These places, most of which have mild climates and pleasant terrain, are in real danger.

# Housing:

## Affording the American Dream

Have you heard the story about the two California contractors who bumped into each other at the lumberyard? It is now being retold in other parts of the United States, with local emphasis.

"Congratulate me, Ralph," one of them says. "I've just sold my first $150,000 house!"

"Holy breezeway, Earl, last time we talked you were building $80,000 houses."

"I still am, but now I get $150,000 for them."

The question is, Who can afford these houses? As the average price of a new house reached an all-time high of $101,000 in May 1984, up from $20,000 in 1965, more prospective buyers got edged out of the market. The average U.S. family now puts 33 percent of its income toward monthly house payments, compared with the 25 percent necessary eight years ago. These figures mean that fewer than three of every ten Americans can afford current mortgage rates and building costs.

The 1980s may well be the era of making do, doubling up with parents, buying a house with several people unrelated to you, making dollhouses livable, learning creative financing tactics, budgeting up to 40 percent of your gross income for shelter costs—or, yes, simply getting used to renting indefinitely.

Most of us change our address several times during our lives. In most metro areas the options are an apartment, a single home, a condominium, or a mobile home. The choices often fall within common life stages and income levels. Here are several possibilities:

- *You are eighteen to twenty-one,* carefully looking at a college or graduate school in Big Ten country. Unless you take a room in a dormitory, the odds are you'll rent an apartment. Small metro areas dominated by a major university tend to have an oversupply of structures with five or more rental units.
- *You are twenty to twenty-five,* single, with a minimum of responsibilities, diligently working at your first job but willing to change employers and move anywhere for a better opportunity. If moving in with Mom and Dad is not your preference, you could take the common tack of renting a studio or one-bedroom apartment; your commitment lasts only as long as the term of the lease.
- *You are twenty-five to thirty-five,* married, with two small children and an offer for a better job in a distant and unfamiliar metro area. Renting a house for a year or so may give you an opportunity to become thoroughly acquaint-

ed with the new area before you invest in a home of your own. You might also consider buying an inexpensive condominium that can easily be resold or rented once you find a house and neighborhood that are right for you.

- *You are thirty-five to forty-five,* married, with children, and have recently taken a promotion in another city with a fat relocation bonus and corresponding pay increase. If you're selling a home, the odds are you'll trade up for a larger house in the suburbs.

- *You are well into your sixth decade,* your children have scattered like tumbleweeds in the wind, and you have an ark of a home that you plan to sell. Your options are wider than those of other age groups: You can rent an apartment or buy a smaller home, condo, or mobile home in town or in another metro area, perhaps one with a milder climate and a lower cost of living.

## MAJOR HOUSING CHOICES

If you're thinking of moving to a metro area hundreds of miles distant, it would help to know what kinds of local shelter choices are available, what the average costs would be for renting, and—because two thirds of us eventually end up buying a single-family home—what are the average homeowner costs you'll encounter there.

### Single Houses

If you walk through the front door of the typical American home, you'll find yourself in a structure that was built in 1964 and has a single-level, 1,600-square-foot floor plan enclosing five rooms (three bedrooms, one bath, a complete kitchen), no basement, and an insulated attic and storm windows to conserve the heat from its gas-fired, warm-air furnace. This house is kept cool during hot spells by a central air-conditioning unit. It is also connected to city water and sewerage lines.

So much for national composites. Among the 57 million single houses in the United States (and particularly among the newer suburban homes), a buyer can choose from many building styles—Cape Cods and Cape Anns, mountain A-frames, cabins of peeled pine log, desert adobes, Greek revivals, American and Dutch colonials, Puget Sounds, catslides, exotic glass solaria, futuristic earth berms, Victorians, plantation cottages, and ubiquitous split-levels and California bungalows.

In the metro areas, the portion of single homes you'll actually find among all the other options—apartments, condos, duplexes, triplexes, and mobile homes—can vary considerably.

---

### The Silent Housing Boom

With all the talk about squeezes, shortages, and crises in American housing, one can easily overlook some remarkable things that happened during the 1970s.

Only 58 of the nation's 3,100 counties lost housing units between 1970 and 1980, and almost all of the net loss was in Bronx and Kings counties, in the New York metro area.

While our population was growing at the second slowest rate per decade in history, housing grew faster than during any decade since 1900. Americans managed to erect 20 million new housing units in those ten years, which amounts to almost one new housing unit for each new person added to the population. These 20 million homes, apartments, condos, and mobile homes exceed the total housing stock of either Canada or Mexico as well as the total number of housing units in Italy, France, or Britain.

---

### Single Houses in the Metro Areas

| Most Single Houses | As % of All Units | Fewest Single Houses | As % of All Units |
|---|---|---|---|
| 1. Joplin, MO | 84 | 1. Jersey City, NJ | 12% |
| 2. Enid, OK | 83 | 2. New York, NY | 17 |
| Huntsville, AL | 83 | 3. Boston, MA | 22 |
| 3. Anderson, SC | 82 | 4. Lewiston–Auburn, ME | 41 |
| Gadsden, AL | 82 | 5. Chicago, IL | 46 |
| Lynchburg, VA | 82 | 5. Lawrence–Haverhill, MA–NH | 46 |
| Parkersburg-Marietta, WV-OH | 82 | 7. Anchorage, AK | 48 |
| 4. Anderson, IN | 81 | 7. Fall River, MA–RI | 48 |
| Dayton-Springfield, OH | 81 | 9. Fort Lauderdale–Hollywood–Pompano Beach, FL | 50 |
| Muskegon, MI | 81 | 9. Honolulu, HI | 50 |
| Sherman-Denison, TX | 81 | 9. Miami–Hialeah, FL | 50 |
| South Bend, IN | 81 | | |

*Source:* U.S. Bureau of the Census, *1980 Census of Population and Housing.*

The national average for single houses as a percentage of all occupied units is 71%.

### Condominiums

"Condominium" was nothing more than an obscure Latin word before a new legal concept for owning real estate was imported from Puerto Rico to the U.S. mainland in 1960. Under the arrangement, you could own outright an apartment, townhouse, or single house in a multiple-unit development. You could also sell, lease, bequeath, and furnish that legally described cube of air space independent of other unit owners.

Moreover, you owned the elevators, heating plant, streets, parking spaces, garden landscaping, tennis courts, swimming pool, lights, and walkways in common with the rest of the development's residents.

Throughout most of the 1970s, condominiums were heavily promoted to either newlywed or nearly dead buyers, as some brokers called them. Indeed, young couples and singles making their way out of the rental market and retired couples who wanted to unload a large house for a smaller one were major reasons for the number of condominium units growing from zero in 1960 to more than 2.5 million today.

If you've been reluctantly tearing rental payments from your checkbook and are weighing the purchase of a home for the first time, you might consider a condominium as a compromise between apartment living and the tax advantages of owning a single-family home. With a condominium, you have freedom from house and yard maintenance, a ready-made social life, and common recreation facilities. You also receive the tax advantages of ownership, often at a lower cost than buying a house would entail.

On the minus side, condo owners sometimes complain of ticky-tacky construction, parking problems, thin party walls, and living cheek by jowl with renters or other unfamiliar neighbors.

Condos can be high-rise (vertical) or low-rise (horizontal), depending on local zoning laws and available land. You'll find residential condominiums in metro areas where land is scarce and where the prices of single detached homes are out of reach for people looking to buy a first home. This form of real estate is most common in the resort-and-vacation metro areas.

### Condominiums in the Metro Areas

| Most Condominiums | As % of All Units |
|---|---|
| 1. West Palm Beach–Boca Raton–Delray Beach, FL | 33% |
| 2. Fort Lauderdale–Hollywood–Pompano Beach, FL | 32 |
| 3. Honolulu, HI | 24 |
| 4. Sarasota, FL | 20 |
| 5. Fort Myers, FL | 18 |
| 6. Bradenton, FL | 16 |
| 7. Fort Pierce, FL | 14 |
| 7. Miami–Hialeah, FL | 14 |
| 9. Anaheim–Santa Ana, CA | 11 |
| 10. Reno, NV | 10 |

*Source:* U.S. Bureau of the Census, *1980 Census of Population and Housing.* (All percent figures are rounded.)

The national average for condominiums as a percentage of all occupied units is 3%. Sixty-eight metro areas have no condominiums.

### Mobile Homes

As you struggle to scrape up the down payment for a suburban ranch or a town house close to work, you may already have the $21,000 needed to buy an average mobile home outright.

The major advantage of a mobile home is price. It takes a typical contractor's crew several months to build a typical three-bedroom house, whereas a mobile home takes 80 to 100 hours. In 1983, when the average cost of building a conventional home was $45 per square foot, exclusive of land, the cost of manufacturing a mobile home was $21 per square foot.

This doesn't mean that mobile homes lack quality. Since World War II, when many defense workers were housed in 300-square-foot sheet-metal boxes with ersatz cooking facilities and no plumbing, mobile homes have gradually shaken their reputation for tackiness. Mobile homes now are at least 14 feet wide. Seventy-foot-long Double Wides can enclose three bedrooms, two baths, a living room, dining room, kitchen, and closets. New mobile homes are usually sold complete; appliances, furniture, draperies, lamps, and carpeting are all included in the price, as are built-in plumbing, heating, air-conditioning, and electrical systems.

Among the attractions of a mobile home are its availability (there are 410 factories around the country where you can buy one) and its affordability (the purchase price is low, and one can be easily financed through a personal property loan or a conventional 30-year VA or FHA loan). It's simple to transport and install at the owner's private acreage or at a well-run park, and inexpensive to maintain.

The value of a mobile home, however, may depreciate in many areas where conventional homes increase in value. Arbitrary evictions from mobile home parks are not uncommon in many states, nor are restrictive zoning laws that confine this kind of housing to the urban/rural fringe.

The only time the mobile home is actually mobile is when it leaves the factory and is towed by a truck in one or more sections to a concrete foundation, whether on the owner's acreage or at one of 24,000 trailer parks in the country. When it arrives, the wheels, axle, and towing tongue are removed, and all that still resembles a trailer is the I-beamed chassis, which quickly becomes hidden structural reinforcement once the unit is winched onto the foundation and plumbed. After that, the mobile home becomes more or less permanent; no more than 3 percent of them are ever moved again.

Last year, half of all new mobile homes were trucked to just eight states: California, Florida, Georgia, Louisiana, North Carolina, Oklahoma, South Carolina, and Texas. You're more likely, in general, to find permissive zoning regulations and a wider choice of mobile home parks in smaller metro areas of the Sun Belt. You're less likely to find them in large metro areas where the high cost of residential land offsets any economic benefits of owning a mobile home.

### Mobile Homes in the Metro Areas

| Most Mobile Homes | As % of All Units |
|---|---|
| 1. Ocala, FL | 20% |
| 2. Jacksonville, NC | 18 |
| 2. Redding, CA | 18 |
| 4. Bradenton, FL | 17 |
| 5. Las Cruces, NM | 16 |
| 6. Fort Myers, FL | 15 |
| 7. Lakeland–Winter Haven, FL | 14 |
| 8. Casper, WY | 13 |
| 8. Chico, CA | 13 |
| 8. Fort Pierce, FL | 13 |

*Source:* U.S. Bureau of the Census, *1980 Census of Population and Housing.* (All percent figures are rounded.)

The national average for mobile homes as a percentage of all occupied units is 5%. Sixteen metro areas have no mobile homes.

## Renting an Apartment

Looking for digs close to work, with reasonable rent, tenants similar to yourself, a pleasant landlord, off-street parking, ambience, and all the other items on your checklist might turn out to be a quest that stops when the lease is signed but starts up again on the lease's anniversary. Still, for most newcomers to a metro area, renting is the main style of housing tenure.

As a renter you remain flexible, since you need not stay in an apartment beyond the term of the lease should your income slump or your job take you to another part of the country. You don't need to come up with a down payment; taxes, insurance, repairs, and sometimes utilities are the landlord's headaches.

But you also miss out on such ownership benefits as growing equity, property appreciation, and tax deductions for mortgage interest, while being subject to condo conversion or arbitrary rent hikes in times of low vacancy rates.

Many of us tend to think that apartments are available only in blocks of large, high-rise tower complexes near a large metro area's central business district. In fact, only one out of 50 apartments is in a building of 13 stories or more, and only one out of ten is in a building higher than three stories. Moreover, apartments make up as large a part of occupied housing in smaller metro areas dominated by state universities as they do in metro areas that are much larger in population.

According to the Census Bureau, an apartment is simply a rental unit in a structure with five or more rental units, which excludes rental duplexes, triplexes, and fourplexes.

### Apartments in the Metro Areas

| Most Apartments | As % of All Units | Fewest Apartments | As % of All Units |
|---|---|---|---|
| 1. New York, NY | 56% | 1. Anderson, SC | 4% |
| 2. Austin, TX | 43 | 1. Florence, SC | 4 |
| 3. Jersey City, NJ | 41 | 1. Hickory, NC | 4 |
| 4. Washington, DC–MD–VA | 34 | 4. Anderson, IN | 5 |
| 5. Los Angeles–Long Beach, CA | 30 | 4. Burlington, NC | 5 |
| 5. Miami–Hialeah, FL | 30 | 4. Dothan, AL | 5 |
| 5. Oakland, CA | 30 | 4. Florence, AL | 5 |
| 8. Ann Arbor, MI | 28 | 4. Gadsden, AL | 5 |
| 8. Honolulu, HI | 28 | 4. Joplin, MO | 5 |
| 8. Iowa City, IA | 28 | 4. Ocala, FL | 5 |

Source: U.S. Bureau of the Census, 1980 Census of Population and Housing. (All percent figures are rounded.)

The national average for apartments as a percentage of all occupied units is 15%.

## BUYING THAT SINGLE-FAMILY HOME . . .

Despite the growing number of options in housing, the single-family house seems to be the most common (87 percent of homeowner units are single-family homes) and the most popular (in a 1983 poll, 81 percent of current owners and 70 percent of renters expecting to move within five years said they planned to buy a detached home). In fact, two thirds of us eventually buy a single-family home.

Where are the best markets for prospective buyers? You might guess that a consequence of the country's west-by-south population shift would be dramatically inflated home prices in the same direction. But some of the highest prices estimated for 1984 are found in places where homes have always been expensive: Anchorage, Honolulu, New York City and its suburbs in Connecticut and New Jersey, the District of Columbia and its environs, and, since 1975, California metro areas.

We may never again experience the explosive 178 percent inflation in market values seen in this country during the 1970s, however. In May of 1984, according to the National Association of Realtors, an existing single house carried a price tag of $87,600. Prices rose 31 percent between 1980 and 1984 in the rebounding East, 28 percent in the South, only 18 percent in the slower-growing North Central states, and 17 percent in the West, where values were historically high. These increases don't mean that an $87,600 house can't be found for half that much. It can, in smaller metro areas of Alabama, Indiana, Missouri, and Texas.

### Average Single-Family House Prices

| Highest | | Lowest | |
|---|---|---|---|
| 1. Stamford, CT | $200,000 | 1. Joplin, MO | $37,600 |
| 2. Norwalk, CT | 168,400 | 2. McAllen–Edinburg– Mission, TX | 39,800 |
| 3. Honolulu, HI | 163,400 | 3. Terre Haute, IN | 40,200 |
| 4. San Francisco, CA | 154,500 | 4. St. Joseph, MO | 40,900 |
| 5. San Jose, CA | 143,900 | 5. Brownsville– Harlingen, TX | 41,100 |
| 6. Anaheim–Santa Ana, CA | 142,300 | 6. Battle Creek, MI | 41,500 |
| 7. Santa Barbara– Santa Maria– Lompoc, CA | 138,100 | 7. Muskegon, MI | 41,900 |
| | | 8. Danville, VA | 42,100 |
| 8. Santa Cruz, CA | 127,300 | 9. Gadsden, AL | 43,400 |
| 9. San Diego, CA | 123,503 | 10. Pine Bluff, AR | 43,500 |
| 10. Salinas–Seaside– Monterey, CA | 122,900 | 11. Altoona, PA | 43,600 |
| 11. Oxnard–Ventura, CA | 122,800 | 11. Sherman– Denison, TX | 43,600 |

Source: U.S. Bureau of the Census, 1980 Census of Population and Housing, and the National Association of Realtors, 1984.

## . . . AND REBUYING IT WITH PROPERTY TAXES

In recent years, homeowners who banded together to protest confiscatory property taxes likened them to a ransom that they were forced to pay to keep their shelter off the local tax assessor's auction block. Using this analogy, homeowners in Islip, New York, buy their homes back from the town every 22 years, since the effective tax rate (a tax on the home's full value) is 4.63 percent. Down in Mobile County, Alabama, on the other hand, the "ransom" period is 526 years because of an extremely low effective rate of 0.19 percent. The difference in these figures illustrates the wide variation in property taxes around the country.

Locally, too, property taxes can vary enormously and be madly confusing to homeowners. In California, two houses on the same block with identical price tags and physical characteristics can have substantially different, yet legally impeccable tax bills if one of them was sold before the approval of Proposition 13 and the other after. In Texas, a home's value can be assessed at different levels at different times of the year by different assessors.

Although residential property taxes aren't collected by metro areas (that is done by 13,527 cities, townships, counties, school districts, sanitary districts, hospital districts, and other special districts), statewide average property tax rates are useful in estimating local property tax bills. Clearly, homeowners in Connecti-cut, Massachusetts, New Jersey, and New York have good reason for envying their counterparts in Alabama and Louisiana.

### House Property Tax Bills

| Highest | | Lowest | |
|---|---|---|---|
| 1. Stamford, CT | $3,061 | 1. Alexandria, LA | $ 75 |
| 2. Bergen–Passaic, NJ | 2,777 | 2. Monroe, LA | 82 |
| 3. Newark, NJ | 2,695 | 3. Shreveport, LA | 88 |
| 4. Norwalk, CT | 2,576 | 4. Lake Charles, LA | 92 |
| 5. New York, NY | 2,462 | 5. Houma–Thibodaux, LA | 97 |
| 6. Middlesex–Somerset–Hunterdon, NJ | 2,253 | 6. Baton Rouge, LA | 111 |
| 6. Monmouth–Ocean, NJ | 2,253 | 7. New Orleans, LA | 118 |
| 8. Ann Arbor, MI | 2,132 | 8. Lafayette, LA | 119 |
| 9. Salem–Gloucester, MA | 2,066 | 9. Gadsden, AL | 178 |
| 10. Danbury, CT | 1,779 | 10. Anniston, AL | 184 |

*Source: Places Rated* estimates based on average market values multiplied by each state's average effective property tax rate as reported by the Advisory Commission on Intergovernmental Relations, *Significant Features of Fiscal Federalism,* 1984.

## WHAT A DIFFERENCE AGE MAKES

Anyone watching the speed at which houses can be put up on pricey lots in suburbia or in cheap-jack developments near the industrial fringe might well agree with old-timers who have seen large, balloon-framed homes built with a good deal of craftsmanship. "They don't build them the way they used to," some of them might mutter.

No, they don't. Wraparound porches are rarely found. A porch is now merely a recessed space at the entrance of a house. The ten-foot interior ceilings common before World War II have been replaced with the eight-foot standard. The kind of formal stairway with well-turned balusters and waxed rails that Andy Hardy used to slide down are no longer necessary—most new homes are built on a single level. Milled red oak fascias and moldings have become too expensive for common use; walls are envelopes of three-eighths inch gypsum board nailed to studs rather than the old "mud jobs" of plaster on lath; and solid six-panel doors have lost out to hollow-core flush doors of hemlock veneer.

On the other hand, copper and polyvinyl chloride water pipes have replaced galvanized iron plumbing; knob-and-tube wiring has surrendered to safer electrical circuitry; cast-iron radiators no longer interfere with furniture arrangement; pressure-treated wood has eliminated termite and dry-rot risks; and the seasonal problem of cellar flooding arises less often because there aren't many cellars being excavated. Indeed, as much as 20 percent of a new home's breathtaking price tag is due to vastly superior building materials, according to a recent Prudential Insurance Company study.

One useful indication of the quality of a metro area's housing stock is the percent of homes put up

---

### The Ground Factor

Any real estate broker touting a suburban ranch or condo can tick off the basic factors that play a part in the price tags for housing. Aside from seller's greed, the factors are quality of original construction, turnover rate in the neighborhood, current upkeep, and location. But all these are of secondary importance to local supply and demand.

Cut off a slice of a tract development in suburban Topeka, Kansas, and drop it in the middle of New Jersey's Morris County, and you can see supply and demand at work. The transplanted homes will double in market value, not because they are roomier and are made with better materials, but because of the more intense competition for housing around much of New York City's periphery. You can find well-cared-for three-bedroom ranches in the Kansas capital for $60,000 and nearly identical homes in suburban Newark for $150,000. The local demand for housing, then, is the single best determinant of a home's price.

Based on Federal Housing Authority data, the value of the ground on which a typical existing house is built represents 22 percent of the price of the home if it were to be sold immediately. The figure varies considerably depending on where in the country this typical house is found. In Hawaii, the true cost of the site is more than half the price of the house; in California, it's 34 percent. Elsewhere, in Michigan or Georgia, for example, it's only 14 percent and 15 percent respectively.

#### Land Costs As Percent of House Prices

| Highest | | Lowest | |
|---|---|---|---|
| 1. Hawaii | 51% | 1. Michigan | 14% |
| 2. California | 34 | 2. Georgia | 15 |
| 3. Oregon | 29 | 2. Indiana | 15 |
| 4. Connecticut | 26 | 2. South Carolina | 15 |
| 4. Florida | 26 | 5. Alabama | 16 |
| 4. Washington | 26 | 5. Kansas | 16 |
| 7. Utah | 25 | 5. Pennsylvania | 16 |
| 8. Nevada | 24 | 5. South Dakota | 16 |

*Source: Federal Housing Authority, Property Characteristics, One-Family Homes, by States,* 1983.

before 1940. Although an older house isn't necessarily on the verge of tumbling down, age can signal functional obsolescence and looming maintenance headaches. Clapboards do need scraping and repainting every three years, clogged sewer drains must be snaked, furnaces do wear out, and storm windows must be retrofitted. These tasks can mean both dollars and difficulties.

### Old and New Metro Areas

| Newest | Houses Built Before 1940 | Oldest | Houses Built Before 1940 |
|---|---|---|---|
| 1. Anchorage, AK | 1.1% | 1. Jersey City, NJ | 60.2% |
| 2. Las Vegas, NV | 1.5 | 2. Scranton–Wilkes-Barre, PA | 56.6 |
| 3. Fort Lauderdale–Hollywood–Pompano Beach, FL | 1.7 | 3. Fall River, MA–RI | 55.2 |
| 4. Melbourne–Titusville–Palm Bay, FL | 3.1 | 4. Pittsfield, MA | 54.1 |
| 5. Fort Walton Beach, FL | 3.4 | 5. Altoona, PA | 54.0 |
| 6. Odessa, TX | 3.6 | 6. New Bedford, MA | 53.8 |
| 7. Anaheim–Santa Ana, CA | 3.7 | 7. Lewiston–Auburn, ME | 52.9 |
| 8. Midland, TX | 3.8 | 8. Cumberland, MD–VA | 52.8 |
| 9. Fort Myers, FL | 3.9 | 9. Salem–Gloucester, MA | 52.4 |
| 10. Sarasota, FL | 4.0 | 10. Glens Falls, NY | 51.5 |
| | | 10. Johnstown, PA | 51.5 |

*Source:* U.S. Bureau of the Census, *1980 Census of Population and Housing.*

The median age of the nation's housing is 23 years, the same as it was in 1970.

## HOME ENERGY REQUIREMENTS

After mortgage interest rates, fuel and electricity for the home have been the fastest-rising items on the Consumer Price Index since 1967. What was once a minor and predictable expense, averaging less than 1 percent of a household's budget 15 years ago, may now amount to more than the cost of medical care or clothing.

There are three reasons for the $656 difference between the annual average residential utility bills in Chicago and Huntsville, Alabama: climate, the form of energy used to maintain comfortable temperatures in the house, and the source of this energy.

### Counting the Hours

Texans say that their Gulf Coast, from Brownsville–Harlingen to Corpus Christi and beyond to Beaumont–Port Arthur, is a place where air-conditioning is a necessity like food and water, without which all mankind becomes delirious, withers, and dies. Here, a meteorologist measuring humidity with a psychrometer whenever the temperature climbs over 80 degrees Fahrenheit will count nearly 2,500 hours every year when the instrument's bulb stays wet from moist air. New Delhi records similar numbers, and so does Kinshasa, capital of Zaire. These 2,500-odd hours are the equivalent of more than 200 days per year with

### Older Isn't Always Cheaper

Most people live in homes built years ago that were bought, lived in, and sold by a succession of owners. We all confirm the "filtering theory" of housing, which states that houses filter down from high-income first owners to middle-income buyers to lower-income owners. To put it another way, many high-income families live in newer homes, and most lower-income households occupy older homes.

So what else is new?

Just that when the weekend real estate sections of the *Boston Globe, Washington Post, Chicago Tribune,* or *San Francisco Chronicle* list old homes in "upscale" neighborhoods on the market for $100,000 or more, you're looking at big exceptions to this theory. Nowhere is this more apparent than in Connecticut's Fairfield County. Stamford and Norwalk homes carry some of the biggest price tags in the country, and most of them were built long before World War II.

Nevertheless, the filtering theory holds true for most of America's 329 metro areas: The older the housing, the lower the price.

uncomfortable, sweaty, 12-hour periods of high humidity.

In such desert metro areas as Las Vegas, Phoenix, and Tucson, the days are much drier, but the number of hours there when the temperature is more than 80 degrees Fahrenheit is even greater than the number found on the Texas Gulf Coast. These hours were first counted by U.S. Defense Department building engineers in the late 1940s and updated in 1978 for a worldwide inventory of air and naval bases, supply depots, and weather stations. Not only are these hours useful for gauging how hot a given place is over time, they are also good indicators of how often your home's air conditioner may be humming.

### Counting the Days

In 1915, Eugene P. Milener, an engineer with the Gas Company of Baltimore, made a discovery for which he received little recognition outside of his industry: The amount of natural gas needed to keep buildings warm can be accurately predicted for every degree that the outdoor temperature falls below 65 degrees. Natural gas utilities still use this measurement, called a degree day, to estimate consumption patterns among their customers.

A heating-degree day is the number of degrees the daily average temperature is below 65. Heating your home isn't usually necessary when the temperature outdoors is more than 65, but furnaces are fired up when the outdoor temperature falls below that mark. Thus, a heating-degree day indicates the number of degrees of heating required to keep a house at 65. If, for example, the temperature on a winter day is 35, that day has 30 heating-degree days, meaning that 30 degrees of heating are called for.

The average for annual heating-degree days (total heating-degree days over one year) in the United States is 4,671, ranging among *Places Rated* metro areas from zero in Honolulu to 10,911 in Anchorage. The number of annual degree days in a given place tells you how cold it gets and also how often you'll need to run a home's heating system to keep the indoors comfortable.

### Household Energy Geography

In the early 1950s, the rumbling of coal trucks along their delivery routes was a familiar urban street sound. Three-dollar-a-ton black anthracite was the dominant home heating fuel everywhere east of the Mississippi except for Florida and New England. The blue flame of piped-in natural gas, the major heating fuel today, was just starting to burn in new refrigerators, stoves, clothes dryers, and in furnaces in new homes. Electric utilities were just beginning to encourage construction of total-electric homes.

Today, coal has virtually disappeared from the home energy scene. In spite of the heavy marketing of airtight coal stoves as an auxiliary means of heating houses, the number of homes burning this fuel declined by more than one million over the past decade. The major options now, from most expensive to least, are electric power, residual fuel oil or kerosene, and piped-in natural gas. And, in some timber country metro areas, there's wood.

*Electricity.* In 1950, the only place where most of the homes were all-electric was the small desert town of Las Vegas, seat of Nevada's Clark County. The power there was the cheapest in the country, simply because it was generated by falling water at the new Boulder Canyon hydroelectric project some 25 miles southeast. It still is cheap, relative to nuclear-generated or fossil fuel–generated power that home-owners pay for elsewhere in the country. So is the power that heats and lights homes in the Pacific Northwest and in certain Alabama and Tennessee metro areas close to TVA projects.

Although most American homes are heated with natural gas, electricity is gaining fast. Between 1970 and 1980, the number of all-electric homes increased by more than 200 percent. The reason: It costs much less to wire a new house for electric resistance heat than to install a gas or oil furnace with piping and sheet-metal hot-air conduits. All-electric homes predominate in 50 of the 329 metro areas. The U.S. Department of Energy surveys average annual household energy consumption and prices, and the following are its figures for electricity in 1983:

- Typical Consumption: 17,287 kilowatt-hours per year
- Average Bill: $1,186 per year
- Cost per Million Btus: $18.51

---

### Air-Conditioning Needs: The Top 11 Hot-Weather Metro Areas

| Metro Area | More than 80° F per Year |
| --- | --- |
| 1. Phoenix, AZ | 2,845 hrs |
| 2. Laredo, TX | 2,736 |
| 3. Galveston–Texas City, TX | 2,639 |
| 4. Corpus Christi, TX | 2,531 |
| 5. Tucson, AZ | 2,445 |
| 6. Miami–Hialeah, FL | 2,388 |
| 7. Las Vegas, NV | 2,360 |
| 8. Dallas, TX | 2,304 |
| 8. Sherman–Denison, TX | 2,304 |
| 10. Brownsville–Harlingen, TX | 2,295 |
| 10. McAllen–Edinburg–Mission, TX | 2,295 |

*Source:* U.S. Department of Defense, *Engineering Weather Data,* 1978.

The above range of hours is the equivalent of between 94 and 119 full days of temperatures of 80 degrees Fahrenheit or higher.

### Heating Needs: The Top 10 Cold-Weather Metro Areas

| Metro Area | Degree Days |
| --- | --- |
| 1. Anchorage, AK | 10,911 |
| 2. Grand Forks, ND | 9,876 |
| 3. Duluth, MN–WI | 9,757 |
| 4. Fargo–Moorhead, ND–MN | 9,271 |
| 5. Bismarck, ND | 9,044 |
| 6. St. Cloud, MN | 8,868 |
| 7. Bangor, ME | 8,648 |
| 8. Wausau, WI | 8,586 |
| 9. Eau Claire, WI | 8,388 |
| 10. Minneapolis–St. Paul, MN–WI | 8,310 |

*Source:* National Oceanic and Atmospheric Administration, *Substation Summaries,* 1951 to date.

---

*Oil and Kerosene.* Though their prices have stabilized because of the current world oil glut, number-two heating oil and kerosene were the only items on the Consumer Price Index to sextuple in cost between 1967 and 1980 (since surpassed by mortgage interest costs). This explains why the number of homes heated with fuel oil or kerosene declined by more than two million since 1970. You won't find the price varying greatly by location, but you will find these distillates of imported crude to be the most common heating fuel in 61 metro areas, most of them in New England and Mid-Atlantic states. The Department of Energy gives these figures for 1983 consumption and prices:

- Typical Consumption: 1,043 gallons per year
- Average Bill: $1,237 per year
- Cost per Million Btus: $8.53

*Natural Gas.* In 228 metro areas, the major source for heating a house is a by-product of oil drilling that for many years flamed at the wellhead for lack of a market. Natural gas, a fossil fuel, has meant inexpensive heat for most householders, mainly because the federal government has regulated its interstate price. It is slowly being deregulated and quickly becoming expensive; some experts predict that its cost per million Btus will equal that of fuel oil or kerosene by 1990.

Natural gas has never been cheap to homeowners at the end of the continental transmission lines that begin in Louisiana and Texas gas fields, however. This explains why natural gas isn't preferred in New England or Mid-Atlantic homes, where oil is the least expensive of fuels; or in the Pacific Northwest, where hydroelectric power costs the least. The Department of Energy provides these figures for natural gas usage in 1983:

- Typical Consumption: 13,100 cubic feet per year
- Average Bill: $724 per year
- Cost per Million Btus: $5.53

*Wood.* Anyone who feeds a wood stove has heard the proverb about this fuel: It warms you twice, first when you cut and stack it, and second when you watch it burn. From Rocky Mountain piñon to hickory and ash from Ozark forests, it is the main heating fuel in 2.6 million homes (up from less than one million in 1970). Among metro areas today, only a small percentage of homes—10 percent or so—in Maine, Oregon, and Vermont burn wood exclusively. The U.S. Forest Service determines energy content for various kinds of wood; consumption and price figures for 1983 come from the Department of Energy:

- Typical Consumption: 2.8 cords per year
- Average Bill: $350 per year
- Cost per Million Btus: $5.34 (hardwood)

### Keeping It All Going

Ever since the Arab oil embargo of late 1973, home energy bills—for heating and cooling, lighting, and running appliances—have skyrocketed. During the winter, this expense is borne mostly by northerners, though many residents of the Sun Belt need winter heat as well. The brunt of energy expenses takes a southerly shift during the summer because of air-conditioning.

If you'd like to dodge both winter heating and summer air-conditioning bills, move to Hawaii. You'll still be writing checks to the local public utility, however. Although Honolulu is the only metro area in the United States with no heated homes and also a place where air-conditioning is considered extravagant, you'll still pay the Hawaiian Electric Company nearly $80 a month to keep your water hot, food cool, and lamps lit.

### JUDGING HOMEOWNING COSTS

On the average, are single homes more expensive in Danbury, Dayton, or Duluth? When it comes to paying property taxes, might you be better off in Birmingham than in Boston? Would a February relocation to a warm metro area haunt you in August when you realize how much air-conditioning costs?

To help you answer these questions, *Places Rated* tallies the three biggest dollar expenses of buying and maintaining a single-family home: utility bills, local property taxes, and mortgage payments. The sum of these three items equals the amount you can expect to pay each year for the basics of homeownership. It also represents each metro area's score. Because the single-family home is the type of housing most commonly bought by Americans, we use it here as the basis of our examination of homeowning costs.

Property taxes and mortgage payments are based on the average market value of owner-occupied single homes within each metro area as reported by the *1980 Census of Population and Housing.* These were owners' estimates of what their home would be worth if they decided to sell immediately. To show realistic 1984 prices, *Places Rated* updated these estimates with regional inflation factors reported by the National Association of Realtors.

Each metro area starts with a base score of zero. Points are added according to the following indicators:

1. *Utility bills.* The utility bills are estimated for a home that uses natural gas for space heating, water heating, and cooking because this fuel is available everywhere and is the most frequently chosen in most of the metro areas. Also included in the utility bills are the costs of electricity for lighting, running appliances, and air-conditioning based on local bills for 750 kilowatt-hours of consumption as reported by the Department of Energy. In metro areas where total-electric homes predominate, utility bills are estimates of annual residential all-electric costs, also from the Department of Energy.
2. *Property taxes.* Property taxes are calculated by multiplying the average market value of a house by the state's average effective tax rate for residential property. For example, the property tax bill in Phoenix of $435 is derived from a 1984 house value of $77,700 times Arizona's effective tax rate of 0.56 percent.
3. *Mortgage payments.* Annual mortgage payments are based on a 12 percent, 25-year loan on the average price of a house, after a one-quarter down payment has been made.

### Sample Comparison: Joplin, Missouri, and Stamford, Connecticut

Does anyone recall J. Blandings? Cary Grant played him in the 1948 movie "Mr. Blandings Builds His Dream House." The film tells the story of a New York City couple, tired of living in a crowded apartment, who one day discover a rambling old house for sale on 50 bucolic acres in nearby Connecticut. They fall in love with the place and take a $10,000 plunge to join the suburban gentry.

The ensuing comedy of Mr. Blandings and his trials with country carpenters, stonemasons, and well-diggers may be familiar to homeowners today who buy a "fixer-upper" and then get into money trouble. At the end of the film, Mr. Blandings adds up what he spent to "put the place in shape" and learns that he is out more than $50,000. He might have been better off with a new Cape Cod–style home then being built on the potato patches of Long Island in a place called Levittown.

Or would he? Today, 50 residential-zoned acres close to New York City would be worth millions, and a restored farmhouse in a good location would bring more than half a million all by itself. Nowhere is this more apparent than in Stamford, a metro area that includes the towns of Greenwich, Darien, and New Canaan. The average market value of local homes in Stamford is $200,000. Utility bills average $1,617, property taxes $3,061, and mortgage payments another $18,962, all of which adds up to an incredible annual housing score of 23,640.

In contrast to Stamford, the lowest basic homeowner costs in metropolitan America are found some 1,100 miles west in the environs of Joplin, a pleasant city in Missouri's southeast Ozark corner. As in Stamford, many of the homes were built before World War II, and most are owned by the people living in them.

But unlike the pricey New York City suburbs of Connecticut, Joplin can boast an average market value for homes of $37,600. Through the 1970s, new homes were added to the local housing stock at a faster rate than in many other places in Missouri. Existing houses now range from nineteenth-century farmhouses in rural sections to fine Victorian homes in town and newer brick-and-frame bi-levels and ranches out along U.S. 71. Estimated utility bills in Joplin amount to $1,156, property taxes $440, and mortgage payments $3,563, totaling a score of 5,159 for homeowning costs, the lowest among the metro areas.

### Housing Winners and Losers

| Least Expensive Metro Areas | Places Rated Score | Most Expensive Metro Areas | Places Rated Score |
|---|---|---|---|
| 1. Joplin, MO | 5,159 | 1. Stamford, CT | 23,640 |
| 2. McAllen–Edinburg–Mission, TX | 5,345 | 2. Norwalk, CT | 20,151 |
| 3. Brownsville–Harlingen, TX | 5,376 | 3. San Francisco, CA | 17,158 |
| 4. Gadsden, AL | 5,382 | 4. Honolulu, HI | 17,021 |
| 5. Terre Haute, IN | 5,527 | 5. San Jose, CA | 16,048 |
| 6. Anniston, AL | 5,530 | 6. Anaheim–Santa Ana, CA | 16,047 |
| 7. St. Joseph, MO | 5,589 | 7. Santa Barbara–Santa Maria–Lompoc, CA | 15,547 |

It's dryly said in California that the only way to make a killing on the sale of your home is to sell it for what it will bring and then skip back East, where you can find twice the home at half the price. The kicker is that you have to live in the cold, cold East.

In fact, a mobile Californian choosing to live in Connecticut's Fairfield County may end up losing money on the move. House prices are higher in this part of the Northeast, as are household energy costs and property taxes.

Although sky-high shelter costs don't always indicate desirable housing, they do indicate the pitch of local supply and demand in desirable locations. The irony is that house prices in these locations are beyond the reach not only of most U.S. households but of most households in the area. A quick look at household incomes in the Economics Place Profiles (later on in this book) shows that the average market values for houses in Southern California, Hawaii, and New York City suburbs are between three and five times the annual household incomes there. So much for the rule of shopping only for homes that cost about two and a half times your gross income.

Smaller metro areas located in the slow-growing Midwest and in historically poor parts of the Sun Belt, on the other hand, are ranked at the top when it comes to affordable houses. Market values in these places are only one and a half to two times local household income. The tired maxim of the real estate broker—Location, location, location—applies not only to neighborhoods but to metro areas across the nation as well.

# Places Rated: Metro Areas Ranked for Homeowning Costs

Three criteria are used to rank the 329 metropolitan areas for basic costs of owning a house over one year: (1) annual average utility bills, (2) annual average property taxes, and (3) annual average mortgage payments. The sum of these three items represents the score for each metropolitan area. Places that receive tie scores are given the same rank and are listed in alphabetical order.

### Metro Areas from Least to Most Expensive

| Places Rated Rank | Places Rated Score | Places Rated Rank | Places Rated Score | Places Rated Rank | Places Rated Score |
|---|---|---|---|---|---|
| 1. Joplin, MO | 5,159 | 3. Brownsville–Harlingen, TX | 5,376 | 6. Anniston, AL | 5,530 |
| 2. McAllen–Edinburg–Mission, TX | 5,345 | 4. Gadsden, AL | 5,382 | 7. St. Joseph, MO | 5,589 |
| | | 5. Terre Haute, IN | 5,527 | 8. Pine Bluff, AR | 5,674 |

| Places Rated Rank | Places Rated Score |
|---|---|
| 9. Anderson, IN | 5,704 |
| 10. Dothan, AL | 5,708 |
| 11. Danville, VA | 5,709 |
| 12. Texarkana, TX–Texarkana, AR | 5,717 |
| 13. Sherman–Denison, TX | 5,722 |
| 14. Anderson, SC | 5,725 |
| 15. Fort Smith, AR–OK | 5,784 |
| 16. Muncie, IN | 5,800 |
| 17. Columbus, GA–AL | 5,817 |
| 18. Alexandria, LA | 5,819 |
| 19. Lawton, OK | 5,850 |
| 20. South Bend–Mishawaka, IN | 5,938 |
| 21. Florence, AL | 5,962 |
| 22. Clarksville–Hopkinsville, TN–KY | 6,007 |
| 23. Duluth, MN–WI | 6,040 |
| 24. Cumberland, MD–WV | 6,054 |
| 25. Waco, TX | 6,106 |
| 26. Jacksonville, NC | 6,111 |
| 27. Johnson City–Kingsport–Bristol, TN–VA | 6,119 |
| 28. Laredo, TX | 6,152 |
| 29. Burlington, NC | 6,179 |
| 30. Chattanooga, TN–GA | 6,189 |
| 31. Monroe, LA | 6,190 |
| 32. Altoona, PA | 6,191 |
| 33. Abilene, TX | 6,200 |
| 34. Macon–Warner Robins, GA | 6,235 |
| 35. Pascagoula, MS | 6,248 |
| 36. Fayetteville, NC | 6,274 |
| 37. Huntsville, AL | 6,283 |
| 38. Beaumont–Port Arthur, TX | 6,288 |
| 39. Augusta, GA–SC | 6,292 |
| 40. San Angelo, TX | 6,321 |
| 41. Greenville–Spartanburg, SC | 6,336 |
| 42. Battle Creek, MI | 6,342 |
| 43. Springfield, MO | 6,343 |
| 44. Panama City, FL | 6,373 |
| 45. Muskegon, MI | 6,391 |
| 46. Wichita Falls, TX | 6,404 |
| 47. Yakima, WA | 6,440 |
| 48. Biloxi–Gulfport, MS | 6,458 |
| 49. Killeen–Temple, TX | 6,463 |
| 50. Tuscaloosa, AL | 6,464 |
| 51. Pensacola, FL | 6,479 |
| 52. Alton–Granite City, IL | 6,487 |
| 53. East St. Louis–Belleville, IL | 6,501 |
| 54. Florence, SC | 6,508 |
| 55. Johnstown, PA | 6,524 |
| 56. Sioux City, IA–NE | 6,528 |
| 57. Shreveport, LA | 6,534 |
| 58. Amarillo, TX | 6,546 |
| 59. Elkhart–Goshen, IN | 6,573 |
| 60. Wheeling, WV–OH | 6,576 |
| 61. Steubenville–Weirton, OH–WV | 6,578 |
| 62. Longview–Marshall, TX | 6,608 |
| 63. Kokomo, IN | 6,616 |
| 64. Jacksonville, FL | 6,626 |
| 65. Huntington–Ashland, WV–KY–OH | 6,632 |
| 66. Pueblo, CO | 6,637 |
| 67. Parkersburg–Marietta, WV–OH | 6,657 |
| 68. Lakeland–Winter Haven, FL | 6,680 |
| 69. Fayetteville–Springdale, AR | 6,686 |
| 70. Odessa, TX | 6,689 |
| 71. Athens, GA | 6,691 |
| 72. Knoxville, TN | 6,692 |
| 73. Scranton–Wilkes-Barre, PA | 6,697 |
| 73. Sharon, PA | 6,697 |
| 75. Mobile, AL | 6,704 |
| 76. Asheville, NC | 6,722 |
| 77. Fort Wayne, IN | 6,733 |
| 78. Evansville, IN–KY | 6,743 |
| 79. Utica–Rome, NY | 6,744 |
| 80. Ocala, FL | 6,750 |
| 81. Montgomery, AL | 6,754 |
| 82. Hickory, NC | 6,760 |
| 82. Owensboro, KY | 6,760 |
| 84. Benton Harbor, MI | 6,761 |
| 85. Jackson, MI | 6,794 |
| 86. Birmingham, AL | 6,811 |
| 87. Louisville, KY–IN | 6,812 |
| 88. Enid, OK | 6,829 |
| 89. Wilmington, NC | 6,858 |
| 90. Lewiston–Auburn, ME | 6,876 |
| 91. Mansfield, OH | 6,881 |
| 92. Savannah, GA | 6,896 |
| 93. San Antonio, TX | 6,898 |
| 94. Lake Charles, LA | 6,921 |
| 95. Spokane, WA | 6,927 |
| 96. Corpus Christi, TX | 6,929 |
| 97. Lynchburg, VA | 6,934 |
| 98. Las Cruces, NM | 6,962 |
| 99. Lima, OH | 6,986 |
| 100. Lubbock, TX | 6,990 |
| 101. Indianapolis, IN | 7,012 |
| 102. Memphis, TN–AR–MS | 7,015 |
| 103. Youngstown–Warren, OH | 7,021 |
| 104. Bloomington, IN | 7,056 |
| 105. Wichita, KS | 7,061 |
| 106. Greensboro–Winston-Salem–High Point, NC | 7,064 |
| 107. Kansas City, MO | 7,076 |
| 108. Eau Claire, WI | 7,078 |
| 108. Elmira, NY | 7,078 |
| 110. Houma–Thibodaux, LA | 7,094 |
| 111. Topeka, KS | 7,110 |
| 112. Glens Falls, NY | 7,120 |
| 113. Omaha, NE–IA | 7,128 |
| 114. Great Falls, MT | 7,143 |
| 114. Victoria, TX | 7,143 |
| 116. Charlotte–Gastonia–Rock Hill, NC–SC | 7,169 |
| 117. Oklahoma City, OK | 7,186 |
| 118. Daytona Beach, FL | 7,203 |
| 119. Flint, MI | 7,204 |
| 120. Kankakee, IL | 7,230 |
| 121. St. Cloud, MN | 7,235 |
| 122. Jackson, MS | 7,245 |
| 123. Little Rock–North Little Rock, AR | 7,270 |
| 124. Bangor, ME | 7,277 |
| 125. Williamsport, PA | 7,284 |
| 126. Vineland–Millville–Bridgeton, NJ | 7,295 |
| 127. Tyler, TX | 7,298 |
| 128. Canton, OH | 7,332 |
| 129. Albany, GA | 7,339 |
| 130. El Paso, TX | 7,343 |
| 131. Saginaw–Bay City–Midland, MI | 7,368 |
| 132. Gainesville, FL | 7,388 |
| 133. Decatur, IL | 7,395 |
| 134. Charleston, SC | 7,402 |
| 135. Tampa–St. Petersburg–Clearwater, FL | 7,442 |
| 136. Janesville–Beloit, WI | 7,447 |
| 137. Roanoke, VA | 7,476 |
| 138. Lawrence, KS | 7,497 |
| 139. Tulsa, OK | 7,498 |
| 140. Columbia, SC | 7,519 |
| 141. Fort Walton Beach, FL | 7,554 |
| 142. Rockford, IL | 7,584 |
| 143. St. Louis, MO–IL | 7,605 |
| 144. Reading, PA | 7,614 |
| 145. Dayton–Springfield, OH | 7,635 |
| 146. Gary–Hammond, IN | 7,641 |
| 147. Wausau, WI | 7,642 |
| 148. Syracuse, NY | 7,670 |
| 149. Niagara Falls, NY | 7,686 |
| 150. Columbia, MO | 7,702 |
| 151. Erie, PA | 7,715 |
| 152. Hagerstown, MD | 7,763 |
| 153. Galveston–Texas City, TX | 7,767 |
| 153. Toledo, OH | 7,767 |
| 155. Tacoma, WA | 7,770 |
| 156. Cedar Rapids, IA | 7,774 |
| 157. Lafayette, IN | 7,778 |
| 157. Visalia–Tulare–Porterville, CA | 7,778 |
| 159. Grand Rapids, MI | 7,780 |
| 160. Charleston, WV | 7,789 |
| 161. Nashville, TN | 7,800 |
| 162. Pittsfield, MA | 7,807 |
| 163. Beaver County, PA | 7,866 |
| 164. Yuba City, CA | 7,875 |
| 165. Appleton–Oshkosh–Neenah, WI | 7,877 |
| 166. Waterloo–Cedar Falls, IA | 7,881 |
| 167. Springfield, IL | 7,882 |
| 168. Harrisburg–Lebanon–Carlisle, PA | 7,891 |
| 169. Grand Forks, ND | 7,898 |
| 170. Lansing–East Lansing, MI | 7,907 |
| 171. Albany–Schenectady–Troy, NY | 7,908 |
| 172. Kalamazoo, MI | 7,919 |
| 173. Wilmington, DE–NJ–MD | 7,927 |
| 174. Fort Worth–Arlington, TX | 7,956 |
| 175. Sioux Falls, SD | 7,983 |
| 176. Dubuque, IA | 7,993 |
| 177. Des Moines, IA | 8,028 |
| 178. Tallahassee, FL | 8,029 |
| 179. Springfield, MA | 8,039 |
| 180. Buffalo, NY | 8,064 |

| Places Rated Rank | Places Rated Score | Places Rated Rank | Places Rated Score | Places Rated Rank | Places Rated Score |
|---|---|---|---|---|---|
| 181. Bakersfield, CA | 8,068 | 232. Chico, CA | 8,587 | 281. Orange County, NY | 10,173 |
| 182. Baton Rouge, LA | 8,083 | 233. Rochester, NY | 8,609 | 282. Milwaukee, WI | 10,176 |
| 182. Davenport–Rock Island– | | 234. Champaign–Urbana– | | 283. Seattle, WA | 10,183 |
| Moline, IA–IL | 8,083 | Rantoul, IL | 8,627 | 284. New London–Norwich, CT–RI | 10,218 |
| 184. New Bedford, MA | 8,087 | 235. Modesto, CA | 8,630 | 285. Miami–Hialeah, FL | 10,267 |
| 185. Columbus, OH | 8,093 | | | | |
| | | 236. Lancaster, PA | 8,631 | 286. Aurora–Elgin, IL | 10,384 |
| 186. Pittsburgh, PA | 8,099 | 237. Bloomington–Normal, IL | 8,654 | 287. Lawrence–Haverhill, MA–NH | 10,414 |
| 187. Portland, ME | 8,100 | 238. Midland, TX | 8,672 | 288. Vallejo–Fairfield–Napa, CA | 10,503 |
| 188. Sheboygan, WI | 8,121 | 239. Worcester, MA | 8,715 | 289. New Britain, CT | 10,509 |
| 189. Kansas City, KS | 8,126 | 240. Melbourne–Titusville– | | 290. West Palm Beach–Boca | |
| 190. Akron, OH | 8,138 | Palm Bay, FL | 8,721 | Raton–Delray Beach, FL | 10,512 |
| 191. Cincinnati, OH–KY–IN | 8,143 | 241. Jersey City, NJ | 8,810 | 291. Trenton, NJ | 10,616 |
| 192. Fargo–Moorhead, ND–MN | 8,168 | 242. Austin, TX | 8,831 | 292. Nashua, NH | 10,757 |
| 193. Orlando, FL | 8,196 | 243. Fort Pierce, FL | 8,842 | 293. Denver, CO | 10,789 |
| 194. Greeley, CO | 8,218 | 244. Phoenix, AZ | 8,921 | 294. Fort Lauderdale–Hollywood– | |
| 195. Boise City, ID | 8,221 | 245. Racine, WI | 8,943 | Pompano Beach, FL | 10,810 |
| | | | | 295. Chicago, IL | 10,913 |
| 196. Hamilton–Middletown, OH | 8,227 | 246. Medford, OR | 9,008 | | |
| 197. Bryan–College Station, TX | 8,228 | 247. Vancouver, WA | 9,015 | 296. Ann Arbor, MI | 11,014 |
| 198. Raleigh–Durham, NC | 8,230 | 248. Fall River, MA–RI | 9,017 | 297. Atlantic City, NJ | 11,074 |
| 199. Bradenton, FL | 8,242 | 249. Bremerton, WA | 9,060 | 298. Nassau–Suffolk, NY | 11,138 |
| 200. Fitchburg–Leominster, MA | 8,252 | 250. Baltimore, MD | 9,148 | 299. New Haven–Meriden, CT | 11,460 |
| | | | | 300. Boston, MA | 11,609 |
| 201. Lincoln, NE | 8,256 | 251. Cleveland, OH | 9,168 | | |
| 202. Binghamton, NY | 8,257 | 252. Rochester, MN | 9,193 | 301. Salem–Gloucester, MA | 11,622 |
| 203. Brockton, MA | 8,263 | 253. Providence, RI | 9,274 | 302. Hartford, CT | 11,652 |
| 203. Olympia, WA | 8,263 | 254. Fresno, CA | 9,291 | 302. Middletown, CT | 11,652 |
| 205. Allentown–Bethlehem, PA–NJ | 8,288 | 255. Fort Myers, FL | 9,298 | 304. Monmouth–Ocean, NJ | 11,660 |
| | | | | 305. Boulder–Longmont, CO | 11,914 |
| 206. Lorain–Elyria, OH | 8,309 | 256. Dallas, TX | 9,318 | | |
| 207. La Crosse, WI | 8,310 | 257. Provo–Orem, UT | 9,321 | 306. Middlesex–Somerset– | |
| 207. Philadelphia, PA–NJ | 8,310 | 258. Joliet, IL | 9,327 | Hunterdon, NJ | 12,135 |
| 209. Billings, MT | 8,315 | 259. Eugene–Springfield, OR | 9,370 | 307. Anchorage, AK | 12,175 |
| 210. Atlanta, GA | 8,316 | 260. Iowa City, IA | 9,429 | 308. Reno, NV | 12,449 |
| | | | | 309. Santa Rosa–Petaluma, CA | 12,931 |
| 211. Bellingham, WA | 8,329 | 261. Pawtucket–Woonsocket– | | 310. Oakland, CA | 13,135 |
| 212. Lexington–Fayette, KY | 8,340 | Attleboro, RI–MA | 9,462 | | |
| 213. Richmond–Petersburg, VA | 8,343 | 262. Salt Lake City–Ogden, UT | 9,466 | 311. Lake County, IL | 13,282 |
| 214. Bismarck, ND | 8,365 | 263. Charlottesville, VA | 9,531 | 312. New York, NY | 13,358 |
| 215. York, PA | 8,371 | 264. Minneapolis–St. Paul, | | 313. Bridgeport–Milford, CT | 13,429 |
| | | MN–WI | 9,559 | 314. Washington, DC–MD–VA | 13,724 |
| 216. Salem, OR | 8,378 | 265. Sarasota, FL | 9,560 | 315. Salinas–Seaside–Monterey, | |
| 217. Peoria, IL | 8,388 | | | CA | 13,838 |
| 218. Albuquerque, NM | 8,393 | 266. Lowell, MA–NH | 9,640 | | |
| 219. Brazoria, TX | 8,394 | 267. Burlington, VT | 9,673 | 316. Los Angeles–Long Beach, | |
| 220. Green Bay, WI | 8,401 | 268. Riverside–San Bernardino, | | CA | 13,868 |
| | | CA | 9,754 | 317. Oxnard–Ventura, CA | 14,000 |
| 221. State College, PA | 8,405 | 269. Houston, TX | 9,760 | 318. Newark, NJ | 14,220 |
| 222. Richland–Kennewick– | | 270. Casper, WY | 9,839 | 319. Santa Cruz, CA | 14,303 |
| Pasco, WA | 8,461 | | | 320. Danbury, CT | 14,420 |
| 223. Stockton, CA | 8,474 | 271. Sacramento, CA | 9,855 | | |
| 224. Colorado Springs, CO | 8,509 | 272. Manchester, NH | 9,860 | 321. San Diego, CA | 14,465 |
| 225. New Orleans, LA | 8,515 | 273. Madison, WI | 9,897 | 322. Bergen–Passaic, NJ | 14,607 |
| | | 274. Las Vegas, NV | 9,906 | 323. Santa Barbara–Santa | |
| 226. Kenosha, WI | 8,516 | 275. Portland, OR | 9,912 | Maria–Lompoc, CA | 15,547 |
| 227. Detroit, MI | 8,525 | | | 324. Anaheim–Santa Ana, CA | 16,047 |
| 228. Tucson, AZ | 8,548 | 276. Fort Collins–Loveland, CO | 9,951 | 325. San Jose, CA | 16,048 |
| 229. Norfolk–Virginia Beach– | | 277. Portsmouth–Dover–Rochester, | | | |
| Newport News, VA | 8,568 | NH–ME | 9,966 | 326. Honolulu, HI | 17,021 |
| 230. Lafayette, LA | 8,572 | 278. Poughkeepsie, NY | 9,981 | 327. San Francisco, CA | 17,158 |
| | | 279. Waterbury, CT | 10,024 | 328. Norwalk, CT | 20,151 |
| 231. Redding, CA | 8,584 | 280. Bristol, CT | 10,041 | 329. Stamford, CT | 23,640 |

## Metro Areas Listed Alphabetically

| Metro Area | Places Rated Rank | Metro Area | Places Rated Rank | Metro Area | Places Rated Rank |
|---|---|---|---|---|---|
| Abilene, TX | 33 | Charleston, WV | 160 | Galveston–Texas City, TX | 153 |
| Akron, OH | 190 | Charlotte–Gastonia–Rock Hill, NC–SC | 116 | Gary–Hammond, IN | 146 |
| Albany, GA | 129 | | | Glens Falls, NY | 112 |
| Albany–Schenectady–Troy, NY | 171 | Charlottesville, VA | 263 | | |
| Albuquerque, NM | 218 | Chattanooga, TN–GA | 30 | Grand Forks, ND | 169 |
| | | Chicago, IL | 295 | Grand Rapids, MI | 159 |
| Alexandria, LA | 18 | | | Great Falls, MT | 114 |
| Allentown–Bethlehem, PA–NJ | 205 | Chico, CA | 232 | Greeley, CO | 194 |
| Alton–Granite City, IL | 52 | Cincinnati, OH–KY–IN | 191 | Green Bay, WI | 220 |
| Altoona, PA | 32 | Clarksville–Hopkinsville, TN–KY | 22 | | |
| Amarillo, TX | 58 | Cleveland, OH | 251 | Greensboro–Winston-Salem– High Point, NC | 106 |
| | | Colorado Springs, CO | 224 | | |
| Anaheim–Santa Ana, CA | 324 | | | Greenville–Spartanburg, SC | 41 |
| Anchorage, AK | 307 | Columbia, MO | 150 | Hagerstown, MD | 152 |
| Anderson, IN | 9 | Columbia, SC | 140 | Hamilton–Middletown, OH | 196 |
| Anderson, SC | 14 | Columbus, GA–AL | 17 | Harrisburg–Lebanon–Carlisle, PA | 168 |
| Ann Arbor, MI | 296 | Columbus, OH | 185 | | |
| | | Corpus Christi, TX | 96 | Hartford, CT | 302 |
| Anniston, AL | 6 | | | Hickory, NC | 82 |
| Appleton–Oshkosh–Neenah, WI | 165 | Cumberland, MD–WV | 24 | Honolulu, HI | 326 |
| Asheville, NC | 76 | Dallas, TX | 256 | Houma–Thibodaux, LA | 110 |
| Athens, GA | 71 | Danbury, CT | 320 | Houston, TX | 269 |
| Atlanta, GA | 210 | Danville, VA | 11 | | |
| | | Davenport–Rock Island–Moline, IA–IL | 182 | Huntington–Ashland, WV–KY–OH | 65 |
| Atlantic City, NJ | 297 | | | Huntsville, AL | 37 |
| Augusta, GA–SC | 39 | | | Indianapolis, IN | 101 |
| Aurora–Elgin, IL | 286 | Dayton–Springfield, OH | 145 | Iowa City, IA | 260 |
| Austin, TX | 242 | Daytona Beach, FL | 118 | Jackson, MI | 85 |
| Bakersfield, CA | 181 | Decatur, IL | 133 | | |
| | | Denver, CO | 293 | Jackson, MS | 122 |
| Baltimore, MD | 250 | Des Moines, IA | 177 | Jacksonville, FL | 64 |
| Bangor, ME | 124 | | | Jacksonville, NC | 26 |
| Baton Rouge, LA | 182 | Detroit, MI | 227 | Janesville–Beloit, WI | 136 |
| Battle Creek, MI | 42 | Dothan, AL | 10 | Jersey City, NJ | 241 |
| Beaumont–Port Arthur, TX | 38 | Dubuque, IA | 176 | | |
| | | Duluth, MN–WI | 23 | Johnson City–Kingsport–Bristol, TN–VA | 27 |
| Beaver County, PA | 163 | East St. Louis–Belleville, IL | 53 | | |
| Bellingham, WA | 211 | | | Johnstown, PA | 55 |
| Benton Harbor, MI | 84 | Eau Claire, WI | 108 | Joliet, IL | 258 |
| Bergen–Passaic, NJ | 322 | El Paso, TX | 130 | Joplin, MO | 1 |
| Billings, MT | 209 | Elkhart–Goshen, IN | 59 | Kalamazoo, MI | 172 |
| | | Elmira, NY | 108 | | |
| Biloxi–Gulfport, MS | 48 | Enid, OK | 88 | Kankakee, IL | 120 |
| Binghamton, NY | 202 | | | Kansas City, KS | 189 |
| Birmingham, AL | 86 | Erie, PA | 151 | Kansas City, MO | 107 |
| Bismarck, ND | 214 | Eugene–Springfield, OR | 259 | Kenosha, WI | 226 |
| Bloomington, IN | 104 | Evansville, IN–KY | 78 | Killeen–Temple, TX | 49 |
| | | Fall River, MA–RI | 248 | | |
| Bloomington–Normal, IL | 237 | Fargo–Moorhead, ND–MN | 192 | Knoxville, TN | 72 |
| Boise City, ID | 195 | | | Kokomo, IN | 63 |
| Boston, MA | 300 | Fayetteville, NC | 36 | La Crosse, WI | 207 |
| Boulder–Longmont, CO | 305 | Fayetteville–Springdale, AR | 69 | Lafayette, IN | 157 |
| Bradenton, FL | 199 | Fitchburg–Leominster, MA | 200 | Lafayette, LA | 230 |
| | | Flint, MI | 119 | | |
| Brazoria, TX | 219 | Florence, AL | 21 | Lake Charles, LA | 94 |
| Bremerton, WA | 249 | | | Lake County, IL | 311 |
| Bridgeport–Milford, CT | 313 | Florence, SC | 54 | Lakeland–Winter Haven, FL | 68 |
| Bristol, CT | 280 | Fort Collins–Loveland, CO | 276 | Lancaster, PA | 236 |
| Brockton, MA | 203 | Fort Lauderdale–Hollywood– Pompano Beach, FL | 294 | Lansing–East Lansing, MI | 170 |
| | | Fort Myers, FL | 255 | | |
| Brownsville–Harlingen, TX | 3 | Fort Pierce, FL | 243 | Laredo, TX | 28 |
| Bryan–College Station, TX | 197 | | | Las Cruces, NM | 98 |
| Buffalo, NY | 180 | Fort Smith, AR–OK | 15 | Las Vegas, NV | 274 |
| Burlington, NC | 29 | Fort Walton Beach, FL | 141 | Lawrence, KS | 138 |
| Burlington, VT | 267 | Fort Wayne, IN | 77 | Lawrence–Haverhill, MA–NH | 287 |
| | | Fort Worth–Arlington, TX | 174 | | |
| Canton, OH | 128 | Fresno, CA | 254 | Lawton, OK | 19 |
| Casper, WY | 270 | | | Lewiston–Auburn, ME | 90 |
| Cedar Rapids, IA | 156 | Gadsden, AL | 4 | Lexington–Fayette, KY | 212 |
| Champaign–Urbana–Rantoul, IL | 234 | Gainesville, FL | 132 | Lima, OH | 99 |
| Charleston, SC | 134 | | | Lincoln, NE | 201 |

| Metro Area | Places Rated Rank | Metro Area | Places Rated Rank | Metro Area | Places Rated Rank |
|---|---|---|---|---|---|
| Little Rock–North Little Rock, AR | 123 | Panama City, FL | 44 | Seattle, WA | 283 |
| Longview–Marshall, TX | 62 | Parkersburg–Marietta, WV–OH | 67 | Sharon, PA | 73 |
| Lorain–Elyria, OH | 206 | Pascagoula, MS | 35 | Sheboygan, WI | 188 |
| Los Angeles–Long Beach, CA | 316 | | | | |
| Louisville, KY–IN | 87 | Pawtucket–Woonsocket–Attleboro, RI–MA | 261 | Sherman–Denison, TX | 13 |
| | | Pensacola, FL | 51 | Shreveport, LA | 57 |
| Lowell, MA–NH | 266 | Peoria, IL | 217 | Sioux City, IA–NE | 56 |
| Lubbock, TX | 100 | Philadelphia, PA–NJ | 207 | Sioux Falls, SD | 175 |
| Lynchburg, VA | 97 | Phoenix, AZ | 244 | South Bend–Mishawaka, IN | 20 |
| Macon–Warner Robins, GA | 34 | | | | |
| Madison, WI | 273 | Pine Bluff, AR | 8 | Spokane, WA | 95 |
| | | Pittsburgh, PA | 186 | Springfield, IL | 167 |
| Manchester, NH | 272 | Pittsfield, MA | 162 | Springfield, MA | 179 |
| Mansfield, OH | 91 | Portland, ME | 187 | Springfield, MO | 43 |
| McAllen–Edinburg–Mission, TX | 2 | Portland, OR | 275 | Stamford, CT | 329 |
| Medford, OR | 246 | | | | |
| Melbourne–Titusville–Palm Bay, FL | 240 | Portsmouth–Dover–Rochester, NH–ME | 277 | State College, PA | 221 |
| | | Poughkeepsie, NY | 278 | Steubenville–Weirton, OH–WV | 61 |
| Memphis, TN–AR–MS | 102 | Providence, RI | 253 | Stockton, CA | 223 |
| Miami–Hialeah, FL | 285 | Provo–Orem, UT | 257 | Syracuse, NY | 148 |
| Middlesex–Somerset– Hunterdon, NJ | 306 | Pueblo, CO | 66 | Tacoma, WA | 155 |
| Middletown, CT | 302 | | | | |
| Midland, TX | 238 | Racine, WI | 245 | Tallahassee, FL | 178 |
| | | Raleigh–Durham, NC | 198 | Tampa–St. Petersburg– Clearwater, FL | 135 |
| Milwaukee, WI | 282 | Reading, PA | 144 | Terre Haute, IN | 5 |
| Minneapolis–St. Paul, MN–WI | 264 | Redding, CA | 231 | Texarkana, TX–Texarkana, AR | 12 |
| Mobile, AL | 75 | Reno, NV | 308 | Toledo, OH | 153 |
| Modesto, CA | 235 | | | | |
| Monmouth–Ocean, NJ | 304 | Richland–Kennewick– Pasco, WA | 222 | Topeka, KS | 111 |
| | | Richmond–Petersburg, VA | 213 | Trenton, NJ | 291 |
| Monroe, LA | 31 | Riverside–San Bernardino, CA | 268 | Tucson, AZ | 228 |
| Montgomery, AL | 81 | Roanoke, VA | 137 | Tulsa, OK | 139 |
| Muncie, IN | 16 | Rochester, MN | 252 | Tuscaloosa, AL | 50 |
| Muskegon, MI | 45 | | | | |
| Nashua, NH | 292 | Rochester, NY | 233 | Tyler, TX | 127 |
| | | Rockford, IL | 142 | Utica–Rome, NY | 79 |
| Nashville, TN | 161 | Sacramento, CA | 271 | Vallejo–Fairfield–Napa, CA | 288 |
| Nassau–Suffolk, NY | 298 | Saginaw–Bay City–Midland, MI | 131 | Vancouver, WA | 247 |
| New Bedford, MA | 184 | St. Cloud, MN | 121 | Victoria, TX | 114 |
| New Britain, CT | 289 | | | | |
| New Haven–Meriden, CT | 299 | St. Joseph, MO | 7 | Vineland–Millville–Bridgeton, NJ | 126 |
| | | St. Louis, MO–IL | 143 | Visalia–Tulare–Porterville, CA | 157 |
| New London–Norwich, CT–RI | 284 | Salem, OR | 216 | Waco, TX | 25 |
| New Orleans, LA | 225 | Salem–Gloucester, MA | 301 | Washington, DC–MD–VA | 314 |
| New York, NY | 312 | Salinas–Seaside–Monterey, CA | 315 | Waterbury, CT | 279 |
| Newark, NJ | 318 | | | | |
| Niagara Falls, NY | 149 | Salt Lake City–Ogden, UT | 262 | Waterloo–Cedar Falls, IA | 166 |
| | | San Angelo, TX | 40 | Wausau, WI | 147 |
| Norfolk–Virginia Beach–Newport News, VA | 229 | San Antonio, TX | 93 | West Palm Beach–Boca Raton– Delray Beach, FL | 290 |
| Norwalk, CT | 328 | San Diego, CA | 321 | Wheeling, WV–OH | 60 |
| Oakland, CA | 310 | San Francisco, CA | 327 | Wichita, KS | 105 |
| Ocala, FL | 80 | | | | |
| Odessa, TX | 70 | San Jose, CA | 325 | Wichita Falls, TX | 46 |
| | | Santa Barbara–Santa Maria– Lompoc, CA | 323 | Williamsport, PA | 125 |
| Oklahoma City, OK | 117 | Santa Cruz, CA | 319 | Wilmington, DE–NJ–MD | 173 |
| Olympia, WA | 203 | Santa Rosa–Petaluma, CA | 309 | Wilmington, NC | 89 |
| Omaha, NE–IA | 113 | Sarasota, FL | 265 | Worcester, MA | 239 |
| Orange County, NY | 281 | | | | |
| Orlando, FL | 193 | Savannah, GA | 92 | Yakima, WA | 47 |
| | | Scranton–Wilkes-Barre, PA | 73 | York, PA | 215 |
| Owensboro, KY | 82 | | | Youngstown–Warren, OH | 103 |
| Oxnard–Ventura, CA | 317 | | | Yuba City, CA | 164 |

# Place Profiles: Housing Features of 329 Metro Areas

The following pages summarize local housing features in each metro area, dividing them into the categories of Local Choices, Houses, Energy Requirements, and Annual Costs.

Data in the first category, Local Choices, show the mix of occupied single houses, condominiums, mobile homes, and apartments (defined here as a rented housing unit in a building with five or more rental units) in each metro area. The sums of these percentages (which are rounded) are not always 100; the balance represents renter-occupied duplexes, triplexes, and fourplexes. Data on average monthly rent come from the *1980 Census of Population and Housing* and are boosted by regional inflation factors as reported in the Bureau of Labor's *Consumer Price Index* for April 1984.

In the Houses category, information on the average price for all owner-occupied houses comes from the *1980 Census of Population and Housing* and is adjusted for inflation with 1984 regional data from the National Association of Realtors. Property taxes are based on statewide average residential rates taken from the 1984 issue of *Significant Features of Fiscal Federalism,* an annual publication of the Advisory Commission on Intergovernmental Relations. The percentages of houses built before 1940 also come from the *1980 Census of Population and Housing.*

The heating season, listed under Energy Requirements, is given in terms of heating-degree days per year, and is derived from NOAA's *Substation Summaries.* The number of hours given for air-conditioning represents the normal number of hours per year when the outside temperature climbs over 80 degrees Fahrenheit. These figures come from the Department of Defense manual *Engineering Weather Data.*

The dollar amounts given for the entry Mortgage and Taxes are the annual sum of property taxes and mortgage payments. Utilities, too, are annual dollar amounts. Typical bills for residential natural gas by state come from the Energy Information Administration's unpublished figures for 1983. The Department of Energy's 1983 publication *Typical Electric Bills* details electricity consumption and cost for each metro area. To reflect realistic 1984 energy costs, data from these sources are adjusted for inflation using the Bureau of Labor's Consumer Price Index for April 1984.

A star preceding a metro area's name highlights it as one of the best 25 places for homeowning costs.

### Abilene, TX
Local Choices
　79% houses, 5% mobile homes, 9% apartments (rent $300/month)
Houses
　Price: $47,900
　Property Taxes: $671
　Built Before 1940: 16.3%
Energy Requirements
　Heating Season: 2,610 degree days
　Major Source: Natural gas/Electricity
　Air-conditioning: 2,005 hours
Annual Costs
　Mortgage and Taxes: $5,213
　Utilities: $987
Places Rated Score: 6,200
Places Rated Rank: 33

### Akron, OH
Local Choices
　74% houses, 2% condos, 2% mobile homes, 12% apartments (rent $305/month)
Houses
　Price: $62,200
　Property Taxes: $715
　Built Before 1940: 29.3%
Energy Requirements
　Heating Season: 6,224 degree days
　Major Source: Natural gas/Electricity
　Air-conditioning: 416 hours
Annual Costs
　Mortgage and Taxes: $6,608
　Utilities: $1,530
Places Rated Score: 8,138
Places Rated Rank: 190

### Albany, GA
Local Choices
　67% houses, 7% mobile homes, 10% apartments (rent $275/month)
Houses
　Price: $60,200
　Property Taxes: $729
　Built Before 1940: 7.2%
Energy Requirements
　Heating Season: 1,872 degree days
　Major Source: Natural gas/Electricity
　Air-conditioning: 420 hours
Annual Costs
　Mortgage and Taxes: $6,439
　Utilities: $900
Places Rated Score: 7,339
Places Rated Rank: 129

### Albany–Schenectady–Troy, NY
Local Choices
　58% houses, 4% mobile homes, 12% apartments (rent $305/month)
Houses
　Price: $55,200
　Property Taxes: $1,418
　Built Before 1940: 46.9%
Energy Requirements
　Heating Season: 6,888 degree days
　Major Source: Natural gas/Electricity
　Air-conditioning: 420 hours
Annual Costs
　Mortgage and Taxes: $6,649
　Utilities: $1,259
Places Rated Score: 7,908
Places Rated Rank: 171

### Albuquerque, NM
Local Choices
　67% houses, 2% condos, 7% mobile homes, 17% apartments (rent $335/month)
Houses
　Price: $69,900
　Property Taxes: $650
　Built Before 1940: 6.7%
Energy Requirements
　Heating Season: 4,292 degree days
　Major Source: Natural gas/Electricity
　Air-conditioning: 1,130 hours
Annual Costs
　Mortgage and Taxes: $7,276
　Utilities: $1,117
Places Rated Score: 8,393
Places Rated Rank: 218

### ★ Alexandria, LA
Local Choices
　79% houses, 1% condos, 6% mobile homes, 6% apartments (rent $265/month)
Houses
　Price: $50,100
　Property Taxes: $75
　Built Before 1940: 14.8%
Energy Requirements
　Heating Season: 2,200 degree days
　Major Source: Natural gas/Electricity
　Air-conditioning: 1,721 hours
Annual Costs
　Mortgage and Taxes: $4,820
　Utilities: $999
Places Rated Score: 5,819
Places Rated Rank: 18

## Allentown–Bethlehem, PA–NJ
Local Choices
74% houses, 1% condos, 2% mobile homes, 11% apartments (rent $310/month)
Houses
Price: $62,800
Property Taxes: $1,024
Built Before 1940: 44.8%
Energy Requirements
Heating Season: 5,827 degree days
Major Source: Oil/Electricity
Air-conditioning: 509 hours
Annual Costs
Mortgage and Taxes: $6,981
Utilities: $1,307
Places Rated Score: 8,288
Places Rated Rank: 205

## Alton–Granite City, IL
Local Choices
79% houses, 4% mobile homes, 6% apartments (rent $275/month)
Houses
Price: $47,700
Property Taxes: $758
Built Before 1940: 30.2%
Energy Requirements
Heating Season: 4,840 degree days
Major Source: Natural gas/Electricity
Air-conditioning: 1,223 hours
Annual Costs
Mortgage and Taxes: $5,278
Utilities: $1,209
Places Rated Score: 6,487
Places Rated Rank: 52

## Altoona, PA
Local Choices
76% houses, 6% mobile homes, 7% apartments (rent $270/month)
Houses
Price: $43,600
Property Taxes: $705
Built Before 1940: 54.0%
Energy Requirements
Heating Season: 6,121 degree days
Major Source: Oil/Electricity
Air-conditioning: 351 hours
Annual Costs
Mortgage and Taxes: $4,806
Utilities: $1,385
Places Rated Score: 6,191
Places Rated Rank: 32

## Amarillo, TX
Local Choices
77% houses, 4% mobile homes, 12% apartments (rent $310/month)
Houses
Price: $50,500
Property Taxes: $707
Built Before 1940: 11.3%
Energy Requirements
Heating Season: 4,183 degree days
Major Source: Natural gas/Electricity
Air-conditioning: 1,176 hours
Annual Costs
Mortgage and Taxes: $5,496
Utilities: $1,050
Places Rated Score: 6,546
Places Rated Rank: 58

## Anaheim–Santa Ana, CA
Local Choices
63% houses, 11% condos, 4% mobile

homes, 20% apartments (rent $510/month)
Houses
Price: $142,300
Property Taxes: $1,466
Built Before 1940: 3.7%
Energy Requirements
Heating Season: 1,675 degree days
Major Source: Natural gas/Electricity
Air-conditioning: 888 hours
Annual Costs
Mortgage and Taxes: $14,953
Utilities: $1,094
Places Rated Score: 16,047
Places Rated Rank: 324

## Anchorage, AK
Local Choices
48% houses, 6% condos, 10% mobile homes, 21% apartments (rent $520/month)
Houses
Price: $111,400
Property Taxes: $702
Built Before 1940: 1.1%
Energy Requirements
Heating Season: 10,911 degree days
Major Source: Natural gas/Electricity
Air-conditioning: 6 hours
Annual Costs
Mortgage and Taxes: $11,261
Utilities: $914
Places Rated Score: 12,175
Places Rated Rank: 307

## ★ Anderson, IN
Local Choices
81% houses, 1% condos, 4% mobile homes, 5% apartments (rent $265/month)
Houses
Price: $43,600
Property Taxes: $519
Built Before 1940: 32.4%
Energy Requirements
Heating Season: 5,580 degree days
Major Source: Natural gas/Electricity
Air-conditioning: 745 hours
Annual Costs
Mortgage and Taxes: $4,653
Utilities: $1,051
Places Rated Score: 5,704
Places Rated Rank: 9

## ★ Anderson, SC
Local Choices
82% houses, 1% condos, 9% mobile homes, 4% apartments (rent $245/month)
Houses
Price: $46,100
Property Taxes: $424
Built Before 1940: 19.9%
Energy Requirements
Heating Season: 2,900 degree days
Major Source: Total electric
Air-conditioning: 1,262 hours
Annual Costs
Mortgage and Taxes: $4,793
Utilities: $932
Places Rated Score: 5,725
Places Rated Rank: 14

## Ann Arbor, MI
Local Choices
60% houses, 3% condos, 2% mobile homes, 28% apartments (rent $385/month)

## Houses
Price: $79,600
Property Taxes: $2,132
Built Before 1940: 20.5%
Energy Requirements
Heating Season: 6,306 degree days
Major Source: Natural gas/Electricity
Air-conditioning: 511 hours
Annual Costs
Mortgage and Taxes: $9,673
Utilities: $1,341
Places Rated Score: 11,014
Places Rated Rank: 296

## ★ Anniston, AL
Local Choices
77% houses, 10% mobile homes, 7% apartments (rent $250/month)
Houses
Price: $44,900
Property Taxes: $184
Built Before 1940: 16.6%
Energy Requirements
Heating Season: 2,820 degree days
Major Source: Natural gas/Electricity
Air-conditioning: 1,251 hours
Annual Costs
Mortgage and Taxes: $4,441
Utilities: $1,089
Places Rated Score: 5,530
Places Rated Rank: 6

## Appleton–Oshkosh–Neenah, WI
Local Choices
76% houses, 1% condos, 2% mobile homes, 8% apartments (rent $275/month)
Houses
Price: $57,200
Property Taxes: $1,150
Built Before 1940: 36.2%
Energy Requirements
Heating Season: 7,665 degree days
Major Source: Natural gas/Electricity
Air-conditioning: 388 hours
Annual Costs
Mortgage and Taxes: $6,574
Utilities: $1,303
Places Rated Score: 7,877
Places Rated Rank: 165

## Asheville, NC
Local Choices
73% houses, 1% condos, 12% mobile homes, 9% apartments (rent $270/month)
Houses
Price: $53,100
Property Taxes: $515
Built Before 1940: 23.1%
Energy Requirements
Heating Season: 4,237 degree days
Major Source: Oil/Electricity
Air-conditioning: 610 hours
Annual Costs
Mortgage and Taxes: $5,546
Utilities: $1,176
Places Rated Score: 6,722
Places Rated Rank: 76

## Athens, GA
Local Choices
64% houses, 1% condos, 11% mobile homes, 14% apartments (rent $265/month)
Houses
Price: $53,300

Property Taxes: $645
Built Before 1940: 15.7%
Energy Requirements
Heating Season: 2,822 degree days
Major Source: Natural gas/Electricity
Air-conditioning: 1,122 hours
Annual Costs
Mortgage and Taxes: $5,699
Utilities: $992
Places Rated Score: 6,691
Places Rated Rank: 71

### Atlanta, GA
Local Choices
66% houses, 2% condos, 3% mobile homes, 21% apartments (rent $330/month)
Houses
Price: $68,500
Property Taxes: $829
Built Before 1940: 10.3%
Energy Requirements
Heating Season: 3,095 degree days
Major Source: Natural gas/Electricity
Air-conditioning: 1,151 hours
Annual Costs
Mortgage and Taxes: $7,324
Utilities: $992
Places Rated Score: 8,316
Places Rated Rank: 210

### Atlantic City, NJ
Local Choices
67% houses, 4% condos, 2% mobile homes, 13% apartments (rent $355/month)
Houses
Price: $79,800
Property Taxes: $2,034
Built Before 1940: 29.4%
Energy Requirements
Heating Season: 4,946 degree days
Major Source: Oil/Electricity
Air-conditioning: 473 hours
Annual Costs
Mortgage and Taxes: $9,596
Utilities: $1,478
Places Rated Score: 11,074
Places Rated Rank: 297

### Augusta, GA–SC
Local Choices
76% houses, 1% condos, 8% mobile homes, 8% apartments (rent $275/month)
Houses
Price: $49,600
Property Taxes: $600
Built Before 1940: 13.2%
Energy Requirements
Heating Season: 2,547 degree days
Major Source: Natural gas/Electricity
Air-conditioning: 1,431 hours
Annual Costs
Mortgage and Taxes: $5,300
Utilities: $992
Places Rated Score: 6,292
Places Rated Rank: 39

### Aurora–Elgin, IL
Local Choices
72% houses, 2% condos, 1% mobile homes, 13% apartments (rent $350/month)
Houses
Price: $81,400
Property Taxes: $1,295

Built Before 1940: 28.8%
Energy Requirements
Heating Season: 6,551 degree days
Major Source: Natural gas/Electricity
Air-conditioning: 549 hours
Annual Costs
Mortgage and Taxes: $9,015
Utilities: $1,369
Places Rated Score: 10,384
Places Rated Rank: 286

### Austin, TX
Local Choices
64% houses, 2% condos, 4% mobile homes, 22% apartments (rent $360/month)
Houses
Price: $73,100
Property Taxes: $1,024
Built Before 1940: 9.2%
Energy Requirements
Heating Season: 1,737 degree days
Major Source: Natural gas/Electricity
Air-conditioning: 2,243 hours
Annual Costs
Mortgage and Taxes: $7,955
Utilities: $876
Places Rated Score: 8,831
Places Rated Rank: 242

### Bakersfield, CA
Local Choices
73% houses, 2% condos, 8% mobile homes, 10% apartments (rent $340/month)
Houses
Price: $68,000
Property Taxes: $700
Built Before 1940: 11.5%
Energy Requirements
Heating Season: 2,185 degree days
Major Source: Natural gas/Electricity
Air-conditioning: 1,648 hours
Annual Costs
Mortgage and Taxes: $7,147
Utilities: $921
Places Rated Score: 8,068
Places Rated Rank: 181

### Baltimore, MD
Local Choices
69% houses, 2% condos, 1% mobile homes, 18% apartments (rent $330/month)
Houses
Price: $73,000
Property Taxes: $1,001
Built Before 1940: 27.7%
Energy Requirements
Heating Season: 4,101 degree days
Major Source: Natural gas/Electricity
Air-conditioning: 833 hours
Annual Costs
Mortgage and Taxes: $7,925
Utilities: $1,223
Places Rated Score: 9,148
Places Rated Rank: 250

### Bangor, ME
Local Choices
60% houses, 8% mobile homes, 11% apartments (rent $295/month)
Houses
Price: $55,600
Property Taxes: $845
Built Before 1940: 49.7%

Energy Requirements
Heating Season: 8,648 degree days
Major Source: Oil/Electricity
Air-conditioning: 181 hours
Annual Costs
Mortgage and Taxes: $6,114
Utilities: $1,163
Places Rated Score: 7,277
Places Rated Rank: 124

### Baton Rouge, LA
Local Choices
73% houses, 2% condos, 6% mobile homes, 14% apartments (rent $325/month)
Houses
Price: $74,000
Property Taxes: $111
Built Before 1940: 8.3%
Energy Requirements
Heating Season: 1,670 degree days
Major Source: Natural gas/Electricity
Air-conditioning: 1,723 hours
Annual Costs
Mortgage and Taxes: $7,128
Utilities: $955
Places Rated Score: 8,083
Places Rated Rank: 182

### Battle Creek, MI
Local Choices
77% houses, 1% condos, 4% mobile homes, 9% apartments (rent $280/month)
Houses
Price: $41,500
Property Taxes: $1,111
Built Before 1940: 38.2%
Energy Requirements
Heating Season: 6,720 degree days
Major Source: Natural gas/Electricity
Air-conditioning: 511 hours
Annual Costs
Mortgage and Taxes: $5,041
Utilities: $1,301
Places Rated Score: 6,342
Places Rated Rank: 42

### Beaumont–Port Arthur, TX
Local Choices
80% houses, 1% condos, 6% mobile homes, 8% apartments (rent $315/month)
Houses
Price: $47,800
Property Taxes: $669
Built Before 1940: 14.3%
Energy Requirements
Heating Season: 1,518 degree days
Major Source: Natural gas/Electricity
Air-conditioning: 1,807 hours
Annual Costs
Mortgage and Taxes: $5,201
Utilities: $1,087
Places Rated Score: 6,288
Places Rated Rank: 38

### Beaver County, PA
Local Choices
77% houses, 1% condos, 4% mobile homes, 8% apartments (rent $290/month)
Houses
Price: $58,400
Property Taxes: $952
Built Before 1940: 37.4%

Energy Requirements
Heating Season: 4,865 degree days
Major Source: Natural gas/Electricity
Air-conditioning: 461 hours
Annual Costs
Mortgage and Taxes: $6,491
Utilities: $1,375
Places Rated Score: 7,866
Places Rated Rank: 163

### Bellingham, WA
Local Choices
73% houses, 2% condos, 6% mobile homes, 13% apartments (rent $350/month)
Houses
Price: $74,100
Property Taxes: $748
Built Before 1940: 27.4%
Energy Requirements
Heating Season: 5,738 degree days
Major Source: Total electric
Air-conditioning: 40 hours
Annual Costs
Mortgage and Taxes: $7,770
Utilities: $559
Places Rated Score: 8,329
Places Rated Rank: 211

### Benton Harbor, MI
Local Choices
77% houses, 1% condos, 4% mobile homes, 8% apartments (rent $295/month)
Houses
Price: $45,700
Property Taxes: $1,224
Built Before 1940: 29.9%
Energy Requirements
Heating Season: 6,296 degree days
Major Source: Natural gas/Electricity
Air-conditioning: 465 hours
Annual Costs
Mortgage and Taxes: $5,555
Utilities: $1,206
Places Rated Score: 6,761
Places Rated Rank: 84

### Bergen–Passaic, NJ
Local Choices
54% houses, 1% condos, 13% apartments (rent $415/month)
Houses
Price: $108,900
Property Taxes: $2,777
Built Before 1940: 35.8%
Energy Requirements
Heating Season: 5,350 degree days
Major Source: Natural gas/Electricity
Air-conditioning: 592 hours
Annual Costs
Mortgage and Taxes: $13,099
Utilities: $1,508
Places Rated Score: 14,607
Places Rated Rank: 322

### Billings, MT
Local Choices
70% houses, 1% condos, 8% mobile homes, 10% apartments (rent $330/month)
Houses
Price: $69,400
Property Taxes: $791
Built Before 1940: 17.3%
Energy Requirements
Heating Season: 7,265 degree days

Major Source: Natural gas/Electricity
Air-conditioning: 515 hours
Annual Costs
Mortgage and Taxes: $7,367
Utilities: $948
Places Rated Score: 8,315
Places Rated Rank: 209

### Biloxi–Gulfport, MS
Local Choices
74% houses, 1% condos, 6% mobile homes, 12% apartments (rent $280/month)
Houses
Price: $53,200
Property Taxes: $404
Built Before 1940: 11.6%
Energy Requirements
Heating Season: 1,496 degree days
Major Source: Natural gas/Electricity
Air-conditioning: 2,052 hours
Annual Costs
Mortgage and Taxes: $5,442
Utilities: $1,016
Places Rated Score: 6,458
Places Rated Rank: 48

### Binghamton, NY
Local Choices
62% houses, 6% mobile homes, 10% apartments (rent $285/month)
Houses
Price: $58,100
Property Taxes: $1,493
Built Before 1940: 44.6%
Energy Requirements
Heating Season: 7,285 degree days
Major Source: Natural gas/Electricity
Air-conditioning: 225 hours
Annual Costs
Mortgage and Taxes: $6,999
Utilities: $1,258
Places Rated Score: 8,257
Places Rated Rank: 202

### Birmingham, AL
Local Choices
74% houses, 1% condos, 6% mobile homes, 13% apartments (rent $290/month)
Houses
Price: $57,900
Property Taxes: $237
Built Before 1940: 19.0%
Energy Requirements
Heating Season: 2,844 degree days
Major Source: Natural gas/Electricity
Air-conditioning: 1,380 hours
Annual Costs
Mortgage and Taxes: $5,722
Utilities: $1,089
Places Rated Score: 6,811
Places Rated Rank: 86

### Bismarck, ND
Local Choices
57% houses, 2% condos, 12% mobile homes, 15% apartments (rent $285/month)
Houses
Price: $66,800
Property Taxes: $735
Built Before 1940: 19.8%
Energy Requirements
Heating Season: 9,044 degree days
Major Source: Natural gas/Electricity
Air-conditioning: 439 hours

Annual Costs
Mortgage and Taxes: $7,067
Utilities: $1,298
Places Rated Score: 8,365
Places Rated Rank: 214

### Bloomington, IN
Local Choices
59% houses, 2% condos, 8% mobile homes, 25% apartments (rent $275/month)
Houses
Price: $54,600
Property Taxes: $649
Built Before 1940: 17.6%
Energy Requirements
Heating Season: 4,905 degree days
Major Source: Natural gas/Electricity
Air-conditioning: 848 hours
Annual Costs
Mortgage and Taxes: $5,822
Utilities: $1,234
Places Rated Score: 7,056
Places Rated Rank: 104

### Bloomington–Normal, IL
Local Choices
68% houses, 2% condos, 5% mobile homes, 15% apartments (rent $315/month)
Houses
Price: $65,300
Property Taxes: $1,038
Built Before 1940: 34.7%
Energy Requirements
Heating Season: 5,648 degree days
Major Source: Natural gas/Electricity
Air-conditioning: 848 hours
Annual Costs
Mortgage and Taxes: $7,226
Utilities: $1,428
Places Rated Score: 8,654
Places Rated Rank: 237

### Boise City, ID
Local Choices
75% houses, 2% condos, 8% mobile homes, 8% apartments (rent $365/month)
Houses
Price: $72,100
Property Taxes: $750
Built Before 1940: 12.8%
Energy Requirements
Heating Season: 5,833 degree days
Major Source: Total electric
Air-conditioning: 706 hours
Annual Costs
Mortgage and Taxes: $7,583
Utilities: $638
Places Rated Score: 8,221
Places Rated Rank: 195

### Boston, MA
Local Choices
22% houses, 2% condos, 23% apartments (rent $375/month)
Houses
Price: $84,300
Property Taxes: $2,047
Built Before 1940: 50.6%
Energy Requirements
Heating Season: 5,621 degree days
Major Source: Oil/Electricity
Air-conditioning: 420 hours

Annual Costs
Mortgage and Taxes: $10,033
Utilities: $1,576
Places Rated Score: 11,609
Places Rated Rank: 300

## Boulder–Longmont, CO
Local Choices
66% houses, 5% condos, 5% mobile homes, 19% apartments (rent $440/month)
Houses
Price: $102,200
Property Taxes: $1,033
Built Before 1940: 12.4%
Energy Requirements
Heating Season: 5,540 degree days
Major Source: Natural gas/Electricity
Air-conditioning: 667 hours
Annual Costs
Mortgage and Taxes: $10,725
Utilities: $1,189
Places Rated Score: 11,914
Places Rated Rank: 305

## Bradenton, FL
Local Choices
60% houses, 16% condos, 17% mobile homes, 7% apartments (rent $350/month)
Houses
Price: $67,700
Property Taxes: $697
Built Before 1940: 7.0%
Energy Requirements
Heating Season: 597 degree days
Major Source: Total electric
Air-conditioning: 2,154 hours
Annual Costs
Mortgage and Taxes: $7,110
Utilities: $1,132
Places Rated Score: 8,242
Places Rated Rank: 199

## Brazoria, TX
Local Choices
72% houses, 1% condos, 12% mobile homes, 12% apartments (rent $385/month)
Houses
Price: $67,600
Property Taxes: $946
Built Before 1940: 5.3%
Energy Requirements
Heating Season: 1,434 degree days
Major Source: Natural gas/Electricity
Air-conditioning: 1,763 hours
Annual Costs
Mortgage and Taxes: $7,350
Utilities: $1,044
Places Rated Score: 8,394
Places Rated Rank: 219

## Bremerton, WA
Local Choices
74% houses, 1% condos, 6% mobile homes, 10% apartments (rent $350/month)
Houses
Price: $81,000
Property Taxes: $819
Built Before 1940: 18.3%
Energy Requirements
Heating Season: 4,350 degree days
Major Source: Total electric
Air-conditioning: 64 hours

Annual Costs
Mortgage and Taxes: $8,501
Utilities: $559
Places Rated Score: 9,060
Places Rated Rank: 249

## Bridgeport–Milford, CT
Local Choices
56% houses, 5% condos, 11% apartments (rent $360/month)
Houses
Price: $107,200
Property Taxes: $1,641
Built Before 1940: 34.2%
Energy Requirements
Heating Season: 5,461 degree days
Major Source: Oil/Electricity
Air-conditioning: 302 hours
Annual Costs
Mortgage and Taxes: $11,806
Utilities: $1,623
Places Rated Score: 13,429
Places Rated Rank: 313

## Bristol, CT
Local Choices
62% houses, 1% condos, 13% apartments (rent $315/month)
Houses
Price: $76,500
Property Taxes: $1,171
Built Before 1940: 29.9%
Energy Requirements
Heating Season: 6,130 degree days
Major Source: Oil/Electricity
Air-conditioning: 292 hours
Annual Costs
Mortgage and Taxes: $8,424
Utilities: $1,617
Places Rated Score: 10,041
Places Rated Rank: 280

## Brockton, MA
Local Choices
54% houses, 1% condos, 1% mobile homes, 16% apartments (rent $330/month)
Houses
Price: $57,100
Property Taxes: $1,388
Built Before 1940: 42.0%
Energy Requirements
Heating Season: 6,517 degree days
Major Source: Oil/Electricity
Air-conditioning: 133 hours
Annual Costs
Mortgage and Taxes: $6,802
Utilities: $1,461
Places Rated Score: 8,263
Places Rated Rank: 203

## ★ Brownsville–Harlingen, TX
Local Choices
71% houses, 2% condos, 6% mobile homes, 12% apartments (rent $260/month)
Houses
Price: $41,100
Property Taxes: $575
Built Before 1940: 12.3%
Energy Requirements
Heating Season: 650 degree days
Major Source: Natural gas/Electricity
Air-conditioning: 2,295 hours
Annual Costs
Mortgage and Taxes: $4,466
Utilities: $910

Places Rated Score: 5,376
Places Rated Rank: 3

## Bryan–College Station, TX
Local Choices
56% houses, 1% condos, 7% mobile homes, 25% apartments (rent $350/month)
Houses
Price: $64,900
Property Taxes: $908
Built Before 1940: 7.4%
Energy Requirements
Heating Season: 1,658 degree days
Major Source: Natural gas/Electricity
Air-conditioning: 1,194 hours
Annual Costs
Mortgage and Taxes: $7,058
Utilities: $1,170
Places Rated Score: 8,228
Places Rated Rank: 197

## Buffalo, NY
Local Choices
55% houses, 1% condos, 1% mobile homes, 10% apartments (rent $290/month)
Houses
Price: $56,600
Property Taxes: $1,454
Built Before 1940: 43.4%
Energy Requirements
Heating Season: 6,927 degree days
Major Source: Natural gas/Electricity
Air-conditioning: 347 hours
Annual Costs
Mortgage and Taxes: $6,818
Utilities: $1,246
Places Rated Score: 8,064
Places Rated Rank: 180

## Burlington, NC
Local Choices
80% houses, 8% mobile homes, 5% apartments (rent $260/month)
Houses
Price: $48,500
Property Taxes: $470
Built Before 1940: 19.8%
Energy Requirements
Heating Season: 3,810 degree days
Major Source: Oil/Electricity
Air-conditioning: 916 hours
Annual Costs
Mortgage and Taxes: $5,067
Utilities: $1,112
Places Rated Score: 6,179
Places Rated Rank: 29

## Burlington, VT
Local Choices
59% houses, 3% condos, 5% mobile homes, 14% apartments (rent $355/month)
Houses
Price: $75,000
Property Taxes: $1,200
Built Before 1940: 32.9%
Energy Requirements
Heating Season: 7,876 degree days
Major Source: Oil/Electricity
Air-conditioning: 263 hours
Annual Costs
Mortgage and Taxes: $8,309
Utilities: $1,364
Places Rated Score: 9,673
Places Rated Rank: 267

### Canton, OH
Local Choices
77% houses, 3% mobile homes, 8% apartments (rent $280/month)
Houses
Price: $56,500
Property Taxes: $650
Built Before 1940: 32.2%
Energy Requirements
Heating Season: 6,224 degree days
Major Source: Natural gas/Electricity
Air-conditioning: 416 hours
Annual Costs
Mortgage and Taxes: $6,004
Utilities: $1,328
Places Rated Score: 7,332
Places Rated Rank: 128

### Casper, WY
Local Choices
66% houses, 1% condos, 13% mobile homes, 10% apartments (rent $445/month)
Houses
Price: $88,700
Property Taxes: $426
Built Before 1940: 16.1%
Energy Requirements
Heating Season: 7,553 degree days
Major Source: Natural gas/Electricity
Air-conditioning: 559 hours
Annual Costs
Mortgage and Taxes: $8,836
Utilities: $1,003
Places Rated Score: 9,839
Places Rated Rank: 270

### Cedar Rapids, IA
Local Choices
74% houses, 1% condos, 4% mobile homes, 14% apartments (rent $315/month)
Houses
Price: $59,300
Property Taxes: $972
Built Before 1940: 29.3%
Energy Requirements
Heating Season: 6,601 degree days
Major Source: Natural gas/Electricity
Air-conditioning: 340 hours
Annual Costs
Mortgage and Taxes: $6,593
Utilities: $1,181
Places Rated Score: 7,774
Places Rated Rank: 156

### Champaign–Urbana–Rantoul, IL
Local Choices
60% houses, 2% condos, 6% mobile homes, 23% apartments (rent $320/month)
Houses
Price: $65,000
Property Taxes: $1,033
Built Before 1940: 21.0%
Energy Requirements
Heating Season: 5,631 degree days
Major Source: Natural gas/Electricity
Air-conditioning: 788 hours
Annual Costs
Mortgage and Taxes: $7,193
Utilities: $1,434
Places Rated Score: 8,627
Places Rated Rank: 234

### Charleston, SC
Local Choices
67% houses, 2% condos, 7% mobile homes, 11% apartments (rent $320/month)
Houses
Price: $60,700
Property Taxes: $559
Built Before 1940: 11.9%
Energy Requirements
Heating Season: 2,146 degree days
Major Source: Natural gas/Electricity
Air-conditioning: 1,252 hours
Annual Costs
Mortgage and Taxes: $6,314
Utilities: $1,088
Places Rated Score: 7,402
Places Rated Rank: 134

### Charleston, WV
Local Choices
75% houses, 1% condos, 8% mobile homes, 7% apartments (rent $280/month)
Houses
Price: $67,500
Property Taxes: $250
Built Before 1940: 25.5%
Energy Requirements
Heating Season: 4,417 degree days
Major Source: Natural gas/Electricity
Air-conditioning: 779 hours
Annual Costs
Mortgage and Taxes: $6,644
Utilities: $1,145
Places Rated Score: 7,789
Places Rated Rank: 160

### Charlotte–Gastonia–Rock Hill, NC–SC
Local Choices
72% houses, 1% condos, 7% mobile homes, 12% apartments (rent $305/month)
Houses
Price: $59,200
Property Taxes: $574
Built Before 1940: 15.4%
Energy Requirements
Heating Season: 3,218 degree days
Major Source: Natural gas/Electricity
Air-conditioning: 1,138 hours
Annual Costs
Mortgage and Taxes: $6,188
Utilities: $981
Places Rated Score: 7,169
Places Rated Rank: 116

### Charlottesville, VA
Local Choices
65% houses, 1% condos, 5% mobile homes, 17% apartments (rent $375/month)
Houses
Price: $75,400
Property Taxes: $1,086
Built Before 1940: 21.3%
Energy Requirements
Heating Season: 4,162 degree days
Major Source: Natural gas/Electricity
Air-conditioning: 826 hours
Annual Costs
Mortgage and Taxes: $8,237
Utilities: $1,294
Places Rated Score: 9,531
Places Rated Rank: 263

### Chattanooga, TN–GA
Local Choices
74% houses, 1% condos, 6% mobile homes, 8% apartments (rent $290/month)
Houses
Price: $50,600
Property Taxes: $627
Built Before 1940: 17.7%
Energy Requirements
Heating Season: 3,505 degree days
Major Source: Total electric
Air-conditioning: 1,250 hours
Annual Costs
Mortgage and Taxes: $5,419
Utilities: $770
Places Rated Score: 6,189
Places Rated Rank: 30

### Chicago, IL
Local Choices
46% houses, 9% condos, 1% mobile homes, 27% apartments (rent $325/month)
Houses
Price: $86,000
Property Taxes: $1,367
Built Before 1940: 34.7%
Energy Requirements
Heating Season: 6,497 degree days
Major Source: Natural gas/Electricity
Air-conditioning: 727 hours
Annual Costs
Mortgage and Taxes: $9,519
Utilities: $1,394
Places Rated Score: 10,913
Places Rated Rank: 295

### Chico, CA
Local Choices
67% houses, 1% condos, 13% mobile homes, 11% apartments (rent $325/month)
Houses
Price: $73,000
Property Taxes: $751
Built Before 1940: 12.9%
Energy Requirements
Heating Season: 2,865 degree days
Major Source: Natural gas/Electricity
Air-conditioning: 1,410 hours
Annual Costs
Mortgage and Taxes: $7,666
Utilities: $921
Places Rated Score: 8,587
Places Rated Rank: 232

### Cincinnati, OH–KY–IN
Local Choices
63% houses, 1% condos, 2% mobile homes, 19% apartments (rent $270/month)
Houses
Price: $63,900
Property Taxes: $735
Built Before 1940: 30.3%
Energy Requirements
Heating Season: 4,844 degree days
Major Source: Natural gas/Electricity
Air-conditioning: 849 hours
Annual Costs
Mortgage and Taxes: $6,791
Utilities: $1,352
Places Rated Score: 8,143
Places Rated Rank: 191

## ★ Clarksville–Hopkinsville, TN–KY

**Local Choices**
70% houses, 1% condos, 8% mobile homes, 9% apartments (rent $290/month)

**Houses**
Price: $48,700
Property Taxes: $604
Built Before 1940: 10.5%

**Energy Requirements**
Heating Season: 3,757 degree days
Major Source: Total electric
Air-conditioning: 1,260 hours

**Annual Costs**
Mortgage and Taxes: $5,222
Utilities: $785

Places Rated Score: 6,007
Places Rated Rank: 22

## Cleveland, OH

**Local Choices**
63% houses, 3% condos, 1% mobile homes, 19% apartments (rent $300/month)

**Houses**
Price: $70,800
Property Taxes: $814
Built Before 1940: 32.8%

**Energy Requirements**
Heating Season: 6,154 degree days
Major Source: Natural gas/Electricity
Air-conditioning: 523 hours

**Annual Costs**
Mortgage and Taxes: $7,523
Utilities: $1,645

Places Rated Score: 9,168
Places Rated Rank: 251

## Colorado Springs, CO

**Local Choices**
67% houses, 3% condos, 4% mobile homes, 19% apartments (rent $330/month)

**Houses**
Price: $72,600
Property Taxes: $734
Built Before 1940: 12.5%

**Energy Requirements**
Heating Season: 6,473 degree days
Major Source: Natural gas/Electricity
Air-conditioning: 644 hours

**Annual Costs**
Mortgage and Taxes: $7,619
Utilities: $890

Places Rated Score: 8,509
Places Rated Rank: 224

## Columbia, MO

**Local Choices**
60% houses, 1% condos, 9% mobile homes, 15% apartments (rent $305/month)

**Houses**
Price: $60,100
Property Taxes: $704
Built Before 1940: 14.1%

**Energy Requirements**
Heating Season: 5,078 degree days
Major Source: Natural gas/Electricity
Air-conditioning: 1,066 hours

**Annual Costs**
Mortgage and Taxes: $6,405
Utilities: $1,297

Places Rated Score: 7,702
Places Rated Rank: 150

## Columbia, SC

**Local Choices**
71% houses, 2% condos, 7% mobile homes, 13% apartments (rent $320/month)

**Houses**
Price: $61,800
Property Taxes: $569
Built Before 1940: 9.7%

**Energy Requirements**
Heating Season: 2,347 degree days
Major Source: Natural gas/Electricity
Air-conditioning: 1,359 hours

**Annual Costs**
Mortgage and Taxes: $6,431
Utilities: $1,088

Places Rated Score: 7,519
Places Rated Rank: 140

## ★ Columbus, GA–AL

**Local Choices**
70% houses, 1% condos, 4% mobile homes, 15% apartments (rent $245/month)

**Houses**
Price: $45,100
Property Taxes: $546
Built Before 1940: 14.6%

**Energy Requirements**
Heating Season: 2,378 degree days
Major Source: Natural gas/Electricity
Air-conditioning: 1,511 hours

**Annual Costs**
Mortgage and Taxes: $4,825
Utilities: $992

Places Rated Score: 5,817
Places Rated Rank: 17

## Columbus, OH

**Local Choices**
68% houses, 2% condos, 2% mobile homes, 16% apartments (rent $290/month)

**Houses**
Price: $62,300
Property Taxes: $716
Built Before 1940: 24.7%

**Energy Requirements**
Heating Season: 5,702 degree days
Major Source: Natural gas/Electricity
Air-conditioning: 759 hours

**Annual Costs**
Mortgage and Taxes: $6,618
Utilities: $1,475

Places Rated Score: 8,093
Places Rated Rank: 185

## Corpus Christi, TX

**Local Choices**
73% houses, 2% condos, 3% mobile homes, 14% apartments (rent $320/month)

**Houses**
Price: $54,300
Property Taxes: $761
Built Before 1940: 9.0%

**Energy Requirements**
Heating Season: 930 degree days
Major Source: Natural gas/Electricity
Air-conditioning: 2,531 hours

**Annual Costs**
Mortgage and Taxes: $5,911
Utilities: $1,018

Places Rated Score: 6,929
Places Rated Rank: 96

## ★ Cumberland, MD–WV

**Local Choices**
77% houses, 4% mobile homes, 6% apartments (rent $230/month)

**Houses**
Price: $45,000
Property Taxes: $617
Built Before 1940: 52.8%

**Energy Requirements**
Heating Season: 5,916 degree days
Major Source: Natural gas/Electricity
Air-conditioning: 596 hours

**Annual Costs**
Mortgage and Taxes: $4,885
Utilities: $1,169

Places Rated Score: 6,054
Places Rated Rank: 24

## Dallas, TX

**Local Choices**
67% houses, 2% condos, 2% mobile homes, 23% apartments (rent $360/month)

**Houses**
Price: $76,600
Property Taxes: $1,073
Built Before 1940: 8.6%

**Energy Requirements**
Heating Season: 2,290 degree days
Major Source: Natural gas/Electricity
Air-conditioning: 2,304 hours

**Annual Costs**
Mortgage and Taxes: $8,338
Utilities: $980

Places Rated Score: 9,318
Places Rated Rank: 256

## Danbury, CT

**Local Choices**
62% houses, 3% condos, 7% apartments (rent $420/month)

**Houses**
Price: $116,300
Property Taxes: $1,779
Built Before 1940: 25.0%

**Energy Requirements**
Heating Season: 6,250 degree days
Major Source: Oil/Electricity
Air-conditioning: 476 hours

**Annual Costs**
Mortgage and Taxes: $12,803
Utilities: $1,617

Places Rated Score: 14,420
Places Rated Rank: 320

## ★ Danville, VA

**Local Choices**
78% houses, 1% condos, 8% mobile homes, 7% apartments (rent $225/month)

**Houses**
Price: $42,100
Property Taxes: $607
Built Before 1940: 24.8%

**Energy Requirements**
Heating Season: 3,702 degree days
Major Source: Oil/Electricity
Air-conditioning: 600 hours

**Annual Costs**
Mortgage and Taxes: $4,602
Utilities: $1,107

Places Rated Score: 5,709
Places Rated Rank: 11

## Davenport–Rock Island–Moline, IA–IL

Local Choices
74% houses, 1% condos, 3% mobile homes, 12% apartments (rent $315/month)

Houses
Price: $62,500
Property Taxes: $1,025
Built Before 1940: 30.3%

Energy Requirements
Heating Season: 6,395 degree days
Major Source: Natural gas/Electricity
Air-conditioning: 703 hours

Annual Costs
Mortgage and Taxes: $6,951
Utilities: $1,132

Places Rated Score: 8,083
Places Rated Rank: 182

## Dayton–Springfield, OH

Local Choices
81% houses, 2% condos, 2% mobile homes, 11% apartments (rent $285/month)

Houses
Price: $57,300
Property Taxes: $659
Built Before 1940: 26.0%

Energy Requirements
Heating Season: 5,641 degree days
Major Source: Natural gas/Electricity
Air-conditioning: 679 hours

Annual Costs
Mortgage and Taxes: $6,092
Utilities: $1,543

Places Rated Score: 7,635
Places Rated Rank: 145

## Daytona Beach, FL

Local Choices
69% houses, 7% condos, 10% mobile homes, 11% apartments (rent $325/month)

Houses
Price: $57,800
Property Taxes: $595
Built Before 1940: 9.4%

Energy Requirements
Heating Season: 987 degree days
Major Source: Total electric
Air-conditioning: 1,597 hours

Annual Costs
Mortgage and Taxes: $6,071
Utilities: $1,132

Places Rated Score: 7,203
Places Rated Rank: 118

## Decatur, IL

Local Choices
78% houses, 4% mobile homes, 10% apartments (rent $300/month)

Houses
Price: $54,000
Property Taxes: $859
Built Before 1940: 32.9%

Energy Requirements
Heating Season: 5,344 degree days
Major Source: Natural gas/Electricity
Air-conditioning: 867 hours

Annual Costs
Mortgage and Taxes: $5,981
Utilities: $1,414

Places Rated Score: 7,395
Places Rated Rank: 133

## Denver, CO

Local Choices
66% houses, 7% condos, 3% mobile homes, 21% apartments (rent $370/month)

Houses
Price: $91,500
Property Taxes: $924
Built Before 1940: 14.4%

Energy Requirements
Heating Season: 6,016 degree days
Major Source: Natural gas/Electricity
Air-conditioning: 659 hours

Annual Costs
Mortgage and Taxes: $9,600
Utilities: $1,189

Places Rated Score: 10,789
Places Rated Rank: 293

## Des Moines, IA

Local Choices
72% houses, 1% condos, 3% mobile homes, 16% apartments (rent $335/month)

Houses
Price: $60,900
Property Taxes: $999
Built Before 1940: 29.4%

Energy Requirements
Heating Season: 6,710 degree days
Major Source: Natural gas/Electricity
Air-conditioning: 738 hours

Annual Costs
Mortgage and Taxes: $6,773
Utilities: $1,255

Places Rated Score: 8,028
Places Rated Rank: 177

## Detroit, MI

Local Choices
74% houses, 3% condos, 2% mobile homes, 13% apartments (rent $330/month)

Houses
Price: $59,100
Property Taxes: $1,583
Built Before 1940: 24.1%

Energy Requirements
Heating Season: 6,228 degree days
Major Source: Natural gas/Electricity
Air-conditioning: 498 hours

Annual Costs
Mortgage and Taxes: $7,184
Utilities: $1,341

Places Rated Score: 8,525
Places Rated Rank: 227

## ★ Dothan, AL

Local Choices
76% houses, 10% mobile homes, 5% apartments (rent $260/month)

Houses
Price: $48,000
Property Taxes: $197
Built Before 1940: 11.3%

Energy Requirements
Heating Season: 958 degree days
Major Source: Total electric
Air-conditioning: 1,406 hours

Annual Costs
Mortgage and Taxes: $4,750
Utilities: $958

Places Rated Score: 5,708
Places Rated Rank: 10

## Dubuque, IA

Local Choices
71% houses, 4% mobile homes, 9% apartments (rent $280/month)

Houses
Price: $61,200
Property Taxes: $1,004
Built Before 1940: 42.6%

Energy Requirements
Heating Season: 7,277 degree days
Major Source: Natural gas/Electricity
Air-conditioning: 381 hours

Annual Costs
Mortgage and Taxes: $6,804
Utilities: $1,189

Places Rated Score: 7,993
Places Rated Rank: 176

## ★ Duluth, MN–WI

Local Choices
70% houses, 5% mobile homes, 12% apartments (rent $265/month)

Houses
Price: $46,900
Property Taxes: $361
Built Before 1940: 47.3%

Energy Requirements
Heating Season: 9,757 degree days
Major Source: Oil/Electricity
Air-conditioning: 132 hours

Annual Costs
Mortgage and Taxes: $4,810
Utilities: $1,230

Places Rated Score: 6,040
Places Rated Rank: 23

## East St. Louis–Belleville, IL

Local Choices
73% houses, 1% condos, 9% mobile homes, 8% apartments (rent $285/month)

Houses
Price: $47,600
Property Taxes: $757
Built Before 1940: 26.4%

Energy Requirements
Heating Season: 4,486 degree days
Major Source: Natural gas/Electricity
Air-conditioning: 941 hours

Annual Costs
Mortgage and Taxes: $5,273
Utilities: $1,228

Places Rated Score: 6,501
Places Rated Rank: 53

## Eau Claire, WI

Local Choices
75% houses, 4% mobile homes, 8% apartments (rent $280/month)

Houses
Price: $50,700
Property Taxes: $1,020
Built Before 1940: 35.5%

Energy Requirements
Heating Season: 8,388 degree days
Major Source: Oil/Electricity
Air-conditioning: 496 hours

Annual Costs
Mortgage and Taxes: $5,829
Utilities: $1,249

Places Rated Score: 7,078
Places Rated Rank: 108

## El Paso, TX
Local Choices
  68% houses, 2% condos, 3% mobile homes, 21% apartments (rent $260/month)
Houses
  Price: $57,800
  Property Taxes: $809
  Built Before 1940: 11.0%
Energy Requirements
  Heating Season: 2,678 degree days
  Major Source: Natural gas/Electricity
  Air-conditioning: 1,860 hours
Annual Costs
  Mortgage and Taxes: $6,288
  Utilities: $1,055
Places Rated Score: 7,343
Places Rated Rank: 130

## Elkhart–Goshen, IN
Local Choices
  77% houses, 6% mobile homes, 8% apartments (rent $280/month)
Houses
  Price: $50,900
  Property Taxes: $606
  Built Before 1940: 32.1%
Energy Requirements
  Heating Season: 6,272 degree days
  Major Source: Natural gas/Electricity
  Air-conditioning: 534 hours
Annual Costs
  Mortgage and Taxes: $5,432
  Utilities: $1,141
Places Rated Score: 6,573
Places Rated Rank: 59

## Elmira, NY
Local Choices
  70% houses, 4% mobile homes, 8% apartments (rent $275/month)
Houses
  Price: $48,300
  Property Taxes: $1,241
  Built Before 1940: 47.2%
Energy Requirements
  Heating Season: 6,642 degree days
  Major Source: Natural gas/Electricity
  Air-conditioning: 420 hours
Annual Costs
  Mortgage and Taxes: $5,820
  Utilities: $1,258
Places Rated Score: 7,078
Places Rated Rank: 108

## Enid, OK
Local Choices
  83% houses, 5% mobile homes, 6% apartments (rent $320/month)
Houses
  Price: $58,000
  Property Taxes: $429
  Built Before 1940: 25.4%
Energy Requirements
  Heating Season: 3,718 degree days
  Major Source: Natural gas/Electricity
  Air-conditioning: 1,521 hours
Annual Costs
  Mortgage and Taxes: $5,925
  Utilities: $904
Places Rated Score: 6,829
Places Rated Rank: 88

## Erie, PA
Local Choices
  70% houses, 1% condos, 5% mobile homes, 8% apartments (rent $290/month)

Houses
  Price: $57,100
  Property Taxes: $930
  Built Before 1940: 40.1%
Energy Requirements
  Heating Season: 6,851 degree days
  Major Source: Natural gas/Electricity
  Air-conditioning: 769 hours
Annual Costs
  Mortgage and Taxes: $6,338
  Utilities: $1,377
Places Rated Score: 7,715
Places Rated Rank: 151

## Eugene–Springfield, OR
Local Choices
  70% houses, 1% condos, 8% mobile homes, 14% apartments (rent $355/month)
Houses
  Price: $76,800
  Property Taxes: $1,581
  Built Before 1940: 10.8%
Energy Requirements
  Heating Season: 4,739 degree days
  Major Source: Total electric
  Air-conditioning: 441 hours
Annual Costs
  Mortgage and Taxes: $8,857
  Utilities: $513
Places Rated Score: 9,370
Places Rated Rank: 259

## Evansville, IN–KY
Local Choices
  76% houses, 1% condos, 4% mobile homes, 10% apartments (rent $275/month)
Houses
  Price: $52,700
  Property Taxes: $627
  Built Before 1940: 31.6%
Energy Requirements
  Heating Season: 4,624 degree days
  Major Source: Natural gas/Electricity
  Air-conditioning: 1,195 hours
Annual Costs
  Mortgage and Taxes: $5,622
  Utilities: $1,121
Places Rated Score: 6,743
Places Rated Rank: 78

## Fall River, MA–RI
Local Choices
  48% houses, 1% mobile homes, 16% apartments (rent $245/month)
Houses
  Price: $63,400
  Property Taxes: $1,542
  Built Before 1940: 55.2%
Energy Requirements
  Heating Season: 5,774 degree days
  Major Source: Natural gas/Electricity
  Air-conditioning: 164 hours
Annual Costs
  Mortgage and Taxes: $7,556
  Utilities: $1,461
Places Rated Score: 9,017
Places Rated Rank: 248

## Fargo–Moorhead, ND–MN
Local Choices
  59% houses, 4% condos, 5% mobile homes, 23% apartments (rent $285/month)
Houses
  Price: $65,500

Property Taxes: $721
  Built Before 1940: 25.8%
Energy Requirements
  Heating Season: 9,271 degree days
  Major Source: Oil/Electricity
  Air-conditioning: 409 hours
Annual Costs
  Mortgage and Taxes: $6,931
  Utilities: $1,237
Places Rated Score: 8,168
Places Rated Rank: 192

## Fayetteville, NC
Local Choices
  72% houses, 1% condos, 10% mobile homes, 9% apartments (rent $300/month)
Houses
  Price: $49,700
  Property Taxes: $482
  Built Before 1940: 5.7%
Energy Requirements
  Heating Season: 3,073 degree days
  Major Source: Total electric
  Air-conditioning: 1,260 hours
Annual Costs
  Mortgage and Taxes: $5,194
  Utilities: $1,080
Places Rated Score: 6,274
Places Rated Rank: 36

## Fayetteville–Springdale, AR
Local Choices
  74% houses, 7% mobile homes, 11% apartments (rent $280/month)
Houses
  Price: $53,900
  Property Taxes: $765
  Built Before 1940: 14.9%
Energy Requirements
  Heating Season: 3,839 degree days
  Major Source: Natural gas/Electricity
  Air-conditioning: 1,207 hours
Annual Costs
  Mortgage and Taxes: $5,873
  Utilities: $813
Places Rated Score: 6,686
Places Rated Rank: 69

## Fitchburg–Leominster, MA
Local Choices
  55% houses, 1% mobile homes, 18% apartments (rent $295/month)
Houses
  Price: $55,900
  Property Taxes: $1,359
  Built Before 1940: 48.2%
Energy Requirements
  Heating Season: 6,475 degree days
  Major Source: Oil/Electricity
  Air-conditioning: 297 hours
Annual Costs
  Mortgage and Taxes: $6,659
  Utilities: $1,593
Places Rated Score: 8,252
Places Rated Rank: 200

## Flint, MI
Local Choices
  78% houses, 1% condos, 5% mobile homes, 11% apartments (rent $320/month)
Houses
  Price: $48,500
  Property Taxes: $1,301
  Built Before 1940: 21.7%

Energy Requirements
Heating Season: 7,041 degree days
Major Source: Natural gas/Electricity
Air-conditioning: 509 hours
Annual Costs
Mortgage and Taxes: $5,903
Utilities: $1,301
Places Rated Score: 7,204
Places Rated Rank: 119

### ★ Florence, AL
Local Choices
58% houses, 6% mobile homes, 5% apartments (rent $265/month)
Houses
Price: $51,800
Property Taxes: $213
Built Before 1940: 14.3%
Energy Requirements
Heating Season: 836 degree days
Major Source: Total electric
Air-conditioning: 1,431 hours
Annual Costs
Mortgage and Taxes: $5,126
Utilities: $836
Places Rated Score: 5,962
Places Rated Rank: 21

### Florence, SC
Local Choices
76% houses, 1% condos, 12% mobile homes, 4% apartments (rent $260/month)
Houses
Price: $52,200
Property Taxes: $480
Built Before 1940: 12.8%
Energy Requirements
Heating Season: 2,669 degree days
Major Source: Total electric
Air-conditioning: 1,210 hours
Annual Costs
Mortgage and Taxes: $5,430
Utilities: $1,078
Places Rated Score: 6,508
Places Rated Rank: 54

### Fort Collins–Loveland, CO
Local Choices
67% houses, 4% condos, 8% mobile homes, 14% apartments (rent $375/month)
Houses
Price: $83,700
Property Taxes: $845
Built Before 1940: 13.9%
Energy Requirements
Heating Season: 6,599 degree days
Major Source: Natural gas/Electricity
Air-conditioning: 647 hours
Annual Costs
Mortgage and Taxes: $8,778
Utilities: $1,173
Places Rated Score: 9,951
Places Rated Rank: 276

### Fort Lauderdale–Hollywood–Pompano Beach, FL
Local Choices
49% houses, 32% condos, 3% mobile homes, 16% apartments (rent $425/month)
Houses
Price: $92,100
Property Taxes: $949
Built Before 1940: 1.7%

Energy Requirements
Heating Season: 244 degree days
Major Source: Total electric
Air-conditioning: 2,342 hours
Annual Costs
Mortgage and Taxes: $9,678
Utilities: $1,132
Places Rated Score: 10,810
Places Rated Rank: 294

### Fort Myers, FL
Local Choices
60% houses, 18% condos, 13% mobile homes, 8% apartments (rent $370/month)
Houses
Price: $77,700
Property Taxes: $800
Built Before 1940: 3.9%
Energy Requirements
Heating Season: 457 degree days
Major Source: Total electric
Air-conditioning: 1,863 hours
Annual Costs
Mortgage and Taxes: $8,166
Utilities: $1,132
Places Rated Score: 9,298
Places Rated Rank: 255

### Fort Pierce, FL
Local Choices
63% houses, 14% condos, 13% mobile homes, 9% apartments (rent $350/month)
Houses
Price: $75,000
Property Taxes: $773
Built Before 1940: 4.8%
Energy Requirements
Heating Season: 503 degree days
Major Source: Total electric
Air-conditioning: 2,276 hours
Annual Costs
Mortgage and Taxes: $7,885
Utilities: $957
Places Rated Score: 8,842
Places Rated Rank: 243

### ★ Fort Smith, AR–OK
Local Choices
80% houses, 6% mobile homes, 8% apartments (rent $245/month)
Houses
Price: $45,000
Property Taxes: $640
Built Before 1940: 18.1%
Energy Requirements
Heating Season: 3,336 degree days
Major Source: Natural gas/Electricity
Air-conditioning: 1,534 hours
Annual Costs
Mortgage and Taxes: $4,912
Utilities: $872
Places Rated Score: 5,784
Places Rated Rank: 15

### Fort Walton Beach, FL
Local Choices
71% houses, 8% condos, 11% mobile homes, 9% apartments (rent $310/month)
Houses
Price: $63,800
Property Taxes: $657
Built Before 1940: 3.4%
Energy Requirements
Heating Season: 1,361 degree days

Major Source: Natural gas/Electricity
Air-conditioning: 1,788 hours
Annual Costs
Mortgage and Taxes: $6,706
Utilities: $848
Places Rated Score: 7,554
Places Rated Rank: 141

### Fort Wayne, IN
Local Choices
76% houses, 1% condos, 4% mobile homes, 10% apartments (rent $285/month)
Houses
Price: $52,200
Property Taxes: $621
Built Before 1940: 30.2%
Energy Requirements
Heating Season: 6,209 degree days
Major Source: Natural gas/Electricity
Air-conditioning: 607 hours
Annual Costs
Mortgage and Taxes: $5,567
Utilities: $1,166
Places Rated Score: 6,733
Places Rated Rank: 77

### Fort Worth–Arlington, TX
Local Choices
75% houses, 1% condos, 4% mobile homes, 14% apartments (rent $350/month)
Houses
Price: $63,700
Property Taxes: $892
Built Before 1940: 10.2%
Energy Requirements
Heating Season: 2,382 degree days
Major Source: Natural gas/Electricity
Air-conditioning: 2,095 hours
Annual Costs
Mortgage and Taxes: $6,932
Utilities: $1,024
Places Rated Score: 7,956
Places Rated Rank: 174

### Fresno, CA
Local Choices
71% houses, 2% condos, 4% mobile homes, 16% apartments (rent $335/month)
Houses
Price: $79,700
Property Taxes: $820
Built Before 1940: 12.6%
Energy Requirements
Heating Season: 2,650 degree days
Major Source: Natural gas/Electricity
Air-conditioning: 1,364 hours
Annual Costs
Mortgage and Taxes: $8,370
Utilities: $921
Places Rated Score: 9,291
Places Rated Rank: 254

### ★ Gadsden, AL
Local Choices
82% houses, 7% mobile homes, 5% apartments (rent $235/month)
Houses
Price: $43,400
Property Taxes: $178
Built Before 1940: 18.9%
Energy Requirements
Heating Season: 3,059 degree days
Major Source: Natural gas/Electricity
Air-conditioning: 1,401 hours

Annual Costs
Mortgage and Taxes: $4,293
Utilities: $1,089
Places Rated Score: 5,382
Places Rated Rank: 4

## Gainesville, FL
Local Choices
59% houses, 1% condos, 11% mobile homes, 20% apartments (rent $335/month)
Houses
Price: $60,600
Property Taxes: $624
Built Before 1940: 8.5%
Energy Requirements
Heating Season: 1,081 degree days
Major Source: Total electric
Air-conditioning: 1,724 hours
Annual Costs
Mortgage and Taxes: $6,366
Utilities: $1,022
Places Rated Score: 7,388
Places Rated Rank: 132

## Galveston–Texas City, TX
Local Choices
73% houses, 1% condos, 5% mobile homes, 14% apartments (rent $335/month)
Houses
Price: $61,800
Property Taxes: $865
Built Before 1940: 15.6%
Energy Requirements
Heating Season: 1,224 degree days
Major Source: Natural gas/Electricity
Air-conditioning: 2,639 hours
Annual Costs
Mortgage and Taxes: $6,723
Utilities: $1,044
Places Rated Score: 7,767
Places Rated Rank: 153

## Gary–Hammond, IN
Local Choices
71% houses, 1% condos, 4% mobile homes, 12% apartments (rent $300/month)
Houses
Price: $57,700
Property Taxes: $687
Built Before 1940: 22.7%
Energy Requirements
Heating Season: 6,165 degree days
Major Source: Natural gas/Electricity
Air-conditioning: 525 hours
Annual Costs
Mortgage and Taxes: $6,160
Utilities: $1,481
Places Rated Score: 7,641
Places Rated Rank: 146

## Glens Falls, NY
Local Choices
71% houses, 6% mobile homes, 6% apartments (rent $295/month)
Houses
Price: $48,800
Property Taxes: $1,253
Built Before 1940: 51.5%
Energy Requirements
Heating Season: 6,421 degree days
Major Source: Oil/Electricity
Air-conditioning: 277 hours

Annual Costs
Mortgage and Taxes: $5,874
Utilities: $1,246
Places Rated Score: 7,120
Places Rated Rank: 112

## Grand Forks, ND
Local Choices
54% houses, 4% condos, 6% mobile homes, 24% apartments (rent $270/month)
Houses
Price: $63,400
Property Taxes: $698
Built Before 1940: 24.3%
Energy Requirements
Heating Season: 9,876 degree days
Major Source: Oil/Electricity
Air-conditioning: 652 hours
Annual Costs
Mortgage and Taxes: $6,709
Utilities: $1,189
Places Rated Score: 7,898
Places Rated Rank: 169

## Grand Rapids, MI
Local Choices
74% houses, 2% condos, 4% mobile homes, 9% apartments (rent $295/month)
Houses
Price: $53,300
Property Taxes: $1,428
Built Before 1940: 29.5%
Energy Requirements
Heating Season: 6,801 degree days
Major Source: Natural gas/Electricity
Air-conditioning: 420 hours
Annual Costs
Mortgage and Taxes: $6,479
Utilities: $1,301
Places Rated Score: 7,780
Places Rated Rank: 159

## Great Falls, MT
Local Choices
67% houses, 2% condos, 8% mobile homes, 13% apartments (rent $280/month)
Houses
Price: $58,300
Property Taxes: $665
Built Before 1940: 24.6%
Energy Requirements
Heating Season: 7,652 degree days
Major Source: Natural gas/Electricity
Air-conditioning: 286 hours
Annual Costs
Mortgage and Taxes: $6,195
Utilities: $948
Places Rated Score: 7,143
Places Rated Rank: 114

## Greeley, CO
Local Choices
67% houses, 1% condos, 10% mobile homes, 13% apartments (rent $315/month)
Houses
Price: $67,400
Property Taxes: $681
Built Before 1940: 22.4%
Energy Requirements
Heating Season: 6,639 degree days
Major Source: Natural gas/Electricity
Air-conditioning: 647 hours

Annual Costs
Mortgage and Taxes: $7,073
Utilities: $1,145
Places Rated Score: 8,218
Places Rated Rank: 194

## Green Bay, WI
Local Choices
71% houses, 2% mobile homes, 11% apartments (rent $285/month)
Houses
Price: $62,100
Property Taxes: $1,248
Built Before 1940: 24.5%
Energy Requirements
Heating Season: 8,098 degree days
Major Source: Natural gas/Electricity
Air-conditioning: 264 hours
Annual Costs
Mortgage and Taxes: $7,136
Utilities: $1,265
Places Rated Score: 8,401
Places Rated Rank: 220

## Greensboro–Winston-Salem–High Point, NC
Local Choices
74% houses, 1% condos, 7% mobile homes, 10% apartments (rent $280/month)
Houses
Price: $58,200
Property Taxes: $565
Built Before 1940: 15.9%
Energy Requirements
Heating Season: 3,825 degree days
Major Source: Oil/Electricity
Air-conditioning: 916 hours
Annual Costs
Mortgage and Taxes: $6,083
Utilities: $981
Places Rated Score: 7,064
Places Rated Rank: 106

## Greenville–Spartanburg, SC
Local Choices
76% houses, 1% condos, 8% mobile homes, 9% apartments (rent $275/month)
Houses
Price: $52,000
Property Taxes: $478
Built Before 1940: 16.1%
Energy Requirements
Heating Season: 3,095 degree days
Major Source: Total electric
Air-conditioning: 1,094 hours
Annual Costs
Mortgage and Taxes: $5,404
Utilities: $932
Places Rated Score: 6,336
Places Rated Rank: 41

## Hagerstown, MD
Local Choices
71% houses, 1% condos, 4% mobile homes, 11% apartments (rent $275/month)
Houses
Price: $61,200
Property Taxes: $838
Built Before 1940: 40.0%
Energy Requirements
Heating Season: 5,152 degree days
Major Source: Natural gas/Electricity
Air-conditioning: 702 hours

Annual Costs
    Mortgage and Taxes: $6,634
    Utilities: $1,129
Places Rated Score: 7,763
Places Rated Rank: 152

## Hamilton–Middletown, OH
Local Choices
    74% houses, 2% condos, 4% mobile
    homes, 11% apartments (rent
    $300/month)
Houses
    Price: $65,300
    Property Taxes: $751
    Built Before 1940: 23.1%
Energy Requirements
    Heating Season: 5,015 degree days
    Major Source: Natural gas/Electricity
    Air-conditioning: 928 hours
Annual Costs
    Mortgage and Taxes: $6,940
    Utilities: $1,287
Places Rated Score: 8,227
Places Rated Rank: 196

## Harrisburg–Lebanon–Carlisle, PA
Local Choices
    72% houses, 1% condos, 5% mobile
    homes, 12% apartments (rent
    $315/month)
Houses
    Price: $59,300
    Property Taxes: $966
    Built Before 1940: 36.3%
Energy Requirements
    Heating Season: 5,224 degree days
    Major Source: Oil/Electricity
    Air-conditioning: 744 hours
Annual Costs
    Mortgage and Taxes: $6,584
    Utilities: $1,307
Places Rated Score: 7,891
Places Rated Rank: 168

## Hartford, CT
Local Choices
    70% houses, 6% condos, 1% mobile
    homes, 20% apartments (rent
    $350/month)
Houses
    Price: $91,100
    Property Taxes: $1,395
    Built Before 1940: 27.1%
Energy Requirements
    Heating Season: 6,350 degree days
    Major Source: Oil/Electricity
    Air-conditioning: 476 hours
Annual Costs
    Mortgage and Taxes: $10,035
    Utilities: $1,617
Places Rated Score: 11,652
Places Rated Rank: 302

## Hickory, NC
Local Choices
    50% houses, 12% mobile homes, 4%
    apartments (rent $265/month)
Houses
    Price: $54,100
    Property Taxes: $524
    Built Before 1940: 15.8%
Energy Requirements
    Heating Season: 3,831 degree days
    Major Source: Oil/Electricity
    Air-conditioning: 1,040 hours

Annual Costs
    Mortgage and Taxes: $5,648
    Utilities: $1,112
Places Rated Score: 6,760
Places Rated Rank: 82

## Honolulu, HI
Local Choices
    48% houses, 24% condos, 28%
    apartments (rent $450/month)
Houses
    Price: $163,400
    Property Taxes: $588
    Built Before 1940: 8.4%
Energy Requirements
    Heating Season: 0 degree days
    Major Source: Total electric
    Air-conditioning: 1,342 hours
Annual Costs
    Mortgage and Taxes: $16,075
    Utilities: $946
Places Rated Score: 17,021
Places Rated Rank: 326

## Houma–Thibodaux, LA
Local Choices
    75% houses, 11% mobile homes, 6%
    apartments (rent $290/month)
Houses
    Price: $64,400
    Property Taxes: $97
    Built Before 1940: 12.3%
Energy Requirements
    Heating Season: 1,215 degree days
    Major Source: Natural gas/Electricity
    Air-conditioning: 1,727 hours
Annual Costs
    Mortgage and Taxes: $6,205
    Utilities: $889
Places Rated Score: 7,094
Places Rated Rank: 110

## Houston, TX
Local Choices
    64% houses, 4% condos, 3% mobile
    homes, 24% apartments (rent
    $390/month)
Houses
    Price: $80,100
    Property Taxes: $1,122
    Built Before 1940: 6.9%
Energy Requirements
    Heating Season: 1,434 degree days
    Major Source: Natural gas/Electricity
    Air-conditioning: 1,894 hours
Annual Costs
    Mortgage and Taxes: $8,716
    Utilities: $1,044
Places Rated Score: 9,760
Places Rated Rank: 269

## Huntington–Ashland, WV–KY–OH
Local Choices
    72% houses, 8% mobile homes, 6%
    apartments (rent $260/month)
Houses
    Price: $55,700
    Property Taxes: $206
    Built Before 1940: 29.5%
Energy Requirements
    Heating Season: 4,073 degree days
    Major Source: Natural gas/Electricity
    Air-conditioning: 979 hours
Annual Costs
    Mortgage and Taxes: $5,487
    Utilities: $1,145
Places Rated Score: 6,632
Places Rated Rank: 65

## Huntsville, AL
Local Choices
    83% houses, 1% condos, 4% mobile
    homes, 12% apartments (rent
    $280/month)
Houses
    Price: $56,100
    Property Taxes: $230
    Built Before 1940: 7.3%
Energy Requirements
    Heating Season: 738 degree days
    Major Source: Total electric
    Air-conditioning: 1,240 hours
Annual Costs
    Mortgage and Taxes: $5,545
    Utilities: $738
Places Rated Score: 6,283
Places Rated Rank: 37

## Indianapolis, IN
Local Choices
    72% houses, 1% condos, 3% mobile
    homes, 16% apartments (rent
    $290/month)
Houses
    Price: $55,100
    Property Taxes: $655
    Built Before 1940: 24.9%
Energy Requirements
    Heating Season: 5,577 degree days
    Major Source: Natural gas/Electricity
    Air-conditioning: 763 hours
Annual Costs
    Mortgage and Taxes: $5,873
    Utilities: $1,139
Places Rated Score: 7,012
Places Rated Rank: 101

## Iowa City, IA
Local Choices
    54% houses, 1% condos, 7% mobile
    homes, 28% apartments (rent
    $320/month)
Houses
    Price: $74,600
    Property Taxes: $1,224
    Built Before 1940: 23.3%
Energy Requirements
    Heating Season: 6,404 degree days
    Major Source: Natural gas/Electricity
    Air-conditioning: 615 hours
Annual Costs
    Mortgage and Taxes: $8,297
    Utilities: $1,132
Places Rated Score: 9,429
Places Rated Rank: 260

## Jackson, MI
Local Choices
    78% houses, 1% condos, 5% mobile
    homes, 7% apartments (rent
    $300/month)
Houses
    Price: $45,200
    Property Taxes: $1,211
    Built Before 1940: 38.3%
Energy Requirements
    Heating Season: 6,755 degree days
    Major Source: Natural gas/Electricity
    Air-conditioning: 511 hours
Annual Costs
    Mortgage and Taxes: $5,493
    Utilities: $1,301
Places Rated Score: 6,794
Places Rated Rank: 85

## Jackson, MS

Local Choices
74% houses, 1% condos, 6% mobile homes, 13% apartments (rent $310/month)
Houses
Price: $61,400
Property Taxes: $467
Built Before 1940: 8.8%
Energy Requirements
Heating Season: 2,300 degree days
Major Source: Natural gas/Electricity
Air-conditioning: 1,611 hours
Annual Costs
Mortgage and Taxes: $6,288
Utilities: $957
Places Rated Score: 7,245
Places Rated Rank: 122

## Jacksonville, FL

Local Choices
68% houses, 2% condos, 8% mobile homes, 15% apartments (rent $325/month)
Houses
Price: $52,400
Property Taxes: $540
Built Before 1940: 11.3%
Energy Requirements
Heating Season: 1,327 degree days
Major Source: Total electric
Air-conditioning: 1,725 hours
Annual Costs
Mortgage and Taxes: $5,507
Utilities: $1,119
Places Rated Score: 6,626
Places Rated Rank: 64

## Jacksonville, NC

Local Choices
70% houses, 1% condos, 18% mobile homes, 6% apartments (rent $295/month)
Houses
Price: $48,400
Property Taxes: $470
Built Before 1940: 4.8%
Energy Requirements
Heating Season: 2,975 degree days
Major Source: Total electric
Air-conditioning: 1,020 hours
Annual Costs
Mortgage and Taxes: $5,062
Utilities: $1,049
Places Rated Score: 6,111
Places Rated Rank: 26

## Janesville–Beloit, WI

Local Choices
76% houses, 2% mobile homes, 8% apartments (rent $285/month)
Houses
Price: $53,900
Property Taxes: $1,083
Built Before 1940: 37.4%
Energy Requirements
Heating Season: 6,563 degree days
Major Source: Natural gas/Electricity
Air-conditioning: 234 hours
Annual Costs
Mortgage and Taxes: $6,193
Utilities: $1,254
Places Rated Score: 7,447
Places Rated Rank: 136

## Jersey City, NJ

Local Choices
12% houses, 2% condos, 41% apartments (rent $305/month)
Houses
Price: $60,700
Property Taxes: $1,548
Built Before 1940: 60.2%
Energy Requirements
Heating Season: 5,238 degree days
Major Source: Oil/Electricity
Air-conditioning: 592 hours
Annual Costs
Mortgage and Taxes: $7,302
Utilities: $1,508
Places Rated Score: 8,810
Places Rated Rank: 241

## Johnson City–Kingsport–Bristol, TN–VA

Local Choices
79% houses, 1% condos, 11% mobile homes, 8% apartments (rent $250/month)
Houses
Price: $50,300
Property Taxes: $624
Built Before 1940: 19.1%
Energy Requirements
Heating Season: 4,306 degree days
Major Source: Total electric
Air-conditioning: 850 hours
Annual Costs
Mortgage and Taxes: $5,392
Utilities: $727
Places Rated Score: 6,119
Places Rated Rank: 27

## Johnstown, PA

Local Choices
74% houses, 6% mobile homes, 6% apartments (rent $260/month)
Houses
Price: $46,300
Property Taxes: $755
Built Before 1940: 51.5%
Energy Requirements
Heating Season: 5,724 degree days
Major Source: Natural gas/Electricity
Air-conditioning: 467 hours
Annual Costs
Mortgage and Taxes: $5,147
Utilities: $1,377
Places Rated Score: 6,524
Places Rated Rank: 55

## Joliet, IL

Local Choices
77% houses, 3% condos, 2% mobile homes, 10% apartments (rent $335/month)
Houses
Price: $71,900
Property Taxes: $1,143
Built Before 1940: 22.2%
Energy Requirements
Heating Season: 6,180 degree days
Major Source: Natural gas/Electricity
Air-conditioning: 632 hours
Annual Costs
Mortgage and Taxes: $7,958
Utilities: $1,369
Places Rated Score: 9,327
Places Rated Rank: 258

## ★ Joplin, MO

Local Choices
84% houses, 5% mobile homes, 5% apartments (rent $220/month)
Houses
Price: $37,600
Property Taxes: $440
Built Before 1940: 37.2%
Energy Requirements
Heating Season: 4,188 degree days
Major Source: Natural gas/Electricity
Air-conditioning: 1,171 hours
Annual Costs
Mortgage and Taxes: $4,003
Utilities: $1,156
Places Rated Score: 5,159
Places Rated Rank: 1

## Kalamazoo, MI

Local Choices
70% houses, 2% condos, 3% mobile homes, 16% apartments (rent $310/month)
Houses
Price: $54,400
Property Taxes: $1,459
Built Before 1940: 27.1%
Energy Requirements
Heating Season: 6,281 degree days
Major Source: Natural gas/Electricity
Air-conditioning: 311 hours
Annual Costs
Mortgage and Taxes: $6,618
Utilities: $1,301
Places Rated Score: 7,919
Places Rated Rank: 172

## Kankakee, IL

Local Choices
73% houses, 5% mobile homes, 9% apartments (rent $310/month)
Houses
Price: $52,700
Property Taxes: $837
Built Before 1940: 28.4%
Energy Requirements
Heating Season: 5,980 degree days
Major Source: Natural gas/Electricity
Air-conditioning: 659 hours
Annual Costs
Mortgage and Taxes: $5,829
Utilities: $1,401
Places Rated Score: 7,230
Places Rated Rank: 120

## Kansas City, KS

Local Choices
77% houses, 2% condos, 2% mobile homes, 11% apartments (rent $360/month)
Houses
Price: $66,600
Property Taxes: $646
Built Before 1940: 19.0%
Energy Requirements
Heating Season: 5,161 degree days
Major Source: Natural gas/Electricity
Air-conditioning: 1,092 hours
Annual Costs
Mortgage and Taxes: $6,956
Utilities: $1,170
Places Rated Score: 8,126
Places Rated Rank: 189

## Kansas City, MO

Local Choices
69% houses, 1% condos, 2% mobile

homes, 16% apartments (rent
$305/month)
**Houses**
  Price: $53,200
  Property Taxes: $623
  Built Before 1940: 27.1%
**Energy Requirements**
  Heating Season: 5,161 degree days
  Major Source: Natural gas/Electricity
  Air-conditioning: 1,092 hours
**Annual Costs**
  Mortgage and Taxes: $5,667
  Utilities: $1,409
Places Rated Score: 7,076
Places Rated Rank: 107

### Kenosha, WI
Local Choices
  70% houses, 1% condos, 3% mobile
    homes, 10% apartments (rent
    $295/month)
**Houses**
  Price: $62,800
  Property Taxes: $1,262
  Built Before 1940: 32.9%
**Energy Requirements**
  Heating Season: 6,765 degree days
  Major Source: Natural gas/Electricity
  Air-conditioning: 358 hours
**Annual Costs**
  Mortgage and Taxes: $7,213
  Utilities: $1,303
Places Rated Score: 8,516
Places Rated Rank: 226

### Killeen–Temple, TX
Local Choices
  65% houses, 1% condos, 7% mobile
    homes, 15% apartments (rent
    $290/month)
**Houses**
  Price: $50,400
  Property Taxes: $706
  Built Before 1940: 9.5%
**Energy Requirements**
  Heating Season: 2,039 degree days
  Major Source: Natural gas/Electricity
  Air-conditioning: 2,194 hours
**Annual Costs**
  Mortgage and Taxes: $5,484
  Utilities: $979
Places Rated Score: 6,463
Places Rated Rank: 49

### Knoxville, TN
Local Choices
  75% houses, 1% condos, 6% mobile
    homes, 12% apartments (rent
    $280/month)
**Houses**
  Price: $55,100
  Property Taxes: $683
  Built Before 1940: 16.5%
**Energy Requirements**
  Heating Season: 3,478 degree days
  Major Source: Total electric
  Air-conditioning: 1,094 hours
**Annual Costs**
  Mortgage and Taxes: $5,907
  Utilities: $785
Places Rated Score: 6,692
Places Rated Rank: 72

### Kokomo, IN
Local Choices
  80% houses, 1% condos, 5% mobile
    homes, 7% apartments (rent
    $280/month)

**Houses**
  Price: $50,400
  Property Taxes: $600
  Built Before 1940: 35.3%
**Energy Requirements**
  Heating Season: 5,585 degree days
  Major Source: Natural gas/Electricity
  Air-conditioning: 700 hours
**Annual Costs**
  Mortgage and Taxes: $5,382
  Utilities: $1,234
Places Rated Score: 6,616
Places Rated Rank: 63

### La Crosse, WI
Local Choices
  70% houses, 4% mobile homes, 11%
    apartments (rent $285/month)
**Houses**
  Price: $61,500
  Property Taxes: $1,235
  Built Before 1940: 36.5%
**Energy Requirements**
  Heating Season: 7,417 degree days
  Major Source: Oil/Electricity
  Air-conditioning: 401 hours
**Annual Costs**
  Mortgage and Taxes: $7,061
  Utilities: $1,249
Places Rated Score: 8,310
Places Rated Rank: 207

### Lafayette, IN
Local Choices
  64% houses, 1% condos, 5% mobile
    homes, 19% apartments (rent
    $290/month)
**Houses**
  Price: $61,300
  Property Taxes: $730
  Built Before 1940: 26.0%
**Energy Requirements**
  Heating Season: 5,603 degree days
  Major Source: Natural gas/Electricity
  Air-conditioning: 1,807 hours
**Annual Costs**
  Mortgage and Taxes: $6,544
  Utilities: $1,234
Places Rated Score: 7,778
Places Rated Rank: 157

### Lafayette, LA
Local Choices
  74% houses, 1% condos, 12% mobile
    homes, 10% apartments (rent
    $355/month)
**Houses**
  Price: $79,100
  Property Taxes: $119
  Built Before 1940: 9.8%
**Energy Requirements**
  Heating Season: 1,551 degree days
  Major Source: Natural gas/Electricity
  Air-conditioning: 1,807 hours
**Annual Costs**
  Mortgage and Taxes: $7,617
  Utilities: $955
Places Rated Score: 8,572
Places Rated Rank: 230

### Lake Charles, LA
Local Choices
  77% houses, 4% condos, 9% mobile
    homes, 7% apartments (rent
    $310/month)
**Houses**
  Price: $61,200

Property Taxes: $92
Built Before 1940: 10.9%
**Energy Requirements**
  Heating Season: 1,498 degree days
  Major Source: Natural gas/Electricity
  Air-conditioning: 1,807 hours
**Annual Costs**
  Mortgage and Taxes: $5,895
  Utilities: $1,026
Places Rated Score: 6,921
Places Rated Rank: 94

### Lake County, IL
Local Choices
  74% houses, 5% condos, 2% mobile
    homes, 12% apartments (rent
    $375/month)
**Houses**
  Price: $107,300
  Property Taxes: $1,707
  Built Before 1940: 18.8%
**Energy Requirements**
  Heating Season: 6,550 degree days
  Major Source: Natural gas/Electricity
  Air-conditioning: 599 hours
**Annual Costs**
  Mortgage and Taxes: $11,881
  Utilities: $1,401
Places Rated Score: 13,282
Places Rated Rank: 311

### Lakeland–Winter Haven, FL
Local Choices
  70% houses, 2% condos, 14% mobile
    homes, 8% apartments (rent
    $295/month)
**Houses**
  Price: $53,500
  Property Taxes: $551
  Built Before 1940: 11.6%
**Energy Requirements**
  Heating Season: 678 degree days
  Major Source: Total electric
  Air-conditioning: 1,759 hours
**Annual Costs**
  Mortgage and Taxes: $5,619
  Utilities: $1,061
Places Rated Score: 6,680
Places Rated Rank: 68

### Lancaster, PA
Local Choices
  73% houses, 5% mobile homes, 9%
    apartments (rent $310/month)
**Houses**
  Price: $65,900
  Property Taxes: $1,075
  Built Before 1940: 40.5%
**Energy Requirements**
  Heating Season: 5,283 degree days
  Major Source: Oil/Electricity
  Air-conditioning: 654 hours
**Annual Costs**
  Mortgage and Taxes: $7,324
  Utilities: $1,307
Places Rated Score: 8,631
Places Rated Rank: 236

### Lansing–East Lansing, MI
Local Choices
  70% houses, 1% condos, 4% mobile
    homes, 17% apartments (rent
    $330/month)
**Houses**
  Price: $54,500
  Property Taxes: $1,459
  Built Before 1940: 27.0%

Energy Requirements
Heating Season: 6,904 degree days
Major Source: Natural gas/Electricity
Air-conditioning: 323 hours
Annual Costs
Mortgage and Taxes: $6,618
Utilities: $1,289
Places Rated Score: 7,907
Places Rated Rank: 170

## Laredo, TX
Local Choices
75% houses, 1% condos, 7% mobile homes, 9% apartments (rent $250/month)
Houses
Price: $47,200
Property Taxes: $661
Built Before 1940: 16.5%
Energy Requirements
Heating Season: 876 degree days
Major Source: Natural gas/Electricity
Air-conditioning: 2,736 hours
Annual Costs
Mortgage and Taxes: $5,134
Utilities: $1,018
Places Rated Score: 6,152
Places Rated Rank: 28

## Las Cruces, NM
Local Choices
65% houses, 1% condos, 16% mobile homes, 9% apartments (rent $285/month)
Houses
Price: $54,500
Property Taxes: $507
Built Before 1940: 10.5%
Energy Requirements
Heating Season: 3,194 degree days
Major Source: Natural gas/Electricity
Air-conditioning: 1,848 hours
Annual Costs
Mortgage and Taxes: $5,675
Utilities: $1,287
Places Rated Score: 6,962
Places Rated Rank: 98

## Las Vegas, NV
Local Choices
56% houses, 6% condos, 11% mobile homes, 22% apartments (rent $430/month)
Houses
Price: $87,300
Property Taxes: $673
Built Before 1940: 1.5%
Energy Requirements
Heating Season: 2,601 degree days
Major Source: Total electric
Air-conditioning: 2,360 hours
Annual Costs
Mortgage and Taxes: $8,954
Utilities: $952
Places Rated Score: 9,906
Places Rated Rank: 274

## Lawrence, KS
Local Choices
61% houses, 1% condos, 6% mobile homes, 20% apartments (rent $310/month)
Houses
Price: $61,200
Property Taxes: $594
Built Before 1940: 24.2%

Energy Requirements
Heating Season: 4,728 degree days
Major Source: Natural gas/Electricity
Air-conditioning: 1,094 hours
Annual Costs
Mortgage and Taxes: $6,394
Utilities: $1,103
Places Rated Score: 7,497
Places Rated Rank: 138

## Lawrence–Haverhill, MA–NH
Local Choices
46% houses, 1% condos, 1% mobile homes, 14% apartments (rent $328/month)
Houses
Price: $74,900
Property Taxes: $1,819
Built Before 1940: 51.3%
Energy Requirements
Heating Season: 6,195 degree days
Major Source: Oil/Electricity
Air-conditioning: 506 hours
Annual Costs
Mortgage and Taxes: $8,916
Utilities: $1,498
Places Rated Score: 10,414
Places Rated Rank: 287

## ★ Lawton, OK
Local Choices
78% houses, 1% condos, 4% mobile homes, 10% apartments (rent $300/month)
Houses
Price: $48,500
Property Taxes: $359
Built Before 1940: 11.7%
Energy Requirements
Heating Season: 3,147 degree days
Major Source: Natural gas/Electricity
Air-conditioning: 2,047 hours
Annual Costs
Mortgage and Taxes: $4,955
Utilities: $895
Places Rated Score: 5,850
Places Rated Rank: 19

## Lewiston–Auburn, ME
Local Choices
41% houses, 4% mobile homes, 18% apartments (rent $250/month)
Houses
Price: $52,900
Property Taxes: $804
Built Before 1940: 52.9%
Energy Requirements
Heating Season: 7,374 degree days
Major Source: Oil/Electricity
Air-conditioning: 298 hours
Annual Costs
Mortgage and Taxes: $5,819
Utilities: $1,057
Places Rated Score: 6,876
Places Rated Rank: 90

## Lexington–Fayette, KY
Local Choices
66% houses, 2% condos, 4% mobile homes, 18% apartments (rent $310/month)
Houses
Price: $69,400
Property Taxes: $770
Built Before 1940: 21.0%
Energy Requirements
Heating Season: 4,729 degree days

Major Source: Natural gas/Electricity
Air-conditioning: 954 hours
Annual Costs
Mortgage and Taxes: $7,347
Utilities: $993
Places Rated Score: 8,340
Places Rated Rank: 212

## Lima, OH
Local Choices
62% houses, 1% condos, 4% mobile homes, 7% apartments (rent $270/month)
Houses
Price: $51,200
Property Taxes: $589
Built Before 1940: 37.5%
Energy Requirements
Heating Season: 5,838 degree days
Major Source: Natural gas/Electricity
Air-conditioning: 665 hours
Annual Costs
Mortgage and Taxes: $5,443
Utilities: $1,543
Places Rated Score: 6,986
Places Rated Rank: 99

## Lincoln, NE
Local Choices
68% houses, 2% condos, 3% mobile homes, 17% apartments (rent $295/month)
Houses
Price: $61,500
Property Taxes: $1,372
Built Before 1940: 25.3%
Energy Requirements
Heating Season: 6,218 degree days
Major Source: Natural gas/Electricity
Air-conditioning: 1,000 hours
Annual Costs
Mortgage and Taxes: $7,205
Utilities: $1,051
Places Rated Score: 8,256
Places Rated Rank: 201

## Little Rock–North Little Rock, AR
Local Choices
74% houses, 1% condos, 7% mobile homes, 11% apartments (rent $300/month)
Houses
Price: $58,200
Property Taxes: $826
Built Before 1940: 11.9%
Energy Requirements
Heating Season: 3,354 degree days
Major Source: Natural gas/Electricity
Air-conditioning: 1,545 hours
Annual Costs
Mortgage and Taxes: $6,341
Utilities: $929
Places Rated Score: 7,270
Places Rated Rank: 123

## Longview–Marshall, TX
Local Choices
77% houses, 7% mobile homes, 8% apartments (rent $310/month)
Houses
Price: $52,300
Property Taxes: $732
Built Before 1940: 14.9%
Energy Requirements
Heating Season: 2,271 degree days
Major Source: Natural gas/Electricity
Air-conditioning: 1,853 hours

Annual Costs
    Mortgage and Taxes: $5,686
    Utilities: $922
Places Rated Score: 6,608
Places Rated Rank: 62

### Lorain–Elyria, OH
Local Choices
    77% houses, 2% condos, 3% mobile
    homes, 10% apartments (rent
    $300/month)
Houses
    Price: $63,800
    Property Taxes: $733
    Built Before 1940: 24.1%
Energy Requirements
    Heating Season: 5,800 degree days
    Major Source: Natural gas/Electricity
    Air-conditioning: 523 hours
Annual Costs
    Mortgage and Taxes: $6,779
    Utilities: $1,530
Places Rated Score: 8,309
Places Rated Rank: 206

### Los Angeles–Long Beach, CA
Local Choices
    57% houses, 4% condos, 2% mobile
    homes, 30% apartments (rent
    $405/month)
Houses
    Price: $122,600
    Property Taxes: $1,263
    Built Before 1940: 17.7%
Energy Requirements
    Heating Season: 1,819 degree days
    Major Source: Natural gas/Electricity
    Air-conditioning: 576 hours
Annual Costs
    Mortgage and Taxes: $12,889
    Utilities: $979
Places Rated Score: 13,868
Places Rated Rank: 316

### Louisville, KY–IN
Local Choices
    73% houses, 2% condos, 3% mobile
    homes, 14% apartments (rent
    $275/month)
Houses
    Price: $54,600
    Property Taxes: $606
    Built Before 1940: 21.7%
Energy Requirements
    Heating Season: 4,640 degree days
    Major Source: Natural gas/Electricity
    Air-conditioning: 1,041 hours
Annual Costs
    Mortgage and Taxes: $5,785
    Utilities: $1,027
Places Rated Score: 6,812
Places Rated Rank: 87

### Lowell, MA–NH
Local Choices
    62% houses, 1% condos, 15%
    apartments (rent $335/month)
Houses
    Price: $68,400
    Property Taxes: $1,661
    Built Before 1940: 38.5%
Energy Requirements
    Heating Season: 6,056 degree days
    Major Source: Natural gas/Electricity
    Air-conditioning: 506 hours

Annual Costs
    Mortgage and Taxes: $8,142
    Utilities: $1,498
Places Rated Score: 9,640
Places Rated Rank: 266

### Lubbock, TX
Local Choices
    71% houses, 1% condos, 4% mobile
    homes, 16% apartments (rent
    $335/month)
Houses
    Price: $55,000
    Property Taxes: $769
    Built Before 1940: 6.1%
Energy Requirements
    Heating Season: 3,545 degree days
    Major Source: Natural gas/Electricity
    Air-conditioning: 1,341 hours
Annual Costs
    Mortgage and Taxes: $5,979
    Utilities: $1,011
Places Rated Score: 6,990
Places Rated Rank: 100

### Lynchburg, VA
Local Choices
    82% houses, 1% condos, 7% mobile
    homes, 8% apartments (rent
    $280/month)
Houses
    Price: $52,800
    Property Taxes: $760
    Built Before 1940: 24.2%
Energy Requirements
    Heating Season: 4,233 degree days
    Major Source: Oil/Electricity
    Air-conditioning: 661 hours
Annual Costs
    Mortgage and Taxes: $5,764
    Utilities: $1,170
Places Rated Score: 6,934
Places Rated Rank: 97

### Macon–Warner Robins, GA
Local Choices
    71% houses, 1% condos, 5% mobile
    homes, 9% apartments (rent
    $255/month)
Houses
    Price: $49,100
    Property Taxes: $594
    Built Before 1940: 13.3%
Energy Requirements
    Heating Season: 2,240 degree days
    Major Source: Natural gas/Electricity
    Air-conditioning: 1,549 hours
Annual Costs
    Mortgage and Taxes: $5,243
    Utilities: $992
Places Rated Score: 6,235
Places Rated Rank: 34

### Madison, WI
Local Choices
    58% houses, 1% condos, 1% mobile
    homes, 26% apartments (rent
    $325/month)
Houses
    Price: $75,700
    Property Taxes: $1,522
    Built Before 1940: 23.1%
Energy Requirements
    Heating Season: 7,730 degree days
    Major Source: Natural gas/Electricity
    Air-conditioning: 485 hours

Annual Costs
    Mortgage and Taxes: $8,699
    Utilities: $1,198
Places Rated Score: 9,897
Places Rated Rank: 273

### Manchester, NH
Local Choices
    65% houses, 2% condos, 4% mobile
    homes, 11% apartments (rent
    $330/month)
Houses
    Price: $70,200
    Property Taxes: $1,677
    Built Before 1940: 40.3%
Energy Requirements
    Heating Season: 7,101 degree days
    Major Source: Oil/Electricity
    Air-conditioning: 506 hours
Annual Costs
    Mortgage and Taxes: $8,327
    Utilities: $1,533
Places Rated Score: 9,860
Places Rated Rank: 272

### Mansfield, OH
Local Choices
    77% houses, 4% mobile homes, 8%
    apartments (rent $260/month)
Houses
    Price: $50,300
    Property Taxes: $579
    Built Before 1940: 30.4%
Energy Requirements
    Heating Season: 6,520 degree days
    Major Source: Natural gas/Electricity
    Air-conditioning: 426 hours
Annual Costs
    Mortgage and Taxes: $5,351
    Utilities: $1,530
Places Rated Score: 6,881
Places Rated Rank: 91

### ★ McAllen–Edinburg–Mission, TX
Local Choices
    72% houses, 1% condos, 8% mobile
    homes, 10% apartments (rent
    $235/month)
Houses
    Price: $39,800
    Property Taxes: $557
    Built Before 1940: 9.0%
Energy Requirements
    Heating Season: 696 degree days
    Major Source: Natural gas/Electricity
    Air-conditioning: 2,295 hours
Annual Costs
    Mortgage and Taxes: $4,327
    Utilities: $1,018
Places Rated Score: 5,345
Places Rated Rank: 2

### Medford, OR
Local Choices
    70% houses, 1% condos, 12% mobile
    homes, 9% apartments (rent
    $355/month)
Houses
    Price: $73,100
    Property Taxes: $1,506
    Built Before 1940: 13.9%
Energy Requirements
    Heating Season: 4,930 degree days
    Major Source: Total electric
    Air-conditioning: 630 hours

Annual Costs
Mortgage and Taxes: $8,435
Utilities: $573
Places Rated Score: 9,008
Places Rated Rank: 246

## Melbourne–Titusville–Palm Bay, FL
Local Choices
69% houses, 8% condos, 10% mobile homes, 12% apartments (rent $355/month)
Houses
Price: $72,200
Property Taxes: $744
Built Before 1940: 3.1%
Energy Requirements
Heating Season: 611 degree days
Major Source: Total electric
Air-conditioning: 2,112 hours
Annual Costs
Mortgage and Taxes: $7,589
Utilities: $1,132
Places Rated Score: 8,721
Places Rated Rank: 240

## Memphis, TN–AR–MS
Local Choices
70% houses, 2% condos, 2% mobile homes, 17% apartments (rent $275/month)
Houses
Price: $57,400
Property Taxes: $712
Built Before 1940: 12.6%
Energy Requirements
Heating Season: 3,227 degree days
Major Source: Natural gas/Electricity
Air-conditioning: 1,509 hours
Annual Costs
Mortgage and Taxes: $6,153
Utilities: $862
Places Rated Score: 7,015
Places Rated Rank: 102

## Miami–Hialeah, FL
Local Choices
50% houses, 14% condos, 2% mobile homes, 30% apartments (rent $375/month)
Houses
Price: $86,900
Property Taxes: $895
Built Before 1940: 7.3%
Energy Requirements
Heating Season: 206 degree days
Major Source: Total electric
Air-conditioning: 2,388 hours
Annual Costs
Mortgage and Taxes: $9,135
Utilities: $1,132
Places Rated Score: 10,267
Places Rated Rank: 285

## Middlesex–Somerset–Hunterdon, NJ
Local Choices
65% houses, 2% condos, 1% mobile homes, 15% apartments (rent $455/month)
Houses
Price: $88,300
Property Taxes: $2,253
Built Before 1940: 24.6%
Energy Requirements
Heating Season: 5,100 degree days
Major Source: Natural gas/Electricity
Air-conditioning: 663 hours

Annual Costs
Mortgage and Taxes: $10,627
Utilities: $1,508
Places Rated Score: 12,135
Places Rated Rank: 306

## Middletown, CT
Local Choices
72% houses, 3% condos, 1% mobile homes, 19% apartments (rent $360/month)
Houses
Price: $91,100
Property Taxes: $1,395
Built Before 1940: 31.8%
Energy Requirements
Heating Season: 5,966 degree days
Major Source: Oil/Electricity
Air-conditioning: 476 hours
Annual Costs
Mortgage and Taxes: $10,035
Utilities: $1,617
Places Rated Score: 11,652
Places Rated Rank: 302

## Midland, TX
Local Choices
75% houses, 1% condos, 6% mobile homes, 12% apartments (rent $390/month)
Houses
Price: $70,300
Property Taxes: $984
Built Before 1940: 3.8%
Energy Requirements
Heating Season: 2,621 degree days
Major Source: Natural gas/Electricity
Air-conditioning: 1,884 hours
Annual Costs
Mortgage and Taxes: $7,648
Utilities: $1,024
Places Rated Score: 8,672
Places Rated Rank: 238

## Milwaukee, WI
Local Choices
59% houses, 2% condos, 17% apartments (rent $320/month)
Houses
Price: $77,200
Property Taxes: $1,552
Built Before 1940: 32.1%
Energy Requirements
Heating Season: 7,444 degree days
Major Source: Natural gas/Electricity
Air-conditioning: 358 hours
Annual Costs
Mortgage and Taxes: $8,873
Utilities: $1,303
Places Rated Score: 10,176
Places Rated Rank: 282

## Minneapolis–St. Paul, MN–WI
Local Choices
66% houses, 2% condos, 2% mobile homes, 22% apartments (rent $330/month)
Houses
Price: $80,600
Property Taxes: $621
Built Before 1940: 26.6%
Energy Requirements
Heating Season: 8,310 degree days
Major Source: Natural gas/Electricity
Air-conditioning: 496 hours

Annual Costs
Mortgage and Taxes: $8,265
Utilities: $1,294
Places Rated Score: 9,559
Places Rated Rank: 264

## Mobile, AL
Local Choices
77% houses, 1% condos, 6% mobile homes, 9% apartments (rent $270/month)
Houses
Price: $56,800
Property Taxes: $233
Built Before 1940: 11.7%
Energy Requirements
Heating Season: 1,684 degree days
Major Source: Natural gas/Electricity
Air-conditioning: 1,844 hours
Annual Costs
Mortgage and Taxes: $5,615
Utilities: $1,089
Places Rated Score: 6,704
Places Rated Rank: 75

## Modesto, CA
Local Choices
77% houses, 1% condos, 5% mobile homes, 10% apartments (rent $340/month)
Houses
Price: $75,200
Property Taxes: $775
Built Before 1940: 13.2%
Energy Requirements
Heating Season: 2,767 degree days
Major Source: Natural gas/Electricity
Air-conditioning: 1,017 hours
Annual Costs
Mortgage and Taxes: $7,907
Utilities: $723
Places Rated Score: 8,630
Places Rated Rank: 235

## Monmouth–Ocean, NJ
Local Choices
76% houses, 6% condos, 2% mobile homes, 12% apartments (rent $395/month)
Houses
Price: $88,300
Property Taxes: $2,253
Built Before 1940: 19.2%
Energy Requirements
Heating Season: 5,128 degree days
Major Source: Natural gas/Electricity
Air-conditioning: 592 hours
Annual Costs
Mortgage and Taxes: $10,132
Utilities: $1,528
Places Rated Score: 11,660
Places Rated Rank: 304

## Monroe, LA
Local Choices
77% houses, 6% mobile homes, 10% apartments (rent $265/month)
Houses
Price: $54,500
Property Taxes: $82
Built Before 1940: 11.1%
Energy Requirements
Heating Season: 2,311 degree days
Major Source: Natural gas/Electricity
Air-conditioning: 1,846 hours

Annual Costs
  Mortgage and Taxes: $5,251
  Utilities: $939
Places Rated Score: 6,190
Places Rated Rank: 31

## Montgomery, AL
Local Choices
  76% houses, 1% condos, 6% mobile
    homes, 10% apartments (rent
    $270/month)
Houses
  Price: $57,300
  Property Taxes: $235
  Built Before 1940: 14.1%
Energy Requirements
  Heating Season: 2,269 degree days
  Major Source: Natural gas/Electricity
  Air-conditioning: 1,743 hours
Annual Costs
  Mortgage and Taxes: $5,665
  Utilities: $1,089
Places Rated Score: 6,754
Places Rated Rank: 81

## ★ Muncie, IN
Local Choices
  78% houses, 4% mobile homes, 8%
    apartments (rent $265/month)
Houses
  Price: $43,700
  Property Taxes: $520
  Built Before 1940: 31.2%
Energy Requirements
  Heating Season: 5,580 degree days
  Major Source: Natural gas/Electricity
  Air-conditioning: 653 hours
Annual Costs
  Mortgage and Taxes: $4,659
  Utilities: $1,141
Places Rated Score: 5,800
Places Rated Rank: 16

## Muskegon, MI
Local Choices
  81% houses, 4% mobile homes, 7%
    apartments (rent $270/month)
Houses
  Price: $41,900
  Property Taxes: $1,122
  Built Before 1940: 28.4%
Energy Requirements
  Heating Season: 6,890 degree days
  Major Source: Natural gas/Electricity
  Air-conditioning: 247 hours
Annual Costs
  Mortgage and Taxes: $5,090
  Utilities: $1,301
Places Rated Score: 6,391
Places Rated Rank: 45

## Nashua, NH
Local Choices
  56% houses, 2% condos, 3% mobile
    homes, 14% apartments (rent
    $400/month)
Houses
  Price: $77,700
  Property Taxes: $1,857
  Built Before 1940: 26.4%
Energy Requirements
  Heating Season: 7,015 degree days
  Major Source: Oil/Electricity
  Air-conditioning: 506 hours
Annual Costs
  Mortgage and Taxes: $9,224

Utilities: $1,533
Places Rated Score: 10,757
Places Rated Rank: 292

## Nashville, TN
Local Choices
  69% houses, 2% condos, 4% mobile
    homes, 15% apartments (rent
    $310/month)
Houses
  Price: $65,700
  Property Taxes: $815
  Built Before 1940: 14.6%
Energy Requirements
  Heating Season: 3,696 degree days
  Major Source: Total electric
  Air-conditioning: 1,295 hours
Annual Costs
  Mortgage and Taxes: $7,046
  Utilities: $754
Places Rated Score: 7,800
Places Rated Rank: 161

## Nassau–Suffolk, NY
Local Choices
  80% houses, 2% condos, 8%
    apartments (rent $475/month)
Houses
  Price: $79,400
  Property Taxes: $2,042
  Built Before 1940: 19.0%
Energy Requirements
  Heating Season: 5,330 degree days
  Major Source: Oil/Electricity
  Air-conditioning: 648 hours
Annual Costs
  Mortgage and Taxes: $9,573
  Utilities: $1,565
Places Rated Score: 11,138
Places Rated Rank: 298

## New Bedford, MA
Local Choices
  51% houses, 1% mobile homes, 11%
    apartments (rent $260/month)
Houses
  Price: $54,800
  Property Taxes: $1,332
  Built Before 1940: 53.8%
Energy Requirements
  Heating Season: 5,395 degree days
  Major Source: Natural gas/Electricity
  Air-conditioning: 164 hours
Annual Costs
  Mortgage and Taxes: $6,528
  Utilities: $1,559
Places Rated Score: 8,087
Places Rated Rank: 184

## New Britain, CT
Local Choices
  52% houses, 1% condos, 2% mobile
    homes, 18% apartments (rent
    $305/month)
Houses
  Price: $80,000
  Property Taxes: $1,236
  Built Before 1940: 34.0%
Energy Requirements
  Heating Season: 6,140 degree days
  Major Source: Oil/Electricity
  Air-conditioning: 476 hours
Annual Costs
  Mortgage and Taxes: $8,892
  Utilities: $1,617
Places Rated Score: 10,509
Places Rated Rank: 289

## New Haven–Meriden, CT
Local Choices
  57% houses, 3% condos, 2% mobile
    homes, 18% apartments (rent
    $355/month)
Houses
  Price: $89,400
  Property Taxes: $1,367
  Built Before 1940: 34.0%
Energy Requirements
  Heating Season: 5,793 degree days
  Major Source: Oil/Electricity
  Air-conditioning: 193 hours
Annual Costs
  Mortgage and Taxes: $9,837
  Utilities: $1,623
Places Rated Score: 11,460
Places Rated Rank: 299

## New London–Norwich, CT–RI
Local Choices
  65% houses, 1% condos, 3% mobile
    homes, 12% apartments (rent
    $340/month)
Houses
  Price: $78,100
  Property Taxes: $1,195
  Built Before 1940: 34.2%
Energy Requirements
  Heating Season: 6,030 degree days
  Major Source: Oil/Electricity
  Air-conditioning: 292 hours
Annual Costs
  Mortgage and Taxes: $8,601
  Utilities: $1,617
Places Rated Score: 10,218
Places Rated Rank: 284

## New Orleans, LA
Local Choices
  62% houses, 1% condos, 3% mobile
    homes, 15% apartments (rent
    $315/month)
Houses
  Price: $78,700
  Property Taxes: $118
  Built Before 1940: 21.1%
Energy Requirements
  Heating Season: 1,465 degree days
  Major Source: Natural gas/Electricity
  Air-conditioning: 1,733 hours
Annual Costs
  Mortgage and Taxes: $7,576
  Utilities: $939
Places Rated Score: 8,515
Places Rated Rank: 225

## New York, NY
Local Choices
  17% houses, 2% condos, 56%
    apartments (rent $360/month)
Houses
  Price: $95,800
  Property Taxes: $2,462
  Built Before 1940: 47.8%
Energy Requirements
  Heating Season: 4,848 degree days
  Major Source: Oil/Electricity
  Air-conditioning: 648 hours
Annual Costs
  Mortgage and Taxes: $11,544
  Utilities: $1,814
Places Rated Score: 13,358
Places Rated Rank: 312

## Newark, NJ

Local Choices
  59% houses, 1% condos, 23%
    apartments (rent $365/month)
Houses
  Price: $105,700
  Property Taxes: $2,695
  Built Before 1940: 37.5%
Energy Requirements
  Heating Season: 5,034 degree days
  Major Source: Oil/Electricity
  Air-conditioning: 592 hours
Annual Costs
  Mortgage and Taxes: $12,712
  Utilities: $1,508
Places Rated Score: 14,220
Places Rated Rank: 318

## Niagara Falls, NY

Local Choices
  67% houses, 3% mobile homes, 9%
    apartments (rent $280/month)
Houses
  Price: $53,400
  Property Taxes: $1,374
  Built Before 1940: 43.0%
Energy Requirements
  Heating Season: 6,927 degree days
  Major Source: Natural gas/Electricity
  Air-conditioning: 350 hours
Annual Costs
  Mortgage and Taxes: $6,440
  Utilities: $1,246
Places Rated Score: 7,686
Places Rated Rank: 149

## Norfolk–Virginia Beach–Newport News, VA

Local Choices
  71% houses, 1% condos, 2% mobile
    homes, 16% apartments (rent
    $340/month)
Houses
  Price: $66,600
  Property Taxes: $959
  Built Before 1940: 12.5%
Energy Requirements
  Heating Season: 3,488 degree days
  Major Source: Natural gas/Electricity
  Air-conditioning: 990 hours
Annual Costs
  Mortgage and Taxes: $7,274
  Utilities: $1,294
Places Rated Score: 8,568
Places Rated Rank: 229

## Norwalk, CT

Local Choices
  70% houses, 5% condos, 11%
    apartments (rent $465/month)
Houses
  Price: $168,400
  Property Taxes: $2,576
  Built Before 1940: 29.5%
Energy Requirements
  Heating Season: 5,900 degree days
  Major Source: Oil/Electricity
  Air-conditioning: 345 hours
Annual Costs
  Mortgage and Taxes: $18,534
  Utilities: $1,617
Places Rated Score: 20,151
Places Rated Rank: 328

## Oakland, CA

Local Choices
  66% houses, 5% condos, 2% mobile

---

homes, 20% apartments (rent
    $400/month)
Houses
  Price: $116,200
  Property Taxes: $1,197
  Built Before 1940: 19.7%
Energy Requirements
  Heating Season: 2,909 degree days
  Major Source: Natural gas/Electricity
  Air-conditioning: 360 hours
Annual Costs
  Mortgage and Taxes: $12,214
  Utilities: $921
Places Rated Score: 13,135
Places Rated Rank: 310

## Ocala, FL

Local Choices
  68% houses, 2% condos, 20% mobile
    homes, 5% apartments (rent
    $290/month)
Houses
  Price: $52,300
  Property Taxes: $538
  Built Before 1940: 7.1%
Energy Requirements
  Heating Season: 700 degree days
  Major Source: Total electric
  Air-conditioning: 1,824 hours
Annual Costs
  Mortgage and Taxes: $5,493
  Utilities: $1,257
Places Rated Score: 6,750
Places Rated Rank: 80

## Odessa, TX

Local Choices
  69% houses, 1% condos, 12% mobile
    homes, 13% apartments (rent
    $345/month)
Houses
  Price: $52,100
  Property Taxes: $729
  Built Before 1940: 3.6%
Energy Requirements
  Heating Season: 2,621 degree days
  Major Source: Natural gas/Electricity
  Air-conditioning: 1,884 hours
Annual Costs
  Mortgage and Taxes: $5,665
  Utilities: $1,024
Places Rated Score: 6,689
Places Rated Rank: 70

## Oklahoma City, OK

Local Choices
  76% houses, 1% condos, 3% mobile
    homes, 13% apartments (rent
    $325/month)
Houses
  Price: $61,500
  Property Taxes: $455
  Built Before 1940: 14.1%
Energy Requirements
  Heating Season: 3,457 degree days
  Major Source: Natural gas/Electricity
  Air-conditioning: 1,439 hours
Annual Costs
  Mortgage and Taxes: $6,282
  Utilities: $904
Places Rated Score: 7,186
Places Rated Rank: 117

## Olympia, WA

Local Choices
  68% houses, 1% condos, 11% mobile

---

homes, 12% apartments (rent
    $365/month)
Houses
  Price: $73,300
  Property Taxes: $740
  Built Before 1940: 13.3%
Energy Requirements
  Heating Season: 5,530 degree days
  Major Source: Total electric
  Air-conditioning: 117 hours
Annual Costs
  Mortgage and Taxes: $7,685
  Utilities: $578
Places Rated Score: 8,263
Places Rated Rank: 203

## Omaha, NE–IA

Local Choices
  73% houses, 1% condos, 2% mobile
    homes, 19% apartments (rent
    $290/month)
Houses
  Price: $52,100
  Property Taxes: $1,162
  Built Before 1940: 28.8%
Energy Requirements
  Heating Season: 6,049 degree days
  Major Source: Natural gas/Electricity
  Air-conditioning: 901 hours
Annual Costs
  Mortgage and Taxes: $6,101
  Utilities: $1,027
Places Rated Score: 7,128
Places Rated Rank: 113

## Orange County, NY

Local Choices
  67% houses, 1% condos, 3% mobile
    homes, 11% apartments (rent
    $355/month)
Houses
  Price: $70,600
  Property Taxes: $1,815
  Built Before 1940: 37.5%
Energy Requirements
  Heating Season: 5,415 degree days
  Major Source: Oil/Electricity
  Air-conditioning: 460 hours
Annual Costs
  Mortgage and Taxes: $8,509
  Utilities: $1,664
Places Rated Score: 10,173
Places Rated Rank: 281

## Orlando, FL

Local Choices
  69% houses, 4% condos, 7% mobile
    homes, 15% apartments (rent
    $340/month)
Houses
  Price: $67,600
  Property Taxes: $697
  Built Before 1940: 6.4%
Energy Requirements
  Heating Season: 710 degree days
  Major Source: Total electric
  Air-conditioning: 1,609 hours
Annual Costs
  Mortgage and Taxes: $7,108
  Utilities: $1,088
Places Rated Score: 8,196
Places Rated Rank: 193

## Owensboro, KY

Local Choices
  78% houses, 4% mobile homes, 8%
    apartments (rent $260/month)

Houses
  Price: $54,900
  Property Taxes: $609
  Built Before 1940: 19.8%
Energy Requirements
  Heating Season: 4,268 degree days
  Major Source: Natural gas/Electricity
  Air-conditioning: 1,195 hours
Annual Costs
  Mortgage and Taxes: $5,813
  Utilities: $947
Places Rated Score: 6,760
Places Rated Rank: 82

### Oxnard–Ventura, CA
Local Choices
  73% houses, 9% condos, 5% mobile
  homes, 13% apartments (rent
  $455/month)
Houses
  Prices: $122,800
  Property Taxes: $1,265
  Built Before 1940: 6.2%
Energy Requirements
  Heating Season: 2,286 degree days
  Major Source: Natural gas/Electricity
  Air-conditioning: 124 hours
Annual Costs
  Mortgage and Taxes: $12,905
  Utilities: $1,095
Places Rated Score: 14,000
Places Rated Rank: 317

### Panama City, FL
Local Choices
  70% houses, 5% condos, 12% mobile
  homes, 8% apartments (rent
  $280/month)
Houses
  Price: $50,400
  Property Taxes: $519
  Built Before 1940: 5.8%
Energy Requirements
  Heating Season: 1,388 degree days
  Major Source: Total electric
  Air-conditioning: 1,884 hours
Annual Costs
  Mortgage and Taxes: $5,293
  Utilities: $1,080
Places Rated Score: 6,373
Places Rated Rank: 44

### Parkersburg–Marietta, WV–OH
Local Choices
  82% houses, 7% mobile homes, 6%
  apartments (rent $265/month)
Houses
  Price: $55,300
  Property Taxes: $205
  Built Before 1940: 49.9%
Energy Requirements
  Heating Season: 4,750 degree days
  Major Source: Natural gas/Electricity
  Air-conditioning: 632 hours
Annual Costs
  Mortgage and Taxes: $5,445
  Utilities: $1,212
Places Rated Score: 6,657
Places Rated Rank: 67

### Pascagoula, MS
Local Choices
  78% houses, 1% condos, 7% mobile
  homes, 7% apartments (rent
  $305/month)

Houses
  Price: $51,100
  Property Taxes: $388
  Built Before 1940: 6.2%
Energy Requirements
  Heating Season: 1,496 degree days
  Major Source: Natural gas/Electricity
  Air-conditioning: 1,844 hours
Annual Costs
  Mortgage and Taxes: $5,232
  Utilities: $1,016
Places Rated Score: 6,248
Places Rated Rank: 35

### Pawtucket–Woonsocket–Attleboro, RI–MA
Local Choices
  59% houses, 2% condos, 15%
  apartments (rent $305/month)
Houses
  Price: $69,300
  Property Taxes: $1,338
  Built Before 1940: 46.8%
Energy Requirements
  Heating Season: 6,199 degree days
  Major Source: Oil/Electricity
  Air-conditioning: 290 hours
Annual Costs
  Mortgage and Taxes: $7,908
  Utilities: $1,554
Places Rated Score: 9,462
Places Rated Rank: 261

### Pensacola, FL
Local Choices
  78% houses, 1% condos, 8% mobile
  homes, 8% apartments (rent
  $300/month)
Houses
  Price: $51,400
  Property Taxes: $529
  Built Before 1940: 8.9%
Energy Requirements
  Heating Season: 1,578 degree days
  Major Source: Total electric
  Air-conditioning: 1,884 hours
Annual Costs
  Mortgage and Taxes: $5,399
  Utilities: $1,080
Places Rated Score: 6,479
Places Rated Rank: 51

### Peoria, IL
Local Choices
  78% houses, 1% condos, 3% mobile
  homes, 11% apartments (rent
  $325/month)
Houses
  Price: $62,900
  Property Taxes: $1,001
  Built Before 1940: 29.1%
Energy Requirements
  Heating Season: 6,098 degree days
  Major Source: Natural gas/Electricity
  Air-conditioning: 617 hours
Annual Costs
  Mortgage and Taxes: $6,967
  Utilities: $1,421
Places Rated Score: 8,388
Places Rated Rank: 217

### Philadelphia, PA–NJ
Local Choices
  72% houses, 2% condos, 1% mobile
  homes, 15% apartments (rent
  $340/month)

Houses
  Price: $61,800
  Property Taxes: $1,008
  Built Before 1940: 42.8%
Energy Requirements
  Heating Season: 4,865 degree days
  Major Source: Natural gas/Electricity
  Air-conditioning: 702 hours
Annual Costs
  Mortgage and Taxes: $6,870
  Utilities: $1,440
Places Rated Score: 8,310
Places Rated Rank: 207

### Phoenix, AZ
Local Choices
  69% houses, 7% condos, 8% mobile
  homes, 15% apartments (rent
  $405/month)
Houses
  Price: $77,700
  Property Taxes: $435
  Built Before 1940: 19.1%
Energy Requirements
  Heating Season: 1,124 degree days
  Major Source: Natural gas/Electricity
  Air-conditioning: 2,845 hours
Annual Costs
  Mortgage and Taxes: $7,797
  Utilities: $1,124
Places Rated Score: 8,921
Places Rated Rank: 244

### ★ Pine Bluff, AR
Local Choices
  79% houses, 6% mobile homes, 7%
  apartments (rent $245/month)
Houses
  Price: $43,500
  Property Taxes: $618
  Built Before 1940: 15.5%
Energy Requirements
  Heating Season: 2,588 degree days
  Major Source: Natural gas/Electricity
  Air-conditioning: 1,641 hours
Annual Costs
  Mortgage and Taxes: $4,745
  Utilities: $929
Places Rated Score: 5,674
Places Rated Rank: 8

### Pittsburgh, PA
Local Choices
  73% houses, 1% condos, 3% mobile
  homes, 12% apartments (rent
  $310/month)
Houses
  Price: $60,500
  Property Taxes: $986
  Built Before 1940: 43.4%
Energy Requirements
  Heating Season: 5,930 degree days
  Major Source: Natural gas/Electricity
  Air-conditioning: 471 hours
Annual Costs
  Mortgage and Taxes: $6,724
  Utilities: $1,375
Places Rated Score: 8,099
Places Rated Rank: 186

### Pittsfield, MA
Local Choices
  69% houses, 1% condos, 2% mobile
  homes, 12% apartments (rent
  $290/month)
Houses
  Price: $52,600

Property Taxes: $1,279
Built Before 1940: 54.1%
**Energy Requirements**
Heating Season: 7,406 degree days
Major Source: Oil/Electricity
Air-conditioning: 199 hours
**Annual Costs**
Mortgage and Taxes: $6,267
Utilities: $1,540
Places Rated Score: 7,807
Places Rated Rank: 162

### Portland, ME
**Local Choices**
57% houses, 1% condos, 3% mobile homes, 16% apartments (rent $320/month)
**Houses**
Price: $64,000
Property Taxes: $973
Built Before 1940: 47.0%
**Energy Requirements**
Heating Season: 7,496 degree days
Major Source: Oil/Electricity
Air-conditioning: 236 hours
**Annual Costs**
Mortgage and Taxes: $7,043
Utilities: $1,057
Places Rated Score: 8,100
Places Rated Rank: 187

### Portland, OR
**Local Choices**
70% houses, 2% condos, 3% mobile homes, 18% apartments (rent $380/month)
**Houses**
Price: $80,800
Property Taxes: $1,664
Built Before 1940: 24.5%
**Energy Requirements**
Heating Season: 4,792 degree days
Major Source: Total electric
Air-conditioning: 208 hours
**Annual Costs**
Mortgage and Taxes: $9,321
Utilities: $591
Places Rated Score: 9,912
Places Rated Rank: 275

### Portsmouth–Dover–Rochester, NH–ME
**Local Choices**
52% houses, 5% mobile homes, 12% apartments (rent $330/month)
**Houses**
Price: $71,100
Property Taxes: $1,698
Built Before 1940: 38.0%
**Energy Requirements**
Heating Season: 7,089 degree days
Major Source: Oil/Electricity
Air-conditioning: 220 hours
**Annual Costs**
Mortgage and Taxes: $8,433
Utilities: $1,533
Places Rated Score: 9,966
Places Rated Rank: 277

### Poughkeepsie, NY
**Local Choices**
65% houses, 1% condos, 4% mobile homes, 15% apartments (rent $360/month)
**Houses**
Price: $69,000
Property Taxes: $1,774
Built Before 1940: 30.6%

**Energy Requirements**
Heating Season: 5,824 degree days
Major Source: Oil/Electricity
Air-conditioning: 623 hours
**Annual Costs**
Mortgage and Taxes: $8,317
Utilities: $1,664
Places Rated Score: 9,981
Places Rated Rank: 278

### Providence, RI
**Local Choices**
56% houses, 1% condos, 15% apartments (rent $295/month)
**Houses**
Price: $68,000
Property Taxes: $1,313
Built Before 1940: 49.5%
**Energy Requirements**
Heating Season: 5,927 degree days
Major Source: Oil/Electricity
Air-conditioning: 316 hours
**Annual Costs**
Mortgage and Taxes: $7,759
Utilities: $1,515
Places Rated Score: 9,274
Places Rated Rank: 253

### Provo–Orem, UT
**Local Choices**
68% houses, 2% condos, 4% mobile homes, 12% apartments (rent $310/month)
**Houses**
Price: $80,300
Property Taxes: $739
Built Before 1940: 15.2%
**Energy Requirements**
Heating Season: 5,463 degree days
Major Source: Natural gas/Electricity
Air-conditioning: 877 hours
**Annual Costs**
Mortgage and Taxes: $8,351
Utilities: $970
Places Rated Score: 9,321
Places Rated Rank: 257

### Pueblo, CO
**Local Choices**
77% houses, 1% condos, 5% mobile homes, 10% apartments (rent $275/month)
**Houses**
Price: $51,800
Property Taxes: $523
Built Before 1940: 26.5%
**Energy Requirements**
Heating Season: 5,394 degree days
Major Source: Natural gas/Electricity
Air-conditioning: 954 hours
**Annual Costs**
Mortgage and Taxes: $5,436
Utilities: $1,201
Places Rated Score: 6,637
Places Rated Rank: 66

### Racine, WI
**Local Choices**
72% houses, 1% condos, 1% mobile homes, 11% apartments (rent $310/month)
**Houses**
Price: $66,500
Property Taxes: $1,337
Built Before 1940: 33.9%
**Energy Requirements**
Heating Season: 6,787 degree days

Major Source: Natural gas/Electricity
Air-conditioning: 358 hours
**Annual Costs**
Mortgage and Taxes: $7,640
Utilities: $1,303
Places Rated Score: 8,943
Places Rated Rank: 245

### Raleigh–Durham, NC
**Local Choices**
67% houses, 1% condos, 6% mobile homes, 16% apartments (rent $320/month)
**Houses**
Price: $68,700
Property Taxes: $667
Built Before 1940: 13.1%
**Energy Requirements**
Heating Season: 3,514 degree days
Major Source: Total electric
Air-conditioning: 1,031 hours
**Annual Costs**
Mortgage and Taxes: $7,181
Utilities: $1,049
Places Rated Score: 8,230
Places Rated Rank: 198

### Reading, PA
**Local Choices**
75% houses, 1% condos, 3% mobile homes, 10% apartments (rent $300/month)
**Houses**
Price: $55,500
Property Taxes: $905
Built Before 1940: 49.3%
**Energy Requirements**
Heating Season: 4,931 degree days
Major Source: Oil/Electricity
Air-conditioning: 788 hours
**Annual Costs**
Mortgage and Taxes: $6,168
Utilities: $1,446
Places Rated Score: 7,614
Places Rated Rank: 144

### Redding, CA
**Local Choices**
64% houses, 18% mobile homes, 10% apartments (rent $335/month)
**Houses**
Price: $75,800
Property Taxes: $780
Built Before 1940: 7.4%
**Energy Requirements**
Heating Season: 2,610 degree days
Major Source: Natural gas/Electricity
Air-conditioning: 1,515 hours
**Annual Costs**
Mortgage and Taxes: $7,961
Utilities: $623
Places Rated Score: 8,584
Places Rated Rank: 231

### Reno, NV
**Local Choices**
57% houses, 10% condos, 10% mobile homes, 23% apartments (rent $490/month)
**Houses**
Price: $108,400
Property Taxes: $835
Built Before 1940: 7.7%
**Energy Requirements**
Heating Season: 6,022 degree days
Major Source: Natural gas/Electricity
Air-conditioning: 647 hours

Annual Costs
Mortgage and Taxes: $11,113
Utilities: $1,336
Places Rated Score: 12,449
Places Rated Rank: 308

### Richland–Kennewick–Pasco, WA
Local Choices
66% houses, 2% condos, 11% mobile homes, 14% apartments (rent $410/month)
Houses
Price: $74,000
Property Taxes: $747
Built Before 1940: 5.5%
Energy Requirements
Heating Season: 4,892 degree days
Major Source: Total electric
Air-conditioning: 689 hours
Annual Costs
Mortgage and Taxes: $7,760
Utilities: $701
Places Rated Score: 8,461
Places Rated Rank: 222

### Richmond–Petersburg, VA
Local Choices
73% houses, 2% condos, 2% mobile homes, 15% apartments (rent $335/month)
Houses
Price: $64,600
Property Taxes: $930
Built Before 1940: 17.9%
Energy Requirements
Heating Season: 3,939 degree days
Major Source: Oil/Electricity
Air-conditioning: 1,006 hours
Annual Costs
Mortgage and Taxes: $7,049
Utilities: $1,294
Places Rated Score: 8,343
Places Rated Rank: 213

### Riverside–San Bernardino, CA
Local Choices
72% houses, 5% condos, 10% mobile homes, 10% apartments (rent $380/month)
Houses
Price: $83,000
Property Taxes: $855
Built Before 1940: 7.6%
Energy Requirements
Heating Season: 1,919 degree days
Major Source: Natural gas/Electricity
Air-conditioning: 1,209 hours
Annual Costs
Mortgage and Taxes: $8,721
Utilities: $1,033
Places Rated Score: 9,754
Places Rated Rank: 268

### Roanoke, VA
Local Choices
73% houses, 1% condos, 2% mobile homes, 15% apartments (rent $280/month)
Houses
Price: $57,700
Property Taxes: $832
Built Before 1940: 21.8%
Energy Requirements
Heating Season: 4,307 degree days
Major Source: Natural gas/Electricity
Air-conditioning: 799 hours

Annual Costs
Mortgage and Taxes: $6,306
Utilities: $1,170
Places Rated Score: 7,476
Places Rated Rank: 137

### Rochester, MN
Local Choices
67% houses, 3% condos, 5% mobile homes, 15% apartments (rent $315/month)
Houses
Price: $77,600
Property Taxes: $597
Built Before 1940: 22.9%
Energy Requirements
Heating Season: 8,227 degree days
Major Source: Natural gas/Electricity
Air-conditioning: 336 hours
Annual Costs
Mortgage and Taxes: $7,952
Utilities: $1,241
Places Rated Score: 9,193
Places Rated Rank: 252

### Rochester, NY
Local Choices
67% houses, 1% condos, 3% mobile homes, 14% apartments (rent $330/month)
Houses
Price: $59,700
Property Taxes: $1,534
Built Before 1940: 39.9%
Energy Requirements
Heating Season: 6,718 degree days
Major Source: Natural gas/Electricity
Air-conditioning: 419 hours
Annual Costs
Mortgage and Taxes: $7,194
Utilities: $1,415
Places Rated Score: 8,609
Places Rated Rank: 233

### Rockford, IL
Local Choices
73% houses, 1% condos, 2% mobile homes, 10% apartments (rent $305/month)
Houses
Price: $58,900
Property Taxes: $936
Built Before 1940: 26.2%
Energy Requirements
Heating Season: 6,845 degree days
Major Source: Natural gas/Electricity
Air-conditioning: 583 hours
Annual Costs
Mortgage and Taxes: $6,215
Utilities: $1,369
Places Rated Score: 7,584
Places Rated Rank: 142

### Sacramento, CA
Local Choices
61% houses, 3% condos, 4% mobile homes, 14% apartments (rent $350/month)
Houses
Price: $87,200
Property Taxes: $898
Built Before 1940: 9.7%
Energy Requirements
Heating Season: 2,843 degree days
Major Source: Natural gas/Electricity
Air-conditioning: 1,006 hours

Annual Costs
Mortgage and Taxes: $9,166
Utilities: $689
Places Rated Score: 9,855
Places Rated Rank: 271

### Saginaw–Bay City–Midland, MI
Local Choices
79% houses, 1% condos, 5% mobile homes, 8% apartments (rent $305/month)
Houses
Price: $49,900
Property Taxes: $1,337
Built Before 1940: 27.8%
Energy Requirements
Heating Season: 7,143 degree days
Major Source: Natural gas/Electricity
Air-conditioning: 392 hours
Annual Costs
Mortgage and Taxes: $6,067
Utilities: $1,301
Places Rated Score: 7,368
Places Rated Rank: 131

### St. Cloud, MN
Local Choices
75% houses, 5% mobile homes, 11% apartments (rent $290/month)
Houses
Price: $58,000
Property Taxes: $446
Built Before 1940: 29.0%
Energy Requirements
Heating Season: 8,868 degree days
Major Source: Oil/Electricity
Air-conditioning: 496 hours
Annual Costs
Mortgage and Taxes: $5,941
Utilities: $1,294
Places Rated Score: 7,235
Places Rated Rank: 121

### ★ St. Joseph, MO
Local Choices
76% houses, 4% mobile homes, 8% apartments (rent $240/month)
Houses
Price: $40,900
Property Taxes: $478
Built Before 1940: 50.0%
Energy Requirements
Heating Season: 5,440 degree days
Major Source: Natural gas/Electricity
Air-conditioning: 1,125 hours
Annual Costs
Mortgage and Taxes: $4,352
Utilities: $1,237
Places Rated Score: 5,589
Places Rated Rank: 7

### St. Louis, MO–IL
Local Choices
68% houses, 2% condos, 2% mobile homes, 13% apartments (rent $300/month)
Houses
Price: $60,500
Property Taxes: $708
Built Before 1940: 26.8%
Energy Requirements
Heating Season: 4,486 degree days
Major Source: Natural gas/Electricity
Air-conditioning: 1,131 hours

Annual Costs
Mortgage and Taxes: $6,447
Utilities: $1,158
Places Rated Score: 7,605
Places Rated Rank: 143

### Salem, OR
Local Choices
74% houses, 1% condos, 7% mobile homes, 12% apartments (rent $345/month)
Houses
Price: $67,300
Property Taxes: $1,387
Built Before 1940: 15.3%
Energy Requirements
Heating Season: 4,852 degree days
Major Source: Total electric
Air-conditioning: 296 hours
Annual Costs
Mortgage and Taxes: $7,771
Utilities: $607
Places Rated Score: 8,378
Places Rated Rank: 216

### Salem–Gloucester, MA
Local Choices
58% houses, 3% condos, 1% mobile homes, 15% apartments (rent $330/month)
Houses
Price: $85,000
Property Taxes: $2,066
Built Before 1940: 52.4%
Energy Requirements
Heating Season: 6,321 degree days
Major Source: Oil/Electricity
Air-conditioning: 152 hours
Annual Costs
Mortgage and Taxes: $10,124
Utilities: $1,498
Places Rated Score: 11,622
Places Rated Rank: 301

### Salinas–Seaside–Monterey, CA
Local Choices
66% houses, 4% condos, 4% mobile homes, 18% apartments (rent $415/month)
Houses
Price: $122,900
Property Taxes: $1,266
Built Before 1940: 13.6%
Energy Requirements
Heating Season: 2,959 degree days
Major Source: Natural gas/Electricity
Air-conditioning: 14 hours
Annual Costs
Mortgage and Taxes: $12,917
Utilities: $921
Places Rated Score: 13,838
Places Rated Rank: 315

### Salt Lake City–Ogden, UT
Local Choices
72% houses, 4% condos, 3% mobile homes, 12% apartments (rent $345/month)
Houses
Price: $78,500
Property Taxes: $722
Built Before 1940: 16.6%
Energy Requirements
Heating Season: 5,983 degree days
Major Source: Natural gas/Electricity
Air-conditioning: 877 hours

Annual Costs
Mortgage and Taxes: $8,159
Utilities: $1,307
Places Rated Score: 9,466
Places Rated Rank: 262

### San Angelo, TX
Local Choices
75% houses, 1% condos, 4% mobile homes, 16% apartments (rent $300/month)
Houses
Price: $48,700
Property Taxes: $682
Built Before 1940: 14.6%
Energy Requirements
Heating Season: 2,240 degree days
Major Source: Natural gas/Electricity
Air-conditioning: 2,082 hours
Annual Costs
Mortgage and Taxes: $5,297
Utilities: $1,024
Places Rated Score: 6,321
Places Rated Rank: 40

### San Antonio, TX
Local Choices
74% houses, 1% condos, 3% mobile homes, 15% apartments (rent $290/month)
Houses
Price: $53,800
Property Taxes: $753
Built Before 1940: 13.0%
Energy Requirements
Heating Season: 1,570 degree days
Major Source: Natural gas/Electricity
Air-conditioning: 2,004 hours
Annual Costs
Mortgage and Taxes: $5,850
Utilities: $1,048
Places Rated Score: 6,898
Places Rated Rank: 93

### San Diego, CA
Local Choices
62% houses, 9% condos, 5% mobile homes, 22% apartments (rent $410/month)
Houses
Price: $123,503
Property Taxes: $1,272
Built Before 1940: 8.9%
Energy Requirements
Heating Season: 1,507 degree days
Major Source: Natural gas/Electricity
Air-conditioning: 130 hours
Annual Costs
Mortgage and Taxes: $12,979
Utilities: $1,486
Places Rated Score: 14,465
Places Rated Rank: 321

### San Francisco, CA
Local Choices
51% houses, 4% condos, 1% mobile homes, 23% apartments (rent $445/month)
Houses
Price: $154,500
Property Taxes: $1,591
Built Before 1940: 34.7%
Energy Requirements
Heating Season: 3,042 degree days
Major Source: Natural gas/Electricity
Air-conditioning: 42 hours

Annual Costs
Mortgage and Taxes: $16,237
Utilities: $921
Places Rated Score: 17,158
Places Rated Rank: 327

### San Jose, CA
Local Choices
66% houses, 6% condos, 4% mobile homes, 20% apartments (rent $480/month)
Houses
Price: $143,900
Property Taxes: $1,483
Built Before 1940: 7.4%
Energy Requirements
Heating Season: 3,184 degree days
Major Source: Natural gas/Electricity
Air-conditioning: 157 hours
Annual Costs
Mortgage and Taxes: $15,127
Utilities: $921
Places Rated Score: 16,048
Places Rated Rank: 325

### Santa Barbara–Santa Maria–Lompoc, CA
Local Choices
61% houses, 5% condos, 5% mobile homes, 22% apartments (rent $440/month)
Houses
Price: $138,100
Property Taxes: $1,423
Built Before 1940: 13.8%
Energy Requirements
Heating Season: 1,980 degree days
Major Source: Natural gas/Electricity
Air-conditioning: 44 hours
Annual Costs
Mortgage and Taxes: $14,514
Utilities: $1,033
Places Rated Score: 15,547
Places Rated Rank: 323

### Santa Cruz, CA
Local Choices
69% houses, 4% condos, 7% mobile homes, 13% apartments (rent $430/month)
Houses
Price: $127,300
Property Taxes: $1,312
Built Before 1940: 18.2%
Energy Requirements
Heating Season: 3,139 degree days
Major Source: Natural gas/Electricity
Air-conditioning: 14 hours
Annual Costs
Mortgage and Taxes: $13,382
Utilities: $921
Places Rated Score: 14,303
Places Rated Rank: 319

### Santa Rosa–Petaluma, CA
Local Choices
74% houses, 3% condos, 7% mobile homes, 10% apartments (rent $410/month)
Houses
Price: $114,300
Property Taxes: $1,177
Built Before 1940: 14.8%
Energy Requirements
Heating Season: 3,065 degree days
Major Source: Natural gas/Electricity
Air-conditioning: 770 hours

Annual Costs
    Mortgage and Taxes: $12,010
    Utilities: $921
Places Rated Score: 12,931
Places Rated Rank: 309

## Sarasota, FL
Local Choices
    62% houses, 20% condos, 10% mobile
    homes, 8% apartments (rent
    $390/month)
Houses
    Price: $80,700
    Property Taxes: $831
    Built Before 1940: 4.0%
Energy Requirements
    Heating Season: 597 degree days
    Major Source: Total electric
    Air-conditioning: 2,154 hours
Annual Costs
    Mortgage and Taxes: $8,480
    Utilities: $1,080
Places Rated Score: 9,560
Places Rated Rank: 265

## Savannah, GA
Local Choices
    71% houses, 1% condos, 6% mobile
    homes, 10% apartments (rent
    $280/month)
Houses
    Price: $53,100
    Property Taxes: $642
    Built Before 1940: 17.6%
Energy Requirements
    Heating Season: 1,952 degree days
    Major Source: Natural gas/Electricity
    Air-conditioning: 1,515 hours
Annual Costs
    Mortgage and Taxes: $5,675
    Utilities: $1,221
Places Rated Score: 6,896
Places Rated Rank: 92

## Scranton–Wilkes-Barre, PA
Local Choices
    69% houses, 4% mobile homes, 7%
    apartments (rent $260/month)
Houses
    Price: $48,500
    Property Taxes: $791
    Built Before 1940: 56.6%
Energy Requirements
    Heating Season: 6,114 degree days
    Major Source: Oil/Electricity
    Air-conditioning: 425 hours
Annual Costs
    Mortgage and Taxes: $5,390
    Utilities: $1,307
Places Rated Score: 6,697
Places Rated Rank: 73

## Seattle, WA
Local Choices
    68% houses, 4% condos, 3% mobile
    homes, 19% apartments (rent
    $400/month)
Houses
    Price: $92,800
    Property Taxes: $937
    Built Before 1940: 20.5%
Energy Requirements
    Heating Season: 4,487 degree days
    Major Source: Total electric
    Air-conditioning: 91 hours
Annual Costs
    Mortgage and Taxes: $9,735

Utilities: $448
Places Rated Score: 10,183
Places Rated Rank: 283

## Sharon, PA
Local Choices
    78% houses, 7% mobile homes, 6%
    apartments (rent $290/month)
Houses
    Price: $47,900
    Property Taxes: $782
    Built Before 1940: 43.0%
Energy Requirements
    Heating Season: 6,350 degree days
    Major Source: Natural gas/Electricity
    Air-conditioning: 371 hours
Annual Costs
    Mortgage and Taxes: $5,327
    Utilities: $1,370
Places Rated Score: 6,697
Places Rated Rank: 73

## Sheboygan, WI
Local Choices
    71% houses, 2% mobile homes, 6%
    apartments (rent $270/month)
Houses
    Price: $59,800
    Property Taxes: $1,201
    Built Before 1940: 47.8%
Energy Requirements
    Heating Season: 7,240 degree days
    Major Source: Natural gas/Electricity
    Air-conditioning: 309 hours
Annual Costs
    Mortgage and Taxes: $6,867
    Utilities: $1,254
Places Rated Score: 8,121
Places Rated Rank: 188

## ★ Sherman–Denison, TX
Local Choices
    81% houses, 5% mobile homes, 6%
    apartments (rent $275/month)
Houses
    Price: $43,600
    Property Taxes: $610
    Built Before 1940: 23.8%
Energy Requirements
    Heating Season: 2,864 degree days
    Major Source: Natural gas/Electricity
    Air-conditioning: 2,304 hours
Annual Costs
    Mortgage and Taxes: $4,743
    Utilities: $979
Places Rated Score: 5,722
Places Rated Rank: 13

## Shreveport, LA
Local Choices
    77% houses, 1% condos, 5% mobile
    homes, 10% apartments (rent
    $270/month)
Houses
    Price: $58,800
    Property Taxes: $88
    Built Before 1940: 14.2%
Energy Requirements
    Heating Season: 2,167 degree days
    Major Source: Natural gas/Electricity
    Air-conditioning: 1,846 hours
Annual Costs
    Mortgage and Taxes: $5,659
    Utilities: $875
Places Rated Score: 6,534
Places Rated Rank: 57

## Sioux City, IA–NE
Local Choices
    76% houses, 5% mobile homes, 10%
    apartments (rent $285/month)
Houses
    Price: $47,000
    Property Taxes: $771
    Built Before 1940: 46.5%
Energy Requirements
    Heating Season: 6,953 degree days
    Major Source: Natural gas/Electricity
    Air-conditioning: 796 hours
Annual Costs
    Mortgage and Taxes: $5,227
    Utilities: $1,301
Places Rated Score: 6,528
Places Rated Rank: 56

## Sioux Falls, SD
Local Choices
    68% houses, 1% condos, 5% mobile
    homes, 17% apartments (rent
    $275/month)
Houses
    Price: $60,900
    Property Taxes: $1,077
    Built Before 1940: 25.6%
Energy Requirements
    Heating Season: 7,838 degree days
    Major Source: Natural gas/Electricity
    Air-conditioning: 498 hours
Annual Costs
    Mortgage and Taxes: $6,847
    Utilities: $1,136
Places Rated Score: 7,983
Places Rated Rank: 175

## ★ South Bend–Mishawaka, IN
Local Choices
    81% houses, 1% condos, 2% mobile
    homes, 6% apartments (rent
    $285/month)
Houses
    Price: $45,000
    Property Taxes: $535
    Built Before 1940: 33.0%
Energy Requirements
    Heating Season: 6,462 degree days
    Major Source: Natural gas/Electricity
    Air-conditioning: 563 hours
Annual Costs
    Mortgage and Taxes: $4,797
    Utilities: $1,141
Places Rated Score: 5,938
Places Rated Rank: 20

## Spokane, WA
Local Choices
    73% houses, 1% condos, 5% mobile
    homes, 14% apartments (rent
    $315/month)
Houses
    Price: $61,300
    Property Taxes: $619
    Built Before 1940: 26.5%
Energy Requirements
    Heating Season: 6,835 degree days
    Major Source: Total electric
    Air-conditioning: 373 hours
Annual Costs
    Mortgage and Taxes: $6,425
    Utilities: $502
Places Rated Score: 6,927
Places Rated Rank: 95

### Springfield, IL
Local Choices
73% houses, 1% condos, 5% mobile homes, 10% apartments (rent $300/month)
Houses
Price: $60,400
Property Taxes: $960
Built Before 1940: 32.9%
Energy Requirements
Heating Season: 5,558 degree days
Major Source: Natural gas/Electricity
Air-conditioning: 867 hours
Annual Costs
Mortgage and Taxes: $6,684
Utilities: $1,198
Places Rated Score: 7,882
Places Rated Rank: 167

### Springfield, MA
Local Choices
59% houses, 1% condos, 1% mobile homes, 19% apartments (rent $295/month)
Houses
Price: $54,600
Property Taxes: $1,326
Built Before 1940: 41.1%
Energy Requirements
Heating Season: 5,844 degree days
Major Source: Oil/Electricity
Air-conditioning: 436 hours
Annual Costs
Mortgage and Taxes: $6,499
Utilities: $1,540
Places Rated Score: 8,039
Places Rated Rank: 179

### Springfield, MO
Local Choices
78% houses, 5% mobile homes, 10% apartments (rent $260/month)
Houses
Price: $48,400
Property Taxes: $566
Built Before 1940: 21.5%
Energy Requirements
Heating Season: 4,570 degree days
Major Source: Natural gas/Electricity
Air-conditioning: 964 hours
Annual Costs
Mortgage and Taxes: $5,151
Utilities: $1,192
Places Rated Score: 6,343
Places Rated Rank: 43

### Stamford, CT
Local Choices
61% houses, 5% condos, 17% apartments (rent $480/month)
Houses
Price: $200,000
Property Taxes: $3,061
Built Before 1940: 31.7%
Energy Requirements
Heating Season: 5,250 degree days
Major Source: Oil/Electricity
Air-conditioning: 345 hours
Annual Costs
Mortgage and Taxes: $22,023
Utilities: $1,617
Places Rated Score: 23,640
Places Rated Rank: 329

### State College, PA
Local Choices
60% houses, 1% condos, 7% mobile

homes, 23% apartments (rent $350/month)
Houses
Price: $64,900
Property Taxes: $1,057
Built Before 1940: 29.5%
Energy Requirements
Heating Season: 6,132 degree days
Major Source: Oil/Electricity
Air-conditioning: 351 hours
Annual Costs
Mortgage and Taxes: $7,205
Utilities: $1,200
Places Rated Score: 8,405
Places Rated Rank: 221

### Steubenville–Weirton, OH–WV
Local Choices
79% houses, 6% mobile homes, 6% apartments (rent $260/month)
Houses
Price: $49,400
Property Taxes: $568
Built Before 1940: 39.2%
Energy Requirements
Heating Season: 5,515 degree days
Major Source: Natural gas/Electricity
Air-conditioning: 471 hours
Annual Costs
Mortgage and Taxes: $5,250
Utilities: $1,328
Places Rated Score: 6,578
Places Rated Rank: 61

### Stockton, CA
Local Choices
73% houses, 2% condos, 4% mobile homes, 14% apartments (rent $320/month)
Houses
Price: $71,900
Property Taxes: $740
Built Before 1940: 16.5%
Energy Requirements
Heating Season: 2,806 degree days
Major Source: Natural gas/Electricity
Air-conditioning: 1,017 hours
Annual Costs
Mortgage and Taxes: $7,553
Utilities: $921
Places Rated Score: 8,474
Places Rated Rank: 223

### Syracuse, NY
Local Choices
64% houses, 1% condos, 4% mobile homes, 16% apartments (rent $310/month)
Houses
Price: $53,300
Property Taxes: $1,370
Built Before 1940: 40.6%
Energy Requirements
Heating Season: 6,678 degree days
Major Source: Natural gas/Electricity
Air-conditioning: 433 hours
Annual Costs
Mortgage and Taxes: $6,424
Utilities: $1,246
Places Rated Score: 7,670
Places Rated Rank: 148

### Tacoma, WA
Local Choices
70% houses, 1% condos, 5% mobile homes, 16% apartments (rent $340/month)

Houses
Price: $70,900
Property Taxes: $716
Built Before 1940: 20.7%
Energy Requirements
Heating Season: 4,835 degree days
Major Source: Total electric
Air-conditioning: 122 hours
Annual Costs
Mortgage and Taxes: $7,432
Utilities: $338
Places Rated Score: 7,770
Places Rated Rank: 155

### Tallahassee, FL
Local Choices
61% houses, 1% condos, 10% mobile homes, 18% apartments (rent $320/month)
Houses
Price: $64,700
Property Taxes: $667
Built Before 1940: 7.5%
Energy Requirements
Heating Season: 1,563 degree days
Major Source: Total electric
Air-conditioning: 1,538 hours
Annual Costs
Mortgage and Taxes: $6,802
Utilities: $1,227
Places Rated Score: 8,029
Places Rated Rank: 178

### Tampa–St. Petersburg–Clearwater, FL
Local Choices
65% houses, 8% condos, 10% mobile homes, 13% apartments (rent $330/month)
Houses
Price: $59,500
Property Taxes: $613
Built Before 1940: 7.0%
Energy Requirements
Heating Season: 717 degree days
Major Source: Total electric
Air-conditioning: 2,154 hours
Annual Costs
Mortgage and Taxes: $6,254
Utilities: $1,188
Places Rated Score: 7,442
Places Rated Rank: 135

### ★ Terre Haute, IN
Local Choices
79% houses, 6% mobile homes, 6% apartments (rent $255/month)
Houses
Price: $40,200
Property Taxes: $479
Built Before 1940: 47.2%
Energy Requirements
Heating Season: 5,351 degree days
Major Source: Natural gas/Electricity
Air-conditioning: 834 hours
Annual Costs
Mortgage and Taxes: $4,293
Utilities: $1,234
Places Rated Score: 5,527
Places Rated Rank: 5

### ★ Texarkana, TX–Texarkana, AR
Local Choices
78% houses, 1% condos, 6% mobile homes, 7% apartments (rent $250/month)

Houses
 Price: $44,100
 Property Taxes: $617
 Built Before 1940: 15.4%
Energy Requirements
 Heating Season: 2,362 degree days
 Major Source: Natural gas/Electricity
 Air-conditioning: 1,730 hours
Annual Costs
 Mortgage and Taxes: $4,795
 Utilities: $922
Places Rated Score: 5,717
Places Rated Rank: 12

### Toledo, OH
Local Choices
 73% houses, 1% condos, 4% mobile
  homes, 12% apartments (rent
  $300/month)
Houses
 Price: $58,700
 Property Taxes: $675
 Built Before 1940: 36.2%
Energy Requirements
 Heating Season: 6,381 degree days
 Major Source: Natural gas/Electricity
 Air-conditioning: 540 hours
Annual Costs
 Mortgage and Taxes: $6,241
 Utilities: $1,526
Places Rated Score: 7,767
Places Rated Rank: 153

### Topeka, KS
Local Choices
 74% houses, 2% condos, 4% mobile
  homes, 13% apartments (rent
  $280/month)
Houses
 Price: $57,500
 Property Taxes: $558
 Built Before 1940: 25.6%
Energy Requirements
 Heating Season: 5,243 degree days
 Major Source: Natural gas/Electricity
 Air-conditioning: 1,154 hours
Annual Costs
 Mortgage and Taxes: $6,007
 Utilities: $1,103
Places Rated Score: 7,110
Places Rated Rank: 111

### Trenton, NJ
Local Choices
 69% houses, 1% condos, 18%
  apartments (rent $365/month)
Houses
 Price: $75,700
 Property Taxes: $1,931
 Built Before 1940: 36.3%
Energy Requirements
 Heating Season: 4,947 degree days
 Major Source: Oil/Electricity
 Air-conditioning: 448 hours
Annual Costs
 Mortgage and Taxes: $9,108
 Utilities: $1,508
Places Rated Score: 10,616
Places Rated Rank: 291

### Tucson, AZ
Local Choices
 66% houses, 5% condos, 11% mobile
  homes, 15% apartments (rent
  $350/month)

Houses
 Price: $75,200
 Property Taxes: $421
 Built Before 1940: 18.6%
Energy Requirements
 Heating Season: 1,002 degree days
 Major Source: Natural gas/Electricity
 Air-conditioning: 2,445 hours
Annual Costs
 Mortgage and Taxes: $7,546
 Utilities: $1,002
Places Rated Score: 8,548
Places Rated Rank: 228

### Tulsa, OK
Local Choices
 75% houses, 1% condos, 5% mobile
  homes, 12% apartments (rent
  $320/month)
Houses
 Price: $64,600
 Property Taxes: $478
 Built Before 1940: 15.9%
Energy Requirements
 Heating Season: 3,680 degree days
 Major Source: Natural gas/Electricity
 Air-conditioning: 1,420 hours
Annual Costs
 Mortgage and Taxes: $6,603
 Utilities: $895
Places Rated Score: 7,498
Places Rated Rank: 139

### Tuscaloosa, AL
Local Choices
 68% houses, 1% condos, 7% mobile
  homes, 15% apartments (rent
  $265/month)
Houses
 Price: $54,400
 Property Taxes: $223
 Built Before 1940: 12.0%
Energy Requirements
 Heating Season: 2,626 degree days
 Major Source: Natural gas/Electricity
 Air-conditioning: 1,533 hours
Annual Costs
 Mortgage and Taxes: $5,375
 Utilities: $1,089
Places Rated Score: 6,464
Places Rated Rank: 50

### Tyler, TX
Local Choices
 79% houses, 6% mobile homes, 9%
  apartments (rent $320/month)
Houses
 Price: $58,100
 Property Taxes: $813
 Built Before 1940: 13.7%
Energy Requirements
 Heating Season: 1,923 degree days
 Major Source: Natural gas/Electricity
 Air-conditioning: 1,855 hours
Annual Costs
 Mortgage and Taxes: $6,319
 Utilities: $979
Places Rated Score: 7,298
Places Rated Rank: 127

### Utica–Rome, NY
Local Choices
 60% houses, 5% mobile homes, 9%
  apartments (rent $265/month)
Houses
 Price: $45,600

Property Taxes: $1,173
 Built Before 1940: 51.0%
Energy Requirements
 Heating Season: 6,520 degree days
 Major Source: Natural gas/Electricity
 Air-conditioning: 301 hours
Annual Costs
 Mortgage and Taxes: $5,498
 Utilities: $1,246
Places Rated Score: 6,744
Places Rated Rank: 79

### Vallejo–Fairfield–Napa, CA
Local Choices
 74% houses, 3% condos, 5% mobile
  homes, 11% apartments (rent
  $370/month)
Houses
 Price: $91,200
 Property Taxes: $939
 Built Before 1940: 12.2%
Energy Requirements
 Heating Season: 3,065 degree days
 Major Source: Natural gas/Electricity
 Air-conditioning: 588 hours
Annual Costs
 Mortgage and Taxes: $9,582
 Utilities: $921
Places Rated Score: 10,503
Places Rated Rank: 288

### Vancouver, WA
Local Choices
 69% houses, 1% condos, 5% mobile
  homes, 9% apartments (rent
  $390/month)
Houses
 Price: $81,700
 Property Taxes: $825
 Built Before 1940: 12.5%
Energy Requirements
 Heating Season: 4,667 degree days
 Major Source: Total electric
 Air-conditioning: 208 hours
Annual Costs
 Mortgage and Taxes: $8,569
 Utilities: $446
Places Rated Score: 9,015
Places Rated Rank: 247

### Victoria, TX
Local Choices
 74% houses, 6% mobile homes, 11%
  apartments (rent $330/month)
Houses
 Price: $56,300
 Property Taxes: $788
 Built Before 1940: 10.5%
Energy Requirements
 Heating Season: 1,227 degree days
 Major Source: Natural gas/Electricity
 Air-conditioning: 1,861 hours
Annual Costs
 Mortgage and Taxes: $6,125
 Utilities: $1,018
Places Rated Score: 7,143
Places Rated Rank: 114

### Vineland–Millville–Bridgeton, NJ
Local Choices
 73% houses, 1% condos, 6% mobile
  homes, 11% apartments (rent
  $315/month)
Houses
 Price: $48,400
 Property Taxes: $1,233
 Built Before 1940: 34.1%

Energy Requirements
Heating Season: 4,750 degree days
Major Source: Oil/Electricity
Air-conditioning: 679 hours
Annual Costs
Mortgage and Taxes: $5,817
Utilities: $1,478
Places Rated Score: 7,295
Places Rated Rank: 126

## Visalia–Tulare–Porterville, CA
Local Choices
78% houses, 6% mobile homes, 8%
apartments (rent $320/month)
Houses
Price: $64,200
Property Taxes: $661
Built Before 1940: 15.1%
Energy Requirements
Heating Season: 2,386 degree days
Major Source: Natural gas/Electricity
Air-conditioning: 1,399 hours
Annual Costs
Mortgage and Taxes: $6,745
Utilities: $1,033
Places Rated Score: 7,778
Places Rated Rank: 157

## ★ Waco, TX
Local Choices
77% houses, 3% mobile homes, 12%
apartments (rent $280/month)
Houses
Price: $46,300
Property Taxes: $648
Built Before 1940: 16.5%
Energy Requirements
Heating Season: 2,058 degree days
Major Source: Natural gas/Electricity
Air-conditioning: 2,194 hours
Annual Costs
Mortgage and Taxes: $5,037
Utilities: $1,069
Places Rated Score: 6,106
Places Rated Rank: 25

## Washington, DC–MD–VA
Local Choices
58% houses, 7% condos, 1% mobile
homes, 31% apartments (rent
$415/month)
Houses
Price: $117,800
Property Taxes: $1,360
Built Before 1940: 19.2%
Energy Requirements
Heating Season: 4,260 degree days
Major Source: Natural gas/Electricity
Air-conditioning: 910 hours
Annual Costs
Mortgage and Taxes: $12,530
Utilities: $1,194
Places Rated Score: 13,724
Places Rated Rank: 314

## Waterbury, CT
Local Choices
60% houses, 3% condos, 2% mobile
homes, 14% apartments (rent
$310/month)
Houses
Price: $76,400
Property Taxes: $1,168
Built Before 1940: 33.2%
Energy Requirements
Heating Season: 6,150 degree days
Major Source: Oil/Electricity
Air-conditioning: 344 hours

Annual Costs
Mortgage and Taxes: $8,407
Utilities: $1,617
Places Rated Score: 10,024
Places Rated Rank: 279

## Waterloo–Cedar Falls, IA
Local Choices
76% houses, 1% condos, 4% mobile
homes, 10% apartments (rent
$320/month)
Houses
Price: $59,300
Property Taxes: $973
Built Before 1940: 32.8%
Energy Requirements
Heating Season: 7,415 degree days
Major Source: Natural gas/Electricity
Air-conditioning: 425 hours
Annual Costs
Mortgage and Taxes: $6,594
Utilities: $1,287
Places Rated Score: 7,881
Places Rated Rank: 166

## Wausau, WI
Local Choices
77% houses, 4% mobile homes, 6%
apartments (rent $280/month)
Houses
Price: $55,500
Property Taxes: $1,116
Built Before 1940: 36.4%
Energy Requirements
Heating Season: 8,586 degree days
Major Source: Natural gas/Electricity
Air-conditioning: 456 hours
Annual Costs
Mortgage and Taxes: $6,377
Utilities: $1,265
Places Rated Score: 7,642
Places Rated Rank: 147

## West Palm Beach–Boca Raton– Delray Beach, FL
Local Choices
51% houses, 33% condos, 5% mobile
homes, 10% apartments (rent
$385/month)
Houses
Price: $89,300
Property Taxes: $919
Built Before 1940: 5.2%
Energy Requirements
Heating Season: 299 degree days
Major Source: Total electric
Air-conditioning: 2,052 hours
Annual Costs
Mortgage and Taxes: $9,380
Utilities: $1,132
Places Rated Score: 10,512
Places Rated Rank: 290

## Wheeling, WV–OH
Local Choices
74% houses, 1% condos, 6% mobile
homes, 7% apartments (rent
$245/month)
Houses
Price: $53,800
Property Taxes: $199
Built Before 1940: 49.9%
Energy Requirements
Heating Season: 5,216 degree days
Major Source: Natural gas/Electricity
Air-conditioning: 471 hours
Annual Costs
Mortgage and Taxes: $5,303

Utilities: $1,273
Places Rated Score: 6,576
Places Rated Rank: 60

## Wichita, KS
Local Choices
74% houses, 1% condos, 4% mobile
homes, 11% apartments (rent
$270/month)
Houses
Price: $56,800
Property Taxes: $551
Built Before 1940: 19.9%
Energy Requirements
Heating Season: 4,687 degree days
Major Source: Natural gas/Electricity
Air-conditioning: 1,280 hours
Annual Costs
Mortgage and Taxes: $5,931
Utilities: $1,130
Places Rated Score: 7,061
Places Rated Rank: 105

## Wichita Falls, TX
Local Choices
77% houses, 1% condos, 4% mobile
homes, 11% apartments (rent
$290/month)
Houses
Price: $49,500
Property Taxes: $692
Built Before 1940: 19.4%
Energy Requirements
Heating Season: 2,904 degree days
Major Source: Natural gas/Electricity
Air-conditioning: 2,047 hours
Annual Costs
Mortgage and Taxes: $5,380
Utilities: $1,024
Places Rated Score: 6,404
Places Rated Rank: 46

## Williamsport, PA
Local Choices
71% houses, 7% mobile homes, 8%
apartments (rent $275/month)
Houses
Price: $53,800
Property Taxes: $877
Built Before 1940: 49.3%
Energy Requirements
Heating Season: 5,981 degree days
Major Source: Oil/Electricity
Air-conditioning: 549 hours
Annual Costs
Mortgage and Taxes: $5,977
Utilities: $1,307
Places Rated Score: 7,284
Places Rated Rank: 125

## Wilmington, DE–NJ–MD
Local Choices
73% houses, 1% condos, 3% mobile
homes, 16% apartments (rent
$335/month)
Houses
Price: $64,100
Property Taxes: $481
Built Before 1940: 23.3%
Energy Requirements
Heating Season: 4,940 degree days
Major Source: Oil/Electricity
Air-conditioning: 683 hours
Annual Costs
Mortgage and Taxes: $6,556
Utilities: $1,371
Places Rated Score: 7,927
Places Rated Rank: 173

## Wilmington, NC

**Local Choices**
74% houses, 1% condos, 6% mobile homes, 10% apartments (rent $280/month)

**Houses**
Price: $55,600
Property Taxes: $539
Built Before 1940: 14.9%

**Energy Requirements**
Heating Season: 2,433 degree days
Major Source: Total electric
Air-conditioning: 683 hours

**Annual Costs**
Mortgage and Taxes: $5,809
Utilities: $1,049
Places Rated Score: 6,858
Places Rated Rank: 89

## Worcester, MA

**Local Choices**
50% houses, 1% mobile homes, 15% apartments (rent $300/month)

**Houses**
Price: $60,600
Property Taxes: $1,473
Built Before 1940: 46.8%

**Energy Requirements**
Heating Season: 6,848 degree days
Major Source: Oil/Electricity
Air-conditioning: 297 hours

**Annual Costs**
Mortgage and Taxes: $7,217
Utilities: $1,498
Places Rated Score: 8,715
Places Rated Rank: 239

## Yakima, WA

**Local Choices**
74% houses, 1% condos, 8% mobile homes, 9% apartments (rent $300/month)

**Houses**
Price: $56,200
Property Taxes: $567
Built Before 1940: 24.5%

**Energy Requirements**
Heating Season: 6,009 degree days
Major Source: Total electric
Air-conditioning: 551 hours

**Annual Costs**
Mortgage and Taxes: $5,891
Utilities: $549
Places Rated Score: 6,440
Places Rated Rank: 47

## York, PA

**Local Choices**
76% houses, 1% condos, 6% mobile homes, 6% apartments (rent $295/month)

**Houses**
Price: $62,300
Property Taxes: $1,016
Built Before 1940: 38.4%

**Energy Requirements**
Heating Season: 5,075 degree days
Major Source: Natural gas/Electricity
Air-conditioning: 744 hours

**Annual Costs**
Mortgage and Taxes: $6,925
Utilities: $1,446
Places Rated Score: 8,371
Places Rated Rank: 215

## Youngstown–Warren, OH

**Local Choices**
78% houses, 1% condos, 3% mobile homes, 10% apartments (rent $280/month)

**Houses**
Price: $51,700
Property Taxes: $594
Built Before 1940: 32.0%

**Energy Requirements**
Heating Season: 6,426 degree days
Major Source: Natural gas/Electricity
Air-conditioning: 388 hours

**Annual Costs**
Mortgage and Taxes: $5,491
Utilities: $1,530
Places Rated Score: 7,021
Places Rated Rank: 103

## Yuba City, CA

**Local Choices**
68% houses, 1% condos, 8% mobile homes, 14% apartments (rent $295/month)

**Houses**
Price: $66,200
Property Taxes: $682
Built Before 1940: 12.9%

**Energy Requirements**
Heating Season: 2,585 degree days
Major Source: Natural gas/Electricity
Air-conditioning: 1,294 hours

**Annual Costs**
Mortgage and Taxes: $6,954
Utilities: $921
Places Rated Score: 7,875
Places Rated Rank: 164

## Et Cetera

## HOME FEATURES: WHERE YOU SEE THEM, WHERE YOU GET THEM

Each year, the Federal Housing Authority reports on the characteristics of single-family homes whose mortgages it insures. Here's a geography of eight selected features.

*Stories.* The use of the word "story" to refer to flights of buildings may have originated with tiers of stained-glass or painted windows that described a special event. The common definition today is the space between the floor and the ceiling, roof, or the floor above, in the case of a multistory home. It has nothing to do with the height of a house; a house that appears from the outside to be two stories may actually be a single-story with a cathedral ceiling. More than 85 percent of new houses have only one story. Older homes with more than one story predominate in Connecticut, Maine, Maryland, Massachusetts, New Jersey, New York, Pennsylvania, and Wisconsin.

*Construction and Exterior.* In frame construction, the wood frame supports the floors and roof; in masonry construction, the exterior masonry wall serves as the support. Masonry construction using local stone has virtually disappeared in new houses. Concrete block construction, however, is a common technique in Arizona (40 percent of new homes have it) and Florida (85 percent), where the exterior is either spray-painted or stuccoed. Everywhere else, the majority of new houses are of frame construction.

Aluminum siding is the preferred exterior in Maryland and Ohio; wood is the choice in Georgia and Washington. The majority (86 percent) of all homes being built with brick exteriors in the United States are in the southern states. Exteriors of brick or stucco are preferred in California and Nevada.

*Basements.* The basement is an area of full-story height below the first floor that is not meant for year-round living. Only a third of new houses have basements, because they are expensive to excavate. In six states, however, two out of three new houses come

## Taxing the Home: Statewide Averages

Although the dollar amount of your home's recent property tax bills may seem to ratchet upward with each reassessment, there is some slight comfort in knowing that the rate at which your home is being taxed is actually going down.

Over the past ten years, while the prices of existing homes rose dramatically, nationwide average effective property tax rates dropped from 2 percent of these values to less than 1.25 percent. Economists expect the trend downward to continue.

Nowhere in the United States can you own a home and entirely escape property taxes (except in Alaska, where you have to be 65). But homeowners in certain states (like Louisiana, where the statewide average property tax rate is 0.15 percent) shoulder less of a burden than do homeowners in other states (such as Michigan, which has an average tax rate of 2.68 percent).

### Property Tax on a $100,000 Home by State

| State | Average Effective Rate | Annual Bill | State | Average Effective Rate | Annual Bill | State | Average Effective Rate | Annual Bill |
|---|---|---|---|---|---|---|---|---|
| Alabama | 0.41% | $ 410 | Louisiana | 0.15% | $ 150 | Ohio | 1.15% | $1,150 |
| Alaska | 1.35 | 1,350 | Maine | 1.52 | 1,520 | | | |
| Arizona | 0.56 | 560 | Maryland | 1.37 | 1,370 | Oklahoma | 0.74 | 740 |
| Arkansas | 1.42 | 1,420 | | | | Oregon | 2.06 | 2,060 |
| California | 1.03 | 1,030 | Massachusetts | 2.43 | 2,430 | Pennsylvania | 1.63 | 1,630 |
| | | | Michigan | 2.68 | 2,680 | Rhode Island | 1.93 | 1,930 |
| Colorado | 1.01 | 1,010 | Minnesota | 0.77 | 770 | South Carolina | 0.92 | 920 |
| Connecticut | 1.53 | 1,530 | Mississippi | 0.76 | 760 | | | |
| Delaware | 0.75 | 750 | Missouri | 1.17 | 1,170 | South Dakota | 1.77 | 1,770 |
| Florida | 1.03 | 1,030 | | | | Tennessee | 1.24 | 1,240 |
| Georgia | | | Montana | 1.14 | 1,140 | Texas | 1.40 | 1,400 |
| | | | Nebraska | 2.23 | 2,230 | Utah | 0.92 | 920 |
| Hawaii | 0.36 | 360 | Nevada | 0.77 | 770 | Vermont | 1.60 | 1,600 |
| Idaho | 1.04 | 1,040 | New Hampshire | 2.39 | 2,390 | | | |
| Illinois | 1.59 | 1,590 | New Jersey | 2.55 | 2,550 | Virginia | 1.44 | 1,440 |
| Indiana | 1.19 | 1,190 | | | | Washington | 1.01 | 1,010 |
| Iowa | 1.64 | 1,640 | New Mexico | 0.93 | 930 | West Virginia | 0.37 | 370 |
| | | | New York | 2.57 | 2,570 | Wisconsin | 2.01 | 2,010 |
| Kansas | 0.97 | 970 | North Carolina | 0.97 | 970 | Wyoming | 0.48 | 480 |
| Kentucky | 1.11 | 1,110 | North Dakota | 1.10 | 1,100 | | | |

*Source:* Advisory Commission on Intergovernmental Relations, *Significant Features of Fiscal Federalism,* 1984.

with some kind of basement, reflecting a pattern of locating the furnace below grade and a preference for extra living space. These states are Illinois, Iowa, Michigan, Minnesota, New York, and Pennsylvania.

Most new houses without basements either have a crawl space (an unfinished, accessible space below the first floor that is usually less than full-story height) or are simply resting on a concrete slab poured on the ground. In the United States, crawl spaces are preferred only in the Pacific Northwest and the Carolinas. Concrete slab footings support almost all new houses in the Sun Belt states of Arizona, Arkansas, Georgia, Louisiana, Mississippi, Oklahoma, and Texas.

*Bathrooms.* Bathrooms are either full (a tub or shower stall, a sink, and a toilet) or half (just a sink and a toilet). All new houses have at least one full bathroom. You'll find the majority of new homes with both a full bathroom and a half-bathroom only in the states of Alabama, Arkansas, Georgia, Louisiana, Maryland, Mississippi, New Jersey, Oklahoma, South Carolina, and Tennessee.

*Fireplaces.* Flueless imitation fireplaces, like dinettes and rumpus rooms, are memories of the 1950s. Half of all new American homes now are built with working fireplaces and chimneys. Unfortunately, many fireplaces in these new homes aren't used, because of smoke problems caused by short chimneys. For a good fireplace draft, the chimney cap should be at least 20 feet above the hearth.

Homes with two fireplaces can be found more frequently in the northern timber states of Idaho, Minnesota, Montana, Oregon, and Washington, and also in North Carolina and Pennsylvania.

*Enclosed Porches.* A porch is a covered addition or recessed space at the entrance of a home. These Main Street lookouts have disappeared from new home markets. You'll find an enclosed porch attached to one out of every 12 older homes in this country. In Connecticut, Iowa, Maine, Massachusetts, New Jersey, and New York, more than one fifth of older homes have them.

*Garages and Carports.* Garages, as everyone knows, are completely enclosed shelters for automobiles; carports are roofed shelters that aren't completely enclosed. Detached garages are a feature of older homes and were typically built behind the home, invisible from the street. Attached two-car garages, which became a popular feature on new homes during the 1950s, now are a standard feature on half of all newly built homes. Today, six out of ten houses, new and old, have garages; just one in ten has a carport. Only in Arizona, Hawaii, Louisiana, and Mississippi is this pattern reversed.

*Swimming Pools.* You won't find new tract houses anywhere with in-ground swimming pools. Builders have learned that few buyers shop for shelter *and* a swimming pool at the same time. Moreover, local ordinances can require expensive liability insurance and a four-foot-high fence around the pool's perimeter to prevent accidents.

Among older homes, fewer than 2 percent have in-ground pools. You'll find at least twice that portion in Arizona, California, Florida, Nevada, and surprisingly, Maine, Massachusetts, and New York.

## HOW MUCH HOUSE CAN YOU AFFORD?

One way of figuring how much house you can afford is to use the 20/25 lending requirements set by the Federal National Mortgage Association, a major purchaser of mortgages in the secondary mortgage market. According to this rule, a family making a 20 percent down payment can finance the rest as long as no more than 25 percent of their gross income (income before taxes) covers the annual principal and interest.

For example, at the average 1983 mortgage rate of 12.85 percent, a family would need a gross income of $30,000 to handle the $620 monthly principal and interest payments on a $70,000 house.

That's one way of looking at it. A far simpler way is to recall the long-standing rule of thumb handed down from parents to children which states that, if you buy a house that costs much more than two and a half times your gross income, you're headed for trouble. For example, if your gross annual income is $25,000, the price range of houses to shop for is $60,000 to $62,500; if your income is $30,000, you can afford a house costing between $70,000 and $75,000.

Based on either of these rules, can a typical American family afford a typical home? Unfortunately, no. According to the National Association of Realtors, the last time a family with the national median income had exactly enough income to qualify for a mortgage on a home priced at the national median was in December of 1978.

## A RENTER'S MISCELLANY

The kind of apartment building you choose to live in definitely makes a difference in your monthly costs. Rents for a typical four-room, 850-square-foot unit are much higher in high-rise elevator buildings (U.S. median $392) than in walk-ups or elevator buildings of three stories or fewer (U.S. median $335), according to

### Rent in the Metro Areas

**Highest**

| | |
|---|---|
| 1. Anchorage, AK | $520 |
| 2. Anaheim–Santa Ana, CA | 510 |
| 3. Reno, NV | 490 |
| 4. San Jose, CA | 480 |
| 4. Stamford, CT | 480 |
| 6. Nassau–Suffolk, NY | 475 |
| 7. Norwalk, CT | 465 |
| 8. Middlesex–Somerset–Hunterdon, NJ | 455 |
| 9. Casper, WY | 445 |
| 10. Las Vegas, NV | 430 |
| 11. Bergen–Passaic, NJ | 415 |
| 12. Richland–Kennewick–Pasco, WA | 410 |
| 13. Seattle, WA | 400 |

**Lowest**

| | |
|---|---|
| 1. Joplin, MO | $220 |
| 2. Danville, VA | 225 |
| 3. Cumberland, MD–WV | 230 |
| 4. Gadsden, AL | 235 |
| 4. McAllen–Edinburg–Mission, TX | 235 |
| 6. St. Joseph, MO | 240 |
| 7. Anderson, SC | 245 |
| 7. Columbus, GA–AL | 245 |
| 7. Fall River, MA–RI | 245 |
| 7. Fort Smith, AR–OK | 245 |
| 7. Pine Bluff, AR | 245 |
| 7. Wheeling, WV–OH | 245 |

*Source: U.S. Bureau of the Census, 1980 Census of Population and Housing.*

Above figures represent 1980 rents boosted by Consumer Price Index inflation factors to show realistic 1984 figures. All figures are rounded to the nearest five dollars.

the latest Institute of Real Estate Management survey. The least expensive kind of building is the garden apartment, defined by the institute as a group of low-rise apartment buildings on a large landscaped lot under one manager. The national median monthly rental for this kind of building is $310.

You'll find that the annual turnover rate, defined as newly occupied apartments as a percent of all the apartments in the building in a year's time, also varies by the kind of building. Around the country, high-rise elevator buildings have the lowest turnover rate (U.S. median 22 percent), whereas the turnover rate in walk-ups and elevator buildings of three or fewer stories is twice this (U.S. median 44 percent). The kind of apartment building with the most transient population is the garden apartment, in which 54 percent of tenants moved in within the previous 12 months.

### The Rule of 156

One useful way of determining the rent for a house is to divide its market value by 156. This rule of 156 was developed by the city of San Francisco as a way of specifying the fair value of an apartment being converted into a condo for a tenant who had been renting it. As the landlord might put it, the price equals 156 times your monthly rent, take it or leave it.

What the rule implies in reverse is that landlords

can expect a 156-month (or 13-year) payback on houses they rent. Using this rule plus the prices of houses given in the Place Profiles, it isn't difficult to figure roughly what it would cost you to rent a house in a given metro area, assuming that the landlord has realistic expectations for the rate of return on property.

In Miami–Hialeah, the rent would be $557; in San Francisco, $990; in Joplin, Missouri, $241. The rule of 156 may seem unfair to landlords, since there is only an 8 percent return from which maintenance and taxes must be paid. Bear in mind, however, that landlords rarely buy houses for the rental income they may bring; rather, they buy them for their market appreciation and rent them during the interim merely to cover expenses.

### The Renter Majority

Today about 60 percent of American households live in urbanized areas, which make up only 1.5 percent of total U.S. land area. Renter households are even more concentrated, with one fourth of total rental units located in just 17 counties, which compose only 0.5 percent of the country's land area. Half of all rental units are found within 84 counties. Yet, of the 3,100 counties in the United States, renters constitute a majority only in the 13 listed below.

**Counties with a Majority of Rental Units**

| County | Rental Units as % of All Units |
| --- | --- |
| 1. New York County, NY | 92.2% |
| 2. Bronx County (New York), NY | 85.4 |
| 3. Kings County (New York), NY | 76.6 |
| 4. Hudson County (Jersey City), NJ | 71.3 |
| 5. Suffolk County (Boston), MA | 70.8 |
| 6. San Francisco County, CA | 66.3 |
| 7. Queens County (New York), NY | 61.9 |
| 8. Orleans Parish (New Orleans), LA | 61.3 |
| 9. Essex County (Newark), NJ | 60.5 |
| 10. Fulton County (Atlanta), GA | 53.5 |
| 11. Baltimore City, MD | 52.8 |
| 12. Los Angeles County, CA | 51.5 |
| 13. Honolulu County, HI | 50.1 |

Source: U.S. Bureau of the Census, *1980 Census of Population and Housing*.

## LEGAL SAFEGUARDS FOR RENTERS AND CONDO BUYERS

If you're thinking of moving to another state and either renting an apartment or buying a condominium, a knowledge of local laws could save you from some potentially expensive surprises.

### Renters' Rights

In many states with large renter populations, laws concerning relations between landlords and tenants give rights to the landlord while imposing obligations on the tenant.

Seventeen states, however, have passed landlord-tenant laws based on the Uniform Residential Land-

lord and Tenant Act (1972), a model law drawn up by the National Conference of Commissioners on Uniform State Laws. These states are Alaska, Arizona, Connecticut, Florida, Hawaii, Iowa, Kansas, Kentucky, Michigan, Montana, Nebraska, New Mexico, Oklahoma, Oregon, Tennessee, Virginia, and Washington.

This law defines rights and obligations of both parties to a lease on an apartment or house, and it also specifies the way disputes can be resolved. Among its provisions are:

- If your dispute with a landlord leads you to complain to the local housing board, to join a tenants' group, or to sue your landlord, the landlord cannot retaliate by cutting services, raising your rent, or evicting you.
- If the landlord doesn't make needed repairs, and the cost of the repairs is no more than $100 or half the rent (whichever is greater), you may make the repairs and deduct the expense from your monthly rent.
- After you vacate the apartment or house, any money you've deposited as security must be returned. If there are any deductions from the deposit for damages or other reasons, these deductions must be itemized.
- If your landlord doesn't live up to the lease's terms, you can recover damages in small claims court.

### Protection for Condo Buyers

During the 1960s and 1970s, condo buyers had little legal protection when they signed a purchase agreement. Over the past four years, nine states have passed comprehensive laws to deal with condominium ownership based on the Uniform Condominium Act (1980), drawn up by the National Conference of Commissioners on Uniform State Laws. These states are Maine, Minnesota, Missouri, Nebraska, New Mexico, Pennsylvania, Rhode Island, Virginia, and West Virginia.

The Uniform Condominium Act covers owners' associations, developers' activities, eminent domain, separate titles and taxation, and safeguards for condo buyers. It stipulates, among other things, that:

- The developer must provide you with a Public Offering Statement, accurately and fully disclosing a schedule for finishing construction, the total number of units, the bylaws of the owners' association, copies of any contracts or leases that you have to sign, a current balance sheet and projected one-year budget for the owners' association, and a statement of the monthly common assessments you'll have to pay.
- After signing a purchase agreement, you are given 15 days to "cool off," after which you

can either cancel the agreement without penalty or accept conveyance of the property.

- If you buy a condominium without first being given a Public Offering Statement, you're entitled to receive from the developer an amount equal to 10 percent of the sales price of the unit you bought.
- The developer and real estate agent must guarantee that the unit you are buying is free from defective materials, is built to sound engineering and construction standards, and conforms to local codes.

## PAYING FOR POWER

Household electric bills around the country vary widely in dollar amounts, for several reasons. Customer density, distance from oil and coal fuel sources, age of the power plant, and the type and size of equipment used in generating electricity all play a part in the charges to consumers. Who owns the company, however, may be the biggest factor in determining the amount of your bill.

The Energy Department's latest nationwide price comparison of electricity shows that, in general, publicly owned (municipal) electric power companies charge much lower rates than their larger, privately owned counterparts.

In communities of 2,500 or more, the ten lowest bills for 750 kilowatt-hours of monthly service range from $203 (Tacoma Department of Public Utilities) to $350 (City of Colorado Springs Department of Public Utilities). In contrast, the ten highest bills for the same service are mailed out by such privately owned giants as Consolidated Edison of New York ($1,318) and Narragansett Electric ($753).

### Annual Electric Bills

#### Highest

| | |
|---|---|
| 1. Consolidated Edison of New York | $1,318 |
| 2. San Diego Gas and Electric (California) | 1,117 |
| 3. Long Island Lighting (New York) | 984 |
| 4. Hawaiian Electric | 953 |
| 5. United Illuminating (Connecticut) | 882 |
| 6. Public Service Electric and Gas (New Jersey) | 877 |
| 7. Northern Indiana Public Service | 856 |
| 8. Connecticut Light and Power | 838 |
| 9. Boston Edison (Massachusetts) | 814 |
| 10. Narragansett Electric (Rhode Island) | 753 |

#### Lowest

| | |
|---|---|
| 1. City of Tacoma (Washington) | $203 |
| 2. City of Palo Alto (California) | 212 |
| 3. City of Seattle (Washington) | 221 |
| 4. Washington Water Power | 290 |
| 5. City of Eugene (Oregon) | 309 |
| 5. Puget Sound Power and Light (Washington) | 309 |
| 7. Portland General Electric (Oregon) | 324 |
| 8. Pacific Power and Light (Oregon) | 328 |
| 9. City of Sacramento (California) | 335 |
| 10. City of Colorado Springs (Colorado) | 350 |

Source: U.S. Department of Energy, Typical Electric Bills, 1983.

The national average electric bill for 750 kilowatt-hours of monthly service is $665 per year.

## NUCLEAR HOT SPOTS:
## A NATIONWIDE LOCATOR

Would you mind living near a nuclear power plant?

Given the record of the industry after 900 reactor-years of commercial operation in this country, even a proponent of nuclear power would admit that fears about a catastrophic meltdown or low-level environmental contamination are legitimate.

Because of a lower demand for electricity, construction and regulatory delays, skyrocketing costs, and concerns about reactor safety after the 1979 Three Mile Island incident, the growth of nuclear power has slowed considerably in recent years. Utility planners are simply not willing to take the risk of investing billions in a 12- to 14-year process of building a nuclear plant and then face the possibility of not being allowed to operate it. As a result, plans for 76 power plants have been canceled over the past decade, and not one nuclear plant has been ordered since 1978.

During 1983, the 292 billion kilowatt-hours produced by nuclear reactors accounted for 13 percent of total U.S. electrical output. In Vermont, 80 percent of electricity consumed comes from nuclear power; in Maine, 65 percent; in Connecticut and Nebraska, 50 percent or more. The state with the greatest generating capacity, however, is Illinois, partly because Chicago-based Commonwealth Edison has built or plans to build more nuclear power plants than any other utility in the country.

The following list ranks, in order of their total generating capacity, the 34 states in which nuclear power plants are found. The generating capacity, or power output, for a typical reactor is 1,000 megawatts (1 million kilowatts) of electricity, or enough to supply the needs of a city of 600,000 people at any given moment. Each plant listed is either operating (84 of them) or under construction (39) as of June 1984. The date of operation—actual or planned—is also given for each unit, along with its county location. Not included in this list are three reactors that are licensed but shut down indefinitely (Dresden #1 near Joliet, Illinois, and Three Mile Island #1 and #2 near Harrisburg, Pennsylvania), and two reactors each in Indiana, Mississippi, Ohio, Tennessee, and Washington on which construction has been postponed indefinitely.

### Nuclear Electric-Generating Units:
### The States Ranked

1. ILLINOIS: 13,015 megawatts total capacity
   De Witt County (Clinton #1), 1986; Grundy County (Dresden #2 and #3), 1970, 1971; Lake County (Zion #1 and #2), 1973, 1974; La Salle County (La Salle #1 and #2), 1982, 1984; Ogle County (Byron #1 and #2), 1984, 1985; Rock Island County (Quad Cities #1 and #2), 1972, 1972; Will County (Braidwood #1 and #2), 1985, 1986.

2. PENNSYLVANIA: 8,025 megawatts total capacity
   Beaver County (Beaver Valley #1 and #2), 1976, 1986; Luzerne County (Susquehanna #1 and #2), 1983, 1984; Montgomery

(continued on page 116)

## Nuclear Power Plants in the United States

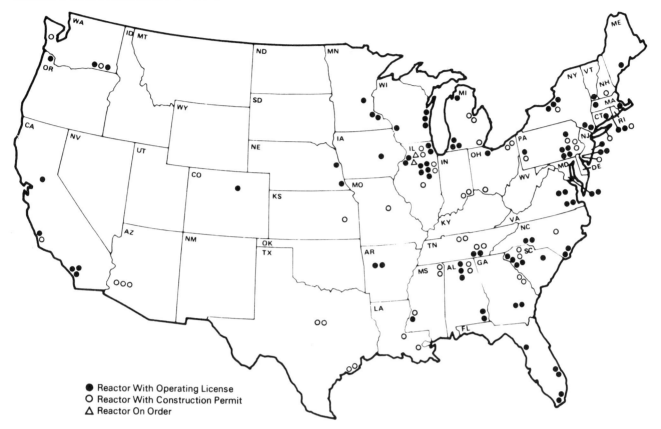

● Reactor With Operating License
○ Reactor With Construction Permit
△ Reactor On Order

*Source:* Atomic Industrial Forum, Inc., January 1984, modified by *Places Rated* to include changes as of August 1984.

## Atomic Metro Areas

| Metro Area | Nuclear Power Plants | Generating Capacity (Megawatts) | Metro Area | Nuclear Power Plants | Generating Capacity (Megawatts) |
|---|---|---|---|---|---|
| Beaver County, PA | 2 | 1,669 | Minneapolis–St. Paul, MN–WI | 1 | 545 |
| Benton Harbor, MI | 2 | 2,130 | Monmouth–Ocean, NJ | 1 | 650 |
| Boston, MA | 1 | 670 | Nassau–Suffolk, NY | 2 | 1,667 |
| Cedar Rapids, IA | 1 | 538 | New London–Norwich, CT–RI | 3 | 2,679 |
| Charlotte–Gastonia–Rock Hill, NC–SC | 4 | 4,650 | | | |
| | | | New Orleans, LA | 1 | 1,104 |
| | | | New York, NY | 2 | 1,838 |
| Chattanooga, TN–GA | 2 | 2,296 | Philadelphia, PA–NJ | 2 | 2,110 |
| Cleveland, OH | 1 | 1,205 | Phoenix, AZ | 3 | 3,810 |
| Davenport–Rock Island– Moline, IA–IL | 2 | 1,578 | Raleigh–Durham, NC | 1 | 900 |
| Detroit, MI | 1 | 1,139 | Richland–Kennewick–Pasco, WA | 2 | 1,960 |
| Dothan, AL | 2 | 1,720 | Rochester, NY | 1 | 470 |
| | | | Sacramento, CA | 1 | 918 |
| Fort Pierce, FL | 2 | 1,608 | Saginaw–Bay City–Midland, MI | 2 | 1,233 |
| Greeley, CO | 1 | 330 | San Diego, CA | 3 | 2,636 |
| Joliet, IL | 4 | 3,828 | | | |
| Lake County, IL | 2 | 2,080 | Scranton–Wilkes-Barre, PA | 2 | 2,100 |
| Lawrence–Haverhill, MA–NH | 1 | 1,150 | Syracuse, NY | 2 | 1,700 |
| | | | Washington, DC–MD–VA | 2 | 1,690 |
| Miami–Hialeah, FL | 2 | 1,332 | Wilmington, DE–NJ–MD | 2 | 2,205 |

*Source:* U.S. Department of Energy, *Inventory of Electric Power Plants in the United States,* 1983.

County (Limerick #1 and #2), 1985, 1988; York County (Peach Bottom #2 and #3), 1974, 1974.

3. ALABAMA: 7,279 megawatts total capacity
Houston County (Farley #1 and #2), 1977, 1981; Jackson County (Bellefonte #1 and #2), 1988, 1990; Morgan County (Browns Ferry #1, #2, and #3), 1974, 1975, 1977.

4. SOUTH CAROLINA: 6,551 megawatts total capacity
Darlington County (Robinson #2), 1971; Fairfield County (Summer), 1984; Oconee County (Oconee #1, #2, and #3), 1973, 1974, 1974; York County (Catawba #1 and #2), 1985, 1987.

5. CALIFORNIA: 5,744 megawatts total capacity
Sacramento County (Rancho Seco), 1975; San Diego County (San Onofre #1, #2, and #3), 1968, 1983, 1984; San Luis Obispo County (Diablo Canyon #1 and #2), 1984, 1985.

6. NEW YORK: 5,668 megawatts total capacity
Oswego County (Nine Mile #1 and #2), 1969, 1986; Suffolk County (FitzPatrick and Shoreham), 1975, 1985; Wayne County (Ginna), 1970; Westchester County (Indian Point #2 and #3), 1973, 1976.

7. MICHIGAN: 5,395 megawatts total capacity
Berrien County (Cook #1 and #2), 1975, 1978; Charlevoix County (Big Rock Point), 1963; Midland County (Midland #1 and #2), 1985, 1985; Monroe County (Fermi #2), 1984; Van Buren County (Palisades), 1971.

8. NORTH CAROLINA: 4,900 megawatts total capacity
Brunswick County (Brunswick #1 and #2), 1975, 1977; Mecklenburg County (McGuire #1 and #2), 1981, 1984; Wake County (Harris #1), 1986.

9. TEXAS: 4,800 megawatts total capacity
Matagorda County (South Texas #1 and #2), 1987, 1989; Somervell County (Comanche Peak #1 and #2), 1985, 1986.

10. TENNESSEE: 4,650 megawatts total capacity
Hamilton County (Sequayah #1 and #2), 1981, 1982; Rhea County (Watts Bar #1 and #2), 1984, 1986.

11. NEW JERSEY: 3,922 megawatts total capacity
Ocean County (Oyster Creek), 1969; Salem County (Salem #1 and #2, Hope Creek), 1977, 1981, 1986.

12. FLORIDA: 3,820 megawatts total capacity
Citrus County (Crystal River #3), 1977; Dade County (Turkey Point #3 and #4), 1972, 1973; St. Lucie County (St. Lucie #1 and #2), 1976, 1983.

13. ARIZONA: 3,810 megawatts total capacity
Maricopa County (Palos Verde #1, #2, and #3), 1984, 1985, 1986.

14. GEORGIA: 3,776 megawatts total capacity
Appling County (Hatch #1 and #2), 1975, 1979; Burke County (Vogtle #1 and #2), 1987, 1988.

15. VIRGINIA: 3,390 megawatts total capacity
Louisa County (North Anna #1 and #2), 1978, 1980; Surry County (Surry #1 and #2), 1972, 1973.

16. CONNECTICUT: 3,261 megawatts total capacity
Middlesex County (Haddam), 1968; New London County (Millstone #1, #2, and #3), 1970, 1975, 1986.

17. MISSISSIPPI: 2,500 megawatts total capacity
Claiborne County (Grand Gulf #1 and #2), 1982, 1990.

18. OHIO: 2,095 megawatts total capacity
Lake County (Perry #1), 1985; Ottawa County (Davis-Besse #1), 1977.

19. LOUISIANA: 2,038 megawatts total capacity
St. Charles Parish (Waterford #3), 1984; West Feliciana Parish (River Bend #1), 1985.

20. WASHINGTON: 1,940 megawatts total capacity
Benton County (Hanford Nuclear and WPSS #2), 1966, 1984.

21. ARKANSAS: 1,762 megawatts total capacity
Pope County (Arkansas Nuclear #1 and #2), 1974, 1980.

22. MARYLAND: 1,690 megawatts total capacity
Calvert County (Calvert Cliffs #1 and #2), 1975, 1977.

23. MINNESOTA: 1,605 megawatts total capacity
Goodhue County (Prairie Island #1 and #2), 1973, 1974; Wright County (Monticello), 1971.

24. WISCONSIN: 1,579 megawatts total capacity
Kewaunee County (Kewaunee), 1974; Manitowoc County (Point Beach #1 and #2), 1970, 1972; Vernon County (La Crosse), 1969.

25. NEBRASKA: 1,256 megawatts total capacity
Nemaha County (Cooper), 1974; Washington County (Fort Calhoun), 1973.

26. KANSAS: 1,150 megawatts total capacity
Coffey County (Wolf Creek), 1985.

26. NEW HAMPSHIRE: 1,150 megawatts total capacity
Rockingham County (Seabrook #1), 1985.

28. OREGON: 1,130 megawatts total capacity
Columbia County (Trojan #1), 1976.

29. MISSOURI: 1,120 megawatts total capacity
Callaway County (Callaway #1), 1984.

30. MAINE: 825 megawatts total capacity
Lincoln County (Maine Yankee), 1972.

31. MASSACHUSETTS: 745 megawatts total capacity
Franklin County (Yankee), 1961; Plymouth County (Pilgrim), 1972.

32. IOWA: 538 megawatts total capacity
Linn County (Arnold #1), 1975.

33. VERMONT: 514 megawatts total capacity
Windham County (Vermont Yankee), 1972.

34. COLORADO: 330 megawatts total capacity
Weld County (Fort St. Vrain), 1979.

*Source:* Atomic Industrial Forum, *Directory,* 1984, and Energy Information Administration, *Inventory of Electric Power Plants,* 1983.

# Health Care & Environment:

## Matters of Life & Death

Americans continue to get healthier. Judging by two universal measures of population health, infant mortality and life expectancy, America is healthier now than it was even a few years ago. Why are life expectancy and infant mortality such commonly accepted indications of the health of general populations? First, because data can be found in almost every developed nation in the form of birth and death certificates. Second, the quality of postpartum and infant care available in a nation (or state or town) generally reflects the quality of other important health services as well. As for life expectancy, it remains a very broad but meaningful indicator of a nation's ability to provide lifelong necessities for health, such as sanitary food and drinking water, proper immunization and disease screening, and a basic measure of professional medical attention when needed.

In January 1984, the U.S. Department of Health and Human Services reported that infant mortality in America had dropped to its lowest level ever, with provisional data showing 11.2 deaths per 1,000 live births in 1982. At the same time, life expectancy had risen to 74.5 years in 1982, with girls born that year likely to live 78.2 years and boys 70.8 years. This represented an overall increase of about two years since 1978, when general life expectancy was 72.5 years, and a gain of nearly 30 years since 1900.

Not all Americans share equally in these statistical gains. The mortality rate for black infants is nearly twice that of white infants; and although in recent years life expectancy has increased at a faster rate for blacks than for whites, blacks on average still live about six years less than whites.

You might assume, given this news about our declining infant mortality rate and rising life expectancy, that America is the world's healthiest nation. But the sobering fact is that we lag behind many developed nations in these basic health indicators. In 1978, the most recent date for which comparable data are available, the United States ranked 16th in infant mortality and 15th in life expectancy.

Why does America, land of plenty, finish behind so many other countries? A 1984 article by John McPhee in the *New Yorker*, describing the lives of several young family physicians in rural Maine, may have one answer. McPhee quotes a well-known Boston-based cardiologist, Dr. Roman DeSanctis, as saying: "Canada has a lower death rate than we do, and broader medical care. Canada has doctors everywhere, in all the small towns. Sweden does, too. Meanwhile, we have all these high-tech doctors in cities with their machines."

Despite our great number of physicians, and their advanced training and technical support, the basic problem could be maldistribution of medical care. Many physicians, for example, want to practice near a major hospital and also wish to live in a city large enough to provide them with the amenities their incomes allow. In general, as *Places Rated*'s examination of the metro areas shows, larger, more affluent places such as Boston, New York, and San Francisco have a greater proportion of health care facilities, whereas more sparsely settled areas have increasingly smaller proportions.

## AMERICA'S LEADING KILLERS

Given the inevitability of death and taxes, it seems likely that we will always have a death rate. The death rate (number of deaths per 100,000 population) changes slightly from year to year, along with the percentage of deaths each year due to different causes, but the

three most common killers of Americans remain heart disease, cancer, and stroke, which make up about 68 percent of all deaths. Altogether the ten leading causes of death accounted for 85 percent of all deaths in 1980.

**The Top 10 Killers**

| Cause of Death | Estimated Rate per 100,000 People |
| --- | --- |
| Heart diseases | 336.0 |
| Malignant neoplasms | 183.9 |
| Cerebrovascular diseases | 75.1 |
| Accidents | 46.7 |
| Chronic obstructive pulmonary conditions | 24.7 |
| Influenza and pneumonia | 24.1 |
| Diabetes mellitus | 15.4 |
| Chronic liver conditions and cirrhosis of the liver | 13.5 |
| Atherosclerosis | 13.0 |
| Suicide | 11.9 |

*Source:* National Center for Health Statistics, *Monthly Vital Statistics Report, Advanced Data: Final Mortality, 1980,* 1983.

When we speak of death rates, we usually mean the number of people who die every year for every 100,000 people in the general population. Death rates may be either unadjusted (crude) or age-adjusted. The latter allow for the fact that a country, state, or metro area with a generally older population will have a higher death rate than places with younger residents. Florida, for example, has a median age of 34.7 years—the oldest in the nation—and 17.3 percent of its total population is aged 65 or over. Alaska, on the other hand, has a median age of only 26.1 years, which is the nation's lowest, and only 2.9 percent of its population is over age 65. Missouri, Arkansas, New York, and Pennsylvania also have relatively old populations, and states in the West, including the Mountain States, have young ones. The discussions and maps in this chapter generally use age-adjusted figures to compensate for these regional differences.

Heart disease is still our number-one killer. More than 760,000 Americans died of heart disease in 1980, which represented almost four out of every ten deaths. Although the age-adjusted death rate from this leading killer increased 1.3 percent between 1979 and 1980, its incidence has fallen since 1950 due to the strides made in prevention, diagnosis, surgery, and treatment. In 1980, roughly twice the number of men died of heart disease as did women.

Although the percentage of deaths caused by heart disease is decreasing, the proportion of deaths caused by the second greatest killer, cancer, is on the rise and has been since 1950. In 1980, cancer (referred to by the National Center for Health Statistics as malignant neoplasms) was responsible for about two of every ten American deaths, or 416,509 victims. The age-adjusted death rate for cancer in 1980 was 1.5 times greater for men than women.

Cerebrovascular disease, or stroke, remains our third greatest killer, accounting for nearly one out of

---

**Life Expectancy in the States**

Life expectancy in America's states shows noticeable variation, with most of the states having the longest life expectancy located in the Great Interior and states having the shortest in the Southeast. The listing below shows average life expectancy for 1970, the most recent year for which complete figures are available. Life expectancies in many states are now considerably longer, but due to the delay in compiling and analyzing statistics, final data for 1980 will not be available until 1985.

**States Ranked for Life Expectancy**

| State | Life Expectancy | State | Life Expectancy |
| --- | --- | --- | --- |
| 1. Hawaii | 73.60 | 26. Missouri | 70.69 |
| 2. Minnesota | 72.96 | 27. Arkansas | 70.66 |
| 3. Utah | 72.90 | 27. Florida | 70.66 |
| 4. North Dakota | 72.79 | 29. Michigan | 70.63 |
| 5. Nebraska | 72.60 | 30. Montana | 70.56 |
| 6. Kansas | 72.58 | 31. Arizona | 70.55 |
| 7. Iowa | 72.56 | 31. New York | 70.55 |
| 8. Connecticut | 72.48 | 33. Pennsylvania | 70.43 |
| 8. Wisconsin | 72.48 | 34. New Mexico | 70.32 |
| 10. Oregon | 72.13 | 35. Wyoming | 70.29 |
| 11. South Dakota | 72.08 | 36. Maryland | 70.22 |
| 12. Colorado | 72.06 | 37. Illinois | 70.14 |
| 13. Rhode Island | 71.90 | 38. Tennessee | 70.11 |
| 14. Idaho | 71.87 | 39. Kentucky | 70.10 |
| 15. Massachusetts | 71.83 | 40. Virginia | 70.08 |
| 16. Washington | 71.72 | 41. Delaware | 70.06 |
| 17. California | 71.71 | 42. West Virginia | 69.48 |
| 18. Vermont | 71.64 | 43. Alaska | 69.31 |
| 19. Oklahoma | 71.42 | 44. North Carolina | 69.21 |
| 20. New Hampshire | 71.23 | 45. Alabama | 69.05 |
| 21. Maine | 70.93 | 46. Nevada | 69.03 |
| 21. New Jersey | 70.93 | 47. Louisiana | 68.76 |
| 23. Texas | 70.90 | 48. Georgia | 68.54 |
| 24. Indiana | 70.88 | 49. Mississippi | 68.09 |
| 25. Ohio | 70.82 | 50. South Carolina | 67.96 |

*Source:* National Center for Health Statistics, *U.S. Decennial Life Tables for 1969–71, Vol. II,* June 1975.

every ten American deaths and claiming 170,225 lives in 1980. It was the only one of the three leading killers to show a decline (2 percent) between 1979 and 1980, which reflects the general downward trend of deaths from stroke since 1950. The age-adjusted death rate for stroke was 1.2 times higher for men than women, and 1.8 times higher for blacks than for whites.

## THE HIGH COSTS OF HEALTH CARE

Life expectancy is rising, but so is the cost of health care. Recent surveys showed that medical costs in the United States climbed to $322.4 billion in 1982, up about 25 percent from the previous year. That 1982 figure amounts to an average of $1,365 per person, or 10.5 percent of the gross national product!

The future promises little improvement. By 1990, government forecasts say, the annual cost of national health care will climb to $756 billion. Standard and Poor's estimates are even higher, putting the total at $480 billion by 1985 and $821 billion by 1990.

One sector of the U.S. business world that gives health care costs particular scrutiny is the insurance industry. For decades, people who have sold health insurance have evaluated the relative health of various parts of the country and the cost of illness care. Every large health insurance company that sells to individuals (and there are fewer and fewer of these companies each year as more and more group plans are sold) issues its agents a rate book, a confidential, in-house tool that enables the agent to quote prices for policies based on the age, health, occupational status, and sex of the proposed insured. In addition to these variables, premiums for policies also vary according to place of residence. Why? Are some places greater health risks?

The answer lies not so much in the varying risks of becoming ill (although the health companies tell us that the frequency with which people get sick *does* vary noticeably around the country) as in the consequent cost of caring for the patient, both in terms of physician's fees and hospital rooms.

*Places Rated* examined six rate books from major companies specializing in health insurance and found that they agree closely on which places in America are good health insurance risks and which aren't. The best place in America to buy health insurance, for example, is the southeastern corner of Pennsylvania, excluding the Philadelphia metro area. York, Lancaster, Lebanon, and Berks counties are the only ones in the rate books to get top-of-the-line ratings. Immediately following this prime location are South Carolina and South Dakota. Next best are North Carolina and Arkansas. Some of the worst places? New York City and Syracuse, New York.

Based on the listings of these six rate books, *Places Rated* devised a system that classifies the relative insurance/hospitalization costs of the 329 metro areas as either Outstanding, Excellent, Good, Fair, Poor, or Unacceptable. (The costs index for each metro area is given in the Place Profiles.) Twenty metro areas receive Outstanding ratings, whereas 13 are classified as Poor and four as Unacceptable.

### Insurance/Hospitalization Costs Index: Best and Worst Metro Areas

| Outstanding Costs Index | Poor Costs Index |
|---|---|
| Anderson, SC | Binghamton, NY |
| Asheville, NC | Buffalo, NY |
| Burlington, NC | Elmira, NY |
| Charleston, SC | Galveston–Texas City, TX |
| Columbia, SC | Glens Falls, NY |
| Cumberland, MD–WV | Houston, TX |
| Fayetteville, NC | Los Angeles–Long Beach, CA |
| Florence, SC | Miami–Hialeah, FL |
| Greenville–Spartanburg, SC | Niagara Falls, NY |
| Hagerstown, MD | Orange County, NY |
| Harrisburg–Lebanon–Carlisle, PA | Poughkeepsie, NY |
| Hickory, NC | Rochester, NY |
| Jacksonville, NC | Utica–Rome, NY |
| Lancaster, PA | |
| Owensboro, KY | **Unacceptable Costs Index** |
| Raleigh–Durham, NC | Albany–Schenectady–Troy, NY |
| Reading, PA | Nassau–Suffolk, NY |
| Sioux Falls, SD | New York, NY |
| Wilmington, NC | Syracuse, NY |
| York, PA | |

## ENVIRONMENT AND DAILY HEALTH

It wasn't until the early 1970s that terms like *ecosystem*, *ecology*, and *environmental hazards* became part of our vocabulary. Before that time, only health specialists and physicians seemed concerned about the potentially lethal effects of pollution, contaminants, and additives. More and more, experts are focusing on environmental factors to explain the distribution and concentration of various ailments and diseases. Where

## Rising Hospital Costs

Hospital care accounted for about 42 percent of total health care costs in 1982, followed by doctors' services at 19 percent, nursing home care 9 percent, and dentists 6 percent, according to a 1984 report from the Department of Health and Human Services.

Hospital costs have increased five and a half times since 1965. The average hospital stay, for example, skyrocketed from $316 in 1965 to $1,844 in 1980. (Consumer costs rose two and a half times during the same period.)

The average daily cost for a semiprivate hospital room in 1982 was $165, with prices generally highest in parts of the West, Midwest, and East, and lowest in the South.

### Average Daily Hospital Room Rates: The States and District of Columbia Ranked

| Place and Rank | Average Daily Room Charge | Place and Rank | Average Daily Room Charge |
|---|---|---|---|
| 1. District of Columbia | $233 | 26. Indiana | $146 |
| 2. Alaska | 217 | 26. Minnesota | 146 |
| 3. California | 215 | 26. Utah | 146 |
| 4. Illinois | 190 | 26. Wisconsin | 146 |
| 5. Pennsylvania | 186 | 30. Arizona | 145 |
| 6. Michigan | 185 | 30. Missouri | 145 |
| 7. New York | 184 | 32. Florida | 140 |
| 8. Oregon | 182 | 32. Kansas | 140 |
| 9. Massachusetts | 180 | 34. Iowa | 139 |
| 10. Hawaii | 177 | 35. West Virginia | 137 |
| 10. Ohio | 177 | 36. Nebraska | 133 |
| 12. Delaware | 172 | 36. Oklahoma | 133 |
| 12. Washington | 172 | 38. Virginia | 132 |
| 14. New Jersey | 171 | 39. South Dakota | 131 |
| 15. Nevada | 169 | 40. Kentucky | 130 |
| 16. Vermont | 168 | 40. Wyoming | 130 |
| 17. Colorado | 167 | 42. Alabama | 124 |
| 17. New Hampshire | 167 | 43. Georgia | 123 |
| 19. Rhode Island | 166 | 44. North Dakota | 122 |
| 20. Connecticut | 162 | 45. Texas | 119 |
| 21. Maine | 159 | 46. Louisiana | 116 |
| 22. New Mexico | 152 | 47. Arkansas | 114 |
| 23. Idaho | 151 | 48. Tennessee | 111 |
| 23. Montana | 151 | 49. North Carolina | 110 |
| 25. Maryland | 148 | 50. South Carolina | 108 |
| | | 51. Mississippi | 94 |

*Source:* Health Insurance Association of America, *Source Book of Health Insurance Data,* annual.

Figures are for 1982 cost to patient for semiprivate room.

dumps, chemical spills, insecticides, industrial wastes, and other contaminants.

In the past 15 years, we've made a lot of progress in cleaning up our soil, air, and water. But problem areas do remain, and they can be health hazards. Water pollution and, to some extent, soil pollution are covered in the chapter "Climate & Terrain." The discussion that follows deals with additional water-related matters and with air pollution.

### Think About Your Drinking Water

Most people are aware that pollution of drinking water constitutes a serious health problem in many American cities. But we sometimes forget that pollutants are not the only things in the water we drink that can affect our health.

About half of all Americans drink water from nearly 9,500 fluoridated community systems. What is fluoride? It is the salt form of the element fluorine, which, like gold, iron, or magnesium, can occur naturally in our soil and water. Natural traces of fluoride are found in many foods and in about a third of the nation's water. Most parts of Texas, Illinois, Iowa, Oklahoma, and Ohio have water that is naturally fluoridated.

Fluoride is ingested much like iron, which is beneficial to the blood and may be obtained by eating certain foods, drinking water with traces of iron in it, or by taking pills, capsules, or liquids that contain iron compounds. You may already be aware that fluoridation benefits young people, whose teeth are developing, but did you know that it can also be important to retirement-aged people, whose bones need the extra protection fluoridation offers?

Fluoride has nothing to do with the taste of water or with other qualities such as softness, hardness, acidity, and so on. Research indicates that some types of hard water—water with large amounts of dissolved salts and minerals—may be helpful in preventing certain cardiovascular problems, principally coronary heart disease and stroke. For reasons that are not clear, the dissolved substances (salts of calcium and magnesium, especially carbonates, as well as sulfates and chlorides) seem to protect people from cardiovascular disease. So if you move to a place with hard water, check with the local or county health department before you install a water purifier or softener. The minerals causing the hard water may actually be good for you.

### Air Quality in the Metro Areas

The bodily harm caused by air pollution has been well documented. Many of us have experienced the watering eyes, shortness of breath, mild chest pain, or burning feeling in throat or lungs that can accompany a day when air pollution is high. Air pollutants have also been known to cause mental retardation, seizures, nerve disorders, damage to heart and lung tissue, and

you live is increasingly a determining factor in what diseases you are susceptible to. It is possible, for example, that drinking chlorinated water (chlorine is used to kill bacteria not only in swimming pools but also in most drinking water) increases the risk of gastrointestinal cancer by between 50 percent and 100 percent. Many birth defects, disorders of the nervous system, and extraordinarily high rates of certain cancers have been linked directly to hazardous waste even death. In 1948, for example, weather conditions trapped polluted air over the city of Donora, Pennsylvania, for nearly a week. Of a population of 8,000, almost 6,000 became ill, complaining of chest pains, headaches, eye irritation, coughing, and dizzy spells, and 20 people died from related causes. Four years later in London, about 4,000 people died from smog that lingered over the city for five days.

In the Place Profiles later in this chapter, *Places Rated* examines the distribution and concentration of the six major air pollutants as defined by the Environmental Protection Agency (EPA).

*Total suspended particulates* (TSP) is a name for any minute particle or group of particles—such as pollen, soot, asbestos, sand, or dust—borne by the wind. Generally speaking, the concentration of particulates increases as one travels from west to east, since that is the direction of the prevailing winds. Like most other pollutants, particulates are found in the greatest concentrations around cities and industrial centers and in the smallest concentrations in rural areas. The great exception is the dry regions of the Southwest, where dust storms create clouds of TSP. The EPA primary standard—the point at which a pollutant begins to affect human health—is 75 micrograms per cubic meter of air for TSP. (A microgram is a millionth of a gram.)

## Pollution Problems

In examining air pollution, *Places Rated* studied the EPA's *Air Quality Data*, 1983, to identify the pollutants for which each metro area's annual mean average exceeded the EPA primary standard. Many metro areas experience problems with total suspended particulates and carbon monoxide, and a few have severe problems with ozone. Below is a list of the 17 metro areas that exceed the EPA primary standard for two or more major pollutants.

### Metro Areas with Air Pollution Problems

| Metro Area | Pollutants |
| --- | --- |
| Albuquerque, NM | TSP, CO |
| Anaheim–Santa Ana, CA | TSP, CO, $O_3$, $NO_2$, Pb |
| Baltimore, MD | TSP, $SO_2$, CO |
| Boise City, ID | TSP, CO |
| Chicago, IL | TSP, CO |
| Denver, CO | TSP, CO |
| Detroit, MI | TSP, CO |
| El Paso, TX | TSP, CO |
| Fresno, CA | CO, $O_3$ |
| Jersey City, NJ | TSP, CO |
| Los Angeles–Long Beach, CA | TSP, CO, $O_3$, $NO_2$, Pb |
| Minneapolis–St. Paul, MN–WI | CO, Pb |
| Nashville, TN | CO, $NO_2$ |
| Phoenix, AZ | TSP, CO |
| Riverside–San Bernardino, CA | TSP, $O_3$ |
| Steubenville–Weirton, OH–WV | TSP, $SO_2$ |
| Tucson, AZ | TSP, CO |

*Sulfur dioxide* ($SO_2$) is an acrid, corrosive gas produced by the burning of coal (particularly soft coal) that is high in sulfur. Coal burning accounts for 60 percent of the $SO_2$ in the air. Most of the $SO_2$ is found, therefore, in the older eastern cities where coal is still used as a major fuel for industry and home heating. The EPA primary standard for concentration of $SO_2$ is 80 micrograms per cubic meter of air, or roughly 0.03 parts per million.

*Carbon monoxide* (CO) is especially deadly. When inhaled in great enough concentrations, it enters the bloodstream and chemically prevents the absorption of oxygen, resulting in death. Carbon monoxide is produced by the incomplete combustion of carbon fuels; about 75 percent of it is produced by automobiles. The EPA primary standard for concentration of CO is 10 milligrams per cubic meter of air, or roughly nine parts per million.

*Photochemical oxidants* are a group of pollutants that combine chemically in the presence of strong sunlight. These chemicals are mostly nitrous oxides, hydrocarbons, and ozone ($O_3$). The common name for photochemical oxidants is *smog*. Because oxidant pollution involves two things that are beyond the scope of most regulations and constraints—sunshine and automobiles—it is the fastest-spreading and hardest to control of all air pollution problems. The EPA primary standard for ozone is 0.12 parts per million, and pollution severity is measured by the mean number of days over a given time during which the standard is exceeded.

*Nitrous oxides* ($NO_2$) are produced when fossil fuels are burned at extremely high temperatures, a process that occurs most often in internal combustion engines. Nitrous oxides are a primary ingredient of photochemical oxidants, or smog. The EPA primary standard for concentration of $NO_2$ is 100 micrograms per cubic meter of air, or about 0.05 parts per million.

*Lead* (Pb) is a poisonous element that usually occurs as a metal. However, traces can be found in living tissue, in soil and water, even in the air we breathe. Fortunately, with the advent of unleaded gasoline, the major source of this airborne poison has been largely controlled. The EPA primary standard for this pollutant is 1.5 micrograms per cubic meter of air.

## JUDGING HEALTH CARE AND ENVIRONMENT

In this age of euphemism, *health* means not only health but also its exact opposite, illness. A hospital is not really a health care institution; its business is to take care of sick people. The truly healthy need little health care, save for an occasional shot or checkup; the unhealthy need a lot.

The health care facilities of different places cannot be rated with total fairness. The quality of care that a patient receives may be largely the luck of the draw. The skill of the doctor and the training, competence, and dedication of the nursing staff can vary, sometimes greatly. But it is possible to compare the places for relative abundance of facilities. For this reason, *Places Rated Almanac* looks at the availability of certain facilities for "illness care," at relative costs for insurance and hospitalization, and at two environmental factors—fluoridation of drinking water and air pollution—in ranking the metro areas.

The first of *Places Rated*'s scoring indicators, the number of physicians for every 100,000 residents, is a general measure of basic health care supply. Where is the greatest concentration of doctors? As mentioned briefly earlier, many are found in large cities, which have numerous hospitals and other facilities. Surprisingly, the two metro areas with the greatest concentration of physicians in the nation are located about 150 miles apart on the plains of the northern Midwest: Rochester, Minnesota, and Iowa City, Iowa. Both have relatively small resident populations and unusually large proportions of physicians, Rochester due to the Mayo Clinic and Iowa City because of the medical complex associated with the University of Iowa and the Veterans Administration.

The next two variables, teaching hospitals and medical schools, are almost universally accepted as indicators of health care quality as well as health care capacity. Medical schools are scarce indeed; there are only about 150 of them in America, and quite a few of these (such as Dartmouth College Medical School in Hanover, New Hampshire) are not located in metro areas. These schools attract every type of medical talent: physicians, diagnosticians, psychiatrists, nurses, teachers, and hospital specialists. Furthermore, these schools give rise to and are integrated with teaching hospitals, where one can receive care supervised by medical school faculty. This interaction between medical school and teaching hospital encourages the development and use of the latest techniques, equipment, and therapy. Constant review and analysis of cases by faculty and students—a necessary part of the teaching process—help prevent sloppy or inept patient care.

Cardiac rehabilitation centers, comprehensive cancer treatment centers, and hospices constitute the next three variables. Their presence serves as an indicator of the availability of a range of specialized health care services within an area. The cardiac rehabilitation units (CRUs) considered by *Places Rated Almanac* are not cardiac intensive care units, which most sizable hospitals have. These rehabilitation centers are actually programs in physical fitness and conditioning for patients who have suffered one or more heart attacks. Likewise, the cancer treatment centers are not to be confused with the cancer wards of major hospitals. They are similar, but the centers listed in the Place Profiles include both those institutions designated by the National Cancer Institute as truly comprehensive

(there are only 20 of these in the metro areas) as well as a number of slightly less comprehensive clinical cancer centers.

Hospices, or care for the terminally ill, originated in Europe and have recently become one of the fastest-growing forms of health care. It is estimated that there are now more than 1,200 throughout the country. To be considered by *Places Rated Almanac,* hospices may be either independent, allied with a major hospital, or located within a hospital under the direction of a hospice team. Given the unique and valuable service rendered by hospices, they are an important addition to the health care network of any metro area.

Along with availability of such facilities, the affordability of health care is a major concern of many Americans. Consequently, *Places Rated* has included a major new ranking variable, the insurance/hospitalization costs index, derived from the rate books of major health insurers. This costs index serves as a basic indicator of insurance costs, frequency of illness in a given place, and relative cost of hospitalization. When the *Places Rated* costs index falls into the Poor and Unacceptable ranges, it is viewed as a negative indicator.

Fluoridation of drinking water remains somewhat controversial despite evidence that it helps prevent tooth decay and hardens and protects bones. Since the publication of the first edition of *Places Rated Almanac,* many large cities have discontinued fluoridation, but until hard evidence emerges that it is harmful to living tissue, *Places Rated* continues to regard it as a positive health care asset. The other environmental variable, air pollution, counts heavily against a metro area.

It should be noted that a number of modifications to the system for rating metro areas for health care and environment have been introduced in this edition of *Places Rated Almanac.* Two changes are of major importance. The first is the addition of the insurance/hospitalization costs index. The second, and one that is applied in a similar fashion in three other chapters of this book, is the CMSA Access factor. Every metro area receives full credit for scored assets within its boundaries, but each metro area that is part of a Consolidated Metropolitan Statistical Area, or CMSA (a full listing of the 22 CMSAs and their 76 component metro areas is given in the Appendix) is also awarded bonus points, as explained below, in recognition of the fact that certain assets of a given metro area can benefit residents of nearby areas as well. The special health care facilities for which residents of more than one metro area share the benefits are identified by *Places Rated* as teaching hospitals, medical schools, cardiac rehabilitation centers, comprehensive cancer treatment centers, and hospices.

Each metro area starts with a base score of zero, and points are either added or subtracted according to the following indicators:

1. *Physicians per 100,000 residents.* One point is awarded for every physician per 100,000 people living within the metro area.
2. *Teaching hospitals.* Each teaching hospital is worth 200 points. A ceiling of 2,000 points is set for teaching hospitals because there can be many of them attached to each medical school, some only marginally involved in teaching. Also, the number of teaching hospitals usually is in almost direct proportion to city size. To be as fair as possible in rating facilities nationwide, therefore, only the first ten teaching hospitals in each metro area are awarded points (although all are listed in the Place Profiles).
3. *Medical schools.* Each medical school receives 300 points.
4. *Cardiac rehabilitation centers, comprehensive cancer treatment centers, and hospices.* Each of these facilities is worth 100 points, with a 1,000-point ceiling for each type of facility. Cancer treatment centers that meet rigorous standards set by the National Cancer Institute are awarded an additional 50 points apiece; they are identified by a bullet (•) in the Place Profiles.
5. *Costs index.* Based on health insurance rate books, *Places Rated* has classified the metro areas according to their relative health care costs. Points are either added or subtracted according to the following designations: Outstanding = 400 points; Excellent = 200; Good = 100; Fair = 0; Poor = −100; Unacceptable = −200. The designation for each metro area is listed in the Place Profiles.
6. *Fluoridation.* A metro area receives 300 points if all its central cities have fluoridated water, either natural or adjusted. If only one central city in a two-city metro area is fluoridated, the metro area receives 150 points; in a three-city metro area, each city with fluoridated water is worth 100 points.
7. *Air pollution.* One hundred points is subtracted for each pollutant that exceeds the EPA primary standard in its annual mean average. In the case of ozone, the number of days exceeding the standard varies enormously from metro area to metro area. Accordingly, the severity of the ozone problem is highlighted by one or more triangles (▲) in the Place Profiles, and an additional 100 points is subtracted for each triangle.
8. *CMSA Access.* Each of the 76 metro areas that is part of a Consolidated Metropolitan Statistical Area is eligible to receive bonus points based on "shared" facilities: teaching hospitals, medical schools, cardiac rehabilitation

centers, comprehensive cancer treatment centers, and hospices. A place receives a bonus of 10 percent of the points accumulated by the *other* metro areas in the CMSA for these facilities. A metro area's *own* points for shared facilities are not considered in calculating its bonus points. Thus, in the Dallas–Fort Worth consolidated area, the Dallas metro area receives a bonus of 40 access points, or 10 percent of the 400 points accumulated by Fort Worth–Arlington, and Fort Worth–Arlington receives 220 access points, based on Dallas's 2,200 points for shared facilities. (Three metro areas receive no access bonus because the other metro area in the CMSA has none of the shared facilities: Buffalo, New York; Pittsburgh; and Portland, Oregon.)

### Sample Comparison: New York, New York, and Glens Falls, New York

As it did in the first edition of *Places Rated Almanac*, New York leads the metro areas in health care facilities and environment. The nation's largest metro area, it consequently has an extensive supply of medical insti-

---

### What Do the Rankings Mean?

It should be underscored that what is being judged in this chapter is health *care* in each of America's metro areas, not health of the resident population. Moreover, *Places Rated* is judging not health care service but health care facilities. And, finally, we are judging not *all* facilities but rather some of the exceptional ones.

Keeping this in mind will help the reader avoid the mistake of assuming that a low score in this chapter means either (1) that the people in X place are unhealthy and don't live very long, or (2) that if one were to relocate to X place, basic health care—including even such complex emergency surgery as a coronary bypass—would be unavailable or inferior. Both of these conclusions are incorrect. A low score or rank in this chapter does indicate, however, that the emphasis in that metro area is probably on basic health care and that the latest techniques, equipment, and personnel trained to implement them are more likely to be found elsewhere.

Affluent, big-city metro areas generally score higher in our rankings than the more sparsely populated metro areas. But this doesn't mean that a person cannot receive excellent medical care in a rural area or a poor state or, conversely, experience medical care that is bad enough to be life-threatening in even the best of hospitals. The quality of medical and nursing care most people receive depends upon a number of variables, including the patient's ability to pay, blind chance, and human error.

tutions to accommodate its millions of inhabitants. Furthermore, many prestigious universities and philanthropic foundations that support the work of these institutions are located in this city, helping to make it one of the leading medical research centers in the world.

The numbers speak for themselves. New York has 370 physicians per 100,000 residents, for 370 points, and 36 teaching hospitals (more than any other metro area; second-place Chicago has 21), good for the maximum possible 2,000 points. Its seven medical schools (again, more than any other metro area) give it another 2,100 points. New York also has 16 cardiac rehabilitation centers (for which it tallies the maximum possible 1,000 points); five cancer treatment centers, two of which receive a 50-point bonus (600 points); and nine hospices (900 points). In the next three categories, the Big Apple loses 200 points for its Unacceptable rating in insurance costs, is awarded 300 points for fluoridated drinking water, and is penalized 100 points for air pollution (for all its great size and traffic, this metro area has a surprisingly small air pollution problem, with only one pollutant—CO).

But New York's scoring does not end here. Under *Places Rated*'s new scoring system, metro areas that compose what the U.S. Bureau of the Census calls Consolidated Metropolitan Statistical Areas share a percentage of the points accumulated by the other members of their CMSA for medical schools, teaching hospitals, cardiac rehabilitation units, cancer treatment centers, and hospices. Altogether 12 metro areas make up the New York–Northern New Jersey–Long Island consolidated area. The points for shared facilities earned by the other 11 metro areas in the CMSA amount to 8,800, resulting in an 880-point bonus for New York. This pushes New York's score to a hefty 7,850 points for an undisputed first place.

About 200 miles north of New York lies the last-place finisher in the health care race, Glens Falls. This metro area has a respectable number of physicians per 100,000 residents, 143, for 143 points. However, that is about all this small, upstate town can boast of in the way of health care. It has no teaching hospitals, medical schools, cardiac rehabilitation centers, comprehensive cancer centers, or hospices. It receives a Poor rating for health insurance costs, which means a loss of 100 points, and it does not fluoridate its water. There is no air pollution in Glens Falls, which is not surprising, considering its location near the 5.6-million-acre Adirondack Park. All this adds up to only 43 points, the lowest score among the metro areas.

It's interesting to note that another New York metro area, Orange County, has a similarly sparse number of health care assets. However, since Orange County is part of the huge New York–Northern New Jersey–Long Island consolidated area, it earns enough bonus points to be propelled into a respectable 79th place.

## Places Rated: Metro Areas Ranked for Health Care and Environment

Nine criteria are used in arriving at a score for the quality of health care and environment in a metro area: (1) physicians per 100,000 residents, (2) teaching hospitals, (3) medical schools, (4) cardiac rehabilitation centers, (5) comprehensive cancer treatment centers, (6) hospices, (7) insurance/hospitalization costs index, (8) fluoridation of drinking water, and (9) air pollution.

Metro areas can also be awarded bonus points for shared facilities—teaching hospitals, medical schools, cardiac rehabilitation centers, cancer treatment centers, and hospices—within their Consolidated Metropolitan Statistical Areas.

Places that receive tie scores are given the same rank and are listed in alphabetical order.

### Metro Areas from Best to Worst

| Places Rated Rank | Places Rated Score | Places Rated Rank | Places Rated Score | Places Rated Rank | Places Rated Score |
|---|---|---|---|---|---|
| 1. New York, NY | 7,850 | 11. San Francisco, CA | 3,726 | 21. Seattle, WA | 2,715 |
| 2. Chicago, IL | 5,766 | 12. Baltimore, MD | 3,562 | 22. Bergen–Passaic, NJ | 2,661 |
| 3. Boston, MA | 5,301 | 13. Raleigh–Durham, NC | 3,476 | 23. Stamford, CT | 2,610 |
| 4. Philadelphia, PA–NJ | 5,158 | 14. Pittsburgh, PA | 3,413 | 24. Middlesex–Somerset–Hunterdon, NJ | 2,589 |
| 5. Los Angeles–Long Beach, CA | 5,153 | 15. Atlanta, GA | 3,195 | 25. New Orleans, LA | 2,586 |
| 6. Washington, DC–MD–VA | 4,361 | 16. Cleveland, OH | 3,167 | 26. Omaha, NE–IA | 2,559 |
| 7. Detroit, MI | 4,142 | 17. Milwaukee, WI | 3,053 | 27. Bridgeport–Milford, CT | 2,550 |
| 8. Newark, NJ | 4,106 | 18. Rochester, MN | 2,966 | 28. Denver, CO | 2,533 |
| 9. Minneapolis–St. Paul, MN–WI | 3,934 | 19. St. Louis, MO–IL | 2,850 | 29. Norwalk, CT | 2,530 |
| 10. Nassau–Suffolk, NY | 3,919 | 20. Dallas, TX | 2,825 | 30. Hartford, CT | 2,521 |

| Places Rated Rank | Places Rated Score | Places Rated Rank | Places Rated Score | Places Rated Rank | Places Rated Score |
|---|---|---|---|---|---|
| 31. Ann Arbor, MI | 2,508 | 88. Lansing–East Lansing, MI | 1,371 | 144. Boulder–Longmont, CO | 962 |
| 32. Monmouth–Ocean, NJ | 2,482 | 89. Gary–Hammond, IN | 1,364 | 145. Knoxville, TN | 960 |
| 33. Houston, TX | 2,467 | 90. Charlottesville, VA | 1,348 | | |
| 33. Providence, RI | 2,467 | | | 146. Muncie, IN | 949 |
| 35. Buffalo, NY | 2,465 | 91. San Antonio, TX | 1,337 | 147. Racine, WI | 931 |
| | | 92. Honolulu, HI | 1,298 | 148. Waterloo–Cedar Falls, IA | 925 |
| 36. Richmond–Petersburg, VA | 2,448 | 93. Grand Rapids, MI | 1,274 | 149. Fargo–Moorhead, ND–MN | 920 |
| 37. Iowa City, IA | 2,437 | 94. Greenville–Spartanburg, SC | 1,260 | 150. Brockton, MA | 916 |
| 38. San Diego, CA | 2,416 | 95. Tucson, AZ | 1,259 | | |
| 39. Oakland, CA | 2,362 | | | 150. Green Bay, WI | 916 |
| 40. Danbury, CT | 2,350 | 96. Des Moines, IA | 1,256 | 152. Battle Creek, MI | 900 |
| | | 97. Fort Lauderdale–Hollywood– | | 152. Fall River, MA–RI | 900 |
| 41. Miami–Hialeah, FL | 2,314 | Pompano Beach, FL | 1,252 | 152. Lubbock, TX | 900 |
| 42. Dayton–Springfield, OH | 2,253 | 98. New Britain, CT | 1,245 | 155. Middletown, CT | 884 |
| 43. Indianapolis, IN | 2,243 | 99. Lake County, IL | 1,237 | | |
| 44. Riverside–San Bernadino, | | 100. Salem–Gloucester, MA | 1,232 | 156. Huntington–Ashland, | |
| CA | 2,201 | | | WV–KY–OH | 875 |
| 45. Madison, WI | 2,168 | 101. Scranton–Wilkes-Barre, PA | 1,219 | 157. Fayetteville, NC | 872 |
| | | 102. Waterbury, CT | 1,218 | 158. Beaver County, PA | 861 |
| 46. Cincinnati, OH–KY–IN | 2,138 | 103. Asheville, NC | 1,204 | 159. Williamsport, PA | 860 |
| 47. San Jose, CA | 2,117 | 104. Aurora–Elgin, IL | 1,203 | 160. Nashua, NH | 853 |
| 48. Louisville, KY–IN | 2,111 | 105. Lawrence–Haverhill, MA–NH | 1,202 | | |
| 49. Harrisburg–Lebanon– | | | | 161. Sioux City, IA–NE | 846 |
| Carlisle, PA | 2,087 | 106. Tampa–St. Petersburg– | | 162. Cedar Rapids, IA | 837 |
| 50. New Haven–Meriden, CT | 2,068 | Clearwater, FL | 1,189 | 163. Portland, ME | 834 |
| | | 107. Peoria, IL | 1,184 | 164. Appleton–Oshkosh– | |
| 51. Memphis, TN–AR–MS | 2,043 | 108. Jacksonville, FL | 1,181 | Neenah, WI | 833 |
| 52. Anaheim–Santa Ana, CA | 2,025 | 109. Duluth, MN–WI | 1,159 | 164. Columbus, GA–AL | 833 |
| 53. Rochester, NY | 1,969 | 110. Reading, PA | 1,154 | | |
| 54. Columbia, MO | 1,951 | | | 166. Montgomery, AL | 832 |
| 55. Kansas City, MO | 1,939 | 111. Johnson City–Kingsport– | | 167. South Bend–Mishawaka, IN | 830 |
| | | Bristol, TN–VA | 1,152 | 168. Anderson, SC | 820 |
| 56. Norfolk–Virginia Beach– | | 112. Topeka, KS | 1,148 | 169. Florence, SC | 818 |
| Newport News, VA | 1,932 | 113. Hamilton–Middletown, OH | 1,135 | 169. Hagerstown, MD | 818 |
| 57. Springfield, IL | 1,877 | 114. Pawtucket–Woonsocket– | | | |
| 58. Little Rock–North Little Rock, | | Attleboro, RI–MA | 1,117 | 169. Wausau, WI | 818 |
| AR | 1,861 | 115. Davenport–Rock Island– | | 172. Bloomington–Normal, IL | 815 |
| 59. Lexington–Fayette, KY | 1,860 | Moline, IA–IL | 1,113 | 173. Owensboro, KY | 812 |
| 60. Albuquerque, NM | 1,853 | | | 174. Vineland–Millville–Bridgeton, | |
| | | 116. Lancaster, PA | 1,111 | NJ | 807 |
| 61. Nashville, TN | 1,850 | 117. Grand Forks, ND | 1,109 | 175. Wichita, KS | 806 |
| 62. Columbus, OH | 1,837 | 118. Oxnard–Ventura, CA | 1,106 | | |
| 63. Burlington, VT | 1,809 | 119. Lorain–Elyria, OH | 1,105 | 176. Bismarck, ND | 804 |
| 64. Worcester, MA | 1,805 | 120. Wilmington, NC | 1,099 | 177. Sarasota, FL | 801 |
| 65. Augusta, GA–SC | 1,798 | | | 178. Eau Claire, WI | 798 |
| | | 121. Youngstown–Warren, OH | 1,097 | 179. Wheeling, WV–OH | 791 |
| 66. Jackson, MS | 1,792 | 122. Savannah, GA | 1,084 | 180. Evansville, IN–KY | 783 |
| 67. Jersey City, NJ | 1,759 | 123. Lowell, MA–NH | 1,083 | | |
| 68. Toledo, OH | 1,738 | 124. Vallejo–Fairfield–Napa, CA | 1,079 | 181. Austin, TX | 782 |
| 69. Gainesville, FL | 1,731 | 125. Kenosha, WI | 1,067 | 182. Bangor, ME | 780 |
| 70. Kansas City, KS | 1,711 | | | 183. Lincoln, NE | 775 |
| | | 126. Fort Wayne, IN | 1,060 | 184. Orlando, FL | 765 |
| 71. Greensboro–Winston-Salem– | | 127. Joliet, IL | 1,058 | 185. Cumberland, MD–WV | 760 |
| High Point, NC | 1,694 | 128. Santa Rosa–Petaluma, CA | 1,052 | | |
| 72. Birmingham, AL | 1,692 | 129. Kalamazoo, MI | 1,043 | 186. Lewiston–Auburn, ME | 759 |
| 73. Akron, OH | 1,656 | 130. Sioux Falls, SD | 1,041 | 187. Salem, OR | 749 |
| 74. Salt Lake City–Ogden, UT | 1,631 | | | 188. Lima, OH | 741 |
| 75. Oklahoma City, OK | 1,623 | 131. Syracuse, NY | 1,040 | 189. Jacksonville, NC | 740 |
| | | 132. Fort Worth–Arlington, TX | 1,038 | 190. Manchester, NH | 737 |
| 76. Portland, OR | 1,590 | 133. Roanoke, VA | 1,036 | | |
| 77. Phoenix, AZ | 1,584 | 134. Santa Cruz, CA | 1,035 | 191. Decatur, IL | 732 |
| 78. Tulsa, OK | 1,581 | 135. Sacramento, CA | 1,027 | 191. Lynchburg, VA | 732 |
| 79. Orange County, NY | 1,574 | | | 193. Bloomington, IN | 731 |
| 80. Mobile, AL | 1,469 | 136. Saginaw–Bay City– | | 193. Fort Collins–Loveland, CO | 731 |
| | | Midland, MI | 1,022 | 193. Johnstown, PA | 731 |
| 81. Charleston, SC | 1,463 | 137. Binghamton, NY | 1,007 | | |
| 82. Shreveport, LA | 1,445 | 138. Hickory, NC | 1,006 | 196. Flint, MI | 724 |
| 82. Wilmington, DE–NJ–MD | 1,445 | 139. Charlotte–Gastonia–Rock Hill, | | 197. Daytona Beach, FL | 723 |
| 84. Galveston–Texas City, TX | 1,437 | NC–SC | 999 | 198. Colorado Springs, CO | 721 |
| 85. Albany–Schenectady– | | 140. Burlington, NC | 994 | 199. York, PA | 713 |
| Troy, NY | 1,431 | | | 200. Springfield, MA | 710 |
| | | 141. Bristol, CT | 975 | | |
| 86. Columbia, SC | 1,421 | 142. Rockford, IL | 969 | 201. Charleston, WV | 708 |
| 87. Trenton, NJ | 1,372 | 143. Alton–Granite City, IL | 965 | 202. Greeley, CO | 706 |

| Places Rated Rank | Places Rated Score | Places Rated Rank | Places Rated Score | Places Rated Rank | Places Rated Score |
|---|---|---|---|---|---|
| 203. Janesville–Beloit, WI | 700 | 246. Las Cruces, NM | 588 | 288. Altoona, PA | 432 |
| 203. Sharon, PA | 700 | 247. Houma–Thibodaux, LA | 583 | 289. Bakersfield, CA | 420 |
| 205. Muskegon, MI | 699 | 248. Anderson, IN | 580 | 290. Las Vegas, NV | 412 |
| | | 249. Springfield, MO | 577 | | |
| 206. Pittsfield, MA | 694 | 250. Benton Harbor, MI | 570 | 291. Killeen–Temple, TX | 398 |
| 207. La Crosse, WI | 686 | | | 292. Sherman–Denison, TX | 394 |
| 208. Huntsville, AL | 685 | 251. Chattanooga, TN–GA | 564 | 293. Utica–Rome, NY | 391 |
| 209. Jackson, MI | 679 | 252. Pensacola, FL | 563 | 294. Odessa, TX | 384 |
| 210. Tuscaloosa, AL | 674 | 253. Elmira, NY | 562 | 295. West Palm Beach–Boca | |
| | | 254. New London–Norwich, CT–RI | 556 | Raton–Delray Beach, FL | 375 |
| 211. Champaign–Urbana– | | 255. Wichita Falls, TX | 549 | | |
| Rantoul, IL | 672 | | | 296. McAllen–Edinburg– | |
| 211. Tyler, TX | 672 | 256. Lafayette, LA | 548 | Mission, TX | 372 |
| 213. Amarillo, TX | 669 | 257. Fort Myers, FL | 546 | 297. Tallahassee, FL | 370 |
| 214. Great Falls, MT | 667 | 258. Eugene–Springfield, OR | 539 | 298. Fresno, CA | 369 |
| 215. Parkersburg–Marietta, | | 258. Tacoma, WA | 539 | 299. Poughkeepsie, NY | 355 |
| WV–OH | 665 | 260. Waco, TX | 538 | 300. Salinas–Seaside–Monterey, | |
| | | | | CA | 352 |
| 216. Fitchburg–Leominster, MA | 655 | 261. Santa Barbara–Santa Maria– | | | |
| 216. Lafayette, IN | 655 | Lompoc, CA | 532 | 301. Modesto, CA | 347 |
| 218. Alexandria, LA | 640 | 262. Erie, PA | 529 | 302. Casper, WY | 345 |
| 218. Bryan–College Station, TX | 640 | 263. El Paso, TX | 528 | 303. Texarkana, TX–Texarkana, AR | 343 |
| 218. Dubuque, IA | 640 | 264. Fort Pierce, FL | 527 | 304. Baton Rouge, LA | 342 |
| | | 265. New Bedford, MA | 519 | 304. Stockton, CA | 342 |
| 221. Atlantic City, NJ | 637 | | | | |
| 222. Enid, OK | 626 | 266. Melbourne–Titusville– | | 306. Olympia, WA | 338 |
| 223. Gadsden, AL | 622 | Palm Bay, FL | 517 | 307. Bradenton, FL | 333 |
| 224. Allentown–Bethlehem, PA–NJ | 621 | 266. Vancouver, WA | 517 | 308. Monroe, LA | 331 |
| 224. Lawrence, KS | 621 | 268. Longview–Marshall, TX | 509 | 309. Lakeland–Winter Haven, FL | 323 |
| | | 269. Niagara Falls, NY | 507 | 310. Yakima, WA | 317 |
| 226. Albany, GA | 618 | 270. Steubenville–Weirton, | | | |
| 227. Pine Bluff, AR | 617 | OH–WV | 505 | 311. Lake Charles, LA | 314 |
| 228. Beaumont–Port Arthur, TX | 616 | | | 312. Bremerton, WA | 310 |
| 229. Reno, NV | 615 | 271. Joplin, MO | 500 | 313. Mansfield, OH | 303 |
| 230. State College, PA | 612 | 272. Spokane, WA | 497 | 314. Richland–Kennewick– | |
| | | 273. Ocala, FL | 489 | Pasco, WA | 300 |
| 231. Kankakee, IL | 609 | 274. Fort Walton Beach, FL | 484 | 315. Redding, CA | 274 |
| 232. Florence, AL | 607 | 275. Billings, MT | 479 | | |
| 233. Athens, GA | 605 | | | 316. Victoria, TX | 260 |
| 234. St. Cloud, MN | 603 | 276. Lawton, OK | 477 | 317. Medford, OR | 256 |
| 235. Anchorage, AK | 601 | 277. Pueblo, CO | 468 | 318. Chico, CA | 243 |
| | | 278. Fort Smith, AR–OK | 466 | 319. Bellingham, WA | 240 |
| 236. Anniston, AL | 598 | 279. Laredo, TX | 465 | 320. Abilene, TX | 237 |
| 237. Elkhart–Goshen, IN | 596 | 280. Corpus Christi, TX | 458 | | |
| 237. Kokomo, IN | 596 | | | 321. San Angelo, TX | 236 |
| 237. Portsmouth–Dover–Rochester, | | 281. Boise City, ID | 453 | 322. St. Joseph, MO | 223 |
| NH–ME | 596 | 281. Terre Haute, IN | 453 | 323. Yuba City, CA | 212 |
| 240. Fayetteville–Springdale, AR | 594 | 283. Clarksville–Hopkinsville, | | 324. Visalia–Tulare–Porterville, CA | 210 |
| | | TN–KY | 446 | 325. Panama City, FL | 201 |
| 241. Danville, VA | 593 | 284. East St. Louis–Belleville, IL | 444 | | |
| 241. Dothan, AL | 593 | 285. Canton, OH | 443 | 326. Provo–Orem, UT | 198 |
| 241. Macon–Warner Robins, GA | 593 | | | 327. Midland, TX | 97 |
| 241. Pascagoula, MS | 593 | 286. Biloxi–Gulfport, MS | 441 | 328. Brownsville–Harlingen, TX | 91 |
| 241. Sheboygan, WI | 593 | 287. Brazoria, TX | 438 | 329. Glens Falls, NY | 43 |

## Metro Areas Listed Alphabetically

| Metro Area | Places Rated Rank | Metro Area | Places Rated Rank | Metro Area | Places Rated Rank |
|---|---|---|---|---|---|
| Abilene, TX | 320 | Anaheim–Santa Ana, CA | 52 | Atlantic City, NJ | 221 |
| Akron, OH | 73 | Anchorage, AK | 235 | Augusta, GA–SC | 65 |
| Albany, GA | 226 | Anderson, IN | 248 | Aurora–Elgin, IL | 104 |
| Albany–Schenectady–Troy, NY | 85 | Anderson, SC | 168 | Austin, TX | 181 |
| Albuquerque, NM | 60 | Ann Arbor, MI | 31 | Bakersfield, CA | 289 |
| Alexandria, LA | 218 | Anniston, AL | 236 | Baltimore, MD | 12 |
| Allentown–Bethlehem, PA–NJ | 224 | Appleton–Oshkosh–Neenah, WI | 164 | Bangor, ME | 182 |
| Alton–Granite City, IL | 143 | Asheville, NC | 103 | Baton Rouge, LA | 304 |
| Altoona, PA | 288 | Athens, GA | 233 | Battle Creek, MI | 152 |
| Amarillo, TX | 213 | Atlanta, GA | 15 | Beaumont–Port Arthur, TX | 228 |

| Metro Area | Places Rated Rank | Metro Area | Places Rated Rank | Metro Area | Places Rated Rank |
|---|---|---|---|---|---|
| Beaver County, PA | 158 | Eau Claire, WI | 178 | Kalamazoo, MI | 129 |
| Bellingham, WA | 319 | El Paso, TX | 263 | | |
| Benton Harbor, MI | 250 | Elkhart–Goshen, IN | 237 | Kankakee, IL | 231 |
| Bergen–Passaic, NJ | 22 | Elmira, NY | 253 | Kansas City, KS | 70 |
| Billings, MT | 275 | Enid, OK | 222 | Kansas City, MO | 55 |
| | | | | Kenosha, WI | 125 |
| Biloxi–Gulfport, MS | 286 | Erie, PA | 262 | Killeen–Temple, TX | 291 |
| Binghamton, NY | 137 | Eugene–Springfield, OR | 258 | | |
| Birmingham, AL | 72 | Evansville, IN–KY | 180 | Knoxville, TN | 145 |
| Bismarck, ND | 176 | Fall River, MA–RI | 152 | Kokomo, IN | 237 |
| Bloomington, IN | 193 | Fargo–Moorhead, ND–MN | 149 | La Crosse, WI | 207 |
| | | | | Lafayette, IN | 216 |
| Bloomington–Normal, IL | 172 | Fayetteville, NC | 157 | Lafayette, LA | 256 |
| Boise City, ID | 281 | Fayetteville–Springdale, AR | 240 | | |
| Boston, MA | 3 | Fitchburg–Leominster, MA | 216 | Lake Charles, LA | 311 |
| Boulder–Longmont, CO | 144 | Flint, MI | 196 | Lake County, IL | 99 |
| Bradenton, FL | 307 | Florence, AL | 232 | Lakeland–Winter Haven, FL | 309 |
| | | | | Lancaster, PA | 116 |
| Brazoria, TX | 287 | Florence, SC | 169 | Lansing–East Lansing, MI | 88 |
| Bremerton, WA | 312 | Fort Collins–Loveland, CO | 193 | | |
| Bridgeport–Milford, CT | 27 | Fort Lauderdale–Hollywood– | | Laredo, TX | 279 |
| Bristol, CT | 141 | Pompano Beach, FL | 97 | Las Cruces, NM | 246 |
| Brockton, MA | 150 | Fort Myers, FL | 257 | Las Vegas, NV | 290 |
| | | Fort Pierce, FL | 264 | Lawrence, KS | 224 |
| Brownsville–Harlingen, TX | 328 | | | Lawrence–Haverhill, MA–NH | 105 |
| Bryan–College Station, TX | 218 | Fort Smith, AR–OK | 278 | | |
| Buffalo, NY | 35 | Fort Walton Beach, FL | 274 | Lawton, OK | 276 |
| Burlington, NC | 140 | Fort Wayne, IN | 126 | Lewiston–Auburn, ME | 186 |
| Burlington, VT | 63 | Fort Worth–Arlington, TX | 132 | Lexington–Fayette, KY | 59 |
| | | Fresno, CA | 298 | Lima, OH | 188 |
| Canton, OH | 285 | | | Lincoln, NE | 183 |
| Casper, WY | 302 | Gadsden, AL | 223 | | |
| Cedar Rapids, IA | 162 | Gainesville, FL | 69 | Little Rock–North Little Rock, AR | 58 |
| Champaign–Urbana–Rantoul, IL | 211 | Galveston–Texas City, TX | 84 | Longview–Marshall, TX | 268 |
| Charleston, SC | 81 | Gary–Hammond, IN | 89 | Lorain–Elyria, OH | 119 |
| | | Glens Falls, NY | 329 | Los Angeles–Long Beach, CA | 5 |
| Charleston, WV | 201 | | | Louisville, KY–IN | 48 |
| Charlotte–Gastonia–Rock Hill, NC–SC | 139 | Grand Forks, ND | 117 | | |
| Charlottesville, VA | 90 | Grand Rapids, MI | 93 | Lowell, MA–NH | 123 |
| Chattanooga, TN–GA | 251 | Great Falls, MT | 214 | Lubbock, TX | 152 |
| Chicago, IL | 2 | Greeley, CO | 202 | Lynchburg, VA | 191 |
| | | Green Bay, WI | 150 | Macon–Warner Robins, GA | 241 |
| Chico, CA | 318 | | | Madison, WI | 45 |
| Cincinnati, OH–KY–IN | 46 | Greensboro–Winston-Salem– High Point, NC | 71 | | |
| Clarksville–Hopkinsville, TN–KY | 283 | Greenville–Spartanburg, SC | 94 | Manchester, NH | 190 |
| Cleveland, OH | 16 | Hagerstown, MD | 169 | Mansfield, OH | 313 |
| Colorado Springs, CO | 198 | Hamilton–Middletown, OH | 113 | McAllen–Edinburg–Mission, TX | 296 |
| | | Harrisburg–Lebanon–Carlisle, PA | 49 | Medford, OR | 317 |
| Columbia, MO | 54 | | | Melbourne–Titusville–Palm Bay, FL | 266 |
| Columbia, SC | 86 | Hartford, CT | 30 | | |
| Columbus, GA–AL | 164 | Hickory, NC | 138 | Memphis, TN–AR–MS | 51 |
| Columbus, OH | 62 | Honolulu, HI | 92 | Miami–Hialeah, FL | 41 |
| Corpus Christi, TX | 280 | Houma–Thibodaux, LA | 247 | Middlesex–Somerset–Hunterdon, NJ | 24 |
| | | Houston, TX | 33 | Middletown, CT | 155 |
| Cumberland, MD–WV | 185 | | | Midland, TX | 327 |
| Dallas, TX | 20 | Huntington–Ashland, WV–KY–OH | 156 | | |
| Danbury, CT | 40 | Huntsville, AL | 208 | Milwaukee, WI | 17 |
| Danville, VA | 241 | Indianapolis, IN | 43 | Minneapolis–St. Paul, MN–WI | 9 |
| Davenport–Rock Island–Moline, IA–IL | 115 | Iowa City, IA | 37 | Mobile, AL | 80 |
| | | Jackson, MI | 209 | Modesto, CA | 301 |
| Dayton–Springfield, OH | 42 | | | Monmouth–Ocean, NJ | 32 |
| Daytona Beach, FL | 197 | Jackson, MS | 66 | | |
| Decatur, IL | 191 | Jacksonville, FL | 108 | Monroe, LA | 308 |
| Denver, CO | 28 | Jacksonville, NC | 189 | Montgomery, AL | 166 |
| Des Moines, IA | 96 | Janesville–Beloit, WI | 203 | Muncie, IN | 146 |
| | | Jersey City, NJ | 67 | Muskegon, MI | 205 |
| Detroit, MI | 7 | | | Nashua, NH | 160 |
| Dothan, AL | 241 | Johnson City–Kingsport–Bristol, TN–VA | 111 | | |
| Dubuque, IA | 218 | Johnstown, PA | 193 | Nashville, TN | 61 |
| Duluth, MN–WI | 109 | Joliet, IL | 127 | Nassau–Suffolk, NY | 10 |
| East St. Louis–Belleville, IL | 284 | Joplin, MO | 271 | New Bedford, MA | 265 |
| | | | | New Britain, CT | 98 |
| | | | | New Haven–Meriden, CT | 50 |

| Metro Area | Places Rated Rank | Metro Area | Places Rated Rank | Metro Area | Places Rated Rank |
|---|---|---|---|---|---|
| New London–Norwich, CT–RI | 254 | Reno, NV | 229 | Stamford, CT | 23 |
| New Orleans, LA | 25 | | | | |
| New York, NY | 1 | Richland–Kennewick–Pasco, WA | 314 | State College, PA | 230 |
| Newark, NJ | 8 | Richmond–Petersburg, VA | 36 | Steubenville–Weirton, OH–WV | 270 |
| Niagara Falls, NY | 269 | Riverside–San Bernardino, CA | 44 | Stockton, CA | 304 |
| | | Roanoke, VA | 133 | Syracuse, NY | 131 |
| Norfolk–Virginia Beach–Newport News, VA | 56 | Rochester, MN | 18 | Tacoma, WA | 258 |
| Norwalk, CT | 29 | | | | |
| Oakland, CA | 39 | Rochester, NY | 53 | Tallahassee, FL | 297 |
| Ocala, FL | 273 | Rockford, IL | 142 | Tampa–St. Petersburg–Clearwater, FL | 106 |
| Odessa, TX | 294 | Sacramento, CA | 135 | Terre Haute, IN | 281 |
| | | Saginaw–Bay City–Midland, MI | 136 | Texarkana, TX–Texarkana, AR | 303 |
| Oklahoma City, OK | 75 | St. Cloud, MN | 234 | Toledo, OH | 68 |
| Olympia, WA | 306 | | | | |
| Omaha, NE–IA | 26 | St. Joseph, MO | 322 | Topeka, KS | 112 |
| Orange County, NY | 79 | St. Louis, MO–IL | 19 | Trenton, NJ | 87 |
| Orlando, FL | 184 | Salem, OR | 187 | Tucson, AZ | 95 |
| | | Salem–Gloucester, MA | 100 | Tulsa, OK | 78 |
| Owensboro, KY | 173 | Salinas–Seaside–Monterey, CA | 300 | Tuscaloosa, AL | 210 |
| Oxnard–Ventura, CA | 118 | | | | |
| Panama City, FL | 325 | Salt Lake City–Ogden, UT | 74 | Tyler, TX | 211 |
| Parkersburg–Marietta, WV–OH | 215 | San Angelo, TX | 321 | Utica–Rome, NY | 293 |
| Pascagoula, MS | 241 | San Antonio, TX | 91 | Vallejo–Fairfield–Napa, CA | 124 |
| | | San Diego, CA | 38 | Vancouver, WA | 266 |
| Pawtucket–Woonsocket–Attleboro, RI–MA | 114 | San Francisco, CA | 11 | Victoria, TX | 316 |
| Pensacola, FL | 252 | San Jose, CA | 47 | Vineland–Millville–Bridgeton, NJ | 174 |
| Peoria, IL | 107 | Santa Barbara–Santa Maria–Lompoc, CA | 261 | Visalia–Tulare–Porterville, CA | 324 |
| Philadelphia, PA–NJ | 4 | Santa Cruz, CA | 134 | Waco, TX | 260 |
| Phoenix, AZ | 77 | Santa Rosa–Petaluma, CA | 128 | Washington, DC–MD–VA | 6 |
| | | Sarasota, FL | 177 | Waterbury, CT | 102 |
| Pine Bluff, AR | 227 | | | | |
| Pittsburgh, PA | 14 | Savannah, GA | 122 | Waterloo–Cedar Falls, IA | 148 |
| Pittsfield, MA | 206 | Scranton–Wilkes-Barre, PA | 101 | Wausau, WI | 169 |
| Portland, ME | 163 | Seattle, WA | 21 | West Palm Beach–Boca Raton–Delray Beach, FL | 295 |
| Portland, OR | 76 | Sharon, PA | 203 | Wheeling, WV–OH | 179 |
| | | Sheboygan, WI | 241 | Wichita, KS | 175 |
| Portsmouth–Dover–Rochester, NH–ME | 237 | Sherman–Denison, TX | 292 | Wichita Falls, TX | 255 |
| Poughkeepsie, NY | 299 | Shreveport, LA | 82 | Williamsport, PA | 159 |
| Providence, RI | 33 | Sioux City, IA–NE | 161 | Wilmington, DE–NJ–MD | 82 |
| Provo–Orem, UT | 326 | Sioux Falls, SD | 130 | Wilmington, NC | 120 |
| Pueblo, CO | 277 | South Bend–Mishawaka, IN | 167 | Worcester, MA | 64 |
| | | | | | |
| Racine, WI | 147 | Spokane, WA | 272 | Yakima, WA | 310 |
| Raleigh–Durham, NC | 13 | Springfield, IL | 57 | York, PA | 199 |
| Reading, PA | 110 | Springfield, MA | 200 | Youngstown–Warren, OH | 121 |
| Redding, CA | 315 | Springfield, MO | 249 | Yuba City, CA | 323 |

## Place Profiles: Health Care Facilities and Environmental Features of 329 Metro Areas

In the pages that follow, some of the health care facilities and environmental characteristics of the 329 metro areas are detailed. The information is derived from a number of sources: American Medical Association, *Physician Characteristics and Distribution in the United States,* 1982; U.S. Department of Commerce, Bureau of the Census, *County and City Data Book,* 1983; Anthony Kruzas, *Medical and Health Information Directory,* 1982; American Heart Association, *Directory of Cardiac Rehabilitation,* 1981; American Cancer Society,

*Cancer Facts and Figures,* 1984; Environmental Protection Agency, *Air Quality Data, 1983;* and U.S. Department of Health and Human Services, *Fluoridation Census,* 1984.

Teaching hospitals that are located in metro areas that have no medical schools are affiliated with schools in other metro areas. Those cancer treatment centers designated as fully comprehensive by the National Cancer Institute are identified by a bullet (•) before their names. The presence of a symbol for a pollutant that picks Pittsburgh PA as the best place to live in America! Philadelphia was #5 overall, w/ good arts & education, poor housing etc.

Have fun. Love
Mary & Jos

MOM —

    I had to use
one of these in
a research project,
& Marg and I had
so much fun with
it, we'd thought you
might enjoy it too.
It is better in detail,
than for overall ranking
-- what else to
conclude from a guide

in the category Air Pollution indicates that this pollutant exceeds the EPA primary standard in its annual mean average. One or more triangles (▲) in this category signal a severe ozone problem. The CMSA Access entry gives the name of the consolidated area to which the metro area belongs and tells how many points it receives for shared assets.

A star preceding a metro area's name highlights it as one of the top 25 places for health care and environment.

**Abilene, TX**
Physicians per 100,000: 137
Costs Index: Good
Fluoridation: None
Air Pollution: Insignificant
Places Rated Score: 237
Places Rated Rank: 320

**Akron, OH**
Physicians per 100,000: 176
Teaching Hospitals:
  Akron City Hospital
  Akron General Medical Center
  St. Thomas Hospital Medical Center
Cardiac Rehabilitation Centers:
  Litchfield Rehabilitation Center CRU
Costs Index: Excellent
Fluoridation: Adjusted
Air Pollution: Insignificant
CMSA Access: CLEVELAND–AKRON–
  LORAIN, OH (280)
Places Rated Score: 1,656
Places Rated Rank: 73

**Albany, GA**
Physicians per 100,000: 118
Costs Index: Excellent
Fluoridation: Adjusted
Air Pollution: Insignificant
Places Rated Score: 618
Places Rated Rank: 226

**Albany–Schenectady–Troy, NY**
Physicians per 100,000: 231
Teaching Hospitals:
  Albany Medical Center Hospital
  VA Medical Center
Medical Schools:
  Albany Medical College of Union
    University
Cardiac Rehabilitation Centers:
  Albany Medical Center Hospital Exercise
    Test Lab
  St. Mary's Hospital CRU
  Samaritan Hospital Coronary Care and
    Rehabilitation Unit
  VA Medical Center CRU
Hospices:
  Hospice of Schenectady
Costs Index: Unacceptable
Fluoridation: Adjusted (Schenectady and
  Troy only)
Air Pollution: Insignificant
Places Rated Score: 1,431
Places Rated Rank: 85

**Albuquerque, NM**
Physicians per 100,000: 253
Teaching Hospitals:
  Bernalillo County Medical Center
  Lovelace-Bataan Medical Center
  VA Medical Center
Medical Schools:
  University of New Mexico School of
    Medicine

Cardiac Rehabilitation Centers:
  Lovelace Medical Center CRU
  New Heart, Inc., Rehabilitation Center
Comprehensive Cancer Treatment
  Centers:
  University of New Mexico Cancer
    Research and Treatment Center
Hospices:
  Hospital Home Health Care–Hospice
    Program
Costs Index: Excellent
Fluoridation: Adjusted
Air Pollution: TSP, CO
Places Rated Score: 1,853
Places Rated Rank: 60

**Alexandria, LA**
Physicians per 100,000: 140
Costs Index: Excellent
Fluoridation: Natural
Air Pollution: Insignificant
Places Rated Score: 640
Places Rated Rank: 218

**Allentown–Bethlehem, PA–NJ**
Physicians per 100,000: 171
Cardiac Rehabilitation Centers:
  Sacred Heart Hospital CRU
Costs Index: Excellent
Fluoridation: Adjusted (Bethlehem only)
Air Pollution: Insignificant
Places Rated Score: 621
Places Rated Rank: 224

**Alton–Granite City, IL**
Physicians per 100,000: 85
Cardiac Rehabilitation Centers:
  St. Elizabeth Medical Center CRU
Hospices:
  Hospice of Madison County
  St. Anthony's Hospital–Home Health
    Agency
Costs Index: Excellent
Fluoridation: Adjusted (Alton only)
Air Pollution: Insignificant
CMSA Access: ST. LOUIS–EAST ST.
  LOUIS–ALTON, MO–IL (230)
Places Rated Score: 965
Places Rated Rank: 143

**Altoona, PA**
Physicians per 100,000: 132
Cardiac Rehabilitation Centers:
  Altoona Hospital Cardiac Rehabilitation
    Program
Costs Index: Excellent
Fluoridation: None
Air Pollution: Insignificant
Places Rated Score: 432
Places Rated Rank: 288

**Amarillo, TX**
Physicians per 100,000: 169
Cardiac Rehabilitation Centers:
  Amarillo Cardiac Program CRU
Costs Index: Good

Fluoridation: Natural
Air Pollution: Insignificant
Places Rated Score: 669
Places Rated Rank: 213

**Anaheim–Santa Ana, CA**
Physicians per 100,000: 205
Teaching Hospitals:
  University of California, Irvine, Medical
    Center
Medical Schools:
  California College of Medicine, Irvine
Cardiac Rehabilitation Centers
  Anaheim Memorial Hospital CRU
  Chapman General Hospital CRU
  Fountain Valley Community Hospital
    CRU
  Fullerton Community Hospital CRU
  Hoag Memorial Presbyterian Hospital
    CRU
  Martin Luther Medical Center CRU
  Mercy General Hospital CRU
  Mission Community Hospital CRU
    Orange CTC
  Palm Harbor General Hospital CRU
  St. Joseph's Hospital CRU
  St. Jude Hospital CRU
  Santa Ana–Tustin Community Hospital
    CTC
  University of California, Irvine, Medical
    Center CRU
Hospices:
  Hospice Orange County, Inc.
Costs Index: Fair
Fluoridation: None
Air Pollution: TSP, CO, O$_3$, NO$_2$, Pb
CMSA Access: LOS ANGELES–ANAHEIM–
  RIVERSIDE, CA (720)
Places Rated Score: 2,025
Places Rated Rank: 52

**Anchorage, AK**
Physicians per 100,000: 201
Cardiac Rehabilitation Centers:
  Alaska Treatment Center CRU
Hospices:
  Hospice of Anchorage
Costs Index: Fair
Fluoridation: Adjusted
Air Pollution: CO
Places Rated Score: 601
Places Rated Rank: 235

**Anderson, IN**
Physicians per 100,000: 80
Costs Index: Excellent
Fluoridation: Adjusted
Air Pollution: Insignificant
Places Rated Score: 580
Places Rated Rank: 248

**Anderson, SC**
Physicians per 100,000: 120
Costs Index: Outstanding
Fluoridation: Adjusted

Air Pollution: Insignificant
Places Rated Score: 820
Places Rated Rank: 168

**Ann Arbor, MI**
Physicians per 100,000: 633
Teaching Hospitals:
St. Joseph Mercy Hospital
University Hospital
VA Medical Center
Medical Schools:
University of Michigan Medical School
Cardiac Rehabilitation Centers:
St. Joseph Mercy Hospital CRU
Hospices:
Hospice of Washtenaw
Costs Index: Good
Fluoridation: Adjusted
Air Pollution: Insignificant
CMSA Access: DETROIT–ANN ARBOR,
MI (375)
Places Rated Score: 2,508
Places Rated Rank: 31

**Anniston, AL**
Physicians per 100,000: 98
Costs Index: Excellent
Fluoridation: Adjusted
Air Pollution: Insignificant
Places Rated Score: 598
Places Rated Rank: 236

**Appleton–Oshkosh–Neenah, WI**
Physicians per 100,000: 133
Cardiac Rehabilitation Centers:
Appleton Memorial Hospital CRU
St. Elizabeth Hospital CRU
Costs Index: Excellent
Fluoridation: Adjusted
Air Pollution: Insignificant
Places Rated Score: 833
Places Rated Rank: 164

**Asheville, NC**
Physicians per 100,000: 204
Cardiac Rehabilitation Centers:
St. Joseph Hospital CRU
VA Medical Center
Hospices:
Mountain Area Hospice
Costs Index: Outstanding
Fluoridation: Adjusted
Air Pollution: Insignificant
Places Rated Score: 1,204
Places Rated Rank: 103

**Athens, GA**
Physicians per 100,000: 105
Costs Index: Excellent
Fluoridation: Adjusted
Air Pollution: Insignificant
Places Rated Score: 605
Places Rated Rank: 233

★ **Atlanta, GA**
Physicians per 100,000: 195
Teaching Hospitals:
Crawford W. Long Memorial Hospital of
Emory University
Emory University Hospital
Grady Memorial Hospital
Henrietta Egleston Hospital for Children
VA Medical Center (Decatur)
Medical Schools:
Emory University School of Medicine
School of Medicine at Morehouse
College

Cardiac Rehabilitation Centers:
Atlanta Jewish Community Center CRU
Clayton General Hospital CRU
De Kalb General Hospital CRU
Georgia Baptist Medical Center CRU
Grady Memorial Hospital CRU
Northside Hospital CRU
Piedmont Hospital CRU
Hospices:
Grady Hospice of Grady Memorial
Hospital
Hospice Atlanta
Wesley Homes, Inc.
Costs Index: Good
Fluoridation: Adjusted
Air Pollution: Insignificant
Places Rated Score: 3,195
Places Rated Rank: 15

**Atlantic City, NJ**
Physicians per 100,000: 137
Costs Index: Excellent
Fluoridation: Adjusted
Air Pollution: Insignificant
Places Rated Score: 637
Places Rated Rank: 221

**Augusta, GA–SC**
Physicians per 100,000: 298
Teaching Hospitals:
Eugene Talmadge Memorial Hospital and
Clinic–Medical College of Georgia
VA Medical Center
Medical Schools:
Medical College of Georgia School of
Medicine
Cardiac Rehabilitation Centers:
Medical College of Georgia CRU
VA Medical Center CRU
Hospices:
St. Joseph's Hospital–Hospice Program
Costs Index: Excellent
Fluoridation: Adjusted
Air Pollution: Insignificant
Places Rated Score: 1,798
Places Rated Rank: 65

**Aurora–Elgin, IL**
Physicians per 100,000: 123
Costs Index: Excellent
Fluoridation: Natural (Aurora); adjusted
(Elgin)
Air Pollution: Insignificant
CMSA Access: CHICAGO–GARY–LAKE
COUNTY, IL–IN–WI (580)
Places Rated Score: 1,203
Places Rated Rank: 104

**Austin, TX**
Physicians per 100,000: 182
Hospices:
Girling and Associates–Home Health
Services, Inc.
Girling and Associates–Home Health
Services (Georgetown)
Costs Index: Good
Fluoridation: Adjusted
Air Pollution: Insignificant
Places Rated Score: 782
Places Rated Rank: 181

**Bakersfield, CA**
Physicians per 100,000: 120
Teaching Hospitals:
Kern Medical Center
Cardiac Rehabilitation Centers:
Mercy Hospital CRU
Costs Index: Good

Fluoridation: None
Air Pollution: TSP
Places Rated Score: 420
Places Rated Rank: 289

★ **Baltimore, MD**
Physicians per 100,000: 312
Teaching Hospitals:
Baltimore City Hospitals
Johns Hopkins Hospital
Maryland General Hospital
Sinai Hospital of Baltimore
Union Memorial Hospital
University of Maryland Hospital
VA Medical Center
Medical Schools:
Johns Hopkins University School of
Medicine
University of Maryland School of Medicine
Cardiac Rehabilitation Centers:
Church Hospital Corporation CRU
Greater Baltimore Medical Center CRU
Maryland General Hospital CRU
St. Agnes Hospital Cardiology
Department
St. Joseph Hospital CRU
Sinai Hospital–Department of Rehabilitative
Medicine
U.S. Public Health Service Hospital CRU
Comprehensive Cancer Treatment
Centers:
• Johns Hopkins Oncology Center
Hospices:
Church Hospital Corporation–Hospice
Care Program
St. Agnes Hospital Home Care Program
Sinai Hospital Home Care Hospice
Costs Index: Good
Fluoridation: Adjusted
Air Pollution: TSP, SO$_2$, CO
Places Rated Score: 3,562
Places Rated Rank: 12

**Bangor, ME**
Physicians per 100,000: 280
Costs Index: Excellent
Fluoridation: Adjusted
Air Pollution: Insignificant
Places Rated Score: 780
Places Rated Rank: 182

**Baton Rouge, LA**
Physicians per 100,000: 142
Costs Index: Excellent
Fluoridation: None
Air Pollution: Insignificant
Places Rated Score: 342
Places Rated Rank: 304

**Battle Creek, MI**
Physicians per 100,000: 100
Cardiac Rehabilitation Centers:
Community Hospital Association
Cardiac Evaluation
Hospices:
Good Samaritan Hospice Care
Visiting Nurse Service of Calhoun
County
Costs Index: Excellent
Fluoridation: Adjusted
Air Pollution: Insignificant
Places Rated Score: 900
Places Rated Rank: 152

**Beaumont–Port Arthur, TX**
Physicians per 100,000: 116
Hospices:
Home Health–Home Care, Inc.

Costs Index: Good
Fluoridation: Adjusted
Air Pollution: Insignificant
Places Rated Score: 616
Places Rated Rank: 228

**Beaver County, PA**
Physicians per 100,000: 81
Costs Index: Excellent
Fluoridation: Adjusted
Air Pollution: Insignificant
CMSA Access: PITTSBURGH–BEAVER
    VALLEY, PA (280)
Places Rated Score: 861
Places Rated Rank: 158

**Bellingham, WA**
Physicians per 100,000: 140
Costs Index: Good
Fluoridation: None
Air Pollution: Insignificant
Places Rated Score: 240
Places Rated Rank: 319

**Benton Harbor, MI**
Physicians per 100,000: 70
Costs Index: Excellent
Fluoridation: Adjusted
Air Pollution: Insignificant
Places Rated Score: 570
Places Rated Rank: 250

**★ Bergen–Passaic, NJ**
Physicians per 100,000: 211
Teaching Hospitals:
    Hackensack Hospital
Cardiac Rehabilitation Centers:
    Bergen County Heart Association CRU
    Pascack Valley Hospital CRU
    Passaic General Hospital CRU
    YM-YWHA of Bergen County CRU
Hospices:
    Hackensack Hospital–Hospice Program
    Tri-Hospital Home Health–Palliative Care
        Program
    Valley Hospital–Northwest Bergen
        Hospice Program
Costs Index: Good
Fluoridation: None
Air Pollution: Insignificant
CMSA Access: NEW YORK–NORTHERN
    NEW JERSEY–LONG ISLAND,
    NY–NJ–CT (1,450)
Places Rated Score: 2,661
Places Rated Rank: 22

**Billings, MT**
Physicians per 100,000: 179
Cardiac Rehabilitation Centers:
    St. Vincent Hospital CRU
Costs Index: Excellent
Fluoridation: None
Air Pollution: Insignificant
Places Rated Score: 479
Places Rated Rank: 275

**Biloxi–Gulfport, MS**
Physicians per 100,000: 141
Cardiac Rehabilitation Centers:
    Keesler Air Force Base Medical
        Center
Costs Index: Excellent
Fluoridation: None
Air Pollution: Insignificant
Places Rated Score: 441
Places Rated Rank: 286

**Binghamton, NY**
Physicians per 100,000: 207
Teaching Hospitals:
    Charles S. Wilson Memorial Hospital
Cardiac Rehabilitation Centers:
    Binghamton General Hospital CRU
    Our Lady of Lourdes Hospital CRU
    Wilson Memorial Hospital CRU
Hospices:
    Our Lady of Lourdes Memorial
        Hospital–Hospice
Costs Index: Poor
Fluoridation: Adjusted
Air Pollution: Insignificant
Places Rated Score: 1,007
Places Rated Rank: 137

**Birmingham, AL**
Physicians per 100,000: 242
Teaching Hospitals:
    Children's Hospital
    University of Alabama Hospitals
    VA Hospital
Medical Schools:
    University of Alabama in Birmingham
        School of Medicine
Cardiac Rehabilitation Centers:
    University of Alabama in Birmingham
        CRU
Comprehensive Cancer Treatment
    Centers:
• University of Alabama in Birmingham–
        Comprehensive Cancer Center
Hospices:
    The Baptist Medical Centers–Hospice
        House Call
Costs Index: Good
Fluoridation: None
Air Pollution: Insignificant
Places Rated Score: 1,692
Places Rated Rank: 72

**Bismarck, ND**
Physicians per 100,000: 204
Cardiac Rehabilitation Centers:
    St. Alexius Hospital CRU
Costs Index: Excellent
Fluoridation: Adjusted
Air Pollution: Insignificant
Places Rated Score: 804
Places Rated Rank: 176

**Bloomington, IN**
Physicians per 100,000: 131
Cardiac Rehabilitation Centers:
    YMCA–Bloomington Hospital CRU
Costs Index: Excellent
Fluoridation: Adjusted
Air Pollution: Insignificant
Places Rated Score: 731
Places Rated Rank: 193

**Bloomington–Normal, IL**
Physicians per 100,000: 115
Cardiac Rehabilitation Centers:
    Brookhaw Hospital CRU
    Mennonite Hospital Cardiac Rehabilitation
        Program
Costs Index: Excellent
Fluoridation: Adjusted
Air Pollution: Insignificant
Places Rated Score: 815
Places Rated Rank: 172

**Boise City, ID**
Physicians per 100,000: 153

Cardiac Rehabilitation Centers:
    Idaho Elks Hospital Rehabilitation
        Program
    St. Alphonsus Hospital CRU
Hospices:
    Mountain States Tumor Institute
Costs Index: Excellent
Fluoridation: None
Air Pollution: TSP, CO
Places Rated Score: 453
Places Rated Rank: 281

**★ Boston, MA**
Physicians per 100,000: 471
Teaching Hospitals:
    Beth Israel Hospital
    Boston Hospital for Women
    Children's Hospital Medical Center
    Faulkner Hospital
    Massachusetts Eye and Ear Infirmary
    Massachusetts General Hospital
    McLean Hospital
    New England Deaconess Hospital
    New England Medical Center Hospital
    Peter Bent Brigham Hospital
    Robert B. Brigham Hospital
    University Hospital
    St. Elizabeth's Hospital
    St. Margaret's Hospital for Women
    VA Medical Center (Boston)
    VA Medical Center (West Roxbury)
Medical Schools:
    Boston University School of Medicine
    Harvard Medical School
    Tufts University School of Medicine
Cardiac Rehabilitation Centers:
    Beth Israel Hospital Exercise Lab
    Faulkner Hospital CRU
    Massachusetts General Hospital CRU
    Massachusetts General Hospital Health
        Enhancement Center
    Massachusetts Rehabilitation Hospital
        CRU
    Mount Auburn Hospital CRU
    New England Heart Center
    New England Medical Center Hospital
        CRU
    New England Memorial Hospital CRU
    New England Rehabilitation Hospital
        CRU
    Norwood Hospital CRU
    University Hospital CRU
Comprehensive Cancer Treatment
    Centers:
• Sidney Farber Cancer Institute
    Tufts–New England Medical Center–Cancer
        Center
Hospices:
    Hospice of the Good Shepherd
    University Hospital–Regional Oncology
        Program
    Youville Rehabilitation and Chronic Disease
        Hospital
Costs Index: Good
Fluoridation: Adjusted
Air Pollution: CO
CMSA Access: BOSTON–LAWRENCE–SALEM,
    MA–NH (80)
Places Rated Score: 5,301
Places Rated Rank: 3

**Boulder–Longmont, CO**
Physicians per 100,000: 167
Hospices:
    Boulder County Hospice
Costs Index: Excellent
Fluoridation: Adjusted

Air Pollution: Insignificant
CMSA Access: DENVER–BOULDER,
 CO (195)
Places Rated Score: 962
Places Rated Rank: 144

**Bradenton, FL**
Physicians per 100,000: 133
Cardiac Rehabilitation Centers:
 L. W. Blake Memorial Hospital CRU
Costs Index: Good
Fluoridation: None
Air Pollution: Insignificant
Places Rated Score: 333
Places Rated Rank: 307

**Brazoria, TX**
Physicians per 100,000: 53
Costs Index: Good
Fluoridation: Almost none
Air Pollution: Insignificant
CMSA Access: HOUSTON–
 GALVESTON–BRAZORIA, TX (285)
Places Rated Score: 438
Places Rated Rank: 287

**Bremerton, WA**
Physicians per 100,000: 110
Costs Index: Excellent
Fluoridation: None
Air Pollution: Insignificant
Places Rated Score: 310
Places Rated Rank: 312

**Bridgeport–Milford, CT**
Physicians per 100,000: 220
Teaching Hospitals:
 Bridgeport Hospital
 St. Vincent's Medical Center
Cardiac Rehabilitation Centers:
 Park City Hospital CRU
 Progressive Cardiac Care Rehabilitation
 Program
Costs Index: Excellent
Fluoridation: Adjusted (Bridgeport only)
Air Pollution: O₃
CMSA Access: NEW YORK–NORTHERN
 NEW JERSEY–LONG ISLAND,
 NY–NJ–CT (1,480)
Places Rated Score: 2,550
Places Rated Rank: 27

**Bristol, CT**
Physicians per 100,000: 265
Costs Index: Excellent
Fluoridation: Adjusted
Air Pollution: Insignificant
CMSA Access: HARTFORD–NEW
 BRITAIN–MIDDLETOWN, CT (210)
Places Rated Score: 975
Places Rated Rank: 141

**Brockton, MA**
Physicians per 100,000: 101
Cardiac Rehabilitation Centers:
 Brockton Hospital–Old Colony YMCA
 CRU
Costs Index: Excellent
Fluoridation: None
Air Pollution: Insignificant
CMSA Access: BOSTON–LAWRENCE–
 SALEM, MA–NH (515)
Places Rated Score: 916
Places Rated Rank: 150

**Brownsville–Harlingen, TX**
Physicians per 100,000: 91
Costs Index: Good
Fluoridation: None
Air Pollution: TSP
Places Rated Score: 91
Places Rated Rank: 328

**Bryan–College Station, TX**
Physicians per 100,000: 90
Medical Schools:
 Texas A & M University College of
 Medicine
Costs Index: Good
Fluoridation: Adjusted (Bryan only)
Air Pollution: Insignificant
Places Rated Score: 640
Places Rated Rank: 218

**Buffalo, NY**
Physicians per 100,000: 215
Teaching Hospitals:
 Deaconess Hospital of Buffalo
 Erie County Medical Center
 Millard Fillmore Hospital
 VA Medical Center
Medical Schools:
 SUNY at Buffalo School of Medicine
Cardiac Rehabilitation Centers:
 Buffalo Cardiac CRU
 Buffalo VA Hospital CRU
 Deaconess Hospital of Buffalo CRU
 DeGraff Memorial Hospital CRU
 Erie County Medical Center CRU
 Millard Fillmore Hospital Exercise
 Laboratory
 St. Joseph Intercommunity Hospital
 CRU
Comprehensive Cancer Treatment
 Centers:
● Roswell Park Memorial Institute–
 Comprehensive Cancer Center
Hospices:
 Hospice Buffalo
Costs Index: Poor
Fluoridation: Adjusted
Air Pollution: Insignificant
Places Rated Score: 2,465
Places Rated Rank: 35

**Burlington, NC**
Physicians per 100,000: 94
Cardiac Rehabilitation Centers:
 Memorial Hospital of Alamance County
 CRU
Hospices:
 Hospice of Alamance County
Costs Index: Outstanding
Fluoridation: Adjusted
Air Pollution: Insignificant
Places Rated Score: 994
Places Rated Rank: 140

**Burlington, VT**
Physicians per 100,000: 509
Teaching Hospitals:
 Medical Center Hospital of Vermont
Medical Schools:
 University of Vermont College of
 Medicine
Cardiac Rehabilitation Centers:
 Mary Fletcher Hospital CRU
Comprehensive Cancer Treatment
 Centers:
 University of Vermont–Vermont Regional
 Cancer Center

Hospices:
 Visiting Nurse Association of Vermont
Costs Index: Excellent
Fluoridation: Adjusted
Air Pollution: Insignificant
Places Rated Score: 1,809
Places Rated Rank: 63

**Canton, OH**
Physicians per 100,000: 143
Cardiac Rehabilitation Centers:
 Doctors Hospital of Stark County CRU
Costs Index: Excellent
Fluoridation: None
Air Pollution: Insignificant
Places Rated Score: 443
Places Rated Rank: 285

**Casper, WY**
Physicians per 100,000: 145
Costs Index: Excellent
Fluoridation: None
Air Pollution: Insignificant
Places Rated Score: 345
Places Rated Rank: 302

**Cedar Rapids, IA**
Physicians per 100,000: 137
Cardiac Rehabilitation Centers:
 Community Hospital CRU
Hospices:
 Mercy Hospital–Hospice of Mercy
Costs Index: Excellent
Fluoridation: Adjusted
Air Pollution: Insignificant
Places Rated Score: 837
Places Rated Rank: 162

**Champaign–Urbana–Rantoul, IL**
Physicians per 100,000: 172
Cardiac Rehabilitation Centers:
 Carle Foundation Hospital CRU
Hospices:
 Mercy Hospice Care Program
Costs Index: Excellent
Fluoridation: Adjusted (Rantoul only)
Air Pollution: Insignificant
Places Rated Score: 672
Places Rated Rank: 211

**Charleston, SC**
Physicians per 100,000: 263
Teaching Hospitals:
 Medical University Hospital of South
 Carolina
 VA Medical Center
Medical Schools:
 Medical University of South
 Carolina–College of Medicine
Cardiac Rehabilitation Centers:
 South Carolina University Hospital CRU
Costs Index: Outstanding
Fluoridation: None
Air Pollution: Insignificant
Places Rated Score: 1,463
Places Rated Rank: 81

**Charleston, WV**
Physicians per 100,000: 208
Teaching Hospitals:
 Charleston Area Medical Center
Cardiac Rehabilitation Centers:
 Charleston Area Medical Center CRU
Costs Index: Excellent
Fluoridation: None
Air Pollution: Insignificant
Places Rated Score: 708
Places Rated Rank: 201

## Charlotte–Gastonia–Rock Hill, NC–SC
Physicians per 100,000: 99
Teaching Hospitals:
  Charlotte Memorial Hospital and
    Medical Center
Cardiac Rehabilitation Centers:
  Charlotte Rehabilitation Hospital CRU
Hospices:
  Hospice at Charlotte
  Hospice of Gastonia
Costs Index: Excellent
Fluoridation: Adjusted
Air Pollution: CO
Places Rated Score: 999
Places Rated Rank: 139

## Charlottesville, VA
Physicians per 100,000: 648
Teaching Hospitals:
  University of Virginia Hospitals
Medical Schools:
  University of Virginia School of
    Medicine
Costs Index: Excellent
Fluoridation: None
Air Pollution: Insignificant
Places Rated Score: 1,348
Places Rated Rank: 90

## Chattanooga, TN–GA
Physicians per 100,000: 164
Teaching Hospitals:
  Erlanger Medical Center
Cardiac Rehabilitation Centers:
  Erlanger Medical Center CRU
Costs Index: Good
Fluoridation: None
Air Pollution: Insignificant
Places Rated Score: 564
Places Rated Rank: 251

## ★ Chicago, IL
Physicians per 100,000: 226
Teaching Hospitals:
  Children's Memorial Hospital
  Christ Hospital
  Cook County Hospital
  Evanston Hospital
  Illinois Masonic Medical Center
  Little Company of Mary Hospital
  Lutheran General Hospital
  MacNeal Memorial Hospital
  McGaw Hospital–Loyola University
    Medical Center
  Mercy Hospital and Medical Center
  Michael Reese Hospital and Medical
    Center
  Mount Sinai Hospital Medical Center
  Northwestern Memorial Hospital
  Rush–Presbyterian–St. Luke's Medical
    Center
  St. Joseph Hospital
  Schwab Rehabilitation Center
  University of Chicago Hospitals and
    Clinics
  University of Illinois Hospital
  VA Medical Center (Hines)
  VA Medical Center (Lakeside)
  VA Medical Center (Westside)
Medical Schools:
  Loyola University of Chicago–Stritch
    School of Medicine
  Northwestern University Medical School
  Rush Medical College
  University of Chicago–Pritzker School of
    Medicine

University of Health Sciences–Chicago
  Medical School
University of Illinois College of Medicine
Cardiac Rehabilitation Centers:
  Alexian Brothers Medical Center CRU
  Gottlieb Memorial Hospital–Special
    Medical Services
  Hinsdale Sanitarium CRU
  Holy Family Hospital CRU
  Lutheran General Hospital CRU
  Marianjoy Hospital Rehabilitation Program
  Memorial Hospital of DuPage–Physical
    Medicine Department
  Northwestern Memorial Hospital CRU
  Oak Forest Hospital–Cardiac Stress Test
    Lab
  St. Anne's Hospital CRU
  St. Francis Hospital CRU (Blue Island)
  St. Francis Hospital CRU (Evanston)
  Skokie Valley Community Hospital CRU
  Swedish Covenant Hospital CRU
  Westlake Community Hospital CRU
Hospices:
  Carestoel Professional Care Center
  Hospice of the North Shore
  Illinois Masonic Medical Center Hospice
    Services
  Lutheran General Hospital–Cancer Care
    Unit
  St. Barnabas Hospice–Glen Ellyn
  St. Barnabas Hospice–Wheaton
Costs Index: Fair
Fluoridation: Adjusted
Air Pollution: TSP, CO
CMSA Access: CHICAGO–GARY–LAKE
  COUNTY, IL–IN–WI (40)
Places Rated Score: 5,766
Places Rated Rank: 2

## Chico, CA
Physicians per 100,000: 143
Costs Index: Good
Fluoridation: None
Air Pollution: Insignificant
Places Rated Score: 243
Places Rated Rank: 318

## Cincinnati, OH–KY–IN
Physicians per 100,000: 198
Teaching Hospitals:
  Christ Hospital
  Cincinnati General Hospital
  Good Samaritan Hospital
  VA Medical Center
Medical Schools:
  University of Cincinnati College of
    Medicine
Cardiac Rehabilitation Centers:
  Bethesda Hospital CRU
  Jewish Community Center CRU
Hospices:
  Hospice of Cincinnati
Costs Index: Excellent
Fluoridation: Adjusted
Air Pollution: Insignificant
CMSA Access: CINCINNATI–HAMILTON,
  OH–KY–IN (40)
Places Rated Score: 2,138
Places Rated Rank: 46

## Clarksville–Hopkinsville, TN–KY
Physicians per 100,000: 96
Costs Index: Excellent
Fluoridation: Adjusted (Clarksville only)
Air Pollution: Insignificant
Places Rated Score: 446
Places Rated Rank: 283

## ★ Cleveland, OH
Physicians per 100,000: 267
Teaching Hospitals:
  Cleveland Clinic Educational Foundation
  Cuyahoga County Hospital
  Highland View Hospital
  Mount Sinai Hospital of Cleveland
  St. Luke's Hospital
  University Hospitals of Cleveland
  VA Medical Center
Medical Schools:
  Case Western Reserve University School
    of Medicine
  Northeastern Ohio Universities College of
    Medicine
Cardiac Rehabilitation Centers:
  Cuyahoga County Hospital CRU
  Lakewood Hospital CRU
  Marymount Hospital Coronary Step-Up
  Parma Community General Hospital CRU
  VA Hospital CRU
Costs Index: Good
Fluoridation: Adjusted
Air Pollution: TSP
CMSA Access: CLEVELAND–AKRON–
  LORAIN, OH (100)
Places Rated Score: 3,167
Places Rated Rank: 16

## Colorado Springs, CO
Physicians per 100,000: 121
Cardiac Rehabilitation Centers:
  Pikes Peak "Y" CRU
Hospices:
  Penrose Hospital–Hospice Program
Costs Index: Excellent
Fluoridation: Natural
Air Pollution: CO
Places Rated Score: 721
Places Rated Rank: 198

## Columbia, MO
Physicians per 100,000: 651
Teaching Hospitals:
  Harry S. Truman Memorial VA Hospital
  University of Missouri Medical Center
Medical Schools:
  University of Missouri, Columbia, School
    of Medicine
Hospices:
  John H. Walters Hospice of Central
    Missouri
Costs Index: Excellent
Fluoridation: Adjusted
Air Pollution: Insignificant
Places Rated Score: 1,951
Places Rated Rank: 54

## Columbia, SC
Physicians per 100,000: 221
Medical Schools:
  University of South Carolina School of
    Medicine
Cardiac Rehabilitation Centers:
  Baptist Medical Center CRU
Hospices:
  South Carolina Baptist Hospital Hospice
Costs Index: Outstanding
Fluoridation: Adjusted
Air Pollution: Insignificant
Places Rated Score: 1,421
Places Rated Rank: 86

## Columbus, GA–AL
Physicians per 100,000: 133
Cardiac Rehabilitation Centers:
  Martin Army Hospital CRU

The Medical Center CRU
Costs Index: Excellent
Fluoridation: Adjusted
Air Pollution: Insignificant
Places Rated Score: 833
Places Rated Rank: 164

## Columbus, OH
Physicians per 100,000: 187
Teaching Hospitals:
Ohio State University Hospitals
Riverside Methodist Hospital
Medical Schools:
Ohio State University College of
Medicine
Cardiac Rehabilitation Centers:
Doctors Hospital CRU
Ohio State University Hospital CRU
Riverside Methodist Hospital CRU
Comprehensive Cancer Treatment
Centers:
• Ohio State University–Comprehensive
Cancer Center
Costs Index: Excellent
Fluoridation: Adjusted
Air Pollution: Insignificant
Places Rated Score: 1,837
Places Rated Rank: 62

## Corpus Christi, TX
Physicians per 100,000: 158
Costs Index: Good
Fluoridation: Adjusted
Air Pollution: TSP
Places Rated Score: 458
Places Rated Rank: 280

## Cumberland, MD–WV
Physicians per 100,000: 160
Cardiac Rehabilitation Centers:
Memorial Hospital CRU
Sacred Heart Hospital CRU
Costs Index: Outstanding
Fluoridation: None
Air Pollution: Insignificant
Places Rated Score: 760
Places Rated Rank: 185

## ★ Dallas, TX
Physicians per 100,000: 185
Teaching Hospitals:
Baylor University Medical Center
Methodist Hospital of Dallas
Parkland Memorial Hospital
Presbyterian Hospital of Dallas
St. Paul Hospital
VA Medical Center
Medical Schools:
University of Texas Southwestern
Medical School at Dallas
Cardiac Rehabilitation Centers:
Baylor University Hospital–Hunt Heart
Center
Dallas Cardiac Institute CRU
Dallas County Hospital
Presbyterian Medical Center CRU
St. Paul Hospital CRU
Hospices:
Ann's Haven–Hospice of Denton County
Hospice–VNA Home Health Care
Costs Index: Good
Fluoridation: Adjusted
Air Pollution: Insignificant
CMSA Access: DALLAS–FORT WORTH,
TX (40)
Places Rated Score: 2,825
Places Rated Rank: 20

## Danbury, CT
Physicians per 100,000: 220
Cardiac Rehabilitation Centers:
Danbury Hospital CRU
Costs Index: Excellent
Fluoridation: Adjusted
Air Pollution: Insignificant
CMSA Access: NEW YORK–NORTHERN
NEW JERSEY–LONG ISLAND,
NY–NJ–CT (1,530)
Places Rated Score: 2,350
Places Rated Rank: 40

## Danville, VA
Physicians per 100,000: 93
Costs Index: Excellent
Fluoridation: Adjusted
Air Pollution: Insignificant
Places Rated Score: 593
Places Rated Rank: 241

## Davenport–Rock Island–
## Moline, IA–IL
Physicians per 100,000: 113
Cardiac Rehabilitation Centers:
Davenport and Scott County Family "Y"
CRU
Franciscan Medical Center CRU (Rock
Island)
Mercy Hospital CRU
Hospices:
Hospice Care Group, Inc.
Lutheran Hospital–Hospice Program
Costs Index: Excellent
Fluoridation: Adjusted
Air Pollution: Insignificant
Places Rated Score: 1,113
Places Rated Rank: 115

## Dayton–Springfield, OH
Physicians per 100,000: 153
Teaching Hospitals:
Good Samaritan Hospital and Health
Center
Kettering Medical Center
Miami Valley Hospital
VA Medical Center
Medical Schools:
Wright State University School of
Medicine
Cardiac Rehabilitation Centers:
Ambulatory Care Center–Grandview
Hospital
Good Samaritan Hospital Cardiac Center
Kettering Medical Center CRU
Hospices:
Christel and Fairborn Manors
Hospice of Dayton
Costs Index: Excellent
Fluoridation: Adjusted
Air Pollution: Insignificant
Places Rated Score: 2,253
Places Rated Rank: 42

## Daytona Beach, FL
Physicians per 100,000: 123
Cardiac Rehabilitation Centers:
Halifax Hospital and Medical Center CRU
Hospices:
Hospice of Volusia
Costs Index: Good
Fluoridation: Adjusted
Air Pollution: Insignificant
Places Rated Score: 723
Places Rated Rank: 197

## Decatur, IL
Physicians per 100,000: 132
Cardiac Rehabilitation Centers:
Decatur Memorial Hospital CRU
Costs Index: Excellent
Fluoridation: Adjusted
Air Pollution: Insignificant
Places Rated Score: 732
Places Rated Rank: 191

## Denver, CO
Physicians per 100,000: 273
Teaching Hospitals:
Colorado General Hospital
Presbyterian Medical Center
VA Medical Center
Medical Schools:
University of Colorado School of
Medicine
Cardiac Rehabilitation Centers:
Denver General Hospital Coronary Care
Unit
Fitzsimmons Army Base Medical Center
Heart-Lung Center CRU
Lutheran Medical Center CRU
St. Joseph Hospital CRU
South Denver Clinic CRU
University of Colorado Health Sciences
Center CRU
Comprehensive Cancer Treatment
Centers:
• Colorado Regional Cancer Center, Inc.
Hospices:
Hospice of Holy Spirit
Hospice of Metro Denver
Costs Index: Excellent
Fluoridation: Adjusted
Air Pollution: TSP, CO
CMSA Access: DENVER–BOULDER,
CO (10)
Places Rated Score: 2,533
Places Rated Rank: 28

## Des Moines, IA
Physicians per 100,000: 156
Teaching Hospitals:
Iowa Methodist Medical Center
Cardiac Rehabilitation Centers:
Iowa Lutheran Hospital CRU
Iowa Methodist Medical Center
Mercy Hospital Medical Center CRU
VA Medical Center CRU
Hospices:
Hospice of Central Iowa
Costs Index: Excellent
Fluoridation: Adjusted
Air Pollution: TSP
Places Rated Score: 1,256
Places Rated Rank: 96

## ★ Detroit, MI
Physicians per 100,000: 182
Teaching Hospitals:
Children's Hospital of Michigan
Detroit General Hospital
Grace Hospital
Harper Hospital
Henry Ford Hospital
Hutzel Hospital
Oakwood Hospital
Providence Hospital
St. John Hospital
St. Joseph Mercy Hospital
Sinai Hospital of Detroit
Wayne County General Hospital
Medical Schools:
Wayne State University School of
Medicine

Cardiac Rehabilitation Centers:
  Annapolis Hospital Cardiac
    Rehabilitation Program
  Bon Secours Hospital CRU
  Downriver Treadmill Team CRU
  Henry Ford Hospital CRU
  Macomb Heart and Rehabilitation
    Institute
  Outer Drive Hospital CRU
  St. Joseph Mercy Hospital CRU
  Sinai Hospital of Detroit CRU
  William Beaumont Hospital CRU
Comprehensive Cancer Treatment
  Centers:
• Comprehensive Cancer Center of
    Metropolitan Detroit
Hospices:
  Cottage Hospital
  Hospice of Southeastern Michigan
  Michigan Cancer Foundation Services
  St. Joseph's Hospital–Hospice Program
Costs Index: Fair
Fluoridation: Adjusted
Air Pollution: TSP, CO
CMSA Access: DETROIT–ANN ARBOR,
  MI (110)
Places Rated Score: 4,142
Places Rated Rank: 7

**Dothan, AL**
Physicians per 100,000: 93
Costs Index: Excellent
Fluoridation: Adjusted
Air Pollution: Insignificant
Places Rated Score: 593
Places Rated Rank: 241

**Dubuque, IA**
Physicians per 100,000: 140
Costs Index: Excellent
Fluoridation: Adjusted
Air Pollution: Insignificant
Places Rated Score: 640
Places Rated Rank: 218

**Duluth, MN–WI**
Physicians per 100,000: 159
Medical Schools:
  University of Minnesota, Duluth, School
    of Medicine
Cardiac Rehabilitation Centers:
  St. Luke's Hospital CRU
  St. Mary's Hospital CRU
Hospices:
  Hospice–Duluth–St. Luke's Hospital
Costs Index: Excellent
Fluoridation: Adjusted
Air Pollution: TSP
Places Rated Score: 1,159
Places Rated Rank: 109

**East St. Louis–Belleville, IL**
Physicians per 100,000: 84
Costs Index: Excellent
Fluoridation: None
Air Pollution: TSP
CMSA Access: ST. LOUIS–EAST ST.
  LOUIS–ALTON, MO–IL (260)
Places Rated Score: 444
Places Rated Rank: 284

**Eau Claire, WI**
Physicians per 100,000: 198
Hospices:
  Sacred Heart Hospital Hospice
Costs Index: Excellent
Fluoridation: Adjusted

Air Pollution: Insignificant
Places Rated Score: 798
Places Rated Rank: 178

**El Paso, TX**
Physicians per 100,000: 128
Cardiac Rehabilitation Centers:
  R. E. Thomason General Hospital CRU
  St. Joseph's Hospital
Costs Index: Good
Fluoridation: Natural
Air Pollution: TSP, CO
Places Rated Score: 528
Places Rated Rank: 263

**Elkhart–Goshen, IN**
Physicians per 100,000: 96
Costs Index: Excellent
Fluoridation: Adjusted
Air Pollution: Insignificant
Places Rated Score: 596
Places Rated Rank: 237

**Elmira, NY**
Physicians per 100,000: 162
Cardiac Rehabilitation Centers:
  St. Joseph Hospital CRU
Hospices:
  Southern Tier Hospice
Costs Index: Poor
Fluoridation: Adjusted
Air Pollution: Insignificant
Places Rated Score: 562
Places Rated Rank: 253

**Enid, OK**
Physicians per 100,000: 126
Costs Index: Excellent
Fluoridation: Adjusted
Air Pollution: Insignificant
Places Rated Score: 626
Places Rated Rank: 222

**Erie, PA**
Physicians per 100,000: 129
Teaching Hospitals:
  Hamot Medical Center
Costs Index: Excellent
Fluoridation: None
Air Pollution: Insignificant
Places Rated Score: 529
Places Rated Rank: 262

**Eugene–Springfield, OR**
Physicians per 100,000: 139
Costs Index: Excellent
Fluoridation: Adjusted
Air Pollution: TSP
Places Rated Score: 539
Places Rated Rank: 258

**Evansville, IN–KY**
Physicians per 100,000: 183
Cardiac Rehabilitation Centers:
  Evansville Internal Medicine Specialists
    CRU
Costs Index: Excellent
Fluoridation: Adjusted
Air Pollution: Insignificant
Places Rated Score: 783
Places Rated Rank: 180

**Fall River, MA–RI**
Physicians per 100,000: 100
Hospices:
  Hospice Outreach, Inc.
Costs Index: Excellent
Fluoridation: Adjusted

Air Pollution: Insignificant
CMSA Access: PROVIDENCE–PAWTUCKET–
  FALL RIVER, RI–MA (200)
Places Rated Score: 900
Places Rated Rank: 152

**Fargo–Moorhead, ND–MN**
Physicians per 100,000: 220
Cardiac Rehabilitation Centers:
  Fargo Clinic CRU
  Rehab Medicine Service, Inc.
Costs Index: Excellent
Fluoridation: Adjusted
Air Pollution: Insignificant
Places Rated Score: 920
Places Rated Rank: 149

**Fayetteville, NC**
Physicians per 100,000: 72
Cardiac Rehabilitation Centers:
  Fayette VA Medical Center CRU
Costs Index: Outstanding
Fluoridation: Adjusted
Air Pollution: Insignificant
Places Rated Score: 872
Places Rated Rank: 157

**Fayetteville–Springdale, AR**
Physicians per 100,000: 144
Hospices:
  Northwest Arkansas Hospice
    Association
Costs Index: Excellent
Fluoridation: Adjusted (Springdale only)
Air Pollution: Insignificant
Places Rated Score: 594
Places Rated Rank: 240

**Fitchburg–Leominster, MA**
Physicians per 100,000: 205
Hospices:
  Burbank Hospital Hospice Care
Costs Index: Excellent
Fluoridation: Adjusted (Fitchburg only)
Air Pollution: Insignificant
Places Rated Score: 655
Places Rated Rank: 216

**Flint, MI**
Physicians per 100,000: 124
Teaching Hospitals:
  Hurley Medical Center
Cardiac Rehabilitation Centers:
  McLaren General Hospital CRU
  St. Joseph Hospital CRU
Hospices:
  Hospice of Flint
Costs Index: Good
Fluoridation: None
Air Pollution: Insignificant
Places Rated Score: 724
Places Rated Rank: 196

**Florence, AL**
Physicians per 100,000: 107
Costs Index: Excellent
Fluoridation: Adjusted
Air Pollution: Insignificant
Places Rated Score: 607
Places Rated Rank: 232

**Florence, SC**
Physicians per 100,000: 118
Costs Index: Outstanding
Fluoridation: Adjusted
Air Pollution: Insignificant
Places Rated Score: 818
Places Rated Rank: 169

## Fort Collins–Loveland, CO
Physicians per 100,000: 131
Hospices:
    Hospice, Inc., of Larimer County
Costs Index: Excellent
Fluoridation: Adjusted
Air Pollution: Insignificant
Places Rated Score: 731
Places Rated Rank: 193

## Fort Lauderdale–Hollywood–Pompano Beach, FL
Physicians per 100,000: 167
Cardiac Rehabilitation Centers:
    Broward General Medical Center CRU
    Florida Medical Center CRU
    Holy Cross Hospital CRU
    North Ridge General Hospital CRU
    South Broward Cardiac Center
        Rehabilitation Program
Hospices:
    Gold Coast Home Health Services
        Hospice Team
    Hospice of Broward
    Hospice of South Florida
Costs Index: Fair
Fluoridation: Adjusted (Hollywood only)
Air Pollution: Insignificant
CMSA Access: MIAMI–FORT
    LAUDERDALE, FL (185)
Places Rated Score: 1,252
Places Rated Rank: 97

## Fort Myers, FL
Physicians per 100,000: 146
Costs Index: Good
Fluoridation: Adjusted
Air Pollution: Insignificant
Places Rated Score: 546
Places Rated Rank: 257

## Fort Pierce, FL
Physicians per 100,000: 127
Costs Index: Good
Fluoridation: Adjusted
Air Pollution: Insignificant
Places Rated Score: 527
Places Rated Rank: 264

## Fort Smith, AR–OK
Physicians per 100,000: 166
Cardiac Rehabilitation Centers:
    St. Edward Mercy Medical Center CRU
Costs Index: Excellent
Fluoridation: None
Air Pollution: Insignificant
Places Rated Score: 466
Places Rated Rank: 278

## Fort Walton Beach, FL
Physicians per 100,000: 84
Costs Index: Good
Fluoridation: Natural
Air Pollution: Insignificant
Places Rated Score: 484
Places Rated Rank: 274

## Fort Wayne, IN
Physicians per 100,000: 160
Cardiac Rehabilitation Centers:
    Fort Wayne Cardiac Rehabilitation
        Program
    Northeastern Indiana Hospital CRU
Hospices:
    Hospice of Fort Wayne
    Parkview Hospice
Costs Index: Excellent

Fluoridation: Adjusted
Air Pollution: Insignificant
Places Rated Score: 1,060
Places Rated Rank: 126

## Fort Worth–Arlington, TX
Physicians per 100,000: 118
Cardiac Rehabilitation Centers:
    All Saints Episcopal Hospital CRU
    St. Joseph's Hospital CRU
Hospices:
    Community Hospice of St. Joseph
    Trinity Valley Hospice Association
Costs Index: Good
Fluoridation: Adjusted
Air Pollution: TSP
CMSA Access: DALLAS–FORT
    WORTH, TX (220)
Places Rated Score: 1,038
Places Rated Rank: 132

## Fresno, CA
Physicians per 100,000: 169
Cardiac Rehabilitation Centers:
    Fresno Community Hospital CRU
    St. Agnes Hospital Cardiac
        Rehabilitation Program
Hospices:
    Hospice of Fresno
Costs Index: Good
Fluoridation: Almost none
Air Pollution: CO, O$_3$
Places Rated Score: 369
Places Rated Rank: 298

## Gadsden, AL
Physicians per 100,000: 122
Cardiac Rehabilitation Centers:
    Baptist Memorial Hospital CRU
Costs Index: Good
Fluoridation: Adjusted
Air Pollution: Insignificant
Places Rated Score: 622
Places Rated Rank: 223

## Gainesville, FL
Physicians per 100,000: 531
Teaching Hospitals:
    Shands Teaching Hospital and
        Clinics
    VA Medical Center
Medical Schools:
    University of Florida College of
        Medicine
Cardiac Rehabilitation Centers:
    Alachua General Hospital CRU
Costs Index: Good
Fluoridation: Adjusted
Air Pollution: Insignificant
Places Rated Score: 1,731
Places Rated Rank: 69

## Galveston–Texas City, TX
Physicians per 100,000: 412
Teaching Hospitals:
    University of Texas Medical Branch at
        Arlington
Medical Schools:
    University of Texas Medical School at
        Galveston
Comprehensive Cancer Treatment
Centers:
    University of Texas Medical Branch
        Hospitals–Cancer Center
Costs Index: Poor
Fluoridation: Natural
Air Pollution: Insignificant

CMSA Access: HOUSTON–GALVESTON–
    BRAZORIA, TX (225)
Places Rated Score: 1,437
Places Rated Rank: 84

## Gary–Hammond, IN
Physicians per 100,000: 114
Cardiac Rehabilitation Centers:
    Porter Memorial Hospital CRU
    St. Anthony Medical Center CRU
    St. Catherine Hospital CRU
Costs Index: Excellent
Fluoridation: Adjusted
Air Pollution: TSP
CMSA Access: CHICAGO–GARY–LAKE
    COUNTY, IL–IN–WI (550)
Places Rated Score: 1,364
Places Rated Rank: 89

## Glens Falls, NY
Physicians per 100,000: 143
Costs Index: Poor
Fluoridation: None
Air Pollution: Insignificant
Places Rated Score: 43
Places Rated Rank: 329

## Grand Forks, ND
Physicians per 100,000: 209
Medical Schools:
    University of North Dakota School of
        Medicine
Cardiac Rehabilitation Centers:
    United Hospital CRU
Costs Index: Excellent
Fluoridation: Adjusted
Air Pollution: Insignificant
Places Rated Score: 1,109
Places Rated Rank: 117

## Grand Rapids, MI
Physicians per 100,000: 174
Teaching Hospitals:
    Blodgett Memorial Medical Center
    Butterworth Hospital
Cardiac Rehabilitation Centers:
    Butterworth Hospital CRU
Hospices:
    Hospice of Greater Grand Rapids
Costs Index: Excellent
Fluoridation: Adjusted
Air Pollution: Insignificant
Places Rated Score: 1,274
Places Rated Rank: 93

## Great Falls, MT
Physicians per 100,000: 167
Costs Index: Excellent
Fluoridation: Natural
Air Pollution: Insignificant
Places Rated Score: 667
Places Rated Rank: 214

## Greeley, CO
Physicians per 100,000: 106
Cardiac Rehabilitation Centers:
    Weld County General Hospital CRU
Costs Index: Excellent
Fluoridation: Adjusted
Air Pollution: Insignificant
Places Rated Score: 706
Places Rated Rank: 202

## Green Bay, WI
Physicians per 100,000: 116
Cardiac Rehabilitation Centers:
    Bellin Memorial Hospital CRU

St. Vincent Hospital CRU
Hospices:
Carl Kouba Hospice–Bellin Memorial
Hospital
Costs Index: Excellent
Fluoridation: Adjusted
Air Pollution: Insignificant
Places Rated Score: 916
Places Rated Rank: 150

## Greensboro–Winston-Salem–High Point, NC
Physicians per 100,000: 194
Teaching Hospitals:
North Carolina Baptist Hospitals, Inc.
Medical Schools:
Bowman Gray School of Medicine of
Wake Forest University
Cardiac Rehabilitation Centers:
Moses Cone Memorial Hospital CRU
Wake Forest Hospital, Department of
Medical and Physical Education
Comprehensive Cancer Treatment
Centers:
Bowman Gray School of Medicine–
Oncology Research Center
Hospices:
Greensboro Hospice
Hospice of Winston-Salem/Forsyth
County, Inc.
Costs Index: Excellent
Fluoridation: Adjusted
Air Pollution: Insignificant
Places Rated Score: 1,694
Places Rated Rank: 71

## Greenville–Spartanburg, SC
Physicians per 100,000: 160
Teaching Hospitals:
Greenville Hospital System
Cardiac Rehabilitation Centers:
Greenville Memorial Hospital CRU
Hospices:
Greenville Hospital System–Hospice
Program
Costs Index: Outstanding
Fluoridation: Adjusted
Air Pollution: Insignificant
Places Rated Score: 1,260
Places Rated Rank: 94

## Hagerstown, MD
Physicians per 100,000: 118
Costs Index: Outstanding
Fluoridation: Adjusted
Air Pollution: Insignificant
Places Rated Score: 818
Places Rated Rank: 169

## Hamilton–Middletown, OH
Physicians per 100,000: 95
Cardiac Rehabilitation Centers:
Fort Hamilton–Hughes Hospital CRU
Middletown Area YMCA CRU
Middletown Hospital CRU
Hospices:
Hospice of Middletown
Costs Index: Excellent
Fluoridation: Adjusted
Air Pollution: Insignificant
CMSA Access: CINCINNATI–HAMILTON,
OH–KY–IN (140)
Places Rated Score: 1,135
Places Rated Rank: 113

## Harrisburg–Lebanon–Carlisle, PA
Physicians per 100,000: 187

Teaching Hospitals:
Harrisburg Hospital
Milton S. Hershey Medical Center
Medical Schools:
Pennsylvania State University College of
Medicine
Cardiac Rehabilitation Centers:
Carlisle Hospital CRU
Holy Spirit Hospital CRU
Milton S. Hershey Medical Center CRU
Hospices:
Harrisburg Hospital Hospice Unit
Hospice of Central Pennsylvania
Costs Index: Outstanding
Fluoridation: Adjusted
Air Pollution: Insignificant
Places Rated Score: 2,087
Places Rated Rank: 49

## Hartford, CT
Physicians per 100,000: 281
Teaching Hospitals:
Hartford Hospital
Mount Sinai Hospital
St. Francis Hospital and Medical Center
University of Connecticut Health
Center–John Dempsey Hospital
VA Medical Center (Newington)
Medical Schools:
University of Connecticut School of
Medicine
Cardiac Rehabilitation Centers:
Hartford Hospital CRU
Mount Sinai Hospital CRU
St. Francis Hospital CRU
Hospices:
Palliative Care Team
Costs Index: Excellent
Fluoridation: Adjusted
Air Pollution: Insignificant
CMSA Access: HARTFORD–NEW
BRITAIN–MIDDLETOWN, CT (40)
Places Rated Score: 2,521
Places Rated Rank: 30

## Hickory, NC
Physicians per 100,000: 106
Cardiac Rehabilitation Centers:
Glenn K. Frye Memorial Hospital CRU
Hospices:
Hospice of Catawba Valley
Costs Index: Outstanding
Fluoridation: Adjusted
Air Pollution: Insignificant
Places Rated Score: 1,006
Places Rated Rank: 138

## Honolulu, HI
Physicians per 100,000: 198
Teaching Hospitals:
Queen's Medical Center
Medical Schools:
University of Hawaii–John A. Burns
School of Medicine
Cardiac Rehabilitation Centers:
Central YMCA CRU
Kaukini Medical Center Cardiac Care
Unit
Tripler Army Base Medical Center
Comprehensive Cancer Treatment
Centers:
University of Hawaii at Manoa–Cancer
Center of Hawaii
Hospices:
St. Francis Hospital–Hospice Program
Costs Index: Good
Fluoridation: Almost none

Air Pollution: Insignificant
Places Rated Score: 1,298
Places Rated Rank: 92

## Houma–Thibodaux, LA
Physicians per 100,000: 83
Costs Index: Excellent
Fluoridation: Adjusted
Air Pollution: Insignificant
Places Rated Score: 583
Places Rated Rank: 247

## Houston, TX
Physicians per 100,000: 207
Teaching Hospitals:
Harris County Hospital District
Hermann Hospital
Texas Children's Hospital
VA Medical Center
Medical Schools:
Baylor College of Medicine
University of Texas Medical School at
Houston
Cardiac Rehabilitation Centers:
Ben Taub General Hospital CRU
Houston Cardiac Rehabilitation Center
CRU
Methodist Hospital Adult Fitness
Program
Rehabilitation Institute CRU
VA Hospital CRU
West Houston Cardiac Rehabilitation
Center CRU
Comprehensive Cancer Treatment
Centers:
• University of Texas Health System
Cancer Center
Hospices:
Houston Institute for Cancer
Costs Index: Poor
Fluoridation: Natural (approximately 50%
of the metro area)
Air Pollution: TSP
CMSA Access: HOUSTON–GALVESTON–
BRAZORIA, TX (60)
Places Rated Score: 2,467
Places Rated Rank: 33

## Huntington–Ashland, WV–KY–OH
Physicians per 100,000: 125
Medical Schools:
Marshall University School of Medicine
Cardiac Rehabilitation Centers:
King's Daughters Hospital CRU
(Ashland)
Costs Index: Excellent
Fluoridation: Adjusted (Huntington only)
Air Pollution: Insignificant
Places Rated Score: 875
Places Rated Rank: 156

## Huntsville, AL
Physicians per 100,000: 185
Costs Index: Excellent
Fluoridation: Adjusted
Air Pollution: Insignificant
Places Rated Score: 685
Places Rated Rank: 208

## Indianapolis, IN
Physicians per 100,000: 243
Teaching Hospitals:
Indiana University Hospitals
Methodist Hospital of Indiana, Inc.
VA Medical Center
William N. Wishard Memorial Hospital

Medical Schools:
Indiana University School of Medicine
Cardiac Rehabilitation Centers:
Methodist Hospital of Indiana CRU
St. Vincent Hospital CRU
Vital Cardiac Rehabilitation Unit
Winona Memorial Hospital CRU
Hospices:
Methodist Hospital Hospice
Costs Index: Excellent
Fluoridation: Adjusted
Air Pollution: CO
Places Rated Score: 2,243
Places Rated Rank: 43

**Iowa City, IA**
Physicians per 100,000: 1,137
Teaching Hospitals:
University of Iowa Hospitals and Clinics
VA Medical Center
Medical Schools:
University of Iowa School of Medicine
Cardiac Rehabilitation Centers:
University of Iowa Hospitals and Clinics
CRU
Costs Index: Excellent
Fluoridation: Adjusted
Air Pollution: Insignificant
Places Rated Score: 2,437
Places Rated Rank: 37

**Jackson, MI**
Physicians per 100,000: 79
Hospices:
Hospice of Jackson
Costs Index: Excellent
Fluoridation: Adjusted
Air Pollution: Insignificant
Places Rated Score: 679
Places Rated Rank: 209

**Jackson, MS**
Physicians per 100,000: 292
Teaching Hospitals:
University of Mississippi Medical Center
VA Medical Center
Medical Schools:
University of Mississippi School of
Medicine
Cardiac Rehabilitation Centers:
Mississippi Methodist Hospital CRU
St. Dominic–Jackson Hospital CRU
VA Medical Center CRU
Costs Index: Excellent
Fluoridation: Adjusted
Air Pollution: Insignificant
Places Rated Score: 1,792
Places Rated Rank: 66

**Jacksonville, FL**
Physicians per 100,000: 181
Teaching Hospitals:
University Hospital of Jacksonville
Cardiac Rehabilitation Centers:
Baptist Medical Center CRU
University Hospital of Jacksonville CRU
Hospices:
Hospice of Northeast Florida
Methodist Hospital Hospice
St. Vincent's Medical Center–Home
Care Program
Costs Index: Good
Fluoridation: Natural
Air Pollution: Pb
Places Rated Score: 1,181
Places Rated Rank: 108

**Jacksonville, NC**
Physicians per 100,000: 40
Costs Index: Outstanding
Fluoridation: Natural
Air Pollution: Insignificant
Places Rated Score: 740
Places Rated Rank: 189

**Janesville–Beloit, WI**
Physicians per 100,000: 100
Cardiac Rehabilitation Centers:
Beloit Memorial Hospital CRU
Costs Index: Excellent
Fluoridation: Adjusted
Air Pollution: Insignificant
Places Rated Score: 700
Places Rated Rank: 203

**Jersey City, NJ**
Physicians per 100,000: 139
Cardiac Rehabilitation Centers:
Morristown Memorial Hospital CRU
St. Mary Hospital CRU
Costs Index: Good
Fluoridation: None
Air Pollution: TSP, CO
CMSA Access: New York–Northern
New Jersey–Long Island,
NY–NJ–CT (1,520)
Places Rated Score: 1,759
Places Rated Rank: 67

**Johnson City–Kingsport–
Bristol, TN–VA**
Physicians per 100,000: 152
Medical Schools:
East Tennessee State University College
of Medicine
Cardiac Rehabilitation Centers:
Bristol Memorial Hospital CRU
Memorial Hospital, Inc., CRU
Costs Index: Excellent
Fluoridation: Adjusted
Air Pollution: Insignificant
Places Rated Score: 1,152
Places Rated Rank: 111

**Johnstown, PA**
Physicians per 100,000: 131
Teaching Hospitals:
Conemaugh Valley Memorial Hospital
Cardiac Rehabilitation Centers:
Mercy Hospital of Johnstown CRU
Hospices:
Mercy Hospital–Hospice Unit
Costs Index: Excellent
Fluoridation: None
Air Pollution: Insignificant
Places Rated Score: 731
Places Rated Rank: 193

**Joliet, IL**
Physicians per 100,000: 78
Costs Index: Good
Fluoridation: Natural
Air Pollution: Insignificant
CMSA Access: Chicago–Gary–Lake
County, IL–IN–WI (580)
Places Rated Score: 1,058
Places Rated Rank: 127

**Joplin, MO**
Physicians per 100,000: 100
Cardiac Rehabilitation Centers:
Freeman Hospital CRU

Hospices:
St. John's Medical Center–Pastoral Care
Department
Costs Index: Excellent
Fluoridation: None
Air Pollution: Insignificant
Places Rated Score: 500
Places Rated Rank: 271

**Kalamazoo, MI**
Physicians per 100,000: 243
Cardiac Rehabilitation Centers:
Borgess Medical Center CRU
Bronson Methodist Hospital CRU
Hospices:
Kalamazoo Hospice
Costs Index: Excellent
Fluoridation: Adjusted
Air Pollution: Insignificant
Places Rated Score: 1,043
Places Rated Rank: 129

**Kankakee, IL**
Physicians per 100,000: 109
Costs Index: Excellent
Fluoridation: Adjusted
Air Pollution: Insignificant
Places Rated Score: 609
Places Rated Rank: 231

**Kansas City, KS**
Physicians per 100,000: 251
Teaching Hospitals:
University of Kansas Medical Center
Medical Schools:
University of Kansas School of Medicine
Cardiac Rehabilitation Centers
Bethany Medical Center Cardiac
Rehabilitation Program
Heart Institute CRU
Providence–St. Margaret Center CRU
Costs Index: Excellent
Fluoridation: Adjusted
Air Pollution: Insignificant
CMSA Access: Kansas City, MO–Kansas
City, KS (160)
Places Rated Score: 1,711
Places Rated Rank: 70

**Kansas City, MO**
Physicians per 100,000: 159
Teaching Hospitals:
St. Luke's Hospital of Kansas City
Truman Medical Center
VA Medical Center
Medical Schools:
University of Missouri at Kansas City
School of Medicine
Cardiac Rehabilitation Centers:
Research Medical Center–Physical
Medicine and Rehabilitation
St. Luke's Hospital CRU
St. Mary's Hospital CRU
Trinity Lutheran Hospital CRU
Truman Medical Center–East–Maximum
Care Unit
Hospices:
Hospice Care of Mid-America
Kansas City Hospice
Costs Index: Good
Fluoridation: None
Air Pollution: Insignificant
CMSA Access: Kansas City, MO–Kansas
City, KS (80)
Places Rated Score: 1,939
Places Rated Rank: 55

**Kenosha, WI**
Physicians per 100,000: 87
Costs Index: Good
Fluoridation: Adjusted
Air Pollution: Insignificant
CMSA Access: CHICAGO–GARY–LAKE
    COUNTY, IL–IN–WI (580)
Places Rated Score: 1,067
Places Rated Rank: 125

**Killeen–Temple, TX**
Physicians per 100,000: 198
Cardiac Rehabilitation Centers:
    Teague VA Center CRU
Costs Index: Good
Fluoridation: None
Air Pollution: Insignificant
Places Rated Score: 398
Places Rated Rank: 291

**Knoxville, TN**
Physicians per 100,000: 160
Cardiac Rehabilitation Centers:
    Fort Sanders Presbyterian Hospital
        Cardiac Rehabilitation Program
    St. Mary's Medical Center CRU
Hospices:
    Fort Sanders Presbyterian
        Hospital–Hospice
Costs Index: Excellent
Fluoridation: Adjusted
Air Pollution: Insignificant
Places Rated Score: 960
Places Rated Rank: 145

**Kokomo, IN**
Physicians per 100,000: 96
Costs Index: Excellent
Fluoridation: Adjusted
Air Pollution: Insignificant
Places Rated Score: 596
Places Rated Rank: 237

**La Crosse, WI**
Physicians per 100,000: 286
Cardiac Rehabilitation Centers:
    La Crosse Exercise Program CRU
    La Crosse Lutheran Hospital CRU
Costs Index: Excellent
Fluoridation: None
Air Pollution: Insignificant
Places Rated Score: 686
Places Rated Rank: 207

**Lafayette, IN**
Physicians per 100,000: 155
Costs Index: Excellent
Fluoridation: Adjusted
Air Pollution: Insignificant
Places Rated Score: 655
Places Rated Rank: 216

**Lafayette, LA**
Physicians per 100,000: 148
Cardiac Rehabilitation Centers:
    Lafayette General Hospital CRU
    Our Lady of Lourdes Hospital Cardiac
        Rehabilitation Program
Costs Index: Excellent
Fluoridation: None
Air Pollution: Insignificant
Places Rated Score: 548
Places Rated Rank: 256

**Lake Charles, LA**
Physicians per 100,000: 114
Costs Index: Excellent

**Fluoridation:** None
Air Pollution: Insignificant
Places Rated Score: 314
Places Rated Rank: 311

**Lake County, IL**
Physicians per 100,000: 167
Hospices:
    Hospice of Highland Park Hospital
Costs Index: Good
Flouridation: Natural and adjusted
Air Pollution: Insignificant
CMSA Access: CHICAGO–GARY–LAKE
    COUNTY, IL–IN–WI (570)
Places Rated Score: 1,237
Places Rated Rank: 99

**Lakeland–Winter Haven, FL**
Physicians per 100,000: 123
Hospices:
    Good Shepherd Hospice
Costs Index: Good
Fluoridation: None
Air Pollution: Insignificant
Places Rated Score: 323
Places Rated Rank: 309

**Lancaster, PA**
Physicians per 100,000: 111
Cardiac Rehabilitation Centers:
    Lancaster General Hospital CRU
    Lancaster Osteopathic Hospital
        CRU
    St. Joseph's Hospital Cardiac Treatment
        Center
Costs Index: Outstanding
Fluoridation: Adjusted
Air Pollution: Insignificant
Places Rated Score: 1,111
Places Rated Rank: 116

**Lansing–East Lansing, MI**
Physicians per 100,000: 171
Teaching Hospitals:
    Edward W. Sparrow Hospital
Medical Schools:
    Michigan State University College of
        Human Medicine
Cardiac Rehabilitation Centers:
    Ingham Medical Center Cardiac
        Rehabilitation Program
    Lansing General Hospital CRU
Costs Index: Excellent
Fluoridation: Adjusted
Air Pollution: Insignificant
Places Rated Score: 1,371
Places Rated Rank: 88

**Laredo, TX**
Physicians per 100,000: 65
Costs Index: Good
Fluoridation: Natural
Air Pollution: Insignificant
Places Rated Score: 465
Places Rated Rank: 279

**Las Cruces, NM**
Physicians per 100,000: 88
Costs Index: Excellent
Fluoridation: Natural
Air Pollution: Insignificant
Places Rated Score: 588
Places Rated Rank: 246

**Las Vegas, NV**
Physicians per 100,000: 112

Cardiac Rehabilitation Centers:
    Southern Nevada Memorial Hospital
        CRU
    Sunrise Hospital CRU
Hospices:
    Nathan Adelson Memorial Hospice
Costs Index: Fair
Fluoridation: None
Air Pollution: Insignificant
Places Rated Score: 412
Places Rated Rank: 290

**Lawrence, KS**
Physicans per 100,000: 121
Costs Index: Excellent
Fluoridation: Adjusted
Air Pollution: Insignificant
Places Rated Score: 621
Places Rated Rank: 224

**Lawrence–Haverhill, MA–NH**
Physicians per 100,000: 147
Cardiac Rehabilitation Centers:
    Lawrence General Hospital–Exercise
        Tolerance Test Lab
Hospices:
    Bon Secours Hospital
Costs Index: Excellent
Fluoridation: Adjusted (Haverhill only)
Air Pollution: Insignificant
CMSA Access: BOSTON–LAWRENCE–
    SALEM, MA–NH (505)
Places Rated Score: 1,202
Places Rated Rank: 105

**Lawton, OK**
Physicians per 100,000: 77
Costs Index: Excellent
Fluoridation: Adjusted
Air Pollution: TSP
Places Rated Score: 477
Places Rated Rank: 276

**Lewiston–Auburn, ME**
Physicians per 100,000: 159
Hospices:
    Clover Manor Hospice
Costs Index: Excellent
Fluoridation: Adjusted
Air Pollution: Insignificant
Places Rated Score: 759
Places Rated Rank: 186

**Lexington–Fayette, KY**
Physicians per 100,000: 360
Teaching Hospitals:
    Albert B. Chandler Medical Center
    VA Medical Center
Medical Schools:
    University of Kentucky College of
        Medicine
Cardiac Rehabilitation Centers:
    Central Baptist Hospital CRU
    Good Samaritan Hospital Cardiac
        Rehabilitation Department
    St. Joseph Hospital CRU
Comprehensive Cancer Treatment
    Centers:
    McDowell Community Cancer Network,
        Inc.
Hospices:
    Community Hospice of Lexington
    McDowell Community Center–Hospice
Costs Index: Excellent
Fluoridation: None

Air Pollution: Insignificant
Places Rated Score: 1,860
Places Rated Rank: 59

## Lima, OH
Physicians per 100,000: 141
Cardiac Rehabilitation Centers:
  Lima Memorial Hospital Cardiac
    Treatment Center
Costs Index: Excellent
Fluoridation: Adjusted
Air Pollution: Insignificant
Places Rated Score: 741
Places Rated Rank: 188

## Lincoln, NE
Physicians per 100,000: 175
Cardiac Rehabilitation Centers:
  Bryan Memorial Hospital CRU
Costs Index: Excellent
Fluoridation: Adjusted
Air Pollution: Insignificant
Places Rated Score: 775
Places Rated Rank: 183

## Little Rock–North Little Rock, AR
Physicians per 100,000: 261
Teaching Hospitals:
  University of Arkansas Hospital
  VA Medical Center
Medical Schools:
  University of Arkansas College of
    Medicine
Cardiac Rehabilitation Centers:
  Human Performance Center CRU
  University of Arkansas Health Sciences
    CRU
  VA Medical Center Cardiology Unit
Hospices:
  Hospice of Arkansas
Costs Index: Excellent
Fluoridation: Adjusted
Air Pollution: Insignificant
Places Rated Score: 1,861
Places Rated Rank: 58

## Longview–Marshall, TX
Physicians per 100,000: 109
Costs Index: Good
Fluoridation: Adjusted
Air Pollution: Insignificant
Places Rated Score: 509
Places Rated Rank: 268

## Lorain–Elyria, OH
Physicians per 100,000: 85
Cardiac Rehabilitation Centers:
  Elyria Memorial Hospital CRU
  Lorain Family and Community Hospital
    Post-Cardiac Rehabilitation Program
Hospices:
  St. Joseph's Hospital–Hospice Unit
Costs Index: Good
Fluoridation: Adjusted
Air Pollution: Insignificant
CMSA Access: CLEVELAND–AKRON–LORAIN,
  OH (320)
Places Rated Score: 1,105
Places Rated Rank: 119

## ★ Los Angeles–Long Beach, CA
Physicians per 100,000: 243
Teaching Hospitals:
  Cedars-Sinai Medical Center
  Children's Hospital of Los Angeles
  Hospital of the Good Samaritan
  Huntington Memorial Hospital

Los Angeles County Harbor General
  Hospital
Martin Luther King Jr. General Hospital
Memorial Hospital Medical Center
Ranchos Los Amigos Hospital
UCLA Hospital
USC Medical Center
VA Medical Center (Brentwood)
VA Medical Center (Long Beach)
VA Medical Center (Sepulveda)
VA Medical Center (Wadsworth)
Medical Schools:
  Charles Drew Postgraduate Medical
    School
  UCLA School of Medicine
  USC School of Medicine
Cardiac Rehabilitation Centers:
  Alhambra Community Hospital CRU
  Antelope Valley Hospital CTC
  Beverly Hospital CRU
  Brotman Medical Center CRU
  California Hospital Medical Center
  Cedars-Sinai Medical Center CRU
  Centinela Hospital Medical Center CRU
  Cerritos Gardens General Hospital CRU
  Daniel Freeman Hospital CRU
  Downey Community Hospital CTC
  Foothill Presbyterian Hospital CTC
  Garfield Medical Center CRU
  Glendale Adventist Medical Center CRU
  Greater El Monte Community Hospital
    CRU
  Harbor General Hospital CRU
  Hawthorne Community Hospital CRU
  Hospital of the Good Samaritan CRU
  Huntington Memorial Hospital
  Kaiser Foundation Hospital CRU
  Little Company of Mary Hospital CRU
  Long Beach Community Hospital CRU
  Long Beach Memorial Medical Center
    CRU
  Martin Luther King Jr. Hospital CRU
  Memorial Hospital of Gardena
  Memorial Hospital of Glendale CRU
  Methodist Hospital of Southern
    California CTC
  Pacific Hospital CRU
  Pomona Valley Community Hospital
    CRU
  Presbyterian Hospital Cardiac
    Rehabilitation Program
  Queen of the Valley Hospital Coronary
    Observation Unit
  Rancho Los Amigos Hospital CRU
  Riverside Hospital CRU
  Ross-Loos Medical Center CRU
  St. John's Hospital CRU
  St. Luke's Hospital CRU
  Santa Monica Hospital CRU
  South Bay Hospital CRU
  Torrance Memorial Hospital CRU
  UCLA Medical Center CRU
  Westside Family YMCA CRU
  Whittier Hospital CRU
Comprehensive Cancer Treatment
  Centers:
  • UCLA Jonsson Comprehensive Cancer
    Center
  • USC–Cancer Research Institute
Hospices:
  Continuity of Life Program
  Granada Hills Hospice
  Hospice in the Home (Visiting Nurse
    Association of Los Angeles)
  Hospice of Pasadena, Inc.
  Hospital Home Health Care
    Agency–Hospice Program

Kaiser Permanente Hospice Program
Long Beach Community
  Hospital–Hospice Program
Los Angeles County–USC Cancer
  Center Hospice Program
Northridge Hospital–Home Health Care
Parkwood Community Hospital–Hospice
  Program
VA Medical Center (Wadsworth)–
  Palliative Treatment Program
Costs Index: Poor
Fluoridation: Adjusted (Long Beach only)
Air Pollution: TSP, CO, O₃ ▲▲, NO₂, Pb
CMSA Access: LOS ANGELES–ANAHEIM–
  RIVERSIDE, CA (360)
Places Rated Score: 5,153
Places Rated Rank: 5

## Louisville, KY–IN
Physicians per 100,000: 211
Teaching Hospitals:
  Jewish Hospital
  Louisville General Hospital
  VA Medical Center
Medical Schools:
  University of Louisville School of
    Medicine
Cardiac Rehabilitation Centers:
  Audubon Hospital CRU
  Highlands Baptist Hospital CRU
  Norton Memorial Infirmary CRU
  St. Anthony Hospital Cardiac Rebound
Hospices:
  Hospice of Louisville and Southern
    Indiana
  Hospice of Southern Indiana
Costs Index: Excellent
Fluoridation: Adjusted
Air Pollution: CO
Places Rated Score: 2,111
Places Rated Rank: 48

## Lowell, MA–NH
Physicians per 100,000: 268
Cardiac Rehabilitation Centers:
  St. John's Hospital CRU
Costs Index: Excellent
Fluoridation: None
Air Pollution: Insignificant
CMSA Access: BOSTON–LAWRENCE–SALEM,
  MA–NH (515)
Places Rated Score: 1,083
Places Rated Rank: 123

## Lubbock, TX
Physicians per 100,000: 200
Medical Schools:
  Texas Tech University School of
    Medicine
Hospices:
  Hospice of the Good Samaritan
Costs Index: Good
Fluoridation: Natural
Air Pollution: TSP
Places Rated Score: 900
Places Rated Rank: 152

## Lynchburg, VA
Physicians per 100,000: 132
Cardiac Rehabilitation Centers:
  Virginia Baptist Hospital CRU
Costs Index: Excellent
Fluoridation: Adjusted
Air Pollution: Insignificant
Places Rated Score: 732
Places Rated Rank: 191

## Macon–Warner Robins, GA

Physicians per 100,000: 143
Cardiac Rehabilitation Centers:
  Medical Center of Central Georgia CRU
Costs Index: Excellent
Fluoridation: Adjusted (Warner Robins
  only)
Air Pollution: Insignificant
Places Rated Score: 593
Places Rated Rank: 241

## Madison, WI

Physicians per 100,000: 418
Teaching Hospitals:
  Madison General Hospital
  University of Wisconsin Hospitals
  William S. Middleton Memorial VA
    Medical Center
Medical Schools:
  University of Wisconsin School of
    Medicine
Cardiac Rehabilitation Centers:
  Biodynamics Lab–University of
    Wisconsin
  University of Wisconsin Hospital CRP
Comprehensive Cancer Treatment
  Centers:
• University of Wisconsin Medical
    Center–Clinical Cancer Center
Hospices:
  Dane County Hospice, Inc.
Costs Index: Good
Fluoridation: Adjusted
Air Pollution: Insignificant
Places Rated Score: 2,168
Places Rated Rank: 45

## Manchester, NH

Physicians per 100,000: 337
Cardiac Rehabilitation Centers:
  Catholic Medical Center CRU
  Easter Seal Rehabilitation Center
Costs Index: Excellent
Fluoridation: None
Air Pollution: Insignificant
Places Rated Score: 737
Places Rated Rank: 190

## Mansfield, OH

Physicians per 100,000: 103
Costs Index: Excellent
Fluoridation: None
Air Pollution: Insignificant
Places Rated Score: 303
Places Rated Rank: 313

## McAllen–Edinburg–Mission, TX

Physicians per 100,000: 72
Costs Index: Good
Fluoridation: Natural (McAllen and Mission
  only)
Air Pollution: Insignificant
Places Rated Score: 372
Places Rated Rank: 296

## Medford, OR

Physicians per 100,000: 156
Costs Index: Excellent
Fluoridation: None
Air Pollution: CO
Places Rated Score: 256
Places Rated Rank: 317

## Melbourne–Titusville– Palm Bay, FL

Physicians per 100,000: 117
Hospices:
  Hospice of St. Francis

Hospice of South Brevard
Costs Index: Good
Fluoridation: Adjusted (Melbourne only)
Air Pollution: Insignificant
Places Rated Score: 517
Places Rated Rank: 266

## Memphis, TN–AR–MS

Physicians per 100,000: 243
Teaching Hospitals:
  Baptist Memorial Hospital
  City of Memphis Hospital
  VA Medical Center
Medical Schools:
  University of Tennessee College of
    Medicine
Cardiac Rehabilitation Centers:
  University of Tennessee, Memphis,
    Hospital CRU
  VA Hospital CRU
Comprehensive Cancer Treatment
  Centers:
  St. Jude Children's Research
    Hospital–Cancer Center
Hospices
  Health and Hospice Services of
    Memphis
  Hospice of Memphis, Inc.
  Mid-South Comprehensive Home and
    Hospice, Inc.
Costs Index: Good
Fluoridation: Adjusted
Air Pollution: CO
Places Rated Score: 2,043
Places Rated Rank: 51

## Miami–Hialeah, FL

Physicians per 100,000: 284
Teaching Hospitals:
  Jackson Memorial Hospital
  Mount Sinai Medical Center
  VA Medical Center
Medical Schools:
  University of Miami School of Medicine
Cardiac Rehabilitation Centers:
  American Hospital Cardiovascular
    Laboratory
  Baptist Hospital of Miami CRU
  Biscayne Medical Center CRU
  Mercy Cardiac Treatment Center CRU
  Mount Sinai Medical Center CRU
  North Miami General Hospital CRU
  Palmetto General Hospital CRU
Comprehensive Cancer Treatment
  Centers:
• University of Miami School of
    Medicine–Comprehensive Cancer
    Center
Hospices:
  Hospice of Miami
Costs Index: Poor
Fluoridation: Adjusted
Air Pollution: CO
CMSA Access: MIAMI–FORT
  LAUDERDALE, FL (80)
Places Rated Score: 2,314
Places Rated Rank: 41

## ★ Middlesex–Somerset–Hunterdon, NJ

Physicians per 100,000: 159
Teaching Hospitals:
  Middlesex General Hospital
Medical Schools:
  College of Medicine and Dentistry of
    New Jersey, Rutgers Medical School
Hospices:
  Somerset County Hospice

Costs Index: Excellent
Fluoridation: Adjusted (approximately 50%
  of the metro area)
Air Pollution: Insignificant
CMSA Access: NEW YORK–NORTHERN
  NEW JERSEY–LONG ISLAND,
  NY–NJ–CT (1,480)
Places Rated Score: 2,589
Places Rated Rank: 24

## Middletown, CT

Physicians per 100,000: 184
Cardiac Rehabilitation Centers:
  Middlesex Memorial Hospital CRU
Costs Index: Excellent
Fluoridation: Adjusted
Air Pollution: O₃
CMSA Access: HARTFORD–NEW
  BRITAIN–MIDDLETOWN, CT (200)
Places Rated Score: 884
Places Rated Rank: 155

## Midland, TX

Physicians per 100,000: 97
Costs Index: Good
Fluoridation: Almost none
Air Pollution: TSP
Places Rated Score: 97
Places Rated Rank: 327

## ★ Milwaukee, WI

Physicians per 100,000: 233
Teaching Hospitals:
  Milwaukee County Medical Complex
  Mount Sinai Medical Center
  VA Medical Center
Medical Schools:
  Medical College of Wisconsin
Cardiac Rehabilitation Centers:
  Columbia Hospital CRU
  Deaconess Hospital CRU
  Lutheran Hospital CRU
  Milwaukee Regional Medical Center
    Fitness Program
  Mount Sinai Medical Center CRP
  St. Francis Hospital CRU
  St. Luke's Hospital CRU
  St. Mary's Hospital CRU
  Southeastern Wisconsin Regional
    Medical Center Curative Workshop
Comprehensive Cancer Treatment
  Centers:
  Milwaukee Children's Hospital–
    Department of Hematology and
    Oncology
Hospices:
  Hospice of Milwaukee
  Milwaukee Hospice, Inc.
  Mount Sinai Medical Center–Ambulatory
    Oncology
  St. Joseph's Hospital
  St. Mary's Hospital
Costs Index: Good
Fluoridation: Adjusted
Air Pollution: Insignificant
CMSA Access: MILWAUKEE–RACINE,
  WI (20)
Places Rated Score: 3,053
Places Rated Rank: 17

## ★ Minneapolis–St. Paul, MN–WI

Physicians per 100,000: 234
Teaching Hospitals:
  Abbott–Northwestern Hospital, Inc.
  Hennepin County Medical Center
  Mount Sinai Hospital
  St. Paul–Ramsey Medical Center

University of Minnesota Hospitals and
  Clinics
VA Medical Center
Medical Schools:
  University of Minnesota, Minneapolis,
    Medical School
Cardiac Rehabilitation Centers:
  Bethesda Lutheran Medical Center CRU
  Eitel Hospital CRU
  Fairview-Southdale Hospital CRU
  Hennepin County Medical Center CRU
  Methodist Hospital CRU
  Midway Hospital CRU
  North Memorial Medical Center–
    Intervention and Rehabilitation
    Program
  St. John's Hospital CRU
  St. Joseph's Hospital CRU
  St. Paul–Ramsey Medical Center
  University of Minnesota CRU
  VA Medical Center CRU
Hospices:
  Abbott–Northwestern Hospital–Hospice
    Program
  Bethesda Lutheran Medical
    Hospital–Hospice (St. Paul)
  Fairview Community Hospitals–Hospice
    Program (Edina)
  Fairview Community Hospitals–Hospice
    Program (Minneapolis)
  Mercy-Unity Home Health Care
  Methodist Hospital–Hospice Program
  Metropolitan Medical Center–Hospice
    Program
  Midway Hospital Hospice Program
  Minnesota Coalition for Terminal Care
  North Memorial Medical
    Center–Hospice Program
  St. John's Hospital–Hospice Program
  St. Joseph's Hospital–Hospice Program
  St. Mary's Hospital–Hospice Program
Costs Index: Good
Fluoridation: Adjusted
Air Pollution: CO, Pb
Places Rated Score: 3,934
Places Rated Rank: 9

**Mobile, AL**
Physicians per 100,000: 169
Teaching Hospitals:
  University of South Alabama Medical
    Center
Medical Schools:
  University of South Alabama School of
    Medicine
Cardiac Rehabilitation Centers:
  Operation Bounce Back, Cardiac
    Therapy, Inc.
Hospices:
  The Hospice of Mobile
  Villa Mercy Hospice
Costs Index: Excellent
Fluoridation: Adjusted
Air Pollution: Insignificant
Places Rated Score: 1,469
Places Rated Rank: 80

**Modesto, CA**
Physicians per 100,000: 147
Hospices:
  Modesto Community Hospice
Costs Index: Good
Fluoridation: None
Air Pollution: Insignificant
Places Rated Score: 347
Places Rated Rank: 301

**Monmouth–Ocean, NJ**
Physicians per 100,000: 142
Teaching Hospitals:
  Jersey Shore Medical Center–Fitkin
    Hospital
  Monmouth Medical Center
Hospices:
  Community Memorial Hospital–Hospice
    Program
Costs Index: Excellent
Fluoridation: Adjusted (Monmouth only)
Air Pollution: Insignificant
CMSA Access: New York–Northern
  New Jersey–Long Island, NY–NJ–CT
  (1,490)
Places Rated Score: 2,482
Places Rated Rank: 32

**Monroe, LA**
Physicians per 100,000: 131
Costs Index: Excellent
Fluoridation: None
Air Pollution: Insignificant
Places Rated Score: 331
Places Rated Rank: 308

**Montgomery, AL**
Physicians per 100,000: 132
Cardiac Rehabilitation Centers:
  Baptist Medical Center CRU
Hospices:
  Hospice of Montgomery
Costs Index: Excellent
Fluoridation: Adjusted
Air Pollution: Insignificant
Places Rated Score: 832
Places Rated Rank: 166

**Muncie, IN**
Physicians per 100,000: 149
Teaching Hospitals:
  Ball Memorial Hospital
Cardiac Rehabilitation Centers:
  Ball Memorial Hospital CRU
Costs Index: Excellent
Fluoridation: Adjusted
Air Pollution: Insignificant
Places Rated Score: 949
Places Rated Rank: 146

**Muskegon, MI**
Physicians per 100,000: 99
Cardiac Rehabilitation Centers:
  Mercy Hospital CRU
Costs Index: Excellent
Fluoridation: Adjusted
Air Pollution: Insignificant
Places Rated Score: 699
Places Rated Rank: 205

**Nashua, NH**
Physicians per 100,000: 128
Costs Index: Excellent
Fluoridation: None
Air Pollution: Insignificant
CMSA Access: Boston–Lawrence–Salem,
  MA–NH (525)
Places Rated Score: 853
Places Rated Rank: 160

**Nashville, TN**
Physicians per 100,000: 250
Teaching Hospitals:
  Hubbard Hospital of the Meharry
    College
  St. Thomas Hospital

VA Medical Center
Vanderbilt University Hospital
Medical Schools:
  Meharry Medical College School of
    Medicine
  Vanderbilt University School of Medicine
Cardiac Rehabilitation Centers:
  Park View Hospital Cardiac
    Conditioning Center
  St. Thomas Hospital CRU
Costs Index: Excellent
Fluoridation: None
Air Pollution: CO, NO$_2$
Places Rated Score: 1,850
Places Rated Rank: 61

★ **Nassau–Suffolk, NY**
Physicians per 100,000: 229
Teaching Hospitals:
  Long Island Jewish–Hillside Medical
    Center
  Nassau County Medical Center
  Nassau Hospital
  North Shore University Hospital
  VA Hospital (Northport)
Medical Schools:
  SUNY at Stony Brook–Health Sciences
    Center–School of Medicine
Cardiac Rehabilitation Centers:
  Adult Fitness Program (Garden City)
  Brookhaven CPR Center CRU (Port
    Jefferson)
  Community Hospital–Department of
    Rehabilitative Medicine (Glen Cove)
  Lydia Hall Hospital CRU (Freeport)
  Nassau Cardiac Rehabilitation and
    Diagnostic Service (Mineola)
  Nassau County Medical Center CRU
    (East Meadow)
  North Shore University Hospital Cardiac
    Exercise Center (Manhasset)
  St. Francis Hospital CRU (Roslyn)
  South Nassau Community Hospital
    Cardiac Work Evaluation Unit
    (Oceanside)
  South Shore Cardiac Clinic CRU (North
    Massapequa)
  Southside Hospital CRU (Bay Shore)
  Suffolk Cardiac Pulmonary Associates,
    Inc. (West Islip)
Hospices:
  Mercy Hospital Hospice
  Nassau Hospital–Hospice Program
Costs Index: Unacceptable
Fluoridation: Adjusted (part of Nassau
  County only)
Air Pollution: Insignificant
CMSA Access: New York–Northern
  New Jersey–Long Island, NY–NJ–CT
  (1,290)
Places Rated Score: 3,919
Places Rated Rank: 10

**New Bedford, MA**
Physicians per 100,000: 319
Costs Index: Excellent
Fluoridation: None
Air Pollution: Insignificant
Places Rated Score: 519
Places Rated Rank: 265

**New Britain, CT**
Physicians per 100,000: 265
Teaching Hospitals:
  New Britain General Hospital
Cardiac Rehabilitation Centers:
  New Britain General Hospital CRU

Costs Index: Excellent
Fluoridation: Adjusted
Air Pollution: Insignificant
CMSA Access: HARTFORD–NEW
  BRITAIN–MIDDLETOWN, CT (180)
Places Rated Score: 1,245
Places Rated Rank: 98

## New Haven–Meriden, CT
Physicians per 100,000: 318
Teaching Hospitals:
  Hospital of St. Raphael
  VA Medical Center–West Haven
  Yale–New Haven Hospital
Medical Schools:
  Yale University School of Medicine
Cardiac Rehabilitation Centers:
  VA Medical Center CRU
  Yale–New Haven Medical Center CRU
Comprehensive Cancer Treatment
  Centers:
• Yale University Comprehensive Cancer
  Center
Hospices:
  Connecticut Hospice, Inc.
  Hospice Institute
Costs Index: Good
Fluoridation: Adjusted
Air Pollution: O$_3$
Places Rated Score: 2,068
Places Rated Rank: 50

## New London–Norwich, CT–RI
Physicians per 100,00: 156
Costs Index: Excellent
Fluoridation: Adjusted
Air Pollution: O$_3$
Places Rated Score: 556
Places Rated Rank: 254

## ★ New Orleans, LA
Physicians per 100,000: 286
Teaching Hospitals:
  Charity Hospital of New Orleans
  Ochsner Medical Foundation Hospital
  Touro Infirmary
  VA Medical Center
Medical Schools:
  Louisiana State University School of
    Medicine in New Orleans
  Tulane University School of Medicine
Cardiac Rehabilitation Centers:
  East Jefferson General Hospital CRU
  F. E. Herbert Outpatient Cardiovascular
    Therapy Program
  Jo Ellen Smith Memorial Hospital
    In-Patient Cardio-Therapy Program
  Ochsner Foundation Hospital CRU
Hospices
  Hospice of Greater New Orleans
Costs Index: Good
Fluoridation: Adjusted
Air Pollution: Insignificant
Places Rated Score: 2,586
Places Rated Rank: 25

## ★ New York, NY
Physicians per 100,000: 370
Teaching Hospitals:
  Beth Israel Medical Center
  Booth Memorial Medical Center
  Bronx-Lebanon Medical Center
  Bronx Municipal Hospital Center
  Brookdale Hospital Medical Center
  Brooklyn Hospital
  Catholic Medical Center of Brooklyn
    and Queens

City Hospital Center at Elmhurst
Cumberland Hospital
Harlem Hospital Center
Hospital for Joint Diseases and Medical
  Center
Hospital for Special Surgery
Hospital of the Albert Einstein School of
  Medicine
Jewish Hospital and Medical Center of
  Brooklyn
Kings County Hospital Center
Lenox Hill Hospital
Long Island College Hospital
Lutheran Medical Center
Memorial Hospital for Cancer and Allied
  Diseases
Methodist Hospital
Misericordia Hospital Medical Center
Montefiore Hospital and Medical Center
Mount Sinai Hospital
New York Hospital
New York Medical College Hospitals
New York University Medical Center
Presbyterian Hospital in the City of New
  York
Roosevelt Hospital
St. John's Episcopal Hospital
St. Luke's Hospital Center
St. Vincent's Hospital and Medical
  Center of New York
St. Vincent's Medical Center of
  Richmond
State University Hospital Downstate
  Medical Center
VA Medical Center (Brooklyn)
VA Medical Center (Manhattan)
Westchester County Medical Center
Medical Schools:
  Albert Einstein College of Medicine of
    Yeshiva University
  Columbia University College of
    Physicians and Surgeons
  Cornell University Medical College
  Mount Sinai School of Medicine, CUNY
  New York Medical College
  New York University School of Medicine
  SUNY Downstate Medical Center
    College of Medicine
Cardiac Rehabilitation Centers:
  Beth Israel Medical Center CRU
  Coronary Exercise Lab CRU
  East Side Cardiopulmonary
    Rehabilitation Department
  Kingsbrook Jewish Medical Center
  Long Island Jewish Medical Center
  Methodist Hospital Reconditioning Lab
  Montefiore Hospital Exercise Lab and
    CRU
  New York Hospital–Cornell Medical
    Center CRU
  New York State University Medical
    Center CRC
  Nyack Hospital CRU
  Phelps Memorial Hospital CRU
  Richmond Cardiological Services CRU
  St. John's Episcopal Hospital CRU
  S. I. Diagnostic and Rehabilitation
    Center
  United Hospital CRU
  Victory Memorial Hospital Cardiological
    Services
Comprehensive Cancer Treatment
  Centers:
  Albert Einstein College of
    Medicine–Cancer Research Center
• College of Physicians and
  Surgeons–Columbia University
  Cancer Research Center

• Memorial Sloan-Kettering Cancer Center
  Mount Sinai School of Medicine–
    Department of Neoplastic Diseases
  New York University Medical
    Center–Cancer Center
Hospices:
  Cabrini Hospice–Cabrini Medical Center
  Calvary Hospital
  Hospice of Rockland, Inc.
  Hospice of St. Luke's–Roosevelt
    Hospital
  Hospice of Westchester
  Metropolitan Jewish Geriatric Center
  New York Infirmary–Beekman Downtown
    Hospital–Hospice Program
  St. Rose's Home
  United Hospital Hospice
Costs Index: Unacceptable
Fluoridation: Adjusted
Air Pollution: CO
CMSA Access: NEW YORK–NORTHERN
  NEW JERSEY–LONG ISLAND, NY–NJ–CT
  (880)
Places Rated Score: 7,850
Places Rated Rank: 1

## ★ Newark, NJ
Physicians per 100,000: 226
Teaching Hospitals:
  Martland Medical Center
  Muhlenberg Hospital
  Newark–Beth Israel Medical Center
  Overlook Hospital
  St. Barnabas Medical Center
  St. Michael's Medical Center
  VA Medical Center (East Orange)
Medical Schools:
  College of Medicine and Dentistry of
    New Jersey–New Jersey Medical
    School
Cardiac Rehabilitation Centers:
  Hospital Center at Orange CRU
  Newark–Beth Israel Medical Center
    Cardiac Rehabilitation Service
  St. Michael's Medical Center CRU
  VA Medical Center CRU (East Orange)
Hospices:
  Hospice, Inc.
  Karen Anne Quinlan Center of Hope
  Muhlenberg Hospital–Home Health Care
    Program
  Overlook Hospital–Hospice Home Care
    Department
  Riverside Hospice
Costs Index: Good
Fluoridation: Almost none
Air Pollution: CO
CMSA Access: NEW YORK–NORTHERN
  NEW JERSEY–LONG ISLAND, NY–NJ–CT
  (1,280)
Places Rated Score: 4,106
Places Rated Rank: 8

## Niagara Falls, NY
Physicians per 100,000: 102
Costs Index: Poor
Fluoridation: Adjusted
Air Pollution: Insignificant
CMSA Access: BUFFALO–NIAGARA FALLS,
  NY (205)
Places Rated Score: 507
Places Rated Rank: 269

## Norfolk–Virginia Beach–
## Newport News, VA
Physicians per 100,000: 132
Teaching Hospitals:
  Medical Center Hospitals

VA Medical Center
Medical Schools:
  Eastern Virginia Medical School
Cardiac Rehabilitation Centers:
  General Hospital of Virginia Beach CRU
  Non-Invasive Cardio Lab CRU
  Norfolk General Hospital CRU
  Riverside Hospital Cardiovascular
    Therapy
Hospices:
  DePaul Hospital
  Edmarc Hospice for Children, Inc.
  Riverside Hospital
Costs Index: Excellent
Fluoridation: Adjusted (Norfolk and
  Newport News only)
Air Pollution: Insignificant
Places Rated Score: 1,932
Places Rated Rank: 56

**Norwalk, CT**
Physicians per 100,000: 220
Teaching Hospitals:
  Norwalk Hospital
Cardiac Rehabilitation Centers:
  Norwalk Hospital CRU
Costs Index: Excellent
Fluoridation: Adjusted
Air Pollution: Insignificant
CMSA Access: NEW YORK–NORTHERN
  NEW JERSEY–LONG ISLAND,
  NY–NJ–CT (1,510)
Places Rated Score: 2,530
Places Rated Rank: 29

**Oakland, CA**
Physicians per 100,000: 212
Teaching Hospitals:
  VA Medical Center (Martinez)
Cardiac Rehabilitation Centers:
  Alta Bates Hospital CRU
  Doctors Hospital CRU
  Eden Hospital CRU
  Herrick Memorial Hospital CRU
  Mount Diablo Medical Center CRU
  Peralta Hospital
Hospices:
  Gray Panther Hospice of Berkeley
  Hospice of Contra Costa (Lafayette)
  Hospice of Contra Costa (Walnut
    Creek)
  Kaiser Permanente Hayward Hospice
  Shanti Project
  Vesper Hospice
Costs Index: Fair
Fluoridation: Adjusted
Air Pollution: Insignificant
CMSA Access: SAN FRANCISCO–
  OAKLAND–SAN JOSE, CA (450)
Places Rated Score: 2,362
Places Rated Rank: 39

**Ocala, FL**
Physicians per 100,000: 89
Costs Index: Good
Fluoridation: Adjusted
Air Pollution: Insignificant
Places Rated Score: 489
Places Rated Rank: 273

**Odessa, TX**
Physicians per 100,000: 84
Costs Index: Good
Fluoridation: Natural
Air Pollution: TSP
Places Rated Score: 384
Places Rated Rank: 294

**Oklahoma City, OK**
Physicians per 100,000: 223
Teaching Hospitals:
  University Hospital and Clinics
  VA Medical Center
Medical Schools:
  University of Oklahoma College of
    Medicine
Cardiac Rehabilitation Centers:
  Baptist Medical Center CRU
  Presbyterian Hospital OMRF CRU
  St. Anthony's Hospital–Progressive CV
    Unit
Costs Index: Excellent
Fluoridation: Adjusted
Air Pollution: TSP
Places Rated Score: 1,623
Places Rated Rank: 75

**Olympia, WA**
Physicians per 100,000: 138
Cardiac Rehabilitation Centers:
  St. Peter Hospital CRU
Costs Index: Good
Fluoridation: None
Air Pollution: Insignificant
Places Rated Score: 338
Places Rated Rank: 306

**Omaha, NE–IA**
Physicians per 100,000: 259
Teaching Hospitals:
  Creighton–Omaha Regional Health Care
    Corporation
  University of Nebraska Hospital and
    Clinics
  VA Medical Center
Medical Schools:
  Creighton University School of Medicine
  University of Nebraska College of
    Medicine
Cardiac Rehabilitation Centers:
  Archbishop Bergan Hospital CRU
  Bishop Clarkson Memorial Hospital CRU
  Immanuel Medical Center Cardiac
    Recovery Program
  Lutheran Medical Center CRU
  Nebraska Methodist Hospital CRU
  St. Joseph Hospital CRU
Hospices:
  Montclair Nursing Center
  Omaha Hospice Organization
Costs Index: Good
Fluoridation: Adjusted
Air Pollution: CO
Places Rated Score: 2,559
Places Rated Rank: 26

**Orange County, NY**
Physicians per 100,000: 134
Costs Index: Poor
Fluoridation: Almost none
Air Pollution: Insignificant
CMSA Access: NEW YORK–NORTHERN
  NEW JERSEY–LONG ISLAND, NY–NJ–CT
  (1,540)
Places Rated Score: 1,574
Places Rated Rank: 79

**Orlando, FL**
Physicians per 100,000: 165
Cardiac Rehabilitation Centers:
  Florida Hospital CRU
Hospices:
  Hospice of Central Florida
Costs Index: Good
Fluoridation: Adjusted

Air Pollution: Insignificant
Places Rated Score: 765
Places Rated Rank: 184

**Owensboro, KY**
Physicians per 100,000: 112
Costs Index: Outstanding
Fluoridation: Adjusted
Air Pollution: Insignificant
Places Rated Score: 812
Places Rated Rank: 173

**Oxnard–Ventura, CA**
Physicians per 100,000: 156
Cardiac Rehabilitation Centers:
  St. John's Hospital CRU
Hospices:
  Conejo Hospice, Inc.
  Mercy Hospice of St. John's Hospital
Costs Index: Good
Fluoridation: None
Air Pollution: $O_3$ ▲▲
CMSA Access: LOS ANGELES–
  ANAHEIM–RIVERSIDE, CA (850)
Places Rated Score: 1,106
Places Rated Rank: 118

**Panama City, FL**
Physicians per 100,000: 101
Costs Index: Good
Fluoridation: None
Air Pollution: Insignificant
Places Rated Score: 201
Places Rated Rank: 325

**Parkersburg–Marietta, WV–OH**
Physicians per 100,000: 115
Cardiac Rehabilitation Centers:
  Camden–Clark Memorial Hospital CRU
  St. Joseph's Hospital CRU
Costs Index: Excellent
Fluoridation: Adjusted (Parkersburg only)
Air Pollution: Insignificant
Places Rated Score: 665
Places Rated Rank: 215

**Pascagoula, MS**
Physicians per 100,000: 93
Costs Index: Excellent
Fluoridation: Adjusted
Air Pollution: Insignificant
Places Rated Score: 593
Places Rated Rank: 241

**Pawtucket–Woonsocket–
Attleboro, RI–MA**
Physicians per 100,000: 237
Teaching Hospitals:
  Memorial Hospital
Cardiac Rehabilitation Centers:
  Memorial Hospital CRU
Costs Index: Good
Fluoridation: Adjusted
Air Pollution: Insignificant
CMSA Access: PROVIDENCE–
  PAWTUCKET–FALL RIVER, RI–MA (180)
Places Rated Score: 1,117
Places Rated Rank: 114

**Pensacola, FL**
Physicians per 100,000: 163
Cardiac Rehabilitation Centers:
  Baptist Hospital CRU
  Heart-Lung Rehabilitation Center
Hospices:
  Hospice of Pensacola

Costs Index: Good
Fluoridation: None
Air Pollution: Insignificant
Places Rated Score: 563
Places Rated Rank: 252

## Peoria, IL
Physicians per 100,000: 184
Teaching Hospitals:
St. Francis Hospital–Medical Center
Cardiac Rehabilitation Centers:
Pekin Memorial Hospital CRU
St. Francis Hospital Medical Center
Health Fitness Unit
Hospices:
Methodist Medical Center of
Illinois–Cancer Care Program
Costs Index: Excellent
Fluoridation: Adjusted
Air Pollution: Insignificant
Places Rated Score: 1,184
Places Rated Rank: 107

## ★ Philadelphia, PA–NJ
Physicians per 100,000: 268
Teaching Hospitals:
Albert Einstein Medical Center
Albert Einstein Medical Center–Daroff
Division
Bryn Mawr Hospital
Children's Hospital of Philadelphia
Cooper Hospital (Camden, NJ)
Crozer-Chester Medical Center
Episcopal Hospital
Graduate Hospital
Hahnemann Medical College and
Hospital of Philadelphia
Hospital of the University of
Pennsylvania
Lankenau Hospital
Medical College of Pennsylvania
Mercy Catholic Medical Center
Pennsylvania Hospital
Presbyterian–University of Pennsylvania
Medical Center
St. Christopher's Hospital for Children
Temple University Hospital
Thomas Jefferson University Hospital
VA Medical Center
Medical Schools:
Hahnemann Medical College
Jefferson Medical College of Thomas
Jefferson University
Medical College of Pennsylvania
Temple University School of Medicine
University of Pennsylvania School of
Medicine
Cardiac Rehabilitation Centers:
Albert Einstein Medical Center CRU
John F. Kennedy Hospital CRU
Naval Regional Medical Center CRU
Pennsylvania Hospital Cardiopulmonary
Rehabilitation Center
Thomas Jefferson University Hospital
CRU
Comprehensive Cancer Treatment
Centers:
• Fox Chase–University of Pennsylvania
Comprehensive Cancer Center
Hospices:
Bryn Mawr Hospital Hospice Program
Paoli Memorial Hospital–Hospice
Program
Pennsylvania Hospital–Hospice Program
Presbyterian–University of Pennsylvania
Medical Center Hospice Program
Costs Index: Excellent

Fluoridation: Adjusted
Air Pollution: CO, Pb
CMSA Access: PHILADELPHIA–WILMINGTON–
TRENTON, PA–NJ–DE–MD (40)
Places Rated Score: 5,158
Places Rated Rank: 4

## Phoenix, AZ
Physicians per 100,000: 184
Teaching Hospitals:
Good Samaritan Hospital
Maricopa County General Hospital
St. Joseph's Hospital and Medical
Center
Cardiac Rehabilitation Centers:
Arizona Heart Institute Preventative
Medicine Department
Good Samaritan Hospital CRU
John C. Lincoln Hospital Cardiac
Fitness Program
Mesa Lutheran Hospital CRU
Phoenix General Hospital CRU
Scottsdale Memorial Hospital CRU
Hospices:
Hospice of the Valley (Mesa)
Hospice of the Valley (Phoenix)
St. Joseph's Hospital and Medical
Center–Oncology Life
Enrichment Program
Samaritan Health Service
Costs Index: Fair
Fluoridation: None
Air Pollution: TSP, CO
Places Rated Score: 1,584
Places Rated Rank: 77

## Pine Bluff, AR
Physicians per 100,000: 117
Costs Index: Excellent
Fluoridation: Adjusted
Air Pollution: Insignificant
Places Rated Score: 617
Places Rated Rank: 227

## ★ Pittsburgh, PA
Physicians per 100,000: 213
Teaching Hospitals:
Allegheny General Hospital
Children's Hospital of Pittsburgh
Eye and Ear Hospital of Pittsburgh
Magee–Women's Hospital
Mercy Hospital of Pittsburgh
Montefiore Hospital Association of
Western Pennsylvania
Presbyterian–University Hospital
St. Francis General Hospital
VA Medical Center
Western Pennsylvania Hospital
Western Psychiatric Institute and Clinic
Medical Schools:
University of Pittsburgh School of
Medicine
Cardiac Rehabilitation Centers:
Human Energy Research Lab–University
of Pittsburgh
Pittsburgh Children's Hospital CRU
St. Francis General Hospital CRU
Shadyside Hospital Progressive
Cardiac Care
Hospices:
Forbes Hospice
Costs Index: Excellent
Fluoridation: Adjusted
Air Pollution: SO₂
Places Rated Score: 3,413
Places Rated Rank: 14

## Pittsfield, MA
Physicians per 100,000: 194
Teaching Hospitals:
Berkshire Medical Center
Cardiac Rehabilitation Centers:
Pittsfield YMCA Cardiac Rehabilitation
Program
Costs Index: Excellent
Fluoridation: None
Air Pollution: Insignificant
Places Rated Score: 694
Places Rated Rank: 206

## Portland, ME
Physicians per 100,000: 334
Teaching Hospitals:
Maine Medical Center
Hospices:
Hospice of Maine
Costs Index: Excellent
Fluoridation: None
Air Pollution: Insignificant
Places Rated Score: 834
Places Rated Rank: 163

## Portland, OR
Physicians per 100,000: 290
Teaching Hospitals:
Emanuel Hospital
University of Oregon Health Sciences
Center
Medical Schools:
University of Oregon Health Sciences
Center
Cardiac Rehabilitation Centers:
Cardio and Pulmonary Rehabilitation
Institute
Portland State University Adult Fitness
Program
YMCA Cardiac Therapy
Hospices:
Hospice of Oregon–Good Samaritan
Hospital
Oregon Comprehensive Cancer
Program–Hospice Program
Providence Hospice–Providence
Medical Center
Costs Index: Good
Fluoridation: None
Air Pollution: Pb
Places Rated Score: 1,590
Places Rated Rank: 76

## Portsmouth–Dover–Rochester, NH–ME
Physicians per 100,000: 96
Hospices:
Seacoast Hospice
Costs Index: Excellent
Fluoridation: Adjusted (Portsmouth and
Rochester only)
Air Pollution: Insignificant
Places Rated Score: 596
Places Rated Rank: 237

## Poughkeepsie, NY
Physicians per 100,000: 155
Costs Index: Poor
Fluoridation: Adjusted
Air Pollution: Insignificant
Places Rated Score: 355
Places Rated Rank: 299

## Providence, RI
Physicians per 100,000: 327
Teaching Hospitals:
Miriam Hospital

Rhode Island Hospital
Roger Williams General Hospital
VA Medical Center
Women and Infants Hospital of Rhode
Island
Medical Schools:
Brown University Program in Medicine
Cardiac Rehabilitation Centers:
Rhode Island Cardiac Rehabilitation
Center
St. Joseph Hospital CRU
Comprehensive Cancer Treatment
Centers:
Roger Williams General
Hospital–Cancer Center
Hospices:
Hospice Care of Rhode Island
Costs Index: Good
Fluoridation: Adjusted
Air Pollution: Insignificant
CMSA Access: PROVIDENCE–
PAWTUCKET–FALL RIVER,
RI–MA (40)
Places Rated Score: 2,467
Places Rated Rank: 33

**Provo–Orem, UT**
Physicians per 100,000: 98
Costs Index: Excellent
Fluoridation: None
Air Pollution: CO
Places Rated Score: 198
Places Rated Rank: 326

**Pueblo, CO**
Physicians per 100,000: 168
Cardiac Rehabilitation Centers:
St. Mary–Corwin Hospital CRU
Costs Index: Excellent
Fluoridation: None
Air Pollution: Insignificant
Places Rated Score: 468
Places Rated Rank: 277

**Racine, WI**
Physicians per 100,000: 91
Cardiac Rehabilitation Centers:
St. Luke's Hospital YMCA
St. Mary's Medical Center CRU
Costs Index: Good
Fluoridation: Adjusted
Air Pollution: Insignificant
CMSA Access: MILWAUKEE–RACINE, WI
(240)
Places Rated Score: 931
Places Rated Rank: 147

★ **Raleigh–Durham, NC**
Physicians per 100,000: 526
Teaching Hospitals:
Duke University Hospital
North Carolina Memorial Hospital
VA Medical Center
Wake County Hospital System, Inc.
Medical Schools:
Duke University School of Medicine
University of North Carolina at Chapel
Hill School of Medicine
Cardiac Rehabilitation Centers:
Duke University Medical Center CRU
North Carolina Memorial Hospital CRU
Raleigh Cardiac Foundation CRU
Wake County Medical Center CRU
Comprehensive Cancer Treatment
Centers:
• Duke University Medical Center–
Comprehensive Cancer Center

University of North Carolina–Cancer
Research Center
Hospices:
Hospice of North Carolina, Inc.
Hospice of Wake County
Triangle Hospice
Costs Index: Outstanding
Fluoridation: Adjusted
Air Pollution: CO
Places Rated Score: 3,476
Places Rated Rank: 13

**Reading, PA**
Physicians per 100,000: 154
Cardiac Rehabilitation Centers:
Community General Hospital CRU
Reading Hospital and Medical Center
CRU
St. Joseph's Hospital CRU
Costs Index: Outstanding
Fluoridation: Adjusted
Air Pollution: Insignificant
Places Rated Score: 1,154
Places Rated Rank: 110

**Redding, CA**
Physicians per 100,000: 174
Costs Index: Good
Fluoridation: None
Air Pollution: Insignificant
Places Rated Score: 274
Places Rated Rank: 315

**Reno, NV**
Physicians per 100,000: 215
Medical Schools:
University of Nevada School of Medical
Sciences
Cardiac Rehabilitation Centers:
Washoe Medical Center CRU
Costs Index: Good
Fluoridation: None
Air Pollution: CO
Places Rated Score: 615
Places Rated Rank: 229

**Richland–Kennewick–Pasco, WA**
Physicians per 100,000: 100
Cardiac Rehabilitation Centers:
Valley General Hospital CRU
Costs Index: Good
Fluoridation: None
Air Pollution: Insignificant
Places Rated Score: 300
Places Rated Rank: 314

**Richmond–Petersburg, VA**
Physicians per 100,000: 248
Teaching Hospitals:
McGuire VA Medical Center
Medical College of Virginia Hospitals
Medical Schools:
Virginia Commonwealth University–
Medical College of Virginia School
of Medicine
Cardiac Rehabilitation Centers:
Chippenham Hospital Cardiac
Treatment Center
Johnston–Willis Hospital CRU
Medical College of Virginia Hospital
CRU
VA Medical Center CRU
Virginia Heart Institute CRU
Wirt Hatcher Memorial–The Retreat
Hospital

Comprehensive Cancer Treatment
Centers:
Medical College of Virginia–Virginia
Commonwealth University Cancer
Center
Hospices:
American Cancer Society–Virginia
Division, Inc.
Medical College of Virginia–Hospice
Program
St. Mary's Hospital
Costs Index: Excellent
Fluoridation: Adjusted
Air Pollution: Insignificant
Places Rated Score: 2,448
Places Rated Rank: 36

**Riverside–San Bernardino, CA**
Physicians per 100,000: 191
Teaching Hospitals:
Jerry L. Pettis Memorial VA Hospital
Loma Linda University Medical Center
Riverside General Hospital–University
Medical Center
Medical Schools:
Loma Linda University School of
Medicine
Cardiac Rehabilitation Centers:
Cardiac Therapy CRU
Cardiopulmonary Stress Test and Work
Evaluation Unit
Eisenhower Medical Center CRU
Jerry L. Pettis VA Hospital CRU
Kaiser Foundation Hospital CRU
Riverside General Hospital CRU
St. Bernardine Hospital CRU
San Antonio Community Hospital CRU
Costs Index: Fair
Fluoridation: None
Air Pollution: TSP, O₃▲▲
CMSA Access: LOS ANGELES–ANAHEIM–
RIVERSIDE, CA (710)
Places Rated Score: 2,201
Places Rated Rank: 44

**Roanoke, VA**
Physicians per 100,000: 236
Cardiac Rehabilitation Centers:
Lewis-Gale Hospital, Inc., CTC
Roanoke Memorial Hospital CRU
Hospices:
Friendship Manor Geriatric Center
Costs Index: Excellent
Fluoridation: Adjusted
Air Pollution: Insignificant
Places Rated Score: 2,201
Places Rated Rank: 44

★ **Rochester, MN**
Physicians per 100,000: 1,516
Teaching Hospitals:
Rochester Methodist Hospital
St. Mary's Hospital of Rochester
Medical Schools:
Mayo Medical School
Cardiac Rehabilitation Centers:
St. Mary's Hospital CRU
Comprehensive Cancer Treatment
Centers:
• Mayo Comprehensive Cancer Center
Costs Index: Excellent
Fluoridation: Adjusted
Air Pollution: Insignificant
Places Rated Score: 2,966
Places Rated Rank: 18

**Rochester, NY**
Physicians per 100,000: 269

Teaching Hospitals:
  Genesee Hospital
  Highland Hospital of Rochester
  Rochester General Hospital
  Rochester St. Mary's Hospital of the
    Sisters of Charity
  Strong Memorial Hospital of the
    University of Rochester
Medical Schools:
  University of Rochester–School of
    Medicine and Dentistry
Cardiac Rehabilitation Centers:
  Strong Memorial Hospital Cardiac
    Rehabilitation Project
Comprehensive Cancer Treatment
  Centers:
  University of Rochester Cancer Center
Hospices:
  Genesee Region Home Care
    Association
Costs Index: Poor
Fluoridation: Adjusted
Air Pollution: TSP
Places Rated Score: 1,969
Places Rated Rank: 53

**Rockford, IL**
Physicians per 100,000: 169
Cardiac Rehabilitation Centers:
  Rockford Memorial Hospital CRU
  St. Anthony Medical Center CRU
Hospices:
  Northern Illinois Hospice Association
Costs Index: Excellent
Fluoridation: Adjusted
Air Pollution: Insignificant
Places Rated Score: 969
Places Rated Rank: 142

**Sacramento, CA**
Physicians per 100,000: 227
Teaching Hospitals:
  University of California,
    Davis–Sacramento Medical Center
Medical Schools:
  University of California, Davis, School of
    Medicine
Cardiac Rehabilitation Centers:
  University of California, Davis, CRU
  University of California, Davis, Pacers
    CRU
Hospices:
  Hospice of Mercy
Costs Index: Good
Fluoridation: None
Air Pollution: Pb
Places Rated Score: 1,027
Places Rated Rank: 135

**Saginaw–Bay City–Midland, MI**
Physicians per 100,000: 122
Cardiac Rehabilitation Centers:
  Midland Hospital Center CRU
  Saginaw General Hospital CRU
  Saginaw Osteopathic Hospital CRU
Hospices:
  Hospice of Saginaw
  The Visiting Nurse Association of
    Midland
Costs Index: Excellent
Fluoridation: Adjusted
Air Pollution: Pb
Places Rated Score: 1,022
Places Rated Rank: 136

**St. Cloud, MN**
Physicians per 100,000: 103
Costs Index: Excellent

Fluoridation: Adjusted
Air Pollution: Insignificant
Places Rated Score: 603
Places Rated Rank: 234

**St. Joseph, MO**
Physicians per 100,000: 123
Cardiac Rehabilitation Centers:
  Methodist Medical Center CRU
Costs Index: Good
Fluoridation: None
Air Pollution: TSP
Places Rated Score: 223
Places Rated Rank: 322

★ **St. Louis, MO–IL**
Physicians per 100,000: 220
Teaching Hospitals:
  St. John's Mercy Medical Center
  St. Louis Children's
    Hospital–Washington University
  St. Louis University Hospitals
  VA Medical Center
  Washington University Medical Center
Medical Schools:
  St. Louis University School of Medicine
  Washington University School of
    Medicine
Cardiac Rehabilitation Centers:
  Deaconess Hospital CRU
  DePaul Community Health Center CRU
  Normandy Osteopathic Hospital
  St. Louis Medical Center Cardiac
    Rehabilitation Program
  Washington University School of
    Medicine CRU
Hospices:
  Lutheran Medical Center–Continuing
    Care Unit
  St. Luke's Hospitals Hospice
Costs Index: Good
Fluoridation: Adjusted
Air Pollution: Pb
CMSA Access: ST. LOUIS–EAST ST.
  LOUIS–ALTON, MO–IL (30)
Places Rated Score: 2,850
Places Rated Rank: 19

**Salem, OR**
Physicians per 100,000: 149
Hospices:
  Mid-Willamette Valley Hospice
Costs Index: Excellent
Fluoridation: Adjusted
Places Rated Score: 749
Places Rated Rank: 187

**Salem–Gloucester, MA**
Physicians per 100,000: 147
Cardiac Rehabilitation Centers:
  Beverly Hospital CRU
  Hunt Memorial Hospital Telemetry
    Department
Hospices:
  Beverly Hospital-Hospice Program
  Hospice of the North Shore
Costs Index: Excellent
Fluoridation: Almost none
Air Pollution: Insignificant
CMSA Access: BOSTON–LAWRENCE–
  SALEM, MA–NH (485)
Places Rated Score: 1,232
Places Rated Rank: 100

**Salinas–Seaside–Monterey, CA**
Physicians per 100,000: 152
Hospices:
  Hospice of the Monterey Peninsula

Costs Index: Good
Fluoridation: None
Air Pollution: Insignificant
Places Rated Score: 352
Places Rated Rank: 300

**Salt Lake City–Ogden, UT**
Physicians per 100,000: 231
Teaching Hospitals:
  Latter-Day Saints Hospital
  University of Utah Hospital
  VA Medical Center
Medical Schools:
  University of Utah College of
    Medicine
Cardiac Rehabilitation Centers:
  Latter-Day Saints Hospital CRU
  McKay Dee Hospital
Hospices:
  Hospice of Northern Utah
  Hospice of Salt Lake
Costs Index: Excellent
Fluoridation: None
Air Pollution: CO
Places Rated Score: 1,631
Places Rated Rank: 74

**San Angelo, TX**
Physicians per 100,000: 136
Costs Index: Good
Fluoridation: None
Air Pollution: Insignificant
Places Rated Score: 236
Places Rated Rank: 321

**San Antonio, TX**
Physicians per 100,000: 237
Teaching Hospitals:
  Audie L. Murphy Memorial Veterans
    Hospital
  Bexar County Hospital District
  Wilford Hall U.S. Air Force Medical
    Center
Medical Schools:
  University of Texas Medical School at
    San Antonio
Cardiac Rehabilitation Centers:
  Baptist Memorial Hospital CRU
Hospices:
  Hospice–St. Benedict Hospital and
    Nursing Home
Costs Index: Good
Fluoridation: None
Air Pollution: TSP
Places Rated Score: 1,337
Places Rated Rank: 91

**San Diego, CA**
Physicians per 100,000: 216
Teaching Hospitals:
  Mercy Hospital and Medical Center
  University Hospital–University of
    California, San Diego, Medical Center
  VA Medical Center
Medical Schools:
  University of California, San Diego,
    School of Medicine
Cardiac Rehabilitation Centers:
  Alvarado Community Hospital CRU
  Cardiopulmonary Rehabilitation Center
  El Cajon Valley CPR Rehabilitation
    Center
  Grossmont Hospital CRU
  Mercy Hospital CRU
  San Diego VA Hospital CRU
  Scripps Memorial Hospital CRU
  Sharp Hospital–San Diego Cardiac
    Center

University of California, San Diego,
Medical Center CRU
**Comprehensive Cancer Treatment
Centers:**
University of California, San Diego,
Cancer Center
**Hospices:**
College Park Hospital–Hospice Program
El Cajon Valley Hospital–Hospice Unit
The Elizabeth Hospice, Inc.
San Diego County Hospice Corporation
**Costs Index:** Fair
**Fluoridation:** None
**Air Pollution:** O₃
**Places Rated Score:** 2,416
**Places Rated Rank:** 38

★ **San Francisco, CA**
**Physicians per 100,000:** 416
**Teaching Hospitals:**
Children's Hospital of San Francisco
Kaiser Foundation Hospital
Mount Zion Hospital and Medical
Center
Presbyterian Hospital of the Pacific
Medical Center
University of California, San Francisco,
Hospitals and Clinics
VA Medical Center
**Medical Schools:**
University of California, San Francisco,
School of Medicine
**Cardiac Rehabilitation Centers:**
Letterman Army Medical Center CRU
North Bay Cardiac Treatment Center
Novato Community Hospital CRU
Peninsula Hospital CRU
San Francisco Central YM Cardiac
Therapy
San Francisco General Hospital
Cardiology Outpatient
Department YM Cardiac Therapy CRU
Sequoia Hospital–YMCA CRU
**Hospices:**
Hospice of Marin (Kentfield)
Hospice of Marin (San Rafael)
Hospice of San Francisco
Mission Hospice, Inc., of San Mateo
County
Sequoia Hospital District–Patient
Support Program
**Costs Index:** Fair
**Fluoridation:** Adjusted
**Air Pollution:** Insignificant
**CMSA Access:** SAN FRANCISCO–OAKLAND–
SAN JOSE, CA (310)
**Places Rated Score:** 3,726
**Places Rated Rank:** 11

**San Jose, CA**
**Physicians per 100,000:** 247
**Teaching Hospitals:**
Stanford University Hospital
VA Medical Center (Palo Alto)
**Medical Schools:**
Stanford University School of Medicine
**Cardiac Rehabilitation Centers:**
Community Hospital of Los Gatos CRU
El Camino Cardiovascular Institute CRU
YM Cardiac Therapy CRU
**Hospices:**
Hospice of the Valley
Visiting Nurses of Santa Clara County
Hospice Program
**Costs Index:** Fair
**Fluoridation:** Adjusted

**Air Pollution:** CO
**CMSA Access:** SAN FRANCISCO–
OAKLAND–SAN JOSE, CA (470)
**Places Rated Score:** 2,117
**Places Rated Rank:** 47

**Santa Barbara–Santa
Maria–Lompoc, CA**
**Physicians per 100,000:** 232
**Cardiac Rehabilitation Centers:**
Marian Hospital CRU
**Hospices:**
Hospice of Santa Barbara
Santa Barbara Visiting Nurse
Association
**Costs Index:** Good
**Fluoridation:** None
**Air Pollution:** TSP
**Places Rated Score:** 532
**Places Rated Rank:** 261

**Santa Cruz, CA**
**Physicians per 100,000:** 165
**Cardiac Rehabilitation Centers:**
Dominican Santa Cruz Hospital
CRU
**Hospices:**
Hospice of Santa Cruz County
**Costs Index:** Good
**Fluoridation:** None
**Air Pollution:** Insignificant
**CMSA Access:** SAN FRANCISCO–
OAKLAND–SAN JOSE, CA (570)
**Places Rated Score:** 1,035
**Places Rated Rank:** 134

**Santa Rosa–Petaluma, CA**
**Physicians per 100,000:** 182
**Hospices:**
Home Hospice of Sonoma County
Valley of the Moon Hospice
**Costs Index:** Good
**Fluoridation:** None
**Air Pollution:** Insignificant
**CMSA Access:** SAN FRANCISCO–
OAKLAND–SAN JOSE, CA (570)
**Places Rated Score:** 1,052
**Places Rated Rank:** 128

**Sarasota, FL**
**Physicians per 100,000:** 201
**Cardiac Rehabilitation Centers:**
Sarasota YMCA Cardiac Rehabilitation
Program
**Hospices:**
Hospice of Sarasota County
**Costs Index:** Good
**Fluoridation:** Natural
**Air Pollution:** Insignificant
**Places Rated Score:** 801
**Places Rated Rank:** 177

**Savannah, GA**
**Physicians per 100,000:** 184
**Cardiac Rehabilitation Centers:**
Chandler General Hospital CRU
Memorial Medical Center CRU
St. Joseph's Hospital CRU
**Hospices:**
Hospice Savannah
**Costs Index:** Excellent
**Fluoridation:** Adjusted
**Air Pollution:** Insignificant
**Places Rated Score:** 1,084
**Places Rated Rank:** 122

**Scranton–Wilkes-Barre, PA**
**Physicians per 100,000:** 119
**Cardiac Rehabilitation Centers:**
Community Medical Center CRU
Mercy Hospital CRU
Moses Taylor Hospital CTC
State General Hospital–Hazleton CPR
Center
**Hospices:**
Hospice of Pennsylvania
Hospice St. John
**Costs Index:** Excellent
**Fluoridation:** Adjusted
**Air Pollution:** Insignificant
**Places Rated Score:** 1,219
**Places Rated Rank:** 101

★ **Seattle, WA**
**Physicians per 100,000:** 245
**Teaching Hospitals:**
Children's Orthopedic Hospital and
Medical Center
University of Washington Hospitals:
Harborview Medical Center
University of Washington Hospitals:
University Hospital
U.S. Public Health Service Hospital
VA Medical Center
**Medical Schools:**
University of Washington School of
Medicine
**Cardiac Rehabilitation Centers:**
Capri CRU
Seattle Public Health Hospital CRU
University of Washington Department of
Physio-Nursing
**Comprehensive Cancer Treatment
Centers:**
• Fred Hutchinson Cancer Research
Center
**Hospices:**
Community Home Health Care
Hospice of Seattle
Hospice of Snohomish County
**Costs Index:** Excellent
**Fluoridation:** Adjusted
**Air Pollution:** CO
**CMSA Access:** SEATTLE–TACOMA,
WA (20)
**Places Rated Score:** 2,715
**Places Rated Rank:** 21

**Sharon, PA**
**Physicians per 100,000:** 100
**Cardiac Rehabilitation Centers:**
Sharon General Hospital CRU
**Costs Index:** Excellent
**Fluoridation:** Adjusted
**Air Pollution:** Insignificant
**Places Rated Score:** 700
**Places Rated Rank:** 203

**Sheboygan, WI**
**Physicians per 100,000:** 93
**Costs Index:** Excellent
**Fluoridation:** Adjusted
**Air Pollution:** Insignificant
**Places Rated Score:** 593
**Places Rated Rank:** 241

**Sherman–Denison, TX**
**Physicians per 100,000:** 144
**Costs Index:** Good
**Fluoridation:** Natural (Sherman only)
**Air Pollution:** Insignificant
**Places Rated Score:** 394
**Places Rated Rank:** 292

**Shreveport, LA**
Physicians per 100,000: 245
Teaching Hospitals:
Louisiana State University Hospital
VA Medical Center
Medical Schools:
Louisiana State University School of
Medicine in Shreveport
Costs Index: Excellent
Fluoridation: Adjusted
Air Pollution: Insignificant
Places Rated Score: 1,445
Places Rated Rank: 82

**Sioux City, IA–NE**
Physicians per 100,000: 146
Cardiac Rehabilitation Centers:
Marian Health Center CRU
Hospices:
Marian Health Center
Costs Index: Excellent
Fluoridation: Adjusted
Air Pollution: Insignificant
Places Rated Score: 846
Places Rated Rank: 161

**Sioux Falls, SD**
Physicians per 100,000: 241
Cardiac Rehabilitation Centers:
Sioux Valley Hospital CRU
Costs Index: Outstanding
Fluoridation: Adjusted
Air Pollution: Insignificant
Places Rated Score: 1,041
Places Rated Rank: 130

**South Bend–Mishawaka, IN**
Physicians per 100,000: 130
Cardiac Rehabilitation Centers:
Cardiac Treatment Center of South
Bend, Inc.
St. Joseph's Hospital
Costs Index: Excellent
Fluoridation: Adjusted
Air Pollution: Insignificant
Places Rated Score: 830
Places Rated Rank: 167

**Spokane, WA**
Physicians per 100,000: 197
Cardiac Rehabilitation Centers:
Deaconess Hospital CRU
Sacred Heart Medical Center CRU
Spokane CRU
Hospices:
Hospice Maranatha
Costs Index: Good
Fluoridation: None
Air Pollution: TSP, CO
Places Rated Score: 497
Places Rated Rank: 272

**Springfield, IL**
Physicians per 100,000: 277
Teaching Hospitals:
Memorial Medical Center
St. John's Hospital
Medical Schools:
Southern Illinois University School of
Medicine
Cardiac Rehabilitation Centers:
Cardiac Rehabilitation for Postcardiac
Patients, Inc.
St. John's Hospital CRU
Springfield Community Hospital
CRU

Hospices:
St. John's Hospital–Department of
Family Practice
Costs Index: Excellent
Fluoridation: Adjusted
Air Pollution: Insignificant
Places Rated Score: 1,877
Places Rated Rank: 57

**Springfield, MA**
Physicians per 100,000: 210
Teaching Hospitals:
Baystate Medical Center
Cardiac Rehabilitation Centers:
Baystate Medical Center CRU
Costs Index: Excellent
Fluoridation: None
Air Pollution: Insignificant
Places Rated Score: 710
Places Rated Rank: 200

**Springfield, MO**
Physicians per 100,000: 177
Cardiac Rehabilitation Centers:
St. John's Hospital–YMCA CRU
Hospices:
Hospice of Southwest Missouri
Costs Index: Excellent
Fluoridation: None
Air Pollution: Insignificant
Places Rated Score: 577
Places Rated Rank: 249

★ **Stamford, CT**
Physicians per 100,000: 220
Teaching Hospitals:
Stamford Hospital
Cardiac Rehabilitation Centers:
Greenwich Hospital Association CRU
St. Joseph Hospital CRU
YMCA Cardiac Rehabilitation Exercise
Program
Costs Index: Excellent
Fluoridation: Adjusted
Air Pollution: CO
CMSA Access: NEW YORK–NORTHERN
NEW JERSEY–LONG ISLAND, NY–NJ–CT
(1,490)
Places Rated Score: 2,610
Places Rated Rank: 23

**State College, PA**
Physicians per 100,000: 112
Costs Index: Excellent
Fluoridation: Adjusted
Air Pollution: Insignificant
Places Rated Score: 612
Places Rated Rank: 230

**Steubenville–Weirton, OH–WV**
Physicians per 100,000: 105
Cardiac Rehabilitation Centers:
St. John Medical Center CRU
Costs Index: Excellent
Fluoridation: Adjusted
Air Pollution: TSP, SO$_2$
Places Rated Score: 505
Places Rated Rank: 270

**Stockton, CA**
Physicians per 100,000: 142
Cardiac Rehabilitation Centers:
San Joaquin Cardiac Clinic
Costs Index: Good
Fluoridation: None
Air Pollution: Insignificant
Places Rated Score: 342
Places Rated Rank: 304

**Syracuse, NY**
Physicians per 100,000: 240
Teaching Hospitals:
State University Hospital of the Upstate
Medical Center
VA Medical Center
Medical Schools:
SUNY Upstate Medical Center College
of Medicine
Costs Index: Unacceptable
Fluoridation: Adjusted
Air Pollution: Insignificant
Places Rated Score: 1,040
Places Rated Rank: 131

**Tacoma, WA**
Physicians per 100,000: 134
Cardiac Rehabilitation Centers:
VA Hospital CRU
Hospices:
Hospice of Tacoma
Costs Index: Good
Fluoridation: None
Air Pollution: CO
CMSA Access: SEATTLE–TACOMA,
WA (205)
Places Rated Score: 539
Places Rated Rank: 258

**Tallahassee, FL**
Physicians per 100,000: 170
Cardiac Rehabilitation Centers:
Tallahassee Physical Therapy Services
CRU
Costs Index: Good
Fluoridation: None
Air Pollution: Insignificant
Places Rated Score: 370
Places Rated Rank: 297

**Tampa–St. Petersburg–
Clearwater, FL**
Physicians per 100,000: 189
Teaching Hospitals:
James E. Haley VA Medical Center
Medical Schools:
University of South Florida College of
Medicine
Cardiac Rehabilitation Centers:
Bayfront Medical Center CRU
Palms of Pasadena Hospital CRU
Tampa Bay Cardiac Prevention CRU
Hospices:
Hospice Care, Inc.
Costs Index: Good
Fluoridation: None
Air Pollution: Insignificant
Places Rated Score: 1,189
Places Rated Rank: 106

**Terre Haute, IN**
Physicians per 100,000: 153
Cardiac Rehabilitation Centers:
Union Hospital CRU
Costs Index: Excellent
Fluoridation: None
Air Pollution: Insignificant
Places Rated Score: 453
Places Rated Rank: 281

**Texarkana, TX–Texarkana, AR**
Physicians per 100,000: 143
Costs Index: Excellent
Fluoridation: None
Air Pollution: Insignificant
Places Rated Score: 343
Places Rated Rank: 303

## Toledo, OH
Physicians per 100,000: 238
Teaching Hospitals:
  Medical College of Ohio Hospital
Medical Schools:
  Medical College of Ohio at Toledo
Cardiac Rehabilitation Centers:
  Flower Hospital CRU
  Medical College of Ohio CRU
  Riverside Hospital Acute Progressive
    Coronary Care
  St. Vincent's Hospital Cardiac
    Conditioning Program
  University of Toledo CRU
Hospices:
  Northwest Ohio Hospice Association
Costs Index: Good
Fluoridation: Adjusted
Air Pollution: Insignificant
Places Rated Score: 1,738
Places Rated Rank: 68

## Topeka, KS
Physicians per 100,000: 248
Cardiac Rehabilitation Centers:
  St. Francis Hospital CRU
  Stormont–Vail Medical Center CRU
  VA Hospital CRU
Hospices:
  Hospice of Topeka
Costs Index: Excellent
Fluoridation: Adjusted
Air Pollution: Insignificant
Places Rated Score: 1,148
Places Rated Rank: 112

## Trenton, NJ
Physicians per 100,000: 287
Cardiac Rehabilitation Centers:
  St. Francis Medical Center–Cardiology
    Section
Costs Index: Excellent
Fluoridation: Adjusted
Air Pollution: Insignificant
CMSA Access: PHILADELPHIA–WILMINGTON–
  TRENTON, PA–NJ–DE–MD (485)
Places Rated Score: 1,372
Places Rated Rank: 87

## Tucson, AZ
Physicians per 100,000: 259
Teaching Hospitals:
  Tucson Medical Center
  University of Arizona Health Services
    Center
  VA Medical Center
Medical Schools:
  University of Arizona College of
    Medicine
Cardiac Rehabilitation Centers:
  St. Joseph's Hospital CRU
Comprehensive Cancer Treatment
  Centers:
  University of Arizona Cancer Center
Hospices:
  Hillhaven Hospice
Costs Index: Fair
Fluoridation: None
Air Pollution: TSP, CO
Places Rated Score: 1,259
Places Rated Rank: 95

## Tulsa, OK
Physicians per 100,000: 181
Medical Schools:
  Oral Roberts University School of
    Medicine

Cardiac Rehabilitation Centers:
  Hillcrest Medical Center CRU
  Oklahoma Osteopathic Hospital
    CRU
  St. Francis Hospital CRU
  St. John's Medical Center Cardiac
    Exercise Lab
  Thornton Family Hospital CRU
Hospices:
  St. Francis Hospital–Hospice Program
Costs Index: Excellent
Fluoridation: Adjusted
Air Pollution: Insignificant
Places Rated Score: 1,581
Places Rated Rank: 78

## Tuscaloosa, AL
Physicians per 100,000: 174
Costs Index: Excellent
Fluoridation: Adjusted
Air Pollution: Insignificant
Places Rated Score: 674
Places Rated Rank: 210

## Tyler, TX
Physicians per 100,000: 172
Cardiac Rehabilitation Centers:
  Mother Francis Hospital CRU
Costs Index: Good
Fluoridation: Adjusted
Air Pollution: Insignificant
Places Rated Score: 672
Places Rated Rank: 211

## Utica–Rome, NY
Physicians per 100,000: 141
Cardiac Rehabilitation Centers:
  St. Luke's Memorial Hospital CRC
Hospices:
  Hospice Care, Inc.
Costs Index: Poor
Fluoridation: Adjusted (Utica only)
Air Pollution: Insignificant
Places Rated Score: 391
Places Rated Rank: 293

## Vallejo–Fairfield–Napa, CA
Physicians per 100,000: 199
Hospices:
  Hospice of Napa Valley
Costs Index: Good
Fluoridation: Adjusted (Vallejo only)
Air Pollution: Insignificant
CMSA Access: SAN FRANCISCO–
  OAKLAND–SAN JOSE, CA (580)
Places Rated Score: 1,079
Places Rated Rank: 124

## Vancouver, WA
Physicians per 100,000: 87
Costs Index: Good
Fluoridation: Adjusted
Air Pollution: TSP
CMSA Access: PORTLAND–VANCOUVER,
  OR–WA (130)
Places Rated Score: 517
Places Rated Rank: 266

## Victoria, TX
Physicians per 100,000: 160
Costs Index: Good
Fluoridation: Almost none
Air Pollution: Insignificant
Places Rated Score: 260
Places Rated Rank: 316

## Vineland–Millville–Bridgeton, NJ
Physicians per 100,000: 112
Costs Index: Excellent
Fluoridation: None
Air Pollution: Insignificant
CMSA Access: PHILADELPHIA–
  WILMINGTON–TRENTON,
  PA–NJ–DE–MD (495)
Places Rated Score: 807
Places Rated Rank: 174

## Visalia–Tulare–Porterville, CA
Physicians per 100,000: 110
Costs Index: Good
Fluoridation: None
Air Pollution: Insignificant
Places Rated Score: 210
Places Rated Rank: 324

## Waco, TX
Physicians per 100,000: 138
Costs Index: Good
Fluoridation: Adjusted
Air Pollution: Insignificant
Places Rated Score: 538
Places Rated Rank: 260

## ★ Washington, DC–MD–VA
Physicians per 100,000: 511
Teaching Hospitals:
  Children's Hospital National Medical
    Center
  George Washington University Hospital
  Georgetown University Hospital
  Howard University Hospital
  VA Medical Center
  Washington Hospital Center
Medical Schools:
  George Washington University School of
    Medicine
  Georgetown University School of
    Medicine
  Howard University College of Medicine
Cardiac Rehabilitation Centers:
  Arlington Hospital Cardiac Exercise
    Clinic
  Arlington Hospital CRU
  Fairfax Hospital Cardiac Therapy
    Program
  George Washington University Hospital
    CRU
  Georgetown University Medical Center
    CRU
  Greater Southeast Community Hospital
    CRU
  Loudoun Memorial Hospital CTC
  Mount Vernon Hospital Ancillary
    Services
  Orthopedic and Rehabilitation Hospital
    CRC
  Washington Adventist Hospital CRU
Comprehensive Cancer Treatment
  Centers:
• Georgetown University–Howard
    University Comprehensive Cancer
    Center
Hospices:
  Hospice Care of the District of
    Columbia
  The Washington Home Hospice
  Washington Hospice Society, Inc.
Costs Index: Good
Fluoridation: Adjusted
Air Pollution: CO
Places Rated Score: 4,361
Places Rated Rank: 6

**Waterbury, CT**
Physicians per 100,000: 318
Teaching Hospitals:
   Waterbury Hospital
Cardiac Rehabilitation Centers:
   St. Mary's Hospital CRU
   Waterbury Hospital CRU
Costs Index: Excellent
Fluoridation: Adjusted
Air Pollution: Insignificant
Places Rated Score: 1,218
Places Rated Rank: 102

**Waterloo–Cedar Falls, IA**
Physicians per 100,000: 125
Cardiac Rehabilitation Centers:
   Allen Memorial Hospital CRU
   St. Francis Hospital CRU
   Schoitz Memorial Hospital
      CRU
Costs Index: Excellent
Fluoridation: Adjusted
Air Pollution: Insignificant
Places Rated Score: 925
Places Rated Rank: 148

**Wausau, WI**
Physicians per 100,000: 118
Cardiac Rehabilitation Centers:
   Wausau Hospital Center CRU
Hospices:
   Wausau Hospice Program
Costs Index: Excellent
Fluoridation: Adjusted
Air Pollution: Insignificant
Places Rated Score: 818
Places Rated Rank: 169

**West Palm Beach–Boca
Raton–Delray Beach, FL**
Physicians per 100,000: 175
Hospices:
   Hospice of Boca Raton
   Hospice of Palm Beach County
Costs Index: Fair
Fluoridation: None
Air Pollution: Insignificant
Places Rated Score: 375
Places Rated Rank: 295

**Wheeling, WV–OH**
Physicians per 100,000: 191
Cardiac Rehabilitation Centers:
   Wheeling Hospital CRU
Hospices:
   Clara Welty Hospice Program
Costs Index: Excellent
Fluoridation: Adjusted
Air Pollution: TSP
Places Rated Score: 791
Places Rated Rank: 179

**Wichita, KS**
Physicians per 100,000: 206

Teaching Hospitals:
   Wesley Medical Center
Cardiac Rehabilitation Centers:
   St. Francis Hospital–Wichita CRU
   St. Joseph Medical Center CRU
   Wesley Medical Center–Wichita
      University CRU
Costs Index: Good
Fluoridation: None
Air Pollution: Insignificant
Places Rated Score: 806
Places Rated Rank: 175

**Wichita Falls, TX**
Physicians per 100,000: 149
Costs Index: Good
Fluoridation: Adjusted
Air Pollution: Insignificant
Places Rated Score: 549
Places Rated Rank: 255

**Williamsport, PA**
Physicians per 100,000: 160
Cardiac Rehabilitation Centers:
   Divine Providence Hospital CRU
   Williamsport Hospital CRU
Costs Index: Excellent
Fluoridation: Adjusted
Air Pollution: Insignificant
Places Rated Score: 860
Places Rated Rank: 159

**Wilmington, DE–NJ–MD**
Physicians per 100,000: 180
Teaching Hospitals:
   Wilmington Medical Center, Inc.
Cardiac Rehabilitation Centers:
   Wilmington Cardiac Treatment
      Center
Costs Index: Excellent
Fluoridation: Adjusted
Air Pollution: Insignificant
CMSA Access: PHILADELPHIA–
   WILMINGTON–TRENTON,
   PA–NJ–DE–MD (465)
Places Rated Score: 1,445
Places Rated Rank: 82

**Wilmington, NC**
Physicians per 100,000: 199
Cardiac Rehabilitation Centers:
   New Hanover Memorial Hospital CRU
Hospices:
   North Cape Fear Hospice
Costs Index: Outstanding
Fluoridation: Adjusted
Air Pollution: Insignificant
Places Rated Score: 1,099
Places Rated Rank: 120

**Worcester, MA**
Physicians per 100,000: 205
Teaching Hospitals:
   Memorial Hospital

St. Vincent Hospital
University of Massachusetts Teaching
   Hospital
Worcester City Hospital
Medical Schools:
   University of Massachusetts, Worcester,
      Medical School
Cardiac Rehabilitation Units:
   St. Vincent Hospital CRU
   University of Massachusetts Medical
      Center CRU
Hospices:
   University of Massachusetts Medical
      Center–Palliative Care, Inc.
Costs Index: Excellent
Fluoridation: None
Air Pollution: Insignificant
Places Rated Score: 1,805
Places Rated Rank: 64

**Yakima, WA**
Physicians per 100,000: 117
Cardiac Rehabilitation Centers:
   Yakima Valley Memorial Hospital CRU
Costs Index: Good
Fluoridation: None
Air Pollution: Insignificant
Places Rated Score: 317
Places Rated Rank: 310

**York, PA**
Physicians per 100,000: 113
Teaching Hospitals:
   York Hospital
Costs Index: Outstanding
Fluoridation: None
Air Pollution: Insignificant
Places Rated Score: 713
Places Rated Rank: 199

**Youngstown–Warren, OH**
Physicians per 100,000: 147
Teaching Hospitals:
   St. Elizabeth Hospital Medical Center
   Youngstown Hospital Association
Cardiac Rehabilitation Centers:
   Professional Cardiac
      Rehabilitation–Procare
   Trumbull Memorial Hospital CRU
Hospices:
   Hospice of Youngstown
Costs Index: Excellent
Fluoridaton: Adjusted (Warren only)
Air Pollution: TSP
Places Rated Score: 1,097
Places Rated Rank: 121

**Yuba City, CA**
Physicians per 100,000: 112
Costs Index: Good
Fluoridation: None
Air Pollution: Insignificant
Places Rated Score: 212
Places Rated Rank: 323

# ARE THERE GEOGRAPHIC PATTERNS OF DISEASE?

A glance at the maps depicting the areas with the highest and the lowest mortality rates for heart disease, cancer, and stroke suggests that there are geographical patterns to the three leading killers. For each of these diseases, the states with the highest death rates lie in the central or eastern section of the country, and the states with the lowest death rates lie in the West. Why these apparent patterns exist can be explained in some instances, but in others the pattern remains an interesting puzzle.

## Heart Disease and Stroke: Perennial Threats

The map "Death Rates: Heart Disease" reflects age-adjusted death rates for white men aged 35 to 74, who experience a higher mortality rate than the population as a whole (nationally the death rate in 1980 for this group was 480.9). West Virginia experienced the highest death rate, 581.0, whereas Hawaii had the lowest, only 321.7. As noted above, all the states with the highest rates of heart disease are in the eastern half of the continent, and all the states with the lowest rates are in the West. Compared with the West, the eastern United States is generally more thickly populated and more industrialized, and it has more large cities and a life-style that is usually faster paced. Perhaps the less hectic, more exercise-filled life common in the western states may account for some of the difference in death rates, as may the drinking water. Recently, studies have revealed at least a tentative correlation between hard drinking water (water with a high percentage of dissolved salts and minerals) and a lower incidence of heart disease.

Another possible factor is diet. The Southwest, traditionally the region with the lowest rates of heart disease, is marked by a diet that is heavily influenced by Mexico. Red meat is eaten seldom, with beans, grains, and cheese providing most of the protein. Such a diet, high in complex carbohydrates, is generally considered by nutritionists to be near the ideal.

Cerebrovascular disease, or stroke, is closely related to and interconnected with heart disease. Like the number-one killer, stroke is aggravated by excess weight, high blood pressure, stress, and a diet high in sodium. Therefore, you could assume that states with high death rates from heart disease would likewise have high death rates from stroke. But in fact, as the map "Death Rates: Stroke" shows, not a single state has very high rates of both heart disease and stroke. The entire southeastern quadrant of the United States seems plagued by high rates of either heart disease or stroke. The fact that the Deep South states of Tennessee, Mississippi, Alabama, and Georgia have very high

stroke death rates comes as no surprise, since these states have large black populations. Blacks, with their predisposition to hypertension, have always had a high incidence of death from stroke. Moreover, the traditional Southern black diet tends to be very high in sodium.

## Tracking the Deadly Cancers

"It's the one John Wayne part nobody wants," mused actor Robert Ryan after learning he had cancer. Certainly none of us wants to get this disease, the number-two killer in America, despite the continual progress that has been made in early diagnosis and effective treatment for most varieties.

Some cancers are not very serious. Skin cancers—with the exception of melanoma—are rarely fatal, and tremendous progress has been made in treating most cancers of the bones and connective tissues. But other forms remain extremely pernicious. Cancer of the esophagus, for example, has a five-year survival rate of only 5 percent. Lung cancer has a five-year survival rate of 12 percent, and the comparable rate for stomach cancer is only 14 percent.

According to the most recent and thoroughly re-

**Death Rates: Heart Disease**

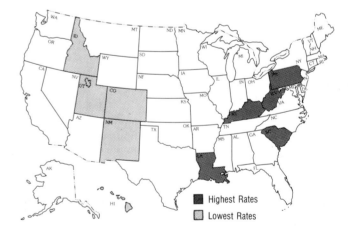

| States with Highest Rates | Estimated Deaths per 100,000* | States with Lowest Rates | Estimated Deaths per 100,000* |
|---|---|---|---|
| 1. West Virginia | 581.0 | 1. Hawaii | 321.7 |
| 2. Kentucky | 561.6 | 2. New Mexico | 324.2 |
| 3. South Carolina | 559.4 | 3. Colorado | 385.8 |
| 4. Louisiana | 537.3 | 4. Utah | 394.8 |
| 5. Pennsylvania | 533.3 | 5. Idaho | 397.0 |

*Source:* Metropolitan Life Insurance Company, *Statistical Bulletin*, July–September 1984.

*Figures represent age-adjusted death rate for white men aged 35 to 74 in 1980.

**Death Rates: Stroke**

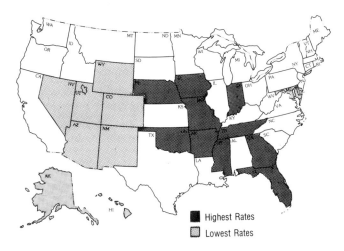

Highest Rates
Lowest Rates

| States with Highest Rates | Estimated Deaths per 100,000* | States with Lowest Rates | Estimated Deaths per 100,000* |
|---|---|---|---|
| 1. Arkansas | 109.8 | 1. Alaska | 18.0 |
| 2. Florida | 100.2 | 2. Hawaii | 40.3 |
| 3. Oklahoma | 98.0 | 3. Utah | 45.8 |
| 4. Mississippi | 97.2 | 4. New Mexico | 50.0 |
| 5. Iowa | 96.9 | 5. Colorado | 51.2 |
| 6. Tennessee | 96.0 | 6. Arizona | 51.8 |
| 7. Nebraska | 92.9 | 7. Wyoming | 54.0 |
| 8. Missouri | 92.2 | 8. Maryland | 55.0 |
| 9. Indiana | 90.5 | 9. Nevada | 55.1 |
| 10. Georgia | 90.1 | 10. Delaware | 55.8 |

Source: National Center for Health Statistics, *Vital Statistics of the United States, Vol. II: Mortality,* 1982.

*Figures are for 1978.

**Death Rates: Cancer**

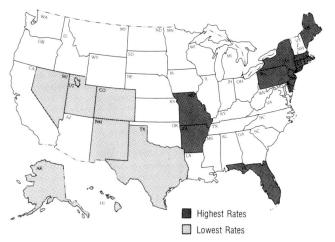

Highest Rates
Lowest Rates

| States with Highest Rates | Estimated Deaths per 100,000* | States with Lowest Rates | Estimated Deaths per 100,000* |
|---|---|---|---|
| 1. Rhode Island | 259 | 1. Alaska | 68 |
| 2. Florida | 244 | 2. Utah | 96 |
| 3. Pennsylvania | 232 | 3. Colorado | 127 |
| 4. New Jersey | 224 | 4. Hawaii | 128 |
| 5. Maine | 217 | 5. New Mexico | 136 |
| 5. Massachusetts | 217 | 6. Texas | 141 |
| 7. Delaware | 215 | 7. Nevada | 144 |
| 7. New York | 215 | | |
| 9. Connecticut | 213 | | |
| 10. Missouri | 212 | | |
| 11. Arkansas | 210 | | |

Source: American Cancer Society, *Cancer Facts and Figures,* 1984.

*Figures are projected death rates for 1984 for all cancers.

searched study of cancer incidence yet undertaken, *U.S. Cancer Mortality Rates and Trends—1950–1979,* published by the Environmental Protection Agency and the National Cancer Institute in 1983, there are definite geographic patterns to many cancers. Although research has not yet pinpointed the cause for cancer in general, some environmental risks related to specific toxins called carcinogens (cancer-causing substances) have been documented. Certain factors, such as occupation, environment, personal habits (such as smoking), and diet, have been shown to induce some types of cancer. A number of these risk factors are more prevalent in the heavily urbanized Northeast than they are in the West, especially those related to the environment. The map "Death Rates: Cancer," based on projections for 1984 by the American Cancer Society, bears out this generalization, showing the highest death rates concentrated in the Northeast.

The best-known link between life-style and cancer has been established in the case of lung cancer, a disease that is not only painful and practically incurable but also largely preventable. Lung cancer caused an estimated 13 deaths per 100,000 people in 1950, and that figure reached 42 deaths per 100,000 in 1979. The American Cancer Society claims that cigarette smoking

is responsible for 83 percent of lung cancer cases in men and 43 percent in women.

Some cancers may possibly be linked to nationality. For example, North Dakota and South Dakota have long shown high incidences of stomach cancer. Many of the residents of the Dakotas are descendants of Finns and White Russians. Interestingly enough, the incidence of stomach cancer is elevated in both Finland and the Soviet Union. Likewise, Hawaii's high rates of stomach cancer may be due to the fact that many of its citizens trace their roots to Japan, a country with elevated rates of this cancer. Pure hereditary susceptibility may be involved, although diet is a more plausible explanation.

## YOU ARE WHAT YOU EAT, SMOKE, DRINK . . .

Do you subscribe to the when-your-number's-up-it's-up theory of life expectancy? Then you may be surprised to learn that, based on recent trends, experts conclude it's less likely to be a stray bullet or virus that kills you than the way you lead your life.

The most common causes of death at the turn of the century—typhoid fever, cholera, tuberculosis, smallpox, gastroenteritis, and nephritis—have been practically eliminated by scientific advances and improved sanitation. Today, more than 70 percent of the two million Americans who die each year are victims of heart disease, cancer, stroke, cirrhosis of the liver, bronchitis, asthma, and emphysema—the so-called life-style diseases that may be aggravated by such behavior as overeating, heavy drinking, smoking, and lack of exercise.

To see how your daily habits measure up, take a look at the table "How Healthy Is Your Life-Style?" The creators of this table warn that since some risk factors are more important than others, an entirely accurate picture of your health may not emerge from this self-analysis. However, they add, changing your habits so that you qualify for the low-risk ratings will result in a longer life.

The following are some suggestions that can help you reduce your health risks.

*Stop smoking and drink only in moderation.* Cigarette smokers run twice the risk that nonsmokers do of death from coronary disease. Smoking also contributes to stroke, lung cancer, emphysema, and bronchitis. Likewise, an excess of alcohol can be dangerous, increasing your chances of developing cirrhosis of the liver (this condition is found six times as frequently among alcoholics as among nonalcoholics) and cardiovascular problems. Drinking combined with driving multiplies the risk of dying in an automobile accident; at least half of such accidents in the United States involve drunk drivers.

*Eat a balanced diet and watch your weight.* Six of the ten leading causes of death have been linked to diet: heart attack, stroke, atherosclerosis, cancer, cirrhosis of the liver, and diabetes. Reducing your intake of refined flour and sugar, salt (which in excess contributes to high blood pressure), and saturated fats (which have been implicated as factors in heart disease and stroke) while choosing from a range of meat, poultry,

## How Healthy Is Your Life-Style?

| Risk Category | No Risk | Slight Risk | Substantial Risk | Heavy Risk | Dangerous Risk |
|---|---|---|---|---|---|
| **Smoking** | No smoking or stopped for at least 10 years | Less than 10 cigarettes, 5 pipes or cigars a day | Half pack a day | 1 pack a day | 2 or more packs a day |
| **Alcohol** | Nondrinker | Stopped drinker | Fewer than 6 drinks per week | More than 6 drinks per week | More than 2 drinks per day |
| **Trimness** | Lean | Slightly plump | Moderately obese | Considerably obese | Grossly obese |
| **Physical activity** | Walk more than 2 miles a day or climb 20 or more flights of stairs a day | Walk 1.5–2 miles a day or climb 15–20 flights of stairs a day | Walk only 0.5 to 1.5 miles a day or climb only 5–15 flights of stairs a day | Walk only 2–5 blocks a day or climb 2–4 flights of stairs a day | Walk less than 2 blocks a day or climb less than 2 flights of stairs a day |
| **Prescription drugs** | With doctor's consent, following orders carefully | Take medication daily without side effects | Take medication when needed with few side effects | Use sleeping and nerve pills regularly without doctor's supervision | Without doctor's consent, mix with other drugs or alcohol |
| **Nonprescription drugs** | Use occasionally only for short periods. Label warnings heeded | | | | Continuing use, drinking or driving despite label warnings |
| **Alcohol and driving —boats, cars, motorcycles, snowmobiles** | Never drink. Drive only with safety aids—seat belt, helmet, life jacket | Never drive after drinking without safety aids | Drive after 2 drinks with safety aids | Drive after 2 drinks without safety aids | Drive after more than 2 drinks without safety aids |
| **Motor vehicle safety** | Always wear seat belt | Wear seat belt more than half of the time | Wear seat belt as a driver half of the time | Wear seat belt as a passenger half of the time | Wear seat belt less than half of the time |
| **Water safety— swimming and boating** | Qualified expert | Know how to swim and the safety rules | Know how to swim and may swim after 1 drink or nerve drug | Do not know how to swim but use life jacket half of the time | Do not know how to swim; never use life jacket |
| **Blood cholesterol** | Less than 180 | 180–220 | 220–280 | 280–320 | 320 and up |
| **Blood pressure** | 120/80 or less | 120/80–140/90 | 140/90–160/100 | 160/100–180/105 | Above 180/105 |
| **Blood sugar** | Less than 120 two hours after a meal of syrup and pancakes | Between 110 and 130 two hours after meals; checked each 3 months | Blood sugar more than 150 without diet control | Blood sugar more than 150 without diet control, doctor's care | Diabetes without doctor's care at less than 45 years of age |
| **FOR WOMEN ONLY** | | | | | |
| **Breast check for lumps** | Monthly self-exam and yearly check by physician | Monthly self-exam but no doctor exam | Self-exam 2–3 times a year but no doctor's exam | 1 time a year by a doctor | Never |
| **Pap smear** | Every year | Every 3 years | Every 4 years | Never | Never; nonmenstrual bleeding |

*Source:* Methodist Hospital of Indianapolis, Inc. Prepared by Pamela Hall under the supervision of Drs. Lewis C. Robbins and Jack H. Hall, developers of the Health Hazard Appraisal System. Used by permission.

fish, fruits, vegetables, and fiber foods is highly recommended. A balanced diet can also help you to lose extra weight, which puts added stress on the heart and organs, aggravating disease conditions.

*Get regular exercise.* Exercise, now seen almost as a miracle drug, can help you maintain proper weight, keep your body in good operating condition, and relieve stress (which contributes to ulcers and high blood pressure). It's also necessary to prevent premature aging and degeneration of muscles and joints. The use-it-or-lose-it maxim definitely applies here.

*Get regular medical care.* Be sure to consult your doctor regularly and have whatever checkups or tests he or she recommends, such as a Pap smear or blood pressure tests.

## SUICIDE IN AMERICA

Suicide tends to be a phenomenon not of the poor, homeless, and downtrodden, but rather of the well-to-do and highly educated professional, usually male and white. In short, suicide occurs predominantly in the upper middle class. It is not in the slums of New York City, Newark, or Chicago that people kill themselves with greatest frequency; rather, it is in the affluent suburbs and the relatively prosperous, wide-open country of the Mountain States and the West. The highest rates of suicide occur in states without many big cities, such as Wyoming and New Mexico; most of these states also have per capita incomes substantially above the nation's average. In contrast, many of the states with the lowest suicide rates (New Jersey, Massachusetts, New York, and Illinois) have large cities, poverty, high crime, and all the other stress-related problems one would normally associate with despair and self-destruction.

There are several theories about why certain places have higher suicide rates than others. Some people point to the substantial percentage of elderly residents in Arizona and Florida as an explanation for their high suicide records. True, suicide is high among older Americans, many of whom suffer constant pain or irreversible declining health due to a chronic or terminal illness. But many of the states with low suicide rates also have a large number of residents who are over 65.

A more reliable indicator of suicide may be relatively young populations. Most of the suicide-prone states, like Alaska, Arizona, Colorado, and New Mexico, have populations with significant percentages of people under 17. Nevada, the state with by far the highest suicide rate, is the second youngest state after Alaska. However, Nevada's legalized gambling, prostitution, dependence on casinos and the entertainment industry, high rates of alcohol consumption and alcoholism, and transient population probably also contribute to its leading suicide rate.

## States Ranked by Suicide Rate

| State | Suicides per 100,000 Population | State | Suicides per 100,000 Population |
|---|---|---|---|
| 1. New Jersey | 7.4 | 24. Ohio | 11.9 |
| 2. Massachusetts | 8.2 | 27. Louisiana | 12.1 |
| 3. Connecticut | 8.9 | 28. Tennessee | 12.2 |
| 4. Mississippi | 9.2 | 29. Texas | 12.3 |
| 5. Illinois | 9.3 | 30. Maine | 12.5 |
| 6. New York | 9.5 | 30. West Virginia | 12.5 |
| 6. South Carolina | 9.5 | 32. Georgia | 12.6 |
| 8. Nebraska | 10.1 | 33. South Dakota | 12.7 |
| 9. Indiana | 10.4 | 34. Kentucky | 12.8 |
| 10. Maryland | 10.8 | 35. Idaho | 13.1 |
| 10. Minnesota | 10.8 | 35. Oklahoma | 13.1 |
| 12. Kansas | 10.9 | 37. Utah | 13.2 |
| 13. Iowa | 11.0 | 38. Washington | 13.3 |
| 13. New Hampshire | 11.0 | 39. Virginia | 13.4 |
| 13. North Dakota | 11.0 | 40. California | 14.5 |
| 16. Pennsylvania | 11.1 | 40. Montana | 14.5 |
| 17. Alabama | 11.2 | 42. Oregon | 14.6 |
| 17. North Carolina | 11.2 | 43. Vermont | 14.7 |
| 17. Rhode Island | 11.2 | 44. Florida | 15.4 |
| 20. Hawaii | 11.4 | 45. Wyoming | 16.0 |
| 21. Michigan | 11.5 | 46. Colorado | 16.3 |
| 22. Arkansas | 11.6 | 47. Alaska | 16.9 |
| 23. Wisconsin | 11.7 | 47. Arizona | 16.9 |
| 24. Delaware | 11.9 | 49. New Mexico | 17.4 |
| 24. Missouri | 11.9 | 50. Nevada | 22.9 |

*Source:* National Center for Health Statistics, unpublished data, 1980.

## WHAT HAVE THEY DONE TO THE RAIN?

The first noticeable effect was the wearing away of detail on stone and marble monuments around the world—the giant obelisk in St. Peter's square in Rome, the Parthenon in Athens, friezes on buildings in Washington, D.C., the intricate carving on many of Northern Europe's fine Gothic cathedrals. But since the discovery of the phenomenon called acid rain in the late 1960s, increasing evidence has shown the caustic precipitation to be harmful to living creatures as well. In the United States, environmentalists warn, vast stretches of forests, important spawning grounds for fish, even the health of a significant number of people could be in grave danger.

### What Is Acid Rain?

Acid rain has been called an insidious form of air pollution, and its poisonous consequences are usually suffered a considerable distance from the source of the problem. The major cause of acid rain is the pollutant sulfur dioxide ($SO_2$), a principal emission of coal burning; other pollutants are also involved. In the United States, 48 million tons of sulfur and nitrogen fumes was spewed into the air in 1980, most of it coming from 31 states bordering on or east of the Mississippi River. Ohio, Illinois, Indiana, Michigan, Kentucky, Tennessee, and West Virginia have generally been pointed to as the most significant sources of $SO_2$ pollution.

## Acid Rain in the Metro Areas

Most of the country's worst areas for acid rain are in non-metropolitan locations, but according to the U.S. Geological Survey's *Water-Supply Paper 2250*, sixteen metro areas have present or potential problems with acid rain:

Albany–Schenectady–Troy, NY
Atlantic City, NJ
Baltimore, MD
Duluth, MN–WI
Eau Claire, WI
Eugene–Springfield, OR
Glens Falls, NY
Hagerstown, MD
Medford, OR
Middlesex–Somerset–
   Hunterdon, NJ

Monmouth–Ocean, NJ
St. Cloud, MN–WI
Salt Lake City–Ogden,
   UT
Trenton, NJ
Vineland–Millville–
   Bridgeton, NJ
Wausau, WI

*Source:* U.S. Geological Survey, *Water-Supply Paper 2250*, 1984.

In measuring acidity of water or soil, the pH scale is used (pH stands for *potential of hydrogen*). This scale has a neutral point of 7; less than 7 means acid, more than 7 means alkaline. The pH scale is logarithmic, so that pH 4.6 is ten times more acid than pH 5.6, and pH 3.6 is 100 times more acidic than pH 4.6. Ordinary rain is somewhat acidic, with a pH of 5.6, but when sulfur and nitrogen oxides react with moisture in the air, they intensify the acidity of rain.

Because of prevailing westerly winds and because most coal burning takes place east of the Mississippi, the effects of acid rain are seen most commonly in the Appalachian Mountains and along the eastern seaboard.

### Destructive Effects

The effects of acid rain on forests have long been documented in Europe but only recently observed in America. All along the Appalachian Mountain chain, from Georgia to Maine, the growth rate of mountain trees is slowing. The rate for red spruce, for example, is now only 74 percent of that recorded in 1965, and the decline is not from logging. In the southern half of the Appalachian chain, the new growth of loblolly pine, backbone of the southeastern timber economy, is creeping to a standstill. Such trees as the beech, sugar maple, and hickory are growing deformed limbs, producing weak and brittle wood, and losing their resistance to insects and disease.

Since the pollutants are carried in clouds, the poisoning effect intensifies with altitude. In addition, hilltop trees tend to "comb" damaging particles from the air. Foresters monitoring mountaintop pH levels claim that a pH of 2 exists in some clouds, an acidity greater than that of table vinegar. Mount Mitchell, near Asheville in western North Carolina, the highest peak in the East, is fast becoming a bald mountain.

For more than a decade, sport and commercial fishermen of the Atlantic have witnessed the decline of the East's greatest saltwater sport fish, the striped bass. The rapid decline of this magnificent fish was assumed for a while to be the result of a natural cycle, and the fish was expected to bounce back in a few years. This hasn't happened, and some marine biologists now fear it never will. The reason: rising acidity in the estuaries of the Chesapeake Bay, premier spawning grounds for the striper. Those spawning grounds are now practically barren, not only of the bass but also of shad, herring, perch, and alewife. Why? Biologists have measured the pH of the freshwater streams and rivers (like the Potomac, Rappahannock, James, and York rivers) that flow into the Chesapeake and discovered that the water of these rivers is terribly acidic, with pH readings as low as 3.8. Fish eggs and larvae are sensitive to changes in the pH; the bass especially likes water that is alkaline (a pH of 8). Acid rain, falling on the coastal plain of Maryland, flows into the streams and creates acid surges that kill the eggs and larvae. Even when the river returns to normal alkalinity, the damage has been done.

The problem of acid lakes and rivers is not confined to the Maryland shore. In the Adirondack Mountains of New York, for example, fish have disappeared from more than 200 lakes due to acidification.

Human life may also be at direct risk. In June 1984, the Office of Technological Assessment concluded a three-year study and reported that clouds bearing acid rain and smog from air pollution could be killing as many as 50,000 Americans and Canadians a year. Most threatened, according to the report, are persons with heart and lung ailments. Both the EPA and utilities industries have contested these findings.

Southern California has a problem of its own, acid fog, which some environmental engineers think may have a greater net impact than acid rain. The fog, which is similar to fogs that contributed to more than 12,000 deaths in London during a three-month period in 1952, is most severe in the Los Angeles Basin and San Joaquin Valley.

## KEEPING AN EYE ON THE ENVIRONMENT

With the establishment of the EPA in 1970, the U.S. government began an active role in protection of the environment, setting and enforcing standards for the cleanliness of air and water. But how have the states responded to the challenge of safeguarding their natural resources?

According to a 1983 study by the Washington-based Conservation Foundation, the most environment-conscious states are Minnesota, California, New Jersey, Massachusetts, and Oregon, whereas the least are Alabama, Missouri, Mississippi, Idaho, and New Mexico. The report uses 23 criteria to judge the states, among them per capita spending on environmental quality control and parks; land-use planning; congressional voting records of state delegations on environmental and energy issues; and whether a state awards tax breaks for solar energy projects.

In general, the Conservation Foundation concludes, the states of New England, the Great Lakes, and the Pacific Coast deserve the highest marks for their efforts to improve and conserve the environment, and those in the South and the Rocky Mountain states the lowest.

Another finding of the study is that those states with stringent environmental laws are not alienating industry, as had been commonly anticipated; in fact, some have been successful in attracting it. The foundation could find no evidence that strict regulations have led to a "widespread exodus of American industry abroad" or even to other states "in search of pollution havens."

## Environmental Effort

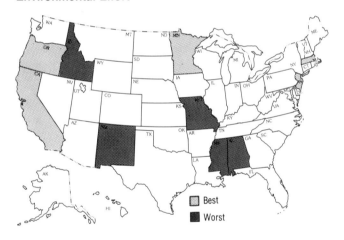

■ Best
■ Worst

### States Ranked for Environmental Effort, from Best to Worst

| | | |
|---|---|---|
| 1. Minnesota | 18. Michigan | 33. Tennessee |
| 2. California | 18. Ohio | |
| 3. New Jersey | 18. South Dakota | 33. Utah |
| 4. Massachusetts | | 33. West Virginia |
| 5. Oregon | 21. Delaware | 33. Wyoming |
| | 21. Iowa | 39. Nebraska |
| 6. Washington | 23. Illinois | 39. Nevada |
| 7. Maryland | 23. Pennsylvania | |
| 7. Montana | 23. Virginia | 39. North Dakota |
| 7. New York | | 39. Texas |
| 7. Wisconsin | 26. Arkansas | 43. Louisiana |
| | 27. Colorado | 43. New Hampshire |
| 11. Indiana | 27. Rhode Island | 45. Oklahoma |
| 12. Hawaii | 29. Georgia | |
| 12. Kentucky | 29. North Carolina | 46. New Mexico |
| 14. Connecticut | | 47. Idaho |
| 14. Maine | 29. South Carolina | 48. Mississippi |
| | 32. Arizona | 49. Missouri |
| 14. Vermont | 33. Alaska | 50. Alabama |
| 17. Florida | 33. Kansas | |

*Source:* Conservation Foundation, 1983.

## HAY FEVER SUFFERERS, TAKE NOTE

It doesn't come from hay, and it doesn't cause a fever, but that's not much consolation to the 18 million Americans afflicted with hay fever. Aside from the personal discomfort it causes, various government agencies estimate that it also results in more than five million workdays lost per year, at a price tag of more than $300 million.

Hay fever is any allergic reaction of the eyes, nose, or throat to certain airborne particles. These particles may be either pollen from seed-bearing trees, grasses, and weeds, or spores from certain molds. The term originated in Britain 150 years ago, when people assumed its feverlike symptoms had something to do with the fall haying. Most individuals might think that once they're into adulthood, they already know whether they have hay fever. But if you were to relocate, would you suddenly and mysteriously develop a continual running nose and minor sore throat? Allergy problems aren't always alleviated by relocation, and sometimes a new allergen—absent where you used to live—can turn up to cause you problems with hay fever.

The incidence of hay fever varies around the world. In the Arctic, for example, it doesn't exist. Because of low temperatures and poor soil, arctic plants are small and primitive. In the tropics and subtropics, there is very little hay fever because the plants are generally flowered and produce pollen that is so heavy it cannot become airborne.

It is in the temperate regions that one finds the greatest amounts of irritating pollen. The worst places in America for hay fever are the middle regions, where grasses and trees without flowers predominate. Because farming continually disrupts the soil and therefore encourages the growth of weeds (especially the most troublesome of them, ragweed), America's heartland is the most hay fever–ridden area. It extends from the Rockies to the Appalachian chain, and from the Canadian border down to the states of the mid-South.

Yet no area of the country except Alaska and the southern half of Florida is free from hay fever—it's simply a question of degree. The West Coast is almost ragweed-free, although it has other allergenic pollens.

Some places that were once havens for asthmatics and hay fever sufferers are now less free of allergens. Examples are many of the fast-growing areas of the Southwest. Thirty years ago, Tucson was virtually free of ragweed pollen. Its desert location precluded the growth of the weeds, grasses, and trees that cause hay fever. But as more and more people moved into the area, more trees were planted and lawns seeded. The result? A pollen index that's still good but not as good as it used to be.

The table on the next page shows the ragweed pollen index for a number of places around the country.

## Counting All Those Pollen Grains

The American Academy of Allergy has devised the Ragweed Pollen Index to indicate the local severity of the pollen problem. This index is derived from (1) length of the season, (2) concentration of pollen grains in the air at the season's peak, and (3) total pollen catch throughout the season. The higher the index number, the worse the problem; an index greater than 10 means lots of discomfort.

### Ragweed Pollen Index for Selected Places

| | | | | | | | |
|---|---|---|---|---|---|---|---|
| **Alabama** | | **Decatur** | 114.0 | **Missouri** | | **Oregon** | |
| Birmingham | 49.0 | East St. Louis | 100.0 | Kansas City | 109.0 | Corvallis | 0 |
| Mobile | 8.0 | Peoria | 122.0 | St. Louis | 78.0 | Portland | 0.5 |
| **Alaska** | | Quincy | 98.0 | **Montana** | | **Pennsylvania** | |
| All cities | 0 | Rockford | 96.0 | Glacier | | Altoona | 52.0 |
| **Arizona** | | Springfield | 72.0 | National Park | 0.1 | Erie | 65.0 |
| Phoenix | 0.2 | **Indiana** | | Yellowstone | | Philadelphia | 55.0 |
| Tucson | 2.0 | Evansville | 136.0 | National Park | 0.2 | Pittsburgh | 90.0 |
| **Arkansas** | | Fort Wayne | 107.0 | **Nebraska** | | **Rhode Island** | |
| Fort Smith | 103.0 | Gary | 62.0 | Lincoln | 63.0 | Providence | 26.0 |
| Little Rock | 62.0 | Indianapolis | 92.0 | North Platte | 13.0 | **South Carolina** | |
| **California** | | **Iowa** | | Omaha | 148.0 | Charleston | 11.0 |
| Alpine | 3.0 | Cedar Rapids | 122.0 | Scottsbluff | 38.0 | Columbia | 40.0 |
| Anaheim | 0.5 | Council Bluffs | 148.0 | **Nevada** | | **South Dakota** | |
| Los Angeles | 0.5 | Davenport | 113.0 | Reno | 0.1 | Aberdeen | 17.0 |
| Sacramento | 0.2 | Des Moines | 69.0 | **New Hampshire** | | Rapid City | 12.0 |
| San Diego | 11.0 | **Kansas** | | Concord | 7.0 | Sioux Falls | 52.0 |
| San Francisco | 0.2 | Kansas City | 101.0 | Conway | 3.0 | **Tennessee** | |
| Santa Barbara | 3.0 | Wichita | 58.0 | Manchester | 9.0 | Johnson City | 51.0 |
| **Colorado** | | **Kentucky** | | Nashua | 29.0 | Knoxville | 49.0 |
| Colorado Springs | 4.0 | Lexington | 151.0 | **New Jersey** | | Memphis | 73.0 |
| Denver | 19.0 | Louisville | 99.0 | Atlantic City | 30.0 | Nashville | 69.0 |
| **Connecticut** | | **Louisiana** | | New Brunswick | 60.0 | **Texas** | |
| Bridgeport | 23.0 | New Orleans | 43.0 | Newark | 18.0 | Amarillo | 41.0 |
| Hartford | 54.0 | Tallulah | 33.0 | Trenton | 26.0 | Brownsville | 24.0 |
| New Haven | 25.0 | **Maine** | | **New Mexico** | | Dallas | 115.0 |
| Waterbury | 27.0 | Lewiston | 13.0 | Albuquerque | 7.0 | El Paso | 15.0 |
| **Delaware** | | Portland | 24.0 | Roswell | 4.0 | Galveston | 36.0 |
| Wilmington | 54.0 | Presque Isle | 0.4 | **New York** | | Houston | 68.0 |
| **District** | | **Maryland** | | Albany | 48.0 | San Antonio | 16.0 |
| of Columbia | 42.0 | Baltimore | 51.0 | Binghamton | 31.0 | **Utah** | |
| **Florida** | | **Massachusetts** | | Buffalo | 59.0 | Salt Lake City | 8.0 |
| Bradenton | 4.0 | Amherst | 25.0 | Elmira | 43.0 | Zion National Park | 0.7 |
| Daytona Beach | 3.0 | Boston | 16.0 | Manhattan | 25.0 | **Vermont** | |
| Fort Lauderdale | 9.0 | Nantucket | 5.0 | Rochester | 60.0 | Burlington | 47.0 |
| Fort Myers | 0.2 | Springfield | 20.0 | Syracuse | 25.0 | **Virginia** | |
| Gainesville | 20.0 | Worcester | 9.0 | Tupper Lake | 8.0 | Charlottesville | 35.0 |
| Jacksonville | 6.0 | **Michigan** | | Utica | 26.0 | Norfolk | 54.0 |
| Melbourne | 21.0 | Ann Arbor | 119.0 | Yonkers | 38.0 | Richmond | 42.0 |
| Miami | 2.0 | Bay City | 72.0 | **North Carolina** | | Roanoke | 85.0 |
| Orlando | 3.0 | Charlevoix | 21.0 | Asheville | 57.0 | **Washington** | |
| Panama City | 32.0 | Detroit | 59.0 | Charlotte | 42.0 | Seattle | 0 |
| Pensacola | 10.0 | Escanaba | 57.0 | Raleigh | 28.0 | Spokane | 0.1 |
| Tallahassee | 6.0 | Flint | 76.0 | **North Dakota** | | Yakima | 0.2 |
| Tampa | 6.0 | Grand Rapids | 126.0 | Fargo | 125.0 | **West Virginia** | |
| West Palm Beach | 5.0 | Lansing | 94.0 | **Ohio** | | Charleston | 31.0 |
| **Georgia** | | Marquette | 12.0 | Akron | 100.0 | **Wisconsin** | |
| Atlanta | 24.0 | Saginaw | 72.0 | Cincinnati | 122.0 | Eagle River | 13.0 |
| Valdosta | 8.0 | **Minnesota** | | Cleveland | 56.0 | Madison | 93.0 |
| **Idaho** | | Duluth | 44.0 | Columbus | 75.0 | Milwaukee | 86.0 |
| Boise City | 5.0 | Minneapolis | 99.0 | Dayton | 90.0 | Sheboygan | 90.0 |
| **Illinois** | | Moorhead | 125.0 | Toledo | 122.0 | Superior | 44.0 |
| Bloomington | 122.0 | Rochester | 88.0 | Youngstown | 70.0 | **Wyoming** | |
| Champaign | 76.0 | **Mississippi** | | **Oklahoma** | | Lander | 23.0 |
| Chicago | 62.0 | Biloxi | 7.0 | Oklahoma City | 73.0 | | |
| | | Vicksburg | 33.0 | Tulsa | 65.0 | | |

*Source:* American Academy of Allergy, 1977.

No figures are given for Hawaii because the academy has no reporting stations there.

# Crime:

## Safe & Not-So-Safe Places

What are the odds that you'll be a victim of crime in the place you live? Obviously, vulnerability to crime varies enormously from metro area to metro area, just as it does among neighborhoods in the same city. Some places are so safe you couldn't pay someone to assault you, while others are just plain dangerous.

In Wheeling, West Virginia–Ohio, for example, the chances of your encountering violent crime—murder, rape, assault, or robbery—are only one in 806 over a year. But move to New York City and those odds skyrocket to one in 62 over the same period, making the Big Apple 13 times more violent than Wheeling.

Chances are that, for the near term at least, Wheeling will remain a safe place and New York a crime-ridden one. According to the FBI, crime rates do not shift significantly in any given place from year to year. Some of the other patterns in crime observed by the FBI in the past decade are the following:

- Rates of all types of crime are highest in big cities, lower in small and medium-sized towns, and lowest in rural areas.
- Criminal behavior is closely related to the economic status, age, race, and sex of given populations.
- High crime rates are associated with increasing populations and large numbers of transients. Conversely, low crime rates are often linked to steady or decreasing populations, even when coupled with adverse economic conditions.
- Incidence of most crimes peaks during the summer months, especially on weekends.
- Robbery, burglary, and larceny are more prevalent in big cities than elsewhere, and the overwhelming majority of these crimes are committed by people with criminal records.
- Murder and aggravated assault are often committed by people without criminal records, probably because they are usually unpremeditated crimes of passion.

### FACTORS LINKED WITH CRIME

What causes crime, and what can be done about it? The FBI has identified several basic factors that are linked with local crime rates:

*Population density,* as well as the overall size of the area's population. This factor does not appear to affect crime rate directly until population density becomes very high. Thus the high crime rate of a metropolitan area like Miami–Hialeah will be partially attributable to pockets of overcrowding, which can spawn violence. A government booklet entitled "City Size and Quality of Life" points out that most cities become ungovernable when their populations exceed about six million.

159

### Murder in America

The pattern of the murder rate in America, rather than reaching one level or gradually increasing or declining, is one of a wave, alternately rising and falling. What is the reason for this fluctuation?

According to C. Ray Jeffries, professor of criminology at the Criminal Justice School of Florida State University, the explanation can be found in a combination of factors. A great deal of variation in the murder rate can be chalked up to police reporting procedures, for example. As a result of improved reporting methods, more murders are reported now than earlier in the century.

Demography also plays a role in the murder rate, specifically the proportion of young men (aged roughly 16 to 21) to the general population. In times when that proportion is high, violent crime rates will also be high. Jeffries attributes the slight decline in murder over the last few years to a corresponding decline in the size of this violence-prone segment of the population.

Another factor is the social climate. With Prohibition came the rise of bootlegging and organized crime; the Depression meant unemployment, poverty, homelessness, and the destruction of family life and communities. It is not too surprising, then, that the murder rate showed a steady increase throughout the twenties and peaked during the height of the Depression. With World War II, unemployment was almost nonexistent—men were either in uniform or stoking the machine of wartime industry. There were almost no young men at home to boost the murder rate.

During the placid Eisenhower years the murder rate leveled out. But the turbulent sixties, a time of strife resulting from the push for civil rights and the controversy over the Vietnam War, and fueled by a surge in the number of teenaged men born of the baby boom, meant a murder rate that climbed to new heights.

When populations reach this level, the social fabric begins to break down.

*Composition* of the population, especially in regard to age, race, and sex. Minority-group men between the ages of 15 and 24 commit a large percentage of crimes. Members of this group who are poor or unemployed account for an even greater percentage. If a city has a large proportion of such individuals among its population, its crime rate will usually be high.

*Economic status* of the population, including job availability. High unemployment, especially when coupled with a large percentage of the population that is unskilled, poor, and uneducated, will result in unacceptably high crime. But unemployment and poverty alone do not predispose a region to crime. Many of the crime-free areas in America are poorer than average, with steady or declining populations. In addition, given similar sets of circumstances, rich people tend to be arrested less frequently than poor ones, especially on suspicion. Once arrested, they are convicted with less frequency. This is especially true in regard to property crimes and crimes committed by juveniles.

*Cultural conditions,* such as educational level and recreational and religious behavior.

*Transience.* One of the greatest deterrents to crime appears to be a strong neighborhood in which people know each other well and watch out for each other's safety and property, regardless of the amount of police protection in the area. This is why high transience rates, which indicate strangers living next to each other, are associated with high crime rates.

*Climate* has a marked relationship with criminal behavior. Crimes increase dramatically during certain weather phases, and violent crime in particular tends to be more frequent in warm climates than cold ones. All crimes except robbery occur most frequently in hot months (July and August) and least frequently in cold ones (January and February). Robbery, the exception, is highest in December, perhaps because during the holiday season pedestrians carrying large amounts of cash and stores doing brisk business make tempting targets.

Other factors the FBI has found to be related to crime rates include strength or weakness of the police force; the policies and attitudes of prosecuting officials, judges, juries, and parole boards; and the attitudes of the community toward crime and its tendency to report crime.

One common misperception about crime and crime prevention is that the safety of a community rises or falls in direct proportion to the size and strength of the local police force. Not so. Police definitely help to fight crime, but most of what police do is after the fact. They respond to complaints or tips; they search for offenders; they apprehend criminals and bring them to trial. A large number of police per capita is usually an

**U.S. Homicide Rate, 1900-1980**

Homicides per 100,000 population

Source: National Center for Health Statistics, *Vital Statistics of the United States.*

indication of a high-crime area rather than an area where crime is being prevented.

The crime rate of an area indicates more than how safe an individual may be there; along with rates of alcoholism, divorce, and suicide, it is one of four social indicators often cited by sociologists that help provide a rough gauge of a place's social solidarity. Areas with high crime rates tend to have a weak social fabric characterized by transience, poverty, and little sense of community. Low-crime areas, whether rich or poor, are generally characterized by some degree of community spirit and, above all, a willingness on the part of residents to watch out for each other's welfare.

## KEEPING TRACK OF CRIME

Every year the FBI collects from more than 15,000 police departments around the country the number of arrests for various crimes. Of all the crimes reported, there are eight that, because of their seriousness,

frequency, and likelihood of being reported to the police, have been chosen to serve as an index for determining crime trends across the nation. These compose the FBI's Crime Index:

| Violent Crimes | Property Crimes |
|---|---|
| murder | burglary |
| forcible rape | larceny-theft |
| robbery | motor vehicle theft |
| aggravated assault | arson |

Many crimes, of course, are never reported to the police, and this affects the accuracy of the Crime Index. And police departments, in turn, often underreport to the FBI to protect or improve their images. In all, it is estimated that only half of all crimes committed are reported to the FBI.

A necessary distinction to make is that between crime incidence and crime rate. The actual number of occurrences of a crime constitutes its *incidence*. For example, in the Pittsburgh metro area a total of 103 murders were committed in the year 1982 (the latest

---

### Violent vs. Property Crime

Violent crimes, which make up only 10 percent of total crime in the United States, involve bodily injury or the threat of injury. The FBI's Crime Index defines the following offenses as violent crimes: murder, forcible rape (including attempts to commit rape), robbery (which differs from burglary and larceny-theft in that its victims are threatened with harm if they do not surrender their property), and aggravated assault (an attack on a person with intent to kill or cause injury).

Below are the metro areas that in 1982 scored highest and lowest in overall violent crime. Seven of the ten most dangerous metro areas were found in the South or the West, and eight of the safest in the East North Central or West North Central regions.

commit a felony or theft), larceny-theft (which includes such diverse offenses as purse-snatching, pocket-picking, shoplifting, and bicycle theft), motor vehicle theft, and arson. Although arson was designated an Index crime in 1979, data on this crime are not yet available for the metro areas. For this reason *Places Rated Almanac* does not include arson in its survey of crime.

The following metro areas were the winners and losers in overall property crime in 1982. Again we see a preponderance of southern and western metro areas in the Most Dangerous list; mostly Middle Atlantic or East North Central metro areas are found under the heading Safest.

#### Violent Crime in the Metro Areas

| Safest Metro Areas | Violent Crime Rate | Most Dangerous Metro Areas | Violent Crime Rate |
|---|---|---|---|
| 1. St. Cloud, MN | 47 | 1. New York, NY | 1,782 |
| 2. Sheboygan, WI | 53 | 2. Miami–Hialeah, FL | 1,589 |
| 3. Bismarck, ND | 56 | 3. Los Angeles–Long Beach, CA | 1,270 |
| 4. Grand Forks, ND | 63 | 4. Baltimore, MD | 1,164 |
| 5. Eau Claire, WI | 87 | 5. Las Vegas, NV | 1,057 |
| 6. Rochester, MN | 89 | 6. New Orleans, LA | 1,007 |
| 7. Binghamton, NY | 94 | 7. West Palm Beach–Boca Raton–Delray Beach, FL | 995 |
| 8. Duluth, MN–WI | 101 | 8. Newark, NJ | 977 |
| 9. Appleton–Oshkosh–Neenah, WI | 106 | 9. San Francisco, CA | 968 |
| 9. Nashua, NH | 106 | 10. Orlando, FL | 956 |

*Source: FBI, Crimes by County—1982 (unpublished report), 1984.*

The FBI lists four offenses in the category of property crime: burglary (the unlawful entry of a building to

#### Property Crime in the Metro Areas

| Safest Metro Areas | Property Crime Rate | Most Dangerous Metro Areas | Property Crime Rate |
|---|---|---|---|
| 1. Johnstown, PA | 1,733 | 1. Atlantic City, NJ | 10,849 |
| 2. Beaver County, PA | 1,810 | 2. Odessa, TX | 10,014 |
| 3. Wheeling, WV–OH | 1,838 | 3. Las Cruces, NM | 9,271 |
| 4. Steubenville–Weirton, OH–WV | 2,292 | 4. Miami–Hialeah, FL | 8,701 |
| 5. Scranton–Wilkes-Barre, PA | 2,356 | 5. Las Vegas, NV | 8,557 |
| 6. Danville, VA | 2,378 | 6. West Palm Beach–Boca Raton–Delray Beach, FL | 7,882 |
| 7. Altoona, PA | 2,381 | 7. Savannah, GA | 7,797 |
| 8. Sharon, PA | 2,528 | 8. Stockton, CA | 7,713 |
| 9. Biloxi–Gulfport, MS | 2,589 | 9. Lubbock, TX | 7,670 |
| 10. Johnson City–Kingsport–Bristol, TN–VA | 2,630 | 10. Tucson, AZ | 7,582 |

*Source: FBI, Crimes by County—1982 (unpublished report), 1984.*

**Regional Crime Rates**

| Region | Violent Crime Rates | | | | Property Crime Rates | | |
|---|---|---|---|---|---|---|---|
| | Murder | Forcible Rape | Robbery | Aggravated Assault | Burglary | Larceny-Theft | Motor Vehicle Theft |
| **U.S. National Average** | 9.1 | 33.6 | 231.9 | 280.8 | 1,475.2 | 3,069.8 | 452.8 |
| **Northeast:** Maine, New Hampshire, Vermont, Massachusetts, Rhode Island, Connecticut | 7.4 | 25.4 | 348.5 | 257.5 | 1,366.0 | 2,664.3 | 626.8 |
| **Middle Atlantic:** New York, New Jersey, Pennsylvania | 8.6 | 26.4 | 409.9 | 266.0 | 1,375.8 | 2,648.2 | 605.8 |
| **East North Central:** Ohio, Indiana, Illinois, Michigan, Wisconsin | 7.2 | 29.1 | 185.9 | 221.2 | 1,294.4 | 3,000.9 | 445.6 |
| **West North Central:** Minnesota, Iowa, Missouri, North Dakota, South Dakota, Nebraska, Kansas | 4.8 | 21.1 | 104.2 | 169.7 | 1,138.7 | 2,746.4 | 238.9 |
| **South Atlantic:** District of Columbia, Delaware, Maryland, Virginia, West Virginia, North Carolina, South Carolina, Georgia, Florida | 10.9 | 37.4 | 214.7 | 376.0 | 1,503.3 | 3,201.0 | 312.3 |
| **East South Central:** Kentucky, Tennessee, Alabama, Mississippi | 10.7 | 27.6 | 121.7 | 220.2 | 1,197.7 | 2,279.1 | 261.2 |
| **West South Central:** Arkansas, Louisiana, Oklahoma, Texas | 14.7 | 41.2 | 194.8 | 302.4 | 1,687.0 | 3,047.3 | 484.0 |
| **Mountain:** Montana, Idaho, Wyoming, Colorado, New Mexico, Arizona, Utah, Nevada | 7.1 | 37.1 | 138.8 | 297.4 | 1,578.2 | 3,951.3 | 341.4 |
| **Pacific:** Washington, Oregon, California, Alaska, Hawaii | 9.7 | 49.2 | 313.4 | 343.3 | 1,936.2 | 3,833.7 | 578.6 |

*Source:* FBI, *Crime in the United States,* 1983.

Regions are those defined by the FBI. Figures are crime rates (incidence per 100,000 population) for 1982.

year for which complete FBI data are available). Therefore, Pittsburgh's incidence of murder is 103. Waco, Texas, had only 33 murders in the same year. Judging from these figures, you might think Pittsburgh is far more dangerous than Waco. However, more than two million people live in Pittsburgh, while only about 170,000 live in Waco.

The best way to compare places of different sizes is to look at the crime *rate,* which is the incidence of crime per year per 100,000 people. Calculating by this method yields a murder rate of 4.5 for Pittsburgh and a rate of 17.9 for Waco. The average murder rate for all U.S. metro areas is 10.0, so Pittsburgh, for all its reputation as a tough steel town, is actually twice as safe from murder as the average metro area, whereas Waco is just about twice as dangerous, a characteristic it shares with most metro areas in the Lone Star State.

The distribution of safe and dangerous places follows traditional patterns that any criminologist would recognize immediately. For example, the northern New England states record consistently low crime rates. Wheeling—ranked by *Places Rated* as the safest metro area in the nation—enjoys the generally favorable social indicators found in much of the Middle South.

At the other end of the spectrum, many of the country's most dangerous metro areas are located on the eastern coast from New Jersey southward. The reason? For one thing, all of these coastal areas have shown tremendous growth rates over the past 30 years. New people moving into an area disrupt neighborhoods and social patterns. Florida especially has had explosive increases in population—including many displaced Caribbean islanders—as has Texas. Both now suffer from the instability and crime that such growth can spawn.

But there are other reasons as well. Professional criminals gravitate to places where the living is easy and the pickings bountiful; they don't stay in the declining industrial towns of the North but head South to warm weather, popular resorts, and tourist towns. This is one reason Las Vegas and Miami–Hialeah have been plagued by high crime for decades.

## JUDGING SAFETY FROM CRIME

In *Places Rated*'s view, a basic flaw in the FBI's Crime Index totals is that they fail to differentiate adequately between property crimes and the less numerous, but far more serious, violent crimes. The most common crime by far is larceny-theft (stealing hubcaps is an example). Yet according to the FBI's statistical method for determining total crime rate, stealing hubcaps is counted as heavily as first-degree murder. This certainly doesn't allow for a realistic estimate of the relative danger levels in the United States.

Eugene–Springfield, Oregon, for instance, has a total crime rate of 6,504, roughly on a par with Lakeland–Winter Haven, Florida, at 6,510. But are the two metro areas equally dangerous? Not by a long shot. Lakeland–Winter Haven's violent crime rate is more than three times as high as Eugene–Springfield's (802 as compared with 249). Although the Oregon metro area has a relatively high property crime rate, it

nevertheless is a comparatively safe city—something you wouldn't guess from looking at its crime rate as shown in the FBI report.

The formula used to rate the 329 U.S. metro areas for safety is simple: *Places Rated Almanac* uses the FBI *Crimes by County* data for violent and property crimes, but since we consider property crimes much less serious than crimes against people, we give them one-tenth the weight of violent crimes. Each metro area starts with a base score of zero, and points are assigned according to the following indicators:

**Crime in the Metro Areas**

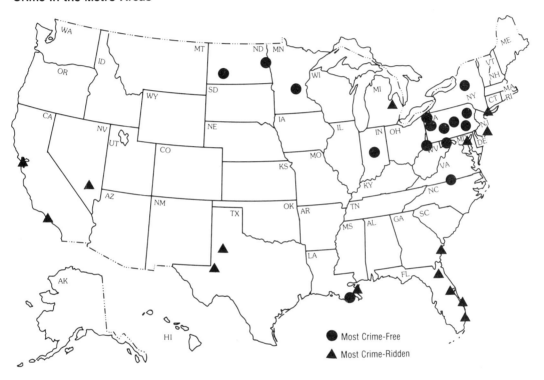

● Most Crime-Free
▲ Most Crime-Ridden

| Most Crime-Free Metro Areas | Places Rated Score | Most Crime-Ridden Metro Areas | Places Rated Score |
|---|---|---|---|
| 1. Wheeling, WV–OH | 308 | 1. New York, NY | 2,498 |
| 2. Beaver County, PA | 310 | 2. Miami–Hialeah, FL | 2,459 |
| 3. Cumberland, MD–WV | 337 | 3. Los Angeles–Long Beach, CA | 1,960 |
| 4. St. Cloud, MN | 343 | 4. Las Vegas, NV | 1,913 |
| 5. Johnstown, PA | 353 | 5. Atlantic City, NJ | 1,878 |
| 6. Scranton–Wilkes-Barre, PA | 372 | 6. West Palm Beach–Boca Raton–Delray Beach, FL | 1,783 |
| 7. Danville, VA | 379 | 7. Baltimore, MD | 1,730 |
| 8. Sharon, PA | 384 | 8. Odessa, TX | 1,698 |
| 9. Altoona, PA | 399 | 9. Orlando, FL | 1,671 |
| 10. Houma–Thibodaux, LA | 400 | 9. Flint, MI | 1,671 |
| 10. Utica–Rome, NY | 400 | 11. Gainesville, FL | 1,658 |
| 12. Grand Forks, ND | 401 | 12. San Francisco, CA | 1,619 |
| 13. Bismarck, ND | 413 | 13. Savannah, GA | 1,614 |
| 13. Kokomo, IN | 413 | 14. Lubbock, TX | 1,608 |
| 13. Lancaster, PA | 413 | 15. New Orleans, LA | 1,604 |

The Places Rated Score is the sum of the violent crime rate and one-tenth the property crime rate.

1. *Violent crime rate.* The rates for all violent crimes—murder, forcible rape, robbery, and aggravated assault—as reported by the FBI are totaled.
2. *Property crime rate.* The FBI rates for burglary, larceny-theft, and motor vehicle theft are added together; the result is divided by 10.

The sum of a metro area's violent crime rate and one-tenth its property crime rate, rounded off, represents the metro area's score. Each metro area's rates for specific crimes are given in the Place Profiles later in this chapter.

### Sample Comparison: Beaver County, Pennsylvania, and Miami–Hialeah, Florida

Beaver County, a residential metro area on Pennsylvania's western edge, ranks second for safety from crime according to the *Places Rated* formula. Adding its violent crime rate (129) to one-tenth its property crime rate (181) results in a total score of 310, second only to that of Wheeling, West Virginia–Ohio. In fact, Beaver County is just one of a handful of very safe places found near the junction of Pennsylvania, Ohio, and West Virginia. Altoona, Pennsylvania; Cumberland, Maryland–West Virginia; Johnstown, Pennsylvania; Steubenville–Weirton, Ohio–West Virginia; and Wheeling—all of which rank in the top 95 percent of the *Places Rated* universe—also profit from neighborhoods that are largely working class and untouched by the problems of urban communities.

In contrast, Miami–Hialeah has a crime score of 2,459, the sum of its violent crime rate (1,589) and one-tenth its property crime rate (870). Thus the Florida metro area ends up 328th overall, just ahead of last-place New York. This sorry finish is hardly surprising considering that Miami–Hialeah placed among the ten worst metro areas in six of the seven Index crimes. Beset by rapid population growth—an increase of some 28 percent between 1970 and 1980—and caught in the crosscurrents of the illegal drug trade, this resort metro area has a serious crime problem.

## Places Rated: Metro Areas Ranked for Safety from Crime

In ranking the 329 metro areas for relative safety, *Places Rated Almanac* uses two criteria: (1) violent crime rate and (2) property crime rate divided by 10. The sum of these rates, rounded off, is the metro area's score. The higher the score, the more dangerous the metro area. Places that receive tie scores are given the same rank and are listed in alphabetical order.

Those scores in parentheses—for Anchorage, Alaska, and Burlington, Vermont—were calculated by different means since data for these metro areas were not given in the FBI's 1984 *Crimes by County*. The figures for Anchorage are based on crime rates for 1982 within the city of Anchorage, whereas Burlington's represent average crime rates for the state of Vermont.

### Metro Areas from Safest to Most Dangerous

| Places Rated Rank | Places Rated Score | Places Rated Rank | Places Rated Score | Places Rated Rank | Places Rated Score |
|---|---|---|---|---|---|
| 1. Wheeling, WV–OH | 308 | 16. Binghamton, NY | 415 | 28. Provo–Orem, UT | 485 |
| 2. Beaver County, PA | 310 | 17. Steubenville–Weirton, OH–WV | 418 | 29. Duluth, MN–WI | 488 |
| 3. Cumberland, MD–WV | 337 | 18. Johnson City–Kingsport–Bristol, TN–VA | 424 | 29. Parkersburg–Marietta, WV–OH | 488 |
| 4. St. Cloud, MN | 343 | 19. Eau Claire, WI | 433 | | |
| 5. Johnstown, PA | 353 | 20. Rochester, MN | 437 | 31. Salem–Gloucester, MA | 490 |
| | | | | 32. Burlington, VT | (494) |
| 6. Scranton–Wilkes-Barre, PA | 372 | 21. York, PA | 440 | 33. Fargo–Moorhead, ND–MN | 503 |
| 7. Danville, VA | 379 | 22. Wausau, WI | 442 | 34. Allentown–Bethlehem, PA–NJ | 514 |
| 8. Sharon, PA | 384 | 23. Sheboygan, WI | 450 | 35. Florence, AL | 516 |
| 9. Altoona, PA | 399 | 24. Nashua, NH | 452 | | |
| 10. Houma–Thibodaux, LA | 400 | 25. Williamsport, PA | 464 | 36. Reading, PA | 522 |
| | | | | 37. Elkhart–Goshen, IN | 524 |
| 10. Utica–Rome, NY | 400 | | | 38. Appleton–Oshkosh–Neenah, WI | 525 |
| 12. Grand Forks, ND | 401 | 26. Lafayette, IN | 465 | | |
| 13. Bismarck, ND | 413 | 27. Portsmouth–Dover–Rochester, NH–ME | 475 | 39. State College, PA | 540 |
| 13. Kokomo, IN | 413 | | | 40. Fort Walton Beach, FL | 544 |
| 13. Lancaster, PA | 413 | | | | |

| Places Rated Rank | Places Rated Score | Places Rated Rank | Places Rated Score | Places Rated Rank | Places Rated Score |
|---|---|---|---|---|---|
| 41. Bristol, CT | 545 | 96. Charlottesville, VA | 756 | 153. Kenosha, WI | 911 |
| 41. Fayetteville–Springdale, AR | 545 | 97. Sioux City, IA–NE | 759 | 154. Santa Rosa–Petaluma, CA | 912 |
| 43. Danbury, CT | 548 | 98. Lewiston–Auburn, ME | 764 | 155. Peoria, IL | 921 |
| 44. Sioux Falls, SD | 556 | 99. Hickory, NC | 765 | | |
| 45. Asheville, NC | 566 | 100. Brazoria, TX | 768 | 156. Abilene, TX | 923 |
| | | | | 157. Huntsville, AL | 924 |
| 45. Nassau–Suffolk, NY | 566 | 101. Niagara Falls, NY | 775 | 158. Dothan, AL | 930 |
| 47. Glens Falls, NY | 568 | 102. Madison, WI | 779 | 159. Athens, GA | 933 |
| 47. Owensboro, KY | 568 | 102. Richland–Kennewick– | | 160. Louisville, KY–IN | 937 |
| 49. Dubuque, IA | 571 | Pasco, WA | 779 | | |
| 50. Elmira, NY | 582 | 104. Macon–Warner Robins, GA | 783 | 161. Youngstown–Warren, OH | 938 |
| | | 104. Muncie, IN | 783 | 162. Sarasota, FL | 939 |
| 51. Green Bay, WI | 583 | | | 163. Bridgeport–Milford, CT | 943 |
| 52. Pascagoula, MS | 591 | 106. Roanoke, VA | 784 | 164. Chattanooga, TN–GA | 946 |
| 53. Lorain–Elyria, OH | 609 | 107. Fort Myers, FL | 787 | 165. Chico, CA | 947 |
| 54. Albany–Schenectady– | | 108. Lincoln, NE | 789 | | |
| Troy, NY | 610 | 108. Waterbury, CT | 789 | 166. Grand Rapids, MI | 952 |
| 55. Knoxville, TN | 622 | 110. Oxnard–Ventura, CA | 791 | 167. Tyler, TX | 955 |
| | | | | 168. Monroe, LA | 957 |
| 56. Norwalk, CT | 625 | 111. Great Falls, MT | 792 | 169. Santa Cruz, CA | 964 |
| 57. Hagerstown, MD | 627 | 112. Orange County, NY | 804 | 169. Vallejo–Fairfield–Napa, CA | 964 |
| 58. Joplin, MO | 628 | 113. Billings, MT | 810 | | |
| 59. Harrisburg–Lebanon–Carlisle, | | 113. Biloxi–Gulfport, MS | 810 | 171. Greensboro–Winston-Salem– | |
| PA | 629 | 115. Montgomery, AL | 815 | High Point, NC | 967 |
| 60. Terre Haute, IN | 630 | | | 171. Jacksonville, NC | 967 |
| | | 116. Lowell, MA–NH | 819 | 173. St. Joseph, MO | 969 |
| 61. Manchester, NH | 633 | 116. Monmouth–Ocean, NJ | 819 | 173. Salt Lake City–Ogden, UT | 969 |
| 61. New London–Norwich, | | 118. Columbus, GA–AL | 820 | 175. Albany, GA | 970 |
| CT–RI | 633 | 119. Aurora–Elgin, IL | 821 | | |
| 61. Poughkeepsie, NY | 633 | 120. Lake County, IL | 822 | 176. Buffalo, NY | 971 |
| 64. Erie, PA | 635 | | | 177. Brownsville–Harlingen, TX | 974 |
| 65. Pittsfield, MA | 638 | 120. Texarkana, TX–Texarkana, | 822 | 178. Anderson, SC | 975 |
| | | AR | | 179. Kankakee, IL | 976 |
| 66. Lynchburg, VA | 643 | 122. Portland, ME | 823 | 179. Longview–Marshall, TX | 976 |
| 67. Middletown, CT | 646 | 123. Bellingham, WA | 825 | | |
| 68. Canton, OH | 650 | 124. Milwaukee, WI | 826 | 181. Cincinnati, OH–KY–IN | 978 |
| 69. Bangor, ME | 651 | 125. Iowa City, IA | 830 | 182. Raleigh–Durham, NC | 981 |
| 69. Bremerton, WA | 651 | | | 183. Anaheim–Santa Ana, CA | 983 |
| | | 126. Davenport–Rock Island– | | 184. Nashville, TN | 984 |
| 71. Fitchburg–Leominster, MA | 655 | Moline, IA–IL | 834 | 185. Casper, WY | 989 |
| 72. Bloomington, IN | 657 | 127. Stamford, CT | 835 | | |
| 73. Fort Smith, AR–OK | 663 | 128. McAllen–Edinburg– | | 186. Greeley, CO | 994 |
| 74. Huntington–Ashland, | | Mission, TX | 836 | 187. Gary–Hammond, IN | 996 |
| WV–KY–OH | 665 | 129. Joliet, IL | 837 | 188. Norfolk–Virginia Beach– | |
| 75. Bloomington–Normal, IL | 673 | 130. Enid, OK | 845 | Newport News, VA | 997 |
| | | | | 189. Providence, RI | 998 |
| 76. La Crosse, WI | 676 | 131. Lima, OH | 855 | 189. Toledo, OH | 998 |
| 77. Worcester, MA | 680 | 132. Bergen–Passaic, NJ | 857 | | |
| 78. Pittsburgh, PA | 687 | 133. Janesville–Beloit, WI | 858 | 191. Topeka, KS | 999 |
| 79. Syracuse, NY | 689 | 134. Fall River, MA–RI | 861 | 192. Indianapolis, IN | 1,000 |
| 80. Middlesex–Somerset– | | 135. Evansville, IN–KY | 864 | 193. Omaha, NE–IA | 1,008 |
| Hunterdon, NJ | 691 | | | 194. New Bedford, MA | 1,012 |
| | | 136. Spokane, WA | 869 | 195. Salem, OR | 1,014 |
| 81. Waterloo–Cedar Falls, IA | 700 | 137. Augusta, GA–SC | 872 | | |
| 82. Alton–Granite City, IL | 706 | 138. Eugene–Springfield, OR | 874 | 195. Tuscaloosa, AL | 1,014 |
| 83. Burlington, NC | 707 | 139. Anderson, IN | 878 | 197. Bryan–College Station, TX | 1,016 |
| 84. Fort Wayne, IN | 710 | 140. Boise City, ID | 880 | 198. Lawrence, KS | 1,018 |
| 85. Cedar Rapids, IA | 714 | | | 199. Jackson, MI | 1,021 |
| | | 141. Akron, OH | 886 | 200. Champaign–Urbana– | |
| 86. Charleston, WV | 721 | 142. Honolulu, HI | 891 | Rantoul, IL | 1,022 |
| 87. Alexandria, LA | 727 | 143. Hamilton–Middletown, OH | 892 | | |
| 88. Medford, OR | 728 | 143. Redding, CA | 892 | 201. Santa Barbara–Santa | |
| 89. Killeen–Temple, TX | 733 | 143. Springfield, MO | 892 | Maria–Lompoc, CA | 1,026 |
| 90. Clarksville–Hopkinsville, | | | | 202. Lafayette, LA | 1,030 |
| TN–KY | 736 | 146. New Haven–Meriden, CT | 893 | 203. Battle Creek, MI | 1,031 |
| | | 147. Lansing–East Lansing, MI | 894 | 204. San Angelo, TX | 1,032 |
| 91. Fort Collins–Loveland, CO | 744 | 147. Rochester, NY | 894 | 205. Chicago, IL | 1,034 |
| 91. Pawtucket–Woonsocket– | | 149. Decatur, IL | 897 | | |
| Attleboro, RI–MA | 744 | 150. New Britain, CT | 903 | 206. Sherman–Denison, TX | 1,035 |
| 93. Gadsden, AL | 749 | | | 207. South Bend–Mishawaka, IN | 1,038 |
| 94. Olympia, WA | 752 | 151. Minneapolis–St. Paul, MN–WI | 906 | 208. Melbourne–Titusville–Palm | |
| 94. Vancouver, WA | 752 | 152. Lawrence–Haverhill, MA–NH | 909 | Bay, FL | 1,039 |

| Places Rated Rank | Places Rated Score | Places Rated Rank | Places Rated Score | Places Rated Rank | Places Rated Score |
|---|---|---|---|---|---|
| 209. Des Moines, IA | 1,044 | 250. Wichita, KS | 1,164 | 290. Tucson, AZ | 1,400 |
| 210. Austin, TX | 1,049 | | | | |
| | | 251. Midland, TX | 1,166 | 291. Fort Pierce, FL | 1,422 |
| 211. Laredo, TX | 1,050 | 251. Waco, TX | 1,166 | 292. Wilmington, NC | 1,423 |
| 212. Lexington–Fayette, KY | 1,055 | 253. Pine Bluff, AR | 1,169 | 293. Jersey City, NJ | 1,434 |
| 212. Racine, WI | 1,055 | 254. Seattle, WA | 1,170 | 294. Las Cruces, NM | 1,457 |
| 214. Philadelphia, PA–NJ | 1,059 | 255. Wichita Falls, TX | 1,179 | 295. Newark, NJ | 1,461 |
| 215. Columbia, MO | 1,065 | | | | |
| | | 255. Yuba City, CA | 1,179 | 296. Kansas City, MO | 1,468 |
| 215. San Jose, CA | 1,065 | 257. Pueblo, CO | 1,181 | 297. Pensacola, FL | 1,472 |
| 217. Ann Arbor, MI | 1,067 | 257. Trenton, NJ | 1,181 | 298. Riverside–San Bernardino, CA | 1,475 |
| 218. Saginaw–Bay City–Midland, MI | 1,068 | 259. Greenville–Spartanburg, SC | 1,185 | 299. Albuquerque, NM | 1,483 |
| 219. Mansfield, OH | 1,072 | 260. Benton Harbor, MI | 1,190 | 299. Fresno, CA | 1,483 |
| 220. Amarillo, TX | 1,073 | | | | |
| | | 261. San Antonio, TX | 1,197 | 301. Memphis, TN–AR–MS | 1,488 |
| 221. Richmond–Petersburg, VA | 1,076 | 261. Shreveport, LA | 1,197 | 302. Tampa–St. Petersburg–Clearwater, FL | 1,493 |
| 222. Tulsa, OK | 1,080 | 263. Jacksonville, FL | 1,211 | 303. Charleston, SC | 1,495 |
| 223. Colorado Springs, CO | 1,086 | 264. Springfield, MA | 1,212 | 304. Houston, TX | 1,499 |
| 224. Boulder–Longmont, CO | 1,088 | 265. Galveston–Texas City, TX | 1,213 | 305. Portland, OR | 1,504 |
| 225. Jackson, MS | 1,091 | | | | |
| | | 266. Boston, MA | 1,215 | 306. Mobile, AL | 1,511 |
| 226. Columbus, OH | 1,092 | 267. Anchorage, AK | (1,223) | 307. Columbia, SC | 1,524 |
| 226. Victoria, TX | 1,092 | 268. Springfield, IL | 1,225 | 308. Dallas, TX | 1,529 |
| 228. Bradenton, FL | 1,093 | 269. Phoenix, AZ | 1,268 | 309. Oakland, CA | 1,533 |
| 228. Lake Charles, LA | 1,093 | 270. Charlotte–Gastonia–Rock Hill, NC–SC | 1,273 | 310. Fort Lauderdale–Hollywood–Pompano Beach, FL | 1,536 |
| 230. East St. Louis–Belleville, IL | 1,096 | | | | |
| | | 271. Hartford, CT | 1,279 | 311. Muskegon, MI | 1,537 |
| 231. San Diego, CA | 1,099 | 272. Oklahoma City, OK | 1,297 | 312. Bakersfield, CA | 1,561 |
| 232. Yakima, WA | 1,106 | 273. St. Louis, MO–IL | 1,306 | 313. Baton Rouge, LA | 1,565 |
| 233. Salinas–Seaside–Monterey, CA | 1,107 | 274. Atlanta, GA | 1,308 | 314. Detroit, MI | 1,587 |
| 234. Wilmington, DE–NJ–MD | 1,115 | 275. Beaumont–Port Arthur, TX | 1,313 | 315. New Orleans, LA | 1,604 |
| 235. Reno, NV | 1,116 | | | | |
| | | 276. Washington, DC–MD–VA | 1,317 | 316. Lubbock, TX | 1,608 |
| 236. Kalamazoo, MI | 1,120 | 277. El Paso, TX | 1,323 | 317. Savannah, GA | 1,614 |
| 237. Birmingham, AL | 1,123 | 278. Ocala, FL | 1,327 | 318. San Francisco, CA | 1,619 |
| 238. Anniston, AL | 1,125 | 279. Little Rock–North Little Rock, AR | 1,328 | 319. Gainesville, FL | 1,658 |
| 239. Visalia–Tulare–Porterville, CA | 1,132 | 280. Florence, SC | 1,334 | 320. Flint, MI | 1,671 |
| 240. Vineland–Millville–Bridgeton, NJ | 1,135 | | | | |
| | | 281. Corpus Christi, TX | 1,335 | 320. Orlando, FL | 1,671 |
| | | 282. Brockton, MA | 1,336 | 322. Odessa, TX | 1,698 |
| 241. Cleveland, OH | 1,138 | 283. Panama City, FL | 1,344 | 323. Baltimore, MD | 1,730 |
| 242. Kansas City, KS | 1,142 | 284. Daytona Beach, FL | 1,347 | 324. West Palm Beach–Boca Raton–Delray Beach, FL | 1,783 |
| 243. Fayetteville, NC | 1,150 | 285. Fort Worth–Arlington, TX | 1,348 | 325. Atlantic City, NJ | 1,878 |
| 244. Dayton–Springfield, OH | 1,151 | | | | |
| 245. Modesto, CA | 1,154 | 286. Sacramento, CA | 1,363 | 326. Las Vegas, NV | 1,913 |
| | | 287. Denver, CO | 1,365 | 327. Los Angeles–Long Beach, CA | 1,960 |
| 246. Lawton, OK | 1,156 | 288. Lakeland–Winter Haven, FL | 1,373 | 328. Miami–Hialeah, FL | 2,459 |
| 246. Rockford, IL | 1,156 | 289. Stockton, CA | 1,395 | 329. New York, NY | 2,498 |
| 248. Tallahassee, FL | 1,161 | | | | |
| 249. Tacoma, WA | 1,162 | | | | |

## Metro Areas Listed Alphabetically

| Metro Area | Places Rated Rank | Metro Area | Places Rated Rank | Metro Area | Places Rated Rank |
|---|---|---|---|---|---|
| Abilene, TX | 156 | Anaheim–Santa Ana, CA | 183 | Atlantic City, NJ | 325 |
| Akron, OH | 141 | Anchorage, AK | 267 | Augusta, GA–SC | 137 |
| Albany, GA | 175 | Anderson, IN | 139 | Aurora–Elgin, IL | 119 |
| Albany–Schenectady–Troy, NY | 54 | Anderson, SC | 178 | Austin, TX | 210 |
| Albuquerque, NM | 299 | Ann Arbor, MI | 217 | Bakersfield, CA | 312 |
| Alexandria, LA | 87 | Anniston, AL | 238 | Baltimore, MD | 323 |
| Allentown–Bethlehem, PA–NJ | 34 | Appleton–Oshkosh–Neenah, WI | 38 | Bangor, ME | 69 |
| Alton–Granite City, IL | 82 | Asheville, NC | 45 | Baton Rouge, LA | 313 |
| Altoona, PA | 9 | Athens, GA | 159 | Battle Creek, MI | 203 |
| Amarillo, TX | 220 | Atlanta, GA | 274 | Beaumont–Port Arthur, TX | 275 |

| Metro Area | Places Rated Rank | Metro Area | Places Rated Rank | Metro Area | Places Rated Rank |
|---|---|---|---|---|---|
| Beaver County, PA | 2 | East St. Louis–Belleville, IL | 230 | Johnstown, PA | 5 |
| Bellingham, WA | 123 | | | Joliet, IL | 129 |
| Benton Harbor, MI | 260 | Eau Claire, WI | 19 | Joplin, MO | 58 |
| Bergen–Passaic, NJ | 132 | El Paso, TX | 277 | Kalamazoo, MI | 236 |
| Billings, MT | 113 | Elkhart–Goshen, IN | 37 | | |
| | | Elmira, NY | 50 | Kankakee, IL | 179 |
| Biloxi–Gulfport, MS | 113 | Enid, OK | 130 | Kansas City, KS | 242 |
| Binghamton, NY | 16 | | | Kansas City, MO | 296 |
| Birmingham, AL | 237 | Erie, PA | 64 | Kenosha, WI | 153 |
| Bismarck, ND | 13 | Eugene–Springfield, OR | 138 | Killeen–Temple, TX | 89 |
| Bloomington, IN | 72 | Evansville, IN–KY | 135 | | |
| | | Fall River, MA–RI | 134 | Knoxville, TN | 55 |
| Bloomington–Normal, IL | 75 | Fargo–Moorhead, ND–MN | 33 | Kokomo, IN | 13 |
| Boise City, ID | 140 | | | La Crosse, WI | 76 |
| Boston, MA | 266 | Fayetteville, NC | 243 | Lafayette, IN | 26 |
| Boulder–Longmont, CO | 224 | Fayetteville–Springdale, AR | 41 | Lafayette, LA | 202 |
| Bradenton, FL | 228 | Fitchburg–Leominster, MA | 71 | | |
| | | Flint, MI | 320 | Lake Charles, LA | 228 |
| Brazoria, TX | 100 | Florence, AL | 35 | Lake County, IL | 120 |
| Bremerton, WA | 69 | | | Lakeland–Winter Haven, FL | 288 |
| Bridgeport–Milford, CT | 163 | Florence, SC | 280 | Lancaster, PA | 13 |
| Bristol, CT | 41 | Fort Collins–Loveland, CO | 91 | Lansing–East Lansing, MI | 147 |
| Brockton, MA | 282 | Fort Lauderdale–Hollywood– Pompano Beach, FL | 310 | Laredo, TX | 211 |
| Brownsville–Harlingen, TX | 177 | Fort Myers, FL | 107 | Las Cruces, NM | 294 |
| Bryan–College Station, TX | 197 | Fort Pierce, FL | 291 | Las Vegas, NV | 326 |
| Buffalo, NY | 176 | | | Lawrence, KS | 198 |
| Burlington, NC | 83 | Fort Smith, AR–OK | 73 | Lawrence–Haverhill, MA–NH | 152 |
| Burlington, VT | 32 | Fort Walton Beach, FL | 40 | | |
| | | Fort Wayne, IN | 84 | Lawton, OK | 246 |
| Canton, OH | 68 | Fort Worth–Arlington, TX | 285 | Lewiston–Auburn, ME | 98 |
| Casper, WY | 185 | Fresno, CA | 299 | Lexington–Fayette, KY | 212 |
| Cedar Rapids, IA | 85 | | | Lima, OH | 131 |
| Champaign–Urbana–Rantoul, IL | 200 | Gadsden, AL | 93 | Lincoln, NE | 108 |
| Charleston, SC | 303 | Gainesville, FL | 319 | | |
| | | Galveston–Texas City, TX | 265 | Little Rock–North Little Rock, AR | 279 |
| Charleston, WV | 86 | Gary–Hammond, IN | 187 | Longview–Marshall, TX | 179 |
| Charlotte–Gastonia–Rock Hill, NC–SC | 270 | Glens Falls, NY | 47 | Lorain–Elyria, OH | 53 |
| Charlottesville, VA | 96 | Grand Forks, ND | 12 | Los Angeles–Long Beach, CA | 327 |
| Chattanooga, TN–GA | 164 | Grand Rapids, MI | 166 | Louisville, KY–IN | 160 |
| Chicago, IL | 205 | Great Falls, MT | 111 | | |
| | | Greeley, CO | 186 | Lowell, MA–NH | 116 |
| Chico, CA | 165 | Green Bay, WI | 51 | Lubbock, TX | 316 |
| Cincinnati, OH–KY–IN | 181 | | | Lynchburg, VA | 66 |
| Clarksville–Hopkinsville, TN–KY | 90 | Greensboro–Winston-Salem– High Point, NC | 171 | Macon–Warner Robins, GA | 104 |
| Cleveland, OH | 241 | Greenville–Spartanburg, SC | 259 | Madison, WI | 102 |
| Colorado Springs, CO | 223 | Hagerstown, MD | 57 | | |
| | | Hamilton–Middletown, OH | 143 | Manchester, NH | 61 |
| Columbia, MO | 215 | Harrisburg–Lebanon–Carlisle, PA | 59 | Mansfield, OH | 219 |
| Columbia, SC | 307 | | | McAllen–Edinburg–Mission, TX | 128 |
| Columbus, GA–AL | 118 | Hartford, CT | 271 | Medford, OR | 88 |
| Columbus, OH | 226 | Hickory, NC | 99 | Melbourne–Titusville–Palm Bay, FL | 208 |
| Corpus Christi, TX | 281 | Honolulu, HI | 142 | | |
| | | Houma–Thibodaux, LA | 10 | Memphis, TN–AR–MS | 301 |
| Cumberland, MD–WV | 3 | Houston, TX | 304 | Miami–Hialeah, FL | 328 |
| Dallas, TX | 308 | | | Middlesex–Somerset–Hunterdon, NJ | 80 |
| Danbury, CT | 43 | Huntington–Ashland, WV–KY–OH | 74 | Middletown, CT | 67 |
| Danville, VA | 7 | Huntsville, AL | 157 | Midland, TX | 251 |
| Davenport–Rock Island–Moline, IA–IL | 126 | Indianapolis, IN | 192 | | |
| | | Iowa City, IA | 125 | Milwaukee, WI | 124 |
| Dayton–Springfield, OH | 244 | Jackson, MI | 199 | Minneapolis–St. Paul, MN–WI | 151 |
| Daytona Beach, FL | 284 | | | Mobile, AL | 306 |
| Decatur, IL | 149 | Jackson, MS | 225 | Modesto, CA | 245 |
| Denver, CO | 287 | Jacksonville, FL | 263 | Monmouth–Ocean, NJ | 116 |
| Des Moines, IA | 209 | Jacksonville, NC | 171 | | |
| | | Janesville–Beloit, WI | 133 | Monroe, LA | 168 |
| Detroit, MI | 314 | Jersey City, NJ | 293 | Montgomery, AL | 115 |
| Dothan, AL | 158 | | | Muncie, IN | 104 |
| Dubuque, IA | 49 | Johnson City–Kingsport–Bristol, TN–VA | 18 | Muskegon, MI | 311 |
| Duluth, MN–WI | 29 | | | Nashua, NH | 24 |

| Metro Area | Places Rated Rank |
|---|---|
| Nashville, TN | 184 |
| Nassau–Suffolk, NY | 45 |
| New Bedford, MA | 194 |
| New Britain, CT | 150 |
| New Haven–Meriden, CT | 146 |
| New London–Norwich, CT–RI | 61 |
| New Orleans, LA | 315 |
| New York, NY | 329 |
| Newark, NJ | 295 |
| Niagara Falls, NY | 101 |
| Norfolk–Virginia Beach–Newport News, VA | 188 |
| Norwalk, CT | 56 |
| Oakland, CA | 309 |
| Ocala, FL | 278 |
| Odessa, TX | 322 |
| Oklahoma City, OK | 272 |
| Olympia, WA | 94 |
| Omaha, NE–IA | 193 |
| Orange County, NY | 112 |
| Orlando, FL | 320 |
| Owensboro, KY | 47 |
| Oxnard–Ventura, CA | 110 |
| Panama City, FL | 283 |
| Parkersburg–Marietta, WV–OH | 29 |
| Pascagoula, MS | 52 |
| Pawtucket–Woonsocket–Attleboro, RI–MA | 91 |
| Pensacola, FL | 297 |
| Peoria, IL | 155 |
| Philadelphia, PA–NJ | 214 |
| Phoenix, AZ | 269 |
| Pine Bluff, AR | 253 |
| Pittsburgh, PA | 78 |
| Pittsfield, MA | 65 |
| Portland, ME | 122 |
| Portland, OR | 305 |
| Portsmouth–Dover–Rochester, NH–ME | 27 |
| Poughkeepsie, NY | 61 |
| Providence, RI | 189 |
| Provo–Orem, UT | 28 |
| Pueblo, CO | 257 |
| Racine, WI | 212 |

| Metro Area | Places Rated Rank |
|---|---|
| Raleigh–Durham, NC | 182 |
| Reading, PA | 36 |
| Redding, CA | 143 |
| Reno, NV | 235 |
| Richland–Kennewick–Pasco, WA | 102 |
| Richmond–Petersburg, VA | 221 |
| Riverside–San Bernardino, CA | 298 |
| Roanoke, VA | 106 |
| Rochester, MN | 20 |
| Rochester, NY | 147 |
| Rockford, IL | 246 |
| Sacramento, CA | 286 |
| Saginaw–Bay City–Midland, MI | 218 |
| St. Cloud, MN | 4 |
| St. Joseph, MO | 173 |
| St. Louis, MO–IL | 273 |
| Salem, OR | 195 |
| Salem–Gloucester, MA | 31 |
| Salinas–Seaside–Monterey, CA | 233 |
| Salt Lake City–Ogden, UT | 173 |
| San Angelo, TX | 204 |
| San Antonio, TX | 261 |
| San Diego, CA | 231 |
| San Francisco, CA | 318 |
| San Jose, CA | 215 |
| Santa Barbara–Santa Maria–Lompoc, CA | 201 |
| Santa Cruz, CA | 169 |
| Santa Rosa–Petaluma, CA | 154 |
| Sarasota, FL | 162 |
| Savannah, GA | 317 |
| Scranton–Wilkes-Barre, PA | 6 |
| Seattle, WA | 254 |
| Sharon, PA | 8 |
| Sheboygan, WI | 23 |
| Sherman–Denison, TX | 206 |
| Shreveport, LA | 261 |
| Sioux City, IA–NE | 97 |
| Sioux Falls, SD | 44 |
| South Bend–Mishawaka, IN | 207 |
| Spokane, WA | 136 |
| Springfield, IL | 268 |
| Springfield, MA | 264 |

| Metro Area | Places Rated Rank |
|---|---|
| Springfield, MO | 143 |
| Stamford, CT | 127 |
| State College, PA | 39 |
| Steubenville–Weirton, OH–WV | 17 |
| Stockton, CA | 289 |
| Syracuse, NY | 79 |
| Tacoma, WA | 249 |
| Tallahassee, FL | 248 |
| Tampa–St. Petersburg–Clearwater, FL | 302 |
| Terre Haute, IN | 60 |
| Texarkana, TX–Texarkana, AR | 120 |
| Toledo, OH | 189 |
| Topeka, KS | 191 |
| Trenton, NJ | 257 |
| Tucson, AZ | 290 |
| Tulsa, OK | 222 |
| Tuscaloosa, AL | 195 |
| Tyler, TX | 167 |
| Utica–Rome, NY | 10 |
| Vallejo–Fairfield–Napa, CA | 169 |
| Vancouver, WA | 94 |
| Victoria, TX | 226 |
| Vineland–Millville–Bridgeton, NJ | 240 |
| Visalia–Tulare–Porterville, CA | 239 |
| Waco, TX | 251 |
| Washington, DC–MD–VA | 276 |
| Waterbury, CT | 108 |
| Waterloo–Cedar Falls, IA | 81 |
| Wausau, WI | 22 |
| West Palm Beach–Boca Raton–Delray Beach, FL | 324 |
| Wheeling, WV–OH | 1 |
| Wichita, KS | 250 |
| Wichita Falls, TX | 255 |
| Williamsport, PA | 25 |
| Wilmington, DE–NJ–MD | 234 |
| Wilmington, NC | 292 |
| Worcester, MA | 77 |
| Yakima, WA | 232 |
| York, PA | 21 |
| Youngstown–Warren, OH | 161 |
| Yuba City, CA | 255 |

## Place Profiles: Crime Rates in 329 Metro Areas

The following charts detail each metro area's rates for seven FBI Crime Index offenses: murder, forcible rape, robbery, aggravated assault, burglary, larceny-theft, and motor vehicle theft. These offenses are divided into violent and property crimes, and a total rate for each of these categories is also given.

All figures are from the FBI's *Crimes by County—1982*, 1984. Two metro areas were not included in this

work: Anchorage, Alaska, and Burlington, Vermont. The crime rates given for Anchorage, therefore, are for the city of Anchorage, and those given for Burlington are the statewide averages. Both these metro areas' rates appear in parentheses.

A star preceding a metro area's name highlights that metro area as one of the top 25 places for safety from crime.

| | Violent Crime Rates | | | | | Property Crime Rates | | | | | | |
|---|---|---|---|---|---|---|---|---|---|---|---|---|
| | Murder | Forcible Rape | Robbery | Aggravated Assault | Total | Burglary | Larceny-Theft | Motor Vehicle Theft | Total | Places Rated Score | Places Rated Rank |
| Metro Area Average | 10.0 | 39.2 | 298.6 | 314.7 | 663 | 1,669.5 | 3,436.3 | 554.3 | 5,660 | 1,229 | — |
| Abilene, TX | 11.7 | 55.2 | 116.3 | 233.4 | 417 | 1,205.7 | 3,557.6 | 301.2 | 5,065 | 923 | 156 |
| Akron, OH | 3.9 | 39.3 | 133.2 | 201.9 | 378 | 1,203.7 | 3,556.8 | 316.1 | 5,077 | 886 | 141 |
| Albany, GA | 17.1 | 81.1 | 116.0 | 203.9 | 418 | 1,830.1 | 3,465.7 | 223.5 | 5,519 | 970 | 175 |
| Albany–Schenectady–Troy, NY | 2.5 | 14.2 | 69.1 | 185.6 | 271 | 1,097.7 | 2,149.0 | 138.7 | 3,385 | 610 | 54 |
| Albuquerque, NM | 9.0 | 59.1 | 232.3 | 479.8 | 780 | 2,145.5 | 4,513.4 | 371.6 | 7,031 | 1,483 | 299 |
| Alexandria, LA | 10.0 | 15.0 | 55.8 | 205.3 | 286 | 1,270.0 | 2,936.4 | 202.5 | 4,409 | 727 | 87 |
| Allentown–Bethlehem, PA–NJ | 4.1 | 16.4 | 72.6 | 101.9 | 195 | 870.6 | 2,173.8 | 146.8 | 3,191 | 514 | 34 |
| Alton–Granite City, IL | 4.5 | 19.7 | 64.8 | 142.2 | 231 | 1,370.8 | 3,166.2 | 212.5 | 4,750 | 706 | 82 |
| ★ Altoona, PA | 5.1 | 16.1 | 53.3 | 86.2 | 161 | 863.4 | 1,364.4 | 152.7 | 2,381 | 399 | 9 |
| Amarillo, TX | 13.4 | 28.9 | 125.0 | 324.3 | 492 | 1,907.6 | 3,601.4 | 305.1 | 5,814 | 1,073 | 220 |
| Anaheim–Santa Ana, CA | 4.1 | 30.0 | 181.1 | 200.3 | 416 | 1,863.7 | 3,346.6 | 466.5 | 5,677 | 983 | 183 |
| Anchorage, AK | (11.6) | (83.0) | (252.6) | (226.3) | (574) | (1,291.1) | (4,615.3) | (588.1) | (6,495) | (1,223) | 267 |
| Anderson, IN | 3.6 | 29.8 | 70.3 | 199.1 | 303 | 1,990.8 | 3,596.5 | 162.1 | 5,749 | 878 | 139 |
| Anderson, SC | 15.3 | 28.4 | 53.8 | 410.9 | 508 | 1,405.0 | 2.950.4 | 306.2 | 4,662 | 975 | 178 |
| Ann Arbor, MI | 2.4 | 48.3 | 99.0 | 336.6 | 486 | 1,326.9 | 4,064.8 | 418.3 | 5,810 | 1,067 | 217 |
| Anniston, AL | 8.2 | 24.5 | 132.4 | 537.9 | 703 | 1,253.1 | 2,749.1 | 222.3 | 4,225 | 1,125 | 238 |
| Appleton–Oshkosh–Neenah, WI | 1.4 | 12.6 | 16.7 | 75.4 | 106 | 922.1 | 3,160.0 | 102.0 | 4,184 | 525 | 38 |
| Asheville, NC | 7.3 | 13.3 | 52.7 | 147.2 | 221 | 885.1 | 2,386.2 | 185.4 | 3,457 | 566 | 45 |
| Athens, GA | 10.4 | 34.1 | 101.4 | 230.2 | 376 | 1,516.0 | 3,775.2 | 275.4 | 5,567 | 933 | 159 |
| Atlanta, GA | 12.5 | 52.9 | 264.3 | 369.0 | 699 | 1,929.6 | 3,693.4 | 469.2 | 6,092 | 1,308 | 274 |
| Atlantic City, NJ | 10.9 | 54.9 | 337.1 | 390.2 | 793 | 2,590.5 | 7,584.7 | 674.2 | 10,849 | 1,878 | 325 |
| Augusta, GA–SC | 11.6 | 41.3 | 99.0 | 294.2 | 446 | 1,588.2 | 2,434.7 | 237.9 | 4,261 | 872 | 137 |
| Aurora–Elgin, IL | 4.5 | 19.4 | 100.4 | 221.7 | 346 | 1,570.3 | 3,004.9 | 171.1 | 4,746 | 821 | 119 |
| Austin, TX | 13.7 | 48.9 | 131.2 | 186.9 | 381 | 1,976.8 | 4,402.0 | 300.4 | 6,679 | 1,049 | 210 |
| Bakersfield, CA | 14.7 | 50.7 | 269.8 | 453.7 | 789 | 2,407.9 | 4,750.8 | 562.7 | 7,721 | 1,561 | 312 |
| Baltimore, MD | 13.3 | 39.6 | 505.2 | 605.9 | 1,164 | 1,548.1 | 3,692.6 | 417.3 | 5,658 | 1,730 | 323 |
| Bangor, ME | 0.0 | 12.2 | 44.3 | 61.1 | 118 | 979.7 | 4,103.9 | 247.6 | 5,331 | 651 | 69 |
| Baton Rouge, LA | 14.1 | 43.4 | 187.7 | 638.0 | 883 | 2,178.3 | 4,281.1 | 363.1 | 6,823 | 1,565 | 313 |
| Battle Creek, M! | 4.3 | 30.2 | 124.4 | 302.7 | 462 | 1,751.9 | 3,762.0 | 182.6 | 5,697 | 1,031 | 203 |
| Beaumont–Port Arthur, TX | 10.6 | 43.5 | 212.3 | 524.8 | 791 | 1,762.1 | 3,116.5 | 336.2 | 5,215 | 1,313 | 275 |
| ★ Beaver County, PA | 3.4 | 15.2 | 37.2 | 73.4 | 129 | 574.8 | 1,045.8 | 189.0 | 1,810 | 310 | 2 |
| Bellingham, WA | 3.7 | 22.1 | 19.3 | 196.2 | 241 | 1,554.8 | 3,968.1 | 313.2 | 5,836 | 825 | 123 |
| Benton Harbor, MI | 4.7 | 56.3 | 120.3 | 452.7 | 634 | 1,523.9 | 3,860.2 | 180.7 | 5,565 | 1,190 | 260 |
| Bergen–Passaic, NJ | 4.0 | 8.8 | 234.5 | 161.2 | 409 | 1,110.7 | 2,700.9 | 677.6 | 4,489 | 857 | 132 |
| Billings, MT | 0.9 | 22.6 | 77.7 | 153.7 | 255 | 1,274.7 | 3,937.0 | 335.4 | 5,547 | 810 | 113 |
| Biloxi–Gulfport, MS | 14.1 | 60.6 | 152.8 | 323.7 | 551 | 1,981.5 | 242.2 | 365.6 | 2,589 | 810 | 113 |
| ★ Binghamton, NY | 1.5 | 11.3 | 25.3 | 56.3 | 94 | 774.3 | 2,272.4 | 157.1 | 3,204 | 415 | 16 |
| Birmingham, AL | 15.2 | 38.7 | 196.6 | 330.0 | 581 | 1,598.9 | 3,223.5 | 599.1 | 5,422 | 1,123 | 237 |
| ★ Bismarck, ND | 1.2 | 11.0 | 13.4 | 30.5 | 56 | 604.4 | 2,783.4 | 176.7 | 3,565 | 413 | 13 |
| Bloomington, IN | 0.0 | 16.4 | 25.6 | 121.7 | 164 | 967.5 | 3,763.7 | 200.5 | 4,932 | 657 | 72 |
| Bloomington–Normal, IL | 3.3 | 15.8 | 45.8 | 171.5 | 236 | 1,207.3 | 3,033.3 | 122.4 | 4,363 | 673 | 75 |
| Boise City, ID | 2.8 | 23.8 | 52.6 | 324.2 | 403 | 1,329.5 | 3,211.2 | 223.5 | 4,764 | 880 | 140 |
| Boston, MA | 5.3 | 24.2 | 306.3 | 344.4 | 680 | 1,387.8 | 2,632.2 | 1,331.1 | 5,351 | 1,215 | 266 |
| Boulder–Longmont, CO | 2.0 | 32.9 | 54.1 | 334.7 | 424 | 1,480.7 | 4,865.3 | 296.7 | 6,643 | 1,088 | 224 |
| Bradenton, FL | 7.4 | 50.7 | 120.0 | 347.7 | 526 | 1,831.4 | 3,588.0 | 256.2 | 5,676 | 1,093 | 228 |
| Brazoria, TX | 15.9 | 24.4 | 53.2 | 172.8 | 266 | 1,130.6 | 3,676.0 | 214.1 | 5,021 | 768 | 100 |
| Bremerton, WA | 3.3 | 35.8 | 51.1 | 169.9 | 260 | 1,245.2 | 2,497.0 | 170.6 | 3,913 | 651 | 69 |
| Bridgeport–Milford, CT | 5.9 | 18.8 | 213.0 | 167.9 | 405 | 1,538.5 | 3,192.1 | 645.6 | 5,376 | 943 | 163 |
| Bristol, CT | 2.9 | 2.9 | 40.5 | 180.7 | 227 | 923.5 | 2,087.0 | 172.0 | 3,183 | 545 | 41 |
| Brockton, MA | 0.0 | 35.6 | 200.4 | 558.1 | 794 | 1,595.7 | 2,802.4 | 1,019.0 | 5,417 | 1,336 | 282 |
| Brownsville–Harlingen, TX | 10.2 | 32.1 | 72.1 | 309.1 | 424 | 1,888.3 | 3,024.9 | 589.2 | 5,502 | 974 | 177 |
| Bryan–College Station, TX | 12.9 | 38.7 | 96.2 | 235.1 | 383 | 1,690.3 | 4,288.2 | 350.2 | 6,329 | 1,016 | 197 |
| Buffalo, NY | 5.3 | 30.0 | 187.3 | 300.3 | 523 | 1,268.6 | 2,724.6 | 488.4 | 4,482 | 971 | 176 |
| Burlington, NC | 10.9 | 16.8 | 48.3 | 282.1 | 358 | 1,064.5 | 2,289.7 | 133.2 | 3,487 | 707 | 83 |
| Burlington, VT | (1.6) | (29.2) | (17.7) | (59.2) | (108) | (1,277.7) | (2,354.1) | (229.3) | (3,861) | (494) | 32 |
| Canton, OH | 4.2 | 27.2 | 107.7 | 144.8 | 284 | 1,077.4 | 2,292.5 | 287.1 | 3,657 | 650 | 68 |
| Casper, WY | 9.1 | 26.1 | 52.2 | 318.4 | 406 | 1,545.0 | 3,923.8 | 366.7 | 5,836 | 989 | 185 |
| Cedar Rapids, IA | 2.4 | 14.2 | 56.0 | 112.1 | 185 | 1,211.4 | 3,860.7 | 222.9 | 5,295 | 714 | 85 |

| | Violent Crime Rates | | | | | Property Crime Rates | | | | | Places Rated Score | Places Rated Rank |
|---|---|---|---|---|---|---|---|---|---|---|---|---|
| | Murder | Forcible Rape | Robbery | Aggravated Assault | Total | Burglary | Larceny-Theft | Motor Vehicle Theft | Total | | | |
| Metro Area Average | 10.0 | 39.2 | 298.6 | 314.7 | 663 | 1,669.5 | 3,436.3 | 554.3 | 5,660 | 1,229 | — |
| Champaign–Urbana–Rantoul, IL | 2.4 | 22.0 | 114.0 | 375.1 | 514 | 1,472.1 | 3,454.0 | 156.1 | 5,082 | 1,022 | 200 |
| Charleston, SC | 12.8 | 52.8 | 261.5 | 592.3 | 919 | 1,813.4 | 3,549.0 | 392.4 | 5,755 | 1,495 | 303 |
| Charleston, WV | 5.0 | 28.2 | 137.0 | 150.3 | 321 | 1,012.7 | 2,681.7 | 312.5 | 4,007 | 721 | 86 |
| Charlotte–Gastonia–Rock Hill, NC–SC | 9.6 | 30.2 | 142.0 | 513.1 | 695 | 1,793.0 | 3,739.4 | 252.7 | 5,785 | 1,273 | 270 |
| Charlottesville, VA | 15.4 | 18.9 | 54.0 | 184.2 | 273 | 738.6 | 3,916.9 | 180.8 | 4,836 | 756 | 96 |
| Chattanooga, TN–GA | 11.3 | 23.0 | 105.6 | 294.1 | 434 | 1,280.0 | 3,478.2 | 365.4 | 5,124 | 946 | 164 |
| Chicago, IL | 12.8 | 24.2 | 313.3 | 210.7 | 561 | 1,068.6 | 2,912.7 | 748.0 | 4,729 | 1,034 | 205 |
| Chico, CA | 6.6 | 44.4 | 69.6 | 265.7 | 386 | 1,842.0 | 3,544.8 | 218.0 | 5,605 | 947 | 165 |
| Cincinnati, OH–KY–IN | 6.0 | 33.4 | 166.7 | 275.0 | 481 | 1,280.1 | 3,427.2 | 262.1 | 4,969 | 978 | 181 |
| Clarksville–Hopkinsville, TN–KY | 11.9 | 25.0 | 98.9 | 247.2 | 383 | 1,171.2 | 2,194.2 | 167.4 | 3,533 | 736 | 90 |
| Cleveland, OH | 13.2 | 42.0 | 333.1 | 281.9 | 670 | 1,418.2 | 2,220.2 | 1,037.3 | 4,676 | 1,138 | 241 |
| Colorado Springs, CO | 4.3 | 61.2 | 150.5 | 256.1 | 472 | 1,812.6 | 4,001.0 | 328.9 | 6,143 | 1,086 | 223 |
| Columbia, MO | 5.9 | 26.7 | 78.0 | 290.4 | 401 | 1,736.2 | 4,740.4 | 159.0 | 6,636 | 1,065 | 215 |
| Columbia, SC | 11.8 | 56.7 | 219.0 | 646.5 | 934 | 1,667.7 | 3,802.2 | 427.4 | 5,897 | 1,524 | 307 |
| Columbus, GA–AL | 10.1 | 34.3 | 156.4 | 196.4 | 397 | 1,351.5 | 2,565.1 | 316.1 | 4,233 | 820 | 118 |
| Columbus, OH | 8.4 | 38.6 | 243.4 | 233.9 | 524 | 1,743.0 | 3,640.8 | 296.0 | 5,680 | 1,092 | 226 |
| Corpus Christi, TX | 15.1 | 46.8 | 158.6 | 423.3 | 644 | 2,135.7 | 4,251.8 | 527.7 | 6,915 | 1,335 | 281 |
| ★ Cumberland, MD–WV | 0.9 | 19.2 | 18.3 | 75.1 | 114 | 501.6 | 1,676.7 | 61.3 | 2,240 | 337 | 3 |
| Dallas, TX | 17.9 | 66.3 | 310.2 | 378.5 | 773 | 2,317.8 | 4,730.8 | 507.7 | 7,556 | 1,529 | 308 |
| Danbury, CT | 2.7 | 24.2 | 57.2 | 118.5 | 203 | 1,088.5 | 2,104.4 | 256.5 | 3,449 | 548 | 43 |
| ★ Danville, VA | 8.7 | 11.3 | 27.8 | 93.0 | 141 | 589.6 | 1,696.5 | 92.2 | 2,378 | 379 | 7 |
| Davenport–Rock Island–Moline, IA–IL | 1.8 | 22.6 | 100.6 | 244.4 | 369 | 1,270.1 | 3,206.2 | 165.3 | 4,642 | 834 | 126 |
| Dayton–Springfield, OH | 7.9 | 37.9 | 306.2 | 231.2 | 583 | 1,661.8 | 3,768.8 | 242.5 | 5,673 | 1,151 | 244 |
| Daytona Beach, FL | 8.8 | 57.1 | 173.4 | 431.2 | 671 | 2,223.4 | 4,218.1 | 327.4 | 6,769 | 1,347 | 284 |
| Decatur, IL | 1.5 | 19.0 | 104.8 | 203.5 | 329 | 1,900.7 | 3,667.7 | 113.9 | 5,682 | 897 | 149 |
| Denver, CO | 7.6 | 53.2 | 233.4 | 324.8 | 619 | 2,065.7 | 4,861.6 | 529.7 | 7,457 | 1,365 | 287 |
| Des Moines, IA | 5.2 | 28.1 | 107.4 | 199.9 | 341 | 1,524.3 | 5,212.2 | 294.8 | 7,031 | 1,044 | 209 |
| Detroit, MI | 14.0 | 48.7 | 462.5 | 344.2 | 869 | 2,211.9 | 3,748.0 | 1,213.7 | 7,174 | 1,587 | 314 |
| Dothan, AL | 6.5 | 15.5 | 76.7 | 434.0 | 533 | 1,235.2 | 2,579.0 | 156.6 | 3,971 | 930 | 158 |
| Dubuque, IA | 0.0 | 1.1 | 37.4 | 69.5 | 108 | 1,162.5 | 3,275.0 | 188.1 | 4,626 | 571 | 49 |
| Duluth, MN–WI | 3.0 | 21.4 | 25.9 | 51.1 | 101 | 956.9 | 2,696.9 | 216.9 | 3,871 | 488 | 29 |
| East St. Louis–Belleville, IL | 19.0 | 43.5 | 142.8 | 552.8 | 758 | 1,170.9 | 1,920.3 | 292.4 | 3,384 | 1,096 | 230 |
| ★ Eau Claire, WI | 2.3 | 11.3 | 19.6 | 54.2 | 87 | 691.9 | 2,670.5 | 93.4 | 3,456 | 433 | 19 |
| El Paso, TX | 8.9 | 46.8 | 184.9 | 562.3 | 803 | 1,488.9 | 3,261.4 | 452.0 | 5,202 | 1,323 | 277 |
| Elkhart–Goshen, IN | 1.5 | 26.3 | 30.7 | 122.7 | 181 | 742.7 | 2,568.4 | 116.8 | 3,428 | 524 | 37 |
| Elmira, NY | 5.1 | 11.2 | 48.8 | 147.3 | 212 | 792.4 | 2,835.4 | 70.1 | 3,698 | 582 | 50 |
| Enid, OK | 12.1 | 19.6 | 72.3 | 182.4 | 286 | 1,627.7 | 3,700.0 | 254.7 | 5,582 | 845 | 130 |
| Erie, PA | 3.2 | 31.4 | 121.3 | 150.9 | 307 | 934.4 | 2,150.7 | 195.5 | 3,281 | 635 | 64 |
| Eugene–Springfield, OR | 5.1 | 35.6 | 93.0 | 115.2 | 249 | 1,602.1 | 4,424.1 | 228.6 | 6,255 | 874 | 138 |
| Evansville, IN–KY | 5.1 | 25.8 | 102.3 | 265.3 | 399 | 1,170.3 | 3,244.8 | 235.4 | 4,651 | 864 | 135 |
| Fall River, MA–RI | 1.3 | 17.9 | 106.8 | 271.3 | 397 | 1,493.2 | 2,492.4 | 647.0 | 4,633 | 861 | 134 |
| Fargo–Moorhead, ND–MN | 0.0 | 24.9 | 31.3 | 65.4 | 122 | 663.6 | 2,972.1 | 176.9 | 3,813 | 503 | 33 |
| Fayetteville, NC | 8.7 | 54.1 | 180.0 | 336.7 | 580 | 2,070.2 | 3,275.8 | 359.6 | 5,706 | 1,150 | 243 |
| Fayetteville–Springdale, AR | 4.0 | 24.1 | 37.2 | 103.6 | 169 | 1,085.1 | 2,474.9 | 200.1 | 3,760 | 545 | 41 |
| Fitchburg–Leominster, MA | 1.1 | 25.4 | 68.8 | 170.5 | 166 | 1,198.7 | 1,397.4 | 296.5 | 3,893 | 655 | 71 |
| Flint, MI | 8.5 | 56.7 | 234.0 | 630.8 | 930 | 2,488.9 | 4,614.3 | 305.7 | 7,409 | 1,671 | 320 |
| Florence, AL | 5.1 | 10.2 | 28.3 | 122.8 | 166 | 943.5 | 2,384.8 | 172.3 | 3,501 | 516 | 35 |
| Florence, SC | 7.0 | 41.7 | 168.7 | 585.1 | 803 | 1,707.5 | 3,305.5 | 306.0 | 5,319 | 1,334 | 280 |
| Fort Collins–Loveland, CO | 1.9 | 29.4 | 28.7 | 137.6 | 198 | 1,227.1 | 4,028.0 | 205.7 | 5,461 | 744 | 91 |
| Fort Lauderdale–Hollywood–Pompano Beach, FL | 13.7 | 46.0 | 368.2 | 376.6 | 805 | 2,190.1 | 4,514.0 | 613.8 | 7,318 | 1,536 | 310 |
| Fort Myers, FL | 5.4 | 35.1 | 150.2 | 226.1 | 417 | 1,301.5 | 2,253.2 | 150.6 | 3,705 | 787 | 107 |
| Fort Pierce, FL | 12.9 | 59.8 | 179.9 | 475.8 | 728 | 2,451.5 | 4,214.0 | 273.6 | 6,939 | 1,422 | 291 |
| Fort Smith, AR–OK | 7.3 | 31.6 | 49.9 | 145.4 | 234 | 1,221.2 | 2,797.7 | 267.1 | 4,286 | 663 | 73 |
| Fort Walton Beach, FL | 7.5 | 20.1 | 70.3 | 147.3 | 245 | 796.1 | 1,975.7 | 221.0 | 2,993 | 544 | 40 |
| Fort Wayne, IN | 7.3 | 27.2 | 120.0 | 110.7 | 265 | 822.1 | 3,377.7 | 243.3 | 4,443 | 710 | 84 |
| Fort Worth–Arlington, TX | 12.6 | 60.1 | 263.3 | 301.6 | 638 | 2,109.6 | 4,404.8 | 585.9 | 7,100 | 1,348 | 285 |
| Fresno, CA | 13.3 | 56.9 | 302.2 | 385.2 | 758 | 2,366.6 | 4,390.9 | 498.4 | 7,256 | 1,483 | 299 |

| | Violent Crime Rates | | | | | Property Crime Rates | | | | | Places Rated Score | Places Rated Rank |
|---|---|---|---|---|---|---|---|---|---|---|---|---|
| | Murder | Forcible Rape | Robbery | Aggravated Assault | Total | Burglary | Larceny-Theft | Motor Vehicle Theft | Total | | | |
| Metro Area Average | 10.0 | 39.2 | 298.6 | 314.7 | 663 | 1,669.5 | 3,436.3 | 554.3 | 5,660 | | 1,229 | — |
| Gadsden, AL | 7.7 | 16.3 | 57.4 | 254.7 | 336 | 1,098.1 | 2,799.4 | 230.7 | 4,128 | | 749 | 93 |
| Gainesville, FL | 10.5 | 78.8 | 164.9 | 680.4 | 935 | 2,025.8 | 4,965.8 | 246.5 | 7,238 | | 1,658 | 319 |
| Galveston–Texas City, TX | 10.5 | 58.6 | 234.3 | 346.3 | 650 | 1,798.9 | 3,314.0 | 521.1 | 5,634 | | 1,213 | 265 |
| Gary–Hammond, IN | 18.3 | 49.1 | 212.3 | 226.7 | 506 | 1,351.2 | 2,653.6 | 886.4 | 4,891 | | 996 | 187 |
| Glens Falls, NY | 1.8 | 7.2 | 8.1 | 225.3 | 242 | 911.0 | 2,199.3 | 149.3 | 3,260 | | 568 | 47 |
| ★ Grand Forks, ND | 1.5 | 5.9 | 16.2 | 39.8 | 63 | 582.0 | 2,639.0 | 154.7 | 3,376 | | 401 | 12 |
| Grand Rapids, MI | 5.7 | 45.8 | 125.8 | 265.3 | 443 | 1,310.8 | 3,588.5 | 194.9 | 5,094 | | 952 | 166 |
| Great Falls, MT | 1.2 | 8.5 | 59.3 | 136.7 | 206 | 1,294.8 | 4,131.1 | 440.5 | 5,866 | | 792 | 111 |
| Greeley, CO | 6.2 | 34.6 | 44.6 | 321.4 | 407 | 1,462.5 | 4,133.7 | 279.1 | 5,875 | | 994 | 186 |
| Green Bay, WI | 0.6 | 3.9 | 29.7 | 84.5 | 119 | 734.5 | 3,754.3 | 157.9 | 4,647 | | 583 | 51 |
| Greensboro–Winston-Salem–High Point, NC | 7.2 | 25.3 | 106.6 | 395.3 | 534 | 1,355.5 | 2,754.5 | 214.7 | 4,325 | | 967 | 171 |
| Greenville–Spartanburg, SC | 7.6 | 41.1 | 101.3 | 524.2 | 674 | 1,468.3 | 3,352.8 | 288.7 | 5,110 | | 1,185 | 259 |
| Hagerstown, MD | 5.2 | 13.1 | 47.1 | 194.4 | 260 | 694.7 | 2,883.7 | 98.5 | 3,677 | | 627 | 57 |
| Hamilton–Middletown, OH | 3.1 | 29.0 | 106.6 | 224.0 | 363 | 1,486.2 | 3,596.6 | 208.2 | 5,291 | | 892 | 143 |
| Harrisburg–Lebanon–Carlisle, PA | 3.8 | 20.8 | 116.2 | 130.2 | 271 | 974.4 | 2,453.5 | 149.9 | 3,578 | | 629 | 59 |
| Hartford, CT | 8.0 | 27.7 | 366.4 | 246.6 | 649 | 1,637.9 | 3,849.3 | 820.0 | 6,307 | | 1,279 | 271 |
| Hickory, NC | 8.6 | 10.6 | 45.1 | 366.1 | 430 | 1,163.7 | 2,046.1 | 141.1 | 3,351 | | 765 | 99 |
| Honolulu, HI | 3.2 | 34.3 | 185.6 | 50.9 | 274 | 1,576.8 | 4,128.5 | 465.1 | 6,170 | | 891 | 142 |
| ★ Houma–Thibodaux, LA | 9.5 | 19.7 | 53.1 | 116.9 | 199 | 743.7 | 1,178.5 | 89.5 | 2,012 | | 400 | 10 |
| Houston, TX | 28.9 | 58.7 | 486.9 | 218.5 | 793 | 2,545.5 | 3,104.1 | 1,405.6 | 7,055 | | 1,499 | 304 |
| Huntington–Ashland, WV–KY–OH | 4.2 | 20.8 | 67.9 | 229.3 | 322 | 1,099.1 | 2,089.6 | 241.5 | 3,430 | | 665 | 74 |
| Huntsville, AL | 8.5 | 32.4 | 107.5 | 187.6 | 336 | 1,410.0 | 4,128.4 | 344.9 | 5,883 | | 924 | 157 |
| Indianapolis, IN | 8.0 | 46.6 | 216.1 | 220.8 | 492 | 1,448.4 | 3,177.0 | 462.6 | 5,088 | | 1,000 | 192 |
| Iowa City, IA | 0.0 | 23.3 | 18.4 | 277.4 | 319 | 1,050.7 | 3,862.8 | 192.7 | 5,106 | | 830 | 125 |
| Jackson, MI | 3.3 | 44.2 | 85.7 | 415.7 | 549 | 1,312.8 | 3,196.7 | 209.5 | 4,719 | | 1,021 | 199 |
| Jackson, MS | 20.0 | 39.9 | 221.7 | 168.6 | 450 | 2,155.0 | 3,942.2 | 309.5 | 6,407 | | 1,091 | 225 |
| Jacksonville, FL | 10.6 | 52.7 | 273.5 | 376.2 | 713 | 1,617.2 | 3,150.3 | 209.8 | 4,977 | | 1,211 | 263 |
| Jacksonville, NC | 6.1 | 19.9 | 109.1 | 489.1 | 624 | 1,028.3 | 2,250.5 | 152.3 | 3,431 | | 967 | 171 |
| Janesville–Beloit, WI | 1.4 | 20.2 | 72.0 | 174.2 | 268 | 1,430.4 | 4,292.7 | 178.5 | 5,902 | | 858 | 133 |
| Jersey City, NJ | 13.2 | 32.9 | 498.5 | 306.0 | 851 | 1,875.5 | 2,717.4 | 1,239.7 | 5,833 | | 1,434 | 293 |
| ★ Johnson City–Kingsport–Bristol, TN–VA | 4.5 | 12.8 | 33.6 | 109.8 | 161 | 791.8 | 1,642.8 | 195.4 | 2,630 | | 424 | 18 |
| ★ Johnstown, PA | 2.3 | 7.5 | 16.2 | 153.5 | 180 | 614.4 | 1,010.1 | 108.6 | 1,733 | | 353 | 5 |
| Joliet, IL | 6.5 | 15.5 | 101.4 | 268.9 | 392 | 1,315.2 | 2,776.8 | 354.6 | 4,447 | | 837 | 129 |
| Joplin, MO | 3.1 | 10.9 | 38.9 | 161.7 | 215 | 1,103.4 | 2,844.3 | 185.8 | 4,134 | | 628 | 58 |
| Kalamazoo, MI | 1.9 | 38.7 | 81.2 | 552.7 | 675 | 1,058.1 | 3,279.5 | 119.4 | 4,457 | | 1,120 | 236 |
| Kankakee, IL | 6.8 | 18.4 | 170.3 | 247.7 | 443 | 1,632.2 | 3,463.7 | 231.2 | 5,327 | | 976 | 179 |
| Kansas City, KS | 7.0 | 31.1 | 153.6 | 376.6 | 568 | 1,840.1 | 3,534.3 | 364.8 | 5,739 | | 1,142 | 242 |
| Kansas City, MO | 11.6 | 49.8 | 331.8 | 469.5 | 863 | 1,932.1 | 3,658.9 | 457.2 | 6,048 | | 1,468 | 296 |
| Kenosha, WI | 4.0 | 29.5 | 151.3 | 108.3 | 293 | 1,557.2 | 4,227.4 | 391.7 | 6,176 | | 911 | 153 |
| Killeen–Temple, TX | 7.8 | 37.7 | 112.2 | 193.6 | 351 | 1,220.6 | 2,405.7 | 189.7 | 3,816 | | 733 | 89 |
| Knoxville, TN | 6.8 | 26.5 | 110.0 | 124.7 | 268 | 1,242.5 | 1,840.3 | 456.0 | 3,539 | | 622 | 55 |
| ★ Kokomo, IN | 3.9 | 11.6 | 29.9 | 69.5 | 115 | 814.2 | 2,020.1 | 142.8 | 2,977 | | 413 | 13 |
| La Crosse, WI | 2.2 | 8.7 | 12.0 | 105.8 | 129 | 1,045.7 | 4,272.1 | 151.6 | 5,469 | | 676 | 76 |
| Lafayette, IN | 4.1 | 19.0 | 33.1 | 78.7 | 135 | 878.7 | 2,269.9 | 154.0 | 3,303 | | 465 | 26 |
| Lafayette, LA | 11.3 | 40.9 | 134.5 | 418.5 | 605 | 1,398.7 | 2,556.9 | 291.6 | 4,247 | | 1,030 | 202 |
| Lake Charles, LA | 11.5 | 32.8 | 111.0 | 375.7 | 531 | 1,792.8 | 3,547.6 | 279.0 | 5,619 | | 1,093 | 228 |
| Lake County, IL | 3.9 | 19.6 | 134.3 | 212.1 | 370 | 1,150.9 | 3,142.4 | 231.5 | 4,525 | | 822 | 120 |
| Lakeland–Winter Haven, FL | 10.3 | 57.3 | 154.1 | 580.3 | 802 | 1,621.5 | 3,808.2 | 278.2 | 5,708 | | 1,373 | 288 |
| ★ Lancaster, PA | 1.1 | 9.6 | 42.7 | 83.1 | 137 | 716.1 | 1,895.6 | 154.7 | 2,766 | | 413 | 13 |
| Lansing–East Lansing, MI | 2.2 | 59.2 | 88.4 | 220.9 | 371 | 1,405.1 | 3,646.2 | 181.2 | 5,233 | | 894 | 147 |
| Laredo, TX | 7.5 | 25.3 | 111.4 | 263.0 | 407 | 2,104.4 | 3,943.8 | 378.2 | 6,426 | | 1,050 | 211 |
| Las Cruces, NM | 6.1 | 42.6 | 111.7 | 369.6 | 530 | 2,258.3 | 6,620.5 | 391.9 | 9,271 | | 1,457 | 294 |
| Las Vegas, NV | 19.8 | 70.2 | 603.2 | 363.8 | 1,057 | 3,076.9 | 4,722.9 | 757.6 | 8,557 | | 1,913 | 326 |
| Lawrence, KS | 2.9 | 30.7 | 65.7 | 258.5 | 358 | 1,747.0 | 4,582.1 | 268.8 | 6,598 | | 1,018 | 198 |
| Lawrence–Haverhill, MA–NH | 2.5 | 15.7 | 93.2 | 314.0 | 426 | 1,586.9 | 2,371.98 | 877.3 | 4,836 | | 909 | 152 |

| | Violent Crime Rates | | | | | Property Crime Rates | | | | | | |
|---|---|---|---|---|---|---|---|---|---|---|---|---|
| | Murder | Forcible Rape | Robbery | Aggravated Assault | Total | Burglary | Larceny-Theft | Motor Vehicle Theft | Total | Places Rated Score | Places Rated Rank |
| Metro Area Average | 10.0 | 39.2 | 298.6 | 314.7 | 663 | 1,669.5 | 3,436.3 | 554.3 | 5,660 | 1,229 | — |
| Lawton, OK | 4.2 | 62.4 | 179.7 | 437.0 | 683 | 1,510.2 | 2,860.9 | 354.3 | 4,725 | 1,156 | 246 |
| Lewiston–Auburn, ME | 3.8 | 8.9 | 57.1 | 205.7 | 275 | 1,255.5 | 3,418.7 | 215.8 | 4,890 | 764 | 98 |
| Lexington–Fayette, KY | 12.6 | 30.5 | 147.0 | 263.8 | 454 | 1,547.3 | 4,144.8 | 318.6 | 6,011 | 1,055 | 212 |
| Lima, OH | 2.0 | 22.4 | 108.7 | 235.1 | 368 | 1,338.7 | 3,383.5 | 144.1 | 4,866 | 855 | 131 |
| Lincoln, NE | 1.0 | 25.6 | 50.6 | 149.4 | 227 | 1,146.8 | 4,270.6 | 207.7 | 5,625 | 789 | 108 |
| Little Rock–North Little Rock, AR | 10.3 | 57.8 | 216.0 | 404.1 | 688 | 1,868.5 | 4,148.4 | 381.2 | 6,398 | 1,328 | 279 |
| Longview–Marshall, TX | 21.6 | 41.3 | 111.4 | 277.3 | 452 | 1,650.1 | 3,221.7 | 376.7 | 5,249 | 976 | 179 |
| Lorain–Elyria, OH | 3.7 | 18.6 | 76.4 | 167.6 | 266 | 1,296.0 | 1,808.6 | 317.8 | 3,422 | 609 | 53 |
| Los Angeles–Long Beach, CA | 18.1 | 67.7 | 651.8 | 532.3 | 1,270 | 2,301.2 | 3,496.8 | 1,104.2 | 6,902 | 1,960 | 327 |
| Louisville, KY–IN | 6.5 | 28.2 | 222.9 | 175.4 | 433 | 1,534.2 | 3,159.1 | 350.5 | 5,044 | 937 | 160 |
| Lowell, MA–NH | 6.4 | 16.9 | 110.7 | 265.3 | 399 | 1,126.0 | 2,458.3 | 615.6 | 4,200 | 819 | 116 |
| Lubbock, TX | 11.4 | 70.3 | 143.2 | 615.7 | 841 | 2,479.6 | 4,790.1 | 400.2 | 7,670 | 1,608 | 316 |
| Lynchburg, VA | 4.8 | 21.9 | 34.3 | 191.3 | 252 | 909.9 | 2,876.5 | 121.4 | 3,908 | 643 | 66 |
| Macon–Warner Robins, GA | 9.9 | 27.5 | 91.6 | 214.8 | 344 | 1,075.8 | 3,007.2 | 304.6 | 4,388 | 783 | 104 |
| Madison, WI | 2.2 | 26.3 | 63.2 | 107.9 | 200 | 1,290.5 | 4,323.6 | 178.9 | 5,793 | 779 | 102 |
| Manchester, NH | 0.8 | 19.9 | 57.3 | 58.8 | 137 | 1,168.6 | 3,410.4 | 383.4 | 4,962 | 633 | 61 |
| Mansfield, OH | 4.6 | 11.4 | 139.2 | 434.9 | 590 | 1,532.2 | 3,049.2 | 235.0 | 4,816 | 1,072 | 219 |
| McAllen–Edinburg–Mission, TX | 5.0 | 25.2 | 41.4 | 324.4 | 396 | 1,566.7 | 2,577.1 | 275.4 | 4,399 | 836 | 128 |
| Medford, OR | 4.5 | 23.2 | 48.0 | 150.0 | 226 | 1,248.4 | 3,596.6 | 181.4 | 5,026 | 728 | 88 |
| Melbourne–Titusville–Palm Bay, FL | 5.8 | 45.5 | 84.2 | 351.8 | 487 | 1,613.7 | 3,626.4 | 280.2 | 5,520 | 1,039 | 208 |
| Memphis, TN–AR–MS | 15.4 | 83.6 | 492.0 | 303.9 | 895 | 2,013.0 | 3,306.6 | 608.3 | 5,928 | 1,488 | 301 |
| Miami–Hialeah, FL | 29.7 | 55.7 | 732.7 | 770.7 | 1,589 | 2,471.2 | 5,331.6 | 897.8 | 8,701 | 2,459 | 328 |
| Middlesex–Somerset–Hunterdon, NJ | 3.0 | 15.6 | 205.5 | 148.2 | 372 | 343.5 | 2,485.4 | 355.9 | 3,185 | 691 | 80 |
| Middletown, CT | 8.2 | 8.2 | 43.3 | 189.7 | 249 | 967.0 | 2,674.1 | 325.8 | 3,967 | 646 | 67 |
| Midland, TX | 18.0 | 42.8 | 74.4 | 465.3 | 601 | 1,998.6 | 3,029.5 | 623.0 | 5,651 | 1,166 | 251 |
| Milwaukee, WI | 5.4 | 17.8 | 165.1 | 126.6 | 315 | 1,129.7 | 3,684.0 | 301.1 | 5,115 | 826 | 124 |
| Minneapolis–St. Paul, MN–WI | 3.2 | 33.4 | 181.4 | 138.0 | 356 | 1,611.4 | 3,559.2 | 328.8 | 5,499 | 906 | 151 |
| Mobile, AL | 16.3 | 51.6 | 261.8 | 504.9 | 835 | 2,338.0 | 4,124.2 | 297.8 | 6,760 | 1,511 | 306 |
| Modesto, CA | 6.1 | 37.6 | 116.8 | 324.6 | 485 | 2,017.4 | 4,363.0 | 312.4 | 6,693 | 1,154 | 245 |
| Monmouth–Ocean, NJ | 2.6 | 24.4 | 94.8 | 233.0 | 355 | 1,176.3 | 3,204.0 | 266.0 | 4,646 | 819 | 116 |
| Monroe, LA | 8.4 | 37.8 | 52.5 | 443.9 | 543 | 1,247.6 | 2,712.2 | 186.9 | 4,147 | 957 | 168 |
| Montgomery, AL | 10.4 | 19.6 | 110.6 | 230.9 | 372 | 1,312.8 | 2,936.1 | 183.5 | 4,433 | 815 | 115 |
| Muncie, IN | 6.3 | 26.6 | 87.7 | 245.1 | 366 | 1,029.9 | 2,936.9 | 209.9 | 4,177 | 783 | 104 |
| Muskegon, MI | 2.6 | 43.8 | 138.6 | 674.4 | 859 | 2,002.6 | 4,596.4 | 179.2 | 6,778 | 1,537 | 311 |
| ★ Nashua, NH | 0.7 | 18.1 | 41.0 | 46.5 | 106 | 1,006.9 | 2,263.1 | 186.8 | 3,457 | 452 | 24 |
| Nashville, TN | 11.9 | 44.5 | 215.7 | 209.3 | 481 | 1,533.6 | 3,193.4 | 303.4 | 5,030 | 984 | 184 |
| Nassau–Suffolk, NY | 2.5 | 8.9 | 113.4 | 86.9 | 212 | 998.1 | 2,169.4 | 375.1 | 3,543 | 566 | 45 |
| New Bedford, MA | 0.8 | 18.0 | 181.9 | 291.2 | 492 | 1,841.1 | 2,798.4 | 566.1 | 5,206 | 1,012 | 194 |
| New Britain, CT | 0.7 | 29.7 | 213.6 | 150.7 | 395 | 1,328.1 | 3,339.3 | 416.9 | 5,084 | 903 | 150 |
| New Haven–Meriden, CT | 5.3 | 23.8 | 221.2 | 122.6 | 373 | 1,499.4 | 3,142.7 | 554.2 | 5,196 | 893 | 146 |
| New London–Norwich, CT–RI | 2.9 | 29.2 | 72.9 | 147.8 | 253 | 1,054.5 | 2,502.6 | 249.5 | 3,807 | 633 | 61 |
| New Orleans, LA | 24.0 | 60.2 | 497.7 | 425.5 | 1,007 | 1,759.5 | 3,579.1 | 630.4 | 5,969 | 1,604 | 315 |
| New York, NY | 20.8 | 45.0 | 1,180.1 | 536.3 | 1,782 | 2,247.5 | 3,556.8 | 1,349.5 | 7,154 | 2,498 | 329 |
| Newark, NJ | 8.8 | 46.0 | 538.5 | 383.6 | 977 | 1,446.1 | 2,672.4 | 726.1 | 4,845 | 1,461 | 295 |
| Niagara Falls, NY | 1.8 | 24.9 | 137.9 | 174.6 | 339 | 1,218.9 | 2,844.5 | 295.4 | 4,359 | 775 | 101 |
| Norfolk–Virginia Beach–Newport News, VA | 9.8 | 39.4 | 203.1 | 227.5 | 480 | 1,240.8 | 3,689.0 | 237.5 | 5,167 | 997 | 188 |
| Norwalk, CT | 2.4 | 19.6 | 87.8 | 69.8 | 180 | 1,244.9 | 2,746.8 | 464.9 | 4,457 | 625 | 56 |
| Oakland, CA | 10.2 | 51.3 | 356.6 | 385.9 | 804 | 2,125.5 | 4,693.5 | 468.8 | 7,288 | 1,533 | 309 |
| Ocala, FL | 10.8 | 34.0 | 132.2 | 508.7 | 686 | 2,140.9 | 3,967.8 | 304.6 | 6,413 | 1,327 | 278 |
| Odessa, TX | 29.8 | 61.2 | 232.6 | 372.7 | 696 | 3,285.8 | 5,893.1 | 834.7 | 10,014 | 1,698 | 322 |
| Oklahoma City, OK | 12.6 | 59.4 | 240.9 | 342.4 | 655 | 2,205.8 | 3,439.6 | 773.4 | 6,419 | 1,297 | 272 |
| Olympia, WA | 1.6 | 41.3 | 40.6 | 145.8 | 229 | 1,477.9 | 3,579.6 | 170.0 | 5,228 | 752 | 94 |
| Omaha, NE–IA | 4.8 | 35.5 | 138.3 | 313.5 | 492 | 1,295.9 | 3,559.7 | 305.3 | 5,161 | 1,008 | 193 |
| Orange County, NY | 3.8 | 13.8 | 117.9 | 274.7 | 410 | 1,277.6 | 2,458.4 | 202.0 | 3,938 | 804 | 112 |
| Orlando, FL | 10.4 | 64.5 | 269.5 | 611.5 | 956 | 2,448.3 | 4,316.6 | 389.8 | 7,155 | 1,671 | 320 |
| Owensboro, KY | 4.6 | 19.7 | 41.7 | 86.9 | 153 | 1,274.6 | 2,684.7 | 195.8 | 4,155 | 568 | 47 |

| | Violent Crime Rates | | | | | Property Crime Rates | | | | Places Rated Score | Places Rated Rank |
|---|---|---|---|---|---|---|---|---|---|---|---|
| | Murder | Forcible Rape | Robbery | Aggravated Assault | Total | Burglary | Larceny-Theft | Motor Vehicle Theft | Total | | |
| Metro Area Average | 10.0 | 39.2 | 298.6 | 314.7 | 663 | 1,669.5 | 3,436.3 | 554.3 | 5,660 | 1,229 | — |
| Oxnard–Ventura, CA | 5.8 | 35.2 | 136.5 | 201.0 | 379 | 1,387.7 | 2,431.2 | 309.0 | 4,128 | 791 | 110 |
| Panama City, FL | 10.4 | 74.7 | 78.5 | 591.7 | 755 | 1,361.1 | 4,262.9 | 264.7 | 5,889 | 1,344 | 283 |
| Parkersburg–Marietta, WV–OH | 1.9 | 15.3 | 46.4 | 97.3 | 161 | 937.6 | 2,157.6 | 176.2 | 3,271 | 488 | 29 |
| Pascagoula, MS | 1.9 | 19.0 | 90.2 | 150.1 | 261 | 1,254.9 | 1,879.0 | 163.4 | 3,297 | 591 | 52 |
| Pawtucket–Woonsocket–Attleboro, RI–MA | 5.1 | 18.2 | 65.2 | 159.3 | 248 | 1,381.4 | 2,979.7 | 598.7 | 4,960 | 744 | 91 |
| Pensacola, FL | 8.1 | 56.8 | 177.9 | 635.9 | 879 | 1,899.3 | 3,678.7 | 352.7 | 5,931 | 1,472 | 297 |
| Peoria, IL | 4.9 | 25.6 | 121.3 | 322.2 | 474 | 1,258.0 | 3,069.4 | 147.2 | 4,475 | 921 | 155 |
| Philadelphia, PA–NJ | 10.1 | 31.5 | 320.3 | 265.9 | 628 | 1,245.9 | 2,483.6 | 579.9 | 4,309 | 1,059 | 214 |
| Phoenix, AZ | 8.5 | 40.1 | 193.7 | 297.3 | 540 | 2,084.6 | 4,767.9 | 427.3 | 7,280 | 1,268 | 269 |
| Pine Bluff, AR | 8.8 | 58.2 | 183.4 | 373.5 | 624 | 1,878.3 | 3,368.9 | 205.4 | 5,453 | 1,169 | 253 |
| Pittsburgh, PA | 4.5 | 21.2 | 226.9 | 142.2 | 395 | 900.4 | 1,552.8 | 461.7 | 2,915 | 687 | 78 |
| Pittsfield, MA | 0.0 | 42.4 | 41.7 | 170.2 | 254 | 1,370.1 | 2,206.3 | 256.4 | 3,833 | 638 | 65 |
| Portland, ME | 3.8 | 23.4 | 65.4 | 201.8 | 294 | 1,510.2 | 3,466.0 | 309.1 | 5,285 | 823 | 122 |
| Portland, OR | 5.9 | 58.8 | 319.8 | 371.7 | 756 | 2,453.0 | 4,603.9 | 424.9 | 7,482 | 1,504 | 305 |
| Portsmouth–Dover–Rochester, NH–ME | 4.5 | 7.9 | 36.3 | 69.8 | 119 | 900.8 | 2,457.3 | 207.0 | 3,565 | 475 | 27 |
| Poughkeepsie, NY | 2.0 | 7.7 | 114.9 | 192.5 | 317 | 1,016.0 | 1,999.1 | 140.5 | 3,156 | 633 | 61 |
| Providence, RI | 3.7 | 22.4 | 150.9 | 291.8 | 469 | 1,484.4 | 2,868.2 | 936.2 | 5,289 | 998 | 189 |
| Provo–Orem, UT | 1.3 | 6.9 | 25.5 | 91.6 | 125 | 501.6 | 2,943.8 | 149.5 | 3,595 | 485 | 28 |
| Pueblo, CO | 6.8 | 39.8 | 126.3 | 408.2 | 581 | 1,862.7 | 3,871.3 | 268.4 | 6,002 | 1,181 | 257 |
| Racine, WI | 3.4 | 18.2 | 130.5 | 330.5 | 483 | 1,588.5 | 3,971.3 | 160.7 | 5,721 | 1,055 | 212 |
| Raleigh–Durham, NC | 10.8 | 32.2 | 129.7 | 235.9 | 409 | 1,601.3 | 3,890.1 | 235.0 | 5,726 | 981 | 182 |
| Reading, PA | 2.6 | 14.7 | 104.6 | 126.3 | 248 | 797.5 | 1,794.7 | 148.9 | 2,741 | 522 | 36 |
| Redding, CA | 4.1 | 36.4 | 61.3 | 294.7 | 397 | 1,307.0 | 3,422.8 | 227.6 | 4,957 | 892 | 143 |
| Reno, NV | 7.5 | 69.3 | 221.2 | 206.2 | 504 | 1,823.7 | 3,921.9 | 367.4 | 6,113 | 1,116 | 235 |
| Richland–Kennewick–Pasco, WA | 6.8 | 24.3 | 44.6 | 203.6 | 279 | 1,159.8 | 3,591.6 | 240.7 | 4,992 | 779 | 102 |
| Richmond–Petersburg, VA | 12.3 | 37.9 | 237.5 | 224.7 | 512 | 1,692.9 | 3,696.9 | 247.1 | 5,637 | 1,076 | 221 |
| Riverside–San Bernardino, CA | 9.9 | 46.4 | 245.0 | 457.5 | 759 | 2,588.0 | 4,013.5 | 557.8 | 7,159 | 1,475 | 298 |
| Roanoke, VA | 7.9 | 13.7 | 107.3 | 122.7 | 252 | 1,304.0 | 3,815.9 | 200.9 | 5,321 | 784 | 106 |
| ★ Rochester, MN | 0.0 | 5.4 | 37.5 | 46.0 | 89 | 809.3 | 2,537.1 | 137.0 | 3,483 | 437 | 20 |
| Rochester, NY | 4.3 | 21.5 | 142.8 | 215.5 | 384 | 1,276.7 | 3,569.7 | 248.9 | 5,095 | 894 | 147 |
| Rockford, IL | 4.6 | 22.8 | 181.1 | 334.4 | 543 | 1,871.8 | 4,058.8 | 204.9 | 6,136 | 1,156 | 246 |
| Sacramento, CA | 8.1 | 45.0 | 273.3 | 281.9 | 608 | 2,239.2 | 4,773.5 | 529.0 | 7,542 | 1,363 | 286 |
| Saginaw–Bay City–Midland, MI | 7.0 | 44.1 | 120.1 | 351.0 | 523 | 1,371.4 | 3,910.5 | 174.6 | 5,457 | 1,068 | 218 |
| ★ St. Cloud, MN | 1.8 | 10.3 | 11.5 | 23.5 | 47 | 555.2 | 2,260.1 | 143.6 | 2,959 | 343 | 4 |
| St. Joseph, MO | 4.5 | 18.1 | 65.5 | 243.8 | 332 | 1,698.5 | 4,441.9 | 229.1 | 6,370 | 969 | 173 |
| St. Louis, MO–IL | 15.5 | 30.6 | 326.1 | 368.7 | 741 | 1,778.6 | 3,321.7 | 549.1 | 5,649 | 1,306 | 273 |
| Salem, OR | 3.2 | 33.2 | 80.7 | 282.9 | 400 | 1,592.8 | 4,302.0 | 243.3 | 6,138 | 1,014 | 195 |
| Salem–Gloucester, MA | 0.0 | 5.1 | 43.4 | 98.1 | 147 | 905.2 | 2,026.8 | 504.4 | 3,436 | 490 | 31 |
| Salinas–Seaside–Monterey, CA | 9.8 | 39.0 | 166.8 | 315.0 | 531 | 1,631.7 | 3,889.2 | 245.1 | 5,766 | 1,107 | 233 |
| Salt Lake City–Ogden, UT | 4.1 | 32.6 | 125.5 | 191.7 | 354 | 1,434.9 | 4,407.3 | 310.8 | 6,153 | 969 | 173 |
| San Angelo, TX | 5.5 | 42.7 | 63.5 | 383.2 | 495 | 1,368.6 | 3,685.3 | 321.9 | 5,376 | 1,032 | 204 |
| San Antonio, TX | 18.5 | 41.4 | 207.4 | 313.9 | 581 | 2,047.9 | 3,586.9 | 523.5 | 6,158 | 1,197 | 261 |
| San Diego, CA | 6.4 | 43.9 | 250.8 | 244.3 | 545 | 1,659.5 | 3,239.4 | 636.7 | 5,536 | 1,099 | 231 |
| San Francisco, CA | 9.9 | 51.5 | 548.6 | 358.0 | 968 | 1,625.1 | 4,282.9 | 606.2 | 6,514 | 1,619 | 318 |
| San Jose, CA | 4.5 | 49.7 | 191.0 | 185.7 | 431 | 1,590.7 | 4,336.6 | 410.0 | 6,337 | 1,065 | 215 |
| Santa Barbara–Santa Maria–Lompoc, CA | 4.8 | 36.8 | 102.3 | 295.1 | 439 | 1,569.1 | 4,029.8 | 269.2 | 5,868 | 1,026 | 201 |
| Santa Cruz, CA | 3.1 | 30.6 | 99.3 | 256.7 | 390 | 1,682.3 | 3,739.1 | 318.8 | 5,740 | 964 | 169 |
| Santa Rosa–Petaluma, CA | 3.6 | 34.5 | 87.3 | 218.8 | 344 | 1,595.7 | 3,763.0 | 319.1 | 5,678 | 912 | 154 |
| Sarasota, FL | 6.0 | 53.0 | 103.2 | 235.5 | 398 | 1,559.3 | 3,642.1 | 208.7 | 5,410 | 939 | 162 |
| Savannah, GA | 16.4 | 84.8 | 303.4 | 430.0 | 835 | 2,027.0 | 5,431.0 | 339.4 | 7,797 | 1,614 | 317 |
| ★ Scranton–Wilkes-Barre, PA | 3.6 | 8.9 | 42.3 | 82.0 | 137 | 739.5 | 1,446.8 | 169.5 | 2,356 | 372 | 6 |
| Seattle, WA | 4.4 | 60.3 | 184.8 | 245.7 | 495 | 1,910.4 | 4,481.2 | 355.1 | 6,747 | 1,170 | 254 |
| ★ Sharon, PA | 2.3 | 12.4 | 35.0 | 81.6 | 131 | 587.7 | 1,743.5 | 196.7 | 2,528 | 384 | 8 |
| ★ Sheboygan, WI | 1.9 | 5.8 | 15.6 | 29.2 | 53 | 846.9 | 3,043.4 | 80.7 | 3,971 | 450 | 23 |
| Sherman–Denison, TX | 9.4 | 20.8 | 62.4 | 454.3 | 547 | 1,624.9 | 3,046.1 | 209.0 | 4,880 | 1,035 | 206 |
| Shreveport, LA | 15.6 | 45.9 | 146.2 | 427.6 | 635 | 1,533.7 | 3,753.0 | 327.4 | 5,614 | 1,197 | 261 |

| | Violent Crime Rates | | | | | Property Crime Rates | | | | Places Rated Score | Places Rated Rank |
|---|---|---|---|---|---|---|---|---|---|---|---|
| | Murder | Forcible Rape | Robbery | Aggravated Assault | Total | Burglary | Larceny-Theft | Motor Vehicle Theft | Total | | |
| Metro Area Average | 10.0 | 39.2 | 298.6 | 314.7 | 663 | 1,669.5 | 3,436.3 | 554.3 | 5,660 | 1,229 | — |
| Sioux City, IA–NE | 4.3 | 23.0 | 35.0 | 133.0 | 195 | 1,323.6 | 4,062.8 | 253.3 | 5,640 | 759 | 97 |
| Sioux Falls, SD | 0.9 | 18.1 | 29.9 | 103.2 | 152 | 849.1 | 3,034.2 | 153.9 | 4,037 | 556 | 44 |
| South Bend–Mishawaka, IN | 4.2 | 39.3 | 179.6 | 165.8 | 389 | 1,857.8 | 4,397.5 | 240.3 | 6,496 | 1,038 | 207 |
| Spokane, WA | 5.1 | 22.4 | 96.0 | 216.2 | 340 | 1,525.4 | 3,513.9 | 252.0 | 5,291 | 869 | 136 |
| Springfield, IL | 2.7 | 35.7 | 170.6 | 429.0 | 638 | 1,673.0 | 3,983.4 | 210.5 | 5,867 | 1,225 | 268 |
| Springfield, MA | 3.5 | 41.6 | 109.6 | 572.9 | 728 | 1,668.4 | 2,640.9 | 538.0 | 4,847 | 1,212 | 264 |
| Springfield, MO | 3.8 | 33.2 | 81.7 | 143.2 | 262 | 1,841.0 | 4,210.5 | 250.8 | 6,302 | 892 | 143 |
| Stamford, CT | 3.0 | 13.5 | 197.4 | 134.6 | 348 | 1,331.8 | 3,107.2 | 428.1 | 4,867 | 835 | 127 |
| State College, PA | 0.9 | 12.4 | 33.5 | 135.9 | 183 | 678.6 | 2,793.1 | 100.6 | 3,572 | 540 | 39 |
| ★ Steubenville–Weirton, OH–WV | 2.7 | 5.5 | 66.6 | 114.1 | 189 | 767.8 | 1,345.7 | 178.9 | 2,292 | 418 | 17 |
| Stockton, CA | 19.5 | 44.4 | 250.2 | 309.4 | 624 | 2,366.4 | 4,929.1 | 417.9 | 7,713 | 1,395 | 289 |
| Syracuse, NY | 2.0 | 21.1 | 132.2 | 109.5 | 265 | 1,328.6 | 2,735.4 | 174.2 | 4,238 | 689 | 79 |
| Tacoma, WA | 5.3 | 67.3 | 157.8 | 306.3 | 537 | 2,196.7 | 3,729.4 | 329.8 | 6,256 | 1,162 | 249 |
| Tallahassee, FL | 9.9 | 54.7 | 110.4 | 426.8 | 602 | 1,721.8 | 3,630.8 | 243.9 | 5,597 | 1,161 | 248 |
| Tampa–St. Petersburg–Clearwater, FL | 8.9 | 61.1 | 231.1 | 569.1 | 870 | 2,037.7 | 3,894.5 | 298.6 | 6,231 | 1,493 | 302 |
| Terre Haute, IN | 0.8 | 15.8 | 60.9 | 133.4 | 211 | 1,456.0 | 2,433.3 | 303.5 | 4,193 | 630 | 60 |
| Texarkana, TX–Texarkana, AR | 4.2 | 20.2 | 52.3 | 284.1 | 361 | 1,191.0 | 3,214.0 | 204.8 | 4,610 | 822 | 120 |
| Toledo, OH | 4.1 | 38.4 | 238.0 | 161.1 | 442 | 1,583.4 | 3,615.5 | 361.5 | 5,560 | 998 | 189 |
| Topeka, KS | 3.8 | 29.3 | 139.3 | 250.7 | 423 | 1,826.8 | 3,740.1 | 194.1 | 5,761 | 999 | 191 |
| Trenton, NJ | 5.2 | 34.9 | 342.9 | 214.1 | 597 | 1,822.0 | 3,502.5 | 518.6 | 5,843 | 1,181 | 257 |
| Tucson, AZ | 9.5 | 55.7 | 189.6 | 387.3 | 642 | 2,223.0 | 4,962.8 | 395.9 | 7,582 | 1,400 | 290 |
| Tulsa, OK | 8.2 | 41.6 | 167.7 | 298.0 | 516 | 1,825.9 | 3,200.0 | 623.5 | 5,649 | 1,080 | 222 |
| Tuscaloosa, AL | 6.5 | 19.4 | 84.7 | 401.9 | 513 | 1,218.6 | 3,516.5 | 275.6 | 5,011 | 1,014 | 195 |
| Tyler, TX | 9.5 | 39.3 | 113.6 | 242.5 | 405 | 1,605.6 | 3,590.6 | 305.8 | 5,502 | 955 | 167 |
| ★ Utica–Rome, NY | 1.9 | 8.1 | 41.3 | 60.8 | 112 | 984.8 | 1,773.3 | 123.2 | 2,881 | 400 | 10 |
| Vallejo–Fairfield–Napa, CA | 6.1 | 40.3 | 114.0 | 307.2 | 468 | 1,348.9 | 3,383.0 | 234.4 | 4,966 | 964 | 169 |
| Vancouver, WA | 4.5 | 37.8 | 66.6 | 138.7 | 248 | 1,628.1 | 3,184.0 | 227.5 | 5,040 | 752 | 94 |
| Victoria, TX | 8.1 | 39.2 | 85.1 | 329.5 | 462 | 2,301.3 | 3,716.7 | 282.3 | 6,300 | 1,092 | 226 |
| Vineland–Millville–Bridgeton, NJ | 6.7 | 18.7 | 135.8 | 334.3 | 496 | 2,026.8 | 4,003.6 | 366.4 | 6,397 | 1,135 | 240 |
| Visalia–Tulare–Porterville, CA | 13.2 | 31.1 | 103.5 | 394.3 | 542 | 1,917.3 | 3,649.3 | 334.3 | 5,901 | 1,132 | 239 |
| Waco, TX | 17.9 | 39.1 | 145.7 | 334.9 | 538 | 1,866.7 | 4,154.2 | 264.2 | 6,285 | 1,166 | 251 |
| Washington, DC–MD–VA | 10.3 | 40.7 | 454.1 | 274.7 | 780 | 1,365.9 | 3,589.5 | 413.8 | 5,369 | 1,317 | 276 |
| Waterbury, CT | 10.8 | 20.4 | 167.4 | 86.3 | 285 | 1,442.0 | 3,175.1 | 421.1 | 5,038 | 789 | 108 |
| Waterloo–Cedar Falls, IA | 1.9 | 14.8 | 51.2 | 141.3 | 209 | 1,213.7 | 3,502.8 | 187.0 | 4,904 | 700 | 81 |
| ★ Wausau, WI | 0.0 | 16.4 | 23.4 | 99.7 | 140 | 532.7 | 2,407.9 | 87.2 | 3,028 | 442 | 22 |
| West Palm Beach–Boca Raton–Delray Beach, FL | 12.5 | 56.7 | 261.3 | 664.3 | 995 | 2,501.9 | 4,896.2 | 484.2 | 7,882 | 1,783 | 324 |
| ★ Wheeling, WV–OH | 4.3 | 11.3 | 63.9 | 44.5 | 124 | 657.5 | 1,052.9 | 127.2 | 1,838 | 308 | 1 |
| Wichita, KS | 10.0 | 51.3 | 170.7 | 263.4 | 495 | 1,761.7 | 4,581.8 | 339.0 | 6,683 | 1,164 | 250 |
| Wichita Falls, TX | 14.6 | 58.5 | 203.4 | 305.0 | 582 | 1,794.1 | 3,787.6 | 389.8 | 5,972 | 1,179 | 255 |
| ★ Williamsport, PA | 3.4 | 9.2 | 31.1 | 98.4 | 142 | 863.4 | 2,201.0 | 157.2 | 3,222 | 464 | 25 |
| Wilmington, DE–NJ–MD | 3.6 | 30.0 | 139.0 | 367.5 | 540 | 1,469.9 | 3,842.8 | 433.7 | 5,746 | 1,115 | 234 |
| Wilmington, NC | 7.6 | 37.8 | 149.3 | 522.5 | 717 | 2,162.7 | 4,575.7 | 316.5 | 7,055 | 1,423 | 292 |
| Worcester, MA | 2.5 | 24.9 | 109.5 | 181.8 | 319 | 1,281.0 | 1,935.5 | 395.0 | 3,611 | 680 | 77 |
| Yakima, WA | 4.5 | 50.5 | 116.3 | 278.0 | 449 | 1,637.6 | 4,692.1 | 237.8 | 6,568 | 1,106 | 232 |
| ★ York, PA | 1.6 | 11.0 | 61.5 | 71.5 | 146 | 736.3 | 2,050.1 | 158.7 | 2,945 | 440 | 21 |
| Youngstown–Warren, OH | 5.5 | 21.5 | 167.4 | 350.6 | 545 | 1,285.3 | 2,268.6 | 371.7 | 3,926 | 938 | 161 |
| Yuba City, CA | 10.3 | 32.7 | 68.1 | 502.0 | 613 | 1,899.8 | 3,493.5 | 268.7 | 5,662 | 1,179 | 255 |

## CRIME ON THE DECLINE?

In 1980, the number of crimes reported to the FBI reached the highest level ever recorded in the bureau's 50-year history of collecting crime figures. Two years later, the numbers took another turn—this time for the better, with a 3 percent overall drop in the eight Index crimes from 1981.

Although it is far too early to conclude that crime is on the decline, officials at the FBI are expressing "cautious optimism" about the findings for 1982: murder down 7 percent, forcible rape down 5 percent, robbery 6 percent, burglary 9 percent, larceny-theft 1 percent, motor vehicle theft 2 percent, and arson 12 percent. The only Index crime whose incidence increased was aggravated assault, and that rise was just 1 percent. The rates of both violent and property crime declined by 4 percent. Overall rates for violent and property crime also fell by 5 percent each in the first six months of 1983, the FBI reported.

The National Crime Survey of the Bureau of Justice Statistics came to similar conclusions. The study, based on twice-yearly interviews with about 130,000 victims of crime, found a 7 percent decrease in serious crimes in 1983. Violent crime fell 10 percent and property crime 8 percent. This marked the second year in a row that the bureau's survey and the FBI reports both showed significant declines.

Despite the unanimity of the two studies, there has been controversy about the findings. Many criminologists are skeptical about lower statistics meaning less crime, pointing to flaws in both systems of gathering data. The FBI reports have been faulted for reflecting only crimes already reported to police and for the fact that their data come from local authorities, who may overreport or underreport for their own reasons. And although the Bureau of Justice Statistics survey overcomes these drawbacks by getting information directly from crime victims, it has been criticized because individual perceptions could skew the results; for instance, a citizen from a small town might describe a purse-snatching as a serious crime, whereas a big-city resident would be liable to dismiss it as part of urban life. Both organizations are presently reevaluating their methods in hopes of improving their reliability.

The real test of whether these studies do presage a downswing will be the pattern of crime rates in the next few years. Still, experts have not been loath to offer explanations for the small dip that has occurred. One is the aging of the baby-boom generation, leaving a smaller proportion of the population in the crime-prone range of ages 18 to 24. Another is the fact that citizens are taking a more active interest in the security of their neighborhoods. Also cited are the increasingly rigorous sentences sought by prosecutors and imposed by judges, and the Justice Department's nationwide campaign to impose stricter penalties on repeat offenders.

### Crime Rates in the Metro Areas

Does this recent drop in crime mean that the 329 metro areas have significantly lower rates than previously? To find out, let's compare these rates with those of the metro areas in the 1981 edition of *Places Rated Almanac*, which used data for 1979. (A note of caution: For two reasons, any comparison of these two sets of data will be imperfect. First, as explained in the Introduction to this book, the names and boundaries of many metro areas have shifted since 1981, so that the exact counterpart of a place described in the earlier edition may no longer exist. Second, unlike the case in this edition, crime data were not available for all the 1981 metro areas; in those places the averages for all metro areas within the state were used.)

As we pointed out early in this chapter, it is unusual for a place's crime rate to alter very much from year to year—safe places tend to remain safe, and dangerous places dangerous. In general, this rule holds true for our 329 metro areas. Of the 15 metro areas that were ranked safest by the 1981 *Places Rated Almanac*, ten also appear in this edition's top 15:

Source: FBI, *Uniform Crime Reports*, 1982, 1983.

Figures are for 1982.

| Altoona, PA | Lancaster, PA |
| Binghamton, NY | St. Cloud, MN |
| Grand Forks, ND | Scranton–Wilkes-Barre, PA |
| Kokomo, IN | Utica–Rome, NY |
| Johnstown, PA | Wheeling, WV–OH |

Likewise, 11 of 1981's fifteen most dangerous metro areas also number among the 15 most crime-ridden places in this edition:

| Baltimore, MD | New York, NY |
| Gainesville, FL | Orlando, FL |
| Las Vegas, NV | San Francisco, CA |
| Los Angeles–Long Beach, CA | Savannah, GA |
| | West Palm Beach– |
| Miami–Hialeah, FL | Boca Raton–Delray |
| New Orleans, LA | Beach, FL |

There were, however, a few startling changes in overall rank. Those metro areas that lost the most ground in relative safety, dropping at least 149 places, were the following: Anniston, Alabama (from 74th to 238th); Brockton, Massachusetts (131st to 282nd); Laredo, Texas (62nd to 211th); Midland, Texas (70th to 251st); Odessa, Texas (169th to 322nd); and Sherman–Denison, Texas (52nd to 206th). Four of them owe their descent in the standings to higher violent crime rates: Anniston's rose by 54 percent, Brockton's by 86 percent, Odessa's by 83 percent, and Sherman–Denison's by a spectacular 141 percent. In Laredo and Midland, property crime rates that had jumped 43 percent and 56 percent, respectively, were the culprits.

Why do four Texas metro areas appear in this group? One possible explanation is the explosive growth that has taken place in the state, undermining the social fabric and placing unusual stress on communities and services.

Of those metro areas whose ranks improved since the last edition, only two recorded significantly large changes: Fort Myers, Florida, which went from 233rd place to 107th, and New London–Norwich, Connecticut–Rhode Island, which leapt from 172nd to 61st.

(Johnson City–Kingsport–Bristol, Tennessee–Virginia, and several New England metro areas also improved their rankings considerably, but these changes do not necessarily reflect a true drop in crime since the 1981 ranks of these places were based on state averages, individual metro area data being unavailable.) Fort Myers saw a 64 percent drop in its violent crime rate and a 35 percent dip in its property crime rate, while New London–Norwich recorded a 50 percent decline in violent crime and one of 31 percent in property crime over the same period.

Fort Myers's turnaround, according to the Lee County sheriff's office, was based on two community action programs, Crime Watch and CRIMESTOP. In Crime Watch, police officers train citizens in the basics of observation and reporting, teaching them what events to be suspicious of and which details they should note to help police track down a suspect. The CRIMESTOP program televises reenactments of unsolved felonies, filmed at the actual sites of the crimes, after which viewers who think they may have a lead are urged to call in. New London–Norwich, too, recently instituted programs that enlisted the aid of the community. Their success proves that citizen involvement is essential in fighting crime.

## WHAT THE STATES SPEND TO FIGHT CRIME

If a state devotes a lot of money to law enforcement and criminal investigations, chances are that crime levels there are low—right?

Wrong. A close examination of justice expenditures and crime rates in the states reveals just the opposite. For example, Alaska, which leads the states in justice spending, has the ninth highest crime rate in the United States. And West Virginia, which devotes less of its budget to justice activities than all but two of the other 49 states, has the nation's lowest crime rate. In

**Justice Spending in the States**

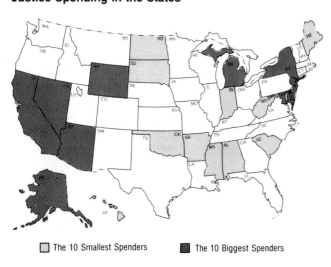

☐ The 10 Smallest Spenders    ■ The 10 Biggest Spenders

**Crime in the States**

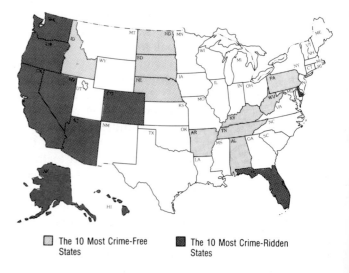

☐ The 10 Most Crime-Free States    ■ The 10 Most Crime-Ridden States

## Justice Spending and Crime Rate by State

| State | Spending per Capita | Rank | Crime Rate | Rank | State | Spending per Capita | Rank | Crime Rate | Rank |
|---|---|---|---|---|---|---|---|---|---|
| Alabama | $ 65 | 44 | 4,134 | 40 | Montana | $ 76 | 31 | 4,444 | 33 |
| Alaska | 275 | 1 | 6,265 | 9 | Nebraska | 78 | 30 | 4,019 | 42 |
| Arizona | 124 | 5 | 7,295 | 2 | Nevada | 150 | 3 | 8,104 | 1 |
| Arkansas | 48 | 50 | 3,479 | 44 | New Hampshire | 70 | 40 | 4,453 | 32 |
| California | 132 | 4 | 7,289 | 3 | New Jersey | 122 | 6 | 5,788 | 16 |
| | | | | | | | | | |
| Colorado | 98 | 16 | 6,861 | 6 | New Mexico | 95 | 18 | 5,608 | 18 |
| Connecticut | 93 | 21 | 5,808 | 15 | New York | 175 | 2 | 6,210 | 11 |
| Delaware | 121 | 7 | 6,341 | 8 | North Carolina | 80 | 28 | 4,225 | 38 |
| Florida | 104 | 15 | 7,192 | 4 | North Dakota | 61 | 46 | 2,777 | 49 |
| Georgia | 76 | 32 | 5,143 | 23 | Ohio | 81 | 26 | 5,098 | 24 |
| | | | | | | | | | |
| Hawaii | 108 | 14 | 6,981 | 5 | Oklahoma | 69 | 42 | 4,580 | 30 |
| Idaho | 73 | 37 | 4,114 | 41 | Oregon | 109 | 11 | 6,247 | 10 |
| Illinois | 109 | 12 | 5,082 | 25 | Pennsylvania | 89 | 22 | 3,453 | 45 |
| Indiana | 62 | 45 | 4,538 | 31 | Rhode Island | 98 | 17 | 5,601 | 19 |
| Iowa | 72 | 38 | 4,281 | 36 | South Carolina | 69 | 41 | 4,812 | 28 |
| | | | | | | | | | |
| Kansas | 75 | 36 | 4,942 | 26 | South Dakota | 66 | 43 | 2,960 | 47 |
| Kentucky | 75 | 34 | 3,082 | 46 | Tennessee | 75 | 35 | 3,878 | 43 |
| Louisiana | 93 | 19 | 5,212 | 21 | Texas | 70 | 39 | 5,711 | 17 |
| Maine | 58 | 47 | 4,200 | 39 | Utah | 79 | 29 | 5,302 | 20 |
| Maryland | 120 | 8 | 6,184 | 12 | Vermont | 76 | 33 | 5,163 | 22 |
| | | | | | | | | | |
| Massachusetts | 109 | 13 | 5,942 | 14 | Virginia | 88 | 23 | 4,256 | 37 |
| Michigan | 114 | 9 | 6,120 | 13 | Washington | 93 | 20 | 6,388 | 7 |
| Minnesota | 85 | 25 | 4,417 | 35 | West Virginia | 53 | 48 | 2,252 | 50 |
| Mississippi | 53 | 49 | 2,840 | 48 | Wisconsin | 87 | 24 | 4,439 | 34 |
| Missouri | 81 | 27 | 4,919 | 27 | Wyoming | 112 | 10 | 4,803 | 29 |

Source: Bureau of Justice Statistics, *Report to the Nation on Crime and Justice*, October 1983.

general, states with high expenditures have high crime rates, and those with low expenditures have low rates. This correlation indicates that states spend in response to crime rather than in hopes of preventing it.

However, other factors besides the crime rate may be at work. A state may owe a high justice expenditure to the fact that it attracts a great number of tourists and must therefore provide more police services, or to the fact that its criminal justice system is inefficient.

The table "Justice Spending and Crime Rate by State" shows how the states stack up in justice expenditures and crime rates. The figures on justice outlays come from the Bureau of Justice Statistics and are for 1979, the most recent year for which data are available. They represent the per capita amount a state spends each year on law enforcement, prosecution, public defense and adjudication, prisons and other forms of corrections, and such miscellaneous activities as victim compensation and criminal justice planning. The state crime rates, from the FBI *Uniform Crime Reports*, are also for 1979 to present a true comparison.

## VICTIMS: ASKING FOR JUSTICE

Everybody wonders what to do about criminals. But only recently has a nationwide wave of anger and frustration addressed the question, What can be done to ease the problems of the victims of crime?

When you become a victim, you may also fall victim to social injustice, police callousness, court delays, and legal tangles. You may even get lost in the human services systems of the country if the crime leaves you hospitalized and unable to work.

### Who Are the Victims?

According to the National Crime Survey of the Bureau of Justice Statistics for 1981, the number of crime victims has held fairly steady at an annual rate of about 35 victims per 1,000 people since 1973.

In 1981, men were victims of violent crime in 48 percent of cases, compared with 28 percent for women, and men were robbed or assaulted about twice as often as women. Blacks suffered greater numbers of crimes than whites—50 percent versus 35 percent—although offenders and their victims were generally of the same race.

For crimes of violence or theft, people between the ages of 12 and 24 had the highest victimization rates and those 65 or older the lowest. Members of families in the lowest income category (less than $3,000 a year) had the highest overall rate of victimization of any income group for crimes of violence, and unemployed persons were victimized more often than those who had jobs. The survey also found that victimization

## State Aid to Victims of Crime

| State | Financial Award | To Qualify, Victim Must . . . | | |
|---|---|---|---|---|
| | | Show Financial Need | Report to Police Within | File Claim Within |
| Alaska | $ 0–40,000 | No | 5 days | 24 mo |
| California | 100–23,000 | Yes | * | 12 |
| Colorado | 25– 1,500 | No | 3 | 6 |
| Connecticut | 100–10,000 | No | 5 | 24 |
| Delaware | 25–10,000 | No | * | 12 |
| District of Columbia | 0–25,000 | Yes | 7 | 6 |
| Florida | 0–10,000 | Yes | 3 | 12 |
| Hawaii | 0–10,000 | No | * | 18 |
| Illinois | 0–15,000 | No | 3 | 12 |
| Indiana | 100–10,000 | No | 2 | 3 |
| Iowa | 0– 2,000 | No | 1 | 6 |
| Kansas | 100–10,000 | Yes | 3 | 12 |
| Kentucky | 100–15,000 | Yes | 2 | 12 |
| Louisiana | 250–10,000 | No | 3 | 12 |
| Maryland | 100–45,000 | Yes | 2 | 6 |
| Massachusetts | 100–10,000 | No | 2 | 12 |
| Michigan | 100–15,000 | Yes | 2 | 1 |
| Minnesota | 100–25,000 | No | 5 | 12 |
| Missouri | 200–10,000 | No | 2 | 12 |
| Montana | 0–25,000 | No | 3 | 12 |
| Nebraska | 0–10,000 | No | 3 | 24 |
| Nevada | 100– 5,000 | Yes | 5 | 12 |
| New Jersey | 100–25,000 | No | 90 | 24 |
| New Mexico | 0–12,500 | No | 30 | 12 |
| New York | 0–20,000† | Yes | 7 | 12 |
| North Dakota | 100–25,000 | No | 3 | 12 |
| Ohio | 0–25,000 | No | 3 | 12 |
| Oklahoma | 0–10,000 | No | 3 | 12 |
| Oregon | 250–23,000 | No | 3 | 6 |
| Pennsylvania | 100–25,000 | No | 3 | 12 |
| Rhode Island | 0–25,000 | No | 10 | 24 |
| South Carolina | 300–10,000 | No | 2 | 6 |
| Tennessee | 100–10,000 | No | 2 | 12 |
| Texas | 0–50,000 | Yes | 3 | 6 |
| Virginia | 100–10,000 | Yes | 2 | 6 |
| Washington | 200–15,000† | No | 3 | 12 |
| West Virginia | 0–20,000 | No | 3 | 24 |
| Wisconsin | 0–12,000 | No | 5 | 24 |

Source: State Legislatures, November/December 1981, with additions from the National Organization of Victim Assistance.

*Must report, but no time limit specified.
†Plus unlimited medical expenses.

rates for violent crime were higher among residents of the central cities than among suburbanites or rural dwellers. In two thirds of all violent crimes in 1981, victims were assaulted by people they did not know.

### Action for Victims

Most people say that the best way to help a crime victim is to catch the criminal. But it's hard to see how this helps victims who may be injured physically, suffering emotionally, and unable to take up their lives. A number of steps have recently been taken to offer victims more satisfaction.

In 1982, Congress responded to the growing con-

cern for victims' rights by passing the Victim and Witness Protection Act. This act imposes heavy penalties on those who threaten or intimidate a witness, instructs federal judges to study a crime's impact upon the victims before passing sentence, and requires many of those convicted to make restitution to their victims.

A restitution law was enacted at the federal level in 1982. Restitution takes three forms: service to the community, service to the victim, or financial payment. Someone found guilty of driving under the influence, for example, might be assigned to work a certain number of hours in a hospital emergency room, observing the results of drunk driving firsthand and also aiding the community. An offender might also be required to pay the victim a stipulated amount or to perform a service for the victim.

Thirty-seven states and the District of Columbia operate programs that compensate victims of violent crime (see the table "State Aid to Victims of Crime"). The funds distributed by the states come from a variety of sources. General revenues, fines, and penalties collected by the state are usually tapped for this purpose. Several states draw a small percentage of the salaries earned by offenders on work release or in prison, and others claim defendants' profits from the sale of books or films based on their criminal exploits.

Another move on behalf of victims was made in California in 1981, when Proposition 8—or Prop 8, as the victims' bill of rights is known—was passed into law by 56 percent of the vote. Some of its provisions were for the elimination of plea bargaining in felony cases, for longer sentences for habitual criminals, and for the admission of previously excluded evidence.

But Prop 8 has not worked the way it was intended. Some attorneys for accused criminals say Prop 8 has actually helped their clients, saving them from what ordinarily would have been convictions. Judges and prosecutors report that there is little evidence of greater number of convictions or of longer sentences. And court officials in some jurisdictions—notably Orange County—claim that the elimination of plea bargaining has aggravated the backlog of criminal cases.

## LIFE BEHIND BARS

A cost of crime not often considered by the general public is the drain on society that occurs *after* the crime has been committed and *after* sentence has been passed—incarceration. Not only does society lose these convicts as full-time members of the work force, but it must also foot the ever-increasing bill for their imprisonment.

### Prison Populations

As of 1983, there were approximately 432,000 inmates in America's 50 federal prisons, 600 state prisons, and 3,900 county and city jails. California, the nation's most populous state, also had the biggest prison population as of mid-1983—just over 37,000. Texas was a close second, its inmate population falling slightly below that mark, while New York (30,000) and Florida (28,000) ranked third and fourth.

If we look beyond prisons and consider all forms of correctional sanction, we find that 2.4 million people—more than 1 percent of the U.S. population—are under some correctional care, custody, or supervision. This figure translates to 1.2 percent of all adults over 18 and one in every 45 adult men.

The numbers are large—and getting larger. The nationwide prison population has doubled since 1973 and jumped by 23 percent since 1982. In 1972, the rate of incarceration across the country was 93 per 100,000 people; it was 177 per 100,000 in 1983, the highest such rate since the government began keeping records in 1925.

The following states, according to the Bureau of Justice Statistics, have seen staggering increases in their numbers of prisoners between the end of 1981 and the end of 1982: Alaska and North Dakota, 28 percent; Nevada, 25 percent; New Mexico, 23 percent; Oklahoma, 21 percent; and Hawaii, 18 percent. Since 1980, Arizona's inmate population has doubled.

Such increases may seem strange considering that the national crime rate has been declining since 1980. Most criminologists attribute them to recent changes made by state legislatures in sentencing. Nearly all states now require some sort of mandatory sentencing, which means that certain offenses automatically mean doing time. Increasing the length of minimum sen-

tences has also compounded the problem, as have the adoption in ten states of determinate sentencing (basing offenders' sentences on the seriousness of their crimes and on their records) and the straitening of parole-release laws in another dozen states.

## Over the Limit

This trend has had immediate and obvious results. With record numbers of prisoners outstripping the resources of jails, inmates in prisons all over the country have been given makeshift cells in corridors, tents, trailers, and gymnasiums. Overcrowding has also meant, in many cases, the suspension of work and education programs for prisoners, leaving them almost exclusively confined to their cells. At San Quentin, California, where the official capacity of 2,700 inmates has been exceeded by 1,200, living conditions are so bad that its warden has described the state prison as a "time bomb."

This phrase might well apply to a great many other institutions, where the situation is such that guards cannot always protect inmates from each other. In 1980, for example, 39 percent of all deaths that occurred behind bars resulted from murder or "unknown causes," according to the Bureau of Justice Statistics. New York State (which includes the infamous Attica Correctional Facility) recorded 40 deaths from unknown causes, Texas 50 such deaths, and New Mexico 39 murders during that year.

## FIREARMS AND CRIME

Although many claim that people rather than guns kill people, it is undisputable that the weapons most commonly used by murderers are firearms. In 1982, according to the FBI, 60 percent of all homicides were committed with either a handgun, shotgun, or rifle.

The handgun is often portrayed as the favorite weapon of the criminal. Easily concealed and extremely lethal, it was by far the most frequently used gun in 1982 homicides, being employed in 43 percent of all such deaths. In 1980, the FBI reported, handguns were used in some 220,000 robberies and 157,000 aggravated assaults. Sixty-six percent of law enforcement officers killed in that same year were slain with handguns. In fact, although handguns make up only 20 percent of the firearms in this country, they account for 90 percent of all firearms misuse, criminal or accidental.

## Ownership of Guns

The table "Who Are the Firearms Owners?" provides a portrait of the Americans who own handguns or long guns (rifles or shotguns), based on a 1978 survey of 1,500 people. The majority of handgun owners in this study were white, male, 36 to 45 years old, graduates of technical or vocational schools, and residents of rural areas of the South. Self-avowed conservative Americans owned the greatest percentage of hand-

---

### Death Row, U.S.A.

The same tough stance recently taken by the judiciary that has contributed to prison overcrowding has also meant a greater willingness to impose the death penalty. As of May 1984 there were 1,351 inmates awaiting execution in the United States, a 27 percent increase over 1982 and the greatest such total ever. Thirty-eight states had the death penalty in mid-1984.

Almost two thirds of those on death row at that time were in southern prisons, with Florida (214), Texas (172), and Georgia (115) reporting the highest totals. The western states recorded approximately another 20 percent of inmates sentenced to death, or 269 prisoners; 157 of these were imprisoned in California. The North Central states had about 11 percent of the total (143), and the northeastern states about 5 percent (62).

Of those 1,351 prisoners awaiting execution, according to the NAACP Legal Defense and Educational Fund, Inc., 701 were white, 562 black, 68 Hispanic, 15 American Indians, and four Asians (the race of one inmate was unknown to NAACP). Only 18 of them were women.

## Who Are the Firearms Owners?

| | "Does anyone living in this immediate household own a handgun or pistol or not?" | | | "How about a long gun—such as a rifle or shotgun—does anyone own one of those or not?" | | |
|---|---|---|---|---|---|---|
| | Yes | No | Not Sure | Yes | No | Not Sure |
| **National Average** | 24% | 72% | 4% | 36% | 62% | 3% |
| **Sex** | | | | | | |
| Male | 29 | 67 | 4 | 43 | 55 | 2 |
| Female | 19 | 77 | 4 | 28 | 68 | 3 |
| **Race** | | | | | | |
| White | 25 | 72 | 3 | 39 | 59 | 2 |
| Black | 23 | 69 | 9 | 20 | 75 | 5 |
| **Education** | | | | | | |
| Some grade school | 21 | 72 | 6 | 23 | 72 | 5 |
| Some high school | 23 | 71 | 6 | 41 | 56 | 3 |
| High school graduate | 24 | 74 | 2 | 38 | 62 | 1 |
| Technical/vocational | 32 | 64 | 4 | 47 | 47 | 6 |
| Some college | 28 | 70 | 2 | 36 | 63 | 2 |
| College graduate | 22 | 73 | 5 | 28 | 68 | 4 |
| Graduate/professional | 20 | 72 | 8 | 42 | 54 | 4 |
| **Income** | | | | | | |
| Under $4,000 | 14 | 81 | 5 | 21 | 77 | 2 |
| $4,000 to $6,999 | 21 | 76 | 2 | 23 | 75 | 1 |
| $7,000 to $9,999 | 21 | 76 | 4 | 29 | 69 | 2 |
| $10,000 to $12,999 | 21 | 78 | 1 | 37 | 62 | 1 |
| $13,000 to $14,999 | 23 | 73 | 4 | 38 | 59 | 3 |
| $15,000 to $19,999 | 24 | 74 | 2 | 40 | 59 | 1 |
| $20,000 to $24,999 | 35 | 63 | 2 | 49 | 49 | 2 |
| $25,000 and over | 30 | 69 | 1 | 45 | 55 | 0 |
| **Age** | | | | | | |
| 18 to 25 years | 21 | 76 | 4 | 34 | 62 | 3 |
| 26 to 35 years | 25 | 72 | 4 | 37 | 61 | 2 |
| 36 to 45 years | 30 | 68 | 3 | 44 | 55 | 1 |
| 46 to 55 years | 29 | 68 | 4 | 41 | 56 | 2 |
| 56 to 65 years | 22 | 76 | 3 | 36 | 62 | 2 |
| 66 years and older | 23 | 74 | 4 | 24 | 73 | 3 |
| **Community size** | | | | | | |
| Urban | 23 | 72 | 6 | 29 | 68 | 3 |
| Suburban | 22 | 76 | 2 | 32 | 66 | 2 |
| Rural | 31 | 66 | 4 | 56 | 43 | 1 |
| **Region** | | | | | | |
| Northeast | 15 | 84 | 1 | 31 | 69 | 0 |
| Industrial | 17 | 78 | 5 | 32 | 65 | 3 |
| Midlands | 16 | 83 | 1 | 38 | 61 | 1 |
| South | 41 | 50 | 9 | 39 | 56 | 5 |
| Central | 34 | 64 | 2 | 53 | 46 | 2 |
| Pacific | 19 | 80 | 2 | 25 | 74 | 2 |
| **Religion** | | | | | | |
| Protestant | 29 | 66 | 5 | 40 | 57 | 3 |
| Catholic | 18 | 81 | 1 | 29 | 70 | 1 |
| Jewish | 11 | 89 | 0 | 20 | 80 | 0 |
| Other | 17 | 82 | 1 | 32 | 67 | 1 |
| None | 24 | 71 | 5 | 37 | 59 | 5 |
| **Politics** | | | | | | |
| Liberal | 20 | 76 | 4 | 31 | 67 | 2 |
| Moderate | 25 | 73 | 3 | 38 | 60 | 2 |
| Conservative | 27 | 70 | 4 | 40 | 58 | 2 |

*Source:* Cambridge Reports, Inc., *An Analysis of Public Attitudes Toward Handgun Control,* 1978. Reprinted by permission.

guns (27 percent), but 20 percent of those people calling themselves liberals owned them, too.

In the case of long guns, the percentage of ownership rose with income up to $25,000 and then fell off slightly. This percentage was nearly twice as high among whites as among blacks, and was highest in rural areas of what the survey designated the Central region, among men between 36 and 45, and among those with technical or vocational degrees.

### State Laws on Handguns

As of March 1982, thirty-six states had a constitutional provision allowing the ownership of handguns. But 41 of the states also had at least two requirements that had to be met before an adult could purchase or carry a handgun, such as undergoing a waiting period or obtaining a license or permit. In several states—Alaska, Kentucky, Nevada, and Oklahoma, for example—the restrictions were minimal, while in such states as Hawaii, Illinois, Massachusetts, and New York they were comprehensive.

Both statewide and national movements urging further control of the sale of handguns have been formed in recent years. Their members cite not only the roughly 11,000 Americans murdered each year by this weapon but also the 1,300 accidental fatalities and 10,000 suicides in which it is involved yearly. Proponents of further restrictions point to the success that legislation banning the sale of handguns has had in reducing murder rates in Boston, the District of Columbia, and South Carolina.

On the other side of the issue are sportsmen, hunters, collectors, and many other law-abiding citizens who use and own handguns. They claim that to disarm honest citizens through gun laws only stacks the odds more in favor of criminals who will not obey such laws.

## DRIVING UNDER THE INFLUENCE

Not all criminals rob banks or commit murder; you might even be one yourself, if you drink and then drive. People who do so may not get caught every time they break the law, any more than speeders do, but they are criminals just the same. And when they do get caught, it's usually because their crime has had a devastating impact.

### The Deadly Statistics

The damage done by those who drive under the influence adds up to some sobering figures: more than 25,000 deaths a year and $5 billion a year lost. Drunk drivers are estimated to cause between 50 percent and 90 percent of all traffic fatalities.

About one of every 50 drivers on the highway at any given time is likely to be legally drunk, and that proportion rises to one in ten on weekend nights. On an average day, intoxicated drivers kill 70 people, one every 20 minutes. Many of them don't think they are drunk—they just had a couple of drinks at a party, that's all.

To be considered legally drunk in most states, a person must have the equivalent of .10 percent alcohol in their blood. Someone who weighs about 150 pounds will attain that level with five drinks over two and a half hours. A drink, strictly defined, is the equivalent of one-half ounce of pure alcohol, found in one mixed drink, one 12-ounce can of beer, or one four-ounce glass of wine. To reach the .05 percent level, the upper limit set by some states, all it takes is three drinks within an hour and a half.

More than half of those persons charged with drunk driving are men between the ages of 18 and 40. The largest group arrested is men between the ages of 25 and 40, the second largest men between 18 and 25. And, although drivers under age 21 represent about 10 percent of all licensed drivers and drive only 9 percent of all vehicle miles driven, they account for fully 21 percent of alcohol-related fatalities.

## U.S. Drinking Ages

Because of the large percentages of young people involved in such accidents, 29 of the 35 states that had lowered their drinking ages in the early 1970s have raised them again. The following information, dated June 1984, comes from the National Transportation Safety Board.

In 23 states, a person must be 21 years old to purchase or consume any alcoholic beverage (Nebraska's law will go into effect on July 1, 1985):

| | | |
|---|---|---|
| Alaska | Marlyland | Oklahoma |
| Arizona | Michigan | Oregon |
| Arkansas | Missouri | Pennsylvania |
| California | Nebraska | Rhode Island |
| Delaware | Nevada | Tennessee |
| Illinois | New Jersey | Utah |
| Indiana | New Mexico | Washington |
| Kentucky | North Dakota | |

In 19 states, the legal minimum age for buying or consuming any alcoholic beverage is 18, 19, or 20:

| | |
|---|---|
| Alabama (19) | Minnesota (19) |
| Connecticut (20) | Montana (19) |
| Florida (19) | New Hampshire (20) |
| Georgia (19) | New York (19) |
| Hawaii (18) | Texas (19) |
| Idaho (19) | Vermont (18) |
| Iowa (19) | West Virginia (19) |
| Louisiana (18) | Wisconsin (19) |
| Maine (20) | Wyoming (19) |
| Massachusetts (20) | |

Three states allow only 3.2 percent beer to people under 21 (Colorado, Kansas, and South Dakota); in two places the legal minimum age for beer and table wine is 18, and 21 for fortified wine and distilled spirits (the District of Columbia and Mississippi); and three states require buyers to be at least 19 for beer and 21 for wine and distilled spirits (North Carolina, Ohio, and Virginia). In South Carolina a person must be at least 20 to purchase beer and wine, and 21 to buy distilled spirits.

In July 1984, a federal law was enacted to penalize states that allow drinking by people under 21; the bill would also reward states with mandatory sentences for drunk drivers. Both penalties and rewards are to be distributed in the form of federal highway funds.

# Transportation:

## Getting In, Out, & Around

Jaded travelers take for granted the vast networks of Interstate highways, airline routes, and Amtrak rails that lace up this country's different points. A look at a national map shows certain metro areas to be hubs with many highway, rail, and air-route spokes, while others appear as lesser intersections, removed from the mainstream of intercity travel.

Population size has something to do with an area's transportation assets, and so do the hazards of geography. There are 26 metro areas larger than Denver, for example, but because the Mile High City is plunked down at the edge of the Rocky Mountains halfway between Chicago and Southern California, and midway from Houston to Seattle, only five airports are busier than Denver's Stapleton International.

Intercity travel is only one part of the picture, of course. Some metro areas have efficient and inexpensive public transit systems relied on by hundreds of thousands of commuters each working day. In other metro areas, older fleets of transit buses with optimistic schedules lurch along routes that rarely reach any neighborhoods but those close to downtown. Still other metro areas have no public transit at all; their residents must get around by car, depending on expressways, commercial arteries, and residential streets.

## GETTING AROUND TOWN

If you are moving to El Paso, can your family get by without a second car? If you are being transferred to your employer's headquarters in Cleveland, will it be more convenient to carpool or to use public transportation if you settle in the suburb of Shaker Heights? How much time might you need to spend each day getting to and from work? Becoming familiar with the local transportation features of a particular metro area will help you answer some of these questions.

### The Commuting Life

Every weekday morning, in cities and towns all over the country, traffic trickles out of suburban streets, flows into arterial roads, and floods freeways to capacity with people bound for work. According to most transportation experts, the morning rush hour lasts 118 minutes, between 7:01 and 8:59. Most workers travel by automobile, alone; one out of five belongs to a car pool; and one out of 15 opts for public transit.

The evening rush hour lasts longer, 150 minutes, from 4:30 to 7:00. There are more traffic delays at this time than in the morning, when people so purposefully leave home and arrive at work in the shortest possible time. In the evening, many commuters stop for a drink, go shopping, run errands, or just dawdle. After all, one can't be fired for being late for supper. In fact, traffic experts say, even if you head straight home, the evening trip not only seems longer than the trip to work, it actually is—20 percent longer.

How much time do metro area dwellers spend going to and from work each day? To allow for the longer trip home in the evening, *Places Rated* multiplies the average journey-to-work figure by 2.2 to estimate the round-trip time in each of the metro areas. As you might suspect, daily commuting time increases with city size. Workers in Grand Forks, North Dakota, for instance, putting in 230 working days a year, spend about 110 hours commuting. New Yorkers spend 310 hours. The contrast between Grand Forks and New York, then, is more than one between a prairie college town and the nation's largest city. Based on commuting time alone, Grand Forkers have more free time than New Yorkers, the equivalent of five 40-hour weeks.

### Getting to Work and Back

| Shortest Commuting Time | Minutes per Day* | Longest Commuting Time | Minutes per Day* |
|---|---|---|---|
| 1. Grand Forks, ND | 28.6 | 1. New York, NY | 81.0 |
| 2. Bismarck, ND | 30.8 | 2. Nassau–Suffolk, NY | 70.6 |
| 2. Rochester, MN | 30.8 | 3. Washington, DC–MD–VA | 64.5 |
| 4. Fargo–Moorhead, ND–MN | 31.5 | 4. Monmouth–Ocean, NJ | 64.0 |
| 4. Lawton, OK | 31.5 | 5. Chicago, IL | 63.8 |
| 6. Lafayette, IN | 31.7 | 6. Houston, TX | 58.5 |
| 6. Sheboygan, WI | 31.7 | 7. Baltimore, MD | 58.3 |
| 8. Appleton–Oshkosh–Neenah, WI | 32.3 | 8. Jersey City, NJ | 57.6 |
| 8. Sioux Falls, SD | 32.3 | 9. Philadelphia, PA–NJ | 56.3 |
| 10. Sioux City, IA–NE | 32.6 | 10. New Orleans, LA | 55.9 |
| | | 10. Newark, NJ | 55.9 |

*Source* (for journey-to-work figures): U.S. Bureau of the Census, *1980 Census of Population and Housing.*

**Places Rated* multiplies journey-to-work minutes by a factor of 2.2 to estimate round-trip daily commuting time.

### Public Mass Transit

One reason for the long commute in big cities is the often onerous job of making linked transit trips to get to work. Nationally, the average duration of an *unlinked* transit trip—a direct route, with no transfers—is 15 minutes. But many big-city commuters have to make *linked* trips—driving to a park-and-ride lot; boarding a train, tram, or bus; and sometimes switching again before finally arriving at work.

Nevertheless, in larger cities where the tab for daily parking in a downtown garage tops ten dollars, where rush hour traffic jams approach grid-lock, where distances are long and time always seems short, public transit really counts. In three of our largest cities—Houston, Los Angeles, and Phoenix—daily driving over long distances is a way of life unrelieved by rapid public transit; taking the bus is the only alternative. In other places such as Atlanta, Washington, and San Francisco, large local bus fleets are complemented by rapid transit rail systems.

Depending on where they want to go, New York City commuters can choose from bus, heavy rail, light rail, commuter railroad, ferryboat, and even aerial tramway service. New York straphangers may not always enjoy their subway ride to work, but few among the jostled riders aboard a rocking, grimy IRT car would ever envy a Houston driver who has missed his or her exit on the Southwest Freeway at rush hour.

### Metro Areas with No Public Transit

| | |
|---|---|
| Anniston, AL | Jacksonville, NC |
| Bismarck, ND | Joplin, MO |
| Brazoria, TX | Kankakee, IL |
| Bryan–College Station, TX | Kokomo, IN |
| Burlington, NC | Las Cruces, NM |
| Casper, WY | Lawton, OK |
| Clarksville–Hopkinsville, TN–KY | Longview–Marshall, TX |
| Dothan, AL | Ocala, FL |
| Elkhart–Goshen, IN | Odessa, TX |
| Enid, OK | Pascagoula, MS |
| Fayetteville–Springdale, AR | Richland–Kennewick–Pasco, WA |
| Florence, AL | Sharon, PA |
| Fort Smith, AR–OK | Sherman–Denison, TX |
| Gadsden, AL | Texarkana, TX–Texarkana, AR |
| Great Falls, MT | Victoria, TX |
| Houma–Thibodaux, LA | Yuba City, CA |
| Huntsville, AL | |

*Source: Places Rated* survey, April 1984.

### The Mass Transit Quarter

Public transit is available in most cities, but it is an option passed up by 93 out of every 100 persons who commute to work because the operating schedule isn't convenient, the system doesn't reach the workplace, or because they prefer the freedom of their own car. In only 17 of the 945 cities with populations over 25,000 does at least one in four workers use public transit.

| City | Commuters Using Public Transit |
|---|---|
| 1. New York, NY | 56% |
| 2. San Francisco, CA | 39 |
| 3. Washington, DC | 38 |
| 4. Boston, MA | 34 |
| 4. Jersey City, NJ | 34 |
| 6. Chicago, IL | 32 |
| 7. Philadelphia, PA | 30 |
| 8. Cambridge, MA | 28 |
| 8. Mount Vernon, NY | 28 |
| 8. Oak Park, IL | 28 |
| 8. Somerville, MA | 28 |
| 12. Evanston, IL | 27 |
| 13. Hoboken, NJ | 26 |
| 13. Newark, NJ | 26 |
| 15. Atlanta, GA | 25 |
| 15. Baltimore, MD | 25 |
| 15. Rockville Centre, NY | 25 |

*Source: U.S. Bureau of the Census, *1980 Census of Population and Housing.*

**By Bus.** In most cities, public transit and "the bus" are synonymous. Unlike rapid rail and trolley networks, a bus system requires no expensive construction, and routes can be easily changed to meet demand.

Each of the country's 1,022 public transit systems puts motor buses on the street, but transit systems do vary in size and type of operation. Several large systems—CTA (Chicago), Southern California RTD (Los Angeles), WMATA (Washington, D.C.), and NYCTA (New York), for example—operate more than 2,000 buses each, 24 hours a day, with less than one minute between buses on the heaviest routes during morning and evening rush hours. At the other extreme are the one- and two-bus "shoppers' specials" that run loops in the central business district of smaller metro areas.

**On the Tracks.** Although buses can meet the demand for public transit nearly everywhere, rail lines are more efficient in carrying large numbers of rush hour commuters in the major cities. Several kinds of rail service are available in the big metro areas, from rapid rail to trolley car to commuter train.

*Rapid rail lines,* owing to their exclusive rights-of-way, are unaffected by traffic jams. Their trains and trams not only carry hundreds of people, they carry them quickly: The average speed of buses during peak rush hour, nationwide, is 11.8 miles per hour. Rapid rail systems average more than 20 miles per hour. There are two types of rapid rail lines in use today in 15 metro areas: heavy rail, which accounts for 2.5 billion passenger trips in a year, and light rail, which accounts for 150 million passenger trips. Both are electrically powered, and both may be found in the same city.

Heavy rail systems—known locally as subways, elevated railways, or Els—have high-level platform stations. The cars are individually powered through the third rail, and are hitched together to form longer trains during rush hours. New York City's heavy rail system, composed of two separate networks, is the world's largest, with 6,263 cars traveling more than 450 miles of track; Philadelphia also has two systems. As of January 1984, ten U.S. metro areas have heavy rail systems:

| | |
|---|---|
| Atlanta, GA | Oakland, CA |
| Boston, MA | Philadelphia, PA–NJ |
| Chicago, IL | (2 systems) |
| Cleveland, OH | San Francisco, CA |
| New York, NY | Seattle, WA |
| (2 systems) | Washington, DC–MD–VA |

Light rail cars, powered by overhead electrical wires, travel at half the speed of heavy rail cars. Because their tracks are laid above ground, they are less expensive to build and therefore are the fastest-growing form of mass transit, currently being planned in 19 cities. Nine metro areas now have light rail transit:

## Rating the Transit Supply

Totting up all of the local buses, rapid rail cars, and trolley coaches will give you the size of a metro area's transportation fleet, but that isn't an accurate measure of transit supply.

A better indicator can be found if you take the number of passengers that a fleet's vehicles can carry at one time, multiply that number by the miles the fleet runs up each day in service, and then divide by the number of people living in the metro area's urban part. The result is known as seat miles per capita.

In Madison, there are slightly more than six bus seats traveling one mile of route for every person in the Wisconsin capital's urbanized area, the best single-mode transit supply of any metro area. But the ultimate record for transportation supply goes to New York. If all vehicles were put in service at the same time, this metro area's multimode fleet would provide more than 23 seat miles for each resident. Not surprisingly, New York is the only city in the United States where a majority of commuters use public transit.

### The Top 10 Metro Areas for Bus Transit Supply

| Metro Area | Buses | Seat Miles per Capita |
|---|---|---|
| 1. Madison, WI | 193 | 6.02 |
| 2. Duluth, MN–WI | 101 | 5.08 |
| 2. Santa Cruz, CA | 94 | 5.08 |
| 4. Honolulu, HI | 406 | 4.64 |
| 5. Portland, OR | 649 | 4.21 |
| 6. Boulder–Longmont, CO | 55 | 3.99 |
| 6. San Jose, CA | 745 | 3.99 |
| 8. Portland, ME | 63 | 3.92 |
| 9. Atlantic City, NJ | 35 | 3.88 |
| 10. Minneapolis–St. Paul, MN–WI | 1,012 | 3.77 |

### The Top 10 Metro Areas for Bus and Rapid Rail Transit Supply

| Metro Area | Seat Miles per Capita |
|---|---|
| 1. New York, NY | 23.49 |
| 2. San Francisco, CA | 11.68 |
| 3. Washington, DC–MD–VA | 8.81 |
| 4. Oakland, CA | 7.18 |
| 5. Cleveland, OH | 6.42 |
| 6. Seattle, WA | 6.37 |
| 7. Boston, MA | 5.60 |
| 8. Atlanta, GA | 4.95 |
| 9. Chicago, IL | 4.68 |
| 10. Philadelphia, PA–NJ | 3.79 |

*Source:* Derived from U.S. Department of Transportation, Urban Mass Transportation Administration, *National Urban Mass Transportation Statistics—Section 15 Report,* 1984.

The average transit supply in the metro areas is 2.43 seat miles per capita.

| | |
|---|---|
| Atlanta, GA | Newark, NJ |
| Boston, MA | Philadelphia, PA–NJ |
| Cleveland, OH | Pittsburgh, PA |
| Detroit, MI | San Francisco, CA |
| New Orleans, LA | |

*Trolley coaches* are street car–type railways that travel on city streets with semiprivate or exclusive rights-of-way. They are a less efficient form of travel than rapid rail since the trams are at the mercy of automobile traffic and, in some cities, must stop for streetlights. Another disadvantage is that their routes cannot be altered. These systems have been largely replaced by bus; in fact, only five metro areas in the United States have trolley coach operations:

| | |
|---|---|
| Boston, MA | San Francisco, CA |
| Dayton–Springfield, OH | Seattle, WA |
| Philadelphia, PA–NJ | |

*Commuter railroads* have been an important form of transportation from more distant suburbs to the central part of major cities since the nineteenth century. Using both locomotive-hauled and self-propelled passenger cars, this service is characterized by multitrip tickets, station-to-station fares, railroad employment practices, and usually only one or two stations in the central business district. Eighteen commuter railroads in 11 metro areas ferry more than a million commuters to and from work. The largest commuter railroad network, made up of seven firms, is found in New York and uses 2,500 cars to move 525,000 riders in a typical weekday. In Chicago, the next largest commuter railroad center, nine carriers operating 850 cars transport 290,000 workers in a typical day.

### Freeway Traffic

Just as most metro area commuters have a car all to themselves on the way to work, most of them drive part of the way on a functionally classified urban freeway, that is, a divided highway with fully controlled access points. The extent to which a metro area is drawn tight by ribbons of freeway is governed by its land area and population. Los Angeles is regarded as a place overburdened with concrete, partly because so many of the innovations of limited-access, high-speed arterial road construction—ramps, trumpets, and cloverleafs—were seen early in Southern California.

In U.S. cities, the length of urban freeways amounts to 3.24 percent of the total road and street mileage. If you look at freeways in this way, Los Angeles may be undeserving of its reputation as the Freeway City since limited-access divided highways there make up only 2.3 percent of the total road mileage.

Nine metro areas have no freeways, and those that have them differ in the amount of traffic their freeways must accommodate. In 21 metro areas, traffic volume averages 90 percent or more of the capacity of the freeways. Most of these congested freeways are in major metro areas or in the East: Seven of the 21 are in the New York–Northern New Jersey–Long Island consolidated area. Surprisingly, traffic volume is also very heavy in some of the less populated metropolitan areas, including Olympia, Washington, and Anchorage, Alaska.

## Most Congested Metro Areas

| | |
|---|---|
| Allentown–Bethlehem, PA | Los Angeles–Long Beach, CA |
| Anchorage, AK | Middlesex–Somerset– |
| Atlanta, GA | Hunterdon, NJ |
| Austin, TX | Monmouth–Ocean, NJ |
| Bergen–Passaic, NJ | New Orleans, LA |
| Birmingham, AL | New York, NY |
| Cleveland, OH | Newark, NJ |
| Denver, CO | Olympia, WA |
| Detroit, MI | Orange County, NY |
| Houston, TX | San Antonio, TX |
| Jersey City, NJ | Wilmington, DE–NJ–MD |

Traffic volume on the freeways in these metro areas averages 90% or more of design capacity.

## INTERCITY TRAVEL

''You can't get there from here'' is the punch line of the old joke about the lost city feller who asked directions of a bemused farmer. The line has little meaning in today's metropolitan areas, given the networks of well-traveled highways, railroads, and airways that connect these places.

Or does it? Obviously, you can neither take to the Interstate nor board a train if your destination is Anchorage or Honolulu. For that matter, you can't get to Bloomington, Indiana; Bremerton, Washington; or Burlington, North Carolina, by the same means. When it comes to intercity travel choices, some metro areas are better off than others.

### Interstate Highways

When President Franklin Roosevelt idly penciled three east-west and five north-south lines on a U.S. map back in 1938 as part of a proposed national highway system, he probably had no idea that his drawing would be so important in determining whether many rural towns would grow and many others would decline. He envisioned a 34,000-mile network of multilane toll roads. Although the concept of collecting tolls was soon dropped by the Bureau of Public Roads, the basic routes on his map foresaw the Interstate Highway System, a river of economic life to cities and towns along the way and possibly a cause of stagnation for those that were bypassed.

The Interstate system is now an almost complete 42,500-mile road network, at least four traffic lanes wide, that spans 48 states and links together nearly every city with a population of more than 50,000. Still, 60 of our metro areas are not on the Interstate network. Even though Interstate routes account for only 1 percent of all road and street mileage in the United States, they carry 25 percent of all the traffic. As the car is the dominant means of intercity travel, so the dominant road is the Interstate.

On any given day, Americans drive more than 870 million miles on Interstate highways. Three out of ten of all those miles are logged in just four states: California, Illinois, Ohio, and Texas. The heaviest traffic can be found on the stretches of the Interstate system that are classified as urban. These cloverleafed freeways, spurs, and beltways in and around cities carry 55 percent of all the travel. The balance is borne by the long, often boringly straight rural routes that make up 77 percent of Interstate mileage.

### Busiest Stretches of Interstate Highways

I-5, I-210, I-405, I-605 in Los Angeles, CA
I-5 in Seattle, WA
I-10, I-45, I-59, I-610 in Houston, TX
I-25 in Denver, CO
I-35E, I-635 in Dallas, TX
I-75 in Atlanta, GA
I-80, I-580 in Oakland, CA
I-80, I-380 in San Francisco, CA
I-90, I-94, I-290 in Chicago, IL
I-95 in New York, NY
I-280 in San Jose, CA
I-395 in Washington, DC–MD–VA

### Loneliest Stretches of Interstate Highways

I-15 between Idaho Falls, ID, and Butte, MT
I-25 between Buffalo, WY, and Casper, WY
I-29 between Grand Forks, ND, and the Canadian border
I-29 between Sioux Falls, SD, and Fargo–Moorhead, ND
I-70 between Cove Fort, Utah, and the Colorado border
I-90 between Buffalo, WY, and Gillette, WY
I-91 between Derby Line, VT, and St. Johnsbury, VT
I-94 between Billings, MT, and the North Dakota border

According to the U.S. Department of Transportation, the busiest stretches on the Interstate carry 150,000 to 250,000 vehicles every 24 hours. The loneliest carry fewer than 2,500.

---

### Decoding the Interstate System

The numbers in the middle of the red-white-and-blue, shield-shaped signs along the Interstate system were developed in 1957 by the American Association of State Highway Transportation Officials. There are 34 odd-numbered routes, which run north and south, and 27 even-numbered routes, which run east and west. The lowest-numbered routes are in the West and the South; I-5, for example, lies along the nation's West Coast and I-10 along the southern border.

In cities, these one- or two-digit numbers don't change as long as they are part of the major traffic stream. Beltways around the city, on the other hand, carry three numbers: the main route number with an even-numbered prefix. For example, I-495, an 88-mile-long route around Boston, and I-287, a 94-mile-long loop skirting New York City, are the two longest beltways in the Interstate system. If a main route carries an odd-numbered prefix (such as I-195 in Miami or I-780 in San Francisco), the route is a spur that connects with the main route at only one end.

Three-digit route numbers are never used twice in the same state. In New York, I-90 runs through Schenectady, Syracuse, Rochester, and Buffalo, and the beltways off this main route in those cities are numbered, respectively, I-890, I-690, I-490, and I-290. This rule isn't carried across state lines, however. Two cities on I-10 but in different states, Houston and New Orleans, have the identical beltway number of I-610.

---

### Boarding Pass, Please

It's said in the South that when you die and are on your way to either heaven or hell, you'll have to make connections in Atlanta. Atlanta's airport, Hartsfield International, is the world's second busiest.

Like other airports that are reached by scheduled airlines, Hartsfield is a twentieth-century urban landmark in the same way the railroad station was a sign of the times in the late nineteenth century. Most of the 595 airports served by domestic carriers in the United States are quiet, even desolate places. But some, like Hartsfield, resemble self-contained cities, and last year 38 of these airports in the nation's large hubs handled 70 percent of the nearly 300 million people who boarded domestic flights. The busiest, Chicago's O'Hare International Airport, boarded more passengers than the 400 smallest U.S. airports combined.

Two hundred and forty-six metro areas have one airport with scheduled service, 19 have two airports, and two—Chicago and Los Angeles–Long Beach—have three. In one day, flights from these 290 airports average one for every 8,862 residents in metro areas that have access to passenger service.

### The Busiest U.S. Airports

| Airport | Annual Passengers |
|---|---|
| 1. Chicago O'Hare International | 42,873,000 |
| 2. Hartsfield International (Atlanta) | 37,919,000 |
| 3. Los Angeles International | 33,426,000 |
| 4. John F. Kennedy International (New York) | 27,904,000 |
| 5. Dallas–Fort Worth Regional | 26,783,000 |
| 6. Stapleton International (Denver) | 25,247,000 |
| 7. San Francisco International | 23,166,000 |
| 8. Miami International | 19,321,000 |
| 9. La Guardia (New York) | 18,183,000 |
| 10. Logan International (Boston) | 17,848,000 |
| 11. Newark International | 17,411,000 |
| 12. Lambert–St. Louis International | 16,241,000 |
| 13. Honolulu International | 15,261,000 |
| 14. Washington National (Washington, D.C.) | 14,166,000 |
| 15. Houston Intercontinental | 12,984,000 |

Source: Airport Operators Council International, 1984.

Figures represent the number of passengers arriving and departing at each airport every year.

You'll stand the best chance of dodging airport jams if you fly on Thursday afternoons and Saturday nights. The worst travel days used to be Fridays and Sundays. Now they are Tuesdays and Wednesdays because more people take advantage of special fares requiring midweek travel.

### Riding the Rails

Sixty years ago, eight out of ten people who had to get from one city in the United States to another did it aboard a train. There were 20,000 different ones from which to choose, if you didn't care where you were going. The *Twentieth Century Limited, El Capitan, Blue Streak*—each had a unique, trademarked name. They still do—*Desert Wind, Sunset Limited, Empire Builder,*

*Silver Palm*—but today there are just 230 of them. Over the years, their share of the commercial passenger traffic has dwindled to 7 percent.

If passenger trains are ever to rise again, the renaissance will be due not to high gasoline prices and spot fuel shortages but to mounting congestion on intercity highways. California traffic experts, for example, foresee a four-hour automobile commute between San Jose and San Francisco by 1990. The railroads have a priceless asset: existing tracks and rights-of-way into the population centers of the nation.

The National Railroad Passenger Corporation, a profit-making body, was created by Congress to subsidize the passenger-carrying business of its member railroads. Better known as Amtrak, it began operation in 1971. Today it carries virtually all of the 25 million passengers who board intercity trains each year.

The passenger rails don't reach everywhere, however. Although Amtrak's timetable boasts stops at hundreds of cities and towns from Aberdeen, Maryland, to Yuma, Arizona, 166 of the 329 metro areas aren't on the route system. The metro areas bypassed include such large places as Tulsa, Louisville, and Des Moines.

On the average, there is a weekday Amtrak train for every 197,497 residents among the 163 metro areas with rail passenger service. Battle Creek, Michigan, ought to be as renowned for passenger trains as for breakfast cereal, since there are more Amtrak departures per capita here than in any other metro area: one for every 17,695 people per weekday. By far the biggest markets for train service are in the northeast quadrant of the United States. But the fastest-growing markets are on the West Coast, particularly for the two-hour-and-forty-minute run between Los Angeles and San Diego and for the six-hour San Francisco–Bakersfield route.

## JUDGING TRANSPORTATION SUPPLY

When it comes to evaluating the supply of travel options in a metro area, a good measure is how many people can be served by a place's transit system and by the number of intercity travel choices. Would urban dwellers in Syracuse or San Angelo have a better chance of finding a seat on a bus? Which metro area airport—Atlanta's or Denver's—has more daily departures per local population?

In rating metro areas for transit supply, *Places Rated*'s approach is similar to that taken in the first edition of this book. As before, we examine three modes of transportation used between cities (Interstate highways, airplane, and passenger train) and one used locally (mass transit). A useful new scoring element introduced for this edition of *Places Rated Almanac* is the daily commute, the average time spent getting to and from work within a metro area. To arrive at a score for each metro area, these five criteria are compared with

### The Busiest Two-Way Air Routes

| Routes | Annual Passengers |
|---|---|
| 1. Boston–New York City | 4,220,250 |
| 2. New York City–Washington, D.C. | 3,807,250 |
| 3. Los Angeles–New York City | 2,453,920 |
| 4. Los Angeles–San Francisco | 2,376,950 |
| 5. Chicago–New York City | 2,332,640 |
| 6. Miami–New York City | 1,658,080 |
| 7. New York City–San Francisco | 1,458,660 |
| 8. Honolulu–Kahului, Maui | 1,366,280 |
| 9. New York City–Pittsburgh | 1,339,940 |
| 10. Fort Lauderdale–New York City | 1,256,990 |
| 11. Las Vegas–Los Angeles | 1,140,000 |
| 12. Detroit–New York City | 983,010 |
| 13. Atlanta–New York City | 964,580 |
| 14. Chicago–Los Angeles | 936,520 |
| 15. Honolulu–Lihue, Kauai | 924,830 |

*Source:* Air Transport Association of America, 1984.

### The Busiest Amtrak Routes

| Northeast Corridor* | Annual Passengers |
|---|---|
| 1. New York–Philadelphia | 2,400,000 |
| 2. Metroliners, Boston–New York–Washington | 1,200,000 |
| 3. Harrisburg–Philadelphia | 760,000 |
| 4. New Haven–Springfield, MA | 260,000 |
| **Short Distance** | |
| 1. Los Angeles–San Diego | 1,064,000 |
| 2. New York–Albany–Niagara Falls | 841,000 |
| 3. Chicago–Detroit–Toledo | 368,000 |
| 4. Chicago–St. Louis | 274,000 |
| 5. Oakland–Bakersfield | 221,000 |
| **Long Distance** | |
| 1. Chicago–Oakland–Los Angeles | 725,000 |
| 2. New York–Florida | 610,000 |
| 3. Los Angeles–Seattle | 485,000 |
| 4. Chicago–New York–Boston | 350,000 |
| 5. New York–New Orleans | 250,000 |

*Source:* Amtrak, *Ridership By Route,* 1984.

*Another 6.1 million passengers a year travel various Amtrak routes along the Northeast Corridor not listed here.

the national metro area averages.

In the case of judging air service, some further adjustments were made in calculating a score for metro areas that are part of a Consolidated Metropolitan Statistical Area (see the Appendix for a list of CMSAs and component metro areas). Because major airports tend to serve a very wide geographical area and are able to accommodate large numbers of travelers, *Places Rated* considers the air service assets of CMSA component metro areas to be shared equally by all members of the CMSA, no matter which metro area the airport(s) may be located in.

Each metro area starts with a base score of zero, to which points are added according to the following indicators:

1. *Daily commute.* The time spent commuting to and from work is almost entirely unproductive—and unavoidable. To rate each

## You're Better Off in Large Hubs

The Federal Aviation Administration (FAA) rates each metro area for its share of airline service by designating it as one of the following: large hub, medium hub, small hub, or non-hub.

| A metro area is a . . . | if passengers leaving its airport(s) total . . . |
|---|---|
| large hub | 1% or more |
| medium hub | 0.25% to 0.99% |
| small hub | 0.05% to 0.24% |
| non-hub | less than 0.05% |
| | **of all U.S. airline passengers in a year.** |

There's one big advantage to living in a large hub besides having a wider choice of carriers with more frequent nonstop flights to more destinations: Flying between large hubs is cheaper.

The cost of an airline ticket into and out of Bismarck, North Dakota (a non-hub), or Charleston, West Virginia (a small hub), helps subsidize the same airline's small profit from a New York vacationer's air travel to Miami or a Los Angeles conventioneer's trip to Chicago. When airlines skirmish with bargain fares between large hubs, travelers in the smaller hubs end up paying part of the tab.

place for commuting time, the U.S. metro area average of 49.7 minutes is divided by the average minutes local workers spend in daily commuting. The result is then multiplied by 1,000. Consequently, the shorter the commuting time, the more points a metro area will receive. Workers in Houston, for instance, spend an average of 58.5 minutes commuting, which works out to 850 points, compared with an average time of only 28.6 minutes in Grand Forks, North Dakota. This daily commute results in a score that is more than twice Houston's.

2. *Mass transit.* Counting the number of motor buses and rapid rail cars in a metro area's transit system won't tell you enough about local transit performance. *Places Rated* instead adopts the urban mass transit industry's measure of *seat miles per capita,* which means the number of transit seats that travel one mile of transit route for each person in the urban core each day.

Among the 296 metro areas with public transit, the average number of seat miles per capita is 2.43. To rate each metro area for transit supply, the local seat mile figure is divided by this 2.43 average and multiplied by 1,000, with a maximum total of 5,000 points per metro area. Chicago's buses and

rapid rail cars provide 4.68 seat miles for each resident. The Second City therefore has a transit supply 1.926 times the metro area average, good for 1,926 points.

3. *Interstate highways.* There are an average of 1.438 main numbered routes for the 269 metro areas reached by the 42,500-mile Interstate system. To rate each metro area in this category, the number of routes in the metro area is divided by the average of 1.438 and multiplied by 1,000. Dallas is reached by four routes—I–20, I–30, I–35, and I–45; the Texas metro area therefore has 2.782 times the national average of Interstate routes, totaling 2,782 points.

4. *Airline flights.* For the 303 metro areas with access to airports with passenger service, the average number of residents per departing flight each day is 8,862. To rate each metro area, this average is divided by the local ratio of residents to departure, then multiplied by 1,000. (In the case of CMSA component metro areas, the ratio of residents per departure is arrived at by dividing the total number of departures in the CMSA by the total CMSA population. Each member metro area receives the same number of points.) The maximum score for each metro area is 3,000 points.

5. *Passenger train (Amtrak) departures.* The average number of residents per Amtrak departure each day for the 163 metro areas served by Amtrak is 197,497. To arrive at a score for each metro area, this average is divided by the local number of residents per daily train departure, then multiplied by 1,000, with a ceiling of 1,500 points.

### Sample Comparison: New York, New York, and Houma–Thibodaux, Louisiana

A premier world port and trade center and a pair of cities in Louisiana bayou country are the best and worst metro areas, respectively, for transportation supply according to *Places Rated*'s criteria.

In Houma–Thibodaux, which comprises Lafourche and Terrebonne parishes, workers take 52.6 minutes to get to and from their jobs each day. Dividing 49.7 minutes, the national average round-trip commuting time for the metro areas, by 52.6 and multiplying by 1,000 yields a score of 945. There is no public transportation in this metro area, nor any Interstate highways linking it with other metro areas along the network.

And despite Houma–Thibodaux's population growth during the 1970s in the midst of the Louisiana oil and natural gas boom, it is served by only one airline. To board a plane for such destinations as Miami, Dallas, or Memphis means driving northeast on U.S. 90 for an hour or so to New Orleans International–Moisant Field. There are just four commuter flights per day out of Houma–Terrebonne Airport, or one flight for every 44,219 people in this small metro area. Houma–Thibodaux's score for this transportation asset is calculated by dividing 8,862, the national average of metro area residents per daily flight, by 44,219 and multiplying by 1,000; the result is 200 points. Amtrak service is also lacking, meaning that the total score for this metro area is the sum of its points for commuting time and air travel—1,145, the lowest of all 329 metro areas.

New York, in contrast, is the core of the country's largest metro complex: the New York–Northern New Jersey–Long Island consolidated area. Workers here spend an average of 81 minutes every day commuting, good for a score of only 614. Most of New York's commuters use public transit, and it is ironic that they spend so much time—the longest daily trip of any metro area—aboard the biggest transit system in the world. New York's 4,662 buses and 6,263 rapid rail cars provide a phenomenal 23.49 seats per mile of route for each resident. When divided by the national metro area average of 2.43 and multiplied by 1,000, this figure results in a score of 9,667, which is trimmed to the maximum number of points *Places Rated* allows for this category, 5,000.

Three Interstate highways reach the nation's largest city, giving it an additional 2,086 points after dividing 3 by 1.438, the national average of Interstate highways per metro area, and multiplying by 1,000. As part of the New York–Northern New Jersey–Long Island consolidated area, made up of 12 metro areas, New York is served by eight passenger airports: Allaire Field, Igor I. Sikorsky Memorial, John F. Kennedy International, La Guardia, Long Island–MacArthur, Newark International, Republic, and Stewart. There are a total of 1,229 airline flights out of these facilities each day, or one flight for every 14,271 people. This results in a score of 621 for air travel.

Amtrak's biggest hub in the United States is at Grand Central Station, in downtown Manhattan. Twenty-seven trains leave here every day, most of which reach other metro areas in the consolidated area, which means one train for every 649,604 people. This works out to a score of 304 when divided into the national average of one daily train for every 197,497 metro area residents and then multiplied by 1,000. The sum of New York's five scores is 8,625, the highest of any metro area in the United States.

# Places Rated: Metro Areas Ranked for Transportation Supply

Determining a score for transportation means looking closely at a metro area's ability to accommodate the transportation needs of its residents, using the following criteria: (1) daily commute, (2) public transportation, (3) Interstate highways, (4) air service, and (5) passenger rail service.

Places that receive tie scores are given the same rank and are listed in alphabetical order.

## Metro Areas from Best to Worst

| Places Rated Rank | Places Rated Score | Places Rated Rank | Places Rated Score | Places Rated Rank | Places Rated Score |
|---|---|---|---|---|---|
| 1. New York, NY | 8,625 | 16. Boston, MA | 6,801 | 31. Springfield, IL | 6,172 |
| 2. Atlanta, GA | 8,409 | 17. Reno, NV | 6,767 | 32. Harrisburg–Lebanon– | |
| 3. San Francisco, CA | 8,299 | 18. Richmond–Petersburg, VA | 6,680 |     Carlisle, PA | 6,164 |
| 4. Washington, DC–MD–VA | 8,236 | 19. Seattle, WA | 6,634 | 33. Springfield, MA | 6,159 |
| 5. Denver, CO | 8,145 | 20. Boise City, ID | 6,575 | 34. Charlotte–Gastonia– | |
| | | | |     Rock Hill, NC–SC | 6,099 |
| 6. Chicago, IL | 7,742 | | | 35. La Crosse, WI | 6,096 |
| 7. Champaign–Urbana– | | | | | |
|     Rantoul, IL | 7,447 | 21. Albuquerque, NM | 6,558 | 36. Madison, WI | 6,084 |
| 8. Baltimore, MD | 7,405 | 22. Raleigh–Durham, NC | 6,544 | 37. Charlottesville, VA | 6,041 |
| 9. Cleveland, OH | 7,333 | 23. East St. Louis–Belleville, IL | 6,539 | 38. Savannah, GA | 5,958 |
| 10. Burlington, VT | 7,146 | 24. Oakland, CA | 6,430 | 39. Portland, OR | 5,947 |
| | | 25. Fargo–Moorhead, ND–MN | 6,325 | 40. New Haven–Meriden, CT | 5,938 |
| 11. Hartford, CT | 7,120 | | | 41. Honolulu, HI | 5,911 |
| 12. St. Louis, MO–IL | 7,119 | 26. Billings, MT | 6,285 | 42. Philadelphia, PA–NJ | 5,903 |
| 13. Boulder–Longmont, CO | 7,108 | 27. Sioux Falls, SD | 6,271 | 43. Las Vegas, NV | 5,900 |
| 14. Syracuse, NY | 6,951 | 28. Memphis, TN–AR–MS | 6,247 | 44. Bloomington–Normal, IL | 5,889 |
| 15. Albany–Schenectady– | | 29. Salt Lake City–Ogden, UT | 6,228 | 45. Orlando, FL | 5,887 |
|     Troy, NY | 6,883 | 30. Dallas, TX | 6,213 | | |

| Places Rated Rank | Places Rated Score |
|---|---|
| 46. Kansas City, MO | 5,869 |
| 47. Columbia, SC | 5,859 |
| 48. Gary–Hammond, IN | 5,855 |
| 49. Omaha, NE–IA | 5,806 |
| 50. Indianapolis, IN | 5,804 |
| 51. Erie, PA | 5,754 |
| 52. Cincinnati, OH–KY–IN | 5,748 |
| 53. Redding, CA | 5,727 |
| 54. Santa Barbara–Santa Maria–Lompoc, CA | 5,662 |
| 55. South Bend–Mishawaka, IN | 5,634 |
| 56. Lincoln, NE | 5,618 |
| 57. Pittsburgh, PA | 5,616 |
| 58. Bangor, ME | 5,613 |
| 59. Jacksonville, FL | 5,611 |
| 60. Minneapolis–St. Paul, MN-WI | 5,606 |
| 61. Tampa–St. Petersburg–Clearwater, FL | 5,588 |
| 62. Grand Forks, ND | 5,587 |
| 63. Niagara Falls, NY | 5,561 |
| 64. Lansing–East Lansing, MI | 5,557 |
| 65. Spokane, WA | 5,534 |
| 66. Tallahassee, FL | 5,530 |
| 67. Des Moines, IA | 5,521 |
| 68. San Diego, CA | 5,489 |
| 69. Providence, RI | 5,474 |
| 70. Charleston, WV | 5,470 |
| 71. Louisville, KY–IN | 5,420 |
| 72. Kalamazoo, MI | 5,419 |
| 73. Fort Wayne, IN | 5,416 |
| 74. San Antonio, TX | 5,387 |
| 75. Buffalo, NY | 5,384 |
| 76. Topeka, KS | 5,348 |
| 77. Toledo, OH | 5,323 |
| 78. Midland, TX | 5,310 |
| 79. Eugene–Springfield, OR | 5,293 |
| 80. Cedar Rapids, IA | 5,270 |
| 81. Lafayette, LA | 5,268 |
| 82. San Jose, CA | 5,224 |
| 83. Duluth, MN–WI | 5,205 |
| 84. Miami–Hialeah, FL | 5,202 |
| 85. West Palm Beach–Boca Raton–Delray Beach, FL | 5,201 |
| 86. Portland, ME | 5,185 |
| 87. Birmingham, AL | 5,177 |
| 88. Rochester, NY | 5,165 |
| 89. Sacramento, CA | 5,097 |
| 90. Anchorage, AK | 5,091 |
| 91. Asheville, NC | 5,086 |
| 92. Nashville, TN | 5,030 |
| 93. Santa Cruz, CA | 5,010 |
| 94. Kansas City, KS | 5,006 |
| 95. Jersey City, NJ | 4,982 |
| 96. Alton–Granite City, IL | 4,975 |
| 97. Florence, SC | 4,963 |
| 98. Lafayette, IN | 4,956 |
| 99. Milwaukee, WI | 4,945 |
| 100. Jackson, MS | 4,917 |
| 101. Flint, MI | 4,912 |
| 102. Lynchburg, VA | 4,909 |
| 103. Amarillo, TX | 4,902 |
| 104. New Britain, CT | 4,900 |

| Places Rated Rank | Places Rated Score |
|---|---|
| 105. Akron, OH | 4,883 |
| 106. Detroit, MI | 4,808 |
| 107. Jackson, MI | 4,800 |
| 108. Trenton, NJ | 4,786 |
| 109. Dayton–Springfield, OH | 4,775 |
| 110. Pawtucket–Woonsocket–Attleboro, RI–MA | 4,738 |
| 111. Salem, OR | 4,732 |
| 112. Tacoma, WA | 4,730 |
| 113. Phoenix, AZ | 4,729 |
| 114. Tuscaloosa, AL | 4,723 |
| 115. Richland–Kennewick–Pasco, WA | 4,714 |
| 116. Battle Creek, MI | 4,652 |
| 117. Joliet, IL | 4,645 |
| 118. Middletown, CT | 4,636 |
| 119. Houston, TX | 4,626 |
| 120. Fall River, MA–RI | 4,602 |
| 121. Manchester, NH | 4,595 |
| 122. Utica–Rome, NY | 4,592 |
| 123. Fort Myers, FL | 4,583 |
| 124. New Orleans, LA | 4,579 |
| 125. St. Cloud, MN | 4,565 |
| 126. Provo–Orem, UT | 4,546 |
| 127. Wilmington, DE–NJ–MD | 4,532 |
| 128. Binghamton, NY | 4,529 |
| 129. New London–Norwich, CT–RI | 4,505 |
| 130. Bristol, CT | 4,495 |
| 131. Kenosha, WI | 4,473 |
| 132. Fort Worth–Arlington, TX | 4,472 |
| 133. Oklahoma City, OK | 4,459 |
| 134. Greensboro–Winston-Salem–High Point, NC | 4,458 |
| 135. Stockton, CA | 4,427 |
| 136. Casper, WY | 4,410 |
| 137. Fayetteville, NC | 4,402 |
| 138. Shreveport, LA | 4,401 |
| 139. Parkersburg–Marietta, WV–OH | 4,399 |
| 139. Rochester, MN | 4,399 |
| 141. Tucson, AZ | 4,397 |
| 142. Fresno, CA | 4,388 |
| 143. Columbus, OH | 4,364 |
| 144. Los Angeles–Long Beach, CA | 4,345 |
| 145. Johnstown, PA | 4,343 |
| 146. Muncie, IN | 4,325 |
| 147. Sioux City, IA–NE | 4,316 |
| 148. Bismarck, ND | 4,303 |
| 149. Canton, OH | 4,279 |
| 150. Knoxville, TN | 4,273 |
| 151. Altoona, PA | 4,246 |
| 152. Charleston, SC | 4,207 |
| 153. Middlesex–Somerset–Hunterdon, NJ | 4,198 |
| 154. Fort Lauderdale–Hollywood–Pompano Beach, FL | 4,186 |
| 154. Little Rock–North Little Rock, AR | 4,186 |
| 156. Elkhart–Goshen, IN | 4,168 |
| 157. Poughkeepsie, NY | 4,166 |
| 158. Salinas–Seaside–Monterey, CA | 4,160 |

| Places Rated Rank | Places Rated Score |
|---|---|
| 159. Lubbock, TX | 4,158 |
| 160. Vallejo–Fairfield–Napa, CA | 4,153 |
| 161. Vineland–Millville–Bridgeton, NJ | 4,133 |
| 162. Daytona Beach, FL | 4,117 |
| 163. Lima, OH | 4,084 |
| 164. Olympia, WA | 4,083 |
| 165. Lexington–Fayette, KY | 4,080 |
| 166. Chico, CA | 4,067 |
| 167. Abilene, TX | 4,031 |
| 168. Huntington–Ashland, WV–KY–OH | 4,001 |
| 169. Anaheim–Santa Ana, CA | 3,954 |
| 170. Greenville–Spartanburg, SC | 3,950 |
| 171. Aurora–Elgin, IL | 3,943 |
| 172. Wichita, KS | 3,933 |
| 173. Lancaster, PA | 3,908 |
| 174. Davenport–Rock Island–Moline, IA–IL | 3,907 |
| 175. Columbia, MO | 3,893 |
| 176. Roanoke, VA | 3,872 |
| 177. Decatur, IL | 3,867 |
| 178. Springfield, MO | 3,828 |
| 179. Lowell, MA–NH | 3,820 |
| 180. Vancouver, WA | 3,817 |
| 181. Brockton, MA | 3,810 |
| 182. Bradenton, FL | 3,805 |
| 183. Ocala, FL | 3,798 |
| 184. Green Bay, WI | 3,793 |
| 185. Bellingham, WA | 3,776 |
| 186. Pittsfield, MA | 3,759 |
| 187. Tulsa, OK | 3,758 |
| 188. Great Falls, MT | 3,747 |
| 189. Sarasota, FL | 3,742 |
| 190. Yakima, WA | 3,731 |
| 191. Bakersfield, CA | 3,725 |
| 192. Cumberland, MD–WV | 3,709 |
| 193. El Paso, TX | 3,705 |
| 194. Scranton–Wilkes-Barre, PA | 3,683 |
| 195. Austin, TX | 3,670 |
| 196. Dubuque, IA | 3,668 |
| 197. Worcester, MA | 3,643 |
| 198. Lorain–Elyria, OH | 3,629 |
| 199. Corpus Christi, TX | 3,626 |
| 200. Monroe, LA | 3,606 |
| 201. Fayetteville–Springdale, AR | 3,581 |
| 202. Lawrence–Haverhill, MA–NH | 3,575 |
| 203. Racine, WI | 3,558 |
| 204. Atlantic City, NJ | 3,556 |
| 205. Terre Haute, IN | 3,550 |
| 206. Lake Charles, LA | 3,549 |
| 207. Norwalk, CT | 3,536 |
| 208. Gainesville, FL | 3,527 |
| 209. Newark, NJ | 3,514 |
| 210. Medford, OR | 3,512 |
| 211. Bergen–Passaic, NJ | 3,511 |
| 212. Montgomery, AL | 3,509 |
| 213. Pueblo, CO | 3,501 |
| 214. Evansville, IN–KY | 3,496 |
| 214. Wausau, WI | 3,496 |
| 216. Tyler, TX | 3,460 |
| 217. Salem–Gloucester, MA | 3,459 |
| 218. Sheboygan, WI | 3,458 |

| Places Rated Rank | Places Rated Score | Places Rated Rank | Places Rated Score | Places Rated Rank | Places Rated Score |
|---|---|---|---|---|---|
| 219. Grand Rapids, MI | 3,454 | 256. Waco, TX | 3,018 | 293. Biloxi–Gulfport, MS | 2,516 |
| 220. Kankakee, IL | 3,444 | 257. Columbus, GA–AL | 2,995 | 294. Wheeling, WV–OH | 2,450 |
| | | 258. Benton Harbor, MI | 2,989 | 295. Alexandria, LA | 2,444 |
| 221. Ann Arbor, MI | 3,433 | 258. Las Cruces, NM | 2,989 | | |
| 222. Hagerstown, MD | 3,431 | 260. Rockford, IL | 2,987 | 296. Waterbury, CT | 2,434 |
| 223. Galveston–Texas City, TX | 3,423 | | | 297. Victoria, TX | 2,407 |
| 224. Lake County, IL | 3,422 | 261. Peoria, IL | 2,967 | 298. Brazoria, TX | 2,391 |
| 225. Lakeland–Winter Haven, FL | 3,412 | 262. Beaver County, PA | 2,960 | 299. Lawton, OK | 2,366 |
| | | 263. Lewiston–Auburn, ME | 2,941 | 300. Joplin, MO | 2,335 |
| 226. Chattanooga, TN–GA | 3,401 | 264. San Angelo, TX | 2,938 | | |
| 227. Colorado Springs, CO | 3,389 | 265. Lawrence, KS | 2,931 | 301. Portsmouth–Dover–Rochester, NH–ME | 2,321 |
| 228. Youngstown–Warren, OH | 3,374 | | | 302. Enid, OK | 2,312 |
| 229. Muskegon, MI | 3,353 | 266. Pensacola, FL | 2,918 | 303. Owensboro, KY | 2,273 |
| 230. Waterloo–Cedar Falls, IA | 3,351 | 267. Wilmington, NC | 2,904 | 304. York, PA | 2,267 |
| | | 268. Fort Walton Beach, FL | 2,886 | 305. Fitchburg–Leominster, MA | 2,244 |
| 231. Mobile, AL | 3,345 | 269. Allentown–Bethlehem, PA–NJ | 2,881 | | |
| 232. Hamilton–Middletown, OH | 3,338 | 270. Mansfield, OH | 2,876 | 306. Glens Falls, NY | 2,241 |
| 233. Baton Rouge, LA | 3,329 | | | 307. Oxnard–Ventura, CA | 2,238 |
| 234. Elmira, NY | 3,324 | 271. Anderson, IN | 2,865 | 308. Dothan, AL | 2,232 |
| 235. Laredo, TX | 3,322 | 272. Killeen–Temple, TX | 2,862 | 309. Clarksville–Hopkinsville, TN–KY | 2,226 |
| | | 273. Wichita Falls, TX | 2,793 | 310. Gadsden, AL | 2,174 |
| 236. Nashua, NH | 3,320 | 274. Beaumont–Port Arthur, TX | 2,782 | | |
| 237. Santa Rosa–Petaluma, CA | 3,313 | 275. Panama City, FL | 2,778 | 311. Fort Pierce, FL | 2,143 |
| 238. Orange County, NY | 3,299 | | | 312. Nassau–Suffolk, NY | 2,119 |
| 239. Appleton–Oshkosh–Neenah, WI | 3,298 | 276. Iowa City, IA | 2,770 | 313. McAllen–Edinburg–Mission, TX | 2,117 |
| 240. New Bedford, MA | 3,219 | 277. Yuba City, CA | 2,768 | 314. Sharon, PA | 2,017 |
| | | 278. State College, PA | 2,740 | 315. Modesto, CA | 2,000 |
| 241. Norfolk–Virginia Beach–Newport News, VA | 3,215 | 279. Danbury, CT | 2,715 | | |
| 242. Bridgeport–Milford, CT | 3,197 | 280. Anderson, SC | 2,707 | 316. Odessa, TX | 1,944 |
| 242. Eau Claire, WI | 3,197 | | | 317. Sherman–Denison, TX | 1,922 |
| 244. Saginaw–Bay City–Midland, MI | 3,186 | 281. Hickory, NC | 2,703 | 318. Burlington, NC | 1,910 |
| 245. Danville, VA | 3,161 | 282. Monmouth–Ocean, NJ | 2,690 | 319. Athens, GA | 1,866 |
| | | 283. St. Joseph, MO | 2,689 | 320. Kokomo, IN | 1,817 |
| 246. Macon–Warner Robins, GA | 3,144 | 284. Longview–Marshall, TX | 2,680 | | |
| 247. Riverside–San Bernardino, CA | 3,141 | 285. Huntsville, AL | 2,661 | 321. Jacksonville, NC | 1,780 |
| 248. Reading, PA | 3,120 | | | 322. Pascagoula, MS | 1,750 |
| 249. Brownsville–Harlingen, TX | 3,119 | 286. Fort Collins–Loveland, CO | 2,637 | 323. Bloomington, IN | 1,746 |
| 250. Stamford, CT | 3,110 | 287. Melbourne–Titusville–Palm Bay, FL | 2,560 | 324. Pine Bluff, AR | 1,671 |
| | | 288. Texarkana, TX–Texarkana, AR | 2,537 | 325. Bremerton, WA | 1,670 |
| 251. Williamsport, PA | 3,097 | 289. Johnson City–Kingsport–Bristol, TN–VA | 2,532 | | |
| 252. Visalia–Tulare–Porterville, CA | 3,094 | 290. Albany, GA | 2,531 | 326. Greeley, CO | 1,641 |
| 253. Fort Smith, AR–OK | 3,092 | | | 327. Steubenville–Weirton, OH–WV | 1,532 |
| 253. Janesville–Beloit, WI | 3,092 | 291. Bryan–College Station, TX | 2,530 | 328. Florence, AL | 1,454 |
| 255. Anniston, AL | 3,051 | 292. Augusta, GA–SC | 2,523 | 329. Houma–Thibodaux, LA | 1,145 |

## Metro Areas Listed Alphabetically

| Metro Area | Places Rated Rank | Metro Area | Places Rated Rank | Metro Area | Places Rated Rank |
|---|---|---|---|---|---|
| Abilene, TX | 167 | Anniston, AL | 255 | Beaver County, PA | 262 |
| Akron, OH | 105 | Appleton–Oshkosh–Neenah, WI | 239 | Bellingham, WA | 185 |
| Albany, GA | 290 | Asheville, NC | 91 | Benton Harbor, MI | 258 |
| Albany–Schenectady–Troy, NY | 15 | Athens, GA | 319 | Bergen–Passaic, NJ | 211 |
| Albuquerque, NM | 21 | Atlanta, GA | 2 | Billings, MT | 26 |
| Alexandria, LA | 295 | Atlantic City, NJ | 204 | Biloxi–Gulfport, MS | 293 |
| Allentown–Bethlehem, PA–NJ | 269 | Augusta, GA–SC | 292 | Binghamton, NY | 128 |
| Alton–Granite City, IL | 96 | Aurora–Elgin, IL | 171 | Birmingham, AL | 87 |
| Altoona, PA | 151 | Austin, TX | 195 | Bismarck, ND | 148 |
| Amarillo, TX | 103 | Bakersfield, CA | 191 | Bloomington, IN | 323 |
| Anaheim–Santa Ana, CA | 169 | Baltimore, MD | 8 | Bloomington–Normal, IL | 44 |
| Anchorage, AK | 90 | Bangor, ME | 58 | Boise City, ID | 20 |
| Anderson, IN | 271 | Baton Rouge, LA | 233 | Boston, MA | 16 |
| Anderson, SC | 280 | Battle Creek, MI | 116 | Boulder–Longmont, CO | 13 |
| Ann Arbor, MI | 221 | Beaumont–Port Arthur, TX | 274 | Bradenton, FL | 182 |

| Metro Area | Places Rated Rank | Metro Area | Places Rated Rank | Metro Area | Places Rated Rank |
|---|---|---|---|---|---|
| Brazoria, TX | 298 | Florence, SC | 97 | Laredo, TX | 235 |
| Bremerton, WA | 325 | Fort Collins–Loveland, CO | 286 | Las Cruces, NM | 258 |
| Bridgeport–Milford, CT | 242 | Fort Lauderdale–Hollywood– | | Las Vegas, NV | 43 |
| Bristol, CT | 130 | Pompano Beach, FL | 154 | Lawrence, KS | 265 |
| Brockton, MA | 181 | Fort Myers, FL | 123 | Lawrence–Haverhill, MA–NH | 202 |
| | | Fort Pierce, FL | 311 | | |
| Brownsville–Harlingen, TX | 249 | | | Lawton, OK | 299 |
| Bryan–College Station, TX | 291 | Fort Smith, AR–OK | 253 | Lewiston–Auburn, ME | 263 |
| Buffalo, NY | 75 | Fort Walton Beach, FL | 268 | Lexington–Fayette, KY | 165 |
| Burlington, NC | 318 | Fort Wayne, IN | 73 | Lima, OH | 163 |
| Burlington, VT | 10 | Fort Worth–Arlington, TX | 132 | Lincoln, NE | 56 |
| | | Fresno, CA | 142 | | |
| Canton, OH | 149 | | | Little Rock–North Little Rock, AR | 154 |
| Casper, WY | 136 | Gadsden, AL | 310 | Longview–Marshall, TX | 284 |
| Cedar Rapids, IA | 80 | Gainesville, FL | 208 | Lorain–Elyria, OH | 198 |
| Champaign–Urbana–Rantoul, IL | 7 | Galveston–Texas City, TX | 223 | Los Angeles–Long Beach, CA | 144 |
| Charleston, SC | 152 | Gary–Hammond, IN | 48 | Louisville, KY–IN | 71 |
| | | Glens Falls, NY | 306 | | |
| Charleston, WV | 70 | | | Lowell, MA–NH | 179 |
| Charlotte–Gastonia–Rock Hill, | | Grand Forks, ND | 62 | Lubbock, TX | 159 |
| NC–SC | 34 | Grand Rapids, MI | 219 | Lynchburg, VA | 102 |
| Charlottesville, VA | 37 | Great Falls, MT | 188 | Macon–Warner Robins, GA | 246 |
| Chattanooga, TN–GA | 226 | Greeley, CO | 326 | Madison, WI | 36 |
| Chicago, IL | 6 | Green Bay, WI | 184 | | |
| | | | | Manchester, NH | 121 |
| Chico, CA | 166 | Greensboro–Winston-Salem– | | Mansfield, OH | 270 |
| Cincinnati, OH–KY–IN | 52 | High Point, NC | 134 | McAllen–Edinburg–Mission, TX | 313 |
| Clarksville–Hopkinsville, TN–KY | 309 | Greenville–Spartanburg, SC | 170 | Medford, OR | 210 |
| Cleveland, OH | 9 | Hagerstown, MD | 222 | Melbourne–Titusville–Palm Bay, FL | 287 |
| Colorado Springs, CO | 227 | Hamilton–Middletown, OH | 232 | | |
| | | Harrisburg–Lebanon–Carlisle, PA | 32 | Memphis, TN–AR–MS | 28 |
| Columbia, MO | 175 | | | Miami–Hialeah, FL | 84 |
| Columbia, SC | 47 | Hartford, CT | 11 | Middlesex–Somerset–Hunterdon, NJ | 153 |
| Columbus, GA–AL | 257 | Hickory, NC | 281 | Middletown, CT | 118 |
| Columbus, OH | 143 | Honolulu, HI | 41 | Midland, TX | 78 |
| Corpus Christi, TX | 199 | Houma–Thibodaux, LA | 329 | | |
| | | Houston, TX | 119 | Milwaukee, WI | 99 |
| Cumberland, MD–WV | 192 | | | Minneapolis–St. Paul, MN–WI | 60 |
| Dallas, TX | 30 | Huntington–Ashland, WV–KY–OH | 168 | Mobile, AL | 231 |
| Danbury, CT | 279 | Huntsville, AL | 285 | Modesto, CA | 315 |
| Danville, VA | 245 | Indianapolis, IN | 50 | Monmouth–Ocean, NJ | 282 |
| Davenport–Rock Island–Moline, | | Iowa City, IA | 276 | | |
| IA–IL | 174 | Jackson, MI | 107 | Monroe, LA | 200 |
| | | | | Montgomery, AL | 212 |
| Dayton–Springfield, OH | 109 | Jackson, MS | 100 | Muncie, IN | 146 |
| Daytona Beach, FL | 162 | Jacksonville, FL | 59 | Muskegon, MI | 229 |
| Decatur, IL | 177 | Jacksonville, NC | 321 | Nashua, NH | 236 |
| Denver, CO | 5 | Janesville–Beloit, WI | 253 | | |
| Des Moines, IA | 67 | Jersey City, NJ | 95 | Nashville, TN | 92 |
| | | | | Nassau-Suffolk, NY | 312 |
| Detroit, MI | 106 | Johnson City–Kingsport–Bristol, | | New Bedford, MA | 240 |
| Dothan, AL | 308 | TN–VA | 289 | New Britain, CT | 104 |
| Dubuque, IA | 196 | Johnstown, PA | 145 | New Haven–Meriden, CT | 40 |
| Duluth, MN–WI | 83 | Joliet, IL | 117 | | |
| East St. Louis–Belleville, IL | 23 | Joplin, MO | 300 | New London–Norwich, CT–RI | 129 |
| | | Kalamazoo, MI | 72 | New Orleans, LA | 124 |
| Eau Claire, WI | 242 | Kankakee, IL | 220 | New York, NY | 1 |
| El Paso, TX | 193 | Kansas City, KS | 94 | Newark, NJ | 209 |
| Elkhart–Goshen, IN | 156 | Kansas City, MO | 46 | Niagara Falls, NY | 63 |
| Elmira, NY | 234 | Kenosha, WI | 131 | | |
| Enid, OK | 302 | Killeen–Temple, TX | 272 | Norfolk–Virginia Beach–Newport | |
| | | | | News, VA | 241 |
| Erie, PA | 51 | Knoxville, TN | 150 | Norwalk, CT | 207 |
| Eugene–Springfield, OR | 79 | Kokomo, IN | 320 | Oakland, CA | 24 |
| Evansville, IN–KY | 214 | La Crosse, WI | 35 | Ocala, FL | 183 |
| Fall River, MA–RI | 120 | Lafayette, IN | 98 | Odessa, TX | 316 |
| Fargo–Moorhead, ND–MN | 25 | Lafayette, LA | 81 | | |
| | | | | Oklahoma City, OK | 133 |
| Fayetteville, NC | 137 | Lake Charles, LA | 206 | Olympia, WA | 164 |
| Fayetteville–Springdale, AR | 201 | Lake County, IL | 224 | Omaha, NE–IA | 49 |
| Fitchburg–Leominster, MA | 305 | Lakeland–Winter Haven, FL | 225 | Orange County, NY | 238 |
| Flint, MI | 101 | Lancaster, PA | 173 | Orlando, FL | 45 |
| Florence, AL | 328 | Lansing–East Lansing, MI | 64 | Owensboro, KY | 303 |

| Metro Area | Places Rated Rank | Metro Area | Places Rated Rank | Metro Area | Places Rated Rank |
|---|---|---|---|---|---|
| Oxnard–Ventura, CA | 307 | St. Joseph, MO | 283 | Tallahassee, FL | 66 |
| Panama City, FL | 275 | St. Louis, MO–IL | 12 | Tampa–St. Petersburg– | |
| Parkersburg–Marietta, WV–OH | 139 | Salem, OR | 111 | Clearwater, FL | 61 |
| Pascagoula, MS | 322 | Salem–Gloucester, MA | 217 | Terre Haute, IN | 205 |
| | | Salinas–Seaside–Monterey, CA | 158 | Texarkana, TX–Texarkana, AR | 288 |
| Pawtucket–Woonsocket–Attleboro, | | | | Toledo, OH | 77 |
| RI–MA | 110 | Salt Lake City–Ogden, UT | 29 | | |
| Pensacola, FL | 266 | San Angelo, TX | 264 | Topeka, KS | 76 |
| Peoria, IL | 261 | San Antonio, TX | 74 | Trenton, NJ | 108 |
| Philadelphia, PA–NJ | 42 | San Diego, CA | 68 | Tucson, AZ | 141 |
| Phoenix, AZ | 113 | San Francisco, CA | 3 | Tulsa, OK | 187 |
| | | | | Tuscaloosa, AL | 114 |
| Pine Bluff, AR | 324 | San Jose, CA | 82 | | |
| Pittsburgh, PA | 57 | Santa Barbara–Santa Maria– | | Tyler, TX | 216 |
| Pittsfield, MA | 186 | Lompoc, CA | 54 | Utica–Rome, NY | 122 |
| Portland, ME | 86 | Santa Cruz, CA | 93 | Vallejo–Fairfield–Napa, CA | 160 |
| Portland, OR | 39 | Santa Rosa–Petaluma, CA | 237 | Vancouver, WA | 180 |
| | | Sarasota, FL | 189 | Victoria, TX | 297 |
| Portsmouth–Dover–Rochester, | | | | | |
| NH–ME | 301 | Savannah, GA | 38 | Vineland–Millville–Bridgeton, NJ | 161 |
| Poughkeepsie, NY | 157 | Scranton–Wilkes-Barre, PA | 194 | Visalia–Tulare–Porterville, CA | 252 |
| Providence, RI | 69 | Seattle, WA | 19 | Waco, TX | 256 |
| Provo–Orem, UT | 126 | Sharon, PA | 314 | Washington, DC–MD–VA | 4 |
| Pueblo, CO | 213 | Sheboygan, WI | 218 | Waterbury, CT | 296 |
| | | | | | |
| Racine, WI | 203 | Sherman–Denison, TX | 317 | Waterloo–Cedar Falls, IA | 230 |
| Raleigh–Durham, NC | 22 | Shreveport, LA | 138 | Wausau, WI | 214 |
| Reading, PA | 248 | Sioux City, IA–NE | 147 | West Palm Beach–Boca Raton– | |
| Redding, CA | 53 | Sioux Falls, SD | 27 | Delray Beach, FL | 85 |
| Reno, NV | 17 | South Bend–Mishawaka, IN | 55 | Wheeling, WV–OH | 294 |
| | | | | Wichita, KS | 172 |
| Richland–Kennewick–Pasco, WA | 115 | Spokane, WA | 65 | | |
| Richmond–Petersburg, VA | 18 | Springfield, IL | 31 | Wichita Falls, TX | 273 |
| Riverside–San Bernardino, CA | 247 | Springfield, MA | 33 | Williamsport, PA | 251 |
| Roanoke, VA | 176 | Springfield, MO | 178 | Wilmington, DE–NJ–MD | 127 |
| Rochester, MN | 139 | Stamford, CT · | 250 | Wilmington, NC | 267 |
| | | | | Worcester, MA | 197 |
| Rochester, NY | 88 | State College, PA | 278 | | |
| Rockford, IL | 260 | Steubenville–Weirton, OH–WV | 327 | Yakima, WA | 190 |
| Sacramento, CA | 89 | Stockton, CA | 135 | York, PA | 304 |
| Saginaw–Bay City–Midland, MI | 244 | Syracuse, NY | 14 | Youngstown–Warren, OH | 228 |
| St. Cloud, MN | 125 | Tacoma, WA | 112 | Yuba City, CA | 277 |

## Place Profiles: Transportation Indicators in 329 Metro Areas

The following pages provide brief summaries of local commuting conditions, mass public transit, and options for intercity transportation in each of the 329 metro areas.

The sources for the information are the U.S. Department of Commerce, Bureau of the Census, *1980 Census of Population and Housing;* American Public Transit Association, *Transit Facts, 1982–1983,* and U.S. Department of Transportation, Urban Mass Transit Administration, *Directory of Regularly Scheduled, Fixed Route, Local Public Transportation Service,* 1981, *Directory of Regularly Scheduled, Fixed Route, Local Rural Public Transportation Service,* 1981, and *National Urban Mass Transportation Statistics—Section 15 Report,* 1984; U.S. Department of Transportation, Federal Highway Administration, unpublished Highway Performance Monitoring System data, 1984, and *Interstate System*

*Route Log and Finder List,* undated; Official Airline Guides, Inc., *Travel Planner,* Spring 1984, and U.S. Department of Transportation, Federal Aviation Administration, *Air Traffic Activity,* fiscal year 1983; and National Railroad Passenger Corporation, *Amtrak Timetable,* 1984.

The first entry in the profiles, Daily Commute, is the average number of minutes that workers in the metro area spend getting to and from work, regardless of the mode of transportation. These figures are the 1980 Census journey-to-work data for each metro area multiplied by 2.2 to represent a round-trip whose return half takes slightly longer than the first half.

Under the heading Public Transportation is the number of mass transit vehicles available during rush hour. Just below this figure appears the seat miles per capita, a measurement common in the transit industry, which is the number of transit seats that travel one mile of transit route daily for each person in the metro area's urban core. In metro areas with more than one mode of public transportation—such as Atlanta and San Francisco—this number is the total for all modes.

Descriptions of freeway traffic are derived from the Federal Highway Administration, which rates urban freeways for their level of service on a scale from "free-flowing" progressing through "flowout capacity" and ending at "congested." *Places Rated* adopts the following simplification, using the Federal Highway Administration's definition of a highway's full capacity as 2,000 vehicles per hour in one 12-foot-wide traffic lane: Freeway traffic is judged *very heavy* if the traffic volume is 90 percent or more of the freeway's capacity, *heavy* if the volume is 50 to 89 percent of capacity, *moderate* if the volume is 34 to 49 percent, and *light* if the volume is 33 percent or less. The entry None indicates a metro area with no freeways.

A major part of a metro area's freeway mileage comes from the beltways, spurs, and heavily traveled routes of the Interstate Highway System. But the 61 two-digit main routes are intercity travel assets, too. Accordingly, each main route in the system that reaches the metro area is listed.

The first item under the heading Air Service is the FAA's hub classification for the metro area: large hub, medium hub, small hub, or non-hub. In most CMSAs, the core metro area is designated a large hub, and other member metro areas are classified as part of that hub. Thus, the entry for Boulder–Longmont, Colorado, reads "Part of Denver hub." The airport's name is listed next. (Because of local boosterism, many airports have the word "international" in their title; the airport in Great Falls, Montana, for example, is named International but has no international flights.) The airport's three-letter identifier, recognized internationally, is enclosed in parentheses next to its title. Every airport in the world with scheduled service has a unique identifier. All airports, including those that *Places Rated* scores as part of the air service "pool" shared by members of a consolidated area, are listed under the metro area in which they are located. In four cases, however, airports are listed under two metro areas and credited to both. Two of these exceptions involve airports that straddle the boundaries of two metro areas (Dallas–Fort Worth Regional, listed under Dallas and Fort Worth, and Sarasota–Bradenton Airport, credited to both Bradenton and Sarasota); the other two are cases of airports located in one metro area but roughly equidistant from two metro areas (Akron–Canton Regional, located in Akron but also close to Canton, and Bradley International of Hartford, about 20 minutes away from both downtown Hartford and Springfield, Massachusetts).

For metro areas that neither have airports nor share them, the location of the nearest airport is given along with its distance and direction from the metro area. Also listed in this category are the number of airlines that serve the airport and the total number of flights departing each day. (*Places Rated* also counts air taxis, or carriers that fly passengers on small aircraft with fewer than 30 seats and a maximum payload of less than 7,500 pounds; and commuter carriers, which are air taxis that make at least five round-trips a week between two or more points under a published flight schedule.)

Finally, figures for Amtrak service are the number of passenger trains departing from the metro area on an average weekday. Metro areas that are part of CMSAs share in the number of Amtrak departures from the major city in the CMSA.

A star preceding a metro area's name highlights it as one of the top 25 places for transportation assets.

| Metro Area | Daily Commute | Public Transportation | Freeway Traffic | Interstate Highways | Air Service | Amtrak Service | Places Rated Score | Places Rated Rank |
|---|---|---|---|---|---|---|---|---|
| Abilene, TX | 34.8 min | 17 city buses<br>Seat miles/capita: 1.14 | Light | I-20 | Non-hub<br>Abilene Municipal (ABI)<br>2 airlines, 18 flights/day | — | 4,031 | 167 |
| Akron, OH | 43.8 min | 135 city buses<br>Seat miles/capita: 1.74 | Heavy | I-76<br>I-77<br>I-80 | Part of Cleveland hub<br>Akron–Canton Regional (CAK)<br>6 airlines, 24 flights/day | — | 4,883 | 105 |
| Albany, GA | 38.9 min | 15 city buses<br>Seat miles/capita: 1.13 | Light | — | Non-hub<br>Albany–Dougherty County (ABY)<br>2 airlines, 10 flights/day | — | 2,531 | 290 |
| ★ Albany–Schenectady–Troy, NY | 43.3 min | 236 city buses<br>Seat miles/capita: 3.21 | Light | I-87<br>I-88<br>I-90 | Medium hub<br>Albany County (ALB)<br>13 airlines, 78 flights/day | 11 trains/day | 6,883 | 15 |
| ★ Albuquerque, NM | 41.6 min | 82 city buses<br>Seat miles/capita: 1.31 | Heavy | I-25<br>I-40 | Medium hub<br>Albuquerque International (ABQ)<br>16 airlines, 118 flights/day | 2 trains/day | 6,558 | 21 |
| Alexandria, LA | 37.8 min | 16 city buses<br>Seat miles/capita: 1.15 | Light | — | Non-hub<br>Esler Regional (ESF)<br>5 airlines, 10 flights/day | — | 2,444 | 295 |

| Metro Area | Daily Commute | Public Transportation | Freeway Traffic | Interstate Highways | Air Service | Amtrak Service | Places Rated Score | Places Rated Rank |
|---|---|---|---|---|---|---|---|---|
| Allentown–Bethlehem, PA–NJ | 41.4 min | 65 city buses<br>Seat miles/capita: 1.14 | Very heavy | I-78 | Small hub<br>Allentown–Bethlehem–Easton (ABE)<br>5 airlines, 37 flights/day | — | 2,881 | 269 |
| Alton–Granite City, IL | 45.1 min | 18 city buses<br>Seat miles/capita: 1.35 | Light | I-55<br>I-70 | Part of St. Louis hub | 6 trains/day | 4,975 | 96 |
| Altoona, PA | 37.0 min | 31 city buses<br>Seat miles/capita: 2.62 | Light | — | Non-hub<br>Altoona–Blair County (AOO)<br>1 airline, 5 flights/day | 4 trains/day | 4,246 | 151 |
| Amarillo, TX | 37.8 min | 39 city buses<br>Seat miles/capita: 1.74 | Moderate | I-27<br>I-40 | Small hub<br>Amarillo International (AMA)<br>6 airlines, 29 flights/day | — | 4,902 | 103 |
| Anaheim–Santa Ana, CA | 51.9 min | 497 city buses<br>Seat miles/capita: 1.71 | Heavy | I-5<br>I-10 | Part of Los Angeles hub<br>John Wayne–Orange County (SNA)<br>12 airlines, 66 flights/day | 6 trains/day | 3,954 | 169 |
| Anchorage, AK | 38.7 min | 50 city buses<br>Seat miles/capita: 1.96 | Very heavy | — | Medium hub<br>Anchorage International (ANC)<br>19 airlines, 185 flights/day | — | 5,091 | 90 |
| Anderson, IN | 40.5 min | 27 city buses<br>Seat miles/capita: 2.29 | Light | I-69 | Nearest airport: Muncie, 20 miles NE | — | 2,865 | 271 |
| Anderson, SC | 40.9 min | 6 city buses<br>Seat miles/capita: 1.45 | Light | I-85 | Non-hub<br>Anderson County (AND)<br>1 airline, 3 flights/day | — | 2,707 | 280 |
| Ann Arbor, MI | 41.4 min | 47 city buses<br>Seat miles/capita: 1.18 | Moderate | I-94 | Part of Detroit hub | 5 trains/day | 3,433 | 221 |
| Anniston, AL | 39.6 min | — | Light | — | Non-hub<br>Anniston–Calhoun County (ANB)<br>1 airline, 4 flights/day | 2 trains/day | 3,051 | 255 |
| Appleton–Oshkosh–Neenah, WI | 32.3 min | 58 city buses<br>Seat miles/capita: 2.72 | Heavy | — | Small hub<br>Outagamie County (ATW)<br>Wittman Field (OSH)<br>3 airlines, 21 flights/day | — | 3,298 | 239 |
| Asheville, NC | 40.7 min | 45 city buses<br>Seat miles/capita: 2.93 | Moderate | I-26<br>I-40 | Small hub<br>Asheville Regional (AVL)<br>4 airlines, 23 flights/day | — | 5.086 | 91 |
| Athens, GA | 40.0 min | 8 city buses<br>Seat miles/capita: .85 | None | — | Non-hub<br>Athens Municipal (AHN)<br>1 airline, 4 flights/day | — | 1,866 | 319 |
| ★ Atlanta, GA | 54.3 min | 885 city buses<br>120 rapid rail cars<br>Seat miles/capita: 4.95 | Very heavy | I-20<br>I-75<br>I-85 | Large hub<br>William B. Hartsfield–Atlanta International (ATL)<br>18 airlines, 765 flights/day | 4 trains/day | 8,409 | 2 |
| Atlantic City, NJ | 44.2 min | 35 city buses<br>Seat miles/capita: 3.88 | Moderate | — | Non-hub<br>Bader Field (AIY)<br>Pomona Field (ACY)<br>5 airlines, 26 flights/day | — | 3,556 | 204 |
| Augusta, GA–SC | 43.6 min | 30 city buses<br>Seat miles/capita: .80 | Moderate | I-20 | Small hub<br>Bush Field (AGS)<br>4 airlines, 14 flights/day | — | 2,523 | 292 |
| Aurora–Elgin, IL | 46.0 min | 59 city buses<br>Seat miles/capita: 1.48 | Heavy | I-90 | Part of Chicago hub | 6 trains/day | 3,943 | 171 |
| Austin, TX | 41.8 min | 71 city buses<br>Seat miles/capita: 1.25 | Very heavy | I-35 | Small hub<br>Robert Mueller Municipal (AUS)<br>11 airlines, 77 flights/day | — | 3,670 | 195 |
| Bakersfield, CA | 38.5 min | 40 city buses<br>Seat miles/capita: 1.20 | Heavy | — | Non-hub<br>Meadows Field (BFL)<br>6 airlines, 20 flights/day | 4 trains/day | 3,725 | 191 |
| ★ Baltimore, MD | 58.3 min | 900 city buses<br>2 commuter railroads<br>Seat miles/capita: 3.42 | Moderate | I-70<br>I-83<br>I-95<br>I-97 | Medium hub<br>Baltimore–Washington International (BWI)<br>26 airlines, 214 flights/day | 31 trains/day | 7,405 | 8 |
| Bangor, ME | 33.0 min | 9 city buses<br>Seat miles/capita: 1.00 | Light | I-95 | Small hub<br>Bangor International (BGR)<br>4 airlines, 29 flights/day | — | 5,613 | 58 |
| Baton Rouge, LA | 50.2 min | 55 city buses<br>Seat miles/capita: 1.04 | Heavy | I-10<br>I-12 | Small hub<br>Baton Rouge Metropolitan–Ryan Field (BTR)<br>5 airlines, 29 flights/day | — | 3,329 | 233 |
| Battle Creek, MI | 37.8 min | 20 city buses<br>Seat miles/capita: 1.71 | Light | I-94 | Small hub<br>W. K. Kellogg Regional (BTL)<br>1 airline, 7 flights/day | 8 trains/day | 4,652 | 116 |

| Metro Area | Daily Commute | Public Transportation | Freeway Traffic | Interstate Highways | Air Service | Amtrak Service | Places Rated Score | Places Rated Rank |
|---|---|---|---|---|---|---|---|---|
| Beaumont–Port Arthur, TX | 42.5 min | 33 city buses Seat miles/capita: .91 | Light | I-10 | Non-hub Jefferson County (BPT) 5 airlines, 23 flights/day | — | 2,782 | 274 |
| Beaver County, PA | 44.7 min | 13 city buses Seat miles/capita: .42 | Heavy | — | Part of Pittsburgh hub Beaver County (BFP) 1 airline, 1 daily flight | — | 2,960 | 262 |
| Bellingham, WA | 35.9 min | 16 city buses Seat miles/capita: 2.71 | Heavy | I-5 | Non-hub Bellingham International (BLI) 1 airline, 7 flights/day | — | 3,776 | 185 |
| Benton Harbor, MI | 36.5 min | 2 city buses Seat miles/capita: .22 | Light | I-94 I-96 | Non-hub Ross Field (BEH) 1 airline, 3 flights/day | — | 2,989 | 258 |
| Bergen–Passaic, NJ | 54.3 min | 460 city buses Seat miles/capita: 2.37 | Very heavy | I-80 | Part of New York hub | — | 3,511 | 211 |
| Billings, MT | 35.4 min | 15 city buses Seat miles/capita: 1.19 | Light | I-90 I-94 | Small hub Billings Logan International (BIL) 5 airlines, 41 flights/day | — | 6,285 | 26 |
| Biloxi–Gulfport, MS | 44.9 min | 18 city buses Seat miles/capita: .67 | Moderate | I-10 | Non-hub Gulfport–Biloxi Regional (GPT) 1 airline, 9 flights/day | — | 2,516 | 293 |
| Binghamton, NY | 38.3 min | 39 city buses Seat miles/capita: 1.61 | Light | I-81 I-88 | Non-hub Edwin A. Link Field–Broom County (BGM) 8 airlines, 35 flights/day | — | 4,529 | 128 |
| Birmingham, AL | 51.3 min | 237 city buses Seat miles/capita: 2.61 | Very heavy | I-20 I-59 I-65 | Medium hub Birmingham Municipal (BHM) 9 airlines, 60 flights/day | 2 trains/day | 5,177 | 87 |
| Bismarck, ND | 30.8 min | — | Light | I-94 | Non-hub Bismarck Municipal (BIS) 5 airlines, 18 flights/day | — | 4,303 | 148 |
| Bloomington, IN | 38.1 min | 4 city buses Seat miles/capita: .42 | None | — | Non-hub Monroe County (BMG) 1 airline, 3 flights/day | — | 1,746 | 323 |
| Bloomington–Normal, IL | 33.4 min | 23 city buses Seat miles/capita: 1.86 | Light | I-55 I-74 | Non-hub Bloomington–Normal (BMI) 1 airline, 10 flights/day | 6 trains/day | 5,889 | 44 |
| ★ Boise City, ID | 36.7 min | 28 city buses Seat miles/capita: 1.38 | Moderate | I-80 | Small hub Boise Air Terminal (BOI) 10 airlines, 48 flights/day | 2 trains/day | 6,575 | 20 |
| ★ Boston, MA | 51.7 min | 1,115 city buses 796 rapid rail cars 50 trolley coaches 2 commuter railroads 2 ferry systems Seat miles/capita: 5.60 | Heavy | I-90 I-93 I-95 | Large hub General Edward Lawrence Logan International (BOS) 42 airlines, 404 flights/day | 11 trains/day | 6,801 | 16 |
| ★ Boulder–Longmont, CO | 45.5 min | 55 city buses Seat miles/capita: 3.99 | Heavy | I-25 | Part of Denver hub Boulder Municipal (WBU) 1 airline, 4 flights/day | — | 7,108 | 13 |
| Bradenton, FL | 41.1 min | 18 city buses Seat miles/capita: .81 | Moderate | I-75 | Small hub Sarasota–Bradenton (SRQ) 11 airlines, 62 flights/day | — | 3,805 | 182 |
| Brazoria, TX | 50.6 min | — | Heavy | — | Part of Houston hub | — | 2,391 | 298 |
| Bremerton, WA | 55.0 min | 18 city buses Seat miles/capita: 1.86 | Light | — | Nearest airport: Seattle, 52 miles SE | — | 1,670 | 325 |
| Bridgeport–Milford, CT | 44.7 min | 70 city buses Seat miles/capita: 1.13 | Heavy | I-95 | Part of New York hub Igor I. Sikorsky Memorial (BDR) 2 airlines, 17 flights/day | 9 trains/day | 3,197 | 242 |
| Bristol, CT | 42.2 min | 3 city buses Seat miles/capita: .24 | Heavy | I-84 | Part of Hartford hub | — | 4,495 | 130 |
| Brockton, MA | 51.0 min | 45 city buses Seat miles/capita: 1.68 | Heavy | I-95 | Part of Boston hub | — | 3,810 | 181 |
| Brownsville–Harlingen, TX | 35.9 min | 24 city buses Seat miles/capita: 1.75 | Light | — | Non-hub Harlingen (HRL) Brownsville–South Padre Island International (BRO) 5 airlines, 24 flights/day | — | 3,119 | 249 |
| Bryan–College Station, TX | 33.4 min | — | None | — | Non-hub Easterwood Field (CLL) 3 airlines, 11 flights/day | — | 2,530 | 291 |

| Metro Area | Daily Commute | Public Transportation | Freeway Traffic | Interstate Highways | Air Service | Amtrak Service | Places Rated Score | Places Rated Rank |
|---|---|---|---|---|---|---|---|---|
| Buffalo, NY | 42.9 min | 393 city buses<br>Seat miles/capita: 2.61 | Moderate | I-90 | Medium hub<br>Greater Buffalo International (BUF)<br>12 airlines, 134 flights/day | 11 trains/day | 5,384 | 75 |
| Burlington, NC | 40.9 min | — | Heavy | I-85 | Nearest airport: Greensboro, 32 miles W | — | 1,910 | 318 |
| ★ Burlington, VT | 38.1 min | 18 city buses<br>Seat miles/capita: 1.57 | Light | I-89 | Non-hub<br>Burlington International (BTV)<br>8 airlines, 43 flights/day | 2 trains/day | 7,146 | 10 |
| Canton, OH | 40.9 min | 60 city buses<br>Seat miles/capita: 1.63 | Heavy | I-77 | Small hub<br>Akron–Canton Regional (CAK)<br>6 airlines, 24 flights/day | 4 trains/day | 4,279 | 149 |
| Casper, WY | 39.8 min | — | Moderate | I-25 | Non-hub<br>Natrona County International (CPR)<br>6 airlines, 20 flights/day | — | 4,410 | 136 |
| Cedar Rapids, IA | 36.3 min | 45 city buses<br>Seat miles/capita: 2.21 | Light | I-80 | Small hub<br>Cedar Rapids Municipal (CID)<br>7 airlines, 44 flights/day | — | 5,270 | 80 |
| ★ Champaign–Urbana–Rantoul, IL | 33.7 min | 51 city buses<br>Seat miles/capita: 3.11 | Moderate | I-57<br>I-72<br>I-74 | Non-hub<br>U. of Illinois–Willard (CMI)<br>4 airlines, 21 flights/day | 2 trains/day | 7,447 | 7 |
| Charleston, SC | 48.6 min | 32 city buses<br>Seat miles/capita: .65 | Light | I-26 | Small hub<br>Charleston AFB International (CHS)<br>4 airlines, 35 flights/day | 4 trains/day | 4,207 | 152 |
| Charleston, WV | 47.5 min | 83 city buses<br>Seat miles/capita: 3.60 | Moderate | I-64<br>I-77<br>I-79 | Small hub<br>Kanawha Airport (CRW)<br>6 airlines, 26 flights/day | — | 5,470 | 70 |
| Charlotte–Gastonia–Rock Hill, NC–SC | 44.4 min | 129 city buses<br>Seat miles/capita: 1.88 | Heavy | I-77<br>I-85 | Medium hub<br>Charlotte–Douglas International (CLT)<br>15 airlines, 264 flights/day | 2 trains/day | 6,099 | 34 |
| Charlottesville, VA | 42.0 min | 12 city buses<br>Seat miles/capita: 1.35 | Light | I-64 | Non-hub<br>Charlottesville–Albemarle (CHO)<br>4 airlines, 27 flights/day | 2 trains/day | 6,041 | 37 |
| Chattanooga, TN–GA | 48.2 min | 71 city buses<br>1 cable incline<br>Seat miles/capita: 1.57 | Heavy | I-24<br>I-75 | Small hub<br>Lovell Field (CHA)<br>4 airlines, 16 flights/day | — | 3,401 | 226 |
| ★ Chicago, IL | 63.8 min | 2,420 city buses<br>1,100 rapid rail cars<br>7 commuter railroads<br>1 ferry system<br>Seat miles/capita: 4.68 | Heavy | I-55<br>I-57<br>I-80<br>I-90<br>I-94 | Large hub<br>Merrill C. Meigs (CGX)<br>Chicago Midway (MDW)<br>Chicago–O'Hare International (ORD)<br>42 airlines, 927 flights/day | 21 trains/day | 7,742 | 6 |
| Chico, CA | 35.4 min | 8 city buses<br>Seat miles/capita: 1.03 | Heavy | — | Non-hub<br>Chico Municipal (CIC)<br>3 airlines, 12 flights/day | 2 trains/day | 4,067 | 166 |
| Cincinnati, OH–KY–IN | 49.3 min | 622 city buses<br>1 ferry system<br>Seat miles/capita: 3.69 | Heavy | I-71<br>I-74<br>I-75 | Medium hub<br>Greater Cincinnati International (CVG)<br>13 airlines, 168 flights/day | 2 trains/day | 5,748 | 52 |
| Clarksville–Hopkinsville, TN–KY | 36.7 min | — | None | I-24 | Non-hub<br>Outlaw Field (CKV)<br>1 airline, 3 flights/day | — | 2,226 | 309 |
| ★ Cleveland, OH | 51.5 min | 1,016 city buses<br>171 rapid rail cars<br>Seat miles/capita: 6.42 | Very heavy | I-71<br>I-77<br>I-80<br>I-90 | Large hub<br>Burke–Lakefront (BKL)<br>Cleveland–Hopkins International (CLE)<br>28 airlines, 211 flights/day | 3 trains/day | 7,333 | 9 |
| Colorado Springs, CO | 38.7 min | 50 city buses<br>Seat miles/capita: 1.20 | Heavy | I-25 | Small hub<br>City of Colorado Springs Municipal (COS)<br>6 airlines, 32 flights/day | — | 3,389 | 227 |
| Columbia, MO | 34.8 min | 19 city buses<br>Seat miles/capita: 1.94 | Light | I-70 | Non-hub<br>Columbia Regional (COU)<br>3 airlines, 11 flights/day | — | 3,893 | 175 |
| Columbia, SC | 44.4 min | 40 city buses<br>Seat miles/capita: .86 | Moderate | I-20<br>I-26<br>I-77 | Small hub<br>Columbia Metropolitan (CAE)<br>5 airlines, 37 flights/day | 4 trains/day | 5,859 | 47 |

| Metro Area | Daily Commute | Public Transportation | Freeway Traffic | Interstate Highways | Air Service | Amtrak Service | Places Rated Score | Places Rated Rank |
|---|---|---|---|---|---|---|---|---|
| Columbus, GA–AL | 38.5 min | 56 city buses<br>Seat miles/capita: 1.73 | Moderate | I-85 | Small hub<br>Columbus Metropolitan (CSG)<br>2 airlines, 8 flights/day | — | 2,995 | 257 |
| Columbus, OH | 45.8 min | 273 city buses<br>Seat miles/capita: 2.06 | Very heavy | I-70<br>I-71 | Medium hub<br>Port Columbus International<br>(CMH)<br>17 airlines, 146 flights/day | — | 4,364 | 143 |
| Corpus Christi, TX | 41.1 min | 52 city buses<br>1 ferry system<br>Seat miles/capita: 1.41 | Moderate | I-37 | Small hub<br>Corpus Christi International (CRP)<br>5 airlines, 42 flights/day | — | 3,626 | 199 |
| Cumberland, MD–WV | 39.6 min | 10 city buses<br>Seat miles/capita: 1.11 | Light | — | Non-hub<br>Cumberland Municipal (CBE)<br>1 airline, 6 flights/day | 2 trains/day | 3,709 | 192 |
| Dallas, TX | 52.8 min | 582 city buses<br>Seat miles/capita: 1.98 | Heavy | I-20<br>I-30<br>I-35E<br>I-45 | Large hub<br>Dallas–Fort Worth Regional<br>(DFW)<br>Dallas Love Field (DAL)<br>37 airlines, 554 flights/day | — | 6,213 | 30 |
| Danbury, CT | 53.9 min | 6 city buses<br>Seat miles/capita: .42 | Heavy | I-84 | Part of New York hub | — | 2,715 | 279 |
| Danville, VA | 43.3 min | 6 city buses<br>Seat miles/capita: .86 | Light | — | Non-hub<br>Danville Municipal (DAN)<br>1 airline, 2 flights/day | 2 trains/day | 3,161 | 245 |
| Davenport–Rock Island–Moline, IA–IL | 38.1 min | 78 city buses<br>Seat miles/capita: 1.82 | Moderate | I-74<br>I-80 | Small hub<br>Quad-City (MLI)<br>6 airlines, 20 flights/day | — | 3,907 | 174 |
| Dayton–Springfield, OH | 42.2 min | 230 city buses<br>80 trolley coaches<br>Seat miles/capita: 2.64 | Very heavy | I-70<br>I-75 | Medium hub<br>James M. Cox–Dayton<br>International (DAY)<br>9 airlines, 119 flights/day | — | 4,775 | 109 |
| Daytona Beach, FL | 39.4 min | 40 city buses<br>Seat miles/capita: 1.56 | Moderate | I-4<br>I-95 | Small hub<br>Daytona Beach Regional (DAB)<br>4 airlines, 24 flights/day | — | 4,117 | 162 |
| Decatur, IL | 34.5 min | 31 city buses<br>Seat miles/capita: 1.91 | Light | I-72 | Non-hub<br>Decatur (DEC)<br>1 airline, 14 flights/day | — | 3,867 | 177 |
| ★ Denver, CO | 48.6 min | 671 city buses<br>Seat miles/capita: 3.31 | Very heavy | I-25<br>I-70<br>I-76 | Large hub<br>Stapleton International (DEN)<br>24 airlines, 533 flights/day | 6 trains/day | 8,145 | 5 |
| Des Moines, IA | 37.8 min | 105 city buses<br>Seat miles/capita: 2.62 | Heavy | I-35<br>I-80 | Small hub<br>Des Moines Municipal (DSM)<br>9 airlines, 72 flights/day | — | 5,521 | 67 |
| Detroit, MI | 51.3 min | 1,347 city buses<br>2 commuter railroads<br>Seat miles/capita: 2.36 | Very heavy | I-75<br>I-94<br>I-96 | Large hub<br>Detroit City (DET)<br>Detroit Metropolitan–Wayne<br>County (DTW)<br>31 airlines, 308 flights/day | 3 trains/day | 4,808 | 106 |
| Dothan, AL | 38.5 min | — | Light | — | Non-hub<br>Dothan (DHN)<br>2 airlines, 13 flights/day | — | 2,232 | 308 |
| Dubuque, IA | 33.4 min | 26 city buses<br>1 cable incline<br>Seat miles/capita: 2.54 | Moderate | — | Non-hub<br>Dubuque Municipal (DBQ)<br>2 airlines, 12 flights/day | — | 3,668 | 196 |
| Duluth, MN–WI | 38.9 min | 101 city buses<br>Seat miles/capita: 5.08 | Moderate | I-35 | Small hub<br>Duluth International (DLH)<br>2 airlines, 12 flights/day | 1 train daily | 5,205 | 83 |
| ★ East St. Louis–Belleville, IL | 45.1 min | 56 city buses<br>Seat miles/capita: 3.46 | Heavy | I-55<br>I-64<br>I-70 | Part of St. Louis hub | — | 6,539 | 23 |
| Eau Claire, WI | 33.2 min | 14 city buses<br>Seat miles/capita: 1.29 | Heavy | I-94 | Non-hub<br>Eau Claire County (EAU)<br>2 airlines, 7 flights/day | — | 3,197 | 242 |
| El Paso, TX | 42.5 min | 115 city buses<br>Seat miles/capita: 1.69 | Heavy | I-10 | Medium hub<br>El Paso International (ELP)<br>8 airlines, 62 flights/day | — | 3,705 | 193 |
| Elkhart–Goshen, IN | 34.1 min | — | Light | I-80 | Non-hub<br>Elkhart Municipal (EKI)<br>1 airline, 8 flights/day | 2 trains/day | 4,168 | 156 |
| Elmira, NY | 36.3 min | 17 city buses<br>Seat miles/capita: 1.66 | Light | — | Non-hub<br>Elmira–Corning Regional (ELM)<br>4 airlines, 14 flights/day | — | 3,324 | 234 |

| Metro Area | Daily Commute | Public Transportation | Freeway Traffic | Interstate Highways | Air Service | Amtrak Service | Places Rated Score | Places Rated Rank |
|---|---|---|---|---|---|---|---|---|
| Enid, OK | 33.9 min | — | Light | — | Non-hub<br>Enid–Woodring Municipal (WDG)<br>1 airline, 6 flights/day | — | 2,312 | 302 |
| Erie, PA | 37.6 min | 77 city buses<br>Seat miles/capita: 2.88 | Moderate | I-79<br>I-90 | Small hub<br>Erie International (ERI)<br>2 airlines, 14 flights/day | 2 trains/day | 5,754 | 51 |
| Eugene–Springfield, OR | 38.7 min | 80 city buses<br>Seat miles/capita: 2.92 | Moderate | I-5 | Small hub<br>Mahlon Sweet Field (EUG)<br>4 airlines, 21 flights/day | 2 trains/day | 5,293 | 79 |
| Evansville, IN–KY | 40.9 min | 24 city buses<br>Seat miles/capita: .89 | Moderate | I-64 | Small hub<br>Evansville Dress Regional (EVV)<br>5 airlines, 38 flights/day | — | 3,496 | 214 |
| Fall River, MA–RI | 42.2 min | 41 city buses<br>Seat miles/capita: 1.93 | Moderate | I-95 | Part of Providence hub | — | 4,602 | 120 |
| ★ Fargo–Moorhead, ND–MN | 31.5 min | 29 city buses<br>Seat miles/capita: 1.85 | Moderate | I-29<br>I-94 | Small hub<br>Hector Field (FAR)<br>3 airlines, 17 flights/day | 2 trains/day | 6,325 | 25 |
| Fayetteville, NC | 38.1 min | 26 city buses<br>Seat miles/capita: .80 | Heavy | I-95 | Small hub<br>Fayetteville Municipal–Grannis Field (FAY)<br>2 airlines, 16 flights/day | 2 trains/day | 4,402 | 137 |
| Fayetteville–Springdale, AR | 36.1 min | — | None | — | Non-hub<br>Drake Field (FYV)<br>3 airlines, 25 flights/day | — | 3,581 | 201 |
| Fitchburg–Leominster, MA | 39.4 min | 8 city buses<br>Seat miles/capita: .70 | None | I-90 | Nearest airport: Boston, 53 miles SE | — | 2,244 | 305 |
| Flint, MI | 42.5 min | 58 city buses<br>Seat miles/capita: 1.16 | Moderate | I-69<br>I-75 | Small hub<br>Bishop (FNT)<br>5 airlines, 19 flights/day | 4 trains/day | 4,912 | 101 |
| Florence, AL | 46.9 min | — | Light | — | Non-hub<br>Muscle Shoals (MSL)<br>2 airlines, 6 flights/day | — | 1,454 | 328 |
| Florence, SC | 41.4 min | 3 city buses<br>Seat miles/capita: .36 | Light | I-20<br>I-95 | Non-hub<br>Florence City–County (FLO)<br>3 airlines, 9 flights/day | 4 trains/day | 4,963 | 97 |
| Fort Collins–Loveland, CO | 38.7 min | 12 city buses<br>Seat miles/capita: 1.02 | Light | I-25 | Non-hub<br>Fort Collins–Loveland Municipal (FTO)<br>1 airline, 4 flights/day | — | 2,637 | 286 |
| Fort Lauderdale–Hollywood–Pompano Beach, FL | 49.7 min | 151 city buses<br>Seat miles/capita: 1.00 | Heavy | I-95 | Part of Miami hub<br>Fort Lauderdale–Hollywood International (FLL)<br>29 airlines, 150 flights/day | 4 trains/day | 4,186 | 154 |
| Fort Myers, FL | 45.5 min | 15 city buses<br>Seat miles/capita: .71 | Moderate | I-75 | Small hub<br>Page Field (FMY)<br>11 airlines, 58 flights/day | — | 4,583 | 123 |
| Fort Pierce, FL | 43.8 min | 8 city buses<br>Seat miles/capita: .76 | Moderate | I-95 | Nearest airport: West Palm Beach, 40 miles S | — | 2,143 | 311 |
| Fort Smith, AR–OK | 41.4 min | — | Light | I-40 | Non-hub<br>Fort Smith Municipal (FSM)<br>4 airlines, 22 flights/day | — | 3,092 | 253 |
| Fort Walton Beach, FL | 38.5 min | 8 city buses<br>Seat miles/capita: .62 | Moderate | I-10 | Non-hub<br>Fort Walton Municipal (VPS)<br>4 airlines, 8 flights/day | — | 2,886 | 268 |
| Fort Wayne, IN | 40.3 min | 98 city buses<br>Seat miles/capita: 2.76 | Light | I-69 | Small hub<br>Fort Wayne Municipal–Baer Field (FWA)<br>4 airlines, 34 flights/day | 4 trains/day | 5,416 | 73 |
| Fort Worth–Arlington, TX | 48.4 min | 135 city buses<br>Seat miles/capita: .92 | Heavy | I-20<br>I-35W | Part of Dallas hub<br>Dallas–Fort Worth Regional (DFW)<br>33 airlines, 554 flights/day | — | 4,472 | 132 |
| Fresno, CA | 40.5 min | 103 city buses<br>Seat miles/capita: 2.07 | Heavy | — | Small hub<br>Fresno Air Terminal (FAT)<br>11 airlines, 47 flights/day | 4 trains/day | 4,388 | 142 |
| Gadsden, AL | 43.8 min | — | Light | I-59 | Non-hub<br>Gadsden Municipal (GAD)<br>1 airline, 4 flights/day | — | 2,174 | 310 |
| Gainesville, FL | 41.1 min | 36 city buses<br>Seat miles/capita: 2.31 | Moderate | I-75 | Non-hub<br>Gainesville Regional (GNV)<br>3 airlines, 13 flights/day | — | 3,527 | 208 |

| Metro Area | Daily Commute | Public Transportation | Freeway Traffic | Interstate Highways | Air Service | Amtrak Service | Places Rated Score | Places Rated Rank |
|---|---|---|---|---|---|---|---|---|
| Galveston–Texas City, TX | 46.2 min | 15 city buses<br>1 ferry system<br>Seat miles/capita: .59 | Heavy | I-45 | Part of Houston hub | — | 3,423 | 223 |
| Gary–Hammond, IN | 49.7 min | 121 city buses<br>Seat miles/capita: 1.25 | Heavy | I-65<br>I-80<br>I-90<br>I-94 | Part of Chicago hub | 4 trains/day | 5,855 | 48 |
| Glens Falls, NY | 38.9 min | 5 city buses<br>Seat miles/capita: .65 | Moderate | I-87 | Nearest airport: Albany, 47 miles S | — | 2,241 | 306 |
| Grand Forks, ND | 28.6 min | 6 city buses<br>Seat miles/capita: .76 | Light | I-29 | Non-hub<br>Grand Forks International (GFK)<br>3 airlines, 10 flights/day | 2 trains/day | 5,587 | 62 |
| Grand Rapids, MI | 37.6 min | 102 city buses<br>Seat miles/capita: 1.81 | Heavy | I-96 | Small hub<br>Kent County International (GRR)<br>7 airlines, 47 flights/day | — | 3,454 | 219 |
| Great Falls, MT | 32.8 min | — | Light | I-15 | Small hub<br>Great Falls International (GTF)<br>4 airlines, 14 flights/day | — | 3,747 | 188 |
| Greeley, CO | 41.4 min | 10 city buses<br>Seat miles/capita: 1.07 | Light | — | Nearest airport: Denver, 50 miles SW | — | 1,641 | 326 |
| Green Bay, WI | 33.4 min | 26 city buses<br>Seat miles/capita: 1.21 | Light | I-43 | Small hub<br>Austin–Straubel Field (GRB)<br>5 airlines, 22 flights/day | — | 3,793 | 184 |
| Greensboro–Winston-Salem–High Point, NC | 40.5 min | 81 city buses<br>Seat miles/capita: 1.22 | Heavy | I-40<br>I-85 | Medium hub<br>Greensboro Regional (GSO)<br>Smith Reynolds (INT)<br>8 airlines, 84 flights/day | 2 trains/day | 4,458 | 134 |
| Greenville–Spartanburg, SC | 41.1 min | 23 city buses<br>Seat miles/capita: .46 | Light | I-26<br>I-85 | Small hub<br>Greenville–Spartanburg (GSP)<br>8 airlines, 30 flights/day | 2 trains/day | 3,950 | 170 |
| Hagerstown, MD | 46.6 min | 14 city buses<br>Seat miles/capita: 1.41 | Light | I-70<br>I-81 | Non-hub<br>Washington County Regional (HGR)<br>2 airlines, 5 flights/day | — | 3,431 | 222 |
| Hamilton–Middletown, OH | 42.9 min | 25 city buses<br>Seat miles/capita: .85 | Light | I-75 | Part of Cincinnati hub | 2 trains/day | 3,338 | 232 |
| Harrisburg–Lebanon–Carlisle, PA | 41.1 min | 82 city buses<br>Seat miles/capita: 1.96 | Moderate | I-76<br>I-81<br>I-83 | Small hub<br>Harrisburg International–Olmsted Field (MDT)<br>7 airlines, 40 flights/day | 4 trains/day | 6,164 | 32 |
| ★ Hartford, CT | 44.4 min | 259 city buses<br>Seat miles/capita: 3.38 | Heavy | I-84<br>I-86<br>I-91 | Medium hub<br>Bradley International (BDL)<br>18 airlines, 117 flights/day | 12 trains/day | 7,120 | 11 |
| Hickory, NC | 38.1 min | 8 city buses<br>Seat miles/capita: .86 | Moderate | I-40 | Non-hub<br>Hickory Municipal (HKY)<br>2 airlines, 8 flights/day | — | 2,703 | 281 |
| Honolulu, HI | 49.7 min | 406 city buses<br>Seat miles/capita: 4.64 | Heavy | I-1 | Large hub<br>Honolulu International (HNL)<br>29 airlines, 290 flights/day | — | 5,911 | 41 |
| Houma–Thibodaux, LA | 52.6 min | — | None | — | Non-hub<br>Houma–Terrebonne (HUM)<br>1 airline, 4 flights/day | — | 1,145 | 329 |
| Houston, TX | 58.5 min | 860 city buses<br>Seat miles/capita: 2.37 | Very heavy | I-10<br>I-45 | Large hub<br>William P. Hobby (HOU)<br>Houston Intercontinental (IAH)<br>35 airlines, 493 flights/day | — | 4,626 | 119 |
| Huntington–Ashland, WV–KY–OH | 44.7 min | 34 city buses<br>Seat miles/capita: 1.26 | Light | I-64 | Non-hub<br>Tri-State–Walker-Long Field (HTS)<br>5 airlines, 19 flights/day | 2 trains/day | 4,001 | 168 |
| Huntsville, AL | 40.7 min | — | Moderate | — | Small hub<br>Huntsville–Madison County (HSV)<br>4 airlines, 32 flights/day | — | 2,661 | 285 |
| Indianapolis, IN | 46.9 min | 227 city buses<br>Seat miles/capita: 1.81 | Heavy | I-65<br>I-69<br>I-70<br>I-74 | Medium hub<br>Indianapolis International (IND)<br>14 airlines, 138 flights/day | 1 train daily | 5,804 | 50 |
| Iowa City, IA | 34.8 min | 14 city buses<br>Seat miles/capita: 1.57 | Light | I-80 | Nearest airport: Cedar Rapids, 22 miles NW | — | 2,770 | 276 |
| Jackson, MI | 39.6 min | 33 city buses<br>Seat miles/capita: 2.71 | Moderate | I-94 | Non-hub<br>Jackson County–Reynolds Field (JXN)<br>1 airline, 4 flights/day | 5 trains/day | 4,800 | 107 |

| Metro Area | Daily Commute | Public Transportation | Freeway Traffic | Interstate Highways | Air Service | Amtrak Service | Places Rated Score | Places Rated Rank |
|---|---|---|---|---|---|---|---|---|
| Jackson, MS | 45.5 min | 42 city buses<br>Seat miles/capita: 1.06 | Moderate | I-20<br>I-55 | Small hub<br>Allen C. Thompson Field (JAN)<br>6 airlines, 37 flights/day | 2 trains/day | 4,917 | 100 |
| Jacksonville, FL | 47.7 min | 206 city buses<br>Seat miles/capita: 2.29 | Heavy | I-10<br>I-95 | Medium hub<br>Jacksonville International (JAX)<br>11 airlines, 93 flights/day | 4 trains/day | 5,611 | 59 |
| Jacksonville, NC | 33.9 min | — | Light | — | Non-hub<br>Albert J. Ellis (OAJ)<br>1 airline, 4 flights/day | — | 1,780 | 321 |
| Janesville–Beloit, WI | 34.5 min | 12 city buses<br>Seat miles/capita: 1.55 | Moderate | I-90 | Non-hub<br>Rock County (JVL)<br>1 airline, 5 flights/day | — | 3,092 | 253 |
| Jersey City, NJ | 57.6 min | 225 city buses<br>1 commuter railroad<br>Seat miles/capita: 2.69 | Very heavy | I-78<br>I-80<br>I-95 | Part of New York hub | — | 4,982 | 95 |
| Johnson City–Kingsport–Bristol, TN–VA | 43.1 min | 14 city buses<br>Seat miles/capita: .42 | Moderate | I-81 | Small hub<br>Tri-City (TRI)<br>5 airlines, 25 flights/day | — | 2,532 | 289 |
| Johnstown, PA | 43.3 min | 45 city buses<br>1 cable incline<br>Seat miles/capita: 3.32 | Light | — | Non-hub<br>Johnstown–Cambria County (JST)<br>1 airline, 10 flights/day | 2 trains/day | 4,343 | 145 |
| Joliet, IL | 53.7 min | 47 city buses<br>Seat miles/capita: 1.87 | Heavy | I-55<br>I-80 | Part of Chicago hub | 8 trains/day | 4,645 | 117 |
| Joplin, MO | 36.5 min | — | Light | I-44 | Non-hub<br>Joplin Municipal (JLN)<br>3 airlines, 4 flights/day | — | 2,335 | 300 |
| Kalamazoo, MI | 37.4 min | 67 city buses<br>Seat miles/capita: 2.88 | Moderate | I-94 | Small hub<br>Kalamazoo Municipal (AZO)<br>3 airlines, 17 flights/day | 7 trains/day | 5,419 | 72 |
| Kankakee, IL | 39.8 min | — | Light | I-57 | Nearest airport: Chicago, 50 miles NE | 5 trains/day | 3,444 | 220 |
| Kansas City, KS | 42.9 min | 12 city buses<br>Seat miles/capita: .15 | Heavy | I-29<br>I-35<br>I-70 | Part of Kansas City, MO, hub | — | 5,006 | 94 |
| Kansas City, MO | 48.0 min | 350 city buses<br>Seat miles/capita: 2.55 | Heavy | I-29<br>I-35<br>I-70 | Large hub<br>Kansas City International (MCI)<br>Kansas City Downtown (MKC)<br>26 airlines, 208 flights/day | 3 trains/day | 5,869 | 46 |
| Kenosha, WI | 40.5 min | 31 city buses<br>Seat miles/capita: 2.41 | Heavy | I-94 | Part of Chicago hub | — | 4,473 | 131 |
| Killeen–Temple, TX | 35.0 min | 9 city buses<br>Seat miles/capita: .81 | Light | I-35 | Non-hub<br>Killeen Municipal (ILE)<br>Draughon–Miller Municipal (TPL)<br>1 airline, 10 flights/day | — | 2,862 | 272 |
| Knoxville, TN | 49.9 min | 121 city buses<br>Seat miles/capita: 2.83 | Heavy | I-40<br>I-75 | Small hub<br>McGhee Tyson (TYS)<br>10 airlines, 46 flights/day | — | 4,273 | 150 |
| Kokomo, IN | 33.7 min | — | Light | — | Non-hub<br>Kokomo Municipal (OKK)<br>1 airline, 4 flights/day | — | 1,817 | 320 |
| La Crosse, WI | 33.9 min | 29 city buses<br>Seat miles/capita: 2.84 | Light | I-90 | Non-hub<br>La Crosse Municipal (LSE)<br>2 airlines, 13 flights/day | 2 trains/day | 6,096 | 35 |
| Lafayette, IN | 31.7 min | 30 city buses<br>Seat miles/capita: 2.19 | Light | I-65 | Non-hub<br>Purdue University (LAF)<br>1 airline, 4 flights/day | 2 trains/day | 4,956 | 98 |
| Lafayette, LA | 47.7 min | 22 city buses<br>Seat miles/capita: 1.29 | Moderate | I-10 | Non-hub<br>Lafayette Regional (LFT)<br>5 airlines, 91 flights/day | — | 5,268 | 81 |
| Lake Charles, LA | 43.3 | 10 city buses<br>Seat miles/capita: .54 | Moderate | I-10 | Non-hub<br>Lake Charles Municipal (LCH)<br>3 airlines, 28 flights/day | — | 3,549 | 206 |
| Lake County, IL | 53.2 | 38 city buses<br>Seat miles/capita: .57 | Heavy | I-94 | Part of Chicago hub | — | 3,422 | 224 |
| Lakeland–Winter Haven, FL | 42.9 min | 4 city buses<br>Seat miles/capita: .14 | Moderate | I-4 | Nearest airport: Tampa, 35 miles SW | 6 trains/day | 3,412 | 225 |
| Lancaster, PA | 37.4 min | 38 city buses<br>Seat miles/capita:1.61 | Moderate | — | Non-hub<br>Lancaster (LNS)<br>1 airline, 17 flights/day | 12 trains/day | 3,908 | 173 |

| Metro Area | Daily Commute | Public Transportation | Freeway Traffic | Interstate Highways | Air Service | Amtrak Service | Places Rated Score | Places Rated Rank |
|---|---|---|---|---|---|---|---|---|
| Lansing–East Lansing, MI | 39.6 min | 76 city buses Seat miles/capita:1.99 | Heavy | I-69 I-96 | Small hub Capital City (LAN) 5 airlines, 28 flights/day | 4 trains/day | 5,557 | 64 |
| Laredo, TX | 37.2 min | 20 city buses Seat miles/capita: 1.40 | Light | I-35 | Non-hub Laredo International (LRD) 3 airlines, 8 flights/day | — | 3,322 | 235 |
| Las Cruces, NM | 37.6 min | — | Moderate | I-10 I-25 | Non-hub Las Cruces–Crawford (LRU) 1 airline, 3 flights/day | — | 2,989 | 258 |
| Las Vegas, NV | 41.6 min | 25 city buses Seat miles/capita: .38 | Moderate | I-15 | Large hub McCarran International (LAS) 26 airlines, 255 flights/day | 2 trains/day | 5,900 | 43 |
| Lawrence, KS | 35.4 min | 16 city buses Seat miles/capita: 2.02 | Moderate | I-70 | Nearest airport: Kansas City, MO, 35 miles NE | — | 2,931 | 265 |
| Lawrence–Haverhill, MA-NH | 44.4 min | 24 city buses Seat miles/capita: .76 | Heavy | I-93 | Part of Boston hub | — | 3,575 | 202 |
| Lawton, OK | 31.5 min | — | Light | I-44 | Non-hub Lawton Municipal (LAW) 1 airline, 10 flights/day | — | 2,366 | 299 |
| Lewiston–Auburn, ME | 35.9 min | 14 city buses Seat miles/capita: 1.33 | Light | I-95 | Non-hub Auburn–Lewiston Municipal (LEW) 1 airline, 3 flights/day | — | 2,941 | 263 |
| Lexington–Fayette, KY | 40.5 min | 52 city buses Seat miles/capita: 1.79 | Heavy | I-64 I-75 | Small hub Blue Grass (LEX) 6 airlines, 26 flights/day | — | 4,080 | 165 |
| Lima, OH | 37.0 min | 11 city buses Seat miles/capita: 1.05 | Light | I-75 | Non-hub Lima–Allen County (LIA) 1 airline, 2 flights/day | 4 trains/day | 4,084 | 163 |
| Lincoln, NE | 34.8 min | 63 city buses Seat miles/capita: 2.39 | Light | I-80 | Small hub Lincoln Municipal (LNK) 4 airlines, 22 flights/day | 4 trains/day | 5,618 | 56 |
| Little Rock–North Little Rock, AR | 43.8 min | 62 city buses Seat miles/capita: 1.40 | Heavy | I-30 I-40 | Small hub Adams Field (LIT) 7 airlines, 58 flights/day | — | 4,186 | 154 |
| Longview–Marshall, TX | 38.7 min | — | Light | I-20 | Non-hub Gregg County (GGG) 3 airlines, 12 flights/day | — | 2,680 | 284 |
| Lorain–Elyria, OH | 42.0 min | 9 city buses Seat miles/capita: .27 | Heavy | I-80 I-90 | Part of Cleveland hub | 2 trains/day | 3,629 | 198 |
| Los Angeles–Long Beach, CA | 53.5 min | 3,465 city buses 1 commuter railroad 1 ferry system Seat miles/capita: 2.80 | Very heavy | I-5 I-10 | Large hub Burbank–Glendale–Pasadena (BUR) Long Beach–Daugherty Field (LGB) Los Angeles International (LAX) 61 airlines, 708 flights/day | 13 trains/day | 4,345 | 144 |
| Louisville, KY–IN | 48.6 min | 318 city buses Seat miles/capita: 2.78 | Heavy | I-64 I-65 I-71 | Medium hub Standiford Field (SDF) 12 airlines, 126 flights/day | — | 5,420 | 71 |
| Lowell, MA–NH | 47.3 min | 36 city buses Seat miles/capita: 1.52 | Heavy | I-95 | Part of Boston hub | — | 3,820 | 179 |
| Lubbock, TX | 35.9 min | 42 city buses Seat miles/capita: 1.59 | Light | I-27 | Small hub Lubbock International (LBB) 5 airlines, 34 flights/day | — | 4,158 | 159 |
| Lynchburg, VA | 35.6 min | 26 city buses Seat miles/capita: 1.84 | Light | — | Non-hub Lynchburg Municipal–Preston Glenn Field (LYN) 2 airlines, 20 flights/day | 2 trains/day | 4,909 | 102 |
| Macon–Warner Robins, GA | 42.9 min | 22 city buses Seat miles/capita: .79 | Heavy | I-16 I-75 | Non-hub Lewis B. Wilson (MCN) 2 airlines, 8 flights/day | — | 3,144 | 246 |
| Madison, WI | 39.6 min | 193 city buses Seat miles/capita: 6.02 | Moderate | I-90 I-94 | Small hub Dane County Regional–Truax Field (MSN) 6 airlines, 35 flights/day | — | 6,084 | 36 |
| Manchester, NH | 42.5 min | 33 city buses Seat miles/capita: 2.14 | Moderate | I-93 | Non-hub Manchester (MHT) 4 airlines, 27 flights/day | — | 4,595 | 121 |
| Mansfield, OH | 36.5 min | 10 city buses Seat miles/capita: .84 | Heavy | I-71 | Non-hub Mansfield–Lahm Municipal (MFD) 1 airline, 7 flights/day | — | 2,876 | 270 |

| Metro Area | Daily Commute | Public Transportation | Freeway Traffic | Interstate Highways | Air Service | Amtrak Service | Places Rated Score | Places Rated Rank |
|---|---|---|---|---|---|---|---|---|
| McAllen–Edinburg–Mission, TX | 37.6 min | 24 city buses Seat miles/capita: 1.02 | Light | — | Non-hub Miller International (MFE) 2 airlines, 12 flights/day | — | 2,117 | 313 |
| Medford, OR | 36.7 min | 5 city buses Seat miles/capita: .63 | Light | I-5 | Non-hub Medford–Jackson County (MRF) 4 airlines, 18 flights/day | — | 3,512 | 210 |
| Melbourne–Titusville–Palm Bay, FL | 44.2 min | 12 city buses Seat miles/capita: .38 | Moderate | I-95 | Small hub Melbourne Regional (MLB) 4 airlines, 18 flights/day | — | 2,560 | 287 |
| Memphis, TN–AR–MS | 48.4 min | 313 city buses Seat miles/capita: 2.69 | Heavy | I-40 I-55 | Medium hub Memphis International (MEM) 13 airlines, 236 flights/day | 2 trains/day | 6,247 | 28 |
| Miami–Hialeah, FL | 52.1 min | 865 city buses Seat miles/capita: 3.58 | Heavy | I-95 | Large hub Miami International (MIA) 61 airlines, 381 flights/day | 4 trains/day | 5,202 | 84 |
| Middlesex–Somerset–Hunterdon, NJ | 53.9 min | 310 city buses Seat miles/capita: 2.33 | Very heavy | I-78 I-80 | Part of New York hub | — | 4,198 | 153 |
| Middletown, CT | 42.0 min | 7 city buses Seat miles/capita: .57 | Heavy | I-91 | Part of Hartford hub | — | 4,636 | 118 |
| Midland, TX | 35.9 min | 6 city buses Seat miles/capita: .56 | Moderate | I-20 | Small hub Midland Regional (MAF) 8 airlines, 39 flights/day | — | 5,310 | 78 |
| Milwaukee, WI | 42.7 min | 631 city buses Seat miles/capita: 3.48 | Heavy | I-43 I-94 | Medium hub General Mitchell Field (MKE) 12 airlines, 125 flights/day | 2 trains/day | 4,945 | 99 |
| Minneapolis–St. Paul, MN–WI | 44.2 min | 1,012 city buses Seat miles/capita: 3.77 | Moderate | I-35 I-94 | Large hub Minneapolis–St. Paul International (MSP) 23 airlines, 304 flights/day | 3 trains/day | 5,606 | 60 |
| Mobile, AL | 51.7 min | 38 city buses Seat miles/capita: .86 | Light | I-10 I-65 | Small hub Bates Field (MOB) 7 airlines, 32 flights/day | — | 3,345 | 231 |
| Modesto, CA | 36.7 min | 20 city buses Seat miles/capita: .84 | Heavy | — | Non-hub Modesto City–County (MOD) 4 airlines, 9 flights/day | — | 2,000 | 315 |
| Monmouth–Ocean, NJ | 64.0 min | 306 city buses Seat miles/capita: 2.40 | Very heavy | — | Part of New York hub Allaire Field (ARX) 2 airlines, 10 flights/day | — | 2,690 | 282 |
| Monroe, LA | 39.4 min | 18 city buses Seat miles/capita: 1.07 | Heavy | I-20 | Non-hub Monroe Regional (MLU) 3 airlines, 19 flights/day | — | 3,606 | 200 |
| Montgomery, AL | 44.7 min | 35 city buses Seat miles/capita: 1.18 | Moderate | I-65 I-85 | Small hub Dannelly Field (MGM) 4 airlines, 16 flights/day | — | 3,509 | 212 |
| Muncie, IN | 36.5 min | 21 city buses Seat miles/capita: 1.53 | Moderate | I-69 | Non-hub Delaware County–Johnson Field (MIE) 1 airline, 2 flights/day | 2 trains/day | 4,325 | 146 |
| Muskegon, MI | 38.7 min | 14 city buses Seat miles/capita: .88 | Moderate | I-96 | Non-hub Muskegon County (MKG) 2 airlines, 18 flights/day | — | 3,353 | 229 |
| Nashua, NH | 43.6 min | 1 city bus Seat miles/capita: .09 | Heavy | I-93 | Part of Boston hub | — | 3,320 | 236 |
| Nashville, TN | 49.3 min | 153 city buses Seat miles/capita: 1.97 | Heavy | I-24 I-40 I-65 | Medium hub Nashville Metropolitan (BNA) 13 airlines, 108 flights/day | — | 5,030 | 92 |
| Nassau–Suffolk, NY | 70.6 min | 940 city buses 1 commuter railroad Seat miles/capita: 1.19 | Heavy | — | Part of New York hub Republic (FRG) Long Island–MacArthur (ISP) 11 airlines, 58 flights/day | — | 2,119 | 312 |
| New Bedford, MA | 39.4 min | 51 city buses Seat miles/capita: 2.55 | Moderate | I-95 | Non-hub New Bedford Municipal (EWB) 1 airline, 4 flights/day | — | 3,219 | 240 |
| New Britain, CT | 38.9 min | 20 city buses Seat miles/capita: .98 | Heavy | I-84 | Part of Hartford hub | 11 trains/day | 4,900 | 104 |
| New Haven–Meriden, CT | 42.9 min | 130 city buses Seat miles/capita: 2.35 | Heavy | I-91 I-95 | Large hub Tweed–New Haven (HVN) 2 airlines, 52 flights/day | 12 trains/day | 5,938 | 40 |
| New London–Norwich, CT–RI | 40.3 min | 24 city buses Seat miles/capita: 1.07 | Heavy | I-95 | Non-hub Groton–New London (GON) 3 airlines, 18 flights/day | 11 trains/day | 4,505 | 129 |

| Metro Area | Daily Commute | Public Transportation | Freeway Traffic | Interstate Highways | Air Service | Amtrak Service | Places Rated Score | Places Rated Rank |
|---|---|---|---|---|---|---|---|---|
| New Orleans, LA | 55.9 min | 568 city buses<br>35 rapid rail cars<br>1 ferry system<br>Seat miles/capita: 3.65 | Very heavy | I-10 | Large hub<br>New Orleans International–<br>Moisant Field (MSY)<br>23 airlines, 167 flights/day | 2 trains/day | 4,579 | 124 |
| ★ New York, NY | 81.0 min | 4,662 buses<br>6,263 rapid rail cars<br>2 ferry systems<br>Seat miles/capita:<br>23.49 | Very heavy | I-78<br>I-87<br>I-95 | Large hub<br>John F. Kennedy International<br>(JFK)<br>La Guardia (LGA)<br>87 airlines, 838 flights/day | 27 trains/day | 8,625 | 1 |
| Newark, NJ | 55.9 min | 677 city buses<br>26 rapid rail cars<br>Seat miles/capita: 2.44 | Very heavy | I-95 | Part of New York hub<br>Newark International (EWR)<br>28 airlines, 304 flights/day | 27 trains/day | 3,514 | 209 |
| Niagara Falls, NY | 37.2 min | 89 city buses<br>Seat miles/capita: 2.61 | Moderate | I-90 | Part of Buffalo hub | 6 trains/day | 5,561 | 63 |
| Norfolk–<br>Virginia Beach–<br>Newport News, VA | 47.1 min | 305 city buses<br>Seat miles/capita: 1.85 | Moderate | I-64 | Medium hub<br>Norfolk International (ORF)<br>Patrick Henry International (PHF)<br>13 airlines, 92 flights/day | — | 3,215 | 241 |
| Norwalk, CT | 54.1 min | 39 city buses<br>Seat miles/capita: 2.42 | Heavy | I-95 | Part of New York hub | — | 3,536 | 207 |
| ★ Oakland, CA | 56.3 min | 886 city buses<br>439 rapid rail cars<br>Seat miles/capita: 7.18 | Heavy | I-80 | Part of San Francisco hub<br>Metropolitan Oakland International<br>(OAK)<br>12 airlines, 118 flights/day | 4 trains/day | 6,430 | 24 |
| Ocala, FL | 42.5 min | — | Moderate | I-75 | Non-hub<br>Ocala Municipal–Jim Taylor Field<br>(OCF)<br>1 airline, 6 flights/day | 2 trains/day | 3,798 | 183 |
| Odessa, TX | 39.8 min | — | Moderate | I-20 | Nearest airport: Midland, 15 miles<br>SW | — | 1,944 | 316 |
| Oklahoma City, OK | 44.9 min | 81 city buses<br>Seat miles/capita: .80 | Moderate | I-35<br>I-40<br>I-44 | Medium hub<br>Will Rogers World (OKC)<br>15 airlines, 91 flights/day | — | 4,459 | 133 |
| Olympia, WA | 44.0 min | 19 city buses<br>Seat miles/capita: 1.84 | Very heavy | I-5 | Nearest airport: Seattle, 30 miles<br>NE | 4 trains/day | 4,083 | 164 |
| Omaha, NE–IA | 38.7 min | 223 city buses<br>Seat miles/capita: 2.89 | Moderate | I-80 | Medium hub<br>Eppley Airfield (OMA)<br>16 airlines, 85 flights/day | 4 trains/day | 5,806 | 49 |
| Orange County, NY | 53.5 min | 5 city buses<br>Seat miles/capita: .13 | Very heavy | I-84<br>I-87 | Part of New York hub<br>Stewart (SWF)<br>1 airline, 2 flights/day | — | 3,299 | 238 |
| Orlando, FL | 45.5 min | 47 city buses<br>Seat miles/capita: .54 | Heavy | I-4 | Medium hub<br>Orlando International (MCO)<br>22 airlines, 188 flights/day | 6 trains/day | 5,887 | 45 |
| Owensboro, KY | 41.1 min | 5 city buses<br>Seat miles/capita: .58 | Light | — | Non-hub<br>Owensboro–Daviess County<br>(OWB)<br>1 airline, 8 flights/day | — | 2,273 | 303 |
| Oxnard–<br>Ventura, CA | 51.0 min | 50 city buses<br>Seat miles/capita: .88 | Heavy | — | Part of Los Angeles hub<br>Oxnard (OXR)<br>2 airlines, 20 flights/day | 2 trains/day | 2,238 | 307 |
| Panama City, FL | 37.8 min | 3 city buses<br>Seat miles/capita: .25 | None | — | Non-hub<br>Panama City–Bay County (PFN)<br>2 airlines, 15 flights/day | — | 2,778 | 275 |
| Parkersburg–<br>Marietta, WV–OH | 43.6 min | 9 city buses<br>Seat miles/capita: .95 | Light | I-77 | Non-hub<br>Wood County (PKB)<br>2 airlines, 12 flights/day | 6 trains/day | 4,399 | 139 |
| Pascagoula, MS | 47.1 min | — | Light | I-10 | Nearest airport: Mobile, AL, 35<br>miles SW | — | 1,750 | 322 |
| Pawtucket–<br>Woonsocket–<br>Attleboro, RI–MA | 40.9 min | 100 city buses<br>Seat miles/capita: 2.17 | Moderate | I-95 | Part of Providence hub | — | 4,738 | 110 |
| Pensacola, FL | 43.8 min | 28 city buses<br>Seat miles/capita: .86 | Moderate | I-10 | Small hub<br>Pensacola Municipal (PNS)<br>7 airlines, 24 flights/day | — | 2,918 | 266 |
| Peoria, IL | 40.7 min | 47 city buses<br>Seat miles/capita: 1.20 | Heavy | I-74 | Small hub<br>Greater Peoria (PIA)<br>5 airlines, 23 flights/day | — | 2,967 | 261 |
| Philadelphia,<br>PA–NJ | 56.3 min | 1,534 city buses<br>808 rapid rail cars<br>174 trolley coaches<br>2 commuter railroads<br>Seat miles/capita: 3.79 | Heavy | I-76<br>I-95 | Large hub<br>North Philadelphia (PNE)<br>Philadelphia International (PHL)<br>31 airlines, 360 flights/day | 42 trains/day | 5,903 | 42 |

| Metro Area | Daily Commute | Public Transportation | Freeway Traffic | Interstate Highways | Air Service | Amtrak Service | Places Rated Score | Places Rated Rank |
|---|---|---|---|---|---|---|---|---|
| Phoenix, AZ | 47.7 min | 245 city buses<br>Seat miles/capita: 1.16 | Heavy | I-10<br>I-17 | Large hub<br>Phoenix Sky Harbor International (PHX)<br>Scottsdale Municipal (SCF)<br>23 airlines, 265 flights/day | 2 trains/day | 4,729 | 113 |
| Pine Bluff, AR | 41.8 min | 11 city buses<br>Seat miles/capita: 1.17 | Light | — | Nearest airport: Little Rock, 45 miles NW | — | 1,671 | 324 |
| Pittsburgh, PA | 50.4 min | 915 city buses<br>92 rapid rail cars<br>2 cable inclines<br>Seat miles/capita: 3.80 | Heavy | I-76<br>I-79 | Large hub<br>Allegheny County (AGC)<br>Greater Pittsburgh International (PIT)<br>19 airlines, 368 flights/day | 4 trains/day | 5,616 | 57 |
| Pittsfield, MA | 33.2 min | 16 city buses<br>Seat miles/capita: 1.85 | None | — | Nearest airport: Albany, NY, 45 miles NW | 2 trains/day | 3,759 | 186 |
| Portland, ME | 37.6 min | 63 city buses<br>1 ferry system<br>Seat miles/capita: 3.92 | Moderate | I-95 | Small hub<br>Portland International Jetport (PWM)<br>5 airlines, 34 flights/day | — | 5,185 | 86 |
| Portland, OR | 45.8 min | 649 city buses<br>Seat miles/capita: 4.21 | Heavy | I-5<br>I-84 | Medium hub<br>Portland International (PDX)<br>19 airlines, 143 flights/day | 5 trains/day | 5,947 | 39 |
| Portsmouth–Dover–Rochester, NH–ME | 39.6 min | 14 city buses<br>Seat miles/capita: .90 | Moderate | I-95 | Nearest airport: Manchester, 47 miles W | — | 2,321 | 301 |
| Poughkeepsie, NY | 49.5 min | 23 city buses<br>Seat miles/capita: 1.12 | Heavy | I-97 | Non-hub<br>Dutchess County (POU)<br>5 airlines, 14 flights/day | 13 trains/day | 4,166 | 157 |
| Providence, RI | 39.6 min | 178 city buses<br>Seat miles/capita: 2.17 | Moderate | I-84<br>I-95 | Small hub<br>Theodore Francis Green State (PVD)<br>9 airlines, 53 flights/day | 11 trains/day | 5,474 | 69 |
| Provo–Orem, UT | 38.3 min | 60 city buses<br>Seat miles/capita: 2.36 | Moderate | I-15 | Non-hub<br>Provo Municipal (PVU)<br>1 airline, 2 flights/day | 4 trains/day | 4,546 | 126 |
| Pueblo, CO | 35.9 min | 23 city buses<br>Seat miles/capita: 1.40 | Moderate | I-25 | Non-hub<br>Pueblo Memorial (PUB)<br>1 airline, 12 flights/day | — | 3,501 | 213 |
| Racine, WI | 37.4 min | 25 city buses<br>Seat miles/capita: 1.40 | Heavy | I-94 | Part of Milwaukee hub | 2 trains/day | 3,558 | 203 |
| ★ Raleigh–Durham, NC | 42.5 min | 132 city buses<br>Seat miles/capita: 2.42 | Heavy | I-40<br>I-85 | Medium hub<br>Raleigh–Durham (RDU)<br>12 airlines, 100 flights/day | 4 trains/day | 6,544 | 22 |
| Reading, PA | 39.4 min | 52 city buses<br>Seat miles/capita: 2.00 | Heavy | I-76 | Non-hub<br>Reading Municipal (RDG)<br>1 airline, 12 flights/day | — | 3,120 | 248 |
| Redding, CA | 33.7 min | 16 city buses<br>Seat miles/capita: 2.02 | Heavy | I-5 | Non-hub<br>Redding Municipal (RDD)<br>6 airlines, 16 flights/day | 2 trains/day | 5,727 | 53 |
| ★ Reno, NV | 36.7 min | 13 city buses<br>Seat miles/capita: .53 | Moderate | I-80 | Medium hub<br>Reno–Cannon International (RNO)<br>14 airlines, 73 flights/day | 2 trains/day | 6,767 | 17 |
| Richland–Kennewick–Pasco, WA | 46.6 min | — | Heavy | — | Non-hub<br>Tri-Cities (PSC)<br>4 airlines, 35 flights/day | 2 trains/day | 4,714 | 115 |
| ★ Richmond–Petersburg, VA | 48.8 min | 222 city buses<br>Seat miles/capita: 2.47 | Heavy | I-64<br>I-85<br>I-95 | Small hub<br>Richard Evelyn Byrd International (RIC)<br>12 airlines, 91 flights/day | 8 trains/day | 6,680 | 18 |
| Riverside–San Bernardino, CA | 48.4 min | 133 city buses<br>Seat miles/capita: 1.26 | Heavy | I-10 | Part of Los Angeles hub<br>Ontario International (ONT)<br>Riverside Municipal (RAL)<br>17 airlines, 85 flights/day | 4 trains/day | 3,141 | 247 |
| Roanoke, VA | 52.4 min | 35 city buses<br>Seat miles/capita: 1.31 | Heavy | I-81 | Small hub<br>Roanoke Regional (ROA)<br>2 airlines, 42 flights/day | — | 3,872 | 176 |
| Rochester, MN | 30.8 min | 10 city buses<br>Seat miles/capita: 1.10 | Light | I-90 | Small hub<br>Rochester Municipal (RST)<br>4 airlines, 17 flights/day | — | 4,399 | 139 |
| Rochester, NY | 42.9 min | 253 city buses<br>Seat miles/capita: 2.78 | Heavy | I-90 | Medium hub<br>Rochester–Monroe County (ROC)<br>10 airlines, 73 flights/day | 8 trains/day | 5,165 | 88 |

| Metro Area | Daily Commute | Public Transportation | Freeway Traffic | Interstate Highways | Air Service | Amtrak Service | Places Rated Score | Places Rated Rank |
|---|---|---|---|---|---|---|---|---|
| Rockford, IL | 37.2 min | 50 city buses<br>Seat miles/capita: 1.63 | Light | I-90 | Non-hub<br>Greater Rockford (RFD)<br>1 airline, 9 flights/day | — | 2,987 | 260 |
| Sacramento, CA | 42.7 min | 238 city buses<br>Seat miles/capita: 1.99 | Heavy | I-5<br>I-80 | Small hub<br>Sacramento Metropolitan (SMF)<br>13 airlines, 80 flights/day | 6 trains/day | 5,097 | 89 |
| Saginaw–Bay City–Midland, MI | 39.4 min | 106 city buses<br>Seat miles/capita: 1.71 | Moderate | I-75 | Small hub<br>Tri-City (MBS)<br>3 airlines, 25 flights/day | — | 3,186 | 244 |
| St. Cloud, MN | 37.2 min | 22 city buses<br>Seat miles/capita: 2.51 | Light | I-94 | Nearest airport: Minneapolis, 68 miles SE | 2 trains/day | 4,565 | 125 |
| St. Joseph, MO | 37.0 min | 19 city buses<br>Seat miles/capita: 1.58 | Light | I-29 | Nearest airport: Kansas City, 30 miles SE | — | 2,689 | 283 |
| ★ St. Louis, MO-IL | 50.6 min | 942 city buses<br>Seat miles/capita. 3.47 | Heavy | I-44<br>I-55<br>I-64<br>I-70 | Large hub<br>Lambert–St. Louis International (STL)<br>26 airlines, 383 flights/day | 6 trains/day | 7,119 | 12 |
| Salem, OR | 40.7 min | 58 city buses<br>Seat miles/capita: 2.85 | Moderate | I-5 | Non-hub<br>McNary Field (SLE)<br>1 airline, 4 flights/day | 2 trains/day | 4,732 | 111 |
| Salem–Gloucester, MA | 52.1 min | 34 city buses<br>1 commuter railroad<br>Seat miles/capita: .88 | Heavy | I-95 | Part of Boston hub | — | 3,459 | 217 |
| Salinas–Seaside–Monterey, CA | 36.1 min | 52 city buses<br>Seat miles/capita: 1.75 | Heavy | — | Small hub<br>Monterey Peninsula (MRY)<br>6 airlines, 23 flights/day | 2 trains/day | 4,160 | 158 |
| Salt Lake City–Ogden, UT | 44.2 min | 307 city buses<br>Seat miles/capita: 2.32 | Heavy | I-15<br>I-80 | Medium hub<br>Salt Lake International (SLC)<br>13 airlines, 194 flights/day | 4 trains/day | 6,228 | 29 |
| San Angelo, TX | 34.5 min | 15 city buses<br>Seat miles/capita: 1.35 | Moderate | — | Non-hub<br>Mathis Field (SJT)<br>2 airlines, 9 flights/day | — | 2,938 | 264 |
| San Antonio, TX | 44.9 min | 454 city buses<br>Seat miles/capita: 3.20 | Very heavy | I-10<br>I-35<br>I-37 | Medium hub<br>San Antonio International (SAT)<br>14 airlines, 106 flights/day | — | 5,387 | 74 |
| San Diego, CA | 43.1 min | 516 city buses<br>Seat miles/capita: 2.02 | Heavy | I-5<br>I-8<br>I-15 | Medium hub<br>San Diego International–Lindbergh Field (SAN)<br>21 airlines, 142 flights/day | 7 trains/day | 5,489 | 68 |
| ★ San Francisco, CA | 55.2 min | 1,082 city buses<br>439 rapid rail cars<br>174 street cars<br>345 trolley coaches<br>4 ferry systems<br>Seat miles/capita: 11.68 | Heavy | I-80 | Large hub<br>San Francisco International (SFO)<br>36 airlines, 406 flights/day | 7 trains/day | 8,299 | 3 |
| San Jose, CA | 50.2 min | 745 city buses<br>Seat miles/capita: 3.99 | Heavy | I-80 | Part of San Francisco hub<br>San Jose Municipal (SJC)<br>16 airlines, 92 flights/day | 2 trains/day | 5,224 | 82 |
| Santa Barbara–Santa Maria–Lompoc, CA | 36.1 min | 76 city buses<br>Seat miles/capita: 2.44 | Heavy | — | Non-hub<br>Santa Barbara Municipal (SBA)<br>8 airlines, 66 flights/day | 2 trains/day | 5,662 | 54 |
| Santa Cruz, CA | 48.6 min | 94 city buses<br>Seat miles/capita: 5.08 | Heavy | — | Part of San Francisco hub | — | 5,010 | 93 |
| Santa Rosa–Petaluma, CA | 49.9 min | 21 city buses<br>Seat miles/capita: 1.02 | Heavy | — | Part of San Francisco hub | — | 3,313 | 237 |
| Sarasota, FL | 38.9 min | 15 city buses<br>Seat miles/capita: .49 | Moderate | I-75 | Small hub<br>Sarasota–Bradenton (SRQ)<br>11 airlines, 62 flights/day | — | 3,742 | 189 |
| Savannah, GA | 47.1 min | 63 city buses<br>Seat miles/capita: 2.25 | Moderate | I-16<br>I-95 | Small hub<br>Savannah International (SAV)<br>4 airlines, 27 flights/day | 8 trains/day | 5,958 | 38 |
| Scranton–Wilkes-Barre, PA | 40.9 min | 102 city buses<br>Seat miles/capita: 1.67 | Moderate | I-81<br>I-84 | Small hub<br>Wilkes-Barre–Scranton International (AVP)<br>6 airlines, 32 flights/day | — | 3,683 | 194 |
| ★ Seattle, WA | 50.8 min | 1,248 city buses<br>115 trolley coaches<br>1 ferry system<br>Seat miles/capita: 6.37 | Heavy | I-5<br>I-90 | Large hub<br>Henry M. Jackson International (SEA)<br>28 airlines, 254 flights/day | 4 trains/day | 6,634 | 19 |
| Sharon, PA | 37.6 min | — | Moderate | I-80 | Nearest airport: Youngstown, OH, 10 miles W | — | 2,017 | 314 |

| Metro Area | Daily Commute | Public Transportation | Freeway Traffic | Interstate Highways | Air Service | Amtrak Service | Places Rated Score | Places Rated Rank |
|---|---|---|---|---|---|---|---|---|
| Sheboygan, WI | 31.7 min | 18 city buses<br>Seat miles/capita: 2.05 | Light | I-43 | Non-hub<br>Sheboygan County Memorial (SBM)<br>1 airline, 4 flights/day | — | 3,458 | 218 |
| Sherman–Denison, TX | 40.5 min | — | Light | I-35 | Nearest airport: Dallas, 65 miles SW | — | 1,922 | 317 |
| Shreveport, LA | 43.6 min | 57 city buses<br>Seat miles/capita: 1.44 | Moderate | I-20<br>I-49 | Small hub<br>Shreveport Regional (SHV)<br>5 airlines, 48 flights/day | — | 4,401 | 138 |
| Sioux City, IA–NE | 32.6 min | 34 city buses<br>Seat miles/capita: 2.34 | Moderate | I-29 | Small hub<br>Sioux City Municipal (SUX)<br>5 airlines, 15 flights/day | — | 4,316 | 147 |
| Sioux Falls, SD | 32.3 min | 31 city buses<br>Seat miles/capita: 2.41 | Moderate | I-29<br>I-90 | Small hub<br>Joe Foss Field (FSD)<br>7 airlines, 29 flights/day | — | 6,271 | 27 |
| South Bend–Mishawaka, IN | 38.1 min | 58 city buses<br>Seat miles/capita: 1.71 | Light | I-80 | Small hub<br>Michiana Regional (SBN)<br>4 airlines, 39 flights/day | 2 trains/day | 5,634 | 55 |
| Spokane, WA | 40.5 min | 80 city buses<br>Seat miles/capita: 2.00 | Heavy | I-90 | Medium hub<br>Spokane International (GEG)<br>8 airlines, 63 flights/day | 2 trains/day | 5,534 | 65 |
| Springfield, IL | 38.1 min | 42 city buses<br>Seat miles/capita: 2.28 | Moderate | I-55<br>I-72 | Non-hub<br>Capital (SPI)<br>3 airlines, 22 flights/day | 6 trains/day | 6,172 | 31 |
| Springfield, MA | 39.8 min | 217 city buses<br>Seat miles/capita: 2.86 | Moderate | I-90<br>I-91 | Medium hub<br>Bradley International (BDL)<br>18 airlines, 117 flights/day | 12 trains/day | 6,159 | 33 |
| Springfield, MO | 39.2 min | 36 city buses<br>Seat miles/capita: 1.73 | Moderate | I-44 | Small hub<br>Springfield Regional (SGF)<br>4 airlines, 27 flights/day | — | 3,828 | 178 |
| Stamford, CT | 53.2 min | 37 city buses<br>Seat miles/capita: 1.35 | Heavy | I-95 | Part of New York hub | 14 trains/day | 3,110 | 250 |
| State College, PA | 38.1 min | 18 city buses<br>Seat miles/capita: 2.34 | Light | — | Non-hub<br>University Park (SCE)<br>1 airline, 6 flights/day | — | 2,740 | 278 |
| Steubenville–Weirton, OH–WV | 42.2 min | 10 city buses<br>Seat miles/capita: .86 | Light | — | Nearest airport: Pittsburgh, PA, 33 miles NE | — | 1,532 | 327 |
| Stockton, CA | 38.5 min | 53 city buses<br>Seat miles/capita: 1.79 | Heavy | I-5 | Non-hub<br>Stockton Metropolitan (SCK)<br>4 airlines, 8 flights/day | 4 trains/day | 4,427 | 135 |
| ★ Syracuse, NY | 41.4 min | 195 city buses<br>Seat miles/capita: 3.43 | Moderate | I-81<br>I-90 | Medium hub<br>Syracuse Hancock International (SYR)<br>11 airlines, 105 flights/day | 10 trains/day | 6,951 | 14 |
| Tacoma, WA | 47.1 min | 191 city buses<br>115 trolley coaches<br>Seat miles/capita: 3.25 | Heavy | I-5 | Part of Seattle hub | 6 trains/day | 4,730 | 112 |
| Tallahassee, FL | 40.9 min | 46 city buses<br>Seat miles/capita: 2.57 | Moderate | I-10 | Small hub<br>Tallahassee Municipal (TLH)<br>8 airlines, 55 flights/day | — | 5,530 | 66 |
| Tampa–St. Petersburg–Clearwater, FL | 45.1 min | 214 city buses<br>Seat miles/capita: 1.05 | Heavy | I-4<br>I-75 | Large hub<br>Tampa International (TPA)<br>St. Petersburg–Clearwater International (PIE)<br>25 airlines, 262 flights/day | 10 trains/day | 5,588 | 61 |
| Terre Haute, IN | 41.1 min | 22 city buses<br>Seat miles/capita: 1.96 | Light | I-70 | Non-hub<br>Hulman Regional (HUF)<br>1 airline, 13 flights/day | — | 3,550 | 205 |
| Texarkana, TX–Texarkana, AR | 40.9 min | — | Light | I-30 | Non-hub<br>Texarkana Municipal (TXK)<br>1 airline, 8 flights/day | — | 2,537 | 288 |
| Toledo, OH | 39.4 min | 211 city buses<br>Seat miles/capita: 2.90 | Heavy | I-75<br>I-80 | Small hub<br>Toledo Express (TOL)<br>9 airlines, 36 flights/day | 3 trains/day | 5,323 | 77 |
| Topeka, KS | 40.5 min | 28 city buses<br>Seat miles/capita: 1.48 | Moderate | I-70 | Non-hub<br>Forbes Field (FOE)<br>3 airlines, 23 flights/day | 2 trains/day | 5,348 | 76 |
| Trenton, NJ | 47.7 min | 93 city buses<br>Seat miles/capita: 2.38 | Moderate | I-95 | Part of Philadelphia hub<br>Mercer County (TTN)<br>2 airlines, 11 flights/day | 43 trains/day | 4,786 | 108 |

| Metro Area | Daily Commute | Public Transportation | Freeway Traffic | Interstate Highways | Air Service | Amtrak Service | Places Rated Score | Places Rated Rank |
|---|---|---|---|---|---|---|---|---|
| Tucson, AZ | 46.4 min | 159 city buses<br>Seat miles/capita: 2.35 | Heavy | I-10<br>I-19 | Medium hub<br>Tucson International (TUS)<br>13 airlines, 58 flights/day | — | 4,397 | 141 |
| Tulsa, OK | 44.7 min | 95 city buses<br>Seat miles/capita: 1.43 | Moderate | I-44 | Medium hub<br>Tulsa International (TUL)<br>14 airlines, 101 flights/day | — | 3,758 | 187 |
| Tuscaloosa, AL | 42.5 min | 10 city buses<br>Seat miles/capita: .67 | Light | I-20<br>I-59 | Non-hub<br>Tuscaloosa Municipal (TCL)<br>2 airlines, 6 flights/day | 2 trains/day | 4,723 | 114 |
| Tyler, TX | 41.1 min | 1 city bus<br>Seat miles/capita: .09 | Light | I-20 | Non-hub<br>Pounds Field (TYR)<br>3 airlines, 22 flights/day | — | 3,460 | 216 |
| Utica–Rome, NY | 37.4 min | 40 city buses<br>Seat miles/capita: 1.72 | Light | I-90 | Non-hub<br>Oneida County (UCA)<br>2 airlines, 13 flights/day | 10 trains/day | 4,592 | 122 |
| Vallejo–Fairfield–Napa, CA | 47.3 min | 24 city buses<br>Seat miles/capita: 1.24 | Heavy | I-80 | Part of San Francisco hub | 2 trains/day | 4,153 | 160 |
| Vancouver, WA | 48.4 min | 25 city buses<br>Seat miles/capita: .87 | Heavy | I-5 | Part of Portland hub | 8 trains/day | 3,817 | 180 |
| Victoria, TX | 44.4 min | — | Light | — | Non-hub<br>Victoria Regional (VCT)<br>3 airlines, 10 flights/day | — | 2,407 | 297 |
| Vineland–Millville–Bridgeton, NJ | 37.6 min | 24 city buses<br>Seat miles/capita: 1.80 | Moderate | — | Part of Philadelphia hub | — | 4,133 | 161 |
| Visalia–Tulare–Porterville, CA | 35.4 min | 1 city bus<br>Seat miles/capita: .11 | Moderate | — | Non-hub<br>Visalia Municipal (VIS)<br>1 airline, 4 flights/day | 3 trains/day | 3,094 | 252 |
| Waco, TX | 36.7 min | 17 city buses<br>Seat miles/capita: .84 | Heavy | I-35 | Non-hub<br>Waco–Madison Cooper (ACT)<br>1 airline, 12 flights/day | — | 3,018 | 256 |
| ★ Washington, DC–MD–VA | 64.5 min | 2,043 city buses<br>296 rapid rail cars<br>Seat miles/capita: 8.81 | Heavy | I-66<br>I-95 | Large hub<br>Dulles International (IAD)<br>Washington National (DCA)<br>40 airlines, 408 flights/day | 22 trains/day | 8,236 | 4 |
| Waterbury, CT | 42.9 min | 34 city buses<br>Seat miles/capita: 1.41 | Heavy | I-84 | Nearest airport: New Haven, 30 miles SE | — | 2,434 | 296 |
| Waterloo–Cedar Falls, IA | 33.4 min | 22 city buses<br>Seat miles/capita: 1.22 | Light | — | Small hub<br>Waterloo Municipal (ALO)<br>5 airlines, 25 flights/day | — | 3,351 | 230 |
| Wausau, WI | 33.2 min | 14 city buses<br>Seat miles/capita: 1.76 | Light | — | Non-hub<br>Central Wisconsin (CWA)<br>2 airlines, 16 flights/day | — | 3,496 | 214 |
| West Palm Beach–Boca Raton–Delray Beach, FL | 43.6 min | 71 city buses<br>Seat miles/capita: .97 | Heavy | I-95 | Medium hub<br>Palm Beach International (PBI)<br>22 airlines, 104 flights/day | 4 trains/day | 5,201 | 85 |
| Wheeling, WV–OH | 45.5 min | 21 city buses<br>Seat miles/capita: 1.38 | Moderate | I-70 | Nearest airport: Pittsburgh, PA, 50 miles NE | — | 2,450 | 294 |
| Wichita, KS | 39.4 min | 74 city buses<br>Seat miles/capita: 1.61 | Heavy | I-35 | Small hub<br>Wichita Mid–Continent (ICT)<br>10 airlines, 61 flights/day | — | 3,933 | 172 |
| Wichita Falls, TX | 34.8 min | 8 city buses<br>Seat miles/capita: .56 | Very heavy | I-44 | Non-hub<br>Wichita Falls Municipal (SPS)<br>2 airlines, 6 flights/day | — | 2,793 | 273 |
| Williamsport, PA | 38.7 min | 18 city buses<br>Seat miles/capita: 2.04 | Light | — | Non-hub<br>Williamsport–Lycoming County (IPT)<br>1 airline, 13 flights/day | — | 3,097 | 251 |
| Wilmington, DE–NJ–MD | 45.5 min | 100 city buses<br>Seat miles/capita: 1.64 | Very heavy | I-95 | Part of Philadelphia hub<br>Greater Wilmington–New Castle County (ILG)<br>1 airline, 5 flights/day | 31 trains/day | 4,532 | 127 |
| Wilmington, NC | 40.9 min | 13 city buses<br>Seat miles/capita: .98 | Heavy | — | Non-hub<br>New Hanover County (ILM)<br>3 airlines, 15 flights/day | — | 2,904 | 267 |
| Worcester, MA | 41.1 min | 61 city buses<br>Seat miles/capita: 1.47 | Heavy | I-90 | Non-hub<br>Worcester Municipal (ORH)<br>3 airlines, 7 flights/day | 2 trains/day | 3,643 | 197 |
| Yakima, WA | 37.8 min | 16 city buses<br>Seat miles/capita: 1.31 | Moderate | I-82 | Non-hub<br>Yakima Air Terminal (YKM)<br>2 airlines, 23 flights/day | — | 3,731 | 190 |

| Metro Area | Daily Commute | Public Transportation | Freeway Traffic | Interstate Highways | Air Service | Amtrak Service | Places Rated Score | Places Rated Rank |
|---|---|---|---|---|---|---|---|---|
| York, PA | 43.3 min | 20 city buses<br>Seat miles/capita: 1.03 | Moderate | I-83 | Nearest airport: Harrisburg, 25 miles NE | — | 2,267 | 304 |
| Youngstown–Warren, OH | 40.9 min. | 75 city buses<br>Seat miles/capita: 1.30 | Moderate | I-76<br>I-80 | Small hub<br>Youngstown Municipal (YNG)<br>4 airlines, 14 flights/day | — | 3,374 | 228 |
| Yuba City, CA | 39.2 min | — | Moderate | — | Nearest airport: Sacramento, 35 miles SE | 2 trains/day | 2,768 | 277 |

# Et Cetera

## MAJOR U.S. AIRLINES

In the early days of U.S. commercial air travel, airlines made most of their money contracting with the Post Office Department to deliver mail, and an adventurous passenger was likely to spend the flight sitting on a pile of mail sacks. A coast-to-coast flight in 1926 took 32 hours, including 14 stops for refueling, and cost the passenger $400. Today that same flight takes a little less than six hours, at a price as low as $99.

Air travel is far more comfortable and efficient than it was in its barnstorming years. Compared with the 13 airlines that operated in 1926 and carried 6,000 passengers, there are now 30 U.S. certified carriers that carry more than 300 million passengers a year. They are ranked below by the number of miles they travel in service per month.

| Major Airlines | Millions of Miles per Month | Aircraft |
|---|---|---|
| 1. United | 33.4 | 317 |
| 2. American | 24.8 | 228 |
| 3. Eastern | 25.1 | 260 |
| 4. Delta | 23.7 | 220 |
| 5. Republic | 13.9 | 163 |
| 6. TWA | 11.5 | 150 |
| 7. USAir | 10.7 | 120 |
| 8. Northwest | 8.2 | 111 |
| 9. Continental | 7.4 | 112 |
| 10. Western | 7.3 | 72 |
| 11. Pan American | 4.3 | NA* |

| National Airlines | | |
|---|---|---|
| 1. Piedmont | 7.5 | 73 |
| 2. Southwest | 5.0 | 37 |
| 3. Frontier | 4.8 | 53 |
| 4. Ozark | 3.9 | 44 |
| 5. Pacific Southwest | 3.0 | 31 |
| 6. AirCal | 1.9 | 22 |

| Large Regional Airlines | | |
|---|---|---|
| 1. People Express | 4.5 | 20 |
| 2. New York Air | 1.2 | NA* |
| 3. Northeastern | 1.1 | NA* |
| 4. Muse Air | 1.0 | 7 |
| 5. Empire | 0.7 | 5 |
| 6. Jet America | 0.6 | 3 |
| 7. Air Wisconsin | 0.5 | 16 |

| Alaskan and Hawaiian Airlines | Millions of Miles per Month | Aircraft |
|---|---|---|
| 1. Alaska Airlines | 2.2 | NA* |
| 2. Wien Air Alaska | 1.4 | 10 |
| 3. Hawaiian | 0.6 | 12 |
| 4. Aloha | 0.4 | 8 |
| 5. Reeve Aleutian | 0.1 | 6 |

Source: Federal Aviation Administration, *Statistical Handbook of Aviation*, 1984, and *Aviation Week and Space Technology*, July 30, 1984.

*Not available.

## FERRYBOATS, CABLE CARS, AND INCLINES

Besides the ubiquitous bus and the different rail systems in larger cities are other types of vehicles operated by U.S. transit systems. Although these modes have little impact on total mass transit, they are by far the most fun to watch and ride, undeniably adding to a city's flavor.

San Francisco has the nation's only cable car system. In operation since the nineteenth century, the 41 cars are the only transit property in the National Register of Historic Places.

The largest transit vehicles in the United States are ferryboats, which range in size up to 380 feet and can carry as many as 2,500 passengers per trip. Eleven metro areas have ferryboat systems:

| | |
|---|---|
| Boston, MA (2 systems) | New York, NY |
| Chicago, IL | (2 systems) |
| Cincinnati, OH–KY–IN | Portland, ME |
| Corpus Christi, TX | San Francisco, CA |
| Galveston–Texas City, TX | (4 systems) |
| Los Angeles–Long Beach, CA | Seattle, WA |
| New Orleans, LA | |

Four metro areas operate cog or cable incline cars that traverse steep hills:

Chattanooga, TN–GA: Lookout Mountain
Dubuque, IA: Fourth Street Elevator
Johnstown, PA: Johnstown-Westmont Incline
Pittsburgh, PA: Monongahela and Duquesne Heights

## WHERE'S THE BUS (OR TRAM, OR STREET CAR)?

If you've got the fare and you know where your transit stops and where it's going, on a darkening and cold winter afternoon the quality of public transportation ultimately comes down to how long you have to stand around waiting for it. Basing our calculations on the assumption that all the vehicles of a transit system are in service and spaced evenly over each mile of their routes, *Places Rated* ranks the 35 largest such systems according to their waiting times.

In the first column of the table are detailed the different modes of transportation in the system. *Route miles* means the number of miles over which a system's fleet travels in service. If a bus or tram travels in only one direction within the right-of-way, each mile is counted once. If a vehicle travels in both directions, each mile is counted twice. For example, a mile of single track over which street cars operate in two directions represents two route miles.

*Fleet age* is simply the average number of years a transit system's collection of vehicles has been in service. The oldest fleets in the United States are the San Francisco Municipal Railway's historic cable cars (87 years old) and the charming street cars (62 years old) operated by the New Orleans Public Service Company. The transit vehicle with the shortest active life is the ever-present diesel-powered bus. By the time these roarers are finally scrapped—after an average of nine years on the street—their odometers may register more than 300,000 miles.

But just because a vehicle is old doesn't necessarily mean it's slow. The *average speed* (the average number of miles traveled per hour including frequent stops for passengers) is governed by local congestion on the roads. Seattle's METRO buses are more than twice as old as the Dallas Transit System's fleet, but they still move faster over their routes.

*Headway* is the distance between vehicles if they are spaced evenly over each mile of route; if you just miss a CTA bus in Chicago, for example, the next one should be only 1.18 miles behind. *Waiting time*, finally, represents the average amount of time you should have to wait for a ride given the number of vehicles in the system, their average speed, and their headway.

The transit systems are presented in order of their average waiting time for all modes of transportation, from shortest to longest. This average is a weighted average and is derived in the following way, using the NYCTA system as an example: The waiting time of 5.96 minutes for buses is multiplied by the number of buses (4,573) and then added to the product of the waiting time for rapid rail cars (0.57 minutes) and the number of cars (6,263). This sum (30,825) is then divided by the total number of transit vehicles within the system (10,836), which results in an average waiting time of 2.84 minutes, second best in this ranking.

Not all the figures for numbers of vehicles jibe with those presented in the Place Profiles. This is because the figures in the profiles are for the entire metro area—which might encompass more than one network —whereas the numbers in this table are for individual transit systems.

### The 35 Largest Transit Systems Ranked by Waiting Time

| System | Number of Vehicles | Route Miles | Fleet Age | Average Speed | Headway | Waiting Time |
|---|---|---|---|---|---|---|
| 1. BART (San Francisco–Oakland) | 450 rapid rail cars | 142 | 9 yr | 27.5 mph | 0.63 mi | 1.38 min |
| 2. NYCTA/MTA (New York) | 4,573 buses | 1,841 | 9 | 8.1 | 0.81 | 5.96 |
|  | 6,263 rapid rail cars | 464 | 21 | 18.4 | 0.15 | 0.57 |
| 3. CTA (Chicago) | 2,420 buses | 1,428 | 10 | 10.1 | 1.18 | 7.01 |
|  | 1,100 rapid rail cars | 175 | 20 | 27.1 | 0.32 | 0.70 |
| 4. WMATA (Washington, D.C.) | 2,043 buses | 1,288 | 9 | 14.0 | 1.26 | 6.36 |
|  | 296 rapid rail cars | 78 | 5 | 17.9 | 0.53 | 1.77 |
| 5. San Francisco Municipal Railway | 526 buses | 445 | 11 | 9.6 | 1.69 | 10.58 |
|  | 174 street cars | 41 | 6 | 11.4 | 0.47 | 2.48 |
|  | 345 trolley coaches | 111 | 20 | 7.4 | 0.64 | 5.22 |
|  | 41 cable cars | 4 | 87 | 4.3 | 0.20 | 2.72 |
| 6. MBTA (Boston) | 1,115 buses | 1,420 | 9 | 12.7 | 2.55 | 12.03 |
|  | 496 rapid rail cars | 78 | 16 | 22.0 | 0.31 | 0.84 |
|  | 300 street cars | 59 | 22 | 15.1 | 0.39 | 1.56 |
|  | 50 trolley coaches | 32 | 14 | 12.8 | 1.28 | 6.00 |
| 7. Greater Cleveland RTA | 1,016 buses | 1,031 | 11 | 12.0 | 2.03 | 9.74 |
|  | 100 rapid rail cars | 38 | 24 | 31.0 | 0.76 | 1.47 |
|  | 71 street cars | 26 | 29 | 16.2 | 0.73 | 2.71 |
| 8. SORTA (Cincinnati) | 528 buses | 586 | 9 | 14.3 | 2.22 | 9.31 |
| 9. SEPTA (Philadelphia) | 1,534 buses | 2,006 | 9 | 10.1 | 2.62 | 15.54 |
|  | 440 rapid rail cars | 106 | 32 | 15.3 | 0.48 | 1.89 |
|  | 368 street cars | 176 | 27 | 9.3 | 0.96 | 6.24 |
|  | 174 trolley coaches | 42 | 14 | 8.0 | 0.48 | 3.62 |

| System | Number of Vehicles | Route Miles | Fleet Age | Average Speed | Headway | Waiting Time |
|---|---|---|---|---|---|---|
| 10. New Orleans Public Service | 505 buses | 507 | 8 yr | 10.4 mph | 2.01 mi | 11.58 min |
| | 35 street cars | 13 | 62 | 8.7 | 0.74 | 5.12 |
| 11. Santa Clara County Transit (San Jose) | 745 buses | 1,112 | 7 | 14.1 | 2.99 | 11.94 |
| 12. Kansas City (MO) Transit Authority | 350 buses | 481 | 9 | 13.6 | 2.75 | 12.22 |
| 13. MTA Harris County (Houston) | 860 buses | 1,372 | 7 | 13.9 | 3.19 | 13.77 |
| 14. Southern California RTD (Los Angeles) | 2,960 buses | 4,901 | 10 | 13.5 | 3.31 | 13.89 |
| 15. Baltimore MTA | 900 buses | 1,274 | 9 | 11.3 | 2.83 | 14.16 |
| 16. Dallas Transit System | 582 buses | 1,015 | 5 | 14.6 | 3.49 | 14.33 |
| 17. Metro Dade County Transit (Miami) | 865 buses | 1,404 | 8 | 12.6 | 3.25 | 14.76 |
| 18. Seattle METRO | 1,027 buses | 1,940 | 11 | 19.1 | 3.78 | 15.96 |
| | 115 trolley coaches | 108 | 5 | 18.6 | 1.88 | 8.05 |
| 19. Honolulu Department of Transportation | 406 buses | 796 | 10 | 14.7 | 3.92 | 15.48 |
| 20. SEMTA (Detroit) | 1,346 buses | 2,984 | 8 | 15.6 | 4.43 | 17.74 |
| 21. Bi-State Transit (St. Louis) | 1,098 buses | 2,131 | 8 | 12.8 | 3.88 | 17.78 |
| 22. Tri-County MTD (Portland, OR) | 649 buses | 1,367 | 9 | 16.2 | 4.21 | 18.05 |
| 23. MARTA (Atlanta) | 885 buses | 2,182 | 10 | 13.4 | 4.93 | 21.29 |
| | 120 rapid rail cars | 31 | 3 | 19.0 | 0.52 | 1.66 |
| 24. Memphis Area Transit | 313 buses | 759 | 13 | 14.7 | 4.85 | 19.80 |
| 25. Milwaukee Transit System | 631 buses | 1,344 | 12 | 12.6 | 4.26 | 20.29 |
| 26. Alameda County Transit (Oakland) | 835 buses | 2,170 | 11 | 14.4 | 5.20 | 21.36 |
| 27. PAT (Pittsburgh) | 903 buses | 2,369 | 10 | 13.2 | 5.25 | 23.85 |
| | 92 street cars | 52 | 37 | 14.9 | 1.13 | 4.55 |
| 28. MTC (Minneapolis–St. Paul) | 1,012 buses | 2,700 | 9 | 13.6 | 5.34 | 22.08 |
| 29. San Diego Transit Authority | 341 buses | 1,063 | 12 | 12.8 | 6.23 | 27.51 |
| 30. VIA MTS (San Antonio) | 454 buses | 1,482 | 8 | 14.0 | 6.53 | 27.98 |
| 31. River City Transit Authority (Louisville) | 318 buses | 995 | 6 | 13.3 | 6.26 | 28.23 |
| 32. Denver RTD | 671 buses | 2,850 | 6 | 16.5 | 8.49 | 35.89 |
| 33. Phoenix Transit | 245 buses | 1,208 | 10 | 16.6 | 9.86 | 38.17 |
| 34. Niagara Frontier Transit (Buffalo) | 482 buses | 1,882 | 12 | 10.9 | 7.81 | 42.99 |
| 35. Orange County Transit (Anaheim) | 497 buses | 2,959 | 6 | 14.4 | 11.91 | 46.70 |

Source: U.S. Department of Transportation, Urban Mass Transit Authority, National Urban Mass Transportation Statistics—Section 15 Report, 1984.

## CONTRADICTORY RULES OF THE ROAD

Except for the national speed limit of 55 miles per hour imposed in 1974, each state regulates what its drivers can and cannot do. Consequently, driving across state boundaries can also mean a brush with contradictory traffic codes. Here are eight examples, with one caveat. The information comes from the National Committee on Uniform Traffic Laws, the National Highway Traffic Safety Administration, and the American Automobile Association's latest Digest of Motor Laws, but it may not reflect recent changes in the law.

*Speed Limits.* There are two kinds of speed limits—absolute and prima facie, a legal phrase meaning "at first view." If the speed limit of 55 is absolute, going 56 means breaking the law. If the speed limit of 55 is prima facie, however, going 56 or even 60 is merely apparent evidence of unreasonable and imprudent speed. Drivers may escape a fine if they can convince the traffic court that their speed was reasonable and safe in light of the highway's condition, traffic, and visibility. All or some speed limits in 16 states are prima facie:

| | |
|---|---|
| Alabama | Michigan |
| Arizona | Minnesota |
| Arkansas | New Hampshire |
| California | Ohio |
| Colorado | Oregon |
| Connecticut | Rhode Island |
| Idaho | Texas |
| Massachusetts | Utah |

*Right and Left Turn on Red.* In 1947, California became the first state to permit drivers to turn right on a red signal after a complete stop. The last was Massachusetts, in 1980. New York City now is the only major jurisdiction that prohibits the turn. According to the Federal Highway Administration, fewer accidents occur when drivers turn right on a red light than when they turn right on a green light. Furthermore, the rule saves each driver an average of 14 seconds at a turn, cuts gasoline consumption and exhaust emissions, and allows intersections to handle more traffic.

---

### Rules of the Road Rated

If your travels take you to Massachusetts, you will find the oddest, most archaic, and most contradictory traffic laws in the United States. In Kansas, on the other hand, the most rational and up-to-date rules of the road have been on the books for years.

These judgments have been made by the National Committee on Uniform Traffic Laws, a semiofficial organization that publishes and continually revises the Uniform Vehicle Code (UVC), a complete set of motor laws designed as a model for the states. The committee—whose members are traffic court judges, state motor vehicle commissioners, and representatives of the automobile manufacturing and insurance industries—rates the states on how closely their statutes agree with the UVC. Complete agreement yields a score of 1,065.

#### States Ranked by Traffic Laws from Best to Worst

| State | Score | State | Score |
|---|---|---|---|
| 1. Kansas | 932 | 26. Montana | 586 |
| 2. Alabama | 911 | 27. Arizona | 579 |
| 3. South Carolina | 862 | 28. Minnesota | 576 |
| 4. Utah | 852 | 29. Ohio | 565 |
| 5. Idaho | 837 | 30. Tennessee | 560 |
| 6. North Dakota | 833 | 31. Rhode Island | 557 |
| 7. Georgia | 827 | 32. Louisiana | 538 |
| 8. Washington | 812 | 33. Oregon | 529 |
| 9. Pennsylvania | 787 | 34. West Virginia | 528 |
| 10. Illinois | 775 | 35. Nevada | 509 |
| 11. Colorado | 747 | 36. South Dakota | 461 |
| 12. Delaware | 720 | 37. California | 454 |
| 13. Maryland | 717 | 38. Kentucky | 448 |
| 14. Nebraska | 714 | 39. Arkansas | 434 |
| 15. Florida | 711 | 40. Iowa | 420 |
| 16. Hawaii | 683 | 41. Connecticut | 415 |
| 17. Texas | 649 | 42. Michigan | 405 |
| 18. New York | 648 | 43. Maine | 398 |
| 19. New Hampshire | 630 | 43. Wisconsin | 398 |
| 19. Vermont | 630 | 45. North Carolina | 344 |
| 21. Alaska | 625 | 46. Mississippi | 318 |
| 22. Wyoming | 620 | 47. Virginia | 315 |
| 23. Oklahoma | 615 | 48. New Jersey | 314 |
| 24. Indiana | 600 | 49. Missouri | 286 |
| 25. New Mexico | 596 | 50. Massachusetts | 253 |

Source: U.S. Department of Transportation, *Rules of the Road Rated*, 1981.

The District of Columbia was awarded 452 points for its traffic laws, a score that would place it 38th among the states.

---

In the past five years, most states have enacted statutes permitting left turns on a red signal, but only after a complete stop and only from a one-way street into another one-way street. Fourteen places still prohibit turning left on red:

| | |
|---|---|
| Arkansas | New Jersey |
| Connecticut | North Carolina |
| District of Columbia | Rhode Island |
| Kansas | South Carolina |
| Maine | Utah |
| Mississippi | Vermont |
| Missouri | Wyoming |

The state of New York permits a left turn on red everywhere except New York City. Tennessee permits the turn when so marked by each city.

*Child Restraints.* Automobile accidents are the leading cause of death among young children. Because standard seat belts are not designed for very small children, and because these children are at greater risk in automobile accidents than adults, 41 states require the use of special restraints when driving with children who are less than preschool age. The nine states without such mandatory restraint laws are:

| | |
|---|---|
| Alaska | Texas |
| Idaho | Utah |
| Iowa | Vermont |
| Louisiana | Wyoming |
| South Dakota | |

*Studded Tires.* Most states allow drivers to mount studded snow tires on their automobiles for better traction during an icy winter. Because the carbide-tipped studs damage road surfaces, nine states prohibit their use:

| | |
|---|---|
| Alabama | Mississippi |
| Hawaii | Texas |
| Illinois | Utah |
| Louisiana | Wisconsin |
| Minnesota | |

*Glass Tinting.* Tinted automobile window glass is a frequently chosen factory option. Over the past five years, however, aftermarket application of black and gunmetal gray plastic sheeting to the inside of car windows has become extremely popular. Because it interferes with night vision, it is prohibited in all but 15 states:

| | |
|---|---|
| Alaska | Montana |
| Arkansas | Nebraska |
| Connecticut | Nevada |
| Georgia | Oklahoma |
| Kentucky | South Carolina |
| Maine | South Dakota |
| Maryland | Wyoming |
| Missouri | |

*Audio Headsets.* The issue here is whether the ears are as necessary for safe driving as the eyes. When you don't hear an ambulance siren, a ticket for failing to yield the right-of-way to an emergency vehicle is the likely consequence. But when you can't hear a train whistle or the air horn of an oncoming 18-wheeler, the result could be far more serious. Accordingly, 11 states prohibit the driver from wearing an audio headset:

| | |
|---|---|
| Alaska | Minnesota |
| California | Pennsylvania |
| Florida | Rhode Island |
| Georgia | Virginia |
| Illinois | Washington |
| Massachusetts | |

*Motorcycle Helmets.* The mileage fatality rate (deaths per 100 million miles) for motorcycle travel is five times that for auto travel, and the major cause is head injuries. Consequently, 41 states require motorcycle riders to wear helmets. Motorcyclists have challenged the law, but state courts have generally upheld it because it affects the biker's right to receive insurance compensation for injuries. Nine states, however, do not require protective headgear of any kind for motorcyclists and passengers:

| | |
|---|---|
| California | Maine |
| Colorado | Nebraska |
| Connecticut | Rhode Island |
| Illinois | Washington |
| Iowa | |

*Mandatory Safety Inspections.* Most states require regular inspection of automobiles to rid the highways of dangerous vehicles with bald tires, wobbly suspensions, smoky exhausts, and defective brakes and lights. But 13 states do not require regular examinations, although their state police may randomly pull cars over for roadside inspections:

| | |
|---|---|
| Alabama | North Dakota |
| Florida | Ohio |
| Idaho | Oregon |
| Illinois | South Dakota |
| Indiana | Washington |
| Nebraska | Wisconsin |
| New Mexico | |

Connecticut, Iowa, Kansas, Maryland, and Nevada require inspections only on newly registered cars or cars that are being sold. In Arizona, Colorado, and Georgia, regular inspections are mandatory only for exhaust emissions.

## FINDING YOUR WAY ON THE INTERSTATE

By staying with a combination of Interstate routes, it is possible to drive from one metro area in the continental United States to almost any other without having to stop for a traffic light.

Five of the principal routes are more than 2,000 miles long. The longest, I–90, stretches 3,088 miles between downtown Boston and Seattle's waterfront. The next longest routes are I–80 (2,909 miles, from San Francisco to Hackensack, New Jersey), I–10 (2,460 miles along the nation's southern border, from Los Angeles to Jacksonville, Florida), I–40 (2,458 miles, from Barstow, California, to Smithfield, North Carolina), and I–70 (2,181 miles from Cove Fort, Utah, to Baltimore). Three of these routes, I–10, I–80, and I–90, cross the country from coast to coast, and I–40 nearly makes it.

Seven Interstate routes span the nation in a north-south direction, or nearly so: I–5 (1,382 miles, from San Diego to Bellingham, Washington), I–15 (1,431 miles, from San Diego to the Montana-Canada border), I–35 (1,572 miles from Laredo, Texas, to Duluth), I–55 (944 miles, from suburban New Orleans to Chicago), I–65 (887 miles, from Mobile, Alabama, to Gary–Hammond, Indiana), I–75 (1,742 miles, from Naples, Florida, to the Michigan-Canada border), and I–95 (1,857 miles, from the city of Miami to the Maine-Canada border).

### The Interstate System: A Route Log and Finder List

| Route | Total Mileage | Mileage by State | | Selected Cities Served |
|---|---|---|---|---|
| I–4 | 132.10 | Florida | 132.10 | Daytona Beach, Lakeland, Orlando, Tampa, Winter Haven |
| I–5 | 1,381.88 | California | 797.00 | Anaheim, Los Angeles, Redding, Sacramento, San Diego, Santa Ana, Stockton |
| | | Oregon | 308.50 | Eugene, Medford, Portland, Salem |
| | | Washington | 276.30 | Bellingham, Olympia, Seattle, Tacoma, Vancouver |
| I–8 | 348.49 | California | 170.00 | San Diego |
| | | Arizona | 178.49 | Casa Grande, Yuma |
| I–10 | 2,460.29 | California | 242.50 | Los Angeles, Riverside, San Bernardino |
| | | Arizona | 392.96 | Phoenix, Tucson |
| | | New Mexico | 164.43 | Las Cruces |
| | | Texas | 880.79 | Beaumont, El Paso, Houston, San Antonio |
| | | Louisiana | 274.42 | Baton Rouge, Lafayette, Lake Charles, New Orleans |
| | | Mississippi | 77.10 | Biloxi, Gulfport, Pascagoula |
| | | Alabama | 66.20 | Mobile |
| | | Florida | 361.89 | Jacksonville, Pensacola, Tallahassee |
| I–12 | 85.59 | Louisiana | 85.59 | Baton Rouge |
| I–15 | 1,430.95 | California | 288.10 | Riverside, San Bernardino, San Diego |
| | | Nevada | 123.77 | Las Vegas |
| | | Arizona | 29.35 | Beaver Dam |
| | | Utah | 398.85 | Ogden, Orem, Provo, Salt Lake City |
| | | Idaho | 195.87 | Blackfoot, Idaho Falls, Pocatello |
| | | Montana | 395.01 | Butte, Great Falls, Helena, Sweetgrass |

| Route | Total Mileage | Mileage by State | | Selected Cities Served |
|---|---|---|---|---|
| I-16 | 165.41 | Georgia | 165.41 | Macon, Savannah |
| I-17 | 145.67 | Arizona | 145.67 | Flagstaff, Phoenix |
| I-19 | 63.13 | Arizona | 63.13 | Tucson |
| I-20 | 1,537.17 | Texas | 634.54 | Abilene, Arlington, Dallas, Fort Worth, Longview, Marshall, Midland, Odessa, Tyler |
| | | Louisiana | 189.87 | Monroe, Shreveport |
| | | Mississippi | 154.50 | Jackson, Meridian, Vicksburg |
| | | Alabama | 215.00 | Anniston, Birmingham, Tuscaloosa |
| | | Georgia | 201.75 | Atlanta, Augusta |
| | | South Carolina | 141.51 | Columbia, Florence |
| I-24 | 316.52 | Illinois | 38.73 | Vienna |
| | | Kentucky | 93.37 | Hopkinsville |
| | | Tennessee | 180.30 | Chattanooga, Clarksville, Nashville |
| | | Georgia | 4.12 | — |
| I-25 | 1,060.62 | New Mexico | 460.76 | Albuquerque, Las Cruces, Santa Fe |
| | | Colorado | 298.94 | Colorado Springs, Denver, Fort Collins, Longmont, Pueblo |
| | | Wyoming | 300.92 | Casper, Cheyenne |
| I-26 | 260.81 | North Carolina | 39.95 | Asheville |
| | | South Carolina | 220.86 | Charleston, Columbia, Spartanburg |
| I-27 | 124.38 | Texas | 124.38 | Amarillo, Lubbock |
| I-29 | 752.34 | Missouri | 130.30 | Kansas City, St. Joseph |
| | | Iowa | 151.81 | Council Bluffs, Sioux City |
| | | South Dakota | 252.70 | Sioux Falls |
| | | North Dakota | 217.53 | Fargo, Grand Forks |
| I-30 | 336.78 | Texas | 193.70 | Dallas, Texarkana |
| | | Arkansas | 143.08 | Little Rock, Texarkana |
| I-35 | 1,572.39 | Texas | 503.82 | Arlington, Austin, Dallas, Fort Worth, Laredo, San Antonio, Temple, Waco |
| | | Oklahoma | 235.96 | Oklahoma City |
| | | Kansas | 235.60 | Kansas City, Lawrence, Topeka, Wichita |
| | | Missouri | 114.80 | Kansas City |
| | | Iowa | 218.51 | Des Moines |
| | | Minnesota | 263.70 | Albert Lea, Duluth, Minneapolis, St. Paul |
| I-37 | 142.96 | Texas | 142.96 | Corpus Christi, San Antonio |
| I-40 | 2,458.14 | California | 154.60 | Barstow, Needles |
| | | Arizona | 359.67 | Flagstaff, Kingman |
| | | New Mexico | 374.11 | Albuquerque, Gallup, Tucumcari |
| | | Texas | 177.00 | Amarillo |
| | | Oklahoma | 331.03 | Clinton, Oklahoma City |
| | | Arkansas | 284.80 | Fort Smith, Little Rock |
| | | Tennessee | 451.60 | Knoxville, Memphis, Nashville |
| | | North Carolina | 325.33 | Asheville, Burlington, Durham, Greensboro, Hickory, Raleigh, Winston-Salem |
| I-43 | 119.58 | Wisconsin | 119.58 | Green Bay, Milwaukee, Sheboygan |
| I-44 | 484.66 | Oklahoma | 193.86 | Oklahoma City, Tulsa |
| | | Missouri | 290.80 | Joplin, Springfield, St. Louis |
| I-45 | 284.99 | Texas | 284.99 | Dallas, Galveston, Houston, Texas City |
| I-49 | 34.08 | Louisiana | 34.08 | Alexandria |
| I-55 | 943.70 | Louisiana | 65.81 | Hammond, La Place |
| | | Mississippi | 289.70 | Grenada, Jackson, McComb |
| | | Tennessee | 12.20 | Memphis |
| | | Arkansas | 72.22 | Blytheville, West Memphis |
| | | Missouri | 209.20 | Cape Girardeau, St. Louis |
| | | Illinois | 294.57 | Bloomington, Chicago, East St. Louis, Joliet, Springfield |
| I-57 | 380.57 | Missouri | 22.00 | — |
| | | Illinois | 358.57 | Champaign, Chicago, Kankakee, Rantoul, Urbana |
| I-59 | 444.12 | Louisiana | 11.48 | New Orleans, Slidell |
| | | Mississippi | 171.20 | Hattiesburg, Laurel, Meridian |
| | | Alabama | 241.50 | Birmingham, Gadsden, Tuscaloosa |
| | | Georgia | 19.94 | — |
| I-64 | 929.33 | Illinois | 128.06 | Belleville, East St. Louis |
| | | Indiana | 124.04 | Evansville, New Albany |
| | | Kentucky | 191.70 | Frankfort, Lexington, Louisville |
| | | West Virginia | 186.55 | Charleston, Huntington |
| | | Virginia | 298.98 | Charlottesville, Newport News, Norfolk, Richmond |
| I-65 | 887.38 | Alabama | 366.30 | Birmingham, Mobile, Montgomery |
| | | Tennessee | 121.40 | Nashville |
| | | Kentucky | 137.60 | Bowling Green, Louisville |
| | | Indiana | 262.08 | Gary, Indianapolis, Lafayette |

*(continued on page 216)*

# Interstate Highways

| Route | Total Mileage | Mileage by State | | Selected Cities Served |
|-------|---------------|------------------|------|------------------------|
| I-66 | 76.70 | Virginia | 75.40 | Arlington, Falls Church |
| | | | 1.30 | Washington, D.C. |
| I-69 | 294.39 | Indiana | 157.79 | Anderson, Fort Wayne, Indianapolis, Muncie |
| | | Michigan | 136.60 | Battle Creek, Flint, Lansing |
| I-70 | 2,180.82 | Utah | 231.10 | Cove Fort, Green River, Richfield |
| | | Colorado | 450.51 | Denver, Grand Junction |
| | | Kansas | 424.20 | Kansas City, Lawrence, Topeka |
| | | Missouri | 251.60 | Columbia, Kansas City, St. Louis |
| | | Illinois | 160.25 | East St. Louis |
| | | Indiana | 156.27 | Indianapolis, Terre Haute |
| | | Ohio | 225.69 | Columbus, Dayton, Springfield |
| | | West Virginia | 14.40 | Wheeling |
| | | Pennsylvania | 169.30 | Pittsburgh |
| | | Maryland | 97.50 | Baltimore, Hagerstown |
| I-71 | 345.58 | Kentucky | 97.92 | Louisville |
| | | Ohio | 247.66 | Akron, Cincinnati, Cleveland, Columbus |
| I-72 | 78.68 | Illinois | 78.68 | Champaign, Springfield |
| I-74 | 416.64 | Iowa | 5.42 | Davenport |
| | | Illinois | 220.10 | Bloomington, Champaign, Moline, Peoria, Rock Island, Urbana |
| | | Indiana | 171.87 | Crawfordsville, Indianapolis |
| | | Ohio | 19.45 | Cincinnati |
| I-75 | 1,742.34 | Florida | 429.19 | Bradenton, Fort Myers, Gainesville, Lakeland, Ocala, St. Petersburg, Sarasota, Tampa |
| | | Georgia | 355.00 | Atlanta, Macon, Valdosta |
| | | Tennessee | 161.40 | Chattanooga, Knoxville |
| | | Kentucky | 191.60 | Covington, Lexington, Richmond |
| | | Ohio | 211.53 | Cincinnati, Dayton, Lima, Middletown, Toledo |
| | | Michigan | 393.62 | Bay City, Detroit, Flint, Saginaw |
| I-76 | 618.48 | Colorado | 184.14 | Denver |
| | | Nebraska | 2.47 | — |
| | | Ohio | 77.82 | Akron, Youngstown |
| | | Pennsylvania | 351.25 | Harrisburg, Lancaster, Philadelphia, Pittsburgh, Reading |
| I-77 | 597.86 | South Carolina | 75.41 | Columbia, Rock Hill |
| | | North Carolina | 105.43 | Charlotte |
| | | Virginia | 67.17 | Wytheville |
| | | West Virginia | 186.75 | Charleston, Parkersburg |
| | | Ohio | 163.10 | Akron, Canton, Cleveland, Marietta |
| I-78 | 143.39 | Pennsylvania | 76.69 | Allentown, Bethlehem |
| | | New Jersey | 66.20 | Jersey City, Newark |
| | | New York | 0.50 | New York City |
| I-79 | 343.56 | West Virginia | 159.85 | Charleston, Morgantown |
| | | Pennsylvania | 183.73 | Erie, Pittsburgh |
| I-80 | 2,909.52 | California | 203.80 | Oakland, Sacramento, San Francisco |
| | | Nevada | 410.66 | Elko, Reno, Winnemucca |
| | | Utah | | Salt Lake City |
| | | Wyoming | 402.82 | Cheyenne, Laramie, Rock Springs |
| | | Nebraska | 455.26 | Grand Island, Lincoln, Omaha |
| | | Iowa | 306.55 | Davenport, Des Moines, Iowa City |
| | | Illinois | 163.52 | Chicago, Joliet, Moline, Rock Island |
| | | Indiana | 151.65 | Elkhart, Gary, Hammond, Mishawaka, South Bend |
| | | Ohio | 237.07 | Cleveland, Elyria, Toledo, Warren, Youngstown |
| | | Pennsylvania | 311.24 | Du Bois, Milton, Sharon, Stroudsburg |
| | | New Jersey | 68.10 | Bergen–Passaic metro area |
| I-81 | 856.08 | Tennessee | 75.30 | Bristol, Johnson City, Kingsport, Knoxville |
| | | Virginia | 325.00 | Bristol, Roanoke |
| | | West Virginia | 25.98 | Martinsburg |
| | | Maryland | 12.00 | Hagerstown |
| | | Pennsylvania | 233.70 | Harrisburg, Scranton, Wilkes-Barre |
| | | New York | 184.10 | Binghamton, Syracuse |
| I-82 | 128.77 | Washington | 113.97 | Kennewick, Pasco, Richland, Yakima |
| | | Oregon | 14.80 | — |
| I-83 | 87.56 | Maryland | 37.50 | Baltimore |
| | | Pennsylvania | 50.06 | Harrisburg, York |
| I-84 | 1,014.60 | Oregon | 369.01 | Baker, Pendleton, Portland |
| | | Idaho | 275.61 | Boise, Twin Falls |
| | | Utah | 120.53 | Ogden |
| | | Pennsylvania | 49.75 | Scranton |
| | | New York | 71.60 | Orange County |
| | | Connecticut | 112.09 | Bristol, Danbury, Hartford, New Britain, Waterbury |
| | | Rhode Island | 16.00 | Providence |

| Route | Total Mileage | Mileage by State | | Selected Cities Served |
|-------|---------------|------------------|------|------------------------|
| I-85 | 668.33 | Alabama | 80.10 | Montgomery |
| | | Georgia | 178.94 | Atlanta |
| | | South Carolina | 106.25 | Anderson, Greenville, Spartanburg |
| | | North Carolina | 233.44 | Burlington, Charlotte, Durham, Gastonia, Greensboro, High Point |
| | | Virginia | 69.60 | Petersburg |
| I-86 | 38.75 | Connecticut | 30.69 | Hartford |
| | | Massachusetts | 8.06 | Sturbridge |
| I-87 | 333.30 | New York | 333.30 | Albany, Glens Falls, New York City, Orange County, Poughkeepsie, Troy |
| I-88 | 117.28 | New York | 117.28 | Binghamton, Schenectady |
| I-89 | 191.33 | New Hampshire | 60.94 | Concord |
| | | Vermont | 130.39 | Burlington, Montpelier |
| I-90 | 3,087.65 | Washington | 296.72 | Seattle, Spokane |
| | | Idaho | 73.77 | Coeur d'Alene, Kellogg |
| | | Montana | 551.20 | Billings, Butte, Missoula |
| | | Wyoming | 208.78 | Sheridan |
| | | South Dakota | 412.85 | Rapid City, Sioux Falls |
| | | Minnesota | 275.58 | Albert Lea, Rochester |
| | | Wisconsin | 187.17 | Beloit, Janesville, La Crosse, Madison |
| | | Illinois | 112.98 | Chicago, Elgin, Rockford |
| | | Indiana | 156.90 | Elkhart, Gary, Hammond, Mishawaka, South Bend |
| | | Ohio | 244.13 | Cleveland, Elyria, Lorain, Toledo |
| | | Pennsylvania | 46.60 | Erie |
| | | New York | 386.77 | Albany, Buffalo, Rochester, Rome, Schenectady, Syracuse, Troy, Utica |
| | | Massachusetts | 134.20 | Boston, Pittsfield, Springfield, Worcester |
| I-91 | 290.70 | Connecticut | 57.98 | Hartford, Meriden, Middletown, New Haven |
| | | Massachusetts | 54.92 | Springfield |
| | | Vermont | 177.80 | Brattleboro, St. Johnsbury |
| I-93 | 174.30 | Massachusetts | 31.37 | Boston, Lawrence, Lowell |
| | | New Hampshire | 131.93 | Concord, Manchester |
| | | Vermont | 11.00 | St. Johnsbury |
| I-94 | 1,607.12 | Montana | 247.93 | Billings, Miles City |
| | | North Dakota | 352.61 | Bismarck, Fargo |
| | | Minnesota | 259.27 | Minneapolis, Moorhead, St. Cloud, St. Paul |
| | | Wisconsin | 348.17 | Eau Claire, Kenosha, Madison, Milwaukee, Racine |
| | | Illinois | 77.37 | Chicago, Lake County |
| | | Indiana | 45.73 | Gary, Hammond |
| | | Michigan | 276.04 | Ann Arbor, Battle Creek, Benton Harbor, Detroit, Jackson, Kalamazoo |
| I-95 | 1,857.44 | Florida | 380.39 | Boca Raton, Daytona Beach, Fort Lauderdale, Fort Pierce, Hialeah, Hollywood, Jacksonville, Melbourne, Miami, Palm Beach, Pompano Beach, Titusville, West Palm Beach |
| | | Georgia | 111.69 | Savannah |
| | | South Carolina | 198.75 | Florence |
| | | North Carolina | 181.22 | Fayetteville |
| | | Virginia | 181.80 | Arlington, Petersburg, Richmond |
| | | | 0.12 | Washington, D.C. |
| | | Maryland | 109.15 | Baltimore |
| | | Delaware | 23.42 | Wilmington |
| | | Pennsylvania | 51.94 | Philadelphia |
| | | New Jersey | 74.20 | Elizabeth, Newark, Trenton |
| | | New York | 23.25 | New York City |
| | | Connecticut | 111.57 | Bridgeport, Milford, New Haven, New London, Norwalk, Stamford |
| | | Rhode Island | 43.33 | Providence |
| | | Massachusetts | 52.56 | Attleboro, Boston |
| | | New Hampshire | 16.15 | Portsmouth |
| | | Maine | 297.89 | Augusta, Bangor, Portland |
| I-96 | 193.10 | Michigan | 193.10 | Detroit, Grand Rapids, Lansing, Muskegon |
| I-97 | 1.90 | Maryland | 1.90 | Washington, D.C., urban area |

*Source:* U.S. Department of Transportation, *Interstate System Route Log and Finder List*, undated.

# Education:

## Where Schools Get Good Marks

Nine months of the year, all day long, three of every ten Americans are either working for an educational institution or being taught in one. Supporting the public side of this endeavor takes billions of tax dollars, and recent reviews of whether the price is worth it have caused educators and parents to tangle.

Education isn't the sacred cow it once was. The achievement of high school students on most standardized tests is lower today than it was in 1957, when the launching of Sputnik also launched an urgent nationwide push to improve education. Among seventeen-year-olds tested in 1982, says a report by the National Commission on Excellence in Education, nearly 40 percent couldn't draw inferences from written material, only one fifth could write a persuasive essay, and only one third could solve a math problem requiring several steps.

Privately, parents and teachers each blame the other. Although parents say they trust teachers more than politicians, journalists, or business people, they don't give teachers high marks. Only half the public gave teachers a grade of B or better when asked in a 1984 Gallup poll to choose either A, B, C, D, or F. For their part, teachers are even stingier graders—only 21 percent gave parents a grade of B or higher.

As for education and the metro areas, two things are certain: (1) If there is one public service in which shoddy performance pushes families to change their address, it is the kind of education their children are getting in public schools, and (2) If schemes for improving the schools—such as merit pay for good teachers, longer days, smaller classes, and an extra month in the academic year—are to be tried, they will require money.

## PUBLIC SCHOOLS AT THE ELEMENTARY AND SECONDARY LEVEL

The quality of the public schools usually tips the balance for a relocating family weighing a neighborhood's good and bad points. Too often, the choice is influenced by a real estate agent's hearsay that the schools are great or ought to be because the town's tax rate is high. Are there ways for parents to compare districts and schools within these districts more objectively? Definitely.

### Shopping for a District

The smallest political unit in the United States has got to be the school district. In the 1930s, the country was fragmented into 128,000 of them. After decades of consolidations, they now number fewer than 16,000 and range in size from the giant New York City Public and Los Angeles Unified school districts to several hundred "paper" ones that don't operate schools themselves, busing children instead to other districts.

Moving into a metro area often means stepping into a thicket of school districts, each with its own politics, funding, philosophy, standards, curricula—and, yes, results. Since your tax dollars will help support the district, you'll want to investigate their differences with a consumer's eye. Visit the district principal or superintendent's office and consider several factors:

• A good district can give you a written philosophy or a statement of educational objectives approved within the last five years by the state board of education. If educational philosophy and objectives are explicit and under constant examination and review, then a district takes its mission seriously.

• The classroom teachers in the district should have not only a standard certificate but also (in 50 percent of the cases or better) at least a master's degree or equivalent in the subject they teach.

• Nationally, only 77 percent of ninth-graders finish high school. A district's holding power—that is, the percent of its ninth-grade pupils who stay in school and graduate—should be at least 90 percent.

• If 95 percent of a district's enrollment is in average daily attendance, that's a good indication of how closely parents and schools keep tabs on children. Nationally, the average daily attendance is 90 percent; in some districts, it is a good deal less.

• Beware of the professional revolving door. A high number of eligible teachers not getting tenure *might* mean that the district has tough standards; but it could also be a sign that the district cuts costs by hiring beginners and then refusing them tenure at the end of their probationary period. Under this scheme, it is possible for a child to progress from kindergarten through high school and have inexperienced, unfamiliar teachers each year.

## Shopping for a School

Moving into a good school district won't necessarily mean that you'll find quality education in all of its schools. Get a district map of neighborhood boundaries for the schools as well as a list of Parent-Teacher Association (PTA) contacts. Talking with a local parent will save you time. Then visit the school's principal or the head guidance counselor to obtain specific information.

• A good high school should have one guidance counselor for every 200 students, and it should also have at least one full-time career counselor.

• Classroom size in high school should average no more than 30 students.

• The size of the senior class should range from 300 to 500 students. If the enrollment is much smaller than that, many worthwhile specialized courses won't be offered.

• A quality high school should offer four years of English, mathematics, and foreign languages; second-year courses in biology, astronomy, chemistry, and

| The 40 Largest Public School Districts | |
|---|---|
| Unit | Students Enrolled |
| 1. New York City Public | 924,123 |
| 2. Los Angeles Unified | 540,903 |
| 3. City of Chicago | 442,889 |
| 4. Dade County (Miami, FL) | 224,580 |
| 5. Philadelphia City | 213,980 |
| 6. Detroit City | 208,656 |
| 7. Houston Independent School District | 193,702 |
| 8. Broward County (Fort Lauderdale, FL) | 127,758 |
| 9. Dallas Independent School District | 127,584 |
| 10. Fairfax County (Fairfax, VA) | 124,631 |
| 11. Baltimore City | 123,376 |
| 12. Prince Georges County (Upper Marlboro, MD) | 116,598 |
| 13. Memphis City | 111,262 |
| 14. San Diego City Unified | 110,904 |
| 15. Hillsborough County (Tampa, FL) | 109,953 |
| 16. Duval County (Jacksonville, FL) | 99,512 |
| 17. Jefferson County (Louisville, KY) | 96,609 |
| 18. Montgomery County (Rockville, MD) | 95,696 |
| 19. District of Columbia | 94,975 |
| 20. Baltimore County (Towson, MD) | 92,387 |
| 21. Clark County (Las Vegas, NV) | 89,547 |
| 22. Milwaukee | 86,312 |
| 23. Pinellas County (Clearwater, FL) | 85,341 |
| 24. Orleans Parish (New Orleans, LA) | 83,391 |
| 25. Orange County (Orlando, FL) | 79,431 |
| 26. Jefferson County (Lakewood, CO) | 77,274 |
| 27. De Kalb County (Decatur, GA) | 76,114 |
| 28. Cleveland | 75,796 |
| 29. Mecklenburg County–Charlotte City (Charlotte, NC) | 72,756 |
| 30. Albuquerque | 72,012 |
| 31. Columbus (Columbus, OH) | 71,594 |
| 32. Atlanta City | 69,977 |
| 33. Palm Beach County (West Palm Beach, FL) | 69,855 |
| 34. Nashville–Davidson County (Nashville, TN) | 67,437 |
| 35. Anne Arundel County (Annapolis, MD) | 67,422 |
| 36. Fort Worth Independent School District | 65,822 |
| 37. Boston | 62,989 |
| 38. Mobile County (Mobile, AL) | 62,641 |
| 39. Denver | 62,438 |
| 40. Granite (Salt Lake City, UT) | 62,129 |

*Source:* U.S. Department of Education, *Universe of Public School Districts,* 1984.

physics; college-preparatory courses in the humanities; at least one year of computer literacy; and Advanced Placement (AP) courses for college credit. (South Carolina recently became the first state to require all its high schools to offer AP courses.)

• A good high school averages ten National Merit Scholarship commendations a year; an excellent school averages 15 or more a year.

• Because one fifth of all four-year public colleges must accept every high school graduate within the state, regardless of program followed or grades earned, it is no longer noteworthy that most of a high school's graduating seniors go on to college. The question to ask is, Which colleges are accepting them —top-rated schools with tough admissions standards or open-admission institutions with no requirements but that the check be good and the diploma in hand?

Don't cross a high school off your list if it doesn't measure up on all of these points. A school can have all but one or two and still be a good one.

Many relocation experts advise their clients that the stability of a town is reflected best in its schools. If the high school is good, chances are that the schools at the lower levels will also be good. In choosing an elementary school or a junior high, again, ask questions of principals and other parents.

• In junior high schools—grades 7, 8, and 9—there should be special provision for both bright students and slow learners.

• In elementary schools, there should be a full-time librarian and a classroom-size library.

• Class size in elementary schools should average no more than 20 pupils.

If you can't investigate schools personally, you can still gauge their quality from afar. Among the standard albeit imperfect yardsticks are pupil/teacher ratio, the amount of money spent on educating one student, teacher salaries, and effort to support the public schools with tax revenue.

## Pupil/Teacher Ratios

Teachers unions bargain as fiercely for smaller classes as they do for more money at contract-renegotiation time. Teaching classes with fewer pupils reduces professional stress, forestalling the gray hair that comes with the career. And such classes insure the need for more teachers at a time when enrollments aren't growing. In addition, testing shows that small classes do make a difference in a child's learning.

Imagine that a child in a typical classroom of 40 children scores at the modest 50th percentile (right in the middle) of an achievement test. The same child taught in a classroom of 15 or 20 would have scored at the 55th percentile; in a group of ten, at the 65th percentile; and a class of five, at the 75th percentile. A child in a group of 40, then, would score 25 percentile points higher if taught in a group of five students. These findings, based on research conducted since 1900 involving one million students, come from the Far West Laboratory for Educational Research and Development, in San Francisco.

Unfortunately, classes averaging five pupils are luxuries that public school districts can't afford. To reduce the average class size in metropolitan Cleveland by just one student would mean hiring 1,200 additional teachers and finding an extra $2.2 million to pay them each month; in metropolitan Dallas, the monthly payroll would climb by $3 million for 2,000 additional teachers.

The number of pupils for each full-time teacher is smaller in some metro areas than in others, and this ratio can be regarded as a rough indicator of how many children there are in a typical classroom, as well as how good an opportunity these children have to learn.

### Metro Area Pupil/Teacher Ratios

| Lowest | | Highest | |
|---|---|---|---|
| 1. Billings, MT | 8.08 | 1. Vancouver, WA | 20.52 |
| 2. Pittsfield, MA | 10.72 | 2. Bremerton, WA | 20.30 |
| 3. Trenton, NJ | 11.07 | 3. Vallejo–Fairfield– Napa, CA | 20.27 |
| 4. Charlottesville, VA | 11.15 | 4. Jacksonville, NC | 20.17 |
| 5. Burlington, VT | 11.43 | 5. Seattle, WA | 20.15 |
| 6. Middlesex– Somerset– Hunterdon, NJ | 11.73 | 6. San Jose, CA | 19.83 |
| | | 7. Las Vegas, NV | 19.62 |
| 7. Bristol, CT | 11.74 | 8. Richland– Kennewick– Pasco, WA | 19.59 |
| 7. Hartford, CT | 11.74 | | |
| 7. Middletown, CT | 11.74 | 9. Provo–Orem, UT | 19.54 |
| 7. New Britain, CT | 11.74 | 10. Dothan, AL | 19.35 |

*Source:* U.S. Bureau of the Census, *Compendium of Public Employment,* forthcoming, and Market Data Retrieval, *National School Market Index,* 1983.

These figures are derived by dividing public school enrollment by the number of "instructional staff," a term that embraces not only teachers but also principals, librarians, guidance counselors, psychological counselors—in other words, everyone involved in teaching or the improvement of education.

The national metro area average for pupil/teacher ratio is 15.12.

## The Cost of Educating One Pupil

Nassau–Suffolk, New York, spends more than three times as much money to educate one pupil as does Dothan, Alabama. Are children better schooled on Long Island? Or is public instruction accomplished more efficiently in southeastern Alabama? Neither, necessarily. There are many items hidden in a metro area's figures for expenses per student, items that either have nothing to do with education or reflect a special need of the metro area. In New York, there is the expense of salaries for security guards in Bronx school hallways; in Miami and Houston, of bilingual instruction for large Hispanic enrollments; in Anchorage, of high energy costs during a long heating season; in St. Louis, of busing children in and out of center-city schools. Living costs are another factor. Much of the difference between Dothan's outlay of $1,505 per student and Nassau–Suffolk's figure of $4,637 represents the gap between what it takes to live in the Northeast and the Deep South.

Just as the cost of educating one student varies between rich and poor states, so it varies between rich and poor districts *within* the states. For example, Odessa, in western Texas, spends almost twice as much money per student as El Paso, about 300 miles away. The variation between the richest school district and the poorest is widest in Georgia, according to a recent U.S. Department of Education survey. In Hawaii, which has the country's only statewide school district, there is no disparity at all. Dollars per pupil becomes a meaningful statistic when data for metro areas within the same state are compared.

## Dollars Spent per Pupil in the Metro Areas

| Most | | Fewest | |
|---|---|---|---|
| 1. Casper, WY | $4,870 | 1. Dothan, AL | $1,505 |
| 2. Middlesex–Somerset–Hunterdon, NJ | 4,869 | 2. Gadsden, AL | 1,537 |
| | | 3. Montgomery, AL | 1,561 |
| 3. Nassau–Suffolk, NY | 4,637 | 4. Mobile, AL | 1,606 |
| 4. San Francisco, CA | 4,001 | 5. Anniston, AL | 1,607 |
| 5. Rochester, NY | 3,992 | 6. Clarksville–Hopkinsville, TN–KY | 1,620 |
| 6. Poughkeepsie, NY | 3,881 | 7. Tuscaloosa, AL | 1,717 |
| 7. Trenton, NJ | 3,873 | 8. Chattanooga, TN–GA | 1,763 |
| 8. Anchorage, AK | 3,843 | 9. Boise City, ID | 1,772 |
| 9. Binghamton, NY | 3,766 | 10. Johnson City–Kingsport–Bristol, TN–VA | 1,776 |
| 10. Niagara Falls, NY | 3,762 | | |

*Source:* U.S. Bureau of the Census, *Compendium of Government Finance,* forthcoming, and Market Data Retrieval, *National School Market Index,* 1983.

The national metro area average for dollars spent per pupil is $2,861.

## What Teachers Earn

Parents tend to think that teachers bail out of their profession because of burnout brought on by semester after semester of unruly and unmotivated pupils. Not entirely, say ex-teachers; it's mainly the money.

Their seventh- and eighth-grade pupils pull down $1.50 an hour for baby-sitting, teachers point out when they negotiate their contracts. If a teacher working five class periods were to be paid $1.50 per day for nothing more than watching over each child in an average-size classroom, he or she would earn $3,750 each month of the academic year. Yet teachers accomplish much more than keeping every five- to seventeen-year-old off the street. They teach them, too, throughout a long, arduous day. Therefore, the argument goes, teachers should be paid more.

Teaching requires formal preparation, certification, and a lifelong perfection of skills. Moreover, teacher earnings have suffered more from inflation than the earnings of other professionals: The average amount of money teachers earn today is no more than what they made in 1973, after adjustment to current dollars. Teachers in some districts can barely stay afloat. According to the National Education Association, classroom teachers who support families in some counties

## Compulsory Education

Most state laws requiring school attendance until a specified age were passed near the beginning of the century and haven't changed much in the decades since. The span of compulsory attendance ranges from six years in Mississippi to 12 in Hawaii, Ohio, and Utah.

| Place | Compulsory Attendance Age Range* | Place | Compulsory Attendance Age Range* |
|---|---|---|---|
| Alabama | Between 7 and 16 | Nebraska | Not less than 7 nor more than 16 |
| Alaska | Between 7 and 16 | Nevada | Between 7 and 17 |
| Arizona | Between 8 and 16 | New Hampshire | Between 6 and 16 |
| Arkansas | Between 7 and 15 (both inclusive) | | |
| California | Between 6 and 16 | New Jersey | Between 6 and 16 |
| | | New Mexico | Attained 6 and until attaining 17 |
| Colorado | Of 7 and under 16 | New York | From 6 to 16 |
| Connecticut | Over 7 and under 16 | North Carolina | Between 7 and 16 |
| Delaware | Between 6 and 16 | North Dakota | Of 7 to 16 |
| District of Columbia | Between 7 and 16 | | |
| Florida | Attained 7 but not 16 | Ohio | Between 6 and 18 |
| | | Oklahoma | Between 8 and 16 |
| Georgia | Between 7th and 16th birthdays | Oregon | Between 7 and 18 |
| Hawaii | At least 6 and not 18 | Pennsylvania | Not later than 8, until 17 |
| Idaho | Of 7 but not 16 | Rhode Island | Completed 7 years of life, not completed 16 years of life |
| Illinois | Between 7 and 16 | | |
| Indiana | Not less than 7, not more than 16 | | |
| | | South Carolina | Of 7 to 16 |
| Iowa | Over 7 and under 16 | South Dakota | Of 7 and not exceeding 16 |
| Kansas | Of 7 and under 16 | Tennessee | Between 7 and 16 |
| Kentucky | Of 7 and under 16 | Texas | As much as 7, not more than 17 |
| Louisiana | Between 7 and 15 | Utah | Between 6 and 18 |
| Maine | Between 7th and 15th anniversaries | | |
| | | Vermont | Between 7 and 16 |
| Maryland | Between 6 and 16 | Virginia | Reached 6th birthday, not passed the 17th birthday |
| Massachusetts | Between 6 and 16 | | |
| Michigan | Between 6 and 16 | Washington | Child 8 and under 15 |
| Minnesota | Between 7 and 16 | West Virginia | Begin with the 7th birthday, continue to the 16th birthday |
| Mississippi | From 7 to 13 | | |
| | | Wisconsin | Between 6 and 16 |
| Missouri | Between 7 and 16 | Wyoming | Between 7 and 16 inclusive |
| Montana | Is 7, not yet reached 16th birthday | | |

*Source:* U.S. Department of Education, *Digest of Education Statistics,* 1984.

*As stated in the state's compulsory attendance laws.

in the Deep South qualify for food stamps under certain conditions. On the other hand, in every one of America's metro areas teachers earn more than uniformed firemen and policemen. Some taxpayers and city managers point out that for nine months' work classroom teachers are the best paid of municipal employees.

The $2,000 difference between the monthly paychecks of Anchorage teachers and those in Wilmington may reflect the value taxpayers and city managers place on teachers as much as differences in the cost of living and average household income.

### Metro Area Average Monthly Teacher Salaries

| Highest | | Lowest | |
|---|---|---|---|
| 1. Anchorage, AK | $2,927 | 1. Wilmington, DE–NJ–MD | $ 929 |
| 2. Detroit, MI | 2,609 | 2. Mobile, AL | 1,063 |
| 3. Santa Barbara–Santa Maria–Lompoc, CA | 2,517 | 3. Augusta, GA–SC | 1,097 |
| | | 4. Charleston, WV | 1,134 |
| 4. Nassau–Suffolk, NY | 2,494 | 5. Richmond–Petersburg, VA | 1,152 |
| 5. Flint, MI | 2,474 | 6. Macon–Warner Robins, GA | 1,181 |
| 6. San Jose, CA | 2,417 | | |
| 7. Anaheim–Santa Ana, CA | 2,416 | 7. Pascagoula, MS | 1,199 |
| 8. San Diego, CA | 2,369 | 8. Houma–Thibodaux, LA | 1,202 |
| 9. Grand Forks, ND | 2,344 | 9. Florence, SC | 1,205 |
| 10. Ann Arbor, MI | 2,327 | 9. Montgomery, AL | 1,205 |

Source: U.S. Bureau of the Census, *Compendium of Public Employment*, forthcoming.

Figures represent the average paycheck for the 2,210,274 teachers in the metro areas in October 1982. It should be noted that different school districts pay their teachers over different time periods; some teachers have nine-month contracts, others ten-month contracts, and still others year-long contracts.

The national metro area average for monthly teacher salaries is $1,778.

### Support Your Public Schools: The Effort Index

Along with the pupil/teacher ratio, the amount of effort a metro area devotes to supporting and improving neighborhood schools may be considered one of the most important reflections of the local quality of education. *Places Rated Almanac* gauges the level of this support by applying a formula to determine each place's effort index.

To calculate effort index, we look at how much revenue a place devotes to public schools relative to its need. Metro areas with many children in private schools, for example, have low public school budget needs, as do metro areas whose populations of school-age children are shrinking. A metro area's relative need is determined by dividing its total population by its public school enrollment and comparing this to the national average. (Nationally the ratio is 5.836 persons for every one in public school.) Finally, we divide this figure for need by the actual proportion of tax revenues given over to public schools as compared to the national average.

This formula (the creation of the Advisory Commission on Intergovernmental Relations) puts all metro areas on an equal footing, offering an effective way to compare them. If a metro's effort index is greater than 1.000, it is giving above-average support to its school system, whereas an index less than 1.000 indicates that the metro area is giving below-average support, possibly falling short of local needs.

### Metro Area Effort Indexes

| Lowest | | Highest | |
|---|---|---|---|
| 1. Richland–Kennewick–Pasco, WA | 0.456 | 1. State College, PA | 1.760 |
| 2. New York, NY | 0.618 | 2. Middlesex–Somerset–Hunterdon, NJ | 1.754 |
| 3. Anchorage, AK | 0.692 | 3. Cumberland, MD–WV | 1.667 |
| 4. Dothan, AL | 0.699 | 4. Fort Pierce, FL | 1.642 |
| 5. Pascagoula, MS | 0.703 | 5. Davenport–Rock Island–Moline, IA–IL | 1.627 |
| 6. Houma–Thibodaux, LA | 0.710 | 6. Salem, OR | 1.605 |
| 7. Visalia–Tulare–Porterville, CA | 0.713 | 7. Burlington, VT | 1.575 |
| 8. Las Vegas, NV | 0.720 | 8. New London–Norwich, CT–RI | 1.543 |
| 9. Huntsville, AL | 0.736 | 9. Bryan–College Station, TX | 1.535 |
| 10. Tuscaloosa, AL | 0.738 | 10. Lancaster, PA | 1.505 |

Source: U.S. Bureau of the Census, *Compendium of Government Finance*, forthcoming, and Market Data Retrieval, *National School Market Index*, 1983.

The national metro area average for effort index is 1.000.

## FOR ONE IN NINE: PRIVATE SCHOOLS

A startling statistic about K–12 education in the United States since 1930 is the nearly 100 percent growth in the number of private schools in contrast to the 75 percent decline in the number of public schools. This isn't to say that public K–12 education is collapsing; most of the schools that have closed are rural one-room buildings. But the statistic does show that private schools have become a thriving alternative. During the 1970s, when school enrollments were dropping, private schools held on to more of their enrollment than did public schools, losing only 6 percent as compared with 11 percent for public schools. Today one out of nine school-age children attends a private or parochial school.

Recent research from the Department of Education shows that students in private high schools take more courses than their public school counterparts and that they take these courses in smaller classes. Critics of public education point out that because private institutions forego the smorgasbord of electives that public schools offer their students, graduates of private high schools have tougher basic courses on their transcripts and are better prepared for college study. (In fact, private school pupils score higher on average on the Scholastic Aptitude Tests than students in public schools.) Not for nothing are private schools a preferred educational option for many families, not all of whom are Catholic or well-to-do.

Most private schools are run by some religious group, accounting for 80 percent of all private schools. The remaining institutions tend to be small schools;

## Private Schools in the Metro Areas

Whatever the reason for the steady enrollments in private school—the desire for religious training or for a more rigorous education—it is undeniable that private schools are a fixture on the American education scene. All of the 329 metro areas have at least one private K–12 school, and only 55 metro areas have fewer than ten. The 20 places below have the greatest proportion of private-school students among their school-age populations.

### The 20 Metro Areas with the Highest Proportion of Students in Private School, K–12

| Metro Area | Percent Students in Private School |
|---|---|
| 1. Dubuque, IA | 35.3% |
| 2. New Orleans, LA | 28.9 |
| 3. Owensboro, KY | 25.0 |
| 4. Jersey City, NJ | 24.8 |
| 4. New York, NY | 24.8 |
| 6. Wilmington, DE–NJ–MD | 23.7 |
| 7. St. Louis, MO–IL | 22.9 |
| 8. Stamford, CT | 22.8 |
| 9. San Francisco, CA | 22.6 |
| 10. Erie, PA | 22.5 |
| 11. Baltimore, MD | 22.4 |
| 11. Trenton, NJ | 22.4 |
| 13. West Palm Beach–Boca Raton– Delray Beach, FL | 22.2 |
| 14. Wheeling, WV–OH | 21.7 |
| 15. Cleveland, OH | 21.3 |
| 16. Savannah, GA | 21.0 |
| 17. Milwaukee, WI | 20.9 |
| 18. Chicago, IL | 20.5 |
| 19. Miami–Hialeah, FL | 20.4 |
| 20. Bristol, CT | 20.1 |

Source: Derived from Market Data Retrieval, National School Market Index, 1983.

they enroll only 16 percent of private school pupils. Among religiously affiliated schools, Catholic schools predominate in number and enrollment, but there are also substantial numbers of pupils in Baptist, Lutheran, Christian, Jewish, Seventh-Day Adventist, and Episcopal schools.

### Private Schools and Enrollments

| Type of School | Schools | Students |
|---|---|---|
| Catholic | 9,660 | 3,190,687 |
| Lutheran | 1,533 | 219,963 |
| Seventh-Day Adventist | 1,092 | 82,609 |
| Baptist | 1,071 | 233,334 |
| Christian | 651 | 112,906 |
| Jewish | 399 | 85,231 |
| Episcopal | 315 | 76,973 |
| Other sectarian | 1,491 | 224,788 |
| Nonsectarian | 4,767 | 802,374 |
| Total | 20,979 | 5,028,865 |

Source: National Center for Education Statistics, unpublished data, 1984.

# BEYOND HIGH SCHOOL: METRO AREA COLLEGES AND UNIVERSITIES

Educators like to say that schooling leads to just three things: more schooling, employment, or unemployment. When high school graduates go on to college or find jobs, the public education system is successful; if they do neither, the system is considered a flop. In fact, nearly half of metro area high school graduates enter college, and six out of ten of these begin their freshman year at an institution within 50 miles of home.

## More than an Education

Everywhere from Abilene to Youngstown, chamber of commerce promotional brochures tout the diversity of local colleges and universities more frequently than other urban assets. And with good reason. Among the 12 million full-time college students in the United States, nine million are studying in metro areas. For 21 million other people, the typical location for their evening or weekend continuing education course is a local college classroom.

But colleges and universities contribute other things besides education. In smaller metro areas, a worthy theatre where a touring group of professional players can stage *Hamlet* or an auditorium where an orchestra and choir can perform *The Messiah* can often only be found at the local college campus. Colleges and universities are stable white-collar employers, too. In Gainesville, Florida; Lawrence, Kansas; and Tuscaloosa, Alabama, they are the major employer. Finally, there is the connection between research-oriented universities and healthy economies. Two prime examples are Stanford University's impetus to the growth of high-tech enterprises in San Jose and the Bay Area, and M.I.T.'s faculty and alumni who have started many thriving electronics firms along Route 128 outside of Boston.

## Metro Area Higher Education Options

Although a metro area may have many colleges and students, it may not necessarily be the home of quality education. But if these colleges are of different kinds and offer different programs—that is, if they provide a number of academic options—then we can conclude that the metro area is meeting the varied needs of a community.

Just as a city's municipal bonds are rated for quality and safety using letter grades, so *Places Rated Almanac* has devised a similar method of assessing options in higher education. (The options rating for each metro area is shown in the Place Profiles later in the chapter.)

*C-Rated Metro Areas.* These metro areas offer limited options. There may either be no public colleges at all (as in Abilene, Texas), only two-year public colleges (as in Bremerton, Washington), or only four-year colleges that may not offer courses at night and on weekends for certification in trade and technical occupations, as most two-year colleges do.

**B-Rated Metro Areas.** The options found here can include private colleges and universities, but there must also be at least one public two-year college and one public four-year college to satisfy the demand for low-cost education, ranging from instruction in the trades and technical occupations to courses leading to a bachelor's degree.

**A-Rated Metro Areas.** In these metro areas there are at least two public junior colleges, two public four-year colleges, and a group of privately controlled colleges and universities, one or more of which must be highly selective in admitting students. Such private schools would appeal to students searching for smaller classes, more individual attention, and specialized courses.

**AA-Rated Metro Areas.** These metro areas have a full complement of professional schools in law, medicine, and business, as well as accredited art and music schools. For undergraduates, there are more than two public junior colleges and more than two public four-year colleges, plus a wide choice of private colleges.

**AAA-Rated Metro Areas.** The handful of top-rated metro areas are the ones with the richest and most varied mix of campuses. They boast of international student populations as well as large numbers of students drawn from everywhere in the country; of universities whose faculty divide their time between research and teaching both there and at other area institutions; of open-admissions junior colleges offering not just instruction in the trades and technical occupations but also traditional courses transferable for credit to senior colleges; of colleges that pool specialized classes, films, and library resources; of professional schools in law, medicine, business, engineering, science, music, and art; and of a wide variety of private colleges with unique cultural and religious programs. The only metro areas in the nation that meet these requirements are Boston, Chicago, Los Angeles–Long Beach, New York, Philadelphia, San Francisco, and Washington.

## JUDGING EDUCATIONAL EFFORT AND OPPORTUNITIES

To measure the chances for quality education in the metro areas, *Places Rated* examines two sides of academic life that affect the community—the K–12 system, which includes public elementary, junior high, and high schools, and the local mix of public and private colleges and universities.

Public K–12 schools are rated by examining two critical factors. The first is the number of pupils for each full-time teacher, or the pupil/teacher ratio. If there is one thing on which parents and educators agree, it is that a child's opportunity to learn improves in small classes. The second factor is the local effort index. A creation of the Advisory Commission on Intergovernmental Relations, this figure indicates how much of a metro area's tax revenue is turned over to support and improve the public schools. Indirectly, the effort index also shows how strongly public schools compete for money with such other municipal services as parks and recreation, fire and police, streets, sanitation, and health care. Although a metro area's effort rating doesn't necessarily tell you how good the schools are, it does suggest how good the metro area's taxpayers expect them to be.

*Places Rated's* tack for scoring local higher education is based on the variety of academic options that can meet the differing needs of a community: night and weekend continuing education courses for people who work, full-time graduate courses in the professions, courses leading to occupational certification in junior colleges, and the traditional bachelor's degree curriculum offered in a four-year college.

Each metro area begins with a base score of zero, to which points are added according to the following indicators:

---

### The College-Educated Majority

The year 1967 was a good one for education. It marked the first time in history that the majority of Americans over 25 had the equivalent of a high school diploma. We won't be seeing a similar year for college, however. In spite of millions of full-time students enrolled in college, only one in six persons over 25 currently has at least 16 years of school, the equivalent of a college degree.

Persons over 25 with 16 or more years of schooling are the rule rather than the exception in only 14 of the 945 cities in the United States with populations over 25,000. Not surprisingly, ten have large university communities.

| City | Percent of Population with 16 Years of Schooling |
|------|-------------------------------------------------|
| 1. Chapel Hill, NC | 68.7% |
| 2. East Lansing, MI | 65.4 |
| 3. Davis, CA | 60.9 |
| 4. State College, PA | 59.5 |
| 5. Ann Arbor, MI | 56.2 |
| 5. Blacksburg, VA | 56.2 |
| 7. College Station, TX | 54.0 |
| 8. Berkeley, CA | 52.3 |
| 9. Upper Arlington, OH | 52.0 |
| 10. Shaker Heights, OH | 50.6 |
| 11. Palo Alto, CA | 54.0 |
| 11. Wilmette, IL | 54.0 |
| 13. Rancho Palos Verdes, CA | 51.2 |
| 14. Boulder, CO | 50.5 |

*Source:* U.S. Bureau of the Census, *1980 Census of Population and Housing.*

1. *Pupil/teacher ratio.* A metro area's number of pupils per full-time teacher in the public schools is divided into the national metro average for this ratio of 15.12. The result is multiplied by 1,000 and added to the score. In Dallas's six counties, for example, the 14.16 pupils for each full-time teacher earns the Texas metro area 1,068 points. There is a ceiling of 1,500 points in this category.

2. *Effort index.* This figure, which represents that portion of a metro area's revenue allotted to supporting and improving public schools, is multiplied by 1,000 and added to the score. Dallas's effort index of 0.951 means an additional 951 points. A ceiling of 1,500 points is also in effect for effort index.

3. *Academic options.* Each metro area earns points on the basis of its letter grade for options in higher education: 1,500 points for an AAA rating, given to those metro areas with the richest and most varied offerings; 1,250 points for AA; 1,000 points for A; 750 for B; and 500 for C.

## Sample Comparison: Philadelphia, Pennsylvania–New Jersey, and Pascagoula, Mississippi

The country's best and worst metro areas for educational opportunities according to *Places Rated*'s scoring system are located in the Northeast and the Deep South, respectively.

The Philadelphia metro area is a multiple-county giant that straddles parts of Pennsylvania and New Jersey. In the category of K–12 quality, its marks exceed the national average, although they're not outstanding: its pupil/teacher ratio is 13.22, slightly better than the national metro area average of 15.12, and its effort index—its proportion of available tax income that goes to support local schools—is 1.137, just an eyelash above the national average of 1.000. Each of these figures is indexed against the appropriate national average and then multiplied by 1,000, resulting in a total of 2,281 points (1,144 for pupil/teacher ratio and 1,137 for effort index). But Philadelphia's prodigious number of colleges and universities, offering a wide range of academic options, propels the metro area into first place. With its 46 four-year institutions and 21 two-year schools—among them the University of Pennsylvania, Temple University, Curtis Institute of Music, and Hahnemann Medical College—Philadelphia earns the highest rating possible in this

## Spanking, Paddling, and Suspensions

During a given school year, one of every 30 pupils is spanked or paddled at least once, and one in 19 is suspended for breaking school rules. According to the Education Department's Office for Civil Rights, the states in which suspensions exceed the national average are all located east of the Mississippi River, with the exception of California. Paddling and spanking, typical forms of discipline in the elementary grades, are concentrated in the Southeast and adjacent southwestern states but are unheard of in New England.

### States Reporting Corporal Punishment Exceeding National Average*

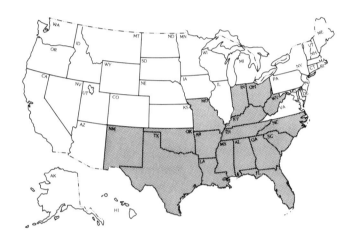

Source: National Center for Education Statistics, *Condition of Education*, 1984.

*The national average for corporal punishment is 3.5% of public elementary and secondary school enrollment. The shaded area of the map shows states exceeding this level.

category, AAA, good for 1,500 points. Its total score is 3,781.

At the other end of the scale is Pascagoula, a fast-growing county in the Gulf South. Its pupil/teacher ratio is 15.15, which yields 998 points after being divided into the national average and then multiplied by 1,000. Its effort index of 0.703 is the fifth lowest among the metro areas and results in 703 points. Pascagoula is one of only two metro areas in the nation with no colleges, either two-year or four-year (the other is Bristol, Connecticut), and so receives no points for higher academic options. Its combined score for pupil/teacher ratio and effort index, then, remains its overall score: 1,701, putting it in last place among the metro areas.

# Places Rated: Metro Areas Ranked for Educational Effort and Opportunities

The following criteria are used to rate a metro area for the educational opportunities it affords its residents: (1) pupil/teacher ratio in the public K–12 system, (2) effort index in K–12, and (3) academic options in higher education. Places that receive tie scores are given the same rank and listed alphabetically.

## Metro Areas from Best to Worst

| Places Rated Rank | Places Rated Score | Places Rated Rank | Places Rated Score | Places Rated Rank | Places Rated Score |
|---|---|---|---|---|---|
| 1. Philadelphia, PA–NJ | 3,781 | 44. Syracuse, NY | 3,144 | 88. Waterbury, CT | 2,995 |
| 2. Bergen–Passaic, NJ | 3,653 | | | 90. Asheville, NC | 2,990 |
| 3. Washington, DC–MD–VA | 3,635 | 46. Jackson, MS | 3,130 | | |
| 4. Hartford, CT | 3,628 | 47. Middletown, CT | 3,128 | 90. Hagerstown, MD | 2,990 |
| 5. Rochester, NY | 3,582 | 47. New Britain, CT | 3,128 | 92. New York, NY | 2,984 |
| | | 49. Chico, CA | 3,126 | 93. Wichita, KS | 2,981 |
| 6. Providence, RI | 3,558 | 50. Buffalo, NY | 3,121 | 94. Orlando, FL | 2,976 |
| 7. Pittsburgh, PA | 3,544 | | | 95. Bryan–College Station, TX | 2,973 |
| 8. Middlesex–Somerset– Hunterdon, NJ | 3,539 | 51. Eugene–Springfield, OR | 3,118 | | |
| 9. St. Louis, MO–IL | 3,530 | 52. Wilmington, DE–NJ–MD | 3,112 | 95. Portland, ME | 2,973 |
| 10. Springfield, MA | 3,525 | 53. Florence, SC | 3,109 | 97. Alexandria, LA | 2,972 |
| | | 54. Lancaster, PA | 3,097 | 97. Cleveland, OH | 2,972 |
| 11. New Haven–Meriden, CT | 3,495 | 55. Gainesville, FL | 3,094 | 99. Utica–Rome, NY | 2,970 |
| 12. Charlottesville, VA | 3,489 | | | 100. Muncie, IN | 2,965 |
| 13. Chicago, IL | 3,486 | 56. Greensboro–Winston-Salem– High Point, NC | 3,090 | | |
| 14. Boston, MA | 3,479 | 57. Springfield, IL | 3,078 | 101. Eau Claire, WI | 2,960 |
| 15. Baltimore, MD | 3,471 | 58. Omaha, NE–IA | 3,069 | 102. Kansas City, MO | 2,949 |
| | | 59. Detroit, MI | 3,064 | 103. Alton–Granite City, IL | 2,945 |
| 16. Raleigh–Durham, NC | 3,455 | 60. Austin, TX | 3,063 | 103. Lafayette, IN | 2,945 |
| 17. Albany–Schenectady– Troy, NY | 3,399 | | | 105. Danville, VA | 2,943 |
| 18. San Francisco, CA | 3,371 | 61. Pawtucket–Woonsocket– Attleboro, RI–MA | 3,058 | | |
| 19. Cumberland, MD–WV | 3,363 | 62. Atlanta, GA | 3,057 | 106. Phoenix, AZ | 2,942 |
| 20. Newark, NJ | 3,362 | 63. Binghamton, NY | 3,052 | 107. Richmond–Petersburg, VA | 2,940 |
| | | 64. Fayetteville, NC | 3,051 | 108. San Antonio, TX | 2,938 |
| 21. Ann Arbor, MI | 3,346 | 65. Jacksonville, FL | 3,048 | 109. Bangor, ME | 2,934 |
| 22. Portland, OR | 3,343 | | | 110. Atlantic City, NJ | 2,929 |
| 23. Burlington, VT | 3,323 | 66. Madison, WI | 3,047 | | |
| 24. Trenton, NJ | 3,311 | 67. Milwaukee, WI | 3,044 | 111. Columbus, OH | 2,928 |
| 25. Worcester, MA | 3,299 | 67. Tampa–St. Petersburg– Clearwater, FL | 3,044 | 112. Fort Smith, AR–OK | 2,927 |
| | | 69. Charlotte–Gastonia– Rock Hill, NC–SC | 3,031 | 112. St. Joseph, MO | 2,927 |
| 26. Tyler, TX | 3,283 | 70. Bridgeport–Milford, CT | 3,029 | 114. Johnson City–Kingsport– Bristol, TN | 2,925 |
| 27. Salem, OR | 3,278 | | | 115. Youngstown–Warren, OH | 2,920 |
| 28. Houston, TX | 3,271 | 70. Danbury, CT | 3,029 | | |
| 29. Dallas, TX | 3,269 | 70. Norwalk, CT | 3,029 | 116. Cincinnati, OH–KY–IN | 2,918 |
| 30. Pittsfield, MA | 3,264 | 70. Stamford, CT | 3,029 | 116. Kenosha, WI | 2,918 |
| | | 74. Kansas City, KS | 3,028 | 118. Augusta, GA–SC | 2,915 |
| 31. New London–Norwich, CT–RI | 3,244 | 74. Louisville, KY–IN | 3,028 | 119. Pensacola, FL | 2,914 |
| 32. Greenville–Spartanburg, SC | 3,236 | | | 120. Columbia, SC | 2,908 |
| 33. Nassau–Suffolk, NY | 3,234 | 74. Reading, PA | 3,028 | | |
| 34. Scranton–Wilkes-Barre, PA | 3,230 | 77. La Crosse, WI | 3,027 | 120. Oklahoma City, OK | 2,908 |
| 35. Harrisburg–Lebanon– Carlisle, PA | 3,224 | 78. Albuquerque, NM | 3,026 | 122. Williamsport, PA | 2,906 |
| | | 78. Portsmouth–Dover– Rochester, NH–ME | 3,026 | 123. Kokomo, IN | 2,904 |
| 35. West Palm Beach–Boca Raton–Delray Beach, FL | 3,224 | 80. Sharon, PA | 3,022 | 124. York, PA | 2,903 |
| 37. Los Angeles–Long Beach, CA | 3,195 | | | 125. Davenport–Rock Island– Moline, IL | 2,901 |
| 38. State College, PA | 3,169 | 81. Norfolk–Virginia Beach– Newport News, VA | 3,014 | | |
| 39. Killeen–Temple, TX | 3,167 | 82. Minneapolis–St. Paul, MN–WI | 3,013 | 126. Texarkana, TX–Texarkana, AR | 2,899 |
| 40. Charleston, SC | 3,164 | 83. Terre Haute, IN | 3,012 | 127. Poughkeepsie, NY | 2,898 |
| | | 84. Billings, MT | 3,008 | 128. Kalamazoo, MI | 2,896 |
| 41. Fort Pierce, FL | 3,154 | 85. Wheeling, WV–OH | 3,002 | 129. Charleston, WV | 2,894 |
| 42. Champaign–Urbana– Rantoul, IL | 3,147 | | | 130. Lansing–East Lansing, MI | 2,891 |
| 43. Denver, CO | 3,145 | 86. Elmira, NY | 3,000 | | |
| 44. Allentown–Bethlehem, PA–NJ | 3,144 | 87. Lakeland–Winter Haven, FL | 2,998 | 131. Waterloo–Cedar Falls, IA | 2,889 |
| | | 88. New Orleans, LA | 2,995 | 132. Miami–Hialeah, FL | 2,879 |
| | | | | 133. Lincoln, NE | 2,878 |
| | | | | 134. Wilmington, NC | 2,876 |
| | | | | 135. South Bend–Mishawaka, IN | 2,874 |

| Places Rated Rank | Places Rated Score |
|---|---|
| 136. Bloomington, IN | 2,873 |
| 137. Joplin, MO | 2,871 |
| 137. Mansfield, OH | 2,871 |
| 139. Joliet, IL | 2,868 |
| 140. Waco, TX | 2,867 |
| 141. Ocala, FL | 2,864 |
| 142. Lexington–Fayette, KY | 2,861 |
| 143. Shreveport, LA | 2,858 |
| 144. Kankakee, IL | 2,855 |
| 145. Bloomington–Normal, IL | 2,854 |
| 145. Greeley, CO | 2,854 |
| 147. Amarillo, TX | 2,852 |
| 147. Toledo, OH | 2,852 |
| 149. Birmingham, AL | 2,851 |
| 150. Appleton–Oshkosh–Neenah, WI | 2,844 |
| 151. Anaheim–Santa Ana, CA | 2,843 |
| 152. Iowa City, IA | 2,842 |
| 153. Corpus Christi, TX | 2,840 |
| 154. Laredo, TX | 2,827 |
| 155. Longview–Marshall, TX | 2,816 |
| 156. Melbourne–Titusville–Palm Bay, FL | 2,814 |
| 157. Fort Walton Beach, FL | 2,809 |
| 157. Galveston–Texas City, TX | 2,809 |
| 159. Memphis, TN–AR–MS | 2,804 |
| 160. Lynchburg, VA | 2,803 |
| 161. Fitchburg–Leominster, MA | 2,799 |
| 162. Evansville, IN–KY | 2,797 |
| 162. Medford, OR | 2,797 |
| 164. Topeka, KS | 2,795 |
| 165. San Diego, CA | 2,794 |
| 166. Sacramento, CA | 2,793 |
| 167. Tallahassee, FL | 2,790 |
| 168. Monmouth–Ocean, NJ | 2,787 |
| 169. Mobile, AL | 2,779 |
| 170. Altoona, PA | 2,778 |
| 170. Bellingham, WA | 2,778 |
| 172. Spokane, WA | 2,774 |
| 173. Anderson, SC | 2,772 |
| 173. Dayton–Springfield, OH | 2,772 |
| 173. Fort Wayne, IN | 2,772 |
| 173. Saginaw–Bay City–Midland, MI | 2,772 |
| 177. Enid, OK | 2,764 |
| 178. Nashville, TN | 2,763 |
| 179. Knoxville, TN | 2,761 |
| 180. Abilene, TX | 2,757 |
| 181. Canton, OH | 2,754 |
| 181. Colorado Springs, CO | 2,754 |
| 181. Orange County, NY | 2,754 |
| 184. Wausau, WI | 2,749 |
| 185. Hamilton–Middletown, OH | 2,747 |
| 185. Vineland–Millville–Bridgeton, NJ | 2,747 |
| 185. Wichita Falls, TX | 2,747 |
| 188. Beaumont–Port Arthur, TX | 2,745 |
| 189. Great Falls, MT | 2,737 |
| 190. Las Cruces, NM | 2,736 |
| 191. Fort Lauderdale–Hollywood–Pompano Beach, FL | 2,734 |
| 192. Racine, WI | 2,732 |

| Places Rated Rank | Places Rated Score |
|---|---|
| 193. Brockton, MA | 2,729 |
| 193. Fort Myers, FL | 2,729 |
| 193. Salem–Gloucester, MA | 2,729 |
| 196. Manchester, NH | 2,728 |
| 196. Nashua, NH | 2,728 |
| 198. Hickory, NC | 2,726 |
| 199. Roanoke, VA | 2,723 |
| 200. Santa Rosa–Petaluma, CA | 2,722 |
| 201. Grand Forks, ND | 2,721 |
| 201. Odessa, TX | 2,721 |
| 203. Santa Barbara–Santa Maria–Lompoc, CA | 2,719 |
| 204. Brazoria, TX | 2,718 |
| 205. Bradenton, FL | 2,712 |
| 206. Seattle, WA | 2,710 |
| 207. San Jose, CA | 2,709 |
| 207. Springfield, MO | 2,709 |
| 209. San Angelo, TX | 2,707 |
| 210. Grand Rapids, MI | 2,705 |
| 211. Dubuque, IA | 2,701 |
| 212. Lawrence, KS | 2,700 |
| 213. Victoria, TX | 2,696 |
| 214. Lewiston–Auburn, ME | 2,694 |
| 215. Johnstown, PA | 2,691 |
| 216. Indianapolis, IN | 2,690 |
| 217. Bismarck, ND | 2,686 |
| 218. Tucson, AZ | 2,685 |
| 219. Decatur, IL | 2,683 |
| 220. Rockford, IL | 2,680 |
| 221. Glens Falls, NY | 2,674 |
| 222. Sioux City, IA–NE | 2,673 |
| 223. Steubenville–Weirton, OH–WV | 2,672 |
| 224. Columbus, GA–AL | 2,665 |
| 225. Clarksville–Hopkinsville, TN–KY | 2,654 |
| 225. Jackson, MI | 2,654 |
| 227. Pueblo, CO | 2,653 |
| 228. Sherman–Denison, TX | 2,652 |
| 229. Macon–Warner Robins, GA | 2,651 |
| 229. Sioux Falls, SD | 2,651 |
| 231. Athens, GA | 2,646 |
| 231. Jacksonville, NC | 2,646 |
| 231. Oakland, CA | 2,646 |
| 234. McAllen–Edinburg–Mission, TX | 2,644 |
| 235. Erie, PA | 2,641 |
| 236. Baton Rouge, LA | 2,635 |
| 237. East St. Louis–Belleville, IL | 2,630 |
| 237. Muskegon, MI | 2,630 |
| 239. Lima, OH | 2,629 |
| 240. Bristol, CT | 2,628 |
| 240. Tulsa, OK | 2,628 |
| 242. Fort Worth–Arlington, TX | 2,627 |
| 243. Sarasota, FL | 2,626 |
| 244. Olympia, WA | 2,625 |
| 245. Green Bay, WI | 2,622 |
| 246. Cedar Rapids, IA | 2,619 |
| 246. Duluth, MN–WI | 2,619 |
| 248. Provo–Orem, UT | 2,618 |
| 249. Modesto, CA | 2,616 |
| 250. Des Moines, IA | 2,613 |

| Places Rated Rank | Places Rated Score |
|---|---|
| 251. Daytona Beach, FL | 2,612 |
| 252. Santa Cruz, CA | 2,611 |
| 253. Lake County, IL | 2,607 |
| 254. Riverside–San Bernardino, CA | 2,596 |
| 255. Biloxi–Gulfport, MS | 2,592 |
| 256. Boulder–Longmont, CO | 2,587 |
| 257. Lorain–Elyria, OH | 2,582 |
| 258. Little Rock–North Little Rock, AR | 2,581 |
| 259. Jersey City, NJ | 2,574 |
| 260. Bakersfield, CA | 2,564 |
| 261. Albany, GA | 2,560 |
| 262. Sheboygan, WI | 2,557 |
| 263. Pine Bluff, AR | 2,554 |
| 264. Tacoma, WA | 2,546 |
| 265. Benton Harbor, MI | 2,545 |
| 265. Lubbock, TX | 2,545 |
| 267. Bremerton, WA | 2,544 |
| 268. Niagara Falls, NY | 2,538 |
| 269. Elkhart–Goshen, IN | 2,537 |
| 270. Beaver County, PA | 2,535 |
| 271. Janesville–Beloit, WI | 2,532 |
| 272. Reno, NV | 2,529 |
| 273. Gary–Hammond, IN | 2,526 |
| 274. Huntington–Ashland, WV–KY–OH | 2,525 |
| 275. Burlington, NC | 2,519 |
| 276. Flint, MI | 2,511 |
| 277. Fargo–Moorhead, ND–MN | 2,506 |
| 278. Parkersburg–Marietta, WV–OH | 2,503 |
| 279. Honolulu, HI | 2,502 |
| 279. St. Cloud, MN | 2,502 |
| 281. Panama City, FL | 2,500 |
| 282. Vallejo–Fairfield–Napa, CA | 2,498 |
| 283. Owensboro, KY | 2,491 |
| 283. Yakima, WA | 2,491 |
| 285. Battle Creek, MI | 2,483 |
| 286. El Paso, TX | 2,479 |
| 286. Lawrence–Haverhill, MA–NH | 2,479 |
| 286. Lowell, MA–NH | 2,479 |
| 289. Redding, CA | 2,471 |
| 290. Anderson, IN | 2,469 |
| 291. Savannah, GA | 2,456 |
| 292. Casper, WY | 2,453 |
| 292. Monroe, LA | 2,453 |
| 294. Peoria, IL | 2,452 |
| 295. Fall River, MA–RI | 2,439 |
| 295. New Bedford, MA | 2,439 |
| 295. Salinas–Seaside–Monterey, CA | 2,439 |
| 298. Akron, OH | 2,438 |
| 299. Florence, AL | 2,427 |
| 300. Midland, TX | 2,416 |
| 301. Chattanooga, TN–GA | 2,415 |
| 302. Anchorage, AK | 2,414 |
| 303. Brownsville–Harlingen, TX | 2,413 |
| 303. Fort Collins–Loveland, CO | 2,413 |
| 305. Fresno, CA | 2,407 |
| 306. Boise City, ID | 2,391 |
| 307. Tuscaloosa, AL | 2,390 |

| Places Rated Rank | Places Rated Score | Places Rated Rank | Places Rated Score | Places Rated Rank | Places Rated Score |
|---|---|---|---|---|---|
| 308. Montgomery, AL | 2,388 | 316. Lafayette, LA | 2,305 | 323. Stockton, CA | 2,155 |
| 309. Yuba City, CA | 2,387 | 317. Gadsden, AL | 2,299 | 325. Rochester, MN | 2,134 |
| 310. Columbia, MO | 2,377 | 318. Huntsville, AL | 2,257 | | |
| | | 319. Las Vegas, NV | 2,241 | 326. Visalia–Tulare–Porterville, CA | 2,128 |
| 311. Lawton, OK | 2,375 | 320. Dothan, AL | 2,230 | 327. Houma–Thibodaux, LA | 1,995 |
| 312. Salt Lake City–Ogden, UT | 2,340 | | | 328. Richland–Kennewick–Pasco, WA | 1,728 |
| 313. Lake Charles, LA | 2,336 | 321. Aurora–Elgin, IL | 2,208 | | |
| 314. Fayetteville–Springdale, AR | 2,334 | 322. Anniston, AL | 2,189 | 329. Pascagoula, MS | 1,701 |
| 315. Vancouver, WA | 2,332 | 323. Oxnard–Ventura, CA | 2,155 | | |

## Metro Areas Listed Alphabetically

| Metro Area | Places Rated Rank | Metro Area | Places Rated Rank | Metro Area | Places Rated Rank |
|---|---|---|---|---|---|
| Abilene, TX | 180 | Bridgeport–Milford, CT | 70 | Elkhart–Goshen, IN | 269 |
| Akron, OH | 298 | Bristol, CT | 240 | Elmira, NY | 86 |
| Albany, GA | 261 | Brockton, MA | 193 | Enid, OK | 177 |
| Albany–Schenectady–Troy, NY | 17 | | | | |
| Albuquerque, NM | 78 | Brownsville–Harlingen, TX | 303 | Erie, PA | 235 |
| | | Bryan–College Station, TX | 95 | Eugene–Springfield, OR | 51 |
| Alexandria, LA | 97 | Buffalo, NY | 50 | Evansville, IN–KY | 162 |
| Allentown–Bethlehem, PA–NJ | 44 | Burlington, NC | 275 | Fall River, MA–RI | 295 |
| Alton–Granite City, IL | 103 | Burlington, VT | 23 | Fargo–Moorhead, ND–MN | 277 |
| Altoona, PA | 170 | | | | |
| Amarillo, TX | 147 | Canton, OH | 181 | Fayetteville, NC | 64 |
| | | Casper, WY | 292 | Fayetteville–Springdale, AR | 314 |
| Anaheim–Santa Ana, CA | 151 | Cedar Rapids, IA | 246 | Fitchburg–Leominster, MA | 161 |
| Anchorage, AK | 302 | Champaign–Urbana–Rantoul, IL | 42 | Flint, MI | 276 |
| Anderson, IN | 290 | Charleston, SC | 40 | Florence, AL | 299 |
| Anderson, SC | 173 | | | | |
| Ann Arbor, MI | 21 | Charleston, WV | 129 | Florence, SC | 53 |
| | | Charlotte–Gastonia–Rock Hill, NC–SC | 69 | Fort Collins–Loveland, CO | 303 |
| Anniston, AL | 322 | Charlottesville, VA | 12 | Fort Lauderdale–Hollywood–Pompano Beach, FL | 191 |
| Appleton–Oshkosh–Neenah, WI | 150 | Chattanooga, TN–GA | 301 | Fort Myers, FL | 193 |
| Asheville, NC | 90 | Chicago, IL | 13 | Fort Pierce, FL | 41 |
| Athens, GA | 231 | | | | |
| Atlanta, GA | 62 | Chico, CA | 49 | Fort Smith, AR–OK | 112 |
| | | Cincinnati, OH–KY–IN | 116 | Fort Walton Beach, FL | 157 |
| Atlantic City, NJ | 110 | Clarksville–Hopkinsville, TN–KY | 225 | Fort Wayne, IN | 173 |
| Augusta, GA–SC | 118 | Cleveland, OH | 97 | Fort Worth–Arlington, TX | 242 |
| Aurora–Elgin, IL | 321 | Colorado Springs, CO | 181 | Fresno, CA | 305 |
| Austin, TX | 60 | | | | |
| Bakersfield, CA | 260 | Columbia, MO | 310 | Gadsden, AL | 317 |
| | | Columbia, SC | 120 | Gainesville, FL | 55 |
| Baltimore, MD | 15 | Columbus, GA–AL | 224 | Galveston–Texas City, TX | 157 |
| Bangor, ME | 109 | Columbus, OH | 111 | Gary–Hammond, IN | 273 |
| Baton Rouge, LA | 236 | Corpus Christi, TX | 153 | Glens Falls, NY | 221 |
| Battle Creek, MI | 285 | | | | |
| Beaumont–Port Arthur, TX | 188 | Cumberland, MD–WV | 19 | Grand Forks, ND | 201 |
| | | Dallas, TX | 29 | Grand Rapids, MI | 210 |
| Beaver County, PA | 270 | Danbury, CT | 70 | Great Falls, MT | 189 |
| Bellingham, WA | 170 | Danville, VA | 105 | Greeley, CO | 145 |
| Benton Harbor, MI | 265 | Davenport–Rock Island–Moline, IA–IL | 125 | Green Bay, WI | 245 |
| Bergen–Passaic, NJ | 2 | | | | |
| Billings, MT | 84 | Dayton–Springfield, OH | 173 | Greensboro–Winston-Salem–High Point, NC | 56 |
| Biloxi–Gulfport, MS | 255 | Daytona Beach, FL | 251 | Greenville–Spartanburg, SC | 32 |
| Binghamton, NY | 63 | Decatur, IL | 219 | Hagerstown, MD | 90 |
| Birmingham, AL | 149 | Denver, CO | 43 | Hamilton–Middletown, OH | 185 |
| Bismarck, ND | 217 | Des Moines, IA | 250 | Harrisburg–Lebanon–Carlisle, PA | 35 |
| Bloomington, IN | 136 | | | | |
| | | Detroit, MI | 59 | Hartford, CT | 4 |
| Bloomington–Normal, IL | 145 | Dothan, AL | 320 | Hickory, NC | 198 |
| Boise City, ID | 306 | Dubuque, IA | 211 | Honolulu, HI | 279 |
| Boston, MA | 14 | Duluth, MN–WI | 246 | Houma–Thibodaux, LA | 327 |
| Boulder–Longmont, CO | 256 | East St. Louis–Belleville, IL | 237 | Houston, TX | 28 |
| Bradenton, FL | 205 | | | | |
| | | Eau Claire, WI | 101 | Huntington–Ashland, WV–KY–OH | 274 |
| Brazoria, TX | 204 | El Paso, TX | 286 | Huntsville, AL | 318 |
| Bremerton, WA | 267 | | | | |

| Metro Area | Places Rated Rank |
|---|---|
| Indianapolis, IN | 216 |
| Iowa City, IA | 152 |
| Jackson, MI | 225 |
| Jackson, MS | 46 |
| Jacksonville, FL | 65 |
| Jacksonville, NC | 231 |
| Janesville–Beloit, WI | 271 |
| Jersey City, NJ | 259 |
| Johnson City–Kingsport–Bristol, TN–VA | 114 |
| Johnstown, PA | 215 |
| Joliet, IL | 139 |
| Joplin, MO | 137 |
| Kalamazoo, MI | 128 |
| Kankakee, IL | 144 |
| Kansas City, KS | 74 |
| Kansas City, MO | 102 |
| Kenosha, WI | 116 |
| Killeen–Temple, TX | 39 |
| Knoxville, TN | 179 |
| Kokomo, IN | 123 |
| La Crosse, WI | 77 |
| Lafayette, IN | 103 |
| Lafayette, LA | 316 |
| Lake Charles, LA | 313 |
| Lake County, IL | 253 |
| Lakeland–Winter Haven, FL | 87 |
| Lancaster, PA | 54 |
| Lansing–East Lansing, MI | 130 |
| Laredo, TX | 154 |
| Las Cruces, NM | 190 |
| Las Vegas, NV | 319 |
| Lawrence, KS | 212 |
| Lawrence–Haverhill, MA–NH | 286 |
| Lawton, OK | 311 |
| Lewiston–Auburn, ME | 214 |
| Lexington–Fayette, KY | 142 |
| Lima, OH | 239 |
| Lincoln, NE | 133 |
| Little Rock–North Little Rock, AR | 258 |
| Longview–Marshall, TX | 155 |
| Lorain–Elyria, OH | 257 |
| Los Angeles–Long Beach, CA | 37 |
| Louisville, KY–IN | 74 |
| Lowell, MA–NH | 286 |
| Lubbock, TX | 265 |
| Lynchburg, VA | 160 |
| Macon–Warner Robins, GA | 229 |
| Madison, WI | 66 |
| Manchester, NH | 196 |
| Mansfield, OH | 137 |
| McAllen–Edinburg–Mission, TX | 234 |
| Medford, OR | 162 |
| Melbourne–Titusville–Palm Bay, FL | 156 |
| Memphis, TN–AR–MS | 159 |
| Miami–Hialeah, FL | 132 |
| Middlesex–Somerset–Hunterdon, NJ | 8 |
| Middletown, CT | 47 |
| Midland, TX | 300 |
| Milwaukee, WI | 67 |
| Minneapolis–St. Paul, MN–WI | 82 |
| Mobile, AL | 169 |
| Modesto, CA | 249 |
| Monmouth–Ocean, NJ | 168 |
| Monroe, LA | 292 |
| Montgomery, AL | 308 |
| Muncie, IN | 100 |
| Muskegon, MI | 237 |
| Nashua, NH | 196 |
| Nashville, TN | 178 |
| Nassau–Suffolk, NY | 33 |
| New Bedford, MA | 295 |
| New Britain, CT | 47 |
| New Haven–Meriden, CT | 11 |
| New London–Norwich, CT–RI | 31 |
| New Orleans, LA | 88 |
| New York, NY | 92 |
| Newark, NJ | 20 |
| Niagara Falls, NY | 268 |
| Norfolk–Virginia Beach–Newport News, VA | 81 |
| Norwalk, CT | 70 |
| Oakland, CA | 231 |
| Ocala, FL | 141 |
| Odessa, TX | 201 |
| Oklahoma City, OK | 120 |
| Olympia, WA | 244 |
| Omaha, NE–IA | 58 |
| Orange County, NY | 181 |
| Orlando, FL | 94 |
| Owensboro, KY | 283 |
| Oxnard–Ventura, CA | 323 |
| Panama City, FL | 281 |
| Parkersburg–Marietta, WV–OH | 278 |
| Pascagoula, MS | 329 |
| Pawtucket–Woonsocket–Attleboro, RI–MA | 61 |
| Pensacola, FL | 119 |
| Peoria, IL | 294 |
| Philadelphia, PA–NJ | 1 |
| Phoenix, AZ | 106 |
| Pine Bluff, AR | 263 |
| Pittsburgh, PA | 7 |
| Pittsfield, MA | 30 |
| Portland, ME | 95 |
| Portland, OR | 22 |
| Portsmouth–Dover–Rochester, NH–ME | 78 |
| Poughkeepsie, NY | 127 |
| Providence, RI | 6 |
| Provo–Orem, UT | 248 |
| Pueblo, CO | 227 |
| Racine, WI | 192 |
| Raleigh–Durham, NC | 16 |
| Reading, PA | 74 |
| Redding, CA | 289 |
| Reno, NV | 272 |
| Richland–Kennewick–Pasco, WA | 328 |
| Richmond–Petersburg, VA | 107 |
| Riverside–San Bernardino, CA | 254 |
| Roanoke, VA | 199 |
| Rochester, MN | 325 |
| Rochester, NY | 5 |
| Rockford, IL | 220 |
| Sacramento, CA | 166 |
| Saginaw–Bay City–Midland, MI | 173 |
| St. Cloud, MN | 279 |
| St. Joseph, MO | 112 |
| St. Louis, MO–IL | 9 |
| Salem, OR | 27 |
| Salem–Gloucester, MA | 193 |
| Salinas–Seaside–Monterey, CA | 295 |
| Salt Lake City–Ogden, UT | 312 |
| San Angelo, TX | 209 |
| San Antonio, TX | 108 |
| San Diego, CA | 165 |
| San Francisco, CA | 18 |
| San Jose, CA | 207 |
| Santa Barbara–Santa Maria–Lompoc, CA | 203 |
| Santa Cruz, CA | 252 |
| Santa Rosa–Petaluma, CA | 200 |
| Sarasota, FL | 243 |
| Savannah, GA | 291 |
| Scranton–Wilkes-Barre, PA | 34 |
| Seattle, WA | 206 |
| Sharon, PA | 80 |
| Sheboygan, WI | 262 |
| Sherman–Denison, TX | 228 |
| Shreveport, LA | 143 |
| Sioux City, IA–NE | 222 |
| Sioux Falls, SD | 229 |
| South Bend–Mishawaka, IN | 135 |
| Spokane, WA | 172 |
| Springfield, IL | 57 |
| Springfield, MA | 10 |
| Springfield, MO | 207 |
| Stamford, CT | 70 |
| State College, PA | 38 |
| Steubenville–Weirton, OH–WV | 223 |
| Stockton, CA | 323 |
| Syracuse, NY | 44 |
| Tacoma, WA | 264 |
| Tallahassee, FL | 167 |
| Tampa–St. Petersburg–Clearwater, FL | 67 |
| Terre Haute, IN | 83 |
| Texarkana, TX–Texarkana, AR | 126 |
| Toledo, OH | 147 |
| Topeka, KS | 164 |
| Trenton, NJ | 24 |
| Tucson, AZ | 218 |
| Tulsa, OK | 240 |
| Tuscaloosa, AL | 307 |
| Tyler, TX | 26 |
| Utica–Rome, NY | 99 |
| Vallejo–Fairfield–Napa, CA | 282 |
| Vancouver, WA | 315 |
| Victoria, TX | 213 |
| Vineland–Millville–Bridgeton, NJ | 185 |

| Metro Area | Places Rated Rank | Metro Area | Places Rated Rank | Metro Area | Places Rated Rank |
|---|---|---|---|---|---|
| Visalia–Tulare–Porterville, CA | 326 | West Palm Beach–Boca Raton–Delray Beach, FL | 35 | Wilmington, NC | 134 |
| Waco, TX | 140 | Wheeling, WV–OH | 85 | Worcester, MA | 25 |
| Washington, DC–MD–VA | 3 | Wichita, KS | 93 | Yakima, WA | 283 |
| Waterbury, CT | 88 | | | York, PA | 124 |
| | | Wichita Falls, TX | 185 | Youngstown–Warren, OH | 115 |
| Waterloo–Cedar Falls, IA | 131 | Williamsport, PA | 122 | | |
| Wausau, WI | 184 | Wilmington, DE–NJ–MD | 52 | Yuba City, CA | 309 |

## Place Profiles: Educational Features of 329 Metro Areas

The following pages outline the main features of the educational landscape in U.S. metro areas: elementary and secondary (public and private schools) and colleges and universities (two- and four-year institutions, both public and private).

Besides the two factors used by *Places Rated Almanac* to rank the performance of public schools—pupil/teacher ratio and effort index for public-school support—information on dollars spent per pupil and average teacher salary are also given. The figures for salary represent the average monthly paycheck paid in October 1982 and have not been standardized to offset possible differences in the length of teachers' pay periods. Figures for New England County Metro Area Standards are used for New England metro areas. Hawaii's statewide averages are used for Honolulu. Figures for the number of private K–12 schools and their total enrollment are included under the heading Private. The number of each metro area's institutions of higher education and their total enrollments are included under the heading Colleges and Universities.

Sources for K–12 data include: U.S. Bureau of the Census, *Compendium of Public Employment* and *Compendium of Government Finances*, both forthcoming as of November 1984. Data on the number of districts, school buildings, and enrollment of metro area public schools come from the National School Market Index, published annually by Market Data Retrieval, Westport, Connecticut, as do figures on metro area private schools and their enrollment. For higher education, the source is the National Center for Education Statistics, *Education Directory, Colleges and Universities, 1983–84*, 1984.

A star preceding a metro area's name highlights it as one of the top 25 places for educational effort and opportunities.

### Abilene, TX
Elementary and Secondary
  Public: 5 districts, 42 schools, 20,409 pupils
    Pupil/Teacher Ratio: 13.29
    Dollars per Pupil: $1,960
    Average Teacher Salary: $1,651
    Effort Index: 1.119
  Private: 4 schools, 908 pupils
Colleges and Universities
  Two-year: None
  Four-year and Beyond: 2 private; 5,847 students
  Degree Options: C
Places Rated Score: 2,757
Places Rated Rank: 180

### Akron, OH
Elementary and Secondary
  Public: 30 districts, 207 schools, 117,740 pupils
    Pupil/Teacher Ratio: 16.79
    Dollars per Pupil: $2,532
    Average Teacher Salary: $2,140
    Effort Index: 1.038

  Private: 45 schools, 12,580 pupils
Colleges and Universities
  Two-year: None
  Four-year and Beyond: 1 private, 2 public; 47,719 students
  Degree Options: C
Places Rated Score: 2,438
Places Rated Rank: 298

### Albany, GA
Elementary and Secondary
  Public: 2 districts, 36 schools, 22,840 pupils
    Pupil/Teacher Ratio: 14.70
    Dollars per Pupil: $1,977
    Average Teacher Salary: $1,305
    Effort Index: 0.781
  Private: 11 schools, 2,667 pupils
Colleges and Universities
  Two-year: 1 public; 1,884 students
  Four-year and Beyond: 1 public; 1,896 students
  Degree Options: B
Places Rated Score: 2,560
Places Rated Rank: 261

### ★ Albany–Schenectady–Troy, NY
Elementary and Secondary
  Public: 56 districts, 237 schools, 132,891 pupils
    Pupil/Teacher Ratio: 15.10
    Dollars per Pupil: $3,607
    Average Teacher Salary: $1,967
    Effort Index: 1,148
  Private: 112 schools, 22,742 pupils
Colleges and Universities
  Two-year: 3 private, 2 public; 13,812 students
  Four-year and Beyond: 8 private, 2 public; 41,853 students
  Degree Options: AA
Places Rated Score: 3,399
Places Rated Rank: 17

### Albuquerque, NM
Elementary and Secondary
  Public: 1 district, 110 schools, 67,073 pupils
    Pupil/Teacher Ratio: 11.78
    Dollars per Pupil: $3,368
    Average Teacher Salary: $1,539
    Effort Index: 1.243

Private: 34 schools, 8,411 pupils
Colleges and Universities
 Two-year: None
 Four-year and Beyond: 1 private, 1
  public; 25,864 students
 Degree Options: C
Places Rated Score: 3,026
Places Rated Rank: 78

### Alexandria, LA
Elementary and Secondary
 Public: 1 district, 52 schools,
 23,083 pupils
  Pupil/Teacher Ratio: 12.28
  Dollars per Pupil: $2,450
  Average Teacher Salary: $1,354
  Effort Index: 1.241
 Private: 11 schools, 4,097 pupils
Colleges and Universities
 Two-year: 1 public; 1,713 students
 Four-year and Beyond: 1 private; 1,049
  students
 Degree Options: C
Places Rated Score: 2,972
Places Rated Rank: 97

### Allentown–Bethlehem, PA–NJ
Elementary and Secondary
 Public: 46 districts, 194 schools,
 100,994 pupils
  Pupil/Teacher Ratio: 13.79
  Dollars per Pupil: $2,903
  Average Teacher Salary: $1,733
  Effort Index: 1.298
 Private: 59 schools, 13,535 pupils
Colleges and Universities
 Two-year: 2 private, 3 public; 9,978
  students
 Four-year and Beyond: 7 private; 15,355
  students
 Degree Options: B
Places Rated Score: 3,144
Places Rated Rank: 44

### Alton–Granite City, IL
Elementary and Secondary
 Public: 16 districts, 112 schools,
 47,900 pupils
  Pupil/Teacher Ratio: 15.80
  Dollars per Pupil: $2,540
  Average Teacher Salary: $1,778
  Effort Index: 1.238
 Private: 36 schools, 6,499 pupils
Colleges and Universities
 Two-year: 1 public; 5,155 students
 Four-year and Beyond: 1 public; 11,098
  students
 Degree Options: B
Places Rated Score: 2,945
Places Rated Rank: 103

### Altoona, PA
Elementary and Secondary
 Public: 7 districts, 42 schools,
 23,064 pupils
  Pupil/Teacher Ratio: 15.29
  Dollars per Pupil: $2,389
  Average Teacher Salary: $1,465
  Effort Index: 1.289
 Private: 19 schools, 3,579 pupils
Colleges and Universities
 Two-year: 1 public; 2,428 students
 Four-year and Beyond: None
 Degree Options: C
Places Rated Score: 2,778
Places Rated Rank: 170

### Amarillo, TX
Elementary and Secondary
 Public: 5 districts, 58 schools,
 32,704 pupils
  Pupil/Teacher Ratio: 14.37
  Dollars per Pupil: $2,624
  Average Teacher Salary: $1,603
  Effort Index: 1.050
 Private: 12 schools, 1,939 pupils
Colleges and Universities
 Two-year: 2 public; 7,121 students
 Four-year and Beyond: 1 public; 6,805
  students
 Degree Options: B
Places Rated Score: 2,852
Places Rated Rank: 147

### Anaheim–Santa Ana, CA
Elementary and Secondary
 Public: 29 districts, 483 schools,
 341,367 pupils
  Pupil/Teacher Ratio: 19.11
  Dollars per Pupil: $3,161
  Average Teacher Salary: $2,416
  Effort Index: 1.052
 Private: 188 schools, 23,674 pupils
Colleges and Universities
 Two-year: 7 public; 146,935 students
 Four-year and Beyond: 6 private, 1
  public; 32,331 students
 Degree Options: A
Places Rated Score: 2,843
Places Rated Rank: 151

### Anchorage, AK
Elementary and Secondary
 Public: 1 district, 74 schools,
 38,745 pupils
  Pupil/Teacher Ratio: 15.55
  Dollars per Pupil: $3,843
  Average Teacher Salary: $2,927
  Effort Index: 0.692
 Private: 13 schools, 2,187 pupils
Colleges and Universities
 Two-year: 1 public; 8,268 students
 Four-year and Beyond: 1 private, 1
  public; 4,252 students
 Degree Options: B
Places Rated Score: 2,414
Places Rated Rank: 302

### Anderson, IN
Elementary and Secondary
 Public: 5 districts, 46 schools,
 27,099 pupils
  Pupil/Teacher Ratio: 16.55
  Dollars per Pupil: $1,961
  Average Teacher Salary: $1,600
  Effort Index: 1.056
 Private: 11 schools, 1,866 pupils
Colleges and Universities
 Two-year: None
 Four-year and Beyond: 1 private; 2,008
  students
 Degree Options: C
Places Rated Score: 2,469
Places Rated Rank: 290

### Anderson, SC
Elementary and Secondary
 Public: 5 districts, 50 schools,
 27,437 pupils
  Pupil/Teacher Ratio: 17.34
  Dollars per Pupil: $1,801
  Average Teacher Salary: $1,361
  Effort Index: 1.400
 Private: 17 schools, 1,469 pupils

Colleges and Universities
 Two-year: None
 Four-year and Beyond: 1 private; 1,048
  students
 Degree Options: C
Places Rated Score: 2,772
Places Rated Rank: 173

### ★ Ann Arbor, MI
Elementary and Secondary
 Public: 10 districts, 80 schools,
 40,532 pupils
  Pupil/Teacher Ratio: 16.23
  Dollars per Pupil: $3,574
  Average Teacher Salary: $2,327
  Effort Index: 1.414
 Private: 33 schools, 4,615 pupils
Colleges and Universities
 Two-year: 1 public; 8,247 students
 Four-year and Beyond: 2 private, 2
  public; 55,696 students
 Degree Options: A
Places Rated Score: 3,346
Places Rated Rank: 21

### Anniston, AL
Elementary and Secondary
 Public: 5 districts, 34 schools,
 22,146 pupils
  Pupil/Teacher Ratio: 18.14
  Dollars per Pupil: $1,607
  Average Teacher Salary: $1,434
  Effort Index: 0.855
 Private: 5 schools, 1,594 pupils
Colleges and Universities
 Two-year: None
 Four-year and Beyond: 1 public; 6,284
  students
 Degree Options: C
Places Rated Score: 2,189
Places Rated Rank: 322

### Appleton–Oshkosh–Neenah, WI
Elementary and Secondary
 Public: 18 districts, 104 schools,
 47,620 pupils
  Pupil/Teacher Ratio: 15.63
  Dollars per Pupil: $2,954
  Average Teacher Salary: $1,800
  Effort Index: 1.127
 Private: 66 schools, 11,899 pupils
Colleges and Universities
 Two-year: 1 public; 5,308 students
 Four-year and Beyond: 1 private, 1
  public; 11,750 students
 Degree Options: B
Places Rated Score: 2,844
Places Rated Rank: 150

### Asheville, NC
Elementary and Secondary
 Public: 2 districts, 49 schools, 28,792
 pupils
  Pupil/Teacher Ratio: 14.86
  Dollars per Pupil: $2,292
  Average Teacher Salary: $1,458
  Effort Index: 1.222
 Private: 13 schools, 2,033 pupils
Colleges and Universities
 Two-year: 3 private, 1 public; 3,499
  students
 Four-year and Beyond: 1 private, 1
  public; 3,067 students
 Degree Options: B
Places Rated Score: 2,990
Places Rated Rank: 90

## Athens, GA

Elementary and Secondary
Public: 6 districts, 40 schools,
21,745 pupils
    Pupil/Teacher Ratio: 13.37
    Dollars per Pupil: $2,103
    Average Teacher Salary: $1,316
    Effort Index: 1.015
Private: 9 schools, 2,013 pupils
Colleges and Universities
Two-year: None
Four-year and Beyond: 1 public; 25,886
  students
Degree Options: C
Places Rated Score: 2,646
Places Rated Rank: 231

## Atlanta, GA

Elementary and Secondary
Public: 24 districts, 650 schools,
413,946 pupils
    Pupil/Teacher Ratio: 15.17
    Dollars per Pupil: $2,267
    Average Teacher Salary: $1,480
    Effort Index: 0.810
Private: 187 schools, 38,020 pupils
Colleges and Universities
Two-year: 2 private, 3 public; 23,517
  students
Four-year and Beyond: 16 private, 4
  public; 65,819 students
Degree Options: AA
Places Rated Score: 3,057
Places Rated Rank: 62

## Atlantic City, NJ

Elementary and Secondary
Public: 42 districts, 111 schools,
45,374 pupils
    Pupil/Teacher Ratio: 12.75
    Dollars per Pupil: $3,596
    Average Teacher Salary: $2,038
    Effort Index: 0.993
Private: 33 schools, 8,784 pupils
Colleges and Universities
Two-year: 1 public; 3,591 students
Four-year and Beyond: 1 public; 5,056
  students
Degree Options: B
Places Rated Score: 2,929
Places Rated Rank: 110

## Augusta, GA–SC

Elementary and Secondary
Public: 4 districts, 110 schools,
61,991 pupils
    Pupil/Teacher Ratio: 13.25
    Dollars per Pupil: $2,235
    Average Teacher Salary: $1,097
    Effort Index: 1.024
Private: 41 schools, 7,442 pupils
Colleges and Universities
Two-year: 1 private, 1 public; 1,670
  students
Four-year and Beyond: 1 private, 3
  public; 8,769 students
Degree Options: B
Places Rated Score: 2,915
Places Rated Rank: 118

## Aurora–Elgin, IL

Elementary and Secondary
Public: 15 districts, 142 schools,
86,769 pupils
    Pupil/Teacher Ratio: 17.80
    Dollars per Pupil: $2,218
    Average Teacher Salary: $1,950
    Effort Index: 0.858

Private: 47 schools, 11,199 pupils
Colleges and Universities
Two-year: 2 public; 12,673 students
Four-year and Beyond: 2 private; 1,728
  students
Degree Options: C
Places Rated Score: 2,208
Places Rated Rank: 321

## Austin, TX

Elementary and Secondary
Public: 21 districts, 160 schools,
94,921 pupils
    Pupil/Teacher Ratio: 12.36
    Dollars per Pupil: $2,815
    Average Teacher Salary: $1,584
    Effort Index: 1.090
Private: 36 schools, 6,865 pupils
Colleges and Universities
Two-year: 1 public; 15,362 students
Four-year and Beyond: 6 private, 1
  public; 52,870 students
Degree Options: B
Places Rated Score: 3,063
Places Rated Rank: 60

## Bakersfield, CA

Elementary and Secondary
Public: 49 districts, 168 schools,
80,367 pupils
    Pupil/Teacher Ratio: 15.79
    Dollars per Pupil: $3,441
    Average Teacher Salary: $2,114
    Effort Index: 0.856
Private: 36 schools, 5,690 pupils
Colleges and Universities
Two-year: 3 public; 15,465 students
Four-year and Beyond: 1 public; 3,641
  students
Degree Options: B
Places Rated Score: 2,564
Places Rated Rank: 260

## ★ Baltimore, MD

Elementary and Secondary
Public: 6 districts, 532 schools,
336,231 pupils
    Pupil/Teacher Ratio: 13.75
    Dollars per Pupil: $3,208
    Average Teacher Salary: $2,079
    Effort Index: 1.121
Private: 228 schools, 96,745 pupils
Colleges and Universities
Two-year: 5 private, 4 public; 53,090
  students
Four-year and Beyond: 10 private, 5
  public; 58,339 students
Degree Options: AA
Places Rated Score: 3,471
Places Rated Rank: 15

## Bangor, ME

Elementary and Secondary
Public: 9 districts, 34 schools,
13,138 pupils
    Pupil/Teacher Ratio: 13.79
    Dollars per Pupil: $2,048
    Average Teacher Salary: $1,396
    Effort Index: 1.088
Private: 8 schools, 1,187 pupils
Colleges and Universities
Two-year: 1 private, 1 public; 1,383
  students
Four-year and Beyond: 1 private, 1
  public; 13,150 students
Degree Options: B
Places Rated Score: 2,934
Places Rated Rank: 109

## Baton Rouge, LA

Elementary and Secondary
Public: 4 districts, 154 schools,
86,188 pupils
    Pupil/Teacher Ratio: 14.09
    Dollars per Pupil: $2,651
    Average Teacher Salary: $1,800
    Effort Index: 1.062
Private: 57 schools, 17,493 pupils
Colleges and Universities
Two-year: None
Four-year and Beyond: 2 public; 40,225
  students
Degree Options: C
Places Rated Score: 2,635
Places Rated Rank: 236

## Battle Creek, MI

Elementary and Secondary
Public: 10 districts, 57 schools,
25,776 pupils
    Pupil/Teacher Ratio: 16.55
    Dollars per Pupil: $2,950
    Average Teacher Salary: $2,247
    Effort Index: 1.070
Private: 10 schools, 1,705 pupils
Colleges and Universities
Two-year: 1 public; 5,193 students
Four-year and Beyond: 1 private; 1,742
  students
Degree Options: C
Places Rated Score: 2,483
Places Rated Rank: 285

## Beaumont–Port Arthur, TX

Elementary and Secondary
Public: 17 districts, 126 schools,
72,795 pupils
    Pupil/Teacher Ratio: 12.92
    Dollars per Pupil: $2,843
    Average Teacher Salary: $1,679
    Effort Index: 1.075
Private: 21 schools, 4,187 pupils
Colleges and Universities
Two-year: None
Four-year and Beyond: 1 public; 14,638
  students
Degree Options: C
Places Rated Score: 2,745
Places Rated Rank: 188

## Beaver County, PA

Elementary and Secondary
Public: 15 districts, 60 schools,
33,905 pupils
    Pupil/Teacher Ratio: 15.99
    Dollars per Pupil: $2,574
    Average Teacher Salary: $1,691
    Effort Index: 1.089
Private: 14 schools, 3,101 pupils
Colleges and Universities
Two-year: 2 public; 3,829 students
Four-year and Beyond: 1 private; 1,267
  students
Degree Options: C
Places Rated Score: 2,535
Places Rated Rank: 270

## Bellingham, WA

Elementary and Secondary
Public: 7 districts, 43 schools,
17,974 pupils
    Pupil/Teacher Ratio: 18.40
    Dollars per Pupil: $2,919
    Average Teacher Salary: $1,984
    Effort Index: 1.206
Private: 9 schools, 1,680 pupils

Colleges and Universities
Two-year: 1 public; 1,920 students
Four-year and Beyond: 1 public; 9,352 students
Degree Options: B
Places Rated Score: 2,778
Places Rated Rank: 170

## Benton Harbor, MI
Elementary and Secondary
Public: 14 districts, 70 schools, 34,784 pupils
Pupil/Teacher Ratio: 17.44
Dollars per Pupil: $2,662
Average Teacher Salary: $1,679
Effort Index: 1.178
Private: 28 schools, 4,736 pupils
Colleges and Universities
Two-year: 1 public; 2,977 students
Four-year and Beyond: 1 private; 2,851 students
Degree Options: C
Places Rated Score: 2,545
Places Rated Rank: 265

## ★ Bergen–Passaic, NJ
Elementary and Secondary
Public: 95 districts, 395 schools, 193,177 pupils
Pupil/Teacher Ratio: 11.98
Dollars per Pupil: $3,556
Average Teacher Salary: $2,210
Effort Index: 1.391
Private: 173 schools, 44,258 pupils
Colleges and Universities
Two-year: 3 private, 2 public; 19,637 students
Four-year and Beyond: 4 private, 2 public; 32,278 students
Degree Options: A
Places Rated Score: 3,653
Places Rated Rank: 2

## Billings, MT
Elementary and Secondary
Public: 15 districts, 58 schools, 20,444 pupils
Pupil/Teacher Ratio: 8.08
Dollars per Pupil: $2,652
Average Teacher Salary: $2,220
Effort Index: 1.008
Private: 11 schools, 1,401 pupils
Colleges and Universities
Two-year: None
Four-year and Beyond: 1 private, 1 public; 4,565 students
Degree Options: C
Places Rated Score: 3,008
Places Rated Rank: 84

## Biloxi–Gulfport, MS
Elementary and Secondary
Public: 7 districts, 54 schools, 29,521 pupils
Pupil/Teacher Ratio: 13.97
Dollars per Pupil: $1,898
Average Teacher Salary: $1,365
Effort Index: 1.010
Private: 6 schools, 662 pupils
Colleges and Universities
Two-year: 1 private; 792 students
Four-year and Beyond: None
Degree Options: C
Places Rated Score: 2,592
Places Rated Rank: 255

## Binghamton, NY
Elementary and Secondary
Public: 18 districts, 76 schools, 47,894 pupils
Pupil/Teacher Ratio: 13.26
Dollars per Pupil: $3,766
Average Teacher Salary: $1,869
Effort Index: 1.161
Private: 24 schools, 4,520 pupils
Colleges and Universities
Two-year: 1 public; 6,833 students
Four-year and Beyond: 1 public; 11,725 students
Degree Options: B
Places Rated Score: 3,052
Places Rated Rank: 63

## Birmingham, AL
Elementary and Secondary
Public: 18 districts, 295 schools, 155,371 pupils
Pupil/Teacher Ratio: 16.55
Dollars per Pupil: $1,832
Average Teacher Salary: $1,694
Effort Index: 0.937
Private: 54 schools, 11,697 pupils
Colleges and Universities
Two-year: 2 private, 2 public; 10,309 students
Four-year and Beyond: 4 private, 2 public; 23,117 students
Degree Options: A
Places Rated Score: 2,851
Places Rated Rank: 149

## Bismarck, ND
Elementary and Secondary
Public: 23 districts, 51 schools, 14,436 pupils
Pupil/Teacher Ratio: 15.44
Dollars per Pupil: $3,118
Average Teacher Salary: $2,131
Effort Index: 1.207
Private: 10 schools, 2,050 pupils
Colleges and Universities
Two-year: 1 public; 2,346 students
Four-year and Beyond: 1 private; 1,121 students
Degree Options: C
Places Rated Score: 2,686
Places Rated Rank: 217

## Bloomington, IN
Elementary and Secondary
Public: 2 districts, 28 schools, 13,580 pupils
Pupil/Teacher Ratio: 17.32
Dollars per Pupil: $2,151
Average Teacher Salary: $1,760
Effort Index: 1.503
Private: 7 schools, 505 pupils
Colleges and Universities
Two-year: None
Four-year and Beyond: 1 public; 32,711 students
Degree Options: C
Places Rated Score: 2,873
Places Rated Rank: 136

## Bloomington–Normal, IL
Elementary and Secondary
Public: 13 districts, 52 schools, 18,670 pupils
Pupil/Teacher Ratio: 14.02
Dollars per Pupil: $2,605
Average Teacher Salary: $1,778
Effort Index: 1.275
Private: 9 schools, 2,261 pupils

Colleges and Universities
Two-year: None
Four-year and Beyond: 1 private, 1 public; 22,232 students
Degree Options: C
Places Rated Score: 2,854
Places Rated Rank: 145

## Boise City, ID
Elementary and Secondary
Public: 3 districts, 64 schools, 34,750 pupils
Pupil/Teacher Ratio: 16.34
Dollars per Pupil: $1,772
Average Teacher Salary: $1,592
Effort Index: 0.966
Private: 13 schools, 1,928 pupils
Colleges and Universities
Two-year: None
Four-year and Beyond: 1 public; 11,092 students
Degree Options: C
Places Rated Score: 2,391
Places Rated Rank: 306

## ★ Boston, MA
Elementary and Secondary
Public: 109 districts, 775 schools, 404,095 pupils
Pupil/Teacher Ratio: 14.46
Dollars per Pupil: $2,707
Average Teacher Salary: $1,964
Effort Index: 0.933
Private: 308 schools, 75,926 pupils
Colleges and Universities
Two-year: 13 private, 6 public; 37,292 students
Four-year and Beyond: 31 private, 3 public; 186,445 students
Degree Options: AAA
Places Rated Score: 3,479
Places Rated Rank: 14

## Boulder–Longmont, CO
Elementary and Secondary
Public: 2 districts, 70 schools, 35,658 pupils
Pupil/Teacher Ratio: 15.10
Dollars per Pupil: $2,773
Average Teacher Salary: $1,472
Effort Index: 1.085
Private: 16 schools, 2,182 pupils
Colleges and Universities
Two-year: None
Four-year and Beyond: 1 private, 1 public; 22,304 students
Degree Options: C
Places Rated Score: 2,587
Places Rated Rank: 256

## Bradenton, FL
Elementary and Secondary
Public: 1 district, 31 schools, 21,229 pupils
Pupil/Teacher Ratio: 12.82
Dollars per Pupil: $3,045
Average Teacher Salary: $1,405
Effort Index: 1.033
Private: 13 schools, 2,313 pupils
Colleges and Universities
Two-year: 1 public; 6,604 students
Four-year and Beyond: None
Degree Options: C
Places Rated Score: 2,712
Places Rated Rank: 205

## Brazoria, TX
Elementary and Secondary
Public: 8 districts, 56 schools,
35,985 pupils
Pupil/Teacher Ratio: 13.85
Dollars per Pupil: $2,927
Average Teacher Salary: $1,667
Effort Index: 1.126
Private: 2 schools, 217 pupils
Colleges and Universities
Two-year: 2 public; 7,412 students
Four-year and Beyond: None
Degree Options: C
Places Rated Score: 2,718
Places Rated Rank: 204

## Bremerton, WA
Elementary and Secondary
Public: 5 districts, 50 schools,
29,068 pupils
Pupil/Teacher Ratio: 20.30
Dollars per Pupil: $2,662
Average Teacher Salary: $1,941
Effort Index: 1.299
Private: 11 schools, 1,422 pupils
Colleges and Universities
Two-year: 1 public; 5,338 students
Four-year and Beyond: None
Degree Options: C
Places Rated Score: 2,544
Places Rated Rank: 267

## Bridgeport–Milford, CT
Elementary and Secondary
Public: 11 districts, 117 schools,
64,086 pupils
Pupil/Teacher Ratio: 12.10
Dollars per Pupil: $3,139
Average Teacher Salary: $1,990
Effort Index: 1.279
Private: 29 schools, 9,741 pupils
Colleges and Universities
Two-year: 1 public; 2,657 students
Four-year and Beyond: 4 private; 17,212
students
Degree Options: C
Places Rated Score: 3,029
Places Rated Rank: 70

## Bristol, CT
Elementary and Secondary
Public: 3 districts, 14 schools,
10,843 pupils
Pupil/Teacher Ratio: 11.74
Dollars per Pupil: $2,994
Average Teacher Salary: $1,770
Effort Index: 1.340
Private: 8 schools, 2,731 pupils
Colleges and Universities
Two-year: None
Four-year and Beyond: None
Degree Options: None
Places Rated Score: 2,628
Places Rated Rank: 240

## Brockton, MA
Elementary and Secondary
Public: 9 districts, 52 schools,
32,321 pupils
Pupil/Teacher Ratio: 14.46
Dollars per Pupil: $2,707
Average Teacher Salary: $1,964
Effort Index: 0.933
Private: 22 schools, 3,272 pupils
Colleges and Universities
Two-year: 1 public; 7,174 students

Four-year and Beyond: 3 private, 2
public; 19,052 students
Degree Options: B
Places Rated Score: 2,729
Places Rated Rank: 193

## Brownsville–Harlingen, TX
Elementary and Secondary
Public: 10 districts, 85 schools,
58,915 pupils
Pupil/Teacher Ratio: 14.22
Dollars per Pupil: $1,962
Average Teacher Salary: $1,257
Effort Index: 0.849
Private: 15 schools, 3,475 pupils
Colleges and Universities
Two-year: 2 public; 6,103 students
Four-year and Beyond: None
Degree Options: C
Places Rated Score: 2,413
Places Rated Rank: 303

## Bryan–College Station, TX
Elementary and Secondary
Public: 2 districts, 19 schools,
14,175 pupils
Pupil/Teacher Ratio: 15.54
Dollars per Pupil: $2,274
Average Teacher Salary: $1,497
Effort Index: 1.535
Private: 7 schools, 993 pupils
Colleges and Universities
Two-year: None
Four-year and Beyond: 1 public; 36,127
students
Degree Options: C
Places Rated Score: 2,973
Places Rated Rank: 95

## Buffalo, NY
Elementary and Secondary
Public: 29 districts, 231 schools,
157,327 pupils
Pupil/Teacher Ratio: 13.30
Dollars per Pupil: $3,746
Average Teacher Salary: $2,194
Effort Index: 0.984
Private: 152 schools, 37,513 pupils
Colleges and Universities
Two-year: 4 private, 3 public; 19,953
students
Four-year and Beyond: 4 private, 3
public; 46,422 students
Degree Options: A
Places Rated Score: 3,121
Places Rated Rank: 50

## Burlington, NC
Elementary and Secondary
Public: 2 districts, 32 schools,
19,624 pupils
Pupil/Teacher Ratio: 15.55
Dollars per Pupil: $2,175
Average Teacher Salary: $1,460
Effort Index: 1.047
Private: 4 schools, 718 pupils
Colleges and Universities
Two-year: 1 public; 2,052 students
Four-year and Beyond: 1 private; 2,625
students
Degree Options: C
Places Rated Score: 2,519
Places Rated Rank: 275

## ★ Burlington, VT
Elementary and Secondary
Public: 20 districts, 51 schools,
21,038 pupils
Pupil/Teacher Ratio: 11.43
Dollars per Pupil: $2,855
Average Teacher Salary: $1,350
Effort Index: 1.575
Private: 13 schools, 2,100 pupils
Colleges and Universities
Two-year: 1 private; 1,605 students
Four-year and Beyond: 3 private, 1
public; 14,104 students
Degree Options: C
Places Rated Score: 3,323
Places Rated Rank: 23

## Canton, OH
Elementary and Secondary
Public: 20 districts, 139 schools,
76,607 pupils
Pupil/Teacher Ratio: 17.09
Dollars per Pupil: $2,185
Average Teacher Salary: $1,669
Effort Index: 1.119
Private: 29 schools, 8,475 pupils
Colleges and Universities
Two-year: 2 public; 4,868 students
Four-year and Beyond: 3 private; 3,003
students
Degree Options: B
Places Rated Score: 2,754
Places Rated Rank: 181

## Casper, WY
Elementary and Secondary
Public: 1 district, 34 schools,
14,002 pupils
Pupil/Teacher Ratio: 14.51
Dollars per Pupil: $4,870
Average Teacher Salary: $2,243
Effort Index: 0.911
Private: 4 schools, 843 pupils
Colleges and Universities
Two-year: 1 public; 3,475 students
Four-year and Beyond: None
Degree Options: C
Places Rated Score: 2,453
Places Rated Rank: 292

## Cedar Rapids, IA
Elementary and Secondary
Public: 11 districts, 68 schools,
32,416 pupils
Pupil/Teacher Ratio: 16.14
Dollars per Pupil: $3,675
Average Teacher Salary: $1,774
Effort Index: 1.182
Private: 17 schools, 3,805 pupils
Colleges and Universities
Two-year: 1 public; 5,928 students
Four-year and Beyond: 3 private; 3,468
students
Degree Options: C
Places Rated Score: 2,619
Places Rated Rank: 246

## Champaign–Urbana–Rantoul, IL
Elementary and Secondary
Public: 17 districts, 58 schools,
23,544 pupils
Pupil/Teacher Ratio: 13.86
Dollars per Pupil: $3,193
Average Teacher Salary: $1,736
Effort Index: 1.306
Private: 5 schools, 1,210 pupils

Colleges and Universities
Two-year: 1 public; 8,441 students
Four-year and Beyond: 1 public; 34,914 students
Degree Options: B
Places Rated Score: 3,147
Places Rated Rank: 42

**Charleston, SC**
Elementary and Secondary
Public: 5 districts, 123 schools, 80,551 pupils
Pupil/Teacher Ratio: 14.71
Dollars per Pupil: $2,167
Average Teacher Salary: $1,388
Effort Index: 1.386
Private: 71 schools, 12,892 pupils
Colleges and Universities
Two-year: 1 private, 1 public; 6,468 students
Four-year and Beyond: 1 private, 3 public; 12,673 students
Degree Options: B
Places Rated Score: 3,164
Places Rated Rank: 40

**Charleston, WV**
Elementary and Secondary
Public: 2 districts, 140 schools, 48,709 pupils
Pupil/Teacher Ratio: 13.82
Dollars per Pupil: $2,483
Average Teacher Salary: $1,134
Effort Index: 1.300
Private: 18 schools, 2,383 pupils
Colleges and Universities
Two-year: None
Four-year and Beyond: 1 private, 2 public; 9,555 students
Degree Options: C
Places Rated Score: 2,894
Places Rated Rank: 129

**Charlotte–Gastonia–Rock Hill, NC–SC**
Elementary and Secondary
Public: 14 districts, 307 schools, 185,578 pupils
Pupil/Teacher Ratio: 14.68
Dollars per Pupil: $2,306
Average Teacher Salary: $1,475
Effort Index: 1.001
Private: 60 schools, 14,195 pupils
Colleges and Universities
Two-year: 2 private, 4 public; 26,761 students
Four-year and Beyond: 10 private, 2 public; 24,951 students
Degree Options: A
Places Rated Score: 3,031
Places Rated Rank: 69

**Charlottesville, VA**
Elementary and Secondary
Public: 4 districts, 43 schools, 17,734 pupils
Pupil/Teacher Ratio: 11.15
Dollars per Pupil: $2,695
Average Teacher Salary: $1,214
Effort Index: 1.383
Private: 18 schools, 2,600 pupils
Colleges and Universities
Two-year: 1 public; 3,348 students
Four-year and Beyond: 1 public; 17,118 students
Degree Options: B
Places Rated Score: 3,489
Places Rated Rank: 12

**Chattanooga, TN–GA**
Elementary and Secondary
Public: 9 districts, 156 schools, 75,934 pupils
Pupil/Teacher Ratio: 17.25
Dollars per Pupil: $1,763
Average Teacher Salary: $1,550
Effort Index: 0.788
Private: 45 schools, 9,931 pupils
Colleges and Universities
Two-year: 2 private, 1 public; 6,110 students
Four-year and Beyond: 3 private, 1 public; 13,087 students
Degree Options: B
Places Rated Score: 2,415
Places Rated Rank: 301

★ **Chicago, IL**
Elementary and Secondary
Public: 201 districts, 1,456 schools, 926,573 pupils
Pupil/Teacher Ratio: 16.21
Dollars per Pupil: $3,242
Average Teacher Salary: $1,995
Effort Index: 1.053
Private: 724 schools, 239,512 pupils
Colleges and Universities
Two-year: 4 private, 18 public; 181,436 students
Four-year and Beyond: 34 private, 3 public; 151,725 students
Degree Options: AAA
Places Rated Score: 3,486
Places Rated Rank: 13

**Chico, CA**
Elementary and Secondary
Public: 15 districts, 56 schools, 23,173 pupils
Pupil/Teacher Ratio: 14.18
Dollars per Pupil: $3,600
Average Teacher Salary: $1,986
Effort Index: 1.310
Private: 21 schools, 1,843 pupils
Colleges and Universities
Two-year: 1 public; 8,402 students
Four-year and Beyond: 1 public; 14,289 students
Degree Options: B
Places Rated Score: 3,126
Places Rated Rank: 49

**Cincinnati, OH–KY–IN**
Elementary and Secondary
Public: 59 districts, 394 schools, 233,481 pupils
Pupil/Teacher Ratio: 16.93
Dollars per Pupil: $2,456
Average Teacher Salary: $1,899
Effort Index: 1.025
Private: 174 schools, 55,195 pupils
Colleges and Universities
Two-year: 2 private, 3 public; 12,924 students
Four-year and Beyond: 7 private, 2 public; 53,468 students
Degree Options: A
Places Rated Score: 2,918
Places Rated Rank: 116

**Clarksville–Hopkinsville, TN–KY**
Elementary and Secondary
Public: 2 districts, 37 schools, 24,039 pupils
Pupil/Teacher Ratio: 15.93
Dollars per Pupil: $1,620

Average Teacher Salary: $1,536
Effort Index: 0.955
Private: 13 schools, 4,384 pupils
Colleges and Universities
Two-year: 1 public; 1,089 students
Four-year and Beyond: 1 public; 3,892 students
Degree Options: B
Places Rated Score: 2,654
Places Rated Rank: 225

**Cleveland, OH**
Elementary and Secondary
Public: 58 districts, 494 schools, 285,993 pupils
Pupil/Teacher Ratio: 16.10
Dollars per Pupil: $3,386
Average Teacher Salary: $1,890
Effort Index: 1.033
Private: 192 schools, 77,384 pupils
Colleges and Universities
Two-year: 3 private, 2 public; 66,614 students
Four-year and Beyond: 11 private, 1 public; 40,875 students
Degree Options: A
Places Rated Score: 2,972
Places Rated Rank: 97

**Colorado Springs, CO**
Elementary and Secondary
Public: 15 districts, 116 schools, 61,116 pupils
Pupil/Teacher Ratio: 15.52
Dollars per Pupil: $2,608
Average Teacher Salary: $1,615
Effort Index: 1.030
Private: 19 schools, 3,883 pupils
Colleges and Universities
Two-year: 2 private, 1 public; 7,079 students
Four-year and Beyond: 2 private, 1 public; 7,851 students
Degree Options: B
Places Rated Score: 2,754
Places Rated Rank: 181

**Columbia, MO**
Elementary and Secondary
Public: 6 districts, 33 schools, 14,520 pupils
Pupil/Teacher Ratio: 15.17
Dollars per Pupil: $2,136
Average Teacher Salary: $1,447
Effort Index: 0.880
Private: 11 schools, 930 pupils
Colleges and Universities
Two-year: None
Four-year and Beyond: 2 private, 1 public; 28,416 students
Degree Options: C
Places Rated Score: 2,377
Places Rated Rank: 310

**Columbia, SC**
Elementary and Secondary
Public: 7 districts, 114 schools, 75,648 pupils
Pupil/Teacher Ratio: 14.43
Dollars per Pupil: $2,367
Average Teacher Salary: $1,455
Effort Index: 1.110
Private: 60 schools, 8,637 pupils
Colleges and Universities
Two-year: 1 private, 1 public; 6,582 students

Four-year and Beyond: 4 private, 1 public; 28,358 students
Degree Options: B
Places Rated Score: 2,908
Places Rated Rank: 120

## Columbus, GA–AL
Elementary and Secondary
Public: 5 districts, 85 schools, 41,771 pupils
Pupil/Teacher Ratio: 14.45
Dollars per Pupil: $2,022
Average Teacher Salary: $1,458
Effort Index: 0.869
Private: 21 schools, 2,928 pupils
Colleges and Universities
Two-year: 2 private, 1 public; 2,412 students
Four-year and Beyond: 1 public; 4,245 students
Degree Options: B
Places Rated Score: 2,665
Places Rated Rank: 224

## Columbus, OH
Elementary and Secondary
Public: 54 districts, 423 schools, 225,330 pupils
Pupil/Teacher Ratio: 16.33
Dollars per Pupil: $2,406
Average Teacher Salary: $1,904
Effort Index: 1.002
Private: 79 schools, 21,892 pupils
Colleges and Universities
Two-year: 3 public; 11,990 students
Four-year and Beyond: 11 private, 2 public; 73,210 students
Degree Options: A
Places Rated Score: 2,928
Places Rated Rank: 111

## Corpus Christi, TX
Elementary and Secondary
Public: 20 districts, 133 schools, 71,194 pupils
Pupil/Teacher Ratio: 13.03
Dollars per Pupil: $2,679
Average Teacher Salary: $1,259
Effort Index: 0.930
Private: 37 schools, 6,841 pupils
Colleges and Universities
Two-year: 1 public; 8,620 students
Four-year and Beyond: 1 public; 3,251 students
Degree Options: B
Places Rated Score: 2,840
Places Rated Rank: 153

## ★ Cumberland, MD–WV
Elementary and Secondary
Public: 2 districts, 45 schools, 18,798 pupils
Pupil/Teacher Ratio: 13.58
Dollars per Pupil: $3,013
Average Teacher Salary: $1,685
Effort Index: 1.667
Private: 9 schools, 1,832 pupils
Colleges and Universities
Two-year: 2 public; 3,097 students
Four-year and Beyond: 1 public; 3,654 students
Degree Options: B
Places Rated Score: 3,363
Places Rated Rank: 19

## Dallas, TX
Elementary and Secondary
Public: 60 districts, 602 schools, 378,453 pupils
Pupil/Teacher Ratio: 14.16
Dollars per Pupil: $2,327
Average Teacher Salary: $1,471
Effort Index: 0.951
Private: 140 schools, 33,575 pupils
Colleges and Universities
Two-year: 2 private, 7 public; 51,164 students
Four-year and Beyond: 10 private, 3 public; 50,620 students
Degree Options: AA
Places Rated Score: 3,269
Places Rated Rank: 29

## Danbury, CT
Elementary and Secondary
Public: 9 districts, 48 schools, 31,451 pupils
Pupil/Teacher Ratio: 12.10
Dollars per Pupil: $3,139
Average Teacher Salary: $1,990
Effort Index: 1.279
Private: 12 schools, 3,327 pupils
Colleges and Universities
Two-year: None
Four-year and Beyond: 1 public; 5,996 students
Degree Options: C
Places Rated Score: 3,029
Places Rated Rank: 70

## Danville, VA
Elementary and Secondary
Public: 2 districts, 40 schools, 21,290 pupils
Pupil/Teacher Ratio: 13.74
Dollars per Pupil: $1,813
Average Teacher Salary: $1,485
Effort Index: 1.342
Private: 9 schools, 2,352 pupils
Colleges and Universities
Two-year: 1 public; 2,377 students
Four-year and Beyond: 1 private; 916 students
Degree Options: C
Places Rated Score: 2,943
Places Rated Rank: 105

## Davenport–Rock Island–Moline, IA–IL
Elementary and Secondary
Public: 23 districts, 150 schools, 72,616 pupils
Pupil/Teacher Ratio: 16.78
Dollars per Pupil: $2,482
Average Teacher Salary: $1,923
Effort Index: 1.627
Private: 16 schools, 4,300 pupils
Colleges and Universities
Two-year: 3 public; 10,659 students
Four-year and Beyond: 3 private; 5,470 students
Degree Options: C
Places Rated Score: 2,901
Places Rated Rank: 125

## Dayton–Springfield, OH
Elementary and Secondary
Public: 43 districts, 284 schools, 174,254 pupils
Pupil/Teacher Ratio: 15.88
Dollars per Pupil: $2,677

Average Teacher Salary: $1,823
Effort Index: 1.070
Private: 60 schools, 18,529 pupils
Colleges and Universities
Two-year: 2 private, 3 public; 24,998 students
Four-year and Beyond: 6 private, 1 public; 21,763 students
Degree Options: B
Places Rated Score: 2,772
Places Rated Rank: 173

## Daytona Beach, FL
Elementary and Secondary
Public: 1 district, 56 schools, 36,076 pupils
Pupil/Teacher Ratio: 16.03
Dollars per Pupil: $3,314
Average Teacher Salary: $1,487
Effort Index: 1.169
Private: 23 schools, 4,556 pupils
Colleges and Universities
Two-year: 1 public; 7,793 students
Four-year and Beyond: 2 private; 4,534 students
Degree Options: C
Places Rated Score: 2,612
Places Rated Rank: 251

## Decatur, IL
Elementary and Secondary
Public: 8 districts, 57 schools, 23,249 pupils
Pupil/Teacher Ratio: 15.14
Dollars per Pupil: $2,370
Average Teacher Salary: $1,945
Effort Index: 1.184
Private: 14 schools, 3,410 pupils
Colleges and Universities
Two-year: 1 public; 3,313 students
Four-year and Beyond: 1 private; 1,547 students
Degree Options: C
Places Rated Score: 2,683
Places Rated Rank: 219

## Denver, CO
Elementary and Secondary
Public: 17 districts, 448 schools, 259,097 pupils
Pupil/Teacher Ratio: 15.42
Dollars per Pupil: $3,035
Average Teacher Salary: $1,849
Effort Index: 0.914
Private: 124 schools, 25,799 pupils
Colleges and Universities
Two-year: 1 private, 3 public; 22,551 students
Four-year and Beyond: 8 private, 4 public; 43,297 students
Degree Options: AA
Places Rated Score: 3,145
Places Rated Rank: 43

## Des Moines, IA
Elementary and Secondary
Public: 22 districts, 159 schools, 66,749 pupils
Pupil/Teacher Ratio: 14.13
Dollars per Pupil: $2,928
Average Teacher Salary: $1,652
Effort Index: 1.043
Private: 25 schools, 5,900 pupils
Colleges and Universities
Two-year: 2 private, 1 public; 8,742 students

Four-year and Beyond: 6 private; 10,095 students
Degree Options: C
Places Rated Score: 2,613
Places Rated Rank: 250

**Detroit, MI**
Elementary and Secondary
Public: 111 districts, 1,288 schools, 827,764 pupils
  Pupil/Teacher Ratio: 18.22
  Dollars per Pupil: $3,236
  Average Teacher Salary: $2,609
  Effort Index: 0.984
Private: 410 schools, 118,345 pupils
Colleges and Universities
Two-year: 2 private, 8 public; 110,220 students
Four-year and Beyond: 14 private, 3 public; 74,030 students
Degree Options: AA
Places Rated Score: 3,064
Places Rated Rank: 59

**Dothan, AL**
Elementary and Secondary
Public: 5 districts, 41 schools, 26,430 pupils
  Pupil/Teacher Ratio: 19.35
  Dollars per Pupil: $1,505
  Average Teacher Salary: $1,450
  Effort Index: 0.699
Private: 8 schools, 2,673 pupils
Colleges and Universities
Two-year: 1 public; 1,971 students
Four-year and Beyond: 1 public; 1,570 students
Degree Options: B
Places Rated Score: 2,230
Places Rated Rank: 320

**Dubuque, IA**
Elementary and Secondary
Public: 2 districts, 30 schools, 14,798 pupils
  Pupil/Teacher Ratio: 16.05
  Dollars per Pupil: $2,800
  Average Teacher Salary: $1,804
  Effort Index: 1.259
Private: 24 schools, 8,079 pupils
Colleges and Universities
Two-year: None
Four-year and Beyond: 4 private; 4,318 students
Degree Options: C
Places Rated Score: 2,701
Places Rated Rank: 211

**Duluth, MN–WI**
Elementary and Secondary
Public: 21 districts, 110 schools, 45,894 pupils
  Pupil/Teacher Ratio: 15.53
  Dollars per Pupil: $3,438
  Average Teacher Salary: $1,943
  Effort Index: 0.895
Private: 19 schools, 2,747 pupils
Colleges and Universities
Two-year: 1 public; 3,724 students
Four-year and Beyond: 1 private, 2 public; 14,208 students
Degree Options: B
Places Rated Score: 2,619
Places Rated Rank: 246

**East St. Louis–Belleville, IL**
Elementary and Secondary
Public: 39 districts, 123 schools, 56,511 pupils
  Pupil/Teacher Ratio: 17.13
  Dollars per Pupil: $2,801
  Average Teacher Salary: $1,888
  Effort Index: 1.247
Private: 44 schools, 8,549 pupils
Colleges and Universities
Two-year: 2 public; 11,930 students
Four-year and Beyond: 1 private; 750 students
Degree Options: C
Places Rated Score: 2,630
Places Rated Rank: 237

**Eau Claire, WI**
Elementary and Secondary
Public: 11 districts, 54 schools, 21,198 pupils
  Pupil/Teacher Ratio: 15.25
  Dollars per Pupil: $3,417
  Average Teacher Salary: $1,675
  Effort Index: 1.219
Private: 28 schools, 3,847 pupils
Colleges and Universities
Two-year: 1 public; 3,146 students
Four-year and Beyond: 1 public; 10,883 students
Degree Options: B
Places Rated Score: 2,960
Places Rated Rank: 101

**El Paso, TX**
Elementary and Secondary
Public: 9 districts, 135 schools, 121,403 pupils
  Pupil/Teacher Ratio: 16.40
  Dollars per Pupil: $1,845
  Average Teacher Salary: $1,496
  Effort Index: 0.807
Private: 29 schools, 6,837 pupils
Colleges and Universities
Two-year: 1 public; 11,206 students
Four-year and Beyond: 1 public; 15,129 students
Degree Options: B
Places Rated Score: 2,479
Places Rated Rank: 286

**Elkhart–Goshen, IN**
Elementary and Secondary
Public: 7 districts, 58 schools, 26,780 pupils
  Pupil/Teacher Ratio: 17.19
  Dollars per Pupil: $2,276
  Average Teacher Salary: $1,653
  Effort Index: 1.157
Private: 18 schools, 2,534 pupils
Colleges and Universities
Two-year: None
Four-year and Beyond: 2 private; 1,113 students
Degree Options: C
Places Rated Score: 2,537
Places Rated Rank: 269

**Elmira, NY**
Elementary and Secondary
Public: 3 districts, 25 schools, 15,477 pupils
  Pupil/Teacher Ratio: 11.89
  Dollars per Pupil: $3,440
  Average Teacher Salary: $1,865
  Effort Index: 1.228
Private: 11 schools, 2,154 pupils

Colleges and Universities
Two-year: None
Four-year and Beyond: 1 private; 2,548 students
Degree Options: C
Places Rated Score: 3,000
Places Rated Rank: 86

**Enid, OK**
Elementary and Secondary
Public: 9 districts, 37 schools, 11,966 pupils
  Pupil/Teacher Ratio: 13.18
  Dollars per Pupil: $2,273
  Average Teacher Salary: $1,495
  Effort Index: 1.117
Private: 3 schools, 494 pupils
Colleges and Universities
Two-year: None
Four-year and Beyond: 1 private; 1,132 students
Degree Options: C
Places Rated Score: 2,764
Places Rated Rank: 177

**Erie, PA**
Elementary and Secondary
Public: 13 districts, 78 schools, 45,548 pupils
  Pupil/Teacher Ratio: 15.88
  Dollars per Pupil: $2,514
  Average Teacher Salary: $1,684
  Effort Index: 1.189
Private: 48 schools, 13,222 pupils
Colleges and Universities
Two-year: 2 private; 592 students
Four-year and Beyond: 3 private, 2 public; 13,849 students
Degree Options: C
Places Rated Score: 2,641
Places Rated Rank: 235

**Eugene–Springfield, OR**
Elementary and Secondary
Public: 16 districts, 112 schools, 44,088 pupils
  Pupil/Teacher Ratio: 15.26
  Dollars per Pupil: $4,060
  Average Teacher Salary: $1,900
  Effort Index: 1.377
Private: 26 schools, 2,921 pupils
Colleges and Universities
Two-year: 1 public; 7,748 students
Four-year and Beyond: 2 private, 1 public; 15,766 students
Degree Options: B
Places Rated Score: 3,118
Places Rated Rank: 51

**Evansville, IN–KY**
Elementary and Secondary
Public: 6 districts, 77 schools, 45,706 pupils
  Pupil/Teacher Ratio: 17.39
  Dollars per Pupil: $2,288
  Average Teacher Salary: $1,816
  Effort Index: 1.177
Private: 29 schools, 6,419 pupils
Colleges and Universities
Two-year: 1 private, 2 public; 3,086 students
Four-year and Beyond: 1 private, 1 public; 8,425 students
Degree Options: B
Places Rated Score: 2,797
Places Rated Rank: 162

## Fall River, MA–RI
Elementary and Secondary
  Public: 6 districts, 61 schools,
  24,503 pupils
    Pupil/Teacher Ratio: 15.79
    Dollars per Pupil: $2,117
    Average Teacher Salary: $1,662
    Effort Index: 0.981
  Private: 20 schools, 4,434 pupils
Colleges and Universities
  Two-year: 1 public; 4,851 students
  Four-year and Beyond: None
  Degree Options: C
Places Rated Score: 2,439
Places Rated Rank: 295

## Fargo–Moorhead, ND–MN
Elementary and Secondary
  Public: 17 districts, 58 schools,
  23,505 pupils
    Pupil/Teacher Ratio: 15.31
    Dollars per Pupil: $2,840
    Average Teacher Salary: $2,153
    Effort Index: 1.019
  Private: 13 schools, 2,556 pupils
Colleges and Universities
  Two-year: None
  Four-year and Beyond: 1 private, 2
  public; 19,119 students
  Degree Options: C
Places Rated Score: 2,506
Places Rated Rank: 277

## Fayetteville, NC
Elementary and Secondary
  Public: 3 districts, 80 schools,
  48,518 pupils
    Pupil/Teacher Ratio: 15.61
    Dollars per Pupil: $2,152
    Average Teacher Salary: $1,408
    Effort Index: 1.332
  Private: 9 schools, 1,858 pupils
Colleges and Universities
  Two-year: 1 private, 1 public; 6,172
  students
  Four-year and Beyond: 1 private, 1
  public; 3,220 students
  Degree Options: B
Places Rated Score: 3,051
Places Rated Rank: 64

## Fayetteville–Springdale, AR
Elementary and Secondary
  Public: 9 districts, 40 schools,
  17,834 pupils
    Pupil/Teacher Ratio: 17.50
    Dollars per Pupil: $1,891
    Average Teacher Salary: $1,280
    Effort Index: 0.970
  Private: 4 schools, 674 pupils
Colleges and Universities
  Two-year: None
  Four-year and Beyond: 1 public; 16,052
  students
  Degree Options: C
Places Rated Score: 2,334
Places Rated Rank: 314

## Fitchburg–Leominster, MA
Elementary and Secondary
  Public: 5 districts, 24 schools,
  12,985 pupils
    Pupil/Teacher Ratio: 13.06
    Dollars per Pupil: $2,524
    Average Teacher Salary: $1,616
    Effort Index: 1.141
  Private: 13 schools, 3,436 pupils

Colleges and Universities
  Two-year: None
  Four-year and Beyond: 1 public; 6,609
  students
  Degree Options: C
Places Rated Score: 2,799
Places Rated Rank: 161

## Flint, MI
Elementary and Secondary
  Public: 21 districts, 161 schools,
  97,060 pupils
    Pupil/Teacher Ratio: 18.74
    Dollars per Pupil: $3,098
    Average Teacher Salary: $2,474
    Effort Index: 0.956
  Private: 30 schools, 7,498 pupils
Colleges and Universities
  Two-year: 1 private, 1 public; 12,627
  students
  Four-year and Beyond: 1 private, 1
  public; 7,458 students
  Degree Options: B
Places Rated Score: 2,511
Places Rated Rank: 276

## Florence, AL
Elementary and Secondary
  Public: 6 districts, 54 schools,
  24,617 pupils
    Pupil/Teacher Ratio: 15.82
    Dollars per Pupil: $1,959
    Average Teacher Salary: $1,335
    Effort Index: 0.971
  Private: 4 schools, 1,181 pupils
Colleges and Universities
  Two-year: None
  Four-year and Beyond: 1 private, 1
  public; 5,395 students
  Degree Options: C
Places Rated Score: 2,427
Places Rated Rank: 299

## Florence, SC
Elementary and Secondary
  Public: 5 districts, 42 schools,
  23,523 pupils
    Pupil/Teacher Ratio: 14.40
    Dollars per Pupil: $1,905
    Average Teacher Salary: $1,205
    Effort Index: 1.309
  Private: 20 schools, 2,765 pupils
Colleges and Universities
  Two-year: 1 public; 2,324 students
  Four-year and Beyond: 1 public; 2,911
  students
  Degree Options: B
Places Rated Score: 3,109
Places Rated Rank: 53

## Fort Collins–Loveland, CO
Elementary and Secondary
  Public: 3 districts, 62 schools,
  26,250 pupils
    Pupil/Teacher Ratio: 15.11
    Dollars per Pupil: $2,768
    Average Teacher Salary: $1,521
    Effort Index: 0.912
  Private: 10 schools, 1,396 pupils
Colleges and Universities
  Two-year: None
  Four-year and Beyond: 1 public; 18,909
  students
  Degree Options: C
Places Rated Score: 2,413
Places Rated Rank: 303

## Fort Lauderdale–Hollywood–Pompano Beach, FL
Elementary and Secondary
  Public: 1 district, 157 schools,
  127,096 pupils
    Pupil/Teacher Ratio: 13.67
    Dollars per Pupil: $3,116
    Average Teacher Salary: $1,416
    Effort Index: 1.128
  Private: 119 schools, 30,735 pupils
Colleges and Universities
  Two-year: 1 private, 1 public; 23,736
  students
  Four-year and Beyond: 2 private; 6,498
  students
  Degree Options: C
Places Rated Score: 2,734
Places Rated Rank: 191

## Fort Myers, FL
Elementary and Secondary
  Public: 1 district, 46 schools,
  30,800 pupils
    Pupil/Teacher Ratio: 13.19
    Dollars per Pupil: $3,183
    Average Teacher Salary: $1,382
    Effort Index: 1.083
  Private: 17 schools, 4,155 pupils
Colleges and Universities
  Two-year: 1 public; 5,647 students
  Four-year and Beyond: None
  Degree Options: C
Places Rated Score: 2,729
Places Rated Rank: 193

## Fort Pierce, FL
Elementary and Secondary
  Public: 2 districts, 31 schools,
  23,513 pupils
    Pupil/Teacher Ratio: 13.11
    Dollars per Pupil: $3,670
    Average Teacher Salary: $1,514
    Effort Index: 1.642
  Private: 21 schools, 3,817 pupils
Colleges and Universities
  Two-year: 1 public; 5,894 students
  Four-year and Beyond: None
  Degree Options: C
Places Rated Score: 3,154
Places Rated Rank: 41

## Fort Smith, AR–OK
Elementary and Secondary
  Public: 24 districts, 83 schools,
  30,773 pupils
    Pupil/Teacher Ratio: 14.25
    Dollars per Pupil: $1,922
    Average Teacher Salary: $1,376
    Effort Index: 1.366
  Private: 9 schools, 1,460 pupils
Colleges and Universities
  Two-year: 1 private, 1 public; 4,218
  students
  Four-year and Beyond: None
  Degree Options: C
Places Rated Score: 2,927
Places Rated Rank: 112

## Fort Walton Beach, FL
Elementary and Secondary
  Public: 1 district, 35 schools,
  23,413 pupils
    Pupil/Teacher Ratio: 14.01
    Dollars per Pupil: $2,558
    Average Teacher Salary: $1,215
    Effort Index: 1.230
  Private: 4 schools, 688 pupils

Colleges and Universities
Two-year: 1 public; 3,638 students
Four-year and Beyond: None
Degree Options: C
Places Rated Score: 2,809
Places Rated Rank: 157

## Fort Wayne, IN

Elementary and Secondary
Public: 20 districts, 108 schools, 62,034 pupils
Pupil/Teacher Ratio: 17.89
Dollars per Pupil: $2,382
Average Teacher Salary: $1,796
Effort Index: 1.177
Private: 57 schools, 14,576 pupils
Colleges and Universities
Two-year: 2 private, 1 public; 5,072 students
Four-year and Beyond: 4 private, 1 public; 12,953 students
Degree Options: B
Places Rated Score: 2,772
Places Rated Rank: 173

## Fort Worth–Arlington, TX

Elementary and Secondary
Public: 36 districts, 313 schools, 189,145 pupils
Pupil/Teacher Ratio: 15.09
Dollars per Pupil: $2,300
Average Teacher Salary: $1,631
Effort Index: 0.875
Private: 57 schools, 12,362 pupils
Colleges and Universities
Two-year: 3 private, 1 public; 28,155 students
Four-year and Beyond: 5 private, 1 public; 35,195 students
Degree Options: B
Places Rated Score: 2,627
Places Rated Rank: 242

## Fresno, CA

Elementary and Secondary
Public: 47 districts, 221 schools, 107,232 pupils
Pupil/Teacher Ratio: 18.11
Dollars per Pupil: $3,118
Average Teacher Salary: $1,905
Effort Index: 0.822
Private: 36 schools, 6,538 pupils
Colleges and Universities
Two-year: 3 public; 20,115 students
Four-year and Beyond: 3 private, 1 public; 17,503 students
Degree Options: B
Places Rated Score: 2,407
Places Rated Rank: 305

## Gadsden, AL

Elementary and Secondary
Public: 3 districts, 40 schools, 18,850 pupils
Pupil/Teacher Ratio: 19.18
Dollars per Pupil: $1,537
Average Teacher Salary: $1,458
Effort Index: 1.011
Private: 6 schools, 1,187 pupils
Colleges and Universities
Two-year: 1 public; 3,572 students
Four-year and Beyond: None
Degree Options: C
Places Rated Score: 2,299
Places Rated Rank: 317

## Gainesville, FL

Elementary and Secondary
Public: 2 districts, 41 schools, 25,331 pupils
Pupil/Teacher Ratio: 14.96
Dollars per Pupil: $3,239
Average Teacher Salary: $1,652
Effort Index: 1.333
Private: 26 schools, 2,691 pupils
Colleges and Universities
Two-year: 1 public; 7,354 students
Four-year and Beyond: 1 public; 34,252 students
Degree Options: B
Places Rated Score: 3,094
Places Rated Rank: 55

## Galveston–Texas City, TX

Elementary and Secondary
Public: 9 districts, 67 schools, 51,418 pupils
Pupil/Teacher Ratio: 12.36
Dollars per Pupil: $2,906
Average Teacher Salary: $1,621
Effort Index: 0.835
Private: 17 schools, 2,889 pupils
Colleges and Universities
Two-year: 2 public; 4,946 students
Four-year and Beyond: 2 public; 2,245 students
Degree Options: B
Places Rated Score: 2,809
Places Rated Rank: 157

## Gary–Hammond, IN

Elementary and Secondary
Public: 22 districts, 199 schools, 122,245 pupils
Pupil/Teacher Ratio: 17.16
Dollars per Pupil: $2,411
Average Teacher Salary: $1,786
Effort Index: 0.895
Private: 63 schools, 17,609 pupils
Colleges and Universities
Two-year: 1 public; 3,294 students
Four-year and Beyond: 1 private, 2 public; 13,885 students
Degree Options: B
Places Rated Score: 2,526
Places Rated Rank: 273

## Glens Falls, NY

Elementary and Secondary
Public: 20 districts, 46 schools, 23,280 pupils
Pupil/Teacher Ratio: 13.19
Dollars per Pupil: $3,394
Average Teacher Salary: $1,911
Effort Index: 1.028
Private: 5 schools, 953 pupils
Colleges and Universities
Two-year: 1 public; 3,019 students
Four-year and Beyond: None
Degree Options: C
Places Rated Score: 2,674
Places Rated Rank: 221

## Grand Forks, ND

Elementary and Secondary
Public: 8 districts, 27 schools, 10,583 pupils
Pupil/Teacher Ratio: 15.16
Dollars per Pupil: $2,758
Average Teacher Salary: $2,344
Effort Index: 1.224
Private: 4 schools, 614 pupils

Colleges and Universities
Two-year: None
Four-year and Beyond: 1 public; 10,905 students
Degree Options: C
Places Rated Score: 2,721
Places Rated Rank: 201

## Grand Rapids, MI

Elementary and Secondary
Public: 28 districts, 138 schools, 114,119 pupils
Pupil/Teacher Ratio: 17.00
Dollars per Pupil: $2,739
Average Teacher Salary: $1,964 ·
Effort Index: 1.066
Private: 92 schools, 25,337 pupils
Colleges and Universities
Two-year: 1 private, 1 public; 13,718 students
Four-year and Beyond: 8 private, 1 public; 11,286 students
Degree Options: B
Places Rated Score: 2,705
Places Rated Rank: 210

## Great Falls, MT

Elementary and Secondary
Public: 10 districts, 35 schools, 14,446 pupils
Pupil/Teacher Ratio: 14.94
Dollars per Pupil: $2,809
Average Teacher Salary: $1,897
Effort Index: 1.225
Private: 9 schools, 1,039 pupils
Colleges and Universities
Two-year: None
Four-year and Beyond: 1 private; 1,272 students
Degree Options: C
Places Rated Score: 2,737
Places Rated Rank: 189

## Greeley, CO

Elementary and Secondary
Public: 12 districts, 56 schools, 20,679 pupils
Pupil/Teacher Ratio: 14.15
Dollars per Pupil: $3,177
Average Teacher Salary: $1,515
Effort Index: 1.036
Private: 7 schools, 610 pupils
Colleges and Universities
Two-year: 1 public; 5,302 students
Four-year and Beyond: 1 public; 9,671 students
Degree Options: B
Places Rated Score: 2,854
Places Rated Rank: 145

## Green Bay, WI

Elementary and Secondary
Public: 8 districts, 60 schools, 32,192 pupils
Pupil/Teacher Ratio: 15.62
Dollars per Pupil: $3,188
Average Teacher Salary: $1,777
Effort Index: 0.904
Private: 35 schools, 7,863 pupils
Colleges and Universities
Two-year: 1 public; 5,540 students
Four-year and Beyond: 1 private, 1 public; 6,353 students
Degree Options: B
Places Rated Score: 2,622
Places Rated Rank: 245

## Greensboro–Winston-Salem–High Point, NC
Elementary and Secondary
   Public: 12 districts, 270 schools,
   156,244 pupils
      Pupil/Teacher Ratio: 15.03
      Dollars per Pupil: $2,328
      Average Teacher Salary: $1,520
      Effort Index: 1.084
   Private: 11 schools, 13,348 pupils
Colleges and Universities
   Two-year: 4 private, 2 public; 9,575
   students
   Four-year and Beyond: 8 private, 4
   public; 28,372 students
   Degree Options: A
Places Rated Score: 3,090
Places Rated Rank: 56

## Greenville–Spartanburg, SC
Elementary and Secondary
   Public: 9 districts, 196 schools,
   106,414 pupils
      Pupil/Teacher Ratio: 14.54
      Dollars per Pupil: $2,147
      Average Teacher Salary: $1,376
      Effort Index: 1.196
   Private: 83 schools, 12,149 pupils
Colleges and Universities
   Two-year: 4 private, 2 public; 10,515
   students
   Four-year and Beyond: 5 private, 2
   public; 24,430 students
   Degree Options: A
Places Rated Score: 3,236
Places Rated Rank: 32

## Hagerstown, MD
Elementary and Secondary
   Public: 1 district, 45 schools,
   19,306 pupils
      Pupil/Teacher Ratio: 14.09
      Dollars per Pupil: $2,802
      Average Teacher Salary: $1,891
      Effort Index: 1.417
   Private: 12 schools, 2,004 pupils
Colleges and Universities
   Two-year: 1 private, 1 public; 2,772
   students
   Four-year and Beyond: None
   Degree Options: C
Places Rated Score: 2,990
Places Rated Rank: 90

## Hamilton–Middletown, OH
Elementary and Secondary
   Public: 10 districts, 80 schools,
   47,902 pupils
      Pupil/Teacher Ratio: 16.91
      Dollars per Pupil: $2,319
      Average Teacher Salary: $1,619
      Effort Index: 1.103
   Private: 14 schools, 4,232 pupils
Colleges and Universities
   Two-year: 2 public; 3,450 students
   Four-year and Beyond: 1 public; 14,872
   students
   Degree Options: B
Places Rated Score: 2,747
Places Rated Rank: 185

## Harrisburg–Lebanon–Carlisle, PA
Elementary and Secondary
   Public: 29 districts, 185 schools,
   95,696 pupils
      Pupil/Teacher Ratio: 14.43
      Dollars per Pupil: $2,617

      Average Teacher Salary: $1,617
      Effort Index: 1.176
   Private: 65 schools, 11,877 pupils
Colleges and Universities
   Two-year: 2 private, 2 public; 14,709
   students
   Four-year and Beyond: 5 private, 3
   public; 14,234 students
   Degree Options: A
Places Rated Score: 3,224
Places Rated Rank: 35

## ★ Hartford, CT
Elementary and Secondary
   Public: 35 districts, 213 schools,
   112,710 pupils
      Pupil/Teacher Ratio: 11.74
      Dollars per Pupil: $2,994
      Average Teacher Salary: $1,770
      Effort Index: 1.340
   Private: 70 schools, 20,704 pupils
Colleges and Universities
   Two-year: 1 private, 5 public; 16,751
   students
   Four-year and Beyond: 6 private, 3
   public; 54,816 students
   Degree Options: A
Places Rated Score: 3,628
Places Rated Rank: 4

## Hickory, NC
Elementary and Secondary
   Public: 5 districts, 72 schools,
   38,819 pupils
      Pupil/Teacher Ratio: 14.42
      Dollars per Pupil: $2,169
      Average Teacher Salary: $1,456
      Effort Index: 1.177
   Private: 8 schools, 1,247 pupils
Colleges and Universities
   Two-year: 2 public; 4,382 students
   Four-year and Beyond: 1 private; 1,382
   students
   Degree Options: C
Places Rated Score: 2,726
Places Rated Rank: 198

## Honolulu, HI
Elementary and Secondary
   Public: 1 district, 162 schools,
   125,774 pupils
      Pupil/Teacher Ratio: 24.77
      Dollars per Pupil: $2,324
      Average Teacher Salary: $2,003
      Effort Index: 0.892
   Private: 89 schools, 27,024 pupils
Colleges and Universities
   Two-year: 4 public; 18,623 students
   Four-year and Beyond: 4 private, 2
   public; 27,473 students
   Degree Options: A
Places Rated Score: 2,502
Places Rated Rank: 279

## Houma–Thibodaux, LA
Elementary and Secondary
   Public: 2 districts, 71 schools,
   41,404 pupils
      Pupil/Teacher Ratio: 19.27
      Dollars per Pupil: $2,179
      Average Teacher Salary: $1,202
      Effort Index: 0.710
   Private: 17 schools, 5,493 pupils
Colleges and Universities
   Two-year: None

   Four-year and Beyond: 1 public; 7,226
   students
   Degree Options: C
Places Rated Score: 1,995
Places Rated Rank: 327

## Houston, TX
Elementary and Secondary
   Public: 40 districts, 673 schools,
   552,216 pupils
      Pupil/Teacher Ratio: 14.30
      Dollars per Pupil: $2,758
      Average Teacher Salary: $1,557
      Effort Index: 0.963
   Private: 156 schools, 38,435 pupils
Colleges and Universities
   Two-year: 5 public; 50,196 students
   Four-year and Beyond: 7 private, 6
   public; 69,740 students
   Degree Options: AA
Places Rated Score: 3,271
Places Rated Rank: 28

## Huntington–Ashland, WV–KY–OH
Elementary and Secondary
   Public: 15 districts, 164 schools,
   66,523 pupils
      Pupil/Teacher Ratio: 15.84
      Dollars per Pupil: $2,001
      Average Teacher Salary: $1,529
      Effort Index: 1.070
   Private: 14 schools, 1,665 pupils
Colleges and Universities
   Two-year: 1 private; 472 students
   Four-year and Beyond: 1 private, 1
   public; 12,189 students
   Degree Options: C
Places Rated Score: 2,525
Places Rated Rank: 274

## Huntsville, AL
Elementary and Secondary
   Public: 2 districts, 57 schools,
   37,671 pupils
      Pupil/Teacher Ratio: 14.80
      Dollars per Pupil: $1,863
      Average Teacher Salary: $1,395
      Effort Index: 0.736
   Private: 18 schools, 3,953 pupils
Colleges and Universities
   Two-year: None
   Four-year and Beyond: 1 private, 2
   public; 11,503 students
   Degree Options: C
Places Rated Score: 2,257
Places Rated Rank: 318

## Indianapolis, IN
Elementary and Secondary
   Public: 44 districts, 341 schools,
   216,048 pupils
      Pupil/Teacher Ratio: 16.11
      Dollars per Pupil: $2,345
      Average Teacher Salary: $1,826
      Effort Index: 1.001
   Private: 106 schools, 25,506 pupils
Colleges and Universities
   Two-year: 2 private, 1 public; 6,306
   students
   Four-year and Beyond: 6 private, 1
   public; 32,400 students
   Degree Options: B
Places Rated Score: 2,690
Places Rated Rank: 216

## Iowa City, IA
Elementary and Secondary
Public: 4 districts, 27 schools,
10,402 pupils
Pupil/Teacher Ratio: 15.62
Dollars per Pupil: $2,687
Average Teacher Salary: $1,696
Effort Index: 1.374
Private: 4 schools, 354 pupils
Colleges and Universities
Two-year: None
Four-year and Beyond: 1 public; 28,948
students
Degree Options: C
Places Rated Score: 2,842
Places Rated Rank: 152

## Jackson, MI
Elementary and Secondary
Public: 12 districts, 50 schools,
26,640 pupils
Pupil/Teacher Ratio: 18.68
Dollars per Pupil: $2,930
Average Teacher Salary: $2,019
Effort Index: 1.345
Private: 13 schools, 3,784 pupils
Colleges and Universities
Two-year: 1 public; 5,259 students
Four-year and Beyond: 1 private; 975
students
Degree Options: C
Places Rated Score: 2,654
Places Rated Rank: 225

## Jackson, MS
Elementary and Secondary
Public: 8 districts, 104 schools,
59,282 pupils
Pupil/Teacher Ratio: 14.64
Dollars per Pupil: $2,446
Average Teacher Salary: $1,237
Effort Index: 1.097
Private: 42 schools, 13,338 pupils
Colleges and Universities
Two-year: 1 private, 2 public; 9,573
students
Four-year and Beyond: 6 private, 2
public; 14,231 students
Degree Options: A
Places Rated Score: 3,130
Places Rated Rank: 46

## Jacksonville, FL
Elementary and Secondary
Public: 4 districts, 189 schools,
130,710 pupils
Pupil/Teacher Ratio: 13.77
Dollars per Pupil: $2,859
Average Teacher Salary: $1,553
Effort Index: 1.200
Private: 72 schools, 18,607 pupils
Colleges and Universities
Two-year: 1 public; 15,661 students
Four-year and Beyond: 4 private, 1
public; 11,308 students
Degree Options: B
Places Rated Score: 3,048
Places Rated Rank: 65

## Jacksonville, NC
Elementary and Secondary
Public: 2 districts, 31 schools,
17,892 pupils
Pupil/Teacher Ratio: 20.17
Dollars per Pupil: $1,947
Average Teacher Salary: $1,556
Effort Index: 1.396

Private: 5 schools, 1,002 pupils
Colleges and Universities
Two-year: 1 public; 2,744 students
Four-year and Beyond: None
Degree Options: C
Places Rated Score: 2,646
Places Rated Rank: 231

## Janesville–Beloit, WI
Elementary and Secondary
Public: 8 districts, 54 schools,
27,025 pupils
Pupil/Teacher Ratio: 14.96
Dollars per Pupil: $2,781
Average Teacher Salary: $1,680
Effort Index: 1.021
Private: 19 schools, 2,644 pupils
Colleges and Universities
Two-year: 1 public; 2,287 students
Four-year and Beyond: 1 private; 1,081
students
Degree Options: C
Places Rated Score: 2,532
Places Rated Rank: 271

## Jersey City, NJ
Elementary and Secondary
Public: 13 districts, 100 schools,
76,503 pupils
Pupil/Teacher Ratio: 13.34
Dollars per Pupil: $3,041
Average Teacher Salary: $1,863
Effort Index: 0.941
Private: 75 schools, 25,231 pupils
Colleges and Universities
Two-year: None
Four-year and Beyond: 2 private, 1
public; 16,203 students
Degree Options: C
Places Rated Score: 2,574
Places Rated Rank: 259

## Johnson City–Kingsport–Bristol, TN–VA
Elementary and Secondary
Public: 13 districts, 183 schools,
83,043 pupils
Pupil/Teacher Ratio: 15.01
Dollars per Pupil: $1,776
Average Teacher Salary: $1,469
Effort Index: 1.168
Private: 13 schools, 2,159 pupils
Colleges and Universities
Two-year: 2 public; 3,393 students
Four-year and Beyond: 5 private, 1
public; 11,968 students
Degree Options: B
Places Rated Score: 2,925
Places Rated Rank: 114

## Johnstown, PA
Elementary and Secondary
Public: 24 districts, 81 schools,
42,464 pupils
Pupil/Teacher Ratio: 16.13
Dollars per Pupil: $2,435
Average Teacher Salary: $1,562
Effort Index: 1.253
Private: 29 schools, 6,299 pupils
Colleges and Universities
Two-year: 1 private; 541 students
Four-year and Beyond: 1 private, 1
public; 4,792 students
Degree Options: C
Places Rated Score: 2,691
Places Rated Rank: 215

## Joliet, IL
Elementary and Secondary
Public: 42 districts, 139 schools,
70,341 pupils
Pupil/Teacher Ratio: 16.00
Dollars per Pupil: $2,701
Average Teacher Salary: $1,746
Effort Index: 1.173
Private: 43 schools, 9,929 pupils
Colleges and Universities
Two-year: 1 public; 11,078 students
Four-year and Beyond: 2 private, 1
public; 11,243 students
Degree Options: B
Places Rated Score: 2,868
Places Rated Rank: 139

## Joplin, MO
Elementary and Secondary
Public: 12 districts, 67 schools,
23,734 pupils
Pupil/Teacher Ratio: 15.70
Dollars per Pupil: $2,077
Average Teacher Salary: $1,386
Effort Index: 1.409
Private: 10 schools, 1,236 pupils
Colleges and Universities
Two-year: None
Four-year and Beyond: 1 private, 1
public; 5,105 students
Degree Options: C
Places Rated Score: 2,871
Places Rated Rank: 137

## Kalamazoo, MI
Elementary and Secondary
Public: 9 districts, 70 schools,
34,564 pupils
Pupil/Teacher Ratio: 17.83
Dollars per Pupil: $3,169
Average Teacher Salary: $2,126
Effort Index: 1.298
Private: 20 schools, 4,365 pupils
Colleges and Universities
Two-year: 1 public; 7,895 students
Four-year and Beyond: 2 private, 1
public; 22,385 students
Degree Options: B
Places Rated Score: 2,896
Places Rated Rank: 128

## Kankakee, IL
Elementary and Secondary
Public: 13 districts, 45 schools,
18,713 pupils
Pupil/Teacher Ratio: 16.52
Dollars per Pupil: $2,742
Average Teacher Salary: $1,745
Effort Index: 1.440
Private: 12 schools, 2,724 pupils
Colleges and Universities
Two-year: 1 public; 3,589 students
Four-year and Beyond: 1 private; 1,907
students
Degree Options: C
Places Rated Score: 2,855
Places Rated Rank: 144

## Kansas City, KS
Elementary and Secondary
Public: 19 districts, 220 schools,
93,531 pupils
Pupil/Teacher Ratio: 12.91
Dollars per Pupil: $2,812
Average Teacher Salary: $1,596
Effort Index: 1.107
Private: 48 schools, 11,656 pupils

Colleges and Universities
   Two-year: 1 private, 2 public; 12,312
      students
   Four-year and Beyond: 4 private, 1
      public; 3,850 students
   Degree Options: B
Places Rated Score: 3,028
Places Rated Rank: 74

## Kansas City, MO
Elementary and Secondary
   Public: 37 districts, 284 schools,
   151,946 pupils
      Pupil/Teacher Ratio: 14.95
      Dollars per Pupil: $2,459
      Average Teacher Salary: $1,615
      Effort Index: 0.938
   Private: 83 schools, 21,581 pupils
Colleges and Universities
   Two-year: 1 private, 4 public; 15,448
      students
   Four-year and Beyond: 10 private, 1
      public; 21,735 students
   Degree Options: A
Places Rated Score: 2,949
Places Rated Rank: 102

## Kenosha, WI
Elementary and Secondary
   Public: 13 districts, 42 schools,
   21,514 pupils
      Pupil/Teacher Ratio: 14.62
      Dollars per Pupil: $3,633
      Average Teacher Salary: $2,166
      Effort Index: 1.133
   Private: 20 schools, 3,623 pupils
Colleges and Universities
   Two-year: 1 public; 6,938 students
   Four-year and Beyond: 1 private, 1
      public; 7,226 students
   Degree Options: B
Places Rated Score: 2,918
Places Rated Rank: 116

## Killeen–Temple, TX
Elementary and Secondary
   Public: 14 districts, 75 schools,
   38,831 pupils
      Pupil/Teacher Ratio: 12.95
      Dollars per Pupil: $2,745
      Average Teacher Salary: $1,335
      Effort Index: 1.589
   Private: 4 schools, 600 pupils
Colleges and Universities
   Two-year: 2 public; 7,614 students
   Four-year and Beyond: 2 private; 1,636
      students
   Degree Options: C
Places Rated Score: 3,167
Places Rated Rank: 39

## Knoxville, TN
Elementary and Secondary
   Public: 12 districts, 198 schools,
   101,464 pupils
      Pupil/Teacher Ratio: 15.76
      Dollars per Pupil: $1,842
      Average Teacher Salary: $1,396
      Effort Index: 1.052
   Private: 21 schools, 3,792 pupils
Colleges and Universities
   Two-year: 4 private, 1 public; 4,282
      students
   Four-year and Beyond: 4 private, 1
      public; 30,224 students
   Degree Options: B
Places Rated Score: 2,761
Places Rated Rank: 179

## Kokomo, IN
Elementary and Secondary
   Public: 7 districts, 38 schools,
   17,819 pupils
      Pupil/Teacher Ratio: 13.46
      Dollars per Pupil: $2,595
      Average Teacher Salary: $1,703
      Effort Index: 1.031
   Private: 9 schools, 1,311 pupils
Colleges and Universities
   Two-year: 1 public; 1,447 students
   Four-year and Beyond: 1 public; 2,808
      students
   Degree Options: B
Places Rated Score: 2,904
Places Rated Rank: 123

## La Crosse, WI
Elementary and Secondary
   Public: 5 districts, 29 schools,
   13,269 pupils
      Pupil/Teacher Ratio: 16.12
      Dollars per Pupil: $3,654
      Average Teacher Salary: $1,620
      Effort Index: 1.339
   Private: 21 schools, 3,325 pupils
Colleges and Universities
   Two-year: 1 public; 4,868 students
   Four-year and Beyond: 1 private, 1
      public; 9,824 students
   Degree Options: B
Places Rated Score: 3,027
Places Rated Rank: 77

## Lafayette, IN
Elementary and Secondary
   Public: 3 districts, 35 schools,
   17,425 pupils
      Pupil/Teacher Ratio: 16.52
      Dollars per Pupil: $2,359
      Average Teacher Salary: $1,786
      Effort Index: 1.280
   Private: 10 schools, 804 pupils
Colleges and Universities
   Two-year: 1 public; 1,482 students
   Four-year and Beyond: 1 public; 32,635
      students
   Degree Options: B
Places Rated Score: 2,945
Places Rated Rank: 103

## Lafayette, LA
Elementary and Secondary
   Public: 2 districts, 59 schools,
   36,075 pupils
      Pupil/Teacher Ratio: 14.66
      Dollars per Pupil: $1,801
      Average Teacher Salary: $1,625
      Effort Index: 0.774
   Private: 21 schools, 6,164 pupils
Colleges and Universities
   Two-year: None
   Four-year and Beyond: 1 public; 15,702
      students
   Degree Options: C
Places Rated Score: 2,305
Places Rated Rank: 316

## Lake Charles, LA
Elementary and Secondary
   Public: 1 district, 64 schools,
   32,682 pupils
      Pupil/Teacher Ratio: 16.50
      Dollars per Pupil: $2,644
      Average Teacher Salary: $1,589
      Effort Index: 0.920
   Private: 5 schools, 607 pupils

Colleges and Universities
   Two-year: None
   Four-year and Beyond: 1 public; 7,270
      students
   Degree Options: C
Places Rated Score: 2,336
Places Rated Rank: 313

## Lake County, IL
Elementary and Secondary
   Public: 51 districts, 167 schools,
   85,912 pupils
      Pupil/Teacher Ratio: 14.83
      Dollars per Pupil: $2,974
      Average Teacher Salary: $1,768
      Effort Index: 1.087
   Private: 45 schools, 10,988 pupils
Colleges and Universities
   Two-year: 1 public; 12,187 students
   Four-year and Beyond: 8 private; 4,671
      students
   Degree Options: C
Places Rated Score: 2,607
Places Rated Rank: 253

## Lakeland–Winter Haven, FL
Elementary and Secondary
   Public: 1 district, 96 schools,
   58,627 pupils
      Pupil/Teacher Ratio: 12.49
      Dollars per Pupil: $2,575
      Average Teacher Salary: $1,339
      Effort Index: 1.288
   Private: 24 schools, 5,071 pupils
Colleges and Universities
   Two-year: 1 private, 1 public; 5,501
      students
   Four-year and Beyond: 4 private; 5,036
      students
   Degree Options: C
Places Rated Score: 2,998
Places Rated Rank: 87

## Lancaster, PA
Elementary and Secondary
   Public: 17 districts, 125 schools, 58,972
   pupils
      Pupil/Teacher Ratio: 13.78
      Dollars per Pupil: $2,574
      Average Teacher Salary: $1,678
      Effort Index: 1.505
   Private: 103 schools, 10,291 pupils
Colleges and Universities
   Two-year: None
   Four-year and Beyond: 4 private, 1
      public; 11,769 students
   Degree Options: C
Places Rated Score: 3,097
Places Rated Rank: 54

## Lansing–East Lansing, MI
Elementary and Secondary
   Public: 25 districts, 167 schools,
   80,055 pupils
      Pupil/Teacher Ratio: 15.31
      Dollars per Pupil: $3,064
      Average Teacher Salary: $1,978
      Effort Index: 1.154
   Private: 31 schools, 5,542 pupils
Colleges and Universities
   Two-year: 1 public; 19,799 students
   Four-year and Beyond: 3 private, 1
      public; 44,582 students
   Degree Options: B
Places Rated Score: 2,891
Places Rated Rank: 130

## Laredo, TX
Elementary and Secondary
Public: 4 districts, 39 schools,
28,747 pupils
  Pupil/Teacher Ratio: 13.77
  Dollars per Pupil: $2,522
  Average Teacher Salary: $1,277
  Effort Index: 0.979
Private: 9 schools, 2,566 pupils
Colleges and Universities
Two-year: 1 public; 3,546 students
Four-year and Beyond: 1 public; 900
  students
Degree Options: B
Places Rated Score: 2,827
Places Rated Rank: 154

## Las Cruces, NM
Elementary and Secondary
Public: 3 districts, 38 schools,
20,862 pupils
  Pupil/Teacher Ratio: 11.93
  Dollars per Pupil: $2,795
  Average Teacher Salary: $1,496
  Effort Index: 0.968
Private: 9 schools, 792 pupils
Colleges and Universities
Two-year: None
Four-year and Beyond: 1 public; 13,395
  students
Degree Options: C
Places Rated Score: 2,736
Places Rated Rank: 190

## Las Vegas, NV
Elementary and Secondary
Public: 1 district, 117 schools,
89,119 pupils
  Pupil/Teacher Ratio: 19.62
  Dollars per Pupil: $2,362
  Average Teacher Salary: $1,920
  Effort Index: 0.720
Private: 24 schools, 4,935 pupils
Colleges and Universities
Two-year: 1 public; 8,340 students
Four-year and Beyond: 1 public; 11,452
  students
Degree Options: B
Places Rated Score: 2,241
Places Rated Rank: 319

## Lawrence, KS
Elementary and Secondary
Public: 3 districts, 28 schools,
8,659 pupils
  Pupil/Teacher Ratio: 15.80
  Dollars per Pupil: $2,372
  Average Teacher Salary: $1,571
  Effort Index: 0.993
Private: 3 schools, 356 pupils
Colleges and Universities
Two-year: 1 public; 879 students
Four-year and Beyond: 1 private, 1
  public; 25,239 students
Degree Options: B
Places Rated Score: 2,700
Places Rated Rank: 212

## Lawrence–Haverhill, MA–NH
Elementary and Secondary
Public: 22 districts, 102 schools,
49,602 pupils
  Pupil/Teacher Ratio: 14.46
  Dollars per Pupil: $2,707
  Average Teacher Salary: $1,964
  Effort Index: 0.933
Private: 52 schools, 13,163 pupils

Colleges and Universities
Two-year: 1 public; 6,782 students
Four-year and Beyond: 1 private; 3,751
  students
Degree Options: C
Places Rated Score: 2,479
Places Rated Rank: 286

## Lawton, OK
Elementary and Secondary
Public: 13 districts, 62 schools,
22,191 pupils
  Pupil/Teacher Ratio: 14.03
  Dollars per Pupil: $2,100
  Average Teacher Salary: $1,532
  Effort Index: 0.797
Private: 1 school, 157 pupils
Colleges and Universities
Two-year: None
Four-year and Beyond: 1 public; 5,497
  students
Degree Options: C
Places Rated Score: 2,375
Places Rated Rank: 311

## Lewiston–Auburn, ME
Elementary and Secondary
Public: 9 districts, 29 schools,
17,838 pupils
  Pupil/Teacher Ratio: 14.91
  Dollars per Pupil: $1,826
  Average Teacher Salary: $1,288
  Effort Index: 1.180
Private: 11 schools, 1,853 pupils
Colleges and Universities
Two-year: 1 private, 1 public; 610
  students
Four-year and Beyond: 1 private; 1,452
  students
Degree Options: C
Places Rated Score: 2,694
Places Rated Rank: 214

## Lexington–Fayette, KY
Elementary and Secondary
Public: 7 districts, 92 schools,
53,222 pupils
  Pupil/Teacher Ratio: 15.82
  Dollars per Pupil: $1,909
  Average Teacher Salary: $2,275
  Effort Index: 1.155
Private: 25 schools, 4,655 pupils
Colleges and Universities
Two-year: 2 private, 1 public; 22,930
  students
Four-year and Beyond: 5 private, 1
  public; 26,201 students
Degree Options: B
Places Rated Score: 2,861
Places Rated Rank: 142

## Lima, OH
Elementary and Secondary
Public: 16 districts, 63 schools,
30,772 pupils
  Pupil/Teacher Ratio: 17.96
  Dollars per Pupil: $2,221
  Average Teacher Salary: $1,635
  Effort Index: 1.037
Private: 11 schools, 3,450 pupils
Colleges and Universities
Two-year: 1 private, 1 public; 4,023
  students
Four-year and Beyond: 1 private, 1
  public; 1,494 students
Degree Options: B
Places Rated Score: 2,629
Places Rated Rank: 239

## Lincoln, NE
Elementary and Secondary
Public: 5 districts, 57 schools,
28,746 pupils
  Pupil/Teacher Ratio: 15.39
  Dollars per Pupil: $3,091
  Average Teacher Salary: $1,678
  Effort Index: 1.145
Private: 21 schools, 3,949 pupils
Colleges and Universities
Two-year: 1 public; 5,559 students
Four-year and Beyond: 2 private, 1
  public; 28,278 students
Degree Options: B
Places Rated Score: 2,878
Places Rated Rank: 133

## Little Rock–North Little Rock, AR
Elementary and Secondary
Public: 20 districts, 165 schools,
85,435 pupils
  Pupil/Teacher Ratio: 16.08
  Dollars per Pupil: $1,977
  Average Teacher Salary: $1,416
  Effort Index: 1.141
Private: 39 schools, 9,287 pupils
Colleges and Universities
Two-year: 3 private; 1,285 students
Four-year and Beyond: 4 private, 3
  public; 18,666 students
Degree Options: C
Places Rated Score: 2,581
Places Rated Rank: 258

## Longview–Marshall, TX
Elementary and Secondary
Public: 13 districts, 60 schools,
33,581 pupils
  Pupil/Teacher Ratio: 13.09
  Dollars per Pupil: $2,843
  Average Teacher Salary: $1,495
  Effort Index: 1.161
Private: 7 schools, 1,169 pupils
Colleges and Universities
Two-year: 1 public; 4,389 students
Four-year and Beyond: 3 private; 2,558
  students
Degree Options: C
Places Rated Score: 2,816
Places Rated Rank: 155

## Lorain–Elyria, OH
Elementary and Secondary
Public: 16 districts, 95 schools,
54,937 pupils
  Pupil/Teacher Ratio: 17.15
  Dollars per Pupil: $2,456
  Average Teacher Salary: $1,699
  Effort Index: 1.200
Private: 24 schools, 7,553 pupils
Colleges and Universities
Two-year: 1 public; 6,692 students
Four-year and Beyond: 1 private; 2,809
  students
Degree Options: C
Places Rated Score: 2,582
Places Rated Rank: 257

## Los Angeles–Long Beach, CA
Elementary and Secondary
Public: 81 districts, 1,601 schools,
1,237,707 pupils
  Pupil/Teacher Ratio: 18.84
  Dollars per Pupil: $3,259
  Average Teacher Salary: $2,213
  Effort Index: 0.892
Private: 920 schools, 211,540 pupils

Colleges and Universities
  Two-year: 3 private, 22 public; 315,228
  students
  Four-year and Beyond: 43 private, 7
  public; 250,435 students
  Degree Options: AAA
Places Rated Score: 3,195
Places Rated Rank: 37

## Louisville, KY–IN
Elementary and Secondary
  Public: 12 districts, 249 schools,
  206,974 pupils
    Pupil/Teacher Ratio: 16.82
    Dollars per Pupil: $2,114
    Average Teacher Salary: $1,803
    Effort Index: 1.129
  Private: 133 schools, 35,873 pupils
Colleges and Universities
  Two-year: 5 private, 2 public; 7,136
  students
  Four-year and Beyond: 4 private, 2
  public; 30,406 students
  Degree Options: A
Places Rated Score: 3,028
Places Rated Rank: 74

## Lowell, MA–NH
Elementary and Secondary
  Public: 7 districts, 66 schools,
  39,615 pupils
    Pupil/Teacher Ratio: 14.46
    Dollars per Pupil: $2,707
    Average Teacher Salary: $1,964
    Effort Index: 0.933
  Private: 30 schools, 5,597 pupils
Colleges and Universities
  Two-year: None
  Four-year and Beyond: 1 private, 1
  public; 15,548 students
  Degree Options: C
Places Rated Score: 2,479
Places Rated Rank: 286

## Lubbock, TX
Elementary and Secondary
  Public: 8 districts, 74 schools,
  41,306 pupils
    Pupil/Teacher Ratio: 15.91
    Dollars per Pupil: $2,187
    Average Teacher Salary: $1,495
    Effort Index: 1.095
  Private: 11 schools, 2,021 pupils
Colleges and Universities
  Two-year: None
  Four-year and Beyond: 1 private, 2
  public; 24,344 students
  Degree Options: C
Places Rated Score: 2,545
Places Rated Rank: 265

## Lynchburg, VA
Elementary and Secondary
  Public: 3 districts, 47 schools,
  24,706 pupils
    Pupil/Teacher Ratio: 14.64
    Dollars per Pupil: $2,148
    Average Teacher Salary: $1,449
    Effort Index: 1.270
  Private: 10 schools, 2,718 pupils
Colleges and Universities
  Two-year: 1 public; 3,683 students
  Four-year and Beyond: 3 private; 7,220
  students
  Degree Options: C
Places Rated Score: 2,803
Places Rated Rank: 160

## Macon–Warner Robins, GA
Elementary and Secondary
  Public: 5 districts, 86 schools,
  49,020 pupils
    Pupil/Teacher Ratio: 14.64
    Dollars per Pupil: $2,037
    Average Teacher Salary: $1,181
    Effort Index: 0.868
  Private: 22 schools, 6,530 pupils
Colleges and Universities
  Two-year: 1 private, 1 public; 3,176
  students
  Four-year and Beyond: 2 private, 1
  public; 4,685 students
  Degree Options: B
Places Rated Score: 2,651
Places Rated Rank: 229

## Madison, WI
Elementary and Secondary
  Public: 16 districts, 105 schools,
  50,909 pupils
    Pupil/Teacher Ratio: 14.17
    Dollars per Pupil: $3,580
    Average Teacher Salary: $1,775
    Effort Index: 1.230
  Private: 31 schools, 5,102 pupils
Colleges and Universities
  Two-year: 2 private, 1 public; 7,909
  students
  Four-year and Beyond: 1 private, 1
  public; 42,980 students
  Degree Options: B
Places Rated Score: 3,047
Places Rated Rank: 66

## Manchester, NH
Elementary and Secondary
  Public: 13 districts, 37 schools,
  28,804 pupils
    Pupil/Teacher Ratio: 13.98
    Dollars per Pupil: $2,252
    Average Teacher Salary: $1,478
    Effort Index: 1.147
  Private: 21 schools, 4,097 pupils
Colleges and Universities
  Two-year: 1 private, 2 public; 2,692
  students
  Four-year and Beyond: 4 private; 9,399
  students
  Degree Options: C
Places Rated Score: 2,728
Places Rated Rank: 196

## Mansfield, OH
Elementary and Secondary
  Public: 10 districts, 54 schools,
  26,355 pupils
    Pupil/Teacher Ratio: 15.75
    Dollars per Pupil: $2,359
    Average Teacher Salary: $1,591
    Effort Index: 1.161
  Private: 9 schools, 2,335 pupils
Colleges and Universities
  Two-year: 1 public; 1,962 students
  Four-year and Beyond: 1 public; 1,095
  students
  Degree Options: B
Places Rated Score: 2,871
Places Rated Rank: 137

## McAllen–Edinburg–Mission, TX
Elementary and Secondary
  Public: 15 districts, 109 schools,
  82,035 pupils
    Pupil/Teacher Ratio: 12.09
    Dollars per Pupil: $2,089

Average Teacher Salary: $1,375
    Effort Index: 0.893
  Private: 16 schools, 2,720 pupils
Colleges and Universities
  Two-year: None
  Four-year and Beyond: 1 public; 8,347
  students
  Degree Options: C
Places Rated Score: 2,644
Places Rated Rank: 234

## Medford, OR
Elementary and Secondary
  Public: 10 districts, 55 schools,
  23,422 pupils
    Pupil/Teacher Ratio: 14.26
    Dollars per Pupil: $3,124
    Average Teacher Salary: $1,731
    Effort Index: 1.237
  Private: 12 schools, 1,516 pupils
Colleges and Universities
  Two-year: None
  Four-year and Beyond: 1 public; 1,326
  students
  Degree Options: C
Places Rated Score: 2,797
Places Rated Rank: 162

## Melbourne–Titusville–Palm Bay, FL
Elementary and Secondary
  Public: 1 district, 62 schools,
  44,524 pupils
    Pupil/Teacher Ratio: 13.86
    Dollars per Pupil: $3,153
    Average Teacher Salary: $1,454
    Effort Index: 1.223
  Private: 25 schools, 5,276 pupils
Colleges and Universities
  Two-year: 1 private, 1 public; 10,861
  students
  Four-year and Beyond: 1 private; 6,963
  students
  Degree Options: C
Places Rated Score: 2,814
Places Rated Rank: 156

## Memphis, TN–AR–MS
Elementary and Secondary
  Public: 10 districts, 239 schools,
  163,121 pupils
    Pupil/Teacher Ratio: 15.29
    Dollars per Pupil: $1,792
    Average Teacher Salary: $1,269
    Effort Index: 0.815
  Private: 100 schools, 28,963 pupils
Colleges and Universities
  Two-year: 2 private, 2 public; 13,966
  students
  Four-year and Beyond: 8 private, 2
  public; 27,593 students
  Degree Options: A
Places Rated Score: 2,804
Places Rated Rank: 159

## Miami–Hialeah, FL
Elementary and Secondary
  Public: 1 district, 252 schools,
  221,039 pupils
    Pupil/Teacher Ratio: 15.96
    Dollars per Pupil: $3,538
    Average Teacher Salary: $1,790
    Effort Index: 0.932
  Private: 210 schools, 56,915 pupils
Colleges and Universities
  Two-year: 4 private, 1 public; 39,237
  students
  Four-year and Beyond: 5 private, 3
  public; 33,049 students

Degree Options: A
Places Rated Score: 2,879
Places Rated Rank: 132

★ **Middlesex–Somerset–
Hunterdon, NJ**
Elementary and Secondary
Public: 71 districts, 294 schools,
146,784 pupils
Pupil/Teacher Ratio: 11.73
Dollars per Pupil: $4,869
Average Teacher Salary: $2,147
Effort Index: 1.754
Private: 30 schools, 4,556 pupils
Colleges and Universities
Two-year: 2 public; 17,411 students
Four-year and Beyond: 1 private, 1
public; 32,932 students
Degree Options: B
Places Rated Score: 3,539
Places Rated Rank: 8

**Middletown, CT**
Elementary and Secondary
Public: 5 districts, 29 schools,
10,997 pupils
Pupil/Teacher Ratio: 11.74
Dollars per Pupil: $2,994
Average Teacher Salary: $1,770
Effort Index: 1.340
Private: 11 schools, 2,769 pupils
Colleges and Universities
Two-year: 1 public; 2,986 students
Four-year and Beyond: 2 private; 3,158
students
Degree Options: C
Places Rated Score: 3,128
Places Rated Rank: 47

**Midland, TX**
Elementary and Secondary
Public: 2 districts, 28 schools,
17,166 pupils
Pupil/Teacher Ratio: 16.40
Dollars per Pupil: $2,921
Average Teacher Salary: $2,020
Effort Index: 0.994
Private: 4 schools, 1,674 pupils
Colleges and Universities
Two-year: 1 public; 3,346 students
Four-year and Beyond: None
Degree Options: C
Places Rated Score: 2,416
Places Rated Rank: 300

**Milwaukee, WI**
Elementary and Secondary
Public: 54 districts, 404 schools,
221,870 pupils
Pupil/Teacher Ratio: 14.73
Dollars per Pupil: $3,535
Average Teacher Salary: $2,163
Effort Index: 1.017
Private: 260 schools, 58,827 pupils
Colleges and Universities
Two-year: 1 private, 2 public; 28,774
students
Four-year and Beyond: 14 private, 1
public; 47,729 students
Degree Options: A
Places Rated Score: 3,044
Places Rated Rank: 67

**Minneapolis–St. Paul, MN–WI**
Elementary and Secondary
Public: 68 districts, 525 schools,
364,331 pupils
Pupil/Teacher Ratio: 17.20

Dollars per Pupil: $3,213
Average Teacher Salary: $2,095
Effort Index: 0.884
Private: 255 schools, 55,650 pupils
Colleges and Universities
Two-year: 5 private, 7 public; 32,096
students
Four-year and Beyond: 16 private, 2
public; 89,990 students
Degree Options: AA
Places Rated Score: 3,013
Places Rated Rank: 82

**Mobile, AL**
Elementary and Secondary
Public: 3 districts, 109 schools,
83,245 pupils
Pupil/Teacher Ratio: 15.37
Dollars per Pupil: $1,606
Average Teacher Salary: $1,063
Effort Index: 1.045
Private: 61 schools, 16,727 pupils
Colleges and Universities
Two-year: 2 public; 2,926 students
Four-year and Beyond: 3 private, 1
public; 11,448 students
Degree Options: B
Places Rated Score: 2,779
Places Rated Rank: 169

**Modesto, CA**
Elementary and Secondary
Public: 27 districts, 109 schools,
50,288 pupils
Pupil/Teacher Ratio: 15.95
Dollars per Pupil: $3,218
Average Teacher Salary: $1,929
Effort Index: 0.918
Private: 28 schools, 5,161 pupils
Colleges and Universities
Two-year: 1 public; 11,379 students
Four-year and Beyond: 1 public; 4,574
students
Degree Options: B
Places Rated Score: 2,616
Places Rated Rank: 249

**Monmouth–Ocean, NJ**
Elementary and Secondary
Public: 80 districts, 258 schools,
152,890 pupils
Pupil/Teacher Ratio: 13.02
Dollars per Pupil: $3,253
Average Teacher Salary: $2,044
Effort Index: 1.126
Private: 63 schools, 22,803 pupils
Colleges and Universities
Two-year: 2 public; 18,089 students
Four-year and Beyond: 4 private; 6,510
students
Degree Options: C
Places Rated Score: 2,787
Places Rated Rank: 168

**Monroe, LA**
Elementary and Secondary
Public: 2 districts, 53 schools, 28,504
pupils
Pupil/Teacher Ratio: 15.78
Dollars per Pupil: $1,988
Average Teacher Salary: $1,338
Effort Index: 0.995
Private: 12 schools, 3,266 pupils
Colleges and Universities
Two-year: None

Four-year and Beyond: 1 public; 11,075
students
Degree Options: C
Places Rated Score: 2,453
Places Rated Rank: 292

**Montgomery, AL**
Elementary and Secondary
Public: 4 districts, 76 schools,
52,897 pupils
Pupil/Teacher Ratio: 17.16
Dollars per Pupil: $1,561
Average Teacher Salary: $1,205
Effort Index: 1.007
Private: 34 schools, 7,706 pupils
Colleges and Universities
Two-year: None
Four-year and Beyond: 2 private; 2
public; 8,427 students
Degree Options: C
Places Rated Score: 2,388
Places Rated Rank: 308

**Muncie, IN**
Elementary and Secondary
Public: 7 districts, 44 schools,
22,574 pupils
Pupil/Teacher Ratio: 14.94
Dollars per Pupil: $2,183
Average Teacher Salary: $1,602
Effort Index: 1.203
Private: 6 schools, 836 pupils
Colleges and Universities
Two-year: 1 public; 2,194 students
Four-year and Beyond: 1 public; 18,208
students
Degree Options: B
Places Rated Score: 2,965
Places Rated Rank: 100

**Muskegon, MI**
Elementary and Secondary
Public: 12 districts, 70 schools,
30,721 pupils
Pupil/Teacher Ratio: 16.71
Dollars per Pupil: $2,966
Average Teacher Salary: $2,015
Effort Index: 1.225
Private: 18 schools, 3,398 pupils
Colleges and Universities
Two-year: 1 private, 1 public; 6,262
students
Four-year and Beyond: None
Degree Options: C
Places Rated Score: 2,630
Places Rated Rank: 237

**Nashua, NH**
Elementary and Secondary
Public: 7 districts, 33 schools,
19,359 pupils
Pupil/Teacher Ratio: 13.98
Dollars per Pupil: $2,252
Average Teacher Salary: $1,478
Effort Index: 1.147
Private: 21 schools, 4,794 pupils
Colleges and Universities
Two-year: 1 public; 1,160 students
Four-year and Beyond: 2 private; 3,272
students
Degree Options: C
Places Rated Score: 2,728
Places Rated Rank: 196

## Nashville, TN
Elementary and Secondary
Public: 11 districts, 264 schools,
145,834 pupils
  Pupil/Teacher Ratio: 17.20
  Dollars per Pupil: $1,782
  Average Teacher Salary: $1,877
  Effort Index: 0.884
Private: 67 schools, 18,644 pupils
Colleges and Universities
  Two-year: 4 private, 1 public; 7,272
  students
  Four-year and Beyond: 10 private, 1
  public; 24,286 students
  Degree Options: A
Places Rated Score: 2,763
Places Rated Rank: 178

## Nassau–Suffolk, NY
Elementary and Secondary
Public: 128 districts, 672 schools,
393,369 pupils
  Pupil/Teacher Ratio: 13.33
  Dollars per Pupil: $4,637
  Average Teacher Salary: $2,494
  Effort Index: 1.099
Private: 222 schools, 71,016 pupils
Colleges and Universities
  Two-year: 4 private, 5 public; 58,932
  students
  Four-year and Beyond: 11 private, 3
  public; 66,701 students
  Degree Options: A
Places Rated Score: 3,234
Places Rated Rank: 33

## New Bedford, MA
Elementary and Secondary
Public: 8 districts, 35 schools,
25,532 pupils
  Pupil/Teacher Ratio: 15.79
  Dollars per Pupil: $2,117
  Average Teacher Salary: $1,662
  Effort Index: 0.981
Private: 11 schools, 2,443 pupils
Colleges and Universities
  Two-year: None
  Four-year and Beyond: 1 private, 1
  public; 7,007 students
  Degree Options: C
Places Rated Score: 2,439
Places Rated Rank: 295

## New Britain, CT
Elementary and Secondary
Public: 4 districts, 36 schools,
19,490 pupils
  Pupil/Teacher Ratio: 11.74
  Dollars per Pupil: $2,994
  Average Teacher Salary: $1,770
  Effort Index: 1.340
Private: 12 schools, 3,254 pupils
Colleges and Universities
  Two-year: 1 private; 383 students
  Four-year and Beyond: 1 public; 12,487
  students
  Degree Options: C
Places Rated Score: 3,128
Places Rated Rank: 47

## ★ New Haven–Meriden, CT
Elementary and Secondary
Public: 17 districts, 143 schools,
74,912 pupils
  Pupil/Teacher Ratio: 12.84
  Dollars per Pupil: $2,815

Average Teacher Salary: $1,660
  Effort Index: 1.317
Private: 49 schools, 12,552 pupils
Colleges and Universities
  Two-year: 1 private, 2 public; 3,656
  students
  Four-year and Beyond: 5 private, 1
  public; 32,683 students
  Degree Options: A
Places Rated Score: 3,495
Places Rated Rank: 11

## New London–Norwich, CT–RI
Elementary and Secondary
Public: 17 districts, 83 schools,
35,063 pupils
  Pupil/Teacher Ratio: 12.16
  Dollars per Pupil: $2,919
  Average Teacher Salary: $1,507
  Effort Index: 1.543
Private: 14 schools, 4,308 pupils
Colleges and Universities
  Two-year: 1 private, 2 public; 5,159
  students
  Four-year and Beyond: 1 private; 1,933
  students
  Degree Options: C
Places Rated Score: 3,244
Places Rated Rank: 31

## New Orleans, LA
Elementary and Secondary
Public: 6 districts, 299 schools,
195,681 pupils
  Pupil/Teacher Ratio: 14.91
  Dollars per Pupil: $2,664
  Average Teacher Salary: $1,323
  Effort Index: 0.981
Private: 205 schools, 79,407 pupils
Colleges and Universities
  Two-year: 1 private, 2 public; 9,709
  students
  Four-year and Beyond: 9 private, 3
  public; 42,117 students
  Degree Options: A
Places Rated Score: 2,995
Places Rated Rank: 88

## New York, NY
Elementary and Secondary
Public: 105 districts, 1,289 schools,
1,109,700 pupils
  Pupil/Teacher Ratio: 17.46
  Dollars per Pupil: $3,104
  Average Teacher Salary: $2,240
  Effort Index: 0.618
Private: 1,025 schools, 366,038 pupils
Colleges and Universities
  Two-year: 30 private, 8 public; 74,567
  students
  Four-year and Beyond: 95 private, 17
  public; 357,769 students
  Degree Options: AAA
Places Rated Score: 2,984
Places Rated Rank: 92

## ★ Newark, NJ
Elementary and Secondary
Public: 111 districts, 565 schools,
314,362 pupils
  Pupil/Teacher Ratio: 12.06
  Dollars per Pupil: $3,442
  Average Teacher Salary: $1,695
  Effort Index: 1.109
Private: 221 schools, 53,452 pupils
Colleges and Universities

Two-year: 1 private, 2 public; 18,097
  students
  Four-year and Beyond: 10 private, 4
  public; 56,303 students
  Degree Options: A
Places Rated Score: 3,362
Places Rated Rank: 20

## Niagara Falls, NY
Elementary and Secondary
Public: 10 districts, 61 schools,
38,340 pupils
  Pupil/Teacher Ratio: 14.97
  Dollars per Pupil: $3,762
  Average Teacher Salary: $2,251
  Effort Index: 1.028
Private: 29 schools, 5,364 pupils
Colleges and Universities
  Two-year: 1 public; 4,375 students
  Four-year and Beyond: 1 private; 3,825
  students
  Degree Options: C
Places Rated Score: 2,538
Places Rated Rank: 268

## Norfolk–Virginia Beach–Newport News, VA
Elementary and Secondary
Public: 11 districts, 302 schools,
219,181 pupils
  Pupil/Teacher Ratio: 13.41
  Dollars per Pupil: $2,118
  Average Teacher Salary: $1,455
  Effort Index: 0.886
Private: 109 schools, 23,891 pupils
Colleges and Universities
  Two-year: 3 public; 22,578 students
  Four-year and Beyond: 5 private, 4
  public; 39,088 students
  Degree Options: A
Places Rated Score: 3,014
Places Rated Rank: 81

## Norwalk, CT
Elementary and Secondary
Public: 4 districts, 37 schools,
20,699 pupils
  Pupil/Teacher Ratio: 12.10
  Dollars per Pupil: $3,139
  Average Teacher Salary: $1,990
  Effort Index: 1.279
Private: 16 schools, 2,364 pupils
Colleges and Universities
  Two-year: 2 public; 5,458 students
  Four-year and Beyond: 2 private; 65
  students
  Degree Options: C
Places Rated Score: 3,029
Places Rated Rank: 70

## Oakland, CA
Elementary and Secondary
Public: 37 districts, 524 schools,
286,408 pupils
  Pupil/Teacher Ratio: 18.27
  Dollars per Pupil: $3,327
  Average Teacher Salary: $2,081
  Effort Index: 0.818
Private: 243 schools, 42,318 pupils
Colleges and Universities
  Two-year: 1 private, 9 public; 96,895
  students
  Four-year and Beyond: 19 private, 2
  public; 48,920 students
  Degree Options: A
Places Rated Score: 2,646
Places Rated Rank: 231

## Ocala, FL
Elementary and Secondary
Public: 1 district, 32 schools, 22,779 pupils
  Pupil/Teacher Ratio: 13.67
  Dollars per Pupil: $2,862
  Average Teacher Salary: $1,506
  Effort Index: 1.259
Private: 9 schools, 2,456 pupils
Colleges and Universities
  Two-year: 1 public; 3,030 students
  Four-year and Beyond: None
  Degree Options: C
Places Rated Score: 2,864
Places Rated Rank: 141

## Odessa, TX
Elementary and Secondary
Public: 1 district, 33 schools, 25,900 pupils
  Pupil/Teacher Ratio: 14.84
  Dollars per Pupil: $3,063
  Average Teacher Salary: $1,842
  Effort Index: 0.952
Private: 6 schools, 1,313 pupils
Colleges and Universities
  Two-year: 1 public; 4,106 students
  Four-year and Beyond: 3 private, 1 public; 3,658 students
  Degree Options: B
Places Rated Score: 2,721
Places Rated Rank: 201

## Oklahoma City, OK
Elementary and Secondary
Public: 60 districts, 346 schools, 159,822 pupils
  Pupil/Teacher Ratio: 14.92
  Dollars per Pupil: $2,365
  Average Teacher Salary: $1,441
  Effort Index: 0.895
Private: 35 schools, 9,206 pupils
Colleges and Universities
  Two-year: 1 private, 4 public; 21,190 students
  Four-year and Beyond: 7 private, 4 public; 44,425 students
  Degree Options: A
Places Rated Score: 2,908
Places Rated Rank: 120

## Olympia, WA
Elementary and Secondary
Public: 8 districts, 48 schools, 25,970 pupils
  Pupil/Teacher Ratio: 18.96
  Dollars per Pupil: $2,696
  Average Teacher Salary: $1,949
  Effort Index: 1.077
Private: 13 schools, 1,126 pupils
Colleges and Universities
  Two-year: 1 public; 2,996 students
  Four-year and Beyond: 1 private, 1 public; 3,128 students
  Degree Options: B
Places Rated Score: 2,625
Places Rated Rank: 244

## Omaha, NE–IA
Elementary and Secondary
Public: 24 districts, 226 schools, 105,152 pupils
  Pupil/Teacher Ratio: 14.29
  Dollars per Pupil: $2,904
  Average Teacher Salary: $1,621
  Effort Index: 1.011

Private: 71 schools, 17,769 pupils
Colleges and Universities
  Two-year: 2 public; 9,561 students
  Four-year and Beyond: 4 private, 2 public; 21,313 students
  Degree Options: A
Places Rated Score: 3,069
Places Rated Rank: 58

## Orange County, NY
Elementary and Secondary
Public: 17 districts, 81 schools, 50,795 pupils
  Pupil/Teacher Ratio: 14.49
  Dollars per Pupil: $3,720
  Average Teacher Salary: $1,835
  Effort Index: 1.210
Private: 31 schools, 6,434 pupils
Colleges and Universities
  Two-year: 1 public; 5,425 students
  Four-year and Beyond: 1 private; 1,038 students
  Degree Options: C
Places Rated Score: 2,754
Places Rated Rank: 181

## Orlando, FL
Elementary and Secondary
Public: 3 districts, 163 schools, 123,920 pupils
  Pupil/Teacher Ratio: 12.97
  Dollars per Pupil: $2,735
  Average Teacher Salary: $1,601
  Effort Index: 1.060
Private: 60 schools, 14,293 pupils
Colleges and Universities
  Two-year: 2 public; 16,018 students
  Four-year and Beyond: 3 private, 1 public; 18,848 students
  Degree Options: B
Places Rated Score: 2,976
Places Rated Rank: 94

## Owensboro, KY
Elementary and Secondary
Public: 2 districts, 29 schools, 13,225 pupils
  Pupil/Teacher Ratio: 15.18
  Dollars per Pupil: $2,060
  Average Teacher Salary: $1,673
  Effort Index: 0.995
Private: 17 schools, 4,415 pupils
Colleges and Universities
  Two-year: 1 private; 274 students
  Four-year and Beyond: 2 private; 1,813 students
  Degree Options: C
Places Rated Score: 2,491
Places Rated Rank: 283

## Oxnard–Ventura, CA
Elementary and Secondary
Public: 20 districts, 170 schools, 106,369 pupils
  Pupil/Teacher Ratio: 19.18
  Dollars per Pupil: $2,918
  Average Teacher Salary: $2,297
  Effort Index: 0.867
Private: 69 schools, 12,557 pupils
Colleges and Universities
  Two-year: 2 public; 18,776 students
  Four-year and Beyond: 1 private; 2,467 students
  Degree Options: C
Places Rated Score: 2,155
Places Rated Rank: 323

## Panama City, FL
Elementary and Secondary
Public: 1 district, 29 schools, 20,000 pupils
  Pupil/Teacher Ratio: 12.92
  Dollars per Pupil: $2,780
  Average Teacher Salary: $1,455
  Effort Index: 0.830
Private: 10 schools, 1,485 pupils
Colleges and Universities
  Two-year: 1 public; 3,913 students
  Four-year and Beyond: None
  Degree Options: C
Places Rated Score: 2,500
Places Rated Rank: 281

## Parkersburg–Marietta, WV–OH
Elementary and Secondary
Public: 8 districts, 83 schools, 31,332 pupils
  Pupil/Teacher Ratio: 14.68
  Dollars per Pupil: $2,155
  Average Teacher Salary: $1,540
  Effort Index: 0.973
Private: 12 schools, 1,305 pupils
Colleges and Universities
  Two-year: 2 public; 4,184 students
  Four-year and Beyond: 2 private; 1,713 students
  Degree Options: C
Places Rated Score: 2,503
Places Rated Rank: 278

## Pascagoula, MS
Elementary and Secondary
Public: 4 districts, 38 schools, 24,420 pupils
  Pupil/Teacher Ratio: 15.15
  Dollars per Pupil: $1,847
  Average Teacher Salary: $1,199
  Effort Index: 0.703
Private: 3 schools, 555 pupils
Colleges and Universities
  Two-year: None
  Four-year and Beyond: None
  Degree Options: C
Places Rated Score: 1,701
Places Rated Rank: 329

## Pawtucket–Woonsocket–Attleboro, RI–MA
Elementary and Secondary
Public: 14 districts, 100 schools, 48,612 pupils
  Pupil/Teacher Ratio: 13.63
  Dollars per Pupil: $2,850
  Average Teacher Salary: $2,081
  Effort Index: 1.449
Private: 23 schools, 6,071 pupils
Colleges and Universities
  Two-year: None
  Four-year and Beyond: 1 private; 6,582 students
  Degree Options: C
Places Rated Score: 3,058
Places Rated Rank: 61

## Pensacola, FL
Elementary and Secondary
Public: 2 districts, 86 schools, 52,995 pupils
  Pupil/Teacher Ratio: 15.61
  Dollars per Pupil: $3,161
  Average Teacher Salary: $1,519
  Effort Index: 1.195
Private: 31 schools, 7,632 pupils

Colleges and Universities
Two-year: 1 public; 8,659 students
Four-year and Beyond: 1 public; 5,294 students
Degree Options: B
Places Rated Score: 2,914
Places Rated Rank: 119

**Peoria, IL**
Elementary and Secondary
Public: 48 districts, 163 schools, 65,481 pupils
  Pupil/Teacher Ratio: 16.72
  Dollars per Pupil: $2,497
  Average Teacher Salary: $1,849
  Effort Index: 1.048
Private: 67 schools, 9,199 pupils
Colleges and Universities
Two-year: 1 private, 1 public; 13,809 students
Four-year and Beyond: 2 private; 6,164 students
Degree Options: C
Places Rated Score: 2,452
Places Rated Rank: 294

★ **Philadelphia, PA–NJ**
Elementary and Secondary
Public: 170 districts, 900 schools, 687,270 pupils
  Pupil/Teacher Ratio: 13.22
  Dollars per Pupil: $3,235
  Average Teacher Salary: $1,975
  Effort Index: 1.137
Private: 659 schools, 139,734 pupils
Colleges and Universities
Two-year: 15 private, 6 public; 69,670 students
Four-year and Beyond: 42 private, 4 public; 135,616 students
Degree Options: AAA
Places Rated Score: 3,781
Places Rated Rank: 1

**Phoenix, AZ**
Elementary and Secondary
Public: 55 districts, 366 schools, 274,189 pupils
  Pupil/Teacher Ratio: 15.56
  Dollars per Pupil: $2,781
  Average Teacher Salary: $1,813
  Effort Index: 0.970
Private: 203 schools, 31,952 pupils
Colleges and Universities
Two-year: 1 private, 6 public; 51,055 students
Four-year and Beyond: 8 private, 2 public; 61,754 students
Degree Options: A
Places Rated Score: 2,942
Places Rated Rank: 106

**Pine Bluff, AR**
Elementary and Secondary
Public: 9 districts, 45 schools, 17,976 pupils
  Pupil/Teacher Ratio: 15.64
  Dollars per Pupil: $1,876
  Average Teacher Salary: $1,211
  Effort Index: 1.088
Private: 4 schools, 761 pupils
Colleges and Universities
Two-year: None
Four-year and Beyond: 1 public; 2,731 students
Degree Options: C
Places Rated Score: 2,554
Places Rated Rank: 263

★ **Pittsburgh, PA**
Elementary and Secondary
Public: 80 districts, 631 schools, 322,010 pupils
  Pupil/Teacher Ratio: 13.83
  Dollars per Pupil: $3,079
  Average Teacher Salary: $1,741
  Effort Index: 1.201
Private: 284 schools, 62,150 pupils
Colleges and Universities
Two-year: 9 private, 10 public; 31,955 students
Four-year and Beyond: 11 private, 2 public; 63,201 students
Degree Options: AA
Places Rated Score: 3,544
Places Rated Rank: 7

**Pittsfield, MA**
Elementary and Secondary
Public: 8 districts, 38 schools, 15,043 pupils
  Pupil/Teacher Ratio: 10.72
  Dollars per Pupil: $2,660
  Average Teacher Salary: $1,419
  Effort Index: 1.354
Private: 17 schools, 2,730 pupils
Colleges and Universities
Two-year: 1 public; 1,988 students
Four-year and Beyond: 1 private; 129 students
Degree Options: C
Places Rated Score: 3,264
Places Rated Rank: 30

**Portland, ME**
Elementary and Secondary
Public: 14 districts, 85 schools, 31,218 pupils
  Pupil/Teacher Ratio: 13.15
  Dollars per Pupil: $2,074
  Average Teacher Salary: $1,411
  Effort Index: 1.073
Private: 23 schools, 3,412 pupils
Colleges and Universities
Two-year: 2 private, 1 public; 2,190 students
Four-year and Beyond: 3 private, 1 public; 13,238 students
Degree Options: B
Places Rated Score: 2,973
Places Rated Rank: 95

★ **Portland, OR**
Elementary and Secondary
Public: 62 districts, 385 schools, 184,007 pupils
  Pupil/Teacher Ratio: 14.02
  Dollars per Pupil: $3,904
  Average Teacher Salary: $1,782
  Effort Index: 1.265
. Private: 124 schools, 19,037 pupils
Colleges and Universities
Two-year: 2 private, 2 public; 12,752 students
Four-year and Beyond: 15 private, 2 public; 27,842 students
Degree Options: A
Places Rated Score: 3,343
Places Rated Rank: 22

**Portsmouth–Dover–Rochester, NH–ME**
Elementary and Secondary
Public: 19 districts, 50 schools, 35,512 pupils
  Pupil/Teacher Ratio: 13.99

Dollars per Pupil: $3,096
Average Teacher Salary: $1,417
Effort Index: 1.195
Private: 17 schools, 3,782 pupils
Colleges and Universities
Two-year: 2 private, 1 public; 3,462 students
Four-year and Beyond: 1 public; 12,415 students
Degree Options: B
Places Rated Score: 3,026
Places Rated Rank: 78

**Poughkeepsie, NY**
Elementary and Secondary
Public: 14 districts, 69 schools, 42,926 pupils
  Pupil/Teacher Ratio: 14.42
  Dollars per Pupil: $3,881
  Average Teacher Salary: $1,979
  Effort Index: 1.349
Private: 34 schools, 6,120 pupils
Colleges and Universities
Two-year: 1 private, 1 public; 9,016 students
Four-year and Beyond: 3 private; 6,247 students
Degree Options: C
Places Rated Score: 2,898
Places Rated Rank: 127

★ **Providence, RI**
Elementary and Secondary
Public: 15 districts, 172 schools, 74,904 pupils
  Pupil/Teacher Ratio: 13.63
  Dollars per Pupil: $2,850
  Average Teacher Salary: $2,081
  Effort Index: 1.449
Private: 76 schools, 20,411 pupils
Colleges and Universities
Two-year: 1 public; 12,149 students
Four-year and Beyond: 10 private, 2 public; 54,731 students
Degree Options: A
Places Rated Score: 3,558
Places Rated Rank: 6

**Provo–Orem, UT**
Elementary and Secondary
Public: 3 districts, 90 schools, 51,790 pupils
  Pupil/Teacher Ratio: 19.54
  Dollars per Pupil: $2,009
  Average Teacher Salary: $1,637
  Effort Index: 1.094
Private: 3 schools, 433 pupils
Colleges and Universities
Two-year: 1 public; 5,593 students
Four-year and Beyond: 1 private; 29,695 students
Degree Options: B
Places Rated Score: 2,618
Places Rated Rank: 248

**Pueblo, CO**
Elementary and Secondary
Public: 2 districts, 50 schools, 24,889 pupils
  Pupil/Teacher Ratio: 15.50
  Dollars per Pupil: $2,742
  Average Teacher Salary: $1,340
  Effort Index: 0.927
Private: 7 schools, 675 pupils
Colleges and Universities
Two-year: 1 public; 1,064 students
Four-year and Beyond: 1 public; 5,432 students

Degree Options: B
Places Rated Score: 2,653
Places Rated Rank: 227

## Racine, WI
Elementary and Secondary
Public: 12 districts, 54 schools,
30,634 pupils
Pupil/Teacher Ratio: 12.42
Dollars per Pupil: $2,821
Average Teacher Salary: $1,272
Effort Index: 1.015
Private: 37 schools, 6,888 pupils
Colleges and Universities
Two-year: None
Four-year and Beyond: 1 private; 60
students
Degree Options: C
Places Rated Score: 2,732
Places Rated Rank: 192

## ★ Raleigh–Durham, NC
Elementary and Secondary
Public: 7 districts, 155 schools,
94,583 pupils
Pupil/Teacher Ratio: 13.16
Dollars per Pupil: $2,440
Average Teacher Salary: $1,429
Effort Index: 1.056
Private: 38 schools, 8,129 pupils
Colleges and Universities
Two-year: 6 private, 2 public; 10,014
students
Four-year and Beyond: 5 private, 3
public; 64,077 students
Degree Options: AA
Places Rated Score: 3,455
Places Rated Rank: 16

## Reading, PA
Elementary and Secondary
Public: 19 districts, 107 schools,
54,190 pupils
Pupil/Teacher Ratio: 14.02
Dollars per Pupil: $2,760
Average Teacher Salary: $1,656
Effort Index: 1.200
Private: 31 schools, 7,467 pupils
Colleges and Universities
Two-year: 2 public; 3,040 students
Four-year and Beyond: 2 private, 1
public; 8,742 students
Degree Options: B
Places Rated Score: 3,028
Places Rated Rank: 74

## Redding, CA
Elementary and Secondary
Public: 28 districts, 63 schools,
22,774 pupils
Pupil/Teacher Ratio: 16.19
Dollars per Pupil: $3,631
Average Teacher Salary: $1,932
Effort Index: 1.037
Private: 19 schools, 2,391 pupils
Colleges and Universities
Two-year: 1 public; 9,462 students
Four-year and Beyond: None
Degree Options: C
Places Rated Score: 2,471
Places Rated Rank: 289

## Reno, NV
Elementary and Secondary
Public: 1 district, 60 schools,
32,006 pupils
Pupil/Teacher Ratio: 14.96
Dollars per Pupil: $2,848

Average Teacher Salary: $1,654
Effort Index: 0.769
Private: 15 schools, 2,300 pupils
Colleges and Universities
Two-year: 1 public; 7,963 students
Four-year and Beyond: 2 private, 1
public; 9,976 students
Degree Options: B
Places Rated Score: 2,529
Places Rated Rank: 272

## Richland–Kennewick–Pasco, WA
Elementary and Secondary
Public: 10 districts, 62 schools,
30,788 pupils
Pupil/Teacher Ratio: 19.59
Dollars per Pupil: $2,683
Average Teacher Salary: $1,868
Effort Index: 0.456
Private: 13 schools, 1,714 pupils
Colleges and Universities
Two-year: 1 public; 5,798 students
Four-year and Beyond: None
Degree Options: C
Places Rated Score: 1,728
Places Rated Rank: 328

## Richmond–Petersburg, VA
Elementary and Secondary
Public: 13 districts, 233 schools,
139,400 pupils
Pupil/Teacher Ratio: 12.95
Dollars per Pupil: $2,421
Average Teacher Salary: $1,152
Effort Index: 1.023
Private: 51 schools, 10,833 pupils
Colleges and Universities
Two-year: 3 public; 15,229 students
Four-year and Beyond: 5 private, 2
public; 30,234 students
Degree Options: B
Places Rated Score: 2,940
Places Rated Rank: 107

## Riverside–San Bernardino, CA
Elementary and Secondary
Public: 57 districts, 493 schools,
299,991 pupils
Pupil/Teacher Ratio: 18.98
Dollars per Pupil: $2,918
Average Teacher Salary: $2,141
Effort Index: 0.799
Private: 134 schools, 19,164 pupils
Colleges and Universities
Two-year: 8 public; 72,523 students
Four-year and Beyond: 3 private, 2
public; 17,745 students
Degree Options: A
Places Rated Score: 2,596
Places Rated Rank: 254

## Roanoke, VA
Elementary and Secondary
Public: 4 districts, 75 schools,
39,208 pupils
Pupil/Teacher Ratio: 13.63
Dollars per Pupil: $2,291
Average Teacher Salary: $1,618
Effort Index: 1.114
Private: 10 schools, 1,855 pupils
Colleges and Universities
Two-year: 1 private, 1 public; 6,436
students
Four-year and Beyond: 1 private; 954
students
Degree Options: C
Places Rated Score: 2,723
Places Rated Rank: 199

## Rochester, MN
Elementary and Secondary
Public: 5 districts, 31 schools,
18,685 pupils
Pupil/Teacher Ratio: 16.91
Dollars per Pupil: $2,635
Average Teacher Salary: $2,062
Effort Index: 0.740
Private: 11 schools, 2,203 pupils
Colleges and Universities
Two-year: 1 public; 3,278 students
Four-year and Beyond: 3 private; 1,196
students
Degree Options: C
Places Rated Score: 2,134
Places Rated Rank: 325

## ★ Rochester, NY
Elementary and Secondary
Public: 50 districts, 252 schools,
164,003 pupils
Pupil/Teacher Ratio: 12.69
Dollars per Pupil: $3,992
Average Teacher Salary: $2,190
Effort Index: 1.140
Private: 103 schools, 27,247 pupils
Colleges and Universities
Two-year: 4 private, 2 public; 14,507
students
Four-year and Beyond: 8 private, 2
public; 42,973 students
Degree Options: AA
Places Rated Score: 3,582
Places Rated Rank: 5

## Rockford, IL
Elementary and Secondary
Public: 13 districts, 101 schools,
50,863 pupils
Pupil/Teacher Ratio: 14.81
Dollars per Pupil: $2,480
Average Teacher Salary: $1,830
Effort Index: 1.159
Private: 25 schools, 7,020 pupils
Colleges and Universities
Two-year: 1 public; 9,985 students
Four-year and Beyond: 1 private; 1,469
students
Degree Options: C
Places Rated Score: 2,680
Places Rated Rank: 220

## Sacramento, CA
Elementary and Secondary
Public: 55 districts, 389 schools,
192,673 pupils
Pupil/Teacher Ratio: 17.10
Dollars per Pupil: $3,234
Average Teacher Salary: $2,028
Effort Index: 0.909
Private: 134 schools, 21,497 pupils
Colleges and Universities
Two-year: 1 private, 4 public; 55,970
students
Four-year and Beyond: 2 public; 40,992
students
Degree Options: A
Places Rated Score: 2,793
Places Rated Rank: 166

## Saginaw–Bay City–Midland, MI
Elementary and Secondary
Public: 21 districts, 161 schools,
79,668 pupils
Pupil/Teacher Ratio: 17.72
Dollars per Pupil: $2,965
Average Teacher Salary: $2,086
Effort Index: 1.169

Private: 57 schools, 13,223 pupils
Colleges and Universities
  Two-year: 1 public; 10,279 students
  Four-year and Beyond: 1 private, 1
  public; 6,489 students
  Degree Options: B
Places Rated Score: 2,772
Places Rated Rank: 173

## St. Cloud, MN
Elementary and Secondary
  Public: 16 districts, 64 schools,
  32,393 pupils
    Pupil/Teacher Ratio: 15.93
    Dollars per Pupil: $2,933
    Average Teacher Salary: $1,857
    Effort Index: 1.053
  Private: 32 schools, 6,807 pupils
Colleges and Universities
  Two-year: None
  Four-year and Beyond: 2 private, 1
  public; 15,845 students
  Degree Options: C
Places Rated Score: 2,502
Places Rated Rank: 279

## St. Joseph, MO
Elementary and Secondary
  Public: 4 districts, 34 schools,
  14,277 pupils
    Pupil/Teacher Ratio: 15.14
    Dollars per Pupil: $2,321
    Average Teacher Salary: $1,368
    Effort Index: 1.428
  Private: 6 schools, 1,322 pupils
Colleges and Universities
  Two-year: None
  Four-year and Beyond: 1 public; 4,269
  students
  Degree Options: C
Places Rated Score: 2,927
Places Rated Rank: 112

## ★ St. Louis, MO–IL
Elementary and Secondary
  Public: 46 districts, 486 schools,
  280,749 pupils
    Pupil/Teacher Ratio: 15.23
    Dollars per Pupil: $2,955
    Average Teacher Salary: $1,837
    Effort Index: 1.287
  Private: 203 schools, 83,423 pupils
Colleges and Universities
  Two-year: 3 private, 5 public; 38,142
  students
  Four-year and Beyond: 21 private, 2
  public; 45,064 students
  Degree Options: AA
Places Rated Score: 3,530
Places Rated Rank: 9

## Salem, OR
Elementary and Secondary
  Public: 40 districts, 120 schools,
  40,300 pupils
    Pupil/Teacher Ratio: 14.71
    Dollars per Pupil: $3,613
    Average Teacher Salary: $1,705
    Effort Index: 1.605
  Private: 47 schools, 5,833 pupils
Colleges and Universities
  Two-year: 1 public; 6,523 students
  Four-year and Beyond: 2 private, 1
  public; 4,598 students
  Degree Options: B
Places Rated Score: 3,278
Places Rated Rank: 27

## Salem–Gloucester, MA
Elementary and Secondary
  Public: 15 districts, 79 schools,
  36,856 pupils
    Pupil/Teacher Ratio: 14.46
    Dollars per Pupil: $2,707
    Average Teacher Salary: $1,964
    Effort Index: 0.933
  Private: 32 schools, 6,774 pupils
Colleges and Universities
  Two-year: 2 private, 1 public; 5,656
  students
  Four-year and Beyond: 2 private, 1
  public; 10,336 students
  Degree Options: B
Places Rated Score: 2,729
Places Rated Rank: 193

## Salinas–Seaside–Monterey, CA
Elementary and Secondary
  Public: 25 districts, 94 schools,
  48,591 pupils
    Pupil/Teacher Ratio: 15.98
    Dollars per Pupil: $3,520
    Average Teacher Salary: $1,961
    Effort Index: 0.993
  Private: 22 schools, 4,448 pupils
Colleges and Universities
  Two-year: 2 public; 14,221 students
  Four-year and Beyond: 1 private; 411
  students
  Degree Options: C
Places Rated Score: 2,439
Places Rated Rank: 295

## Salt Lake City–Ogden, UT
Elementary and Secondary
  Public: 7 districts, 317 schools,
  211,280 pupils
    Pupil/Teacher Ratio: 19.24
    Dollars per Pupil: $2,183
    Average Teacher Salary: $1,707
    Effort Index: 0.804
  Private: 26 schools, 4,820 pupils
Colleges and Universities
  Two-year: 2 private, 1 public; 8,773
  students
  Four-year and Beyond: 1 private, 2
  public; 35,958 students
  Degree Options: B
Places Rated Score: 2,340
Places Rated Rank: 312

## San Angelo, TX
Elementary and Secondary
  Public: 6 districts, 36 schools,
  15,482 pupils
    Pupil/Teacher Ratio: 14.22
    Dollars per Pupil: $2,009
    Average Teacher Salary: $1,546
    Effort Index: 1.143
  Private: 4 schools, 531 pupils
Colleges and Universities
  Two-year: None
  Four-year and Beyond: 1 public; 5,834
  students
  Degree Options: C
Places Rated Score: 2,707
Places Rated Rank: 209

## San Antonio, TX
Elementary and Secondary
  Public: 2 districts, 312 schools,
  216,678 pupils
    Pupil/Teacher Ratio: 13.88
    Dollars per Pupil: $2,371

Average Teacher Salary: $1,486
    Effort Index: 1.098
  Private: 86 schools, 22,383 pupils
Colleges and Universities
  Two-year: 2 public; 27,344 students
  Four-year and Beyond: 6 private, 1
  public; 20,985 students
  Degree Options: B
Places Rated Score: 2,938
Places Rated Rank: 108

## San Diego, CA
Elementary and Secondary
  Public: 43 districts, 473 schools,
  309,642 pupils
    Pupil/Teacher Ratio: 18.90
    Dollars per Pupil: $3,271
    Average Teacher Salary: $2,369
    Effort Index: 0.994
  Private: 198 schools, 33,065 pupils
Colleges and Universities
  Two-year: 1 private, 7 public; 89,353
  students
  Four-year and Beyond: 9 private, 1
  public; 52,143 students
  Degree Options: A
Places Rated Score: 2,794
Places Rated Rank: 165

## ★ San Francisco, CA
Elementary and Secondary
  Public: 43 districts, 330 schools,
  166,566 pupils
    Pupil/Teacher Ratio: 15.98
    Dollars per Pupil: $4,001
    Average Teacher Salary: $2,181
    Effort Index: 0.925
  Private: 252 schools, 48,593 pupils
Colleges and Universities
  Two-year: 1 private, 6 public; 61,998
  students
  Four-year and Beyond: 20 private, 3
  public; 56,160 students
  Degree Options: AAA
Places Rated Score: 3,371
Places Rated Rank: 18

## San Jose, CA
Elementary and Secondary
  Public: 33 districts, 343 schools,
  241,008 pupils
    Pupil/Teacher Ratio: 19.38
    Dollars per Pupil: $3,497
    Average Teacher Salary: $2,417
    Effort Index: 0.929
  Private: 99 schools, 11,946 pupils
Colleges and Universities
  Two-year: 4 private, 7 public; 87,550
  students
  Four-year and Beyond: 5 private, 1
  public; 48,108 students
  Degree Options: A
Places Rated Score: 2,709
Places Rated Rank: 207

## Santa Barbara–Santa Maria–
## Lompoc, CA
Elementary and Secondary
  Public: 23 districts, 92 schools,
  45,512 pupils
    Pupil/Teacher Ratio: 17.91
    Dollars per Pupil: $3,656
    Average Teacher Salary: $2,517
    Effort Index: 1.125
  Private: 39 schools, 7,050 pupils
Colleges and Universities
  Two-year: 2 public; 17,404 students

Four-year and Beyond: 3 private, 1 public; 18,358 students
Degree Options: B
Places Rated Score: 2,719
Places Rated Rank: 203

**Santa Cruz, CA**
Elementary and Secondary
Public: 10 districts, 53 schools, 34,229 pupils
  Pupil/Teacher Ratio: 19.05
  Dollars per Pupil: $2,916
  Average Teacher Salary: $1,873
  Effort Index: 1.067
Private: 29 schools, 3,977 pupils
Colleges and Universities
Two-year: 1 public; 10,483 students
Four-year and Beyond: 1 private, 1 public; 7,326 students
Degree Options: B
Places Rated Score: 2,611
Places Rated Rank: 252

**Santa Rosa–Petaluma, CA**
Elementary and Secondary
Public: 6 districts, 77 schools, 46,949 pupils
  Pupil/Teacher Ratio: 16.30
  Dollars per Pupil: $3,375
  Average Teacher Salary: $2,012
  Effort Index: 1.044
Private: 24 schools, 4,276 pupils
Colleges and Universities
Two-year: 1 public; 20,138 students
Four-year and Beyond: 1 public; 6,664 students
Degree Options: B
Places Rated Score: 2,722
Places Rated Rank: 200

**Sarasota, FL**
Elementary and Secondary
Public: 1 district, 28 schools, 24,684 pupils
  Pupil/Teacher Ratio: 14.86
  Dollars per Pupil: $2,765
  Average Teacher Salary: $1,482
  Effort Index: 1.109
Private: 19 schools, 3,065 pupils
Colleges and Universities
Two-year: None
Four-year and Beyond: 2 private; 624 students
Degree Options: C
Places Rated Score: 2,626
Places Rated Rank: 243

**Savannah, GA**
Elementary and Secondary
Public: 2 districts, 62 schools, 35,371 pupils
  Pupil/Teacher Ratio: 14.18
  Dollars per Pupil: $2,124
  Average Teacher Salary: $1,470
  Effort Index: 0.889
Private: 27 schools, 9,410 pupils
Colleges and Universities
Two-year: 1 private; 654 students
Four-year and Beyond: 1 private, 2 public; 5,559 students
Degree Options: C
Places Rated Score: 2,456
Places Rated Rank: 291

**Scranton–Wilkes-Barre, PA**
Elementary and Secondary
Public: 35 districts, 201 schools, 108,967 pupils

Pupil/Teacher Ratio: 14.55
Dollars per Pupil: $2,559
Average Teacher Salary: $1,567
Effort Index: 1.441
Private: 93 schools, 19,490 pupils
Colleges and Universities
Two-year: 4 private, 4 public; 14,919 students
Four-year and Beyond: 6 private, 2 public; 22,969 students
Degree Options: B
Places Rated Score: 3,230
Places Rated Rank: 34

**Seattle, WA**
Elementary and Secondary
Public: 34 districts, 481 schools, 267,266 pupils
  Pupil/Teacher Ratio: 20.15
  Dollars per Pupil: $2,917
  Average Teacher Salary: $2,211
  Effort Index: 0.959
Private: 169 schools, 32,674 pupils
Colleges and Universities
Two-year: 9 public; 49,769 students
Four-year and Beyond: 9 private, 1 public; 47,411 students
Degree Options: A
Places Rated Score: 2,710
Places Rated Rank: 206

**Sharon, PA**
Elementary and Secondary
Public: 12 districts, 47 schools, 21,915 pupils
  Pupil/Teacher Ratio: 13.73
  Dollars per Pupil: $2,859
  Average Teacher Salary: $1,625
  Effort Index: 1.421
Private: 12 schools, 2,179 pupils
Colleges and Universities
Two-year: 1 public; 922 students
Four-year and Beyond: 2 private; 3,007 students
Degree Options: C
Places Rated Score: 3,022
Places Rated Rank: 80

**Sheboygan, WI**
Elementary and Secondary
Public: 9 districts, 45 schools, 17,824 pupils
  Pupil/Teacher Ratio: 15.45
  Dollars per Pupil: $3,288
  Average Teacher Salary: $1,703
  Effort Index: 1.078
Private: 24 schools, 3,465 pupils
Colleges and Universities
Two-year: None
Four-year and Beyond: 1 private; 809 students
Degree Options: C
Places Rated Score: 2,557
Places Rated Rank: 262

**Sherman–Denison, TX**
Elementary and Secondary
Public: 13 districts, 45 schools, 16,386 pupils
  Pupil/Teacher Ratio: 13.82
  Dollars per Pupil: $2,572
  Average Teacher Salary: $1,541
  Effort Index: 1.058
Private: 4 schools, 358 pupils
Colleges and Universities
Two-year: 1 public; 4,559 students

Four-year and Beyond: 1 private; 1,186 students
Degree Options: C
Places Rated Score: 2,652
Places Rated Rank: 228

**Shreveport, LA**
Elementary and Secondary
Public: 2 districts, 102 schools, 62,370 pupils
  Pupil/Teacher Ratio: 13.41
  Dollars per Pupil: $2,523
  Average Teacher Salary: $1,539
  Effort Index: 0.980
Private: 37 schools, 9,977 pupils
Colleges and Universities
Two-year: 2 public; 2,157 students
Four-year and Beyond: 1 private, 1 public; 5,721 students
Degree Options: B
Places Rated Score: 2,858
Places Rated Rank: 143

**Sioux City, IA–NE**
Elementary and Secondary
Public: 9 districts, 56 schools, 19,619 pupils
  Pupil/Teacher Ratio: 15.13
  Dollars per Pupil: $3,071
  Average Teacher Salary: $1,719
  Effort Index: 1.173
Private: 15 schools, 3,383 pupils
Colleges and Universities
Two-year: 1 public; 1,461 students
Four-year and Beyond: 2 private; 2,513 students
Degree Options: C
Places Rated Score: 2,673
Places Rated Rank: 222

**Sioux Falls, SD**
Elementary and Secondary
Public: 7 districts, 48 schools, 18,502 pupils
  Pupil/Teacher Ratio: 14.28
  Dollars per Pupil: $2,280
  Average Teacher Salary: $1,313
  Effort Index: 1.092
Private: 23 schools, 3,034 pupils
Colleges and Universities
Two-year: 1 private; 364 students
Four-year and Beyond: 3 private; 2,985 students
Degree Options: C
Places Rated Score: 2,651
Places Rated Rank: 229

**South Bend–Mishawaka, IN**
Elementary and Secondary
Public: 5 districts, 67 schools, 39,010 pupils
  Pupil/Teacher Ratio: 18.10
  Dollars per Pupil: $2,424
  Average Teacher Salary: $1,926
  Effort Index: 1.289
Private: 29 schools, 8,625 pupils
Colleges and Universities
Two-year: 1 private, 1 public; 2,626 students
Four-year and Beyond: 3 private, 1 public; 17,389 students
Degree Options: B
Places Rated Score: 2,874
Places Rated Rank: 135

## Spokane, WA
Elementary and Secondary
  Public: 14 districts, 122 schools,
  61,742 pupils
    Pupil/Teacher Ratio: 18.93
    Dollars per Pupil: $2,601
    Average Teacher Salary: $1,940
    Effort Index: 1.225
  Private: 34 schools, 5,872 pupils
Colleges and Universities
  Two-year: 2 public; 14,621 students
  Four-year and Beyond: 2 private, 1
  public; 13,449 students
  Degree Options: B
Places Rated Score: 2,774
Places Rated Rank: 172

## Springfield, IL
Elementary and Secondary
  Public: 15 districts, 69 schools,
  28,505 pupils
    Pupil/Teacher Ratio: 15.23
    Dollars per Pupil: $2,762
    Average Teacher Salary: $1,694
    Effort Index: 1.335
  Private: 29 schools, 6,922 pupils
Colleges and Universities
  Two-year: 1 private, 1 public; 7,509
  students
  Four-year and Beyond: 1 public; 3,327
  students
  Degree Options: B
Places Rated Score: 3,078
Places Rated Rank: 57

## ★ Springfield, MA
Elementary and Secondary
  Public: 20 districts, 153 schools,
  76,705 pupils
    Pupil/Teacher Ratio: 13.54
    Dollars per Pupil: $3,088
    Average Teacher Salary: $1,762
    Effort Index: 1.408
  Private: 64 schools, 15,734 pupils
Colleges and Universities
  Two-year: 1 private, 2 public; 12,634
  students
  Four-year and Beyond: 7 private, 1
  public; 20,040 students
  Degree Options: A
Places Rated Score: 3,525
Places Rated Rank: 10

## Springfield, MO
Elementary and Secondary
  Public: 15 districts, 85 schools,
  36,564 pupils
    Pupil/Teacher Ratio: 15.36
    Dollars per Pupil: $1,921
    Average Teacher Salary: $1,454
    Effort Index: 1.224
  Private: 15 schools, 1,778 pupils
Colleges and Universities
  Two-year: 1 private, 1 public; 2,489
  students
  Four-year and Beyond: 4 private, 1
  public; 19,416 students
  Degree Options: C
Places Rated Score: 2,709
Places Rated Rank: 207

## Stamford, CT
Elementary and Secondary
  Public: 4 districts, 42 schools,
  27,737 pupils
    Pupil/Teacher Ratio: 12.10
    Dollars per Pupil: $3,139
    Average Teacher Salary: $1,990

Effort Index: 1.279
  Private: 35 schools, 8,234 pupils
Colleges and Universities
  Two-year: None
  Four-year and Beyond: 2 private; 66
  students
  Degree Options: C
Places Rated Score: 3,029
Places Rated Rank: 70

## State College, PA
Elementary and Secondary
  Public: 4 districts, 31 schools,
  14,890 pupils
    Pupil/Teacher Ratio: 12.94
    Dollars per Pupil: $3,057
    Average Teacher Salary: $1,485
    Effort Index: 1.760
  Private: 10 schools, 1,034 pupils
Colleges and Universities
  Two-year: None
  Four-year and Beyond: 1 public; 36,162
  students
  Degree Options: C
Places Rated Score: 3,169
Places Rated Rank: 38

## Steubenville–Weirton, OH–WV
Elementary and Secondary
  Public: 8 districts, 75 schools,
  29,262 pupils
    Pupil/Teacher Ratio: 15.38
    Dollars per Pupil: $2,376
    Average Teacher Salary: $1,631
    Effort Index: 1.189
  Private: 16 schools, 3,238 pupils
Colleges and Universities
  Two-year: 1 public; 1,789 students
  Four-year and Beyond: 2 private; 1,693
  students
  Degree Options: C
Places Rated Score: 2,672
Places Rated Rank: 223

## Stockton, CA
Elementary and Secondary
  Public: 17 districts, 127 schools,
  66,565 pupils
    Pupil/Teacher Ratio: 18.17
    Dollars per Pupil: $3,177
    Average Teacher Salary: $2,113
    Effort Index: 0.823
  Private: 38 schools, 7,277 pupils
Colleges and Universities
  Two-year: 1 private; 265 students
  Four-year and Beyond: 1 private; 5,997
  students
  Degree Options: C
Places Rated Score: 2,155
Places Rated Rank: 323

## Syracuse, NY
Elementary and Secondary
  Public: 37 districts, 194 schools,
  119,713 pupils
    Pupil/Teacher Ratio: 13.03
    Dollars per Pupil: $3,470
    Average Teacher Salary: $1,839
    Effort Index: 0.983
  Private: 55 schools, 12,319 pupils
Colleges and Universities
  Two-year: 3 private, 2 public; 12,802
  students
  Four-year and Beyond: 3 private, 3
  public; 36,262 students
  Degree Options: A
Places Rated Score: 3,144
Places Rated Rank: 44

## Tacoma, WA
Elementary and Secondary
  Public: 15 districts, 187 schools,
  89,823 pupils
    Pupil/Teacher Ratio: 17.65
    Dollars per Pupil: $3,215
    Average Teacher Salary: $2,053
    Effort Index: 1.189
  Private: 32 schools, 6,452 pupils
Colleges and Universities
  Two-year: 1 public; 3,973 students
  Four-year and Beyond: 2 private; 7,782
  students
  Degree Options: C
Places Rated Score: 2,546
Places Rated Rank: 264

## Tallahassee, FL
Elementary and Secondary
  Public: 2 districts, 49 schools,
  36,135 pupils
    Pupil/Teacher Ratio: 15.32
    Dollars per Pupil: $2,412
    Average Teacher Salary: $1,232
    Effort Index: 1.053
  Private: 19 schools, 5,728 pupils
Colleges and Universities
  Two-year: 1 public; 4,871 students
  Four-year and Beyond: 2 public; 26,847
  students
  Degree Options: B
Places Rated Score: 2,790
Places Rated Rank: 167

## Tampa–St. Petersburg–Clearwater, FL
Elementary and Secondary
  Public: 4 districts, 283 schools, 224,517
  pupils
    Pupil/Teacher Ratio: 14.06
    Dollars per Pupil: $2,932
    Average Teacher Salary: $1,579
    Effort Index: 1.219
  Private: 158 schools, 34,380 pupils
Colleges and Universities
  Two-year: 3 private, 2 public; 31,361
  students
  Four-year and Beyond: 5 private, 1
  public; 35,492 students
  Degree Options: B
Places Rated Score: 3,044
Places Rated Rank: 67

## Terre Haute, IN
Elementary and Secondary
  Public: 2 districts, 43 schools,
  23,053 pupils
    Pupil/Teacher Ratio: 17.79
    Dollars per Pupil: $2,445
    Average Teacher Salary: $1,634
    Effort Index: 1.412
  Private: 12 schools, 1,191 pupils
Colleges and Universities
  Two-year: 1 public; 1,559 students
  Four-year and Beyond: 2 private, 1
  public; 13,917 students
  Degree Options: B
Places Rated Score: 3,012
Places Rated Rank: 83

## Texarkana, TX–Texarkana, AR
Elementary and Secondary
  Public: 18 districts, 58 schools,
  23,561 pupils
    Pupil/Teacher Ratio: 14.95
    Dollars per Pupil: $2,039
    Average Teacher Salary: $1,392
    Effort Index: 1.138

Private: 1 school, 182 pupils
Colleges and Universities
Two-year: 1 public; 3,553 students
Four-year and Beyond: 1 public; 1,142 students
Degree Options: B
Places Rated Score: 2,899
Places Rated Rank: 126

## Toledo, OH
Elementary and Secondary
Public: 25 districts, 191 schools, 104,464 pupils
Pupil/Teacher Ratio: 17.44
Dollars per Pupil: $2,513
Average Teacher Salary: $1,745
Effort Index: 0.985
Private: 69 schools, 21,583 pupils
Colleges and Universities
Two-year: 1 private, 1 public; 4,918 students
Four-year and Beyond: 1 private, 3 public; 39,882 students
Degree Options: A
Places Rated Score: 2,852
Places Rated Rank: 147

## Topeka, KS
Elementary and Secondary
Public: 5 districts, 67 schools, 25,335 pupils
Pupil/Teacher Ratio: 14.30
Dollars per Pupil: $3,404
Average Teacher Salary: $1,330
Effort Index: 1.237
Private: 15 schools, 2,880 pupils
Colleges and Universities
Two-year: None
Four-year and Beyond: 1 public; 6,515 students
Degree Options: C
Places Rated Score: 2,795
Places Rated Rank: 164

## ★ Trenton, NJ
Elementary and Secondary
Public: 11 districts, 89 schools, 47,402 pupils
Pupil/Teacher Ratio: 11.07
Dollars per Pupil: $3,873
Average Teacher Salary: $1,976
Effort Index: 1.195
Private: 49 schools, 13,701 pupils
Colleges and Universities
Two-year: 1 public; 10,248 students
Four-year and Beyond: 4 private, 2 public; 26,496 students
Degree Options: B
Places Rated Score: 3,311
Places Rated Rank: 24

## Tucson, AZ
Elementary and Secondary
Public: 14 districts, 160 schools, 121,136 pupils
Pupil/Teacher Ratio: 16.74
Dollars per Pupil: $2,858
Average Teacher Salary: $2,311
Effort Index: 1.032
Private: 79 schools, 10,329 pupils
Colleges and Universities
Two-year: 1 public; 21,780 students
Four-year and Beyond: 1 public; 30,669 students
Degree Options: B
Places Rated Score: 2,685
Places Rated Rank: 218

## Tulsa, OK
Elementary and Secondary
Public: 46 districts, 387 schools, 126,163 pupils
Pupil/Teacher Ratio: 17.33
Dollars per Pupil: $2,421
Average Teacher Salary: $1,666
Effort Index: 1.006
Private: 25 schools, 7,058 pupils
Colleges and Universities
Two-year: 1 private, 2 public; 17,925 students
Four-year and Beyond: 2 private, 1 public; 10,227 students
Degree Options: B
Places Rated Score: 2,628
Places Rated Rank: 240

## Tuscaloosa, AL
Elementary and Secondary
Public: 2 districts, 42 schools, 23,433 pupils
Pupil/Teacher Ratio: 16.76
Dollars per Pupil: $1,717
Average Teacher Salary: $1,505
Effort Index: 0.738
Private: 4 schools, 1,752 pupils
Colleges and Universities
Two-year: 1 public; 3,206 students
Four-year and Beyond: 1 private, 1 public; 16,510 students
Degree Options: B
Places Rated Score: 2,390
Places Rated Rank: 307

## Tyler, TX
Elementary and Secondary
Public: 8 districts, 45 schools, 25,265 pupils
Pupil/Teacher Ratio: 14.07
Dollars per Pupil: $2,666
Average Teacher Salary: $1,476
Effort Index: 1.458
Private: 10 schools, 1,213 pupils
Colleges and Universities
Two-year: 1 public; 7,217 students
Four-year and Beyond: 1 private, 1 public; 3,242 students
Degree Options: B
Places Rated Score: 3,283
Places Rated Rank: 26

## Utica–Rome, NY
Elementary and Secondary
Public: 29 districts, 108 schools, 56,738 pupils
Pupil/Teacher Ratio: 13.75
Dollars per Pupil: $3,380
Average Teacher Salary: $1,812
Effort Index: 1.120
Private: 30 schools, 5,904 pupils
Colleges and Universities
Two-year: 1 private, 2 public; 9,381 students
Four-year and Beyond: 3 private, 1 public; 7,094 students
Degree Options: B
Places Rated Score: 2,970
Places Rated Rank: 99

## Vallejo–Fairfield–Napa, CA
Elementary and Secondary
Public: 11 districts, 114 schools, 61,260 pupils
Pupil/Teacher Ratio: 20.27
Dollars per Pupil: $3,023

Average Teacher Salary: $2,076
Effort Index: 1.002
Private: 40 schools, 7,313 pupils
Colleges and Universities
Two-year: 2 public; 16,040 students
Four-year and Beyond: 1 private, 1 public; 2,080 students
Degree Options: B
Places Rated Score: 2,498
Places Rated Rank: 282

## Vancouver, WA
Elementary and Secondary
Public: 9 districts, 79 schools, 42,405 pupils
Pupil/Teacher Ratio: 20.52
Dollars per Pupil: $2,543
Average Teacher Salary: $2,007
Effort Index: 1.095
Private: 14 schools, 2,017 pupils
Colleges and Universities
Two-year: 1 public; 5,731 students
Four-year and Beyond: None
Degree Options: C
Places Rated Score: 2,332
Places Rated Rank: 315

## Victoria, TX
Elementary and Secondary
Public: 4 districts, 30 schools, 14,257 pupils
Pupil/Teacher Ratio: 14.84
Dollars per Pupil: $2,328
Average Teacher Salary: $1,302
Effort Index: 0.927
Private: 6 schools, 687 pupils
Colleges and Universities
Two-year: 1 public; 2,529 students
Four-year and Beyond: 1 public; 936 students
Degree Options: B
Places Rated Score: 2,696
Places Rated Rank: 213

## Vineland–Millville–Bridgeton, NJ
Elementary and Secondary
Public: 16 districts, 59 schools, 27,171 pupils
Pupil/Teacher Ratio: 12.76
Dollars per Pupil: $2,936
Average Teacher Salary: $1,728
Effort Index: 1.062
Private: 16 schools, 3,398 pupils
Colleges and Universities
Two-year: 1 public; 2,419 students
Four-year and Beyond: None
Degree Options: C
Places Rated Score: 2,747
Places Rated Rank: 185

## Visalia–Tulare–Porterville, CA
Elementary and Secondary
Public: 48 districts, 120 schools, 59,887 pupils
Pupil/Teacher Ratio: 16.52
Dollars per Pupil: $2,861
Average Teacher Salary: $1,865
Effort Index: 0.713
Private: 16 schools, 1,838 pupils
Colleges and Universities
Two-year: 2 public; 9,317 students
Four-year and Beyond: None
Degree Options: C
Places Rated Score: 2,128
Places Rated Rank: 326

## Waco, TX
Elementary and Secondary
  Public: 18 districts, 75 schools,
  28,704 pupils
    Pupil/Teacher Ratio: 13.68
    Dollars per Pupil: $2,362
    Average Teacher Salary: $1,462
    Effort Index: 1.261
  Private: 13 schools, 2,191 pupils
Colleges and Universities
  Two-year: 2 public; 9,272 students
  Four-year and Beyond: 1 private; 467
    students
  Degree Options: C
Places Rated Score: 2,867
Places Rated Rank: 140

## ★ Washington, DC–MD–VA
Elementary and Secondary
  Public: 16 districts, 939 schools,
  568,828 pupils
    Pupil/Teacher Ratio: 15.43
    Dollars per Pupil: $2,681
    Average Teacher Salary: $2,223
    Effort Index: 1.155
  Private: 505 schools, 101,086 pupils
Colleges and Universities
  Two-year: 1 private, 6 public; 73,681
    students
  Four-year and Beyond: 26 private, 5
    public; 155,068 students
  Degree Options: AAA
Places Rated Score: 3,635
Places Rated Rank: 3

## Waterbury, CT
Elementary and Secondary
  Public: 9 districts, 65 schools,
  31,717 pupils
    Pupil/Teacher Ratio: 12.84
    Dollars per Pupil: $2,815
    Average Teacher Salary: $1,660
    Effort Index: 1.317
  Private: 15 schools, 6,077 pupils
Colleges and Universities
  Two-year: 2 public; 5,565 students
  Four-year and Beyond: 1 private; 1,484
    students
  Degree Options: C
Places Rated Score: 2,995
Places Rated Rank: 88

## Waterloo–Cedar Falls, IA
Elementary and Secondary
  Public: 12 districts, 69 schools,
  27,883 pupils
    Pupil/Teacher Ratio: 16.26
    Dollars per Pupil: $3,025
    Average Teacher Salary: $1,723
    Effort Index: 1.209
  Private: 16 schools, 4,396 pupils
Colleges and Universities
  Two-year: 1 public; 1,897 students
  Four-year and Beyond: 1 private, 1
    public; 11,437 students
  Degree Options: B
Places Rated Score: 2,889
Places Rated Rank: 131

## Wausau, WI
Elementary and Secondary
  Public: 8 districts, 39 schools,
  17,931 pupils
    Pupil/Teacher Ratio: 14.30
    Dollars per Pupil: $3,241
    Average Teacher Salary: $1,583
    Effort Index: 1.192

Private: 22 schools, 4,012 pupils
Colleges and Universities
  Two-year: 1 public; 3,521 students
  Four-year and Beyond: None
  Degree Options: C
Places Rated Score: 2,749
Places Rated Rank: 184

## West Palm Beach–Boca Raton–Delray Beach, FL
Elementary and Secondary
  Public: 1 district, 91 schools,
  70,243 pupils
    Pupil/Teacher Ratio: 12.36
    Dollars per Pupil: $3,471
    Average Teacher Salary: $1,402
    Effort Index: 1.250
  Private: 79 schools, 20,120 pupils
Colleges and Universities
  Two-year: 1 public; 11,954 students
  Four-year and Beyond: 3 private, 1
    public; 10,327 students
  Degree Options: B
Places Rated Score: 3,224
Places Rated Rank: 35

## Wheeling, WV–OH
Elementary and Secondary
  Public: 2 districts, 41 schools,
  15,658 pupils
    Pupil/Teacher Ratio: 14.94
    Dollars per Pupil: $2,296
    Average Teacher Salary: $1,707
    Effort Index: 1.240
  Private: 27 schools, 4,343 pupils
Colleges and Universities
  Two-year: 3 public; 5,775 students
  Four-year and Beyond: 1 private, 1
    public; 3,503 students
  Degree Options: B
Places Rated Score: 3,002
Places Rated Rank: 85

## Wichita, KS
Elementary and Secondary
  Public: 19 districts, 182 schools,
  71,777 pupils
    Pupil/Teacher Ratio: 12.54
    Dollars per Pupil: $2,702
    Average Teacher Salary: $1,435
    Effort Index: 1.025
  Private: 35 schools, 8,513 pupils
Colleges and Universities
  Two-year: 1 public; 2,985 students
  Four-year and Beyond: 2 private, 1
    public; 18,204 students
  Degree Options: B
Places Rated Score: 2,981
Places Rated Rank: 93

## Wichita Falls, TX
Elementary and Secondary
  Public: 5 districts, 43 schools,
  21,165 pupils
    Pupil/Teacher Ratio: 12.52
    Dollars per Pupil: $2,231
    Average Teacher Salary: $1,479
    Effort Index: 1.039
  Private: 7 schools, 1,067 pupils
Colleges and Universities
  Two-year: None
  Four-year and Beyond: 1 public; 4,818
    students
  Degree Options: C
Places Rated Score: 2,747
Places Rated Rank: 185

## Williamsport, PA
Elementary and Secondary
  Public: 8 districts, 40 schools,
  21,622 pupils
    Pupil/Teacher Ratio: 13.62
    Dollars per Pupil: $3,290
    Average Teacher Salary: $1,501
    Effort Index: 1.296
  Private: 11 schools, 1,463 pupils
Colleges and Universities
  Two-year: 1 public; 3,701 students
  Four-year and Beyond: 1 private; 1,192
    students
  Degree Options: C
Places Rated Score: 2,906
Places Rated Rank: 122

## Wilmington, DE–NJ–MD
Elementary and Secondary
  Public: 21 districts, 149 schools,
  84,377 pupils
    Pupil/Teacher Ratio: 14.30
    Dollars per Pupil: $2,827
    Average Teacher Salary: $929
    Effort Index: 1.285
  Private: 35 schools, 26,171 pupils
Colleges and Universities
  Two-year: 3 public; 7,198 students
  Four-year and Beyond: 2 private, 1
    public; 21,561 students
  Degree Options: B
Places Rated Score: 3,112
Places Rated Rank: 52

## Wilmington, NC
Elementary and Secondary
  Public: 1 district, 30 schools,
  19,888 pupils
    Pupil/Teacher Ratio: 14.91
    Dollars per Pupil: $2,404
    Average Teacher Salary: $1,442
    Effort Index: 1.265
  Private: 11 schools, 1,589 pupils
Colleges and Universities
  Two-year: 1 public; 1,927 students
  Four-year and Beyond: 1 public; 5,766
    students
  Degree Options: B
Places Rated Score: 2,876
Places Rated Rank: 134

## ★ Worcester, MA
Elementary and Secondary
  Public: 33 districts, 154 schools,
  65,992 pupils
    Pupil/Teacher Ratio: 13.06
    Dollars per Pupil: $2,524
    Average Teacher Salary: $1,616
    Effort Index: 1.141
  Private: 51 schools, 12,162 pupils
Colleges and Universities
  Two-year: 3 private, 1 public; 7,281
    students
  Four-year and Beyond: 7 private, 1
    public; 21,756 students
  Degree Options: A
Places Rated Score: 3,299
Places Rated Rank: 25

## Yakima, WA
Elementary and Secondary
  Public: 15 districts, 77 schools,
  34,259 pupils
    Pupil/Teacher Ratio: 17.96
    Dollars per Pupil: $2,618
    Average Teacher Salary: $1,940
    Effort Index: 1.149

Private: 16 schools, 2,162 pupils
Colleges and Universities
    Two-year: 1 public; 2,997 students
    Four-year and Beyond: 1 private; 292
        students
    Degree Options: C
Places Rated Score: 2,491
Places Rated Rank: 283

**York, PA**
Elementary and Secondary
    Public: 15 districts, 99 schools,
        50,225 pupils
        Pupil/Teacher Ratio: 14.47
        Dollars per Pupil: $2,297
        Average Teacher Salary: $1,600
        Effort Index: 1.359
    Private: 38 schools, 6,811 pupils
Colleges and Universities
    Two-year: 1 public; 1,341 students

Four-year and Beyond: 3 private; 6,565
    students
Degree Options: C
Places Rated Score: 2,903
Places Rated Rank: 124

**Youngstown–Warren, OH**
Elementary and Secondary
    Public: 37 districts, 183 schools,
        94,885 pupils
        Pupil/Teacher Ratio: 16.48
        Dollars per Pupil: $2,404
        Average Teacher Salary: $1,728
        Effort Index: 1.253
    Private: 43 schools, 13,331 pupils
Colleges and Universities
    Two-year: 2 private, 1 public; 2,705
        students
    Four-year and Beyond: 1 public; 15,590
        students

Degree Options: B
Places Rated Score: 2,920
Places Rated Rank: 115

**Yuba City, CA**
Elementary and Secondary
    Public: 17 districts, 59 schools,
        20,293 pupils
        Pupil/Teacher Ratio: 17.21
        Dollars per Pupil: $3,727
        Average Teacher Salary: $1,888
        Effort Index: 1.009
    Private: 13 schools, 1,459 pupils
Colleges and Universities
    Two-year: 1 public; 8,192 students
    Four-year and Beyond: None
    Degree Options: C
Places Rated Score: 2,387
Places Rated Rank: 309

# Et Cetera

## SOLVING THE SAT PUZZLE . . . OR TRYING

After 17 years of unbroken decline, the average scores of students on the Scholastic Aptitude Tests (SAT), given by the College Entrance Examination Board (CEEB), bottomed out in 1980 and started slowly upward in 1982. "We now think that we have a trend," CEEB President George Hanford told the *Chronicle of Higher Education*. At the current rate of recovery, however, math scores won't match their 1963 high until the year 2000 and verbal scores not until well into the next century. Although CEEB officials don't know why the scores have risen recently, they do suggest that recent high school seniors have enjoyed better instruction in the lower grades and have taken more courses in high school than the students who graduated before them.

Two researchers pointed out in a 1982 issue of *Phi Delta Kappan* that SAT scores started declining 18 years after the 1945 atomic bomb tests and began rising 18 years after the United States suspended all but underground atomic testing in 1963. The steepest drops in scores occurred in states nearest the bomb detonations, especially Nevada and Utah; smaller declines occurred in the northeastern and southeastern states that were far from the proving grounds. According to these researchers, those who blame the drop in SAT scores on television viewing, the Vietnam War, the child-spacing effect, changes in the number and mix of students taking the test, and poorer performance of schools are overlooking the effects of atomic fallout on the cognitive abilities of children.

But in Texas two other scholars of SAT trends have a different theory. The states that have the records of the highest scores, they claim, are not those that spend the most money for education, nor those with a long

tradition of quality public education, but those with the coldest winters: Average scores from cold-weather states are consistently higher than scores from warm-weather states. They offer two explanations for the link between cold weather and high SAT scores: (1) research on thermal conditions and human behavior suggests that cool room temperatures reduce mistakes on tests, and (2) long winters force children to remain inside after school and on weekends, thereby favoring family interaction, which is critical for pupil achievement.

Nonsense, another researcher points out. If one were to rank the states by their average total SATs, one would be ranking the states by the percent of college-bound seniors who actually took the test. In general, the larger the group tested, the lower the average level of performance.

**Average SAT Scores: The States Ranked**

| State | Percent of College-Bound Seniors Tested | Average Score | | |
|---|---|---|---|---|
| | | Verbal | Math | Total |
| 1. Iowa | 3% | 519 | 570 | 1,089 |
| 2. South Dakota | 3 | 520 | 566 | 1,086 |
| 3. North Dakota | 3 | 500 | 554 | 1,054 |
| 4. Kansas | 5 | 502 | 549 | 1,051 |
| 5. Utah | 4 | 503 | 542 | 1,045 |
| 6. Nebraska | 6 | 493 | 548 | 1,041 |
| 7. Montana | 9 | 490 | 544 | 1,034 |
| 7. Wyoming | 5 | 489 | 545 | 1,034 |
| 9. Minnesota | 7 | 481 | 539 | 1,020 |
| 10. New Mexico | 8 | 487 | 527 | 1,014 |
| 11. Oklahoma | 5 | 484 | 525 | 1,009 |
| 11. Tennessee | 8 | 486 | 523 | 1,009 |
| 13. Wisconsin | 10 | 475 | 532 | 1,007 |
| 14. Arkansas | 4 | 482 | 521 | 1,003 |
| 15. Kentucky | 6 | 479 | 518 | 997 |

| State | Percent of College-Bound Seniors Tested | Average Score Verbal | Average Score Math | Average Score Total |
|-------|------------------|--------|------|-------|
| 16. Idaho | 7% | 480 | 512 | 992 |
| 16. Mississippi | 3 | 480 | 512 | 992 |
| 18. Colorado | 17 | 468 | 514 | 982 |
| 19. Illinois | 14 | 463 | 518 | 981 |
| 19. Missouri | 11 | 469 | 512 | 981 |
| 21. Louisiana | 5 | 472 | 508 | 980 |
| 22. Michigan | 11 | 461 | 515 | 976 |
| 22. West Virginia | 7 | 466 | 510 | 976 |
| 24. Alabama | 6 | 467 | 503 | 970 |
| 25. Ohio | 16 | 460 | 508 | 968 |
| 25. Washington | 19 | 463 | 505 | 968 |
| 27. Nevada | 17 | 442 | 489 | 931 |
| 27. New Hampshire | 57 | 448 | 483 | 931 |
| 29. Alaska | 30 | 443 | 471 | 914 |
| 30. Oregon | 42 | 435 | 472 | 907 |
| 30. Vermont | 54 | 437 | 470 | 907 |
| 32. Connecticut | 69 | 436 | 468 | 904 |
| 33. Delaware | 50 | 433 | 469 | 902 |
| 34. Maryland | 50 | 429 | 469 | 898 |
| 35. California | 38 | 421 | 476 | 897 |
| 36. Massachusetts | 66 | 429 | 467 | 896 |
| 37. New York | 62 | 424 | 470 | 894 |
| 37. Virginia | 51 | 428 | 466 | 894 |
| 39. Maine | 46 | 429 | 463 | 892 |
| 40. Florida | 38 | 423 | 467 | 890 |
| 41. Pennsylvania | 52 | 425 | 462 | 887 |
| 42. Rhode Island | 61 | 424 | 461 | 885 |
| 43. New Jersey | 65 | 418 | 458 | 876 |
| 44. Hawaii | 47 | 395 | 474 | 869 |
| 45. Texas | 32 | 413 | 453 | 866 |
| 46. Indiana | 47 | 410 | 454 | 864 |
| 47. North Carolina | 47 | 395 | 432 | 827 |
| 48. Georgia | 49 | 392 | 430 | 822 |
| 49. South Carolina | 49 | 384 | 419 | 803 |
| 50. Arizona | 11 | 169 | 509 | 678 |

Source: College Entrance Examination Board, unpublished data, 1984.

## CERTIFYING PUPILS . . .

In the late 1970s, parents became convinced that teachers were neglecting the primary subjects, particularly reading, writing, and mathematics. Moreover, it wasn't possible to tell from a report card just how well a child was doing in relation to other children. Students were being promoted from grade to grade regardless of accomplishment. The result: Elementary pupils and even high school graduates who couldn't read a newspaper, write an intelligent sentence, address a postcard, or balance a checkbook.

This concern about students being ill prepared for adulthood led to a movement among taxpayers for accountability, or the holding of school districts responsible for teaching basic skills. One form of accountability is mandatory competency testing, an exam taken by each pupil to certify whether he or she can actually read, write, and solve mathematical problems.

Competency testing is a sensitive issue among educators, many of whom have been embarrassed by the results. When the tests were first administered to

pupils in the Florida public schools in 1978, the results were shocking. Thirty-seven percent failed a reading test for which the passing score was two and a half years below their grade level. In Kansas in 1981, nearly four out of ten high school juniors scored below the minimum level for reading and mathematics.

Forty states employ competency tests mainly to identify students who need "remediation," a term that means tutoring or retaking a course. Twenty-one states, however, use the test to certify pupils for grade promotion in elementary school and for high school graduation.

### Grade Promotion and High School Graduation: The 21 States That Certify Students

| State | Test Required for: Grade Promotion | Test Required for: High School Graduation | First Graduating Class Assessed |
|-------|-----------------|--------------------|------------------|
| Alabama | | • | 1985 |
| Arizona | | • | 1976 |
| Arkansas | • | | |
| California | • | • | 1979 |
| Delaware | | • | 1981 |
| Florida | • | • | 1983 |
| Georgia | | • | 1985 |
| Hawaii | | • | 1983 |
| Louisiana | • | | 1992 |
| Maryland | | • | 1982 |
| Nevada | | • | 1982 |
| New Jersey | | • | 1985 |
| New York | | • | 1979 |
| North Carolina | | • | 1980 |
| Oregon | | • | 1978 |
| South Carolina | • | • | 1990 |
| Tennessee | | • | 1982 |
| Texas | | • | 1986 |
| Utah | | • | 1980 |
| Vermont | | • | 1981 |
| Virginia | | • | 1981 |

Source: Education Commission of the States, States Activity—Minimum Competency Testing, 1984.

## . . . AND TESTING THE TEACHERS

Pupils in public schools aren't the only ones encountering competency tests. To identify candidates who have neither an aptitude for teaching nor skill in an academic discipline, 20 states require new teachers to take a competency test before they get their first license. Some of these states administer the test before the candidate enters a teacher-training program, while other states test the candidate after the training sequence but before the license is awarded.

That's not the end of teacher accountability. Thirty-nine states require teachers to renew their licenses, or become recertified, by taking continuing education courses. The renewal period is usually every three to five years, though some states allow longer periods based on the candidate's successful teaching experience. Thirty-four of these states will issue no lifetime licenses. Five states—Indiana, Michigan, Rhode Island, Texas, and Washington—have periodic renewal

## Raising Standards: The New Basics

The National Commission on Excellence in Education recommends that all college-bound high school seniors be required to take at least 16 units of the New Basics before qualifying for their diplomas. The commission defines these New Basics as one year of computer science, two years of a foreign language, four years of English, three years of mathematics, three years of science, and three years of social studies.

In ranking the states by the number of such courses their legislatures or state boards of education require of college-bound seniors, only Texas and Virginia come close to the recommended standard.

Seven states—Colorado, Iowa, Maine, Massachusetts, Michigan, Nebraska, and Wyoming—have their own graduation requirements, determined by local boards, that do not necessarily conform to the New Basics formula.

### High School Courses Required for Graduation: The States Ranked

| State | New Basics Units | Computer | Foreign Language | English | Mathematics | Science | Social Studies | Physical Education | Electives | Effective Class of |
|-------|------------------|----------|------------------|---------|-------------|---------|----------------|--------------------|-----------|--------------------|
| 1. Virginia | 16.0 | | 3.0 | 4.0 | 3.0 | 3.0 | 3.0 | 2.0 | 4.0 | 1985 |
| 2. Texas | 15.5 | 1.0 | 2.0 | 4.0 | 3.0 | 3.0 | 2.5 | 2.0 | 3.0 | 1988 |
| 3. New Hampshire | 14.0 | 0.5 | 3.0 | 4.0 | 2.0 | 2.0 | 2.5 | 1.25 | 4.0 | 1989 |
| 4. Louisiana | 13.5 | 0.5 | | 4.0 | 3.0 | 3.0 | 3.0 | 2.0 | 7.5 | 1990 |
| 4. Rhode Island | 13.5 | 0.5 | 2.0 | 4.0 | 3.0 | 2.0 | 2.0 | | 4.0 | 1988 |
| 6. Florida | 13.0 | | | 4.0 | 3.0 | 3.0 | 3.0 | 1.0 | 9.0 | 1987 |
| 6. Missouri | 13.0 | | | 4.0 | 3.0 | 3.0 | 3.0 | 1.0 | 8.0 | 1985 |
| 6. Pennsylvania | 13.0 | | | 4.0 | 3.0 | 3.0 | 3.0 | 1.0 | | 1989 |
| 6. Vermont | 13.0 | | | 4.0 | 3.0 | 3.0 | 3.0 | 1.5 | | 1989 |
| 10. Arkansas | 12.0 | | | 4.0 | 2.0 | 3.0 | 3.0 | 1.0 | 6.5 | 1988 |
| 10. Connecticut | 12.0 | | | 4.0 | 3.0 | 2.0 | 3.0 | 1.0 | 6.0 | 1988 |
| 10. Georgia | 12.0 | 1.0 | | 4.0 | 2.0 | 2.0 | 3.0 | 1.0 | 8.0 | 1988 |
| 10. Hawaii | 12.0 | | | 4.0 | 2.0 | 2.0 | 4.0 | 1.5 | 6.0 | 1983 |
| 10. South Carolina | 12.0 | | | 4.0 | 3.0 | 2.0 | 3.0 | 1.0 | 7.0 | 1987 |
| 15. Oregon | 11.5 | | 1.0 | 3.0 | 2.0 | 2.0 | 3.5 | 2.0 | 8.0 | 1988 |
| 15. South Dakota | 11.5 | 0.5 | | 4.0 | 2.0 | 2.0 | 3.0 | | 8.0 | 1989 |
| 15. Wisconsin | 11.5 | 0.5 | | 4.0 | 2.0 | 2.0 | 3.0 | 2.0 | | 1989 |
| 18. Alaska | 11.0 | | | 4.0 | 2.0 | 2.0 | 3.0 | 1.0 | 9.0 | 1985 |
| 18. California | 11.0 | | 1.0 | 3.0 | 2.0 | 2.0 | 3.0 | 2.0 | | 1987 |
| 18. Delaware | 11.0 | | | 4.0 | 2.0 | 2.0 | 3.0 | 1.5 | 6.5 | 1987 |
| 18. Kansas | 11.0 | | | 4.0 | 2.0 | 2.0 | 3.0 | 1.0 | 8.0 | 1988 |
| 18. Kentucky | 11.0 | | | 4.0 | 3.0 | 2.0 | 2.0 | 1.0 | 7.0 | 1987 |
| 18. Maryland | 11.0 | | | 4.0 | 2.0 | 2.0 | 3.0 | 1.0 | 8.0 | * |
| 18. North Dakota | 11.0 | | | 4.0 | 2.0 | 2.0 | 3.0 | 1.0 | 5.0 | 1984 |
| 18. West Virginia | 11.0 | | 1.0 | 4.0 | 2.0 | 1.0 | 3.0 | 2.0 | 7.0 | 1985 |
| 26. Utah | 10.5 | 0.5 | | 3.0 | 2.0 | 2.0 | 3.0 | 2.0 | 9.0 | 1988 |
| 27. Alabama | 10.0 | | | 4.0 | 2.0 | 1.0 | 3.0 | 3.5 | 6.5 | 1985 |
| 27. Arizona | 10.0 | | | 4.0 | 2.0 | 2.0 | 2.0 | | 9.5 | 1987 |
| 27. Idaho | 10.0 | | | 4.0 | 2.0 | 2.0 | 2.0 | 1.5 | 6.0 | 1988 |
| 27. Indiana | 10.0 | | | 4.0 | 2.0 | 2.0 | 2.0 | 1.5 | 8.0 | 1989 |
| 27. New Mexico | 10.0 | | | 4.0 | 2.0 | 2.0 | 2.0 | 1.0 | 9.0 | 1987 |
| 27. North Carolina | 10.0 | | | 4.0 | 2.0 | 2.0 | 2.0 | 1.0 | 9.0 | 1987 |
| 27. Oklahoma | 10.0 | | | 4.0 | 2.0 | 2.0 | 2.0 | | 10.0 | 1987 |
| 34. Tennessee | 9.5 | | | 4.0 | 2.0 | 2.0 | 1.5 | 1.5 | 9.0 | 1987 |
| 34. Washington | 9.5 | | | 3.0 | 2.0 | 2.0 | 2.5 | 2.0 | 5.5 | 1989 |
| 36. Illinois | 9.0 | | 1.0 | 3.0 | 2.0 | 1.0 | 2.0 | 4.5 | 2.25 | 1988 |
| 36. Minnesota | 9.0 | | | 4.0 | 1.0 | 1.0 | 3.0 | 1.5 | 9.5 | 1982 |
| 36. Montana | 9.0 | | | 4.0 | 2.0 | 1.0 | 2.0 | 1.0 | 10.0 | 1986 |
| 36. New Jersey | 9.0 | | | 4.0 | 2.0 | 1.0 | 2.0 | 4.0 | 4.0 | * |
| 36. New York | 9.0 | | | 4.0 | 1.0 | 1.0 | 3.0 | 0.5 | 8.5 | * |
| 41. Nevada | 8.0 | | | 3.0 | 2.0 | 1.0 | 2.0 | 2.5 | 9.5 | 1986 |
| 41. Ohio | 8.0 | | | 3.0 | 2.0 | 1.0 | 2.0 | 1.0 | 9.0 | 1988 |
| 43. Mississippi | 7.5 | | | 3.0 | 1.0 | 1.0 | 2.5 | | 8.5 | * |

*Source: Places Rated rankings derived from Education Commission of the States, Minimum High School Graduation Course Requirements in the States, August 1984.*

*Graduation requirements have been in effect for a number of years.

leading to life certificates, which are increasingly being linked to advanced professional training.

## Testing the Teachers

| State | Competency | | Recertification | |
|---|---|---|---|---|
| | Test | Starting | Required | Every . . . |
| Alabama | Yes | 1981 | Yes | 8–12 yr* |
| Alaska | No | | Yes | 5 |
| Arizona | Yes | 1980 | Yes | 6 |
| Arkansas | Yes | 1983 | Yes | 6–10* |
| California | Yes | 1982 | Yes | 5 |
| Colorado | Yes | 1983 | Yes | 5 |
| Connecticut | Yes | 1985 | No | |
| Delaware | Yes | 1983 | No | |
| Florida | Yes | 1980 | Yes | 6 |
| Georgia | Yes | 1979 | Yes | 5–10* |
| Hawaii | No | | No | |
| Idaho | No | | No | |
| Illinois | No | | No | |
| Indiana | No | | Yes | 5–10* |
| Iowa | No | | Yes | 6–10* |
| Kansas | No | | Yes | 3–5* |
| Kentucky | No | | Yes | 10 |
| Louisiana | Yes | 1979 | No | |
| Maine | No | | Yes | 5 |
| Maryland | No | | Yes | 5–10* |
| Massachusetts | No | | No | |
| Michigan | No | | Yes | 6 |
| Minnesota | No | | Yes | 5 |
| Mississippi | Yes | 1977 | Yes | 5–10* |
| Missouri | No | | No | |
| Montana | No | | Yes | 5 |
| Nebraska | No | | Yes | 3 |
| Nevada | No | | Yes | 5–6* |
| New Hampshire | No | | Yes | 3 |
| New Jersey | No | | No | |
| New Mexico | Yes | 1983 | Yes | 4–10* |
| New York | Yes | 1984 | No | |
| North Carolina | Yes | 1981 | Yes | 5 |
| North Dakota | No | | Yes | 5 |
| Ohio | No | | Yes | 4–8* |
| Oklahoma | Yes | 1982 | Yes | 5 |
| Oregon | No | | Yes | 3–5* |
| Pennsylvania | No | | Yes | 6 |
| Rhode Island | No | | Yes | 3–5* |
| South Carolina | Yes | 1982 | Yes | 5 |
| South Dakota | No | | Yes | 5 |
| Tennessee | Yes | 1981 | Yes | 10 |
| Texas | Yes | 1985 | Yes | 3–5* |
| Utah | No | | Yes | 5 |
| Vermont | No | | Yes | 5 |
| Virginia | Yes | 1981 | Yes | 5 |
| Washington | No | | Yes | 4 |
| West Virginia | Yes | 1985 | Yes | 3–5* |
| Wisconsin | No | | No | |
| Wyoming | No | | Yes | 5–10* |

Source: Education Commission of the States, Clearinghouse Notes, and Phi Delta Kappan, October 1984.

*Certification interval depends on years of successful teaching experience.

## OUTSTANDING PUBLIC SECONDARY SCHOOLS

In 1983 and again in 1984, the Department of Education asked the chief education officer of each state to name the best public secondary schools in his or her state.

Of the nearly 1,000 schools so nominated, 354 have received official recognition for excellence in education. These schools had to pass a rigorous screening process, which included a careful look at curricula and academic achievement; inspection of buildings, classrooms, and facilities; informal observations of classes, lunch periods, and assemblies; and interviews with students, parents, teachers, and administrators. The evaluators, none of whom worked for the federal government, were specialists in public-school improvement and accreditation.

Two hundred seventy-five of these outstanding secondary schools are located in metro areas. The schools include 123 junior high schools (JHS), middle schools (MS), and intermediate schools (IS), as well as 152 high schools (HS).

### The Best Secondary Schools in the Metro Areas

**Akron, OH**
Hudson HS, Hudson
Hudson JHS, Hudson
Perkins JHS, Akron

**Albany–Schenectady–Troy, NY**
Niskayuna HS, Schenectady

**Albuquerque, NM**
Albuquerque HS, Albuquerque
Hoover MS, Albuquerque
Jefferson MS, Albuquerque
Manzano HS, Albuquerque
Taft MS, Albuquerque
West Mesa HS, Albuquerque

**Anaheim–Santa Ana, CA**
Venado MS, Irvine

**Ann Arbor, MI**
Huron HS, Ann Arbor
Slauson IS, Ann Arbor

**Atlanta, GA**
Douglass HS, Atlanta
Garrett MS, Austell
Walton HS, Marietta

**Austin, TX**
Austin HS, Austin

**Baton Rouge, LA**
Baton Rouge HS, Baton Rouge
McKinley MS, Baton Rouge

**Birmingham, AL**
Bush MS, Birmingham
Homewood HS, Homewood
Homewood MS, Homewood
Mountain Brook HS, Mountain Brook

**Boston, MA**
Acton–Boxborough HS, Acton
Rockland JHS, Rockland

**Bridgeport–Milford, CT**
Flood IS, Stratford
Wooster IS, Stratford

**Casper, WY**
Walsh HS, Casper

**Cedar Rapids, IA**
Franklin JHS, Cedar Rapids
Linn-Mar JHS, Cedar Rapids
Washington HS, Cedar Rapids

**Charleston, WV**
Washington HS, Charleston

**Charlotte–Gastonia–Rock Hill, NC–SC**
Carmel JHS, Charlotte, NC
Rock Hill HS, Rock Hill, SC

**Chicago, IL**
Community HS North, Downers Grove
Glenbrook North HS, Northbrook
Glenbrook South HS, Glenview
Homewood-Flossmoor HS, Flossmoor
Medinah ES, Roselle
Old Orchard JHS, Skokie
Rich Township HS, Richton Park
Thomas JHS, Arlington Heights
York Community HS, Elmhurst

**Cincinnati, OH–KY–IN**
Harrison JHS, Harrison, OH
Indian Hill HS, Cincinnati
Princeton HS, Cincinnati
Princeton JHS, Cincinnati
Wyoming HS, Wyoming, OH

**Cleveland, OH**
Shaker Heights HS, Shaker Heights
Woodbury JHS, Shaker Heights

**Colorado Springs, CO**
Cheyenne Mountain HS, Colorado Springs
Holmes JHS, Colorado Springs

**Columbia, SC**
Irmo HS, Columbia
Spring Valley HS, Columbia
Wright MS, Columbia

**Columbus, OH**
Jones MS, Columbus

**Dallas, TX**
Richardson HS, Richardson

**Dayton–Springfield, OH**
Ankeny JHS, Beavercreek
Centerville HS, Centerville

**Daytona Beach, FL**
Mainland HS, Daytona Beach

**Denver, CO**
Carmody JHS, Lakewood
Mrachek MS, Aurora
Wheat Ridge HS, Wheat Ridge

**Des Moines, IA**
Indian Hills JHS, Des Moines
Valley HS, West Des Moines

**Detroit, MI**
Andover HS, Bloomfield Hills
Cass Technical HS, Detroit
Grosse Point South HS,
   Grosse Point
Lahser HS, Bloomfield Hills
Southfield HS, Southfield

**Eau Claire, WI**
Memorial HS, Eau Claire

**El Paso, TX**
Desert View MS, El Paso

**Eugene–Springfield, OR**
Monroe MS, Eugene
Oaklea MS, Junction City
South Eugene HS, Eugene

**Fargo–Moorhead, ND–MN**
Franklin JHS, Fargo

**Fort Lauderdale–Hollywood–
Pompano Beach, FL**
South Plantation HS, Plantation

**Fort Smith, AR–OK**
Gans JHS, Muldrow, OK
Muldrow HS, Muldrow, OK
Southside HS, Fort Smith, AR

**Gary–Hammond, IN**
Valparaiso HS, Valparaiso
Westchester MS, Chesterton

**Grand Rapids, MI**
Northview HS, Grand Rapids
West Ottawa MS, Holland

**Greenville–Spartanburg, SC**
League MS, Greenville
Spartanburg Senior HS, Spar-
   tanburg

**Hartford, CT**
Illing JHS, Manchester

**Houma–Thibodaux, LA**
Raceland JHS, Raceland

**Houston, TX**
Bellaire HS, Bellaire
Bleyl JHS, Houston
Stratford HS, Houston

**Indianapolis, IN**
Carmel HS, Carmel
Clay JHS, Carmel
Davis HS, Indianapolis
Lawrence North HS, India-
   napolis
North Central HS, Indianapolis
Warren Central HS, India-
   napolis
Westland MS, Indianapolis

**Iowa City, IA**
South East JHS, Iowa City

**Jackson, MS**
Clinton HS, Clinton

**Jacksonville, FL**
Gorris JHS, Jacksonville
Davis JHS, Jacksonville
Parker HS, Jacksonville
Ribault HS, Jacksonville

**Kansas City, KS**
Oregon Trail JHS, Olathe
Shawnee Mission South HS,
   Shawnee Mission
Shawnee Mission West HS,
   Shawnee Mission

**Kansas City, MO**
Blue Springs HS, Blue Springs
Lewis MS, Excelsior Springs

**Lafayette, LA**
Lafayette MS, Lafayette

**Lake County, IL**
Elm Place MS, Highland Park
Wilmot JHS, Deerfield

**Lansing–East Lansing, MI**
Okemos HS, Okemos

**Las Vegas, NV**
Cannon JHS, Las Vegas
Guinn JHS, Las Vegas

**Lewiston–Auburn, ME**
Auburn MS, Auburn

**Lincoln, NE**
East HS, Lincoln
Lincoln HS, Lincoln

**Los Angeles–Long Beach,
CA**
Artesia HS, Lakewood
Montebello MS, Montebello
Pioneer HS, Whittier
West HS, Torrance

**Lynchburg, VA**
Glass HS, Lynchburg

**Madison, WI**
LaFollette HS, Madison

**Medford, OR**
Crater HS, Central Point

**Melbourne–Titusville–
Palm Bay, FL**
Jefferson JHS, Merritt Island

**Memphis, TN–AR–MS**
Collierville MS, Collierville, TN
Snowden MS, Memphis

**Miami–Hialeah, FL**
American HS, Hialeah
Highland Oaks JHS, North
   Miami Beach

**Milwaukee, WI**
Brown Deer HS, Brown Deer
Burroughs MS, Milwaukee
King HS, Milwaukee
Webster Transitional MS,
   Cedarburg

**Minneapolis–St. Paul, MN–WI**
Edina HS, Edina, MN
Hopkins HS, Minnetonka, MN
Hopkins North JHS, Minneton-
   ka, MN
Hopkins West JHS, Minneton-
   ka, MN
Oak-Land JHS, Lake Elmo, MN
Richfield HS, Richfield, MN
Stillwater JHS, Stillwater, MN

**Mobile, AL**
Vigor HS, Prichard

**Nassau–Suffolk, NY**
Miller Place HS, Miller Place
Murphy JHS, Stony Brook
Northport HS, Northport
Shoreham–Wading River MS,
   Shoreham

**New Bedford, MA**
New Bedford HS, New Bedford

**New Haven–Meriden, CT**
Amity Regional HS, Orange
Conte Arts MS, New Haven

**New Orleans, LA**
King HS, Metairie
Lakewood JHS, Luling

**New York, NY**
Blue Mountain MS, Peekskill
Bronx HS of Science, Bronx
Brooklyn Technical HS,
   Brooklyn
Cardozo HS, Bayside
Edgemont HS, Scarsdale
Fox Lane MS, Bedford
New Rochelle HS, New Ro-
   chelle
Scarsdale HS, Scarsdale
Stuyvesant HS, New York

**Norfolk–Virginia Beach–
Newport News, VA**
Dunbar-Erwin MS, Newport
   News
Menchville HS, Newport News

**Norwalk, CT**
Middlebrook MS, Wilton
Wilton HS, Wilton

**Oakland, CA**
Alvarado MS, Union City
Logan HS, Union City

**Oklahoma City, OK**
Marshall HS, Oklahoma City
Millwood HS, Oklahoma City
Northeast HS, Oklahoma City

**Olympia, WA**
Jefferson MS, Olympia

**Omaha, NE–IA**
Arbor Heights JHS, Omaha
Burke HS, Omaha
Kirn JHS, Council Bluffs, IA
Millard North HS, Omaha
Millard South HS, Omaha
Westside HS, Omaha

**Pawtucket–Woonsocket–
Attleboro, RI–MA**
Lincoln HS, Lincoln, RI

**Philadelphia, PA–NJ**
Bala-Cynwyd MS, Bala-
   Cynwyd, PA
Conestoga HS, Berwyn, PA
Harriton HS, Rosemont, PA
Radnor HS, Radnor, PA
Welsh Valley MS, Narberth, PA

**Phoenix, AZ**
Agua Fria Union HS, Avondale
Chandler HS, Chandler
Foston JHS, Mesa
Mesa HS, Mesa
Rhodes JHS, Mesa
Shea MS, Phoenix
Westwood HS, Mesa
Willis JHS, Chandler

**Pine Bluff, AR**
White Hall HS, Pine Bluff

**Pittsburgh, PA**
Mount Lebanon HS, Pittsburgh
Upper St. Clair HS, Pittsburgh

**Portland, ME**
Deering HS, Portland
King MS, Portland
Portland HS, Portland

**Portland, OR**
Cedar Park IS, Beaverton
Clackamas HS, Milwaukie
Lake Oswego HS, Lake
   Oswego

Light MS, Portland
McLoughlin JHS, Milwaukie
Renne IS, Newburg
Sunset HS, Beaverton
West Linn HS, West Linn

**Portsmouth–Dover–
Rochester, NH–ME**
Exeter JHS, Exeter, NH

**Providence, RI**
Bain JHS, Cranston
East Greenwich HS, East
   Greenwich
Western Hills JHS, Cranston

**Provo–Orem, UT**
Timpview HS, Provo

**Raleigh–Durham, NC**
Broughton HS, Raleigh
Enloe HS, Raleigh

**Reno, NV**
Reno HS, Reno
Swope MS, Reno

**Richland–Kennewick–Pasco,
WA**
Hanford HS, Richland
Pasco HS, Pasco

**Richmond–Petersburg, VA**
Hermitage HS, Richmond

**Riverside–San Bernardino,
CA**
Mission JHS, Riverside
Terrace Hills JHS, Grand
   Terrace

**Roanoke, VA**
Breckinridge JHS, Roanoke
Cave Spring HS, Roanoke
Hidden Valley JHS, Roanoke

**Rochester, MN**
Adams JHS, Rochester

**Rochester, NY**
Greece Athena HS,
   Rochester

**St. Louis, MO–IL**
Brentwood JHS, Brentwood,
   MO
Ladue JHS, Ladue, MO
McCluer North HS, Florissant,
   MO
Parkway West Senior HS,
   Ballwin, MO
Patonville Heights MS,
   Maryland Heights, MO
Watkins HS, St. Louis

**Salt Lake City–Ogden, UT**
Bountiful HS, Bountiful
Brighton HS, Salt Lake City
Butler MS, Salt Lake City
Eastmont MS, Sandy
Highland HS, Salt Lake City
South HS, Salt Lake City

**San Antonio, TX**
Churchill HS, San Antonio

**San Diego, CA**
Chula Vista HS, Chula Vista
Fallbrook Union HS, Fallbrook
Santana HS, Santee
Twin Peaks MS, Poway

**San Francisco, CA**
Borel MS, San Mateo
Crocker JHS, Hillsborough
Davidson MS, San Rafael
Lowell HS, San Francisco

**San Jose, CA**
Leyva JHS, San Jose

**Seattle, WA**
Lindbergh HS, Renton
Redmond HS, Redmond
Shorewood HS, Seattle

**Shreveport, LA**
Captain Shreve HS, Shreveport
Youree Drive MS, Shreveport

**Spokane, WA**
Sacajawea JHS, Spokane

**Springfield, MO**
Kickapoo HS, Springfield

**Tacoma, WA**
Curtis HS, Tacoma
Curtis JHS, Tacoma

**Tampa–St. Petersburg–Clearwater, FL**
Brandon HS, Brandon
Hollins HS, St. Petersburg
Largo MS, Largo

**Toledo, OH**
Arbor Hills JHS, Sylvania

**Topeka, KS**
Topeka West HS, Topeka

**Tucson, AZ**
Amphitheatre HS, Tucson
Utterback JHS, Tucson

**Tulsa, OK**
Washington HS, Tulsa

**Vancouver, WA**
Battle Ground HS, Battle Ground

**Washington, DC–MD–VA**
Alice Deal JHS, Washington
Brookland JHS, Washington
George Mason HS, Falls Church, VA

Hobson MS, Washington
Jefferson JHS, Washington
Williams HS, Alexandria, VA

**Wheeling, WV–OH**
Bridge Street JHS, Wheeling
Triadelphia JHS, Wheeling
Wheeling JHS, Wheeling
Wheeling Park HS, Wheeling

**Wichita, KS**
Horace Mann MS, Wichita

**Wilmington, DE–NJ–MD**
Brandywine HS, Wilmington

*Source:* U.S. Department of Education, press releases from the Secondary School Recognition Program, 1983 and 1984.

## THE HIGH COST OF COLLEGE

Some say that in the future white-collar workplace, only those who have college degrees will get the nod for new slots in management training, or even entry-level jobs behind the counter or in the mail room. But coming up with four years of tuition and fees to help their children launch a career is breaking a lot of middle-income families. To go away to college and make it through in standard time, most students need at least two out of these three sources of money (aside from parental largesse): a scholarship, a student loan, and a part-time job.

The best way to cut costs at the very start is to do some sharp thinking when choosing a college. If you are planning on college, consider your options. You can:

• Live at home, enroll in a low-cost two-year college that offers courses good toward a bachelor's degree, and then transfer to a local four-year state college for your junior and senior years. This is the least expensive way to get a college education.

• Enroll in a public four-year college or university in your home state. The tuition will definitely be higher than that of a two-year college. And if you decide to live on campus, it will cost you $2,500 more per year than attending college while living at home.

• Enroll in a public college or university outside your home state. This will mean paying stiff tuition charges. But establishing legal residency could save you a significant amount. Tuitions in California public colleges, for example, are one fifth what you'd pay in several northeastern states.

• Register at a private college or university. This is the most expensive option, even if you live at home.

### Private vs. Public Tuition

The costs for a room and daily meals on campus aren't much greater at private colleges than they are at state institutions. The average $16,400 extra that a student pays for choosing a private over a state college is entirely in the tuition.

Students at private colleges pay two thirds of the real cost of their education; the rest comes from gifts and earnings from the school's endowment. At state-run colleges, the student pays only one fifth of the real cost, the slack being taken up by state government money. But private colleges spend a great deal more to educate each student than do public colleges since they offer unique cultural and religious environments, smaller classes, and special programs not available at state schools. In paying more for tuition at a private school, the student often gets more.

### Tuition, Room, and Board:
#### The Most Expensive Colleges and Universities

| East | Total |
|---|---|
| 1. Harvard University (Cambridge, MA) | $13,185 |
| 2. Barnard College (New York, NY) | 13,165 |
| 3. Yale University (New Haven, CT) | 13,160 |
| 4. Sarah Lawrence College (Bronxville, NY) | 13,130 |
| 5. Princeton University (Princeton, NJ) | 12,910 |
| 6. Smith College (Northampton, MA) | 12,740 |
| 7. Bard College (Annandale-on-Hudson, NY) | 12,680 |
| 8. Dartmouth College (Hanover, NH) | 12,580 |
| 9. Tufts University (Medford, MA) | 12,534 |
| 10. Brown University (Providence, RI) | 12,495 |

| South | Total |
|---|---|
| 1. Tulane University of Louisiana (New Orleans, LA) | $10,450 |
| 2. Vanderbilt University (Nashville, TN) | 10,071 |
| 3. Emory University (Atlanta, GA) | 9,970 |
| 4. Duke University (Durham, NC) | 9,969 |
| 5. Sweet Briar College (Sweet Briar, VA) | 9,650 |
| 6. Hollins College (Hollins College, VA) | 9,600 |
| 7. Southern Methodist University (Dallas, TX) | 9,585 |
| 8. Randolph-Macon Woman's College (Lynchburg, VA) | 9,580 |
| 9. University of Miami (Coral Gables, FL) | 9,328 |
| 10. Rollins College (Winter Park, FL) | 9,251 |

| West | Total |
|---|---|
| 1. Stanford University (Stanford, CA) | $12,839 |
| 2. Harvey Mudd College (Claremont, CA) | 11,710 |
| 3. Scripps College (Claremont, CA) | 11,460 |
| 4. University of Southern California (Los Angeles, CA) | 11,350 |
| 5. Occidental College (Los Angeles, CA) | 11,298 |
| 6. University of the Pacific (Stockton, CA) | 11,297 |
| 7. Pomona College (Claremont, CA) | 11,200 |
| 8. Pepperdine University (Malibu, CA) | 11,064 |
| 9. Mills College (Oakland, CA) | 10,500 |
| 10. University of Redlands (Redlands, CA) | 10,375 |

| Midwest | Total |
|---|---|
| 1. Northwestern University (Evanston, IL) | $12,291 |
| 2. University of Chicago | 12,136 |
| 3. Oberlin College (Oberlin, OH) | 11,425 |
| 4. Washington University (St. Louis, MO) | 11,320 |
| 5. Kenyon College (Gambier, OH) | 10,500 |
| 6. Carleton College (Northfield, MN) | 10,149 |
| 7. Denison University (Granville, OH) | 10,020 |
| 7. Lake Forest College (Lake Forest, IL) | 10,020 |
| 9. Case Western Reserve University (Cleveland, OH) | 9,870 |
| 10. College of Wooster (Wooster, OH) | 9,650 |

Source: National Center for Education Statistics, *Basic Student Charges, 1983–84*, 1984.

## In-State and Out-of-State Tuition

Each fall, 300,000 freshmen head for colleges outside their home state. Half enroll in private schools, and the other half enter state colleges at which tuition for nonresidents often equals tuition they would pay at any private school. It isn't accidental that states showing net gains from the annual freshman migration have a good supply of private schools within their borders, or are noted for downhill skiing, or are simply located in the best parts of the Sun Belt. The states that lose the most students are found in the cold Midwest and Northeast.

The biggest dollar differences between in-state and out-of-state tuition are found at each of the California State University and Colleges 14 campuses, at each of the University of California's nine campuses, the three campuses of the University of Colorado, the University of Michigan's main campus, and the University of Vermont. At these 28 schools, nonresident tuition is at least $3,000 more than in-state tuition.

Paying the out-of-state tuition differential has been challenged in the courts by students claiming discrimination. Others simply change their legal residence by re-registering their cars in the new state and taking part-time jobs in which state taxes are withheld, thus qualifying for the lower rate.

### The Annual Freshman Exchange

| Losers | Outgoing Freshmen | Winners | Incoming Freshmen |
|---|---|---|---|
| 1. New York | 31,000 | 1. California | 25,500 |
| 2. New Jersey | 28,300 | 2. Massachusetts | 20,800 |
| 3. Illinois | 19,800 | 3. New York | 18,500 |
| 4. Pennsylvania | 16,400 | 4. Pennsylvania | 17,400 |
| 5. Connecticut | 13,700 | 5. Texas | 14,500 |
| 6. Ohio | 12,000 | 6. Florida | 13,900 |

Source: National Center for Education Statistics, *Condition of Education*, 1984.

## TOP-RANKED PH.D. PROGRAMS

The following rankings are derived from the five-volume *Assessment of Research-Doctorate Programs in the United States*. Institutions are ranked by the number of programs in five basic fields—physical sciences and

### Basic Yearly Student Charges in Public Colleges by State

| | Tuition | Room | Board | Total | | Tuition | Room | Board | Total |
|---|---|---|---|---|---|---|---|---|---|
| U.S. Average | $870 | $1,140 | $1,250 | $3,260 | U.S. Average | $870 | $1,140 | $1,250 | $3,260 |
| 1. Hawaii | 340 | 900 | 900 | 2,140 | 26. Iowa | 990 | 900 | 1,140 | 3,030 |
| 2. Mississippi | 830 | 660 | 900 | 2,390 | 27. Wisconsin | 990 | 1,080 | 1,110 | 3,180 |
| 3. Oklahoma | 610 | 840 | 1,010 | 2,460 | 28. Alaska | 600 | 920 | 1,760 | 3,280 |
| 4. North Dakota | 850 | 600 | 1,070 | 2,520 | 29. Washington | 810 | 1,160 | 1,330 | 3,300 |
| 5. New Mexico | 770 | 880 | 880 | 2,530 | 30. Oregon | 970 | 1,000 | 1,350 | 3,320 |
| 6. North Carolina | 500 | 910 | 1,140 | 2,550 | 31. Minnesota | 1,160 | 980 | 1,190 | 3,330 |
| 7. Arkansas | 820 | 730 | 1,070 | 2,620 | 31. Virginia | 980 | 1,150 | 1,200 | 3,330 |
| 8. Arizona | 560 | 1,010 | 1,060 | 2,630 | 33. Nevada | 850 | 1,190 | 1,340 | 3,380 |
| 9. Louisiana | 690 | 980 | 980 | 2,650 | 34. Utah | 880 | 970 | 1,540 | 3,390 |
| 10. Missouri | 790 | 950 | 950 | 2,690 | 35. Illinois | 880 | 1,220 | 1,300 | 3,400 |
| 10. Texas | 420 | 1,040 | 1,230 | 2,690 | 36. Indiana | 1,280 | 880 | 1,320 | 3,480 |
| 12. Kentucky | 740 | 870 | 1,110 | 2,720 | 37. Colorado | 1,020 | 1,100 | 1,430 | 3,550 |
| 13. Florida | 730 | 1,030 | 1,020 | 2,780 | 38. Connecticut | 870 | 1,520 | 1,370 | 3,760 |
| 14. Tennessee | 750 | 960 | 1,100 | 2,810 | 39. Delaware | 1,210 | 1,460 | 1,100 | 3,770 |
| 15. Kansas | 860 | 910 | 1,050 | 2,820 | 40. Michigan | 1,310 | 1,060 | 1,420 | 3,790 |
| 16. Alabama | 880 | 800 | 1,150 | 2,830 | 41. New Jersey | 1,130 | 1,420 | 1,260 | 3,810 |
| 17. South Dakota | 1,120 | 830 | 950 | 2,900 | 42. Maine | 1,430 | 1,290 | 1,290 | 4,010 |
| 18. Nebraska | 1,000 | 830 | 1,080 | 2,910 | 43. Massachusetts | 1,060 | 1,500 | 1,500 | 4,060 |
| 18. Wyoming | 580 | 960 | 1,370 | 2,910 | 44. New York | 1,240 | 1,460 | 1,380 | 4,080 |
| 20. California | 280 | 1,280 | 1,430 | 2,990 | 45. Maryland | 1,080 | 1,510 | 1,510 | 4,100 |
| 21. Georgia | 860 | 880 | 1,260 | 3,000 | 46. Ohio | 1,500 | 1,490 | 1,130 | 4,120 |
| 21. Montana | 780 | 800 | 1,420 | 3,000 | 47. Pennsylvania | 1,760 | 1,250 | 1,180 | 4,190 |
| 23. South Carolina | 960 | 910 | 1,140 | 3,010 | 48. Rhode Island | 1,180 | 1,560 | 1,560 | 4,300 |
| 24. Idaho | 790 | 760 | 1,470 | 3,020 | 49. New Hampshire | 1,810 | 1,350 | 1,330 | 4,490 |
| 24. West Virginia | 600 | 1,150 | 1,270 | 3,020 | 50. Vermont | 2,180 | 1,450 | 1,270 | 4,900 |

Source: National Center for Education Statistics, unpublished data, 1984.

mathematics, humanities, engineering, biological sciences, and social and behavioral sciences—that scored 60 or higher in reputation for "faculty quality." A rating of 50 represented the mean; a score of 75 would be considered exceptional.

The table "Top-Ranked Ph.D.-Granting Institutions" details how many programs in each field scored at least 60 points and also indicates how many of those programs also ranked at the higher level of 70 points or above. The entry Overall Score represents the total number of both these kinds of programs.

It's interesting to note that five of the top ten institutions for Ph.D. programs are also among the nation's most expensive places at which to get an education: Harvard, Princeton, Stanford, University of Chicago, and Yale.

### Top-Ranked Ph.D.-Granting Institutions

| | Programs Rated 60 or Above | | | | | | Programs Rated 70 or Above | Overall Score |
|---|---|---|---|---|---|---|---|---|
| Institution | Physics, Science, Mathematics | Humanities | Engineering | Biology | Social Science | Total | | |
| 1. University of California, Berkeley | 6 | 9 | 4 | 4 | 7 | 30 | 15 | 45 |
| 2. Stanford University (Stanford, CA) | 6 | 4 | 4 | 4 | 6 | 24 | 10 | 34 |
| 3. Harvard University (Cambridge, MA) | 5 | 5 | — | 4 | 6 | 20 | 12 | 32 |
| 3. Yale University (New Haven, CT) | 6 | 7 | — | 6 | 6 | 25 | 7 | 32 |
| 5. Massachusetts Institute of Technology (Cambridge, MA) | 5 | 2 | 4 | 3 | 3 | 17 | 12 | 29 |
| 6. Princeton University (Princeton, NJ) | 5 | 7 | 4 | — | 5 | 21 | 7 | 28 |
| 7. University of Chicago | 5 | 4 | — | 4 | 7 | 20 | 7 | 27 |
| 8. University of California, Los Angeles | 5 | 5 | 2 | 6 | 6 | 24 | — | 24 |
| 8. University of Michigan | 2 | 6 | 3 | 4 | 6 | 21 | 3 | 24 |
| 8. University of Wisconsin | 5 | 3 | 2 | 5 | 6 | 21 | 3 | 24 |
| 11. Columbia University (New York, NY) | 5 | 6 | — | 4 | 6 | 21 | 2 | 23 |
| 12. Cornell University (Ithaca, NY) | 6 | 6 | 3 | 4 | 3 | 22 | 1 | 23 |
| 13. University of Illinois (Champaign, IL) | 4 | 2 | 4 | 4 | 3 | 17 | 2 | 19 |
| 14. University of Pennsylvania (Philadelphia, PA) | 2 | 5 | 1 | 3 | 5 | 16 | 1 | 17 |
| 15. California Institute of Technology (Pasadena, CA) | 4 | — | 4 | 1 | — | 9 | 6 | 15 |
| 16. University of Minnesota | 3 | — | 2 | 2 | 4 | 11 | 2 | 13 |
| 16. University of Texas (Austin, TX) | 3 | 3 | 3 | 2 | 2 | 13 | — | 13 |
| 18. University of North Carolina (Chapel Hill, NC) | 2 | 3 | — | 2 | 4 | 11 | — | 11 |
| 18. Northwestern University (Evanston, IL) | 1 | 1 | 3 | 1 | 5 | 11 | — | 11 |
| 20. University of Washington (Seattle, WA) | 2 | — | 1 | 5 | 2 | 10 | — | 10 |

*Source:* David S. Webster, *Change,* May/June 1983; derived from *Assessment of Research-Doctorate Programs in the United States.*

# The Arts:
## Where the Cultural Action Is

Sure you want to escape from your gigantic metro area to a serene spot that's uncrowded, crime-free, and inexpensive. Who doesn't? So when the chance arrives, either in the form of a company relocation, a mid-life change, or retirement, you pack up and make your break. And you're delighted to find that rural or small-town life is all it's cracked up to be. There is a sense of cohesion, of continuity and tradition, of community spirit and neighborliness that you thought had died in America. You're happier than you've been in years.

For about four months.

Because in your rush to leave behind all the unpleasant and dangerous aspects of big-city life, you forgot the museum done in neoclassical stone that you passed twice each day in the crush of commuter traffic. You overlooked the several libraries offering not only books but also filmstrips and movies, records and tapes, and free lectures and exhibits. And then there were the big universities, three of them, that you tended to take for granted yet that provided so much for you and your family. And what about the symphony and the two repertory theatres?

You trot down to the public library in your new town, only to find a well-worn selection of fiction, mostly published in the fifties, and a few back issues of *Family Circle* and *Field & Stream*. You search for a theatre or musical event and find your only choice is a

concert stop by touring country-and-western performer Clyde McFritter and His Heavy Haulers.

Of all the categories that form the composite known as quality of life, the one called the arts is singularly and inevitably associated with big cities. Of course, this is true for some recreational facilities as well—professional sports teams, zoos, amusement parks. However, many of the most valuable recreational facilities, such as lakes, hiking trails, campgrounds, and national forests, are found far from cities; in fact, they *must* be far from cities. The arts alone are big-city phenomena. Therefore, it should come as no surprise that *Places Rated*'s top three metro areas for the arts are New York, Chicago, and Los Angeles, which are also our three most populous. Yet this is not to say that culture cannot be found in many smaller places in America. Although it's fairly safe to assume that the bigger a met is, the more cultural facilities it will have, there are interesting exceptions to this rule, as we will discover later in the chapter.

## WHAT *ARE* THE ARTS, ANYWAY?

The answer to the question of what makes up art or the arts is simple: Nobody can agree. But even though people can't get together on a single definition, or on one thing that all art is, most people do concur that certain specific things are indeed included in the broad category called the arts. For example, the following two lists draw a distinction that most of us would recognize:

| Definitely Art | Possibly Art |
| --- | --- |
| paintings, frescoes, murals | sidewalk drawing |
| ballet | break dancing |
| stained glass | monogrammed glasses |
| Placido Domingo | The Who |
| Chicago Symphony Orchestra | folk music, blues, jazz |
| Chinese bronzes | comic books |

It is not within *Places Rated Almanac*'s purview to decide which, if any, of the items in the right-hand list are art. Rather, we choose to confine our survey of cultural amenities in the metro areas to items identical with or related to those in the first list, those which most people agree have artistic or cultural merit. Whether any or all of the items in the second list are art is a moot question today; most are controversial or dubious simply because they have not yet withstood the test of time. It can be argued that at least some of them may be considered folk art, which is increasingly popular and will be discussed in another section of this chapter.

The broad categories of cultural wealth that *Places Rated* has selected to survey include museums, fine arts radio and public television, universities, symphony orchestras, theatres, opera companies, dance troupes, and public libraries. Singly, each represents either an important facet of artistic achievement or the transmission of, or learning about, that achievement. Together, they reflect the cultural and intellectual tone of a metro area. Finally, their presence indicates a second layer of cultural life: the specialty shops catering to lovers of classical music or fine paintings and prints; the ethnic restaurants, literary clubs, and lecture societies that flourish in the atmosphere produced by artists, musicians, professors, and others of similar bent; perhaps even the kind of conversation made at a bridge party, cookout, or day at the beach.

## MUSEUMS: CULTURAL STOREHOUSES

The artistic elements of city life might be broken down into two categories: performances and possessions. The performing arts and broadcasts that feature fine music or cultural fare belong in the first group. The collected arts, such as those found in museums, belong in the second.

A. Bartlett Giamatti, president of Yale University, once referred to museums and libraries as "institutions that mediate between the past and the future." Whether it is through a collection of artifacts in history museums, or the paintings and sculpture in an art museum, or the technologically entertaining displays in a science museum, these institutions give us an opportunity to benefit from the accomplishments of others and participate in a cultural life far beyond our own immediate experience.

### The Arts and the Electronic Revolution

Even though most cultural facilities are found in big cities, a revolution in communication is under way that is making the arts accessible to those who live in remote rural areas. Even if you, as a recent refugee from a huge metro area, have given up live performances of the theatre, symphony, ballet, and opera, a whole world of artistic enjoyment is still available to you in your new home in small-town America. Recorded performances, both audio and visual, are available on cable television, public radio and television, and commercially sold cassettes.

What will this electronic revolution mean? Will videocassette recorders, cable television, satellite reception, and digital laser disks render the arts universal and homogeneous? A 1984 Harris poll reported that ownership of videocassette recorders has increased to 17 percent of Americans, many of them people who frequently attend arts performances; it concluded that a continuation of this trend "could become a threat instead of a boon to the arts." Will "cultural" cities become a thing of the past, totally replaced by broadcasting and recording sites?

Most arts lovers and critics think not. They make the point that a symphony in residence enriches a town just by being there—even when it's not performing or recording. Likewise, a community that is willing to support a theatre, dance company, or opera shows its dedication to the arts by the mere fact of this support, which reflects the community's values and priorities.

The first public museum in America was the Charleston Museum, still in existence, organized in 1773 by the Charleston, South Carolina, Library Society. Since that time, nearly 5,000 more museums have been established in this country; the number varies according to whose definition you use. A museum can be simply a collection of objects on view to the public on an occasional basis, or a treasure trove of artistic, scientific, or historic artifacts housed in a magnificent public building, looked after by hundreds of employees and supported by millions of dollars annually.

The most prevalent type of museum in the United States is the history museum. The greatest number can be found in the eastern half of the country. Approximately half of all museums are run by private, nonprofit organizations. Most museums in the country were started in the 1900s, with a huge escalation in the 1950s and 1960s, when more than a third of all museums existing today were built.

Since data on the operating and acquisitions budgets of museums are not available in all cases, determining a museum's relative size and scope is a problem. However, after reviewing data from the American Association of Museums (AAM) and the National Council on the Arts, *Places Rated* has prepared a basic set of requirements. To qualify for inclusion in this almanac, a museum first must comply with the AAM's official definition: "An organized and permanent non-profit institution, essentially educational or aesthetic in purpose, with professional staff, which owns and utilizes tangible objects, cares for them, and exhibits them to the public on some regular schedule." Furthermore, each museum must have a minimum of three curators, or equivalents, each in charge of an internal department or field. It must also have a regular publication and/or a library of 5,000 volumes or more, although this requirement is waived if the museum has five or more curators.

In all, 100 metro areas have museums that meet these requirements, and 13 metro areas have four or more qualifying museums. New York is far and away the leader in this category, with 18 major museums.

### Major Museums: The Top 13 Metro Areas

| Metro Area | Qualifying Museums | Metro Area | Qualifying Museums |
|---|---|---|---|
| 1. New York, NY | 18 | 8. Ann Arbor, MI | 4 |
| 2. Washington, DC–MD–VA | 10 | 8. Dallas, TX | 4 |
| | | 8. Detroit, MI | 4 |
| 3. Boston, MA | 6 | 8. Minneapolis–St. Paul, MN–WI | 4 |
| 3. Chicago, IL | 6 | | |
| 3. Los Angeles–Long Beach, CA | 6 | 8. New Haven–Meriden, CT | 4 |
| 3. Philadelphia, PA–NJ | 6 | 8. Seattle, WA | 4 |
| 7. San Francisco, CA | 5 | | |

Source: American Association of Museums, *Official Museum Directory*, National Register Publishing Company, 1982.

## TUNING IN TO CULTURE: PUBLIC TELEVISION AND FINE ARTS RADIO

When television channels were first allocated, certain of them were reserved by the Federal Communications Commission for nonprofit "educational" television stations, which were to be extensions of the classroom. Gradually the concept was broadened. "Educational television" became "public television," which grew to include all kinds of artistic and intellectual fare not readily available on commercial television: discussion programs, opera, symphony, Shakespeare, engrossing explanations of science and the universe, and creative and intellectually stimulating children's shows. The finest programs of the various stations were shared through a national network—the Public Broadcasting Service (PBS). And the audience increased.

During the month of March 1980, for example, A. C. Nielsen reported that more than 52 million U.S. households (68.2 percent of all American television-owning families) watched an average of 9 hours and 25 minutes of public television. The viewing time was an hour and a half longer than had been reported just two years before. And the total audience had doubled since 1975. Today, there are more than 290 U.S. public television stations broadcasting a total of more than 30,000 hours per week, nearly twice as many hours as a decade ago.

What are all these stations showing and their audiences so eagerly watching? In many cases, the arts. During the course of a television season, public television will broadcast performances of many major U.S. symphony orchestras, such as those of Boston, Los Angeles, Chicago, Minnesota, Cleveland, Philadelphia, Detroit, New York, and Washington, D.C. Also televised will be presentations by nearly every major dance company and choreographer, performances by major opera companies, and a wide range of theatre productions.

Virtually every metro area in the country has access to public television by way of cable, and 148 of 329 metro areas have at least one such station broadcasting from within their boundaries. Sixteen metro areas have two public TV stations, and two—New York and San Francisco—have three.

In addition to public television, many metro areas support their own public radio stations. These stations belong to the National Public Radio (NPR) network, sharing collectively programs that may originate in one station or another around the country. NPR, like PBS, is supported by the Corporation for Public Broadcasting, an independent federal agency that relies on matching grants to finance noncommercial broadcasting. Fine arts and public radio stations are found in 136 metro areas; 21 metro areas have two stations, and 12 have three or more:

| | |
|---|---|
| Buffalo, NY (3) | Minneapolis–St. Paul, MN–WI (3) |
| Chicago, IL (3) | |
| Columbus, OH (3) | New York, NY (3) |
| Los Angeles–Long Beach, CA (4) | Portland, OR (3) |
| | San Francisco, CA (3) |
| Louisville, KY–IN (3) | Washington, DC–MD–VA (3) |
| Madison, WI (3) | Waterloo–Cedar Falls, IA (3) |

## COLLEGES AND UNIVERSITIES: CULTURAL MICROCOSMS

Although universities are primarily educational institutions, they are cultural microcosms as well. Within their walls, one can usually find a symphony orchestra, a dance company or two, at least one theatre, and a fine arts radio station and/or a culturally oriented television station. A large and prestigious university needs all these facilities.

These institutions offer many cultural advantages to the local resident. University-produced symphony concerts and plays are almost always much less expensive than their professional counterparts. Also, they are usually less crowded and are located where parking and crowds are less of a problem. Ask the people who live in medium-sized metro areas, such as Ann Arbor, Michigan; Madison, Wisconsin; Austin, Texas; or Raleigh–Durham, North Carolina, what helps make their localities so special. Before long, they'll mention the universities—and they don't have to be students to appreciate them.

All institutions of higher learning contribute to the

cultural level of a metro area, but the larger ones, with more students, will have more extensive and varied cultural facilities and programs. Furthermore, it seems obvious that schools offering degrees in the fine and performing arts will have more programs and events for the community's benefit. In an attempt to limit our survey to institutions making a special cultural contribution to the community, *Places Rated* therefore considers only four-year schools having undergraduate enrollments of 2,000 students or more and offering at least one degree in one of the following fields (not to be confused with arts *courses,* which almost all universities have): Art/Art History, Creative Writing, Dance, Drama/Theatre, Music, and Voice/Opera.

Qualifying colleges and universities are found in 205 metro areas, and 65 of these universities offer degrees in four or more of the named fields. There are 19 metro areas enjoying the cultural benefits of four or more qualifying universities, and an elite group of ten have five or more.

### Fine Arts Universities: The Top 10 Metro Areas

| Metro Area | Qualifying Universities | Metro Area | Qualifying Universities |
|---|---|---|---|
| 1. New York, NY | 12 | 7. Minneapolis–St. Paul, MN–WI | 5 |
| 2. Boston, MA | 11 | 7. New Orleans, LA | 5 |
| 3. Chicago, IL | 10 | 7. Norfolk–Virginia Beach–Newport News, VA | 5 |
| 4. Philadelphia, PA–NJ | 9 | | |
| 4. Washington, DC–MD–VA | 9 | 7. Providence, RI | 5 |
| 6. Los Angeles–Long Beach, CA | 8 | | |

Source: *Lovejoy's College Guide,* 16th ed.

## THE PERFORMING ARTS: SYMPHONY, THEATRE, OPERA, AND DANCE

To say that the American performing arts underwent a renaissance in the 1970s would be an understatement. More surprising has been the continued flourishing of the arts in the early 1980s, given the dramatic decline in government funding. In addition to increased corporate support, there has been an unparalleled interest on the part of individual Americans in participating in the arts, whether as professionals, amateurs, or spectators. Symphony attendance, for example, rose from 12.7 million in 1970 to 22 million in 1982; opera attendance, in the same period, from 4.6 million to 10.1 million. And according to a Harris poll released in late 1984, more Americans went to performances of theatre, dance, opera, and music in 1984 than in 1980. The biggest winners were ballet and opera, whose attendance rates jumped from 25 percent of the population in 1980 to 34 percent and 35 percent, respectively, in 1984. These gains in arts attendance occurred despite a drop in the amount of leisure time adult Americans have, from an average of 19.2 hours a week in 1980 to 18.1 hours a week in 1984.

### Symphony Orchestras

Concerts by symphony orchestras in this country date back to a performance in 1731 in Charleston, South Carolina. More than 100 years later, in 1842, the New York Philharmonic became America's first organized symphony. Today, the American Symphony Orchestra League estimates that there are 1,500 orchestras in the United States and Canada, half of which are members of the league. Thirty-four orchestras are classified by the league as Major; that is, each has an annual operating income of more than $3.25 million. Four Major orchestras are located in Canada, and the rest are in the United States.

---

### Performing Arts on Campus

If you live in a college town, you already have more cultural activities to choose from than someone who lives in a town without a college or university. But if your home also happens to be home to a school with one or more highly rated programs in the performing arts, the variety of offerings may amount to an arts Eden.

Listed below are the ten best schools in America for three of the performing arts according to *The Gourman Report,* which evaluates schools on the basis of the strength of departments and the academic performance of students.

#### The 10 Best Universities for Art

1. New York University (New York)
2. Harvard University (Cambridge, MA)
3. Princeton University (Princeton, NJ)
4. Yale University (New Haven, CT)
5. University of California, Berkeley
6. University of Chicago
7. University of Pennsylvania (Philadelphia)
8. Cornell University (Ithaca, NY)
9. Stanford University (Stanford, CA)
10. University of California, Los Angeles

#### The 10 Best Universities for Drama/Theatre

1. Northwestern University (Evanston, IL)
2. University of California, Los Angeles
3. Yale University (New Haven, CT)
4. Cornell University (Ithaca, NY)
5. Stanford University (Stanford, CA)
6. University of Denver
7. Indiana University (Bloomington)
8. University of Washington (Seattle)
9. University of Iowa (Iowa City)
10. Carnegie-Mellon (Pittsburgh, PA)

#### The 10 Best Universities for Music

1. Harvard University (Cambridge, MA)
2. Yale University (New Haven, CT)
3. University of California, Berkeley
4. University of California, Los Angeles
5. University of Chicago
6. University of Michigan (Ann Arbor)
7. University of Illinois (Urbana)
8. Princeton University (Princeton, NJ)
9. New York University (New York)
10. Columbia University (New York)

Source: Dr. Jack Gourman, *The Gourman Report: A Rating of Undergraduate Programs in American and International Universities,* 4th ed. National Education Standards (Los Angeles), 1984.

## Major American Symphony Orchestras

Atlanta Symphony Orchestra
Baltimore Symphony Orchestra
Boston Symphony Orchestra
Buffalo Philharmonic Orchestra
Chicago Symphony Orchestra
Cincinnati Symphony Orchestra
Cleveland Orchestra
Dallas Symphony Orchestra
Denver Symphony Orchestra
Detroit Symphony Orchestra
Houston Symphony Orchestra
Indianapolis Symphony Orchestra
Los Angeles Philharmonic
Milwaukee Symphony Orchestra
Minnesota Orchestra (Minneapolis)
National Symphony Orchestra (Washington, D.C.)
New Orleans Philharmonic Symphony Orchestra
New York Philharmonic (New York City)
Oregon Symphony Orchestra (Portland)
Philadelphia Orchestra
Pittsburgh Symphony Orchestra
Rochester Philharmonic Orchestra (Rochester, NY)
St. Louis Symphony Orchestra
St. Paul Chamber Orchestra
San Antonio Symphony Orchestra
San Diego Symphony Orchestra
San Francisco Symphony
Seattle Symphony Orchestra
Syracuse Symphony Orchestra
Utah Symphony Orchestra (Salt Lake City)

Source: American Symphony Orchestra League, *Symphony Magazine*, Vol. 34, No. 6, December 1983.

The other categories of orchestras delineated by the league are Regional (those with annual budgets between $900,000 and $3.25 million), Metropolitan (with budgets between $250,000 and $900,000), Urban (with budgets between $115,000 and $250,000), Community (with budgets less than $115,000), College (composed exclusively of faculty and students of a college or university), and Youth (made up of junior high, high school, and/or college students and not exclusively affiliated with one educational institution).

Orchestras are far from uncommon in the metro areas; 257 claim at least one. Thirty-three of these places have four or more orchestras, and ten metro areas have six or more.

### Symphony Orchestras: The Top 10 Metro Areas

| Metro Area | Qualifying Orchestras | Metro Area | Qualifying Orchestras |
|---|---|---|---|
| 1. New York, NY | 21 | 6. Baltimore, MD | 7 |
| 2. Los Angeles–Long Beach, CA | 15 | 6. San Francisco, CA | 7 |
| 3. Chicago, IL | 14 | 8. Houston, TX | 6 |
| 4. Boston, MA | 10 | 8. Oakland, CA | 6 |
| 5. Pittsburgh, PA | 9 | 8. Seattle, WA | 6 |

Source: American Symphony Orchestra League, *Symphony Magazine*, Vol. 34, No. 6, December 1983.

## Repertory Theatre

Theatre has taken many forms in America over the years, from traditional Shakespearean plays, to vaudeville in the late 1800s and early 1900s, to musicals, to college and community productions. A profound change in American theatre occurred with the rise of the motion picture. From 1900 to 1920, the number of legitimate theatres in the country fell from 1,500 to 500. Yet, a rebound occurred during the prosperous 1920s on Broadway: 150 were added in 1920–21, and another 280 in 1927–28. Broadway reigned supreme from the late 1920s to the early 1950s, when "off-Broadway" productions started to appear in reaction to plays that many producers and theatregoers felt were too commercial and unartistic.

According to Peter Zeisler, in the introduction to *Theatre Profiles/3* (1977), "Until the 1950s, what professional theatre the American public saw was that which had been deemed 'successful' in London or New York. Professional theatre production was centered in New York, just as film and television is centered in California. Missouri could not see new work until it had been 'proved' in New York and, even then, not until it chugged into town as a 'road show'—often two years later. . . . Today, as much is going to New York as is coming from New York." *Theatre Profiles* is an annual publication of the Theatre Communications Group of New York City that lists all the repertory theatres in the country. Repertory theatres are those with a professional staff of actors in residence whose full-time job is acting. This differs of course from community theatres, whose actors are part-time, usually unpaid amateurs. In its survey of theatre in the metro areas, *Places Rated* includes only those theatres with annual budgets of $250,000 or more.

There are only 125 companies in the United States with such large budgets, and they are found in just 69 metro areas. Nineteen of these places have two or more qualifying companies; six have four or more.

### Theatre: The Top 6 Metro Areas

| Metro Area | Qualifying Theatres | Metro Area | Qualifying Theatres |
|---|---|---|---|
| 1. New York, NY | 21 | 4. Washington, DC–MD–VA | 5 |
| 2. Chicago, IL | 7 | 5. Los Angeles–Long Beach, CA | 4 |
| 3. Minneapolis–St. Paul, MN–WI | 6 | 5. Seattle, WA | 4 |

Source: Theatre Communications Group, *Theatre Profiles/6*, New York, 1984.

## Opera

Opera lovers boast that theirs is the greatest of the performing arts, for it combines orchestral and vocal music with theatre and often the dance. The first opera performed in America was the ballad opera *Flora, or Hob in the Well,* in 1735, at Charleston, South Carolina. The first grand opera was performed in 1825, at New York City's Park Theatre, Rossini's *Barber of Seville*. New York has continued to be the country's most important center for opera, but the art form has spread to all quadrants of the nation. From about 650 performing groups in 1969–70, opera expanded to nearly 1,000 groups in 1982, reaching an audience of more than ten million people.

Some of these performing groups are college and university workshops, whereas others are local clubs and choruses. But approximately 130 are companies with annual budgets exceeding $100,000. Full-scale opera productions using professional orchestras and bringing the world's leading singers to the stage are a costly business, and most metro areas haven't the resources or the audiences needed to support this performing art.

In surveying opera in the metropolitan areas, *Places Rated* relied on Opera America, an association of professional opera companies, and its *Profile: 1983,* which lists its members as of that year. The 68 opera companies that qualify by being so listed are fairly evenly distributed, with 59 metro areas having at least one company. Only eight metro areas have two or more opera companies:

| | |
|---|---|
| Baltimore, MD (2) | New York, NY (3) |
| Boston, MA (2) | Philadelphia, PA–NJ (2) |
| Chicago, IL (2) | San Francisco, CA (2) |
| Houston, TX (2) | San Jose, CA (2) |

## Dance

Modern dance and ballet groups flourish throughout America. Ballet is most often found in big cities, but there are regional ballet associations with annual festivals in several parts of the country as well. The first was the Southeast Regional Ballet Festival Association, located in Atlanta, followed by similar groups in the Northeast and Southwest and on the West Coast. A tremendous boost to dance in this country came from the companies of Martha Graham, Merce Cunningham, and the Joffrey Ballet, and more lately from the "Dance in America" series on public television.

Many dance companies are small, because of the nature of the art form. Jazz and modern dance troupes, for example, seldom exceed ten dancers, and many "companies" are composed of between six and eight performers. To exclude these small companies purely on the basis of size would do an injustice to both the art form and the metro areas that are home to the troupes. Therefore, *Places Rated* has included even small groups and companies in its inventory of the arts, using *Dance Magazine Annual, '84* as a source.

Dance companies are one of the most common features on the American arts scene, numbering 400 shared among 133 metro areas. Of these places, 23 have five or more dance groups. The list below shows the metro areas with at least eight companies.

### Dance Companies:
### The Top 9 Metro Areas

| Metro Area | Dance Companies |
|---|---|
| 1. New York, NY | 149 |
| 2. San Francisco, CA | 22 |
| 3. Los Angeles–Long Beach, CA | 20 |
| 4. Chicago, IL | 18 |
| 5. Washington, DC–MD–VA | 16 |
| 6. Philadelphia, PA–NJ | 11 |
| 7. Boston, MA | 9 |
| 7. Houston, TX | 9 |
| 9. Oakland, CA | 8 |

Source: *Dance Magazine, Dance Magazine Annual, '84,* 1983.

## THE PUBLIC LIBRARY: SOMETHING FOR EVERYONE

Every metro area—no matter how small, poor, or isolated—has at least one public library. The public library is the one cultural facility that we have all experienced, regardless of educational background, income, or artistic enthusiasm. Besides books, most libraries also contain records, slides, filmstrips, magazines, and other items that may be used in the building or borrowed for free.

There are more than 8,500 public libraries in the United States, 5,500 of which are branch libraries of a city, county, or regional library system. When the libraries found on college campuses are included, the total comes to over 12,000. This figure, however, does not include the many thousands of libraries in elementary and high schools.

The largest public library system is the New York Public Library, which encompasses more than seven million volumes stored in 80 neighborhood branches. Yet, huge as it is, New York's library offers its citizens less than one volume per person. Although Boston has a smaller library (still impressive with almost five million volumes), it provides more than one and a half books per person. Buffalo's libraries supply nearly three and a half per person.

### Public Libraries:
### The 16 Metro Areas with the Most Volumes

| Metro Area | Number of Volumes | Volumes per Capita |
|---|---|---|
| 1. New York, NY | 7,271,592 | 0.88 |
| 2. Boston, MA | 4,916,277 | 1.75 |
| 3. Los Angeles–Long Beach, CA | 4,602,998 | 0.62 |
| 4. Chicago, IL | 4,383,710 | 0.72 |
| 5. Cleveland, OH | 4,089,384 | 2.15 |
| 6. Buffalo, NY | 3,467,124 | 3.41 |
| 7. Cincinnati, OH–KY–IN | 3,332,926 | 2.38 |
| 8. Houston, TX | 3,156,063 | 1.15 |
| 9. St. Louis, MO–IL | 3,025,890 | 1.67 |
| 10. Philadelphia, PA–NJ | 2,947,727 | 0.63 |
| 11. Detroit, MI | 2,408,863 | 0.54 |
| 12. Honolulu, HI | 2,241,156 | 2.94 |
| 13. Newark, NJ | 2,231,560 | 1.19 |
| 14. Dallas, TX | 2,105,231 | 1.08 |
| 15. Milwaukee, WI | 2,096,002 | 1.50 |
| 16. Pittsburgh, PA | 2,039,057 | 0.92 |

Source: R. R. Bowker, *American Library Directory,* 1983.

The number of volumes in a metro area's library tells only half the story of a place's reading habits; how much *use* those volumes get, or the library's circulation, is the other half. Circulation is expressed in terms of yearly checkouts. When we add that number to the number of library volumes and divide the sum by the population served by the library system, the result is what *Places Rated* calls the reading quotient, which may serve as a rough indicator of the reading habits of a given place. The reading quotients for the metro areas are given in the Place Profiles later in the chapter.

Most big cities have a reading quotient of between 3.0 and 5.0; the general metro area average is between 4.0 and 7.0. In the 12 metro areas that have reading quotients of 3.0 or lower, reading, at least as expressed in visits to and use of public libraries, is not a major pastime. But the 11 metro areas with reading quotients above 12.0 are places where the local libraries are used and used often.

## Reading Quotients in the Metro Areas

| Highest | Reading Quotient | Lowest | Reading Quotient |
|---|---|---|---|
| 1. Bangor, ME | 30.0 | 1. Canton, OH | 2.0 |
| 2. Salem–Gloucester, MA | 21.1 | 2. Binghamton, NY | 2.1 |
| 3. Champaign–Urbana–Rantoul, IL | 17.3 | 3. Longview–Marshall, TX | 2.4 |
| | | 4. Fitchburg–Leominster, MA | 2.6 |
| 4. Pittsfield, MA | 15.0 | 4. Fort Lauderdale–Hollywood–Pompano Beach, FL | 2.6 |
| 5. Madison, WI | 14.0 | | |
| 6. Bloomington–Normal, IL | 13.8 | 6. Biloxi–Gulfport, MS | 2.7 |
| 7. Columbia, MO | 13.7 | 7. Harrisburg–Lebanon–Carlisle, PA | 2.8 |
| 7. Duluth, MN–WI | 13.7 | | |
| 9. Salinas–Seaside–Monterey, CA | 13.2 | 7. Williamsport, PA | 2.8 |
| 10. Bellingham, WA | 12.3 | 9. Birmingham, AL | 2.9 |
| 11. Salem, OR | 12.2 | 10. Allentown–Bethlehem, PA–NJ | 3.0 |
| | | 10. Scranton–Wilkes-Barre, PA | 3.0 |
| | | 10. Wichita Falls, TX | 3.0 |

Source: R. R. Bowker, *American Library Directory*, 1983, provided the information used to calculate the reading quotients.

What, if anything, can we surmise from the above tables? For one thing, it seems that the metro areas with the highest reading quotients tend to be small or medium-sized. Fairly heavy concentrations of avid readers are found in New England and the northern Midwest, whereas five of the metro areas with the lowest reading quotients are in the South. Climate may be a partial reason for differences in reading habits. Perhaps time spent reading increases as "ideal" outdoor weather decreases. This would explain the high reading quotients in the cold Midwest and New England, and generally lower scores in the South.

## JUDGING SUPPLY OF CULTURAL FACILITIES

The nine categories of arts facilities we have described above include not hundreds but thousands of institutions throughout the country. To list all the facilities in each category for each metro area would require several books the size of this one. For example, the *Official Museum Directory* compiled by the American Association of Museums lists more than 3,000 museums in the United States; many are very specialized or are maintained by corporations for specific purposes. Many are very small and exist solely to make money or to serve as a tax shelter for those who own and operate them. Only a small portion are big enough in size and scope to be of real interest or importance to most people.

How can the significant institutions be winnowed out and used to assess the cultural climate of a place? Generally, we start by excluding institutions run for profit. Therefore, commercial television, commercial theatres and supper clubs, and libraries and museums that are appendages of corporations are not included. In addition, whenever possible, we rely on ratings and classifications devised and used by appropriate associations or accrediting bodies, such as the American Symphony Orchestra League and the American Association of Museums.

It can be argued that it is not possible to rank metro areas according to their cultural facilities with total fairness. Nevertheless, one can examine selected cultural variables and indicate their *supply* in the metro areas. We do not attempt here to judge the relative artistic merit of individual symphonies, museums, or operas but rather to indicate how they compare in size, frequency of performance, duration of broadcast, number of productions, and so forth.

In addition to the supply of the various facilities, *ease of access* to them is important. In a sense, the question is asked: How much of a thing can be used, seen, heard, enjoyed, visited, and how often, for how long, and how easily? Some facilities (museums, libraries, and fine arts radio stations, for example) have much more "use potential" than do others. Accordingly, their point potential is high.

In rating the metro areas for supply of cultural facilities, *Places Rated*'s approach is very similar to that taken in the first edition of this book. The nine categories of facilities are the same, although some adjustments have been made in how they are rated. One notable change was improving the criteria used to identify and evaluate universities for their cultural roles. Many more orchestras and dance companies are included.

A major new element is the addition of CMSA Access points, awarded in recognition of the fact that metro areas in close proximity tend to share certain major facilities such as airports, professional sports arenas, and outstanding health care facilities. In the case of the arts, each metro area that is part of a Consolidated Metropolitan Statistical Area (see the Appendix for a complete list) is eligible to receive bonus points for exceptional cultural facilities found in nearby metro areas, as explained in item 10 below.

Each metro area starts with a base score of zero, to which points are added according to the following indicators:

1. *Museums.* All museums meeting the basic criteria outlined earlier in this chapter receive a base score of 500 points. One hundred points is added to the score for each additional curator over the required minimum of three. The ceiling score for any museum is 2,000 points, which is quite

high. *Places Rated* believes that this high point potential accurately reflects the tremendous breadth of exhibits and collections of our major museums, as well as their accessibility to the general public.

2. *Fine arts and public radio.* Along with public television stations, these facilities offer an endless variety of cultural information and entertainment. Because of the scope of their subject matter and their extreme accessibility, their point potential is high. Radio stations receive from 200 to 500 points each, depending on their weekly broadcast time.

| Weekly air time: | Points: |
| --- | --- |
| Less than 120 hours | 200 |
| 120–140 hours | 300 |
| 141–160 hours | 400 |
| More than 160 hours | 500 |

If broadcast information is incomplete, stations receive the minimum 200 points.

3. *Public television.* Public television stations receive a constant score of 500 points each.

4. *Universities.* Four-year colleges and universities with enrollments of 2,000 students or more and offering at least one degree in the arts are eligible for points. The school's enrollment, divided by 100, is the number of points each institution contributes; universities have a point ceiling of 1,000.

5. *Symphony orchestras.* In this edition of *Places Rated Almanac*, from 100 to 500 points are awarded to each type of symphony orchestra recognized by the American Symphony Orchestra League. They are Major, Regional, Metropolitan, Urban, Community, College, and Youth. In the Place Profiles, four of the categories are readily identified by the number of stars that follow their names.

| Type of orchestra: | Points: |
| --- | --- |
| Community, College, Youth | 100 |
| Urban (★) | 200 |
| Metropolitan (★★) | 300 |
| Regional (★★★) | 400 |
| Major (★★★★) | 500 |

6. *Theatres.* Professional nonprofit repertory theatres listed in *Theatre Profiles/6* and having annual budgets of $250,000 or more receive points on the basis of their annual operating expenses. In the Place Profiles, the stars following a theatre's name indicate its budget level.

| Annual budget: | Points: |
| --- | --- |
| Less than $1,000,000 | 100 |
| $1,000,000 to $2,000,000 (★) | 200 |
| $2,000,000 to $3,000,000 (★★) | 300 |
| $3,000,000 to $4,000,000 (★★★) | 400 |
| $4,000,000 and over (★★★★) | 500 |

7. *Opera companies.* Opera companies identified in Opera America's *Profile: 1983* as current and corresponding members receive a base score of 200 points. To this additional points are awarded according to the number of productions and performances. Some opera companies boast of many performances yet produce only two or three operas each season. To reflect this, the product of productions times performances is added to the base score. For example, the Mobile, Alabama, opera has three productions and ten performances. Thus its score is 200 plus 3 x 10, or 230 points. The ceiling for any opera company is 500 points.

8. *Dance companies.* *Places Rated* has identified 400 dance companies eligible for inclusion in the Place Profiles, drawing upon *Dance Magazine Annual, '84*. Each company so listed is awarded a minimum of 50 points. Additional points are awarded to some dance categories on the basis of the size of the troupe; one or two stars following a company's name in the Place Profiles indicate its troupe size and the number of points awarded. The ceiling for any dance company is 200 points.

| Type of troupe: | Number of dancers: | Points: |
| --- | --- | --- |
| All categories | No lower limit | 50 |
| Ethnic-Folk, Modern (★) | More than 15 | 100 |
| Ballet (★) | More than 15 | 100 |
| Ballet (★★) | 40 or more | 200 |

9. *Public libraries.* The points awarded for libraries are determined by their size as expressed in thousands of volumes. America's largest public library system is New York's, with 7,271,592 volumes. The New York metro area therefore receives 7,272 points for its libraries.

10. *CMSA Access.* Each of the 76 metro areas that is part of a Consolidated Metropolitan Statistical Area is eligible for bonus points based on certain outstanding or easily shared cultural facilities: major museums receiving 1,000 or more points; all public radio and television stations; four-star (Major) symphonies; theatres receiving one or more stars; all opera companies; and two-star dance companies. A place receives a bonus of 30 percent of the points accumulated by the *other* metro areas in the CMSA for these facilities; a metro area's *own* points are not considered in calculating its bonus. Thus, in the Detroit–Ann Arbor consolidated area, Ann Arbor receives 894 access points based on Detroit's 2,980 points for

**Outstanding Cultural Assets**

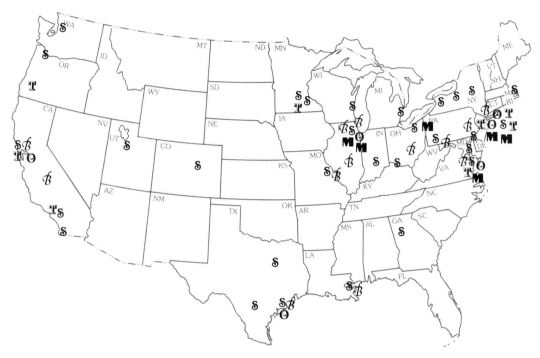

**S**   Major Symphony
**B**   Best Ballet
**O**   Grand Opera
**T**   Outstanding Theatre
**M**   Elite Museum

## America's Cultural Elite

In its inventory of the arts in America, *Places Rated* has compiled thousands of names of museums, symphony orchestras, theatres, operas, and ballet companies. But only a relative handful qualify as members of the cultural elite, receiving from *Places Rated* the maximum points for their respective categories.

The map shows, as might be expected, a large number of these institutions located in the Northeast. However, small pockets of cultural excellence also appear in the Midwest, Texas, and the West Coast. The symphony orchestras indicated on the map are the 30 Major symphonies listed on page 267.

### Elite Museums

Below are the only museums in America that earn *Places Rated*'s highest possible score of 2,000 points:

American Museum of Natural History (New York, NY)
Art Institute of Chicago (Chicago, IL)
Cleveland Museum of Art (Cleveland, OH)
Field Museum of Natural History (Chicago, IL)
Metropolitan Museum of Art (New York, NY)
Smithsonian Institution (Washington, DC–MD–VA)

### Outstanding Theatres

These theatres have annual operating budgets of more than $4 million, the highest in the country:

American Conservatory Theatre (San Francisco, CA)
Arena Stage (Washington, DC–MD–VA)
Circle in the Square (New York, NY)
Guthrie Theatre (Minneapolis–St. Paul, MN–WI)
Mark Taper Forum (Los Angeles–Long Beach, CA)
New York Shakespeare Festival (New York, NY)
Oregon Shakespeare Festival (Medford, OR)
Paper Mill Playhouse (Newark, NJ)

### Grand Opera

The opera companies listed below were awarded the maximum number of points based on their number of productions and performances:

Houston Grand Opera (Houston, TX)
Lyric Opera of Chicago (Chicago, IL)
Metropolitan Opera (New York, NY)
New York City Opera (New York, NY)
San Francisco Opera (San Francisco, CA)
Washington Opera (Washington, DC–MD–VA)

### Best Ballet Companies

The ballet companies that qualify for *Places Rated*'s highest rating with at least 40 dancers are the following:

American Ballet Theatre (New York, NY)
Ballet des Jeunes (Philadelphia, PA–NJ)
Bethesda Ballet Company (Washington, DC–MD–VA)
Columbus Theatre Ballet Association (Columbus, OH)
Crescent Ballet Company (New Orleans, LA)
Fresno Ballet (Fresno, CA)
Houston Ballet (Houston, TX)
Kasamon Ballet (Pittsburgh, PA)
Le Ballet Petit Dance Ensemble (Chicago, IL)
Rockford Company (Rockford, IL)
St. Charles Civic Ballet (St. Louis, MO–IL)
San Francisco Ballet (San Francisco, CA)
Springfield Ballet Company (Springfield, IL)

shared facilities, and Detroit receives a 750-point bonus thanks to Ann Arbor's total of 2,500 points for eligible facilities. Thirteen metro areas receive no access bonus because the other metro area(s) in the CMSA have none of the shared facilities.

## Sample Comparison: Anaheim–Santa Ana, California, and Raleigh–Durham, North Carolina

Anaheim–Santa Ana ranks 49th in the arts; Raleigh–Durham, across the continent in North Carolina, ranks 47th. Only 98 points separate the two. How do they compare in cultural facilities?

In the inventory of museums, the first category, we see that whereas Anaheim–Santa Ana has none, Raleigh–Durham has the North Carolina Museum of Art (worth 600 points) and the North Carolina State Museum (1,000 points). So Raleigh–Durham chalks up an early lead, 1,600 points to zero.

The North Carolina metro area also has two fine arts and public radio stations, WSHA-FM and WUNC-FM, worth 500 and 300 points, respectively. Again, Anaheim–Santa Ana has none. Neither metro area has a public television station.

Both of our sample places do quite well as far as universities are concerned. Anaheim–Santa Ana is home to the Irvine branch of the University of California, worth 849 points, and the Fullerton campus of California State University, which contributes 1,000 points. Raleigh–Durham counters with Duke University (937 points) and the University of North Carolina at Chapel Hill (1,000 points). The standings for this scoring element are close, with Anaheim–Santa Ana raking in 1,849 points and Raleigh–Durham 1,937.

But in the next category, Symphony Orchestras, Anaheim–Santa Ana has the advantage. It earns 300 points for its one College and two Youth symphonies. Additionally, it receives 200 points for its Urban symphony and 300 points for its Metropolitan orchestra, the Orange County Pacific Symphony, for a total of 800 points. Raleigh–Durham comes up with only 500 points for its two symphonies, a Community orchestra (100 points) and a Regional one (400).

Each metro area has a repertory theatre. However, the South Coast Repertory Theatre in Anaheim–Santa Ana has a larger budget and therefore contributes more points (300) than does Raleigh–Durham's Playmakers Repertory Company (100). At this point the working total for our two places is 4,837 for Raleigh–Durham and 2,949 for Anaheim–Santa Ana.

There are no opera companies in these two metro areas. In supply of dance companies, they are fairly even. Neither has a major ballet, and the dance companies each does possess are rather small, adding only the minimum 50 points apiece. The three companies in Anaheim–Santa Ana yield 150 points, and the four in Raleigh–Durham 200.

### New York, New York

"New York, New York, it's a wonderful town!" says the song from the musical *On the Town*. When it comes to the arts and the supply of cultural facilities, this certainly is true, for New York is far and away the winner in this category. Even a brief glance at this metro area's cultural assets reveals it to be the cultural capital of the United States, and perhaps the world:

- *Museums:* New York has no fewer than 18 major museums. Its total for museums alone is 17,600 points! That is only a few hundred points less than sixth-place Philadelphia's score for *all* cultural facilities.
- *Fine Arts Public Radio and Television:* New York has three stations in each category; no other metro area has as many.
- *Universities:* These cultural microcosms, the scoring element with perhaps the broadest cultural effect on a city, are plentiful here. Twelve qualifying colleges and universities contribute 10,017 points to this giant metro area—more than the total arts score posted by 15th-place Baltimore.
- *Symphony Orchestras:* New York has 21 symphony orchestras, including one Major symphony, one Regional symphony, and three Metropolitan symphonies.
- *Theatres:* Who knows the actual number of all the theatres in New York? The Big Apple has 21 that qualify for inclusion in *Places Rated Almanac*.
- *Opera Companies:* With three major professional opera companies, New York is far and away America's opera capital and one of the great opera centers of the world.
- *Dance Companies:* There are 149 dance companies in New York that meet *Places Rated*'s qualifications. Their total point contribution is 8,650, a figure greater than the overall arts score of 308 of the 329 metro areas.

These facilities, representing an unrivaled cornucopia of artistic and cultural riches, together with a library system of more than seven million volumes, combine to give the New York metro area a grand total of 56,745 points. Second-place Chicago, which earns 24,846 points, is not even close.

Public libraries, which represent the next-to-last category, are scored on the basis of their total volumes, with one point awarded for every 1,000 volumes. Anaheim–Santa Ana gains more points here since its library has 725,268 volumes (good for 725 points) compared with the 592,800 in Raleigh–Durham's (593 points). This disparity can be explained by the size of Anaheim–Santa Ana's population, which at 1,932,709 is nearly four times that of Raleigh–Durham's (561,222).

So far Raleigh–Durham is clearly in the lead, 5,730

to 3,824. Not only does it have more facilities; it also provides more relative to its size than does Anaheim–Santa Ana.

But adding in points for the tenth category, CMSA Access, nearly bridges the gap between the two metro areas. As part of the Los Angeles–Anaheim–Riverside consolidated area, Anaheim–Santa Ana is eligible for

30 percent of the total points earned for designated cultural facilities by the other three metro areas in the CMSA, which amounts to 1,808 points. This boosts Anaheim–Santa Ana's total score for the arts to 5,632 and puts it only two places behind Raleigh–Durham. Since Raleigh–Durham is not a member of a CMSA, it earns no points in this category.

## Places Rated: Metro Areas Ranked for Supply of Cultural Facilities

Nine kinds of institutions or facilities are evaluated in arriving at a score for a metro area's cultural assets: (1) museums; (2) fine arts and public radio stations; (3) public television stations; (4) universities offering a degree or degrees in the arts; (5) symphony orchestras; (6) theatres; (7) opera companies; (8) dance companies; and (9) public libraries. Metro areas can also earn

bonus points for shared facilities—major museums, public radio and television stations, major symphonies, certain theatres, operas, and selected dance companies—within their Consolidated Metropolitan Statistical Areas.

Places that receive tie scores are given the same rank and are listed in alphabetical order.

### Metro Areas from Best to Worst

| Places Rated Rank | Places Rated Score | Places Rated Rank | Places Rated Score | Places Rated Rank | Places Rated Score |
|---|---|---|---|---|---|
| 1. New York, NY | 56,745 | 31. Ann Arbor, MI | 7,559 | 60. Louisville, KY–IN | 4,916 |
| 2. Chicago, IL | 24,846 | 31. Atlanta, GA | 7,559 | | |
| 3. Los Angeles–Long Beach, CA | 23,567 | 33. Jersey City, NJ | 7,420 | 61. Tucson, AZ | 4,889 |
| 4. Washington, DC–MD–VA | 21,701 | 34. Danbury, CT | 7,415 | 62. Oklahoma City, OK | 4,843 |
| 5. Boston, MA | 21,042 | 35. Norwalk, CT | 7,273 | 63. Miami–Hialeah, FL | 4,837 |
| | | | | 64. Albany–Schenectady–Troy, NY | 4,655 |
| 6. Philadelphia, PA–NJ | 17,270 | 36. Honolulu, HI | 7,168 | 65. Phoenix, AZ | 4,573 |
| 7. San Francisco, CA | 14,226 | 37. Norfolk–Virginia Beach–Newport News, VA | 7,087 | | |
| 8. Newark, NJ | 14,224 | 38. Orange County, NY | 6,987 | 66. Wilmington, DE–NJ–MD | 4,545 |
| 9. Cleveland, OH | 12,679 | 39. Rochester, NY | 6,956 | 67. Lincoln, NE | 4,523 |
| 10. Minneapolis–St. Paul, MN–WI | 11,714 | 40. Dayton–Springfield, OH | 6,935 | 68. Albuquerque, NM | 4,496 |
| | | | | 69. Memphis, TN–AR–MS | 4,486 |
| 11. Houston, TX | 11,073 | 41. Columbus, OH | 6,648 | 70. Sacramento, CA | 4,483 |
| 12. Pittsburgh, PA | 11,069 | 42. Fort Worth–Arlington, TX | 6,466 | | |
| 13. Dallas, TX | 10,438 | 43. San Jose, CA | 6,446 | 71. Toledo, OH | 4,389 |
| 14. Detroit, MI | 10,389 | 44. Indianapolis, IN | 6,348 | 72. Nashville, TN | 4,342 |
| 15. Baltimore, MD | 9,788 | 45. Oakland, CA | 6,162 | 73. Charlotte–Gastonia–Rock Hill, NC–SC | 4,313 |
| 16. Cincinnati, OH–KY–IN | 9,688 | 46. Providence, RI | 6,152 | 74. Tacoma, WA | 4,297 |
| 17. Seattle, WA | 9,577 | 47. Raleigh–Durham, NC | 5,730 | 75. San Antonio, TX | 4,295 |
| 18. Bergen–Passaic, NJ | 9,304 | 48. Richmond–Petersburg, VA | 5,697 | | |
| 19. St. Louis, MO–IL | 8,896 | 49. Anaheim–Santa Ana, CA | 5,632 | 76. Tulsa, OK | 4,248 |
| 20. San Diego, CA | 8,818 | 50. Akron, OH | 5,564 | 77. Baton Rouge, LA | 4,237 |
| | | | | 78. Lansing–East Lansing, MI | 4,206 |
| 21. Milwaukee, WI | 8,766 | 51. Kansas City, MO | 5,553 | 79. Greensboro–Winston-Salem–High Point, NC | 4,188 |
| 22. Nassau–Suffolk, NY | 8,640 | 52. Salt Lake City–Ogden, UT | 5,528 | 80. Gary–Hammond, IN | 4,115 |
| 23. Buffalo, NY | 8,567 | 53. Austin, TX | 5,355 | | |
| 24. Denver, CO | 8,477 | 54. Riverside–San Bernardino, CA | 5,327 | 81. Birmingham, AL | 3,958 |
| 25. Bridgeport–Milford, CT | 8,368 | 55. Portland, OR | 5,160 | 82. Aurora–Elgin, IL | 3,857 |
| | | | | 83. Kenosha, WI | 3,844 |
| 26. Middlesex–Somerset–Hunterdon, NJ | 8,058 | 56. Madison, WI | 5,123 | 84. El Paso, TX | 3,800 |
| 27. New Orleans, LA | 7,978 | 57. Syracuse, NY | 5,080 | 85. Omaha, NE–IA | 3,787 |
| 28. Stamford, CT | 7,865 | 58. Tampa–St. Petersburg–Clearwater, FL | 5,040 | | |
| 29. New Haven–Meriden, CT | 7,852 | 59. Trenton, NJ | 5,029 | 86. Santa Cruz, CA | 3,748 |
| 30. Monmouth–Ocean, NJ | 7,563 | | | 87. Lake County, IL | 3,746 |

| Places Rated Rank | Places Rated Score | Places Rated Rank | Places Rated Score | Places Rated Rank | Places Rated Score |
|---|---|---|---|---|---|
| 88. Boulder–Longmont, CO | 3,663 | 144. Jacksonville, FL | 2,162 | 201. Pueblo, CO | 1,307 |
| 89. Hartford, CT | 3,616 | 145. Bloomington, IN | 2,152 | 202. Bellingham, WA | 1,302 |
| 90. Fresno, CA | 3,596 | | | 203. San Angelo, TX | 1,301 |
| | | 146. Nashua, NH | 2,122 | 204. Beaver County, PA | 1,284 |
| 90. Lexington–Fayette, KY | 3,596 | 147. Fargo–Moorhead, ND–MN | 2,111 | 205. Lawton, OK | 1,280 |
| 92. Athens, GA | 3,546 | 147. Lawrence–Haverhill, MA–NH | 2,111 | | |
| 93. Springfield, MA | 3,466 | 149. Vineland–Millville–Bridgeton, | | 206. State College, PA | 1,271 |
| 94. Santa Rosa–Petaluma, CA | 3,457 | NJ | 2,097 | 207. Roanoke, VA | 1,263 |
| 95. Lubbock, TX | 3,402 | 150. Kalamazoo, MI | 2,071 | 208. Greeley, CO | 1,254 |
| | | | | 209. Amarillo, TX | 1,235 |
| 96. Gainesville, FL | 3,335 | 151. Erie, PA | 2,032 | 210. McAllen–Edinburg– | |
| 97. Knoxville, TN | 3,309 | 152. Fort Lauderdale–Hollywood– | | Mission, TX | 1,231 |
| 98. Salem–Gloucester, MA | 3,276 | Pompano Beach, FL | 2,027 | | |
| 99. Grand Rapids, MI | 3,255 | 153. Bryan–College Station, TX | 2,002 | 211. Terre Haute, IN | 1,226 |
| 100. Jackson, MS | 3,209 | 154. Brockton, MA | 2,001 | 212. Bakersfield, CA | 1,222 |
| | | 155. Bangor, ME | 1,995 | 213. Bismarck, ND | 1,211 |
| 101. Joliet, IL | 3,177 | | | 214. Racine, WI | 1,171 |
| 102. Lawrence, KS | 3,150 | 156. Corpus Christi, TX | 1,992 | 215. Kansas City, KS | 1,167 |
| 103. Harrisburg–Lebanon– | | 157. Provo–Orem, UT | 1,985 | | |
| Carlisle, PA | 3,083 | 158. Springfield, IL | 1,983 | 216. Appleton–Oshkosh– | |
| 104. Lowell, MA–NH | 3,057 | 159. Pensacola, FL | 1,954 | Neenah, WI | 1,166 |
| 105. Waterloo–Cedar Falls, IA | 3,000 | 160. Johnson City–Kingsport– | | 217. New London–Norwich, CT–RI | 1,164 |
| | | Bristol, TN–VA | 1,925 | 218. Waco, TX | 1,141 |
| 106. Charleston, SC | 2,993 | | | 219. Reading, PA | 1,108 |
| 107. Spokane, WA | 2,988 | 161. Grand Forks, ND | 1,921 | 220. Janesville–Beloit, WI | 1,092 |
| 108. Wichita, KS | 2,987 | 161. Huntsville, AL | 1,921 | | |
| 109. Vallejo–Fairfield–Napa, CA | 2,962 | 163. Fayetteville–Springdale, AR | 1,915 | 221. Lynchburg, VA | 1,079 |
| 110. West Palm Beach–Boca | | 164. Evansville, IN–KY | 1,876 | 222. Wilmington, NC | 1,077 |
| Raton–Delray Beach, FL | 2,888 | 165. St. Cloud, MN | 1,871 | 223. Elmira, NY | 1,048 |
| | | | | 224. Augusta, GA–SC | 1,047 |
| 111. Columbia, MO | 2,882 | 166. Columbus, GA–AL | 1,861 | 225. Rockford, IL | 1,026 |
| 112. Fort Wayne, IN | 2,846 | 167. Des Moines, IA | 1,857 | | |
| 113. Shreveport, LA | 2,826 | 168. Medford, OR | 1,856 | 226. York, PA | 1,022 |
| 114. Las Cruces, NM | 2,804 | 169. Scranton–Wilkes-Barre, PA | 1,832 | 227. Florence, AL | 1,021 |
| 115. Youngstown–Warren, OH | 2,797 | 170. Eau Claire, WI | 1,807 | 228. Davenport–Rock Island– | |
| | | | | Moline, IA–IL | 1,017 |
| 116. Oxnard–Ventura, CA | 2,769 | 171. Beaumont–Port Arthur, TX | 1,795 | 229. Lancaster, PA | 1,015 |
| 117. Santa Barbara– | | 172. Worcester, MA | 1,784 | 230. Salinas–Seaside–Monterey, | |
| Santa Maria–Lompoc, CA | 2,684 | 173. Lafayette, LA | 1,772 | CA | 1,004 |
| 118. Orlando, FL | 2,681 | 174. Mobile, AL | 1,764 | | |
| 119. South Bend–Mishawaka, IN | 2,672 | 175. Galveston–Texas City, TX | 1,756 | 231. Abilene, TX | 996 |
| 120. Eugene–Springfield, OR | 2,631 | | | 231. Yakima, WA | 996 |
| | | 176. Colorado Springs, CO | 1,749 | 233. Canton, OH | 989 |
| 121. Charleston, WV | 2,605 | 177. Burlington, VT | 1,741 | 234. Niagara Falls, NY | 966 |
| 122. Greenville–Spartanburg, SC | 2,569 | 178. Saginaw–Bay City– | | 235. Killeen–Temple, TX | 920 |
| 123. Lorain–Elyria, OH | 2,565 | Midland, MI | 1,708 | | |
| 124. Green Bay, WI | 2,547 | 179. Chico, CA | 1,647 | 236. Cedar Rapids, IA | 904 |
| 125. Muncie, IN | 2,498 | 180. Springfield, MO | 1,634 | 236. East St. Louis–Belleville, IL | 904 |
| | | | | 238. St. Joseph, MO | 879 |
| 126. Columbia, SC | 2,489 | 181. Topeka, KS | 1,632 | 239. Utica–Rome, NY | 858 |
| 127. Chattanooga, TN–GA | 2,483 | 182. Fort Collins–Loveland, CO | 1,609 | 240. Redding, CA | 845 |
| 128. Boise City, ID | 2,385 | 183. Binghamton, NY | 1,599 | | |
| 129. Duluth, MN–WI | 2,377 | 184. Las Vegas, NV | 1,586 | 241. Fayetteville, NC | 844 |
| 130. Portland, ME | 2,351 | 185. Stockton, CA | 1,579 | 242. Hagerstown, MD | 825 |
| | | | | 243. Sarasota, FL | 817 |
| 131. Anchorage, AK | 2,346 | 186. Vancouver, WA | 1,557 | 244. Daytona Beach, FL | 809 |
| 132. Allentown–Bethlehem, PA–NJ | 2,333 | 187. Monroe, LA | 1,528 | 245. Owensboro, KY | 804 |
| 133. Hamilton–Middletown, OH | 2,316 | 188. Brazoria, TX | 1,506 | | |
| 134. Peoria, IL | 2,294 | 189. Alton–Granite City, IL | 1,487 | 246. Poughkeepsie, NY | 785 |
| 135. Savannah, GA | 2,262 | 190. Bloomington–Normal, IL | 1,470 | 247. Billings, MT | 778 |
| | | | | 248. Rochester, MN | 769 |
| 136. Iowa City, IA | 2,255 | 191. La Crosse, WI | 1,466 | 249. New Bedford, MA | 766 |
| 137. Lafayette, IN | 2,236 | 192. Lake Charles, LA | 1,456 | 250. Wausau, WI | 761 |
| 138. Reno, NV | 2,210 | 193. Macon–Warner Robins, | | | |
| 139. Champaign–Urbana– | | GA | 1,435 | 251. Panama City, FL | 755 |
| Rantoul, IL | 2,203 | 194. Tuscaloosa, AL | 1,432 | 252. Fall River, MA–RI | 749 |
| 140. Huntington–Ashland, | | 195. Charlottesville, VA | 1,422 | 253. Lewiston–Auburn, ME | 736 |
| WV–KY–OH | 2,195 | | | 254. Middletown, CT | 730 |
| | | 196. Sioux City, IA–NE | 1,393 | 255. Houma–Thibodaux, LA | 725 |
| 141. Tallahassee, FL | 2,181 | 197. Asheville, NC | 1,391 | | |
| 142. Little Rock–North Little Rock, | | 198. Montgomery, AL | 1,374 | 256. Olympia, WA | 708 |
| AR | 2,180 | 199. New Britain, CT | 1,360 | 257. Salem, OR | 691 |
| 143. Flint, MI | 2,163 | 200. Lima, OH | 1,352 | 258. Biloxi–Gulfport, MS | 679 |

| Places Rated Rank | Places Rated Score | Places Rated Rank | Places Rated Score | Places Rated Rank | Places Rated Score |
|---|---|---|---|---|---|
| 259. Johnstown, PA | 666 | 282. Cumberland, MD–WV | 373 | 308. Portsmouth–Dover–Rochester, NH–ME | 165 |
| 260. Modesto, CA | 631 | 282. Pine Bluff, AR | 373 | 309. Brownsville–Harlingen, TX | 162 |
| | | 284. Fort Pierce, FL | 368 | 310. Pascagoula, MS | 155 |
| 261. Florence, SC | 628 | 285. Battle Creek, MI | 354 | | |
| 262. Atlantic City, NJ | 621 | | | 311. Bradenton, FL | 154 |
| 263. Glens Falls, NY | 603 | 286. Elkhart–Goshen, IN | 353 | 312. Gadsden, AL | 153 |
| 264. Wichita Falls, TX | 599 | 287. Dubuque, IA | 340 | 313. Laredo, TX | 150 |
| 265. Jacksonville, NC | 567 | 288. Alexandria, LA | 334 | 314. Steubenville–Weirton, OH–WV | 147 |
| | | 288. Longview–Marshall, TX | 334 | | |
| 266. Mansfield, OH | 554 | 290. Jackson, MI | 323 | 315. Fort Smith, AR–OK | 145 |
| 267. Muskegon, MI | 529 | | | | |
| 267. Richland–Kennewick–Pasco, WA | 529 | 291. Waterbury, CT | 318 | 316. Burlington, NC | 131 |
| | | 292. Lakeland–Winter Haven, FL | 309 | 317. Yuba City, CA | 122 |
| 269. Bristol, CT | 514 | 293. Casper, WY | 303 | 318. Dothan, AL | 117 |
| 270. Visalia–Tulare–Porterville, CA | 511 | 294. Decatur, IL | 298 | 319. Clarksville–Hopkinsville, TN–KY | 111 |
| | | 295. Kokomo, IN | 285 | | |
| 271. Pawtucket–Woonsocket–Attleboro, RI–MA | 480 | 296. Fitchburg–Leominster, MA | 270 | 320. Parkersburg–Marietta, WV–OH | 91 |
| 272. Manchester, NH | 475 | 297. Anniston, AL | 268 | | |
| 273. Sioux Falls, SD | 465 | 297. Sheboygan, WI | 268 | 321. Fort Walton Beach, FL | 87 |
| 274. Midland, TX | 438 | 299. Ocala, FL | 266 | 321. Victoria, TX | 87 |
| 275. Melbourne–Titusville–Palm Bay, FL | 437 | 300. Odessa, TX | 259 | 323. Danville, VA | 85 |
| | | | | 324. Joplin, MO | 80 |
| 276. Anderson, IN | 430 | 301. Altoona, PA | 256 | 325. Benton Harbor, MI | 79 |
| 277. Wheeling, WV–OH | 422 | 302. Albany, GA | 237 | | |
| 278. Tyler, TX | 404 | 303. Pittsfield, MA | 228 | 326. Kankakee, IL | 75 |
| 279. Great Falls, MT | 401 | 304. Enid, OK | 215 | 327. Sherman–Denison, TX | 68 |
| 280. Bremerton, WA | 382 | 305. Williamsport, PA | 196 | 328. Texarkana, TX–Texarkana, AR | 63 |
| | | | | | |
| 281. Fort Myers, FL | 380 | 306. Hickory, NC | 188 | 329. Sharon, PA | 52 |
| | | 307. Anderson, SC | 169 | | |

## Metro Areas Listed Alphabetically

| Metro Area | Places Rated Rank | Metro Area | Places Rated Rank | Metro Area | Places Rated Rank |
|---|---|---|---|---|---|
| Abilene, TX | 231 | Beaumont–Port Arthur, TX | 171 | Cedar Rapids, IA | 236 |
| Akron, OH | 50 | | | Champaign–Urbana–Rantoul, IL | 139 |
| Albany, GA | 302 | Beaver County, PA | 204 | Charleston, SC | 106 |
| Albany–Schenectady–Troy, NY | 64 | Bellingham, WA | 202 | | |
| Albuquerque, NM | 68 | Benton Harbor, MI | 325 | Charleston, WV | 121 |
| | | Bergen–Passaic, NJ | 18 | Charlotte–Gastonia–Rock Hill, NC–SC | 73 |
| Alexandria, LA | 288 | Billings, MT | 247 | Charlottesville, VA | 195 |
| Allentown–Bethlehem, PA–NJ | 132 | | | Chattanooga, TN–GA | 127 |
| Alton–Granite City, IL | 189 | Biloxi–Gulfport, MS | 258 | Chicago, IL | 2 |
| Altoona, PA | 301 | Binghamton, NY | 183 | | |
| Amarillo, TX | 209 | Birmingham, AL | 81 | Chico, CA | 179 |
| | | Bismarck, ND | 213 | Cincinnati, OH–KY–IN | 16 |
| Anaheim–Santa Ana, CA | 49 | Bloomington, IN | 145 | Clarksville–Hopkinsville, TN–KY | 319 |
| Anchorage, AK | 131 | | | Cleveland, OH | 9 |
| Anderson, IN | 276 | Bloomington–Normal, IL | 190 | Colorado Springs, CO | 176 |
| Anderson, SC | 307 | Boise City, ID | 128 | | |
| Ann Arbor, MI | 31 | Boston, MA | 5 | Columbia, MO | 126 |
| | | Boulder–Longmont, CO | 88 | Columbia, SC | 125 |
| Anniston, AL | 297 | Bradenton, FL | 311 | Columbus, GA–AL | 166 |
| Appleton–Oshkosh–Neenah, WI | 216 | | | Columbus, OH | 41 |
| Asheville, NC | 197 | Brazoria, TX | 188 | Corpus Christi, TX | 156 |
| Athens, GA | 92 | Bremerton, WA | 280 | | |
| Atlanta, GA | 31 | Bridgeport–Milford, CT | 25 | Cumberland, MD–WV | 282 |
| | | Bristol, CT | 269 | Dallas, TX | 13 |
| Atlantic City, NJ | 262 | Brockton, MA | 154 | Danbury, CT | 34 |
| Augusta, GA–SC | 224 | | | Danville, VA | 323 |
| Aurora–Elgin, IL | 82 | Brownsville–Harlingen, TX | 309 | Davenport–Rock Island–Moline, IA–IL | 228 |
| Austin, TX | 53 | Bryan–College Station, TX | 153 | | |
| Bakersfield, CA | 212 | Buffalo, NY | 23 | Dayton–Springfield, OH | 39 |
| | | Burlington, NC | 316 | Daytona Beach, FL | 244 |
| Baltimore, MD | 15 | Burlington, VT | 177 | Decatur, IL | 294 |
| Bangor, ME | 155 | | | Denver, CO | 24 |
| Baton Rouge, LA | 77 | Canton, OH | 233 | | |
| Battle Creek, MI | 285 | Casper, WY | 293 | | |

| Metro Area | Places Rated Rank | Metro Area | Places Rated Rank | Metro Area | Places Rated Rank |
|---|---|---|---|---|---|
| Des Moines, IA | 167 | Jersey City, NJ | 33 | Nashville, TN | 72 |
| | | | | Nassau–Suffolk, NY | 22 |
| Detroit, MI | 14 | Johnson City–Kingsport–Bristol, | | New Bedford, MA | 249 |
| Dothan, AL | 318 | TN–VA | 160 | New Britain, CT | 199 |
| Dubuque, IA | 287 | Johnstown, PA | 259 | New Haven–Meriden, CT | 29 |
| Duluth, MN–WI | 129 | Joliet, IL | 101 | | |
| East St. Louis–Belleville, IL | 236 | Joplin, MO | 324 | New London–Norwich, CT–RI | 217 |
| | | Kalamazoo, MI | 150 | New Orleans, LA | 27 |
| Eau Claire, WI | 170 | | | New York, NY | 1 |
| El Paso, TX | 84 | Kankakee, IL | 326 | Newark, NJ | 8 |
| Elkhart–Goshen, IN | 286 | Kansas City, KS | 215 | Niagara Falls, NY | 234 |
| Elmira, NY | 223 | Kansas City, MO | 51 | | |
| Enid, OK | 304 | Kenosha, WI | 83 | Norfolk–Virginia Beach– | |
| | | Killeen–Temple, TX | 235 | Newport News, VA | 37 |
| Erie, PA | 151 | | | Norwalk, CT | 35 |
| Eugene–Springfield, OR | 120 | Knoxville, TN | 97 | Oakland, CA | 45 |
| Evansville, IN–KY | 164 | Kokomo, IN | 295 | Ocala, FL | 299 |
| Fall River, MA–RI | 252 | La Crosse, WI | 191 | Odessa, TX | 300 |
| Fargo–Moorhead, ND–MN | 147 | Lafayette, IN | 137 | | |
| | | Lafayette, LA | 173 | Oklahoma City, OK | 62 |
| Fayetteville, NC | 241 | | | Olympia, WA | 256 |
| Fayetteville–Springdale, AR | 163 | Lake Charles, LA | 192 | Omaha, NE–IA | 85 |
| Fitchburg–Leominster, MA | 296 | Lake County, IL | 87 | Orange County, NY | 38 |
| Flint, MI | 143 | Lakeland–Winter Haven, FL | 292 | Orlando, FL | 118 |
| Florence, AL | 227 | Lancaster, PA | 229 | | |
| | | Lansing–East Lansing, MI | 78 | Owensboro, KY | 245 |
| Florence, SC | 261 | | | Oxnard–Ventura, CA | 116 |
| Fort Collins–Loveland, CO | 182 | Laredo, TX | 313 | Panama City, FL | 251 |
| Fort Lauderdale–Hollywood– | | Las Cruces, NM | 114 | Parkersburg–Marietta, WV–OH | 320 |
| Pompano Beach, FL | 152 | Las Vegas, NV | 184 | Pascagoula, MS | 310 |
| Fort Myers, FL | 281 | Lawrence, KS | 102 | | |
| Fort Pierce, FL | 284 | Lawrence–Haverhill, MA–NH | 147 | Pawtucket–Woonsocket–Attleboro, | |
| | | | | RI–MA | 271 |
| Fort Smith, AR–OK | 315 | Lawton, OK | 205 | Pensacola, FL | 159 |
| Fort Walton Beach, FL | 321 | Lewiston–Auburn, ME | 253 | Peoria, IL | 134 |
| Fort Wayne, IN | 112 | Lexington–Fayette, KY | 90 | Philadelphia, PA–NJ | 6 |
| Fort Worth–Arlington, TX | 42 | Lima, OH | 200 | Phoenix, AZ | 65 |
| Fresno, CA | 90 | Lincoln, NE | 67 | | |
| | | | | Pine Bluff, AR | 282 |
| Gadsden, AL | 312 | Little Rock–North Little Rock, AR | 142 | Pittsburgh, PA | 12 |
| Gainesville, FL | 96 | Longview–Marshall, TX | 288 | Pittsfield, MA | 303 |
| Galveston–Texas City, TX | 175 | Lorain–Elyria, OH | 123 | Portland, ME | 130 |
| Gary–Hammond, IN | 80 | Los Angeles–Long Beach, CA | 3 | Portland, OR | 55 |
| Glens Falls, NY | 263 | Louisville, KY–IN | 60 | | |
| | | | | Portsmouth–Dover–Rochester, | |
| Grand Forks, ND | 161 | Lowell, MA–NH | 104 | NH–ME | 308 |
| Grand Rapids, MI | 99 | Lubbock, TX | 95 | Poughkeepsie, NY | 246 |
| Great Falls, MT | 279 | Lynchburg, VA | 221 | Providence, RI | 46 |
| Greeley, CO | 208 | Macon–Warner Robins, GA | 193 | Provo–Orem, UT | 157 |
| Green Bay, WI | 124 | Madison, WI | 56 | Pueblo, CO | 201 |
| | | | | | |
| Greensboro–Winston-Salem– | | Manchester, NH | 272 | Racine, WI | 214 |
| High Point, NC | 79 | Mansfield, OH | 266 | Raleigh–Durham, NC | 47 |
| Greenville–Spartanburg, SC | 122 | McAllen–Edinburg–Mission, TX | 210 | Reading, PA | 219 |
| Hagerstown, MD | 242 | Medford, OR | 168 | Redding, CA | 240 |
| Hamilton–Middletown, OH | 133 | Melbourne–Titusville–Palm Bay, FL | 275 | Reno, NV | 138 |
| Harrisburg–Lebanon–Carlisle, PA | 103 | | | | |
| | | Memphis, TN–AR–MS | 69 | Richland–Kennewick–Pasco, WA | 267 |
| Hartford, CT | 89 | Miami–Hialeah, FL | 63 | Richmond–Petersburg, VA | 48 |
| Hickory, NC | 306 | Middlesex–Somerset–Hunterdon, NJ | 26 | Riverside–San Bernardino, CA | 54 |
| Honolulu, HI | 36 | Middletown, CT | 254 | Roanoke, VA | 207 |
| Houma–Thibodaux, LA | 255 | Midland, TX | 274 | Rochester, MN | 248 |
| Houston, TX | 11 | | | | |
| | | Milwaukee, WI | 21 | Rochester, NY | 39 |
| Huntington–Ashland, WV–KY–OH | 140 | Minneapolis–St. Paul, MN–WI | 10 | Rockford, IL | 225 |
| Huntsville, AL | 161 | Mobile, AL | 174 | Sacramento, CA | 70 |
| Indianapolis, IN | 44 | Modesto, CA | 260 | Saginaw–Bay City–Midland, MI | 178 |
| Iowa City, IA | 136 | Monmouth–Ocean, NJ | 30 | St. Cloud, MN | 165 |
| Jackson, MI | 290 | | | | |
| | | Monroe, LA | 187 | St. Joseph, MO | 238 |
| Jackson, MS | 100 | Montgomery, AL | 198 | St. Louis, MO–IL | 19 |
| Jacksonville, FL | 144 | Muncie, IN | 125 | Salem, OR | 257 |
| Jacksonville, NC | 265 | Muskegon, MI | 267 | Salem–Gloucester, MA | 98 |
| Janesville–Beloit, WI | 220 | Nashua, NH | 146 | Salinas–Seaside–Monterey, CA | 230 |

| Metro Area | Places Rated Rank | Metro Area | Places Rated Rank | Metro Area | Places Rated Rank |
|---|---|---|---|---|---|
| Salt Lake City–Ogden, UT | 52 | Springfield, MA | 93 | Vancouver, WA | 186 |
| San Angelo, TX | 203 | Springfield, MO | 180 | Victoria, TX | 321 |
| San Antonio, TX | 75 | Stamford, CT | 28 | | |
| San Diego, CA | 20 | | | Vineland–Millville– | |
| San Francisco, CA | 7 | State College, PA | 206 | Bridgeton, NJ | 149 |
| | | Steubenville–Weirton, | | Visalia–Tulare–Porterville, CA | 270 |
| San Jose, CA | 43 | OH–WV | 314 | Waco, TX | 218 |
| Santa Barbara–Santa Maria– | | Stockton, CA | 185 | Washington, DC–MD–VA | 4 |
| Lompoc, CA | 117 | Syracuse, NY | 57 | Waterbury, CT | 291 |
| Santa Cruz, CA | 86 | Tacoma, WA | 74 | | |
| Santa Rosa–Petaluma, CA | 94 | | | Waterloo–Cedar Falls, IA | 105 |
| Sarasota, FL | 243 | Tallahassee, FL | 141 | Wausau, WI | 250 |
| | | Tampa–St. Petersburg– | | West Palm Beach–Boca Raton– | |
| Savannah, GA | 135 | Clearwater, FL | 58 | Delray Beach, FL | 110 |
| Scranton–Wilkes-Barre, PA | 169 | Terre Haute, IN | 211 | Wheeling, WV–OH | 277 |
| Seattle, WA | 17 | Texarkana, TX–Texarkana, AR | 328 | Wichita, KS | 108 |
| Sharon, PA | 329 | Toledo, OH | 71 | | |
| Sheboygan, WI | 297 | | | Wichita Falls, TX | 264 |
| | | Topeka, KS | 181 | Williamsport, PA | 305 |
| Sherman–Denison, TX | 327 | Trenton, NJ | 59 | Wilmington, DE–NJ–MD | 66 |
| Shreveport, LA | 113 | Tucson, AZ | 61 | Wilmington, NC | 222 |
| Sioux City, IA–NE | 196 | Tulsa, OK | 76 | Worcester, MA | 172 |
| Sioux Falls, SD | 273 | Tuscaloosa, AL | 194 | | |
| South Bend–Mishawaka, IN | 119 | | | Yakima, WA | 231 |
| | | Tyler, TX | 278 | York, PA | 226 |
| Spokane, WA | 107 | Utica–Rome, NY | 239 | Youngstown–Warren, OH | 115 |
| Springfield, IL | 158 | Vallejo–Fairfield–Napa, CA | 109 | Yuba City, CA | 317 |

# Place Profiles: Cultural Facilities of 329 Metro Areas

In the pages that follow, some of the cultural facilities of the 329 metropolitan areas are profiled. The information is derived from a number of sources: American Association of Museums, *Official Museum Directory*, National Register Publishing Company, 1982; Corporation for Public Broadcasting, *CPB Public Broadcasting Directory, 1983–84*, Washington, 1983, and unpublished data, 1984; *Lovejoy's College Guide*, 16th ed., and *College Blue Book*, 19th ed.; American Symphony Orchestra League, *Symphony Magazine*, Vol. 34, No. 6, December 1983; Theatre Communications Group, *Theatre Profiles/6*, New York, 1984; Opera America, *Profile: 1983*, Washington, 1984; *Dance Magazine, Dance Magazine Annual, '84*, 1983; and R. R. Bowker, *American Library Directory*, 1983.

Under the heading Museums are listed the institutions meeting the *Places Rated Almanac* guidelines. The number in parentheses following the museum's name shows the points awarded according to *Places Rated's* scoring criteria.

Fine arts and public radio stations are listed by their identifying call letters and dial number. East of the Mississippi River, call letters begin with a W; west of the Mississippi, they begin with a K. When such information is available, the station's broadcast radius and average weekly air time are also given. In many instances, a station's broadcast range is great enough that its programs may be received in metro areas other than the originating one. This is also the case with public television stations.

The colleges and universities named are the four-year institutions of higher learning that meet *Places Rated's* requirements: an undergraduate enrollment of 2,000 or more students, and degree programs in any of six arts-related courses of study. Each university's name is followed by the number of points it contributes to its metro area's score. A bullet (•) in an institution's listing means that it offers degrees in four of the six possible arts-related fields; two bullets indicate degree programs available in five or more fields.

Symphony orchestras listed are members of the American Symphony Orchestra League. Community, College, and Youth orchestras are listed by name only. Other categories recognized by the league may be identified by the stars appended to their names: ⋆ = Urban; ⋆⋆ = Metropolitan; ⋆⋆⋆ = Regional; ⋆⋆⋆⋆ = Major.

Only nonprofit professional theatres with an annual budget of $250,000 or more are included in the profiles. If a theatre's budget is $1 million or more, its budget range is indicated by the stars following its name: ⋆ = $1 million to $2 million; ⋆⋆ = $2 million to $3 million; ⋆⋆⋆ = $3 million to $4 million; ⋆⋆⋆⋆ = $4 million or more.

Opera companies that appear in the profiles are members of Opera America. Their names are accompanied by the yearly number of productions and performances. Four-star opera companies are those that receive the maximum number of points possible under *Places Rated*'s system.

If the name of a dance company does not indicate its principal artistic focus, the company's name is followed by a letter or letters in parentheses: B = ballet; E-F = ethnic-folk; J = jazz; and M = modern. Most dance companies have only a few full-time dancers; classical ballet typically requires the greatest number and jazz the smallest. In the profiles, larger dance companies are identified by a star or stars. A single star indicates 25 to 39 dancers for a ballet company and 15 or more dancers for an ethnic-folk or modern dance troupe. A ballet company that employs 40 or more dancers is indicated by two stars.

Circulation figures given for public libraries represent total number of annual checkouts. The reading quotient for each metro area is calculated by adding library volumes to circulation and dividing by population served (this is not always the same as the metro area population); an NA indicates that available data are insufficient for deriving the reading quotient.

A star preceding a metro area's name highlights it as one of the top 25 places for cultural facilities.

**Abilene, TX**
Universities:
   Abilene Christian University (350)
   Hardin-Simmons University (210)
Symphony Orchestras:
   Abilene Philharmonic★
Public Libraries:
   235,894 volumes; circulation 273,656
Reading Quotient: 4.6
Places Rated Score: 996
Places Rated Rank: 231

**Akron, OH**
Public Television:
   WEAO Channel 49
Universities:
   Kent State University (1,000)
   University of Akron (1,000)
Symphony Orchestras:
   Akron Symphony Orchestra★★
   Akron Youth Symphony
Dance Companies:
   Ohio Ballet
Public Libraries:
   1,073,099 volumes; circulation
      2,014,701
Reading Quotient: 7.1
CMSA Access: CLEVELAND–AKRON–
   LORAIN, OH (1,541)
Places Rated Score: 5,564
Places Rated Rank: 50

**Albany, GA**
Symphony Orchestras:
   Albany Symphony Orchestra
      (Community)
Public Libraries:
   136,882 volumes; circulation NA
Reading Quotient: NA
Places Rated Score: 237
Places Rated Rank: 302

**Albany–Schenectady–Troy, NY**
Museums:
   New York State Museum (700)
   Schenectady Museum (600)
Fine Arts and Public Radio:
   WAMC-FM 90.3 (110 mi; 84 hrs)
   WMHT-FM 89.1 (70 mi; 168 hrs)
Public Television:
   WMNT Channel 17
Universities:
   SUNY at Albany (1,000)
   Union College (200)

Symphony Orchestras:
   Albany Symphony Orchestra★★
   Empire State Youth Orchestra
Theatres:
   Capitol Repertory Company
Public Libraries:
   454,546 volumes; circulation 1,114,735
Reading Quotient: 7.6
Places Rated Score: 4,655
Places Rated Rank: 64

**Albuquerque, NM**
Museums:
   Albuquerque Museum (600)
   Maxwell Museum of Anthropology (900)
Fine Arts and Public Radio:
   KUNM-FM 90.1 (100 mi; 163 hrs)
Public Television:
   KNME Channel 22
Universities:
   University of Albuquerque (206)
   University of New Mexico (785)••
Symphony Orchestras:
   Albuquerque Youth Symphony
   Chamber Orchestra of Albuquerque
      (Community)
   New Mexico Symphony Orchestra★★★
Public Libraries:
   404,782 volumes; circulation 1,725,000
Reading Quotient: 5.2
Places Rated Score: 4,496
Places Rated Rank: 68

**Alexandria, LA**
Symphony Orchestras:
   Rapides Symphony Orchestra
      (Community)
Public Libraries:
   233,781 volumes; circulation 538,760
Reading Quotient: 5.7
Places Rated Score: 334
Places Rated Rank: 288

**Allentown–Bethlehem, PA–NJ**
Museums:
   Allentown Art Museum (500)
Public Television:
   WLVT Channel 39
Universities:
   Lafayette College (205)
   Lehigh University (432)
Symphony Orchestras:
   Allentown Symphony (Community)
Theatres:
   Pennsylvania Stage Company

Dance Companies:
   Ballet Guild of Lehigh Valley★
Public Libraries:
   395,750 volumes; circulation 1,324,584
Reading Quotient: 3.0
Places Rated Score: 2,333
Places Rated Rank: 132

**Alton–Granite City, IL**
Universities:
   Southern Illinois University, Edwardsville
      (602)
Public Libraries:
   217,464 volumes; circulation 463,767
Reading Quotient: 9.5
CMSA Access: ST. LOUIS–EAST ST.
   LOUIS–ALTON, MO–IL (668)
Places Rated Score: 1,487
Places Rated Rank: 189

**Altoona, PA**
Symphony Orchestras:
   Altoona Symphony Orchestra
      (Community)
Public Libraries:
   156,065 volumes; circulation 314,817
Reading Quotient: 6.7
Places Rated Score: 256
Places Rated Rank: 301

**Amarillo, TX**
Universities:
   West Texas State University (546)
Symphony Orchestras:
   Amarillo Symphony★★
Public Libraries:
   389,007 volumes; circulation 788,537
Reading Quotient: 7.6
Places Rated Score: 1,235
Places Rated Rank: 209

**Anaheim–Santa Ana, CA**
Universities:
   California State University, Fullerton
      (1,000)
   University of California, Irvine (849)
Symphony Orchestras:
   Chapman Symphony Orchestra
      (College)
   Orange County Pacific Symphony★★
   Orange County Youth Symphony
   Southeast Youth Symphony Orchestra
   Symphony West★
Theatres:
   South Coast Repertory Theatre★★

Dance Companies:
Gloria Newman Dance Theatre (M)
Matti Lascoe Dance Theatre
Company (M)
Penrod–Plastino Movement Theatre (M)
Public Libraries:
725,268 volumes; circulation 2,197,160
Reading Quotient: 6.7
CMSA Access: LOS ANGELES–ANAHEIM–
RIVERSIDE, CA (1,808)
Places Rated Score: 5,632
Places Rated Rank: 49

**Anchorage, AK**
Fine Arts and Public Radio:
KSKA-FM 91.1 (147 hrs)
Public Television:
KAKM Channel 7
Universities:
University of Alaska (363)
Symphony Orchestras:
Anchorage Symphony Orchestra
(Community)
Anchorage Youth Symphony
Theatres:
Alaska Repertory Theatre★★
Opera Companies:
Anchorage Civic Opera
3 productions; 18 performances
Dance Companies:
Anchorage Civic Ballet
Public Libraries:
278,580 volumes; circulation 698,424
Reading Quotient: 5.2
Places Rated Score: 2,346
Places Rated Rank: 131

**Anderson, IN**
Symphony Orchestras:
Anderson Symphony Orchestra
(Community)
Public Libraries:
330,252 volumes; circulation 371,515
Reading Quotient: 9.7
Places Rated Score: 430
Places Rated Rank: 276

**Anderson, SC**
Public Libraries:
169,406 volumes; circulation 404,923
Reading Quotient: 4.3
Places Rated Score: 169
Places Rated Rank: 307

**Ann Arbor, MI**
Museums:
Herbarium of the University of Michigan
(1,000)
Kelsey Museum of Ancient and
Medieval Archeology (600)
University of Michigan Museum of
Anthropology (1,200)
University of Michigan Museum of
Zoology (500)
Fine Arts and Public Radio:
WUOM-FM 91.7 (41 mi; 135 hrs)
Universities:
Eastern Michigan University (1,000)
University of Michigan (1,000)••
Symphony Orchestras:
Ann Arbor Chamber Orchestra★
Michigan Youth Orchestra
University of Michigan Orchestra
Dance Companies:
Ann Arbor Ballet Theatre★
Ann Arbor Civic Ballet★
Malini's Dances of India Troupe (E-F)

University of Michigan Dance
Company (M)
Public Libraries:
125,000 volumes; circulation 919,317
Reading Quotient: 7.9
CMSA Access: DETROIT–ANN ARBOR,
MI (894)
Places Rated Score: 7,559
Places Rated Rank: 31

**Anniston, AL**
Theatres:
Alabama Shakespeare Festival
Public Libraries:
167,856 volumes; circulation 233,896
Reading Quotient: 3.4
Places Rated Score: 268
Places Rated Rank: 297

**Appleton–Oshkosh–Neenah, WI**
Universities:
University of Wisconsin, Oshkosh (696)
Symphony Orchestras:
Oshkosh Symphony Orchestra
(Community)
Public Libraries:
370,343 volumes; circulation 946,231
Reading Quotient: 11.3
Places Rated Score: 1,166
Places Rated Rank: 216

**Asheville, NC**
Fine Arts and Public Radio:
WCQS-FM 88.5 (72 hrs)
Public Television:
WUNF Channel 33
Universities:
University of North Carolina, Asheville
(227)
Symphony Orchestras:
Asheville Symphony Orchestra ★
Public Libraries:
264,023 volumes; circulation 726,126
Reading Quotient: 6.2
Places Rated Score: 1,391
Places Rated Rank: 197

**Athens, GA**
Museums:
Clarke Heritage Foundation (500)
University of Georgia Museum of Art
(500)
University of Georgia Museum of
Natural History (800)
Public Television:
WGTV Channel 8
Universities:
University of Georgia (1,000)
Dance Companies:
Athens Ballet Theatre
Public Libraries:
195,937 volumes; circulation NA
Reading Quotient: NA
Places Rated Score: 3,546
Places Rated Rank: 92

**Atlanta, GA**
Museums:
Fernbank Science Center (500)
High Museum of Art (700)
Fine Arts and Public Radio:
WABE-FM 90.1 (45 mi; 168 hrs)
WCLK-FM 91.9 (20 mi; 168 hrs)
Public Television:
WETV Channel 30
Universities:
Clark College (204)
Emory University (308)

Georgia State University (934)•
Kennesaw College (413)
Symphony Orchestras:
Atlanta Community Orchestra
Atlanta Symphony Orchestra ★★★★
Atlanta Symphony Youth Orchestra
Atlanta–Emory Orchestra (College)
Georgia State University Orchestra
Theatres:
Academy Theatre
Alliance Theatre Company/Atlanta
Children's Theatre★★
Dance Companies:
Atlanta Ballet
Carl Ratcliff Dance Theatre (M)
Gwinnett Ballet Theatre
Ruth Mitchell Dance Company
Public Libraries:
1,500,000 volumes; circulation
4,500,000
Reading Quotient: 10.3
Places Rated Score: 7,559
Places Rated Rank: 31

**Atlantic City, NJ**
Universities:
Stockton State College (494)
Dance Companies:
Atlantic Contemporary Ballet Theatre
Public Libraries:
76,851 volumes; circulation 115,533
Reading Quotient: 4.8
Places Rated Score: 621
Places Rated Rank: 262

**Augusta, GA–SC**
Universities:
Augusta College (208)
Symphony Orchestras:
Augusta Symphony Orchestra★
Opera Companies:
Augusta Opera Association, Inc.
2 productions; 4 performances
Dance Companies:
Augusta Ballet Company
Public Libraries:
380,788 volumes; circulation 771,571
Reading Quotient: 4.2
Places Rated Score: 1,047
Places Rated Rank: 224

**Aurora–Elgin, IL**
Symphony Orchestras:
Elgin Area Youth Orchestra
Elgin Symphony Orchestra★
Fox River Symphony Orchestra
(Community)
Public Libraries:
411,122 volumes; circulation 1,067,685
Reading Quotient: 9.5
CMSA Access: CHICAGO–GARY–LAKE
COUNTY, IL–IN–WI (3,046)
Places Rated Score: 3,857
Places Rated Rank: 82

**Austin, TX**
Museums:
Texas Memorial Museum (2,000)
Fine Arts and Public Radio:
KUT-FM 90.5 (42 mi; 168 hrs)
Public Television:
KLRU Channel 18
Universities:
University of Texas (1,000)•
Symphony Orchestras:
Austin Community Orchestra
Austin Symphony Orchestra★★★

Dance Companies:
  Austin Ballet Theatre
  Ballet Austin
  Sharir Dance Company (E-F)
Public Libraries:
  704,652 volumes; circulation 2,066,326
Reading Quotient: 7.4
Places Rated Score: 5,355
Places Rated Rank: 53

## Bakersfield, CA

Universities:
  California State College, Bakersfield
    (258)
Symphony Orchestras:
  Bakersfield Symphony Orchestra★★
Public Libraries:
  663,522 volumes; circulation 1,708,983
Reading Quotient: 5.6
Places Rated Score: 1,222
Places Rated Rank: 212

## ★ Baltimore, MD

Museums:
  Baltimore Museum of Art (1,000)
  Museum and Library of Maryland
    History (700)
  Walter's Art Gallery (600)
Fine Arts and Public Radio:
  WBJC-FM 91.5 (39 mi; 164 hrs)
  WEAA-FM 88.9 (40 mi; 165 hrs)
Public Television:
  WMPS Channel 67
Universities:
  Johns Hopkins University (225)
  Morgan State University (362)
  Towson State University (1,000)•
  University of Maryland, Baltimore City
    (487)
Symphony Orchestras:
  Baltimore Symphony Orchestra★★★★
  Gettysburg Symphony Orchestra
    (Community)
  Greater Baltimore Youth Orchestra
  Hopkins Symphony Orchestra
    (Community)
  New Harbor Chamber Orchestra
    (Community)
  Peabody Symphony Orchestra (College)
  UMBC Symphony
Theatres:
  Center Stage★
Opera Companies:
  Annapolis Opera, Inc.
    3 productions; 13 performances
  Baltimore Opera Company
    5 productions; 15 performances
Dance Companies:
  Ballet Theatre of Annapolis★
  Baltimore Ballet
  Towson State University Dance
    Company (M)
Public Libraries:
  1,900,197 volumes; circulation
    2,124,114
Reading Quotient: 5.1
Places Rated Score: 9,788
Places Rated Rank: 15

## Bangor, ME

Fine Arts and Public Radio:
  WMEH-FM 90.9 (31 mi; 133 hrs)
Universities:
  University of Maine, Orono (972)
Symphony Orchestras:
  Bangor Symphony Orchestra★
Dance Companies:
  Umo Dance Company (M)

Public Libraries:
  472,840 volumes; circulation 461,334
Reading Quotient: 30.0
Places Rated Score: 1,995
Places Rated Rank: 155

## Baton Rouge, LA

Museums:
  Louisiana Arts and Science Center
    (700)
Fine Arts and Public Radio:
  WRKF-FM 89.3 (35 mi; 168 hrs)
Public Television:
  WLPB Channel 27
Universities:
  Louisiana State University and
    Agriculture and Mechanical College
    (1,000)
  Southern University of Agriculture and
    Mechanical College (693)
Symphony Orchestras:
  Baton Rouge Symphony Orchestra★★
Dance Companies:
  Baton Rouge Ballet Theatre★
Public Libraries:
  443,983 volumes; circulation 1,429,408
Reading Quotient: 5.0
Places Rated Score: 4,237
Places Rated Rank: 77

## Battle Creek, MI

Symphony Orchestras:
  Battle Creek Symphony Orchestra★
Public Libraries:
  154,446 volumes; circulation 417,752
Reading Quotient: 5.7
Places Rated Score: 354
Places Rated Rank: 285

## Beaumont–Port Arthur, TX

Fine Arts and Public Radio:
  KVLU-FM 91.3 (25 mi; 139 hrs)
Universities:
  Lamar University (896)
Symphony Orchestras:
  Beaumont Symphony Orchestra★
Dance Companies:
  Beaumont Civic Ballet Company★
Public Libraries:
  298,884 volumes; circulation NA
Reading Quotient: NA
Places Rated Score: 1,795
Places Rated Rank: 171

## Beaver County, PA

Public Libraries:
  31,955 volumes; circulation 95,941
Reading Quotient: 7.7
CMSA Access: PITTSBURGH–BEAVER
  VALLEY, PA (1,252)
Places Rated Score: 1,284
Places Rated Rank: 204

## Bellingham, WA

Universities:
  Western Washington State College
    (1,000)•
Public Libraries:
  301,950 volumes; circulation 1,016,380
Reading Quotient: 12.3
Places Rated Score: 1,302
Places Rated Rank: 202

## Benton Harbor, MI

Public Libraries:
  78,796 volumes; circulation 64,099
Reading Quotient: 4.2
Places Rated Score: 79
Places Rated Rank: 325

## ★ Bergen–Passaic, NJ

Universities:
  Fairleigh Dickinson University (658)
  Ramapo College of New Jersey (430)
  William Patterson College of New Jersey
    (682)
Symphony Orchestras:
  Bergen Philharmonic Orchestra
    (Community)
  Bergen Youth Orchestra
  Garden State Chamber Orchestra
    (Community)
  New Jersey Philharmonic (Community)
Dance Companies:
  Acanthus Ballet
  Baron Ballet Company
  Dance Inc's "Classical Jazz Theatre"
  Irine Fokine Ballet Company
  Joan Wolf Ballet Company
Public Libraries:
  169,249 volumes; circulation 207,250
Reading Quotient: 7.3
CMSA Access: NEW YORK–NORTHERN
  NEW JERSEY–LONG ISLAND, NY–NJ–
  CT (6,715)
Places Rated Score: 9,304
Places Rated Rank: 18

## Billings, MT

Fine Arts and Public Radio:
  KEMC-FM 91.7 (131 hrs)
Symphony Orchestras:
  Billings Symphony Orchestra★
Public Libraries:
  277,995 volumes; circulation 583,000
Reading Quotient: 8.0
Places Rated Score: 778
Places Rated Rank: 247

## Biloxi–Gulfport, MS

Public Television:
  WMAH Channel 19
Public Libraries:
  178,770 volumes; circulation 401,055
Reading Quotient: 2.7
Places Rated Score: 679
Places Rated Rank: 258

## Binghamton, NY

Fine Arts and Public Radio:
  WSKG-FM 89.3 (60 mi; 138 hrs)
Public Television:
  WSKG Channel 46
Symphony Orchestras:
  Binghamton Symphony and Choral
    Society★
  Binghamton Youth Symphony
Opera Companies:
  Tri-Cities Opera Company, Inc.
    3 productions; 12 performances
Public Libraries:
  262,578 volumes; circulation 501,190
Reading Quotient: 2.1
Places Rated Score: 1,599
Places Rated Rank: 183

## Birmingham, AL

Museums:
  Birmingham Museum of Art (600)
Fine Arts and Public Radio:
  WBHM-FM 90.3 (41 mi; 131 hrs)
Public Television:
  WBIQ Channel 10
Universities:
  University of Alabama, Birmingham
    (624)
  Samford University (214)

Symphony Orchestras:
  Alabama Symphony Orchestra★★★
  Alabama Youth Symphony
Dance Companies:
  Ballet UAB★
  Birmingham Creative Dance
    Company (M)
  State of Alabama Ballet
Public Libraries:
  1,019,818 volumes; circulation
    1,023,841
Reading Quotient: 2.9
Places Rated Score: 3,958
Places Rated Rank: 81

## Bismarck, ND
Fine Arts and Public Radio:
  WCND-FM 90.5 (80 mi; 129 hrs)
Public Television:
  KBME Channel 3
Symphony Orchestras:
  Bismarck–Mandan Symphony
    Orchestra★
Public Libraries:
  211,000 volumes; circulation 466,714
Reading Quotient: 5.8
Places Rated Score: 1,211
Places Rated Rank: 213

## Bloomington, IN
Fine Arts and Public Radio:
  WFIU-FM 103.7 (45 mi; 131 hrs)
Public Television:
  WTIU Channel 30
Universities:
  Indiana University (1,000)
Symphony Orchestras:
  Bloomington Symphony Orchestra
    (Community)
  Indiana University Orchestra
Public Libraries:
  152,000 volumes; circulation 572,318
Reading Quotient: 7.4
Places Rated Score: 2,152
Places Rated Rank: 145

## Bloomington–Normal, IL
Fine Arts and Public Radio:
  WGLT-FM 89.1 (35 mi; 133 hrs)
Universities:
  Illinois State University (1,000)●
Symphony Orchestras:
  Bloomington–Normal Symphony
    (Community)
Public Libraries:
  69,565 volumes; circulation 420,000
Reading Quotient: 13.8
Places Rated Score: 1,470
Places Rated Rank: 190

## Boise City, ID
Museums:
  Idaho State Historical Museum (500)
Public Television:
  KAID Channel 4
Universities:
  Boise State University (774)●
Symphony Orchestras:
  Boise Philharmonic★★
  Treasure Valley Youth Symphony
Public Libraries:
  211,376 volumes; circulation 573,278
Reading Quotient: 7.7
Places Rated Score: 2,385
Places Rated Rank: 128

## ★ Boston, MA
Museums:
  Botanical Museum of Harvard (700)
  Fogg Art Museum (1,000)
  Gray Herbarium (500)
  Museum of Fine Arts (1,200)
  Museum of Science (700)
  Peabody Museum of Archeology and
    Ethnology (500)
Fine Arts and Public Radio:
  WBUR-FM 90.9 (100 mi; 165 hrs)
  WGBH-FM 89.7 (90 mi; 168 hrs)
Public Television:
  WEBX Channel 44
  WGBH Channel 2
Universities:
  Berklee College of Music (246)
  Boston College (898)
  Boston University (1,000)●
  Brandeis University (249)
  Framingham State College (312)
  Harvard and Radcliffe Colleges (650)
  Northeastern University (1,000)
  Simmons College (192)
  Tufts University (431)
  University of Massachusetts (1,000)
  Wellesley College (206)
Symphony Orchestras:
  Boston Symphony Orchestra★★★★
  Boston University/Tanglewood/Young
    Artists Orchestra
  Concord Orchestra (Community)
  Greater Boston Youth Symphony
  Handel and Haydn Society★★
  Harvard–Radcliffe Orchestra
  MIT Symphony Orchestra
  Mystic Valley Orchestra (Community)
  New England Symphony Orchestra
    (Community)
  Northeastern University Symphony
Theatres:
  American Repertory Theatre★★
  Boston Shakespeare Company
  Huntington Theatre Company★
Opera Companies:
  Opera Company of Boston
    4 productions; 16 performances
  Boston Lyric Opera
    8 productions; 16 performances
Dance Companies:
  Art of Black Dance and Music (E-F)
  Beth Soll and Company (M)
  Boston Ballet★
  Boston Flamenco Ballet (E-F)
  Concert Dance Company of Boston (M)
  Mandala Folk Dance Ensemble (E-F)★
  MIT Dance Company (M)
  New England Dinosaur (M)
  Ramon de los Reyes Spanish Dance
    Theatre (E-F)
Public Libraries:
  4,916,277 volumes; circulation
    1,454,414
Reading Quotient: 11.3
Places Rated Score: 21,042
Places Rated Rank: 5

## Boulder–Longmont, CO
Museums:
  Boulder Historical Museum (500)
  University of Colorado Museum (700)
Universities:
  University of Colorado (1,000)●
Symphony Orchestras:
  Boulder Chamber Orchestra
    (Community)

Boulder Philharmonic★
Colorado Music Festival★★
Dance Companies:
  Nancy Spanier Dance Theatre of
    Colorado (M)
Public Libraries:
  184,991 volumes; circulation 703,000
Reading Quotient: 8.3
CMSA Access: DENVER–BOULDER,
  CO (628)
Places Rated Score: 3,663
Places Rated Rank: 88

## Bradenton, FL
Public Libraries:
  154,149 volumes; circulation 762,542
Reading Quotient: 5.8
Places Rated Score: 154
Places Rated Rank: 311

## Brazoria, TX
Public Libraries:
  215,523 volumes; circulation 588,992
Reading Quotient: 3.5
CMSA Access: HOUSTON–GALVESTON–
  BRAZORIA, TX (1,290)
Places Rated Score: 1,506
Places Rated Rank: 188

## Bremerton, WA
Symphony Orchestras:
  Bremerton Symphony Orchestra
    (Community)
Public Libraries:
  282,227 volumes; circulation 905,114
Reading Quotient: 7.5
Places Rated Score: 382
Places Rated Rank: 280

## ★ Bridgeport–Milford, CT
Public Television:
  WEDW Channel 49
Universities:
  Fairfield University (283)
  University of Bridgeport (305)
Symphony Orchestras:
  Greater Bridgeport Symphony
    Orchestra★
Public Libraries:
  515,328 volumes; circulation 411,229
Reading Quotient: 6.5
CMSA Access: NEW YORK–NORTHERN
  NEW JERSEY–LONG ISLAND, NY–NJ–
  CT (6,565)
Places Rated Score: 8,368
Places Rated Rank: 25

## Bristol, CT
Public Libraries:
  140,000 volumes; circulation 201,659
Reading Quotient: 5.9
CMSA Access: HARTFORD–NEW
  BRITAIN–MIDDLETOWN, CT (374)
Places Rated Score: 514
Places Rated Rank: 269

## Brockton, MA
Public Libraries:
  262,879 volumes; circulation 495,458
Reading Quotient: 7.9
CMSA Access: BOSTON–LAWRENCE–
  SALEM, MA–NH (1,738)
Places Rated Score: 2,001
Places Rated Rank: 154

## Brownsville–Harlingen, TX
Public Libraries:
    161,781 volumes; circulation
    274,166
Reading Quotient: 3.4
Places Rated Score: 162
Places Rated Rank: 309

## Bryan–College Station, TX
Fine Arts and Public Radio:
    KAMU-FM 90.9 (16 mi; 128 hrs)
Public Television:
    KAMU Channel 15
Universities:
    Texas A&M University (1,000)
Symphony Orchestras:
    Brazos Valley Symphony Orchestra
    (Community)
Public Libraries:
    102,000 volumes; circulation 310,000
Reading Quotient: 4.2
Places Rated Score: 2,002
Places Rated Rank: 153

## ★ Buffalo, NY
Museums:
    Albright Knox Art Gallery (700)
    Buffalo Museum of Science (700)
Fine Arts and Public Radio:
    WBFO-FM 88.7 (22 mi; 168 hrs)
    WEBR-AM 970 (90 mi; 168 hrs)
    WNED-FM 94.5 (100 mi; 133 hrs)
Public Television:
    WNED Channel 17
Universities:
    SUNY at Buffalo (1,000)
Symphony Orchestras:
    Buffalo Philharmonic Orchestra★★★★
    Greater Buffalo Youth Orchestra
Theatres:
    Studio Arena Theatre★★
Public Libraries:
    3,467,124 volumes; circulation
    5,849,765
Reading Quotient: 9.2
Places Rated Score: 8,567
Places Rated Rank: 23

## Burlington, NC
Public Libraries:
    131,082 volumes; circulation
    329,699
Reading Quotient: 3.5
Places Rated Score: 131
Places Rated Rank: 316

## Burlington, VT
Public Television:
    WETK Channel 33
Universities:
    University of Vermont (768)
Symphony Orchestras:
    Vermont Symphony Orchestra★★
    Vermont Youth Orchestra
Public Libraries:
    73,000 volumes; circulation 180,000
Reading Quotient: 6.7
Places Rated Score: 1,741
Places Rated Rank: 177

## Canton, OH
Symphony Orchestras:
    Canton Symphony Orchestra★★
    Canton Youth Symphony
Dance Companies:
    Canton Ballet Company

Public Libraries:
    539,309 volumes; circulation 2,071,389
Reading Quotient: 2.0
Places Rated Score: 989
Places Rated Rank: 233

## Casper, WY
Symphony Orchestras:
    Casper Symphony Orchestra★
Public Libraries:
    103,260 volumes; circulation 307,827
Reading Quotient: 5.7
Places Rated Score: 303
Places Rated Rank: 293

## Cedar Rapids, IA
Fine Arts and Public Radio:
    KCCK-FM 89.5 (25 mi; 126 hrs)
Symphony Orchestras:
    Cedar Rapids Symphony Orchestra★★
    Cedar Rapids Youth Symphony
Public Libraries:
    204,492 volumes; circulation 646,496
Reading Quotient: 7.7
Places Rated Score: 904
Places Rated Rank: 236

## Champaign–Urbana–Rantoul, IL
Fine Arts and Public Radio:
    WILL-AM 580 (150 mi; 82 hrs)
    WILL-FM 90.9 (85 mi; 133 hrs)
Universities:
    University of Illinois (1,000)
Symphony Orchestras:
    Champaign County Youth Symphony
    Champaign–Urbana Symphony
    Orchestra★
Dance Companies:
    Beverly Blossom and Company (M)
Public Libraries:
    353,063 volumes; circulation 1,672,167
Reading Quotient: 17.3
Places Rated Score: 2,203
Places Rated Rank: 139

## Charleston, SC
Museums:
    Charleston Museum (600)
Fine Arts and Public Radio:
    WSCI-FM 89.3 (100 mi; 130 hrs)
Public Television:
    WITV Channel 7
Universities:
    Baptist College (244)
    Charleston College (385)
Symphony Orchestras:
    Charleston Symphony Orchestra★★
Opera Companies:
    Spoletto Festival, U.S.A.
    3 productions; 9 performances
Dance Companies:
    Robert Ivey Ballet
Public Libraries:
    387,332 volumes; circulation 722,006
Reading Quotient: 4.0
Places Rated Score: 2,993
Places Rated Rank: 106

## Charleston, WV
Museums:
    Sunrise Foundation (700)
Fine Arts and Public Radio:
    WVPN-FM 88.5 (50 mi; 132 hrs)
Universities:
    West Virginia State College (449)
Symphony Orchestras:
    Charleston Symphony Orchestra★★

    Charleston Symphony Youth Orchestra
    Lilliput Orchestra (Community)
Dance Companies:
    Charleston Ballet★
    Charleston Ballet Company
Public Libraries:
    506,159 volumes; circulation 982,892
Reading Quotient: 6.9
Places Rated Score: 2,605
Places Rated Rank: 121

## Charlotte–Gastonia–Rock Hill, NC–SC
Museums:
    Mint Museum of Art (500)
Fine Arts and Public Radio:
    WFAE-FM 90.7 (65 mi; 127 hrs)
Public Television:
    WTVI Channel 42
Universities:
    University of North Carolina, Charlotte
    (854)••
Symphony Orchestras:
    Charlotte Symphony Orchestra★★★
    Youth Symphony of the Carolinas
Opera Companies:
    Charlotte Opera Association
    3 productions; 6 performances
Dance Companies:
    Dance Gallery/Charlotte (M)
Public Libraries:
    1,391,441 volumes; circulation
    3,637,272
Reading Quotient: 6.5
Places Rated Score: 4,313
Places Rated Rank: 73

## Charlottesville, VA
Universities:
    University of Virginia (1,000)
Symphony Orchestras:
    Charlottesville University Community
    Symphony
    Youth Orchestra of Charlottesville–
    Albemarle
Public Libraries:
    221,845 volumes; circulation 710,249
Reading Quotient: 6.9
Places Rated Score: 1,422
Places Rated Rank: 195

## Chattanooga, TN–GA
Public Television:
    WTCI Channel 45
Universities:
    Tennessee Temple University (338)
    University of Tennessee, Chattanooga
    (754)
Symphony Orchestras:
    Chattanooga Symphony Orchestra★★
Opera Companies:
    Chattanooga Opera Association
    3 productions; 6 performances
Public Libraries:
    373,482 volumes; circulation 920,992
Reading Quotient: 4.5
Places Rated Score: 2,483
Places Rated Rank: 127

## ★ Chicago, IL
Museums:
    Art Institute of Chicago (2,000)
    Balzekas Museum of Lithuanian Culture
    (700)
    Chicago Historical Society (1,000)
    Field Museum of Natural History (2,000)
    Museum of Science and Industry
    (1,100)

Oriental Institute of the University of
Chicago (700)
**Fine Arts and Public Radio:**
WBEZ-FM 91.5 (100 mi; 162 hrs)
WFMT-FM 98.7 (150 mi; 168 hrs)
WNIB-FM 97.1 (45 mi; 168 hrs)
**Public Television:**
WTTW Channel 11
**Universities:**
Chicago State University (744)
De Paul University (516)
Loyola University (664)
Northeastern Illinois University (467)
Northwestern University (1,000)
Roosevelt University (668)
St. Xavier College (217)
University of Chicago (285)
University of Illinois (1,000)
Wheaton College (207)
**Symphony Orchestras:**
American Conservatory of Music
Orchestra (College)
Chicago Chamber Orchestra★
Chicago Pops Orchestra (Community)
Chicago String Ensemble (Community)
Chicago Symphony Orchestra★★★★
Chicago Symphony Wind Ensemble
(Community)
Civic Orchestra of Chicago (Youth)
Classical Youth Symphony
De Paul University Symphony
Evanston Symphony Orchestra
(Community)
Music of the Baroque★★
Orchestra of Illinois★★
Skokie Valley Symphony Orchestra
(Community)
Youth Symphony Orchestra of Greater
Chicago
**Theatres:**
Body Politic Theatre
Goodman Theatre★★
Northlight Repertory
Organic Theatre Company
Steppenwolf Theatre Company
Victory Gardens Theatre
Wisdom Bridge Theatre
**Opera Companies:**
Chicago Opera Theatre
3 productions; 18 performances
Lyric Opera of Chicago★★★★
8 productions; 62 performances
**Dance Companies:**
Akasha and Company (M)
American Dance Center Ballet
Company
Arve Connection Dance Company (M)
Chicago City Ballet★
Chicago Contemporary Dance
Theatre (M)
Chicago Dance Laboratory (M)
Chicago Dance Medium (M)
Chicago Repertory Dance
Ensemble (M)
Ensemble Español (E-F)
Gus Giordano Jazz Dance Chicago
Joel Hall Dancers (J)
Joseph Holmes Dance Theatre (M)
Le Ballet Petit Dance Ensemble★★
Margot Grimmer American Dance
Company
Mordine and Company (M)
Muntu Dance Theatre (E-F)★
Nana Solbrig and the Chicago Moving
Company (M)
Venetia Stifler and Concert Dance,
Inc. (M)

**Public Libraries:**
4,383,710 volumes; circulation
7,811,071
Reading Quotient: 4.1
CMSA Access: CHICAGO–GARY–LAKE
COUNTY, IL–IN–WI (90)
Places Rated Score: 24,846
Places Rated Rank: 2

## Chico, CA
**Fine Arts and Public Radio:**
KCHO-FM 91.1 (130 mi; 152 hrs)
**Universities:**
California State University, Chico (1,000)
**Public Libraries:**
246,895 volumes; circulation 710,849
Reading Quotient: 6.2
Places Rated Score: 1,647
Places Rated Rank: 179

## ★ Cincinnati, OH–KY–IN
**Museums:**
Cincinnati Art Museum (700)
Cincinnati Historical Society (500)
Cincinnati Museum of Natural History
(500)
**Fine Arts and Public Radio:**
WGUC-FM 90.9 (50 mi; 164 hrs)
WVXU-FM 91.7 (30 mi; 168 hrs)
**Public Television:**
WCET Channel 48
**Universities:**
Northern Kentucky University (400)
University of Cincinnati (1,000)•
Xavier University (255)
**Symphony Orchestras:**
Cincinnati Symphony Orchestra★★★★
Cincinnati Youth Symphony Orchestra
Philharmonic and Concert Orchestras
(College)
**Theatres:**
Cincinnati Playhouse in the Park★
**Opera Companies:**
Cincinnati Opera Association
8 productions; 25 performances
**Dance Companies:**
Cheryl Wallace Dance Works (M)
Cincinnati/New Orleans City Ballet
Company★
Contemporary Dance Theatre (M)
**Public Libraries:**
3,332,926 volumes; circulation
6,166,548
Reading Quotient: 10.9
Places Rated Score: 9,688
Places Rated Rank: 16

## Clarksville–Hopkinsville, TN–KY
**Public Libraries:**
110,701 volumes; circulation 568,257
Reading Quotient: 9.7
Places Rated Score: 111
Places Rated Rank: 319

## ★ Cleveland, OH
**Museums:**
Cleveland Museum of Art (2,000)
Cleveland Museum of Natural History
(1,400)
Western Reserve Historical Society
(800)
**Public Television:**
WVIZ Channel 25
**Universities:**
Case-Western Reserve University (394)•
Cleveland State University (1,000)
John Carroll University (260)

**Symphony Orchestras:**
Cleveland Institute of Music Youth
Orchestra
Cleveland Orchestra★★★★
Ohio Chamber Orchestra★★
**Theatres:**
Cleveland Playhouse★★
Great Lakes Shakespeare Festival★
**Opera Companies:**
Cleveland Opera
3 productions; 12 performances
**Dance Companies:**
Cleveland Ballet★
Cleveland State University Dance
Committee (M)★
Footpath Dance Company (M)
Hungarian Theatre and Dance
Company of Cleveland (E-F)★
North Coast Ballet Theatre
Shalhevet (E-F)
**Public Libraries:**
4,089,384 volumes; circulation
8,085,150
Reading Quotient: 10.2
CMSA Access: CLEVELAND–AKRON–
LORAIN, OH (150)
Places Rated Score: 12,679
Places Rated Rank: 9

## Colorado Springs, CO
**Museums:**
Colorado Springs Fine Arts Center (500)
**Universities:**
University of Colorado, Colorado
Springs (203)
**Symphony Orchestras:**
Colorado Springs Symphony
Orchestra★★★
**Opera Companies:**
Colorado Opera Festival
2 productions; 6 performances
**Dance Companies:**
Rocky Mountain Ballet
**Public Libraries:**
383,644 volumes; circulation 1,001,448
Reading Quotient: 8.3
Places Rated Score: 1,749
Places Rated Rank: 176

## Columbia, MO
**Museums:**
University of Missouri Museum of Art
and Archeology (800)
**Fine Arts and Public Radio:**
KBIA-FM 91.3 (80 mi; 133 hrs)
KOPN-FM 89.5 (40 mi; 160 hrs)
**Universities:**
University of Missouri (1,000)
**Symphony Orchestras:**
Missouri Symphony Orchestra
(Community)
**Public Libraries:**
282,245 volumes; circulation 1,505,191
Reading Quotient: 13.7
Places Rated Score: 2,882
Places Rated Rank: 111

## Columbia, SC
**Fine Arts and Public Radio:**
WLTR-FM 91.3 (42 mi; 130 hrs)
**Public Television:**
WRLK Channel 35
**Universities:**
University of South Carolina (1,000)
**Symphony Orchestras:**
Columbia Youth Orchestra
Palmetto State Orchestra Association
(College)

Dance Companies:
Columbia City Ballet★
Public Libraries:
388,860 volumes; circulation 944,385
Reading Quotient: 5.7
Places Rated Score: 2,489
Places Rated Rank: 126

## Columbus, GA–AL

Museums:
Columbus Museum of Art and Science,
Inc. (500)
Public Television:
WJSP Channel 28
Universities:
Columbus College (230)
Symphony Orchestras:
Columbus Symphony Orchestra★
Public Libraries:
431,118 volumes; circulation 701,436
Reading Quotient: 5.4
Places Rated Score: 1,861
Places Rated Rank: 166

## Columbus, OH

Museums:
Ohio Historical Center (500)
Fine Arts and Public Radio:
WCBE-FM 90.5 (50 mi; 126 hrs)
WOSU-AM 820 (95 mi; 91 hrs)
WOSU-FM 89.7 (60 mi; 133 hrs)
Public Television:
WOSU Channel 34
WPBO Channel 42
Universities:
Capital University (257)
Denison University (310)●
Ohio State University (1,000)●
Ohio Wesleyan University (226)
Symphony Orchestras:
Columbus Symphony Orchestra★★★
Columbus Symphony Youth Orchestra
Pro Musica Chamber Orchestra of
Columbus★
Dance Companies:
Allan Miles Ballet
Ballet Metropolitan
Columbus Theatre Ballet Association★★
Dancentral (M)
Les Danseurs Noir (J)
Ohio State University Dance
Company (M)★
Zivili (E-F)★
Public Libraries:
1,255,000 volumes; circulation 3,866,356
Reading Quotient: 6.0
Places Rated Score: 6,648
Places Rated Rank: 41

## Corpus Christi, TX

Museums:
Corpus Christi Museum (500)
Fine Arts and Public Radio:
KKED-FM 90.3 (70 mi; 131 hrs)
Public Television:
KEDT Channel 16
Symphony Orchestras:
Corpus Christi Symphony Orchestra★★
Dance Companies:
Corpus Christi Ballet Theatre★
Public Libraries:
292,193 volumes; circulation 614,641
Reading Quotient: 3.8
Places Rated Score: 1,992
Places Rated Rank: 156

## Cumberland, MD–WV

Universities:
Frostburg State College (210)
Public Libraries:
163,231 volumes; circulation 602,684
Reading Quotient: 9.6
Places Rated Score: 373
Places Rated Rank: 282

## ★ Dallas, TX

Museums:
Dallas Historical Society (500)
Dallas Museum of Fine Art (800)
Dallas Museum of Natural History
(1,100)
International Museum of Cultures (500)
Fine Arts and Public Radio:
KERA-FM 90.1 (60 mi; 163 hrs)
Public Television:
KERA Channel 13
Universities:
North Texas State University (1,000)
Southern Methodist University (550)
Texas Women's University (445)●
University of Dallas (282)
Symphony Orchestras:
AIMS Orchestra (College)
Dallas Symphony Orchestra★★★★
Greater Dallas Youth Orchestra
Theatres:
Dallas Theatre Center★★★
Theatre Three
Opera Companies:
Dallas Opera
6 productions; 23 performances
Dance Companies:
American Dancing (E-F)★
Dallas Ballet★
Dallas Black Dance Theatre (M)★
Dallas Metropolitan Ballet★
Dancers Unlimited Repertory
Company (M)
Garland Ballet Association
Plana Ballet Theatre
Public Libraries:
2,105,231 volumes; circulation
3,983,961
Reading Quotient: 5.9
CMSA Access: DALLAS–FORT WORTH,
TX (68)
Places Rated Score: 10,438
Places Rated Rank: 13

## Danbury, CT

Universities:
Western Connecticut State College
(274)
Symphony Orchestras:
Connecticut Symphony Orchestra
(Community)
Ridgefield Orchestra (Community)
Ridgefield Youth Orchestra
Public Libraries:
126,132 volumes; circulation 334,518
Reading Quotient: 7.7
CMSA Access: NEW YORK–NORTHERN
NEW JERSEY–LONG ISLAND, NY–NJ–
CT (6,715)
Places Rated Score: 7,415
Places Rated Rank: 34

## Danville, VA

Public Libraries:
85,294 volumes; circulation 193,019
Reading Quotient: 6.1
Places Rated Score: 85
Places Rated Rank: 323

## Davenport–Rock Island–Moline, IA–IL

Universities:
St. Ambrose College (213)
Symphony Orchestras:
Augustana College Symphony
Tri-City Symphony Orchestra★★
Tri-City Youth Symphony Orchestra
Public Libraries:
304,064 volumes; circulation 600,000
Reading Quotient: 8.8
Places Rated Score: 1,017
Places Rated Rank: 228

## Dayton–Springfield, OH

Museums:
Dayton Art Institute (600)
Dayton Museum of Natural History (900)
Public Television:
WPTD Channel 16
WPTO Channel 14
Universities:
Central State University (219)
University of Dayton (634)
Wittenberg University (225)
Wright State University (779)●
Symphony Orchestras:
Allegro Chamber Players (Youth)
Dayton Philharmonic Orchestra★★
Dayton Philharmonic Youth Orchestra
Springfield Symphony Orchestra★
Dance Companies:
Antioch College Dance Ensemble (M)
Dance Theatre Dayton
Dayton Ballet
Dayton Contemporary Dance
Company (M)
Sinclair Dance Ensemble (M)
Public Libraries:
1,677,923 volumes; circulation
5,652,877
Reading Quotient: 10.2
Places Rated Score: 6.,935
Places Rated Rank: 40

## Daytona Beach, FL

Universities:
Stetson University (200)
Dance Companies:
Atlantic Dance Company
Ballet Guild of Sanford–Seminole
Rozak Dancers (E-F)
Public Libraries:
458,802 volumes; circulation 1,716,516
Reading Quotient: 8.0
Places Rated Score: 809
Places Rated Rank: 244

## Decatur, IL

Symphony Orchestras:
Millikin–Decatur Civic Symphony
(Community)
Public Libraries:
197,955 volumes; circulation NA
Reading Quotient: NA
Places Rated Score: 298
Places Rated Rank: 294

## ★ Denver, CO

Museums:
Colorado Historical Society (700)
Denver Art Museum (800)
Denver Museum of Natural History (800)
Fine Arts and Public Radio:
KCFR-FM 90.1 (70 mi; 152 hrs)
Public Television:
KRMA Channel 6

Universities:
Metropolitan State College (637)
University of Colorado, Denver (785)
University of Denver (440)
Symphony Orchestras:
Denver Chamber Orchestra
(Community)
Denver Symphony Orchestra★★★★
Young Artists Orchestra of Denver
Theatres:
Denver Center Theatre Company★★★
Opera Companies:
Central City Opera House Association
3 productions; 31 performances
Dance Companies:
Changing Scene Dance Company (E-F)
Cleo Parker Robinson Dance
Ensemble (M)
Colorado Ballet
Premiere Dance Art Company (B)
Public Libraries:
1,822,111 volumes; circulation NA
Reading Quotient: NA
Places Rated Score: 8,477
Places Rated Rank: 24

**Des Moines, IA**
Public Television:
KDIN Channel 11
Universities:
Drake University (586)●
Symphony Orchestras:
Des Moines Community Orchestra
Drake University Symphony Orchestra
Greater Des Moines Youth Symphony
Opera Companies:
Des Moines Metropolitan Opera
3 productions; 16 performances
Dance Companies:
Des Moines Ballet Company
Public Libraries:
172,965 volumes; circulation 1,234,390
Reading Quotient: 7.4
Places Rated Score: 1,857
Places Rated Rank: 167

★ **Detroit, MI**
Museums:
Cranbrook Institute of Science (800)
Detroit Historical Museum (700)
Detroit Institute of Arts (1,200)
Greenfield Village/Ford Museum (800)
Fine Arts and Public Radio:
WDET-FM 101.9 (35 mi; 168 hrs)
Public Television:
WTVS Channel 56
Universities:
University of Detroit (250)
Wayne State University (1,000)
Symphony Orchestras:
Allen Park Symphony (Community)
Dearborn Symphony Orchestra★
Detroit Symphony Orchestra★★★★
Livonia Youth Symphony Society
Opera Companies:
Michigan Opera Theatre
4 productions; 20 performances
Dance Companies:
Body Electric Company (E-F)
Detroit City Ballet
Michigan Ballet Theatre
Northern Ballet Theatre of Livonia
Nritya Sudha's Hindu Temple Rhythms
(E-F)★
Public Libraries:
2,408,863 volumes; circulation NA

Reading Quotient: NA
CMSA Access: DETROIT–ANN ARBOR,
MI (750)
Places Rated Score: 10,389
Places Rated Rank: 14

**Dothan, AL**
Public Libraries:
117,477 volumes; circulation 312,167
Reading Quotient: 5.8
Places Rated Score: 117
Places Rated Rank: 318

**Dubuque, IA**
Symphony Orchestras:
Dubuque Symphony Orchestra★
Public Libraries:
140,000 volumes; circulation 409,020
Reading Quotient: 8.5
Places Rated Score: 340
Places Rated Rank: 287

**Duluth, MN–WI**
Fine Arts and Public Radio:
KUMD-FM 103.3 (60 mi; 136 hrs)
WSCD-FM 92.9 (50 mi; 140 hrs)
Public Television:
WDSE Channel 8
Universities:
University of Minnesota (661)
Symphony Orchestras:
Duluth–Superior Symphony Orchestra★★
Public Libraries:
315,634 volumes; circulation 959,251
Reading Quotient: 13.7
Places Rated Score: 2,377
Places Rated Rank: 129

**East St. Louis–Belleville, IL**
Public Libraries:
235,621 volumes; circulation 349,503
Reading Quotient: 6.0
CMSA Access: ST. LOUIS–EAST ST.
LOUIS–ALTON, MO–IL (668)
Places Rated Score: 904
Places Rated Rank: 236

**Eau Claire, WI**
Public Television:
WHWC Channel 28
Universities:
University of Wisconsin, Eau Claire
(942)
Symphony Orchestras:
Chippewa Valley Symphony
(Community)
University of Wisconsin, Eau Claire,
Symphony
Public Libraries:
164,957 volumes; circulation 533,734
Reading Quotient: 13.6
Places Rated Score: 1,807
Places Rated Rank: 170

**El Paso, TX**
Museums:
El Paso Museum of Art (600)
Fine Arts and Public Radio:
KTEP-FM 88.5 (100 mi; 164 hrs)
Public Television:
KCOS Channel 13
Universities:
University of Texas, El Paso (1,000)
Symphony Orchestras:
El Paso Symphony Orchestra★★
El Paso Youth Symphony
Irving Symphony Orchestra
(Community)

University of Texas, El Paso, Symphony
Dance Companies:
Antonio Triana–Ballet Español (E-F)
Ballet El Paso
Susan Francis Dancers (J)
Public Libraries:
450,000 volumes; circulation 1,200,000
Reading Quotient: 3.8
Places Rated Score: 3,800
Places Rated Rank: 84

**Elkhart–Goshen, IN**
Symphony Orchestras:
Elkhart Symphony Orchestra★
Public Libraries:
153,109 volumes; circulation 412,881
Reading Quotient: 8.3
Places Rated Score: 353
Places Rated Rank: 286

**Elmira, NY**
Universities:
Elmira College (293)
Symphony Orchestras:
Elmira Symphony and Choral Society★
Dance Companies:
Elmira Corning Ballet★
Public Libraries:
455,196 volumes; circulation 412,712
Reading Quotient: 8.9
Places Rated Score: 1,048
Places Rated Rank: 223

**Enid, OK**
Symphony Orchestras:
Enid–Phillips Symphony (Community)
Public Libraries:
114,943 volumes; circulation 214,269
Reading Quotient: 5.2
Places Rated Score: 215
Places Rated Rank: 304

**Erie, PA**
Fine Arts and Public Radio:
WQLN-FM 91.3 (NW PA; 126 hrs)
Public Television:
WQLN Channel 54
Universities:
Edinboro State College (442)
Symphony Orchestras:
Erie Philharmonic Orchestra★★
Erie Philharmonic Youth Orchestra
Public Libraries:
390,000 volumes; circulation 1,308,199
Reading Quotient: 6.0
Places Rated Score: 2,032
Places Rated Rank: 151

**Eugene–Springfield, OR**
Fine Arts and Public Radio:
KLCC-FM 89.7 (65 mi; 140 hrs)
KWAX-FM 91.1 (58 mi; 133 hrs)
Universities:
University of Oregon (1,000)●●
Symphony Orchestras:
Eugene Symphony Orchestra★★
Eugene Youth Symphony
Dance Companies:
Concert Dance Theatre (M)★
Dobre Folk Ensemble (E-F)★
Eugene Ballet Company★
Oslund and Company Dance (M)
Public Libraries:
281,271 volumes; circulation 1,384,166
Reading Quotient: 11.4
Places Rated Score: 2,631
Places Rated Rank: 120

## Evansville, IN–KY
Public Television:
  WNIN Channel 9
Universities:
  University of Evansville (294)
Symphony Orchestras:
  Evansville Philharmonic Orchestra★★
  University of Evansville Symphony
Public Libraries:
  681,710 volumes; circulation NA
Reading Quotient: NA
Places Rated Score: 1,876
Places Rated Rank: 164

## Fall River, MA–RI
Symphony Orchestras:
  Greater Fall River Symphony Orchestra
    (Community)
Public Libraries:
  308,699 volumes; circulation 291,887
Reading Quotient: 6.0
CMSA Access: PROVIDENCE–PAWTUCKET–
  FALL RIVER, RI–MA (340)
Places Rated Score: 749
Places Rated Rank: 252

## Fargo–Moorhead, ND–MN
Fine Arts and Public Radio:
  KDSU-FM 91.9 (90 mi; 134 hrs)
Public Television:
  KFME Channel 13
Universities:
  North Dakota State University (800)
Symphony Orchestras:
  Fargo–Moorhead Symphony Orchestra★
Public Libraries:
  311,196 volumes; circulation 410,000
Reading Quotient: 11.8
Places Rated Score: 2,111
Places Rated Rank: 147

## Fayetteville, NC
Fine Arts and Public Radio:
  WFSS-FM 89.1 (65 mi; 126 hrs)
Universities:
  Pembroke State University (219)
Symphony Orchestras:
  Fayetteville Symphony Orchestra
    (Community)
Public Libraries:
  225,132 volumes; circulation 564,272
Reading Quotient: 3.2
Places Rated Score: 844
Places Rated Rank: 241

## Fayetteville–Springdale, AR
Public Television:
  KAFT Channel 13
Universities:
  University of Arkansas (1,000)●
Symphony Orchestras:
  North Arkansas Symphony Orchestra★
Public Libraries:
  215,000 volumes; circulation 800,000
Reading Quotient: 6.8
Places Rated Score: 1,915
Places Rated Rank: 163

## Fitchburg–Leominster, MA
Public Libraries:
  269,921 volumes; circulation 497,041
Reading Quotient: 2.6
Places Rated Score: 270
Places Rated Rank: 296

## Flint, MI
Fine Arts and Public Radio:
  WFBE-FM 95.1 (17 mi; 130 hrs)

Public Television:
  WFUM Channel 28
Universities:
  University of Michigan, Flint (237)
Symphony Orchestras:
  Flint Community Music School
    Orchestra (College)
  Flint Symphony Orchestra★★★
Dance Companies:
  Dance Repertory Company
  Flint Ballet Theatre★
Public Libraries:
  475,604 volumes; circulation 898,907
Reading Quotient: 8.6
Places Rated Score: 2,163
Places Rated Rank: 143

## Florence, AL
Public Television:
  WFIQ Channel 36
Universities:
  University of Northern Alabama (475)
Public Libraries:
  45,963 volumes; circulation 150,806
Reading Quotient: 4.3
Places Rated Score: 1,021
Places Rated Rank: 227

## Florence, SC
Public Television:
  WJPM Channel 33
Public Libraries:
  128,156 volumes; circulation 355,893
Reading Quotient: 4.4
Places Rated Score: 628
Places Rated Rank: 261

## Fort Collins–Loveland, CO
Fine Arts and Public Radio:
  KCSU-FM 90.9 (30 mi; 133 hrs)
Universities:
  Colorado State University (1,000)
Symphony Orchestras:
  Fort Collins Symphony Orchestra
    (Community)
Public Libraries:
  208,554 volumes; circulation 725,650
Reading Quotient: 8.0
Places Rated Score: 1,609
Places Rated Rank: 182

## Fort Lauderdale–Hollywood–
Pompano Beach, FL
Symphony Orchestras:
  Broward Community College Youth
    Symphony
  Broward Symphony Orchestra
    (Community)
  Florida Chamber Orchestra★★
  Fort Lauderdale Symphony Orchestra★★
Public Libraries:
  597,296 volumes; circulation 2,067,553
Reading Quotient: 2.6
CMSA Access: MIAMI–FORT LAUDERDALE,
  FL (630)
Places Rated Score: 2,027
Places Rated Rank: 152

## Fort Myers, FL
Symphony Orchestras:
  Southwest Florida Symphony
    Orchestra★
Public Libraries:
  179,987 volumes; circulation 1,008,711
Reading Quotient: 5.4
Places Rated Score: 380
Places Rated Rank: 281

## Fort Pierce, FL
Fine Arts and Public Radio:
  WQCS-FM 88.3 (40 mi; 126 hrs)
Public Libraries:
  67,500 volumes; circulation 337,500
Reading Quotient: 3.9
Places Rated Score: 368
Places Rated Rank: 284

## Fort Smith, AR–OK
Symphony Orchestras:
  Fort Smith Symphony (Community)
Public Libraries:
  45,000 volumes; circulation 170,000
Reading Quotient: 6.7
Places Rated Score: 145
Places Rated Rank: 315

## Fort Walton Beach, FL
Dance Companies:
  Fort Walton Beach Ballet Association
Public Libraries:
  36,755 volumes; circulation 118,032
Reading Quotient: 5.1
Places Rated Score: 87
Places Rated Rank: 321

## Fort Wayne, IN
Universities:
  Indiana University–Purdue University at
    Fort Wayne (915)
Symphony Orchestras:
  Fort Wayne Philharmonic★★
Dance Companies:
  Fort Wayne Ballet★
  Fort Wayne Dance Collective (M)
Public Libraries:
  1,481,309 volumes; circulation
    1,755,443
Reading Quotient: 11.0
Places Rated Score: 2,846
Places Rated Rank: 112

## Fort Worth–Arlington, TX
Museums:
  Amon Carter Museum of Western Art
    (500)
  Fort Worth Museum of Science and
    History (500)
  Kimball Art Museum (700)
Universities:
  Texas Christian University (664)●
  University of Texas, Arlington (1,000)
Symphony Orchestras:
  Fort Worth Civic Orchestra (Community)
  Fort Worth Symphony Orchestra★★★
  University of Texas, Arlington,
    Symphony
  Youth Orchestra of Greater Fort Worth
Opera Companies:
  Fort Worth Opera Association
    4 productions; 7 performances
Dance Companies:
  Ballet Concerto
  Fort Worth Ballet
  TCU Modern Dance Lab Company★
Public Libraries:
  973,187 volumes; circulation 3,271,279
Reading Quotient: 4.0
CMSA Access: DALLAS–FORT WORTH,
  TX (1,001)
Places Rated Score: 6,466
Places Rated Rank: 42

## Fresno, CA
Fine Arts and Public Radio:
  KSJV-FM 91.5 (70 mi; 140 hrs)
  KVPR-FM 89.3 (85 mi; 126 hrs)

Public Television:
 KMTF Channel 18
Universities:
 California State University, Fresno
  (1,000)
Symphony Orchestras:
 Fresno Junior Philharmonic Orchestra
 Fresno Philharmonic Orchestra★★
Dance Companies:
 Fresno Ballet★★
Public Libraries:
 895,926 volumes; circulation 2,057,677
Reading Quotient: 5.7
Places Rated Score: 3,596
Places Rated Rank: 90

**Gadsden, AL**
Public Libraries:
 153,170 volumes; circulation 310,924
Reading Quotient: 4.5
Places Rated Score: 153
Places Rated Rank: 312

**Gainesville, FL**
Museums:
 Florida State Museum (1,000)
Fine Arts and Public Radio:
 WUFT-FM 89.1 (42 mi; 168 hrs)
Public Television:
 WUFT Channel 5
Universities:
 University of Florida (1,000)
Symphony Orchestras:
 University of Florida Symphony
  Orchestra
Theatres:
 Hippodrome Street Theatre
Dance Companies:
 Dance Alive!(B)
Public Libraries:
 85,437 volumes; circulation 752,513
Reading Quotient: 5.4
Places Rated Score: 3,335
Places Rated Rank: 96

**Galveston–Texas City, TX**
Symphony Orchestras:
 Galveston Symphony Orchestra
  (Community)
Public Libraries:
 366,013 volumes; circulation 334,873
Reading Quotient: 3.3
CMSA Access: HOUSTON–GALVESTON–
 BRAZORIA, TX (1,290)
Places Rated Score: 1,756
Places Rated Rank: 175

**Gary–Hammond, IN**
Symphony Orchestras:
 Northwest Indiana Symphony★
 Northwest Indiana Youth Orchestra
Public Libraries:
 768,715 volumes; circulation 1,002,000
Reading Quotient: 7.2
CMSA Access: CHICAGO–GARY–LAKE
 COUNTY, IL–IN–WI (3,046)
Places Rated Score: 4,115
Places Rated Rank: 80

**Glens Falls, NY**
Symphony Orchestras:
 Glens Falls Symphony Orchestra
  (Community)
Opera Companies:
 Lake George Opera Festival
  4 productions; 32 performances

Public Libraries:
 174,866 volumes; circulation 269,311
Reading Quotient: 9.6
Places Rated Score: 603
Places Rated Rank: 263

**Grand Forks, ND**
Fine Arts and Public Radio:
 KFJM-AM 1370 (75 mi; 91 hrs)
Public Television:
 KGFE Channel 2
Universities:
 University of North Dakota (1,000)
Symphony Orchestras:
 Greater Grand Forks Symphony
  (Community)
Public Libraries:
 120,695 volumes; circulation 374,755
Reading Quotient: 7.5
Places Rated Score: 1,921
Places Rated Rank: 161

**Grand Rapids, MI**
Museums:
 Grand Rapids Public Museum (600)
Public Television:
 WGVC Channel 35
Universities:
 Aquinas College (272)
 Calvin College (397)
 Grand Valley State College (366)
 Hope College (220)
Symphony Orchestras:
 Grand Rapids Symphony Orchestra★★★
 Grand Rapids Youth Symphony
Dance Companies:
 Grand Rapids Civic Ballet Company★
Public Libraries:
 300,000 volumes; circulation 1,878,000
Reading Quotient: 5.0
Places Rated Score: 3,255
Places Rated Rank: 99

**Great Falls, MT**
Symphony Orchestras:
 Great Falls Symphony Orchestra★
Public Libraries:
 201,152 volumes; circulation 510,791
Reading Quotient: 4.9
Places Rated Score: 401
Places Rated Rank: 279

**Greeley, CO**
Fine Arts and Public Radio:
 KUNC-FM 91.5 (50 mi; 132 hrs)
Universities:
 University of Northern Colorado (839)
Public Libraries:
 114,622 volumes; circulation 390,875
Reading Quotient: 7.6
Places Rated Score: 1,254
Places Rated Rank: 208

**Green Bay, WI**
Museums:
 Neville Public Museum (600)
Public Television:
 WPNE Channel 38
Universities:
 University of Wisconsin, Green Bay
  (899)
Symphony Orchestras:
 Green Bay Symphony Orchestra★
Public Libraries:
 347,926 volumes; circulation 1,255,375
Reading Quotient: 9.1
Places Rated Score: 2,547
Places Rated Rank: 124

**Greensboro–Winston-Salem–
High Point, NC**
Fine Arts and Public Radio:
 WFDD-FM 88.5 (40 mi; 126 hrs)
Public Television:
 WUNL Channel 26
Universities:
 University of North Carolina,
  Greensboro (823)••
 Wake Forest University (308)
Symphony Orchestras:
 Eastern Philharmonic Orchestra★★
 Greensboro Civic Orchestra
  (Community)
 Greensboro Symphony Orchestra★★
 Winston-Salem Symphony Orchestra★★
Theatres:
 North Carolina Shakespeare Festival
Dance Companies:
 North Carolina Dance Theatre
Public Libraries:
 1,106,807 volumes; circulation
  2,837,111
Reading Quotient: 7.0
Places Rated Score: 4,188
Places Rated Rank: 79

**Greenville–Spartanburg, SC**
Public Television:
 WNTV Channel 29
 WRET Channel 49
Universities:
 Furman University (238)
Symphony Orchestras:
 Carolina Youth Symphony
 Greenville Symphony Orchestra★
 Spartanburg Symphony Orchestra
  (Community)
Dance Companies:
 Carolina Ballet Theatre★★
Public Libraries:
 730,921 volumes; circulation 1,677,501
Reading Quotient: 5.0
Places Rated Score: 2,569
Places Rated Rank: 122

**Hagerstown, MD**
Public Television:
 WWPB Channel 31
Symphony Orchestras:
 Maryland Symphony Orchestra
  (Community)
Public Libraries:
 224,999 volumes; circulation 718,484
Reading Quotient: 8.3
Places Rated Score: 825
Places Rated Rank: 242

**Hamilton–Middletown, OH**
Universities:
 Miami University (1,000)
Symphony Orchestras:
 Hamilton–Fairfield Symphony
  (Community)
 Middletown Symphony Orchestra
  (Community)
Dance Companies:
 Miami University Dance Theatre (M)★
Public Libraries:
 235,919 volumes; circulation NA
Reading Quotient: NA
CMSA Access: CINCINNATI–HAMILTON,
 OH–KY–IN (780)
Places Rated Score: 2,316
Places Rated Rank: 133

## Harrisburg–Lebanon–Carlisle, PA
Museums:
Pennsylvania Historical and Museum
Commission (700)
William Penn Memorial Museum (700)
Fine Arts and Public Radio:
WITF-FM 89.5 (50 mi; 131 hrs)
Public Television:
WITF Channel 33
Symphony Orchestras:
Harrisburg Symphony Orchestra★★
Harrisburg Youth Symphony Orchestra
Public Libraries:
482,949 volumes; circulation 1,169,069
Reading Quotient: 2.8
Places Rated Score: 3,083
Places Rated Rank: 103

## Hartford, CT
Museums:
Wadsworth Atheneum (600)
Fine Arts and Public Radio:
WPBH-FM 90.5 (19 mi; 140 hrs)
Public Television:
WEDH Channel 24
Universities:
University of Hartford (401)
Symphony Orchestras:
Hartford Chamber Orchestra★★
Hartford Symphony Orchestra★★★
Hartford Symphony Orchestra (Youth)
Theatres:
Hartford Stage Company★
Opera Companies:
Connecticut Opera
4 productions; 12 performances
Dance Companies:
Connecticut Jazz Dance Company
Hartford Conservatory Modern Dance
Ensemble
Public Libraries:
466,653 volumes; circulation 547,866
Reading Quotient: 7.4
Places Rated Score: 3,616
Places Rated Rank: 89

## Hickory, NC
Symphony Orchestras:
Western Piedmont Symphony
(Community)
Public Libraries:
87,917 volumes; circulation 177,346
Reading Quotient: 5.3
Places Rated Score: 188
Places Rated Rank: 306

## Honolulu, HI
Museums:
Bernice Pauahi Bishop Museum (800)
Honolulu Academy of the Arts (800)
Fine Arts and Public Radio:
KHPR-FM 88.1 (50 mi; 168 hrs)
Public Television:
KHET Channel 11
KMEB Channel 10
Universities:
University of Hawaii (1,000)
Symphony Orchestras:
Honolulu Symphony Orchestra★★★
Theatres:
Honolulu Theatre for Youth
Opera Companies:
Hawaii Opera Theatre
3 productions; 9 performances
Dance Companies:
Ballet Hawaii
Dances We Dance Company (M)

Public Libraries:
2,241,156 volumes; circulation
5,200,000
Reading Quotient: 7.7
Places Rated Score: 7,168
Places Rated Rank: 36

## Houma–Thibodaux, LA
Universities:
Nicholls State University (468)
Public Libraries:
256,983 volumes; circulation 407,258
Reading Quotient: 3.7
Places Rated Score: 725
Places Rated Rank: 255

## ★ Houston, TX
Museums:
Houston Museum of Natural Science
(1,100)
Museum of Fine Art (700)
Fine Arts and Public Radio:
KPFT-FM 90.1 (45 mi; 168 hrs)
KUHF-FM 88.7 (48 mi; 145 hrs)
Public Television:
KUHT Channel 8
Universities:
Houston Baptist University (222)
Rice University (245)
University of Houston (1,000)
Symphony Orchestras:
Clear Lake Symphony (Community)
Houston Pops Orchestra★★
Houston Symphony Orchestra★★★★
Houston Youth Symphony and Ballet
Symphony North of Houston
(Community)
Texas Chamber Orchestra★
Theatres:
Alley Theatre★★★
Opera Companies:
Houston Grand Opera★★★★
10 productions; 54 performances
Texas Opera Theatre
2 productions; 100 performances
Dance Companies:
Allegro Ballet of Houston
Delia Stewart Dance Company (J)
Discovery Dance Group
Encore Jazz Dancers
Greater Houston Civic Ballet Company★
Houston Ballet★★
Royal Ballet Theatre of Texas
Southwest Jazz Ballet Company
Space/Dance/Theatre
Public Libraries:
3,156,063 volumes; circulation
8,414,755
Reading Quotient: 3.8
Places Rated Score: 11,073
Places Rated Rank: 11

## Huntington–Ashland, WV–KY–OH
Museums:
Huntington Galleries (500)
Public Television:
WPBY Channel 33
Universities:
Marshall University (835)
Symphony Orchestras:
Huntington Chamber Orchestra
(Community)
Public Libraries:
260,000 volumes; circulation 656,431
Reading Quotient: 8.6
Places Rated Score: 2,195
Places Rated Rank: 140

## Huntsville, AL
Fine Arts and Public Radio:
WLRH-FM 89.3 (60 mi; 130 hrs)
Public Television:
WHIQ Channel 25
Universities:
University of Alabama, Huntsville (546)
Symphony Orchestras:
Huntsville Symphony Orchestra★
Huntsville Youth Orchestra
Dance Companies:
Huntsville Civic Ballet
Public Libraries:
225,170 volumes; circulation 461,000
Reading Quotient: 3.5
Places Rated Score: 1,921
Places Rated Rank: 161

## Indianapolis, IN
Museums:
Children's Museum (500)
Indianapolis Museum of Art (900)
Fine Arts and Public Radio:
WAJC-FM 104.5 (65 mi; 126 hrs)
WIAN-FM 90.1 (27 mi; 162 hrs)
Public Television:
WFYI Channel 20
Universities:
Butler University (208)
Indiana University–Purdue University at
Indianapolis (919)
Symphony Orchestras:
Butler University Symphony Orchestra
Indianapolis Symphony Orchestra★★★★
Theatres:
Indiana Repertory Theatre★
Opera Companies:
Indianapolis Opera
3 productions; 6 performances
Dance Companies:
Dance Kaleidoscope (M)
Indianapolis Ballet Theatre
Public Libraries:
1,403,317 volumes; circulation
3,829,511
Reading Quotient: NA
Places Rated Score: 6,348
Places Rated Rank: 44

## Iowa City, IA
Fine Arts and Public Radio:
KSUI-AM 910 (120 mi; 131 hrs)
KSUI-FM 91.7 (70 mi; 134 hrs)
Public Television:
KIIN Channel 12
Universities:
University of Iowa (1,000)
Public Libraries:
155,000 volumes; circulation 487,000
Reading Quotient: 10.4
Places Rated Score: 2,255
Places Rated Rank: 136

## Jackson, MI
Symphony Orchestras:
Jackson Symphony Orchestra
(Community)
Public Libraries:
222,550 volumes; circulation 685,322
Reading Quotient: 6.0
Places Rated Score: 323
Places Rated Rank: 290

## Jackson, MS
Fine Arts and Public Radio:
WJSU-FM (126 hrs)

Public Television:
  WMAA Channel 29
Universities·
  Jackson State University (710)
  Mississippi College (143)
Symphony Orchestras:
  Jackson State University Orchestra
  Jackson Symphony Orchestra★★
  Jackson Symphony Youth Orchestra
Opera Companies:
  Mississippi Opera Association
    2 productions; 4 performances
Dance Companies:
  Ballet Mississippi
Public Libraries:
  797,748 volumes; circulation 1,268,369
Reading Quotient: 4.7
Places Rated Score: 3,209
Places Rated Rank: 100

**Jacksonville, FL**
Fine Arts and Public Radio:
  WJCT-FM 89.9 (125 mi; 133 hrs)
Public Television:
  WJCT Channel 7
Universities:
  Jacksonville University (302)●
Symphony Orchestras:
  Jacksonville Symphony Orchestra★★★
Dance Companies:
  Ballet Guild of Jacksonville★
  Florida Ballet at Jacksonville
  Jacksonville Ballet Theatre★
Public Libraries:
  410,433 volumes; circulation 2,026,528
Reading Quotient: 4.0
Places Rated Score: 2,162
Places Rated Rank: 144

**Jacksonville, NC**
Public Television:
  WUNM Channel 19
Public Libraries:
  67,000 volumes; circulation 300,000
Reading Quotient: 3.3
Places Rated Score: 567
Places Rated Rank: 265

**Janesville–Beloit, WI**
Universities:
  University of Wisconsin, Janesville (899)
Symphony Orchestras:
  Beloit–Janesville Symphony Orchestra
    (Community)
Public Libraries:
  92,535 volumes; circulation NA
Reading Quotient: NA
Places Rated Score: 1,092
Places Rated Rank: 220

**Jersey City, NJ**
Universities:
  Jersey City State College (461)
Public Libraries:
  243,777 volumes; circulation NA
Reading Quotient: NA
CMSA Access: NEW YORK–NORTHERN
  NEW JERSEY–LONG ISLAND, NY–NJ–
  CT (6,715)
Places Rated Score: 7,420
Places Rated Rank: 33

**Johnson City–Kingsport–Bristol, TN–VA**
Fine Arts and Public Radio:
  WETS-FM 89.5 (65 mi; 126 hrs)

Universities:
  East Tennessee State University (792)
Symphony Orchestras:
  Jackson Symphony Orchestra★
  Johnson City Symphony (Community)
  Kingsport Symphony Orchestra
    (Community)
Theatres:
  Barter Theatre★
Dance Companies:
  Bristol Ballet Company★
Public Libraries:
  133,162 volumes; circulation 371,312
Reading Quotient: 6.5
Places Rated Score: 1,925
Places Rated Rank: 160

**Johnstown, PA**
Universities:
  University of Pittsburgh, Johnstown
    (240)
Symphony Orchestras:
  Johnstown Symphony Orchestra★
  Johnstown Youth Symphony
Public Libraries:
  126,209 volumes; circulation NA
Reading Quotient: NA
Places Rated Score: 666
Places Rated Rank: 259

**Joliet, IL**
Public Libraries:
  130,588 volumes; circulation 245,685
Reading Quotient: 4.8
CMSA Access: CHICAGO–GARY–LAKE
  COUNTY, IL–IN–WI (3,046)
Places Rated Score: 3,177
Places Rated Rank: 101

**Joplin, MO**
Public Libraries:
  80,000 volumes; circulation NA
Reading Quotient: NA
Places Rated Score: 80
Places Rated Rank: 324

**Kalamazoo, MI**
Fine Arts and Public Radio:
  WMUK-FM 102.1 (33 mi; 127 hrs)
Universities:
  Western Michigan University (1,000)●
Symphony Orchestras:
  Kalamazoo Junior Symphony
  Kalamazoo Symphony Orchestra★★
Dance Companies:
  Kalamazoo Ballet Company★
Public Libraries:
  270,589 volumes; circulation 721,512
Reading Quotient: 8.0
Places Rated Score: 2,071
Places Rated Rank: 150

**Kankakee, IL**
Public Libraries:
  74,824 volumes; circulation 174,989
Reading Quotient: 8.3
Places Rated Score: 75
Places Rated Rank: 326

**Kansas City, KS**
Universities:
  Pittsburg State University (317)
Symphony Orchestras:
  Youth Symphony of Kansas City
Public Libraries:
  342,720 volumes; circulation 444,019

Reading Quotient: 4.6
CMSA Access: KANSAS CITY, MO–KANSAS
  CITY, KS (407)
Places Rated Score: 1,167
Places Rated Rank: 215

**Kansas City, MO**
Museums:
  Nelson/Atkins Museum of Fine Art (700)
Fine Arts and Public Radio:
  KCUR-FM 89.3 (45 mi; 136 hrs)
Public Television:
  KCPT Channel 19
Universities:
  Avila College (197)
  Central Missouri State University (816)
  University of Missouri, Kansas City (612)
Symphony Orchestras:
  Independence Symphony Orchestra
    (Community)
  Kansas City Symphony★★★
  Northland Symphony Orchestra
    (Community)
Theatres:
  Missouri Repertory Theatre★
Opera Companies:
  Lyric Opera of Kansas City
    6 productions; 26 performances
Dance Companies:
  Kansas City Ballet
Public Libraries:
  1,221,854 volumes; circulation 975,000
Reading Quotient: 7.4
Places Rated Score: 5,553
Places Rated Rank: 51

**Kenosha, WI**
Fine Arts and Public Radio:
  WGTD-FM 91.1 (129 hrs)
Universities:
  University of Wisconsin, Kenosha (281)
Symphony Orchestras:
  Kenosha Symphony (Community)
Public Libraries:
  207,038 volumes; circulation 719,926
Reading Quotient: 11.5
CMSA Access: CHICAGO–GARY–LAKE
  COUNTY, IL–IN–WI (2,956)
Places Rated Score: 3,844
Places Rated Rank: 83

**Killeen–Temple, TX**
Fine Arts and Public Radio:
  KNCT-FM 91.3 (8,846.5 sq mi; 131 hrs)
Public Television:
  KNCT Channel 46
Public Libraries:
  119,714 volumes; circulation NA
Reading Quotient: NA
Places Rated Score: 920
Places Rated Rank: 235

**Knoxville, TN**
Fine Arts and Public Radio:
  WUOT-FM 91.9 (41 mi; 168 hrs)
Public Television:
  WSJK Channel 2
Universities:
  University of Tennessee (1,000)
Symphony Orchestras:
  Knoxville Symphony Orchestra★★
  Knoxville Symphony Youth Orchestra
Dance Companies:
  Appalachian Ballet Company★
  Oak Ridge Civic Ballet Association★
  Tennessee Festival Ballet★

Public Libraries:
608,546 volumes; circulation 1,489,422
Reading Quotient: 6.6
Places Rated Score: 3,309
Places Rated Rank: 97

### Kokomo, IN
Symphony Orchestras:
Kokomo Symphony Orchestra
(Community)
Public Libraries:
185,000 volumes; circulation 498,058
Reading Quotient: 7.2
Places Rated Score: 285
Places Rated Rank: 295

### La Crosse, WI
Fine Arts and Public Radio:
WLSU-FM 88.9 (25 mi; 134 hrs)
Public Television:
WHLA Channel 31
Symphony Orchestras:
La Crosse Symphony Orchestra
(Community)
La Crosse Youth Symphony
Symphony School of America Orchestra
(Youth)
University of Wisconsin, La Crosse,
Symphony
Public Libraries:
265,737 volumes; circulation 206,843
Reading Quotient: 5.0
Places Rated Score: 1,466
Places Rated Rank: 191

### Lafayette, IN
Museums:
Tippecanoe County Historical Museum
(600)
Fine Arts and Public Radio:
WBAA-AM 920 (65 mi; 126 hrs)
Universities:
Purdue University (1,000)
Symphony Orchestras:
Lafayette Symphony (Community)
Purdue University Symphony Orchestra
Public Libraries:
135,518 volumes; circulation 317,543
Reading Quotient: 4.5
Places Rated Score: 2,236
Places Rated Rank: 137

### Lafayette, LA
Fine Arts and Public Radio:
KRVS-FM 88.7 (78 mi; 164 hrs)
Universities:
University of Southwestern Louisiana
(991)
Symphony Orchestras:
L'Orchestre (College)
Public Libraries:
180,064 volumes; circulation 558,469
Reading Quotient: 4.9
Places Rated Score: 1,772
Places Rated Rank: 173

### Lake Charles, LA
Public Television:
KLTL Channel 18
Universities:
McNeese State University (470)
Symphony Orchestras:
Lake Charles Symphony Orchestra
(Community)
Dance Companies:
Lake Charles Ballet Joyeux
Lake Charles Civic Ballet Company★

Public Libraries:
235,695 volumes; circulation NA
Reading Quotient: NA
Places Rated Score: 1,456
Places Rated Rank: 192

### Lake County, IL
Symphony Orchestras:
Flute and Fiddle Club Orchestra
(Community)
Waukegan Symphony Orchestra
(Community)
Public Libraries:
499,676 volumes; circulation 402,289
Reading Quotient: 7.6
CMSA Access: CHICAGO–GARY–LAKE
COUNTY, IL–IN–WI (3,046)
Places Rated Score: 3,746
Places Rated Rank: 87

### Lakeland–Winter Haven, FL
Symphony Orchestras:
Lakeland Symphony Orchestra
(Community)
Winter Haven Youth Symphony
Public Libraries:
108,719 volumes; circulation 334,873
Reading Quotient: 8.5
Places Rated Score: 309
Places Rated Rank: 292

### Lancaster, PA
Universities:
Franklin and Marshall College (206)
Millersville State College (459)
Public Libraries:
350,000 volumes; circulation 690,000
Reading Quotient: 2.8
Places Rated Score: 1,015
Places Rated Rank: 229

### Lansing–East Lansing, MI
Museums:
Michigan State University Museum
(1,200)
Fine Arts and Public Radio:
WKAR-AM 870 (70 mi; 86 hrs)
WKAR-FM 90.5 (80 mi; 132 hrs)
Public Television:
WKAR Channel 23
Universities:
Michigan State University (1,000)
Symphony Orchestras:
Lansing Symphony Orchestra★★
Theatres:
Boarshead–Michigan Public Theatre
Opera Companies:
Opera Company of Greater Lansing
1 production; 2 performances
Dance Companies:
Lansing Ballet Company
Public Libraries:
354,226 volumes; circulation 771,212
Reading Quotient: 5.9
Places Rated Score: 4,206
Places Rated Rank: 78

### Laredo, TX
Symphony Orchestras:
Laredo Philharmonic Orchestra
(Community)
Public Libraries:
50,152 volumes; circulation NA
Reading Quotient: NA
Places Rated Score: 150
Places Rated Rank: 313

### Las Cruces, NM
Museums:
New Mexico State University Museum
(900)
Fine Arts and Public Radio:
KRWG-FM 90.7 (100 mi; 133 hrs)
Public Television:
KRWG Channel 22
Universities:
New Mexico State University (901)
Symphony Orchestras:
Las Cruces Symphony (Community)
Public Libraries:
103,282 volumes; circulation 235,535
Reading Quotient: 3.5
Places Rated Score: 2,804
Places Rated Rank: 114

### Las Vegas, NV
Fine Arts and Public Radio:
KNPR-FM 89.5 (40 mi; 147 hrs)
Public Television:
KLVX Channel 10
Symphony Orchestras:
Las Vegas Chamber Symphony
Orchestra (Community)
Las Vegas Civic Symphony
(Community)
Dance Companies:
Nevada Dance Theatre
Public Libraries:
436,172 volumes; circulation 1,605,667
Reading Quotient: 5.3
Places Rated Score: 1,586
Places Rated Rank: 184

### Lawrence, KS
Museums:
Spencer Museum of Art (600)
University of Kansas Systematics
Museums (1,000)
Fine Arts and Public Radio:
KANU-FM 91.5 (40 mi; 139 hrs)
Universities:
University of Kansas (1,000)●
Symphony Orchestras:
Lawrence Chamber Players
(Community)
Public Libraries:
150,000 volumes; circulation 426,000
Reading Quotient: 11.5
Places Rated Score: 3,150
Places Rated Rank: 102

### Lawrence–Haverhill, MA–NH
Public Libraries:
373,017 volumes; circulation 325,794
Reading Quotient: 6.4
CMSA Access: BOSTON–LAWRENCE–
SALEM, MA–NH (1,738)
Places Rated Score: 2,111
Places Rated Rank: 147

### Lawton, OK
Museums:
Museum of the Great Plains (700)
Universities:
Cameron University (282)
Symphony Orchestras:
Lawton Philharmonic Orchestra★
Public Libraries:
98,000 volumes; circulation 240,000
Reading Quotient: 3.1
Places Rated Score: 1,280
Places Rated Rank: 205

## Lewiston–Auburn, ME
Public Television:
  WCBB Channel 10
Public Libraries:
  236,000 volumes; circulation 128,000
Reading Quotient: 5.8
Places Rated Score: 736
Places Rated Rank: 253

## Lexington–Fayette, KY
Fine Arts and Public Radio:
  WBKY 91.3 (80 mi; 138 hrs)
Public Television:
  WKLE Channel 46
Universities:
  Kentucky State University (120)
  Eastern Kentucky University (1,000)
  University of Kentucky (1,000)
Symphony Orchestras:
  Central Kentucky Youth Orchestra
  Lexington Philharmonic Orchestra★★
Dance Companies:
  Lexington Ballet Company
Public Libraries:
  226,065 volumes; circulation 836,456
Reading Quotient: 5.1
Places Rated Score: 3,596
Places Rated Rank: 90

## Lima, OH
Museums:
  Allen County Museum (700)
Universities:
  Ohio Northern University (218)
Symphony Orchestras:
  Lima Symphony Orchestra★
Public Libraries:
  234,312 volumes; circulation 476,950
Reading Quotient: 6.5
Places Rated Score: 1,352
Places Rated Rank: 200

## Lincoln, NE
Museums:
  State Historical Museum (1,100)
  University of Nebraska State Museum
    (600)
Fine Arts and Public Radio:
  KUCV-FM 90.9 (60 mi; 131 hrs)
Public Television:
  KUON Channel 12
Universities:
  University of Nebraska (1,000)●
Symphony Orchestras:
  Lincoln Civic Orchestra (Community)
  Lincoln Symphony Orchestra★★
  Lincoln Youth Symphony Orchestra
  Nebraska Chamber Orchestra
    (Community)
Public Libraries:
  423,386 volumes; circulation 1,192,394
Reading Quotient: 8.4
Places Rated Score: 4,523
Places Rated Rank: 67

## Little Rock–North Little Rock, AR
Public Television:
  KETS Channel 2
Universities:
  University of Arkansas, Little Rock
    (540)●
Symphony Orchestras:
  Arkansas Symphony Orchestra★★
Theatres:
  Arkansas Repertory Theatre

Opera Companies:
  The Arkansas Opera Theatre
    2 productions; 4 performances
Dance Companies:
  Ballet Arkansas
Public Libraries:
  481,860 volumes; circulation 704,965
Reading Quotient: 4.2
Places Rated Score: 2,180
Places Rated Rank: 142

## Longview–Marshall, TX
Symphony Orchestras:
  Longview Symphony Orchestra
    (Community)
  Marshall Symphony Orchestra
    (Community)
Public Libraries:
  134,182 volumes; circulation 190,525
Reading Quotient: 2.4
Places Rated Score: 334
Places Rated Rank: 288

## Lorain–Elyria, OH
Universities:
  Oberlin College (368)●
Dance Companies:
  Oberlin Dance Company (M)★
Public Libraries:
  406,057 volumes; circulation 940,772
Reading Quotient: 6.1
CMSA Access: CLEVELAND–AKRON–
  LORAIN, OH (1,691)
Places Rated Score: 2,565
Places Rated Rank: 123

## ★ Los Angeles–Long Beach, CA
Museums:
  California Museum of Science and
    Industry (600)
  J. Paul Getty Museum (500)
  Los Angeles County Museum of Art
    (1,000)
  Los Angeles State and County
    Arboretum (750)
  Natural History Museum of Los Angeles
    County (700)
  Southwest Museum (500)
Fine Arts and Public Radio:
  KLON-FM 88.1 (18 mi; 164 hrs)
  KPCC-FM 89.3 (30 mi; 131 hrs)
  KPFK-FM 90.7 (64 mi; 168 hrs)
  KUSC-FM 91.5 (32 mi; 168 hrs)
Public Television:
  KCET Channel 28
  KLCS Channel 58
Universities:
  California State Polytechnic University,
    Pomona (1,000)
  California State University, Long Beach
    (1,000)●
  California State University, Los Angeles
    (858)
  California State University, Northridge
    (1,000)
  Loyola Marymount University (372)
  Pepperdine University (217)
  UCLA (1,000)●
  University of Southern California
    (1,000)●
Symphony Orchestras:
  American Youth Symphony
  Glendale Symphony Orchestra★★
  Long Beach Symphony Orchestra★★★
  Los Angeles Chamber Orchestra★★★
  Los Angeles Philharmonic★★★★

  Los Angeles Solo Repertory Orchestra
    (Community)
  Loyola Marymount University Symphony
    Orchestra
  New American Orchestra (Community)
  Pasadena Chamber Orchestra★
  Pasadena Symphony Orchestra★★
  Pasadena Young Musicians Orchestra★
  Pasadena Youth Symphony Orchestra
  Symphony of the Verdugos
    (Community)
  University of Southern California
    Symphony
  Young Musicians Foundation Debut
    Orchestra
Theatres:
  Los Angeles Actor's Theatre
  Los Angeles Stage Company★
  Los Angeles Theatre Works
  Mark Taper Forum★★★★
Opera Companies:
  Los Angeles Opera Theatre
    3 productions; 9 performances
Dance Companies:
  Avaz International Dance Theatre (E-F)★
  Ballet Pacifica
  Bella Lewitzky Dance Company (M)
  Benn Howard Dance Company (M)
  Bethune Ballet
  Black Ballet Jazz, USA
  Elle Johnson Dance Company (M)
  Gene Maribaccio Ballet Company of
    Los Angeles
  "Koroyar" Folklore Ensemble (E-F)★
  Landrum Dance Theatre (J)
  Lola Montes and Her Spanish Dancers
    (E-F)
  Los Angeles Ballet★
  Margalit Dance Theatre Company (M)
  Newport Ballet
  Pasadena Dance Theatre (B)
  Rudy Perez Performance Ensemble (M)
  R'Wanda Lewis Afro-American Dance
    Company (E-F)
  Shale: Mary Jane Eisenberg Company
  TNR/The New Repertory (M)
  Valentina Oumansky Dramatic Dance
    Ensemble (M)
Public Libraries:
  4,602,998 volumes; circulation
    10,364,280
Reading Quotient: 4.9
CMSA Access: LOS ANGELES–ANAHEIM–
  RIVERSIDE, CA (340)
Places Rated Score: 23,567
Places Rated Rank: 3

## Louisville, KY–IN
Fine Arts and Public Radio:
  WFPK-FM 91.9 (70 mi; 126 hrs)
  WFPL-FM 89.3 (70 mi; 132 hrs)
  WUOL-FM 90.5 (70 mi; 130 hrs)
Public Television:
  WKMJ Channel 68
  WKPC Channel 15
Universities:
  Bellarmine College (115)
  University of Louisville (488)
Symphony Orchestras:
  Louisville–Jefferson County Youth
    Orchestra
  Louisville Orchestra★★★
Theatres:
  Actor's Theatre of Louisville★★★
  Stage One

Opera Companies:
  Kentucky Opera Association
    4 productions; 11 performances
Dance Companies:
  Louisville Ballet
Public Libraries:
  1,119,771 volumes; circulation
    2,627,899
Reading Quotient: 5.5
Places Rated Score: 4,916
Places Rated Rank: 60

## Lowell, MA–NH
Universities:
  University of Lowell (878)
Theatres:
  Merrimack Regional Theatre
Public Libraries:
  340,792 volumes; circulation 303,611
Reading Quotient: 6.8
CMSA Access: BOSTON–LAWRENCE–
  SALEM, MA–NH (1,738)
Places Rated Score: 3,057
Places Rated Rank: 104

## Lubbock, TX
Museums:
  Texas Technical University Museum
    (1,300)
Public Television:
  KTXT Channel 5
Universities:
  Texas Tech University (1,000)
Symphony Orchestras:
  Lubbock Symphony Orchestra★★
Public Libraries:
  302,264 volumes; circulation NA
Reading Quotient: NA
Places Rated Score: 3,402
Places Rated Rank: 95

## Lynchburg, VA
Universities:
  Liberty Baptist College (334)
  Lynchburg College (245)
  Washington and Lee University (300)
Symphony Orchestras:
  Lynchburg Symphony Orchestra
    (Community)
Public Libraries:
  99,546 volumes; circulation 239,291
Reading Quotient: 5.1
Places Rated Score: 1,079
Places Rated Rank: 221

## Macon–Warner Robins, GA
Museums:
  Museum of Arts and Sciences (600)
Universities:
  Mercer University (350)●
Symphony Orchestras:
  Macon Symphony Orchestra
    (Community)
Dance Companies:
  Macon Ballet Company
Public Libraries:
  335,000 volumes; circulation 1,550,000
Reading Quotient: 7.5
Places Rated Score: 1,435
Places Rated Rank: 193

## Madison, WI
Museums:
  Elvehjem Museum of Art (600)
  State Historical Society of Wisconsin
    (800)

Fine Arts and Public Radio:
  WERN-FM 88.7 (70 mi; 126 hrs)
  WHA-AM 970 (60 mi; 88 hrs)
  WORT-FM 89.9 (22 mi; 142 hrs)
Public Television:
  WHA Channel 21
Universities:
  University of Wisconsin (1,000)●
Symphony Orchestras:
  Madison Symphony Orchestra★★
  University of Wisconsin Symphony
  Wisconsin Chamber Orchestra
    (Community)
  Wisconsin Youth Symphony Orchestras
Dance Companies:
  Kanopy Dance Theatre (M)
  Wisconsin Dance Ensemble★
Public Libraries:
  572,909 volumes; circulation 1,945,587
Reading Quotient: 14.0
Places Rated Score: 5,123
Places Rated Rank: 56

## Manchester, NH
Symphony Orchestras:
  New Hampshire Symphony Orchestra★
Public Libraries:
  274,684 volumes; circulation 931,178
Reading Quotient: 7.0
Places Rated Score: 475
Places Rated Rank: 272

## Mansfield, OH
Symphony Orchestras:
  Mansfield Symphony Orchestra★
  Mansfield Symphony Youth Orchestra
Public Libraries:
  253,895 volumes; circulation 596,003
Reading Quotient: 6.5
Places Rated Score: 554
Places Rated Rank: 266

## McAllen–Edinburg–Mission, TX
Universities:
  Pan American University (904)
Symphony Orchestras:
  Valley Symphony Orchestra
    (Community)
Dance Companies:
  Edinburg Dance Theatre
Public Libraries:
  176,607 volumes; circulation 620,359
Reading Quotient: 5.8
Places Rated Score: 1,231
Places Rated Rank: 210

## Medford, OR
Public Television:
  KSYS Channel 8
Universities:
  Southern Oregon State College (393)
Symphony Orchestras:
  Peter Britt Gardens Music & Arts
    Festival★
Theatres:
  Oregon Shakespeare Festival★★★★
Public Libraries:
  263,159 volumes; circulation 1,018,741
Reading Quotient: 9.7
Places Rated Score: 1,856
Places Rated Rank: 168

## Melbourne–Titusville–Palm Bay, FL
Symphony Orchestras:
  Brevard Symphony Orchestra★

Public Libraries:
  237,069 volumes; circulation 646,557
Reading Quotient: 5.4
Places Rated Score: 437
Places Rated Rank: 275

## Memphis, TN–AR–MS
Museums:
  Memphis Pink Palace Museum (500)
Fine Arts and Public Radio:
  WKNO-FM 90.1 (120 mi; 126 hrs)
Public Television:
  WKNO Channel 10
Universities:
  Memphis State University (1,000)
Symphony Orchestras:
  Memphis Symphony Orchestra★★★
  Memphis Youth Symphony Orchestra
Theatres:
  Playhouse on the Square
Opera Companies:
  Opera Memphis
    4 productions; 8 performances
Public Libraries:
  1,354,000 volumes; circulation
    2,545,404
Reading Quotient: 4.9
Places Rated Score: 4,486
Places Rated Rank: 69

## Miami–Hialeah, FL
Fine Arts and Public Radio:
  WLRN-FM 91.3 (34 mi; 164 hrs)
Public Television:
  WLRN Channel 17
  WPBT Channel 2
Universities:
  Barry University (168)
  University of Miami (1,000)●
Symphony Orchestras:
  Central Miami Youth Symphony
  Miami Beach Symphony Orchestra★★
  Miami Chamber Symphony (Community)
  South Florida Youth Symphony
Theatres:
  Coconut Grove Playhouse★
Opera Companies:
  Greater Miami Opera Association
    4 productions; 50 performances
Dance Companies:
  Miami Ballet★
Public Libraries:
  869,238 volumes; circulation 2,051,604
Reading Quotient: NA
Places Rated Score: 4,837
Places Rated Rank: 63

## Middlesex–Somerset–
## Hunterdon, NJ
Public Television:
  WNJB Channel 58
Universities:
  Douglass College (449)●
  Rutgers State University of New Jersey
    (225)
Theatres:
  Crossroads Theatre Company
  George Street Playhouse
Public Libraries:
  119,300 volumes; circulation 258,853
Reading Quotient: 8.0
CMSA Access: NEW YORK–NORTHERN
  NEW JERSEY–LONG ISLAND, NY–NJ–
  CT (6,565)
Places Rated Score: 8,058
Places Rated Rank: 26

## Middletown, CT
Universities:
  Wesleyan University (256)
Public Libraries:
  99,766 volumes; circulation NA
Reading Quotient: NA
CMSA Access: HARTFORD–NEW
  BRITAIN–MIDDLETOWN, CT (374)
Places Rated Score: 730
Places Rated Rank: 254

## Midland, TX
Symphony Orchestras:
  Midland–Odessa Symphony and
    Chorale★★
Public Libraries:
  138,472 volumes; circulation NA
Reading Quotient: NA
Places Rated Score: 438
Places Rated Rank: 274

## ★ Milwaukee, WI
Museums:
  Milwaukee Art Museum (600)
  Milwaukee County Historical Society
    (500)
  Milwaukee Public Museum (500)
Fine Arts and Public Radio:
  WUWM-FM 89.7 (metro Milwaukee;
    147 hrs)
  WYMS-FM 88.9 (20.5 mi; 126 hrs)
Public Television:
  WMVS Channel 10
  WMVT Channel 36
Universities:
  University of Wisconsin, Milwaukee
    (1,000)●
  Marquette University (793)
Symphony Orchestras:
  Milwaukee Symphony Orchestra★★★★
  Music for Youth
  Wisconsin Conservatory of Music
    Chamber Orchestra (College)
Theatres:
  Great American Children's Theatre
    Company
  Milwaukee Repertory Theatre★★
Opera Companies:
  Florentine Opera Company
    3 productions; 9 performances
Dance Companies:
  Bauer Dance Ensemble (M)
  JoJean Retrum Dance Company (J)
  Ko-Thi Dance Company (E-F)
  Milwaukee Ballet Company★
Public Libraries:
  2,096,002 volumes; circulation
    3,350,664
Reading Quotient: 5.3
Places Rated Score: 8,766
Places Rated Rank: 21

## Minneapolis–St. Paul, MN–WI
Museums:
  Bell Museum of Natural History (1,100)
  Minneapolis Institute of Arts (800)
  Science Museum of Minnesota (600)
  Walker Art Center (600)
Fine Arts and Public Radio:
  KSJN–AM 1330 (40 mi; 131 hrs)
  KSJN–FM 91.1 (54 mi; 133 hrs)
  KUOM–AM 770 (86 mi; 48 hrs)
Public Television:
  KTCA Channel 2
  KTCI Channel 17
Universities:
  Bethel College (219)

College of St. Thomas (323)
  Gustavus Adolphus College (225)
  St. Olaf College (404)●
  University of Minnesota, Twin Cities
    (1,000)
Symphony Orchestras:
  Bloomington Symphony Orchestra
    (Community)
  Civic Orchestra of Minneapolis
    (Community)
  Minnesota Orchestra★★★★
  Minnesota Youth Orchestra
  St. Paul Chamber Orchestra★★★★
Theatres:
  Actor's Theatre of St. Paul
  Children's Theatre Company★★
  Cricket Theatre
  Guthrie Theatre★★★★
  Illusion Theatre
  Playwright's Center
Opera Companies:
  Minnesota Opera Company
    4 productions; 13 performances
Dance Companies:
  Ethnic Dance Theatre (E-F)★
  Minnesota Dance Theatre (M)★
  Minnesota Jazz Company
  Nancy Hauser Dance Company (M)
  New Dance Ensemble (M)
Public Libraries:
  1,541,423 volumes; circulation
    4,446,249
Reading Quotient: 9.4
Places Rated Score: 11,714
Places Rated Rank: 10

## Mobile, AL
Fine Arts and Public Radio:
  WHIL-FM 91.3 (84 mi; 132 hrs)
Public Television:
  WEIQ Channel 42
Universities:
  University of South Alabama (609)
Opera Companies:
  Mobile Opera, Inc.
    3 productions; 10 performances
Public Libraries:
  124,585 volumes; circulation 944,514
Reading Quotient: 3.4
Places Rated Score: 1,764
Places Rated Rank: 174

## Modesto, CA
Dance Companies:
  Central Valley Dance Company
  Modesto Civic Ballet Company★
Public Libraries:
  530,752 volumes; circulation 1,501,284
Reading Quotient: 7.6
Places Rated Score: 631
Places Rated Rank: 260

## Monmouth–Ocean, NJ
Universities:
  Monmouth College (315)
Symphony Orchestras:
  Garden State Philharmonic Symphony
    Orchestra (Community)
  Garden State Philharmonic Youth
    Orchestra
  Monmouth Symphony Orchestra
    (Community)
Dance Companies:
  Shore Ballet Company★
  Dorothy Pons Dance Company (J)
Public Libraries:
  82,795 volumes; circulation NA

Reading Quotient: NA
CMSA Access: NEW YORK–NORTHERN
  NEW JERSEY–LONG ISLAND, NY–NJ–
  CT (6,715)
Places Rated Score: 7,563
Places Rated Rank: 30

## Monroe, LA
Public Television:
  KLTM Channel 13
Universities:
  Northeast Louisiana University (767)
Public Libraries:
  257,740 volumes; circulation 680,611
Reading Quotient: 7.1
Places Rated Score: 1,528
Places Rated Rank: 187

## Montgomery, AL
Fine Arts and Public Radio:
  WTSU-FM 89.9 (43 mi; 126 hrs)
Public Television:
  WAIQ Channel 26
Universities:
  Alabama State University (342)
Symphony Orchestras:
  Montgomery Symphony (Community)
Dance Companies:
  Montgomery Civic Ballet
Public Libraries:
  82,252 volumes; circulation NA
Reading Quotient: NA
Places Rated Score: 1,374
Places Rated Rank: 198

## Muncie, IN
Fine Arts and Public Radio:
  WBST-FM 92.1 (15 mi; 163 hrs)
Public Television:
  WIPS Channel 49
Universities:
  Ball State University (1,000)
Symphony Orchestras:
  Muncie Symphony Orchestra★
Public Libraries:
  297,543 volumes; circulation 447,636
Reading Quotient: 9.3
Places Rated Score: 2,498
Places Rated Rank: 125

## Muskegon, MI
Symphony Orchestras:
  West Shore Symphony Orchestra★
  West Shore Youth Symphony Orchestra
Public Libraries:
  229,086 volumes; circulation 546,159
Reading Quotient: 5.0
Places Rated Score: 529
Places Rated Rank: 267

## Nashua, NH
Symphony Orchestras:
  Nashua Symphony Orchestra
    (Community)
Theatres:
  American Stage Festival
Public Libraries:
  184,119 volumes; circulation 523,648
Reading Quotient: 10.4
CMSA Access: BOSTON–LAWRENCE–
  SALEM, MA–NH (1,738)
Places Rated Score: 2,122
Places Rated Rank: 146

## Nashville, TN
Museums:
  Country Music Hall of Fame (500)

Tennessee Botanical Gardens and Fine
Art Center (500)
Fine Arts and Public Radio:
WPLN-FM 90.3 (34 mi; 131 hrs)
Public Television:
WDCN Channel 8
Universities:
Middle Tennessee State University (824)
Vanderbilt University (541)
Symphony Orchestras:
Nashville Community Orchestra
Nashville Symphony Orchestra★★★
Nashville Youth Symphony
Dance Companies:
The Dancers' Studio Theatre Company
(J)
Public Libraries:
527,152 volumes; circulation 1,965,307
Reading Quotient: 5.2
Places Rated Score: 4,342
Places Rated Rank: 72

★ **Nassau–Suffolk, NY**
Universities:
Adelphi University (454)
Hofstra University (599)
Symphony Orchestras:
Great Neck Symphony (Community)
Nassau Symphony (Community)
Theatres:
Nassau Repertory Theatre
Dance Companies:
Eglevsky Ballet Company★
Long Island Dance Company (M)
New York Dance Theatre
Public Libraries:
372,035 volumes; circulation 11,993,867
Reading Quotient: 8.4
CMSA Access: NEW YORK–NORTHERN
NEW JERSEY–LONG ISLAND, NY–NJ–
CT (6,715)
Places Rated Score: 8,640
Places Rated Rank: 22

**New Bedford, MA**
Museums:
New Bedford Whaling Museum (500)
Symphony Orchestras:
New Bedford Symphony Orchestra
(Community)
Public Libraries:
165,539 volumes; circulation 407,388
Reading Quotient: 5.7
Places Rated Score: 766
Places Rated Rank: 249

**New Britain, CT**
Universities:
Central Connecticut State University
(660)
Symphony Orchestras:
New Britain Symphony Orchestra
(Community)
Public Libraries:
226,130 volumes; circulation 318,218
Reading Quotient: 7.5
CMSA Access: HARTFORD–NEW
BRITAIN–MIDDLETOWN, CT (374)
Places Rated Score: 1,360
Places Rated Rank: 199

**New Haven–Meriden, CT**
Museums:
New Haven Colony Historical Society
(600)

Peabody Museum of Natural History
(1,000)
Yale Center for British Art (500)
Yale University Art Gallery (900)
Public Television:
WEDY Channel 24
Universities:
Southern Connecticut State College
(660)
University of New Haven (753)
Yale University (613)●
Symphony Orchestras:
Chamber Orchestra of New England★
Meriden Symphony Orchestra★
New Haven Symphony Orchestra★★
Philharmonic Orchestra of Yale
University
Young Artists Philharmonic
Theatres:
Long Wharf Theatre★★
Yale Repertory Theatre★
Dance Companies:
Connecticut Ballet Company
Margo Knis Dance Ensemble (M)★
Margo Knis Jazz Dance Ensemble
Public Libraries:
726,403 volumes; circulation 666,376
Reading Quotient: 7.6
Places Rated Score: 7,852
Places Rated Rank: 29

**New London–Norwich, CT–RI**
Public Television:
WEDH Channel 53
Symphony Orchestras:
Eastern Connecticut Symphony★
Theatres:
O'Neill Theatre Center★★
Public Libraries:
164,000 volumes; circulation 301,000
Reading Quotient: 7.6
Places Rated Score: 1,164
Places Rated Rank: 217

**New Orleans, LA**
Museums:
Historic New Orleans Collection (600)
Louisiana State Museum (1,200)
New Orleans Museum of Art (700)
Fine Arts and Public Radio:
WWNO-FM 89.9 (70 mi; 133 hrs)
Public Television:
WYES Channel 12
Universities:
Loyola University (245)
Southeastern Louisiana University (899)
Tulane University of Louisiana (487)
University of New Orleans (820)
Xavier University of Louisiana (222)
Symphony Orchestras:
New Orleans Philharmonic Symphony
Orchestra★★★★
New Orleans Symphony Youth
Orchestra
Opera Companies:
New Orleans Opera Association
4 productions; 13 performances
Dance Companies:
Crescent Ballet Company★★
Delta Festival Ballet of New Orleans
New Orleans City/Cincinnati Ballet
Company★
Public Libraries:
802,934 volumes; circulation 1,176,304
Reading Quotient: 3.5
Places Rated Score: 7,978
Places Rated Rank: 27

★ **New York, NY**
Museums:
American Museum of Natural History
(2,000)
American Numismatic Society (800)
Brooklyn Art Museum (1,300)
Brooklyn Botanic Garden (1,200)
Brooklyn Children's Museum (600)
Cooper-Hewitt Museum of Design (500)
Hall of Science (500)
Hispanic Society of America (1,000)
Metropolitan Museum of Art (2,000)
Museum of the American Indian (900)
Museum of the City of New York (700)
Museum of Modern Art (900)
New York Botanical Gardens (1,300)
New York Historical Society (600)
Pierpont Morgan Library and Art
Museum (1,100)
Solomon R. Guggenheim Museum (600)
Staten Island Institute of Arts and
Sciences (600)
Whitney Museum of American Art
(1,000)
Fine Arts and Public Radio:
WBAI-FM 99.5 (60 mi; 168 hrs)
WNYC-AM 830 (115 hrs)
WNYC-FM 93.9 (35 mi; 168 hrs)
Public Television:
WNET Channel 13
WNYC Channel 31
WNYE Channel 25
Universities:
Barnard College (250)
Bernard Baruch College (1,000)
Brooklyn College (1,000)●
City College (1,000)●
Columbia University (1,000)
Fordham University (599)
Hunter College (940)
New York University (1,000)
Queens College (1,000)●
St. Johns University (1,000)
Staten Island College (564)
Yeshiva University (664)
Symphony Orchestras:
American Composers Orchestra★
American Symphony Orchestra★★★
Bronx Philharmonic (Community)
Bronx Symphony Orchestra
(Community)
Brooklyn Philharmonic Symphony
Orchestra★★
Camerata Youth Symphony
City Symphony of Westchester★★
Columbia University Orchestra
Doctors Orchestra Society of New York
(Community)
Downeast Chamber Orchestra (Youth)
Greenwich House Orchestra (College)
Independent School Orchestras (Youth)
Jupiter Symphony Orchestra★
Levite Symphony Orchestra
(Community)
Little Orchestra Society★★
New York Chamber Symphony
(Community)
New York Philharmonic★★★★
New York University Symphony
Orchestra
Staten Island Symphony (Community)
West End Symphony (Community)
Youth Symphony Orchestra of New York
Theatres:
The Acting Company★
American Jewish Theatre

American Place Theatre
Circle in the Square★★★★
Circle Repertory Company★
CSC Repertory
Empire State Institute for the Performing
 Arts
Ensemble Studio Theatre
First All Children's Theatre
INTAR
Mabou Mines
Manhattan Theatre Club★
Music-Theatre Group, Lenox Arts
 Center
New Dramatists
New Federal Theatre
New York Shakespeare Festival★★★★
Playwrights Horizons★★★
Puerto Rican Traveling Theatre
 Company
Repertorio Español
Roundabout Theatre Company★★
Theatre for the New City
Opera Companies:
 Chamber Opera Theatre of New York
  3 productions; 18 performances
 Metropolitan Opera★★★★
  23 productions; 210 performances
 New York City Opera★★★★
  19 productions; 134 performances
Dance Companies:*
 Alvin Ailey American Dance Theatre
  (M)★
 American Ballet Theatre★★
 American Ballet Theatre II★
 Bronx Dance Theatre★
 Chuck Davis Dance Company (E-F)★
 Dance Theatre of Harlem★
 Feld Ballet★
 Festival Dance Theatre★
 George Tomov Yugoslav Folkdance
  Ensemble (E-F)★
 Harkness Ballet of New York★
 Heritage Festivals (E-F)★
 Joffrey Ballet★
 Juilliard Dance Ensemble (M)★
 Martha Graham Dance Company (M)★
 Mayiri Armenian Folk Dance Group
  (E-F)★
 Metropolitan Opera Ballet★
 Paul Taylor Dance Company (M)★
 Pearl Lang Dance Company (M)★
 Philippine Dance Company of New York
  (E-F)★
 Polish American Folk Dance Company
  (E-F)★
 Twyla Tharp Dance (M)★
 U.S. Terpsichore★
 Westchester Ballet Company★
 Windmere Ballet Theatre★
Public Libraries:
 7,271,592 volumes; circulation NA
Reading Quotient: NA
CMSA Access: NEW YORK–NORTHERN
 NEW JERSEY–LONG ISLAND, NY–NJ–
 CT (1,596)
Places Rated Score: 56,745
Places Rated Rank: 1

*A total of 149 dance companies qualified for inclusion in New York's profile, but for reasons of space only those receiving one or two stars are listed.

★ **Newark, NJ**
Museums:
 Newark Museum (1,100)
Fine Arts and Public Radio:
 WBGO-FM 88.3 (40 mi; 164 hrs)
Public Television:
 WNJM Channel 50
Universities:
 Kean College of New Jersey (611)
 Montclair State College (750)
 Newark College of Arts and Sciences
  (331)
 Seton Hall (569)
Symphony Orchestras:
 New Jersey Symphony Orchestra★★★
 New Philharmonic of North West New
  Jersey (Community)
Theatres:
 New Jersey Shakespeare Festival
 Paper Mill Playhouse★★★★
 The Whole Theatre Company
Opera Companies:
 New Jersey State Opera
  3 productions; 3 performances
Dance Companies:
 Garden State Ballet★
 Judith Janus and Contemporary
  Dancers (M)
 New Jersey Ballet Company
 Newark Dance Theatre (J)
 Renate Booue Dance Company (M)
 Westminster Dance Theatre
Public Libraries:
 2,231,560 volumes; circulation
  1,770,831
Reading Quotient: 10.5
CMSA Access: NEW YORK–NORTHERN
 NEW JERSEY–LONG ISLAND, NY–NJ–
 CT (5,872)
Places Rated Score: 14,224
Places Rated Rank: 8

**Niagara Falls, NY**
Public Libraries:
 186,056 volumes; circulation 298,317
Reading Quotient: 6.9
CMSA Access: BUFFALO–NIAGARA FALLS,
 NY (780)
Places Rated Score: 966
Places Rated Rank: 234

**Norfolk–Virginia Beach–Newport
News, VA**
Museums:
 Chrysler Museum (700)
Fine Arts and Public Radio:
 WHRO-FM 89.5 (25 mi; 133 hrs)
Public Television:
 WHRO Channel 15
Universities:
 College of William and Mary (461)
 Hampton Institute (323)
 Norfolk State University (726)
 Old Dominion University (1,000)
 Virginia Commonwealth University
  (1,000)
Symphony Orchestras:
 Old Dominion University Symphony
 Peninsula Symphony of Virginia
  (Community)
 Virginia Beach Community Orchestra
 Virginia Beach Pops★
 Virginia Orchestra Group★★★
Theatres:
 Virginia Stage Company

Opera Companies:
 Virginia Opera Association
  7 productions; 38 performances
Dance Companies:
 Old Dominion University Ballet
  Company
Public Libraries:
 560,856 volumes; circulation 3,117,007
Reading Quotient: 5.3
Places Rated Score: 7,087
Places Rated Rank: 37

**Norwalk, CT**
Symphony Orchestras:
 Norwalk Symphony Orchestra
  (Community)
 Norwalk Youth Symphony
Theatres:
 Westport County Playhouse★
Dance Companies:
 Ballet Etudes Repertory Company
 Nikki Williams Dancers (J)
 Westport Dance Center (M)
Public Libraries:
 68,326 volumes; circulation 277,064
Reading Quotient: 4.5
CMSA Access: NEW YORK–NORTHERN
 NEW JERSEY–LONG ISLAND, NY–NJ–
 CT (6,655)
Places Rated Score: 7,273
Places Rated Rank: 35

**Oakland, CA**
Museums:
 Lawrence Hall of Science (600)
Universities:
 University of California, Berkeley
  (1,000)●
Symphony Orchestras:
 Berkeley Youth Orchestra
 Contra Costa Chamber Orchestra
  (Community)
 Diablo Youth Orchestra
 Oakland Symphony Orchestra★★★
 Oakland Symphony Youth Orchestra
 Young People's Symphony Orchestra
Theatres:
 Berkeley Repertory Theatre★
 Berkeley Shakespeare Festival
Dance Companies:
 Ballet Joyeux
 Berkeley Conservatory Ballet
 Dimensions Dance Theatre (E-F)
 Khadra International Folk Ballet (E-F)★
 Nancy Karp and Dancers (M)
 Oakland Ballet Company★
 Oakland Theatre of Dance
 Terry Meyers Dancers Company (M)
Public Libraries:
 748,377 volumes; circulation 1,618,201
Reading Quotient: 6.6
CMSA Access: SAN FRANCISCO–OAKLAND–
 SAN JOSE, CA (2,114)
Places Rated Score: 6,162
Places Rated Rank: 45

**Ocala, FL**
Symphony Orchestras:
 CFCC Aeolian Players (College)
Public Libraries:
 165,811 volumes; circulation 732,758
Reading Quotient: 4.3
Places Rated Score: 266
Places Rated Rank: 299

## Odessa, TX
Symphony Orchestras:
   West Texas Youth Orchestra
Public Libraries:
   159,355 volumes; circulation 694,158
Reading Quotient: 7.4
Places Rated Score: 259
Places Rated Rank: 300

## Oklahoma City, OK
Museums:
   Oklahoma Historical Society (600)
Public Television:
   KETA Channel 13
Universities:
   Central State University (1,000)
   Oklahoma City University (404)••
   University of Oklahoma (1,000)
Symphony Orchestras:
   Chamber Orchestra of Oklahoma
      (Community)
   Oklahoma City Junior Symphony
   Oklahoma Symphony Orchestra★★★
Dance Companies:
   Ballet Oklahoma★
   University of Oklahoma Ballet
Public Libraries:
   588,872 volumes; circulation 1,913,671
Reading Quotient: 4.2
Places Rated Score: 4,843
Places Rated Rank: 62

## Olympia, WA
Symphony Orchestras:
   Olympia Symphony Orchestra
      (Community)
Public Libraries:
   607,803 volumes; circulation 1,981,858
Reading Quotient: 9.1
Places Rated Score: 708
Places Rated Rank: 256

## Omaha, NE–IA
Museums:
   Joslyn Art Museum (1,200)
Fine Arts and Public Radio:
   KIOS-FM 91.5 (75 mi; 138 hrs)
   KVNO-FM 90.7 (50 mi; 140 hrs)
Universities:
   Creighton University (450)•
Symphony Orchestras:
   Omaha Area Youth Orchestras
   Omaha Symphony Orchestra★★★
Theatres:
   Nebraska Theatre Caravan
   Omaha Magic Theatre
Opera Companies:
   Opera Omaha, Inc.
   3 productions; 10 performances
Dance Companies:
   A Company of Dancers from Creighton
      University
Public Libraries:
   557,237 volumes; circulation 1,771,537
Reading Quotient: 7.1
Places Rated Score: 3,787
Places Rated Rank: 85

## Orange County, NY
Symphony Orchestras:
   Orange County Symphony Orchestra
      (Community)
Public Libraries:
   172,166 volumes; circulation 256,682
Reading Quotient: NA
CMSA Access: New York–Northern
   New Jersey–Long Island, NY–NJ–
   CT (6,715)
Places Rated Score: 6,987
Places Rated Rank: 38

## Orlando, FL
Fine Arts and Public Radio:
   WMFE-FM 90.7 (80 mi; 129 hrs)
Public Television:
   WMFE Channel 24
Universities:
   Rollins College (215)
Symphony Orchestras:
   Florida Symphony Orchestra★★★
   Florida Symphony Youth Orchestra
   University of Central Florida Community
      Symphony
Opera Companies:
   Orlando Opera Company
   3 productions; 7 performances
Dance Companies:
   Ballet Royal★
   Southern Ballet Theatre★
Public Libraries:
   644,525 volumes; circulation
      2,315,900
Reading Quotient: 6.2
Places Rated Score: 2,681
Places Rated Rank: 118

## Owensboro, KY
Public Television:
   WKOH Channel 31
Symphony Orchestras:
   Owensboro Symphony Orchestra★
Public Libraries:
   103,914 volumes; circulation
      323,000
Reading Quotient: 5.0
Places Rated Score: 804
Places Rated Rank: 245

## Oxnard–Ventura, CA
Symphony Orchestras:
   CLC Conejo Symphony Orchestra
      (Community)
   Ventura County Symphony Orchestra★
Public Libraries:
   560,927 volumes; circulation
      1,698,156
Reading Quotient: 7.1
CMSA Access: Los Angeles–Anaheim–
   Riverside, CA (1,908)
Places Rated Score: 2,769
Places Rated Rank: 116

## Panama City, FL
Fine Arts and Public Radio:
   WKGC-AM 1480 (50 mi; 130 hrs)
   WKGC-FM 90.7 (50 mi; 140 hrs)
Public Libraries:
   154,596 volumes; circulation
      488,210
Reading Quotient: 4.3
Places Rated Score: 755
Places Rated Rank: 251

## Parkersburg–Marietta, WV–OH
Public Libraries:
   91,150 volumes; circulation 258,962
Reading Quotient: 3.7
Places Rated Score: 91
Places Rated Rank: 320

## Pascagoula, MS
Public Libraries:
   154,596 volumes; circulation 488,210
Reading Quotient: 4.3
Places Rated Score: 155
Places Rated Rank: 310

## Pawtucket–Woonsocket–Attleboro, RI–MA
Public Libraries:
   239,500 volumes; circulation 300,000
Reading Quotient: 6.1
CMSA Access: Providence–Pawtucket–
   Fall River, RI–MA (240)
Places Rated Score: 480
Places Rated Rank: 271

## Pensacola, FL
Fine Arts and Public Radio:
   WUWF-FM 88.1 (100 mi; 168 hrs)
Public Television:
   WSRE Channel 23
Universities:
   University of West Florida (535)
Symphony Orchestras:
   Greater Pensacola Symphony Orchestra
      (Community)
Public Libraries:
   318,766 volumes; circulation 1,231,903
Reading Quotient: 5.3
Places Rated Score: 1,954
Places Rated Rank: 159

## Peoria, IL
Fine Arts and Public Radio:
   WCBU-FM 89.9 (34 mi; 150 hrs)
Public Television:
   WTVP Channel 47
Universities:
   Bradley University (459)
Symphony Orchestras:
   Central Illinois Youth Symphony
   Peoria Symphony Orchestra★★
Dance Companies:
   Peoria Civic Ballet
Public Libraries:
   485,000 volumes; circulation 900,000
Reading Quotient: 11.1
Places Rated Score: 2,294
Places Rated Rank: 134

## ★ Philadelphia, PA–NJ
Museums:
   Academy of Natural Sciences of
      Philadelphia (800)
   Franklin Institute of Science (500)
   Independence National Historical Park
      (500)
   Pennsylvania Academy of the Fine Arts
      (700)
   Philadelphia Museum of Art (900)
   University of Pennsylvania Museum
      (1,400)
Fine Arts and Public Radio:
   WUHY-FM 90.0 (35 mi; 131 hrs)
Public Television:
   WHVY Channel 12
   WNJS Channel 23
Universities:
   Beaver College (218)
   Bryn Mawr University (293)
   Cheyney State College (250)
   Glassboro State College (597)
   LaSalle College (382)

Temple University (1,000)●
University of Pennsylvania (972)●
Villanova University (630)
West Chester State College (628)
Symphony Orchestras:
Concerto Soloists of Philadelphia★★
New School of Music Orchestra
Philadelphia Orchestra★★★★
Philadelphia Youth Orchestra
Temple University Symphony Orchestra
Theatres:
Philadelphia Drama Guild★
Opera Companies:
Opera Company of Philadelphia
5 productions; 10 performances
Pennsylvania Opera Theatre
2 productions; 6 performances
Dance Companies:
Agape Dancers (M)
Ann Vaachon/Dance Candait (M)
Arthur Hall's Afro-American Dance
Ensemble★
Ballet des Jeunes★★
Camargo Ballet
Germantown Dance Theatre
Group Motion Dance Theatre (M)
Philadanco/Philadelphia Dance
Company (M)★
Schuylkill Valley Regional Dance
Company
South Street Dance Company (M)
Zero Moving Dance Company (M)
Public Libraries:
2,947,727 volumes; circulation
4,960,439
Reading Quotient: NA
CMSA Access: PHILADELPHIA–WILMINGTON–
TRENTON, PA–NJ–DE–MD (690)
Places Rated Score: 17,270
Places Rated Rank: 6

## Phoenix, AZ
Museums:
Heard Museum (700)
Phoenix Art Museum (500)
Fine Arts and Public Radio:
KMCR-FM 91.5 (126 hrs)
Universities:
Arizona State University (1,000)●
Symphony Orchestras:
Phoenix College Orchestra
Phoenix Symphony Orchestra★★★
Phoenix Symphony Youth Orchestra
Scottsdale Symphony Orchestra
(Community)
Sun City Symphony Orchestra
(Community)
Dance Companies:
Arizona Metropolitan Ballet
Yelena Ballet and Dance Theatre
Public Libraries:
1,173,000 volumes; circulation
3,600,000
Reading Quotient: 5.8
Places Rated Score: 4,573
Places Rated Rank: 65

## Pine Bluff, AR
Universities:
University of Arkansas, Pine Bluff (255)
Public Libraries:
117,923 volumes; circulation NA
Reading Quotient: NA
Places Rated Score: 373
Places Rated Rank: 282

## ★ Pittsburgh, PA
Museums:
Buhl Planetarium and Institute of
Popular Science (700)
Carnegie Museum of Natural History
(1,300)
Museum of Art, Carnegie Institute (700)
Fine Arts and Public Radio:
WDUG-FM 90.5 (35 mi; 133 hrs)
WQED-FM 89.3 (60 mi; 139 hrs)
Public Television:
WQED Channel 13
WQEV Channel 16
Universities:
California State College (442)
Carnegie-Mellon University (408)
Duquesne University (458)
University of Pittsburgh (1,000)
Symphony Orchestras:
American Youth Symphony and Chorus
Duquesne University Symphony
McKeesport Symphony Orchestra
(Community)
New Pittsburgh Chamber Orchestra
(Community)
Pittsburgh Civic Orchestra (Community)
Pittsburgh Symphony Orchestra★★★★
Pittsburgh Youth Symphony Orchestra
Three Rivers Training Orchestra (Youth)
University of Pittsburgh Orchestra
Theatres:
Pittsburgh Public Theatre★★
Opera Companies:
Pittsburgh Opera, Inc.
6 productions; 12 performances
Dance Companies:
American Dance Ensemble
The Extension (J)
Kasamon Ballet★★
Pittsburgh Ballet Theatre★
Pittsburgh Dance Alley (M)
The Tamburitzanc (E-F)★
Public Libraries:
2,039,057 volumes; circulation
3,221,558
Reading Quotient: 3.5
Places Rated Score: 11,069
Places Rated Rank: 12

## Pittsfield, MA
Dance Companies:
Berkshire Ballet
Public Libraries:
178,448 volumes; circulation 601,186
Reading Quotient: 15.0
Places Rated Score: 228
Places Rated Rank: 303

## Portland, ME
Fine Arts and Public Radio:
WMEA-FM 90.1 (58 mi; 133 hrs)
Public Television:
WMEG Channel 26
Universities:
University of Southern Maine (820)
Symphony Orchestras:
Portland Symphony Orchestra★★
Theatres:
Portland Stage Company
Dance Companies:
Ram Island Dance Company (M)
Public Libraries:
281,359 volumes; circulation 441,689
Reading Quotient: NA
Places Rated Score: 2,351
Places Rated Rank: 130

## Portland, OR
Museums:
Oregon Museum of Science and
Industry (600)
Fine Arts and Public Radio:
KBOO-FM 90.7 (30 mi; 168 hrs)
KBPS-AM 1450 (30 mi; 126 hrs)
KCAP-FM 91.5 (90 mi; 126 hrs)
Public Television:
KOAP Channel 10
Universities:
Portland State University (728)●
University of Portland (200)
Symphony Orchestras:
Oregon Symphony Orchestra★★★★
Portland Youth Philharmonic Association
Opera Companies:
Portland Opera Association
4 productions; 12 performances
Public Libraries:
1,184,232 volumes; circulation
3,244,838
Reading Quotient: 7.5
Places Rated Score: 5,160
Places Rated Rank: 55

## Portsmouth–Dover–Rochester, NH–ME
Theatres:
Theatre by the Sea
Public Libraries:
65,319 volumes; circulation NA
Reading Quotient: NA
Places Rated Score: 165
Places Rated Rank: 308

## Poughkeepsie, NY
Universities:
Vassar College (222)
Symphony Orchestras:
Hudson Valley Philharmonic
Orchestra★★
Dance Companies:
Mid-Hudson Ballet Company
Orange County Ballet Theatre
Poughkeepsie Civic Ballet
Public Libraries:
113,407 volumes; circulation 312,772
Reading Quotient: 5.1
Places Rated Score: 785
Places Rated Rank: 246

## Providence, RI
Museums:
Rhode Island Historical Society (700)
Rhode Island School of Design Museum
of Art (700)
Public Television:
WSBE Channel 36
Universities:
Brown University (523)
Providence College (459)
Rhode Island College (438)
Roger Williams College (240)
University of Rhode Island (852)
Symphony Orchestras:
Brown University Orchestra
Rhode Island Philharmonic Orchestra★★
Rhode Island Philharmonic Youth
Orchestra
Young Peoples Symphony of Rhode
Island
Theatres:
Trinity Square Repertory Company★★
Dance Companies:
State Ballet of Rhode Island★

Public Libraries:
  739,773 volumes; circulation NA
Reading Quotient: NA
Places Rated Score: 6,152
Places Rated Rank: 46

### Provo–Orem, UT
Fine Arts and Public Radio:
  KBYU-FM 88.9 (150 mi; 140 hrs)
Public Television:
  KBYU Channel 11
Universities:
  Brigham Young University (1,000)
Symphony Orchestras:
  Utah Valley Youth Symphony Orchestra
Public Libraries:
  85,000 volumes; circulation NA
Reading Quotient: NA
Places Rated Score: 1,985
Places Rated Rank: 157

### Pueblo, CO
Public Television:
  KTSC Channel 8
Universities:
  University of Southern Colorado (457)
Symphony Orchestras:
  Pueblo Symphony Orchestra★
Public Libraries:
  150,000 volumes; circulation 383,376
Reading Quotient: 4.2
Places Rated Score: 1,307
Places Rated Rank: 201

### Racine, WI
Symphony Orchestras:
  Racine Symphony Orchestra
  (Community)
Public Libraries:
  252,717 volumes; circulation 668,226
Reading Quotient: 5.3
CMSA Access: MILWAUKEE–RACINE,
  WI (818)
Places Rated Score: 1,171
Places Rated Rank: 214

### Raleigh–Durham, NC
Museums:
  North Carolina Museum of Art (600)
  North Carolina State Museum (1,000)
Fine Arts and Public Radio:
  WSHA-FM 88.9 (18 mi; 168 hrs)
  WUNC-FM 91.5 (135 hrs)
Universities:
  Duke University (937)
  University of North Carolina (1,000)
Symphony Orchestras:
  Durham Symphony Orchestra
  (Community)
  North Carolina Symphony Orchestra★★★
Theatres:
  Playmakers Repertory Company
Dance Companies:
  Bryce Wagner Dance Project (M)
  Concert Dancers of Raleigh
  New Performers Dance Company (M)
  Synergic Theatre/Delta Carnival (M)
Public Libraries:
  592,800 volumes; circulation 1,803,578
Reading Quotient: 5.3
Places Rated Score: 5,730
Places Rated Rank: 47

### Reading, PA
Universities:
  Kutztown State College (568)

Symphony Orchestras:
  Reading Symphony Orchestra★
Public Libraries:
  339,786 volumes; circulation NA
Reading Quotient: NA
Places Rated Score: 1,108
Places Rated Rank: 219

### Redding, CA
Public Television:
  KIXE-TV Channel 9
Symphony Orchestras:
  Shasta Symphony Orchestra
  (Community)
Public Libraries:
  245,426 volumes; circulation 480,034
Reading Quotient: 6.3
Places Rated Score: 845
Places Rated Rank: 240

### Reno, NV
Museums:
  Nevada Historical Society (500)
Fine Arts and Public Radio:
  KUNR-FM 88.7 (49 mi; 133 hrs)
Universities:
  University of Nevada (554)
Symphony Orchestras:
  Reno Chamber Orchestra (Community)
  Reno Philharmonic Association★
Opera Companies:
  Nevada Opera Association
    3 productions; 9 performances
Public Libraries:
  328,831 volumes; circulation 931,178
Reading Quotient: 6.5
Places Rated Score: 2,210
Places Rated Rank: 138

### Richland–Kennewick–Pasco, WA
Symphony Orchestras:
  Mid-Columbia Symphony Orchestra★
Public Libraries:
  328,688 volumes; circulation 797,489
Reading Quotient: 7.4
Places Rated Score: 529
Places Rated Rank: 267

### Richmond–Petersburg, VA
Museums:
  Association for the Preservation of
    Virginia Antiquities (500)
  Valentine Museum (600)
  Virginia Museum of Fine Art (600)
Fine Arts and Public Radio:
  WRFK-FM 106.5 (50 mi; 132 hrs)
Public Television:
  WCVE Channel 23
  WCVW Channel 57
Universities:
  University of Richmond (247)
  Virginia State University (456)
Symphony Orchestras:
  Richmond Community Orchestra
  Richmond Symphony Orchestra★★★
  Richmond Symphony Youth Orchestra
Theatres:
  Virginia Museum Theatre
Dance Companies:
  Concert Ballet of Virginia★
  Richmond Ballet Company
Public Libraries:
  1,143,881 volumes; circulation
    2,457,422
Reading Quotient: 8.2
Places Rated Score: 5,697
Places Rated Rank: 48

### Riverside–San Bernardino, CA
Museums:
  San Bernardino County Museum (800)
Fine Arts and Public Radio:
  KVCR-FM 91.9 (18 mi; 126 hrs)
Public Television:
  KVCR-TV Channel 24
Universities:
  California State College, San Bernardino
    (346)
  University of California, Riverside (412)●
Symphony Orchestras:
  Inland Empire Symphony Orchestra
    (Community)
  San Bernardino Chamber Orchestra
    (College)
Dance Companies:
  Concert Dance Theatre
  Riverside Ballet Theatre
Public Libraries:
  1,001,162 volumes; circulation
    2,771,041
Reading Quotient: 5.0
CMSA Access: LOS ANGELES–ANAHEIM–
  RIVERSIDE, CA (1,668)
Places Rated Score: 5,327
Places Rated Rank: 54

### Roanoke, VA
Fine Arts and Public Radio:
  WVTF-FM 89.1 (100 mi; 128 hrs)
Public Television:
  WBCA Channel 15
Symphony Orchestras:
  Roanoke Symphony Orchestra
Public Libraries:
  363,216 volumes; circulation NA
Reading Quotient: NA
Places Rated Score: 1,263
Places Rated Rank: 207

### Rochester, MN
Fine Arts and Public Radio:
  KLSE-FM 91.7 (40 mi; 131 hrs)
Symphony Orchestras:
  Rochester Symphony Orchestra★★
Public Libraries:
  168,745 volumes; circulation 696,036
Reading Quotient: 9.4
Places Rated Score: 769
Places Rated Rank: 248

### Rochester, NY
Museums:
  International Museum of Photography
    (500)
  Rochester Museum and Science Center
    (1,100)
  Strong Museum (500)
Fine Arts and Public Radio:
  WXXI-FM 91.5 (45 mi; 168 hrs)
Public Television:
  WXXI Channel 21
Universities:
  Nazareth College of Rochester (313)
  SUNY at Brockport (646)●
  SUNY at Geneseo (448)
  University of Rochester (450)
Symphony Orchestras:
  Brighton Symphony Orchestra
    (Community)
  Rochester Philharmonic Orchestra★★★★
  Rochester Philharmonic Youth
    Orchestra
Theatres:
  Ge Va Theatre

Opera Companies:
 Opera Theatre of Rochester
  3 productions; 5 performances
Dance Companies:
 Bucket Dance Company (M)
Public Libraries:
 934,083 volumes; circulation 1,409,352
Reading Quotient: 9.7
Places Rated Score: 6,956
Places Rated Rank: 39

### Rockford, IL
Symphony Orchestras:
 Rockford Area Youth Symphony
 Rockford Symphony Orchestra★★
Theatres:
 New American Theatre
Dance Companies:
 Rockford Company (B)★★
Public Libraries:
 326,389 volumes; circulation 873,929
Reading Quotient: 8.6
Places Rated Score: 1,026
Places Rated Rank: 225

### Sacramento, CA
Fine Arts and Public Radio:
 KXPR-FM 90.9 (60 mi; 145 hrs)
Public Television:
 KVIE Channel 6
Universities:
 California State University, Sacramento
  (1,000)●
Symphony Orchestras:
 Camellia Symphony Orchestra
  (Community)
 Sacramento Symphony Orchestra★★★
 Sacramento Youth Symphony
Opera Companies:
 Sacramento Opera
  2 productions; 4 performances
Dance Companies:
 Capitol City Ballet
 Sacramento Ballet
 Theatre Ballet of Sacramento
Public Libraries:
 1,625,000 volumes; circulation NA
Reading Quotient: NA
Places Rated Score: 4,483
Places Rated Rank: 70

### Saginaw–Bay City–Midland, MI
Symphony Orchestras:
 Midland Symphony Orchestra★★
 Northwood Orchestra★
 Saginaw Symphony Orchestra★★
 Saginaw Symphony Youth Orchestra
Public Libraries:
 808,165 volumes; circulation 2,074,128
Reading Quotient: 7.7
Places Rated Score: 1,708
Places Rated Rank: 178

### St. Cloud, MN
Fine Arts and Public Radio:
 KSJR-FM 91.1 (44 mi; 168 hrs)
Universities:
 St. Cloud State University (952)
Symphony Orchestras:
 St. Cloud Civic Orchestra (Community)
Public Libraries:
 319,142 volumes; circulation 1,047,972
Reading Quotient: 5.2
Places Rated Score: 1,871
Places Rated Rank: 165

### St. Joseph, MO
Museums:
 St. Joseph Museum (500)
Symphony Orchestras:
 St. Joseph Symphony Orchestra
  (Community)
Public Libraries:
 278,748 volumes; circulation 467,049
Reading Quotient: 7.6
Places Rated Score: 879
Places Rated Rank: 238

### ★ St. Louis, MO–IL
Museums:
 Missouri Historical Society (500)
 St. Louis Art Museum (800)
Fine Arts and Public Radio:
 KWMU-FM 90.7 (100 mi; 168 hrs)
Public Television:
 KETC Channel 9
Universities:
 University of Missouri, St. Louis (1,000)
 Washington University (945)●
Symphony Orchestras:
 St. Louis Symphony Orchestra★★★★
 St. Louis Symphony Youth Orchestra
Theatres:
 Repertory Theatre of St. Louis★
Opera Companies:
 Opera Theatre of St. Louis
  5 productions; 25 performances
Dance Companies:
 Metropolitan Ballet of St. Louis★
 Mid-America Dance Company (M)
 Missouri Concert Ballet Company
 St. Charles Civic Ballet★★
 St. Louis Civic Ballet
 St. Louis Repertory Dancers (M)
Public Libraries:
 3,025,890 volumes; circulation
  8,639,769
Reading Quotient: 9.2
Places Rated Score: 8,896
Places Rated Rank: 19

### Salem, OR
Public Television:
 KVDO Channel 3
Public Libraries:
 191,035 volumes; circulation 911,000
Reading Quotient: 12.2
Places Rated Score: 691
Places Rated Rank: 257

### Salem–Gloucester, MA
Museums:
 Peabody Museum of Salem (500)
Universities:
 Salem State College (512)
Symphony Orchestras:
 Cape Ann Symphony Orchestra
  (Community)
 Sinfonie-by-the-Sea (Community)
Dance Companies:
 North Shore Civic Ballet
Public Libraries:
 276,006 volumes; circulation 1,121,522
Reading Quotient: 21.1
CMSA Access: BOSTON–LAWRENCE–SALEM,
 MA–NH (1,738)
Places Rated Score: 3,276
Places Rated Rank: 98

### Salinas–Seaside–Monterey, CA
Fine Arts and Public Radio:
 KUBO-FM 90.9 (40 mi; 140 hrs)

Symphony Orchestras:
 Monterey County Symphony
  Orchestra★★
Theatres:
 El Teatro Campesino
Public Libraries:
 304,040 volumes; circulation 1,136,685
Reading Quotient: 13.2
Places Rated Score: 1,004
Places Rated Rank: 230

### Salt Lake City–Ogden, UT
Museums:
 Utah Museum of Fine Art (600)
 Utah Museum of Natural History (600)
Fine Arts and Public Radio:
 KUER-FM 90.4 (65 mi; 126 hrs)
Public Television:
 KUED Channel 7
Universities:
 University of Utah (1,000)●
Symphony Orchestras:
 Golden Spike Youth Symphony
  Orchestra
 Murray Symphony Orchestra
  (Community)
 Rocky Mountain Symphony
  (Community)
 Utah Symphony Orchestra★★★★
 Utah Youth Symphony
Opera Companies:
 Utah Opera Company
  4 productions; 15 performances
Dance Companies:
 Ballet West★
Public Libraries:
 1,268,310 volumes; circulation
  3,810,272
Reading Quotient: 5.0
Places Rated Score: 5,528
Places Rated Rank: 52

### San Angelo, TX
Museums:
 Fort Concho National Historic Landmark
  (500)
Universities:
 Angelo State University (425)
Symphony Orchestras:
 San Angelo Symphony Orchestra★
Public Libraries:
 175,903 volumes; circulation 452,696
Reading Quotient: 8.3
Places Rated Score: 1,301
Places Rated Rank: 203

### San Antonio, TX
Museums:
 San Antonio Museum of Art (600)
Public Television:
 KLRN Channel 9
Universities:
 Southwest Texas State University
  (1,000)
 Trinity University (238)
Symphony Orchestras:
 San Antonio Symphony Orchestra★★★★
 Youth Orchestras of San Antonio
Dance Companies:
 San Antonio Ballet Company★
 Texas Civic Ballet
Public Libraries:
 1,207,133 volumes; circulation
  2,217,603
Reading Quotient: 3.5
Places Rated Score: 4,295
Places Rated Rank: 75

## ★ San Diego, CA

Museums:
  Natural History Museum (600)
  San Diego Museum of Art (700)
  San Diego Museum of Man (500)
Fine Arts and Public Radio:
  KPBS-FM 89.5 (50 mi; 131 hrs)
Public Television:
  KPBS Channel 15
Universities:
  San Diego State University (1,000)
  University of California, La Jolla (1,000)
  University of San Diego (295)
Symphony Orchestras:
  Jewish Community Center Symphony
    Orchestra (Community)
  San Diego Symphony Orchestra★★★★
  Heartland Youth Philharmonic
  San Diego Youth Symphony
Theatres:
  Old Globe Theatre★★★
  San Diego Repertory Theatre
Opera Companies:
  San Diego Opera
    8 productions; 30 performances
Dance Companies:
  All That Jazz Dancers
  California Ballet Company★
  National Ballet of San Diego
  Stage Seven Dance Theatre (B)★
  Three's Company (M)
  Victor Moreno Dance Theatre★
Public Libraries:
  1,733,387 volumes; circulation
    4,235,888
Reading Quotient: 6.6
Places Rated Score: 8,818
Places Rated Rank: 20

## ★ San Francisco, CA

Museums:
  Asian Art Museum of San Francisco
    (800)
  California Academy of Sciences (1,200)
  California Division of Mines and
    Geology (500)
  California Historical Society (600)
  Fine Arts Museum of San Francisco
    (900)
Fine Arts and Public Radio:
  KALW-FM 91.7 (50 mi; 126 hrs)
  KPFA-FM 94.1 (Bay Area; 168 hrs)
  KQED-FM 88.5 (50 mi; 133 hrs)
Public Television:
  KCSM Channel 60
  KQEC Channel 32
  KQED Channel 9
Universities:
  San Francisco State University (1,000)●
  University of San Francisco (282)
Symphony Orchestras:
  Bay Area Women's Philharmonic
    (Community)
  Chamber Symphony of San Francisco
    (Community)
  San Francisco Chamber Players
    (Community)
  San Francisco Conservatory of Music
    Orchestra (College)
  San Francisco State University
    Symphony Orchestra
  San Francisco Symphony★★★★
  San Francisco Symphony Youth
    Orchestra
·Theatres:
  American Conservatory Theatre★★★★
  Magic Theatre

One Act Theatre Company of San
  Francisco
Opera Companies:
  San Francisco Opera★★★★
    14 productions; 101 performances
  San Rafael–Marin Opera Company
    3 productions; 9 performances
Dance Companies:
  Bagong Diwa Dance Company (E-F)
  Ballet Theatre West
  Bay Area Repertory Dance
    Company (M)
  Christopher Beck and Company
    Dance/Theatre (M)
  Dionysian Duncan Dancers (M)
  Ed Mack Dance Studio Theatre (J)
  Ethnic Music and Dance Ensemble
    (E-F)★
  Jan Van Dyke and Dancers (M)
  Margaret Jenkins Dance Company (M)
  Marika Sakellariou Dance Company (M)
  Marin Ballet★
  Mixed Bag Productions (M)
  Oberlin Dance Collective (M)
  Peninsula Ballet Theatre★
  Rosa Montoya Bailes Flamencos (E-F)
  San Francisco Ballet★★
  San Francisco Ballet Celeste
    International
  Sarh Dances–Motion Arts Company (M)
  Tance Johnson Dancers (M)
  Theatre Ballet of San Francisco
  Theatre Flamenco of San Francisco
    (E-F)
  Westwood International Folk Ensemble
    (E-F)★
Public Libraries:
  1,761,025 volumes; circulation
    2,470,091
Reading Quotient: 6.2
CMSA Access: SAN FRANCISCO–OAKLAND–
  SAN JOSE, CA (606)
Places Rated Score: 14,226
Places Rated Rank: 7

## San Jose, CA

Public Television:
  KTEH Channel 54
Universities:
  San Jose University (1,000)
  Stanford University (659)
Symphony Orchestras:
  San Jose Symphony Orchestra★★
Theatres:
  San Jose Repertory Company
Opera Companies:
  Palo Alto Scholar Opera
    2 productions; 8 performances
  San Jose Symphony Opera
    1 production; 3 performances
Dance Companies:
  City Center Ballet of San Jose
  Janlyn Dance Company (M)
  Los Lupenos de San Jose (E-F)★
  Margaret Wingrove and Dancers (M)
  San Jose Dance Theatre★
  Santa Clara Ballet Company
Public Libraries:
  1,230,000 volumes; circulation
    2,300,000
Reading Quotient: 5.4
CMSA Access: SAN FRANCISCO–OAKLAND–
  SAN JOSE, CA (1,838)
Places Rated Score: 6,446
Places Rated Rank: 43

## Santa Barbara–Santa Maria–Lompoc, CA

Museums:
  Santa Barbara Museum of Natural
    History (800)
Universities:
  University of California, Santa Barbara
    (1,000)●
Symphony Orchestras:
  Santa Barbara Symphony Orchestra★★
Dance Companies:
  Santa Barbara Ballet
Public Libraries:
  533,679 volumes; circulation 1,807,736
Reading Quotient: 7.8
Places Rated Score: 2,684
Places Rated Rank: 117

## Santa Cruz, CA

Fine Arts and Public Radio:
  KUSP-FM 88.9 (155 hrs)
Universities:
  University of California, Santa Cruz
    (633)
Symphony Orchestras:
  Santa Cruz County Symphony★
  Santa Cruz County Youth Symphony
Dance Companies:
  Tandy Beal and Company (M)
Public Libraries:
  311,000 volumes; circulation 975,000
Reading Quotient: 7.8
CMSA Access: SAN FRANCISCO–OAKLAND–
  SAN JOSE, CA (2,054)
Places Rated Score: 3,748
Places Rated Rank: 86

## Santa Rosa–Petaluma, CA

Fine Arts and Public Radio:
  KBBF-FM 89.1 (50 mi; 126 hrs)
Symphony Orchestras:
  Santa Rosa Symphony★★
  Sonoma County Junior Symphony
Dance Companies:
  Ann Woodhead Dance Company (M)
Public Libraries:
  622,954 volumes; circulation 1,635,000
Reading Quotient: 7.4
CMSA Access: SAN FRANCISCO–OAKLAND–
  SAN JOSE, CA (2,084)
Places Rated Score: 3,457
Places Rated Rank: 94

## Sarasota, FL

Symphony Orchestras:
  Florida West Coast Symphony
    Orchestra★★
  Florida West Coast Youth Orchestra
  Sarasota Community Orchestra
Theatres:
  Asolo State Theatre★
Public Libraries:
  117,000 volumes; circulation 687,543
Reading Quotient: 6.4
Places Rated Score: 817
Places Rated Rank: 243

## Savannah, GA

Museums:
  Old Fort Jackson (500)
Fine Arts and Public Radio:
  WSVH 91.1 (90 mi; 127 hrs)
Public Television:
  WVAN Channel 9
Universities:
  Savannah State College (230)

Symphony Orchestras:
    Savannah Symphony Orchestra★★
Dance Companies:
    Savannah Ballet
Public Libraries:
    382,224 volumes; circulation 960,522
Reading Quotient: 5.2
Places Rated Score: 2,262
Places Rated Rank: 135

**Scranton–Wilkes-Barre, PA**
Museums:
    Everhart Museum of Natural History,
        Science and Art (600)
Fine Arts and Public Radio:
    WVIA-FM 89.9 (65 mi; 126 hrs)
Universities:
    Marywood College (310)
    Wilkes College (208)
Dance Companies:
    Wilkes-Barre Ballet Theatre Company
Public Libraries:
    363,572 volumes; circulation 285,293
Reading Quotient: 3.0
Places Rated Score: 1,832
Places Rated Rank: 169

★ **Seattle, WA**
Museums:
    Museum of History and Industry (500)
    Seattle Aquarium (500)
    Seattle Art Museum (600)
    Thomas Burke Memorial Washington
        State Museum (1,000)
Fine Arts and Public Radio:
    KUOW-FM 94.9 (40 mi; 156 hrs)
Public Television:
    KCTS Channel 9
Universities:
    Seattle Pacific University (212)
    Seattle University (464)
    University of Washington (1,000)●
Symphony Orchestras:
    Bellevue Philharmonic Orchestra
        (Community)
    Northwest Chamber Orchestra★★
    Olympic Youth Symphonies
    Seattle Symphony Orchestra★★★★
    Seattle Youth Symphony
    Thalia Symphony and Chamber
        Symphony (Community)
Theatres:
    A Contemporary Theatre★
    The Empty Space
    Intiman Theatre Company
    Seattle Repertory Theatre★★
Opera Companies:
    Seattle Opera
    5 productions; 25 performances
Dance Companies:
    Cornish Dance Theatre
    Kinetics Company (M)
    Martha Nishitani Modern Dance
        Company
    Pacific Northwest Ballet★
    Skinner Releasing Dance Company (M)
Public Libraries:
    1,546,110 volumes; circulation
        4,229,140
Reading Quotient: 11.7
CMSA Access: SEATTLE–TACOMA,
    WA (330)
Places Rated Score: 9,577
Places Rated Rank: 17

**Sharon, PA**
Public Libraries:
    52,400 volumes; circulation 76,000
Reading Quotient: 6.7
Places Rated Score: 52
Places Rated Rank: 329

**Sheboygan, WI**
Public Libraries:
    267,711 volumes; circulation 917,733
Reading Quotient: 11.7
Places Rated Score: 268
Places Rated Rank: 297

**Sherman–Denison, TX**
Public Libraries:
    68,357 volumes; circulation 324,108
Reading Quotient: 5.9
Places Rated Score: 68
Places Rated Rank: 327

**Shreveport, LA**
Public Television:
    KLTS Channel 24
Universities:
    Grambling State University (324)
    Louisiana State University, Shreveport
        (202)
    Louisiana Technical University (855)
Symphony Orchestras:
    Shreveport Symphony Orchestra★★
Opera Companies:
    Shreveport Opera Association
    5 productions; 12 performances
Dance Companies:
    Ballet Lyrique★
Public Libraries:
    284,739 volumes; circulation NA
Reading Quotient: NA
Places Rated Score: 2,826
Places Rated Rank: 113

**Sioux City, IA–NE**
Fine Arts and Public Radio:
    KWIT 90.3 (100 mi; 133 hrs)
Public Television:
    KSIN Channel 27
Symphony Orchestras:
    Sioux City Symphony Orchestra★★
    Siouxland Youth Symphony
Public Libraries:
    192,946 volumes; circulation 478,440
Reading Quotient: 8.2
Places Rated Score: 1,393
Places Rated Rank: 196

**Sioux Falls, SD**
Symphony Orchestras:
    South Dakota Symphony★★
Public Libraries:
    164,818 volumes; circulation 540,539
Reading Quotient: 8.7
Places Rated Score: 465
Places Rated Rank: 273

**South Bend–Mishawaka, IN**
Public Television:
    WNIT Channel 34
Universities:
    Andrews University (200)
    Indiana University, South Bend (392)
    University of Notre Dame (715)
Symphony Orchestras:
    South Bend Symphony Orchestra★★
Dance Companies:
    Patchwork Dance Company (J)

Public Libraries:
    514,756 volumes; circulation 1,747,716
Reading Quotient: 10
Places Rated Score: 2,672
Places Rated Rank: 119

**Spokane, WA**
Fine Arts and Public Radio:
    KBPX-FM 91.1 (100 mi; 129 hrs)
Public Television:
    KSPS Channel 7
Universities:
    Eastern Washington University (734)●
    Gonzaga University (221)
Symphony Orchestras:
    Spokane Junior Symphony
    Spokane Symphony Orchestra★★★
Dance Companies:
    Spokane Ballet
Public Libraries:
    683,396 volumes; circulation 2,307,961
Reading Quotient: 8.7
Places Rated Score: 2,988
Places Rated Rank: 107

**Springfield, IL**
Museums:
    Illinois State Museum (850)
Fine Arts and Public Radio:
    WSSR-FM 91.9 (50 mi; 145 hrs)
Symphony Orchestras:
    Springfield Symphony Orchestra★
Dance Companies:
    Springfield Ballet Company★★
Public Libraries:
    333,133 volumes; circulation 837,784
Reading Quotient: 11.7
Places Rated Score: 1,983
Places Rated Rank: 158

**Springfield, MA**
Museums:
    Museum of Fine Arts (500)
    Springfield Science Museum (600)
Public Television:
    WGBY Channel 57
Universities:
    Westfield State College (290)
Symphony Orchestras:
    Holyoke College Civic Orchestra
    Springfield Symphony Orchestra★★★
    Western Massachusetts Young People's
        Symphony
Theatres:
    Stage West
Dance Companies:
    Amherst Ballet Theatre Company
    Dance Gallery (M)
    Pioneer Valley Ballet
Public Libraries:
    726,410 volumes; circulation 963,394
Reading Quotient: 11.1
Places Rated Score: 3,466
Places Rated Rank: 93

**Springfield, MO**
Fine Arts and Public Radio:
    KSMU-FM 91.1 (15 mi; 133 hrs)
Public Television:
    KOZK Channel 21
Symphony Orchestras:
    Southwest Missouri State University
        Symphony
    Springfield Symphony Orchestra★
Opera Companies:
    Springfield Regional Opera
    3 productions; 10 performances

Public Libraries:
  304,307 volumes; circulation 1,109,925
Reading Quotient: 7.7
Places Rated Score: 1,634
Places Rated Rank: 180

## Stamford, CT
Symphony Orchestras:
  Connecticut Philharmonic Orchestra
    (Community)
  Greenwich Symphony Orchestra★
  Stamford Symphony Orchestra★
Theatres:
  Hartman Theatre★
Opera Companies:
  Stamford State Opera, Inc.
    3 productions; 3 performances
Public Libraries:
  364,123 volumes; circulation 677,775
Reading Quotient: 10.2
CMSA Access: NEW YORK–NORTHERN
  NEW JERSEY–LONG ISLAND, NY–NJ–
  CT (6,592)
Places Rated Score: 7,865
Places Rated Rank: 28

## State College, PA
Universities:
  Pennsylvania State University (1,000)●
Symphony Orchestras:
  Nittany Valley Symphony (Community)
Dance Companies:
  Contemporary Dance Company (M)★
Public Libraries:
  71,003 volumes; circulation 268,290
Reading Quotient: 5.5
Places Rated Score: 1,271
Places Rated Rank: 206

## Steubenville–Weirton, OH–WV
Public Libraries:
  146,637 volumes; circulation 360,209
Reading Quotient: 5.5
Places Rated Score: 147
Places Rated Rank: 314

## Stockton, CA
Fine Arts and Public Radio:
  KUOP-FM 91.3 (70 mi; 153 hrs)
Universities:
  University of the Pacific (351)
Symphony Orchestras:
  Stockton Symphony★★
Dance Companies:
  San Joaquin Ballet
Public Libraries:
  478,266 volumes; circulation 1,110,919
Reading Quotient: 4.8
Places Rated Score: 1,579
Places Rated Rank: 185

## Syracuse, NY
Museums:
  Everson Museum of Art (500)
Fine Arts and Public Radio:
  WCNY-FM 91.3 (60 mi; 154 hrs)
Public Television:
  WCNY Channel 24
Universities:
  Colgate University (260)
  SUNY at Oswego (669)
  Syracuse University (1,000)
Symphony Orchestras:
  Onondaga Civic Symphony Orchestra
    (Community)
  Syracuse Symphony Orchestra★★★★
  Syracuse Symphony Youth Orchestra

Theatres:
  Syracuse Stage★
Opera Companies:
  Opera Theatre of Syracuse
    3 productions; 6 performances
Public Libraries:
  632,534 volumes; circulation 1,063,057
Reading Quotient: 3.7
Places Rated Score: 5,080
Places Rated Rank: 57

## Tacoma, WA
Museums:
  Puget Sound Museum of Natural History
    (700)
Fine Arts and Public Radio:
  KPLU-FM 88.5 (76 mi; 138 hrs)
  KTOY-FM 91.7 (30 mi; 138 hrs)
Public Television:
  KTPS Channel 28
Universities:
  Pacific Lutheran University (269)
  University of Puget Sound (278)
Symphony Orchestras:
  Tacoma Symphony Orchestra★★
  Tacoma Youth Symphony
Theatres:
  Tacoma Actors Guild
Dance Companies:
  Balletacoma★
  Tacoma Performance Dance Company★
Public Libraries:
  282,256 volumes; circulation 1,107,650
Reading Quotient: 4.5
CMSA Access: SEATTLE–TACOMA,
  WA (968)
Places Rated Score: 4,297
Places Rated Rank: 74

## Tallahassee, FL
Fine Arts and Public Radio:
  WFSU-FM 90.5 (35 mi; 140 hrs)
Public Television:
  WFSU Channel 11
Universities:
  Florida State University (1,000)●
Symphony Orchestras:
  Florida State University Symphony
Dance Companies:
  Dance Arts Guild of Tallahassee
  Tallahassee Civic Ballet
Public Libraries:
  181,219 volumes; circulation 644,958
Reading Quotient: 5.3
Places Rated Score: 2,181
Places Rated Rank: 141

## Tampa–St. Petersburg– Clearwater, FL
Fine Arts and Public Radio:
  WUSF-FM 89.7 (47 mi; 148 hrs)
Public Television:
  WEDU Channel 3
  WUSF Channel 16
Universities:
  University of South Florida (1,000)●
  University of Tampa (158)
Symphony Orchestras:
  Florida Gulf Coast Symphony★★★
  Pinellas Youth Symphony
  St. Petersburg Community Symphony
Opera Companies:
  Florida Opera West, Inc.
    3 productions; 4 performances
Dance Companies:
  City Center Ballet, Inc.★
  Dancemakers (J)

Firethorn (M)
Florida Ballet Theatre★
Tampa Ballet★
Public Libraries:
  1,270,096 volumes; circulation
    3,781,383
Reading Quotient: 5.2
Places Rated Score: 5,040
Places Rated Rank: 58

## Terre Haute, IN
Universities:
  Indiana State University (938)
Symphony Orchestras:
  Terre Haute Symphony★
Public Libraries:
  88,247 volumes; circulation 702,624
Reading Quotient: 7.1
Places Rated Score: 1,226
Places Rated Rank: 211

## Texarkana, TX–Texarkana, AR
Public Libraries:
  63,072 volumes; circulation 160,547
Reading Quotient: 4.3
Places Rated Score: 63
Places Rated Rank: 328

## Toledo, OH
Museums:
  Toledo Museum of Art (700)
Fine Arts and Public Radio:
  WGTE-FM 91.3 (45 mi; 135 hrs)
Public Television:
  WGTE Channel 30
Universities:
  University of Toledo (1,000)
Symphony Orchestras:
  Toledo Symphony Orchestra★★★
  Toledo Youth Orchestra
Dance Companies:
  Cassandra Civic Ballet Company
  Toledo Ballet★
  Valois Company of Dancers (M)
Public Libraries:
  1,188,510 volumes; circulation
    3,783,282
Reading Quotient: 10.5
Places Rated Score: 4,389
Places Rated Rank: 71

## Topeka, KS
Public Television:
  KTWU Channel 11
Universities:
  Emporia State University (362)
  Washburn University of Topeka (488)
Public Libraries:
  281,934 volumes; circulation 958,317
Reading Quotient: 10.7
Places Rated Score: 1,632
Places Rated Rank: 181

## Trenton, NJ
Museums:
  New Jersey State Museum (1,200)
Fine Arts and Public Radio:
  WWFM-FM 89.1 (11 mi; 130 hrs)
Public Television:
  WNJT Channel 52
Universities:
  Princeton University (446)
  Rider College (333)
Theatres:
  McCarter Theatre Company★★
Dance Companies:
  Princeton Ballet Society★

Public Libraries:
630,820 volumes; circulation 924,584
Reading Quotient: 7.7
CMSA Access: PHILADELPHIA–WILMINGTON–
TRENTON, PA–NJ–DE–MD (1,219)
Places Rated Score: 5,029
Places Rated Rank: 59

## Tucson, AZ
Museums:
Arizona Heritage Center (500)
Sonora Desert Museum (600)
Fine Arts and Public Radio:
KUAT-AM 1550 (65 mi; 84 hrs)
KUAT-FM 90.5 (60 mi; 126 hrs)
Public Television:
KUAT Channel 6
Universities:
University of Arizona (1,000)•
Symphony Orchestras:
Tucson Symphony Orchestra★★★★
Theatres:
Arizona Theatre Company★
Opera Companies:
Arizona Opera Company
3 productions; 11 performances
Dance Companies:
Tucson Metropolitan Ballet★
Territory Dance Theatre (M)
Public Libraries:
698,800 volumes; circulation 3,600,000
Reading Quotient: 7.6
Places Rated Score: 4,889
Places Rated Rank: 61

## Tulsa, OK
Museums:
Gilcrease Institute of American History
and Art (500)
Philbrook Art Center (500)
Fine Arts and Public Radio:
KWGS-FM 89.5 (30 mi; 145 hrs)
Public Television:
KOED Channel 4
Universities:
Oral Roberts University (304)
University of Tulsa (413)
Symphony Orchestras:
Oklahoma Sinfonia and Chorale★
Tulsa Philharmonic Orchestra★★★
Tulsa Youth Symphony Orchestra
Theatres:
American Theatre Company
Opera Companies:
Tulsa Opera
3 productions; 9 performances
Dance Companies:
Tulsa Ballet Theatre★
Public Libraries:
503,824 volumes; circulation 1,760,920
Reading Quotient: 4.9
Places Rated Score: 4,248
Places Rated Rank: 76

## Tuscaloosa, AL
Fine Arts and Public Radio:
WUAL-FM 91.5 (80 mi; 138 hrs)
Universities:
University of Alabama (1,000)
Public Libraries:
132,000 volumes; circulation 463,213
Reading Quotient: 4.4
Places Rated Score: 1,432
Places Rated Rank: 194

## Tyler, TX
Symphony Orchestras:
East Texas Symphony Orchestra★
Tyler Youth Symphony Orchestra
Public Libraries:
104,396 volumes; circulation 325,000
Reading Quotient: 5.7
Places Rated Score: 404
Places Rated Rank: 278

## Utica–Rome, NY
Museums:
Munson/Williams/Proctor Institute of Art
(500)
Symphony Orchestras:
Utica Symphony Orchestra★
Public Libraries:
158,030 volumes; circulation 251,566
Reading Quotient: 2.5
Places Rated Score: 858
Places Rated Rank: 239

## Vallejo–Fairfield–Napa, CA
Symphony Orchestras:
Napa Valley Symphony Association★
Public Libraries:
587,966 volumes; circulation 1,413,471
Reading Quotient: 6.3
CMSA Access: SAN FRANCISCO–OAKLAND–
SAN JOSE, CA (2,174)
Places Rated Score: 2,962
Places Rated Rank: 109

## Vancouver, WA
Museums:
Clark County Historical Museum (600)
Public Libraries:
312,762 volumes; circulation 1,291,533
Reading Quotient: 7.4
CMSA Access: PORTLAND–VANCOUVER,
OR–WA (644)
Places Rated Score: 1,557
Places Rated Rank: 186

## Victoria, TX
Public Libraries:
87,000 volumes; circulation NA
Reading Quotient: NA
Places Rated Score: 87
Places Rated Rank: 321

## Vineland–Millville–Bridgeton, NJ
Public Libraries:
187,568 volumes; circulation 329,523
Reading Quotient: 5.3
CMSA Access: PHILADELPHIA–WILMINGTON–
TRENTON, PA–NJ–DE–MD (1,909)
Places Rated Score: 2,097
Places Rated Rank: 149

## Visalia–Tulare–Porterville, CA
Public Libraries:
510,987 volumes; circulation 931,044
Reading Quotient: 6.3
Places Rated Score: 511
Places Rated Rank: 270

## Waco, TX
Universities:
Baylor University (873)
Symphony Orchestras:
Waco Symphony Orchestra
(Community)
Public Libraries:
168,350 volumes; circulation 578,255
Reading Quotient: 4.4
Places Rated Score: 1,141
Places Rated Rank: 218

## ★ Washington, DC–MD–VA
Museums:
Daughters of the American Revolution
Museum (600)
Freer Gallery of Art (600)
Library of Congress Collections (600)
National Archives (700)
National Gallery of Art (1,600)
National Museum of American Art
(1,100)
National Museum of Natural History
(900)
National Portrait Gallery (900)
Smithsonian Institution (including Air
and Space Museum) (2,000)
U.S. Marine Corps Museum (800)
Fine Arts and Public Radio:
WAMU-FM 88.5 (50 mi; 168 hrs)
WETA-FM 90.9 (125 mi; 138 hrs)
WPFW-FM 89.3 (100 mi; 168 hrs)
Public Television:
WETA Channel 26
WHMM Channel 32
Universities:
American University (453)
Bowie State College (288)
Catholic University (259)
George Mason University (625)
George Washington University (740)•
Georgetown University (524)
Howard University (565)
University of D.C. (400)
University of Maryland (1,000)•
Symphony Orchestras:
D.C. Youth Orchestra
Georgetown Symphony (Community)
Handel Festival Orchestra★
National Symphony Orchestra★★★★
Theatres:
Arena Stage★★★★
Folger Theatre★
Living Stage Theatre Company
New Playwright's Theatre
Round House Theatre
Opera Companies:
Washington Opera★★★★
8 productions; 63 performances
Dance Companies:
African Heritage Dancers and
Drummers (E-F)★
Ava-Teri Dance Theatre (M)
Bethesda Ballet Company★★
Capitol Ballet Company
Center Dance Ensemble (M)
Dance Exchange (M)
Fairfax Ballet Company
Kinor Dance Company (E-F)
Maida Withers and The Dance
Construction Company (M)
Maryland Dance Theatre (M)
Montgomery Ballet Company
Murray Spalding Dance Theatre (M)
Perle/Bloom and Company (M)
Prochotsky Ballet Theatre
Richard Cunningham Dance
Company (M)
Washington Ballet
Public Libraries:
1,346,723 volumes; circulation
1,487,009
Reading Quotient: 4.4
Places Rated Score: 21,701
Places Rated Rank: 4

## Waterbury, CT
Symphony Orchestras:
Waterbury Symphony Orchestra
(Community)

Dance Companies:
   Nutmeg Ballet Company
Public Libraries:
   167,852 volumes; circulation
   179,988
Reading Quotient: 3.4
Places Rated Score: 318
Places Rated Rank: 291

**Waterloo–Cedar Falls, IA**
Fine Arts and Public Radio:
   KBBG-FM 88.1 (60 mi; 138 hrs)
   KHKE-FM 89.5 (42 mi; 131 hrs)
   KUNI-FM 90.9 (74 mi; 168 hrs)
Public Television
   KRIN Channel 32
Universities:
   University of Northern Iowa (820)
Symphony Orchestras:
   Waterloo–Cedar Falls Symphony
   Orchestra★
Public Libraries:
   380,243 volumes; circulation 1,202,664
Reading Quotient: 8.5
Places Rated Score: 3,000
Places Rated Rank: 105

**Wausau, WI**
Public Television:
   WHRM Channel 20
Public Libraries:
   261,415 volumes; circulation 766,030
Reading Quotient: 9.3
Places Rated Score: 761
Places Rated Rank: 250

**West Palm Beach–Boca Raton–
Delray Beach, FL**
Fine Arts and Public Radio:
   WHRS-FM 90.7 (50 mi; 126 hrs)
Public Television:
   WHRS Channel 42
Universities:
   Florida Atlantic University (830)
Symphony Orchestras:
   Greater Palm Beach Symphony★★
   Boca Raton Symphony Orchestra★
Theatres:
   Caldwell Playhouse
Opera Companies:
   Palm Beach Opera, Inc.
   2 productions; 4 performances
Public Libraries:
   449,559 volumes; circulation 2,136,233
Reading Quotient: 5.4
Places Rated Score: 2,888
Places Rated Rank: 110

**Wheeling, WV–OH**
Symphony Orchestras:
   Wheeling Symphony Orchestra★★
Public Libraries:
   121,760 volumes; circulation 213,000
Reading Quotient: 5.5
Places Rated Score: 422
Places Rated Rank: 277

**Wichita, KS**
Fine Arts and Public Radio:
   KMUW-FM 89.1 (40 mi; 165 hrs)

Public Television:
   KPTS Channel 8
Universities:
   Wichita State University (860)●●
Symphony Orchestras:
   Wichita State University Symphony
   Orchestra
   Wichita Symphony Orchestra★★★
   Wichita Youth Orchestra
Dance Companies:
   Mid-America Dance Company (M)
Public Libraries:
   476,906 volumes; circulation 1,139,428
Reading Quotient: 5.9
Places Rated Score: 2,987
Places Rated Rank: 108

**Wichita Falls, TX**
Universities:
   Midwestern State University (241)
Symphony Orchestras:
   Wichita Falls Symphony Orchestra★
Dance Companies:
   Wichita Falls Ballet Theatre
Public Libraries:
   108,247 volumes; circulation 169,456
Reading Quotient: 3.0
Places Rated Score: 599
Places Rated Rank: 264

**Williamsport, PA**
Symphony Orchestras:
   Susquehanna Valley Symphony
   Orchestra (Community)
Public Libraries:
   96,013 volumes; circulation 240,688
Reading Quotient: 2.8
Places Rated Score: 196
Places Rated Rank: 305

**Wilmington, DE–NJ–MD**
Museums:
   Hagley Museum (600)
Universities:
   University of Delaware (1,000)
Symphony Orchestras:
   Delaware Symphony Orchestra★★
Theatres:
   Delaware Theatre Company
Public Libraries:
   635,627 volumes; circulation 1,593,392
Reading Quotient: 5.6
CMSA Access: PHILADELPHIA–
   WILMINGTON–TRENTON, PA–NJ–DE–
   MD (1,909)
Places Rated Score: 4,545
Places Rated Rank: 66

**Wilmington, NC**
Public Television:
   WUNJ Channel 39
Universities:
   University of North Carolina, Wilmington
   (406)
Public Libraries:
   171,165 volumes; circulation 355,620
Reading Quotient: 5.1
Places Rated Score: 1,077
Places Rated Rank: 222

**Worcester, MA**
Museums:
   Worcester Art Museum (800)
Universities:
   Clark University (203)
Theatres:
   Worcester Foothills Theatre Company
Dance Companies:
   Pyramid Dance Company (M)
Public Libraries:
   631,307 volumes; circulation 904,278
Reading Quotient: 9.5
Places Rated Score: 1,784
Places Rated Rank: 172

**Yakima, WA**
Public Television:
   KXVE Channel 47
Symphony Orchestras:
   Yakima Symphony Orchestra
   (Community)
   Yakima Youth Orchestra
Public Libraries:
   296,189 volumes; circulation 870,154
Reading Quotient: 6.9
Places Rated Score: 996
Places Rated Rank: 231

**York, PA**
Museums:
   Historical Society of York County (500)
Symphony Orchestras:
   York Junior Symphony
   York Symphony Association★
   York Youth Symphony
Public Libraries:
   122,000 volumes; circulation 330,000
Reading Quotient: 4.1
Places Rated Score: 1,022
Places Rated Rank: 226

**Youngstown–Warren, OH**
Fine Arts and Public Radio:
   WYSO-FM 91.3 (60 mi; 162 hrs)
Universities:
   Youngstown State University (990)
Symphony Orchestras:
   Dana Symphony Orchestra (College)
   Warren Chamber Orchestra
   (Community)
   Youngstown Symphony Orchestra
   (Youth)
Dance Companies:
   Ballet Midwest
   Ballet Western Reserve
Public Libraries:
   906,848 volumes; circulation 430,444
Reading Quotient: 5.4
Places Rated Score: 2,797
Places Rated Rank: 115

**Yuba City, CA**
Public Libraries:
   122,101 volumes; circulation 231,133
Reading Quotient: 6.7
Places Rated Score: 122
Places Rated Rank: 317

## Et Cetera

## A DAVID AND GOLIATH PROPOSITION

Show us the biggest metro areas and we'll show you the best places to live for the arts: New York, Chicago, Los Angeles, Washington, D.C., and Boston. The fairly consistent relationship between a metro area's size and its supply of cultural facilities might lead you to believe that such places as Bangor, Maine, and Bloomington, Indiana—both with populations under 100,000 and ranking 155th and 145th, respectively, in the arts—must resign themselves to being cultural underdogs. But think again.

### Pick On Someone Your Own Size

What would happen if Bangor and Bloomington, remembering the old playground maxim, were to say to New York, "Go pick on someone your own size"? By grouping metro areas according to their populations, we are able to explore which ones have a large supply of cultural assets relative to their size and which might be considered culturally deficient. *Places Rated* divides the metro areas into four competitive population groups, based on criteria established by the federal government.

The following lists show how the metro areas rank in the arts when they are measured against similarly sized places.

### Metro Areas and the Arts: Some Size Comparisons

#### Largest Metro Areas
(Population 1,000,000 or More)

| Best Metro Areas | Places Rated Score | Worst Metro Areas | Places Rated Score |
|---|---|---|---|
| 1. New York, NY | 56,745 | 1. Fort Lauderdale–Hollywood–Pompano Beach, FL | 2,027 |
| 2. Chicago, IL | 24,846 | 2. San Antonio, TX | 4,295 |
| 3. Los Angeles–Long Beach, CA | 23,567 | 3. Sacramento, CA | 4,483 |
| 4. Washington, DC–MD–VA | 21,701 | 4. Phoenix, AZ | 4,573 |
| 5. Boston, MA | 21,042 | 5. Miami–Hialeah, FL | 4,837 |
| 6. Philadelphia, PA–NJ | 17,270 | 6. Tampa–St. Petersburg–Clearwater, FL | 5,040 |
| 7. San Francisco, CA | 14,226 | 7. Portland, OR | 5,160 |
| 8. Newark, NJ | 14,224 | 8. Riverside–San Bernardino, CA | 5,327 |
| 9. Cleveland, OH | 12,679 | 9. Anaheim–Santa Ana, CA | 5,632 |
| 10. Minneapolis–St. Paul, MN–WI | 11,714 | 10. Oakland, CA | 6,162 |

#### Medium-Sized Metro Areas
(Population 250,000 to 1,000,000)

| Best Metro Areas | Places Rated Score | Worst Metro Areas | Places Rated Score |
|---|---|---|---|
| 1. Bridgeport–Milford, CT | 8.368 | 1. Lakeland–Winter Haven, FL | 309 |
| 2. Middlesex–Somerset–Hunterdon, NJ | 8,058 | 2. Melbourne–Titusville–Palm Bay, FL | 437 |

| Best Metro Areas | Places Rated Score | Worst Metro Areas | Places Rated Score |
|---|---|---|---|
| 3. New Haven–Meriden, CT | 7,852 | 3. Pawtucket–Woonsocket–Attleboro, RI–MA | 480 |
| 4. Monmouth–Ocean, NJ | 7,563 | 4. Atlantic City, NJ | 621 |
| 5. Ann Arbor, MI | 7,559 | 5. Modesto, CA | 631 |
| 6. Jersey City, NJ | 7,420 | 6. Johnstown, PA | 666 |
| 7. Honolulu, HI | 7,168 | 7. Daytona Beach, FL | 809 |
| 8. Orange County, NY | 6,987 | 8. Utica–Rome, NY | 858 |
| 9. Rochester, NY | 6,956 | 9. East St. Louis–Belleville, IL | 904 |
| 10. Dayton–Springfield, OH | 6,935 | 10. Canton, OH | 989 |

#### Small Metro Areas
(Population 100,000 to 250,000)

| Best Metro Areas | Places Rated Score | Worst Metro Areas | Places Rated Score |
|---|---|---|---|
| 1. Stamford, CT | 7,865 | 1. Sharon, PA | 52 |
| 2. Danbury, CT | 7,415 | 2. Texarkana, TX–Texarkana, AR | 63 |
| 3. Norwalk, CT | 7,273 | 3. Kankakee, IL | 75 |
| 4. Lincoln, NE | 4,523 | 4. Benton Harbor, MI | 79 |
| 5. Kenosha, WI | 3,844 | 5. Joplin, MO | 80 |
| 6. Santa Cruz, CA | 3,748 | 6. Danville, VA | 85 |
| 7. Boulder–Longmont, CO | 3,663 | 7. Fort Walton Beach, FL | 87 |
| 8. Athens, GA | 3,546 | 8. Parkersburg–Marietta, WV–OH | 91 |
| 9. Lubbock, TX | 3,402 | 9. Clarksville–Hopkinsville, TN–KY | 111 |
| 10. Gainesville, FL | 3,335 | 10. Dothan, AL | 117 |

#### Smallest Metro Areas
(Population Less than 100,000)

| Best Metro Areas | Places Rated Score | Worst Metro Areas | Places Rated Score |
|---|---|---|---|
| 1. Lawrence, KS | 3,150 | 1. Sherman–Denison, TX | 68 |
| 2. Las Cruces, NM | 2,804 | 2. Victoria, TX | 87 |
| 3. Iowa City, IA | 2,255 | 3. Burlington, NC | 131 |
| 4. Bloomington, IN | 2,152 | 4. Laredo, TX | 150 |
| 5. Bryan–College Station, TX | 2,002 | 5. Enid, OK | 215 |
| 6. Bangor, ME | 1,995 | 6. Pittsfield, MA | 228 |
| 7. Grand Forks, ND | 1,921 | 7. Fitchburg–Leominster, MA | 270 |
| 8. La Crosse, WI | 1,466 | 8. Casper, WY | 303 |
| 9. San Angelo, TX | 1,301 | 9. Dubuque, IA | 340 |
| 10. Bismarck, ND | 1,211 | 10. Pine Bluff, AR | 373 |

Going one step further, there is a way that metro areas with populations below 100,000 can stand up to and even defeat arts giants like New York and Chicago. It's the culture per capita score, the weapon with which small places can bring metropolitan Goliaths to their knees.

### Determining Culture per Capita

Applying the culture per capita scoring system will prove to a transferring executive who loves the arts or to a retired theatergoer that a move to the Great Plains

## Apples and Oranges

Critics might call it comparing apples to oranges, but applying the per capita scoring principles to the metro area of your choice can result in interesting and sometimes upsetting conclusions.

Casper, Wyoming, and Enid, Oklahoma, for instance, should be delighted to discover where their per capita scores rank them in relation to Chicago and Los Angeles–Long Beach.

Here is a sample of what might be found when the per capita scores of smaller places are compared with those of the cultural leaders.

### Per Capita Comparisons: A Sampler

| Metro Area | Per Capita Score | Overall Arts Rank |
|---|---|---|
| Boston, MA | 750 | 5 |
| New York, NY | 685 | 1 |
| Washington, DC–MD–VA | 668 | 4 |
| Casper, WY | 422 | 293 |
| Pine Bluff, AR | 411 | 282 |
| Chicago, IL | 410 | 2 |
| Dubuque, IA | 363 | 287 |
| Enid, OK | 342 | 304 |
| Los Angeles–Long Beach, CA | 315 | 3 |

does not mean leaving all that wonderful entertainment back home in the big city. Of course, the largest places will still have the most resources, but per capita, places like Bryan–College Station, Texas; Grand Forks, North Dakota; and Lawrence, Kansas, make quite an effort—in fact, might be considered overachievers—in providing their citizens with culture and art.

To evaluate a metro area in terms of cultural facilities per capita, each metro area's *Places Rated* score is divided by its population. This number is then multiplied by 100,000 to do away with the decimal point; the resulting number is the score. For example, New York's overall arts score of 56,745 is divided by the metro area population of 8,274,961, yielding .00680. Multiplying this figure by 100,000 results in a culture per capita score of 680 for New York.

When we compare the 329 metro areas on the basis of culture per capita, the usual megalopolitan leaders fade from view, and Bangor, Bloomington, Grand Forks, and Lawrence have their chance to shine.

### Culture per Capita: The Top 20 Metro Areas

| Metro Area | Per Capita Score | Metro Area | Per Capita Score |
|---|---|---|---|
| 1. Norwalk, CT | 5,741 | 12. Orange County, NY | 2,691 |
| 2. Lawrence, KS | 4,657 | 13. Bangor, ME | 2,377 |
| 3. Danbury, CT | 4,352 | 14. Lincoln, NE | 2,345 |
| 4. Stamford, CT | 3,955 | 15. Bloomington, IN | 2,178 |
| 5. Kenosha, WI | 3,122 | 16. Bryan–College Station, TX | 2,139 |
| 6. Las Cruces, NM | 2,911 | 17. Santa Cruz, CA | 1,992 |
| 7. Grand Forks, ND | 2,906 | 18. Bridgeport–Milford, CT | 1,980 |
| 8. Columbia, MO | 2,871 | 19. Gainesville, FL | 1,946 |
| 9. Ann Arbor, MI | 2,855 | 20. Muncie, IN | 1,943 |
| 10. Iowa City, IA | 2,760 | | |
| 11. Athens, GA | 2,727 | | |

A closer look at the top 20 places for culture per capita reveals that although the largest metro areas are absent from the list, they do have far-reaching effects, even on per capita scores. Eight of the 20 metro areas are actually components of Consolidated Metropolitan Statistical Areas (CMSAs) and draw much of their strength from the metro areas of New York, Chicago, Detroit, and San Francisco. As a matter of fact, the

high-ranking Connecticut metro areas of Norwalk, Danbury, and Stamford each receive more than 6,000 bonus points as part of the New York–Northern New Jersey–Long Island consolidated area.

By disregarding all metro areas with CMSA access, we can discover which are meeting the cultural needs of their populations on their own.

### The 21 Best Non-CMSA Metro Areas in Culture per Capita

| Metro Area | Per Capita Score | Metro Area | Per Capita Score |
|---|---|---|---|
| 1. Lawrence, KS | 4,657 | 13. Fayetteville–Springdale, AR | 1,906 |
| 2. Las Cruces, NM | 2,911 | 14. Waterloo–Cedar Falls, IA | 1,843 |
| 3. Grand Forks, ND | 2,906 | 15. Lafayette, IN | 1,837 |
| 4. Columbia, MO | 2,871 | 16. La Crosse, WI | 1,610 |
| 5. Iowa City, IA | 2,760 | 17. Lubbock, TX | 1,608 |
| 6. Athens, GA | 2,727 | 18. Madison, WI | 1,583 |
| 7. Bangor, ME | 2,377 | 19. New Haven–Meriden, CT | 1,569 |
| 8. Lincoln, NE | 2,345 | 20. Fargo–Moorhead, ND–MN | 1,534 |
| 9. Bloomington, IN | 2,178 | 20. San Angelo, TX | 1,534 |
| 10. Bryan–College Station, TX | 2,139 | | |
| 11. Gainesville, FL | 1,946 | | |
| 12. Muncie, IN | 1,943 | | |

What sparks these smaller metro areas to achieve in the arts? Just as every metro area exists for a different reason, so the local types of support for the arts also differ. In centers for manufacturing and retail trade, this support may be in the form of grants and endowments; in agricultural areas, it may come from individuals. With the exception of La Crosse, Wisconsin, the metro areas listed above all have one source of aid in common: Each is home to a university offering majors in the performing arts. As with nearly every college or university, support for the arts runs high both within the walls of the school and in the community itself.

## FOLK ART IN AMERICA

Folk art is where you find it. And in one form or another—be it music, ethnic food traditions, games, sayings, rhymes, crafts, or simple street pastimes—that's just about everywhere you care to look.

Interest in folk art currently is greater than it has ever been in America, as shown by the remarkable upsurge in the number of folk festivals throughout the country. Many of these festivals are ethnic in origin. The Midwest has numerous festivals celebrating the customs of such places as Germany, Sweden, Norway, Poland, and Lithuania. In the East, similar festivals honoring the Greeks, Italians, and Portuguese are common. Almost every state has at least one gathering of Scottish clans. Black Americans celebrate their history in the traditional musical forms of ballads, blues, and gospel songs. In New Orleans, these old oral traditions combine with instrumentation and more modern city blues to create the world-renowned sound of New Orleans jazz.

Some festivals center on events. There are festivals celebrating the harvest, the making of wine, the departure of fishing fleets, or the butchering of whales. Some festivals are religious; others honor national or local heroes; still others reflect the livelihood of a region, such as the logging festivals of the Northwest,

and the steam-thresher revivals of the Great Plains.

The list of festivals that follows has been compiled with the help of the National Council for the Traditional Arts, in Washington, D.C., and the various folk arts coordinators at the state level. In choosing these festivals, careful attention was paid to include only those faithful to the traditional folk arts. Size and duration of the festivals were considered, as was breadth of appeal. However, some of the biggest festivals were excluded because of their commercial orientation. Finally, whenever possible, we included festivals that occur at different times of the year and at different locations in each state. In many instances a phone number has been included after the festival name to provide further information to those interested.

In most cases, the reader can get a good idea of what each festival is like simply from the festival's name. When the nature of the festival is not obvious, a short explanation is provided. Almost all of the festivals on the list provide music and food—either free or for a nominal charge—in addition to the main event.

## Selected Folk Festivals, by State

**ALABAMA**
Mobile Jazz Festival
Mobile
Early May    (205) 343-4420

Tennessee Valley Old Time Fiddlers
    Convention
Athens
Early October    (205) 837-4235

**ALASKA**
Little Norway Festival
Petersburg
Mid-May    (907) 772-3646

**ARIZONA**
"Tucson Meet Yourself"
A celebration of traditions of the Southwest
Tucson
2nd weekend in October

WA:K Annual Pow Wow
Authentic Indian ceremonies and crafts fair
Tucson
Early to mid-March

**ARKANSAS**
Arkansas Folk Festival
Traditional music, bluegrass
Mountain View
Mid-April    (501) 269-3851

"Back in the Hills" Antique Show and Folklife
    Fair
Crafts, demonstrations, games
War Eagle (near Hindsville)
Early May    (501) 789-5398

**CALIFORNIA**
*Fiesta de la Primavera*
Mexican mariachi bands and Spanish
    dancers
Old Town, San Diego
Mid-May    (714) 297-2219

Ghost Mountain Bluegrass Festival
Pollock Pines
Late May    (916) 487-9761

**COLORADO**
Colorado State Fair
Crafts, music, Western skills competition
Pueblo
Late August

Rocky Mountain Bluegrass Festival
Henderson
Late August    (303) 771-2410

**CONNECTICUT**
Danbury State Fair
Danbury State Fairgrounds
Mid-July    (203) 748-3535

**DELAWARE**
Delaware State Fair
Harrington
3rd week in July    (302) 398-3269

**DISTRICT OF COLUMBIA**
Festival of American Folk Life
Sponsored by the Smithsonian Institution
Washington Monument grounds
Early October    (202) 381-6532

**FLORIDA**
Florida Folk Festival
Native American folklore, crafts,
    demonstrations
White Springs
3rd week in May    (904) 397-2192

Pioneer Days Festival
Traditional music, arts and crafts
Pine Castle Center of the Arts, Orlando
Last weekend in October    (305) 855-7461

**GEORGIA**
Chattahoochee Folk Festival
Columbus
Last week in September    (404) 323-3617

Georgia Sea Island Festival
Music of the Georgia coast
St. Simons Island
Mid-August    (912) 265-9545

**HAWAII**
King Kamehameha Celebration
Traditional Hawaiian dances, storytelling
Honolulu
Early June    (808) 548-4512

**IDAHO**
National Oldtime Fiddlers Contest
Weiser
Mid-June    (208) 549-0452

**ILLINOIS**
International Folk Fair
Celebration of Chicago's ethnic diversity
Chicago
October    (312) 744-3315

Pilsen Community *Fiesta del Sol*
Hispanic neighborhood celebration
Chicago
August    (312) 666-2663

Southern Illinois Folk Festival
Emphasis on Indian and German-American
    traditions
Du Quoin
Late September    (618) 542-5484

**INDIANA**
Annual Duneland Folk Festival
Chesterton and Porter
Mid-July    (219) 926-7561

Annual Indiana Fiddlers Gathering
Battleground
Early September

Bean Blossom Festival
Bill Monroe's famous bluegrass festival
Bean Blossom
Mid-June

**IOWA**
Council Bluffs Old-Time Country Music
    Contest
Council Bluffs
Late August    (712) 366-1136

Midwest Old Settlers and Threshers Reunion
Antique farm machinery, demonstrations, music
Mount Pleasant
Late August    (319) 385-8937

Nordic Fest
One of the largest Norwegian-American celebrations in the country
Decorah
Late July    (319) 382-4147

**KANSAS**
After Harvest Czech Festival
Wilson
3rd week in July    (913) 658-2965

National Flat-Picking Championship
Guitar-playing competition
Winfield
Fall    (316) 221-3250

Smoky Hill River Festival
Crafts, children's games
Salina
Mid-June    (913) 827-4640

**KENTUCKY**
Celebration of Traditional Music
Berea
Late October    (606) 986-9341

Kentucky Folklife Celebration
Traditional mountain music and dances
Louisville
Early June

**LOUISIANA**
Baton Rouge Blues Festival
Mostly black blues and gospel
Baton Rouge
Late April    (504) 344-8558

Cajun Music Festival
Food, music
Lafayette
3rd week in September

Lagniappe on the Bayou
Cajun-Creole celebration
Chauvin
Mid-October    (504) 594-5859

New Orleans Jazz and Heritage Festival
New Orleans
Mid-April    (504) 522-4786

**MAINE**
Annual Fishermen's Festival
Blessing of the fleet, nautical contests
Boothbay Harbor
Late March    (207) 633-4232

Heritage Days
Community celebration
Bath
Early July    (207) 443-9751

**MARYLAND**
Colonial Highland Gathering
Scottish games, music, dances
Fair Hill
Early June    (302) 731-5100

**MASSACHUSETTS**
Feast of St. Anthony
Italian religious feast
Boston (North End)
July    (617) 742-9547

St. Peter's Fiesta
Italian-Portuguese fishing celebration
Gloucester
3rd week in June    (617) 283-1601

**MICHIGAN**
Ann Arbor Council of Traditional Music and Dance
Ann Arbor
Early September

Wheatland Bluegrass and Old Time Music Festival
Remus
Early September

**MINNESOTA**
Forestville Arts and Crafts Festival
Forestville State Park, Preston
Early June    (507) 765-2219

*Laskiainen*
Finnish celebration: logging, games, music
Palo–Markham
1st weekend in February

Paul Bunyan Festival
Brainerd
Late September    (218) 829-0097

**MISSISSIPPI**
Delta Blues Festival
Black blues, spirituals
Greenville
Early September    (601) 335-3523

Northeast Mississippi Blues and Gospel Festival
Traditional black music
Rust College, Holly Springs
Late September

**MISSOURI**
Frontier Folklife Festival
St. Louis
Mid-September

Missouri State Fiddling Championship
Columbia
Late August

Mountain Folks Music Festival
Music of the Ozarks
Silver Dollar City, Branson
Mid-June    (417) 338-2611

**MONTANA**
Homesteaders Days
Hot Springs
Mid-June    (406) 741-3494

**NEBRASKA**
Camp Creek Antique Machinery and Threshing Show
Old farm machinery, music, games, crafts
Waverly
3rd weekend in July

Kolachs Days
Czech celebration
Verdigre
Mid-June    (402) 668-2266

Wilber Czech Festival
Wilber
Early August    (402) 821-2283

**NEVADA**
Basque Festival
Elko
Early July

**NEW HAMPSHIRE**
Annual League of New Hampshire Craftsman's Fair
Carpentry, musical instruments, stained glass
Mount Sunapee State Park, Newbury
1st week in August    (603) 224-3375

Canterbury Fair
Canterbury Center
Late July

New Hampshire Folk Festival
Concord
Last Sunday in August    (603) 224-2508

**NEW JERSEY**
Middletown Folk Festival
Middletown
Mid-June    (201) 291-9200

New Jersey Folk Festival at Douglass College
New Brunswick
Late April    (201) 745-0077

**NEW MEXICO**
*Feria de Artesanos*
Arts and crafts show
Albuquerque
Late August

Indian Market
Native American crafts show
Santa Fe
Late August    (505) 983-5220

*Jickarilla* Apache Tribal Fair
Dulce
Mid-July

Shalako Dance
Authentic religious ceremony
Zuni Pueblo
1st week in December    (505) 782-4481

**NEW YORK**
Berkshire Mountains Bluegrass Festival
Ancram and Hillsdale
Late July    (617) 492-0415

Festival of North Country Folklife
Robert Moses State Park, Massena
Early August

*Scampagnata Folcloristica Italiana*
Italian-American celebration
ARTPARK, Lewiston
Late June

**NORTH CAROLINA**
Annual Mountain Dance and Folk Festival
Asheville
Early August    (704) 254-1981

Bascom Lamar Lunsford Mountain Music and Dance Festival
One of the oldest folk festivals in America
Mars Hill
Early October    (704) 689-1330

World Champion Old Time Fiddlers Convention
Union Grove
1st week in April    (704) 539-4934

**NORTH DAKOTA**
North Dakota Roughrider Days
Dickinson
Early July    (701) 225-5115

## OHIO

Gambier Folk Festival
Kenyon College, Gambier
Late October    (614) 427-4875

Kent State Folk Festival
Kent
Late February

## OKLAHOMA

American Indian Exposition
Anadarko
Mid-August    (405) 247-3424

Grant's Annual Bluegrass and Oldtime
    Festival
Salt Creek Park, Hugo
Early August    (405) 326-5598

World Series of Fiddling and Bluegrass
    Festival
Powderhorn Park, Langley
Late August    (405) 732-3964

## OREGON

State of Jefferson Days
Historic celebration
Klamath Falls
3 weekends in August    (503) 884-5193

Willamette Valley Folk Festival
University of Oregon, Eugene
Mid-May    (503) 686-4373

## PENNSYLVANIA

Brandywine Mountain Music Convention
Concordville
Mid- to late July    (302) 654-3930

Goshenhoppen Folk Festival
Small authentic Pennsylvania Dutch festival
East Greenville
2nd weekend in August    (215) 754-6013

Harvest Days Festival
Landis Valley Farm Museum
Lancaster
Early October    (717) 569-0401

Pittsburgh Folk Festival
Multi-ethnic celebration
Pittsburgh
Memorial Day weekend    (412) 227-6812

## RHODE ISLAND

Annual Usquepaug Johnnycake Festival
Historic festival
Richmond–South Kingstown
Late October

Blessing of the Fleet Festival
Newport
Late July    (401) 847-1600

Cranberry Festival of the Tomaquag Indians
Exeter
Early October    (401) 539-7795

## SOUTH CAROLINA

Lee County Cotton Pickin Festival
Square dances, cotton picking, gospel music
Bishopville
Mid-October    (803) 484-5302

Piccolo Spoleto Traditional Music Festival
One of the best festivals for fine arts
    lovers
Charleston
Late May–early June

## SOUTH DAKOTA

Black Hills Bluegrass Festival
Nemo
July

Black Hills Steam Show and Threshing Bee
Antique farm machinery, music
Sturgis
Mid-August

South Dakota and Open Fiddling Contest
Yankton
3rd week in September    (605) 665-7290

Steam Threshing Jamboree
Madison
3rd week in August

## TENNESSEE

National Storytelling Festival
Jonesboro
Mid-September    (615) 753-2171

Tennessee Grassroots Days
Centennial Park, Nashville
Late September–early October
    (615) 331-0602

Uncle Dave Macon Days
Traditional music and crafts
Murfreesboro
Early to mid-September    (615) 898-2300

## TEXAS

Annual Border Festival
Music, crafts, Mexican rodeo
El Paso
Early October    (915) 543-7780

Texas Folklife Festival
Mexican and native American folklore,
    crafts
San Antonio
Late July    (512) 226-7651

## UTAH

Festival of the American West
Logan
Early August    (801) 750-1145

Southern Utah Folklife Festival
Springdale
Early September    (801) 328-9681

## VERMONT

"Midsummer"
Traditional music, games, dances
Montpelier
Mid-July    (802) 229-9408

Tunbridge Fair
Tunbridge
September

## VIRGINIA

Blue Ridge Folklife Festival
Ferrum College, Ferrum
Late October    (703) 365-2121

Sara–Maybelle Carter Memorial Festival
Abingdon
Late July–early August    (703) 386-9480

## WASHINGTON

The Festival of American Fiddle Tunes
Port Townsend
Late June–early July    (206) 385-5021

Northwest Regional Folklife Festival
Seattle
3rd week in May    (206) 625-5050

## WEST VIRGINIA

Augusta Festival
Elkins
Early August    (304) 636-0006

Vandalia Gathering
Traditional music, storytelling
State Capitol, Charleston
3rd week in May    (304) 348-0220

## WISCONSIN

Lakefront Summerfest
Multi-ethnic celebration
Summerfest Grounds, Milwaukee
Weekends, July-September
    (414) 273-2680

Polka Festival
Merrill
Mid-June    (715) 536-2974

Swiss Volksfest
Swiss-American celebration
New Glarus
Early August    (608) 527-2095

## WYOMING

Cheyenne Frontier Days
Rodeo, horse racing, covered wagons
Cheyenne
3rd week in July    (307) 634-3321

Wyoming State Fiddle Contest
Shoshoni
Memorial Day weekend

YWCA Ethnic Fest
Rock Springs
Mid-May

## HITTING THE BOOKS

In which states do people read the most? Where do they read the least? Where are the greatest concentrations of books found? Which state spends the most money per capita on its libraries, and which spends the least?

Circulation rate is one way to find out which are America's "readingest" states. Library circulation rates —that is, annual number of checkouts per resident— indicate both how much people read and how successful local libraries are in serving their communities. According to R. R. Bowker's *American Library Directory*, the annual per capita circulation rate in the United States ranges from a low of 1.71 books per person in Mississippi to a high of 9.15 books per person in Iowa.

## Library Circulation Rates in the States

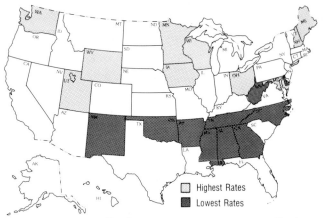

|  | Highest Rates |
|---|---|
| ▩ | Lowest Rates |

| Highest Rates | Checkouts per Capita | Lowest Rates | Checkouts per Capita |
|---|---|---|---|
| 1. Iowa | 9.15 | 1. Mississippi | 1.71 |
| 2. Maryland | 8.10 | 2. Alabama | 2.90 |
| 3. Wyoming | 7.49 | 3. Oklahoma | 2.98 |
| 4. Utah | 6.62 | 4. New Mexico | 3.00 |
| 5. Ohio | 6.60 | 4. Tennessee | 3.00 |
| 6. Minnesota | 6.50 | 6. Arkansas | 3.34 |
| 7. Washington | 6.48 | 7. Georgia | 3.58 |
| 8. New Hampshire | 6.30 | 8. North Carolina | 3.62 |
| 9. Maine | 6.26 | 9. West Virginia | 3.73 |
| 10. Wisconsin | 6.20 | 10. Delaware | 3.80 |

Source: R. R. Bowker, American Library Directory, 1983.

Listed above are states with circulation rates higher than 6.00 and lower than 4.00.

Do circulation rates reflect the availability of library volumes, or does the number of public library books reveal the importance that people in an area attach to collecting and disseminating knowledge? In any event, it is interesting to note that the two states providing the greatest number of public library volumes per capita—Maine and New Hampshire—are also among the states with the highest circulation rates, whereas four of the five states with the fewest library volumes per capita are among those with the lowest circulation rates.

### Per Capita Library Holdings in the States

| Most Books | Volumes per Capita | Fewest Books | Volumes per Capita |
|---|---|---|---|
| 1. Maine | 4.67 | 1. South Carolina | 1.30 |
| 2. New Hampshire | 4.60 | 2. Oklahoma | 1.33 |
| 3. Massachusetts | 4.54 | 3. Tennessee | 1.40 |
| 4. Vermont | 4.01 | 4. Alabama | 1.45 |
|  |  | 4. North Carolina | 1.45 |

Source: R. R. Bowker, American Library Directory, 1983.

Another reflection of how important a region considers its libraries is its annual library expenditures, since library services are often among the first to be cut when a community is looking for ways to reduce expenses. Wyoming leads the states in this category, spending an average of $16.21 per person per year on its libraries; Arkansas spends the least, only $2.94 per person.

### Library Expenditures in the States

| Biggest Spenders | Dollars per Capita per Year | Smallest Spenders | Dollars per Capita per Year |
|---|---|---|---|
| 1. Wyoming | $16.21 | 1. Arkansas | $2.94 |
| 2. New York | 15.42 | 2. South Carolina | 4.01 |
| 3. Maryland | 12.69 | 3. Alabama | 4.67 |
| 4. Connecticut | 12.49 | 4. Tennessee | 4.79 |
| 5. Iowa | 11.93 | 5. Kentucky | 5.00 |
| 6. Washington | 11.71 |  |  |
| 7. Hawaii | 11.70 |  |  |

Source: R. R. Bowker, American Library Directory, 1983.

## A LIBRARY WITH A SURPLUS?

A growing problem in the nation's capital, besides the budget deficit and the national debt, is one of space: many government museums and libraries are running out of room for the mountains of publicly owned artifacts and relics, according to a 1984 issue of U.S. News & World Report.

The Smithsonian Institution, nicknamed the Nation's Attic, has only enough room in its dozen museums open to the public for 1 percent of its possessions. After conducting its first total inventory in 1983 (the project took five years), it discovered 100 million items it didn't know it had. Among the Smithsonian's treasure troves are thousands of preserved fish and birds, which have been laid to rest in liquid-filled bottles and trays. In 20 aircraft hangars outside Washington that are owned by the institution rest spare parts for its antique planes: rotary piston engines, fabric-covered wooden wings, and old propellers and fuselages. There is also a special section housing 10,000 American Indian pots from the nineteenth century.

The National Archives, whose most famous documents are the Declaration of Independence and the Constitution, also has a few other pieces of paper lying around, to wit: three billion documents, five million still pictures, 91 million feet of movie film, and 11 million maps.

The Library of Congress, in the true tradition of great libraries the world over, has a good deal more under its roof than books. But it has some of those, too: 20 million, which sit on 535 *miles* of shelf space. It also has ten million prints and photographs, three million musical scores, 3.8 million maps, 47,000 atlases, and 400,000 newspapers. So you think you've got storage problems?

# Recreation:

## The Best Places to Play

After "Where's that?", the question that chamber of commerce brochure writers find people ask most often about an unfamiliar place is "Is there anything to do there?" No matter where they live, Americans want to make the most of their leisure time. Not for nothing are billions spent each year on everything from video games to insulated jogging clothes, from season tickets at the ballpark to European vacations, from down-filled sleeping bags to graphite fishing rods.

But not everyone can take advantage of the myriad opportunities for recreation. A ski trip to Aspen or a golf weekend at Hilton Head Island is too costly for most people's budgets, and even a backpacking trip in a national park where entrance fees and camping charges are nominal might be out of the question due to the dollars and time it takes to get there and back.

Fortunately, there are many other things to do that are inexpensive and close by. Movies, golf, bowling, and even good restaurants are available nearly every-place in the country; in fact, people living in smaller metro areas usually have better access to these than residents of bigger metro areas. On the other hand, urban crowd pleasers such as zoos, family theme parks, professional sports arenas, and racetracks en-hance leisure living in larger places. For some of us, convenient outdoor recreation in a national forest or along a wild and scenic river is a lucky geographical circumstance; the protected outdoors is a part of the landscape just as developed urban land is. *Places Rated Almanac* looks at each of these kinds of recreation in finding the best places to play in the United States.

## COMMON DENOMINATORS

For scuba diving, the coasts of Florida, California, and Hawaii are your best bets. When it comes to skiing on powdery snow, certain parts of the country are better suited than others because of local topography and climate. The weather and the winds turn other areas into premier places for soaring in gliders. But there are certain kinds of recreation that you can find every-where: dining out at a quality restaurant, a round of weekend golf, bowling at a local tenpin center, or moviegoing at a downtown picture palace or a subur-ban shopping mall.

### Food, Glorious Food

If you're among the one in ten people who enjoys getting out of the house at least once a week for dinner, you might as well go to a worthwhile eatery instead of a portion-controlled Casa de la Maison where distantly prepared frozen packages of beef Wellington and veal *cordon bleu* are microwaved, dished out, and priced at ten times what the restaurant paid for them.

To determine the best metro areas in America for

eating out, *Places Rated* consulted the seven-volume *Mobil Travel Guide,* which since 1958 has rated restaurants across the country. The ratings are derived from two sources: an extensive review of consumer comments, and the inspection reports of field representatives who dine anonymously at establishments throughout the year.

Restaurants are judged on the basis of their food, service, and ambience. Ratings range from one star for a "good, better-than-average" restaurant to five stars for "one of the country's best." Only a very few restaurants receive the coveted five stars in any given year; there were just 11 top-rated restaurants across the nation in 1984.

*Places Rated* gauges access to good restaurants by dividing the resident population by the total number of quality stars awarded by *Mobil Travel Guide* to metro area restaurants. Four one-star restaurants and one three-star restaurant, for example, would yield seven quality stars. Therefore, even though Reno has just 39 rated restaurants—not an overwhelming number when compared with the 249 found in New York, the most of any metro area—it can boast one quality star for every 2,226 residents, the best ratio among the metro areas.

### The 12 Best Metro Areas for Dining Out

| Metro Area | Quality Stars | Residents per Star |
|---|---|---|
| 1. Reno, NV | 87 | 2,226 |
| 2. Salinas–Seaside–Monterey, CA | 87 | 3,338 |
| 3. Portsmouth–Dover–Rochester, NH–ME | 52 | 3,672 |
| 4. Las Vegas, NV | 109 | 4,249 |
| 5. Glens Falls, NY | 22 | 4,984 |
| 6. San Francisco, CA | 286 | 5,030 |
| 7. Rochester, MN | 18 | 5,111 |
| 8. Atlantic City, NJ | 53 | 5,215 |
| 9. Fort Myers, FL | 36 | 5,702 |
| 10. Portland, ME | 32 | 6,057 |
| 11. Burlington, VT | 18 | 6,406 |
| 12. Salem–Gloucester, MA | 38 | 6,797 |

*Source:* Rand McNally & Company, *Mobil Travel Guide* (7 vols.), 1984.

Sixteen metro areas have no restaurants awarded quality ratings by *Mobil Travel Guide:* Anderson, IN; Anderson, SC; Brazoria, TX; Burlington, NC; Danville, VA; Gadsden, AL; Hamilton–Middletown, OH; Houma–Thibodaux, LA; Jacksonville, NC; Jersey City, NJ; Muncie, IN; Panama City, FL; Texarkana, TX–Texarkana, AR; Tyler, TX; Waterbury, CT; and Yakima, WA.

## Public Golf Links

Certainly golf is a common denominator; the game is played in every U.S. metro area, including Anchorage, Alaska. You've got three options when it comes to finding a local golf course on an idle, sunny weekend: the private equity course, which is typically part of a country club open only to members and their guests; daily-fee operations open to all players; and city-built and -operated courses, again open to everyone.

If you're a golfer who can afford to join a private country club with an 18-hole course, you've got one big advantage aside from all the dances and dinners you're paying dues for: You belong to the fortunate 14 percent of golfers who don't have to wait to tee off at a crowded municipal or daily-fee course. Two Florida metro areas (Fort Pierce and West Palm Beach–Boca Raton–Delray Beach) and two affluent suburban metro areas (Lake County, north of Chicago, and Stamford, Connecticut, near New York) have the most 18-hole private equity courses per capita in the nation.

On the other hand, if you're one of the country's 12 million avid golfers who regularly play a round at a local municipal or daily-fee course, only six out of every ten of the nation's 12,000 courses are open to you. Interestingly, the best access to city-owned and -operated courses is not in the upscale metro areas of Texas, California, or the Pacific Northwest but in the small metro areas of the Heartland, in Bismarck, North Dakota; Terre Haute, Indiana; and Waterloo–Cedar Falls, Iowa.

Because access to public golf is an excellent reflection of recreation opportunities in metro areas, *Places Rated* counts the number of local municipal and daily-fee 18-hole (or equivalent) courses per capita.

### Access to Public Links

| The 10 Best Metro Areas | Residents per 18-Hole Course | The 10 Worst Metro Areas | Residents per 18-Hole Course |
|---|---|---|---|
| 1. Sarasota, FL | 10,932 | 1. Anderson, SC | * |
| 2. Jackson, MI | 13,173 | 2. Bristol, CT | * |
| 3. Fort Walton Beach, FL | 13,740 | 3. Gadsden, AL | * |
| 4. Lorain–Elyria, OH | 15,273 | 4. Jersey City, NJ | 1,113,944 |
| 5. Lewiston–Auburn, ME | 16,938 | 5. Portsmouth–Dover–Rochester, NH–ME | 381,876 |
| 6. Grand Rapids, MI | 16,949 | 6. New York, NY | 359,781 |
| 7. Benton Harbor, MI | 17,128 | 7. Houma–Thibodaux, LA | 353,752 |
| 8. Kenosha, WI | 17,591 | 8. Montgomery, AL | 272,867 |
| 9. Rochester, MN | 18,401 | 9. Hagerstown, MD | 226,172 |
| 10. Kalamazoo, MI | 18,468 | 10. Texarkana, TX–Texarkana, AR | 226,134 |

*Source:* National Golf Foundation, unpublished administrative records, 1984.

The national average for public golf is 23,177 residents per 18-hole course.

*These metro areas have no public golf courses.

## Tenpin Bowling

In "Rip Van Winkle," Washington Irving compared the sound of a hardwood ball striking hardwood pins to an ominous clap of thunder. This short story first appeared in 1819, a few years before the sport moved indoors to lanes built in the larger American cities for bowlers, typically Germans, who wanted to play year-round. Bowling has been around a long, long time indeed, and, in all its variations—skittles, fivepins, ninepins, tenpins, candlepins, duckpins—is probably played by more of the world's people than any other game, with the possible exception of soccer.

Nearly 70 million people in the United States take a turn each year at tenpins, the dominant bowling variation. But if the 8,500 bowling centers in this country had to depend solely on this kind of casual participation, many might quickly convert to tanning salons or microcomputer showrooms for a steadier income. The credit for keeping bowling alleys in business goes to such highly organized competitive associations as the American Bowling Congress (ABC), to which 4.5 million men belong, and the Women's International Bowling Congress, with 3.9 million female members, which promote frequent tournaments throughout the country.

Ninety-nine percent of the tenpin bowling centers in this country are certified by the ABC for tournament competition. To rate metro areas for access to tenpin bowling, *Places Rated* compares the number of lanes with the local population. Metro areas that lead the country in this common denominator are typically smaller, blue-collar metro areas in the Frost Belt, where indoor sports and active teams thrive.

### Access to Tenpin Bowling

| The 10 Best Metro Areas | Residents per Lane | The 10 Worst Metro Areas | Residents per Lane |
|---|---|---|---|
| 1. Green Bay, WI | 487 | 1. Boston, MA | 16,313 |
| 2. Milwaukee, WI | 489 | 2. Portland, ME | 13,845 |
| 3. Daytona Beach, FL | 520 | 3. Birmingham, AL | 6,596 |
| 4. Appleton–Oshkosh–Neenah, WI | 540 | 4. Galveston–Texas City, TX | 6,123 |
| 5. Ocala, FL | 572 | 5. Jackson, MS | 5,839 |
| 6. Kalamazoo, MI | 625 | 6. Fresno, CA | 5,306 |
| 7. Elmira, NY | 660 | 7. Laredo, TX | 4,962 |
| 8. Davenport–Rock Island–Moline, IA–IL | 676 | 8. McAllen–Edinburg–Mission, TX | 4,720 |
| 9. Canton, OH | 679 | 9. Springfield, IL | 4,694 |
| 10. Erie, PA | 682 | 10. Florence, SC | 4,590 |

*Source:* American Bowling Congress, unpublished data, 1984.

The national average for tenpin bowling lanes is one for every 1,556 people.

## Moviegoing

Does anyone remember when John Huston won two Academy Awards—best director and best screenplay—for *The Treasure of Sierra Madre?* And his father, Walter, was named best supporting actor for his performance as the grizzled old prospector in the same film? The year was 1948. Jane Wyman won an Oscar that year, too, for her role in *Johnny Belinda; Hamlet* got best picture, and its star, Laurence Olivier, was named best actor.

Thirty plus years ago, moviegoing was the American thing to do of an evening, any evening. Spilled popcorn was regularly swept up from the aisles between shows, the next John Wayne or Spencer Tracy film was announced on a large easel near the candy counter in the lobby, ushers in uniform took you to your seat with a red-lensed flashlight, and you always got a Fox Movietone or Pathé newsreel with the film. There were 18,631 motion picture theaters in 1948, most of them small neighborhood houses, with a few downtown palaces for premieres and first-run screenings. Never again would there be so many, for 1948 also marked the commercial appearance of television.

Today there are fewer than 8,000 commercial four-

wall (as opposed to drive-in) movie theaters in the United States. If you adjust for ticket-price inflation, paid attendance has declined from $4.1 billion in the late 1940s to $1.1 billion in the last few years.

*Places Rated* divides a metro area's population by the number of four-wall theaters to determine local access to movies. Many of these establishments may be of the multiscreen, Cinema Six variety found in suburban shopping malls, but most are still the single-screen Bijou or Strand kind of neighborhood theater.

### Access to Movie Theaters

| The 10 Best Metro Areas | Residents per Theater | The 10 Worst Metro Areas | Residents per Theater |
|---|---|---|---|
| 1. Grand Forks, ND | 11,017 | 1. Utica–Rome, NY | 160,090 |
| 2. Killeen–Temple, TX | 13,416 | 2. Scranton–Wilkes-Barre, PA | 104,114 |
| 3. Des Moines, IA | 14,137 | 3. Pittsfield, MA | 83,490 |
| 4. Charlottesville, VA | 14,196 | 4. Lowell, MA–NH | 81,047 |
| 5. San Francisco, CA | 15,039 | 5. Niagara Falls, NY | 75,785 |
| 6. Bellingham, WA | 15,243 | 6. Washington, DC–MD–VA | 73,882 |
| 7. Abilene, TX | 15,847 | 7. Bristol, CT | 73,762 |
| 8. Salinas–Seaside–Monterey, CA | 16,136 | 8. Louisville, KY–IN | 73,597 |
| 9. Iowa City, IA | 16,343 | 9. Lancaster, PA | 72,469 |
| 10. Eau Claire, WI | 16,367 | 10. Chattanooga, TN–GA | 71,090 |

*Source:* Derived from the U.S. Bureau of the Census, *1977 Census of Selected Service Establishments,* 1981, and *County Business Patterns,* 1983–1984.

The national average is 24,580 residents per theater.

## CROWD PLEASERS

At different times of the year, a resident of the Los Angeles–Long Beach metro area can view the animals at the Los Angeles Zoo; sample the varied offerings at Marineland of the Pacific and the Universal Studios Tour; watch auto racing at the Long Beach Grand Prix; bet on the horses at two racetracks; or take in professional baseball, football, basketball, and hockey, as well as NCAA Division I competition.

Few metro areas have as varied a supply of crowd pleasers as Los Angeles–Long Beach, but some of these opportunities are common in many of the larger metro areas. From Disneyland in Anaheim to New York's Bronx Zoo, these assets offer Americans interesting ways to spend their leisure time.

### Seeing the Animals: Zoos and Aquariums

The two best metro areas for seeing the animals are Chicago and San Diego. Each has not one but two of the country's top-ranked zoological parks. Altogether, 114 metro areas have at least one zoo. The idea that zoos enhance people's lives is a European one that flourishes especially well in America's Midwest. Besides Chicago's two great zoos, the Cincinnati, Cleveland, Detroit, Milwaukee, and St. Louis zoological parks are among the best in the United States. It is not coincidental that the working-class citizens of these cities can trace their roots to European countries—particularly Germany—that also have great zoos.

"Postage-stamp collecting" is the name that zookeepers give to the assembling of colorful animal specimens without regard to whether the animals would fit and thrive in a zoo's limited space. This was once a sure way of drawing more patrons and carving out a reputation as an outstanding institution. Today, professionally run zoos have fewer species on exhibit but more specimens of each. The standard phylogenetic exhibits (grouping African lions with Bengal tigers, timber wolves with hyenas) are being replaced with ecological displays (wildlife in desert or mountain environments) and behavioral exhibits (hibernation, burrowing, nocturnalism) that group specimens more creatively and openly.

This isn't to say that zoos no longer maintain large, diverse collections, for the best American zoos are those with the biggest animal populations. But today the benchmark of a zoo's quality isn't simply how many animals it can keep or breed; just as important is how creatively and naturally the animals are exhibited.

Fifteen American zoos are visited by at least a million people each year. All of them are city- or society-owned, and several are so well known that they attract many tourists.

### The 15 Most Popular Zoos

| | Visitors per Year |
|---|---|
| 1. Lincoln Park Zoo (Chicago) | 4,800,000 |
| 2. National Zoological Park (Washington, D.C.) | 3,300,000 |
| 3. San Diego Zoo | 3,000,000 |
| 4. Bronx Zoo (New York) | 2,000,000 |
| 4. Forest Park Zoo (St. Louis) | 2,000,000 |
| 6. Houston Zoological Gardens | 1,800,000 |
| 7. Brookfield Zoo (Brookfield, IL) | 1,700,000 |
| 8. Los Angeles Zoo | 1,414,000 |
| 9. Wild Animal Park (San Diego) | 1,300,000 |
| 10. Honolulu Zoo | 1,100,000 |
| 10. Milwaukee County Zoo | 1,100,000 |
| 10. Philadelphia Zoological Gardens | 1,100,000 |
| 13. Denver Zoological Gardens | 1,000,000 |
| 13. Minnesota Zoological Gardens (Minneapolis) | 1,000,000 |
| 13. San Antonio Zoo and Aquarium | 1,000,000 |

*Source:* American Association of Zoological Parks and Aquariums, *Zoological Parks and Aquariums in the Americas, 1982–83,* 1983.

Aquariums are far less common than zoos in the United States; in fact, only ten of the 329 metro areas can boast one: Baltimore, Boston, Chicago, Cleveland, Dallas, Honolulu, New York, San Francisco, Seattle, and Tacoma. Not surprisingly, seven of these metro areas are found in states with ocean coastlines. Unlike the great zoological parks, which are run municipally or by societies, some of the best aquariums (including Boston's New England Aquarium) are owned and operated for profit by private firms.

### Family Theme Parks

The person who started it all was Walter Elias Disney; his creation was Disneyland. Because he ignored such time-honored features as a waterfront location and games of chance and skill, the amusement park indus-

try viewed his 180-acre playland skeptically when it opened in Anaheim, California, in 1954. Disney's purpose was to use his famous cartoon characters and feature films as themes to structure a family-centered park more carefully than such parks as Chicago's Riverview or Ocean Park in Santa Monica, places avoided by families because of their tawdriness and cheap, carny atmosphere. That he succeeded is obvious; today, Disneyland and Walt Disney World in Florida—which includes the Magic Kingdom, opened in 1971, and Epcot Center, opened in 1982—together attract more than 22 million people a year.

Of the nearly 100 parks in the United States that market themselves as family theme parks, there are 25 that each draw more than one million visitors a year. Twenty-two metro areas have at least one theme park with this many annual visitors. These extremely popular parks are located near or in large metro areas, but they aren't havens for locals in the way that traditional parks such as Elitch Gardens in Denver, Salt Lake City's Lagoon Amusement Park, or Lake Pontchartrain Beach in New Orleans still are. Rather, theme parks are nationally advertised vacation-industry attractions.

Two "vacation" states—California and Florida—have ten of the top 25 theme parks, attracting more than half of the country's annual 75 million theme-park visitors. In these states, some parks' owners have chosen their locations strategically. The Orlando metro area, for example, is home not only to Walt Disney World & Epcot Center but also Sea World of Florida, which located there to take advantage of Disney World's draw. In Southern California, Knott's Berry Farm, a traditional roadside attraction since 1920, converted to theme-park format and joined Sea World of California and Six Flags Magic Mountain in trying to capitalize on Disneyland's crowds.

### The Auto-Racing Circuit

America's celebrated love affair with fast cars started in Providence, Rhode Island, where the first automobile track race was sponsored in 1896. The affair hasn't ended, at least not for cars that hit 200 miles an hour on oval tracks. Last year, the 250,000 reserved seats for the Indianapolis 500 were sold out weeks before the race, in most instances at $55 per ticket. Whether on a "short eight" crash track in rural Oregon or a banked concrete oval in the Deep South, auto racing in all its variations draws millions each year.

Of the 1,100 auto racetracks in the United States, only a fraction are sanctioned by one or more of the three leading racing organizations: NASCAR, SCCA, and USAC. NASCAR, the National Association for Stock Car Racing, sanctions late-model and modified stock-car racing; SCCA, the Sports Car Club of America, has jurisdiction over sports-car events; and USAC, the United States Automobile Club, sanctions Indy, dirt-car, sprint-car, midget, and late-model racing.

Among the 58 metro areas with sanctioned tracks,

## The 25 Most Popular Theme Parks

| Park (Opening Year) | Operating Schedule | Annual Visitors | Park (Opening Year) | Operating Schedule | Annual Visitors |
|---|---|---|---|---|---|
| 1. **Walt Disney World & Epcot Center** (1971)—Orlando, FL | 365 days | 12,560,000 | 14. **Opryland USA** (1972) Nashville, TN | 140 days | 2,290,000 |
| 2. **Disneyland** (1954) Anaheim, CA | 303 days | 10,420,000 | 15. **Six Flags Over Georgia** (1967)—Atlanta, GA | 148 days | 2,180,000 |
| 3. **Knott's Berry Farm** (1920) Buena Park, CA | 365 days | 4,000,000 | 16. **Busch Gardens—The Old Country** (1975) Williamsburg, VA | 137 days | 1,920,000 |
| 4. **Universal Studios Tour** (1964)—Los Angeles, CA | 365 days | 3,450,000 | 17. **Marriott's Great America** (1976)—Santa Clara, CA | 141 days | 1,760,000 |
| 5. **Busch Gardens—The Dark Continent** (1959)—Tampa, FL | 365 days | 3,080,000 | 18. **Astroworld** (1968) Houston, TX | 159 days | 1,660,000 |
| 6. **Sea World of Florida** (1973) Orlando, FL | 365 days | 3,000,000 | 19. **Hersheypark** (1907) Hershey, PA | 120 days | 1,480,000 |
| 7. **Six Flags Great Adventure** (1974)—Jackson, NJ | 163 days | 2,760,000 | 20. **Worlds of Fun** (1973) Kansas City, MO · | 140 days | 1,400,000 |
| 8. **Cedar Point** (1960) Sandusky, OH | 119 days | 2,630,000 | 21. **Sea World of Ohio** (1970) Aurora, OH | 100 days | 1,170,000 |
| 9. **Kings Island** (1972) Cincinnati, OH | 126 days | 2,601,000 | 22. **Six Flags Over Mid-America** (1971)—St. Louis, MO | 140 days | 1,120,000 |
| 10. **Six Flags Magic Mountain** (1971)—Valencia, CA | 185 days | 2,570,000 | 23. **Carowinds** (1973) Charlotte, NC | 121 days | 1,113,000 |
| 11. **Sea World of California** (1964)—San Diego, CA | 365 days | 2,560,000 | 24. **Cypress Gardens** (1936) Winter Haven, FL | 365 days | 1,112,000 |
| 12. **Six Flags Great America** (1976)—Gurnee, IL | 120 days | 2,370,000 | 25. **Kings Dominion** (1975) Richmond, VA | 121 days | 1,011,000 |
| 13. **Six Flags Over Texas** (1961) Arlington, TX | 146 days | 2,330,000 | | | |

*Source:* Kings Entertainment Company, 1984, and Merrill Lynch, *Theme Park Industry Survey*, 1983.

Indianapolis deserves its title of automobile-racing center. Besides the famous Brickyard—the Indianapolis Motor Speedway—the Hoosier capital has three other sanctioned tracks. Nine other metro areas have two tracks: Colorado Springs, Colorado; Flint, Michigan; Greensboro–Winston-Salem–High Point, North Carolina; Johnson City–Kingsport–Bristol, Tennessee–Virginia; Las Vegas; Nassau–Suffolk, New York; Portland, Oregon; Richmond–Petersburg, Virginia; and Seattle.

### Pari-Mutuel Betting: Win, Place, or Show Payoffs

The biggest spectator sport in the United States is pari-mutuel racing at the track. Based on a system in which the players who bet on the first-, second-, and third-place finishers share the total amount of money bet, pari-mutuel racing draws nearly 100 million people each year. Eighty-six metro areas offer pari-mutuel betting.

Thoroughbred racing dominates the American racing scene. There are 4,967 days of racing at the country's 83 Thoroughbred tracks, exclusive of county fairs. The ten listed nearby draw the biggest daily crowds. Number 10, Ak-Sar-Ben (Nebraska spelled backwards), is an 85-day, nonprofit civic meet held near downtown Omaha that usually attracts more than a million racegoers. In the Los Angeles–Long Beach metro area, Santa Anita Park's two-part season draws close to four million spectators. Aqueduct's three-part season is one of the longest in Thoroughbred racing, and although attendance has fallen over the years, the track still draws more spectators than do the New York Yankees across town in the Bronx.

Standardbred horses are entered in harness racing; jockeys ride behind the horses in small, two-wheeled carts. Harness racing competes with Thoroughbred racing for the racegoer's wager in 13 states. Its annual following at the track is a good deal smaller than that of Thoroughbred racing (45 million versus 26 million racegoers). However, in Delaware, upstate New York, Michigan, and the Chicago environs, pacing and trotting races attract more bettors and a greater cash total in bets than their Thoroughbred competition, and in Canada they outdraw Thoroughbred races two to one.

The country cousin of the more citified and patrician Thoroughbred contests, quarter-horse racing usually takes place at state and county fairs. It gets its name from the wide-open quarter-mile sprint the horses run on the track. Sixteen states permit betting on quarter-horse races, usually on mixed programs with Thoroughbred races. The sport is more popular in the West and Northwest than in any other region.

Dog racing evolved from the early sport of coursing, in which two greyhounds were released together in pursuit of a hare. Modern greyhound racing stems from a 1904 coursing contest held in South Dakota. Its sponsor, Owen Patrick Smith, developed a strong distaste for the killing of hares and spent the next 15 years adapting a mechanical lure to the inside rail of an oval track. The lure now resembles a rabbit and moves around the track on an electric rail. Since greyhounds chase by sight rather than scent, it has proven to be effective.

Of the country's 45 greyhound tracks, there are ten that account for half of dog racing's 23 million annual

### The 10 Most Popular Thoroughbred Tracks

| Track | Average Daily Attendance | Average Bet |
|---|---|---|
| 1. Santa Anita Park (Arcadia, CA) | 32,013 | $163 |
| 2. Hollywood Park (Inglewood, CA) | 28,891 | 180 |
| 3. Saratoga (Saratoga Springs, NY) | 26,644 | 112 |
| 4. Oaklawn Jockey Club (Hot Springs, AR) | 23,271 | 129 |
| 5. Del Mar (Del Mar, CA) | 19,584 | 167 |
| 6. Belmont Park (Elmont, NY) | 19,530 | 177 |
| 7. Aqueduct (New York) | 14,749 | 204 |
| 8. Meadowlands (East Rutherford, NJ) | 14,233 | 151 |
| 9. Gulfstream Park (Hallandale, FL) | 14,074 | 151 |
| 10. Ak-Sar-Ben (Omaha) | 13,655 | 118 |

Source: *Daily Racing Form*, March 26, 1984, and Thoroughbred Racing Associations of North America, Inc., *Directory and Record Book*, 1984.

### The 10 Most Popular Harness Tracks

| Track | Average Daily Attendance | Average Bet |
|---|---|---|
| 1. Meadowlands (East Rutherford, NJ) | 16,010 | $145 |
| 2. Sportsman's Park (Cicero, IL) | 8,988 | 132 |
| 3. Roosevelt Raceway (Westbury, NY) | 7,873 | 168 |
| 4. Hollywood Park (Inglewood, CA) | 7,805 | 127 |
| 5. Hawthorne (Cicero, IL) | 7,179 | 150 |
| 6. Yonkers Raceway (Yonkers, NY) | 6,441 | 204 |
| 7. Maywood Park (Maywood, IL) | 6,135 | 139 |
| 8. Los Alamitos (Cypress, CA) | 5,499 | 150 |
| 9. Pompano Park (Pompano Beach, FL) | 5,492 | 88 |
| 10. Hazel Park (Hazel Park, MI) | 5,200 | 140 |

Source: U.S. Trotting Association, *Trotting and Pacing Guide*, 1984.

### The 10 Most Popular Greyhound Tracks

| Track | Average Daily Attendance | Average Bet |
|---|---|---|
| 1. Wonderland (Revere, MA) | 1,247,653 | $119 |
| 2. Southland Greyhound Park (West Memphis, AR) | 1,189,108 | 108 |
| 3. Lincoln Greyhound Park (Lincoln, RI) | 1,159,070 | 101 |
| 4. St. Petersburg Kennel Club (St. Petersburg) | 1,045,078 | 92 |
| 5. Hollywood Greyhound Track (Hallandale, FL) | 1,043,201 | 108 |
| 6. Wheeling Downs Greyhound Park (Wheeling, WV) | 929,243 | 118 |
| 7. Plainfield Greyhound Park (Plainfield, CT) | 867,773 | 131 |
| 8. Biscayne Greyhound Park (Miami, FL) | 832,963 | 125 |
| 9. Tampa Greyhound Park (Tampa) | 749,318 | 114 |
| 10. Mobile Greyhound Park (Mobile) | 728,305 | 106 |

Source: American Greyhound Track Operators Association, *Directory*, 1984.

attendance. Wonderland is a ten-minute subway ride from downtown Boston. Plainfield Greyhound Park, near Hartford, is Connecticut's sole pari-mutuel racetrack. The only place where people in western Tennessee, northern Mississippi, and northeastern Arkansas can make a legal bet is at Southland Greyhound Park, on the Arkansas side of the Mississippi River, near Memphis.

### Rooting for the Home Team

A frequent topic of discussion on talk shows, in bars, and at work is where the "good" sports towns are. The question is usually argued from one of two perspectives: whether a town has teams with winning records, or whether fans turn out to root for the teams. These two trends are often linked: Over the regular seasons, the clubs with the best attendance usually also have had some of the best records.

Another way to find the best sports towns is to measure the access that a metro area's fans have to regular-season games. "Game seats per capita" is an elementary measurement used most often in professional sports franchising and marketing, especially at expansion time. This figure is found by multiplying the number of home games played by all the teams in a metro area (for example, 81 baseball; 41 basketball; 8 football) by the combined seating capacity of the teams' playing arenas and then dividing that number by the metro area's population.

*Professional Sports.* In arriving at a figure for game seats per capita at professional sporting events, *Places Rated* surveyed each of the 132 metro areas with major-league or minor-league teams in any of four sports: baseball, basketball, football, and hockey. For example, the number of regular-season football games played by the Indianapolis Colts multiplied by the Hoosier Dome's capacity is 480,000. The same calculations yield a figure of 1,037,000 for NBA Pacers basketball and Checkers minor-league hockey games played in Market Square Arena, and 995,918 for Indians minor-league baseball games played at Bush Stadium. The sum of these four figures divided by Indianapolis's metro area population is 2.154, or a little more than two game seats for everyone in the eight-county metro area. Other metro areas have better averages, and in each of them the presence of a baseball team, with its large stadium and long playing season, makes a good deal of difference.

The New York State metro area of Glens Falls has the highest figure for game seats per capita of any metro area due to its White Sox baseball team and Adirondack Reds hockey club, both minor league, combined with its population of 109,649. But if you're interested in major-league sports, consider Denver: Its NBA Nuggets, USFL Gold, and NFL Broncos—as well as minor-league baseball and hockey teams—give it the best game-seats rating of metro areas with major-league clubs.

**Access to Professional Sports:
The Top 15 Metro Areas**

| Metro Area | Game Seats per Capita | Metro Area | Game Seats per Capita |
|---|---|---|---|
| 1. Glens Falls, NY* | 9.421 | 9. Cleveland, OH | 3.926 |
| 2. Denver, CO | 5.890 | 10. Milwaukee, WI | 3.824 |
| 3. Kansas City, MO | 5.030 | 11. Hagerstown, MD* | 3.714 |
| 4. Honolulu, HI* | 4.721 | 12. San Francisco, CA | 3.484 |
| 5. Billings, MT* | 4.716 | | |
| 6. Buffalo, NY | 4.608 | 13. Burlington, VT* | 3.460 |
| 7. Seattle, WA | 4.405 | 14. Cincinnati, OH–KY–IN | 3.369 |
| 8. Fort Worth–Arlington, TX | 4.161 | | |
| | | 15. Portland, ME* | 3.304 |

*Source:* Derived from professional sports media guides.

One hundred thirty-two metro areas have professional sports teams.

*These metro areas have only minor-league teams.

*Collegiate Sports.* Among the biggest crowd pleasers around are the varsity teams fielded by American colleges and universities. The cream of those is generally found among the teams classified Division I (split into Divisions I–A and I–AA for football only) by the National Collegiate Athletic Association (NCAA). Eligibility for this division is based on the quality of a school's typical opponent, or "schedule strength," and game attendance figures.

Nearly 37 million fans attended the 3,224 regular-season games played by the 649 colleges and universities with varsity football teams in 1983. Although the 189 Division I–A and I–AA teams played only one third of these games, they drew 83 percent of the attendance that year. Basketball is even more widely available. Some 32 million fans came out for the 16,108 regular-season and tournament games played by the 1,266 schools that had men's varsity basketball teams in 1983. The 274 NCAA Division I teams played one quarter of these games, yet they accounted for 65 percent of total attendance.

Division I football or basketball is on view in 150 of

the 329 metro areas, from the Cowboys of Hardin-Simmons in Abilene to the Penguins of Youngstown State. Using game seats per capita as the criterion, the best metro area for NCAA Division I football and basketball is Lawrence, Kansas. The number of University of Kansas Jayhawks games played at home multiplied by the seating capacities of Memorial Stadium (football) and Allen Fieldhouse (basketball) yield a figure of 465,498, or almost seven game seats for everyone in town and in surrounding Douglas County.

**Access to NCAA Division I Sports:
The Top 15 Metro Areas**

| Metro Area | Game Seats per Capita | Metro Area | Game Seats per Capita |
|---|---|---|---|
| 1. Lawrence, KS | 6.882 | 9. Tuscaloosa, AL | 3.752 |
| 2. Iowa City, IA | 5.863 | 10. Fayetteville–Springdale, AR | 3.533 |
| 3. Columbia, MO | 5.212 | | |
| 4. Bloomington, IN | 4.953 | 11. Champaign–Urbana–Rantoul, IL | 3.357 |
| 5. Bryan–College Station, TX | 4.888 | | |
| | | 12. Las Cruces, NM | 3.341 |
| 6. State College, PA | 4.545 | 13. Ann Arbor, MI | 3.264 |
| 7. Lafayette, IN | 4.351 | 14. Gainesville, FL | 3.011 |
| 8. Athens, GA | 4.131 | 15. Charlottesville, VA | 2.902 |

*Source:* National Collegiate Athletic Association, *NCAA Basketball* and *NCAA Football*, 1984.

One hundred fifty metro areas have NCAA Division I football or basketball teams.

## OUTDOOR RECREATION ASSETS

To many people, recreation is not something that takes place within four walls or in the middle of a crowded city. Instead, it means turning to the open spaces for fishing, boating, swimming, hiking, running, picnicking, or getting away from it all. Just as some metro areas have more to offer in urban recreation, others undeniably are richer in access to the great outdoors.

### Coastlines and Inland Water

Sooners boast that Oklahoma has so many impounded lakes of every size that if you were to tip the state to the south a bit, the water would flow out and flood Texas for a good while. And Maryland crabbers point out to newcomers that the true length of estuarine shore reached by the Chesapeake Bay's tide would total more than 8,000 miles if all the bends and kinks were straightened out.

You'll spot inland water in nine out of ten of America's metro areas. Aside from being a basic necessity of life, water can be a scenic and recreational amenity if there is enough of it to fish in, boat on, and swim in if the temperature is right. Where would Reno be without Lake Tahoe?

Or Nassau–Suffolk, New York, without Long Island Sound? Four of every five Americans today are congregated together in metro areas within 100 miles of an ocean or Great Lakes coastline; by the end of the decade, the U.S. Department of the Interior predicts, three of every four will live within 50 miles of a

---

**Average Ticket Prices for Professional Sports**

**Baseball**
Highest: $6.75 (Baltimore Orioles, Milwaukee Brewers, New York Yankees)
Lowest: $4.00 (Toronto Blue Jays)

**Basketball**
Highest: $15.50 (Los Angeles Lakers)
Lowest: $6.60 (Indiana Pacers)

**Football**
Highest: $17.75 (Los Angeles Raiders, San Diego Chargers)
Lowest: $10.75 (Cincinnati Bengals)

**Hockey**
Highest: $16.84 (New York Islanders)
Lowest: $8.50 (Buffalo Sabres)

*Source:* H. L. Klein, *People and Properties*, 1984.

Prices are for the 1983 season.

coastline. Ocean or Great Lakes coastlines form part of the peripheries of 84 metro areas and 100 percent of one, Honolulu.

### Large Areas of Inland Water

| Metro Area | Inland Water Area | Percent of Total Surface Area |
|---|---|---|
| 1. Galveston–Texas City, TX | 265 sq mi | 66% |
| 2. New Orleans, LA | 1,265 | 53 |
| 3. Jersey City, NJ | 16 | 34 |
| 4. Melbourne–Titusville– Palm Bay, FL | 299 | 30 |
| 5. Brownsville–Harlingen, TX | 263 | 29 |
| 5. Burlington, VT | 132 | 29 |
| 5. Salt Lake City–Ogden, UT | 478 | 29 |
| 8. West Palm Beach–Boca Raton– Delray Beach, FL | 555 | 28 |
| 9. Fort Myers, FL | 220 | 27 |
| 10. Houma–Thibodaux, LA | 633 | 25 |
| 10. San Francisco, CA | 250 | 25 |
| 12. Nassau–Suffolk, NY | 290 | 24 |
| 13. Portland, ME | 113 | 20 |
| 14. Bremerton, WA | 77 | 19 |
| 14. Wilmington, NC | 34 | 19 |

Source: U.S. Bureau of the Census, Area Measurements, Series G-20, 1962–67.

Inland water area includes ponds and lakes of surface area greater than 40 acres; streams, canals, and rivers if width is one eighth of a mile or greater; water area along irregular Great Lakes and ocean coastlines, if bays, inlets, and estuaries are between one and ten miles wide.

### National Forests, Parks, and Wildlife Refuges

Some of the most popular outdoor activities—driving for pleasure, walking, picnicking, sight-seeing, bird watching, nature walking, and fishing—would probably be even more enjoyable in the country's splendid system of national forests, parks, and wildlife refuges.

There are 155 national forests and 19 national grasslands on 191 million acres in the United States. The main purpose of the National Forest System is silviculture: growing wood, harvesting it carefully, and preserving naturally beautiful areas. Within the forest system are more than a quarter of a million miles of roads, built not only for loggers but for everyone. They lead to a wide variety of recreation outlets: ski resorts, marinas, fishing lakes and streams, hiking trails, and campgrounds.

In contrast to the National Forest System, the National Park System is meant expressly for recreation. The founding of Yellowstone National Park in 1872 marked the beginning of the oldest and now the largest national park system in the world. It comprises 334 national parks, preserves, monuments, memorials, battlefields, seashores, riverways, and trails that together cover some 79 million acres.

Whereas the National Park System acts to keep irreplaceable geographical and historical treasures in the public domain, the national wildlife refuges protect native flora and fauna from people. There are 413 of these remarkable sanctuaries throughout the country,

embracing more than 87 million acres. Most of them are open to the public for a variety of wildlife activities, particularly photography and nature observation. In certain of the refuges and at irregular times, fishing and hunting are permitted, depending on the size of the wild populations. Although the majority of the nation's wildlife refuges are located in open, sometimes remote country, they aren't exclusively a rural amenity. Several can be found within metropolitan areas, such as the Nisqually National Wildlife Refuge in Olympia, Washington, and San Pablo Bay National Wildlife Refuge in the California metro area of Santa Rosa–Petaluma.

## JUDGING RECREATIONAL OPPORTUNITIES

Is there more to do in Houston than in Dallas? How do the California rivals of Los Angeles and San Francisco compare for recreation? Or Jacksonville and Tampa–St. Pete? To answer these questions, Places Rated Almanac examines three categories of assets—Common Denominators (quality restaurants, golf, bowling, and movies), Crowd Pleasers (zoos, aquariums, theme parks, automobile racing, pari-mutuel betting, and professional and collegiate sports), and Outdoor Recreation Assets (miles of coastline, inland water area,

### Outdoor Recreation Assets: 17 Outstanding Metro Areas

| Metro Area | Coastline (mi) | Inland Water Area (sq mi) | Acres in National Parks, Forests, Wildlife Refuges |
|---|---|---|---|
| Anchorage, AK | 90 | 36.0 | 275,000 |
| Bellingham, WA | — | 53.7 | 841,958 |
| Brownsville–Harlingen, TX | 31 | 262.9 | 45,451 |
| Eugene–Springfield, OR | 30 | 48.1 | 1,416,153 |
| Fort Collins–Loveland, CO | — | 29.7 | 766,568 |
| Galveston–Texas City, TX | 25 | 165.0 | — |
| Houma–Thibodaux, LA | 79 | 632.8 | — |
| Melbourne–Titusville– Palm Bay, FL | 72 | 299.0 | 35,733 |
| Miami–Hialeah, FL | 84 | 67.1 | 605,117 |
| New Orleans, LA | 75 | 1,265.2 | 32,948 |
| Provo–Orem, UT | — | 126.9 | 485,642 |
| Salt Lake City–Ogden, UT | — | 477.5 | 201,480 |
| San Francisco, CA | 75 | 249.6 | 127,278 |
| Santa Barbara–Santa Maria–Lompoc, CA | 78 | 7.5 | 754,425 |
| Seattle, WA | 70 | 89.1 | 966,533 |
| Tacoma, WA | 15 | 113.1 | 365,990 |
| Visalia–Tulare– Porterville, CA | — | 3.0 | 1,403,459 |

Listed above in alphabetical order are the metro areas earning the maximum 2,000 points for their supply of Outdoor Recreation Assets. (See the section "Judging Recreational Opportunities," below, for an explanation of how Places Rated points are calculated.)

and acreage in national forests, parks, and wildlife refuges).

In rating the metro areas for their recreational opportunities, *Places Rated* has introduced a number of elements that were not included in the first edition of this book. In the Common Denominators category, access to good restaurants has replaced access to neighborhood bars. The Crowd Pleasers category has been expanded to include minor-league teams and NCAA Division I basketball and football. The all-new category of Outdoor Recreation Assets provides a more well rounded view of an area's leisure-time options.

Like the chapters on health care, transportation, and the arts, this chapter's rating system now allows for bonus points to be awarded to metro areas that are part of a Consolidated Metropolitan Statistical Area (a complete list is in the Appendix). CMSA Access points are *Places Rated*'s way of recognizing that certain outstanding facilities can be enjoyed by people within a relatively wide radius. In the case of recreation, each metro area that is part of a CMSA is eligible to receive points for the Crowd Pleasers assets located in neighboring metro areas, as explained in item 15 below.

In the categories of Common Denominators and Crowd Pleasers, metro areas are awarded points not for their number of facilities but rather for how available these facilities are to residents. Access to these different events is given a rating of AA, A, B, or C (AA indicating the best access and C the worst), and those ratings mean a certain number of points for the metro area: 400 for an AA rating, 300 for A, 200 for B, and 100 for C. The exceptions to this rule—zoos, aquariums, and auto racing—are explained below. For Outdoor Recreation Assets, metro areas earn points according to a different system, also delineated below.

Each metro area starts with a base score of zero, to which points are added according to the following criteria:

1. *Good restaurants.*

| A metro area gets a rating of: | If there is one quality star for every: |
|---|---|
| AA | 14,000 or fewer people |
| A | 14,001–20,000 people |
| B | 20,001–32,500 people |
| C | 32,501 or more people |

2. *Public golf courses.*

| A metro area gets a rating of: | If there is one 18-hole course for every: |
|---|---|
| AA | 20,000 or fewer people |
| A | 20,001–25,000 people |
| B | 25,001–40,000 people |
| C | 40,001 or more people |

3. *Certified tenpin bowling lanes.*

| A metro area gets a rating of: | If there is one lane for every: |
|---|---|
| AA | 950 or fewer people |
| A | 951–1,300 people |
| B | 1,301–3,000 people |
| C | 3,001 or more people |

4. *Movie theaters.*

| A metro area gets a rating of: | If there is one theater for every: |
|---|---|
| AA | 25,000 or fewer people |
| A | 25,001–32,500 people |
| B | 32,501–45,000 people |
| C | 45,001 or more people |

5. *Zoos.* Metro areas with zoos are rated by criteria based on the size of their collections as listed in the directory of member zoos of the American Association of Zoological Parks and Aquariums.

| A metro area gets a rating of: | If the collections in its zoo(s) include: |
|---|---|
| AA | 1,500 or more specimens, of which 500 are mammals of at least 250 species, and its annual operating budget exceeds $4 million |
| A | 750 to 1,499 specimens, of which 300 are mammals of at least 150 species, and its annual operating budget falls between $1.5 and $3.9 million |
| B | 300 to 749 specimens, of which 150 are mammals of at least 50 species, and its annual operating budget falls between $750,000 and $1.49 million |
| C | Fewer than 300 specimens, and its annual operating budget is less than $749,999 |

These standards apply to the total collections of *all* the zoos in a metro area.

6. *Aquariums.* Ten metro areas receive an A rating for having an aquarium certified by the American Association of Zoological Parks and Aquariums.

7. *Family theme parks.* Theme parks drawing more than one million visitors per year are awarded points as follows:

| A metro area gets a rating of: | If there is one open day for every: |
|---|---|
| AA | 4,500 or fewer people |
| A | 4,501–6,500 people |
| B | 6,501–10,000 people |
| C | 10,001 or more people |

8. *Auto racing.* Metro areas earn points for having one or more sanctioned speedways as follows: AA for four speedways, A for three speedways, B for two speedways, and C for one speedway.

9. *Pari-mutuel betting.* Tracks for Thoroughbred, harness, and greyhound racing, as well as jai alai frontons, are scored as follows:

| A metro area gets a rating of: | If there is one racing/open day for every: |
|---|---|
| AA | 2,000 or fewer people |
| A | 2,001–3,500 people |
| B | 3,501–9,500 people |
| C | 9,501 or more people |

## A Baseball Odyssey

Quick—What major-league baseball team is descended from the old Beaneaters? It's not the Boston Red Sox; in fact, it's not even an American League team. It's the Atlanta Braves.

This is just one of many odd and intriguing changes major-league teams have undergone since 1876, when eight professional clubs joined forces to form the National League. Twenty-five years later, in 1901, the American League began play, also with eight teams. Since that time, many of the teams have changed names and moved from one city to another, and the leagues have expanded the number of franchises. The list below shows which of today's American League (AL) and National League (NL) teams have moved to another city and/or changed their name since their founding date.*

**Atlanta Braves (NL)**—*1876*, began as Boston Red Caps; *1883*, renamed Beaneaters; *1907*, renamed Doves; *1909*, renamed Pilgrims; *1936*, renamed Bees; *1941*, renamed Braves; *1953*, moved to Milwaukee and renamed Milwaukee Braves; *1966*, moved to Atlanta and renamed Atlanta Braves.

**Baltimore Orioles (AL)**—*1901*, began as Milwaukee Brewers; *1902*, moved to St. Louis and renamed St. Louis Browns; *1954*, moved to Baltimore and renamed Baltimore Orioles.

**Boston Red Sox (AL)**—*1901*, began as Somersets; *1905*, renamed Puritans; *1907*, renamed Red Sox.

**California Angels (AL)**—*1961*, began as Los Angeles Angels; *1965*, renamed California Angels.

**Chicago Cubs (NL)**—*1876*, began as White Stockings; *1894*, renamed Colts; *1898*, renamed Orphans; *1899*, renamed Cubs.

**Cleveland Indians (AL)**—*1901*, began as Bronchos; *1902*, renamed Blues; *1905*, renamed Naps; *1912*, renamed Molly McGuires; *1914*, renamed Indians.

**Houston Astros (NL)**—*1962*, began as Houston Colt .45's; *1964*, renamed Astros.

**Los Angeles Dodgers (NL)**—*1890*, began as Brooklyn Bridegrooms; *1898*, renamed Superbas; *1911*, renamed Dodgers; *1958*, moved to Los Angeles and renamed Los Angeles Dodgers.

**Milwaukee Brewers (AL)**—*1969*, began as Seattle Pilots; *1970*, moved to Milwaukee and renamed Milwaukee Brewers.

**Minnesota Twins (AL)**—*1901*, began as Washington Senators; *1960*, moved to Minneapolis–St. Paul and renamed Minnesota Twins.

**New York Yankees (AL)**—*1901*, began as Baltimore Orioles; *1903*, moved to New York and renamed New York Highlanders; *1912*, renamed Yankees.

**Oakland A's (AL)**—*1901*, began as Philadelphia Athletics; *1955*, moved to Kansas City and renamed Kansas City Athletics; *1968*, moved to Oakland and renamed Oakland Athletics; *1974*, renamed Oakland A's.

**Pittsburgh Pirates (NL)**—*1887*, began as Alleghenys; *1890*, renamed Innocents; *1891*, renamed Pirates.

**San Francisco Giants (NL)**—*1879*, began as Troy (NY) Trojans; *1883*, moved to New York City and renamed New York Gothams; *1886*, renamed Giants; *1958*, moved to San Francisco and renamed San Francisco Giants.

**Texas Rangers (AL)**—*1961*, began as Washington Senators; *1971*, moved to Arlington and renamed Texas Rangers.

Source: Joseph L. Reichler, ed., *Baseball Encyclopedia*, 1982.

*The Cincinnati Reds (NL, 1876), Philadelphia Phillies (NL, 1883), St. Louis Cardinals (NL, 1892), Chicago White Sox (AL, 1901), Detroit Tigers (AL, 1901), New York Mets (NL, 1962), Kansas City Royals (AL, 1969), Montreal Expos (NL, 1969), San Diego Padres (NL, 1969), Seattle Mariners (AL, 1977), and Toronto Blue Jays (AL, 1977) have neither changed their name nor moved.

10. *Professional sports.*

| A metro area gets a rating of: | If local major- and minor-league teams provide: |
|---|---|
| AA | 2.500 or more game seats per capita |
| A | 1.500–2.499 game seats per capita |
| B | .750–1.499 game seats per capita |
| C | .749 or fewer game seats per capita |

11. *NCAA Division I football and basketball.*

| A metro area gets a rating of: | If local NCAA Division I teams provide: |
|---|---|
| AA | 1.500 or more game seats per capita |
| A | .700–1.499 game seats per capita |
| B | .300–.699 game seats per capita |
| C | .299 or fewer game seats per capita |

12. *Coastlines.* Each mile of general coastline, whether on the ocean or on the Great Lakes, gets 10 points. For example, the 84 miles of Atlantic coastline east of Miami–Hialeah earn the Florida metro area 840 points.

13. *Inland water area.* The percent of a metro area's total surface area that is classified as inland water is multiplied by 50. In Chicago, 9.6 of the 1,902 square miles of surface area are inland water. That works out to 0.5 percent inland water, or 25 points.

14. *National forests, parks, and wildlife refuges.* The percent of a metro area's total acreage that is set aside for national forests, parks, or wildlife refuges is multiplied by 50. Seattle has more than 2,704,640 total acres, 35.74 percent of which composes the Mount Baker and Snoqualmie national forests (966,533 acres), giving the Washington metro area 1,787 points.

15. *CMSA Access.* The 76 metro areas that are part of America's 22 CMSA complexes are eligible for bonus points based on the total number of points amassed for Crowd Pleasers by the other metro areas in its

CMSA. A metro area's own points are not considered in calculating its access bonus.

| A metro area gets a rating of: | If points for Crowd Pleasers earned by CMSA partner(s) total: |
|---|---|
| AA | 1,000 or more |
| A | 700–999 |
| B | 400–699 |
| C | 100–399 |

Four eligible metro areas receive no access bonus because the other area or areas in their CMSA have no Crowd Pleasers.

To maintain relative parity among the three major recreation categories—Common Denominators, Crowd Pleasers, and Outdoor Recreation Assets—a ceiling of 2,000 points is applied to the total for outdoor assets (items 12, 13, and 14 above).

### Sample Comparison: Seattle, Washington, and Danville, Virginia

As it did in the first edition of *Places Rated Almanac,* Seattle wins top honors among the metro areas for recreational facilities. Danville—which did not exist as a metro area in 1981—finishes next to last, with just more than a tenth of the points earned by Seattle.

The Washington metro area receives either A or B ratings for all its Common Denominators, adding up to 1,000 points for this category. Its Crowd Pleasers are equally impressive: There is a premier AA-rated zoo, Woodland Park; an A-rated aquarium; and supplies of auto racing and pari-mutuel betting that earn B and C ratings, respectively. Seattle's ratio of game seats to local residents ranks seventh among the 132 metro areas with major- and minor-league professional sports. The AL Mariners, NFL Seahawks, and NBA SuperSonics play a total of 130 home games in the Kingdome; and 25 miles north of downtown, the Everett Giants, a San Francisco Giants farm club, play 37 baseball games in Memorial Stadium. Although the University of Washington Huskies play the only NCAA Division I basketball and football games in town, the crowds at Husky Stadium and Edmundson Fieldhouse on the west bank of Lake Washington add to Seattle's reputation as a partisan sports town. The

access to all these Crowd Pleasers earns Seattle a hefty 1,500 points for this category.

Manufactured recreation amenities tend to crop up with population density; that's an elementary marketing rule. But no other populous metro area has as splendid a combination of outdoor recreation endowments as Seattle. For openers, there's a 70-mile shoreline frontage on Puget Sound and nearly 90 square miles of inland water, including giant Lake Washington and suburban Lake Sammamish. An hour's drive east on I-90 will get you to several challenging Cascade ski slopes in the midst of Snoqualmie National Forest. North on I-5 and then east on state roads is a big chunk of Mount Baker National Forest. Taken together, these natural facilities earn Seattle 2,000 points, the maximum for Outdoor Recreation Assets. Seattle also is eligible for a bonus of 300 points because it shares the Crowd Pleasers of nearby Tacoma, its partner in the Seattle–Tacoma consolidated area. The total recreation score for Seattle, then, is 4,800.

Danville, in contrast, ranks 328th in recreation outlets. There are no restaurants here rated for quality by the *Mobil Travel Guide,* nor are there any municipal golf courses. On the other hand, the 27 holes of daily-fee golf and 46 lanes of tenpin bowling give the Virginia metro area respectable B ratings in both those categories. The supply of movie theaters is good for only a C rating, bringing Danville's total for Common Denominators to 500 points. In Crowd Pleasers, the metro area comes up empty; it has no zoos, aquariums, theme parks, racetracks, not even a Class A Carolina League baseball team like the ones in Lynchburg and Roanoke.

Although Danville's natural setting east of the Blue Ridge Mountains is pleasant, there are no large lakes for water sports in surrounding Pittsylvania County; the metro area's one tenth of a square mile of inland water is good for just 1 point. Likewise, there are no acres set aside as national parks, national forests, or national wildlife refuges. Danville's 1 point for outdoor recreation, added to its previous total of 500 points, yields a recreation score of 501. The only metro area to score lower is Gadsden, Alabama, with 300 points.

## Places Rated: Metro Areas Ranked for Recreational Opportunities

Fourteen criteria are used to rate a metro area's supply of recreation assets: (1) good restaurants, (2) public golf courses, (3) certified lanes for tenpin bowling, (4) movie theaters, (5) zoos, (6) aquariums, (7) family theme parks, (8) sanctioned automobile racetracks, (9) pari-mutuel betting attractions, (10) major- and minor-league professional sports teams, (11) NCAA Division I football and basketball teams, (12) miles of ocean or Great Lakes coastline, (13) inland water, and (14) national forests, national parks, or national wildlife refuges. The 76 metro areas that belong to a Consolidated Metropolitan Statistical Area can also earn points for shared recreation assets found in other metro areas within that consolidated area. Metro areas that receive tie scores are given the same rank and listed alphabetically.

## Metro Areas from Best to Worst

| Places Rated Rank | Places Rated Score | Places Rated Rank | Places Rated Score | Places Rated Rank | Places Rated Score |
|---|---|---|---|---|---|
| 1. Seattle, WA | 4,800 | 47. Houma–Thibodaux, LA | 2,700 | 96. Saginaw–Bay City– Midland, MI | 2,059 |
| 2. San Francisco, CA | 4,600 | 48. Wilmington, NC | 2,668 | 97. Fort Pierce, FL | 2,058 |
| 3. Miami–Hialeah, FL | 4,300 | 49. Muskegon, MI | 2,666 | 98. Billings, MT | 2,046 |
| 4. Fort Collins–Loveland, CO | 4,200 | 50. Rochester, NY | 2,659 | 99. Kansas City, MO | 2,043 |
| 5. Boulder–Longmont, CO | 4,012 | | | 100. Corpus Christi, TX | 2,037 |
| | | 51. Akron, OH | 2,632 | | |
| 6. Fort Myers, FL | 4,005 | 52. Albuquerque, NM | 2,612 | 101. Roanoke, VA | 2,036 |
| 7. Tacoma, WA | 4,000 | 53. Charleston, SC | 2,561 | 102. Tulsa, OK | 2,024 |
| 8. Las Vegas, NV | 3,996 | 54. Sarasota, FL | 2,535 | 103. Columbus, OH | 2,020 |
| 9. Daytona Beach, FL | 3,967 | 55. Portland, OR | 2,532 | 104. Racine, WI | 2,016 |
| 10. Los Angeles–Long Beach, CA | 3,948 | 56. Knoxville, TN | 2,514 | 105. Fall River, MA–RI | 2,005 |
| | | 57. Lakeland–Winter Haven, FL | 2,513 | | |
| 11. Salt Lake City–Ogden, UT | 3,900 | 58. Detroit, MI | 2,483 | 106. Memphis, TN–AR–MS | 1,994 |
| 12. Melbourne–Titusville– Palm Bay, FL | 3,800 | 59. Phoenix, AZ | 2,472 | 107. Bloomington, IN | 1,990 |
| 13. West Palm Beach–Boca Raton–Delray Beach, FL | 3,772 | 60. Fort Lauderdale–Hollywood– Pompano Beach, FL | 2,455 | 108. Philadelphia, PA–NJ | 1,979 |
| 14. Nassau–Suffolk, NY | 3,705 | | | 109. Omaha, NE–IA | 1,977 |
| 15. Honolulu, HI | 3,703 | 61. Cincinnati, OH–KY–IN | 2,451 | 110. Bremerton, WA | 1,973 |
| | | 62. Buffalo, NY | 2,441 | | |
| 16. New York, NY | 3,579 | 63. Lake County, IL | 2,435 | 111. San Jose, CA | 1,964 |
| 17. Monmouth–Ocean, NJ | 3,544 | 64. Redding, CA | 2,424 | 112. Pascagoula, MS | 1,956 |
| 18. New Orleans, LA | 3,500 | 65. Oakland, CA | 2,394 | 113. La Crosse, WI | 1,953 |
| 19. Eugene–Springfield, OR | 3,400 | | | 114. Toledo, OH | 1,952 |
| 20. Portland, ME | 3,366 | 66. Reno, NV | 2,386 | 115. Madison, WI | 1,944 |
| | | 67. Colorado Springs, CO | 2,375 | | |
| 21. Burlington, VT | 3,357 | 68. Fort Worth–Arlington, TX | 2,366 | 116. Richmond–Petersburg, VA | 1,943 |
| 22. San Diego, CA | 3,347 | 69. Denver, CO | 2,324 | 117. Louisville, KY–IN | 1,942 |
| 23. Cleveland, OH | 3,300 | 70. Appleton–Oshkosh– Neenah, WI | 2,315 | 118. Gary–Hammond, IN | 1,940 |
| 23. Provo–Orem, UT | 3,300 | | | 119. Tallahassee, FL | 1,936 |
| 23. Santa Barbara–Santa Maria–Lompoc, CA | 3,300 | 71. Dallas, TX | 2,310 | 120. Jackson, MI | 1,933 |
| 26. Bellingham, WA | 3,200 | 72. Sacramento, CA | 2,306 | 121. Green Bay, WI | 1,925 |
| 27. Salinas–Seaside–Monterey, CA | 3,179 | 73. Ann Arbor, MI | 2,288 | 122. Wilmington, DE–NJ–MD | 1,923 |
| 28. Anaheim–Santa Ana, CA | 3,156 | 74. New London–Norwich, CT–RI | 2,281 | 123. Davenport–Rock Island– Moline, IA–IL | 1,920 |
| 29. Tucson, AZ | 3,131 | 75. Norwalk, CT | 2,268 | 124. Bergen–Passaic, NJ | 1,918 |
| 30. Duluth, MN–WI | 3,107 | | | 124. Riverside–San Bernardino, CA | 1,918 |
| | | 76. Providence, RI | 2,263 | | |
| 31. Ocala, FL | 3,095 | 77. Santa Rosa–Petaluma, CA | 2,255 | 126. Bridgeport–Milford, CT | 1,913 |
| 32. Boston, MA | 3,066 | 78. St. Louis, MO–IL | 2,243 | 127. Grand Rapids, MI | 1,909 |
| 33. Anchorage, AK | 3,000 | 79. Savannah, GA | 2,237 | 128. Indianapolis, IN | 1,906 |
| 33. Brownsville–Harlingen, TX | 3,000 | 80. Salem–Gloucester, MA | 2,234 | 129. Waterloo–Cedar Falls, IA | 1,900 |
| 33. Galveston–Texas City, TX | 3,000 | | | 130. Glens Falls, NY | 1,883 |
| | | 81. Kenosha, WI | 2,224 | | |
| 36. Fresno, CA | 2,984 | 82. Clarksville–Hopkinsville, TN–KY | 2,219 | 131. Lawrence–Haverhill, MA–NH | 1,879 |
| 37. Norfolk–Virginia Beach– Newport News, VA | 2,964 | 83. Great Falls, MT | 2,176 | 132. Niagara Falls, NY | 1,873 |
| 38. Tampa–St. Petersburg– Clearwater, FL | 2,943 | 84. Mobile, AL | 2,164 | 132. Salem, OR | 1,873 |
| 39. Baltimore, MD | 2,925 | 85. Kalamazoo, MI | 2,163 | 134. Orange County, NY | 1,866 |
| 40. Milwaukee, WI | 2,902 | | | 135. Lake Charles, LA | 1,855 |
| | | 86. Pensacola, FL | 2,160 | | |
| 41. Jacksonville, FL | 2,884 | 87. Minneapolis–St. Paul, MN–WI | 2,158 | 136. Lewiston–Auburn, ME | 1,853 |
| 42. Orlando, FL | 2,881 | 88. Johnson City–Kingsport– Bristol, TN–VA | 2,155 | 137. Nashville, TN | 1,849 |
| 43. Chicago, IL | 2,856 | 89. Bangor, ME | 2,148 | 138. Houston, TX | 1,825 |
| 44. Syracuse, NY | 2,851 | 90. Pittsburgh, PA | 2,145 | 139. South Bend–Mishawaka, IN | 1,819 |
| 45. Visalia–Tulare–Porterville, CA | 2,800 | | | 140. Newark, NJ | 1,818 |
| | | 91. Yakima, WA | 2,140 | | |
| 46. Atlantic City, NJ | 2,711 | 92. Oxnard–Ventura, CA | 2,135 | 141. Lafayette, IN | 1,814 |
| | | 93. Biloxi–Gulfport, MS | 2,106 | 142. Beaumont–Port Arthur, TX | 1,813 |
| | | 94. Fort Walton Beach, FL | 2,092 | 143. Lincoln, NE | 1,804 |
| | | 95. Panama City, FL | 2,089 | 144. Des Moines, IA | 1,802 |
| | | | | 145. Aurora–Elgin, IL | 1,800 |

| Places Rated Rank | Places Rated Score | Places Rated Rank | Places Rated Score | Places Rated Rank | Places Rated Score |
|---|---|---|---|---|---|
| 146. Hartford, CT | 1,790 | 202. Pawtucket–Woonsocket–Attleboro, RI–MA | 1,513 | 258. Brockton, MA | 1,217 |
| 147. Lawton, OK | 1,757 | 203. Brazoria, TX | 1,512 | 258. New Britain, CT | 1,217 |
| 148. Lawrence, KS | 1,752 | 204. San Antonio, TX | 1,509 | 260. Columbus, GA–AL | 1,214 |
| 149. Utica–Rome, NY | 1,750 | 205. Wichita, KS | 1,508 | | |
| 150. Oklahoma City, OK | 1,742 | | | 261. Altoona, PA | 1,210 |
| | | 206. Iowa City, IA | 1,506 | 262. Macon–Warner Robins, GA | 1,204 |
| 151. Springfield, MO | 1,737 | 207. Rochester, MN | 1,503 | 262. Richland–Kennewick–Pasco, WA | 1,204 |
| 152. Fort Smith, AR–OK | 1,736 | 208. Midland, TX | 1,502 | 264. Enid, OK | 1,200 |
| 153. Lafayette, LA | 1,734 | 209. Cedar Rapids, IA | 1,501 | 264. State College, PA | 1,200 |
| 154. Stamford, CT | 1,729 | 210. Hagerstown, MD | 1,491 | | |
| 155. Binghamton, NY | 1,722 | | | 266. Jacksonville, NC | 1,177 |
| | | 211. Columbia, SC | 1,484 | 267. Anniston, AL | 1,165 |
| 156. Fort Wayne, IN | 1,711 | 212. Beaver County, PA | 1,480 | 268. Canton, OH | 1,157 |
| 157. Charlottesville, VA | 1,704 | 213. Benton Harbor, MI | 1,477 | 269. Parkersburg–Marietta, WV–OH | 1,148 |
| 158. Santa Cruz, CA | 1,703 | 214. Vineland–Millville–Bridgeton, NJ | 1,474 | 270. Lancaster, PA | 1,147 |
| 159. Lubbock, TX | 1,702 | 215. Vancouver, WA | 1,464 | | |
| 160. Champaign–Urbana–Rantoul, IL | 1,700 | | | 271. Topeka, KS | 1,141 |
| | | 216. Little Rock–North Little Rock, AR | 1,462 | 272. San Angelo, TX | 1,136 |
| 161. Fayetteville–Springdale, AR | 1,695 | 217. Steubenville–Weirton, OH–WV | 1,460 | 273. Mansfield, OH | 1,133 |
| 162. Peoria, IL | 1,688 | 218. Olympia, WA | 1,451 | 274. Lowell, MA–NH | 1,129 |
| 163. Middletown, CT | 1,682 | 219. New Bedford, MA | 1,450 | 275. Wichita Falls, TX | 1,126 |
| 164. Boise City, ID | 1,672 | 220. Lynchburg, VA | 1,439 | | |
| 165. Poughkeepsie, NY | 1,670 | | | 276. Dayton–Springfield, OH | 1,122 |
| | | 221. Casper, WY | 1,435 | 277. Kankakee, IL | 1,119 |
| 166. Wausau, WI | 1,654 | 222. Lima, OH | 1,428 | 278. Allentown–Bethlehem, PA–NJ | 1,117 |
| 167. Greensboro–Winston-Salem–High Point, NC | 1,651 | 222. Muncie, IN | 1,428 | 279. Montgomery, AL | 1,112 |
| 168. Battle Creek, MI | 1,648 | 224. Jackson, MS | 1,427 | 280. Amarillo, TX | 1,109 |
| 169. Trenton, NJ | 1,646 | 225. Pittsfield, MA | 1,420 | | |
| 170. Joliet, IL | 1,636 | | | 281. El Paso, TX | 1,101 |
| | | 226. Medford, OR | 1,416 | 282. Sharon, PA | 1,100 |
| 171. Bismarck, ND | 1,630 | 227. Fargo–Moorhead, ND–MN | 1,414 | 283. Tuscaloosa, AL | 1,090 |
| 171. Stockton, CA | 1,630 | 228. Baton Rouge, LA | 1,413 | 284. Huntsville, AL | 1,075 |
| 173. Evansville, IN–KY | 1,622 | 228. Bryan–College Station, TX | 1,413 | 285. Austin, TX | 1,063 |
| 174. Pueblo, CO | 1,619 | 230. Greenville–Spartanburg, SC | 1,410 | | |
| 175. Albany–Schenectady–Troy, NY | 1,617 | 230. Victoria, TX | 1,410 | 286. McAllen–Edinburg–Mission, TX | 1,059 |
| | | 232. Abilene, TX | 1,405 | 287. Kansas City, KS | 1,045 |
| 176. Janesville–Beloit, WI | 1,615 | 233. Lexington–Fayette, KY | 1,403 | 288. Cumberland, MD–WV | 1,036 |
| 177. East St. Louis–Belleville, IL | 1,610 | 234. Terre Haute, IN | 1,401 | 289. Elkhart–Goshen, IN | 1,023 |
| 178. Lansing–East Lansing, MI | 1,609 | 235. Eau Claire, WI | 1,397 | 290. Alexandria, LA | 1,018 |
| 178. Las Cruces, NM | 1,609 | | | | |
| 180. Raleigh–Durham, NC | 1,606 | 236. Portsmouth–Dover–Rochester, NH–ME | 1,390 | 291. Athens, GA | 1,001 |
| | | 237. Shreveport, LA | 1,389 | 291. Jersey City, NJ | 1,001 |
| 181. Bloomington–Normal, IL | 1,605 | 238. Scranton–Wilkes-Barre, PA | 1,386 | 293. Kokomo, IN | 1,000 |
| 182. Hamilton–Middletown, OH | 1,604 | 239. Atlanta, GA | 1,362 | 294. Florence, AL | 994 |
| 182. New Haven–Meriden, CT | 1,604 | 240. Sioux City, IA–NE | 1,359 | 295. Waterbury, CT | 946 |
| 184. Lorain–Elyria, OH | 1,602 | | | | |
| 185. Elmira, NY | 1,600 | 241. Flint, MI | 1,355 | 296. Sherman–Denison, TX | 937 |
| | | 242. Bradenton, FL | 1,349 | 297. Rockford, IL | 933 |
| 186. Middlesex–Somerset–Hunterdon, NJ | 1,596 | 243. Erie, PA | 1,340 | 298. Killeen–Temple, TX | 931 |
| 187. Dubuque, IA | 1,587 | 244. Columbia, MO | 1,331 | 299. Yuba City, CA | 918 |
| 188. Washington, DC–MD–VA | 1,578 | 245. Youngstown–Warren, OH | 1,327 | 300. Augusta, GA–SC | 913 |
| 189. Danbury, CT | 1,572 | | | | |
| 189. St. Cloud, MN | 1,572 | 246. Sioux Falls, SD | 1,324 | 301. Worcester, MA | 910 |
| | | 247. Sheyboygan, WI | 1,316 | 302. Johnstown, PA | 903 |
| 191. Bakersfield, CA | 1,568 | 248. Grand Forks, ND | 1,304 | 303. Odessa, TX | 900 |
| 192. Vallejo–Fairfield–Napa, CA | 1,559 | 249. Alton–Granite City, IL | 1,280 | 304. Albany, GA | 859 |
| 193. Reading, PA | 1,549 | 250. Wheeling, WV–OH | 1,271 | 305. Owensboro, KY | 852 |
| 194. Chico, CA | 1,543 | | | | |
| 195. Asheville, NC | 1,542 | 251. St. Joseph, MO | 1,265 | 306. Charleston, WV | 844 |
| | | 252. Waco, TX | 1,248 | 307. York, PA | 842 |
| 196. Monroe, LA | 1,541 | 253. Chattanooga, TN–GA | 1,238 | 308. Huntington–Ashland, WV–KY–OH | 840 |
| 197. Springfield, IL | 1,536 | 254. Gainesville, FL | 1,237 | 309. Anderson, IN | 838 |
| 198. Harrisburg–Lebanon–Carlisle, PA | 1,532 | 255. Charlotte–Gastonia–Rock Hill, NC–SC | 1,236 | 310. Manchester, NH | 837 |
| 199. Nashua, NH | 1,523 | | | | |
| 200. Spokane, WA | 1,517 | 256. Birmingham, AL | 1,234 | 311. Longview–Marshall, TX | 834 |
| | | 257. Decatur, IL | 1,222 | 312. Modesto, CA | 833 |
| 201. Springfield, MA | 1,514 | | | 313. Joplin, MO | 801 |
| | | | | 314. Florence, SC | 800 |

| Places Rated Rank | Places Rated Score | Places Rated Rank | Places Rated Score | Places Rated Rank | Places Rated Score |
|---|---|---|---|---|---|
| 315. Hickory, NC | 797 | 320. Williamsport, PA | 726 | 325. Texarkana, TX–Texarkana, AR | 669 |
| 316. Pine Bluff, AR | 793 | 321. Dothan, AL | 714 | 326. Tyler, TX | 631 |
| 317. Fitchburg–Leominster, MA | 790 | 322. Fayetteville, NC | 709 | 327. Anderson, SC | 613 |
| 318. Bristol, CT | 777 | 323. Laredo, TX | 702 | 328. Danville, VA | 501 |
| 319. Greeley, CO | 739 | 324. Burlington, NC | 701 | 329. Gadsden, AL | 300 |

## Metro Areas Listed Alphabetically

| Metro Area | Places Rated Rank | Metro Area | Places Rated Rank | Metro Area | Places Rated Rank |
|---|---|---|---|---|---|
| Abilene, TX | 232 | Brownsville–Harlingen, TX | 33 | Fargo–Moorhead, ND–MN | 227 |
| Akron, OH | 51 | Bryan–College Station, TX | 228 | | |
| Albany, GA | 304 | Buffalo, NY | 62 | Fayetteville, NC | 322 |
| Albany–Schenectady–Troy, NY | 175 | Burlington, NC | 324 | Fayetteville–Springdale, AR | 161 |
| Albuquerque, NM | 52 | Burlington, VT | 21 | Fitchburg–Leominster, MA | 327 |
| | | | | Flint, MI | 241 |
| Alexandria, LA | 290 | Canton, OH | 268 | Florence, AL | 294 |
| Allentown–Bethlehem, PA–NJ | 278 | Casper, WY | 221 | | |
| Alton–Granite City, IL | 249 | Cedar Rapids, IA | 209 | Florence, SC | 314 |
| Altoona, PA | 261 | Champaign–Urbana–Rantoul, IL | 160 | Fort Collins–Loveland, CO | 4 |
| Amarillo, TX | 280 | Charleston, SC | 53 | Fort Lauderdale–Hollywood–Pompano Beach, FL | 60 |
| Anaheim–Santa Ana, CA | 28 | Charleston, WV | 306 | Fort Myers, FL | 6 |
| Anchorage, AK | 33 | Charlotte–Gastonia–Rock Hill, NC–SC | 255 | Fort Pierce, FL | 97 |
| Anderson, IN | 309 | Charlottesville, VA | 157 | Fort Smith, AR–OK | 152 |
| Anderson, SC | 327 | Chattanooga, TN–GA | 253 | Fort Walton Beach, FL | 94 |
| Ann Arbor, MI | 73 | Chicago, IL | 43 | Fort Wayne, IN | 156 |
| | | | | Fort Worth–Arlington, TX | 68 |
| Anniston, AL | 267 | Chico, CA | 194 | Fresno, CA | 36 |
| Appleton–Oshkosh–Neenah, WI | 70 | Cincinnati, OH–KY–IN | 61 | | |
| Asheville, NC | 195 | Clarksville–Hopkinsville, TN–KY | 82 | Gadsden, AL | 329 |
| Athens, GA | 291 | Cleveland, OH | 23 | Gainesville, FL | 254 |
| Atlanta, GA | 239 | Colorado Springs, CO | 67 | Galveston–Texas City, TX | 33 |
| | | | | Gary–Hammond, IN | 118 |
| Atlantic City, NJ | 46 | Columbia, MO | 244 | Glens Falls, NY | 130 |
| Augusta, GA–SC | 300 | Columbia, SC | 211 | | |
| Aurora–Elgin, IL | 145 | Columbus, GA–AL | 260 | Grand Forks, ND | 248 |
| Austin, TX | 285 | Columbus, OH | 103 | Grand Rapids, MI | 127 |
| Bakersfield, CA | 191 | Corpus Christi, TX | 100 | Great Falls, MT | 83 |
| | | | | Greeley, CO | 319 |
| Baltimore, MD | 39 | Cumberland, MD–WV | 288 | Green Bay, WI | 121 |
| Bangor, ME | 89 | Dallas, TX | 71 | | |
| Baton Rouge, LA | 228 | Danbury, CT | 189 | Greensboro–Winston-Salem–High Point, NC | 167 |
| Battle Creek, MI | 168 | Danville, VA | 328 | Greenville–Spartanburg, SC | 230 |
| Beaumont–Port Arthur, TX | 142 | Davenport–Rock Island–Moline, IA–IL | 123 | Hagerstown, MD | 210 |
| | | | | Hamilton–Middletown, OH | 182 |
| Beaver County, PA | 212 | Dayton–Springfield, OH | 276 | Harrisburg–Lebanon–Carlisle, PA | 198 |
| Bellingham, WA | 26 | Daytona Beach, FL | 9 | | |
| Benton Harbor, MI | 213 | Decatur, IL | 257 | Hartford, CT | 146 |
| Bergen–Passaic, NJ | 124 | Denver, CO | 69 | Hickory, NC | 315 |
| Billings, MT | 98 | Des Moines, IA | 144 | Honolulu, HI | 15 |
| | | | | Houma–Thibodaux, LA | 47 |
| Biloxi–Gulfport, MS | 93 | Detroit, MI | 58 | Houston, TX | 138 |
| Binghamton, NY | 155 | Dothan, AL | 321 | | |
| Birmingham, AL | 256 | Dubuque, IA | 187 | Huntington–Ashland, WV–KY–OH | 308 |
| Bismarck, ND | 171 | Duluth, MN–WI | 30 | Huntsville, AL | 284 |
| Bloomington, IN | 107 | East St. Louis–Belleville, IL | 177 | Indianapolis, IN | 128 |
| | | | | Iowa City, IA | 206 |
| Bloomington–Normal, IL | 181 | Eau Claire, WI | 235 | Jackson, MI | 120 |
| Boise City, ID | 164 | El Paso, TX | 281 | | |
| Boston, MA | 32 | Elkhart–Goshen, IN | 289 | Jackson, MS | 224 |
| Boulder–Longmont, CO | 5 | Elmira, NY | 185 | Jacksonville, FL | 41 |
| Bradenton, FL | 242 | Enid, OK | 264 | Jacksonville, NC | 266 |
| | | | | Janesville–Beloit, WI | 176 |
| Brazoria, TX | 203 | Erie, PA | 243 | Jersey City, NJ | 291 |
| Bremerton, WA | 110 | Eugene–Springfield, OR | 19 | | |
| Bridgeport–Milford, CT | 126 | Evansville, IN–KY | 173 | Johnson City–Kingsport–Bristol, TN–VA | 88 |
| Bristol, CT | 318 | Fall River, MA–RI | 105 | | |
| Brockton, MA | 258 | | | | |

| Metro Area | Places Rated Rank | Metro Area | Rank Places Rank | Metro Area | Places Rated Rank |
|---|---|---|---|---|---|
| Johnstown, PA | 302 | New Haven–Meriden, CT | 182 | San Francisco, CA | 2 |
| Joliet, IL | 170 | | | | |
| Joplin, MO | 313 | New London–Norwich, CT–RI | 74 | San Jose, CA | 111 |
| Kalamazoo, MI | 85 | New Orleans, LA | 18 | Santa Barbara–Santa Maria– | |
| | | New York, NY | 16 | Lompoc, CA | 23 |
| Kankakee, IL | 277 | Newark, NJ | 140 | Santa Cruz, CA | 158 |
| Kansas City, KS | 287 | Niagara Falls, NY | 132 | Santa Rosa–Petaluma, CA | 77 |
| Kansas City, MO | 99 | | | Sarasota, FL | 54 |
| Kenosha, WI | 81 | Norfolk–Virginia Beach– | | | |
| Killeen–Temple, TX | 298 | Newport News, VA | 37 | Savannah, GA | 79 |
| | | Norwalk, CT | 75 | Scranton–Wilkes-Barre, PA | 238 |
| Knoxville, TN | 56 | Oakland, CA | 65 | Seattle, WA | 1 |
| Kokomo, IN | 293 | Ocala, FL | 31 | Sharon, PA | 282 |
| La Crosse, WI | 113 | Odessa, TX | 303 | Sheboygan, WI | 247 |
| Lafayette, IN | 141 | | | | |
| Lafayette, LA | 153 | Oklahoma City, OK | 150 | Sherman–Denison, TX | 296 |
| | | Olympia, WA | 218 | Shreveport, LA | 237 |
| Lake Charles, LA | 135 | Omaha, NE–IA | 109 | Sioux City, IA–NE | 240 |
| Lake County, IL | 63 | Orange County, NY | 134 | Sioux Falls, SD | 246 |
| Lakeland–Winter Haven, FL | 57 | Orlando, FL | 42 | South Bend–Mishawaka, IN | 139 |
| Lancaster, PA | 270 | | | | |
| Lansing–East Lansing, MI | 178 | Owensboro, KY | 305 | Spokane, WA | 200 |
| | | Oxnard–Ventura, CA | 92 | Springfield, IL | 197 |
| Laredo, TX | 323 | Panama City, FL | 95 | Springfield, MA | 201 |
| Las Cruces, NM | 178 | Parkersburg–Marietta, WV–OH | 269 | Springfield, MO | 151 |
| Las Vegas, NV | 8 | Pascagoula, MS | 112 | Stamford, CT | 154 |
| Lawrence, KS | 148 | | | | |
| Lawrence–Haverhill, MA–NH | 131 | Pawtucket–Woonsocket– | | State College, PA | 264 |
| | | Attleboro, RI–MA | 202 | Steubenville–Weirton, OH–WV | 217 |
| Lawton, OK | 147 | Pensacola, FL | 86 | Stockton, CA | 171 |
| Lewiston–Auburn, ME | 136 | Peoria, IL | 162 | Syracuse, NY | 44 |
| Lexington–Fayette, KY | 233 | Philadelphia, PA–NJ | 108 | Tacoma, WA | 7 |
| Lima, OH | 222 | Phoenix, AZ | 59 | | |
| Lincoln, NE | 143 | | | Tallahassee, FL | 119 |
| | | Pine Bluff, AR | 316 | Tampa–St. Petersburg– | |
| Little Rock–North Little Rock, AR | 216 | Pittsburgh, PA | 90 | Clearwater, FL | 38 |
| Longview–Marshall, TX | 311 | Pittsfield, MA | 225 | Terre Haute, IN | 234 |
| Lorain–Elyria, OH | 184 | Portland, ME | 20 | Texarkana, TX–Texarkana, AR | 325 |
| Los Angeles–Long Beach, CA | 10 | Portland, OR | 55 | Toledo, OH | 114 |
| Louisville, KY–IN | 117 | | | | |
| | | Portsmouth–Dover– | | Topeka, KS | 271 |
| Lowell, MA–NH | 274 | Rochester, NH–ME | 236 | Trenton, NJ | 169 |
| Lubbock, TX | 159 | Poughkeepsie, NY | 165 | Tucson, AZ | 29 |
| Lynchburg, VA | 220 | Providence, RI | 76 | Tulsa, OK | 102 |
| Macon–Warner Robins, GA | 262 | Provo–Orem, UT | 23 | Tuscaloosa, AL | 283 |
| Madison, WI | 115 | Pueblo, CO | 174 | | |
| | | | | Tyler, TX | 326 |
| Manchester, NH | 310 | Racine, WI | 104 | Utica–Rome, NY | 149 |
| Mansfield, OH | 273 | Raleigh–Durham, NC | 180 | Vallejo–Fairfield–Napa, CA | 192 |
| McAllen–Edinburg–Mission, TX | 286 | Reading, PA | 193 | Vancouver, WA | 215 |
| Medford, OR | 226 | Redding, CA | 64 | Victoria, TX | 230 |
| Melbourne–Titusville–Palm Bay, FL | 12 | Reno, NV | 66 | | |
| | | | | Vineland–Millville–Bridgeton, NJ | 214 |
| Memphis, TN–AR–MS | 106 | Richland–Kennewick–Pasco, WA | 262 | Visalia–Tulare–Porterville, CA | 45 |
| Miami–Hialeah, FL | 3 | Richmond–Petersburg, VA | 116 | Waco, TX | 252 |
| Middlesex–Somerset–Hunterdon, NJ | 186 | Riverside–San Bernardino, CA | 124 | Washington, DC–MD–VA | 188 |
| Middletown, CT | 163 | Roanoke, VA | 101 | Waterbury, CT | 295 |
| Midland, TX | 208 | Rochester, MN | 207 | | |
| | | | | Waterloo–Cedar Falls, IA | 129 |
| Milwaukee, WI | 40 | Rochester, NY | 50 | Wausau, WI | 166 |
| Minneapolis–St. Paul, MN–WI | 87 | Rockford, IL | 297 | West Palm Beach–Boca Raton– | |
| Mobile, AL | 84 | Sacramento, CA | 72 | Delray Beach, FL | 13 |
| Modesto, CA | 312 | Saginaw–Bay City–Midland, MI | 96 | Wheeling, WV–OH | 250 |
| Monmouth–Ocean, NJ | 17 | St. Cloud, MN | 189 | Wichita, KS | 205 |
| | | | | | |
| Monroe, LA | 196 | St. Joseph, MO | 251 | Wichita Falls, TX | 275 |
| Montgomery, AL | 279 | St. Louis, MO–IL | 78 | Williamsport, PA | 320 |
| Muncie, IN | 222 | Salem, OR | 132 | Wilmington, DE–NJ–MD | 122 |
| Muskegon, MI | 49 | Salem–Gloucester, MA | 80 | Wilmington, NC | 48 |
| Nashua, NH | 199 | Salinas–Seaside–Monterey, CA | 27 | Worcester, MA | 301 |
| | | | | | |
| Nashville, TN | 137 | Salt Lake City–Ogden, UT | 11 | Yakima, WA | 91 |
| Nassau–Suffolk, NY | 14 | San Angelo, TX | 272 | York, PA | 307 |
| New Bedford, MA | 219 | San Antonio, TX | 204 | Youngstown–Warren, OH | 245 |
| New Britain, CT | 258 | San Diego, CA | 22 | Yuba City, CA | 299 |

The following profiles are a selective catalogue of recreation features in each metro area.

The profiles begin with the category Common Denominators, specific options for urban recreation that ought to be available everywhere; the access rating for each item is shown in the right-hand column. The Good Restaurants entry tells how many restaurants at each quality level are in a metro area ("4 ★★" means, for example, that the place has four two-star restaurants). An NA indicates that the *Mobil Travel Guide* does not rate restaurants in that area.

The Crowd Pleasers category lists local zoos, aquariums, theme parks, automobile racecourses (along with sanctioning organization), and pari-mutuel betting attractions. Also included are the days per year that theme parks and pari-mutuel tracks are open along with their access rating. Under the heading Professional Sports, the names of major- and minor-league baseball, basketball, football, and hockey teams are given along with the total game seats per capita and access rating. Major-league team names are in capital letters. Local colleges and universities that field NCAA Division I teams in football and/or basketball are also listed, with separate total game seats per capita and access rating. If the school has only a basketball *or* football team at the Division I level, the team's name is followed by (b) or (f).

The third category, Outdoor Recreation Assets, counts the metro area's number of miles of ocean or Great Lakes coastline, its square miles of inland water, and the acreage for all national forests, parks, and wildlife refuges located there. The figures for inland water come from a series of U.S. Census Bureau geographic reports from the 1960s (still the best source for measurement of water surface areas in each of the nation's metropolitan counties). Ponds and lakes are counted if their surface areas are 40 acres or more; streams, canals, and rivers are also counted if their width is one eighth of a mile or more. The water area along irregular Great Lakes and ocean coastlines is counted, too, if the bays, inlets, and estuaries are between one and ten miles in width. Lengths of ocean and Great Lakes coastlines are estimated from state totals measured by the National Oceanic and Atmospheric Administration. A number of abbreviations are used in this section:

| | | | |
|---|---|---|---|
| NF | National Forest | NP | National Park |
| NHP | National Historic Park | NRA | National Recreation Area |
| NHS | National Historic Site | NSR | National Scenic River |
| NMP | National Military Park | NS | National Seashore |
| NM | National Monument | NWR | National Wildlife Refuge |

The figure in parentheses beside each major heading represents the number of *Places Rated* points awarded the metro area for assets in that category. If the metro area is part of a CMSA complex and receives bonus points for shared recreation assets, the number of access points is shown in parentheses following the name of the consolidated area. A star preceding a metro area's name highlights it as one of the top 25 places for recreation.

Information comes from these sources: American Association of Zoological Parks and Aquariums, *Zoological Parks and Aquariums in the Americas, 1982–1983,* 1983; American Baseball League, unpublished data, 1984; American Bowling Congress, unpublished data, 1984; American Greyhound Track Operators Association, *Directory,* 1984; American Hockey League, *Media Guide,* 1984; Brown Publishing Company, *National Speedway Directory,* 1984; Central Hockey League, *Media Guide,* 1984; Continental Basketball Association, unpublished data, 1984; Daily Racing Form, March 26, 1984; International Hockey League, *Media Guide,* 1984; Kings Entertainment Company, 1984; Merrill Lynch, *Theme Park Industry Survey,* 1983; National Association of Collegiate Directors of Athletics, *The 1983–1984 National Directory of College Athletics,* 1983; National Association of Professional Baseball Leagues, unpublished data, 1984; National Basketball Association, *Media Guide,* 1983; National Collegiate Athletic Association, *National Collegiate Championships,* 1984, *NCAA Basketball,* 1984, and *NCAA Football,* 1984; National Football League, unpublished data, 1984; National Golf Foundation, unpublished administrative records, 1984; National Hockey League, unpublished data, 1984; National League of Professional Baseball Teams, unpublished data, 1984; Rand McNally & Company, *Mobil Travel Guide* (7 vols.), 1984; Thoroughbred Racing Associations of North America, Inc., *Directory and Record Book,* 1983; U.S. Department of Agriculture, Forest Service, *Land Areas of the National Forest System,* 1984; U.S. Department of Commerce: Bureau of the Census, *Area Measurements, Series G-20,* 1962–1967, *County Business Patterns,* 1983–1984, *1977 Census of Selected Service Establishments,* 1981, and National Oceanic and Atmospheric Administration, *The Coastline of the United States,* 1975; U.S. Department of the Interior: Fish and Wildlife Service, unpublished master deed listing, 1984, and National Park Service, *Index to the National Park System and Related Areas,* 1983, and unpublished master deed listing, 1984; United States Football League, unpublished data, 1984; and U.S. Trotting Association, *Trotting and Pacing Guide,* 1984.

## Abilene, TX

Rating

Common Denominators (1,000)
  Good Restaurants: 1 ★, 2 ★★ — **B**
  Golf Courses: 4 private; 1 municipal — **C**
  Bowling Lanes: 108 — **A**
  Movie Theaters: 7 — **AA**
Crowd Pleasers (400)
  Zoos: Abilene Zoological Gardens — **C**
  NCAA Division I: .914 game seats per capita — **A**
    Hardin-Simmons Cowboys (b)
Outdoor Recreation Assets (5)
  Inland Water Area: 2.9 square miles
Places Rated Score: 1,405          Places Rated Rank: 232

## Akron, OH

Common Denominators (1,200)
  Good Restaurants: 1 ★, 4 ★★, 1 ★★★★ — **C**
  Golf Courses: 10 private; 28.5 daily fee; 2.5 — **AA**
    municipal
  Bowling Lanes: 804 — **AA**
  Movie Theaters: 22 — **A**
Crowd Pleasers (800)
  Zoos: Akron Children's Zoo — **C**
  Theme Parks: Sea World of Ohio (100 days) — **B**
  Auto Racing: Nelson Ledges (SCCA) — **C**
  Pari-mutuel Betting: Northfield Harness (89 days) — **B**
  NCAA Division I: .667 game seats per capita — **B**
    Kent State Golden Flashes, University of Akron
    Zips
Outdoor Recreation Assets (232)
  Inland Water Area: 17 square miles
  National Forests, Parks, Wildlife Refuges:
    Cuyahoga Valley NRA (16,074 acres)
CMSA Access: CLEVELAND–AKRON–LORAIN, OH (400)
Places Rated Score: 2,632          Places Rated Rank: 51

## Albany, GA

Common Denominators (700)
  Good Restaurants: 1 ★★ — **C**
  Golf Courses: 2.5 private; 1 municipal — **C**
  Bowling Lanes: 78 — **B**
  Movie Theaters: 4 — **A**
Crowd Pleasers (100)
  Zoos: Chehaw Wild Animal Park — **C**
Outdoor Recreation Assets (59)
  Inland Water Area: 8.1 square miles
Places Rated Score: 859          Places Rated Rank: 304

## Albany–Schenectady–Troy, NY

Common Denominators (1,100)
  Good Restaurants: 10 ★★, 8 ★★★ — **A**
  Golf Courses: 18 private; 15.5 daily fee; 6.5 — **A**
    municipal
  Bowling Lanes: 1,000 — **AA**
  Movie Theaters: 18 — **C**
Crowd Pleasers (400)
  Pari-mutuel Betting: Saratoga (harness, 202 days; — **B**
    Thoroughbred, 24 days)
  Professional Sports: .595 game seats per capita — **C**
    Albany A's (baseball), Patroons (basketball)
  NCAA Division I: .039 game seats per capita — **C**
    Siena College Indians (b)
Outdoor Recreation Assets (117)
  Inland Water Area: 71.8 square miles
  National Forests, Parks, Wildlife Refuges:
    Saratoga NHP (2,605 acres)
Places Rated Score: 1,617          Places Rated Rank: 175

## Albuquerque, NM

Common Denominators (1,000)
  Good Restaurants: 1★, 5 ★★, 3 ★★★ — **B**
  Golf Courses: 6.5 private; 1 daily fee; 3.5 — **C**
    municipal
  Bowling Lanes: 300 — **A**
  Movie Theaters: 18 — **AA**
Crowd Pleasers (1,100)
  Zoos: Rio Grande Zoological Park — **A**
  Auto Racing: Seven Flags Raceway (NASCAR) — **C**
  Pari-mutuel Betting: New Mexico State Fair — **C**
    (Thoroughbred, 17 days)
  Professional Sports: 2.101 game seats per capita — **A**
    Dukes (baseball), Silvers (basketball)
  NCAA Division I: .889 game seats per capita — **A**
    University of New Mexico Lobos
Outdoor Recreation Assets (512)
  National Forest, Parks, Wildlife Refuges:
    Cibola NF (76,588 acres)
Places Rated Score: 2,612          Places Rated Rank: 52

## Alexandria, LA

Common Denominators (500)
  Good Restaurants: 1 ★★★ — **C**
  Golf Courses: 2.5 private; 1 daily fee — **C**
  Bowling Lanes: 40 — **C**
  Movie Theaters: 4 — **B**
Crowd Pleasers (100)
  Zoos: Alexandria Zoological Park — **C**
Outdoor Recreation Assets (418)
  Inland Water Area: 8.6 square miles
  National Forests, Parks, Wildlife Refuges:
    Kisatchie NF (101,221 acres)
Places Rated Score: 1,018          Places Rated Rank: 290

## Allentown–Bethlehem, PA–NJ

Common Denominators (800)
  Good Restaurants: 2 ★, 1 ★★★, 1 ★★★★ — **C**
  Golf Courses: 13 private; 7.5 daily fee; 2 municipal — **B**
  Bowling Lanes: 600 — **A**
  Movie Theaters: 17 — **B**
Crowd Pleasers (200)
  NCAA Division I: .373 game seats per capita — **B**
    Lafayette College Leopards, Lehigh Engineers
Outdoor Recreation Assets (117)
  Inland Water Area: 2.2 square miles
  National Forests, Parks, Wildlife Refuges:
    Appalachian Trail (4,079 acres)
    Delaware NSR (368 acres)
    Delaware Water Gap NRA (16,066 acres)
Places Rated Score: 1,117          Places Rated Rank: 278

## Alton–Granite City, IL

Common Denominators (800)
  Good Restaurants: 1 ★★ — **C**
  Golf Courses: 4.5 private; 3 daily fee; 2 municipal — **B**
  Bowling Lanes: 272 — **A**
  Movie Theaters: 6 — **B**
Outdoor Recreation Assets (80)
  Inland Water Area: 17.6 square miles
CMSA Access: ST. LOUIS–EAST ST. LOUIS–
  ALTON, MO–IL (400)
Places Rated Score: 1,280          Places Rated Rank: 249

## Altoona, PA

Common Denominators (1,200)
  Good Restaurants: 2 ★★, 2 ★★★ — **AA**
  Golf Courses: 3 private; 3 daily fee — **B**
  Bowling Lanes: 133 — **A**
  Movie Theaters: 5 — **A**
Outdoor Recreation Assets (10)
  Inland Water Area: .2 square miles
  National Forests, Parks, Wildlife Refuges:
    Allegheny Portage NHS (517 acres)
Places Rated Score: 1,210          Places Rated Rank: 261

## Amarillo, TX

Common Denominators (1,000)
  Good Restaurants: 1 ★, 3 ★★ — **B**
  Golf Courses: 4 private; 2 daily fee; 2 municipal — **B**
  Bowling Lanes: 112 — **B**
  Movie Theaters: 7 — **AA**

Rating

## Outdoor Recreation Assets (109)
Inland Water Area: 25.9 square miles
National Forests, Parks, Wildlife Refuges:
Alibates Flint Quarries NM (1,079 acres)
Buffalo Lake NWR (7,664 acres)
Lake Meredith NRA (23,379 acres)
Places Rated Score: 1,109          Places Rated Rank: 280

## Anaheim–Santa Ana, CA
Common Denominators (800)
Good Restaurants: 2 ★, 33 ★★, 26 ★★★, 2 ★★★★     AA
Golf Courses: 16 private; 11 daily fee; 7 municipal     C
Bowling Lanes: 1,182     B
Movie Theaters: 38     C
Crowd Pleasers (1,000)     AA
Theme Parks:
Disneyland (303 days)
Knott's Berry Farm (365 days)
Six Flags Magic Mountain (185 days)     C
Pari-mutuel Betting:
Los Alamitos (harness, 19 days; Thoroughbred, 13 days)
Professional Sports: 3.108 game seats per capita     AA
CALIFORNIA ANGELS (baseball), LOS ANGELES RAMS (football)
NCAA Division I: .076 game seats per capita     C
Fullerton State Titans, University of California (Irvine) Anteaters (b)
Outdoor Recreation Assets (956)
Pacific Coastline: 40 miles
Inland Water Area: 3.9 square miles
National Forests, Parks, Wildlife Refuges:
Cleveland NF (54,281 acres)
CMSA Access: LOS ANGELES–ANAHEIM–RIVERSIDE, CA (400)
Places Rated Score: 3,156          Places Rated Rank: 28

## Anchorage, AK
Common Denominators (900)
Good Restaurants: NA     A
Golf Courses: 1 private; 1 daily fee     C
Bowling Lanes: 160     A
Movie Theaters: 5     B
Crowd Pleasers (100)
Zoos: Alaska Zoo     C
Outdoor Recreation Assets (2,000)
Pacific Coastline: 90 miles
Inland Water Area: 36 square miles
National Forests, Parks, Wildlife Refuges:
Chugach NF (275,000 acres)
Places Rated Score: 3,000          Places Rated Rank: 33

## Anderson, IN
Common Denominators (700)
Golf Courses: 4.5 private; 1.5 daily fee; 1 municipal     B
Bowling Lanes: 160     AA
Movie Theaters: 3     C
Outdoor Recreation Assets (138)
Inland Water Area: 12.5 square miles
Places Rated Score: 838          Places Rated Rank: 309

## Anderson, SC
Common Denominators (300)
Golf Courses: 5 private     —
Bowling Lanes: 32     C
Movie Theaters: 3     B
Crowd Pleasers (300)
Professional Sports: 2.162 game seats per capita     A
Braves (baseball)
Outdoor Recreation Assets (13)
Inland Water Area: 1.9 square miles
Places Rated Score: 613          Places Rated Rank: 327

## Ann Arbor, MI
Common Denominators (1,400)
Good Restaurants: 4 ★, 6 ★★, 1 ★★★     AA
Golf Courses: 7 private; 5.5 daily fee; 3 municipal     AA
Bowling Lanes: 318     AA
Movie Theaters: 7     B
Crowd Pleasers (400)
NCAA Division I: 3.264 game seats per capita     AA
Eastern Michigan Hurons, University of Michigan Wolverines
Outdoor Recreation Assets (88)
Inland Water Area: 12.5 square miles
CMSA Access: DETROIT–ANN ARBOR, MI (400)
Places Rated Score: 2,288          Places Rated Rank: 73

## Anniston, AL
Common Denominators (900)
Good Restaurants: 1 ★★★     C
Golf Courses: 3 private; 2 daily fee; 0.5 municipal     B
Bowling Lanes: 44     B
Movie Theaters: 5     AA
Outdoor Recreation Assets (265)
Inland Water Area: 1.2 square miles
National Forests, Parks, Wildlife Refuges:
Talladega NF (19,985 acres)
Places Rated Score: 1,165          Places Rated Rank: 267

## Appleton–Oshkosh–Neenah, WI
Common Denominators (1,300)
Good Restaurants: 5 ★★, 2 ★★★     A
Golf Courses: 6 private; 11.5 daily fee; 2 municipal     AA
Bowling Lanes: 540     AA
Movie Theaters: 8     B
Crowd Pleasers (300)
Professional Sports: 1.531 game seats per capita     A
Foxes (baseball), Wisconsin Fliers (basketball)
Outdoor Recreation Assets (715)
Inland Water Area: 202.9 square miles
Places Rated Score: 2,315          Places Rated Rank: 70

## Asheville, NC
Common Denominators (700)
Good Restaurants: 1 ★, 1 ★★★     C
Golf Courses: 5 private; 1.5 daily fee; 2 municipal     B
Bowling Lanes: 48     C
Movie Theaters: 6     A
Crowd Pleasers (400)
Auto Racing: Asheville (NASCAR)     C
Professional Sports: 1.566 game seats per capita     A
Tourists (baseball)
Outdoor Recreation Assets (442)
Inland Water Area: .8 square miles
National Forests, Parks, Wildlife Refuges:
Blue Ridge Parkway (5,411 acres)
Pisgah NF (31,390 acres)
Places Rated Score: 1,542          Places Rated Rank: 195

## Athens, GA
Common Denominators (600)
Good Restaurants: 1 ★     C
Golf Courses: 1.5 private; 2 daily fee; 1 municipal     B
Bowling Lanes: 36     C
Movie Theaters: 4     B
Crowd Pleasers (400)
NCAA Division I: 4.131 game seats per capita     AA
University of Georgia Bulldogs
Outdoor Recreation Assets (1)
National Forests, Parks, Wildlife Refuges:
Oconee NF (112 acres)
Places Rated Score: 1,001          Places Rated Rank: 291

## Atlanta, GA
Common Denominators (600)
Good Restaurants: 1 ★, 19 ★★, 20 ★★★, 1 ★★★★     B

|  | Rating |
|---|---|
| Golf Courses: 45.5 private; 14 daily fee; 9 municipal | C |
| Bowling Lanes: 656 | C |
| Movie Theaters: 64 | B |
| Crowd Pleasers (700) | |
| Theme Parks: Six Flags Over Georgia (148 days) | C |
| Auto Racing: Atlanta International (NASCAR) | C |
| Professional Sports: 2.534 game seats per capita BRAVES (baseball), HAWKS (basketball), FALCONS (football) | AA |
| NCAA Division I: .212 game seats per capita Georgia Tech Yellow Jackets, Georgia State Panthers (b) | C |

Outdoor Recreation Assets (62)
Inland Water Area: 50.2 square miles
National Forests, Parks, Wildlife Refuges:
Chattahoochee River NRA (5,968 acres)
Kennesaw Mountain National Battlefield Park
(2,884 acres)
Martin Luther King, Jr., NHS (8 acres)
Places Rated Score: 1,362          Places Rated Rank: 239

### Atlantic City, NJ

Common Denominators (1,200)

| | Rating |
|---|---|
| Good Restaurants: 1 ★, 12 ★★, 8 ★★★, 1 ★★★★ | AA |
| Golf Courses: 6 private; 6.5 daily fee; 0.5 municipal | A |
| Bowling Lanes: 90 | C |
| Movie Theaters: 27 | AA |
| Crowd Pleasers (400) | |
| Pari-mutuel Betting: Atlantic City (harness, 145 days; Thoroughbred, 93 days) | AA |

Outdoor Recreation Assets (1,111)
Atlantic Coastline: 52 miles
Inland Water Area: 67.2 square miles
National Forests, Parks, Wildlife Refuges:
Brigantine NWR (19,840 acres)
Places Rated Score: 2,711          Places Rated Rank: 46

### Augusta, GA–SC

Common Denominators (800)

| | Rating |
|---|---|
| Good Restaurants: 1 ★★ | C |
| Golf Courses: 12 private; 3.5 daily fee; 1 municipal | B |
| Bowling Lanes: 158 | B |
| Movie Theaters: 11 | A |

Outdoor Recreation Assets (113)
Inland Water Area: 35 square miles
National Forests, Parks, Wildlife Refuges:
Sumter NF (6,021 acres)
Places Rated Score: 913          Places Rated Rank: 300

### Aurora–Elgin, IL

Common Denominators (1,400)

| | Rating |
|---|---|
| Good Restaurants: 6 ★, 9 ★★, 4 ★★★ | AA |
| Golf Courses: 3.5 private; 3 daily fee; 6 municipal | A |
| Bowling Lanes: 346 | AA |
| Movie Theaters: 12 | A |

CMSA Access: CHICAGO–GARY–LAKE COUNTY,
IL–IN–WI (400)
Places Rated Score: 1,800          Places Rated Rank: 145

### Austin, TX

Common Denominators (700)

| | Rating |
|---|---|
| Good Restaurants: 2 ★, 3 ★★, 1 ★★★ | C |
| Golf Courses: 11.5 private; 5 daily fee; 3 municipal | B |
| Bowling Lanes: 254 | B |
| Movie Theaters: 16 | B |
| Crowd Pleasers (300) | |
| NCAA Division I: 1.096 game seats per capita University of Texas Longhorns | A |

Outdoor Recreation Assets (63)
Inland Water Area: 35.3 square miles
Places Rated Score: 1,063          Places Rated Rank: 285

### Bakersfield, CA

Common Denominators (1,000)

| | Rating |
|---|---|
| Good Restaurants: 1 ★, 4 ★★, 2 ★★★ | B |
| Golf Courses: 4.5 private; 7 daily fee; 4 municipal | A |
| Bowling Lanes: 204 | B |
| Movie Theaters: 15 | A |
| Crowd Pleasers (200) | |
| Professional Sports: .781 game seats per capita Dodgers (baseball) | B |

Outdoor Recreation Assets (368)
Inland Water Area: 19.6 square miles
National Forests, Parks, Wildlife Refuges:
Kern–Pixley NWR (10,618 acres)
Los Padres NF (64,803 acres)
Sequoia NF (294,917 acres)
Places Rated Score: 1,568          Places Rated Rank: 191

### Baltimore, MD

Common Denominators (600)

| | Rating |
|---|---|
| Good Restaurants: 9 ★, 10 ★★, 10 ★★★ | C |
| Golf Courses: 32.5 private; 4 daily fee; 8.5 municipal | C |
| Bowling Lanes: 983 | B |
| Movie Theaters: 62 | B |
| Crowd Pleasers (1,100) | |
| Zoos: Baltimore Zoo | A |
| Aquariums: National Aquarium in Baltimore | A |
| Pari-mutuel Betting: Pimlico (Thoroughbred, 76 days) Trimonium (Thoroughbred, 42 days) | C |
| Professional Sports: 2.347 game seats per capita ORIOLES (baseball), STARS (football), Skipjacks (hockey) | A |
| NCAA Division I: .140 game seats per capita Towson State Tigers (b), U.S. Naval Academy Midshipmen, University of Baltimore Super Bees (b) | C |

Outdoor Recreation Assets (1,225)
Chesapeake Bay Coastline: 96 miles
Inland Water Area: 137.9 square miles
National Forests, Parks, Wildlife Refuges:
Fort McHenry NM (43 acres)
Hampton NHS (59 acres)
National Capital Park (432 acres)
Susquehanna NWR (4 acres)
Places Rated Score: 2,925          Places Rated Rank: 39

### Bangor, ME

Common Denominators (1,200)

| | Rating |
|---|---|
| Good Restaurants: 1 ★, 3 ★★, 1 ★★★ | AA |
| Golf Courses: 3.5 daily fee; 1 municipal | AA |
| Bowling Lanes: 20 | C |
| Movie Theaters: 3 | A |
| Crowd Pleasers (600) | |
| Pari-mutuel Betting: Bangor Raceway (harness, 37 days) | A |
| NCAA Division I: .971 game seats per capita University of Maine Black Bears | A |

Outdoor Recreation Assets (348)
Inland Water Area: 25.3 square miles
Places Rated Score: 2,148          Places Rated Rank: 89

### Baton Rouge, LA

Common Denominators (700)

| | Rating |
|---|---|
| Good Restaurants: 6 ★★, 5 ★★★, 2 ★★★★ | A |
| Golf Courses: 9.5 private; 4 municipal | C |
| Bowling Lanes: 160 | C |
| Movie Theaters: 14 | B |
| Crowd Pleasers (500) | |
| Zoos: Greater Baton Rouge Zoo | B |
| NCAA Division I: 1.145 game seats per capita Louisiana State Fighting Tigers | A |

Outdoor Recreation Assets (213)
Inland Water Area: 68.4 square miles
Places Rated Score: 1,413          Places Rated Rank: 228

Rating

## Battle Creek, MI
Common Denominators (1,500)
Good Restaurants: 1 ★, 3 ★★, 1 ★★★    A
Golf Courses: 6 private; 5.5 daily fee; 1.5    AA
  municipal
Bowling Lanes: 202    AA
Movie Theaters: 7    AA
Crowd Pleasers (100)
Zoos: Binder Park Zoo    C
Outdoor Recreation Assets (48)
Inland Water Area: 6.9 square miles
Places Rated Score: 1,648      Places Rated Rank: 168

## Beaumont–Port Arthur, TX
Common Denominators (600)
Good Restaurants: 2 ★, 3 ★★★    C
Golf Courses: 7.5 private; 2.5 daily fee; 3    B
  municipal
Bowling Lanes: 122    C
Movie Theaters: 11    B
Crowd Pleasers (400)
Professional Sports: .815 game seats per capita    B
  Golden Gators (baseball)
NCAA Division I: .401 game seats per capita    B
  Lamar Cardinals
Outdoor Recreation Assets (813)
Gulf of Mexico Coastline: 32 miles
Inland Water Area: 72.3 square miles
National Forests, Parks, Wildlife Refuges:
  Big Thicket National Preserve (41,730 acres)
  McFaddin NWR (41,682 acres)
  Texas Point NWR (8,952 acres)
Places Rated Score: 1,813      Places Rated Rank: 142

## Beaver County, PA
Common Denominators (1,000)
Good Restaurants: 1 ★★★    C
Golf Courses: 4 private; 5.5 daily fee    A
Bowling Lanes: 242    AA
Movie Theaters: 5    B
Outdoor Recreation Assets (80)
Inland Water Area: 7 square miles
CMSA Access: PITTSBURGH–BEAVER VALLEY, PA (400)
Places Rated Score: 1,480      Places Rated Rank: 212

## Bellingham, WA
Common Denominators (1,100)
Good Restaurants: 2 ★★, 1 ★★★    A
Golf Courses: 2 private; 1.5 daily fee; 1 municipal    B
Bowling Lanes: 76    B
Movie Theaters: 7    AA
Crowd Pleasers (100)
Professional Sports: .416 game seats per capita    C
  Mariners (baseball)
Outdoor Recreation Assets (2,000)
Inland Water Area: 53.7 square miles
National Forests, Parks, Wildlife Refuges:
  Mount Baker NF (452,909 acres)
  North Cascades NP (281,413 acres)
  Ross Lake NRA (107,633 acres)
  San Juan Island NWR (3 acres)
Places Rated Score: 3,200      Places Rated Rank: 26

## Benton Harbor, MI
Common Denominators (1,000)
Good Restaurants: 1 ★, 1 ★★, 1 ★★★    B
Golf Courses: 4.5 private; 9 daily fee; 1 municipal    AA
Bowling Lanes: 114    B
Movie Theaters: 4    B
Outdoor Recreation Assets (477)
Great Lakes Coastline: 44 miles
Inland Water Area: 4.3 square miles
Places Rated Score: 1,477      Places Rated Rank: 213

Rating

## Bergen–Passaic, NJ
Common Denominators (600)
Good Restaurants: 3 ★, 9 ★★, 6 ★★★    C
Golf Courses: 17 private; 4.5 daily fee; 6.5    C
  municipal
Bowling Lanes: 858    B
Movie Theaters: 36    B
Crowd Pleasers (700)
Zoos:    C
  Bergen County Wildlife Center
  Van Saun Park Zoo
Pari-mutuel Betting: Meadowlands (harness, 185    B
  days; Thoroughbred, 99 days)
Professional Sports: 1.654 game seats per capita    A
  NETS (basketball), GENERALS, GIANTS
  (football), DEVILS (hockey)
NCAA Division I: .013 game seats per capita    C
  Fairleigh Dickinson Knights (b)
Outdoor Recreation Assets (218)
Inland Water Area: 18.1 square miles
National Forests, Parks, Wildlife Refuges:
  Appalachian Trail (255 acres)
CMSA Access: NEW YORK–NORTHERN NEW
JERSEY–LONG ISLAND, NY–NJ–CT (400)
Places Rated Score: 1,918      Places Rated Rank: 124

## Billings, MT
Common Denominators (1,300)
Good Restaurants: 1 ★, 4 ★★, 1 ★★★    AA
Golf Courses: 3.5 private; 1.5 daily fee    B
Bowling Lanes: 100    A
Movie Theaters: 5    AA
Crowd Pleasers (700)
Pari-mutuel Betting: Yellowstone Exhibition    A
  (Thoroughbred, 38 days)
Professional Sports: 4.716 game seats per capita    AA
  Mustangs (baseball), Montana Magic (hockey)
Outdoor Recreation Assets (46)
Inland Water Area: 24.1 square miles
Places Rated Score: 2,046      Places Rated Rank: 98

## Biloxi–Gulfport, MS
Common Denominators (1,100)
Good Restaurants: 3 ★, 8 ★★, 2 ★★★    AA
Golf Courses: 4.5 private; 5 daily fee    A
Bowling Lanes: 188    B
Movie Theaters: 5    B
Outdoor Recreation Assets (1,006)
Gulf of Mexico Coastline: 30 miles
Inland Water Area: 22.4 square miles
National Forests, Parks, Wildlife Refuges:
  De Soto NF (61,389 acres)
  Gulf Islands NS (19,997 acres)
Places Rated Score: 2,106      Places Rated Rank: 93

## Binghamton, NY
Common Denominators (1,500)
Good Restaurants: 1 ★, 2 ★★, 4 ★★★    A
Golf Courses: 4.5 private; 8 daily fee; 3 municipal    AA
Bowling Lanes: 364    AA
Movie Theaters: 12    AA
Crowd Pleasers (200)
Zoos: Ross Park Zoo    C
Professional Sports: .737 game seats per capita    C
  Whalers (hockey)
Outdoor Recreation Assets (22)
Inland Water Area: 5.5 square miles
Places Rated Score: 1,722      Places Rated Rank: 155

## Birmingham, AL
Common Denominators (400)
Good Restaurants: 7 ★★, 4 ★★★    C
Golf Courses: 20 private; 5 daily fee; 5    C
  municipal
Bowling Lanes: 134    C

| | Rating |
|---|---|
| Movie Theaters: 19 | C |

Crowd Pleasers (800)

| | |
|---|---|
| Zoos: Birmingham Zoo | B |
| Auto Racing: Birmingham International (NASCAR) | C |
| Professional Sports: 1.692 game seats per capita | A |

Barons (baseball), STALLIONS (football)

| | |
|---|---|
| NCAA Division I: .618 game seats per capita | B |

Samford University Bulldogs (b), University of
Alabama Blazers (b)

Outdoor Recreation Assets (34)
Inland Water Area: 27.5 square miles
National Forests, Parks, Wildlife Refuges:
Watercress NWR (7 acres)
Places Rated Score: 1,234          Places Rated Rank: 256

### Bismarck, ND
Common Denominators (1,400)

| | |
|---|---|
| Good Restaurants: 5 ★★ | AA |
| Golf Courses: 1 private; 2.5 municipal | A |
| Bowling Lanes: 100 | AA |
| Movie Theaters: 3 | A |

Crowd Pleasers (100)

| | |
|---|---|
| Zoos: Dakota Zoo | C |

Outdoor Recreation Assets (130)
Inland Water Area: 73.5 square miles
National Forests, Parks, Wildlife Refuges:
Canfield Lake NWR (3 acres)
Florence Lake NWR (1,468 acres)
Long Lake NWR (10,330 acres)
Places Rated Score: 1,630          Places Rated Rank: 171

### Bloomington, IN
Common Denominators (1,100)

| | |
|---|---|
| Good Restaurants: 2 ★★★ | A |
| Golf Courses: 2 private; 1 daily fee; 1 municipal | B |
| Bowling Lanes: 42 | B |
| Movie Theaters: 5 | AA |

Crowd Pleasers (400)

| | |
|---|---|
| NCAA Division I: 4.953 game seats per capita | AA |

Indiana University Fightin' Hoosiers

Outdoor Recreation Assets (490)
Inland Water Area: 9.1 square miles
National Forests, Parks, Wildlife Refuges:
Hoosier NF (18,317 acres)
Places Rated Score: 1,990          Places Rated Rank: 107

### Bloomington–Normal, IL
Common Denominators (1,100)

| | |
|---|---|
| Good Restaurants: 1 ★, 2 ★★ | B |
| Golf Courses: 2.5 private; 1.5 daily fee; 2 municipal | A |
| Bowling Lanes: 104 | A |
| Movie Theaters: 4 | A |

Crowd Pleasers (500)

| | |
|---|---|
| Zoos: Miller Park Zoo | C |
| NCAA Division I: 1.502 game seats per capita | AA |

Illinois State Redbirds

Outdoor Recreation Assets (5)
Inland Water Area: 1.1 square miles
Places Rated Score: 1,605          Places Rated Rank: 181

### Boise City, ID
Common Denominators (800)

| | |
|---|---|
| Good Restaurants: 2 ★, 1 ★★★ | C |
| Golf Courses: 4 private; 2.5 daily fee; 0.5 municipal | B |
| Bowling Lanes: 122 | B |
| Movie Theaters: 6 | A |

Crowd Pleasers (800)

| | |
|---|---|
| Zoos: Boise City Zoo | C |
| Pari-mutuel Betting: Les Bois Park | A |

(Thoroughbred, 51 days)

| | |
|---|---|
| NCAA Division I: 1.522 game seats per capita | AA |

Boise State Broncos

Outdoor Recreation Assets (72)
Inland Water Area: 8.6 square miles

National Forests, Parks, Wildlife Refuges:
Boise NF (4,211 acres)
Places Rated Score: 1,672          Places Rated Rank: 164

### Boston, MA
Common Denominators (800)

| | |
|---|---|
| Good Restaurants: 21 ★, 34 ★★, 15 ★★★, 3 ★★★★ | A |
| Golf Courses: 32 private; 21.5 daily fee; 11.5 municipal | C |
| Bowling Lanes: 172 | C |
| Movie Theaters: 94 | A |

Crowd Pleasers (1,300)

| | |
|---|---|
| Zoos: | A |

Franklin Park Zoo
Stone Zoo

| | |
|---|---|
| Aquariums: New England Aquarium | A |
| Pari-mutuel Betting: | A |

Foxboro Raceway (harness, 288 days)
Raynham (greyhound, 135 days)
Suffolk Downs (Thoroughbred, 244 days)
Wonderland (greyhound, 310 days)

| | |
|---|---|
| Professional Sports: 1.575 game seats per capita | A |

RED SOX (baseball), CELTICS (basketball),
PATRIOTS (football), BRUINS (hockey)

| | |
|---|---|
| NCAA Division I: .275 game seats per capita | C |

Boston College Eagles, Boston University
Terriers, Harvard Crimson, Northeastern
University Huskies

Outdoor Recreation Assets (666)
Atlantic Coastline: 41 miles
Inland Water Area: 87.8 square miles
National Forests, Parks, Wildlife Refuges:
Adams NHS (9 acres)
Boston NHP (41 acres)
Frederick Law Olmstead NHS (2 acres)
Great Meadows NWR (1,526 acres)
John F. Kennedy NHS (0.09 acres)
Longfellow NHS (2 acres)
Minute Man NHP (712 acres)
Oxbow NWR (662 acres)
Saugus Iron Works NHS (9 acres)
CMSA Access: BOSTON–LAWRENCE–SALEM, MA–NH (300)
Places Rated Score: 3,066          Places Rated Rank: 32

### ★ Boulder–Longmont, CO
Common Denominators (1,300)

| | |
|---|---|
| Good Restaurants: 4 ★★, 2 ★★★, 2 ★★★★ | AA |
| Golf Courses: 2 private; 1.5 daily fee; 2.5 municipal | B |
| Bowling Lanes: 142 | A |
| Movie Theaters: 8 | AA |

Crowd Pleasers (500)

| | |
|---|---|
| Auto Racing: Colorado National (NASCAR) | C |
| NCAA Division I: 2.141 game seats per capita | AA |

University of Colorado Buffalos

Outdoor Recreation Assets (1,812)
Inland Water Area: 9.7 square miles
National Forests, Parks, Wildlife Refuges:
Rocky Mountain NP (27,259 acres)
Roosevelt NF (138,624 acres)
CMSA Access: DENVER–BOULDER, CO (400)
Places Rated Score: 4,012          Places Rated Rank: 5

### Bradenton, FL
Common Denominators (800)

| | |
|---|---|
| Good Restaurants: 1 ★, 1 ★★ | C |
| Golf Courses: 2.5 private; 3 daily fee; 1 municipal | A |
| Bowling Lanes: 64 | B |
| Movie Theaters: 4 | B |

Outdoor Recreation Assets (549)
Gulf of Mexico Coastline: 24 miles
Inland Water Area: 46 square miles
National Forests, Parks, Wildlife Refuges:
DeSoto National Monument (25 acres)
Passage Key NWR (36 acres)
Places Rated Score: 1,349          Places Rated Rank: 242

## Brazoria, TX

| | Rating |
|---|---|
| **Common Denominators (400)** | |
| Golf Courses: 3.5 private; 0.5 daily fee; 1 municipal | C |
| Bowling Lanes: 68 | B |
| Movie Theaters: 3 | C |
| **Outdoor Recreation Assets (812)** | |
| Gulf of Mexico Coastline: 35 miles | |
| Inland Water Area: 79.8 square miles | |
| National Forests, Parks, Wildlife Refuges: | |
| Brazoria NWR (10,361 acres) | |
| San Bernard NWR (21,783 acres) | |
| CMSA Access: HOUSTON–GALVESTON–BRAZORIA, TX (300) | |

Places Rated Score: 1,512   Places Rated Rank: 203

## Bremerton, WA

| | Rating |
|---|---|
| **Common Denominators (700)** | |
| Good Restaurants: 1 ★★★ | C |
| Golf Courses: 2 private; 2 daily fee; 1 municipal | B |
| Bowling Lanes: 68 | B |
| Movie Theaters: 4 | B |
| **Outdoor Recreation Assets (1,273)** | |
| Puget Sound Coastline: 30 miles | |
| Inland Water Area: 76.5 square miles | |

Places Rated Score: 1,973   Places Rated Rank: 110

## Bridgeport–Milford, CT

| | Rating |
|---|---|
| **Common Denominators (600)** | |
| Good Restaurants: 1 ★, 5 ★★, 1 ★★★ | B |
| Golf Courses: 6.5 private; 1 daily fee; 2.5 municipal | C |
| Bowling Lanes: 260 | B |
| Movie Theaters: 9 | C |
| **Crowd Pleasers (600)** | |
| Zoos: Beardsley Zoological Gardens | C |
| Pari-mutuel Betting: | AA |
| Bridgeport Jai Alai (187 days) | |
| Milford Jai Alai (177 days) | |
| NCAA Division I: .089 game seats per capita | C |
| Fairfield University Stags (b) | |
| **Outdoor Recreation Assets (313)** | |
| Atlantic Coastline: 17 miles | |
| Inland Water Area: 7.9 square miles | |
| CMSA Access: NEW YORK–NORTHERN NEW JERSEY–LONG ISLAND, NY–NJ–CT (400) | |

Places Rated Score: 1,913   Places Rated Rank: 126

## Bristol, CT

| | Rating |
|---|---|
| **Common Denominators (400)** | |
| Good Restaurants: 1 ★ | C |
| Golf Courses: 1 private | — |
| Bowling Lanes: 40 | B |
| Movie Theaters: 1 | C |
| **Outdoor Recreation Assets (77)** | |
| Inland Water Area: 1.2 square miles | |
| CMSA Access: HARTFORD–NEW BRITAIN–MIDDLETOWN, CT (300) | |

Places Rated Score: 777   Places Rated Rank: 318

## Brockton, MA

| | Rating |
|---|---|
| **Common Denominators (600)** | |
| Good Restaurants: 1 ★★ | C |
| Golf Courses: 1.5 private; 3 daily fee; 1 municipal | B |
| Bowling Lanes: 56 | C |
| Movie Theaters: 5 | B |
| **Crowd Pleasers (100)** | |
| Professional Sports: .451 game seats per capita | C |
| Bay State Bombardiers (b) | |
| **Outdoor Recreation Assets (117)** | |
| Inland Water Area: 3.5 square miles | |
| CMSA Access: BOSTON–LAWRENCE–SALEM, MA–NH (400) | |

Places Rated Score: 1,217   Places Rated Rank: 258

## Brownsville–Harlingen, TX

| | Rating |
|---|---|
| **Common Denominators (700)** | |
| Good Restaurants: 2 ★, 3 ★★, 2 ★★★ | A |

| | Rating |
|---|---|
| Golf Courses: 3 private; 3 daily fee; 1.5 municipal | B |
| Bowling Lanes: 52 | C |
| Movie Theaters: 4 | C |
| **Crowd Pleasers (300)** | |
| Zoos: Gladys Porter Zoo | A |
| **Outdoor Recreation Assets (2,000)** | |
| Gulf of Mexico Coastline: 31 miles | |
| Inland Water Area: 262.9 square miles | |
| National Forests, Parks, Wildlife Refuges: | |
| Laguna Atascosa NWR (44,940 acres) | |
| Lower Rio Grande Valley NWR (511 acres) | |

Places Rated Score: 3,000   Places Rated Rank: 33

## Bryan–College Station, TX

| | Rating |
|---|---|
| **Common Denominators (1,000)** | |
| Good Restaurants: 2 ★, 1 ★★ | B |
| Golf Courses: 1 private; 1 daily fee; 1 municipal | B |
| Bowling Lanes: 38 | B |
| Movie Theaters: 4 | AA |
| **Crowd Pleasers (400)** | |
| NCAA Division I: 4.888 game seats per capita | AA |
| Texas A & M Aggies | |
| **Outdoor Recreation Assets (13)** | |
| Inland Water Area: 1.5 square miles | |

Places Rated Score: 1,413   Places Rated Rank: 228

## Buffalo, NY

| | Rating |
|---|---|
| **Common Denominators (900)** | |
| Good Restaurants: 1 ★, 6 ★★, 8 ★★★ | B |
| Golf Courses: 13 private; 7.5 daily fee; 9 municipal | B |
| Bowling Lanes: 1,272 | AA |
| Movie Theaters: 21 | C |
| **Crowd Pleasers (1,100)** | |
| Zoos: Buffalo Zoological Gardens | A |
| Auto Racing: Holland International (NASCAR) | C |
| Pari-mutuel Betting: Buffalo Raceway (harness, 143 days) | B |
| Professional Sports: 4.608 game seats per capita | AA |
| Bisons (baseball), BILLS (football), SABRES (hockey) | |
| NCAA Division I: .023 game seats per capita | C |
| Canisius College Golden Griffins (b) | |
| **Outdoor Recreation Assets (341)** | |
| Great Lakes Coastline: 29 miles | |
| Inland Water Area: 10.6 square miles | |
| National Forests, Parks, Wildlife Refuges: | |
| Theodore Roosevelt Inaugural NHS (1 acre) | |
| CMSA Access: BUFFALO–NIAGARA FALLS, NY (100) | |

Places Rated Score: 2,441   Places Rated Rank: 62

## Burlington, NC

| | Rating |
|---|---|
| **Common Denominators (700)** | |
| Golf Courses: 2 private; 4 daily fee; 1 municipal | AA |
| Bowling Lanes: 32 | C |
| Movie Theaters: 3 | B |
| **Outdoor Recreation Assets (1)** | |
| Inland Water Area: .1 square miles | |

Places Rated Score: 701   Places Rated Rank: 324

## ★ Burlington, VT

| | Rating |
|---|---|
| **Common Denominators (1,200)** | |
| Good Restaurants: 1 ★, 4 ★★, 3 ★★★ | AA |
| Golf Courses: 1 private; 3.5 daily fee | A |
| Bowling Lanes: 78 | B |
| Movie Theaters: 4 | A |
| **Crowd Pleasers (700)** | |
| Auto Racing: Catamount International (NASCAR) | C |
| Professional Sports: 3.460 game seats per capita | AA |
| Reds (baseball) | |
| NCAA Division I: .358 game seats per capita | B |
| University of Vermont Catamounts (b) | |
| **Outdoor Recreation Assets (1,457)** | |
| Inland Water Area: 132.3 square miles | |

Places Rated Score: 3,357   Places Rated Rank: 21

## Canton, OH
Common Denominators (1,100)
Good Restaurants: 4 ★★, 1 ★★★ — C
Golf Courses: 6 private; 17 daily fee — AA
Bowling Lanes: 596 — AA
Movie Theaters: 10 — B
Outdoor Recreation Assets (57)
Inland Water Area: 11.1 square miles
Places Rated Score: 1,157    Places Rated Rank: 268

## Casper, WY
Common Denominators (1,000)
Good Restaurants: 1 ★★ — C
Golf Courses: 2 private; 0.5 daily fee; 1 municipal — B
Bowling Lanes: 70 — A
Movie Theaters: 3 — AA
Crowd Pleasers (400)
Professional Sports: 3.076 game seats per capita — AA
Wildcats (basketball)
Outdoor Recreation Assets (35)
Inland Water Area: 26.7 square miles
National Forests, Parks, Wildlife Refuges:
Medicine Bow NF (5,614 acres)
Pathfinder NWR (1,535 acres)
Places Rated Score: 1,435    Places Rated Rank: 221

## Cedar Rapids, IA
Common Denominators (1,100)
Good Restaurants: 2 ★★ — C
Golf Courses: 2.5 private; 3 daily fee; 3.5 municipal — AA
Bowling Lanes: 194 — AA
Movie Theaters: 5 — B
Crowd Pleasers (400)
Auto Racing: Hawkeye Downs (NASCAR) — C
Professional Sports: 2.474 game seats per capita — A
Reds (baseball)
Outdoor Recreation Assets (1)
Inland Water Area: .2 square miles
Places Rated Score: 1,501    Places Rated Rank: 209

## Champaign–Urbana–Rantoul, IL
Common Denominators (1,300)
Good Restaurants: 1 ★, 6 ★★, 3 ★★★ — AA
Golf Courses: 4 private; 2 daily fee; 2 municipal — B
Bowling Lanes: 128 — A
Movie Theaters: 8 — AA
Crowd Pleasers (400)
NCAA Division I: 3.357 game seats per capita — AA
University of Illinois Fighting Illini
Places Rated Score: 1,700    Places Rated Rank: 160

## Charleston, SC
Common Denominators (900)
Good Restaurants: 1 ★, 2 ★★, 6 ★★★ — A
Golf Courses: 12.5 private; 5.5 daily fee; 1 municipal — B
Bowling Lanes: 256 — B
Movie Theaters: 12 — B
Crowd Pleasers (400)
Professional Sports: 1.004 game seats per capita — B
Royals (baseball)
NCAA Division I: .494 game seats per capita — B
Baptist College Buccaneers (b), The Citadel Bulldogs
Outdoor Recreation Assets (1,261)
Atlantic Coastline: 75 miles
Inland Water Area: 217.1 square miles
National Forests, Parks, Wildlife Refuges:
Cape Romain NWR (34,049 acres)
Fort Sumter NM (67 acres)
Francis Marion NF (250,005 acres)
Santee NWR (2 acres)
Places Rated Score: 2,561    Places Rated Rank: 53

## Charleston, WV
Common Denominators (800)
Good Restaurants: 3 ★★, 2 ★★★ — B
Golf Courses: 5 private; 2 daily fee; 2 municipal — B
Bowling Lanes: 128 — B
Movie Theaters: 7 — B
Outdoor Recreation Assets (44)
Inland Water Area: 11.1 square miles
Places Rated Score: 844    Places Rated Rank: 306

## Charlotte–Gastonia–Rock Hill, NC–SC
Common Denominators (600)
Good Restaurants: 3 ★★, 2 ★★★ — C
Golf Courses: 21.5 private; 15.5 daily fee; 2.5 municipal — B
Bowling Lanes: 356 — B
Movie Theaters: 20 — C
Crowd Pleasers (600)
Theme Parks: Carowinds (121 days) — B
Auto Racing: Charlotte (SCCA, NASCAR) — C
Professional Sports: .754 game seats per capita — B
Charlotte O's, Gastonia Expos (baseball)
NCAA Division I: .207 game seats per capita — C
Davidson College Wildcats, University of North Carolina 49ers (b)
Outdoor Recreation Assets (36)
Inland Water Area: 20.2 square miles
National Forests, Parks, Wildlife Refuges:
Kings Mountain NMP (2,529 acres)
Places Rated Score: 1,236    Places Rated Rank: 255

## Charlottesville, VA
Common Denominators (1,100)
Good Restaurants: 2 ★★, 3 ★★★ — AA
Golf Courses: 3.5 private; 1 municipal — C
Bowling Lanes: 40 — B
Movie Theaters: 8 — AA
Crowd Pleasers (400)
NCAA Division I: 2.902 game seats per capita — AA
University of Virginia Cavaliers
Outdoor Recreation Assets (204)
Inland Water Area: .3 square miles
National Forests, Parks, Wildlife Refuges:
Appalachian Trail (926 acres)
Shenandoah NP (29,786 acres)
Places Rated Score: 1,704    Places Rated Rank: 157

## Chattanooga, TN–GA
Common Denominators (700)
Good Restaurants: 4 ★, 8 ★★, 3 ★★★ — A
Golf Courses: 8 private; 3.5 daily fee; 1.5 municipal — C
Bowling Lanes: 152 — B
Movie Theaters: 6 — C
Crowd Pleasers (400)
Professional Sports: 1.369 game seats per capita — B
Lookouts (baseball)
NCAA Division I: .465 game seats per capita — B
University of Tennessee Moccasins
Outdoor Recreation Assets (138)
Inland Water Area: 45.3 square miles
National Forests, Parks, Wildlife Refuges:
Chickamauga and Chattanooga NMP (8,085 acres)
Places Rated Score: 1,238    Places Rated Rank: 253

## Chicago, IL
Common Denominators (1,000)
Good Restaurants: 18 ★, 94 ★★, 34 ★★★, 7 ★★★★, 2 ★★★★★ — A
Golf Courses: 49 private; 59 daily fee; 33 municipal — A
Bowling Lanes: 4,328 — B
Movie Theaters: 145 — B

| | Rating |
|---|---|
| **Crowd Pleasers (1,100)** | |
| Zoos: | **AA** |
| Brookfield Zoo | |
| Lincoln Park Zoo | |
| Aquariums: Shedd Aquarium | **A** |
| Pari-mutuel Betting: | **C** |
| Arlington Park (Thoroughbred, 109 days) | |
| Associates (harness, 21 days) | |
| Egyptian Trotting (21 days) | |
| Hawthorne (harness, 48 days; Thoroughbred, 85 days) | |
| Maywood Park (harness, 76 days) | |
| Sportsman's Park (Thoroughbred, 75 days) | |
| Suburban Downs (harness, 48 days) | |
| Washington Park (harness, 27 days) | |
| Professional Sports: 1.403 game seats per capita | **B** |
| CUBS, WHITE SOX (baseball), BULLS (basketball), BEARS (football), BLACK HAWKS (hockey) | |
| NCAA Division I: .109 game seats per capita | **C** |
| DePaul University Blue Demons (b), Loyola University Ramblers (b), Northwestern University Wildcats, University of Illinois Flames (b) | |
| **Outdoor Recreation Assets (356)** | |
| Great Lakes Coastline: 33 miles | |
| Inland Water Area: 9.6 square miles | |
| National Forests, Parks, Wildlife Refuges: | |
| Chicago Portage NHS (91 acres) | |
| CMSA Access: CHICAGO–GARY–LAKE COUNTY, IL–IN–WI (400) | |
| Places Rated Score: 2,856 | Places Rated Rank: 43 |

### Chico, CA

| | |
|---|---|
| **Common Denominators (900)** | |
| Good Restaurants: 1 ★★★ | **C** |
| Golf Courses: 1 private; 1 daily fee; 2 municipal | **B** |
| Bowling Lanes: 74 | **B** |
| Movie Theaters: 7 | **AA** |
| **Outdoor Recreation Assets (643)** | |
| Inland Water Area: 6.8 square miles | |
| National Forests, Parks, Wildlife Refuges: | |
| Lassen NF (49,239 acres) | |
| Plumas NF (81,972 acres) | |
| Places Rated Score: 1,543 | Places Rated Rank: 194 |

### Cincinnati, OH–KY–IN

| | |
|---|---|
| **Common Denominators (1,100)** | |
| Good Restaurants: 3 ★, 20 ★★, 21 ★★★, 2 ★★★★, 1 ★★★★★ | **AA** |
| Golf Courses: 24.5 private; 10.5 daily fee; 16.5 municipal | **B** |
| Bowling Lanes: 1,260 | **A** |
| Movie Theaters: 43 | **B** |
| **Crowd Pleasers (1,200)** | |
| Zoos: Cincinnati Zoo | **A** |
| Theme Parks: Kings Island (126 days) | **C** |
| Pari-mutuel Betting: | **A** |
| Latonia (Thoroughbred, 131 days) | |
| Latonia Trots (67 days) | |
| Lebanon Raceway (harness, 65 days) | |
| Miami Valley Trotting (61 days) | |
| River Downs (Thoroughbred, 117 days) | |
| Professional Sports: 3.369 game seats per capita | **AA** |
| REDS (baseball), BENGALS (football) | |
| NCAA Division I: .291 game seats per capita | **C** |
| University of Cincinnati Bearcats, Xavier Musketeers (b) | |
| **Outdoor Recreation Assets (51)** | |
| Inland Water Area: 21.8 square miles | |
| National Forests, Parks, Wildlife Refuges: | |
| William Howard Taft NHS (3 acres) | |
| CMSA Access: CINCINNATI–HAMILTON, OH–KY–IN (100) | |
| Places Rated Score: 2,451 | Places Rated Rank: 61 |

### Clarksville–Hopkinsville, TN–KY

| | |
|---|---|
| **Common Denominators (700)** | |
| Good Restaurants: 1 ★, 1 ★★★ | **C** |

| | Rating |
|---|---|
| Golf Courses: 3.5 private; 2 municipal | **B** |
| Bowling Lanes: 72 | **B** |
| Movie Theaters: 4 | **B** |
| **Crowd Pleasers (300)** | |
| NCAA Division I: 1.111 game seats per capita | **A** |
| Austin Peay Governors | |
| **Outdoor Recreation Assets (1,219)** | |
| Inland Water Area: 4.8 square miles | |
| National Forests, Parks, Wildlife Refuges: | |
| Cherokee NF (193,640 acres) | |
| Places Rated Score: 2,219 | Places Rated Rank: 82 |

### ★ Cleveland, OH

| | |
|---|---|
| **Common Denominators (1,200)** | |
| Good Restaurants: 3 ★, 24 ★★, 8 ★★★ | **B** |
| Golf Courses: 27 private; 37 daily fee; 12 municipal | **A** |
| Bowling Lanes: 2,076 | **AA** |
| Movie Theaters: 63 | **A** |
| **Crowd Pleasers (1,200)** | |
| Zoos: Cleveland Metroparks Zoo | **A** |
| Aquariums: Cleveland Aquarium | **A** |
| Pari-mutuel Betting: Thistledown (Thoroughbred, 94 days) | **C** |
| Professional Sports: 3.926 game seats per capita | **AA** |
| INDIANS (baseball), CAVALIERS (basketball), BROWNS (football) | |
| NCAA Division I: .021 game seats per capita | **C** |
| Cleveland State Vikings (b) | |
| **Outdoor Recreation Assets (600)** | |
| Great Lakes Coastline: 56 miles | |
| Inland Water Area: 2.1 square miles | |
| National Forests, Parks, Wildlife Refuges: | |
| Cuyahoga Valley NRA (6,469 acres) | |
| CMSA Access: CLEVELAND–AKRON–LORAIN, OH (300) | |
| Places Rated Score: 3,300 | Places Rated Rank: 23 |

### Colorado Springs, CO

| | |
|---|---|
| **Common Denominators (1,200)** | |
| Good Restaurants: 3 ★, 6 ★★, 4 ★★★ | **AA** |
| Golf Courses: 11.5 private; 1.5 daily fee; 2.5 municipal | **B** |
| Bowling Lanes: 310 | **A** |
| Movie Theaters: 11 | **A** |
| **Crowd Pleasers (800)** | |
| Zoos: Cheyenne Mountain Zoo | **A** |
| Auto Racing: | **B** |
| Pikes Peak Hill Climb (SCCA) | |
| Colorado Springs International (NASCAR) | |
| Pari-mutuel Betting: Rocky Mountain Greyhound Park (72 days) | **B** |
| NCAA Division I: 1.006 game seats per capita | **A** |
| U.S. Air Force Academy Falcons | |
| **Outdoor Recreation Assets (375)** | |
| Inland Water Area: 2.1 square miles | |
| National Forests, Parks, Wildlife Refuges: | |
| Pike NF (100,726 acres) | |
| Places Rated Score: 2,375 | Places Rated Rank: 67 |

### Columbia, MO

| | |
|---|---|
| **Common Denominators (900)** | |
| Good Restaurants: 2 ★, 1 ★★ | **B** |
| Golf Courses: 2.5 private; 1 daily fee; 2 municipal | **B** |
| Bowling Lanes: 24 | **C** |
| Movie Theaters: 6 | **AA** |
| **Crowd Pleasers (400)** | |
| NCAA Division I: 5.212 game seats per capita | **AA** |
| University of Missouri Tigers | |
| **Outdoor Recreation Assets (31)** | |
| Inland Water Area: 4.2 square miles | |
| Places Rated Score: 1,331 | Places Rated Rank: 244 |

### Columbia, SC

| | |
|---|---|
| **Common Denominators (600)** | |
| Good Restaurants: 2 ★, 1 ★★ | **C** |
| Golf Courses: 8.5 private; 4 daily fee; 1 municipal | **B** |

|  | Rating |
|---|---|
| Bowling Lanes: 140 | B |
| Movie Theaters: 9 | C |

Crowd Pleasers (600)
  Zoos: Riverbanks Zoological Park                           B
  Professional Sports: .702 game seats per capita           C
    Pros (baseball)
  NCAA Division I: 1.276 game seats per capita              A
    University of South Carolina Gamecocks
Outdoor Recreation Assets (284)
  Inland Water Area: 59.9 square miles
  National Forests, Parks, Wildlife Refuges:
    Congaree Swamp NM (15,138 acres)
Places Rated Score: 1,484          Places Rated Rank: 211

### Columbus, GA–AL
Common Denominators (900)
  Good Restaurants: 2 ★★★                                   C
  Golf Courses: 4.5 private; 1 daily fee; 2 municipal       B
  Bowling Lanes: 172                                        A
  Movie Theaters: 8                                         A
Crowd Pleasers (300)
  Professional Sports: 1.831 game seats per capita          A
    Astros (baseball)
Outdoor Recreation Assets (14)
  Inland Water Area: 3 square miles
Places Rated Score: 1,214          Places Rated Rank: 260

### Columbus, OH
Common Denominators (1,100)
  Good Restaurants: 2 ★, 10 ★★, 6 ★★★                        B
  Golf Courses: 23 private, 26.5 daily fee; 5               A
    municipal
  Bowling Lanes: 1,260                                      A
  Movie Theaters: 41                                        A
Crowd Pleasers (900)
  Zoos: Columbus Zoological Gardens                         A
  Pari-mutuel Betting:                                      B
    Beulah Racetrack (Thoroughbred, 22 days)
    MARA (harness, 60 days)
    Scioto Downs (harness, 61 days)
  Professional Sports: .844 game seats per capita           B
    Clippers (baseball)
  NCAA Division I: .467 game seats per capita               B
    Ohio State Buckeyes
Outdoor Recreation Assets (20)
  Inland Water Area: 14.3 square miles
Places Rated Score: 2,020          Places Rated Rank: 103

### Corpus Christi, TX
Common Denominators (900)
  Good Restaurants: 3 ★, 3 ★★, 1 ★★★                         B
  Golf Courses: 5 private; 2 daily fee; 2 municipal         B
  Bowling Lanes: 172                                        B
  Movie Theaters: 11                                        A
Outdoor Recreation Assets (1,137)
  Gulf of Mexico Coastline: 25 miles
  Inland Water Area: 273.3 square miles
Places Rated Score: 2,037          Places Rated Rank: 100

### Cumberland, MD–WV
Common Denominators (1,000)
  Good Restaurants: 1 ★★, 1 ★★★                              AA
  Golf Courses: 2 private; 1 daily fee                      C
  Bowling Lanes: 54                                         B
  Movie Theaters: 4                                         A
Outdoor Recreation Assets (36)
  National Forests, Parks, Wildlife Refuges:
    Chesapeake and Ohio Canal NHP (3,494 acres)
Places Rated Score: 1,036          Places Rated Rank: 288

### Dallas, TX
Common Denominators (700)
  Good Restaurants: 12 ★, 9 ★★, 15 ★★★, 3 ★★★★              B
  Golf Courses: 33 private; 4.5 daily fee;                 C
    15 municipal

|  | Rating |
|---|---|
| Bowling Lanes: 672 | B |
| Movie Theaters: 54 | B |

Crowd Pleasers (1,100)
  Zoos: Dallas Zoo                                          A
  Aquariums: Dallas Aquarium                               A
  Professional Sports: 2.331 game seats per capita          A
    MAVERICKS (basketball), COWBOYS (football)
  NCAA Division I: .347 game seats per capita              B
    North Texas State Mean Green, Southern
    Methodist Mustangs
Outdoor Recreation Assets (110)
  Inland Water Area: 98.8 square miles
CMSA Access: DALLAS–FORT WORTH, TX (400)
Places Rated Score: 2,310          Places Rated Rank: 71

### Danbury, CT
Common Denominators (1,000)
  Good Restaurants: 1 ★, 2 ★★, 3 ★★★                         AA
  Golf Courses: 3.5 private; 1 daily fee; 1.5              B
    municipal
  Bowling Lanes: 70                                         B
  Movie Theaters: 5                                         B
Outdoor Recreation Assets (172)
  Inland Water Area: 9.9 square miles
CMSA Access: NEW YORK–NORTHERN NEW JERSEY–
  LONG ISLAND, NY–NJ–CT (400)
Places Rated Score: 1,572          Places Rated Rank: 189

### Danville, VA
Common Denominators (500)
  Golf Courses: 4 private; 1.5 daily fee                   B
  Bowling Lanes: 46                                         B
  Movie Theaters: 2                                         C
Outdoor Recreation Assets (1)
  Inland Water Area: .1 square miles
Places Rated Score: 501            Places Rated Rank: 328

### Davenport–Rock Island–Moline, IA–IL
Common Denominators (1,400)
  Good Restaurants: 2 ★, 8 ★★, 1 ★★★                         A
  Golf Courses: 8 private; 3.5 daily fee; 7 municipal       A
  Bowling Lanes: 568                                        AA
  Movie Theaters: 16                                        AA
Crowd Pleasers (400)
  Zoos: Weed Park Zoo                                       C
  Professional Sports: 1.550 game seats per capita          A
    Quad City Cubs (baseball)
Outdoor Recreation Assets (120)
  Inland Water Area: 40.3 square miles
  National Forests, Parks, Wildlife Refuges:
    Upper Mississippi NWR (398 acres)
Places Rated Score: 1,920          Places Rated Rank: 123

### Dayton–Springfield, OH
Common Denominators (900)
  Good Restaurants: 5 ★★, 2 ★★★, 2 ★★★★                      C
  Golf Courses: 16.5 private; 6.5 daily fee;               B
    11 municipal
  Bowling Lanes: 1,118                                      AA
  Movie Theaters: 25                                        B
Crowd Pleasers (200)
  Zoos:                                                     C
    Animal Fair
    Dayton Museum of Natural History
  NCAA Division I: .186 game seats per capita              C
    University of Dayton Flyers (b)
Outdoor Recreation Assets (22)
  Inland Water Area: 7.4 square miles
Places Rated Score: 1,122          Places Rated Rank: 276

### ★ Daytona Beach, FL
Common Denominators (1,600)
  Good Restaurants: 1 ★, 7 ★★, 4 ★★★                         AA
  Golf Courses: 2 private; 9.5 daily fee; 3 municipal       AA
  Bowling Lanes: 498                                        AA
  Movie Theaters: 11                                        AA

|  | Rating |
|---|---|
| **Crowd Pleasers (900)** | |
| Auto Racing: Daytona International (SCCA, NASCAR) | C |
| Pari-mutuel Betting: | AA |
| Daytona Beach Kennel Club (106 days) | |
| Volusia Jai Alai (181 days) | |
| Professional Sports: 1.270 game seats per capita | B |
| Astros (baseball) | |
| NCAA Division I: .477 game seats per capita | B |
| Bethune-Cookman Wildcats, Stetson University | |
| Hatters (b) | |
| **Outdoor Recreation Assets (1,467)** | |
| Atlantic Coastline: 49 miles | |
| Inland Water Area: 145 square miles | |
| National Forests, Parks, Wildlife Refuges: | |
| Canaveral NS (28,148 acres) | |
| Lake Woodruff NWR (18,225 acres) | |
| Places Rated Score: 3,967    Places Rated Rank: 9 | |

## Decatur, IL

|  | Rating |
|---|---|
| **Common Denominators (1,100)** | |
| Good Restaurants: 3 ★★ | B |
| Golf Courses: 2 private; 0.5 daily fee; 3 municipal | A |
| Bowling Lanes: 156 | AA |
| Movie Theaters: 3 | B |
| **Crowd Pleasers (100)** | |
| Zoos: Scoville Farm Zoo | C |
| **Outdoor Recreation Assets (22)** | |
| Inland Water Area: 2.6 square miles | |
| Places Rated Score: 1,222    Places Rated Rank: 257 | |

## Denver, CO

|  | Rating |
|---|---|
| **Common Denominators (1,100)** | |
| Good Restaurants: 5 ★, 18 ★★, 9 ★★★, 1 ★★★★ | A |
| Golf Courses: 18.5 private; 4 daily fee; 16 municipal | B |
| Bowling Lanes: 1,332 | A |
| Movie Theaters: 47 | A |
| **Crowd Pleasers (1,000)** | |
| Zoos: Denver Zoological Gardens | A |
| Auto Racing: Continental Divide (SCCA) | C |
| Pari-mutuel Betting: | B |
| Centennial (Thoroughbred, 117 days) | |
| Mile High Kennel Club (72 days) | |
| Professional Sports: 5.890 game seats per capita | AA |
| Bears (baseball), NUGGETS (basketball), GOLD, BRONCOS (football), Colorado Flames (hockey) | |
| **Outdoor Recreation Assets (24)** | |
| Inland Water Area: 18.3 square miles | |
| CMSA Access: DENVER–BOULDER, CO (200) | |
| Places Rated Score: 2,324    Places Rated Rank: 69 | |

## Des Moines, IA

|  | Rating |
|---|---|
| **Common Denominators (1,200)** | |
| Good Restaurants: 2 ★, 7 ★★ | B |
| Golf Courses: 8.5 private; 6.5 daily fee; 4.5 municipal | A |
| Bowling Lanes: 266 | A |
| Movie Theaters: 26 | AA |
| **Crowd Pleasers (600)** | |
| Professional Sports: 1.592 game seats per capita | A |
| Cubs (baseball) | |
| NCAA Division I: .722 game seats per capita | A |
| Drake University Bulldogs | |
| **Outdoor Recreation Assets (2)** | |
| Inland Water Area: .8 square miles | |
| Places Rated Score: 1,802    Places Rated Rank: 144 | |

## Detroit, MI

|  | Rating |
|---|---|
| **Common Denominators (700)** | |
| Good Restaurants: 11 ★, 35 ★★, 6 ★★★, 1 ★★★★ | C |
| Golf Courses: 40 private; 78 daily fee; 26 municipal | B |
| Bowling Lanes: 4,517 | A |
| Movie Theaters: 80 | C |

|  | Rating |
|---|---|
| **Crowd Pleasers (1,000)** | |
| Zoos: | AA |
| Belle Isle Zoo and Aquarium | |
| Detroit Zoological Park | |
| Auto Racing: Mount Clemens Race Track (NASCAR) | C |
| Pari-mutuel Betting: | C |
| Detroit Race Course (Thoroughbred, 90 days) | |
| Hazel Park (harness, 84 days; Thoroughbred, 108 days) | |
| Northville Downs (harness, 78 days) | |
| Wolverine Raceway (harness, 84 days) | |
| Professional Sports: 1.538 game seats per capita | A |
| TIGERS (baseball), Spirits, PISTONS (basketball), LIONS (football), RED WINGS (hockey) | |
| NCAA Division I: .029 game seats per capita | C |
| University of Detroit Titans (b) | |
| **Outdoor Recreation Assets (583)** | |
| Great Lakes Coastline: 48 miles | |
| Inland Water Area: 92.9 square miles | |
| CMSA Access: DETROIT–ANN ARBOR, MI (200) | |
| Places Rated Score: 2,483    Places Rated Rank: 58 | |

## Dothan, AL

|  | Rating |
|---|---|
| **Common Denominators (700)** | |
| Good Restaurants: 1 ★★, 1 ★★★ | B |
| Golf Courses: 3 private; 1 daily fee | C |
| Bowling Lanes: 56 | B |
| Movie Theaters: 3 | B |
| **Outdoor Recreation Assets (14)** | |
| Inland Water Area: 3.3 square miles | |
| Places Rated Score: 714    Places Rated Rank: 321 | |

## Dubuque, IA

|  | Rating |
|---|---|
| **Common Denominators (1,500)** | |
| Good Restaurants: 4 ★★ | AA |
| Golf Courses: 2.5 private; 1 daily fee; 1.5 municipal | A |
| Bowling Lanes: 132 | AA |
| Movie Theaters: 5 | AA |
| **Outdoor Recreation Assets (87)** | |
| Inland Water Area: 9.8 square miles | |
| National Forests, Parks, Wildlife Refuges: | |
| Upper Mississippi NWR (476 acres) | |
| Places Rated Score: 1,587    Places Rated Rank: 187 | |

## Duluth, MN–WI

|  | Rating |
|---|---|
| **Common Denominators (1,500)** | |
| Good Restaurants: 1 ★, 8 ★★, 2 ★★★ | AA |
| Golf Courses: 4 private; 2 daily fee; 5.5 municipal | A |
| Bowling Lanes: 284 | AA |
| Movie Theaters: 14 | AA |
| **Crowd Pleasers (100)** | |
| Zoos: Duluth Zoological Gardens | C |
| **Outdoor Recreation Assets (1,507)** | |
| Great Lakes Coastline: 36 miles | |
| Inland Water Area: 656.1 square miles | |
| National Forests, Parks, Wildlife Refuges: | |
| Superior NF (670,753 acres) | |
| Places Rated Score: 3,107    Places Rated Rank: 30 | |

## East St. Louis–Belleville, IL

|  | Rating |
|---|---|
| **Common Denominators (800)** | |
| Good Restaurants: 1 ★★, 1 ★★★ | C |
| Golf Courses: 3 private; 6 daily fee; 1 municipal | B |
| Bowling Lanes: 242 | A |
| Movie Theaters: 9 | B |
| **Crowd Pleasers (400)** | |
| Pari-mutuel Betting: Fairmount Park (Thoroughbred, 165 days) | AA |
| **Outdoor Recreation Assets (10)** | |
| Inland Water Area: 2.3 square miles | |
| CMSA Access: St. Louis–East St. Louis–Alton, MO–IL (400) | |
| Places Rated Score: 1,610    Places Rated Rank: 177 | |

Rating

## Eau Claire, WI
Common Denominators (1,300)
 Good Restaurants: 2 ★, 4 ★★, 1 ★★★    AA
 Golf Courses: 2.5 private; 2 daily fee    B
 Bowling Lanes: 128    A
 Movie Theaters: 8    AA
Outdoor Recreation Assets (97)
 Inland Water Area: 32.1 square miles
Places Rated Score: 1,397    Places Rated Rank: 235

## El Paso, TX
Common Denominators (500)
 Golf Courses:  5 private; 2.5 municipal    C
 Bowling Lanes: 262    B
 Movie Theaters: 12    B
Crowd Pleasers (600)
 Zoos: El Paso Zoological Park    C
 Professional Sports: .992 game seats per capita    B
  Diablos (baseball)
 NCAA Division I: .877 game seats per capita    A
  University of Texas Miners
Outdoor Recreation Assets (1)
 National Forests, Parks, Wildlife Refuges:
  Chamizal National Memorial (55 acres)
Places Rated Score: 1,101    Places Rated Rank: 281

## Elkhart–Goshen, IN
Common Denominators (1,000)
 Good Restaurants: 1 ★, 1 ★★, 1 ★★★    B
 Golf Courses: 3 private; 1.5 daily fee; 1.5    B
  municipal
 Bowling Lanes: 148    AA
 Movie Theaters: 4    B
Outdoor Recreation Assets (23)
 Inland Water Area: 2.1 square miles
Places Rated Score: 1,023    Places Rated Rank: 289

## Elmira, NY
Common Denominators (1,300)
 Good Restaurants: 1 ★, 2 ★★, 1 ★★★★    AA
 Golf Courses: 1 private; 3.5 daily fee; 1 municipal    AA
 Bowling Lanes: 148    AA
 Movie Theaters: 2    C
Crowd Pleasers (300)
 Professional Sports: 1.985 game seats per capita    A
  Suns (baseball)
Places Rated Score: 1,600    Places Rated Rank: 185

## Enid, OK
Common Denominators (1,200)
 Good Restaurants: 1 ★, 1 ★★★    A
 Golf Courses: 1 private; 0.5 daily fee    C
 Bowling Lanes: 68    AA
 Movie Theaters: 3    AA
Places Rated Score: 1,200    Places Rated Rank: 264

## Erie, PA
Common Denominators (1,200)
 Good Restaurants: 1 ★, 2 ★★    C
 Golf Courses: 4 private; 7 daily fee; 3.5 municipal    AA
 Bowling Lanes: 410    AA
 Movie Theaters: 9    A
Crowd Pleasers (100)
 Zoos: Erie Zoo    C
Outdoor Recreation Assets (40)
 Inland Water Area: 6.4 square miles
Places Rated Score: 1,340    Places Rated Rank: 243

## ◄ Eugene–Springfield, OR
Common Denominators (900)
 Good Restaurants: 2 ★, 4 ★★, 3 ★★★    A
 Golf Courses: 2.5 private; 4.5 daily fee; 0.5    B
  municipal
 Bowling Lanes: 166    B
 Movie Theaters: 8    B

Rating

 Crowd Pleasers (500)
  Professional Sports: .860 game seats per capita    B
   Emeralds (baseball)
  NCAA Division I: 1.235 game seats per capita    A
   University of Oregon Ducks
Outdoor Recreation Assets (2,000)
 Pacific Coastline: 30 miles
 Inland Water Area: 48.1 square miles
 National Forests, Parks, Wildlife Refuges:
  Oregon Islands NWR (6 acres)
  Siuslaw NF (242,790 acres)
  Umpqua NF (151,588 acres)
  Willamette NF (1,021,769 acres)
Places Rated Score: 3,400    Places Rated Rank: 19

## Evansville, IN–KY
Common Denominators (700)
 Good Restaurants: 2 ★★, 1 ★★★    C
 Golf Courses: 5 private; 3.5 daily fee; 3 municipal    B
 Bowling Lanes: 184    B
 Movie Theaters: 8    B
Crowd Pleasers (800)
 Zoos: Mesker Park Zoo    C
 Pari-mutuel Betting:    A
  Audubon Raceway (harness, 46 days)
  Ellis Park (Thoroughbred, 59 days)
 Professional Sports: 1.477 game seats per capita    B
  Triplets (baseball)
 NCAA Division I: .579 game seats per capita    B
  University of Evansville Purple Aces (b)
Outdoor Recreation Assets (122)
 Inland Water Area: 36 square miles
Places Rated Score: 1,622    Places Rated Rank: 173

## Fall River, MA–RI
Common Denominators (700)
 Good Restaurants: 1 ★★    C
 Golf Courses: 2.5 private; 1.5 daily fee    C
 Bowling Lanes: 64    B
 Movie Theaters: 5    A
Outdoor Recreation Assets (1,005)
 Atlantic Coastline: 18 miles
 Inland Water Area: 27.9 square miles
CMSA Access: PROVIDENCE–PAWTUCKET–
 FALL RIVER, RI–MA (300)
Places Rated Score: 2,005    Places Rated Rank: 105

## Fargo–Moorhead, ND–MN
Common Denominators (1,400)
 Good Restaurants: 2 ★, 3 ★★    A
 Golf Courses: 3.5 private; 1.5 daily fee; 2.5    A
  municipal
 Bowling Lanes: 154    AA
 Movie Theaters: 6    AA
Outdoor Recreation Assets (14)
 Inland Water Area: 7.7 square miles
Places Rated Score: 1,414    Places Rated Rank: 227

## Fayetteville, NC
Common Denominators (700)
 Good Restaurants: 1 ★★    C
 Golf Courses: 5 private; 3 daily fee    B
 Bowling Lanes: 192    A
 Movie Theaters: 4    C
Outdoor Recreation Assets (9)
 Inland Water Area: 1.2 square miles
Places Rated Score: 709    Places Rated Rank: 322

## Fayetteville–Springdale, AR
Common Denominators (1,100)
 Good Restaurants: 1 ★, 1 ★★, 1 ★★★    A
 Golf Courses: 1 private; 2 daily fee    B
 Bowling Lanes: 92    A
 Movie Theaters: 4    A

| | Rating |
|---|---|
| Crowd Pleasers (400) | |
| NCAA Division I: 3.533 game seats per capita | AA |
| University of Arkansas Razorbacks | |
| Outdoor Recreation Assets (195) | |
| Inland Water Area: .8 square miles | |
| National Forests, Parks, Wildlife Refuges: | |
| Ozark NF (23,247 acres) | |
| Places Rated Score: 1,695 | Places Rated Rank: 161 |

## Fitchburg–Leominster, MA

| | Rating |
|---|---|
| Common Denominators (400) | |
| Good Restaurants: 1 ★★★ | B |
| Golf Courses: 1 private; 3 daily fee | A |
| Movie Theaters: 2 | C |
| Outdoor Recreation Assets (190) | |
| Inland Water Area: 6.8 square miles | |
| Places Rated Score: 790 | Places Rated Rank: 317 |

## Flint, MI

| | Rating |
|---|---|
| Common Denominators (1,000) | |
| Good Restaurants: 1 ★, 1 ★★, 1 ★★★ | C |
| Golf Courses: 10 private; 8 daily fee; 4 municipal | A |
| Bowling Lanes: 612 | AA |
| Movie Theaters: 12 | B |
| Crowd Pleasers (300) | |
| Auto Racing: | B |
| Auto City (NASCAR) | |
| Waterford Hills (SCCA) | |
| Professional Sports: .390 game seats per capita | C |
| Generals (hockey) | |
| Outdoor Recreation Assets (55) | |
| Inland Water Area: 7 square miles | |
| Places Rated Score: 1,355 | Places Rated Rank: 241 |

## Florence, AL

| | Rating |
|---|---|
| Common Denominators (600) | |
| Good Restaurants: 3 ★★ | B |
| Golf Courses: 4.5 private; 0.5 daily fee; 2.5 municipal | B |
| Bowling Lanes: 36 | C |
| Movie Theaters: 3 | C |
| Outdoor Recreation Assets (394) | |
| Inland Water Area: 92.1 square miles | |
| National Forests, Parks, Wildlife Refuges: | |
| Natchez Trace Parkway (4,176 acres) | |
| Places Rated Score: 994 | Places Rated Rank: 294 |

## Florence, SC

| | Rating |
|---|---|
| Common Denominators (400) | |
| Golf Courses: 5 private; 1 daily fee | C |
| Bowling Lanes: 24 | C |
| Movie Theaters: 3 | B |
| Crowd Pleasers (400) | |
| Auto Racing: Darlington Raceway (NASCAR) | C |
| Professional Sports: 2.446 game seats per capita | A |
| Blue Jays (baseball) | |
| Places Rated Score: 800 | Places Rated Rank: 314 |

## ★ Fort Collins–Loveland, CO

| | Rating |
|---|---|
| Common Denominators (1,400) | |
| Good Restaurants: 1 ★, 4 ★★, 4 ★★★ | AA |
| Golf Courses: 2 private; 3.5 municipal | B |
| Bowling Lanes: 160 | AA |
| Movie Theaters: 6 | AA |
| Crowd Pleasers (800) | |
| Pari-mutuel Betting: Cloverleaf Kennel Club (69 days) | AA |
| NCAA Division I: 1.877 game seats per capita | AA |
| Colorado State Rams | |
| Outdoor Recreation Assets (2,000) | |
| Inland Water Area: 29.7 square miles | |
| National Forests, Parks, Wildlife Refuges: | |
| Rocky Mountain NP (143,434 acres) | |
| Roosevelt NF (623,134 acres) | |
| Places Rated Score: 4,200 | Places Rated Rank: 4 |

## Fort Lauderdale–Hollywood– Pompano Beach, FL

| | Rating |
|---|---|
| Common Denominators (1,200) | |
| Good Restaurants: 9 ★, 16 ★★, 21 ★★★, 1 ★★★★ | AA |
| Golf Courses: 20 private; 25 daily fee; 4 municipal | A |
| Bowling Lanes: 802 | A |
| Movie Theaters: 23 | B |
| Crowd Pleasers (600) | |
| Zoos: Markham Park Zoo | C |
| Pari-mutuel Betting: | AA |
| Dania Jai Alai (290 days) | |
| Gulfstream Park (Thoroughbred, 50 days) | |
| Hollywood Greyhound Track (105 days) | |
| Pompano Park (harness, 108 days) | |
| Professional Sports: .538 game seats per capita | C |
| Yankees (baseball) | |
| Outdoor Recreation Assets (255) | |
| Atlantic Coastline: 25 miles | |
| Inland Water Area: 1.3 square miles | |
| CMSA Access: Miami–Fort Lauderdale, FL (400) | |
| Places Rated Score: 2,455 | Places Rated Rank: 60 |

## ★ Fort Myers, FL

| | Rating |
|---|---|
| Common Denominators (1,500) | |
| Good Restaurants: 7 ★, 10 ★★, 3 ★★★ | AA |
| Golf Courses: 8.5 private; 9 daily fee; 2 municipal | AA |
| Bowling Lanes: 266 | AA |
| Movie Theaters: 7 | A |
| Crowd Pleasers (700) | |
| Pari-mutuel Betting: Naples–Fort Myers Kennel Club (109 days) | AA |
| Professional Sports: 1.849 game seats per capita | A |
| Royals (baseball) | |
| Outdoor Recreation Assets (1,805) | |
| Gulf of Mexico Coastline: 38 miles | |
| Inland Water Area: 220 square miles | |
| National Forests, Parks, Wildlife Refuges: | |
| Caloosahatchee NWR (140 acres) | |
| J.N. "Ding" Darling NWR (4,960 acres) | |
| Matlacha Pass NWR (231 acres) | |
| Pine Island NWR (404 acres) | |
| Places Rated Score: 4,005 | Places Rated Rank: 6 |

## Fort Pierce, FL

| | Rating |
|---|---|
| Common Denominators (900) | |
| Good Restaurants: 2 ★★ | C |
| Golf Courses: 12 private; 6 daily fee | AA |
| Bowling Lanes: 92 | B |
| Movie Theaters: 4 | B |
| Crowd Pleasers (400) | |
| Pari-mutuel Betting: Fort Pierce Jai Alai (180 days) | AA |
| Outdoor Recreation Assets (758) | |
| Atlantic Coastline: 45 miles | |
| Inland Water Area: 68.4 square miles | |
| National Forests, Parks, Wildlife Refuges: | |
| Hobe Sound NWR (960 acres) | |
| Places Rated Score: 2,058 | Places Rated Rank: 97 |

## Fort Smith, AR–OK

| | Rating |
|---|---|
| Common Denominators (1,200) | |
| Good Restaurants: 1 ★, 3 ★★, 1 ★★★ | A |
| Golf Courses: 2.5 private; 4.5 daily fee; 1 municipal | AA |
| Bowling Lanes: 96 | B |
| Movie Theaters: 6 | A |
| Outdoor Recreation Assets (536) | |
| Inland Water Area: 37.8 square miles | |
| National Forests, Parks, Wildlife Refuges: | |
| Fort Smith NHS (23 acres) | |
| Ouachita NF (15,128 acres) | |
| Ozark NF (84,547 acres) | |
| Places Rated Score: 1,736 | Places Rated Rank: 152 |

## Fort Walton Beach, FL

| | Rating |
|---|---|
| Common Denominators (1,400) | |
| Good Restaurants: 4 ★★, 1 ★★★ | AA |

| | Rating |
|---|---|
| Golf Courses: 2.5 private; 6.5 daily fee; 1.5 municipal | AA |
| Bowling Lanes: 92 | A |
| Movie Theaters: 4 | A |

Outdoor Recreation Assets (692)
Gulf of Mexico Coastline: 24 miles
Inland Water Area: 58.7 square miles
National Forests, Parks, Wildlife Refuges:
Choctawhatchee NF (675 acres)
Gulf Islands NS (15,910 acres)
Places Rated Score: 2,092          Places Rated Rank: 94

### Fort Wayne, IN
Common Denominators (1,300)

| | Rating |
|---|---|
| Good Restaurants: 2 ★★, 1 ★★★, 1 ★★★★ | B |
| Golf Courses: 5 private; 11 daily fee; 1 municipal | AA |
| Bowling Lanes: 428 | AA |
| Movie Theaters: 13 | A |

Crowd Pleasers (400)

| | |
|---|---|
| Zoos: Fort Wayne Children's Zoo | C |
| Auto Racing: Allen County Memorial Coliseum (USAC) | C |
| Professional Sports: .906 game seats per capita Komets (hockey) | B |

Outdoor Recreation Assets (11)
Inland Water Area: 2.9 square miles
Places Rated Score: 1,711          Places Rated Rank: 156

### Fort Worth–Arlington, TX
Common Denominators (800)

| | Rating |
|---|---|
| Good Restaurants: 5 ★, 21 ★★, 5 ★★★ | A |
| Golf Courses: 20 private; 1 daily fee; 8 municipal | C |
| Bowling Lanes: 404 | B |
| Movie Theaters: 29 | B |

Crowd Pleasers (1,100)

| | |
|---|---|
| Zoos: Fort Worth Zoological Park | A |
| Theme Parks: Six Flags Over Texas (146 days) | B |
| Professional Sports: 4.161 game seats per capita TEXAS RANGERS (baseball) | AA |
| NCAA Division I: .466 game seats per capita Texas Christian Horned Frogs, University of Texas Mavericks | B |

Outdoor Recreation Assets (66)
Inland Water Area: 33 square miles
CMSA Access: DALLAS–FORT WORTH, TX (400)
Places Rated Score: 2,366          Places Rated Rank: 68

### Fresno, CA
Common Denominators (700)

| | Rating |
|---|---|
| Good Restaurants: 4 ★★, 1 ★★★ | C |
| Golf Courses: 6 private; 5.5 daily fee; 2 municipal | B |
| Bowling Lanes: 97 | C |
| Movie Theaters: 20 | A |

Crowd Pleasers (500)

| | |
|---|---|
| Zoos: Roeding Park Zoo | B |
| Professional Sports: .354 game seats per capita Giants (baseball) | C |
| NCAA Division I: .456 game seats per capita California State Bulldogs | B |

Outdoor Recreation Assets (1,784)
Inland Water Area: 37.6 square miles
National Forests, Parks, Wildlife Refuges:
Kings Canyon NP (354,828 acres)
Sequoia NF (130,641 acres)
Sierra NF (855,231 acres)
Places Rated Score: 2,984          Places Rated Rank: 36

### Gadsden, AL
Common Denominators (300)

| | Rating |
|---|---|
| Golf Courses: 4 private | — |
| Bowling Lanes: 32 | C |
| Movie Theaters: 3 | B |

Places Rated Score: 300          Places Rated Rank: 329

### Gainesville, FL
Common Denominators (500)

| | Rating |
|---|---|
| Good Restaurants: 2 ★, 1 ★★★ | C |
| Golf Courses: 3 private; 1.5 daily fee | C |
| Bowling Lanes: 56 | C |
| Movie Theaters: 5 | B |

Crowd Pleasers (500)

| | |
|---|---|
| Zoos: | C |
| Santa Fe Teaching Zoo | |
| Skye Hye Zoological Park | |
| NCAA Division I: 3.011 game seats per capita University of Florida Gators | AA |

Outdoor Recreation Assets (237)
Inland Water Area: 56.6 square miles
Places Rated Score: 1,237          Places Rated Rank: 254

### Galveston–Texas City, TX
Common Denominators (700)

| | Rating |
|---|---|
| Good Restaurants: 1 ★, 2 ★★, 2 ★★★ | A |
| Golf Courses: 3.5 private; 2 daily fee; 2 municipal | B |
| Bowling Lanes: 32 | C |
| Movie Theaters: 3 | C |

Outdoor Recreation Assets (2,000)
Gulf of Mexico Coastline: 25 miles
Inland Water Area: 165 square miles
CMSA Access: HOUSTON–GALVESTON–BRAZORIA, TX (300)
Places Rated Score: 3,000          Places Rated Rank: 33

### Gary–Hammond, IN
Common Denominators (1,000)

| | Rating |
|---|---|
| Good Restaurants: 3 ★, 4 ★★, 3 ★★★ | B |
| Golf Courses: 7 private; 14.5 daily fee; 4 municipal | A |
| Bowling Lanes: 617 | A |
| Movie Theaters: 16 | B |

Crowd Pleasers (100)

| | |
|---|---|
| NCAA Division I: .087 game seats per capita Valparaiso Crusaders (b) | C |

Outdoor Recreation Assets (440)
Great Lakes Coastline: 32 miles
Inland Water Area: 5 square miles
National Forests, Parks, Wildlife Refuges:
Indiana Dunes National Lakeshore (10,948 acres)
CMSA Access: CHICAGO–GARY–LAKE COUNTY, IL–IN–WI (400)
Places Rated Score: 1,940          Places Rated Rank: 118

### Glens Falls, NY
Common Denominators (1,300)

| | Rating |
|---|---|
| Good Restaurants: 2 ★, 4 ★★, 4 ★★★ | AA |
| Golf Courses: 1 private; 5 daily fee | AA |
| Bowling Lanes: 146 | AA |
| Movie Theaters: 2 | C |

Crowd Pleasers (400)

| | |
|---|---|
| Professional Sports: 9.421 game seats per capita White Sox (baseball), Adirondack Reds (hockey) | AA |

Outdoor Recreation Assets (183)
Inland Water Area: 63 square miles
Places Rated Score: 1,883          Places Rated Rank: 130

### Grand Forks, ND
Common Denominators (1,300)

| | Rating |
|---|---|
| Good Restaurants: 1 ★, 1 ★★ | B |
| Golf Courses: 1.5 private; 1.5 daily fee; 1 municipal | AA |
| Bowling Lanes: 54 | A |
| Movie Theaters: 6 | AA |

Outdoor Recreation Assets (4)
National Forests, Parks, Wildlife Refuges:
Kelly's Slough NWR (680 acres)
Places Rated Score: 1,304          Places Rated Rank: 248

### Grand Rapids, MI
Common Denominators (1,400)

| | Rating |
|---|---|
| Good Restaurants: 5 ★, 17 ★★, 4 ★★★, 1 ★★★★ | AA |

|  | Rating |
|---|---|
| Golf Courses: 9 private; 33.5 daily fee; 2 municipal | AA |
| Bowling Lanes: 674 | AA |
| Movie Theaters: 16 | B |

Crowd Pleasers (200)
| Zoos: John Ball Zoological Gardens | B |

Outdoor Recreation Assets (309)
Great Lakes Coastline: 24 miles
Inland Water Area: 19.6 square miles

Places Rated Score: 1,909        Places Rated Rank: 127

## Great Falls, MT
Common Denominators (1,400)
| Good Restaurants: 3 ★★ | AA |
| Golf Courses: 1 private; 1.5 municipal | B |
| Bowling Lanes: 114 | AA |
| Movie Theaters: 4 | AA |

Crowd Pleasers (200)
| Professional Sports: 1.490 game seats per capita | B |
| Dodgers (baseball) | |

Outdoor Recreation Assets (576)
Inland Water Area: 12.4 square miles
National Forests, Parks, Wildlife Refuges:
Benton Lake NWR (11,955 acres)
Lewis and Clark NF (197,103 acres)

Places Rated Score: 2,176        Places Rated Rank: 83

## Greeley, CO
Common Denominators (700)
| Good Restaurants: 1 ★, 1 ★★★ | B |
| Golf Courses: 2 private; 1 municipal | C |
| Bowling Lanes: 78 | B |
| Movie Theaters: 3 | B |

Outdoor Recreation Assets (39)
Inland Water Area: 31.5 square miles

Places Rated Score: 739        Places Rated Rank: 319

## Green Bay, WI
Common Denominators (1,300)
| Good Restaurants: 1 ★, 4 ★★ | A |
| Golf Courses: 1 private; 6.5 daily fee; 1 municipal | AA |
| Bowling Lanes: 360 | AA |
| Movie Theaters: 5 | B |

Crowd Pleasers (400)
| Professional Sports: 1.282 game seats per capita | B |
| PACKERS (football) | |
| NCAA Division I: .445 game seats per capita | B |
| University of Wisconsin Phoenix (b) | |

Outdoor Recreation Assets (225)
Great Lakes Coastline: 18 miles
Inland Water Area: 4.7 square miles

Places Rated Score: 1,925        Places Rated Rank: 121

## Greensboro–Winston-Salem–High Point, NC
Common Denominators (800)
| Good Restaurants: 2 ★★ | C |
| Golf Courses: 19 private; 20 daily fee; 9 municipal | AA |
| Bowling Lanes: 314 | B |
| Movie Theaters: 12 | C |

Crowd Pleasers (800)
| Zoos: North Carolina Zoological Park | B |
| Auto Racing: | B |
| Bowman Gray Stadium (NASCAR) | |
| Caraway (NASCAR) | |
| Professional Sports: 1.200 game seats per capita | B |
| Greensboro Hornets, Winston-Salem Spirits | |
| (baseball) | |
| NCAA Division I: .524 game seats per capita | B |
| North Carolina A & T Aggies, Wake Forest | |
| Demon Deacons | |

Outdoor Recreation Assets (51)
Inland Water Area: 19.3 square miles
National Forests, Parks, Wildlife Refuges:
Guilford Courthouse NMP (220 acres)
Uwharrie NF (9,807 acres)

Places Rated Score: 1,651        Places Rated Rank: 167

## Greenville–Spartanburg, SC
Common Denominators (700)
| Good Restaurants: 3 ★★, 1 ★★★ | C |
| Golf Courses: 12 private; 12.5 daily fee | B |
| Bowling Lanes: 234 | B |
| Movie Theaters: 16 | B |

Crowd Pleasers (700)
| Zoos: Greenville Zoo | C |
| Auto Racing: Greenville–Pickens Speedway | C |
| (NASCAR) | |
| Professional Sports: 1.344 game seats per capita | B |
| Greenville Braves, Spartanburg Suns (baseball) | |
| NCAA Division I: 1.004 game seats per capita | A |
| Clemson Tigers, Furman Paladins | |

Outdoor Recreation Assets (10)
Inland Water Area: 4.3 square miles

Places Rated Score: 1,410        Places Rated Rank: 230

## Hagerstown, MD
Common Denominators (800)
| Good Restaurants: 1 ★, 2 ★★ | B |
| Golf Courses: 2 private; 0.5 municipal | C |
| Bowling Lanes: 42 | B |
| Movie Theaters: 4 | A |

Crowd Pleasers (400)
| Professional Sports: 3.714 game seats per capita | AA |
| Suns (baseball) | |

Outdoor Recreation Assets (291)
Inland Water Area: 12.1 square miles
National Forests, Parks, Wildlife Refuges:
Antietam National Battlefield (1,764 acres)
Appalachian Trail (22 acres)
Catoctin Mountain Park (75 acres)
Chesapeake and Ohio Canal NHP (6,557 acres)
Harper's Ferry NHP (765 acres)

Places Rated Score: 1,491        Places Rated Rank: 210

## Hamilton–Middletown, OH
Common Denominators (900)
| Golf Courses: 4.5 private; 6.5 daily fee; 4 municipal | AA |
| Bowling Lanes: 236 | A |
| Movie Theaters: 6 | B |

Crowd Pleasers (300)
| NCAA Division I: .750 game seats per capita | A |
| Miami University Redskins | |

Outdoor Recreation Assets (4)
Inland Water Area: .4 square miles
CMSA Access: CINCINNATI–HAMILTON, OH–KY–IN (400)

Places Rated Score: 1,604        Places Rated Rank: 182

## Harrisburg–Lebanon–Carlisle, PA
Common Denominators (800)
| Good Restaurants: 4 ★★, 1 ★★★ | C |
| Golf Courses: 10 private; 13 daily fee; 2 municipal | A |
| Bowling Lanes: 496 | A |
| Movie Theaters: 9 | C |

Crowd Pleasers (600)
| Theme Parks: Hersheypark (120 days) | A |
| Pari-mutuel Betting: Penn National (Thoroughbred, | B |
| 92 days) | |
| Professional Sports: .525 game seats per capita | C |
| Hershey Bears (hockey) | |

Outdoor Recreation Assets (132)
Inland Water Area: 32.6 square miles
National Forests, Parks, Wildlife Refuges:
Appalachian Trail (8,363 acres)

Places Rated Score: 1,532        Places Rated Rank: 198

## Hartford, CT
Common Denominators (1,000)
| Good Restaurants: 1 ★, 7 ★★, 6 ★★★, 1 ★★★★ | A |
| Golf Courses: 15 private; 13.5 daily fee; 5.5 municipal | A |
| Bowling Lanes: 386 | B |
| Movie Theaters: 17 | B |

| | Rating |
|---|---|
| **Crowd Pleasers (600)** | |
| Zoos: Children's Zoo | C |
| Pari-mutuel Betting: Hartford Jai Alai (300 days) | A |
| Professional Sports: .848 game seats per capita | B |
| WHALERS (hockey) | |
| **Outdoor Recreation Assets (90)** | |
| Inland Water Area: 19.4 square miles | |
| CMSA Access: HARTFORD–NEW BRITAIN– | |
| MIDDLETOWN, CT (100) | |
| Places Rated Score: 1,790 | Places Rated Rank: 146 |

### Hickory, NC

| | Rating |
|---|---|
| **Common Denominators (600)** | |
| Good Restaurants: 1 ★★ | C |
| Golf Courses: 5.5 private; 4.5 daily fee | B |
| Bowling Lanes: 80 | B |
| Movie Theaters: 3 | C |
| **Crowd Pleasers (100)** | |
| Auto Racing: Hickory (NASCAR) | C |
| **Outdoor Recreation Assets (97)** | |
| Inland Water Area: 22.6 square miles | |
| Places Rated Score: 797 | Places Rated Rank: 315 |

### ★ Honolulu, HI

| | Rating |
|---|---|
| **Common Denominators (1,000)** | |
| Good Restaurants: NA | A |
| Golf Courses: 11 private; 10 daily fee; 3.5 | B |
| municipal | |
| Bowling Lanes: 534 | B |
| Movie Theaters: 29 | A |
| **Crowd Pleasers (1,200)** | |
| Zoos: Honolulu Zoo | A |
| Aquariums: Waikiki Aquarium | A |
| Professional Sports: 4.721 game seats per capita | AA |
| Islanders (baseball) | |
| NCAA Division I: .457 game seats per capita | B |
| University of Hawaii Rainbow Warriors | |
| **Outdoor Recreation Assets (1,503)** | |
| Pacific Coastline: 135 miles | |
| Inland Water Area: 15.2 square miles | |
| National Forests, Parks, Wildlife Refuges: | |
| Hawaiian Islands NWR (1,907 acres) | |
| Places Rated Score: 3,703 | Places Rated Rank: 15 |

### Houma–Thibodaux, LA

| | Rating |
|---|---|
| **Common Denominators (500)** | |
| Golf Courses: 2 private; 0.5 daily fee | C |
| Bowling Lanes: 70 | B |
| Movie Theaters: 4 | B |
| **Crowd Pleasers (200)** | |
| NCAA Division I: .612 game seats per capita | B |
| Nicholls State Colonels | |
| **Outdoor Recreation Assets (2,000)** | |
| Gulf of Mexico Coastline: 79 miles | |
| Inland Water Area: 632.8 square miles | |
| Places Rated Score: 2,700 | Places Rated Rank: 47 |

### Houston, TX

| | Rating |
|---|---|
| **Common Denominators (800)** | |
| Good Restaurants: 8 ★, 26 ★★, 31 ★★★, 1 ★★★★ | A |
| Golf Courses: 50 private; 9.5 daily fee; 7 municipal | C |
| Bowling Lanes: 1,190 | B |
| Movie Theaters: 67 | B |
| **Crowd Pleasers (900)** | |
| Zoos: Houston Zoological Gardens | A |
| Theme Parks: Astroworld (159 days) | C |
| Professional Sports: 1.764 game seats per capita | A |
| ASTROS (baseball), ROCKETS (basketball), | |
| GAMBLERS, OILERS (football) | |
| NCAA Division I: .323 game seats per capita | B |
| Houston Baptist Huskies (b), Rice Owls, Texas | |
| Southern Tigers (b), University of Houston | |
| Cougars | |
| **Outdoor Recreation Assets (125)** | |
| Inland Water Area: 57.6 square miles | |

| | Rating |
|---|---|
| National Forests, Parks, Wildlife Refuges: | |
| Big Thicket National Preserve (1,348 acres) | |
| Sam Houston NF (47,358 acres) | |
| Places Rated Score: 1,825 | Places Rated Rank: 138 |

### Huntington–Ashland, WV–KY–OH

| | Rating |
|---|---|
| **Common Denominators (600)** | |
| Good Restaurants: 2 ★★★ | C |
| Golf Courses: 4.5 private; 7.5 daily fee; 0.5 | B |
| municipal | |
| Bowling Lanes: 146 | B |
| Movie Theaters: 5 | C |
| **Crowd Pleasers (200)** | |
| NCAA Division I: .664 game seats per capita | B |
| Marshall Thundering Herd | |
| **Outdoor Recreation Assets (40)** | |
| Inland Water Area: 17.1 square miles | |
| Places Rated Score: 840 | Places Rated Rank: 308 |

### Huntsville, AL

| | Rating |
|---|---|
| **Common Denominators (900)** | |
| Good Restaurants: 4 ★★, 1 ★★★ | A |
| Golf Courses: 3.5 private; 2.5 daily fee; 2 | B |
| municipal | |
| Bowling Lanes: 118 | B |
| Movie Theaters: 6 | B |
| **Crowd Pleasers (100)** | |
| Auto Racing: Huntsville International (NASCAR) | C |
| **Outdoor Recreation Assets (75)** | |
| Inland Water Area: 7.4 square miles | |
| National Forests, Parks, Wildlife Refuges: | |
| Wheeler NWR (3,019 acres) | |
| Places Rated Score: 1,075 | Places Rated Rank: 284 |

### Indianapolis, IN

| | Rating |
|---|---|
| **Common Denominators (900)** | |
| Good Restaurants: 2 ★, 6 ★★ 4 ★★★, 2 ★★★★ | C |
| Golf Courses: 21 private; 15.5 daily fee; 11.5 | B |
| municipal | |
| Bowling Lanes: 1,084 | A |
| Movie Theaters: 36 | A |
| **Crowd Pleasers (1,000)** | |
| Zoos: Indianapolis Zoo | B |
| Auto Racing: | AA |
| Indiana State Fairgrounds (USAC) | |
| Indianapolis Motor Speedway (USAC) | |
| Indianapolis Raceway (SCCA, USAC) | |
| Speedrome (USAC) | |
| Professional Sports: 2.154 game seats per capita | A |
| Indians (baseball), PACERS (basketball), | |
| COLTS (football), Checkers (hockey) | |
| NCAA Division I: .167 game seats per capita | C |
| Butler University Bulldogs (b) | |
| **Outdoor Recreation Assets (6)** | |
| Inland Water Area: 3.8 square miles | |
| Places Rated Score: 1,906 | Places Rated Rank: 128 |

### Iowa City, IA

| | Rating |
|---|---|
| **Common Denominators (1,100)** | |
| Good Restaurants: 2 ★★ | B |
| Golf Courses: 0.5 private; 1.5 daily fee; 1 | A |
| municipal | |
| Bowling Lanes: 56 | B |
| Movie Theaters: 5 | AA |
| **Crowd Pleasers (400)** | |
| NCAA Division I: 5.863 game seats per capita | AA |
| University of Iowa Hawkeyes | |
| **Outdoor Recreation Assets (6)** | |
| Inland Water Area: .7 square miles | |
| Places Rated Score: 1,506 | Places Rated Rank: 206 |

### Jackson, MI

| | Rating |
|---|---|
| **Common Denominators (1,300)** | |
| Good Restaurants: 1 ★, 3 ★★ | B |
| Golf Courses: 3.5 private; 9.5 daily fee; 2 | AA |
| municipal | |

| | Rating |
|---|---|
| Bowling Lanes: 180 | **AA** |
| Movie Theaters: 6 | **A** |

Crowd Pleasers (500)

| | |
|---|---|
| Auto Racing: Michigan International (NASCAR) | **C** |
| Pari-mutuel Betting: Jackson Raceway (harness, 141 days) | **AA** |

Outdoor Recreation Assets (133)
Inland Water Area: 18.8 square miles

Places Rated Score: 1,933          Places Rated Rank: 120

## Jackson, MS

Common Denominators (700)

| | |
|---|---|
| Good Restaurants: 3 ★, 8 ★★, 3 ★★★ | **AA** |
| Golf Courses: 11.5 private; 1 daily fee; 2 municipal | **C** |
| Bowling Lanes: 62 | **C** |
| Movie Theaters: 7 | **C** |

Crowd Pleasers (700)

| | |
|---|---|
| Zoos: Jackson Zoological Park | **B** |
| Professional Sports: .977 game seats per capita Mets (baseball) | **B** |
| NCAA Division I: .807 game seats per capita Jackson State Tigers | **A** |

Outdoor Recreation Assets (27)
Inland Water Area: 1.2 square miles
National Forests, Parks, Wildlife Refuges:
Natchez Trace Parkway (7,352 acres)

Places Rated Score: 1,427          Places Rated Rank: 224

## Jacksonville, FL

Common Denominators (800)

| | |
|---|---|
| Good Restaurants: 1 ★, 5 ★★, 5 ★★★ | **B** |
| Golf Courses: 19.5 private; 8 daily fee; 2.5 municipal | **B** |
| Bowling Lanes: 452 | **B** |
| Movie Theaters: 20 | **B** |

Crowd Pleasers (900)

| | |
|---|---|
| Zoos: Jacksonville Zoological Park | **B** |
| Pari-mutuel Betting: Bayard Greyhound Park (150 days) Jacksonville Kennel Club (84 days) Orange Park Kennel Club (77 days) | **A** |
| Professional Sports: 1.636 game seats per capita Suns (baseball), BULLS (football) | **A** |
| NCAA Division I: .180 game seats per capita University of Jacksonville Dolphins (b) | **C** |

Outdoor Recreation Assets (1,184)
Atlantic Coastline: 80 miles
Inland Water Area: 201.6 square miles
National Forests, Parks, Wildlife Refuges:
Castillo de San Marcos NM (21 acres)
Fort Caroline National Memorial (132 acres)
Fort Matanzas NM (299 acres)

Places Rated Score: 2,884          Places Rated Rank: 41

## Jacksonville, NC

Common Denominators (500)

| | |
|---|---|
| Golf Courses: 3 private; 1 daily fee | **C** |
| Bowling Lanes: 48 | **B** |
| Movie Theaters: 3 | **B** |

Outdoor Recreation Assets (677)
Atlantic Coastline: 30 miles
Inland Water Area: 57.6 square miles

Places Rated Score: 1,177          Places Rated Rank: 266

## Janesville–Beloit, WI

Common Denominators (1,300)

| | |
|---|---|
| Good Restaurants: 2 ★, 4 ★★ | **AA** |
| Golf Courses: 2.5 private; 2 daily fee; 2.5 municipal | **A** |
| Bowling Lanes: 186 | **AA** |
| Movie Theaters: 4 | **B** |

Crowd Pleasers (300)

| | |
|---|---|
| Professional Sports: 1.908 game seats per capita Brewers (baseball) | **A** |

Outdoor Recreation Assets (15)
Inland Water Area: 2.1 square miles

Places Rated Score: 1,615          Places Rated Rank: 176

## Jersey City, NJ

Common Denominators (500)

| | |
|---|---|
| Golf Courses: 0.5 daily fee | **C** |
| Bowling Lanes: 320 | **B** |
| Movie Theaters: 17 | **B** |

Crowd Pleasers (100)

| | |
|---|---|
| NCAA Division I: .075 game seats per capita St. Peter's College Peacocks (b) | **C** |

Outdoor Recreation Assets (1)
National Forests, Parks, Wildlife Refuges:
Statue of Liberty NM (45 acres)
CMSA Access: NEW YORK–NORTHERN NEW JERSEY–
LONG ISLAND, NY–NJ–CT (400)

Places Rated Score: 1,001          Places Rated Rank: 291

## Johnson City–Kingsport–Bristol, TN–VA

Common Denominators (1,000)

| | |
|---|---|
| Good Restaurants: 6 ★★, 5 ★★★ | **A** |
| Golf Courses: 4 private; 5 daily fee; 4 municipal | **B** |
| Bowling Lanes: 156 | **B** |
| Movie Theaters: 17 | **A** |

Crowd Pleasers (400)

| | |
|---|---|
| Auto Racing: Bristol International (NASCAR) Kingsport International (NASCAR) | **B** |
| Professional Sports: .582 game seats per capita Bristol Tigers, Johnson City Cardinals, Kingsport Mets (baseball) | **C** |
| NCAA Division I: .288 game seats per capita East Tennessee State Buccaneers | **C** |

Outdoor Recreation Assets (755)
Inland Water Area: 40.8 square miles
National Forests, Parks, Wildlife Refuges:
Appalachian Trail (966 acres)
Cherokee NF (193,640 acres)
Jefferson NF (55,961 acres)

Places Rated Score: 2,155          Places Rated Rank: 88

## Johnstown, PA

Common Denominators (800)

| | |
|---|---|
| Good Restaurants: 1 ★, 1 ★★★ | **C** |
| Golf Courses: 4.5 private; 6 daily fee; 0.5 municipal | **B** |
| Bowling Lanes: 172 | **B** |
| Movie Theaters: 10 | **A** |

Crowd Pleasers (100)

| | |
|---|---|
| NCAA Division I: .197 game seats per capita St. Francis College Red Flash (b) | **C** |

Outdoor Recreation Assets (3)
Inland Water Area: .1 square miles
National Forests, Parks, Wildlife Refuges:
Allegheny Portage Railroad NHS (330 acres)
Appalachian Trail (79 acres)
Johnstown Flood National Memorial (164 acres)

Places Rated Score: 903          Places Rated Rank: 302

## Joliet, IL

Common Denominators (1,000)

| | |
|---|---|
| Good Restaurants: 1 ★, 1 ★★, 2 ★★★ | **C** |
| Golf Courses: 6 private; 9.5 daily fee; 3 municipal | **AA** |
| Bowling Lanes: 268 | **A** |
| Movie Theaters: 9 | **B** |

Crowd Pleasers (200)

| | |
|---|---|
| Pari-mutuel Betting: Balmoral Park (Thoroughbred, 61 days) | **B** |

Outdoor Recreation Assets (36)
Inland Water Area: 9 square miles
CMSA Access: CHICAGO–GARY–LAKE COUNTY,
IL–IN–WI (400)

Places Rated Score: 1,636          Places Rated Rank: 170

## Joplin, MO

Common Denominators (800)

| | |
|---|---|
| Good Restaurants: 2 ★★★ | **B** |
| Golf Courses: 3.5 private; 2 municipal | **B** |
| Bowling Lanes: 82 | **B** |
| Movie Theaters: 3 | **B** |

| | Rating |
|---|---|
| **Outdoor Recreation Assets (1)** | |
| National Forests, Parks, Wildlife Refuges: | |
| George Washington Carver NM (210 acres) | |
| Places Rated Score: 801 | Places Rated Rank: 313 |

## Kalamazoo, MI
Common Denominators (1,500)
| | |
|---|---|
| Good Restaurants: 2 ★, 3 ★★, 2 ★★★ | A |
| Golf Courses: 4 private; 9 daily fee; 2.5 municipal | AA |
| Bowling Lanes: 340 | AA |
| Movie Theaters: 10 | AA |

Crowd Pleasers (500)
| | |
|---|---|
| Professional Sports: .965 game seats per capita | B |
| Wings (hockey) | |
| NCAA Division I: 1.093 game seats per capita | A |
| Western Michigan Broncos | |

Outdoor Recreation Assets (163)
Inland Water Area: 18.3 square miles
Places Rated Score: 2,163          Places Rated Rank: 85

## Kankakee, IL
Common Denominators (1,100)
| | |
|---|---|
| Good Restaurants: 1 ★★, 1 ★★★ | B |
| Golf Courses: 1 private; 5 daily fee; 0.5 municipal | AA |
| Bowling Lanes: 96 | A |
| Movie Theaters: 3 | B |

Outdoor Recreation Assets (19)
Inland Water Area: 2.6 square miles
Places Rated Score: 1,119          Places Rated Rank: 277

## Kansas City, KS
Common Denominators (700)
| | |
|---|---|
| Good Restaurants: 2 ★★, 3 ★★★ | C |
| Golf Courses: 15.5 private; 2.5 daily fee; 5 municipal | B |
| Bowling Lanes: 370 | B |
| Movie Theaters: 14 | B |

Outdoor Recreation Assets (45)
Inland Water Area: 15.1 square miles
CMSA Access: KANSAS CITY, MO–KANSAS CITY, KS (300)
Places Rated Score: 1,045          Places Rated Rank: 287

## Kansas City, MO
Common Denominators (1,200)
| | |
|---|---|
| Good Restaurants: 2 ★, 18 ★★, 14 ★★★, 3 ★★★★ | AA |
| Golf Courses: 9 private; 13 daily fee; 6.5 municipal | B |
| Bowling Lanes: 668 | B |
| Movie Theaters: 37 | AA |

Crowd Pleasers (800)
| | |
|---|---|
| Zoos: Swope Park Zoo | B |
| Theme Parks: Worlds of Fun (140 days) | B |
| Professional Sports: 5.030 game seats per capita | AA |
| ROYALS (baseball), KINGS (basketball), CHIEFS (football) | |

Outdoor Recreation Assets (43)
Inland Water Area: 28.4 square miles
Places Rated Score: 2,043          Places Rated Rank: 99

## Kenosha, WI
Common Denominators (1,300)
| | |
|---|---|
| Good Restaurants: 1 ★, 1 ★★, 1 ★★★ | B |
| Golf Courses: 1 private; 4 daily fee; 3 municipal | AA |
| Bowling Lanes: 148 | AA |
| Movie Theaters: 4 | A |

Crowd Pleasers (300)
| | |
|---|---|
| Professional Sports: 1.990 game seats per capita | A |
| Twins (baseball) | |

Outdoor Recreation Assets (224)
Great Lakes Coastline: 12 miles
Inland Water Area: 5.7 square miles
CMSA Access: CHICAGO–GARY–LAKE COUNTY, IL–IN–WI (400)
Places Rated Score: 2,224          Places Rated Rank: 81

## Killeen–Temple, TX
Common Denominators (900)
| | |
|---|---|
| Good Restaurants: 2 ★, 1 ★★★ | C |
| Golf Courses: 4.5 private; 1.5 daily fee; 2 municipal | B |
| Bowling Lanes: 84 | B |
| Movie Theaters: 16 | AA |

Outdoor Recreation Assets (31)
Inland Water Area: 13.2 square miles
Places Rated Score: 931          Places Rated Rank: 298

## Knoxville, TN
Common Denominators (900)
| | |
|---|---|
| Good Restaurants: 7 ★★, 5 ★★★, 1 ★★★★ | A |
| Golf Courses: 7 private; 12 daily fee; 2 municipal | B |
| Bowling Lanes: 196 | B |
| Movie Theaters: 14 | B |

Crowd Pleasers (700)
| | |
|---|---|
| Zoos: Knoxville Zoological Park | B |
| Professional Sports: 1.032 game seats per capita | B |
| Blue Jays (baseball) | |
| NCAA Division I: 1.098 game seats per capita | A |
| University of Tennessee Volunteers | |

Outdoor Recreation Assets (914)
Inland Water Area: 149.1 square miles
National Forests, Parks, Wildlife Refuges:
Appalachian Trail (640 acres)
Great Smoky Mountains NP (225,193 acres)
Places Rated Score: 2,514          Places Rated Rank: 56

## Kokomo, IN
Common Denominators (900)
| | |
|---|---|
| Good Restaurants: 1 ★★ | C |
| Golf Courses: 1 private; 3 daily fee; 1 municipal | AA |
| Bowling Lanes: 72 | B |
| Movie Theaters: 3 | B |

Crowd Pleasers (100)
| | |
|---|---|
| Auto Racing: Kokomo Speedway (USAC) | C |

Places Rated Score: 1,000          Places Rated Rank: 293

## La Crosse, WI
Common Denominators (1,500)
| | |
|---|---|
| Good Restaurants: 1 ★, 1 ★★, 2 ★★★ | AA |
| Golf Courses: 1 private; 2.5 daily fee | A |
| Bowling Lanes: 96 | AA |
| Movie Theaters: 4 | AA |

Outdoor Recreation Assets (453)
Inland Water Area: 23.2 square miles
National Forests, Parks, Wildlife Refuges:
Upper Mississippi River NWR (11,666 acres)
Places Rated Score: 1,953          Places Rated Rank: 113

## Lafayette, IN
Common Denominators (1,300)
| | |
|---|---|
| Good Restaurants: 2 ★★, 1 ★★★ | A |
| Golf Courses: 2.5 private; 3 daily fee; 1 municipal | A |
| Bowling Lanes: 104 | A |
| Movie Theaters: 5 | AA |

Crowd Pleasers (500)
| | |
|---|---|
| Zoos: Columbian Park Zoo | C |
| NCAA Division I: 4.351 game seats per capita | AA |
| Purdue Boilermakers | |

Outdoor Recreation Assets (14)
Inland Water Area: 1.4 square miles
Places Rated Score: 1,814          Places Rated Rank: 141

## Lafayette, LA
Common Denominators (700)
| | |
|---|---|
| Good Restaurants: 3 ★★, 7 ★★★ | AA |
| Golf Courses: 2 private; 2 municipal | C |
| Bowling Lanes: 56 | C |
| Movie Theaters: 4 | C |

Crowd Pleasers (700)
| | |
|---|---|
| Pari-mutuel Betting: Evangeline Downs | AA |
| (Thoroughbred, 109 days) | |

| | Rating |
|---|---|
| NCAA Division I: 1.312 game seats per capita<br>Southwestern Louisiana Ragin' Cajuns | A |

Outdoor Recreation Assets (334)
Inland Water Area: 68 square miles
Places Rated Score: 1,734          Places Rated Rank: 153

## Lake Charles, LA
Common Denominators (1,100)

| | |
|---|---|
| Good Restaurants: 1 ★★★ | C |
| Golf Courses: 2 private; 1 daily fee; 2 municipal | A |
| Bowling Lanes: 76 | AA |
| Movie Theaters: 6 | A |

Crowd Pleasers (700)

| | |
|---|---|
| Pari-mutuel Betting: Delta Downs (Thoroughbred,<br>105 days) | AA |
| NCAA Division I: 1.103 game seats per capita<br>McNeese State Cowboys | A |

Outdoor Recreation Assets (55)
Inland Water Area: 12 square miles
Places Rated Score: 1,855          Places Rated Rank: 135

## Lake County, IL
Common Denominators (1,200)

| | |
|---|---|
| Good Restaurants: 3 ★, 6 ★★, 1 ★★★ | B |
| Golf Courses: 23 private; 10.5 daily fee; 9.5<br>municipal | AA |
| Bowling Lanes: 322 | A |
| Movie Theaters: 15 | A |

Crowd Pleasers (400)

| | |
|---|---|
| Theme Parks: Six Flags Great America (120 days) | AA |

Outdoor Recreation Assets (435)
Great Lakes Coastline: 25 miles
Inland Water Area: 16.8 square miles
CMSA Access: CHICAGO–GARY–LAKE COUNTY,
IL–IN–WI (400)
Places Rated Score: 2,435          Places Rated Rank: 63

## Lakeland–Winter Haven, FL
Common Denominators (1,300)

| | |
|---|---|
| Good Restaurants: 2 ★★, 6 ★★★, 1 ★★★★ | AA |
| Golf Courses: 6.5 private; 9 daily fee; 3.5<br>municipal | AA |
| Bowling Lanes: 206 | B |
| Movie Theaters: 11 | A |

Crowd Pleasers (700)

| | |
|---|---|
| Theme Parks: Cypress Gardens (365 days) | AA |
| Professional Sports: 2.383 game seats per capita<br>Lakeland Tigers, Winter Haven Red Sox<br>(baseball) | A |

Outdoor Recreation Assets (513)
Inland Water Area: 187.2 square miles
Places Rated Score: 2,513          Places Rated Rank: 57

## Lancaster, PA
Common Denominators (900)

| | |
|---|---|
| Good Restaurants: 4 ★, 6 ★★, 1 ★★★, 1 ★★★★ | A |
| Golf Courses: 4.5 private; 5 daily fee | B |
| Bowling Lanes: 284 | A |
| Movie Theaters: 5 | C |

Crowd Pleasers (100)

| | |
|---|---|
| Professional Sports: .214 game seats per capita<br>Lightning (basketball) | C |

Outdoor Recreation Assets (147)
Inland Water Area: 27.9 square miles
Places Rated Score: 1,147          Places Rated Rank: 270

## Lansing–East Lansing, MI
Common Denominators (1,200)

| | |
|---|---|
| Good Restaurants: 2 ★, 4 ★★, 3 ★★★ | B |
| Golf Courses: 2.5 private; 18 daily fee; 2.5<br>municipal | AA |
| Bowling Lanes: 440 | A |
| Movie Theaters: 14 | A |

Crowd Pleasers (400)

| | |
|---|---|
| Zoos: Potter Park Zoo | C |

| | Rating |
|---|---|
| NCAA Division I: 1.215 game seats per capita<br>Michigan State Spartans | A |

Outdoor Recreation Assets (9)
Inland Water Area: 3.1 square miles
Places Rated Score: 1,609          Places Rated Rank: 178

## Laredo, TX
Common Denominators (700)

| | |
|---|---|
| Good Restaurants: 1 ★, 3 ★★ | A |
| Golf Courses: 1 private; 1 municipal | C |
| Bowling Lanes: 20 | C |
| Movie Theaters: 3 | B |

Outdoor Recreation Assets (2)
Inland Water Area: 1.4 square miles
Places Rated Score: 702          Places Rated Rank: 323

## Las Cruces, NM
Common Denominators (1,100)

| | |
|---|---|
| Good Restaurants: 2 ★★, 1 ★★★ | AA |
| Golf Courses: 5 private; 2 daily fee | B |
| Bowling Lanes: 50 | B |
| Movie Theaters: 3 | A |

Crowd Pleasers (400)

| | |
|---|---|
| NCAA Division I: 3.341 game seats per capita<br>New Mexico State Aggies | AA |

Outdoor Recreation Assets (109)
National Forests, Parks, Wildlife Refuges:
San Andres NWR (2 acres)
White Sands NM (53,059 acres)
Places Rated Score: 1,609          Places Rated Rank: 178

## ★ Las Vegas, NV
Common Denominators (1,300)

| | |
|---|---|
| Good Restaurants: 4 ★, 16 ★★, 23 ★★★, 1 ★★★★ | AA |
| Golf Courses: 2 private; 7 daily fee; 2.5 municipal | B |
| Bowling Lanes: 400 | A |
| Movie Theaters: 27 | AA |

Crowd Pleasers (1,100)

| | |
|---|---|
| Zoos: Las Vegas Valley Zoo | C |
| Auto Racing:<br>Caesar's Palace Grand Prix (SCCA)<br>Craig Road Speedway (NASCAR) | B |
| Pari-mutuel Betting: MGM Grand Jai Alai<br>(365 days) | AA |
| Professional Sports: 1.457 game seats per capita<br>Stars (baseball) | B |
| NCAA Division I: .524 game seats per capita<br>University of Nevada Rebels | B |

Outdoor Recreation Assets (1,596)
Inland Water Area: 209.8 square miles
National Forests, Parks, Wildlife Refuges:
Desert NWR (828,766 acres)
Lake Mead NRA (588,785 acres)
Moapa Valley NWR (11 acres)
Toiyabe NF (58,040 acres)
Places Rated Score: 3,996          Places Rated Rank: 8

## Lawrence, KS
Common Denominators (1,300)

| | |
|---|---|
| Good Restaurants: 1 ★★ | C |
| Golf Courses: 1 private; 2.5 daily fee | AA |
| Bowling Lanes: 80 | AA |
| Movie Theaters: 4 | AA |

Crowd Pleasers (400)

| | |
|---|---|
| NCAA Division I: 6.882 game seats per capita<br>University of Kansas Jayhawks | AA |

Outdoor Recreation Assets (52)
Inland Water Area: 3.2 square miles
Places Rated Score: 1,752          Places Rated Rank: 148

## Lawrence–Haverhill, MA–NH
Common Denominators (600)

| | |
|---|---|
| Good Restaurants: 3 ★★, 5 ★★★ | A |
| Golf Courses: 2.5 private; 7.5 daily fee | B |
| Movie Theaters: 7 | C |

| | Rating |
|---|---|
| Crowd Pleasers (400) | |
| Pari-mutuel Betting: | **AA** |
| Rockingham (Thoroughbred, 143 days) | |
| Seabrook Greyhound Park (144 days) | |

**Outdoor Recreation Assets (479)**
Atlantic Coastline: 13 miles
Inland Water Area: 27.8 square miles
National Forests, Parks, Wildlife Refuges:
Parker River NWR (2,321 acres)
CMSA Access: BOSTON–LAWRENCE–SALEM, MA–NH (400)

Places Rated Score: 1,879     Places Rated Rank: 131

### Lawton, OK

| Common Denominators (1,300) | Rating |
|---|---|
| Good Restaurants: 3 ★, 5 ★★, 1 ★★★ | **AA** |
| Golf Courses: 2 private; 1 daily fee; 1 municipal | **B** |
| Bowling Lanes: 154 | **AA** |
| Movie Theaters: 4 | **A** |

**Outdoor Recreation Assets (457)**
Inland Water Area: 5.4 square miles
National Forests, Parks, Wildlife Refuges:
Wichita Mountains NWR (59,019 acres)

Places Rated Score: 1,757     Places Rated Rank: 147

### Lewiston–Auburn, ME

| Common Denominators (1,200) | Rating |
|---|---|
| Good Restaurants: 3 ★★ | **A** |
| Golf Courses: 5 daily fee | **AA** |
| Bowling Lanes: 32 | **B** |
| Movie Theaters: 3 | **A** |
| Crowd Pleasers (400) | |
| Pari-mutuel Betting: Lewiston Raceway (harness, 81 days) | **AA** |

**Outdoor Recreation Assets (253)**
Inland Water Area: 12.1 square miles

Places Rated Score: 1,853     Places Rated Rank: 136

### Lexington–Fayette, KY

| Common Denominators (800) | Rating |
|---|---|
| Good Restaurants: 4 ★★, 2 ★★★, 2 ★★★★ | **A** |
| Golf Courses: 9 private; 6 daily fee; 1 municipal | **B** |
| Bowling Lanes: 168 | **B** |
| Movie Theaters: 6 | **C** |
| Crowd Pleasers (600) | |
| Pari-mutuel Betting: | **B** |
| Keeneland (Thoroughbred, 32 days) | |
| The Red Mile (harness, 52 days) | |
| NCAA Division I: 1.834 game seats per capita | **AA** |
| University of Kentucky Wildcats | |

**Outdoor Recreation Assets (3)**
Inland Water Area: .8 square miles

Places Rated Score: 1,403     Places Rated Rank: 233

### Lima, OH

| Common Denominators (1,300) | Rating |
|---|---|
| Good Restaurants: 2 ★★★ | **B** |
| Golf Courses: 3.5 private; 6 daily fee | **AA** |
| Bowling Lanes: 182 | **AA** |
| Movie Theaters: 6 | **A** |
| Crowd Pleasers (100) | |
| Professional Sports: .614 game seats per capita | **C** |
| Ohio Mixers (basketball) | |

**Outdoor Recreation Assets (28)**
Inland Water Area: 4.5 square miles

Places Rated Score: 1,428     Places Rated Rank: 222

### Lincoln, NE

| Common Denominators (1,100) | Rating |
|---|---|
| Good Restaurants: 1 ★, 1 ★★, 2 ★★★ | **B** |
| Golf Courses: 2 private; 1 daily fee; 3 municipal | **B** |
| Bowling Lanes: 164 | **A** |
| Movie Theaters: 8 | **AA** |
| Crowd Pleasers (700) | |
| Zoos: Folsom Children's Zoo | **C** |
| Pari-mutuel Betting: Nebraska State Fair (Thoroughbred, 43 days) | **B** |

| | Rating |
|---|---|
| NCAA Division I: 2.657 game seats per capita | **AA** |
| University of Nebraska Cornhuskers | |

**Outdoor Recreation Assets (4)**
Inland Water Area: .6 square miles

Places Rated Score: 1,804     Places Rated Rank: 143

### Little Rock–North Little Rock, AR

| Common Denominators (800) | Rating |
|---|---|
| Good Restaurants: 2 ★, 3 ★★, 1 ★★★, 1 ★★★★ | **B** |
| Golf Courses: 13 private; 3 daily fee; 4.5 municipal | **B** |
| Bowling Lanes: 202 | **B** |
| Movie Theaters: 12 | **B** |
| Crowd Pleasers (400) | |
| Zoos: Little Rock Zoological Park | **C** |
| Professional Sports: .874 game seats per capita | **B** |
| Arkansas Travelers (baseball) | |
| NCAA Division I: .066 game seats per capita | **C** |
| University of Arkansas Trojans (b) | |

**Outdoor Recreation Assets (262)**
Inland Water Area: 69.6 square miles
National Forests, Parks, Wildlife Refuges:
Ouachita NF (53,357 acres)

Places Rated Score: 1,462     Places Rated Rank: 216

### Longview–Marshall, TX

| Common Denominators (800) | Rating |
|---|---|
| Good Restaurants: 2 ★, 2 ★★ | **B** |
| Golf Courses: 4.5 private; 2.5 daily fee | **B** |
| Bowling Lanes: 80 | **B** |
| Movie Theaters: 4 | **B** |

**Outdoor Recreation Assets (34)**
Inland Water Area: 8.1 square miles

Places Rated Score: 834     Places Rated Rank: 311

### Lorain–Elyria, OH

| Common Denominators (1,000) | Rating |
|---|---|
| Good Restaurants: 1 ★, 2 ★★ | **C** |
| Golf Courses: 6 private; 17 daily fee; 1 municipal | **AA** |
| Bowling Lanes: 332 | **AA** |
| Movie Theaters: 6 | **C** |

**Outdoor Recreation Assets (202)**
Great Lakes Coastline: 20 miles
Inland Water Area: .2 square miles
CMSA Access: CLEVELAND–AKRON–LORAIN, OH (400)

Places Rated Score: 1,602     Places Rated Rank: 184

### ★ Los Angeles–Long Beach, CA

| Common Denominators (700) | Rating |
|---|---|
| Good Restaurants: 2 ★, 46 ★★, 29 ★★★, 4 ★★★★ | **C** |
| Golf Courses: 31.5 private; 8 daily fee; 34.5 municipal | **C** |
| Bowling Lanes: 2,809 | **B** |
| Movie Theaters: 269 | **A** |
| Crowd Pleasers (1,000) | |
| Zoos: Los Angeles Zoo | **AA** |
| Theme Parks: | **C** |
| Marineland of the Pacific (300 days) | |
| Universal Studios Tour (365 days) | |
| Auto Racing: Long Beach Grand Prix (SCCA) | **C** |
| Pari-mutuel Betting: | **C** |
| Hollywood Park (harness, 53 days; Thoroughbred, 98 days) | |
| Santa Anita Park (Thoroughbred, 121 days) | |
| Professional Sports: 1.002 game seats per capita | **B** |
| DODGERS (baseball), CLIPPERS, LAKERS (basketball), EXPRESS, RAIDERS (football), KINGS (hockey) | |
| NCAA Division I: .255 game seats per capita | **C** |
| Long Beach State 49ers, Loyola Marymount University Lions (b), Pepperdine University Waves (b), University of California Bruins, University of Southern California Trojans | |

**Outdoor Recreation Assets (1,848)**
Pacific Coastline: 55 miles
Inland Water Area: 11.1 square miles

Rating

National Forests, Parks, Wildlife Refuges:
  Angeles NF (642,260 acres)
  Santa Monica Mountains NRA (26,734 acres)
CMSA Access: LOS ANGELES–ANAHEIM–
RIVERSIDE, CA (400)
Places Rated Score: 3,948          Places Rated Rank: 10

## Louisville, KY–IN
Common Denominators (800)
  Good Restaurants: 1 ★, 6 ★★, 7 ★★★, 1 ★★★★          B
  Golf Courses: 15 private; 5 daily fee; 8 municipal          B
  Bowling Lanes: 958          A
  Movie Theaters: 13          C
Crowd Pleasers (1,100)
  Zoos: Louisville Zoological Gardens          A
  Pari-mutuel Betting:          B
    Churchill Downs (Thoroughbred, 117 days)
    Louisville Downs (harness, 153 days)
  Professional Sports: 2.558 game seats per capita          AA
    Redbirds (baseball), Catbirds (basketball)
  NCAA Division I: .422 game seats per capita          B
    University of Louisville Cardinals
Outdoor Recreation Assets (42)
  Inland Water Area: 19.3 square miles
Places Rated Score: 1,942          Places Rated Rank: 117

## Lowell, MA–NH
Common Denominators (600)
  Good Restaurants: 1 ★★          C
  Golf Courses: 2 private; 3.5 daily fee          B
  Bowling Lanes: 104          B
  Movie Theaters: 3          C
Outdoor Recreation Assets (129)
  Inland Water Area: 5.6 square miles
  National Forests, Parks, Wildlife Refuges:
    Lowell NHP (4 acres)
CMSA Access: BOSTON–LAWRENCE–SALEM, MA–NH (400)
Places Rated Score: 1,129          Places Rated Rank: 274

## Lubbock, TX
Common Denominators (1,300)
  Good Restaurants: 1 ★, 5 ★★, 4 ★★★          AA
  Golf Courses: 3 private; 0.5 daily fee; 3 municipal          B
  Bowling Lanes: 152          A
  Movie Theaters: 11          AA
Crowd Pleasers (400)
  NCAA Division I: 1.725 game seats per capita          AA
    Texas Tech Red Raiders
Outdoor Recreation Assets (2)
  Inland Water Area: .3 square miles
  National Forests, Parks, Wildlife Refuges:
    Lower Rio Grande Valley NWR (118 acres)
Places Rated Score: 1,702          Places Rated Rank: 159

## Lynchburg, VA
Common Denominators (700)
  Good Restaurants: 1 ★★, 2 ★★★          A
  Golf Courses: 4 private; 1 daily fee          C
  Bowling Lanes: 64          B
  Movie Theaters: 3          C
Crowd Pleasers (300)
  Professional Sports: 2.081 game seats per capita          A
    Mets (baseball)
Outdoor Recreation Assets (439)
  Inland Water Area: .7 square miles
  National Forests, Parks, Wildlife Refuges:
    Blue Ridge Parkway (2,037 acres)
    George Washington NF (55,587 acres)
Places Rated Score: 1,439          Places Rated Rank: 220

## Macon–Warner Robins, GA
Common Denominators (500)
  Good Restaurants: 2 ★★, 1 ★★★          C
  Golf Courses: 8.5 private; 0.5 daily fee;          C
    1.5 municipal
  Bowling Lanes: 100          B

Rating

  Movie Theaters: 5          C
Crowd Pleasers (400)
  Professional Sports: 1.093 game seats per capita          B
    Pirates (baseball)
  NCAA Division I: .444 game seats per capita          B
    Mercer University Bears (b)
Outdoor Recreation Assets (304)
  Inland Water Area: .1 square miles
  National Forests, Parks, Wildlife Refuges:
    Ocmulgee NM (683 acres)
    Oconee NF (16,570 acres)
    Piedmont NWR (28,503 acres)
Places Rated Score: 1,204          Places Rated Rank: 262

## Madison, WI
Common Denominators (1,000)
  Good Restaurants: 3 ★, 5 ★★          B
  Golf Courses: 3.5 private; 6 daily fee; 3.5          A
    municipal
  Bowling Lanes: 386          AA
  Movie Theaters: 7          C
Crowd Pleasers (800)
  Zoos: Henry Vilas Park Zoo          B
  Professional Sports: .849 game seats per capita          B
    Muskies (baseball)
  NCAA Division I: 1.711 game seats per capita          AA
    University of Wisconsin Badgers
Outdoor Recreation Assets (144)
  Inland Water Area: 34.7 square miles
Places Rated Score: 1,944          Places Rated Rank: 115

## Manchester, NH
Common Denominators (700)
  Good Restaurants: 2 ★★, 1 ★★★          A
  Golf Courses: 1 daily fee; 1 municipal          B
  Movie Theaters: 3          B
Outdoor Recreation Assets (137)
  Inland Water Area: 6.5 square miles
Places Rated Score: 837          Places Rated Rank: 310

## Mansfield, OH
Common Denominators (1,000)
  Good Restaurants: 1 ★★, 2 ★★★          A
  Golf Courses: 2 private; 3 daily fee          B
  Bowling Lanes: 134          A
  Movie Theaters: 3          B
Crowd Pleasers (100)
  Auto Racing: Mid-Ohio Racetrack (SCCA)          C
Outdoor Recreation Assets (33)
  Inland Water Area: 3.3 square miles
Places Rated Score: 1,133          Places Rated Rank: 273

## McAllen–Edinburg–Mission, TX
Common Denominators (900)
  Good Restaurants: 3 ★, 9 ★★          AA
  Golf Courses: 1 private; 2 daily fee; 3 municipal          B
  Bowling Lanes: 60          C
  Movie Theaters: 8          B
Crowd Pleasers (100)
  NCAA Division I: .229 game seats per capita          C
    Pan American University Broncs (b)
Outdoor Recreation Assets (59)
  Inland Water Area: 12.4 square miles
  National Forests, Parks, Wildlife Refuges:
    Santa Anna NWR (3,769 acres)
Places Rated Score: 1,059          Places Rated Rank: 286

## Medford, OR
Common Denominators (1,100)
  Good Restaurants: 4 ★★, 2 ★★★          AA
  Golf Courses: 1.5 private; 0.5 daily fee;          C
    0.5 municipal
  Bowling Lanes: 74          B
  Movie Theaters: 7          AA
Crowd Pleasers (300)
  Auto Racing: Medford Raceway (NASCAR)          C

| | Rating |
|---|---|
| Professional Sports: .838 game seats per capita | B |
| A's (baseball) | |

Outdoor Recreation Assets (16)
  Inland Water Area: 9 square miles
Places Rated Score: 1,416          Places Rated Rank: 226

### ★ Melbourne–Titusville–Palm Bay, FL

Common Denominators (1,400)

| | Rating |
|---|---|
| Good Restaurants: 1 ★, 8 ★★, 1 ★★★ | AA |
| Golf Courses: 4.5 private; 4 daily fee; 3 municipal | A |
| Bowling Lanes: 196 | A |
| Movie Theaters: 12 | AA |

Crowd Pleasers (400)

| | |
|---|---|
| Pari-mutuel Betting: Melbourne Sports Palace | AA |
| (jai alai, 150 days) | |

Outdoor Recreation Assets (2,000)
  Atlantic Coastline: 72 miles
  Inland Water Area: 299 square miles
  National Forests, Parks, Wildlife Refuges:
    Canaveral NS (29,479 acres)
    St. John's NWR (6,254 acres)
Places Rated Score: 3,800          Places Rated Rank: 12

### Memphis, TN–AR–MS

Common Denominators (800)

| | Rating |
|---|---|
| Good Restaurants: 7 ★★, 5 ★★★ | B |
| Golf Courses: 19 private; 1 daily fee; 9 municipal | C |
| Bowling Lanes: 384 | B |
| Movie Theaters: 30 | A |

Crowd Pleasers (1,000)

| | |
|---|---|
| Zoos: Memphis Zoo and Aquarium | A |
| Pari-mutuel Betting: Southland Greyhound Park (136 days) | B |
| Professional Sports: 1.294 game seats per capita | A |
| Chicks (baseball), SHOWBOATS (football) | |
| NCAA Division I: .434 game seats per capita | B |
| Memphis State Tigers | |

Outdoor Recreation Assets (194)
  Inland Water Area: 80.8 square miles
  National Forests, Parks, Wildlife Refuges:
    Lower Hatchie NWR (346 acres)
    Wapanocca NWR (5,484 acres)
Places Rated Score: 1,994          Places Rated Rank: 106

### ★ Miami–Hialeah, FL

Common Denominators (1,100)

| | Rating |
|---|---|
| Good Restaurants: 8 ★, 16 ★★, 15 ★★★, 2 ★★★★, 1 ★★★★★ | A |
| Golf Courses: 16.5 private; 12.5 daily fee; 8 municipal | B |
| Bowling Lanes: 654 | B |
| Movie Theaters: 69 | AA |

Crowd Pleasers (1,000)

| | |
|---|---|
| Zoos: Miami Metro Zoo | A |
| Pari-mutuel Betting: | A |
| Biscayne Greyhound Park (102 days) | |
| Calder (Thoroughbred, 189 days) | |
| Flagler Greyhound Park (104 days) | |
| Hialeah (Thoroughbred, 50 days) | |
| Miami Jai Alai (242 days) | |
| Professional Sports: .800 game seats per capita | B |
| Marlins (baseball), DOLPHINS (football) | |
| NCAA Division I: .321 game seats per capita | B |
| University of Miami Hurricanes (f) | |

Outdoor Recreation Assets (2,000)
  Atlantic Coastline: 84 miles
  Inland Water Area: 67.1 square miles
  National Forests, Parks, Wildlife Refuges:
    Big Cypress National Preserve (18,628 acres)
    Biscayne NP (170,773 acres)
    Everglades NP (415,716 acres)
CMSA Access: MIAMI–FORT LAUDERDALE, FL (200)
Places Rated Score: 4,300          Places Rated Rank: 3

### Middlesex–Somerset–Hunterdon, NJ

Common Denominators (900)

| | Rating |
|---|---|
| Good Restaurants: 2 ★, 10 ★★, 1 ★★★ | C |
| Golf Courses: 12 private; 8.5 daily fee; 5.5 municipal | B |
| Bowling Lanes: 640 | A |
| Movie Theaters: 29 | A |

Crowd Pleasers (200)

| | |
|---|---|
| NCAA Division I: .660 game seats per capita | B |
| Rutgers Scarlet Knights | |

Outdoor Recreation Assets (96)
  Atlantic Coastline: 6 miles
  Inland Water Area: 7.3 square miles
  National Forests, Parks, Wildlife Refuges:
    Morristown NHP (188 acres)
CMSA Access: NEW YORK–NORTHERN NEW
  JERSEY–LONG ISLAND, NY–NJ–CT (400)
Places Rated Score: 1,596          Places Rated Rank: 186

### Middletown, CT

Common Denominators (1,200)

| | Rating |
|---|---|
| Good Restaurants: 1 ★★★ | B |
| Golf Courses: 3.5 daily fee | AA |
| Bowling Lanes: 46 | B |
| Movie Theaters: 4 | AA |

Outdoor Recreation Assets (182)
  Inland Water Area: 7.7 square miles
CMSA Access: HARTFORD–NEW BRITAIN–
  MIDDLETOWN, CT (300)
Places Rated Score: 1,682          Places Rated Rank: 163

### Midland, TX

Common Denominators (1,200)

| | Rating |
|---|---|
| Good Restaurants: 1 ★, 1 ★★ | B |
| Golf Courses: 2 private; 1.5 municipal | B |
| Bowling Lanes: 106 | AA |
| Movie Theaters: 5 | AA |

Crowd Pleasers (300)

| | |
|---|---|
| Professional Sports: 2.477 game seats per capita | A |
| Cubs (baseball) | |

Outdoor Recreation Assets (2)
  Inland Water Area: .3 square miles
Places Rated Score: 1,502          Places Rated Rank: 208

### Milwaukee, WI

Common Denominators (1,200)

| | Rating |
|---|---|
| Good Restaurants: 1 ★, 21 ★★, 10 ★★★, 2 ★★★★ | A |
| Golf Courses: 17 private; 18.5 daily fee; 12.5 municipal | B |
| Bowling Lanes: 2,864 | AA |
| Movie Theaters: 43 | A |

Crowd Pleasers (1,000)

| | |
|---|---|
| Zoos: Milwaukee County Zoo | AA |
| Auto Racing: Road America (SCCA) | C |
| Professional Sports: 3.824 game seats per capita | AA |
| BREWERS (baseball), BUCKS (basketball), Admirals (hockey) | |
| NCAA Division I: .103 game seats per capita | C |
| Marquette Warriors (b) | |

Outdoor Recreation Assets (602)
  Great Lakes Coastline: 49 miles
  Inland Water Area: 32.6 square miles
CMSA Access: MILWAUKEE–RACINE, WI (100)
Places Rated Score: 2,902          Places Rated Rank: 40

### Minneapolis–St. Paul, MN–WI

Common Denominators (1,000)

| | Rating |
|---|---|
| Good Restaurants: 19 ★, 40 ★★, 16 ★★★, 1 ★★★★ | A |
| Golf Courses: 29.5 private; 28 daily fee; 22 municipal | B |
| Bowling Lanes: 1,886 | A |
| Movie Theaters: 56 | B |

Crowd Pleasers (900)

| | |
|---|---|
| Zoos: | AA |
| Como Zoo | |
| Minnesota Zoological Gardens | |

|  | Rating |
|---|---|
| Professional Sports: 2.613 game seats per capita | **AA** |
| TWINS (baseball), VIKINGS (football), NORTH STARS (hockey) | |
| NCAA Division I: .248 game seats per capita | **C** |
| University of Minnesota Golden Gophers | |
| Outdoor Recreation Assets (258) | |
| Inland Water Area: 240.8 square miles | |
| National Forests, Parks, Wildlife Refuges: | |
| Lower St. Croix NSR (5,178 acres) | |
| St. Croix NSR (5,673 acres) | |
| Places Rated Score: 2,158    Places Rated Rank: 87 | |

**Mobile, AL**

| Common Denominators (800) | |
|---|---|
| Good Restaurants: 3 ★★, 5 ★★★ | **B** |
| Golf Courses: 9 private; 3 daily fee; 3 municipal | **B** |
| Bowling Lanes: 160 | **B** |
| Movie Theaters: 10 | **B** |
| Crowd Pleasers (600) | |
| Auto Racing: Mobile International (NASCAR) | **C** |
| Pari-mutuel Betting: Mobile Greyhound Park (286 days) | **AA** |
| NCAA Division I: .299 game seats per capita | **C** |
| University of South Alabama Jaguars (b) | |
| Outdoor Recreation Assets (764) | |
| Gulf of Mexico Coastline: 53 miles | |
| Inland Water Area: 128.9 square miles | |
| National Forests, Parks, Wildlife Refuges: | |
| Bon Secour NWR (2,168 acres) | |
| Places Rated Score: 2,164    Places Rated Rank: 84 | |

**Modesto, CA**

| Common Denominators (700) | |
|---|---|
| Good Restaurants: 2 ★★ | **C** |
| Golf Courses: 2 private; 1.5 daily fee; 1.5 municipal | **C** |
| Bowling Lanes: 106 | **B** |
| Movie Theaters: 9 | **A** |
| Crowd Pleasers (100) | |
| Professional Sports: .658 game seats per capita | **C** |
| A's (baseball) | |
| Outdoor Recreation Assets (33) | |
| Inland Water Area: 10 square miles | |
| Places Rated Score: 833    Places Rated Rank: 312 | |

**★ Monmouth–Ocean, NJ**

| Common Denominators (1,000) | |
|---|---|
| Good Restaurants: 3 ★, 17 ★★, 3 ★★★ | **A** |
| Golf Courses: 13.5 private; 7 daily fee; 6 municipal | **B** |
| Bowling Lanes: 540 | **B** |
| Movie Theaters: 28 | **A** |
| Crowd Pleasers (700) | |
| Theme Parks: Six Flags Great Adventure (163 days) | **A** |
| Pari-mutuel Betting: | **A** |
| Freehold Raceway (harness, 148 days) | |
| Monmouth Park (Thoroughbred, 110 days) | |
| NCAA Division I: .043 game seats per capita | **C** |
| Monmouth College Hawks (b) | |
| Outdoor Recreation Assets (1,444) | |
| Atlantic Coastline: 80 miles | |
| Inland Water Area: 124.8 square miles | |
| National Forests, Parks, Wildlife Refuges: | |
| Barnegat NWR (7,427 acres) | |
| Brigantine NWR (256 acres) | |
| Gateway NRA (4,169 acres) | |
| CMSA Access: NEW YORK–NORTHERN NEW JERSEY–LONG ISLAND, NY–NJ–CT (400) | |
| Places Rated Score: 3,544    Places Rated Rank: 17 | |

**Monroe, LA**

| Common Denominators (800) | |
|---|---|
| Good Restaurants: 1 ★★, 2 ★★★ | **A** |
| Golf Courses: 2.5 private; 2 municipal | **B** |
| Bowling Lanes: 72 | **B** |
| Movie Theaters: 2 | **C** |

|  | Rating |
|---|---|
| Crowd Pleasers (600) | |
| Zoos: Louisiana Purchase Gardens and Zoo | **A** |
| NCAA Division I: 1.465 game seats per capita | **A** |
| Northeast Louisiana Indians | |
| Outdoor Recreation Assets (141) | |
| Inland Water Area: 5.4 square miles | |
| National Forests, Parks, Wildlife Refuges: | |
| D'Arbonne NWR (7,859 acres) | |
| Places Rated Score: 1,541    Places Rated Rank: 196 | |

**Montgomery, AL**

| Common Denominators (700) | |
|---|---|
| Good Restaurants: 5 ★★★ | **A** |
| Golf Courses: 11 private; 1 municipal | **C** |
| Bowling Lanes: 88 | **C** |
| Movie Theaters: 7 | **B** |
| Crowd Pleasers (300) | |
| Zoos: Montgomery Zoo | **B** |
| NCAA Division I: .172 game seats per capita | **C** |
| Alabama State Hornets (b) | |
| Outdoor Recreation Assets (112) | |
| Inland Water Area: 45.1 square miles | |
| Places Rated Score: 1,112    Places Rated Rank: 279 | |

**Muncie, IN**

| Common Denominators (1,100) | |
|---|---|
| Golf Courses: 2 private; 4.5 daily fee | **AA** |
| Bowling Lanes: 180 | **AA** |
| Movie Theaters: 5 | **A** |
| Crowd Pleasers (300) | |
| NCAA Division I: 1.342 game seats per capita | **A** |
| Ball State Cardinals | |
| Outdoor Recreation Assets (28) | |
| Inland Water Area: 2.2 square miles | |
| Places Rated Score: 1,428    Places Rated Rank: 222 | |

**Muskegon, MI**

| Common Denominators (1,500) | |
|---|---|
| Good Restaurants: 3 ★, 4 ★★ | **A** |
| Golf Courses: 4 private; 5 daily fee; 1 municipal | **AA** |
| Bowling Lanes: 228 | **AA** |
| Movie Theaters: 7 | **AA** |
| Crowd Pleasers (200) | |
| Professional Sports: 1.285 game seats per capita | **B** |
| Mohawks (hockey) | |
| Outdoor Recreation Assets (966) | |
| Great Lakes Coastline: 30 miles | |
| Inland Water Area: 17.6 square miles | |
| National Forests, Parks, Wildlife Refuges: | |
| Manistee NF (12,500 acres) | |
| Places Rated Score: 2,666    Places Rated Rank: 49 | |

**Nashua, NH**

| Common Denominators (700) | |
|---|---|
| Good Restaurants: 3 ★★ | **B** |
| Golf Courses: 1 private; 4 daily fee | **A** |
| Bowling Lanes: 40 | **C** |
| Movie Theaters: 3 | **C** |
| Crowd Pleasers (400) | |
| Professional Sports: 3.192 game seats per capita | **AA** |
| Pirates (baseball) | |
| Outdoor Recreation Assets (23) | |
| Inland Water Area: 1.2 square miles | |
| CMSA Access: BOSTON–LAWRENCE–SALEM, MA–NH (400) | |
| Places Rated Score: 1,523    Places Rated Rank: 199 | |

**Nashville, TN**

| Common Denominators (1,000) | |
|---|---|
| Good Restaurants: 4 ★, 5 ★★, 9 ★★★, 3 ★★★★ | **A** |
| Golf Courses: 15.5 private; 3 daily fee; 9.5 municipal | **B** |
| Bowling Lanes: 426 | **B** |
| Movie Theaters: 27 | **A** |
| Crowd Pleasers (800) | |
| Theme Parks: Opryland USA (140 days) | **A** |

| | Rating |
|---|---|
| Professional Sports: 1.330 game seats per capita | B |
| Sounds (baseball) | |
| NCAA Division I: .991 game seats per capita | A |
| Middle Tennessee State Blue Raiders, | |
| Tennessee State Tigers, Vanderbilt | |
| Commodores | |

Outdoor Recreation Assets (49)
Inland Water Area: 37.3 square miles
National Forests, Parks, Wildlife Refuges:
Natchez Trace Parkway (1,132 acres)
Stones River National Battlefield (351 acres)
Places Rated Score: 1,849          Places Rated Rank: 137

### ★ Nassau–Suffolk, NY

| | Rating |
|---|---|
| Common Denominators (1,200) | |
| Good Restaurants: 6 ★, 44 ★★, 23 ★★★ | A |
| Golf Courses: 59 private; 14.5 daily fee; | B |
| 23 municipal | |
| Bowling Lanes: 2,137 | A |
| Movie Theaters: 122 | AA |
| Crowd Pleasers (500) | |
| Auto Racing: | B |
| Islip (NASCAR) | |
| Riverhead (NASCAR) | |
| Pari-mutuel Betting: | C |
| Belmont Park (Thoroughbred, 108 days) | |
| Roosevelt Raceway (harness, 158 days) | |
| Professional Sports: .249 game seats per capita | C |
| ISLANDERS (hockey) | |
| NCAA Division I: .021 game seats per capita | C |
| Hofstra Flying Dutchmen (b) | |

Outdoor Recreation Assets (1,605)
Atlantic Coastline: 170 miles
Inland Water Area: 89.6 square miles
National Forests, Parks, Wildlife Refuges:
Amagansett NWR (36 acres)
Conscience Point NWR (60 acres)
E.A. Norton NWR (187 acres)
Fire Island NS (18,606 acres)
Oyster Bay NWR (3,204 acres)
Sagamore Hill NHS (78 acres)
Seatuck NWR (183 acres)
Target Rock NWR (80 acres)
Wertheim NWR (2,235 acres)
CMSA Access: NEW YORK–NORTHERN NEW
JERSEY–LONG ISLAND, NY–NJ–CT (400)
Places Rated Score: 3,705          Places Rated Rank: 14

### New Bedford, MA

| | Rating |
|---|---|
| Common Denominators (600) | |
| Good Restaurants: 2 ★, 1 ★★ | C |
| Golf Courses: 1.5 private; 0.5 daily fee; | C |
| 1 municipal | |
| Bowling Lanes: 84 | B |
| Movie Theaters: 5 | B |
| Crowd Pleasers (100) | |
| Zoos: Buttonwood Park Zoo | C |

Outdoor Recreation Assets (750)
Atlantic Coastline: 26 miles
Inland Water Area: 20.4 square miles
Places Rated Score: 1,450          Places Rated Rank: 219

### New Britain, CT

| | Rating |
|---|---|
| Common Denominators (700) | |
| Good Restaurants: 2 ★★ | C |
| Golf Courses: 2 daily fee; 1.5 municipal | B |
| Bowling Lanes: 92 | B |
| Movie Theaters: 4 | B |
| Crowd Pleasers (300) | |
| Professional Sports: 1.722 game seats per capita | A |
| Red Sox (baseball) | |

Outdoor Recreation Assets (17)
Inland Water Area: .3 square miles
CMSA Access: HARTFORD–NEW BRITAIN–
MIDDLETOWN, CT (200)
Places Rated Score: 1,217          Places Rated Rank: 258

### New Haven–Meriden, CT

| | Rating |
|---|---|
| Common Denominators (800) | |
| Good Restaurants: 3 ★, 6 ★★ | C |
| Golf Courses: 11 private; 2 daily fee; 3 municipal | C |
| Bowling Lanes: 304 | B |
| Movie Theaters: 22 | AA |
| Crowd Pleasers (400) | |
| Professional Sports: .450 game seats per capita | C |
| Nighthawks (hockey) | |
| NCAA Division I: .901 game seats per capita | A |
| Yale Bulldogs | |

Outdoor Recreation Assets (404)
Atlantic Coastline: 30 miles
Inland Water Area: 8.7 square miles
Places Rated Score: 1,604          Places Rated Rank: 182

### New London–Norwich, CT–RI

| | Rating |
|---|---|
| Common Denominators (1,000) | |
| Good Restaurants: 2 ★, 2 ★★, 2 ★★★ | B |
| Golf Courses: 4 private; 3 daily fee; 2 municipal | B |
| Bowling Lanes: 172 | B |
| Movie Theaters: 11 | AA |
| Crowd Pleasers (600) | |
| Zoos: Moran Nature Center and Zoo | C |
| Auto Racing: Stafford (NASCAR) | C |
| Pari-mutuel Betting: Plainfield Greyhound Park | AA |
| (212 days) | |

Outdoor Recreation Assets (681)
Atlantic Coastline: 35 miles
Inland Water Area: 33.4 square miles
Places Rated Score: 2,281          Places Rated Rank: 74

### ★ New Orleans, LA

| | Rating |
|---|---|
| Common Denominators (800) | |
| Good Restaurants: 8 ★, 16 ★★, 18 ★★★, 7 ★★★★ | AA |
| Golf Courses: 17.5 private; 4.5 daily fee; | C |
| 6 municipal | |
| Bowling Lanes: 406 | C |
| Movie Theaters: 29 | B |
| Crowd Pleasers (700) | |
| Zoos: Audubon Park Zoo | A |
| Pari-mutuel Betting: | B |
| Fair Grounds (Thoroughbred, 97 days) | |
| Jefferson Downs (Thoroughbred, 137 days) | |
| Professional Sports: .463 game seats per capita | C |
| SAINTS (football) | |
| NCAA Division I: .116 game seats per capita | C |
| Tulane Green Wave, University of New Orleans | |
| Privateers (b) | |

Outdoor Recreation Assets (2,000)
Gulf of Mexico Coastline: 75 miles
Inland Water Area: 1,265.2 square miles
National Forests, Parks, Wildlife Refuges:
Boguechito NWR (16,792 acres)
Breton NWR (8,402 acres)
Jean Lafitte NHP (7,754 acres)
Places Rated Score: 3,500          Places Rated Rank: 18

### ★ New York, NY

| | Rating |
|---|---|
| Common Denominators (1,000) | |
| Good Restaurants: 41 ★, 118 ★★, 81 ★★★, 8 ★★★★, | A |
| 1 ★★★★★ | |
| Golf Courses: 49 private; 3 daily fee; 20 municipal | C |
| Bowling Lanes: 2,824 | B |
| Movie Theaters: 356 | AA |
| Crowd Pleasers (1,100) | |
| Zoos: | AA |
| Bronx Zoo | |
| Staten Island Zoo | |
| Aquariums: New York Aquarium | A |
| Pari-mutuel Betting: | C |
| Aqueduct (Thoroughbred, 176 days) | |
| Yonkers Raceway (harness, 77 days) | |
| Professional Sports: 1.340 game seats per capita | B |
| METS, YANKEES (baseball), KNICKER- | |
| BOCKERS (basketball), JETS (football), | |
| RANGERS (hockey) | |

Rating

NCAA Division I: .047 game seats per capita    **C**
  Brooklyn College Kingsmen (b), Columbia
  University Lions, Fordham Rams (b), Iona
  College Gaels (b), Long Island University
  (Brooklyn) Blackbirds (b), Manhattan College
  Jaspers (b), St. Francis College Terriers (b),
  Wagner College Seahawks (b)
Outdoor Recreation Assets (1,079)
  Atlantic Coastline: 27 miles
  Inland Water Area: 149.8 square miles
  National Forests, Parks, Wildlife Refuges:
    Appalachian Trail (960 acres)
    Castle Clinton NM (1 acre)
    Federal Hall NM (0.45 acres)
    Gateway NRA (21,715 acres)
    General Grant National Memorial (0.76 acres)
    Hamilton Grange National Memorial (0.71 acres)
    Statue of Liberty NM (13 acres)
    Theodore Roosevelt Birthplace NHS (0.11
      acres)
  CMSA Access: New York–Northern New
    Jersey–Long Island, NY–NJ–CT (400)
Places Rated Score: 3,579          Places Rated Rank: 16

## Newark, NJ
Common Denominators (700)
  Good Restaurants: 4 ★, 6 ★★, 10 ★★★, 1 ★★★★    **C**
  Golf Courses: 36 private; 7 daily fee;    **C**
    13.5 municipal
  Bowling Lanes: 1,077    **B**
  Movie Theaters: 69    **A**
Crowd Pleasers (300)
  Zoos: Turtle Back Zoo    **B**
  NCAA Division I: .022 game seats per capita    **C**
    Seton Hall Pirates (b)
Outdoor Recreation Assets (418)
  Inland Water Area: 25 square miles
  National Forests, Parks, Wildlife Refuges:
    Appalachian Trail (3,211 acres)
    Delaware NSR (684 acres)
    Delaware Water Gap NRA (37,398 acres)
    Edison NHS (21 acres)
    Great Swamp NWR (6,792 acres)
    Morristown NHP (1,488 acres)
  CMSA Access: New York–Northern New
    Jersey–Long Island, NY–NJ–CT (400)
Places Rated Score: 1,818          Places Rated Rank: 140

## Niagara Falls, NY
Common Denominators (900)
  Good Restaurants: 5 ★★, 1 ★★★    **A**
  Golf Courses: 3.5 private; 3 daily fee; 4 municipal    **A**
  Bowling Lanes: 88    **B**
  Movie Theaters: 3    **C**
Crowd Pleasers (200)
  Professional Sports: .699 game seats per capita    **C**
    White Sox (baseball)
  NCAA Division I: .212 game seats per capita    **C**
    Niagara University Purple Eagles (b)
Outdoor Recreation Assets (373)
  Great Lakes Coastline: 31 miles
  Inland Water Area: 6.6 square miles
  CMSA Access: Buffalo–Niagara Falls, NY (400)
Places Rated Score: 1,873          Places Rated Rank: 132

## Norfolk–Virginia Beach–Newport News, VA
Common Denominators (800)
  Good Restaurants: 13 ★★, 17 ★★★, 1 ★★★★    **A**
  Golf Courses: 10 private; 5.5 daily fee; 6 municipal    **C**
  Bowling Lanes: 708    **B**
  Movie Theaters: 35    **B**
Crowd Pleasers (600)
  Zoos: Lafayette Zoological Park    **C**
  Theme Parks: Busch Gardens–The Old Country    **B**
    (137 acres)
  Auto Racing: Langley Speedway (NASCAR)    **C**

Rating

Professional Sports: .613 game seats per capita    **C**
  Peninsula Pilots, Tidewater Tides (baseball)
NCAA Division I: .299 game seats per capita    **C**
  Old Dominion Monarchs (b), William and Mary
  Indians
Outdoor Recreation Assets (1,564)
  Atlantic Coastline: 69 miles
  Inland Water Area: 151.1 square miles
  National Forests, Parks, Wildlife Refuges:
    Back Bay NWR (4,589 acres)
    Colonial NHP (8,814 acres)
    Great Dismal Swamp NWR (77,733 acres)
    Jamestown NHS (21 acres)
    Mackay Island NWR (874 acres)
    Nansemond NWR (208 acres)
    Plum Tree Island NWR (3,276 acres)
    Yorktown National Cemetery (3 acres)
Places Rated Score: 2,964          Places Rated Rank: 37

## Norwalk, CT
Common Denominators (1,300)
  Good Restaurants: 2 ★, 5 ★★    **AA**
  Golf Courses: 3.5 private; 2 municipal    **B**
  Bowling Lanes: 104    **A**
  Movie Theaters: 9    **AA**
Outdoor Recreation Assets (568)
  Atlantic Coastline: 9 miles
  Inland Water Area: 8.5 square miles
  CMSA Access: New York–Northern New
    Jersey–Long Island, NY–NJ–CT (400)
Places Rated Score: 2,268          Places Rated Rank: 75

## Oakland, CA
Common Denominators (600)
  Good Restaurants: 1 ★, 14 ★★, 3 ★★★, 1 ★★★★    **C**
  Golf Courses: 14 private; 11.5 daily fee;    **C**
    8.5 municipal
  Bowling Lanes: 1,036    **B**
  Movie Theaters: 50    **B**
Crowd Pleasers (800)
  Zoos:    **B**
    Knowland Park Zoo
    Oakland Baby Zoo
  Pari-mutuel Betting: Golden Gate Fields    **C**
    (Thoroughbred, 100 days)
  Professional Sports: 2.898 game seats per capita    **AA**
    A'S (baseball), GOLDEN STATE WARRIORS
    (basketball), INVADERS (football)
  NCAA Division I: .267 game seats per capita    **C**
    St. Mary's College Gaels (b), University of
    California Golden Bears
Outdoor Recreation Assets (594)
  Inland Water Area: 157.4 square miles
  National Forests, Parks, Wildlife Refuges:
    Antioch Dunes NWR (55 acres)
    Eugene O'Neill NHS (13 acres)
    John Muir NHS (9 acres)
    San Francisco Bay NWR (10,620 acres)
  CMSA Access: San Francisco–Oakland–
    San Jose, CA (400)
Places Rated Score: 2,394          Places Rated Rank: 65

## Ocala, FL
Common Denominators (1,300)
  Good Restaurants: 2 ★, 2 ★★    **B**
  Golf Courses: 2 private; 2.5 daily fee;    **A**
    1.5 municipal
  Bowling Lanes: 214    **AA**
  Movie Theaters: 5    **AA**
Crowd Pleasers (300)
  Pari-mutuel Betting: Ocala Jai Alai (60 days)    **A**
Outdoor Recreation Assets (1,495)
  Inland Water Area: 52.5 square miles
  National Forests, Parks, Wildlife Refuges:
    Ocala NF (274,383 acres)
Places Rated Score: 3,095          Places Rated Rank: 31

Rating

## Odessa, TX
Common Denominators (900)
   Good Restaurants: 3 ★★                    **A**
   Golf Courses: 2 private; 1 daily fee        **C**
   Bowling Lanes: 80                          **B**
   Movie Theaters: 4                         **A**
Places Rated Score: 900        Places Rated Rank: 303

## Oklahoma City, OK
Common Denominators (1,000)
   Good Restaurants: 4 ★, 10 ★★, 10 ★★★, 1 ★★★★   **A**
   Golf Courses: 10.5 private; 6 daily fee;       **B**
     11.5 municipal
   Bowling Lanes: 494                 **B**
   Movie Theaters: 27                 **A**
Crowd Pleasers (700)
   Zoos: Oklahoma City Zoo            **A**
   Professional Sports: .984 game seats per capita  **B**
    89ers (baseball)
   NCAA Division I: .599 game seats per capita   **B**
    University of Oklahoma Sooners
Outdoor Recreation Assets (42)
   Inland Water Area: 35.7 square miles
Places Rated Score: 1,742     Places Rated Rank: 150

## Olympia, WA
Common Denominators (1,000)
   Good Restaurants: 2 ★★              **B**
   Golf Courses: 1 private; 4 daily fee     **A**
   Bowling Lanes: 80                  **B**
   Movie Theaters: 4                   **A**
Outdoor Recreation Assets (451)
   Puget Sound Coastline: 10 miles
   Inland Water Area: 47 square miles
   National Forests, Parks, Wildlife Refuges:
    Nisqually NWR (1,985 acres)
    Olympic NF (10 acres)
    Snoqualmie NF (612 acres)
Places Rated Score: 1,451     Places Rated Rank: 218

## Omaha, NE–IA
Common Denominators (1,100)
   Good Restaurants: 1 ★, 9 ★★, 8 ★★★     **AA**
   Golf Courses: 10.5 private; 3.5 daily fee;   **B**
    7.5 municipal
   Bowling Lanes: 606                **A**
   Movie Theaters: 18                **B**
Crowd Pleasers (800)
   Zoos: Henry Doorly Zoo             **B**
   Pari-mutuel Betting: Ak-Sar-Ben (Thoroughbred,  **B**
    85 days)
   Professional Sports: 1.974 game seats per capita  **A**
    Royals (baseball)
   NCAA Division I: .222 game seats per capita   **C**
    Creighton University Bluejays (b)
Outdoor Recreation Assets (77)
   Inland Water Area: 29.5 square miles
   National Forests, Parks, Wildlife Refuges:
    De Soto NWR (4,324 acres)
Places Rated Score: 1,977     Places Rated Rank: 109

## Orange County, NY
Common Denominators (1,000)
   Good Restaurants: 4 ★, 4 ★★, 1 ★★★     **A**
   Golf Courses: 7.5 private; 5 daily fee; 1 municipal  **B**
   Bowling Lanes: 232                **A**
   Movie Theaters: 6                  **B**
Crowd Pleasers (300)
   NCAA Division I: .978 game seats per capita   **A**
    U.S. Military Academy Cadets
Outdoor Recreation Assets (166)
   Inland Water Area: 13.4 square miles
   National Forests, Parks, Wildlife Refuges:
    Appalachian Trail (2,422 acres)
    Upper Delaware NSR (6,559 acres)

Rating

CMSA Access: New York–Northern New Jersey–
  Long Island, NY–NJ–CT (400)
Places Rated Score: 1,866     Places Rated Rank: 134

## Orlando, FL
Common Denominators (1,300)
   Good Restaurants: 5 ★, 17 ★★, 10 ★★★, 2 ★★★★  **AA**
   Golf Courses: 8 private; 25.5 daily fee; 7 municipal  **AA**
   Bowling Lanes: 570                **A**
   Movie Theaters: 19                **B**
Crowd Pleasers (1,000)
   Zoos: Central Florida Zoological Park    **C**
   Theme Parks:                   **AA**
    Sea World of Florida (365 days)
    Walt Disney World & Epcot Center (365 days)
   Pari-mutuel Betting:              **A**
    Sanford–Orlando Kennel Club (106 days)
    Seminole Greyhound Park (105 days)
   Professional Sports: 1.268 game seats per capita  **B**
    Twins (baseball), RENEGADES (football)
Outdoor Recreation Assets (581)
   Inland Water Area: 297.1 square miles
Places Rated Score: 2,881     Places Rated Rank: 42

## Owensboro, KY
Common Denominators (700)
   Good Restaurants: 1 ★★              **C**
   Golf Courses: 2 private; 0.5 daily fee;     **B**
    1.5 municipal
   Bowling Lanes: 36                  **B**
   Movie Theaters: 2                  **B**
Outdoor Recreation Assets (152)
   Inland Water Area: 14.1 square miles
Places Rated Score: 852        Places Rated Rank: 305

## Oxnard–Ventura, CA
Common Denominators (1,000)
   Good Restaurants: 12 ★★, 5 ★★★       **AA**
   Golf Courses: 3.5 private; 4.5 daily fee; 4   **B**
    municipal
   Bowling Lanes: 236                **B**
   Movie Theaters: 15                **B**
Outdoor Recreation Assets (735)
   Pacific Coastline: 37 miles
   Inland Water Area: 1.5 square miles
   National Forests, Parks, Wildlife Refuges:
    Angeles NF (1,473 acres)
    Channel Islands NP (9,905 acres)
    Hopper Mountain NWR (1,871 acres)
    Los Padres NF (556,632 acres)
    Santa Monica Mountains NRA (17,165 acres)
CMSA Access: Los Angeles–Anaheim–
  Riverside, CA (400)
Places Rated Score: 2,135     Places Rated Rank: 92

## Panama City, FL
Common Denominators (900)
   Golf Courses: 3.5 private; 2.5 daily fee    **A**
   Bowling Lanes: 56                  **B**
   Movie Theaters: 4                  **AA**
Outdoor Recreation Assets (1,189)
   Gulf of Mexico Coastline: 44 miles
   Inland Water Area: 113.6 square miles
Places Rated Score: 2,089     Places Rated Rank: 95

## Parkersburg–Marietta, WV–OH
Common Denominators (1,100)
   Good Restaurants: 1 ★★, 2 ★★★        **A**
   Golf Courses: 2 private; 6 daily fee      **AA**
   Bowling Lanes: 71                  **B**
   Movie Theaters: 4                  **B**
Outdoor Recreation Assets (48)
   Inland Water Area: 9.6 square miles
Places Rated Score: 1,148     Places Rated Rank: 269

Rating

## Pascagoula, MS
Common Denominators (1,000)
Good Restaurants: 1 ★, 2 ★★, 1 ★★★                    B
Golf Courses: 1.5 private; 3 daily fee;               A
   0.5 municipal
Bowling Lanes: 40                                     B
Movie Theaters: 4                                     A
Outdoor Recreation Assets (956)
Gulf of Mexico Coastline: 25 miles
Inland Water Area: 25.3 square miles
National Forests, Parks, Wildlife Refuges:
   Gulf Islands NS (49,873 acres)
Places Rated Score: 1,956          Places Rated Rank: 112

## Pawtucket–Woonsocket–Attleboro, RI–MA
Common Denominators (700)
Good Restaurants: 1 ★                                 C
Golf Courses: 4.5 private; 8.5 daily fee             A
Bowling Lanes: 72                                     C
Movie Theaters: 8                                     B
Crowd Pleasers (600)
Pari-mutuel Betting: Lincoln Greyhound Park          AA
   (248 days)
Professional Sports: 1.323 game seats per capita     B
   Red Sox (baseball)
Outdoor Recreation Assets (113)
Inland Water Area: 7 square miles
National Forests, Parks, Wildlife Refuges:
   Trustom Pond NWR (579 acres)
CMSA Access: PROVIDENCE–PAWTUCKET–
   FALL RIVER, RI–MA (100)
Places Rated Score: 1,513          Places Rated Rank: 202

## Pensacola, FL
Common Denominators (700)
Good Restaurants: 2 ★★★                               C
Golf Courses: 6 private; 5 daily fee; 1 municipal    B
Bowling Lanes: 186                                    B
Movie Theaters: 7                                     B
Crowd Pleasers (400)
Auto Racing: Five Flags (NASCAR)                     C
Pari-mutuel Betting: Pensacola Greyhound Park        A
   (104 days)
Outdoor Recreation Assets (1,060)
Gulf of Mexico Coastline: 43 miles
Inland Water Area: 212.2 square miles
Places Rated Score: 2,160          Places Rated Rank: 86

## Peoria, IL
Common Denominators (1,100)
Good Restaurants: 2 ★★, 1 ★★★                         C
Golf Courses: 6 private; 4.5 daily fee;              A
   6.5 municipal
Bowling Lanes: 439                                    AA
Movie Theaters: 13                                    A
Crowd Pleasers (500)
Zoos: Glen Oak Zoo                                    C
Professional Sports: 1.886 game seats per capita     A
   Chiefs (baseball), Prancers (hockey)
NCAA Division I: .259 game seats per capita          C
   Bradley University Braves (b)
Outdoor Recreation Assets (88)
Inland Water Area: 31.8 square miles
Places Rated Score: 1,688          Places Rated Rank: 162

## Philadelphia, PA–NJ
Common Denominators (700)
Good Restaurants: 27 ★, 54 ★★, 18 ★★★, 4 ★★★★,       B
   1 ★★★★★
Golf Courses: 67.5 private; 48 daily fee;            B
   13 municipal
Bowling Lanes: 1,756                                  B
Movie Theaters: 98                                    C
Crowd Pleasers (900)
Zoos: Philadelphia Zoological Gardens                AA

Rating

Pari-mutuel Betting:                                  C
   Continental (Thoroughbred, 135 days)
   Keystone (Thoroughbred, 135 days)
   Liberty Bell (harness, 135 days)
   William Penn (harness, 87 days)
Professional Sports: 1.574 game seats per capita     A
   PHILLIES (baseball), 76ERS (basketball),
   EAGLES (football), FLYERS (hockey)
NCAA Division I: .205 game seats per capita          C
   Drexel Dragons (b), LaSalle College Explorers
   (b), St. Joseph Hawks (b), Temple Owls,
   University of Pennsylvania Quakers, Villanova
   Wildcats (b)
Outdoor Recreation Assets (79)
Inland Water Area: 50.1 square miles
National Forests, Parks, Wildlife Refuges:
   Brigantine NWR (97 acres)
   Edgar Allen Poe House NHS (0.52 acres)
   Hopewell Village NHS (320 acres)
   Independence NHP (2,814 acres)
   Thaddeus Kosciuszko NM (0.02 acres)
   Valley Forge NHP (2,988 acres)
CMSA Access: PHILADELPHIA–WILMINGTON–
   TRENTON, PA–NJ–DE–MD (300)
Places Rated Score: 1,979          Places Rated Rank: 108

## Phoenix, AZ
Common Denominators (800)
Good Restaurants: 2 ★, 18 ★★, 12 ★★★, 3 ★★★★         A
Golf Courses: 29.5 private; 23 daily fee;            B
   6 municipal
Bowling Lanes: 820                                    B
Movie Theaters: 33                                    C
Crowd Pleasers (1,100)
Zoos: Phoenix Zoo                                    A
Auto Racing: Phoenix International (NASCAR)          C
Pari-mutuel Betting:                                  A
   Phoenix Greyhound Park (294 days)
   Turf Paradise (Thoroughbred, 158 days)
Professional Sports: 1.174 game seats per capita     B
   Giants (baseball), SUNS (basketball),
   ARIZONA WRANGLERS (football)
NCAA Division I: .356 game seats per capita          B
   Arizona State Sun Devils
Outdoor Recreation Assets (572)
Inland Water Area: 14.9 square miles
National Forests, Parks, Wildlife Refuges:
   Tonto NF (658,436 acres)
Places Rated Score: 2,472          Places Rated Rank: 59

## Pine Bluff, AR
Common Denominators (600)
Good Restaurants: 1 ★                                 C
Golf Courses: 2 private; 1 municipal                 C
Bowling Lanes: 68                                     A
Movie Theaters: 2                                     C
Outdoor Recreation Assets (193)
Inland Water Area: 34.1 square miles
Places Rated Score: 793           Places Rated Rank: 316

## Pittsburgh, PA
Common Denominators (1,000)
Good Restaurants: 2 ★, 11 ★★, 22 ★★★                  B
Golf Courses: 40 private; 44 daily fee;              B
   6.5 municipal
Bowling Lanes: 1,656                                  A
Movie Theaters: 71                                    A
Crowd Pleasers (1,100)
Zoos:                                                 AA
   Pittsburgh Aviary
   Pittsburgh Zoo
Pari-mutuel Betting:                                  B
   Mountain Laurel (harness, 248 days)
   The Meadows (harness, 63 days)

Rating

Professional Sports: 2.470 game seats per capita    **A**
   PIRATES (baseball), STEELERS (football),
   PENGUINS (hockey)
NCAA Division I: .358 game seats per capita    **B**
   Duquesne Dukes (b), Robert Morris College
   Colonials (b), University of Pittsburgh Panthers
Outdoor Recreation Assets (45)
   Inland Water Area: 28.1 square miles
   National Forests, Parks, Wildlife Refuges:
     Fort Necessity National Battlefield (903 acres)
     Friendship Hill NHS (661 acres)
Places Rated Score: 2,145    Places Rated Rank: 90

### Pittsfield, MA
Common Denominators (1,100)
   Good Restaurants: 1 ★★, 2 ★★★    **AA**
   Golf Courses: 4 private; 4 daily fee    **AA**
   Bowling Lanes: 58    **B**
   Movie Theaters: 1    **C**
Crowd Pleasers (200)
   Pari-mutuel Betting:    **B**
     Berkshire Downs (Thoroughbred, 6 days)
     Great Barrington (Thoroughbred, 16 days)
Outdoor Recreation Assets (120)
   Inland Water Area: 5.5 square miles
Places Rated Score: 1,420    Places Rated Rank: 225

### ★ Portland, ME
Common Denominators (1,200)
   Good Restaurants: 3 ★, 13 ★★, 1 ★★★    **AA**
   Golf Courses: 4 private; 5 daily fee; 2.5 municipal    **AA**
   Bowling Lanes: 14    **C**
   Movie Theaters: 7    **A**
Crowd Pleasers (800)
   Pari-mutuel Betting: Scarborough Downs    **AA**
     (harness, 123 days)
   Professional Sports: 3.304 game seats per capita    **AA**
     Maine Guides (baseball), Maine Mariners
     (hockey)
Outdoor Recreation Assets (1,366)
   Atlantic Coastline: 36 miles
   Inland Water Area: 112.7 square miles
   National Forests, Parks, Wildlife Refuges:
     Rachel Carson NWR (144 acres)
Places Rated Score: 3,366    Places Rated Rank: 20

### Portland, OR
Common Denominators (1,100)
   Good Restaurants: 13 ★, 26 ★★, 19 ★★★    **AA**
   Golf Courses: 9.5 private; 16.5 daily fee;    **B**
     4 municipal
   Bowling Lanes: 744    **B**
   Movie Theaters: 44    **A**
Crowd Pleasers (1,100)
   Zoos: Washington Park Zoo    **A**
   Auto Racing:    **B**
     Portland International (SCCA)
     Rose City (NASCAR)
   Pari-mutuel Betting:    **B**
     Multnomah Kennel Club (80 days)
     Portland Meadows (Thoroughbred, 92 days)
   Professional Sports: 2.425 game seats per capita    **A**
     Beavers (baseball), TRAIL BLAZERS
     (basketball), BREAKERS (football)
   NCAA Division I: .027 game seats per capita    **C**
     Portland State Vikings (b)
Outdoor Recreation Assets (332)
   Inland Water Area: 46.4 square miles
   National Forests, Parks, Wildlife Refuges:
     Eagle Creek NWR (166 acres)
     McLoughlin House NHS (0.63 acres)
     Mount Hood NF (72,415 acres)
     Siuslaw NF (25,440 acres)
     Willamette NF (856 acres)
Places Rated Score: 2,532    Places Rated Rank: 55

### Portsmouth–Dover–Rochester, NH–ME
Common Denominators (700)
   Good Restaurants: 3 ★, 17 ★★, 5 ★★★    **AA**
   Golf Courses: 0.5 daily fee    **C**
   Bowling Lanes: 58    **C**
   Movie Theaters: 4    **C**
Crowd Pleasers (200)
   NCAA Division I: .592 game seats per capita    **B**
     University of New Hampshire Wildcats
Outdoor Recreation Assets (490)
   Atlantic Coastline: 26 miles
   Inland Water Area: 24.6 square miles
   National Forests, Parks, Wildlife Refuges:
     Rachel Carson NWR (1,748 acres)
Places Rated Score: 1,390    Places Rated Rank: 236

### Poughkeepsie, NY
Common Denominators (1,400)
   Good Restaurants: 6 ★★, 3 ★★★, 1 ★★★★, 1 ★★★★★    **AA**
   Golf Courses: 5.5 private; 5 daily fee;    **AA**
     3.5 municipal
   Bowling Lanes: 328    **AA**
   Movie Theaters: 6    **B**
Crowd Pleasers (100)
   NCAA Division I: .159 game seats per capita    **C**
     Marist College Red Foxes (b)
Outdoor Recreation Assets (170)
   Inland Water Area: 20.7 square miles
   National Forests, Parks, Wildlife Refuges:
     Appalachian Trail (3,619 acres)
     Eleanor Roosevelt NHS (181 acres)
     Home of Franklin D. Roosevelt NHS (264 acres)
     Vanderbilt Mansion NHS (212 acres)
Places Rated Score: 1,670    Places Rated Rank: 165

### Providence, RI
Common Denominators (800)
   Good Restaurants: 1 ★, 3 ★★, 5 ★★★    **B**
   Golf Courses: 9.5 private; 9.5 daily fee;    **B**
     1.5 municipal
   Bowling Lanes: 234    **B**
   Movie Theaters: 16    **B**
Crowd Pleasers (300)
   Zoos: Roger Williams Park Zoo    **C**
   NCAA Division I: .477 game seats per capita    **B**
     Brown Bruins, Providence College Friars (b)
Outdoor Recreation Assets (963)
   Atlantic Coastline: 12 miles
   Inland Water Area: 103.6 square miles
   National Forests, Parks, Wildlife Refuges:
     Roger Williams National Memorial (5 acres)
CMSA Access: PROVIDENCE–PAWTUCKET–FALL
RIVER, RI–MA (200)
Places Rated Score: 2,263    Places Rated Rank: 76

### ★ Provo–Orem, UT
Common Denominators (900)
   Good Restaurants: 1 ★★    **C**
   Golf Courses: 3 private; 0.5 daily fee; 3.5    **B**
     municipal
   Bowling Lanes: 104    **B**
   Movie Theaters: 9    **AA**
Crowd Pleasers (400)
   NCAA Division I: 2.843 game seats per capita    **AA**
     Brigham Young Cougars
Outdoor Recreation Assets (2,000)
   Inland Water Area: 126.9 square miles
   National Forests, Parks, Wildlife Refuges:
     Ashley NF (3,885 acres)
     Manti-La Sal NF (91,292 acres)
     Timpanogos Cave NM (250 acres)
     Uinta NF (390,215 acres)
Places Rated Score: 3,300    Places Rated Rank: 23

Rating

## Pueblo, CO
Common Denominators (1,100)
Good Restaurants: 1 ★, 3 ★★ — A
Golf Courses: 1 private; 1.5 daily fee; — B
1.5 municipal
Bowling Lanes: 118 — A
Movie Theaters: 5 — A
Crowd Pleasers (500)
Auto Racing: Pueblo Motorsports (SCCA) — C
Pari-mutuel Betting: Pueblo Greyhound Park — AA
(74 days)
Outdoor Recreation Assets (19)
Inland Water Area: 8.8 square miles
Places Rated Score: 1,619 — Places Rated Rank: 174

## Racine, WI
Common Denominators (1,300)
Good Restaurants: 4 ★, 1 ★★, 1 ★★★ — A
Golf Courses: 2 private; 2 daily fee; 4 municipal — AA
Bowling Lanes: 224 — AA
Movie Theaters: 4 — B
Crowd Pleasers (100)
Zoos: Racine Zoological Garden — C
Outdoor Recreation Assets (216)
Great Lakes Coastline: 12 miles
Inland Water Area: 6.4 square miles
CMSA Access: MILWAUKEE–RACINE, WI (400)
Places Rated Score: 2,016 — Places Rated Rank: 104

## Raleigh–Durham, NC
Common Denominators (1,100)
Good Restaurants: 1 ★, 2 ★★, 6 ★★★ — B
Golf Courses: 14.5 private; 15.5 daily fee — A
Bowling Lanes: 236 — B
Movie Theaters: 34 — AA
Crowd Pleasers (500)
Professional Sports: .624 game seats per capita — C
Durham Bulls (baseball)
NCAA Division I: 1.826 game seats per capita — AA
Duke Blue Devils, North Carolina State
Wolfpack, University of North Carolina Tarheels
Outdoor Recreation Assets (6)
Inland Water Area: 2.5 square miles
Places Rated Score: 1,606 — Places Rated Rank: 180

## Reading, PA
Common Denominators (1,200)
Good Restaurants: 2 ★, 1 ★★, 1 ★★★, 2 ★★★★ — B
Golf Courses: 5 private; 11 daily fee — AA
Bowling Lanes: 270 — A
Movie Theaters: 11 — A
Crowd Pleasers (300)
Professional Sports: 1.837 game seats per capita — A
Phillies (baseball)
Outdoor Recreation Assets (49)
Inland Water Area: 1.9 square miles
National Forests, Parks, Wildlife Refuges:
Appalachian Trail (3,703 acres)
Hopewell Village NHS (529 acres)
Places Rated Score: 1,549 — Places Rated Rank: 193

## Redding, CA
Common Denominators (800)
Good Restaurants: 1 ★, 1 ★★ — C
Golf Courses: 2.5 private; 1.5 daily fee — B
Bowling Lanes: 76 — B
Movie Theaters: 4 — A
Crowd Pleasers (100)
Auto Racing: Shasta (NASCAR) — C
Outdoor Recreation Assets (1,524)
Inland Water Area: 62.8 square miles
National Forests, Parks, Wildlife Refuges:
Lassen NF (149,931 acres)
Lassen Volcanic NP (4,200 acres)
Shasta NF (471,224 acres)

Trinity NF (30,626 acres)
Whiskeytown–Shasta–Trinity NRA (42,488 acres)
Places Rated Score: 2,424 — Places Rated Rank: 64

## Reno, NV
Common Denominators (1,400)
Good Restaurants: 8 ★, 16 ★★, 13 ★★★, 2 ★★★★ — AA
Golf Courses: 1 private; 2 daily fee; 3.5 municipal — A
Bowling Lanes: 166 — A
Movie Theaters: 8 — AA
Crowd Pleasers (500)
Professional Sports: 1.627 game seats per capita — A
Padres (Padres)
NCAA Division I: .697 game seats per capita — B
University of Nevada Wolf Pack
Outdoor Recreation Assets (486)
Inland Water Area: 232.9 square miles
National Forests, Parks, Wildlife Refuges:
Anaho Island NWR (248 acres)
Sheldon NWR (187,200 acres)
Toiyabe NF (56,087 acres)
Places Rated Score: 2,386 — Places Rated Rank: 66

## Richland–Kennewick–Pasco, WA
Common Denominators (900)
Good Restaurants: 1 ★★ — C
Golf Courses: 2 private; 3.5 daily fee; 1 municipal — A
Bowling Lanes: 132 — A
Movie Theaters: 4 — B
Crowd Pleasers (200)
Professional Sports: .768 game seats per capita — B
Tri-Cities Triplets (baseball)
Outdoor Recreation Assets (104)
Inland Water Area: 61.3 square miles
Places Rated Score: 1,204 — Places Rated Rank: 262

## Richmond–Petersburg, VA
Common Denominators (900)
Good Restaurants: 2 ★, 7 ★★, 3 ★★★ — B
Golf Courses: 14.5 private; 11.5 daily fee — B
Bowling Lanes: 330 — B
Movie Theaters: 26 — A
Crowd Pleasers (900)
Theme Parks: Kings Dominion (121 days) — A
Auto Racing: — B
Richmond Fairgrounds (NASCAR)
Southside Speedway (NASCAR)
Professional Sports: .873 game seats per capita — B
Braves (baseball)
NCAA Division I: .498 game seats per capita — B
University of Richmond Spiders, Virginia
Commonwealth University Rams (b)
Outdoor Recreation Assets (143)
Inland Water Area: 78.2 square miles
National Forests, Parks, Wildlife Refuges:
Harrison Lake NWR (445 acres)
Maggie L. Walker NHS (1.28 acres)
Petersburg National Battlefield (1,524 acres)
Poplar Grove National Cemetery (9 acres)
Presquile NWR (1,329 acres)
Richmond National Battlefield Park (771 acres)
Places Rated Score: 1,943 — Places Rated Rank: 116

## Riverside–San Bernardino, CA
Common Denominators (900)
Good Restaurants: 4 ★, 19 ★★, 14 ★★★. — A
Golf Courses: 49.5 private; 30 daily fee; 5 — B
municipal
Bowling Lanes: 956 — B
Movie Theaters: 37 — B
Crowd Pleasers (200)
Zoos: Living Desert Reserve — C
Auto Racing: Riverside International (NASCAR, — C
SCCA)

Rating

Outdoor Recreation Assets (418)
Inland Water Area: 108.1 square miles
National Forests, Parks, Wildlife Refuges:
Angeles NF (10,129 acres)
Cleveland NF (77,977 acres)
Death Valley NM (85,152 acres)
Joshua Tree NM (556,995 acres)
San Bernardino NF (658,645 acres)
CMSA Access: LOS ANGELES–ANAHEIM–
RIVERSIDE, CA (400)
Places Rated Score: 1,918          Places Rated Rank: 124

**Roanoke, VA**
Common Denominators (1,000)
Good Restaurants: 1 ★★, 1 ★★★, 1 ★★★★          B
Golf Courses: 6.5 private; 2.5 daily fee          C
Bowling Lanes: 202          A
Movie Theaters: 13          AA
Crowd Pleasers (200)
Professional Sports: 1.270 game seats per capita          B
Salem Redbirds (baseball)
Outdoor Recreation Assets (836)
Inland Water Area: 1.2 square miles
National Forests, Parks, Wildlife Refuges:
Appalachian Trail (3,458 acres)
Blue Ridge Parkway (5,661 acres)
George Washington NF (13,520 acres)
Jefferson NF (67,819 acres)
Places Rated Score: 2,036          Places Rated Rank: 101

**Rochester, MN**
Common Denominators (1,500)
Good Restaurants: 3 ★, 3 ★★, 3 ★★★          AA
Golf Courses: 1 private; 2 daily fee; 3 municipal          AA
Bowling Lanes: 72          A
Movie Theaters: 5          AA
Outdoor Recreation Assets (3)
Inland Water Area: .4 square miles
Places Rated Score: 1,503          Places Rated Rank: 207

**Rochester, NY**
Common Denominators (1,200)
Good Restaurants: 3 ★, 22 ★★, 17 ★★★, 1 ★★★★          AA
Golf Courses: 17 private; 26.5 daily fee;          A
5 municipal
Bowling Lanes: 1,260          AA
Movie Theaters: 19          C
Crowd Pleasers (500)
Auto Racing: Spencer Speedway (NASCAR)          C
Pari-mutuel Betting: Finger Lakes (Thoroughbred,          B
153 days)
Professional Sports: 1.236 game seats per capita          B
Red Wings (baseball), Americans (hockey)
Outdoor Recreation Assets (959)
Great Lakes Coastline: 90 miles
Inland Water Area: 34.5 square miles
Places Rated Score: 2,659          Places Rated Rank: 50

**Rockford, IL**
Common Denominators (800)
Good Restaurants: 4 ★★          C
Golf Courses: 4 private; 6.5 municipal          B
Bowling Lanes: 422          AA
Movie Theaters: 6          C
Crowd Pleasers (100)
Auto Racing: Blackhawk Farms Raceway (SCCA)          C
Outdoor Recreation Assets (33)
Inland Water Area: 5.2 square miles
Places Rated Score: 933          Places Rated Rank: 297

**Sacramento, CA**
Common Denominators (700)
Good Restaurants: 3 ★, 7 ★★, 5 ★★★          C
Golf Courses: 11.5 private; 11.5 daily fee;          B
6.5 municipal

Rating

Bowling Lanes: 554          B
Movie Theaters: 29          B
Crowd Pleasers (200)
Zoos: Sacramento Zoo          C
Pari-mutuel Betting:          C
California State Fair (Thoroughbred, 14 days)
Golden Bear Raceway (harness, 35 days)
Outdoor Recreation Assets (1,406)
Inland Water Area: 174.5 square miles
National Forests, Parks, Wildlife Refuges:
Eldorado NF (539,658 acres)
Tahoe NF (269,335 acres)
Places Rated Score: 2,306          Places Rated Rank: 72

**Saginaw–Bay City–Midland, MI**
Common Denominators (1,200)
Good Restaurants: 3 ★, 6 ★★, 4 ★★★          A
Golf Courses: 5.5 private; 15 daily fee;          AA
2.5 municipal
Bowling Lanes: 560          AA
Movie Theaters: 9          C
Crowd Pleasers (400)
Zoos: Saginaw Children's Zoo          C
Auto Racing: Dixie (NASCAR)          C
Pari-mutuel Betting: Saginaw Valley Trotting          B
(67 days)
Outdoor Recreation Assets (459)
Great Lakes Coastline: 40 miles
Inland Water Area: 7.2 square miles
National Forests, Parks, Wildlife Refuges:
Shiawassee NWR (8,984 acres)
Places Rated Score: 2,059          Places Rated Rank: 96

**St. Cloud, MN**
Common Denominators (1,300)
Good Restaurants: 2 ★★          C
Golf Courses: 1.5 private; 5 daily fee;          AA
1 municipal
Bowling Lanes: 174          AA
Movie Theaters: 7          AA
Outdoor Recreation Assets (272)
Inland Water Area: 72.8 square miles
National Forests, Parks, Wildlife Refuges:
Sherburne NWR (29,406 acres)
Places Rated Score: 1,572          Places Rated Rank: 189

**St. Joseph, MO**
Common Denominators (1,200)
Good Restaurants: 1 ★★, 1 ★★★          A
Golf Courses: 2 private; 1 municipal          C
Bowling Lanes: 106          AA
Movie Theaters: 4          AA
Outdoor Recreation Assets (65)
Inland Water Area: 5.3 square miles
Places Rated Score: 1,265          Places Rated Rank: 251

**St. Louis, MO–IL**
Common Denominators (800)
Good Restaurants: 1 ★, 13 ★★, 14 ★★★, 3 ★★★★,          B
1 ★★★★★
Golf Courses: 22.5 private; 16 daily fee;          C
2.5 municipal
Bowling Lanes: 1,244          B
Movie Theaters: 67          A
Crowd Pleasers (1,100)
Zoos: Forest Park Zoo          AA
Theme Parks: Six Flags Over Mid-America          C
(140 days)
Auto Racing: Mid-America Raceway (SCCA)          C
Professional Sports: 2.884 game seats per capita          AA
CARDINALS (baseball, football), BLUES
(hockey)
NCAA Division I: .036 game seats per capita          C
St. Louis Billikens (b)

**Rating**

Outdoor Recreation Assets (143)
 Inland Water Area: 77.2 square miles
 National Forests, Parks, Wildlife Refuges:
  Jefferson National Expansion Memorial NHS
  (91 acres)
CMSA Access: St. Louis–East St. Louis–
 Alton, MO–IL (200)
Places Rated Score: 2,243    Places Rated Rank: 78

## Salem, OR
Common Denominators (900)
 Good Restaurants: 1 ★, 2 ★★    C
 Golf Courses: 2 private; 5.5 daily fee    B
 Bowling Lanes: 160    B
 Movie Theaters: 11    AA
Crowd Pleasers (100)
 Professional Sports: .370 game seats per capita    C
  Angels (baseball)
Outdoor Recreation Assets (873)
 Inland Water Area: 14 square miles
 National Forests, Parks, Wildlife Refuges:
  Ankeny NWR (2,796 acres)
  Baskett Slough NWR (2,492 acres)
  Mount Hood NF (65,872 acres)
  Willamette NF (135,004 acres)
Places Rated Score: 1,873    Places Rated Rank: 132

## Salem–Gloucester, MA
Common Denominators (900)
 Good Restaurants: 6 ★, 10 ★★, 4 ★★★    AA
 Golf Courses: 7 private; 3 daily fee; 1.5 municipal    B
 Movie Theaters: 8    A
Outdoor Recreation Assets (934)
 Atlantic Coastline: 33 miles
 Inland Water Area: 22.3 square miles
 National Forests, Parks, Wildlife Refuges:
  Parker River NWR (2,330 acres)
  Salem Maritime NHS (9 acres)
  Thatcher Island NWR (22 acres)
CMSA Access: Boston–Lawrence–Salem, MA–NH (400)
Places Rated Score: 2,234    Places Rated Rank: 80

## Salinas–Seaside–Monterey, CA
Common Denominators (1,300)
 Good Restaurants: 7 ★, 11 ★★, 14 ★★★, 4 ★★★★    AA
 Golf Courses: 10 private; 7.5 daily fee;    A
  2 municipal
 Bowling Lanes: 136    B
 Movie Theaters: 18    AA
Crowd Pleasers (300)
 Auto Racing: Laguna Seca (NASCAR, SCCA)    C
 Professional Sports: .844 game seats per capita    B
  Salinas Spurs (baseball)
Outdoor Recreation Assets (1,579)
 Pacific Coastline: 85 miles
 Inland Water Area: 3 square miles
 National Forests, Parks, Wildlife Refuges:
  Los Padres NF (304,578 acres)
  Pinnacles NM (1,283 acres)
  Salinas River NWR (364 acres)
Places Rated Score: 3,179    Places Rated Rank: 27

## ★ Salt Lake City–Ogden, UT
Common Denominators (1,000)
 Good Restaurants: 6 ★, 10 ★★, 3 ★★★, 1 ★★★★    B
 Golf Courses: 11 private; 5.5 daily fee;    B
  10.5 municipal
 Bowling Lanes: 574    B
 Movie Theaters: 45    AA
Crowd Pleasers (900)
 Zoos:    A
  Hogle Zoological Garden
  Tracy Aviary
 Professional Sports: 1.845 game seats per capita    A
  Gulls (baseball), JAZZ (basketball), Golden
  Eagles (hockey)

**Rating** (right column)

NCAA Division I: .717 game seats per capita    A
 University of Utah Utes, Utah State Aggies
Outdoor Recreation Assets (2,000)
 Inland Water Area: 477.5 square miles
 National Forests, Parks, Wildlife Refuges:
  Cache NF (67,554 acres)
  Wasatch NF (133,926 acres)
Places Rated Score: 3,900    Places Rated Rank: 11

## San Angelo, TX
Common Denominators (1,100)
 Good Restaurants: 1 ★, 1 ★★    B
 Golf Courses: 1 private; 1 daily fee; 0.5 municipal    B
 Bowling Lanes: 68    A
 Movie Theaters: 4    AA
Outdoor Recreation Assets (36)
 Inland Water Area: 10.9 square miles
Places Rated Score: 1,136    Places Rated Rank: 272

## San Antonio, TX
Common Denominators (900)
 Good Restaurants: 11 ★, 15 ★★, 7 ★★★, 2 ★★★★    A
 Golf Courses: 13.5 private; 2 daily fee;    C
  5.5 municipal
 Bowling Lanes: 660    B
 Movie Theaters: 33    A
Crowd Pleasers (600)
 Zoos: San Antonio Zoo and Aquarium    A
 Professional Sports: 1.095 game seats per capita    B
  Dodgers (baseball), SPURS (basketball),
  GUNSLINGERS (football)
 NCAA Division I: .055 game seats per capita    C
  University of Texas Roadrunners (b)
Outdoor Recreation Assets (9)
 Inland Water Area: 3.7 square miles
 National Forests, Parks, Wildlife Refuges:
  San Antonio Missions NHP (463 acres)
Places Rated Score: 1,509    Places Rated Rank: 204

## ★ San Diego, CA
Common Denominators (900)
 Good Restaurants: 3 ★, 38 ★★, 14 ★★★    A
 Golf Courses; 17.5 private; 24 daily fee;    B
  6 municipal
 Bowling Lanes: 928    B
 Movie Theaters: 56    B
Crowd Pleasers (1,300)
 Zoos:    AA
  San Diego Zoo
  Wild Animal Park
 Theme Parks: Sea World of California (365 days)    A
 Pari-mutuel Betting: Del Mar (Thoroughbred,    C
  43 days)
 Professional Sports: 2.762 game seats per capita    AA
  PADRES (baseball), CHARGERS (football)
 NCAA Division I: .264 game seats per capita    C
  San Diego State Aztecs, U.S. International
  University Soaring Gulls (b), University of San
  Diego Toreros (b)
Outdoor Recreation Assets (1,147)
 Pacific Coastline: 55 miles
 Inland Water Area: 52.2 square miles
 National Forests, Parks, Wildlife Refuges:
  Cabrillo NM (144 acres)
  Cleveland NF (288,125 acres)
  Tijuana Slough NWR (407 acres)
Places Rated Score: 3,347    Places Rated Rank: 22

## ★ San Francisco, CA
Common Denominators (1,100)
 Good Restaurants: 2 ★, 34 ★★, 52 ★★★, 15 ★★★★,    AA
  2 ★★★★★
 Golf Courses: 15 private; 4 daily fee; 6 municipal    C
 Bowling Lanes: 572    B
 Movie Theaters: 99    AA

| | Rating |
|---|---|
| **Crowd Pleasers (1,100)** | |
| Zoos: San Francisco Zoological Gardens | A |
| Aquariums: Steinhart Aquarium | A |
| Pari-mutuel Betting: Bay Meadows (Thoroughbred, 111 days) | C |
| Professional Sports: 3.484 game seats per capita GIANTS (baseball), 49ERS (football) | AA |
| **Outdoor Recreation Assets (2,000)** | |
| Pacific Coastline: 75 miles | |
| Inland Water Area: 249.6 square miles | |
| National Forests, Parks, Wildlife Refuges: | |
| Farallon NWR (91 acres) | |
| Fort Point NHS (29 acres) | |
| Golden Gate NRA (60,788 acres) | |
| Muir Woods NM (554 acres) | |
| Point Reyes NS (63,953 acres) | |
| San Francisco Bay NWR (1,863 acres) | |
| CMSA Access: SAN FRANCISCO–OAKLAND– SAN JOSE, CA (400) | |
| Places Rated Score: 4,600 Places Rated Rank: 2 | |

### San Jose, CA

| | Rating |
|---|---|
| **Common Denominators (800)** | |
| Good Restaurants: 2 ★, 11 ★★, 7 ★★★ | B |
| Golf Courses: 8.5 private; 7.5 daily fee; 6.5 municipal | C |
| Bowling Lanes: 648 | B |
| Movie Theaters: 46 | A |
| **Crowd Pleasers (700)** | |
| Zoos: | C |
| Applegate Zoo | |
| San Jose Baby Zoo | |
| Theme Parks: Marriott's Great America (141 days) | B |
| Auto Racing: San Jose Fairgrounds (NASCAR) | C |
| Professional Sports: .281 game seats per capita Bees (baseball) | C |
| NCAA Division I: .568 game seats per capita San Jose State Spartans, Stanford University Cardinals, University of Santa Clara Broncos (b) | B |
| **Outdoor Recreation Assets (64)** | |
| Inland Water Area: 11.6 square miles | |
| National Forests, Parks, Wildlife Refuges: | |
| San Francisco NWR (3,156 acres) | |
| CMSA Access: SAN FRANCISCO–OAKLAND– SAN JOSE, CA (400) | |
| Places Rated Score: 1,964 Places Rated Rank: 111 | |

### ★ Santa Barbara–Santa Maria–Lompoc, CA

| | Rating |
|---|---|
| **Common Denominators (1,100)** | |
| Good Restaurants: 2 ★, 10 ★★, 4 ★★★ | AA |
| Golf Courses: 7 private; 2.5 daily fee; 1 municipal | C |
| Bowling Lanes: 164 | B |
| Movie Theaters: 13 | AA |
| **Crowd Pleasers (200)** | |
| Zoos: Santa Barbara Zoological Gardens | C |
| NCAA Division I: .131 game seats per capita University of California Gauchos (b) | C |
| **Outdoor Recreation Assets (2,000)** | |
| Pacific Coastline: 78 miles | |
| Inland Water Area: 7.5 square miles | |
| National Forests, Parks, Wildlife Refuges: | |
| Channel Islands NP (125,539 acres) | |
| Los Padres NF (628,886 acres) | |
| Places Rated Score: 3,300 Places Rated Rank: 23 | |

### Santa Cruz, CA

| | Rating |
|---|---|
| **Common Denominators (800)** | |
| Good Restaurants: 2 ★★ | C |
| Golf Courses: 3 daily fee; 1 municipal | B |
| Bowling Lanes: 60 | C |
| Movie Theaters: 11 | AA |
| **Crowd Pleasers (100)** | |
| Auto Racing: Watsonville Fairgrounds (NASCAR) | C |

| | Rating |
|---|---|
| **Outdoor Recreation Assets (403)** | |
| Pacific Coastline: 40 miles | |
| Inland Water Area: .1 square miles | |
| CMSA Access: SAN FRANCISCO–OAKLAND– SAN JOSE, CA (400) | |
| Places Rated Score: 1,703 Places Rated Rank: 158 | |

### Santa Rosa–Petaluma, CA

| | Rating |
|---|---|
| **Common Denominators (1,100)** | |
| Good Restaurants: 8 ★★, 6 ★★★ | AA |
| Golf Courses: 2 private; 3.5 daily fee; 3.5 municipal | B |
| Bowling Lanes: 186 | B |
| Movie Theaters: 10 | A |
| **Crowd Pleasers (300)** | |
| Auto Racing: Sears Point International (NASCAR, SCCA) | C |
| Pari-mutuel Betting: Sonoma County Fair (Thoroughbred, 13 days) | C |
| Professional Sports: .514 game seats per capita Santa Rosa Redwood Pioneers (baseball) | C |
| **Outdoor Recreation Assets (455)** | |
| Pacific Coastline: 44 miles | |
| Inland Water Area: 4.5 square miles | |
| National Forests, Parks, Wildlife Refuges: | |
| San Pablo Bay NWR (249 acres) | |
| CMSA Access: SAN FRANCISCO–OAKLAND– SAN JOSE, CA (400) | |
| Places Rated Score: 2,255 Places Rated Rank: 77 | |

### Sarasota, FL

| | Rating |
|---|---|
| **Common Denominators (1,500)** | |
| Good Restaurants: 5 ★, 3 ★★, 5 ★★★ | AA |
| Golf Courses: 7 private; 16.5 daily fee; 2 municipal | AA |
| Bowling Lanes: 204 | A |
| Movie Theaters: 9 | AA |
| **Crowd Pleasers (400)** | |
| Pari-mutuel Betting: Sarasota Kennel Club (101 days) | A |
| Professional Sports: .402 game seats per capita Stingers (basketball) | C |
| **Outdoor Recreation Assets (635)** | |
| Gulf of Mexico Coastline: 35 miles | |
| Inland Water Area: 32.7 square miles | |
| Places Rated Score: 2,535 Places Rated Rank: 54 | |

### Savannah, GA

| | Rating |
|---|---|
| **Common Denominators (900)** | |
| Good Restaurants: 1 ★, 4 ★★, 2 ★★★ | A |
| Golf Courses: 5 private; 1.5 daily fee; 1 municipal | C |
| Bowling Lanes: 116 | B |
| Movie Theaters: 8 | A |
| **Crowd Pleasers (500)** | |
| Auto Racing: Roebling Road (SCCA) | C |
| Professional Sports: 2.514 game seats per capita Cardinals (baseball) | AA |
| **Outdoor Recreation Assets (837)** | |
| Atlantic Coastline: 30 miles | |
| Inland Water Area: 57 square miles | |
| National Forests, Parks, Wildlife Refuges: | |
| Fort Pulaski NM (5,623 acres) | |
| Savannah NWR (11,499 acres) | |
| Wassaw NWR (10,050 acres) | |
| Places Rated Score: 2,237 Places Rated Rank: 79 | |

### Scranton–Wilkes-Barre, PA

| | Rating |
|---|---|
| **Common Denominators (900)** | |
| Good Restaurants: 5 ★, 2 ★★ | C |
| Golf Courses: 12 private; 25 daily fee; 1.5 municipal | AA |
| Bowling Lanes: 600 | A |
| Movie Theaters: 7 | C |
| **Crowd Pleasers (400)** | |
| Zoos: Nay Aug Zoo | C |
| Auto Racing: Pocono International (NASCAR, SCCA) | C |

Rating

Pari-mutuel Betting: Pocono Downs (harness,    **B**
    150 days)
Outdoor Recreation Assets (86)
    Inland Water Area: 35.4 square miles
    National Forests, Parks, Wildlife Refuges:
        Delaware NSR (372 acres)
        Delaware Water Gap NRA (6,662 acres)
Places Rated Score: 1,386        Places Rated Rank: 238

## ★ Seattle, WA
Common Denominators (1,000)
    Good Restaurants: 5 ★, 22 ★★, 14 ★★★, 2 ★★★★    **A**
    Golf Courses: 17 private; 14 daily fee;    **B**
        10.5 municipal
    Bowling Lanes: 916    **B**
    Movie Theaters: 56    **A**
Crowd Pleasers (1,500)
    Zoos: Woodland Park Zoo    **AA**
    Aquariums: Seattle Aquarium    **A**
    Auto Racing:    **B**
        Evergreen Speedway (NASCAR)
        Seattle International (SCCA)
    Pari-mutuel Betting: Longacres (Thoroughbred,    **C**
        131 days)
    Professional Sports: 4.405 game seats per capita    **AA**
        Everett Giants, MARINERS (baseball),
        SUPERSONICS (basketball), SEAHAWKS
        (football)
    NCAA Division I: .259 game seats per capita    **C**
        University of Washington Huskies
Outdoor Recreation Assets (2,000)
    Puget Sound Coastline: 70 miles
    Inland Water Area: 89.1 square miles
    National Forests, Parks, Wildlife Refuges:
        Mount Baker NF (462,209 acres)
        Snoqualmie NF (504,324 acres)
CMSA Access: SEATTLE–TACOMA, WA (300)
Places Rated Score: 4,800        Places Rated Rank: 1

## Sharon, PA
Common Denominators (1,100)
    Good Restaurants: 2 ★★    **B**
    Golf Courses: 3.5 private; 6.5 daily fee    **AA**
    Bowling Lanes: 150    **AA**
    Movie Theaters: 2    **C**
Places Rated Score: 1,100        Places Rated Rank: 282

## Sheboygan, WI
Common Denominators (1,000)
    Good Restaurants: 1 ★★    **C**
    Golf Courses: 1 private; 3 daily fee    **A**
    Bowling Lanes: 150    **AA**
    Movie Theaters: 3    **B**
Outdoor Recreation Assets (316)
    Great Lakes Coastline: 29 miles
    Inland Water Area: 2.7 square miles
Places Rated Score: 1,316        Places Rated Rank: 247

## Sherman–Denison, TX
Common Denominators (700)
    Good Restaurants: 1 ★★★    **B**
    Golf Courses: 3 private; 0.5 daily fee; 0.5    **C**
        municipal
    Bowling Lanes: 40    **B**
    Movie Theaters: 2    **B**
Outdoor Recreation Assets (237)
    Inland Water Area: 44.2 square miles
Places Rated Score: 937        Places Rated Rank: 296

## Shreveport, LA
Common Denominators (700)
    Good Restaurants: 5 ★★, 3 ★★★    **A**
    Golf Courses: 5.5 private; 1 daily fee;    **C**
        2.5 municipal
    Bowling Lanes: 114    **B**
    Movie Theaters: 5    **C**

Rating

Crowd Pleasers (500)
    Pari-mutuel Betting: Louisiana Downs    **A**
        (Thoroughbred, 125 days)
    Professional Sports: .612 game seats per capita    **C**
        Captains (baseball)
    NCAA Division I: .136 game seats per capita    **C**
        Centenary College Gentlemen (b)
Outdoor Recreation Assets (189)
    Inland Water Area: 65.6 square miles
Places Rated Score: 1,389        Places Rated Rank: 237

## Sioux City, IA–NE
Common Denominators (1,000)
    Good Restaurants: 1 ★, 2 ★★    **B**
    Golf Courses: 4.5 private; 1.5 daily fee;    **B**
        1 municipal
    Bowling Lanes: 106    **A**
    Movie Theaters: 4    **A**
Crowd Pleasers (300)
    Pari-mutuel Betting: Akotad Park (Thoroughbred,    **A**
        37 days)
Outdoor Recreation Assets (59)
    Inland Water Area: 13.4 square miles
Places Rated Score: 1,359        Places Rated Rank: 240

## Sioux Falls, SD
Common Denominators (1,200)
    Good Restaurants: 1 ★, 2 ★★    **B**
    Golf Courses: 3 private; 0.5 daily fee; 2 municipal    **B**
    Bowling Lanes: 182    **AA**
    Movie Theaters: 5    **AA**
Crowd Pleasers (100)
    Zoos: Great Plains Zoo    **C**
Outdoor Recreation Assets (24)
    Inland Water Area: 3.9 square miles
Places Rated Score: 1,324        Places Rated Rank: 246

## South Bend–Mishawaka, IN
Common Denominators (1,200)
    Good Restaurants: 1 ★, 5 ★★, 3 ★★★    **AA**
    Golf Courses: 4.5 private; 2 daily fee; 3 municipal    **B**
    Bowling Lanes: 312    **AA**
    Movie Theaters: 6    **B**
Crowd Pleasers (600)
    Zoos: Potawatomi Park Zoo    **B**
    NCAA Division I: 1.833 game seats per capita    **AA**
        University of Notre Dame Fighting Irish
Outdoor Recreation Assets (19)
    Inland Water Area: 1.7 square miles
Places Rated Score: 1,819        Places Rated Rank: 139

## Spokane, WA
Common Denominators (900)
    Good Restaurants: 1 ★, 5 ★★, 3 ★★★    **A**
    Golf Courses: 2 private; 2 daily fee; 5 municipal    **B**
    Bowling Lanes: 256    **A**
    Movie Theaters: 5    **C**
Crowd Pleasers (500)
    Zoos: Walk in the Wild    **C**
    Pari-mutuel Betting: Playfair Race Course    **A**
        (Thoroughbred, 98 days)
    NCAA Division I: .152 game seats per capita    **C**
        Gonzaga Zags (b)
Outdoor Recreation Assets (117)
    Inland Water Area: 18.6 square miles
    National Forests, Parks, Wildlife Refuges:
        Turnbull NWR (14,489 acres)
Places Rated Score: 1,517        Places Rated Rank: 200

## Springfield, IL
Common Denominators (1,100)
    Good Restaurants: 2 ★, 3 ★★, 5 ★★★    **AA**
    Golf Courses: 3 private; 1.5 daily fee;    **B**
        2.5 municipal
    Bowling Lanes: 40    **C**
    Movie Theaters: 10    **AA**

**Rating**

Crowd Pleasers (400)
Zoos: Henson C. Robinson Children's Zoo — **C**
Professional Sports: 1.864 game seats per capita — **A**
Cardinals (baseball)
Outdoor Recreation Assets (36)
Inland Water Area: 8.5 square miles
National Forests, Parks, Wildlife Refuges:
Lincoln Home NHS (12 acres)
Places Rated Score: 1,536 — Places Rated Rank: 197

## Springfield, MA
Common Denominators (800)
Good Restaurants: 2 ★, 4 ★★, 4 ★★★ — **B**
Golf Courses: 9 private; 12.5 daily fee; 4 municipal — **A**
Bowling Lanes: 192 — **B**
Movie Theaters: 10 — **C**
Crowd Pleasers (600)
Theme Parks: Riverside (120 days) — **AA**
Pari-mutuel Betting: Northampton (Thoroughbred, — **C**
10 days)
Professional Sports: .576 game seats per capita — **C**
Indians (hockey)
Outdoor Recreation Assets (114)
Inland Water Area: 13.4 square miles
National Forests, Parks, Wildlife Refuges:
Springfield Armory NHS (55 acres)
Places Rated Score: 1,514 — Places Rated Rank: 201

## Springfield, MO
Common Denominators (1,000)
Good Restaurants: 2 ★★, 3 ★★★ — **A**
Golf Courses: 4 private; 2 daily fee; 2 municipal — **B**
Bowling Lanes: 140 — **B**
Movie Theaters: 7 — **A**
Crowd Pleasers (400)
Zoos: Dickerson Park Zoo — **C**
NCAA Division I: .713 game seats per capita — **A**
Southwest Missouri State Bears
Outdoor Recreation Assets (337)
Inland Water Area: .6 square miles
National Forests, Parks, Wildlife Refuges:
Mark Twain NF (51,327 acres)
Wilson's Creek National Battlefield (1,749 acres)
Places Rated Score: 1,737 — Places Rated Rank: 151

## Stamford, CT
Common Denominators (1,000)
Good Restaurants: 2 ★, 4 ★★, 1 ★★★ — **A**
Golf Courses: 9.5 private; 2 municipal — **C**
Bowling Lanes: 80 — **B**
Movie Theaters: 9 — **AA**
Outdoor Recreation Assets (329)
Atlantic Coastline: 11 miles
Inland Water Area: 5.6 square miles
CMSA Access: NEW YORK–NORTHERN NEW JERSEY–
LONG ISLAND, NY–NJ–CT (400)
Places Rated Score: 1,729 — Places Rated Rank: 154

## State College, PA
Common Denominators (800)
Good Restaurants: 1 ★★, 1 ★★★ — **B**
Golf Courses: 3 private; 3 daily fee — **A**
Bowling Lanes: 55 — **B**
Movie Theaters: 2 — **C**
Crowd Pleasers (400)
NCAA Division I: 4.545 game seats per capita — **AA**
Pennsylvania State Nittany Lions
Places Rated Score: 1,200 — Places Rated Rank: 264

## Steubenville–Weirton, OH–WV
Common Denominators (1,000)
Good Restaurants: 1 ★ — **C**
Golf Courses: 4.5 private; 4 daily fee; — **A**
0.5 municipal
Bowling Lanes: 118 — **A**
Movie Theaters: 6 — **A**

**Rating**

Crowd Pleasers (400)
Pari-mutuel Betting: Waterford Park — **AA**
(Thoroughbred, 151 days)
Outdoor Recreation Assets (60)
Inland Water Area: 7 square miles
Places Rated Score: 1,460 — Places Rated Rank: 217

## Stockton, CA
Common Denominators (800)
Good Restaurants: 1 ★, 2 ★★, 1 ★★★ — **C**
Golf Courses: 6 private; 2 daily fee; 3 municipal — **B**
Bowling Lanes: 170 — **B**
Movie Theaters: 11 — **A**
Crowd Pleasers (800)
Auto Racing: Stockton 99 (NASCAR) — **C**
Pari-mutuel Betting: Ruidoso Downs — **B**
(Thoroughbred, 74 days)
Professional Sports: 1.572 game seats per capita — **A**
Lodi Crushers, Stockton Mudville Nine
(baseball)
NCAA Division I: .619 game seats per capita — **B**
University of the Pacific Tigers
Outdoor Recreation Assets (30)
Inland Water Area: 8.5 square miles
Places Rated Score: 1,630 — Places Rated Rank: 171

## Syracuse, NY
Common Denominators (1,600)
Good Restaurants: 2 ★, 17 ★★, 10 ★★★ — **AA**
Golf Courses: 16 private; 25.5 daily fee; — **AA**
2 municipal
Bowling Lanes: 764 — **AA**
Movie Theaters: 28 — **AA**
Crowd Pleasers (700)
Zoos: Burnet Park Zoo — **C**
Auto Racing: Shangri-La (NASCAR) — **C**
Professional Sports: 1.143 game seats per capita — **B**
Chiefs (baseball)
NCAA Division I: .739 game seats per capita — **A**
Colgate University Red Raiders, Syracuse
University Orangemen
Outdoor Recreation Assets (551)
Great Lakes Coastline: 36 miles
Inland Water Area: 91.5 square miles
Places Rated Score: 2,851 — Places Rated Rank: 44

## ★ Tacoma, WA
Common Denominators (900)
Good Restaurants: 2 ★, 2 ★★, 4 ★★★ — **B**
Golf Courses: 6.5 private; 6 daily fee; — **B**
2.5 municipal
Bowling Lanes: 344 — **B**
Movie Theaters: 17 — **A**
Crowd Pleasers (700)
Zoos: Point Defiance Zoo — **B**
Aquarium: Point Defiance Aquarium — **A**
Professional Sports: 1.186 game seats per capita — **B**
Tigers (baseball)
Outdoor Recreation Assets (2,000)
Puget Sound Coastline: 15 miles
Inland Water Area: 113.1 square miles
National Forests, Parks, Wildlife Refuges:
Mount Rainier NP (235,239 acres)
Nisqually NWR (813 acres)
Snoqualmie NF (129,938 acres)
CMSA Access: SEATTLE–TACOMA, WA (400)
Places Rated Score: 4,000 — Places Rated Rank: 7

## Tallahassee, FL
Common Denominators (700)
Good Restaurants: 2 ★★, 1 ★★★ — **B**
Golf Courses: 4.5 private; 2 daily fee; — **B**
0.5 municipal
Bowling Lanes: 44 — **C**
Movie Theaters: 5 — **B**

Rating

Crowd Pleasers (400)
  NCAA Division I: 3.305 game seats per capita          **AA**
    Florida A & M Rattlers, Florida State Seminoles
Outdoor Recreation Assets (836)
  Inland Water Area: 36.5 square miles
  National Forests, Parks, Wildlife Refuges:
    Apalachicola NF (104,405 acres)
Places Rated Score: 1,936          Places Rated Rank: 119

### Tampa–St. Petersburg–Clearwater, FL
Common Denominators (900)
  Good Restaurants: 26 ★, 21 ★★, 6 ★★★, 4 ★★★★     **A**
  Golf Courses: 27.5 private; 38 daily fee;            **A**
    5 municipal
  Bowling Lanes: 1,042                                **B**
  Movie Theaters: 30                                  **C**
Crowd Pleasers (1,000)
  Theme Parks: Busch Gardens—The Dark                 **AA**
    Continent (365 days)
  Pari-mutuel Betting:                                **A**
    St. Petersburg Kennel Club (101 days)
    Tampa Bay Downs (Thoroughbred, 80 days)
    Tampa Greyhound Park (104 days)
    Tampa Jai Alai (150 days)
  Professional Sports: 1.479 game seats per capita    **B**
    Tampa Tarpons, St. Petersburg Cardinals
    (baseball), BANDITS, BUCCANEERS (football)
  NCAA Division I: .040 game seats per capita          **C**
    University of South Florida Bulls (b)
Outdoor Recreation Assets (1,043)
  Gulf of Mexico Coastline: 78 miles
  Inland Water Area: 122.8 square miles
  National Forests, Parks, Wildlife Refuges:
    Chassahowitzka NWR (6,707 acres)
    Egmont Key NWR (328 acres)
    Pinellas NWR (15 acres)
Places Rated Score: 2,943          Places Rated Rank: 38

### Terre Haute, IN
Common Denominators (1,000)
  Good Restaurants: 1 ★, 1 ★★                          **C**
  Golf Courses: 1.5 private; 0.5 daily fee;            **A**
    3.5 municipal
  Bowling Lanes: 144                                  **A**
  Movie Theaters: 5                                   **A**
Crowd Pleasers (400)
  NCAA Division I: 1.715 game seats per capita        **AA**
    Indiana State Sycamores
Outdoor Recreation Assets (1)
  Inland Water Area: .1 square miles
Places Rated Score: 1,401          Places Rated Rank: 234

### Texarkana, TX–Texarkana, AR
Common Denominators (500)
  Golf Courses: 2 private; 0.5 daily fee               **C**
  Bowling Lanes: 78                                   **B**
  Movie Theaters: 3                                   **B**
Outdoor Recreation Assets (169)
  Inland Water Area: 51 square miles
Places Rated Score: 669          Places Rated Rank: 325

### Toledo, OH
Common Denominators (900)
  Good Restaurants: 2 ★, 11 ★★, 2 ★★★                  **B**
  Golf Courses: 8.5 private; 8 daily fee; 4 municipal  **B**
  Bowling Lanes: 610                                  **A**
  Movie Theaters: 17                                  **B**
Crowd Pleasers (800)
  Zoos: Toledo Zoological Gardens                      **A**
  Pari-mutuel Betting: Raceway Park (harness,          **C**
    61 days)
  Professional Sports: 1.48 game seats per capita      **B**
    Mud Hens (baseball), Goaldiggers (hockey)

Rating

NCAA Division I: .654 game seats per capita            **B**
  Bowling Green State Falcons, University of
  Toledo Rockets
Outdoor Recreation Assets (252)
  Great Lakes Coastline: 19 miles
  Inland Water Area: 9.7 square miles
  National Forests, Parks, Wildlife Refuges:
    Cedar Point NWR (2,445 acres)
    Ottawa NWR (2,078 acres)
    West Sister Island NWR (82 acres)
Places Rated Score: 1,952          Places Rated Rank: 114

### Topeka, KS
Common Denominators (900)
  Good Restaurants: 1 ★★                               **C**
  Golf Courses: 4 private; 0.5 daily fee;              **B**
    2.5 municipal
  Bowling Lanes: 152                                  **A**
  Movie Theaters: 6                                   **A**
Crowd Pleasers (200)
  Zoos: Topeka Zoological Park                         **B**
Outdoor Recreation Assets (41)
  Inland Water Area: 4.5 square miles
Places Rated Score: 1,141          Places Rated Rank: 271

### Trenton, NJ
Common Denominators (800)
  Good Restaurants: 1 ★, 5 ★★                          **B**
  Golf Courses: 7 private; 2 daily fee; 2 municipal    **B**
  Bowling Lanes: 268                                  **A**
  Movie Theaters: 6                                   **C**
Crowd Pleasers (400)
  Auto Racing: New Egypt Speedway (NASCAR)            **C**
  NCAA Division I: 1.154 game seats per capita         **A**
    Princeton Tigers, Rider College Broncs (b)
Outdoor Recreation Assets (46)
  Inland Water Area: 2.1 square miles
CMSA Access: PHILADELPHIA–WILMINGTON–
  TRENTON, PA–NJ–DE–MD (400)
Places Rated Score: 1,646          Places Rated Rank: 169

### Tucson, AZ
Common Denominators (900)
  Good Restaurants: 5 ★★, 1 ★★★★, 1 ★★★★★              **B**
  Golf Courses: 7 private; 5 daily fee; 6 municipal    **B**
  Bowling Lanes: 340                                  **B**
  Movie Theaters: 17                                  **A**
Crowd Pleasers (1,200)
  Zoos:                                                **A**
    Gene Reid Zoological Gardens
    Arizona-Sonora Desert Museum
  Pari-mutuel Betting: Tucson Greyhound Park           **A**
    (235 days)
  Professional Sports: 1.287 game seats per capita     **A**
    Toros (baseball)
  NCAA Division I: .886 game seats per capita          **A**
    University of Arizona Wildcats
Outdoor Recreation Assets (1,031)
  Inland Water Area: 1.1 square miles
  National Forests, Parks, Wildlife Refuges:
    Cabeza Prieta NWR (416,210 acres)
    Coronado NF (382,093 acres)
    Organ Pipe Cactus NM (330,479 acres)
    Saguaro NM (83,337 acres)
Places Rated Score: 3,131          Places Rated Rank: 29

### Tulsa, OK
Common Denominators (1,100)
  Good Restaurants: 1 ★, 14 ★★, 9 ★★★                  **AA**
  Golf Courses: 9.5 private; 5 daily fee; 6 municipal  **B**
  Bowling Lanes: 368                                  **B**
  Movie Theaters: 22                                  **A**
Crowd Pleasers (800)
  Zoos: Tulsa Zoological Park                          **B**
  Auto Racing: Hallett Racing Circuit (SCCA)           **C**

| | Rating |
|---|---|
| Professional Sports: 1.637 game seats per capita | **A** |
|   Drillers (baseball), OUTLAWS (football), Oilers | |
|   (hockey) | |
| NCAA Division I: .620 game seats per capita | **B** |
|   University of Tulsa Golden Hurricane, Oral | |
|   Roberts Titans (b) | |
| Outdoor Recreation Assets (124) | |
|   Inland Water Area: 123.7 square miles | |
| Places Rated Score: 2,024      Places Rated Rank: 102 | |

### Tuscaloosa, AL

| | Rating |
|---|---|
| Common Denominators (600) | |
|   Good Restaurants: 1 ★★, 1 ★★★ | **B** |
|   Golf Courses: 5 private; 1 daily fee | **C** |
|   Bowling Lanes: 64 | **B** |
|   Movie Theaters: 3 | **C** |
| Crowd Pleasers (400) | |
|   NCAA Division I: 3.752 game seats per capita | **AA** |
|     University of Alabama Crimson Tide | |
| Outdoor Recreation Assets (90) | |
|   Inland Water Area: 10.6 square miles | |
|   National Forests, Parks, Wildlife Refuges: | |
|     Talladega NF (8,562 acres) | |
| Places Rated Score: 1,090      Places Rated Rank: 283 | |

### Tyler, TX

| | Rating |
|---|---|
| Common Denominators (500) | |
|   Golf Courses: 5.5 private; 2 daily fee | **B** |
|   Bowling Lanes: 32 | **C** |
|   Movie Theaters: 3 | **B** |
| Crowd Pleasers (100) | |
|   Zoos: Caldwell Children's Zoo | **C** |
| Outdoor Recreation Assets (31) | |
|   Inland Water Area: 5.7 square miles | |
| Places Rated Score: 631      Places Rated Rank: 326 | |

### Utica–Rome, NY

| | Rating |
|---|---|
| Common Denominators (1,300) | |
|   Good Restaurants: 1 ★, 8 ★★, 5 ★★★ | **AA** |
|   Golf Courses: 11.5 private; 14.5 daily fee; | **AA** |
|     1.5 municipal | |
|   Bowling Lanes: 408 | **AA** |
|   Movie Theaters: 2 | **C** |
| Crowd Pleasers (300) | |
|   Zoos: Utica Zoo | **C** |
|   Professional Sports: .712 game seats per capita | **C** |
|     Utica Blue Sox, Twin Falls Mets (baseball) | |
|   NCAA Division I: .122 game seats per capita | **C** |
|     Utica College Pioneers (b) | |
| Outdoor Recreation Assets (150) | |
|   Inland Water Area: 78.9 square miles | |
|   National Forests, Parks, Wildlife Refuges: | |
|     Fort Stanwix NM (16 acres) | |
| Places Rated Score: 1,750      Places Rated Rank: 149 | |

### Vallejo–Fairfield–Napa, CA

| | Rating |
|---|---|
| Common Denominators (800) | |
|   Good Restaurants: 3 ★, 7 ★★, 4 ★★★, 2 ★★★★ | **AA** |
|   Golf Courses: 5.5 private; 1.5 daily fee; | **C** |
|     2 municipal | |
|   Bowling Lanes: 144 | **B** |
|   Movie Theaters: 7 | **C** |
| Crowd Pleasers (100) | |
|   Pari-mutuel Betting: Solano County Fair | **C** |
|     (Thoroughbred, 12 days) | |
| Outdoor Recreation Assets (259) | |
|   Inland Water Area: 81.7 square miles | |
| CMSA Access: SAN FRANCISCO–OAKLAND– | |
|   SAN JOSE, CA (400) | |
| Places Rated Score: 1,559      Places Rated Rank: 192 | |

### Vancouver, WA

| | Rating |
|---|---|
| Common Denominators (800) | |
|   Good Restaurants: 1 ★, 1 ★★, 1 ★★★ | **B** |
|   Golf Courses: 2 private; 2 daily fee | **C** |
|   Bowling Lanes: 132 | **B** |
|   Movie Theaters: 6 | **A** |
| Outdoor Recreation Assets (264) | |
|   Inland Water Area: 31 square miles | |
|   National Forests, Parks, Wildlife Refuges: | |
|     Fort Vancouver NHS (209 acres) | |
|     Gifford Pinchot NF (1,150 acres) | |
| CMSA Access: PORTLAND–VANCOUVER, OR–WA (400) | |
| Places Rated Score: 1,464      Places Rated Rank: 215 | |

### Victoria, TX

| | Rating |
|---|---|
| Common Denominators (1,300) | |
|   Good Restaurants: 1 ★★, 1 ★★★ | **AA** |
|   Golf Courses: 0.5 private; 1 municipal | **B** |
|   Bowling Lanes: 58 | **A** |
|   Movie Theaters: 3 | **AA** |
| Crowd Pleasers (100) | |
|   Zoos: Texas Zoo | **C** |
| Outdoor Recreation Assets (10) | |
|   Inland Water Area: 1.8 square miles | |
| Places Rated Score: 1,410      Places Rated Rank: 230 | |

### Vineland–Millville–Bridgeton, NJ

| | Rating |
|---|---|
| Common Denominators (600) | |
|   Good Restaurants: 1 ★★ | **C** |
|   Golf Courses: 1 daily fee | **C** |
|   Bowling Lanes: 72 | **B** |
|   Movie Theaters: 4 | **B** |
| Crowd Pleasers (100) | |
|   Zoos: Cohanzick Zoo | **C** |
| Outdoor Recreation Assets (374) | |
|   Atlantic Coastline: 30 miles | |
|   Inland Water Area: 7.4 square miles | |
| CMSA Access: PHILADELPHIA–WILMINGTON– | |
|   TRENTON, PA–NJ–DE–MD (400) | |
| Places Rated Score: 1,474      Places Rated Rank: 214 | |

### Visalia–Tulare–Porterville, CA

| | Rating |
|---|---|
| Common Denominators (700) | |
|   Good Restaurants: 1 ★ | **C** |
|   Golf Courses: 1 private; 4.5 daily fee; | **B** |
|     1.5 municipal | |
|   Bowling Lanes: 132 | **B** |
|   Movie Theaters: 6 | **B** |
| Crowd Pleasers (100) | |
|   Professional Sports: .399 game seats per capita | **C** |
|     Visalia Oaks (baseball) | |
| Outdoor Recreation Assets (2,000) | |
|   Inland Water Area: 3 square miles | |
|   National Forests, Parks, Wildlife Refuges: | |
|     Blue Ridge NWR (577 acres) | |
|     Inyo NF (190,574 acres) | |
|     Kings Canyon NP (105,252 acres) | |
|     Pixley NWR (5,147 acres) | |
|     Sequoia NF (700,135 acres) | |
|     Sequoia NP (401,774 acres) | |
| Places Rated Score: 2,800      Places Rated Rank: 45 | |

### Waco, TX

| | Rating |
|---|---|
| Common Denominators (700) | |
|   Good Restaurants: 3 ★★, 1 ★★★ | **A** |
|   Golf Courses: 4 private; 1 daily fee; 1 municipal | **C** |
|   Bowling Lanes: 56 | **C** |
|   Movie Theaters: 5 | **B** |
| Crowd Pleasers (500) | |
|   Zoos: Central Texas Zoo | **C** |
|   NCAA Division I: 2.120 game seats per capita | **AA** |
|     Baylor Bears | |
| Outdoor Recreation Assets (48) | |
|   Inland Water Area: 9.8 square miles | |
| Places Rated Score: 1,248      Places Rated Rank: 252 | |

### Washington, DC–MD–VA

| | Rating |
|---|---|
| Common Denominators (600) | |
|   Good Restaurants: 10 ★, 42 ★★, 30 ★★★, 6 ★★★★ | **A** |
|   Golf Courses: 59 private; 9 daily fee; 19 municipal | **C** |

|  | Rating |
|---|---|
| Bowling Lanes: 1,032 | C |
| Movie Theaters: 44 | C |

**Crowd Pleasers (700)**

| | |
|---|---|
| Zoos: National Zoological Park | AA |
| Pari-mutuel Betting: | C |

Bowie (Thoroughbred, 114 days)
Freestate (harness, 85 days)
Laurel (Thoroughbred, 75 days)
Rosecroft (harness, 85 days)

| | |
|---|---|
| Professional Sports: .499 game seats per capita | C |

Prince William Pirates (baseball), BULLETS
(basketball), REDSKINS (football), CAPITALS
(hockey)

| | |
|---|---|
| NCAA Division I: .215 game seats per capita | C |

American University Eagles (b), George Mason
University Patriots (b), George Washington
University Colonials (b), Georgetown University
Hoyas (b), Howard University Bisons, University
of Maryland Terps

**Outdoor Recreation Assets (278)**

Inland Water Area: 129 square miles
National Forests, Parks, Wildlife Refuges:
Antietam National Battlefield (0.22 acres)
Appalachian Trail (1,061 acres)
Battleground National Cemetery (1 acre)
Catoctin Mountain Park (5,694 acres)
Chesapeake and Ohio Canal NHP (4,761 acres)
Clara Barton NHS (9 acres)
Ford's Theatre NHS (0.29 acres)
Fort Washington Park (341 acres)
Frederick Douglass Home (8 acres)
Fredericksburg and Spotsylvania County
   Battlefields NMP (84 acres)
George Washington Parkway (7,045 acres)
Greenbelt Park (1,176 acres)
Harpers Ferry NHP (370 acres)
John F. Kennedy Center for the Performing Arts
   (18 acres)
Lincoln Memorial (164 acres)
Lyndon B. Johnson Memorial Grove (17 acres)
Manassas National Battlefield Park (3,021 acres)
Marumsco NWR (63 acres)
Mason Neck NWR (1,131 acres)
Monocacy National Battlefield (422 acres)
National Capital Parks (6,036 acres)
National Mall (146 acres)
Piscataway Park (4,210 acres)
Presquile NWR (1,329 acres)
Prince William Forest Park (17,410 acres)
Robert E. Lee Memorial (28 acres)
Rock Creek Park (1,754 acres)
Theodore Roosevelt Island (89 acres)
Thomas Jefferson Memorial (18 acres)
Thomas Stone NHS (322 acres)
Washington Monument (106 acres)
White House (18 acres)
Wolf Trap Farm Park for the Performing Arts
   (130 acres)

Places Rated Score: 1,578          Places Rated Rank: 188

## Waterbury, CT

**Common Denominators (600)**

| | |
|---|---|
| Golf Courses: 2 private; 2 municipal | C |
| Bowling Lanes: 126 | B |
| Movie Theaters: 7 | A |

**Crowd Pleasers (300)**

| | |
|---|---|
| Professional Sports: 1.708 game seats per capita | A |

Angels (baseball)

**Outdoor Recreation Assets (46)**

Inland Water Area: 2.1 square miles

Places Rated Score: 946          Places Rated Rank: 295

## Waterloo–Cedar Falls, IA

**Common Denominators (1,300)**

| | |
|---|---|
| Good Restaurants: 2 ★★, 1 ★★★ | B |

|  | Rating |
|---|---|
| Golf Courses: 3.5 private; 1 daily fee; | AA |
| 5.5 municipal | |
| Bowling Lanes: 182 | AA |
| Movie Theaters: 6 | A |

**Crowd Pleasers (600)**

| | |
|---|---|
| Professional Sports: 2.365 game seats per capita | A |

Waterloo Indians (baseball)

| | |
|---|---|
| NCAA Division I: .755 game seats per capita | A |

University of Northern Iowa Panthers

Places Rated Score: 1,900          Places Rated Rank: 129

## Wausau, WI

**Common Denominators (1,300)**

| | |
|---|---|
| Good Restaurants: 1 ★, 4 ★★ | AA |
| Golf Courses: 1 private; 2.5 daily fee | B |
| Bowling Lanes: 118 | AA |
| Movie Theaters: 4 | A |

**Crowd Pleasers (300)**

| | |
|---|---|
| Professional Sports: 1.573 game seats per capita | A |

Timbers (baseball)

**Outdoor Recreation Assets (54)**

Inland Water Area: 16.7 square miles

Places Rated Score: 1,654          Places Rated Rank: 166

## ★ West Palm Beach–Boca Raton– Delray Beach, FL

**Common Denominators (1,300)**

| | |
|---|---|
| Good Restaurants: 8 ★, 12 ★★, 5 ★★★, 1 ★★★★, | AA |
| 1 ★★★★★ | |
| Golf Courses: 62.5 private; 14.5 daily fee; | AA |
| 5.5 municipal | |
| Bowling Lanes: 420 | A |
| Movie Theaters: 16 | B |

**Crowd Pleasers (600)**

| | |
|---|---|
| Zoos: Dreher Park Zoo | C |
| Auto Racing: Moroso Motorsports (SCCA) | C |
| Pari-mutuel Betting: | A |

Palm Beach Kennel Club (114 days)
West Palm Beach Fronton (155 days)

| | |
|---|---|
| Professional Sports: .633 game seats per capita | C |

West Palm Beach Expos (baseball)

**Outdoor Recreation Assets (1,872)**

Atlantic Coastline: 47 miles
Inland Water Area: 555 square miles
National Forests, Parks, Wildlife Refuges:
Loxahatchee NWR (2,550 acres)

Places Rated Score: 3,772          Places Rated Rank: 13

## Wheeling, WV–OH

**Common Denominators (700)**

| | |
|---|---|
| Good Restaurants: 1 ★, 2 ★★ | C |
| Golf Courses: 3 private; 0.5 daily fee; | B |
| 2.5 municipal | |
| Bowling Lanes: 118 | B |
| Movie Theaters: 5 | B |

**Crowd Pleasers (500)**

| | |
|---|---|
| Zoos: Oglebay's Good Zoo | C |
| Pari-mutuel Betting: Wheeling Downs Greyhound | AA |
| Park (303 days) | |

**Outdoor Recreation Assets (71)**

Inland Water Area: 13.5 square miles

Places Rated Score: 1,271          Places Rated Rank: 250

## Wichita, KS

**Common Denominators (700)**

| | |
|---|---|
| Good Restaurants: 1 ★★, 3 ★★★ | C |
| Golf Courses: 6 private; 5 daily fee; 4 municipal | B |
| Bowling Lanes: 414 | A |
| Movie Theaters: 9 | C |

**Crowd Pleasers (800)**

| | |
|---|---|
| Zoos: Sedgwick County Zoo | A |
| Professional Sports: 1.404 game seats per capita | B |
| Aeros (baseball) | |
| NCAA Division I: .720 game seats per capita | A |

Wichita State Shockers

Rating

Outdoor Recreation Assets (8)
Inland Water Area: 4.2 square miles
Places Rated Score: 1,508     Places Rated Rank: 205

## Wichita Falls, TX
Common Denominators (1,100)
Good Restaurants: 3 ★★     B
Golf Courses: 3.5 private; 0.5 daily fee;     B
2 municipal
Bowling Lanes: 100     A
Movie Theaters: 5     AA
Outdoor Recreation Assets (26)
Inland Water Area: 3.1 square miles
Places Rated Score: 1,126     Places Rated Rank: 275

## Williamsport, PA
Common Denominators (700)
Good Restaurants: 1 ★★, 1 ★★★     B
Golf Courses: 1 private; 1 municipal     C
Bowling Lanes: 96     A
Movie Theaters: 2     C
Outdoor Recreation Assets (26)
Inland Water Area: 6.5 square miles
Places Rated Score: 726     Places Rated Rank: 320

## Wilmington, DE–NJ–MD
Common Denominators (800)
Good Restaurants: 4 ★★, 1 ★★★     C
Golf Courses: 11.5 private; 5.5 daily fee;     B
2 municipal
Bowling Lanes: 444     A
Movie Theaters: 16     B
Crowd Pleasers (400)
Zoos: Brandywine Zoo     C
Pari-mutuel Betting: Brandywine (harness,     B
139 days)
NCAA Division I: .294 game seats per capita     C
University of Delaware Blue Hens
Outdoor Recreation Assets (323)
Inland Water Area: 68 square miles
National Forests, Parks, Wildlife Refuges:
Supawna Meadow NWR (1,716 acres)
CMSA Access: PHILADELPHIA–WILMINGTON–
TRENTON, PA–NJ–DE–MD (400)
Places Rated Score: 1,923     Places Rated Rank: 122

## Wilmington, NC
Common Denominators (1,200)
Good Restaurants: 3 ★★, 1 ★★★     AA
Golf Courses: 4 private; 1 daily fee; 1 municipal     B
Bowling Lanes: 50     B
Movie Theaters: 5     AA
Crowd Pleasers (300)
NCAA Division I: .766 game seats per capita     A
University of North Carolina Seahawks (b)
Outdoor Recreation Assets (1,168)
Atlantic Coastline: 26 miles
Inland Water Area: 33.6 square miles
Places Rated Score: 2,668     Places Rated Rank: 48

## Worcester, MA
Common Denominators (600)
Good Restaurants: 3 ★★, 2 ★★★     C
Golf Courses: 3.5 private; 8.5 daily fee;     A
2 municipal

Rating

Bowling Lanes: 126     C
Movie Theaters: 6     C
Crowd Pleasers (100)
NCAA Division I: .194 game seats per capita     C
Holy Cross Crusaders
Outdoor Recreation Assets (210)
Inland Water Area: 29.1 square miles
Places Rated Score: 910     Places Rated Rank: 301

## Yakima, WA
Common Denominators (800)
Golf Courses: 3 private; 2 daily fee     C
Bowling Lanes: 142     A
Movie Theaters: 8     AA
Crowd Pleasers (400)
Auto Racing: Yakima Speedway (NASCAR)     C
Pari-mutuel Betting: Yakima Meadows     A
(Thoroughbred, 84 days)
Outdoor Recreation Assets (940)
Inland Water Area: 15.3 square miles
National Forests, Parks, Wildlife Refuges:
Gifford Pinchot NF (37,552 acres)
Snoqualmie NF (466,801 acres)
Toppenish NWR (1,763 acres)
Places Rated Score: 2,140     Places Rated Rank: 91

## York, PA
Common Denominators (800)
Good Restaurants: 5 ★★, 2 ★★★     B
Golf Courses: 5.5 private; 8.5 daily fee     B
Bowling Lanes: 332     A
Movie Theaters: 7     C
Outdoor Recreation Assets (42)
Inland Water Area: 5.1 square miles
National Forests, Parks, Wildlife Refuges:
Eisenhower NHS (690 acres)
Gettysburg National Cemetery (21 acres)
Gettysburg NMP (3,689 acres)
Places Rated Score: 842     Places Rated Rank: 307

## Youngstown–Warren, OH
Common Denominators (1,100)
Good Restaurants: 1 ★, 4 ★★, 2 ★★★     C
Golf Courses: 6.5 private; 20 daily fee;     AA
2.5 municipal
Bowling Lanes: 606     AA
Movie Theaters: 13     B
Crowd Pleasers (100)
NCAA Division I: .297 game seats per capita     C
Youngstown State Penguins
Outdoor Recreation Assets (127)
Inland Water Area: 26.1 square miles
Places Rated Score: 1,327     Places Rated Rank: 245

## Yuba City, CA
Common Denominators (600)
Good Restaurants: 1 ★     C
Golf Courses: 1 private; 1.5 daily fee     B
Movie Theaters: 4     A
Outdoor Recreation Assets (318)
Inland Water Area: 9.6 square miles
National Forests, Parks, Wildlife Refuges:
Plumas NF (23,885 acres)
Tahoe NF (20,494 acres)
Places Rated Score: 918     Places Rated Rank: 299

## WHERE ARE THE BEST SPORTS TOWNS?

There are as many ways to determine the best sports towns in America as there are sports fans. Earlier in this chapter, *Places Rated* looked at major spectator sports from the point of view of the fan's ease of access and on this basis found the best metro areas to be Glens Falls, New York; Denver; and Kansas City, Missouri.

Obviously, though, being able to attend a game easily is not the only thing a fan aspires to. Rooting for the home team is fun, but rooting for a *winning* home team is ecstasy. In the lists that follow, *Places Rated* looks at the metro areas to find which have the winningest teams.

### Major-League Title Towns

For baseball fans in the mid-1970s, the place to be was Oakland, California, as the A's hauled in three straight World Series championships. In the 1960s, football fans found a warm welcome in frosty Green Bay, where the Packers took five NFL Championships over a seven-year span. And if basketball is your sport, you won't go far wrong anytime if you back the Boston Celtics, winners of more titles than any other team in NBA history.

Our survey of metro areas with major professional championships looks at the winners in four team sports: baseball, football, basketball, and ice hockey. In the cases of baseball and ice hockey, we include the winners of the World Series (since 1903) and Stanley Cup (since 1894), respectively. For football and basketball, we include the Super Bowl and NBA Championship winners as well as the champions of the predecessors of the modern NFL (the National Football League, 1933–1969, and American Football League, 1960–1969) and the NBA (the Basketball Association of America, 1947–1949). The NFL and AFL champions of 1966, 1967, and 1968 met in the Super Bowls of 1967, 1968, and 1969, before the formation of the modern NFL; for those years, we name the winners of both the individual league championships and the Super Bowl.

If a team has changed names or towns, we list it with the name and in the town where it played at the time it won the championship in question.

### Professional Championships in the Metro Areas

**Anaheim–Santa Ana, CA**
*NFL Championship:* Los Angeles Rams, 1951

**Baltimore, MD**
*World Series:* Orioles, 1966, 1970, 1983
*Super Bowl:* Colts, 1971
*NFL Championship:* Colts, 1958, 1959, 1968
*BAA Championship:* Bullets, 1948

**Boston, MA**
*World Series:* Somersets, 1903; Pilgrims, 1911; Red Sox, 1912, 1914, 1915, 1916, 1918

*NBA Championship:* Celtics, 1957, 1959, 1960, 1961, 1962, 1963, 1964, 1965, 1966, 1968, 1969, 1974, 1976, 1981, 1984
*Stanley Cup:* Bruins, 1929, 1939, 1941, 1970, 1972

**Buffalo, NY**
*AFL Championship:* Bills, 1964, 1965

**Chicago, IL**
*World Series:* White Sox, 1906, 1917; Cubs, 1907, 1908
*NFL Championship:* Bears, 1933, 1940, 1941, 1943, 1946, 1963; Cardinals, 1947
*Stanley Cup:* Black Hawks, 1934, 1938, 1961

**Cincinnati, OH–KY–IN**
*World Series:* Reds, 1919, 1940, 1975, 1976

**Cleveland, OH**
*World Series:* Indians, 1920, 1948
*NFL Championship:* Rams, 1945; Browns, 1950, 1954, 1955, 1964

**Dallas, TX**
*Super Bowl:* Cowboys, 1972, 1978
*AFL Championship:* Texans, 1962

**Detroit, MI**
*World Series:* Tigers, 1935, 1945, 1968, 1984
*NFL Championship:* Lions, 1935, 1952, 1953, 1957
*Stanley Cup:* Red Wings, 1936, 1937, 1943, 1950, 1952, 1954, 1955

**Green Bay, WI**
*Super Bowl:* Packers, 1967, 1968
*NFL Championship:* Packers, 1936, 1937, 1939, 1944, 1961, 1962, 1965, 1966, 1967

**Houston, TX**
*AFL Championship:* Oilers, 1960, 1961

**Kansas City, MO**
*Super Bowl:* Chiefs, 1970
*AFL Championship:* Chiefs, 1966, 1969

**Los Angeles–Long Beach, CA**
*World Series:* Dodgers, 1959, 1963, 1965, 1981
*Super Bowl:* Raiders, 1984
*NFL Championship:* Rams, 1951
*NBA Championship:* Lakers, 1972, 1980, 1982

**Miami–Hialeah, FL**
*Super Bowl:* Dolphins, 1973, 1974

**Milwaukee, WI**
*World Series:* Braves, 1957
*NBA Championship:* Bucks, 1971

**Minneapolis–St. Paul, MN–WI**
*NFL Championship:* Minnesota Vikings, 1969
*BAA Championship:* Minneapolis Lakers, 1949
*NBA Championship:* Minneapolis Lakers, 1950, 1952, 1953, 1954

**Nassau–Suffolk, NY**
*Stanley Cup:* New York Islanders, 1980, 1981, 1982, 1983

**New York, NY**
*World Series:* Giants, 1905, 1921, 1922, 1933, 1954; Yankees, 1923, 1927, 1928, 1932, 1936, 1937, 1938, 1939, 1941, 1943, 1947, 1949, 1950, 1951, 1952, 1953, 1956, 1958, 1961, 1962, 1977, 1978; Brooklyn Dodgers, 1955; Mets, 1969
*Super Bowl:* Jets, 1969
*AFL Championship:* Jets, 1968
*NFL Championship:* Giants, 1934, 1938, 1944, 1956
*NBA Championship:* Knickerbockers, 1970, 1973
*Stanley Cup:* Rangers, 1928, 1933, 1940

**Oakland, CA**
*World Series:* Athletics, 1972, 1973; A's, 1974
*Super Bowl:* Raiders, 1977, 1981
*AFL Championship:* Raiders, 1967
*NBA Championship:* Golden State Warriors, 1975

**Philadelphia, PA–NJ**
*World Series:* Athletics, 1910, 1911, 1913, 1929, 1930; Phillies, 1980
*NFL Championship:* Eagles, 1948, 1949, 1960
*BAA Championship:* Warriors, 1947
*NBA Championship:* Warriors, 1956; 76ers, 1967, 1983
*Stanley Cup:* Flyers, 1974, 1975

**Pittsburgh, PA**
*World Series:* Pirates, 1909, 1925, 1960, 1971, 1979
*Super Bowl:* Steelers, 1975, 1976, 1979, 1980

**Portland, OR**
*NBA Championship:* Trail Blazers, 1977

**Rochester, NY**
*NBA Championship:* Royals, 1951

**St. Louis, MO–IL**
*World Series:* Cardinals, 1926, 1931, 1934, 1942, 1944, 1946, 1964, 1967, 1982
*NBA Championship:* Hawks, 1958

**San Diego, CA**
*AFL Championship:* Chargers, 1963

**San Francisco, CA**
*Super Bowl:* 49ers, 1982

**Seattle, WA**
*NBA Championship:* SuperSonics, 1979
*Stanley Cup:* Metropolitans, 1917

**Syracuse, NY**
*NBA Championship:* Nationals, 1955

**Washington, DC–MD–VA**
*World Series:* Senators, 1924
*Super Bowl:* Redskins, 1983
*NFL Championship:* Redskins, 1937, 1942
*NBA Championship:* Bullets, 1978

*Source:* Official league histories.

## Collegiate Title Towns

The 1984–1985 academic year marks the 103rd season of college athletic championships that began all the way back when Harvard University's J. S. Clark captured the first singles title in college tennis in 1883. Founded in 1906, the National Collegiate Athletic Association (NCAA) began administering collegiate athletic championships in 1921, beginning with its first outdoor track meet. In 1981, the association initiated women's championships. Some 600 colleges and universities have been named national champion in each of the NCAA's three divisions over the years. What follows is a list of the 45 metro area locations of the Division I champions for the past five years.

Many NCAA sports, such as basketball and volleyball, have both men's and women's championships. An M or W after the sport indicates whether the title was in men's or women's competition. Sports such as baseball, football, and wrestling are played at the championship level by men only, whereas field hockey and softball championships are for women only; accordingly, no M or W designation is given. Ski teams are coed.

### NCAA Championships in the Metro Areas

**Alton–Granite City, IL**
*Southern Illinois University, Edwardsville:* Soccer (M), 1979

**Anaheim–Santa Ana, CA**
*California State University, Fullerton:* Baseball, 1984
*University of California, Irvine:* Water Polo, 1982

**Athens, GA**
*University of Georgia:* Football (Division I–A), 1980

**Austin, TX**
*University of Texas:* Baseball, 1983; Swimming and Diving (M), 1981; Swimming and Diving (W), 1984

**Baltimore, MD**
*Johns Hopkins University:* Lacrosse (M), 1980, 1984

**Bloomington, IN**
*Indiana University:* Basketball (M), 1981; Soccer (M), 1982, 1983, 1984

**Boise City, ID**
*Boise State University:* Football (Division I–AA), 1980

**Boulder–Longmont, CO**
*University of Colorado:* Skiing, 1982

**Bryan–College Station, TX**
*Texas A & M University:* Softball, 1983

**Burlington, VT**
*University of Vermont:* Skiing, 1980

**Charlottesville, VA**
*University of Virginia:* Cross-Country Track (W), 1981, 1982

---

## Pro Sports Franchising

All the 88 major-league professional sports teams in the United States play at home in only 38 of the country's 329 metro areas. The greatest number of franchises, six, is found in the Los Angeles–Long Beach metro area.

In professional sports marketing, the largest metro areas are the ones that get the teams. In such places as Los Angeles–Long Beach, local governments can afford to underwrite stadiums and arenas, and ticket-buying fans can be found in the greatest number. But what about a small major-league metro area, such as Green Bay? The Packers are one of the oldest franchises in the NFL. The team divides its eight regular-season home games between Milwaukee's County Stadium and Lambeau Field in Green Bay. The Pack is also the only municipally owned team in professional sports; therefore, it is the only club whose owners can't threaten to move it.

There are large metro areas, however, that either have no professional sports franchises or could support more teams than they already do. The owners of major-league baseball's 26 franchises appointed a committee in 1983 to identify likely places that could put together publicly financed stadiums and blue-ribbon groups of prospective owners. Nine cities were mentioned for expansion: Denver, Phoenix, Washington, Miami, Buffalo, New Orleans, Indianapolis, Vancouver, and Tampa. Milwaukee has expressed interest in a hockey team. But while it may be true, as some studies show, that big-time professional football could easily expand into eight more cities and major-league baseball into six, the number of franchises is strictly controlled by owners. In fact, this control is so powerful that professional sports has been called the only unregulated monopoly allowed to operate in the United States. If there is to be any expansion, it probably will occur at a glacial rate because club owners, like classic monopolists, do not care for the idea of anyone encroaching on their territorial rights.

**Dallas, TX**
*Southern Methodist University:* Outdoor Track (M), 1983

**Denver, CO**
*University of Denver:* Gymnastics (W), 1983

**Detroit, MI**
*Wayne State University:* Fencing (M), 1980, 1982, 1983, 1984; Fencing (W), 1982, 1984

**El Paso, TX**
*University of Texas, El Paso:* Cross-Country Track (M), 1980, 1981, 1984; Outdoor Track (M), 1980, 1981, 1982

**Eugene–Springfield, OR**
*University of Oregon:* Cross-Country Track (W), 1984; Outdoor Track (M), 1984

**Fort Worth–Arlington, TX**
*Texas Christian University:* Golf (W), 1983

**Gainesville, FL**
*University of Florida:* Swimming and Diving (M), 1983, 1984; Swimming and Diving (W), 1982

**Grand Forks, ND**
*University of North Dakota:* Ice Hockey, 1980, 1982

**Greenville–Spartanburg, SC**
*Clemson University:* Football (Division I–A), 1981

**Honolulu, HI**
*University of Hawaii:* Volleyball (W), 1982

**Houston, TX**
*University of Houston:* Golf (M), 1982, 1984

**Iowa City, IA**
*University of Iowa:* Wrestling, 1980, 1981, 1982, 1983, 1984

**Lincoln, NE**
*University of Nebraska:* Gymnastics (M), 1980, 1981, 1982, 1983, 1984

**Los Angeles–Long Beach, CA**
*California State University, Northridge:* Gymnastics (W), 1982
*University of California, Los Angeles:* Softball, 1982; Swimming and Diving (M), 1982; Tennis (M), 1982, 1984; Volleyball (M), 1981, 1982, 1983
*University of Southern California:* Basketball (W), 1983, 1984; Outdoor Track (W), 1982, 1983; Tennis (W), 1983; Volleyball (W), 1983

**Louisville, KY–IN**
*University of Louisville:* Basketball (M), 1980

**Madison, WI**
*University of Wisconsin:* Cross-Country Track (M), 1982; Ice Hockey, 1981, 1983

**Miami–Hialeah, FL**
*University of Miami:* Baseball, 1982; Football (Division I–A), 1983; Golf (W), 1984

**Norfolk–Virginia Beach–Newport News, VA**
*Old Dominion University:* Field Hockey, 1982, 1983, 1984

**Oakland, CA**
*University of California, Berkeley:* Swimming and Diving (M), 1980

**Philadelphia, PA–NJ**
*Temple University:* Lacrosse (W), 1984
*University of Pennsylvania:* Fencing (M), 1981

**Phoenix, AZ**
*Arizona State University:* Baseball, 1981

**Provo–Orem, UT**
*Brigham Young University:* Golf (M), 1981

**Raleigh–Durham, NC**
*North Carolina State University:* Basketball (M), 1983
*University of North Carolina:* Basketball (M), 1982; Lacrosse (M), 1981, 1982; Soccer (W), 1982

---

## A Football Odyssey

The first NFL franchise in Cleveland, Ohio, belonged not to the Browns but to the Rams, who played such opponents as the Brooklyn Dodgers, Chicago Cardinals, and Pittsburgh Pirates back in the 1930s.

Organized professional football as we know it today began to take shape in 1922 with the establishment of the National Football League, although the early teams seem ragtag in comparison to the computerized juggernauts of the 1980s. Through a series of splits and mergers with other leagues over the years, the NFL has remained the dominant pro football organization, and presently consists of 28 teams. The list below recaps which of today's NFL teams have moved to another city and/or changed their name since their founding date.*

**Detroit Lions**—*1930*, began as the NFL Portsmouth (OH) Spartans; *1934*, moved to Detroit and renamed Detroit Lions.
**Indianapolis Colts**—*1952*, defunct Dallas Texans of the All-America Football Conference moved to Baltimore, renamed Baltimore Colts, and joined the NFL; *1983*, moved to Indianapolis and renamed Indianapolis Colts.
**Kansas City Chiefs**—*1959*, began as the Dallas Texans of the American Football League; *1963*, moved to Kansas City and renamed Kansas City Chiefs; *1970*, joined NFL.
**Los Angeles Raiders**—*1959*, began as Oakland Raiders of the American Football League; *1970*, joined NFL; *1982*, moved to Los Angeles and renamed Los Angeles Raiders.
**Los Angeles Rams**—*1937*, began as Cleveland Rams; *1946*, moved to Los Angeles and renamed Los Angeles Rams.

**New England Patriots**—*1959*, began as Boston Patriots of the American Football League; *1970*, joined NFL; *1971*, renamed New England Patriots.
**New York Jets**—*1959*, began as New York Titans of the American Football League; *1963*, renamed New York Jets; *1970*, joined NFL.
**St. Louis Cardinals**—*1913*, began as Racine Avenue (Chicago) Cardinals; *1922*, renamed Chicago Cardinals; *1960*, moved to St. Louis and renamed St. Louis Cardinals.
**San Diego Chargers**—*1959*, franchised as the AFL Los Angeles Chargers; *1961*, moved to San Diego and renamed San Diego Chargers; *1970*, joined NFL.
**Washington Redskins**—*1932*, began as Boston Braves; *1933*, renamed Boston Redskins; *1937*, moved to Washington and renamed Washington Redskins.

*Source: NFL Properties, NFL Record and Fact Book, 1984.*

*The Chicago Bears (1922), Green Bay Packers (1922), New York Giants (1925), Philadelphia Eagles (1933), Pittsburgh Steelers (1933), Dallas Cowboys (1960), Minnesota Vikings (1960), Atlanta Falcons (1965), New Orleans Saints (1966), Seattle Seahawks (1974), and Tampa Bay Buccaneers (1974) began as NFL teams and have neither moved nor changed their team name.

The Cleveland Browns (1946) and San Francisco 49ers (1946) are former All-America Football Conference teams that joined the NFL in 1949.

The Buffalo Bills (1959), Denver Broncos (1959), Houston Oilers (1959), Miami Dolphins (1965), and Cincinnati Bengals (1967) are former American Football League franchises that merged with the NFL in 1970.

**Salt Lake City–Ogden, UT**
*University of Utah:* Skiing, 1981, 1983, 1984

**San Francisco, CA**
*University of San Francisco:* Soccer (M), 1980

**San Jose, CA**
*Stanford University:* Tennis (M), 1980, 1981; Tennis (W), 1982, 1984; Swimming and Diving (W), 1983; Water Polo (M), 1980, 1981

**State College, PA**
*Pennsylvania State University:* Fencing (W), 1983; Football (Division I-A), 1982

**Syracuse, NY**
*Syracuse University:* Lacrosse (M), 1983

**Tallahassee, FL**
*Florida State University:* Outdoor Track (W), 1984

**Tucson, AZ**
*University of Arizona:* Baseball, 1980

**Tulsa, OK**
*University of Tulsa:* Golf (W), 1982

**Tuscaloosa, AL**
*University of Alabama:* Football (Division I-A), 1979

**Washington, DC–MD–VA**
*Georgetown University:* Basketball (M), 1984

**Wilmington, DE–NJ–MD**
*University of Delaware:* Lacrosse (W), 1983

*Source:* National Collegiate Athletic Association, *College Champions,* 1984.

In Division I-A Football, the NCAA recognizes as unofficial national champion the team selected each year by the Associated Press poll of sportswriters and the United Press International poll of coaches.

## LEGAL HOLIDAYS

Properly speaking, there aren't any national holidays in the United States. A day off on Independence Day, Thanksgiving, or Christmas comes by the grace of state legislatures rather than a presidential proclamation or an act of Congress.

The only thing "national" about your holiday calendar is the nine days off given to everyone who works for the federal government: Christmas, Independence Day, Labor Day, New Year's Day, Thanksgiving, and four Mondays—Columbus Day, Memorial Day, Veterans Day, and Washington's Birthday—that were approved in 1968 to create predictable long weekends. Beginning in 1986, Martin Luther King Day will be observed on the third Monday of January, increasing the number of federal holidays to ten.

Although lawmakers in many states have since adopted these same days as legal holidays for their local constituencies, many have not. In 1978, for instance, the federal government moved Veterans Day from the second Monday in November back to its original date, November 11, because few states wanted to be completely in step with Washington's calendar.

The Civil War era gave us more events and heroes to honor with holidays than any other period in American history. However, they aren't all celebrated nationwide. Just as no former secessionist state takes notice of Lincoln's birthday, so none of the Union states honors Robert E. Lee's birthday. Memorial Day, a date originally created to mourn those who died for the Union cause, isn't observed in Alabama, Mississip-

pi, or South Carolina. Those states, as well as Florida, Georgia, Kentucky, and Louisiana, celebrate Confederate Memorial Day instead. So if the calendars of some states have more holidays on them than others, it reflects which local heroes and events their lawmakers think worthy of commemoration.

For traveling salespeople who have found themselves all dressed up with no place to go in Boston on Evacuation Day or in Omaha on Arbor Day, and for anyone who wonders whether there are more long weekends in Florida than in California or Texas, we present a comprehensive list of days, fixed and movable, that are legal holidays somewhere in the United States.

### An American List of Days

#### JANUARY

**Fixed Dates**

*January 1,* New Year's Day: All states
*January 8,* Battle of New Orleans Day: Louisiana
*January 15,* Martin Luther King Day: Connecticut, District of Columbia, Florida, Illinois, Kentucky, Louisiana, Maryland, Massachusetts, Michigan, New Jersey, Pennsylvania, South Carolina
*January 19,* Robert E. Lee's Birthday: Arkansas, Florida, Georgia, Kentucky, Louisiana, South Carolina
*January 30,* Franklin D. Roosevelt Day: Kentucky

**Movable Feasts**

*Third Sunday,* Martin Luther King Day: New York
*Third Monday,* Martin Luther King Day: Ohio
  Robert E. Lee's Birthday: Alabama, Mississippi
  Lee-Jackson Day: Virginia

#### FEBRUARY

**Fixed Dates**

*February 12,* Lincoln's Birthday: Alaska, California, Colorado, Connecticut, Florida, Illinois, Indiana, Iowa, Kansas, Kentucky, Maryland, Missouri, Montana, New Jersey, New Mexico, New York, Utah, Vermont, Washington, West Virginia
*February 19,* Robert E. Lee Day: Kentucky

**Movable Feasts**

*First Monday,* Lincoln's Birthday: Delaware, Oregon
*Second Monday,* Lincoln Day: Arizona
*Third Monday,* Washington's Birthday: All states
*Tuesday before Ash Wednesday,* Mardi Gras: Alabama, Florida (some counties), Louisiana (some parishes)

#### MARCH

**Fixed Dates**

*March 2,* Texas Independence Day: Texas
*March 17,* Evacuation Day: Massachusetts (Suffolk County only)
*March 20,* Youth Day: Oklahoma
*March 25,* Maryland Day: Maryland
*March 26,* Prince Jonah Kuhio Kalanianaole Day: Hawaii

**Movable Feasts**

*First Tuesday,* Town Meeting Day: Vermont
*Two days before Easter,* Good Friday: Connecticut, Delaware, Florida, Hawaii, Indiana, Louisiana, Maryland, New Jersey, North Dakota, Pennsylvania, Tennessee, Wisconsin (11 A.M.–3 P.M.)
*One day after Easter,* Easter Monday: North Carolina
*Last Monday,* Seward's Day: Alaska

#### APRIL

**Fixed Dates**

*April 2,* Pascua Florida Day: Florida
*April 3,* Arbor Day: Arizona

*April 13*, Thomas Jefferson's Birthday: Alabama, Oklahoma
*April 21*, San Jacinto Day: Texas
*April 22*, Arbor Day: Delaware, Nebraska
   Oklahoma Day: Oklahoma
*April 26*, Confederate Memorial Day: Florida, Georgia

**Movable Feasts**

*Third Monday*, Patriot's Day: Maine, Massachusetts
*Fourth Monday*, Fast Day: New Hampshire
*Last Monday*, Confederate Memorial Day: Alabama, Mississippi
*Last Friday*, Arbor Day: Utah

### MAY

**Fixed Dates**

*May 1*, Bird Day: Oklahoma
*May 4*, Rhode Island Independence Day: Rhode Island
*May 8*, Truman Day: Missouri
*May 10*, Confederate Memorial Day: South Carolina
*May 11*, Minnesota Day: Minnesota
*May 20*, Mecklenburg Independence Day: North Carolina
*May 25*, Memorial Day: New Mexico, South Dakota, Vermont
*May 30*, Memorial Day: Delaware, Illinois, Maryland, New
   Hampshire

**Movable Feasts**

*First Tuesday after first Monday*, Primary Election Day: Indiana
*Second Sunday*, Mother's Day: Arizona, Oklahoma
*Last Monday*, Memorial Day: All states except Alabama, Mississippi,
   South Carolina, and those celebrating on May 30

### JUNE

**Fixed Dates**

*June 3*, Jefferson Davis's Birthday: Florida, Georgia, South Carolina
   Confederate Memorial Day: Kentucky, Louisiana
*June 9*, Senior Citizens Day: Oklahoma
*June 11*, King Kamehameha I Day: Hawaii
*June 14*, Flag Day: Pennsylvania
*June 15*, Separation Day: Delaware
*June 17*, Bunker Hill Day: Massachusetts (Suffolk County only)
*June 19*, Emancipation Day: Texas
*June 20*, West Virginia Day: West Virginia

**Movable Feasts**

*First Monday*, Jefferson Davis's Birthday: Alabama, Mississippi
*Second Sunday*, Flag Day: New York
*Third Sunday*, Father's Day: Arizona

### JULY

**Fixed Dates**

*July 4*, Independence Day: All states
*July 24*, Pioneer Day: Utah

**Movable Feasts:** None

### AUGUST

**Fixed Dates**

*August 16*, Bennington Battle Day: Vermont
*August 27*, Lyndon B. Johnson's Birthday: Texas
*August 30*, Huey P. Long Day: Louisiana

**Movable Feasts**

*First Sunday*, American Family Day: Arizona, Minnesota
*First Monday*, Colorado Day: Colorado
*Second Monday*, Victory Day: Rhode Island
*Third Friday*, Admission Day: Hawaii

### SEPTEMBER

**Fixed Dates**

*September 9*, Admission Day: California
*September 12*, Defenders' Day: Maryland
*September 16*, Cherokee Strip Day: Oklahoma

**Movable Feasts**

*First Monday*, Labor Day: All states
*First Tuesday*, Primary Election Day: Wisconsin
*Second Tuesday*, Primary Election Day: Wyoming
*First Saturday after full moon*, Indian Day: Oklahoma

### OCTOBER

**Fixed Dates**

*October 10*, Oklahoma Historical Day: Oklahoma
*October 12*, Columbus Day: Maryland
*October 18*, Alaska Day: Alaska
*October 31*, Nevada Day: Nevada

**Movable Feasts**

*Second Monday*, Columbus Day: All states except Alaska, Iowa,
   Maryland, Michigan, Mississippi, Nevada, North Carolina, North
   Dakota, Oregon, South Carolina, Washington
*Fourth Monday*, Veterans Day: Arkansas, Montana, North Carolina,
   Utah

### NOVEMBER

**Fixed Dates**

*November 1*, All Saints' Day: Louisiana
*November 4*, Will Rogers Day: Oklahoma
*November 11*, Veterans Day: All states except those celebrating in
   October
*November 29*, Nellie Tayloe Ross's Birthday: Wyoming

**Movable Feasts**

*First Tuesday after first Monday*, General Election Day: Arkansas,
   California, Colorado, District of Columbia, Delaware, Florida,
   Hawaii, Idaho, Illinois, Kentucky, Louisiana, Maryland, Missouri,
   Montana, New Jersey, New York, Oklahoma, Pennsylvania,
   Rhode Island, South Carolina, Tennessee, Texas, Virginia,
   West Virginia, Wisconsin, Wyoming

### DECEMBER

**Fixed Dates**

*December 7*, Delaware Day: Delaware
*December 10*, Wyoming Day: Wyoming
*December 25*, Christmas: All states

**Movable Feasts:** None

## LEGALIZED GAMBLING IN THE STATES

None of the 50 states has legalized gambling. What 46 of them do is to make certain forms of gambling legitimate and to authorize the state's right to run them as profitable enterprises, a right they steadfastly withhold from others. Nevada's constitution prohibits lotteries not because they are another form of gambling but because they would compete with the state's cut from casino gambling. A bettor who places twenty dollars on a horse with a bookie would break the law in New York or California—the number-one and number-two horse-racing states—just as he or she would anywhere else.

States permit certain forms of gambling to raise revenue. Seven states—California, Connecticut, Florida, Illinois, Massachusetts, New Jersey, and New York—each take in more money from lotteries or pari-mutuel betting on horses and dogs than Nevada does from its amusement tax on the tables, slot machines, sports-card betting shops, jai alai matches, and occasional horse races combined.

Another reason states sanction certain forms of gambling is to reduce illegal betting by offering comparable alternatives. But it is very difficult for states to raise money through legal gambling and control illegal operations at the same time. The illicit forms of gam-

## Legalized Gambling by State

| State | Horse Racing | Off-Track Betting | Dog Racing | Jai Alai | Lotteries | Bingo | Raffles | Casinos | Numbers | Sports Betting |
|---|---|---|---|---|---|---|---|---|---|---|
| Alabama | | | • | | | • | | | | |
| Alaska | | | | | | • | • | | | |
| Arizona | • | * | • | | • | • | | | | |
| Arkansas | • | | • | | | | | | | |
| California | • | | | | | • | | | | |
| Colorado | • | • | • | | • | • | • | | | |
| Connecticut | | • | • | • | • | • | • | | • | |
| Delaware | • | | | | • | • | | | • | * |
| Florida | • | • | • | • | | • | | | | |
| Georgia | | | | | | • | | | | |
| Hawaii | | | | | | | | | | |
| Idaho | • | | | | | | | | | |
| Illinois | • | • | | | | • | • | | • | |
| Indiana | | | | | | | | | | |
| Iowa | | * | * | | | • | • | | | |
| Kansas | | | | | | • | | | | |
| Kentucky | • | • | | | | | | | | |
| Louisiana | • | • | | | | • | • | | | |
| Maine | • | | | | • | • | • | | | |
| Maryland | • | | | | • | • | • | | | |
| Massachusetts | • | • | • | | • | • | | | • | |
| Michigan | • | | | | • | • | | | • | |
| Minnesota | * | | | | | • | | | | |
| Mississippi | | | | | | | | | | |
| Missouri | | | | | | • | | | | |
| Montana | • | | | | | • | • | | | • |
| Nebraska | • | | | | | • | • | | | |
| Nevada | • | • | • | • | | | | • | | • |
| New Hampshire | • | | • | | • | • | • | | • | |
| New Jersey | • | | | | • | • | • | • | • | |
| New Mexico | • | | | | | • | • | | | |
| New York | • | • | | | • | • | | | | |
| North Carolina | | | | | | • | | | | |
| North Dakota | | | | | | • | | | | |
| Ohio | • | | | | • | • | | | • | |
| Oklahoma | * | * | | | | • | • | | | |
| Oregon | • | | • | | | • | • | | | |
| Pennsylvania | • | • | | | | • | • | | • | |
| Rhode Island | • | | • | • | • | • | • | | • | |
| South Carolina | | | | | | • | | | | |
| South Dakota | • | | • | | | • | • | | | |
| Tennessee | | | | | | • | | | | |
| Texas | | | | | | • | | | | |
| Utah | | | | | | | | | | |
| Vermont | • | | • | | • | • | • | | | |
| Virginia | | | | | | • | • | | | |
| Washington | • | • | | | • | • | • | | | • |
| West Virginia | • | • | • | | | • | | | | |
| Wisconsin | | | | | | • | | | | |
| Wyoming | • | | | | | • | • | | | |

*Source:* National Association of State Racing Commissioners, 1984, and Public Gaming Research Institute, 1984.

• Indicates legal and operating.
*Indicates legal but not now operating.

Propositions for state lotteries in California, Missouri, Oregon, and West Virginia were approved by voters in November 1984. Missouri voters also approved horse racing.

bling are usually more popular: The payoff from an illegal bookmaking shop, floating dice and card games, or the numbers game is greater than that from sanctioned operations because there is no government takeout, and because the winnings are hidden from the tax collector. The stories about bookmakers setting up shop next door to New York City Off-Track Betting parlors are true, just as illegal numbers games still thrive in Massachusetts and New Jersey, two states with daily numbers games of their own.

## WHAT IT TAKES FOR THE BEST SKIING

If you were to draw a line on a map of the United States separating states with the best conditions for skiing from those with poor conditions or no facilities, the result would be a jagged northward arc. It would begin in the Great Smoky Mountains of North Carolina and run due north to Lake Erie, west to the foothills of the Rockies, and then south along the Rocky Mountain cordillera to northern New Mexico and Arizona. Next it would reappear in the California Sierra Nevada, dropping southwest to end in the San Bernardino National Forest an hour and a half out of Los Angeles. Although there are ski areas south of this imaginary curve, the ideal conditions are north of it: rolling, rugged terrain and predictable winter weather that everyone except skiers would call bad.

By definition, a ski area is a hill or mountain with some form of developed trails and lift machinery. Usually there is a lodge for meals and overnight stays. If the area is large and popular, there is also après-ski —nighttime entertainment that can range from music to movies to disco—that to many skiers is as critical as fresh snow and challenging runs.

Of the 587 U.S. ski areas, more than half are found in eight northeastern and Great Lakes states—Massachusetts, Michigan, Minnesota, New Hampshire, New York, Pennsylvania, Vermont, and Wisconsin—because of harsh, long winters and large, recreation-hungry urban populations.

But if you're a skier with time and money, skiing Hanley's Happy Hill in Pennsylvania, Little Switzerland in Wisconsin, or even Vermont's Killington or Stowe isn't quite the same as skiing "destination" areas in the West such as Aspen, Park City, or Jackson Hole. Ski areas are where you find them, but the best *skiing* is in the highest part of the country: the Rocky Mountain West and the Sierra Nevada near Lake Tahoe.

The above statement is not purely a matter of opinion. According to ski-industry surveys, most of the eight to ten million skiers in the United States are of intermediate ability, tending toward advanced. If they could ski anywhere, they would choose areas that enhance their ability; that is, places with high mountains, great vertical rises, long runs, and heavy powder

## The 15 Busiest Ski Areas

America's busiest ski areas, determined by a measurement known as a ski occasion (one ascent and descent of the mountain by a skier), are all located within national forests.

| Ski Area | Ski Occasions |
|---|---|
| 1. Mammoth Mountain, CA | 1,536,214 |
| 2. Breckenridge, CO | 763,200 |
| 3. Steamboat, CO | 743,200 |
| 4. Keystone, CO | 732,200 |
| 5. Snowmass, CO | 679,800 |
| 6. Copper Mountain, CO | 651,800 |
| 7. Taos Ski Valley, NM | 624,235 |
| 8. Mount Bachelor, OR | 603,918 |
| 9. Crystal Mountain, WA | 600,000 |
| 10. Santa Fe Ski Area, NM | 590,000 |
| 11. Alta, UT | 533,536 |
| 12. Snow Summit, CA | 503,571 |
| 13. Sugarbush Valley, VT | 501,000 |
| 14. Bald Mountain, ID | 444,227 |
| 15. Snowbird, UT | 415,111 |

Source: U.S. Forest Service, *National Forest Recreation Use Reports,* 1984.

snowfalls that begin early in winter and last into spring. You'll find more of these qualities within short drives of Denver, Boulder, Reno, Salt Lake City, Seattle, Tacoma, and Spokane than anywhere else.

## The 10 States with the Most Ski Areas

| State | Ski Areas |
|---|---|
| 1. New York | 63 |
| 2. Wisconsin | 48 |
| 3. Michigan | 42 |
| 4. Colorado | 41 |
| 5. California | 37 |
| 5. Pennsylvania | 37 |
| 7. New Hampshire | 31 |
| 8. Vermont | 28 |
| 9. Massachusetts | 26 |
| 10. Minnesota | 25 |

Source: Inter-Ski Services, Inc., *The White Book of Ski Areas,* 1983.

## Vertical Rise . . .

The perpendicular distance from the base to the highest skiable point on a hill or mountain is a ski area's "vertical." Utah's 14 ski areas average 1,826 feet, whereas Alabama's single ski area has a rise of only 150 feet. Although vertical rise has little to do with the quality of the trails, it is a good indication of length of the runs and the mountain's challenge. More than one optimistic ski-area promoter has stretched the distance a bit—some, allegedly, by measuring from the top of the tallest tree on the crest to the surface of the highway below the base lodge.

## The 9 Greatest Vertical Rises

| Ski Area | Height |
|---|---|
| 1. Jackson Hole, WY | 4,139 ft |
| 2. Aspen Highlands, CO | 3,800 |
| 3. High Wallowas, OR | 3,700 |
| 4. Heavenly Valley, CA | 3,600 |
| 4. Snowmass, CO | 3,600 |
| 4. Steamboat, CO | 3,600 |
| 7. Timberline, OR | 3,500 |
| 8. Sun Valley, ID | 3,400 |
| 9. Beaver Creek, CO | 3,340 |

Source: Inter-Ski Services, Inc., *The White Book of Ski Areas,* 1983.

## . . . and Longest Runs . . .

The highest vertical is found at Wyoming's Jackson Hole, but the longest ski run is at Killington, in Vermont. The longest run is the longest continuous trail on the mountain, from the top to the runout, which is usually in the base lodge's parking lot.

## The 9 Longest Ski Runs

| Ski Area | Length |
|---|---|
| 1. Killington, VT | 10.2 mi |
| 2. Jackson Hole, WY | 7.0 |
| 3. Heavenly Valley, CA | 5.5 |
| 3. Taos Ski Valley, NM | 5.5 |
| 5. Mission Ridge, WA | 5.0 |
| 6. Okemo Mountain, VT | 4.5 |
| 6. Stowe, VT | 4.5 |
| 6. Vail, CO | 4.5 |
| 9. Stratton, VT | 4.0 |

Source: Inter-Ski Services, Inc., *The White Book of Ski Areas,* 1983.

## . . . and Lift Capacities

A ski area's lift capacity is the number of people that can be moved up the mountain in one hour. Lifts can be elementary rope or cable tows, bars (T-bars, J-bars, pomalifts, or platterpulls), chairs, trams, or gondolas. Whatever the mix of lifts at a ski resort, the total lift capacity is a good indication of how developed the ski area is and often of how efficient the lift lines are. Twenty-five U.S. ski areas have lift capacities of at least 15,000 skiers per hour, and ten of these can move 20,000 or more up the mountain every hour.

## The 10 Best Ski Areas for Lift Capacity

| Ski Area | Skiers per Hour |
|---|---|
| 1. Mammoth Mountain, CA | 36,000 |
| 2. Squaw Valley, CA | 27,100 |
| 3. Heavenly Valley, CA | 26,500 |
| 4. Killington, VT | 22,800 |
| 5. Sun Valley, ID | 22,204 |
| 6. Steamboat, CO | 22,000 |
| 7. Vail, CO | 21,430 |
| 8. Afton Alps, MN | 20,000 |
| 8. Brandywine, OH | 20,000 |
| 8. Wilmot Mountain, WI | 20,000 |

Source: Inter-Ski Services, Inc., *The White Book of Ski Areas,* 1983.

# Economics:

## Living Costs, Incomes, Taxes, Jobs

In the detached view of some economists, we humans are little more than living resources continually searching for our highest valued use. After all, we switch jobs readily if the money is right. We'll change careers, too, if the prospects are more promising. And we may risk these changes even if it means packing up and moving far away.

For Americans, this is nothing new. Over three centuries our ancestors redistributed themselves as much for the main chance as for elbowroom. In the 1700s they jostled each other in steerage during the long ocean passage to the New World. Around 1800, they climbed aboard creaking wagons in Pennsylvania to make the hard, one-way trip to the Northwest Territory, where farmland was opening up. In this century they bundled their things together and trucked away from southern sharecropped farms for an hourly wage in Detroit automobile factories.

We are still at it, for similar reasons. Periodic Census Bureau surveys find that most people who quit one state for another are either tracking down a better job (or *any* job, period), being transferred by their employer, or fleeing high taxes and day-to-day living costs. By now, everyone knows that the southern and western states were the preferred destinations during the 1970s. If the consensus of public and private forecasters is correct, the migration to the sun will continue into the twenty-first century.

But not every Sun Belt metro area is an unbridled boomtown. Many are saddled with sunset industries. Some suffer recessions more deeply than the rest of the country and consistently bounce back more slowly. Others, owing to their rapid population growth, are now experiencing rapidly climbing living costs. Nor are all Frost Belt metro areas going under or even languishing. Having endured the collapse of their historic industries in recent years, many are now making up for lost time. Some currently enjoy the lowest unemployment rates in the nation and have enviable track records for income growth and job expansion.

"Money's no problem," an accountant will tell you. "Lack of money. . . now *that's* a problem." As is the case for most people, your short-term economic frets probably center on the price of hamburger, jeans, laundry detergent, or haircuts. Over the long run, your concerns may focus on tax bites, jobs, and boosting your income at least to the level where it beats inflation.

## LOCAL LIVING COSTS

Get ready for some surprising answers should you ask experts why and how much living costs vary among metro areas.

Some home economists argue that the only accu-

371

rate way to compare expenses in different metro areas is to trundle a shopping cart around each place and fill it with the packaged goods you'd regularly consume; check the asking prices for homes in the Sunday paper's real estate section; call the gas and electric utility for the cost of residential service; and find out from the tax office just how homes are assessed and when the bill comes due. According to this theory, when you add up the costs of all these items and budget the amount over 12 months, you've got a rough idea of how much annual income you'd need in each metro area.

But after months of pondering such topics as the tastiness of food and physical standards of housing, a committee appointed in 1980 by the U.S. Department of Labor to recommend better ways to measure living costs threw in the towel. Given the infinite variety of consumer preferences, they reported, the only acceptable way to pin down why life in one city was more expensive than in another was to focus on climate's effect on clothing costs and home heating bills.

According to one national clothing retailer, however, the cost difference between a double-knit Sun Belt wardrobe and a woolen Frost Belt wardrobe complete with down-filled outerwear can amount to less than 1 percent of a household's annual budget. As for the comparative costs of keeping warm in Duluth's winter and staying cool in Waco's summer, often the only difference is the season during which local residents pay most of the bill.

One consulting firm that specializes in relocating transferred employees adopts a simple rule of thumb. In its experience, 80 percent of the difference in living costs between metro areas typically comes down to two items: the price of housing and the direct taxes people may encounter in their new area. The other 20 percent comes from local prices for consumer packaged goods and personal services.

To gauge living costs in each metro area, *Places Rated* compares the costs of housing, food, and miscellaneous goods and services against a national yardstick of 100. We also borrow a weighting rule from government surveys, which states that a middle-class family spends 33 percent of its income on homeownership expenses, 30 percent on services, and 17 percent on food. (The remaining 20 percent goes for transportation and health care.)

*Housing.* By *Places Rated* estimates, the average metro area housing costs for utilities, property taxes, and paying off a 25-year, 12 percent mortgage on an existing single-family house after making a one-quarter down payment are $8,340 a year. (For a more detailed analysis of homeownership costs, see the chapter "Housing: Affording the American Dream," pp. 70–116.) Using $8,340 as a norm equal to 100, the housing cost index in Stamford, Connecticut, is 283, while in Joplin, Missouri, it is 62.

## Homeownership Costs in the Metro Areas

| Lowest Costs | Cost Index (U.S. Avg. = 100) | Highest Costs | Cost Index (U.S. Avg. = 100) |
|---|---|---|---|
| 1. Joplin, MO | 62 | 1. Stamford, CT | 283 |
| 2. Brownsville–Harlingen, TX | 64 | 2. Norwalk, CT | 242 |
| 2. McAllen–Edinburg–Mission, TX | 64 | 3. San Francisco, CA | 206 |
| 4. Gadsden, AL | 65 | 4. Honolulu, HI | 204 |
| 5. Anniston, AL | 66 | 5. Anaheim–Santa Ana, CA | 192 |
| 5. Terre Haute, IN | 66 | 5. San Jose, CA | 192 |
| 7. St. Joseph, MO | 67 | 7. Santa Barbara–Santa Maria–Lompoc, CA | 186 |
| 8. Anderson, IN | 68 | 8. Bergen–Passaic, NJ | 175 |
| 8. Danville, VA | 68 | 9. Danbury, CT | 173 |
| 8. Dothan, AL | 68 | 9. San Diego, CA | 173 |

Source: *Places Rated* figures, based on average homeownership costs as calculated in the chapter "Housing: Affording the American Dream."

*Food.* Every three months, the American Chamber of Commerce Researchers Association (ACCRA) prices a carefully selected list of consumer goods and services with the consumption habits of a typical middle-management executive's family in mind. This survey measures relative price levels in more than 200 participating cities, as compared with the national average of 100 for all the cities.

Twenty-seven items are on ACCRA's food list, including meats, fresh produce, dairy products, bread, and a variety of packaged food from frozen orange juice and coffee, to number-303 cans of sweet peas and tomatoes, to an 18-ounce box of Post Toasties. When ACCRA's survey results are applied to the metro areas, we find the lowest food costs in Springfield, Illinois, and the highest, not surprisingly, in Anchorage, Alaska.

## Food Prices in the Metro Areas

| Lowest Prices | Cost Index (U.S. Avg. = 100) | Highest Prices | Cost Index (U.S. Avg. = 100) |
|---|---|---|---|
| 1. Springfield, IL | 87 | 1. Anchorage, AK | 139 |
| 2. Canton, OH | 89 | 2. Honolulu, HI | 125† |
| 3. Columbia, MO | 91 | 3. New York, NY | 112 |
| 3. Dubuque, IA | 91 | 4. Billings, MT | 110 |
| 3. Joplin, MO | 91 | 4. Bridgeport–Milford, CT | 110* |
| 6. Davenport–Rock Island–Moline, IA–IL | 92* | 4. Bristol, CT | 110* |
| 6. Fort Smith, AR–OK | 92 | 4. Casper, WY | 110 |
| 6. Greensboro–Winston-Salem–High Point, NC | 92 | 4. Danbury, CT | 110* |
| 6. Hickory, NC | 92 | 4. Eugene–Springfield, OR | 110* |
| 6. Sioux City, IA–NE | 92* | 4. Hartford, CT | 110 |
| | | 4. Middletown, CT | 110* |
| | | 4. New Britain, CT | 110* |
| | | 4. New Haven–Meriden, CT | 110* |
| | | 4. Stamford, CT | 110* |
| | | 4. Waterbury, CT | 110* |

Source: American Chamber of Commerce Researchers Association, "Inter-City Cost of Living Index," first quarter, 1984.

*Figures derived from prices in nearest metro area or city due to lack of data for metro area itself.

†Honolulu's figure is based on a cost-of-living premium for food awarded federal government employees living in Hawaii.

*Miscellaneous Goods and Services.* Eating out at McDonald's, Pizza Hut, or Kentucky Fried Chicken is a service on ACCRA's shopping list. So are cash-and-carry charges for dry cleaning a man's two-piece suit, visiting a barber for a basic haircut (no styling), and visiting a beauty salon for a shampoo, trim, and blow-dry. ACCRA's list also includes a six-ounce tube of Crest, an 11-ounce bottle of Johnson's Baby Shampoo, a can of Wilson tennis balls, a number-9 standard edition of Parker Brothers Monopoly, and a six-pack of 12-ounce Schlitz or Budweiser beer.

Anchorage again tops the metro areas in this category of living costs, while metro areas in the Mid-South and Midwest enjoy the lowest prices.

**Miscellaneous Goods and Services Prices in the Metro Areas**

| Lowest Prices | Cost Index (U.S. Avg. = 100) | Highest Prices | Cost Index (U.S. Avg. = 100) |
|---|---|---|---|
| 1. Jacksonville, NC | 89* | 1. Anchorage, AK | 138 |
| 2. Anniston, AL | 90* | 2. Honolulu, HI | 125† |
| 2. Gadsden, AL | 90 | 3. Oakland, CA | 120* |
| 4. Canton, OH | 91 | 3. San Francisco, CA | 120 |
| 4. Fort Wayne, IN | 91 | 3. Santa Rosa– Petaluma, CA | 120* |
| 4. Pine Bluff, AR | 91* | | |
| 7. Anderson, SC | 92* | 6. New York, NY | 114 |
| 7. Burlington, NC | 92 | 7. Bremerton, WA | 112* |
| 7. Dothan, AL | 92 | 7. Olympia, WA | 112* |
| 7. Elkhart– Goshen, IN | 92* | 7. Portland, OR | 112 |
| | | 7. Seattle, WA | 112* |
| 7. Florence, SC | 92* | 7. Tacoma, WA | 112 |
| 7. Indianapolis, IN | 92 | 7. Vancouver, WA | 112* |
| 7. Kokomo, IN | 92* | 13. Reno, NV | 111 |
| 7. Lafayette, IN | 92* | 14. Fresno, CA | 110 |
| 7. South Bend– Mishawaka, IN | 92 | 14. Las Vegas, NV | 110 |
| | | 14. Modesto, CA | 110 |
| 7. Steubenville– Weirton, OH–WV | 92 | | |

Source: American Chamber of Commerce Researchers Association, "Inter-City Cost of Living Index," first quarter, 1984.

*Figures derived from prices in nearest metro area or city due to lack of data for metro area itself.

†Honolulu's figure is based on a cost-of-living premium for miscellaneous goods awarded federal government employees living in Hawaii.

## SCRAPING BY ON $33,121 A YEAR

If budgeting the costs of all the things your household needs will give you a rough idea of how much income you'll have to earn to pay for it all, then you might ask whether average household incomes in different parts of the country indicate local living costs. For the most part, they do. According to a recent U.S. Labor Department report, two thirds of the difference in personal incomes between, say, Atlanta and Seattle reflects their different costs of living; the other third reflects their different employers, worker skills, and prevailing wages. (See "Income and Expenses: A Close Connection" on page 374 for more on this subject.)

Households aren't always made up of families. According to the 1984 Census Bureau survey on living arrangements, one quarter of all households are composed either of one person or of several people unrelated to one another (including two million POSSLQs: Persons of Opposite Sex Sharing Living Quarters). There are 12 million single-parent households with at least one child present, and two million of them are headed by men. The rest of the households comprise married couples, some with children, some childless, and some whose children have scattered from the nest.

Like being married 1.2 times and having 2.5 children in the bargain, 2.8 persons per household is an odd statistic. Yet that's roughly what you get when you divide the population of U.S. metro areas by the number of metro area households (figures are from the Rand McNally *1984 Commercial Atlas & Marketing Guide*).

When it comes to a statistic like per capita personal income in a given place, we know the textbook definition, but we also know that a corporate marketing vice president pulling down $100,000 a year plus five field hands earning $10,000 apiece doesn't really add up to six persons with average earnings of $25,000 each. Nonetheless, whether we talk of social phenomena, the stock market, or the strengths of major-league pitchers, we can seldom sidestep statistical averages.

To determine average household incomes in each of the 329 metro areas, *Places Rated Almanac* starts with per capita personal income. This includes not only paychecks but also money from such sources as interest and dividends, rents, alimony, and pensions—in short, the gross sum that you would record on your income tax return before claiming deductions. Per capita personal incomes are then multiplied by 2.8, the average number of persons in a metro area household. The average household income for all U.S. metro areas is currently $33,121, ranging from $51,601 in Anchorage to $16,478 in McAllen–Edinburg–Mission, in historically poor southernmost Texas.

**Average Household Incomes in the Metro Areas**

| Highest | | Lowest | |
|---|---|---|---|
| 1. Anchorage, AK | $51,601 | 1. McAllen– Edinburg– Mission, TX | $16,478 |
| 2. San Francisco, CA | 47,967 | 2. Laredo, TX | 17,287 |
| 3. Bridgeport– Milford, CT | 47,258 | 3. Brownsville– Harlingen, TX | 17,903 |
| 3. Danbury, CT | 47,258 | 4. Provo–Orem, UT | 18,390 |
| 3. Norwalk, CT | 47,258 | 5. Las Cruces, NM | 21,641 |
| 3. Stamford, CT | 47,258 | 6. Bloomington, IN | 21,851 |
| 7. Midland, TX | 46,458 | 7. El Paso, TX | 21,929 |
| 8. Casper, WY | 43,388 | 8. Anniston, AL | 22,254 |
| 9. Bergen–Passaic, NJ | 43,240 | 9. Fayetteville, NC | 22,291 |
| 10. Nassau–Suffolk, NY | 43,075 | 10. Jacksonville, NC | 22,358 |

Source: U.S. Bureau of Economic Analysis, *Survey of Current Business*, April 1984.

The national metro area average for household income is $33,121.

## Income and Expenses: A Close Connection

It may be true, as one Roman philosopher claimed, that money has no odor, but it does have a recognizable pattern: High incomes are usually found where the cost of living is high, and low incomes where living is cheap.

By "cost of living," *Places Rated* means the income required for homeownership, food, and miscellaneous goods and services. Each of these criteria is multiplied by a number that reflects its percentage of a middle-class family's income. Thus we multiply the cost index for homeownership, which consumes one third of an average budget, by 33; the index for food by 17; and the index for miscellaneous goods by 30. The total is then divided by 80, the sum of the three weighted numbers, to represent the overall cost of living.

Five of the 15 metro areas with the highest cost indexes also place among the top metro areas for income, including several in Connecticut. And five of the places where it's cheapest to live—some of them in Alabama and North Carolina—have among the lowest incomes. (A list of highest and lowest household incomes is on page 373.)

### Household Income in the Metro Areas

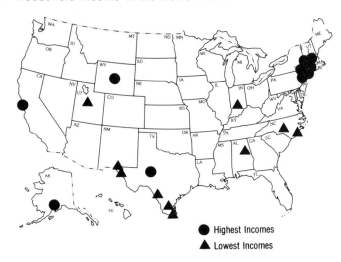

● Highest Incomes
▲ Lowest Incomes

### Overall Cost of Living in the Metro Areas

| Lowest Costs | Cost Index (U.S. Avg. = 100) | Highest Costs | Cost Index (U.S. Avg. = 100) |
|---|---|---|---|
| 1. Joplin, MO | 80 | 1. Stamford, CT | 179 |
| 2. Anniston, AL | 81 | 2. Oxnard– Ventura, CA | 177 |
| 2. Gadsden, AL | 81 | 3. Norwalk, CT | 162 |
| 4. Anderson, SC | 83 | 4. Honolulu, HI | 158 |
| 4. Dothan, AL | 83 | 5. San Francisco, CA | 153 |
| 6. Brownsville– Harlingen, TX | 84 | 6. Anchorage, AK | 142 |
| 6. Florence, AL | 84 | 7. San Jose, CA | 140 |
| 6. Jacksonville, NC | 84 | 8. Anaheim– Santa Ana, CA | 139 |
| 6. Pine Bluff, AR | 84 | 9. Santa Barbara– Santa Maria– Lompoc, CA | 136 |
| 6. St. Joseph, MO | 84 | 10. Bergen–Passaic, NJ | 135 |
| 6. South Bend– Mishawaka, IN | 84 | | |
| 12. Burlington, NC | 85 | 11. Danbury, CT | 133 |
| 12. Fayetteville, NC | 85 | 11. New York, NY | 133 |
| 12. McAllen–Edinburg– Mission, TX | 85 | 11. Newark, NJ | 133 |
| 12. Texarkana, TX– Texarkana, AR | 85 | 11. Oakland, CA | 133 |
| | | 15. Santa Rosa– Petaluma, CA | 132 |

### Cost of Living in the Metro Areas

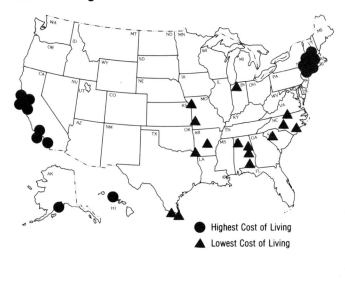

● Highest Cost of Living
▲ Lowest Cost of Living

## TAXES: ONE OF LIFE'S CERTAINTIES

In a calendar year, May 1 marks the mythical Tax Freedom Day on which we stop handing over all of our earnings to federal, state, and local tax collectors and begin pocketing that money for ourselves. Looking at it another way, we spend two hours and 40 minutes of every eight-hour working day earning enough money to pay taxes, according to the District of Columbia–based Tax Foundation, and that amounts to $24 a day for each employed person.

No matter where you live, Social Security taxes hit you with the same impact. So can federal personal income taxes. But state and local taxes differ tremendously. To determine the relative tax bite among metro areas, *Places Rated* focuses on the two most common direct levies: state personal income taxes and state sales taxes. Based on a metro area's average household income, state income taxes are estimated for a two-paycheck couple with one child, filing either a joint or a combined separate return (whichever would result in the smaller amount of taxes owed in each state), after taking typical exemptions and deductions. The taxes that a family pays throughout the year in the store on retail sales are also based on the household's average income, using the optional general sales tax table found in the tax return mailed to taxpayers each year by the Internal Revenue Service.

As a percentage of average household incomes, state income and sales taxes take some of the biggest bites from household incomes in the District of Columbia, Massachusetts, Michigan, Minnesota, New York, Oregon, Utah, and Wisconsin. In Connecticut, Florida, New Hampshire, New Mexico, Texas, and Wyoming, the bite is smallest. And in Alaska and New Hampshire, there is no bite at all.

## The Bite State Taxes Take from Household Income

| Smallest Bites | | Biggest Bites | |
|---|---|---|---|
| 1. Anchorage, AK | 0% | 1. Washington, DC-MD-VA | 5.66% |
| 1. Manchester, NH | 0 | 2. Honolulu, HI | 5.38 |
| 1. Nashua, NH | 0 | 3. Nassau-Suffolk, NY | 5.18 |
| 1. Portsmouth-Dover-Rochester, NH-ME | 0 | 4. Minneapolis-St. Paul, MN-WI | 5.08 |
| 5. Las Cruces, NM | 0.62 | 5. Rochester, MN | 5.04 |
| 6. Brazoria, TX | 0.72 | 6. Provo-Orem, UT | 4.85 |
| 6. Lubbock, TX | 0.72 | 7. Milwaukee, WI | 4.83 |
| 8. Corpus Christi, TX | 0.73 | 8. Salt Lake City-Ogden, UT | 4.82 |
| 8. Sherman-Denison, TX | 0.73 | 9. Portland, OR | 4.70 |
| 10. Killeen-Temple, TX | 0.74 | 10. Madison, WI | 4.69 |
| 10. Texarkana, TX-Texarkana, AR | 0.74 | | |
| 10. Waco, TX | 0.74 | | |

*Source*: Derived from Advisory Commission on Intergovernmental Relations, "Tax Burdens for Families Residing in the Largest City in Each State," 1984.

## WEATHERING THE RECESSION: JOB AND INCOME TRACK RECORDS

New Year's Day 1978 didn't seem to be a particularly notable date in the history of the American economy. Some 75 million residents of metro areas, the highest number ever, had a job to go back to after the holidays; the energy crisis was all but forgotten; food prices were creeping upward.

But over the next 60 months, something happened that was unforeseen by sanguine and cautious business forecasters alike. Not only did the nation experience ruinous inflation, we also suffered back-to-back business slumps far worse than any since the Great Depression.

Not all metro areas were equally stricken. Between 1978 and 1982, consumer prices rose 47.95 percent. Personal income growth in 103 metro areas either kept abreast of or outpaced that figure; incomes in 226 metro areas, however, lagged. During the same period, 167 metro areas outran the economy's job-formation record, while 162 metro areas fell behind it, with 74 of these actually losing jobs.

Clearly, some places hardly felt the recession, whereas others took it on the chin. And some of the latter group still haven't fully recovered. Let's look at their track records in income and job growth over the 60-month period from the relative flush times of January 1978 through the recession's onset, depth, and "official" end in November-December of 1982.

### Income Growth

The cost of living has a broader meaning than the estimate based on pushing a shopping cart around a metro area and pricing its theater tickets, oil changes, T-shirts, shampoo, and other consumer packaged goods and services. Nationally, it is a measurement of what dollars can buy at different times.

Using the U.S. Bureau of Labor Statistics price index for city consumers fixed at 100 for the base year 1967, the cost of living started at 60 in 1920, dropped to 42 by 1940, rebounded to 116 in 1970, and had skyrocketed to 310 by August 1984. Clearly, inflation plays a big role in the nation's cost of living. Not for nothing are the dollar amounts of everything from pension checks, union wages, and apartment rents tied to the cost-of-living index.

Are you better off today than you were a few years ago? This familiar refrain is sounded during political

---

**Tax Facts**

- A typical family earning $25,000 a year pays nearly 20 percent of its income in sales and income taxes to federal, state, and local collectors. For a family earning $50,000, these same taxes take 27 percent. Families in the $75,000-and-over bracket are stuck with a tax bite of 40 percent.

- The median federal tax bite (income and Social Security taxes) is almost six times that of the median state-local sales and income tax bite. For the family earning $25,000 a year, taxes imposed by Washington take 16.6 percent of family income, whereas state-local taxes subtract 2.8 percent. For families earning $50,000, the figures are 23.2 percent and 3.6 percent, respectively.

- Usually the lowest family tax burdens are found in metro areas with unique revenue advantages. Families living in Anchorage, Casper, Las Vegas, and New Orleans shoulder light tax burdens because their home states tap revenue from outsiders—severance taxes and mineral royalties from mining and lumber companies in Alaska, Louisiana, and Wyoming, and amusement and sales taxes from visiting gamblers in Nevada.

- Alaska and New Hampshire are the only states in which residents pay no sales taxes or income taxes. And living in Alaska carries an additional benefit: Each resident receives an annual check from the state's $5.5 billion permanent fund, a savings account from oil and gas fees and royalty payments from North Slope drillers. In 1984, the bonus amounted to $358 per person.

campaigns, which invariably focus on the twin issues of income and joblessness. If voters are disheartened by paltry rises in their real income, then the politician looking to stay in office may be in trouble. And metro areas can be in trouble, too, if local personal incomes don't stay ahead of inflation. When consumers have no money to spend, a litany of trouble begins: Retail stores close up for lack of trade; real estate investments aren't sure things; property crime increases; and municipal services are cut.

## Personal Income Growth in the Metro Areas

| Greatest | Growth, 1978–82 | Least | Growth, 1978–82 |
|---|---|---|---|
| 1. Lafayette, LA | 76.22% | 1. Williamsport, PA | 20.24% |
| 2. Enid, OK | 65.91 | 2. Kokomo, IN | 21.00 |
| 3. Jacksonville, NC | 61.84 | 3. Eugene–Springfield, OR | 24.33 |
| 4. Midland, TX | 60.56 | 4. Flint, MI | 25.49 |
| 5. Bryan–College Station, TX | 60.35 | 5. Elkhart–Goshen, IN | 26.03 |
| 6. Atlantic City, NJ | 59.84 | 6. Texarkana, TX–Texarkana, AR | 26.39 |
| 7. Oklahoma City, OK | 59.48 | 7. Redding, CA | 26.60 |
| 8. New London–Norwich, CT–RI | 58.43 | 8. Steubenville–Weirton, OH–WV | 26.67 |
| 9. Boulder–Longmont, CO | 58.27 | 9. Detroit, MI | 27.24 |
| 10. Colorado Springs, CO | 58.05 | 10. Anderson, IN | 27.67 |

Source: U.S. Bureau of Economic Analysis, unpublished metro area personal income data for 1978–82, 1984.

The national metro area average for income growth is 43.34%.

### Job Expansion

In the midst of the back-to-back recessions of 1980 and 1981–82, it was easy to wonder whether we would ever again hear the buzz saws shriek in Oregon sawmills or the whistles signal a shift change in Pennsylvania ironworks; indeed, whether we would ever again see large numbers of workers troop past the gates of low-tech factories in full production.

Michigan, Indiana, Ohio, and Illinois were particularly hard hit. Between 1980 and 1982, nearly 100,000 jobs disappeared in these four states due to the slump in domestic automobile production and its effect on nearby employers. For every 10,000 jobs lost at Chrysler, Ford, and General Motors, an additional 20,000 were lost in other industries, including 4,500 in iron and steel, 2,500 in wholesale trade, and 900 in business services.

A look at the metro areas with the greatest loss of jobs between the flush times of early 1978 and the recession that bottomed out in November 1982 shows a group lumped in the Rust Bowl section of the United States. Here, in the graying, muscle-bound, blue-collar metro areas of the Great Lakes, firms that produce autos, steel, tires, and machinery predominate.

In contrast, metro areas with the biggest expansion in jobs during the same period were smaller metro areas that either benefited from a rise in light-manufacturing employment—particularly in electronics and instrument firms—or in petroleum refining or other energy production. Atlantic City owes its rebirth to amusement services.

## Job Growth in the Metro Areas

| Greatest | Growth, 1978–82 | Least | Growth, 1978–82 |
|---|---|---|---|
| 1. Portsmouth–Dover–Rochester, NH–ME | 62.51% | 1. Beaver County, PA | −22.73% |
| 2. Fort Pierce, FL | 54.05 | 2. Syracuse, NY | −22.15 |
| 3. Bryan–College Station, TX | 52.53 | 3. Anderson, IN | −20.47 |
| 4. Lafayette, LA | 48.25 | 4. Kokomo, IN | −17.89 |
| 5. Midland, TX | 47.62 | 5. Peoria, IL | −16.28 |
| 6. Atlantic City, NJ | 46.69 | 6. Benton Harbor, MI | −15.87 |
| 7. Ocala, FL | 39.38 | 7. Lorain–Elyria, OH | −15.36 |
| 8. Orlando, FL | 38.53 | 8. Flint, MI | −15.30 |
| 9. Colorado Springs, CO | 38.49 | 8. Muskegon, MI | −15.30 |
| 10. West Palm Beach–Boca Raton–Delray Beach, FL | 38.48 | 10. Battle Creek, MI | −14.97 |

Source: U.S. Bureau of Labor Statistics, unpublished ES–202 records, 1984.

The national metro area average for job growth is 9.45%.

## JUDGING PERSONAL ECONOMIC OUTLOOK

If the annual income in your household is $30,000, would you be better off in Dallas or Denver when it comes to paying state sales and income taxes? If you're out of work, would you find the prospects for landing a job more promising in Seattle or San Francisco? Even if you think you've found a likely metro area with a record of rapid job expansion and a modest tax bite, can you still afford to live and work there given the local costs for housing, groceries, and clothing?

To help you answer these questions, *Places Rated* compares five factors in each metro area: average household income, state sales and income tax bite, costs of living (a scoring element introduced in this edition), and recent five-year rates for income growth and job expansion. Figures for these last two factors also represent a change from the 1981 *Places Rated Almanac*, in which we presented projections for growth rather than actual trends.

Each metro area starts with a base score of zero, to which points are added according to the following indicators:

1. *Average household income adjusted for taxes and living costs.* The average annual household income is reduced by the estimated dollars paid out in state sales and income taxes at that income level. After-tax income is then divided by the local cost-of-living index (see page 374 for an explanation of how costs for housing, food, and miscellaneous items are combined to calculate a metro area's overall cost-of-living index). For example, Chicago's household income after taxes—$35,422—is divided by its cost-of-living index of 115. The result is multiplied by 10 and added to the

base score of zero; in Chicago's case, this works out to 3,080 points.

2. *Income growth.* The local growth rate for personal income over the five-year period between January 1978 and December 1982 (the latest available figures) is multiplied by 50 and added to the score.

3. *Job growth.* The percentage of growth in local number of jobs between January 1978 and December 1982 is multiplied by 50 and added to the total.

## Sample Comparison: Midland, Texas, and Eugene–Springfield, Oregon

The two areas compared here for cost of living, household income, tax bite, and the impact of the last recession illustrate not just the economic extremes among the 329 metro areas but also how *Places Rated*'s scoring method has changed since 1981, when both places were rated in the book's first edition.

Financially, people do quite well in Midland. In 1981, the small metro area in the Permian oil basin of West Texas was ranked 29th of 277 metro areas, mainly

## An Occupational Directory

Using "white collar" or "blue collar" to differentiate between a job that deals either with information or things, is physical or mental, clean or messy, salaried or nonsalaried, high-paying or low-paying, seasonal or year-round, skilled or unskilled, unionized or professional, is somewhat imprecise.

According to U.S. Standard Occupational Classification (SOC) definitions, white-collar jobs include professional and technical workers, managers and administrators, sales workers, and clerical workers. Blue-collar occupations include craftsworkers, operatives, drivers, and nonfarm laborers.

But a quick look at some of the white-collar clerical job titles shows that many of them can be as unskilled, nonsalaried, and seasonal as jobs in the laboring category, while many blue-collar craftsworker jobs can be as skilled, salaried, and highly paid as those in the professional and technical category.

The SOC also identifies two other categories of occupations: service workers and farm workers. Service jobs include police and health-service, food-service, and child-care workers; farmers, farm laborers, and farm managers compose the farm workers category.

### White Collar

**Professional and Technical**
Accountants
Computer specialists
Engineers
Health technologists and technicians
Lawyers and judges
Librarians, archivists, and curators
Life and physical scientists
Personnel and labor relations workers
Physicians, dentists, and related practitioners
Registered nurses, dietitians, and therapists
Religious workers
Research workers
Social scientists
Social and recreation workers
Teachers
Technicians (except health)
Vocational and educational counselors
Writers, artists, and entertainers

**Managers and Administrators (Except Farm)**
Bank officers and financial managers
Building managers and superintendents
Buyers, wholesale and retail trade
Health administrators
Office managers
Officials and administrators
Restaurant, cafeteria, and bar managers
Sales managers
School administrators

**Sales Workers**
Hucksters and peddlers
Insurance agents, brokers, and underwriters
Real estate agents and brokers
Retail store sales clerks
Stock and bond sales agents
Sales representatives
Salespeople

**Clerical Workers**
Bank tellers
Billing clerks
Bookkeepers
Cashiers
Clerical supervisors
Counter clerks, except food
Estimators and investigators
File clerks
Insurance adjusters, examiners, and investigators
Postal clerks and mail carriers
Receptionists
Secretaries
Shipping and receiving clerks
Statistical clerks
Stenographers
Stock clerks and storekeepers
Telephone operators
Typists and office-machine operators

### Blue Collar

**Craftsworkers**
Carpenters
Construction craftsworkers
Machinists and job-setters
Metalcraft workers
Mechanics
Other craftsworkers
Print craftsworkers

**Operatives (Except Transport)**
Assemblers
Checkers, examiners, and inspectors of manufactured goods
Cutters

Dressmakers and seamstresses, except factory
Garage workers and gas station attendants
Laundry and dry-cleaning operatives
Machine operatives
Meat cutters and butchers
Miners
Packers and wrappers
Painters of manufactured goods
Precision machine operatives
Punch and stamping press operatives
Sewers and stitchers

Textile operatives
Welders and flame cutters

**Transport Equipment Operatives**
Bus drivers
Delivery and route workers
Forklift and tow motor operators
Taxi drivers and chauffeurs
Truck drivers

**Laborers (Except Farm)**
Construction laborers
Freight, material, and stock handlers
Gardeners and groundskeepers

*Source:* U.S. Standard Occupational Classification.

because of its high personal income, light tax bite, and rosy outlook for personal income and jobs through the end of the decade. Little has changed. Midland's average household income—$46,458—ranks first in Texas and seventh in the country. The Texas tax bite is just as forgiving now as it was in 1981. There are no levies on personal income nor any on interest and dividends, and while no one is forgiven retail sales taxes, these take only $291 out of average household incomes. When Midland's after-tax household income is divided by its cost-of-living index of 101, the result is 457.1; multiplying this figure by 10 yields 4,571 points.

Instead of looking at the forecast for job and income growth over the rest of the decade, as we did in the 1981 edition, *Places Rated* now examines actual growth over the latest five-year period for which data are available. From 1978 through 1982, the number of workers on the payroll of Midland's employers increased by nearly 47.62 percent. Personal income also shot up, by 60.56 percent, during that time. Not all of the growth came from the oil patch. Midland also produces semiconductors and is a thriving service center in an otherwise empty part of Texas. Multiplying Midland's percentages for job and income growth by 50 yields 5,409 points. This total, when added to the 4,571 points for adjusted household income, earns for Midland the highest score of any metro area, 9,980 points.

In contrast, Eugene–Springfield's economics rating plunged from 44th in *Places Rated*'s 1981 edition to the very bottom in this edition, basically because of recession. If there is one area in the United States where the local economy depends on a vulnerable industry, it is the timbered parts of the Pacific Northwest. Between 1978 and 1982, some 8,317 jobs departed from Eugene–Springfield. Some say these jobs, mainly in logging and in saw and planing mills, may never return. Even though home building has turned around, the Pacific Northwest lumber industry hasn't, due to stiff price competition from Canadian and southeastern producers. Job losses and shorter hours severely dampened household income growth here, too. Multiplying the sum of Eugene–Springfield's percentages for income growth (24.33) and job loss (−8.98) by 50 works out to only 768 points.

Oregon is one of five states that do not collect sales taxes. But what it passes up at the store, it collects every April 15 from residents filing their income tax returns. Accordingly, Eugene–Springfield's average $25,698 household income figure is reduced by $1,102, to reflect the Oregon personal income tax bite. Dividing after-tax income by the cost-of-living index of 108 and then multiplying by 10 yields 2,277 points. Adding this to the 768 points earned for income and job growth gives the Oregon metro area a score of 3,045, putting it in 329th place.

## Places Rated: Metro Areas Ranked for Personal Economic Outlook

*Places Rated Almanac* focuses on three major criteria to rank metro areas for their economic promise: (1) average household income adjusted for taxes and living costs, (2) rate of income growth, and (3) rate of job expansion. Places that receive tie scores are given the same rank and are listed in alphabetical order.

### Metro Areas from Best to Worst

| Places Rated Rank | Places Rated Score | Places Rated Rank | Places Rated Score | Places Rated Rank | Places Rated Score |
|---|---|---|---|---|---|
| 1. Midland, TX | 9,980 | 13. Colorado Springs, CO | 7,699 | 26. Bridgeport–Milford, CT | 7,197 |
| 2. Lafayette, LA | 9,702 | 14. Anchorage, AK | 7,668 | 27. Fort Myers, FL | 7,166 |
| 3. Portsmouth–Dover– | | 15. Abilene, TX | 7,633 | 28. Denver, CO | 7,164 |
| Rochester, NH–ME | 8,367 | | | 29. Fort Lauderdale–Hollywood– | |
| 4. Enid, OK | 8,268 | 16. Victoria, TX | 7,599 | Pompano Beach, FL | 7,136 |
| 5. Oklahoma City, OK | 8,119 | 17. Odessa, TX | 7,565 | 30. Boulder–Longmont, CO | 7,127 |
| | | 18. Houston, TX | 7,464 | | |
| 6. Atlantic City, NJ | 8,107 | 19. Austin, TX | 7,439 | 31. Tulsa, OK | 7,115 |
| 7. Bryan–College Station, TX | 8,040 | 20. Bradenton, FL | 7,437 | 32. Manchester, NH | 7,101 |
| 8. West Palm Beach–Boca | | | | 33. Melbourne–Titusville– | |
| Raton–Delray Beach, FL | 7,992 | 21. Orlando, FL | 7,413 | Palm Bay, FL | 7,089 |
| 9. Fort Pierce, FL | 7,973 | 22. Nassau–Suffolk, NY | 7,371 | 34. Danbury, CT | 7,060 |
| 10. San Angelo, TX | 7,720 | 23. Tyler, TX | 7,327 | 34. Ocala, FL | 7,060 |
| | | 24. San Jose, CA | 7,270 | | |
| 11. Sarasota, FL | 7,715 | 25. Tampa–St. Petersburg– | | 36. Nashua, NH | 6,962 |
| 12. Dallas, TX | 7,710 | Clearwater, FL | 7,256 | 37. Brockton, MA | 6,900 |

| Places Rated Rank | Places Rated Score | Places Rated Rank | Places Rated Score | Places Rated Rank | Places Rated Score |
|---|---|---|---|---|---|
| 38. Longview–Marshall, TX | 6,898 | 98. Beaumont–Port Arthur, TX | 6,019 | 154. Champaign–Urbana– Rantoul, IL | 5,485 |
| 39. San Antonio, TX | 6,873 | 98. Bismarck, ND | 6,019 | 155. Pittsfield, MA | 5,483 |
| 40. Fort Worth–Arlington, TX | 6,862 | 100. Bergen–Passaic, NJ | 6,016 | | |
| | | | | 156. New Haven–Meriden, CT | 5,478 |
| 41. Wichita Falls, TX | 6,805 | 101. St. Joseph, MO | 5,991 | 157. Topeka, KS | 5,464 |
| 42. Poughkeepsie, NY | 6,746 | 102. Nashville, TN | 5,938 | 158. Oakland, CA | 5,457 |
| 43. Burlington, VT | 6,726 | 103. Springfield, MO | 5,932 | 159. Dothan, AL | 5,453 |
| 44. Corpus Christi, TX | 6,690 | 104. Lubbock, TX | 5,923 | 160. Madison, WI | 5,448 |
| 45. New London–Norwich, CT–RI | 6,672 | 105. Billings, MT | 5,913 | | |
| | | | | 161. Greeley, CO | 5,443 |
| 46. Houma–Thibodaux, LA | 6,662 | 106. Seattle, WA | 5,901 | 162. Augusta, GA–SC | 5,431 |
| 47. Lowell, MA–NH | 6,651 | 107. Lake Charles, LA | 5,872 | 163. Louisville, KY–IN | 5,402 |
| 48. Fort Collins–Loveland, CO | 6,631 | 108. Richmond–Petersburg, VA | 5,870 | 164. Wilmington, NC | 5,390 |
| 49. Daytona Beach, FL | 6,592 | 109. Norfolk–Virginia Beach– Newport News, VA | 5,866 | 165. Springfield, IL | 5,384 |
| 50. Shreveport, LA | 6,585 | 110. Albany–Schenectady– Troy, NY | 5,864 | 166. Eau Claire, WI | 5,348 |
| 51. Bristol, CT | 6,527 | | | 167. Des Moines, IA | 5,346 |
| 51. Lawrence–Haverhill, MA–NH | 6,527 | 111. Bloomington–Normal, IL | 5,863 | 168. Las Cruces, NM | 5,341 |
| 53. New Britain, CT | 6,470 | 112. Omaha, NE–IA | 5,853 | 169. New York, NY | 5,338 |
| 54. New Orleans, LA | 6,453 | 113. Minneapolis–St. Paul, MN–WI | 5,843 | 170. Santa Cruz, CA | 5,335 |
| 55. Norwalk, CT | 6,432 | 114. Miami–Hialeah, FL | 5,840 | | |
| | | 115. Orange County, NY | 5,822 | 171. Richland–Kennewick– Pasco, WA | 5,326 |
| 56. Phoenix, AZ | 6,415 | | | 172. Joplin, MO | 5,324 |
| 57. Huntsville, AL | 6,412 | 116. Santa Barbara–Santa Maria–Lompoc, CA | 5,821 | 173. Harrisburg–Lebanon– Carlisle, PA | 5,322 |
| 58. Raleigh–Durham, NC | 6,405 | 117. Vallejo–Fairfield–Napa, CA | 5,819 | 174. Los Angeles–Long Beach, CA | 5,316 |
| 59. Jacksonville, NC | 6,386 | 118. Biloxi–Gulfport, MS | 5,801 | | |
| 60. Boston, MA | 6,363 | 119. St. Louis, MO–IL | 5,800 | 175. Sacramento, CA | 5,309 |
| | | 120. Alton–Granite City, IL | 5,795 | | |
| 61. Fort Walton Beach, FL | 6,342 | | | 176. Chico, CA | 5,307 |
| 62. Killeen–Temple, TX | 6,331 | 121. Trenton, NJ | 5,772 | 177. Springfield, MA | 5,289 |
| 63. Middlesex–Somerset– Hunterdon, NJ | 6,324 | 122. Lake County, IL | 5,755 | 178. Roanoke, VA | 5,287 |
| 64. Atlanta, GA | 6,315 | 123. Fresno, CA | 5,746 | 179. Columbia, SC | 5,279 |
| 65. Salem–Gloucester, MA | 6,309 | 124. Gainesville, FL | 5,739 | 180. Appleton–Oshkosh– Neenah, WI | 5,275 |
| | | 124. McAllen–Edinburg– Mission, TX | 5,739 | | |
| 66. Baton Rouge, LA | 6,308 | | | 181. Little Rock– North Little Rock, AR | 5,273 |
| 67. Hartford, CT | 6,307 | 126. Albuquerque, NM | 5,727 | 182. Cincinnati, OH–KY–IN | 5,270 |
| 67. Middletown, CT | 6,307 | 127. Santa Rosa–Petaluma, CA | 5,703 | 183. Laredo, TX | 5,264 |
| 69. Rochester, NY | 6,304 | 128. Newark, NJ | 5,690 | 184. Pittsburgh, PA | 5,261 |
| 70. Casper, WY | 6,303 | 129. Burlington, NC | 5,680 | 185. Charleston, WV | 5,257 |
| | | 130. Reno, NV | 5,677 | | |
| 71. Waco, TX | 6,259 | | | 186. Fayetteville, NC | 5,255 |
| 72. Lexington–Fayette, KY | 6,245 | 131. Stockton, CA | 5,672 | 187. Alexandria, LA | 5,254 |
| 73. Amarillo, TX | 6,241 | 132. Bremerton, WA | 5,671 | 188. Albany, GA | 5,250 |
| 74. Anaheim–Santa Ana, CA | 6,220 | 132. Charlotte–Gastonia– Rock Hill, NC–SC | 5,671 | 189. Utica–Rome, NY | 5,226 |
| 75. Sherman–Denison, TX | 6,213 | 134. Macon–Warner Robins, GA | 5,659 | 190. Evansville, IN–KY | 5,206 |
| | | 135. Salinas–Seaside– Monterey, CA | 5,656 | | |
| 76. Portland, ME | 6,186 | | | 191. Chicago, IL | 5,205 |
| 77. Wilmington, DE–NJ–MD | 6,174 | 135. Waterbury, CT | 5,656 | 192. Greensboro–Winston– Salem–High Point, NC | 5,204 |
| 78. Kansas City, KS | 6,166 | 137. Green Bay, WI | 5,650 | 192. Sioux Falls, SD | 5,204 |
| 79. Stamford, CT | 6,158 | 138. La Crosse, WI | 5,648 | 194. Asheville, NC | 5,196 |
| 80. Monmouth–Ocean, NJ | 6,154 | 139. Grand Forks, ND | 5,646 | 195. Athens, GA | 5,193 |
| | | 140. Philadelphia, PA–NJ | 5,638 | | |
| 81. Tucson, AZ | 6,147 | | | 196. Honolulu, HI | 5,187 |
| 82. Jacksonville, FL | 6,139 | 141. Binghamton, NY | 5,614 | 196. Parkersburg–Marietta, WV–OH | 5,187 |
| 83. East St. Louis–Belleville, IL | 6,113 | 142. Fargo–Moorhead, ND–MN | 5,594 | 198. Jackson, MS | 5,186 |
| 84. Lawton, OK | 6,105 | 142. Lakeland–Winter Haven, FL | 5,594 | 199. Kenosha, WI | 5,176 |
| 85. Rochester, MN | 6,099 | 144. Savannah, GA | 5,591 | 200. Bangor, ME | 5,172 |
| | | 145. Reading, PA | 5,587 | | |
| 86. Panama City, FL | 6,083 | | | 201. Glens Falls, NY | 5,166 |
| 87. Washington, DC–MD–VA | 6,072 | 146. Kankakee, IL | 5,579 | 202. Columbus, OH | 5,165 |
| 88. San Francisco, CA | 6,063 | 147. Visalia–Tulare–Porterville, CA | 5,563 | 202. Iowa City, IA | 5,165 |
| 89. Owensboro, KY | 6,062 | 148. Knoxville, TN | 5,537 | 204. Memphis, TN–AR–MS | 5,160 |
| 90. Bakersfield, CA | 6,056 | 148. Monroe, LA | 5,537 | 205. Pawtucket–Woonsocket– Attleboro, RI–MA | 5,154 |
| | | 150. Oxnard–Ventura, CA | 5,514 | | |
| 91. Charlottesville, VA | 6,055 | | | | |
| 92. Wichita, KS | 6,036 | 151. Baltimore, MD | 5,503 | | |
| 93. Las Vegas, NV | 6,035 | 152. San Diego, CA | 5,489 | | |
| 94. Pensacola, FL | 6,029 | 153. St. Cloud, MN | 5,488 | 205. Providence, RI | 5,154 |
| 95. Galveston–Texas City, TX | 6,026 | | | | |
| 96. Tallahassee, FL | 6,021 | | | | |
| 97. Brazoria, TX | 6,020 | | | | |

| Places Rated Rank | Places Rated Score | Places Rated Rank | Places Rated Score | Places Rated Rank | Places Rated Score |
|---|---|---|---|---|---|
| 207. Charleston, SC | 5,153 | 246. Birmingham, AL | 4,843 | 289. Huntington–Ashland, WV–KY–OH | 4,383 |
| 208. Columbia, MO | 5,147 | 247. Florence, SC | 4,842 | 290. Janesville–Beloit, WI | 4,371 |
| 209. Lancaster, PA | 5,120 | 248. Bloomington, IN | 4,829 | | |
| 210. Modesto, CA | 5,107 | 249. Elmira, NY | 4,813 | 291. Terre Haute, IN | 4,353 |
| | | 250. Columbus, GA–AL | 4,812 | 292. Akron, OH | 4,350 |
| 211. Fitchburg–Leominster, MA | 5,098 | | | 293. Lafayette, IN | 4,333 |
| 212. Allentown–Bethlehem, PA–NJ | 5,097 | 251. Kalamazoo, MI | 4,794 | 294. Lima, OH | 4,313 |
| 212. Aurora–Elgin, IL | 5,097 | 252. Texarkana, TX–Texarkana, AR | 4,772 | 295. Wausau, WI | 4,300 |
| 214. Indianapolis, IN | 5,082 | 253. Sheboygan, WI | 4,765 | | |
| 215. El Paso, TX | 5,080 | 254. Lansing–East Lansing, MI | 4,747 | 296. Erie, PA | 4,299 |
| | | 255. Cumberland, MD–WV | 4,741 | 297. Decatur, IL | 4,274 |
| 216. South Bend–Mishawaka, IN | 5,056 | | | 298. Anderson, SC | 4,262 |
| 217. Buffalo, NY | 5,047 | 256. Wheeling, WV–OH | 4,740 | 299. Bellingham, WA | 4,247 |
| 218. Worcester, MA | 5,040 | 257. Anniston, AL | 4,730 | 299. Pine Bluff, AR | 4,247 |
| 219. Vineland–Millville–Bridgeton, NJ | 5,023 | 258. Hickory, NC | 4,728 | | |
| | | 259. Spokane, WA | 4,722 | 301. Altoona, PA | 4,230 |
| 220. Greenville–Spartanburg, SC | 5,012 | 260. Great Falls, MT | 4,697 | 302. Gadsden, AL | 4,220 |
| | | | | 303. Elkhart–Goshen, IN | 4,214 |
| 221. Cedar Rapids, IA | 5,009 | 261. Yuba City, CA | 4,694 | 304. Fort Wayne, IN | 4,195 |
| 222. Davenport–Rock Island–Moline, IA–IL | 4,997 | 262. State College, PA | 4,677 | 305. Johnstown, PA | 4,181 |
| 223. Yakima, WA | 4,986 | 263. Sioux City, IA–NE | 4,648 | | |
| 224. Milwaukee, WI | 4,982 | 264. Pueblo, CO | 4,646 | 306. Peoria, IL | 4,073 |
| 225. Brownsville–Harlingen, TX | 4,968 | 265. Boise City, ID | 4,633 | 307. Sharon, PA | 4,055 |
| | | | | 308. Battle Creek, MI | 4,008 |
| 226. York, PA | 4,946 | 266. Fayetteville–Springdale, AR | 4,631 | 309. Muncie, IN | 3,980 |
| 227. Salt Lake City–Ogden, UT | 4,942 | 266. Joliet, IL | 4,631 | 310. Dubuque, IA | 3,949 |
| 228. New Bedford, MA | 4,937 | 268. Hamilton–Middletown, OH | 4,618 | | |
| 229. Lynchburg, VA | 4,926 | 269. Rockford, IL | 4,592 | 311. Duluth, MN–WI | 3,922 |
| 230. Riverside–San Bernardino, CA | 4,923 | 270. Ann Arbor, MI | 4,579 | 312. Detroit, MI | 3,904 |
| | | | | 313. Youngstown–Warren, OH | 3,894 |
| 231. Olympia, WA | 4,912 | 271. Lawrence, KS | 4,573 | 314. Salem, OR | 3,835 |
| 232. Lincoln, NE | 4,908 | 272. Vancouver, WA | 4,571 | 315. Gary–Hammond, IN | 3,826 |
| 233. Scranton–Wilkes-Barre, PA | 4,907 | 273. Mobile, AL | 4,565 | | |
| 234. Johnson City–Kingsport–Bristol, TN–VA | 4,903 | 274. Portland, OR | 4,535 | 316. Jackson, MI | 3,822 |
| 235. Tuscaloosa, AL | 4,900 | 275. Toledo, OH | 4,534 | 317. Steubenville–Weirton, OH–WV | 3,744 |
| | | 276. Dayton–Springfield, OH | 4,532 | 318. Flint, MI | 3,724 |
| 236. Montgomery, AL | 4,892 | 277. Florence, AL | 4,492 | 319. Saginaw–Bay City–Midland, MI | 3,709 |
| 237. Jersey City, NJ | 4,889 | 278. Danville, VA | 4,491 | 320. Muskegon, MI | 3,708 |
| 238. Tacoma, WA | 4,887 | 278. Pascagoula, MS | 4,491 | | |
| 239. Fall River, MA–RI | 4,884 | 280. Chattanooga, TN–GA | 4,487 | 321. Medford, OR | 3,692 |
| 240. Clarksville–Hopkinsville, TN–KY | 4,880 | 281. Hagerstown, MD | 4,477 | 322. Benton Harbor, MI | 3,635 |
| | | 282. Syracuse, NY | 4,474 | 323. Provo–Orem, UT | 3,459 |
| 241. Cleveland, OH | 4,879 | 283. Niagara Falls, NY | 4,463 | 324. Kokomo, IN | 3,429 |
| 242. Kansas City, MO | 4,865 | 284. Redding, CA | 4,459 | 325. Anderson, IN | 3,370 |
| 243. Fort Smith, AR–OK | 4,849 | 285. Lewiston–Auburn, ME | 4,444 | | |
| 244. Grand Rapids, MI | 4,848 | | | 326. Lorain–Elyria, OH | 3,301 |
| 245. Canton, OH | 4,847 | 286. Racine, WI | 4,415 | 327. Williamsport, PA | 3,288 |
| | | 287. Waterloo–Cedar Falls, IA | 4,407 | 328. Beaver County, PA | 3,119 |
| | | 288. Mansfield, OH | 4,386 | 329. Eugene–Springfield, OR | 3,045 |

## Metro Areas Listed Alphabetically

| Metro Area | Places Rated Rank | Metro Area | Places Rated Rank | Metro Area | Places Rated Rank |
|---|---|---|---|---|---|
| Abilene, TX | 15 | Anaheim–Santa Ana, CA | 74 | Atlantic City, NJ | 6 |
| Akron, OH | 292 | Anchorage, AK | 14 | Augusta, GA–SC | 162 |
| Albany, GA | 188 | Anderson, IN | 325 | Aurora–Elgin, IL | 212 |
| Albany–Schenectady–Troy, NY | 110 | Anderson, SC | 298 | Austin, TX | 19 |
| Albuquerque, NM | 126 | Ann Arbor, MI | 270 | Bakersfield, CA | 90 |
| Alexandria, LA | 187 | Anniston, AL | 257 | Baltimore, MD | 151 |
| Allentown–Bethlehem, PA–NJ | 212 | Appleton–Oshkosh–Neenah, WI | 180 | Bangor, ME | 200 |
| Alton–Granite City, IL | 120 | Asheville, NC | 194 | Baton Rouge, LA | 66 |
| Altoona, PA | 301 | Athens, GA | 195 | Battle Creek, MI | 308 |
| Amarillo, TX | 73 | Atlanta, GA | 64 | Beaumont–Port Arthur, TX | 98 |

| Metro Area | Places Rated Rank | Metro Area | Places Rated Rank | Metro Area | Places Rated Rank |
|---|---|---|---|---|---|
| Beaver County, PA | 328 | Eau Claire, WI | 166 | Kankakee, IL | 146 |
| Bellingham, WA | 299 | El Paso, TX | 215 | Kansas City, KS | 78 |
| Benton Harbor, MI | 322 | Elkhart–Goshen, IN | 303 | Kansas City, MO | 242 |
| Bergen–Passaic, NJ | 100 | Elmira, NY | 249 | Kenosha, WI | 199 |
| Billings, MT | 105 | Enid, OK | 4 | Killeen–Temple, TX | 62 |
| Biloxi–Gulfport, MS | 118 | Erie, PA | 296 | Knoxville, TN | 148 |
| Binghamton, NY | 141 | Eugene–Springfield, OR | 329 | Kokomo, IN | 324 |
| Birmingham, AL | 246 | Evansville, IN–KY | 190 | La Crosse, WI | 138 |
| Bismarck, ND | 98 | Fall River, MA–RI | 239 | Lafayette, IN | 293 |
| Bloomington, IN | 248 | Fargo–Moorhead, ND–MN | 142 | Lafayette, LA | 2 |
| Bloomington–Normal, IL | 111 | Fayetteville, NC | 186 | Lake Charles, LA | 107 |
| Boise City, ID | 265 | Fayetteville–Springdale, AR | 266 | Lake County, IL | 122 |
| Boston, MA | 60 | Fitchburg–Leominster, MA | 211 | Lakeland–Winter Haven, FL | 142 |
| Boulder–Longmont, CO | 30 | Flint, MI | 318 | Lancaster, PA | 209 |
| Bradenton, FL | 20 | Florence, AL | 277 | Lansing–East Lansing, MI | 254 |
| Brazoria, TX | 97 | Florence, SC | 247 | Laredo, TX | 183 |
| Bremerton, WA | 132 | Fort Collins–Loveland, CO | 48 | Las Cruces, NM | 168 |
| Bridgeport–Milford, CT | 26 | Fort Lauderdale–Hollywood–Pompano Beach, FL | 29 | Las Vegas, NV | 93 |
| Bristol, CT | 51 | Fort Myers, FL | 27 | Lawrence, KS | 271 |
| Brockton, MA | 37 | Fort Pierce, FL | 9 | Lawrence–Haverhill, MA–NH | 51 |
| Brownsville–Harlingen, TX | 225 | Fort Smith, AR–OK | 243 | Lawton, OK | 84 |
| Bryan–College Station, TX | 7 | Fort Walton Beach, FL | 61 | Lewiston–Auburn, ME | 285 |
| Buffalo, NY | 217 | Fort Wayne, IN | 304 | Lexington–Fayette, KY | 72 |
| Burlington, NC | 129 | Fort Worth–Arlington, TX | 40 | Lima, OH | 294 |
| Burlington, VT | 43 | Fresno, CA | 123 | Lincoln, NE | 232 |
| Canton, OH | 245 | Gadsden, AL | 302 | Little Rock–North Little Rock, AR | 181 |
| Casper, WY | 70 | Gainesville, FL | 124 | Longview–Marshall, TX | 38 |
| Cedar Rapids, IA | 221 | Galveston–Texas City, TX | 95 | Lorain–Elyria, OH | 326 |
| Champaign–Urbana–Rantoul, IL | 154 | Gary–Hammond, IN | 315 | Los Angeles–Long Beach, CA | 174 |
| Charleston, SC | 207 | Glens Falls, NY | 201 | Louisville, KY–IN | 163 |
| Charleston, WV | 185 | Grand Forks, ND | 139 | Lowell, MA–NH | 47 |
| Charlotte–Gastonia–Rock Hill, NC–SC | 132 | Grand Rapids, MI | 244 | Lubbock, TX | 104 |
| Charlottesville, VA | 91 | Great Falls, MT | 260 | Lynchburg, VA | 229 |
| Chattanooga, TN–GA | 280 | Greeley, CO | 161 | Macon–Warner Robins, GA | 134 |
| Chicago, IL | 191 | Green Bay, WI | 137 | Madison, WI | 160 |
| Chico, CA | 176 | Greensboro–Winston-Salem–High Point, NC | 192 | Manchester, NH | 32 |
| Cincinnati, OH–KY–IN | 182 | Greenville–Spartanburg, SC | 220 | Mansfield, OH | 288 |
| Clarksville–Hopkinsville, TN–KY | 240 | Hagerstown, MD | 281 | McAllen–Edinburg–Mission, TX | 124 |
| Cleveland, OH | 241 | Hamilton–Middletown, OH | 268 | Medford, OR | 321 |
| Colorado Springs, CO | 13 | Harrisburg–Lebanon–Carlisle, PA | 173 | Melbourne–Titusville–Palm Bay, FL | 33 |
| Columbia, MO | 208 | Hartford, CT | 67 | Memphis, TN–AR–MS | 204 |
| Columbia, SC | 179 | Hickory, NC | 258 | Miami–Hialeah, FL | 114 |
| Columbus, GA–AL | 250 | Honolulu, HI | 196 | Middlesex–Somerset–Hunterdon, NJ | 63 |
| Columbus, OH | 202 | Houma–Thibodaux, LA | 46 | Middletown, CT | 67 |
| Corpus Christi, TX | 44 | Houston, TX | 18 | Midland, TX | 1 |
| Cumberland, MD–WV | 255 | Huntington–Ashland, WV–KY–OH | 289 | Milwaukee, WI | 224 |
| Dallas, TX | 12 | Huntsville, AL | 57 | Minneapolis–St. Paul, MN–WI | 113 |
| Danbury, CT | 34 | Indianapolis, IN | 214 | Mobile, AL | 273 |
| Danville, VA | 278 | Iowa City, IA | 202 | Modesto, CA | 210 |
| Davenport–Rock Island–Moline, IA–IL | 222 | Jackson, MI | 316 | Monmouth–Ocean, NJ | 80 |
| Dayton–Springfield, OH | 276 | Jackson, MS | 198 | Monroe, LA | 148 |
| Daytona Beach, FL | 49 | Jacksonville, FL | 82 | Montgomery, AL | 236 |
| Decatur, IL | 297 | Jacksonville, NC | 59 | Muncie, IN | 309 |
| Denver, CO | 28 | Janesville–Beloit, WI | 290 | Muskegon, MI | 320 |
| Des Moines, IA | 167 | Jersey City, NJ | 237 | Nashua, NH | 36 |
| Detroit, MI | 312 | Johnson City–Kingsport–Bristol, TN–VA | 234 | Nashville, TN | 102 |
| Dothan, AL | 159 | Johnstown, PA | 305 | Nassau–Suffolk, NY | 22 |
| Dubuque, IA | 310 | Joliet, IL | 266 | New Bedford, MA | 228 |
| Duluth, MN–WI | 311 | Joplin, MO | 172 | New Britain, CT | 53 |
| East St. Louis–Belleville, IL | 83 | Kalamazoo, MI | 251 | New Haven–Meriden, CT | 156 |
|  |  |  |  | New London–Norwich, CT–RI | 45 |
|  |  |  |  | New Orleans, LA | 54 |

| Metro Area | Places Rated Rank | Metro Area | Places Rated Rank | Metro Area | Places Rated Rank |
|---|---|---|---|---|---|
| New York, NY | 169 | Richland–Kennewick–Pasco, WA | 171 | State College, PA | 262 |
| Newark, NJ | 128 | Richmond–Petersburg, VA | 108 | Steubenville–Weirton, OH–WV | 317 |
| Niagara Falls, NY | 283 | Riverside–San Bernardino, CA | 230 | Stockton, CA | 131 |
| | | Roanoke, VA | 178 | Syracuse, NY | 282 |
| Norfolk–Virginia Beach–Newport News, VA | 109 | Rochester, MN | 85 | Tacoma, WA | 238 |
| Norwalk, CT | 55 | Rochester, NY | 69 | Tallahassee, FL | 96 |
| Oakland, CA | 158 | Rockford, IL | 269 | Tampa–St. Petersburg– Clearwater, FL | 25 |
| Ocala, FL | 34 | Sacramento, CA | 175 | Terre Haute, IN | 291 |
| Odessa, TX | 17 | Saginaw–Bay City–Midland, MI | 319 | Texarkana, TX–Texarkana, AR | 252 |
| | | St. Cloud, MN | 153 | Toledo, OH | 275 |
| Oklahoma City, OK | 5 | | | | |
| Olympia, WA | 231 | St. Joseph, MO | 101 | Topeka, KS | 157 |
| Omaha, NE–IA | 112 | St. Louis, MO–IL | 119 | Trenton, NJ | 121 |
| Orange County, NY | 115 | Salem, OR | 314 | Tucson, AZ | 81 |
| Orlando, FL | 21 | Salem–Gloucester, MA | 65 | Tulsa, OK | 31 |
| | | Salinas–Seaside–Monterey, CA | 135 | Tuscaloosa, AL | 235 |
| Owensboro, KY | 89 | | | | |
| Oxnard–Ventura, CA | 150 | Salt Lake City–Ogden, UT | 227 | Tyler, TX | 23 |
| Panama City, FL | 86 | San Angelo, TX | 10 | Utica–Rome, NY | 189 |
| Parkersburg–Marietta, WV–OH | 196 | San Antonio, TX | 39 | Vallejo–Fairfield–Napa, CA | 117 |
| Pascagoula, MS | 278 | San Diego, CA | 152 | Vancouver, WA | 272 |
| | | San Francisco, CA | 88 | Victoria, TX | 16 |
| Pawtucket–Woonsocket– Attleboro, RI–MA | 205 | San Jose, CA | 24 | Vineland–Millville–Bridgeton, NJ | 219 |
| Pensacola, FL | 94 | Santa Barbara–Santa Maria– Lompoc, CA | 116 | Visalia–Tulare–Porterville, CA | 147 |
| Peoria, IL | 306 | Santa Cruz, CA | 170 | Waco, TX | 71 |
| Philadelphia, PA–NJ | 140 | Santa Rosa–Petaluma, CA | 127 | Washington, DC–MD–VA | 87 |
| Phoenix, AZ | 56 | Sarasota, FL | 11 | Waterbury, CT | 135 |
| Pine Bluff, AR | 299 | | | | |
| Pittsburgh, PA | 184 | Savannah, GA | 144 | Waterloo–Cedar Falls, IA | 287 |
| Pittsfield, MA | 155 | Scranton–Wilkes-Barre, PA | 233 | Wausau, WI | 295 |
| Portland, ME | 76 | Seattle, WA | 106 | West Palm Beach–Boca Raton– Delray Beach, FL | 8 |
| Portland, OR | 274 | Sharon, PA | 307 | Wheeling, WV–OH | 256 |
| | | Sheboygan, WI | 253 | Wichita, KS | 92 |
| Portsmouth–Dover–Rochester, NH–ME | 3 | Sherman–Denison, TX | 75 | Wichita Falls, TX | 41 |
| Poughkeepsie, NY | 42 | Shreveport, LA | 50 | Williamsport, PA | 327 |
| Providence, RI | 205 | Sioux City, IA–NE | 263 | Wilmington, DE–NJ–MD | 77 |
| Provo–Orem, UT | 323 | Sioux Falls, SD | 192 | Wilmington, NC | 164 |
| Pueblo, CO | 264 | South Bend–Mishawaka, IN | 216 | Worcester, MA | 218 |
| | | Spokane, WA | 259 | | |
| Racine, WI | 286 | Springfield, IL | 165 | Yakima, WA | 223 |
| Raleigh–Durham, NC | 58 | Springfield, MA | 177 | York, PA | 226 |
| Reading, PA | 145 | Springfield, MO | 103 | Youngstown–Warren, OH | 313 |
| Redding, CA | 284 | Stamford, CT | 79 | Yuba City, CA | 261 |
| Reno, NV | 130 | | | | |

## Place Profiles: Economic Life in 329 Metro Areas

The following profiles highlight certain economic features in the metro areas. These include the factors used to rank the metro areas—indexes for the costs of housing, food, and miscellaneous goods and services (the last given under the entry Other); household income; local tax bite; income growth; and job growth —along with information about white- and blue-collar workers, cyclical threat of unemployment (see pages 408–409 for more about this), and goods produced.

The information comes from these sources: American Chamber of Commerce Researchers Association,

"Inter-City Cost of Living Index," first quarter, 1984; U.S. Department of Commerce, Bureau of the Census, *1980 Census of Population and Housing*, and Bureau of Economic Analysis, "County and Metropolitan Area Personal Income," *Survey of Current Business*, May 1984; Commerce Clearing House, *State Tax Guide*, 1984, and Internal Revenue Service, *Your Individual Income Tax*, 1984; U.S. Department of Labor, Bureau of Labor Statistics Employment and Earnings branch, unpublished data, 1984.

New England metro area figures for household

income and for recent five-year growth in personal income and jobs are derived from New England County Metropolitan Area figures.

Asterisks beside figures for cost indexes of food and miscellaneous goods indicate that these numbers were derived from prices in the nearest metro area or city, since information was not available for the metro area in question. Honolulu's figures for these indexes were based on cost-of-living premiums paid to government employees in Hawaii.

A star preceding a metro area's name highlights it as one of the top 25 places for economic outlook.

| Metro Area | Living Costs (U.S. Avg.=100) | Average Household Income and Taxes | Occupations (U.S. Avg.=100) | Five-Year Growth Income and Jobs | Places Rated Score | Places Rated Rank |
|---|---|---|---|---|---|---|
| ★ Abilene, TX | Housing: 74<br>Food: 104<br>Other: 97 | Income: $32,262<br>Taxes: $235<br>Bite: 0.73% | Blue-Collar Index: 105<br>White-Collar Index: 95<br>Unemployment Threat: Moderate | Income: 52.45%<br>Jobs: 28.24% | 7,633 | 15 |
| | Goods: Food products, musical instruments, women's sportswear, tire retreads, candy, ice cream, fishing tackle, cotton, cattle | | | | | |
| Akron, OH | Housing: 98<br>Food: 103<br>Other: 100 | Income: $29,560<br>Taxes: $832<br>Bite: 2.81% | Blue-Collar Index: 106<br>White-Collar Index: 94<br>Unemployment Threat: Moderate | Income: 35.10%<br>Jobs: −5.56% | 4,350 | 292 |
| | Goods: Rubber and rubber products, rubberized fabric, fishing tackle, surgical instruments, clay, storm windows, chemicals | | | | | |
| Albany, GA | Housing: 88<br>Food: 99<br>Other: 98 | Income: $24,234<br>Taxes: $856<br>Bite: 3.53% | Blue-Collar Index: 109<br>White-Collar Index: 91<br>Unemployment Threat: Moderate | Income: 43.41%<br>Jobs: 11.84% | 5,250 | 188 |
| | Goods: Textile products, paper, rubber and plastic products, thread, golf clubs, cartons, pecans, peanuts | | | | | |
| Albany–Schenectady–Troy, NY | Housing: 95<br>Food: 99<br>Other: 98 | Income: $31,458<br>Taxes: $1,304<br>Bite: 4.15% | Blue-Collar Index: 92<br>White-Collar Index: 108<br>Unemployment Threat: Low | Income: 48.63%<br>Jobs: 6.48% | 5,864 | 110 |
| | Goods: Pork products, sausage, paper, men's shirts, billiard balls, electrical equipment and appliances, motors and generators, axle grease, steam and gas turbines, blankets | | | | | |
| Albuquerque, NM | Housing: 101<br>Food: 99*<br>Other: 100* | Income: $29,753<br>Taxes: $248<br>Bite: 0.83% | Blue-Collar Index: 90<br>White-Collar Index: 110<br>Unemployment Threat: Low | Income: 42.69%<br>Jobs: 12.84% | 5,727 | 126 |
| | Goods: Neon and electric signs, hardware, machine tools, stone, clay | | | | | |
| Alexandria, LA | Housing: 70<br>Food: 107<br>Other: 101 | Income: $23,078<br>Taxes: $220<br>Bite: 0.95% | Blue-Collar Index: 106<br>White-Collar Index: 94<br>Unemployment Threat: Moderate | Income: 48.32%<br>Jobs: 5.39% | 5,254 | 187 |
| | Goods: Fabricated metal, sashes and doors, valves, corn, sugarcane, meat products, lumber and wood products (especially furniture and wood flooring) | | | | | |
| Allentown–Bethlehem, PA–NJ | Housing: 99<br>Food: 99*<br>Other: 106* | Income: $31,856<br>Taxes: $954<br>Bite: 2.99% | Blue-Collar Index: 120<br>White-Collar Index: 80<br>Unemployment Threat: High | Income: 42.57%<br>Jobs: −1.22% | 5,097 | 212 |
| | Goods: Steel and primary metals, electrical appliances, autos, trucks, buses, textiles, blasting powder, hats, marine pumps | | | | | |
| Alton–Granite City, IL | Housing: 78<br>Food: 95*<br>Other: 101* | Income: $30,680<br>Taxes: $994<br>Bite: 3.24% | Blue-Collar Index: 113<br>White-Collar Index: 87<br>Unemployment Threat: Moderate | Income: 38.71%<br>Jobs: 11.22% | 5,795 | 120 |
| | Goods: Coal mining, railway equipment, corn syrup, firebrick, tar and creosote | | | | | |
| Altoona, PA | Housing: 74<br>Food: 98<br>Other: 100 | Income: $24,181<br>Taxes: $747<br>Bite: 3.09% | Blue-Collar Index: 121<br>White-Collar Index: 79<br>Unemployment Threat: High | Income: 39.04%<br>Jobs: −7.10% | 4,230 | 301 |
| | Goods: Candy, potato chips, meat and meat products, dairy products, paper, locomotives, shuttlecocks, copper and aluminum tubes, bathing suits | | | | | |
| Amarillo, TX | Housing: 78<br>Food: 103<br>Other: 104 | Income: $32,452<br>Taxes: $235<br>Bite: 0.72% | Blue-Collar Index: 106<br>White-Collar Index: 94<br>Unemployment Threat: Moderate | Income: 41.15%<br>Jobs: 14.39% | 6,241 | 73 |
| | Goods: Flour, wheat, corn, sorghum, clothing, lumber, printing, carbon black, helium, zinc | | | | | |
| Anaheim–Santa Ana, CA | Housing: 192<br>Food: 95<br>Other: 105 | Income: $38,996<br>Taxes: $1,387<br>Bite: 3.56% | Blue-Collar Index: 92<br>White-Collar Index: 108<br>Unemployment Threat: Low | Income: 48.32%<br>Jobs: 21.97% | 6,220 | 74 |
| | Goods: Computer components, fire alarms, electric meters, hand tools, aircraft parts, mobile homes | | | | | |

| Metro Area | Living Costs (U.S. Avg.=100) | Average Household Income and Taxes | Occupations (U.S. Avg.=100) | Five-Year Growth Income and Jobs | Places Rated Score | Places Rated Rank |
|---|---|---|---|---|---|---|
| ★ Anchorage, AK | Housing: 146<br>Food: 139<br>Other: 138 | Income: $51,601<br>Taxes: None<br>Bite: None | Blue-Collar Index: 84<br>White-Collar Index: 116<br>Unemployment Threat: Low | Income: 51.44%<br>Jobs: 29.24% | 7,668 | 14 |
| | Goods: Printing and publishing, seafood, lumber and wood products, furs | | | | | |
| Anderson, IN | Housing: 68<br>Food: 96*<br>Other: 99* | Income: $26,765<br>Taxes: $883<br>Bite: 3.30% | Blue-Collar Index: 126<br>White-Collar Index: 74<br>Unemployment Threat: High | Income: 27.67%<br>Jobs: −20.47% | 3,370 | 325 |
| | Goods: Auto electrical equipment, glass and brick, clay, pumps, playground equipment | | | | | |
| Anderson, SC | Housing: 69<br>Food: 95*<br>Other: 92* | Income: $23,038<br>Taxes: $727<br>Bite: 3.16% | Blue-Collar Index: 134<br>White-Collar Index: 66<br>Unemployment Threat: High | Income: 34.53%<br>Jobs: −3.06% | 4,262 | 298 |
| | Goods: Lumber, textiles, vacuum cleaners, waxing machines, fiberglass | | | | | |
| Ann Arbor, MI | Housing: 132<br>Food: 100*<br>Other: 102* | Income: $32,556<br>Taxes: $1,530<br>Bite: 4.70% | Blue-Collar Index: 89<br>White-Collar Index: 111<br>Unemployment Threat: Low | Income: 32.96%<br>Jobs: 4.19% | 4,579 | 270 |
| | Goods: Transportation equipment, bearings and springs, precision instruments, drill heads, awnings, cameras | | | | | |
| Anniston, AL | Housing: 66<br>Food: 94*<br>Other: 90* | Income: $22,254<br>Taxes: $714<br>Bite: 3.21% | Blue-Collar Index: 120<br>White-Collar Index: 80<br>Unemployment Threat: High | Income: 38.73%<br>Jobs: 2.69% | 4,730 | 257 |
| | Goods: Textiles, shirts, cloth, cast-iron pipe and other metals, fire hydrants, refrigerators | | | | | |
| Appleton–Oshkosh–Neenah, WI | Housing: 94<br>Food: 94<br>Other: 102 | Income: $30,444<br>Taxes: $1,362<br>Bite: 4.47% | Blue-Collar Index: 115<br>White-Collar Index: 85<br>Unemployment Threat: Moderate | Income: 39.02%<br>Jobs: 6.53% | 5,275 | 180 |
| | Goods: Paper, paper products, farm machinery, wire, canned food, garbage trucks, autos, overalls, plastic buoys | | | | | |
| Asheville, NC | Housing: 81<br>Food: 93*<br>Other: 93* | Income: $25,990<br>Taxes: $964<br>Bite: 3.71% | Blue-Collar Index: 115<br>White-Collar Index: 85<br>Unemployment Threat: Moderate | Income: 41.43%<br>Jobs: 5.62% | 5,196 | 194 |
| | Goods: Electrical equipment, textiles (especially nylon, rayon, and cotton), baby food, dresses, cigarette paper, burley tobacco | | | | | |
| Athens, GA | Housing: 80<br>Food: 96<br>Other: 99 | Income: $23,251<br>Taxes: $808<br>Bite: 3.48% | Blue-Collar Index: 106<br>White-Collar Index: 94<br>Unemployment Threat: Moderate | Income: 39.00%<br>Jobs: 15.54% | 5,193 | 195 |
| | Goods: Hosiery, tapestries, fertilizer, overalls, clocks, electric motors | | | | | |
| Atlanta, GA | Housing: 100<br>Food: 104<br>Other: 100 | Income: $32,452<br>Taxes: $1,239<br>Bite: 3.82% | Blue-Collar Index: 75<br>White-Collar Index: 125<br>Unemployment Threat: Low | Income: 44.10%<br>Jobs: 20.40% | 6,315 | 64 |
| | Goods: Automobiles, airplanes, candy, cottonseed oil, flour, printing and publishing, furniture | | | | | |
| ★ Atlantic City, NJ | Housing: 133<br>Food: 108*<br>Other: 105* | Income: $33,424<br>Taxes: $898<br>Bite: 2.69% | Blue-Collar Index: 100<br>White-Collar Index: 100<br>Unemployment Threat: Moderate | Income: 59.84%<br>Jobs: 46.69% | 8,107 | 6 |
| | Goods: Clothing, bottles and glassware, rubber and plastics, saltwater taffy, reed furniture, baby carriages, distilling | | | | | |
| Augusta, GA–SC | Housing: 75<br>Food: 98<br>Other: 97 | Income: $25,813<br>Taxes: $917<br>Bite: 3.55% | Blue-Collar Index: 110<br>White-Collar Index: 90<br>Unemployment Threat: Moderate | Income: 44.93%<br>Jobs: 7.12% | 5,431 | 162 |
| | Goods: Cotton textiles and cloth, rayon, fertilizer, brick and tile | | | | | |
| Aurora–Elgin, IL | Housing: 125<br>Food: 100*<br>Other: 106* | Income: $35,552<br>Taxes: $1,121<br>Bite: 3.15% | Blue-Collar Index: 112<br>White-Collar Index: 88<br>Unemployment Threat: Moderate | Income: 40.89%<br>Jobs: 0.11% | 5,097 | 212 |
| | Goods: Railroad coaches, sand and gravel, furniture, skirts and shirts, street sweepers, watches | | | | | |
| ★ Austin, TX | Housing: 106<br>Food: 105*<br>Other: 95* | Income: $31,497<br>Taxes: $225<br>Bite: 0.71% | Blue-Collar Index: 88<br>White-Collar Index: 112<br>Unemployment Threat: Low | Income: 51.60%<br>Jobs: 35.85% | 7,439 | 19 |
| | Goods: Electrical instruments, semiconductors, furniture, turkeys, dairy products, fiberglass boats | | | | | |
| Bakersfield, CA | Housing: 97<br>Food: 98<br>Other: 109 | Income: $28,958<br>Taxes: $800<br>Bite: 2.76% | Blue-Collar Index: 106<br>White-Collar Index: 94<br>Unemployment Threat: Moderate | Income: 43.26%<br>Jobs: 22.64% | 6,056 | 90 |
| | Goods: Oil-well tools, paint, pumps, fruit, potatoes, wheat, rubber and plastic goods, guitars | | | | | |

| Metro Area | Living Costs (U.S. Avg.=100) | Average Household Income and Taxes | Occupations (U.S. Avg.=100) | Five-Year Growth Income and Jobs | Places Rated Score | Places Rated Rank |
|---|---|---|---|---|---|---|
| Baltimore, MD | Housing: 110<br>Food: 99*<br>Other: 106* | Income: $32,368<br>Taxes: $1,267<br>Bite: 3.91% | Blue-Collar Index: 98<br>White-Collar Index: 102<br>Unemployment Threat: Low | Income: 44.52%<br>Jobs: 6.86% | 5,503 | 151 |
| | Goods: Electrical appliances, iron and steel, copper, wire and cable, ships, spices and flavorings | | | | | |
| Bangor, ME | Housing: 87<br>Food: 94*<br>Other: 97* | Income: $24,256<br>Taxes: $646<br>Bite: 2.66% | Blue-Collar Index: 96<br>White-Collar Index: 104<br>Unemployment Threat: Low | Income: 42.37%<br>Jobs: 9.76% | 5,172 | 200 |
| | Goods: Writing paper, lumber, canoes, potato chips, shoes | | | | | |
| Baton Rouge, LA | Housing: 97<br>Food: 98<br>Other: 95 | Income: $30,867<br>Taxes: $319<br>Bite: 1.03% | Blue-Collar Index: 103<br>White-Collar Index: 97<br>Unemployment Threat: Moderate | Income: 47.48%<br>Jobs: 15.05% | 6,308 | 66 |
| | Goods: Petrochemicals, acids, alcohol, coke, soda ash, synthetic rubber | | | | | |
| Battle Creek, MI | Housing: 76<br>Food: 95*<br>Other: 106* | Income: $29,868<br>Taxes: $1,387<br>Bite: 4.64% | Blue-Collar Index: 116<br>White-Collar Index: 84<br>Unemployment Threat: High | Income: 32.53%<br>Jobs: −14.97% | 4,008 | 308 |
| | Goods: Breakfast cereals, pumps, auto valves, steel and wire | | | | | |
| Beaumont–Port Arthur, TX | Housing: 75<br>Food: 104<br>Other: 107 | Income: $33,398<br>Taxes: $235<br>Bite: 0.70% | Blue-Collar Index: 120<br>White-Collar Index: 80<br>Unemployment Threat: High | Income: 45.41%<br>Jobs: 3.64% | 6,019 | 98 |
| | Goods: Petrochemicals, ships, oil-well equipment, wood products, rice, agricultural equipment | | | | | |
| Beaver County, PA | Housing: 94<br>Food: 107<br>Other: 106 | Income: $27,695<br>Taxes: $837<br>Bite: 3.02% | Blue-Collar Index: 126<br>White-Collar Index: 74<br>Unemployment Threat: High | Income: 31.93%<br>Jobs: −22.73% | 3,119 | 328 |
| | Goods: Steel tubing, ceramics, paint, cork, coal | | | | | |
| Bellingham, WA | Housing: 100<br>Food: 109*<br>Other: 106* | Income: $27,140<br>Taxes: $443<br>Bite: 1.63% | Blue-Collar Index: 106<br>White-Collar Index: 94<br>Unemployment Threat: Moderate | Income: 31.34%<br>Jobs: 2.25% | 4,247 | 299 |
| | Goods: Salmon packing, shingles, paper, cement, frozen food | | | | | |
| Benton Harbor, MI | Housing: 81<br>Food: 99<br>Other: 104 | Income: $27,401<br>Taxes: $1,268<br>Bite: 4.63% | Blue-Collar Index: 114<br>White-Collar Index: 86<br>Unemployment Threat: Moderate | Income: 32.36%<br>Jobs: −15.87% | 3,635 | 322 |
| | Goods: Washing machines, fruit packing, recreational vehicles, steel castings, vacuum pumps | | | | | |
| Bergen–Passaic, NJ | Housing: 175<br>Food: 108*<br>Other: 105* | Income: $43,240<br>Taxes: $1,201<br>Bite: 2.78% | Blue-Collar Index: 94<br>White-Collar Index: 106<br>Unemployment Threat: Low | Income: 49.18%<br>Jobs: 8.86% | 6,016 | 100 |
| | Goods: Scales, bowling balls, precision instruments, light fixtures, auto seat covers, freight cars, underwear | | | | | |
| Billings, MT | Housing: 100<br>Food: 110<br>Other: 104 | Income: $31,592<br>Taxes: $759<br>Bite: 2.40% | Blue-Collar Index: 97<br>White-Collar Index: 103<br>Unemployment Threat: Low | Income: 41.44%<br>Jobs: 17.51% | 5,913 | 105 |
| | Goods: Sugar, flour, beets, wheat, beans, beef, refined oil, printing, metal ornaments | | | | | |
| Biloxi–Gulfport, MS | Housing: 77<br>Food: 107*<br>Other: 95* | Income: $23,274<br>Taxes: $558<br>Bite: 2.40% | Blue-Collar Index: 107<br>White-Collar Index: 93<br>Unemployment Threat: Moderate | Income: 46.70%<br>Jobs: 18.84% | 5,801 | 118 |
| | Goods: Cat food, seafood canning, wood building products, clothing, tents and awnings, ships and boats | | | | | |
| Binghamton, NY | Housing: 99<br>Food: 96<br>Other: 104 | Income: $30,318<br>Taxes: $1,234<br>Bite: 4.07% | Blue-Collar Index: 101<br>White-Collar Index: 99<br>Unemployment Threat: Moderate | Income: 48.23%<br>Jobs: 5.89% | 5,614 | 141 |
| | Goods: Electrical equipment, instruments, shoes, photographic goods, stereo equipment, fast-freezer units, flexible shafting | | | | | |
| Birmingham, AL | Housing: 82<br>Food: 95<br>Other: 108 | Income: $27,835<br>Taxes: $876<br>Bite: 3.15% | Blue-Collar Index: 105<br>White-Collar Index: 95<br>Unemployment Threat: Moderate | Income: 37.40%<br>Jobs: 2.70% | 4,843 | 245 |
| | Goods: Primary metals (especially iron and steel), pipes and plates, stoves, caskets, truck trailers, airplanes | | | | | |
| Bismarck, ND | Housing: 100<br>Food: 100*<br>Other: 96* | Income: $32,077<br>Taxes: $468<br>Bite: 1.46% | Blue-Collar Index: 88<br>White-Collar Index: 112<br>Unemployment Threat: Low | Income: 42.47%<br>Jobs: 14.05% | 6,019 | 98 |
| | Goods: Farm machinery, woodworking, printing, food processing | | | | | |

| Metro Area | Living Costs (U.S. Avg.=100) | Average Household Income and Taxes | Occupations (U.S. Avg.=100) | Five-Year Growth Income and Jobs | Places Rated Score | Places Rated Rank |
|---|---|---|---|---|---|---|
| Bloomington, IN | Housing: 85<br>Food: 95<br>Other: 102 | Income: $21,851<br>Taxes: $796<br>Bite: 3.64% | Blue-Collar Index: 91<br>White-Collar Index: 109<br>Unemployment Threat: Low | Income: 39.43%<br>Jobs: 12.35% | 4,829 | 248 |
| | Goods: Radios, televisions, railroad ties, elevators, printing and publishing, limestone | | | | | |
| Bloomington–Normal, IL | Housing: 104<br>Food: 105*<br>Other: 98* | Income: $30,713<br>Taxes: $995<br>Bite: 3.24% | Blue-Collar Index: 91<br>White-Collar Index: 109<br>Unemployment Threat: Low | Income: 42.29%<br>Jobs: 16.69% | 5,863 | 111 |
| | Goods: Vacuum cleaners, farm machinery, feeds, dairy products | | | | | |
| Boise City, ID | Housing: 99<br>Food: 104*<br>Other: 99* | Income: $30,736<br>Taxes: $1,406<br>Bite: 4.57% | Blue-Collar Index: 88<br>White-Collar Index: 112<br>Unemployment Threat: Low | Income: 31.56%<br>Jobs: 2.44% | 4,633 | 265 |
| | Goods: Machinery, lumber and wood products, food (especially potatoes and grain) | | | | | |
| Boston, MA | Housing: 139<br>Food: 94*<br>Other: 97* | Income: $36,644<br>Taxes: $1,695<br>Bite: 4.63% | Blue-Collar Index: 89<br>White-Collar Index: 111<br>Unemployment Threat: Low | Income: 53.86%<br>Jobs: 12.08% | 6,363 | 60 |
| | Goods: Computers, missiles and missile-guidance systems, ships, shoes and boots, medical and navigational instruments, textile products; nation's foremost fishing port and wool market | | | | | |
| Boulder–Longmont, CO | Housing: 143<br>Food: 105<br>Other: 102 | Income: $35,599<br>Taxes: $870<br>Bite: 2.44% | Blue-Collar Index: 90<br>White-Collar Index: 110<br>Unemployment Threat: Low | Income: 58.27%<br>Jobs: 26.38% | 7,127 | 30 |
| | Goods: Copy machines, space hardware, electronic equipment, backpacks | | | | | |
| ★ Bradenton, FL | Housing: 99<br>Food: 97*<br>Other: 101* | Income: $30,831<br>Taxes: $324<br>Bite: 1.05% | Blue-Collar Index: 103<br>White-Collar Index: 97<br>Unemployment Threat: Moderate | Income: 52.72%<br>Jobs: 34.38% | 7,437 | 20 |
| | Goods: Fresh vegetables, flowers, soft drinks, bottles, transportation equipment | | | | | |
| Brazoria, TX | Housing: 101<br>Food: 103*<br>Other: 107* | Income: $31,055<br>Taxes: $225<br>Bite: 0.72% | Blue-Collar Index: 120<br>White-Collar Index: 80<br>Unemployment Threat: High | Income: 42.94%<br>Jobs: 18.18% | 6,020 | 97 |
| | Goods: Chemical oil and gas production, cotton, rice and soybeans | | | | | |
| Bremerton, WA | Housing: 109<br>Food: 103*<br>Other: 112* | Income: $32,631<br>Taxes: $506<br>Bite: 1.55% | Blue-Collar Index: 107<br>White-Collar Index: 93<br>Unemployment Threat: Moderate | Income: 38.87%<br>Jobs: 15.60% | 5,671 | 132 |
| | Goods: Shipbuilding, meat packing, lumber, dairy products | | | | | |
| Bridgeport–Milford, CT | Housing: 161<br>Food: 110*<br>Other: 103* | Income: $47,258<br>Taxes: $546<br>Bite: 1.16% | Blue-Collar Index: 104<br>White-Collar Index: 96<br>Unemployment Threat: Moderate | Income: 53.37%<br>Jobs: 17.60% | 7,197 | 26 |
| | Goods: Airplane engines, firearms, ammunition, knives, adding machines, girdles, helicopters | | | | | |
| Bristol, CT | Housing: 120<br>Food: 110*<br>Other: 103* | Income: $37,565<br>Taxes: $477<br>Bite: 1.27% | Blue-Collar Index: 120<br>White-Collar Index: 80<br>Unemployment Threat: High | Income: 52.28%<br>Jobs: 12.04% | 6,527 | 51 |
| | Goods: Screw machine products, glass cutters, knives, sporting equipment, ball bearings, watches | | | | | |
| Brockton, MA | Housing: 99<br>Food: 94*<br>Other: 97* | Income: $36,644<br>Taxes: $1,695<br>Bite: 4.63% | Blue-Collar Index: 106<br>White-Collar Index: 94<br>Unemployment Threat: Moderate | Income: 53.86%<br>Jobs: 12.08% | 6,900 | 37 |
| | Goods: Shoe welts, soles and heels, garments, boxes, machine tools | | | | | |
| Brownsville–Harlingen, TX | Housing: 64<br>Food: 99<br>Other: 98 | Income: $17,903<br>Taxes: $146<br>Bite: 0.82% | Blue-Collar Index: 111<br>White-Collar Index: 89<br>Unemployment Threat: Moderate | Income: 41.05%<br>Jobs: 16.03% | 4,968 | 225 |
| | Goods: Palm-leaf hats, clothing, cotton bandages | | | | | |
| ★ Bryan–College Station, TX | Housing: 99<br>Food: 103*<br>Other: 100* | Income: $24,156<br>Taxes: $192<br>Bite: 0.79% | Blue-Collar Index: 92<br>White-Collar Index: 108<br>Unemployment Threat: Low | Income: 60.35%<br>Jobs: 52.53% | 8,040 | 7 |
| | Goods: Cotton gins, aluminum windows, concrete blocks, printing and publishing, corn, cotton, cattle, poultry | | | | | |
| Buffalo, NY | Housing: 97<br>Food: 104<br>Other: 97 | Income: $31,248<br>Taxes: $1,291<br>Bite: 4.13% | Blue-Collar Index: 104<br>White-Collar Index: 96<br>Unemployment Threat: Moderate | Income: 42.38%<br>Jobs: −2.57% | 5,047 | 217 |
| | Goods: Steel, steel rolling and finishing, cast metals, aircraft parts, electrical goods | | | | | |
| Burlington, NC | Housing: 74<br>Food: 96<br>Other: 92 | Income: $26,662<br>Taxes: $1,007<br>Bite: 3.78% | Blue-Collar Index: 127<br>White-Collar Index: 73<br>Unemployment Threat: High | Income: 42.97%<br>Jobs: 10.26% | 5,680 | 129 |
| | Goods: Textiles, apparel, electrical goods, tobacco products, lumber | | | | | |

| Metro Area | Living Costs (U.S. Avg.=100) | Average Household Income and Taxes | Occupations (U.S. Avg.=100) | Five-Year Growth Income and Jobs | Places Rated Score | Places Rated Rank |
|---|---|---|---|---|---|---|
| Burlington, VT | Housing: 116<br>Food: 99*<br>Other: 98* | Income: $29,582<br>Taxes: $935<br>Bite: 3.16% | Blue-Collar Index: 89<br>White-Collar Index: 111<br>Unemployment Threat: Low | Income: 51.67%<br>Jobs: 28.79% | 6,726 | 43 |
| | Goods: Machine guns, maple furniture, kitchen equipment, printing and publishing, computer parts | | | | | |
| Canton, OH | Housing: 88<br>Food: 89<br>Other: 91 | Income: $29,089<br>Taxes: $818<br>Bite: 2.81% | Blue-Collar Index: 118<br>White-Collar Index: 82<br>Unemployment Threat: High | Income: 37.53%<br>Jobs: −4.14% | 4,847 | 245 |
| | Goods: Ball and roller bearings, safes, locks, office equipment, gasoline and diesel engines, electric sweepers | | | | | |
| Casper, WY | Housing: 118<br>Food: 110<br>Other: 106 | Income: $43,389<br>Taxes: $302<br>Bite: 0.70% | Blue-Collar Index: 106<br>White-Collar Index: 94<br>Unemployment Threat: Moderate | Income: 37.38%<br>Jobs: 11.74% | 6,303 | 70 |
| | Goods: Mining, food processing, bottling, ships, oil | | | | | |
| Cedar Rapids, IA | Housing: 93<br>Food: 94<br>Other: 97 | Income: $33,166<br>Taxes: $1,131<br>Bite: 3.41% | Blue-Collar Index: 105<br>White-Collar Index: 95<br>Unemployment Threat: Moderate | Income: 35.25%<br>Jobs: −2.52% | 5,009 | 221 |
| | Goods: Cereal grains, syrups, dairy products, radio and electronic equipment, road machinery, cranes, gravel crushers | | | | | |
| Champaign–Urbana–Rantoul, IL | Housing: 103<br>Food: 96<br>Other: 102 | Income: $26,695<br>Taxes: $875<br>Bite: 3.28% | Blue-Collar Index: 86<br>White-Collar Index: 114<br>Unemployment Threat: Low | Income: 39.26%<br>Jobs: 19.33% | 5,485 | 154 |
| | Goods: Paper cups, bleacher seats, railroad registers, soybean oil | | | | | |
| Charleston, SC | Housing: 89<br>Food: 95*<br>Other: 102* | Income: $24,038<br>Taxes: $779<br>Bite: 3.24% | Blue-Collar Index: 107<br>White-Collar Index: 93<br>Unemployment Threat: Moderate | Income: 43.23%<br>Jobs: 10.87% | 5,153 | 207 |
| | Goods: Pulp and paper, baking powder, machinery, textiles and apparel, creosoted timber, canned oysters | | | | | |
| Charleston, WV | Housing: 93<br>Food: 108<br>Other: 101 | Income: $30,775<br>Taxes: $994<br>Bite: 3.23% | Blue-Collar Index: 102<br>White-Collar Index: 98<br>Unemployment Threat: Moderate | Income: 36.74%<br>Jobs: 8.24% | 5,257 | 185 |
| | Goods: Flat glass, mining equipment, chemicals, coal, oil, bricks, armored cars | | | | | |
| Charlotte–Gastonia–Rock Hill, NC–SC | Housing: 86<br>Food: 93<br>Other: 93 | Income: $28,904<br>Taxes: $1,121<br>Bite: 3.88% | Blue-Collar Index: 115<br>White-Collar Index: 85<br>Unemployment Threat: Moderate | Income: 41.29%<br>Jobs: 10.39% | 5,671 | 132 |
| | Goods: Hosiery, yarn, cotton textiles, farm implements, flour, detergents, rope, iron pipe, meat products, chlorine | | | | | |
| Charlottesville, VA | Housing: 114<br>Food: 103*<br>Other: 102* | Income: $28,468<br>Taxes: $1,019<br>Bite: 3.58% | Blue-Collar Index: 91<br>White-Collar Index: 109<br>Unemployment Threat: Low | Income: 50.31%<br>Jobs: 19.50% | 6,055 | 91 |
| | Goods: Telephone and telegraph apparatus, semiconductors, ice cream, soft drinks | | | | | |
| Chattanooga, TN–GA | Housing: 74<br>Food: 98<br>Other: 97 | Income: $25,782<br>Taxes: $314<br>Bite: 1.22% | Blue-Collar Index: 114<br>White-Collar Index: 86<br>Unemployment Threat: Moderate | Income: 32.68%<br>Jobs: −0.82% | 4,487 | 280 |
| | Goods: Carpets, food and beverages, auto seat covers, textiles, fabricated metal products | | | | | |
| Chicago, IL | Housing: 131<br>Food: 100<br>Other: 106 | Income: $36,593<br>Taxes: $1,171<br>Bite: 3.20% | Blue-Collar Index: 98<br>White-Collar Index: 102<br>Unemployment Threat: Low | Income: 37.01%<br>Jobs: 5.48% | 5,205 | 191 |
| | Goods: Meat products, radios, televisions, musical instruments, candy, furniture, diesel engines, auto accessories | | | | | |
| Chico, CA | Housing: 103<br>Food: 99*<br>Other: 100* | Income: $26,863<br>Taxes: $699<br>Bite: 2.60% | Blue-Collar Index: 97<br>White-Collar Index: 103<br>Unemployment Threat: Low | Income: 37.25%<br>Jobs: 17.09% | 5,307 | 176 |
| | Goods: Pruning saws, almonds, conveyers, fruit drying | | | | | |
| Cincinnati, OH–KY–IN | Housing: 98<br>Food: 102*<br>Other: 96* | Income: $31,427<br>Taxes: $902<br>Bite: 2.87% | Blue-Collar Index: 104<br>White-Collar Index: 96<br>Unemployment Threat: Moderate | Income: 38.72%<br>Jobs: 4.37% | 5,270 | 182 |
| | Goods: Machine tools, robots, chemicals, soap, refrigerators, bread, beverages, transportation equipment | | | | | |
| Clarksville–Hopkinsville, TN–KY | Housing: 72<br>Food: 98*<br>Other: 102* | Income: $22,884<br>Taxes: $299<br>Bite: 1.31% | Blue-Collar Index: 112<br>White-Collar Index: 88<br>Unemployment Threat: Moderate | Income: 38.71%<br>Jobs: 8.14% | 4,880 | 240 |
| | Goods: Shoes, cowboy boots, cigars, meat, snuff, hogsheads, appliance parts | | | | | |

| Metro Area | Living Costs (U.S. Avg.=100) | Average Household Income and Taxes | Occupations (U.S. Avg.=100) | Five-Year Growth Income and Jobs | Places Rated Score | Places Rated Rank |
|---|---|---|---|---|---|---|
| Cleveland, OH | Housing: 110<br>Food: 99<br>Other: 105 | Income: $35,720<br>Taxes: $1,067<br>Bite: 2.99% | Blue-Collar Index: 104<br>White-Collar Index: 96<br>Unemployment Threat: Moderate | Income: 37.41%<br>Jobs: −5.21% | 4,879 | 241 |
| | Goods: Machine tools, nuts and bolts, iron and steel, auto parts, paints and lacquers, chemicals | | | | | |
| ★ Colorado Springs, CO | Housing: 102<br>Food: 102<br>Other: 97 | Income: $29,380<br>Taxes: $660<br>Bite: 2.25% | Blue-Collar Index: 95<br>White-Collar Index: 105<br>Unemployment Threat: Low | Income: 58.05%<br>Jobs: 38.49% | 7,699 | 13 |
| | Goods: Electronic components, shell fuses, animal vaccines, brooms, engine mounts, motors, instruments | | | | | |
| Columbia, MO | Housing: 92<br>Food: 91<br>Other: 94 | Income: $25,813<br>Taxes: $631<br>Bite: 2.44% | Blue-Collar Index: 81<br>White-Collar Index: 119<br>Unemployment Threat: Low | Income: 38.94%<br>Jobs: 9.83% | 5,147 | 208 |
| | Goods: Electronic products, pool tables, plastic pipe, printing and publishing, corn, wheat, oats | | | | | |
| Columbia, SC | Housing: 90<br>Food: 95*<br>Other: 102* | Income: $26,838<br>Taxes: $909<br>Bite: 3.39% | Blue-Collar Index: 93<br>White-Collar Index: 107<br>Unemployment Threat: Low | Income: 41.75%<br>Jobs: 9.82% | 5,279 | 179 |
| | Goods: Cameras, microcomputers, cotton textiles, fertilizer, chemicals | | | | | |
| Columbus, GA–AL | Housing: 70<br>Food: 103<br>Other: 99 | Income: $23,962<br>Taxes: $846<br>Bite: 3.53% | Blue-Collar Index: 109<br>White-Collar Index: 91<br>Unemployment Threat: Moderate | Income: 38.48%<br>Jobs: 5.23% | 4,812 | 250 |
| | Goods: Bricks, hand tools, textiles, cast iron, farm implements | | | | | |
| Columbus, OH | Housing: 97<br>Food: 100<br>Other: 99 | Income: $29,761<br>Taxes: $838<br>Bite: 2.82% | Blue-Collar Index: 96<br>White-Collar Index: 104<br>Unemployment Threat: Low | Income: 38.94%<br>Jobs: 5.35% | 5,165 | 202 |
| | Goods: Refrigerators, ranges, auto parts, roller bearings, meat products, stone, airplanes | | | | | |
| Corpus Christi, TX | Housing: 83<br>Food: 104<br>Other: 104 | Income: $29,229<br>Taxes: $214<br>Bite: 0.73% | Blue-Collar Index: 109<br>White-Collar Index: 91<br>Unemployment Threat: Moderate | Income: 50.44%<br>Jobs: 22.29% | 6,690 | 44 |
| | Goods: Oil, chemicals, grain, cotton, soda ash, zinc, chlorine, shrimp | | | | | |
| Cumberland, MD–WV | Housing: 73<br>Food: 98*<br>Other: 102* | Income: $23,369<br>Taxes: $869<br>Bite: 3.72% | Blue-Collar Index: 118<br>White-Collar Index: 82<br>Unemployment Threat: High | Income: 39.61%<br>Jobs: 4.65% | 4,741 | 255 |
| | Goods: Railroad equipment, beer, macaroni, underwear, glassware | | | | | |
| ★ Dallas, TX | Housing: 112<br>Food: 105*<br>Other: 105* | Income: $38,769<br>Taxes: $265<br>Bite: 0.68% | Blue-Collar Index: 93<br>White-Collar Index: 107<br>Unemployment Threat: Low | Income: 53.40%<br>Jobs: 29.51% | 7,710 | 12 |
| | Goods: Aluminum doors and windows, oil, gas, wall coverings, food products, frozen foods, potato and corn chips, tools and dies, jigs, farm and construction machinery and equipment, wooden truck trailers, lumber, printing, handbags, concrete | | | | | |
| Danbury, CT | Housing: 173<br>Food: 110*<br>Other: 103* | Income: $47,258<br>Taxes: $546<br>Bite: 1.16% | Blue-Collar Index: 98<br>White-Collar Index: 102<br>Unemployment Threat: Low | Income: 53.37%<br>Jobs: 17.60% | 7,060 | 34 |
| | Goods: Surgical instruments, hat-making machinery, aluminum foil, railroad-testing equipment, aircraft parts, electrical products | | | | | |
| Danville, VA | Housing: 68<br>Food: 100*<br>Other: 98* | Income: $22,758<br>Taxes: $775<br>Bite: 3.41% | Blue-Collar Index: 135<br>White-Collar Index: 65<br>Unemployment Threat: High | Income: 37.65%<br>Jobs: 1.05% | 4,491 | 278 |
| | Goods: Truck tires, broad silk, tobacco, mattresses, fertilizer | | | | | |
| Davenport–Rock Island–Moline, IA–IL | Housing: 97<br>Food: 92*<br>Other: 97* | Income: $32,402<br>Taxes: $1,167<br>Bite: 3.60% | Blue-Collar Index: 110<br>White-Collar Index: 90<br>Unemployment Threat: Moderate | Income: 36.90%<br>Jobs: −2.04% | 4,997 | 222 |
| | Goods: Farm tractors, cookies, cast metal, macaroni, candy | | | | | |
| Dayton–Springfield, OH | Housing: 92<br>Food: 105<br>Other: 97 | Income: $30,232<br>Taxes: $865<br>Bite: 2.86% | Blue-Collar Index: 103<br>White-Collar Index: 97<br>Unemployment Threat: Moderate | Income: 34.69%<br>Jobs: −4.60% | 4,532 | 276 |
| | Goods: Cash registers, computers, aircraft parts, bicycles, rubber and plastics, industrial belts, paper and paper-making machinery | | | | | |
| Daytona Beach, FL | Housing: 86<br>Food: 102<br>Other: 108 | Income: $27,255<br>Taxes: $295<br>Bite: 1.08% | Blue-Collar Index: 97<br>White-Collar Index: 103<br>Unemployment Threat: Low | Income: 49.39%<br>Jobs: 27.43% | 6,592 | 49 |
| | Goods: Electronic components, transportation equipment, fabricated metals, truck farming | | | | | |

| Metro Area | Living Costs (U.S. Avg.=100) | Average Household Income and Taxes | Occupations (U.S. Avg.=100) | Five-Year Growth Income and Jobs | Places Rated Score | Places Rated Rank |
|---|---|---|---|---|---|---|
| Decatur, IL | Housing: 89<br>Food: 96*<br>Other: 102* | Income: $30,663<br>Taxes: $993<br>Bite: 3.24% | Blue-Collar Index: 110<br>White-Collar Index: 90<br>Unemployment Threat: Moderate | Income: 33.71%<br>Jobs: −10.68% | 4,274 | 297 |
| | Goods: Earth movers, carburetors, pumps, valves, tanks, corn, soybeans | | | | | |
| Denver, CO | Housing: 129<br>Food: 104<br>Other: 103 | Income: $39,099<br>Taxes: $1,002<br>Bite: 2.56% | Blue-Collar Index: 91<br>White-Collar Index: 109<br>Unemployment Threat: Low | Income: 53.38%<br>Jobs: 23.07% | 7,164 | 28 |
| | Goods: Beer, mining and farm machinery, coffee roasters, meat products, stone and clay products, printing and publishing | | | | | |
| Des Moines, IA | Housing: 96<br>Food: 93*<br>Other: 100* | Income: $34,622<br>Taxes: $1,205<br>Bite: 3.48% | Blue-Collar Index: 91<br>White-Collar Index: 109<br>Unemployment Threat: Low | Income: 38.08%<br>Jobs: −0.06% | 5,346 | 167 |
| | Goods: Refrigerators, tires, crackers, biscuits, meat products, farming implements, printing and publishing | | | | | |
| Detroit, MI | Housing: 102<br>Food: 100*<br>Other: 102* | Income: $33,858<br>Taxes: $1,589<br>Bite: 4.69% | Blue-Collar Index: 105<br>White-Collar Index: 95<br>Unemployment Threat: Moderate | Income: 27.24%<br>Jobs: −12.44% | 3,904 | 312 |
| | Goods: Autos and auto products, ranges and heating devices, paper, twine, bolts and screws, ball bearings, boilers, ships | | | | | |
| Dothan, AL | Housing: 68<br>Food: 97<br>Other: 92 | Income: $24,024<br>Taxes: $769<br>Bite: 3.20% | Blue-Collar Index: 114<br>White-Collar Index: 86<br>Unemployment Threat: Moderate | Income: 45.18%<br>Jobs: 7.85% | 5,453 | 159 |
| | Goods: Fertilizer, hosiery, vaults, mirrors, toys, steel tubing, pajamas, cooking oil | | | | | |
| Dubuque, IA | Housing: 96<br>Food: 91<br>Other: 101 | Income: $28,904<br>Taxes: $935<br>Bite: 3.23% | Blue-Collar Index: 113<br>White-Collar Index: 87<br>Unemployment Threat: Moderate | Income: 27.95%<br>Jobs: −6.63% | 3,949 | 310 |
| | Goods: Furniture, cabinets, caskets, tractors, meat products | | | | | |
| Duluth, MN–WI | Housing: 72<br>Food: 100<br>Other: 95 | Income: $26,712<br>Taxes: $1,124<br>Bite: 4.21% | Blue-Collar Index: 110<br>White-Collar Index: 90<br>Unemployment Threat: Moderate | Income: 30.10%<br>Jobs: −10.49% | 3,922 | 311 |
| | Goods: Fish, frozen and canned food, mining and construction equipment, lumber, peat, farm tractors | | | | | |
| East St. Louis–Belleville, IL | Housing: 78<br>Food: 95*<br>Other: 100* | Income: $28,176<br>Taxes: $923<br>Bite: 3.28% | Blue-Collar Index: 109<br>White-Collar Index: 91<br>Unemployment Threat: Moderate | Income: 39.82%<br>Jobs: 21.88% | 6,113 | 83 |
| | Goods: Plumbers' supplies, rubber reclaiming, roofing materials, paint, stoves, drinking fountains | | | | | |
| Eau Claire, WI | Housing: 85<br>Food: 96*<br>Other: 102* | Income: $25,388<br>Taxes: $1,029<br>Bite: 4.05% | Blue-Collar Index: 103<br>White-Collar Index: 97<br>Unemployment Threat: Moderate | Income: 43.10%<br>Jobs: 12.05% | 5,348 | 166 |
| | Goods: Tires, inner tubes, golf carts, beer, dairy products, pressure cookers, sawmill and railroad equipment | | | | | |
| El Paso, TX | Housing: 88<br>Food: 96<br>Other: 101 | Income: $21,930<br>Taxes: $170<br>Bite: 0.78% | Blue-Collar Index: 105<br>White-Collar Index: 95<br>Unemployment Threat: Moderate | Income: 43.26%<br>Jobs: 12.52% | 5,080 | 215 |
| | Goods: Clothing, cattle, pecans, rice, maize, feeds, copper, sulfur, bricks and cement | | | | | |
| Elkhart–Goshen, IN | Housing: 79<br>Food: 97*<br>Other: 92* | Income: $29,417<br>Taxes: $959<br>Bite: 3.26% | Blue-Collar Index: 120<br>White-Collar Index: 80<br>Unemployment Threat: High | Income: 26.03%<br>Jobs: −6.43% | 4,214 | 303 |
| | Goods: Band instruments, mobile homes, burlap bags, lightning rods, pharmaceuticals | | | | | |
| Elmira, NY | Housing: 85<br>Food: 100*<br>Other: 94* | Income: $27,683<br>Taxes: $1,055<br>Bite: 3.81% | Blue-Collar Index: 105<br>White-Collar Index: 95<br>Unemployment Threat: Moderate | Income: 43.96%<br>Jobs: −5.58% | 4,813 | 249 |
| | Goods: Gliders, prefabricated homes, trucks, fire-fighting equipment, hydrants | | | | | |
| Enid, OK | Housing: 82<br>Food: 100*<br>Other: 94* | Income: $36,198<br>Taxes: $920<br>Bite: 2.54% | Blue-Collar Index: 112<br>White-Collar Index: 88<br>Unemployment Threat: Moderate | Income: 65.91%<br>Jobs: 21.06% | 8,268 | 4 |
| | Goods: Oil refining, well-drilling and farm machinery, dairy products | | | | | |
| Erie, PA | Housing: 93<br>Food: 101<br>Other: 104 | Income: $28,129<br>Taxes: $860<br>Bite: 3.06% | Blue-Collar Index: 114<br>White-Collar Index: 86<br>Unemployment Threat: Moderate | Income: 37.37%<br>Jobs: −6.47% | 4,299 | 296 |
| | Goods: Gas engines, electric locomotives, wringers, turbines, pipes, tools, vises | | | | | |

| Metro Area | Living Costs (U.S. Avg.=100) | Average Household Income and Taxes | Occupations (U.S. Avg.=100) | Five-Year Growth Income and Jobs | Places Rated Score | Places Rated Rank |
|---|---|---|---|---|---|---|
| Eugene–Springfield, OR | Housing: 112<br>Food: 110*<br>Other: 103* | Income: $25,698<br>Taxes: $1,102<br>Bite: 4.29% | Blue-Collar Index: 102<br>White-Collar Index: 98<br>Unemployment Threat: Moderate | Income: 24.33%<br>Jobs: −8.98% | 3,045 | 329 |
| | Goods: Plywood, canned fruits and vegetables, meat products, grass seed, sheep, poultry | | | | | |
| Evansville, IN–KY | Housing: 81<br>Food: 104<br>Other: 94 | Income: $30,181<br>Taxes: $991<br>Bite: 3.28% | Blue-Collar Index: 118<br>White-Collar Index: 82<br>Unemployment Threat: High | Income: 37.24%<br>Jobs: 2.73% | 5,206 | 190 |
| | Goods: Appliances, aluminum, vegetables, baby food, chemicals, plastics | | | | | |
| Fall River, MA–RI | Housing: 108<br>Food: 94*<br>Other: 97* | Income: $27,591<br>Taxes: $1,198<br>Bites: 4.34% | Blue-Collar Index: 125<br>White-Collar Index: 75<br>Unemployment Threat: High | Income: 43.46%<br>Jobs: 1.96% | 4,884 | 239 |
| | Goods: Dresses, suits, sportswear, thread, yarn, light fixtures, rubber goods | | | | | |
| Fargo–Moorhead, ND–MN | Housing: 98<br>Food: 100*<br>Other: 96* | Income: $30,094<br>Taxes: $424<br>Bite: 1.41% | Blue-Collar Index: 91<br>White-Collar Index: 109<br>Unemployment Threat: Low | Income: 35.95%<br>Jobs: 15.38% | 5,594 | 142 |
| | Goods: Luggage, fur coats, neon signs, meat and dairy products, jewelry | | | | | |
| Fayetteville, NC | Housing: 75<br>Food: 96*<br>Other: 95* | Income: $22,291<br>Taxes: $800<br>Bite: 3.59% | Blue-Collar Index: 105<br>White-Collar Index: 95<br>Unemployment Threat: Moderate | Income: 42.75%<br>Jobs: 12.94% | 5,255 | 186 |
| | Goods: Tobacco loopers, feeds, tires, lace, dolls, asphalt, plywood | | | | | |
| Fayetteville–Springdale, AR | Housing: 80<br>Food: 101<br>Other: 98 | Income: $23,251<br>Taxes: $562<br>Bite: 2.42% | Blue-Collar Index: 108<br>White-Collar Index: 92<br>Unemployment Threat: Moderate | Income: 37.89%<br>Jobs: 4.88% | 4,631 | 266 |
| | Goods: Electric organs, wagons, poultry packing, pipe fittings, sporting goods | | | | | |
| Fitchburg–Leominster, MA | Housing: 99<br>Food: 94*<br>Other: 97* | Income: $29,375<br>Taxes: $1,292<br>Bite: 4.40% | Blue-Collar Index: 115<br>White-Collar Index: 85<br>Unemployment Threat: Moderate | Income: 44.94%<br>Jobs: −0.87% | 5,098 | 211 |
| | Goods: Turbines, paper, saws and knives, handbags and luggage, shoes, hardware | | | | | |
| Flint, MI | Housing: 86<br>Food: 100<br>Other: 102 | Income: $32,000<br>Taxes: $1,454<br>Bite: 4.68% | Blue-Collar Index: 124<br>White-Collar Index: 76<br>Unemployment Threat: High | Income: 25.49%<br>Jobs: −15.30% | 3,724 | 318 |
| | Goods: Pickup trucks, autos, recreational vehicles, plumbing fixtures, structural steel, tents | | | | | |
| Florence, AL | Housing: 71<br>Food: 93*<br>Other: 93* | Income: $24,595<br>Taxes: $783<br>Bite: 3.18% | Blue-Collar Index: 122<br>White-Collar Index: 78<br>Unemployment Threat: High | Income: 34.23%<br>Jobs: −1.09% | 4,492 | 277 |
| | Goods: Primary metals (especially aluminum), chlorides, fertilizer, textiles | | | | | |
| Florence, SC | Housing: 78<br>Food: 95*<br>Other: 92* | Income: $22,498<br>Taxes: $706<br>Bite: 3.14% | Blue-Collar Index: 113<br>White-Collar Index: 87<br>Unemployment Threat: Moderate | Income: 41.34%<br>Jobs: 5.40% | 4,842 | 247 |
| | Goods: Welding equipment, mobile radios, fertilizer, clothing, furniture | | | | | |
| Fort Collins–Loveland, CO | Housing: 119<br>Food: 103<br>Other: 102 | Income: $29,487<br>Taxes: $365<br>Bite: 2.25% | Blue-Collar Index: 97<br>White-Collar Index: 103<br>Unemployment Threat: Low | Income: 54.75%<br>Jobs: 24.44% | 6,631 | 48 |
| | Goods: Dental appliances, instruments, pine timber, lamb, sugar, beets | | | | | |
| Fort Lauderdale–Hollywood–Pompano Beach, FL | Housing: 130<br>Food: 99<br>Other: 98 | Income: $36,655<br>Taxes: $365<br>Bite: 1.00% | Blue-Collar Index: 94<br>White-Collar Index: 106<br>Unemployment Threat: Low | Income: 51.03%<br>Jobs: 26.30% | 7,136 | 29 |
| | Goods: Electronic components, fiberglass, aircraft fittings, boats, oranges | | | | | |
| Fort Myers, FL | Housing: 111<br>Food: 97*<br>Other: 101* | Income: $30,786<br>Taxes: $324<br>Bite: 1.05% | Blue-Collar Index: 100<br>White-Collar Index: 100<br>Unemployment Threat: Moderate | Income: 48.18%<br>Jobs: 36.55% | 7,166 | 27 |
| | Goods: Concrete blocks, surgical and medical supplies, boats, fruits and vegetables | | | | | |
| ★ Fort Pierce, FL | Housing: 106<br>Food: 102*<br>Other: 108* | Income: $28,792<br>Taxes: $310<br>Bite: 1.08% | Blue-Collar Index: 106<br>White-Collar Index: 94<br>Unemployment Threat: Moderate | Income: 51.67%<br>Jobs: 54.05% | 7,973 | 9 |
| | Goods: Barrels, plastic pipe, boats, fertilizer, fruit canning | | | | | |
| Fort Smith, AR–OK | Housing: 69<br>Food: 92<br>Other: 101 | Income: $24,405<br>Taxes: $610<br>Bite: 2.50% | Blue-Collar Index: 119<br>White-Collar Index: 81<br>Unemployment Threat: High | Income: 40.54%<br>Jobs: 1.10% | 4,849 | 243 |
| | Goods: Refrigerators, air conditioners, kitchen cabinets, caskets, food processing | | | | | |

| Metro Area | Living Costs (U.S. Avg.=100) | Average Household Income and Taxes | Occupations (U.S. Avg.=100) | Five-Year Growth Income and Jobs | Places Rated Score | Places Rated Rank |
|---|---|---|---|---|---|---|
| Fort Walton Beach, FL | Housing: 91<br>Food: 98*<br>Other: 96* | Income: $25,466<br>Taxes: $280<br>Bite: 1.10% | Blue-Collar Index: 98<br>White-Collar Index: 102<br>Unemployment Threat: Low | Income: 49.64%<br>Jobs: 23.62% | 6,342 | 61 |
| | Goods: Fish, beverages, pine lumber | | | | | |
| Fort Wayne, IN | Housing: 81<br>Food: 94<br>Other: 91 | Income: $29,182<br>Taxes: $954<br>Bite: 3.27% | Blue-Collar Index: 101<br>White-Collar Index: 99<br>Unemployment Threat: Moderate | Income: 28.16%<br>Jobs: −8.41% | 4,195 | 304 |
| | Goods: Televisions, radios, auto axles, mobile homes, public-address systems, pistons, gasoline pumps | | | | | |
| Fort Worth–Arlington, TX | Housing: 95<br>Food: 105<br>Other: 105 | Income: $33,384<br>Taxes: $235<br>Bite: 0.70% | Blue-Collar Index: 104<br>White-Collar Index: 96<br>Unemployment Threat: Moderate | Income: 47.84%<br>Jobs: 23.75% | 6,862 | 40 |
| | Goods: Pharmaceuticals, oil and gas, aluminum, steel, titanium and brass forgings, salad dressing, pickles, preserves, jams and jellies, grain, leather, electronic and computer parts, printed circuit boards, antennae and cables, wire, soap | | | | | |
| Fresno, CA | Housing: 111<br>Food: 98*<br>Other: 110* | Income: $30,047<br>Taxes: $864<br>Bite: 2.88% | Blue-Collar Index: 98<br>White-Collar Index: 102<br>Unemployment Threat: Low | Income: 41.18%<br>Jobs: 19.70% | 5,746 | 123 |
| | Goods: Wines, dried fruits, poultry, feeds, olive oil, vending machines, plastics | | | | | |
| Gadsden, AL | Housing: 65<br>Food: 94<br>Other: 90 | Income: $23,136<br>Taxes: $735<br>Bite: 3.18% | Blue-Collar Index: 126<br>White-Collar Index: 74<br>Unemployment Threat: High | Income: 35.59%<br>Jobs: −6.51% | 4,220 | 302 |
| | Goods: Food products, iron, wire, coat hangers, ammunition fuses, knives | | | | | |
| Gainesville, FL | Housing: 89<br>Food: 98<br>Other: 99 | Income: $22,756<br>Taxes: $265<br>Bite: 1.16% | Blue-Collar Index: 85<br>White-Collar Index: 115<br>Unemployment Threat: Moderate | Income: 44.38%<br>Jobs: 23.05% | 5,739 | 124 |
| | Goods: Electronic tubes, tung oil, petrochemicals, lumber, meat products | | | | | |
| Galveston–Texas City, TX | Housing: 93<br>Food: 103*<br>Other: 107* | Income: $34,208<br>Taxes: $245<br>Bite: 0.72% | Blue-Collar Index: 108<br>White-Collar Index: 92<br>Unemployment Threat: Moderate | Income: 47.57%<br>Jobs: 5.02% | 6,026 | 95 |
| | Goods: Petrochemicals, barges, pleasure craft, packing plants, dry docks, fish | | | | | |
| Gary–Hammond, IN | Housing: 92<br>Food: 100*<br>Other: 106* | Income: $29,669<br>Taxes: $965<br>Bite: 3.25% | Blue-Collar Index: 123<br>White-Collar Index: 77<br>Unemployment Threat: High | Income: 30.48%<br>Jobs: −11.94% | 3,826 | 315 |
| | Goods: Steel, tinplate, axles, coke, sulfates, bridges, railroad cars, autos, jet engines, light fixtures | | | | | |
| Glens Falls, NY | Housing: 85<br>Food: 99*<br>Other: 98* | Income: $25,539<br>Taxes: $927<br>Bite: 3.63% | Blue-Collar Index: 111<br>White-Collar Index: 89<br>Unemployment Threat: Moderate | Income: 44.69%<br>Jobs: 5.69% | 5,166 | 201 |
| | Goods: Book paper, color pigments, lace, shirts and dresses | | | | | |
| Grand Forks, ND | Housing: 95<br>Food: 100*<br>Other: 96* | Income: $26,636<br>Taxes: $349<br>Bite: 1.31% | Blue-Collar Index: 94<br>White-Collar Index: 106<br>Unemployment Threat: Low | Income: 43.31%<br>Jobs: 14.85% | 5,646 | 139 |
| | Goods: Flour, potato products, beet sugar, wheat, livestock | | | | | |
| Grand Rapids, MI | Housing: 93<br>Food: 95*<br>Other: 105* | Income: $29,915<br>Taxes: $1,389<br>Bite: 4.64% | Blue-Collar Index: 111<br>White-Collar Index: 89<br>Unemployment Threat: Moderate | Income: 33.85%<br>Jobs: 4.89% | 4,848 | 244 |
| | Goods: Furniture, typewriters, calculators, welding equipment, bathroom fixtures, varnishes, lacquers | | | | | |
| Great Falls, MT | Housing: 86<br>Food: 108<br>Other: 102 | Income: $28,120<br>Taxes: $632<br>Bite: 2.25% | Blue-Collar Index: 92<br>White-Collar Index: 108<br>Unemployment Threat: Low | Income: 39.18%<br>Jobs: −1.91% | 4,697 | 260 |
| | Goods: Wheat, barley, oats, hay, linseed oil, copper and zinc, livestock | | | | | |
| Greeley, CO | Housing: 99<br>Food: 103*<br>Other: 102* | Income: $29,151<br>Taxes: $653<br>Bite: 2.24% | Blue-Collar Index: 108<br>White-Collar Index: 92<br>Unemployment Threat: Moderate | Income: 42.17%<br>Jobs: 10.26% | 5,443 | 161 |
| | Goods: Sugar, soft drinks, meat products, potatoes and potato sorters | | | | | |
| Green Bay, WI | Housing: 101<br>Food: 95<br>Other: 95 | Income: $30,282<br>Taxes: $1,352<br>Bite: 4.46% | Blue-Collar Index: 104<br>White-Collar Index: 96<br>Unemployment Threat: Moderate | Income: 43.02%<br>Jobs: 10.34% | 5,650 | 137 |
| | Goods: Paper, tissue paper, cheese, fish, cranes, gloves, fertilizer | | | | | |

| Metro Area | Living Costs (U.S. Avg.=100) | Average Household Income and Taxes | Occupations (U.S. Avg.=100) | Five-Year Growth Income and Jobs | Places Rated Score | Places Rated Rank |
|---|---|---|---|---|---|---|
| Greensboro–Winston-Salem–High Point, NC | Housing: 85 Food: 92 Other: 104 | Income: $29,450 Taxes: $1,147 Bite: 3.89% | Blue-Collar Index: 118 White-Collar Index: 82 Unemployment Threat: High | Income: 38.50% Jobs: 5.36% | 5,204 | 192 |
| | Goods: Wood furniture, loom reeds, burial vaults, cellophane, cigarettes, cotton goods, hosiery | | | | | |
| Greenville–Spartanburg, SC | Housing: 76 Food: 95 Other: 102 | Income: $26,152 Taxes: $879 Bite: 3.36% | Blue-Collar Index: 122 White-Collar Index: 78 Unemployment Threat: High | Income: 40.22% Jobs: 3.85% | 5,012 | 220 |
| | Goods: Textiles, cotton, mill supplies, chemicals, timber, clothing | | | | | |
| Hagerstown, MD | Housing: 93 Food: 99* Other: 106* | Income: $26,880 Taxes: $1,020 Bite: 3.79% | Blue-Collar Index: 120 White-Collar Index: 80 Unemployment Threat: High | Income: 38.21% Jobs: −0.91% | 4,477 | 281 |
| | Goods: Pipe organs, dresses, dust collectors, cold-storage doors, mayonnaise | | | | | |
| Hamilton–Middletown, OH | Housing: 99 Food: 102* Other: 96* | Income: $28,448 Taxes: $799 Bite: 2.81% | Blue-Collar Index: 110 White-Collar Index: 90 Unemployment Threat: Moderate | Income: 36.45% Jobs: 0.05% | 4,618 | 268 |
| | Goods: Safes, printing presses, oil tanks, paper, coke, cast metals | | | | | |
| Harrisburg–Lebanon–Carlisle, PA | Housing: 95 Food: 98 Other: 106 | Income: $31,447 Taxes: $945 Bite: 3.01% | Blue-Collar Index: 102 White-Collar Index: 98 Unemployment Threat: Moderate | Income: 42.24% Jobs: 3.21% | 5,322 | 173 |
| | Goods: Meat and dairy products, steel, road machinery, cotton clothing | | | | | |
| Hartford, CT | Housing: 140 Food: 110 Other: 103 | Income: $37,565 Taxes: $477 Bite: 1.27% | Blue-Collar Index: 93 White-Collar Index: 107 Unemployment Threat: Low | Income: 52.28% Jobs: 12.04% | 6,307 | 67 |
| | Goods: Airplane engines, propellers, revolvers, tobacco, dishwashers, machine tools, glass-making machines | | | | | |
| Hickory, NC | Housing: 81 Food: 92 Other: 99 | Income: $25,203 Taxes: $931 Bite: 3.69% | Blue-Collar Index: 139 White-Collar Index: 61 Unemployment Threat: High | Income: 35.97% Jobs: 4.65% | 4,728 | 258 |
| | Goods: Hosiery, twine, clotheslines, wagons, soft drinks | | | | | |
| Honolulu, HI | Housing: 204 Food: 125 Other: 125 | Income: $33,964 Taxes: $1,828 Bite: 5.38% | Blue-Collar Index: 90 White-Collar Index: 110 Unemployment Threat: Low | Income: 39.55% Jobs: 23.52% | 5,187 | 196 |
| | Goods: Pineapples, pineapple products, sugar, clothing, awnings, tents, fish, cement | | | | | |
| Houma–Thibodaux, LA | Housing: 85 Food: 104* Other: 101* | Income: $29,350 Taxes: $296 Bite: 1.01% | Blue-Collar Index: 124 White-Collar Index: 76 Unemployment Threat: High | Income: 52.95% Jobs: 19.12% | 6,662 | 46 |
| | Goods: Shrimp, oysters, crabs, sugar products, oil and gas, sugarcane | | | | | |
| ★ Houston, TX | Housing: 117 Food: 103 Other: 107 | Income: $39,558 Taxes: $265 Bite: 0.67% | Blue-Collar Index: 100 White-Collar Index: 100 Unemployment Threat: Moderate | Income: 50.35% Jobs: 27.49% | 7,464 | 18 |
| | Goods: Oil-field equipment, synthetic rubber, fertilizer, refineries, steel, pulp and paper, rice mills | | | | | |
| Huntington–Ashland, WV–OH–KY | Housing: 80 Food: 103 Other: 94 | Income: $24,307 Taxes: $744 Bite: 3.06% | Blue-Collar Index: 113 White-Collar Index: 87 Unemployment Threat: Moderate | Income: 32.78% Jobs: 2.52% | 4,383 | 289 |
| | Goods: Glass, dye, stoves, auto bumpers, insulators | | | | | |
| Huntsville, AL | Housing: 75 Food: 93 Other: 93 | Income: $30,470 Taxes: $968 Bite: 3.18% | Blue-Collar Index: 94 White-Collar Index: 106 Unemployment Threat: Low | Income: 47.03% Jobs: 12.26% | 6,412 | 57 |
| | Goods: Telephones, acoustic instruments, rockets, boats, trailers, cotton clothing | | | | | |
| Indianapolis, IN | Housing: 84 Food: 96 Other: 92 | Income: $31,461 Taxes: $1,021 Bite: 3.25% | Blue-Collar Index: 103 White-Collar Index: 97 Unemployment Threat: Moderate | Income: 34.07% Jobs: −0.08% | 5,082 | 214 |
| | Goods: Automotive products, electrical equipment, heavy machinery, drugs | | | | | |
| Iowa City, IA | Housing: 113 Food: 93 Other: 101 | Income: $28,904 Taxes: $935 Bite: 3.23% | Blue-Collar Index: 82 White-Collar Index: 118 Unemployment Threat: Low | Income: 38.75% Jobs: 10.76% | 5,165 | 202 |
| | Goods: Brushes, toothpaste, adhesive paper, foam rubber | | | | | |
| Jackson, MI | Housing: 81 Food: 100 Other: 99 | Income: $27,580 Taxes: $1,276 Bite: 4.63% | Blue-Collar Index: 113 White-Collar Index: 87 Unemployment Threat: Moderate | Income: 30.27% Jobs: −11.01% | 3,822 | 316 |
| | Goods: Grinding wheels, air conditioners, extracts and flavorings, auto and aircraft parts | | | | | |

| Metro Area | Living Costs (U.S. Avg.=100) | Average Household Income and Taxes | Occupations (U.S. Avg.=100) | Five-Year Growth Income and Jobs | Places Rated Score | Places Rated Rank |
|---|---|---|---|---|---|---|
| Jackson, MS | Housing: 87<br>Food: 107*<br>Other: 95* | Income: $27,499<br>Taxes: $683<br>Bite: 2.48% | Blue-Collar Index: 95<br>White-Collar Index: 105<br>Unemployment Threat: Low | Income: 38.01%<br>Jobs: 8.66% | 5,186 | 198 |
| | Goods: Cottonseed oil, furniture, desks, caskets, incubators, hydraulic aircraft and missile parts, work clothes | | | | | |
| Jacksonville, FL | Housing: 79<br>Food: 97<br>Other: 103 | Income: $29,352<br>Taxes: $310<br>Bite: 1.06% | Blue-Collar Index: 99<br>White-Collar Index: 101<br>Unemployment Threat: Low | Income: 44.37%<br>Jobs: 15.27% | 6,139 | 82 |
| | Goods: Pulp and paper, ships, food products | | | | | |
| Jacksonville, NC | Housing: 73<br>Food: 95*<br>Other: 89* | Income: $22,358<br>Taxes: $802<br>Bite: 3.59% | Blue-Collar Index: 112<br>White-Collar Index: 88<br>Unemployment Threat: Moderate | Income: 61.84%<br>Jobs: 14.55% | 6,386 | 59 |
| | Goods: Tobacco products, lumber, boats | | | | | |
| Janesville–Beloit, WI | Housing: 89<br>Food: 94<br>Other: 94 | Income: $28,375<br>Taxes: $1,225<br>Bite: 4.32% | Blue-Collar Index: 118<br>White-Collar Index: 82<br>Unemployment Threat: High | Income: 30.95%<br>Jobs: −2.56% | 4,371 | 290 |
| | Goods: Fountain pens, machine tools, church furniture, room dividers | | | | | |
| Jersey City, NJ | Housing: 106<br>Food: 108*<br>Other: 105* | Income: $32,004<br>Taxes: $864<br>Bite: 2.70% | Blue-Collar Index: 113<br>White-Collar Index: 87<br>Unemployment Threat: Moderate | Income: 41.81%<br>Jobs: −2.79% | 4,889 | 237 |
| | Goods: Soap, cork, cosmetics, macaroni, egg noodles, slippers and sandals | | | | | |
| Johnson City–Kingsport–Bristol, TN–VA | Housing: 73<br>Food: 98*<br>Other: 107* | Income: $23,531<br>Taxes: $299<br>Bite: 1.27% | Blue-Collar Index: 122<br>White-Collar Index: 78<br>Unemployment Threat: High | Income: 40.32%<br>Jobs: 6.68% | 4,903 | 234 |
| | Goods: Chemicals, electrical products, silk and rayon textiles, hosiery, bricks, cheese, cigarette filters, hardwood flooring | | | | | |
| Johnstown, PA | Housing: 78<br>Food: 98*<br>Other: 100* | Income: $25,514<br>Taxes: $776<br>Bite: 3.04% | Blue-Collar Index: 124<br>White-Collar Index: 76<br>Unemployment Threat: High | Income: 37.89%<br>Jobs: −8.68% | 4,181 | 305 |
| | Goods: Mining equipment, girdles, mattresses, soft drinks | | | | | |
| Joliet, IL | Housing: 112<br>Food: 101*<br>Other: 106* | Income: $30,590<br>Taxes: $992<br>Bite: 3.24% | Blue-Collar Index: 114<br>White-Collar Index: 86<br>Unemployment Threat: Moderate | Income: 30.60%<br>Jobs: 6.70% | 4,631 | 266 |
| | Goods: Wallpaper, earth-moving equipment, firebrick, barrels | | | | | |
| Joplin, MO | Housing: 62<br>Food: 91<br>Other: 94 | Income: $23,517<br>Taxes: $567<br>Bite: 2.41% | Blue-Collar Index: 118<br>White-Collar Index: 82<br>Unemployment Threat: High | Income: 42.33%<br>Jobs: 6.77% | 5,324 | 172 |
| | Goods: Furniture, dog food, explosives, engraving and typesetting equipment, store fixtures | | | | | |
| Kalamazoo, MI | Housing: 95<br>Food: 95<br>Other: 105 | Income: $31,276<br>Taxes: $1,462<br>Bite: 4.67% | Blue-Collar Index: 104<br>White-Collar Index: 96<br>Unemployment Threat: Moderate | Income: 35.86%<br>Jobs: −0.21% | 4,794 | 251 |
| | Goods: Paper, silos, fishing tackle, furnace blowers, printing ink, guitars and banjos, drugs | | | | | |
| Kankakee, IL | Housing: 87<br>Food: 99*<br>Other: 104* | Income: $30,022<br>Taxes: $978<br>Bite: 3.26% | Blue-Collar Index: 115<br>White-Collar Index: 85<br>Unemployment Threat: Moderate | Income: 40.74%<br>Jobs: 10.34% | 5,579 | 146 |
| | Goods: Industrial batteries, soybeans, corn products, water heaters, farming implements, hydraulic tools | | | | | |
| Kansas City, KS | Housing: 97<br>Food: 102<br>Other: 105 | Income: $37,268<br>Taxes: $1,021<br>Bite: 2.74% | Blue-Collar Index: 93<br>White-Collar Index: 107<br>Unemployment Threat: Low | Income: 39.56%<br>Jobs: 11.98% | 6,166 | 78 |
| | Goods: Fiberglass, tile, autos, soap, meat packing | | | | | |
| Kansas City, MO | Housing: 85<br>Food: 102*<br>Other: 105* | Income: $30,783<br>Taxes: $789<br>Bite: 2.56% | Blue-Collar Index: 102<br>White-Collar Index: 98<br>Unemployment Threat: Moderate | Income: 37.41%<br>Jobs: −2.60% | 4,865 | 242 |
| | Goods: Ammunition, autos and trucks, greeting cards, valve fittings, tile and brick, work garments | | | | | |
| Kenosha, WI | Housing: 102<br>Food: 94*<br>Other: 94* | Income: $31,752<br>Taxes: $1,442<br>Bite: 4.54% | Blue-Collar Index: 120<br>White-Collar Index: 80<br>Unemployment Threat: High | Income: 41.01%<br>Jobs: 0.01% | 5,176 | 199 |
| | Goods: Autos, musical instruments, tools, wire, rope, underwear, fire-fighting equipment, cranberries | | | | | |

| Metro Area | Living Costs (U.S. Avg.=100) | Average Household Income and Taxes | Occupations (U.S. Avg.=100) | Five-Year Growth Income and Jobs | Places Rated Score | Places Rated Rank |
|---|---|---|---|---|---|---|
| Killeen–Temple, TX | Housing: 77<br>Food: 100<br>Other: 93 | Income: $25,810<br>Taxes: $192<br>Bite: 0.74% | Blue-Collar Index: 104<br>White-Collar Index: 96<br>Unemployment Threat: Moderate | Income: 52.26%<br>Jobs: 16.13% | 6,331 | 62 |
| | Goods: School desks and chairs, theater seats, farm machinery, plastics | | | | | |
| Knoxville, TN | Housing: 80<br>Food: 98<br>Other: 107 | Income: $26,454<br>Taxes: $329<br>Bite: 1.24% | Blue-Collar Index: 105<br>White-Collar Index: 95<br>Unemployment Threat: Moderate | Income: 42.91%<br>Jobs: 12.25% | 5,537 | 148 |
| | Goods: Hosiery, burley tobacco, chemicals, rolled aluminum, cast metals, marble, soft coal | | | | | |
| Kokomo, IN | Housing: 79<br>Food: 96*<br>Other: 92* | Income: $29,439<br>Taxes: $959<br>Bite: 3.26% | Blue-Collar Index: 125<br>White-Collar Index: 75<br>Unemployment Threat: High | Income: 21.00%<br>Jobs: −17.89% | 3,429 | 324 |
| | Goods: Electric signs, radios, playground equipment, auto transmissions, high-performance alloys | | | | | |
| La Crosse, WI | Housing: 100<br>Food: 97<br>Other: 93 | Income: $28,554<br>Taxes: $1,235<br>Bite: 4.33% | Blue-Collar Index: 104<br>White-Collar Index: 96<br>Unemployment Threat: Moderate | Income: 44.88%<br>Jobs: 11.76% | 5,648 | 138 |
| | Goods: Beer, dairy pumps, rubber boots, gauges, sheet metal, cast metals | | | | | |
| Lafayette, IN | Housing: 93<br>Food: 96*<br>Other: 92* | Income: $26,146<br>Taxes: $1,173<br>Bite: 4.48% | Blue-Collar Index: 94<br>White-Collar Index: 106<br>Unemployment Threat: Low | Income: 36.38%<br>Jobs: −3.42% | 4,333 | 293 |
| | Goods: Soap, tools and gears, electric meters, meat products, aluminum, drugs | | | | | |
| ★ Lafayette, LA | Housing: 103<br>Food: 106<br>Other: 101 | Income: $36,089<br>Taxes: $261<br>Bite: 0.70% | Blue-Collar Index: 97<br>White-Collar Index: 103<br>Unemployment Threat: Low | Income: 76.22%<br>Jobs: 48.25% | 9,702 | 2 |
| | Goods: Coffee roasters, aluminum windows, rice, sugar, corn, dairy products | | | | | |
| Lake Charles, LA | Housing: 83<br>Food: 104<br>Other: 101 | Income: $29,288<br>Taxes: $296<br>Bite: 1.01% | Blue-Collar Index: 119<br>White-Collar Index: 81<br>Unemployment Threat: High | Income: 45.44%<br>Jobs: 10.31% | 5,872 | 107 |
| | Goods: Ammonia, chlorine, soda ash, coke, gasoline, synthetic rubber, plastics | | | | | |
| Lake County, IL | Housing: 159<br>Food: 101*<br>Other: 106* | Income: $38,912<br>Taxes: $1,228<br>Bite: 3.16% | Blue-Collar Index: 75<br>White-Collar Index: 125<br>Unemployment Threat: Low | Income: 38.47%<br>Jobs: 17.29% | 5,755 | 122 |
| | Goods: Asbestos, gypsum products, outboard motors, candy, machine tools, brass casting, pharmaceutical manufacturing | | | | | |
| Lakeland–Winter Haven, FL | Housing: 80<br>Food: 97<br>Other: 101 | Income: $25,833<br>Taxes: $280<br>Bite: 1.08% | Blue-Collar Index: 112<br>White-Collar Index: 88<br>Unemployment Threat: Moderate | Income: 39.98%<br>Jobs: 15.74% | 5,594 | 142 |
| | Goods: Citrus fruits, fertilizer, ceramic tile, beverages | | | | | |
| Lancaster, PA | Housing: 103<br>Food: 99<br>Other: 106 | Income: $30,248<br>Taxes: $918<br>Bite: 3.03% | Blue-Collar Index: 122<br>White-Collar Index: 78<br>Unemployment Threat: High | Income: 39.65%<br>Jobs: 5.81% | 5,120 | 209 |
| | Goods: Electric razors, ball bearings, boilers, tin cans, asbestos belting, shoes | | | | | |
| Lansing–East Lansing, MI | Housing: 95<br>Food: 100<br>Other: 100 | Income: $30,439<br>Taxes: $1,425<br>Bite: 4.68% | Blue-Collar Index: 100<br>White-Collar Index: 100<br>Unemployment Threat: Moderate | Income: 34.96%<br>Jobs: 0.76% | 4,747 | 254 |
| | Goods: Autos, auto wheels, tools and dies, aerial-photography equipment | | | | | |
| Laredo, TX | Housing: 74<br>Food: 100*<br>Other: 100* | Income: $17,287<br>Taxes: $146<br>Bite: 0.84% | Blue-Collar Index: 101<br>White-Collar Index: 99<br>Unemployment Threat: Moderate | Income: 46.51%<br>Jobs: 20.24% | 5,264 | 183 |
| | Goods: Cattle, vegetables, citrus fruits, coal, natural gas, oil | | | | | |
| Las Cruces, NM | Housing: 83<br>Food: 96*<br>Other: 101* | Income: $21,641<br>Taxes: $134<br>Bite: 0.62% | Blue-Collar Index: 108<br>White-Collar Index: 92<br>Unemployment Threat: Moderate | Income: 43.29%<br>Jobs: 17.29% | 5,341 | 168 |
| | Goods: Cottonseed oil, alfalfa, melons, livestock | | | | | |
| Las Vegas, NV | Housing: 119<br>Food: 101<br>Other: 110 | Income: $32,626<br>Taxes: $331<br>Bite: 1.01% | Blue-Collar Index: 93<br>White-Collar Index: 107<br>Unemployment Threat: Low | Income: 36.99%<br>Jobs: 26.04% | 6,035 | 93 |
| | Goods: Printing and publishing, foods, primary metals | | | | | |
| Lawrence, KS | Housing: 90<br>Food: 102<br>Other: 103 | Income: $24,836<br>Taxes: $585<br>Bite: 2.36% | Blue-Collar Index: 91<br>White-Collar Index: 109<br>Unemployment Threat: Low | Income: 40.37%<br>Jobs: 1.10% | 4,573 | 271 |
| | Goods: Pipe organs, creameries, milled alfalfa | | | | | |

| Metro Area | Living Costs (U.S. Avg.=100) | Average Household Income and Taxes | Occupations (U.S. Avg.=100) | Five-Year Growth Income and Jobs | Places Rated Score | Places Rated Rank |
|---|---|---|---|---|---|---|
| Lawrence–Haverhill, MA–NH | Housing: 125<br>Food: 94*<br>Other: 97* | Income: $36,644<br>Taxes: $1,695<br>Bite: 4.63% | Blue-Collar Index: 109<br>White-Collar Index: 91<br>Unemployment Threat: Moderate | Income: 53.86%<br>Jobs: 12.08% | 6,527 | 51 |
| | Goods: Gym lockers, paper boxes, textiles, electronic equipment, mattresses, cans | | | | | |
| Lawton, OK | Housing: 70<br>Food: 108*<br>Other: 101* | Income: $23,775<br>Taxes: $409<br>Bite: 1.72% | Blue-Collar Index: 102<br>White-Collar Index: 98<br>Unemployment Threat: Moderate | Income: 52.30%<br>Jobs: 17.88% | 6,105 | 84 |
| | Goods: Men's hats and slacks, cement, tile, greenhouses, hatcheries, cattle, wheat | | | | | |
| Lewiston–Auburn, ME | Housing: 82<br>Food: 94*<br>Other: 97* | Income: $24,447<br>Taxes: $653<br>Bite: 2.67% | Blue-Collar Index: 123<br>White-Collar Index: 77<br>Unemployment Threat: High | Income: 36.27%<br>Jobs: −0.26% | 4,444 | 285 |
| | Goods: Shoes and boots, belting, leather and plastic soles and heels, cotton, rayon, woolen goods | | | | | |
| Lexington–Fayette, KY | Housing: 100<br>Food: 97<br>Other: 101 | Income: $30,570<br>Taxes: $924<br>Bite: 3.02% | Blue-Collar Index: 95<br>White-Collar Index: 105<br>Unemployment Threat: Low | Income: 45.94%<br>Jobs: 19.68% | 6,245 | 72 |
| | Goods: Crop dryers, whiskey, tobacco, electric typewriters, neon signs, parachutes, peanut butter | | | | | |
| Lima, OH | Housing: 84<br>Food: 99<br>Other: 96 | Income: $28,445<br>Taxes: $799<br>Bite: 2.81% | Blue-Collar Index: 125<br>White-Collar Index: 75<br>Unemployment Threat: High | Income: 32.28%<br>Jobs: −6.11% | 4,313 | 294 |
| | Goods: School buses, ambulances, hearses, auto engines, aircraft parts, power shovels, cranes and derricks, stone, neon signs | | | | | |
| Lincoln, NE | Housing: 99<br>Food: 97<br>Other: 99 | Income: $30,514<br>Taxes: $734<br>Bite: 2.41% | Blue-Collar Index: 94<br>White-Collar Index: 106<br>Unemployment Threat: Low | Income: 32.87%<br>Jobs: 5.13% | 4,908 | 232 |
| | Goods: Flour and feed mills, meat products, office supplies, motor scooters, wax | | | | | |
| Little Rock–North Little Rock, AR | Housing: 87<br>Food: 100<br>Other: 104 | Income: $28,686<br>Taxes: $779<br>Bite: 2.72% | Blue-Collar Index: 102<br>White-Collar Index: 98<br>Unemployment Threat: Moderate | Income: 39.81%<br>Jobs: 7.51% | 5,273 | 181 |
| | Goods: Light bulbs, cameras, teletype machinery, fertilizer, cottonseed products, meat products | | | | | |
| Longview–Marshall, TX | Housing: 79<br>Food: 102*<br>Other: 104* | Income: $30,159<br>Taxes: $225<br>Bite: 0.75% | Blue-Collar Index: 118<br>White-Collar Index: 82<br>Unemployment Threat: High | Income: 50.41%<br>Jobs: 23.17% | 6,898 | 38 |
| | Goods: Road-building equipment, beer, plastics, mufflers, pruning saws, attic fans, valve regulators | | | | | |
| Lorain–Elyria, OH | Housing: 100<br>Food: 99*<br>Other: 106* | Income: $27,700<br>Taxes: $764<br>Bite: 2.76% | Blue-Collar Index: 121<br>White-Collar Index: 79<br>Unemployment Threat: High | Income: 28.56%<br>Jobs: −15.36% | 3,301 | 326 |
| | Goods: Cars and trucks, machine tools, plasterboard, primary metals | | | | | |
| Los Angeles–Long Beach, CA | Housing: 166<br>Food: 95*<br>Other: 105* | Income: $36,624<br>Taxes: $1,237<br>Bite: 3.38% | Blue-Collar Index: 100<br>White-Collar Index: 100<br>Unemployment Threat: Moderate | Income: 44.04%<br>Jobs: 6.98% | 5,316 | 174 |
| | Goods: Aircraft, missiles, electronic components, lumber and wood products, clothing, computers | | | | | |
| Louisville, KY–IN | Housing: 82<br>Food: 97<br>Other: 97 | Income: $29,621<br>Taxes: $880<br>Bite: 2.97% | Blue-Collar Index: 107<br>White-Collar Index: 93<br>Unemployment Threat: Moderate | Income: 37.32%<br>Jobs: 7.56% | 5,402 | 163 |
| | Goods: Electrical appliances, auto bodies, beer, biscuits, tanks, baseball bats, whiskey, cigarettes, racehorses | | | | | |
| Lowell, MA–NH | Housing: 116<br>Food: 94*<br>Other: 97* | Income: $36,644<br>Taxes: $1,695<br>Bite: 4.63% | Blue-Collar Index: 110<br>White-Collar Index: 90<br>Unemployment Threat: Moderate | Income: 53.86%<br>Jobs: 12.08% | 6,651 | 47 |
| | Goods: Textiles, yarns and threads, textile machinery, knitwear, wire and cable, printing, computers | | | | | |
| Lubbock, TX | Housing: 84<br>Food: 102<br>Other: 103 | Income: $29,523<br>Taxes: $214<br>Bite: 0.72% | Blue-Collar Index: 97<br>White-Collar Index: 103<br>Unemployment Threat: Low | Income: 47.74%<br>Jobs: 9.01% | 5,923 | 104 |
| | Goods: Dairy products, poultry, grain, livestock, cotton | | | | | |
| Lynchburg, VA | Housing: 83<br>Food: 100*<br>Other: 98* | Income: $26,124<br>Taxes: $919<br>Bite: 3.52% | Blue-Collar Index: 113<br>White-Collar Index: 87<br>Unemployment Threat: High | Income: 40.17%<br>Jobs: 3.56% | 4,926 | 229 |
| | Goods: Batteries, nuclear reactors, furniture, overalls, hosiery, shoes, chemicals | | | | | |

| Metro Area | Living Costs (U.S. Avg.=100) | Average Household Income and Taxes | Occupations (U.S. Avg.=100) | Five-Year Growth Income and Jobs | Places Rated Score | Places Rated Rank |
|---|---|---|---|---|---|---|
| Macon–Warner Robins, GA | Housing: 75<br>Food: 101<br>Other: 96 | Income: $26,944<br>Taxes: $972<br>Bite: 3.61% | Blue-Collar Index: 106<br>White-Collar Index: 94<br>Unemployment Threat: Moderate | Income: 46.69%<br>Jobs: 7.46% | 5,659 | 134 |
| | Goods: Cottonseed oil, flour, pulp wood, cardboard containers, ceramics, overalls, drugs | | | | | |
| Madison, WI | Housing: 119<br>Food: 94*<br>Other: 102* | Income: $33,569<br>Taxes: $1,574<br>Bite: 4.69% | Blue-Collar Index: 82<br>White-Collar Index: 118<br>Unemployment Threat: Low | Income: 40.95%<br>Jobs: 8.21% | 5,448 | 160 |
| | Goods: Hot dogs, sausages, dry-cell batteries, farm machinery, lenses, printing and publishing | | | | | |
| Manchester, NH | Housing: 118<br>Food: 94*<br>Other: 97* | Income: $32,245<br>Taxes: None<br>Bite: None | Blue-Collar Index: 106<br>White-Collar Index: 94<br>Unemployment Threat: Moderate | Income: 49.04%<br>Jobs: 31.57% | 7,101 | 32 |
| | Goods: Knitting and textile machinery, textiles and clothing, boots and shoes, electronic components, lumber and wood products | | | | | |
| Mansfield, OH | Housing: 83<br>Food: 99*<br>Other: 98* | Income: $27,594<br>Taxes: $761<br>Bite: 2.76% | Blue-Collar Index: 121<br>White-Collar Index: 79<br>Unemployment Threat: High | Income: 33.55%<br>Jobs: −4.16% | 4,386 | 288 |
| | Goods: Instruments, fire alarms, thermostats, generators, gasoline engines, tires, steel tubes | | | | | |
| McAllen–Edinburg–Mission, TX | Housing: 64<br>Food: 100<br>Other: 100 | Income: $16,478<br>Taxes: $146<br>Bite: 0.89% | Blue-Collar Index: 110<br>White-Collar Index: 90<br>Unemployment Threat: Moderate | Income: 48.69%<br>Jobs: 27.67% | 5,739 | 124 |
| | Goods: Grapefruit, oranges, clothing, ready-mix concrete, oil, natural gas | | | | | |
| Medford, OR | Housing: 108<br>Food: 109*<br>Other: 103* | Income: $24,699<br>Taxes: $1,046<br>Bite: 4.23% | Blue-Collar Index: 103<br>White-Collar Index: 97<br>Unemployment Threat: Moderate | Income: 29.08%<br>Jobs: 0.12% | 3,692 | 321 |
| | Goods: Lumber, raisins, wine | | | | | |
| Melbourne–Titusville–Palm Bay, FL | Housing: 105<br>Food: 102*<br>Other: 108* | Income: $29,646<br>Taxes: $310<br>Bite: 1.05% | Blue-Collar Index: 95<br>White-Collar Index: 105<br>Unemployment Threat: Low | Income: 49.80%<br>Jobs: 36.11% | 7,089 | 33 |
| | Goods: Electrical equipment, transportation equipment, seafood, citrus fruit | | | | | |
| Memphis, TN–AR–MS | Housing: 84<br>Food: 103<br>Other: 97 | Income: $27,910<br>Taxes: $329<br>Bite: 1.18% | Blue-Collar Index: 101<br>White-Collar Index: 99<br>Unemployment Threat: Moderate | Income: 38.21%<br>Jobs: 5.67% | 5,160 | 204 |
| | Goods: Farm machinery, truck trailers, drugs, paper, furniture, feeds, cosmetics, cotton, lumber | | | | | |
| Miami–Hialeah, FL | Housing: 123<br>Food: 96<br>Other: 107 | Income: $32,808<br>Taxes: $338<br>Bite: 1.03% | Blue-Collar Index: 96<br>White-Collar Index: 104<br>Unemployment Threat: Low | Income: 43.64%<br>Jobs: 14.65% | 5,840 | 114 |
| | Goods: Clothing, drugs, mattresses, water heaters, shutters, ships | | | | | |
| Middlesex–Somerset–Hunterdon, NJ | Housing: 146<br>Food: 108*<br>Other: 105* | Income: $40,205<br>Taxes: $1,121<br>Bite: 2.79% | Blue-Collar Index: 97<br>White-Collar Index: 103<br>Unemployment Threat: Low | Income: 49.65%<br>Jobs: 13.28% | 6,324 | 63 |
| | Goods: Adhesive bandages, baby powder, baby products, paper machinery, wire, needles, auto parts | | | | | |
| Middletown, CT | Housing: 140<br>Food: 110*<br>Other: 103* | Income: $37,565<br>Taxes: $477<br>Bite: 1.27% | Blue-Collar Index: 89<br>White-Collar Index: 111<br>Unemployment Threat: Low | Income: 52.28%<br>Jobs: 12.04% | 6,307 | 67 |
| | Goods: Jet engines, leather gaskets, office supplies, brake linings | | | | | |
| ★ Midland, TX | Housing: 104<br>Food: 103*<br>Other: 97* | Income: $46,458<br>Taxes: $291<br>Bite: 0.63% | Blue-Collar Index: 96<br>White-Collar Index: 104<br>Unemployment Threat: Low | Income: 60.56%<br>Jobs: 47.62% | 9,980 | 1 |
| | Goods: Machinery, oil-field supplies, electrical components, boats, printing and publishing | | | | | |
| Milwaukee, WI | Housing: 122<br>Food: 94*<br>Other: 94* | Income: $35,272<br>Taxes: $1,703<br>Bite: 4.83% | Blue-Collar Index: 106<br>White-Collar Index: 94<br>Unemployment Threat: Moderate | Income: 40.33%<br>Jobs: −4.03% | 4,982 | 224 |
| | Goods: Engines, auto frames, truck bodies, beer, heavy pumping machinery, mine shovels, outboard motors, motorcycles, earphones, cheese, sausage | | | | | |
| Minneapolis–St. Paul, MN–WI | Housing: 115<br>Food: 96<br>Other: 95 | Income: $35,871<br>Taxes: $1,822<br>Bite: 5.08% | Blue-Collar Index: 94<br>White-Collar Index: 106<br>Unemployment Threat: Low | Income: 42.52%<br>Jobs: 8.22% | 5,843 | 113 |
| | Goods: Computers, lawn mowers, sprinklers, dairy products, canned and frozen food, grains, flour, cereals, farm machinery | | | | | |

| Metro Area | Living Costs (U.S. Avg.=100) | Average Household Income and Taxes | Occupations (U.S. Avg.=100) | Five-Year Growth Income and Jobs | Places Rated Score | Places Rated Rank |
|---|---|---|---|---|---|---|
| Mobile, AL | Housing: 80<br>Food: 97<br>Other: 99 | Income: $24,839<br>Taxes: $789<br>Bite: 3.18% | Blue-Collar Index: 111<br>White-Collar Index: 89<br>Unemployment Threat: Moderate | Income: 37.49%<br>Jobs: 0.95% | 4,565 | 273 |
| | Goods: Pitch pine, petrochemicals, wood furniture, ships and barges | | | | | |
| Modesto, CA | Housing: 103<br>Food: 98*<br>Other: 110* | Income: $29,641<br>Taxes: $829<br>Bite: 2.80% | Blue-Collar Index: 110<br>White-Collar Index: 90<br>Unemployment Threat: Moderate | Income: 36.86%<br>Jobs: 10.40% | 5,107 | 210 |
| | Goods: Meat, poultry, dairy products, wine, olive oil, nuts, fruit, crates and bags, dehydrators | | | | | |
| Monmouth–Ocean, NJ | Housing: 140<br>Food: 108*<br>Other: 105* | Income: $34,367<br>Taxes: $933<br>Bite: 2.71% | Blue-Collar Index: 94<br>White-Collar Index: 106<br>Unemployment Threat: Low | Income: 49.81%<br>Jobs: 17.55% | 6,154 | 80 |
| | Goods: Venetian blinds, televisions, candy, clothing | | | | | |
| Monroe, LA | Housing: 74<br>Food: 104*<br>Other: 101* | Income: $24,906<br>Taxes: $243<br>Bite: 0.98% | Blue-Collar Index: 102<br>White-Collar Index: 98<br>Unemployment Threat: Moderate | Income: 46.32%<br>Jobs: 10.22% | 5,537 | 148 |
| | Goods: Paper, boxes, beverages, awnings, ink, bricks | | | | | |
| Montgomery, AL | Housing: 81<br>Food: 100<br>Other: 98 | Income: $26,827<br>Taxes: $851<br>Bite: 3.17% | Blue-Collar Index: 99<br>White-Collar Index: 101<br>Unemployment Threat: High | Income: 36.62%<br>Jobs: 4.13% | 4,892 | 236 |
| | Goods: Canned food, syrup, soft drinks, pickles, clothing, air conditioners | | | | | |
| Muncie, IN | Housing: 70<br>Food: 96<br>Other: 99 | Income: $25,032<br>Taxes: $829<br>Bite: 3.31% | Blue-Collar Index: 110<br>White-Collar Index: 90<br>Unemployment Threat: Moderate | Income: 33.65%<br>Jobs: −10.33% | 3,980 | 309 |
| | Goods: Auto parts, jet-engine parts, wire, fencing, fruit jars, lawn mowers | | | | | |
| Muskegon, MI | Housing: 77<br>Food: 99*<br>Other: 104* | Income: $26,438<br>Taxes: $1,227<br>Bite: 4.64% | Blue-Collar Index: 118<br>White-Collar Index: 82<br>Unemployment Threat: High | Income: 34.65%<br>Jobs: −15.30% | 3,708 | 320 |
| | Goods: Iron castings, auto and airplane engines, furniture, boilers, bearings, bowling and billiard balls, chlorine gas | | | | | |
| Nashua, NH | Housing: 129<br>Food: 94*<br>Other: 97* | Income: $32,245<br>Taxes: None<br>Bite: None | Blue-Collar Index: 103<br>White-Collar Index: 97<br>Unemployment Threat: Moderate | Income: 49.04%<br>Jobs: 31.57% | 6,962 | 36 |
| | Goods: Paper, pulp, electronic components, molding machinery, caskets, greeting cards, beer, disinfectants, bronze and brass products | | | | | |
| Nashville, TN | Housing: 94<br>Food: 99<br>Other: 99 | Income: $28,641<br>Taxes: $344<br>Bite: 1.20% | Blue-Collar Index: 102<br>White-Collar Index: 98<br>Unemployment Threat: Moderate | Income: 41.30%<br>Jobs: 19.12% | 5,938 | 102 |
| | Goods: Boats and barges, coffee, spices, cereals, printing and publishing, hosiery, bridges, electronic equipment | | | | | |
| ★ Nassau–Suffolk, NY | Housing: 134<br>Food: 101*<br>Other: 103* | Income: $43,075<br>Taxes: $2,230<br>Bite: 5.18% | Blue-Collar Index: 90<br>White-Collar Index: 110<br>Unemployment Threat: Low | Income: 56.31%<br>Jobs: 20.07% | 7,371 | 22 |
| | Goods: Aircraft, computers, fabricated metals, salad dressing, ticket punchers, pianos | | | | | |
| New Bedford, MA | Housing: 97<br>Food: 100*<br>Other: 100* | Income: $27,591<br>Taxes: $1,198<br>Bite: 4.34% | Blue-Collar Index: 123<br>White-Collar Index: 77<br>Unemployment Threat: High | Income: 43.46%<br>Jobs: 1.96% | 4,937 | 228 |
| | Goods: Golf balls, fish, mortar-shell casings, ball bearings, instant color film, cotton and silk goods, tire fabric | | | | | |
| New Britain, CT | Housing: 126<br>Food: 110*<br>Other: 103* | Income: $37,565<br>Taxes: $477<br>Bite: 1.27% | Blue-Collar Index: 113<br>White-Collar Index: 87<br>Unemployment Threat: Moderate | Income: 52.28%<br>Jobs: 12.04% | 6,470 | 53 |
| | Goods: Automatic doors, machine tools, hand tools, chucks, specialty meats | | | | | |
| New Haven–Meriden, CT | Housing: 137<br>Food: 110*<br>Other: 103* | Income: $34,364<br>Taxes: $458<br>Bite: 1.33% | Blue-Collar Index: 98<br>White-Collar Index: 102<br>Unemployment Threat: Low | Income: 47.49%<br>Jobs: 5.08% | 5,478 | 156 |
| | Goods: Firearms, ammunition, tools, clocks and watches, lamps, silverware, airplane parts, oil filters, telephones, cutlery, chocolate | | | | | |
| New London–Norwich, CT–RI | Housing: 123<br>Food: 100*<br>Other: 103* | Income: $32,922<br>Taxes: $438<br>Bite: 1.29% | Blue-Collar Index: 109<br>White-Collar Index: 91<br>Unemployment Threat: Moderate | Income: 58.43%<br>Jobs: 16.48% | 6,672 | 45 |
| | Goods: Submarines, ships, safety razors, toothpaste, underwear, engines and turbines | | | | | |

| Metro Area | Living Costs (U.S. Avg.=100) | Average Household Income and Taxes | Occupations (U.S. Avg.=100) | Five-Year Growth Income and Jobs | Places Rated Score | Places Rated Rank |
|---|---|---|---|---|---|---|
| New Orleans, LA | Housing: 102<br>Food: 98<br>Other: 98 | Income: $32,704<br>Taxes: $346<br>Bite: 1.06% | Blue-Collar Index: 99<br>White-Collar Index: 101<br>Unemployment Threat: Low | Income: 52.66%<br>Jobs: 11.68% | 6,453 | 54 |
| | Goods: Ships and barges, molasses and syrups, beer, burlap, roofing, luggage, clothing, asbestos | | | | | |
| New York, NY | Housing: 160<br>Food: 112<br>Other: 114 | Income: $36,047<br>Taxes: $1,637<br>Bite: 4.54% | Blue-Collar Index: 88<br>White-Collar Index: 112<br>Unemployment Threat: Moderate | Income: 46.85%<br>Jobs: 8.16% | 5,338 | 169 |
| | Goods: Clothing, printing and publishing, metal and machine-shop products, chemicals, paint, textiles, foods, beverages | | | | | |
| Newark, NJ | Housing: 171<br>Food: 108<br>Other: 105 | Income: $38,279<br>Taxes: $1,056<br>Bite: 2.76% | Blue-Collar Index: 96<br>White-Collar Index: 104<br>Unemployment Threat: Low | Income: 50.55%<br>Jobs: 7.29% | 5,690 | 128 |
| | Goods: Paint, varnish, perfume, cosmetics, liquor, gold, silver, electrical machinery | | | | | |
| Niagara Falls, NY | Housing: 92<br>Food: 104*<br>Other: 97* | Income: $29,123<br>Taxes: $1,151<br>Bite: 3.95% | Blue-Collar Index: 118<br>White-Collar Index: 82<br>Unemployment Threat: High | Income: 40.82%<br>Jobs: −9.84% | 4,463 | 283 |
| | Goods: Abrasives, record players, business forms, helicopters, paint | | | | | |
| Norfolk–<br>Virginia Beach–<br>Newport News, VA | Housing: 103<br>Food: 102<br>Other: 100 | Income: $29,375<br>Taxes: $1,054<br>Bite: 3.59% | Blue-Collar Index: 103<br>White-Collar Index: 97<br>Unemployment Threat: Moderate | Income: 49.38%<br>Jobs: 12.41% | 5,866 | 109 |
| | Goods: Ships, beverages, candy, peanuts, lawn mowers, electric motors, woodworking machinery, printing, furniture | | | | | |
| Norwalk, CT | Housing: 242<br>Food: 110*<br>Other: 103* | Income: $47,258<br>Taxes: $546<br>Bite: 1.16% | Blue-Collar Index: 83<br>White-Collar Index: 117<br>Unemployment Threat: Low | Income: 53.37%<br>Jobs: 17.60% | 6,432 | 55 |
| | Goods: Astronomic instruments, electric signals, office machines, duplicators, bathrobes, boats, oysters and lobsters, X-ray tubes | | | | | |
| Oakland, CA | Housing: 157<br>Food: 108*<br>Other: 120* | Income: $38,279<br>Taxes: $1,345<br>Bite: 3.51% | Blue-Collar Index: 93<br>White-Collar Index: 107<br>Unemployment Threat: Low | Income: 45.00%<br>Jobs: 8.60% | 5,457 | 158 |
| | Goods: Glass, aluminum, electric cable, cement, rubber goods, wheat, barley, paper products, publishing, clothing, candy, household products, oil, gas | | | | | |
| Ocala, FL | Housing: 81<br>Food: 97*<br>Other: 101* | Income: $23,777<br>Taxes: $265<br>Bite: 1.11% | Blue-Collar Index: 108<br>White-Collar Index: 92<br>Unemployment Threat: Moderate | Income: 50.70%<br>Jobs: 39.38% | 7,060 | 34 |
| | Goods: Meat and meat products, citrus fruits, frozen foods, drugs, air compressors, air-purification machinery, electronic equipment, lumber | | | | | |
| ★ Odessa, TX | Housing: 80<br>Food: 103<br>Other: 97 | Income: $34,591<br>Taxes: $245<br>Bite: 0.71% | Blue-Collar Index: 117<br>White-Collar Index: 83<br>Unemployment Threat: High | Income: 50.38%<br>Jobs: 25.44% | 7,565 | 17 |
| | Goods: Oil-field supplies, elevators, welding equipment, brass, cattle, sheep, petrochemicals | | | | | |
| ★ Oklahoma City, OK | Housing: 86<br>Food: 100<br>Other: 94 | Income: $35,773<br>Taxes: $894<br>Bite: 2.50% | Blue-Collar Index: 99<br>White-Collar Index: 101<br>Unemployment Threat: Low | Income: 59.48%<br>Jobs: 27.09% | 8,119 | 5 |
| | Goods: Aircraft, fabricated metal, computers, clothing, oil-field equipment, crude oil | | | | | |
| Olympia, WA | Housing: 99<br>Food: 103*<br>Other: 112* | Income: $30,467<br>Taxes: $458<br>Bite: 1.59% | Blue-Collar Index: 91<br>White-Collar Index: 109<br>Unemployment Threat: Low | Income: 29.84%<br>Jobs: 11.25% | 4,912 | 231 |
| | Goods: Shingles, belting, beer, oysters, farm machinery | | | | | |
| Omaha, NE–IA | Housing: 85<br>Food: 97*<br>Other: 99* | Income: $31,912<br>Taxes: $784<br>Bite: 2.46% | Blue-Collar Index: 94<br>White-Collar Index: 106<br>Unemployment Threat: Low | Income: 41.05%<br>Jobs: 9.07% | 5,853 | 112 |
| | Goods: Beer, paint and varnish, ball bearings, farm machinery, electric signs, dairy products, grain, feeds, livestock | | | | | |
| Orange County, NY | Housing: 122<br>Food: 101<br>Other: 103 | Income: $30,218<br>Taxes: $1,227<br>Bite: 4.06% | Blue-Collar Index: 103<br>White-Collar Index: 97<br>Unemployment Threat: Moderate | Income: 49.29%<br>Jobs: 14.44% | 5,822 | 115 |
| | Goods: Shirts, hats, boxes, purses, imitation leather, radio parts | | | | | |
| ★ Orlando, FL | Housing: 98<br>Food: 102*<br>Other: 108* | Income: $29,896<br>Taxes: $310<br>Bite: 1.04% | Blue-Collar Index: 95<br>White-Collar Index: 105<br>Unemployment Threat: Moderate | Income: 52.27%<br>Jobs: 38.53% | 7,413 | 21 |
| | Goods: Missiles, candy, coffee, orange-juice concentrate, yachts | | | | | |

| Metro Area | Living Costs (U.S. Avg.=100) | Average Household Income and Taxes | Occupations (U.S. Avg.=100) | Five-Year Growth Income and Jobs | Places Rated Score | Places Rated Rank |
|---|---|---|---|---|---|---|
| Owensboro, KY | Housing: 81 Food: 104* Other: 94* | Income: $28,708 Taxes: $852 Bite: 2.97% | Blue-Collar Index: 116 White-Collar Index: 84 Unemployment Threat: High | Income: 40.55% Jobs: 19.48% | 6,062 | 89 |
| | Goods: Whiskey, cheese, canned foods, flour, oil, meat and poultry, radio tubes, cigars | | | | | |
| Oxnard–Ventura, CA | Housing: 168 Food: 101* Other: 104* | Income: $32,304 Taxes: $984 Bite: 3.05% | Blue-Collar Index: 97 White-Collar Index: 103 Unemployment Threat: Low | Income: 43.91% Jobs: 18.18% | 5,514 | 150 |
| | Goods: Aircraft components, trailers, seafood, tomatoes, petroleum products, electronic components | | | | | |
| Panama City, FL | Housing: 76 Food: 98* Other: 96* | Income: $24,570 Taxes: $280 Bite: 1.14% | Blue-Collar Index: 100 White-Collar Index: 100 Unemployment Threat: Moderate | Income: 45.57% Jobs: 20.88% | 6,083 | 86 |
| | Goods: Paper and paperboard, lawn mowers, boats, cypress shingles, cabinets | | | | | |
| Parkersburg–Marietta, WV–OH | Housing: 80 Food: 103* Other: 94* | Income: $26,852 Taxes: $836 Bite: 3.11% | Blue-Collar Index: 115 White-Collar Index: 85 Unemployment Threat: Moderate | Income: 37.31% Jobs: 8.61% | 5,187 | 196 |
| | Goods: Steel castings, nylon, fiberglass, plastics, glass tubing | | | | | |
| Pascagoula, MS | Housing: 75 Food: 107* Other: 95* | Income: $25,410 Taxes: $620 Bite: 2.44% | Blue-Collar Index: 117 White-Collar Index: 83 Unemployment Threat: High | Income: 44.09% Jobs: −9.99% | 4,491 | 278 |
| | Goods: Ships, paper bags, boxes, underwear, bricks, fertilizer, petrochemicals | | | | | |
| Pawtucket–Woonsocket–Attleboro, RI–MA | Housing: 113 Food: 100* Other: 100* | Income: $30,094 Taxes: $1,003 Bite: 3.33% | Blue-Collar Index: 130 White-Collar Index: 70 Unemployment Threat: High | Income: 43.96% Jobs: 3.72% | 5,154 | 205 |
| | Goods: Thread, lace, fiberglass, toys, wire and cable, gold and silver plate, nuclear fuel, jewelry | | | | | |
| Pensacola, FL | Housing: 78 Food: 98 Other: 96 | Income: $25,032 Taxes: $280 Bite: 1.12% | Blue-Collar Index: 104 White-Collar Index: 96 Unemployment Threat: Moderate | Income: 48.11% Jobs: 16.85% | 6,029 | 94 |
| | Goods: Fertilizer, nylon, tar, creosote, wallboard | | | | | |
| Peoria, IL | Housing: 101 Food: 105 Other: 98 | Income: $35,552 Taxes: $1,074 Bite: 3.20% | Blue-Collar Index: 108 White-Collar Index: 92 Unemployment Threat: Moderate | Income: 29.46% Jobs: −16.28% | 4,073 | 306 |
| | Goods: Bulldozers, earth-movers, castings, oil burners, beer and liquor, caskets | | | | | |
| Philadelphia, PA–NJ | Housing: 100 Food: 98* Other: 106* | Income: $33,449 Taxes: $1,001 Bite: 2.99% | Blue-Collar Index: 101 White-Collar Index: 99 Unemployment Threat: Moderate | Income: 44.64% Jobs: 4.50% | 5,638 | 140 |
| | Goods: Machinery, printing and publishing, drugs | | | | | |
| Phoenix, AZ | Housing: 107 Food: 105 Other: 108 | Income: $31,041 Taxes: $1,019 Bite: 3.28% | Blue-Collar Index: 96 White-Collar Index: 104 Unemployment Threat: Low | Income: 45.18% Jobs: 27.00% | 6,415 | 56 |
| | Goods: Aircraft parts, radios, publishing, beer and liquor, fruit juices, pickles and olives, sugar | | | | | |
| Pine Bluff, AR | Housing: 68 Food: 102* Other: 91* | Income: $23,108 Taxes: $558 Bite: 2.41% | Blue-Collar Index: 115 White-Collar Index: 85 Unemployment Threat: Moderate | Income: 32.15% Jobs: −0.89% | 4,247 | 299 |
| | Goods: Towboats, cotton-picking equipment, paper bags, newsprint, transformers, beef, pork, rice, soybeans | | | | | |
| Pittsburgh, PA | Housing: 97 Food: 107* Other: 107* | Income: $32,934 Taxes: $990 Bite: 3.01% | Blue-Collar Index: 105 White-Collar Index: 95 Unemployment Threat: Moderate | Income: 44.83% Jobs: −1.64% | 5,261 | 184 |
| | Goods: Steel, iron, aluminum, rolling-mill machinery, coke, oil, foods, plate glass, chemicals | | | | | |
| Pittsfield, MA | Housing: 94 Food: 94* Other: 97* | Income: $30,537 Taxes: $1,358 Bite: 4.45% | Blue-Collar Index: 101 White-Collar Index: 99 Unemployment Threat: Moderate | Income: 49.07% Jobs: −0.83% | 5,483 | 155 |
| | Goods: Plastics, paper, electrical products, missiles | | | | | |
| Portland, ME | Housing: 97 Food: 94* Other: 97* | Income: $30,794 Taxes: $999 Bite: 3.24% | Blue-Collar Index: 99 White-Collar Index: 101 Unemployment Threat: Low | Income: 46.99% Jobs: 14.66% | 6,186 | 76 |
| | Goods: Paper and wooden boxes, shoes and boots, threads and yarn, potato chips, burial cases, fish packing | | | | | |
| Portland, OR | Housing: 119 Food: 106 Other: 112 | Income: $33,020 Taxes: $1,553 Bite: 4.70% | Blue-Collar Index: 97 White-Collar Index: 103 Unemployment Threat: Low | Income: 32.64% Jobs: 2.85% | 4,535 | 274 |
| | Goods: Instruments, ships, fuel stokers, lumber, furniture, paper, woolen products | | | | | |

| Metro Area | Living Costs (U.S. Avg.=100) | Average Household Income and Taxes | Occupations (U.S. Avg.=100) | Five-Year Growth Income and Jobs | Places Rated Score | Places Rated Rank |
|---|---|---|---|---|---|---|
| ★ Portsmouth–Dover–Rochester, NH–ME | Housing: 119 Food: 94* Other: 97* | Income: $30,170 Taxes: None Bite: None | Blue-Collar Index: 112 White-Collar Index: 88 Unemployment Threat: Moderate | Income: 47.36% Jobs: 62.51% | 8,367 | 3 |
| | Goods: Microwave parts, tools and dies, drinks, buttons, reaming tools | | | | | |
| Poughkeepsie, NY | Housing: 120 Food: 101* Other: 103* | Income: $34,616 Taxes: $1,537 Bite: 4.44% | Blue-Collar Index: 93 White-Collar Index: 107 Unemployment Threat: Low | Income: 55.84% Jobs: 18.94% | 6,746 | 42 |
| | Goods: Cream separators, milking equipment, business machines, electrical insulators, lingerie, precision gauges | | | | | |
| Providence, RI | Housing: 111 Food: 100* Other: 100* | Income: $30,094 Taxes: $1,003 Bite: 3.33% | Blue-Collar Index: 112 White-Collar Index: 88 Unemployment Threat: Moderate | Income: 43.96% Jobs: 3.72% | 5,154 | 205 |
| | Goods: Valves, jewelry, machine tools, woolens and worsteds, plastics, electronic parts | | | | | |
| Provo–Orem, UT | Housing: 112 Food: 100 Other: 105 | Income: $18,390 Taxes: $892 Bite: 4.85% | Blue-Collar Index: 106 White-Collar Index: 94 Unemployment Threat: Moderate | Income: 29.52% Jobs: 6.96% | 3,459 | 323 |
| | Goods: Pig iron, cast iron, women's clothing, steel pipes, tanks, sporting goods | | | | | |
| Pueblo, CO | Housing: 80 Food: 100 Other: 96 | Income: $27,499 Taxes: $601 Bite: 2.19% | Blue-Collar Index: 108 White-Collar Index: 92 Unemployment Threat: Moderate | Income: 40.46% Jobs: −7.31% | 4,646 | 264 |
| | Goods: Iron, steel, aluminum, auto pistons, storm sashes, brooms, tents, saddles, beer | | | | | |
| Racine, WI | Housing: 107 Food: 95* Other: 99* | Income: $31,511 Taxes: $1,427 Bite: 4.53% | Blue-Collar Index: 118 White-Collar Index: 82 Unemployment Threat: High | Income: 33.23% Jobs: −4.49% | 4,415 | 286 |
| | Goods: Floor and furniture waxes, playing cards, lawn mowers, luggage, tractors, books | | | | | |
| Raleigh–Durham, NC | Housing: 99 Food: 96 Other: 95 | Income: $30,489 Taxes: $1,209 Bite: 3.97% | Blue-Collar Index: 88 White-Collar Index: 112 Unemployment Threat: Low | Income: 45.95% Jobs: 21.76% | 6,405 | 58 |
| | Goods: Cigarettes, tobacco products, textiles, generators, pillowcases, steel tanks, surgical instruments, hosiery | | | | | |
| Reading, PA | Housing: 91 Food: 98* Other: 106* | Income: $32,449 Taxes: $979 Bite: 3.02% | Blue-Collar Index: 122 White-Collar Index: 78 Unemployment Threat: High | Income: 44.50% Jobs: 3.02% | 5,587 | 145 |
| | Goods: Auto frames, hardware, lace machines, optical goods, steel alloys, women's underwear | | | | | |
| Redding, CA | Housing: 103 Food: 99* Other: 100* | Income: $26,348 Taxes: $679 Bite: 2.58% | Blue-Collar Index: 99 White-Collar Index: 101 Unemployment Threat: Low | Income: 26.60% Jobs: 11.75% | 4,459 | 284 |
| | Goods: Timber, wood products, beverage bottling | | | | | |
| Reno, NV | Housing: 149 Food: 102 Other: 111 | Income: $38,472 Taxes: $374 Bite: 0.97% | Blue-Collar Index: 91 White-Collar Index: 109 Unemployment Threat: Low | Income: 32.32% Jobs: 20.26% | 5,677 | 130 |
| | Goods: Microwave equipment, suntan lotion, valves, labeling devices | | | | | |
| Richland–Kennewick–Pasco, WA | Housing: 101 Food: 100 Other: 99 | Income: $32,404 Taxes: $506 Bite: 1.56% | Blue-Collar Index: 102 White-Collar Index: 98 Unemployment Threat: Moderate | Income: 30.03% Jobs: 12.69% | 5,326 | 171 |
| | Goods: Chemicals, foods, printing and publishing | | | | | |
| Richmond–Petersburg, VA | Housing: 100 Food: 103 Other: 102 | Income: $33,510 Taxes: $1,248 Bite: 3.72% | Blue-Collar Index: 99 White-Collar Index: 101 Unemployment Threat: Low | Income: 44.80% Jobs: 8.71% | 5,870 | 108 |
| | Goods: Cigarettes, cigars, pipe and chewing tobacco, fountain pens, luggage, nylon, cellophane, drugs, peanuts, railroad-car bearings | | | | | |
| Riverside–San Bernardino, CA | Housing: 117 Food: 99 Other: 102 | Income: $28,257 Taxes: $771 Bite: 2.73% | Blue-Collar Index: 106 White-Collar Index: 94 Unemployment Threat: Moderate | Income: 37.19% Jobs: 10.38% | 4,923 | 230 |
| | Goods: Orchard heaters, wire-tying machinery, primary metals, tree protectors, citrus fruits | | | | | |
| Roanoke, VA | Housing: 90 Food: 100 Other: 98 | Income: $29,094 Taxes: $1,083 Bite: 3.62% | Blue-Collar Index: 102 White-Collar Index: 98 Unemployment Threat: Moderate | Income: 41.72% Jobs: 5.05% | 5,287 | 178 |
| | Goods: Locks, hydraulic drills, fiberglass, electronic components, textiles | | | | | |
| Rochester, MN | Housing: 110 Food: 96 Other: 102 | Income: $35,344 Taxes: $1,781 Bite: 5.04% | Blue-Collar Index: 82 White-Collar Index: 118 Unemployment Threat: Low | Income: 45.08% Jobs: 12.36% | 6,099 | 85 |
| | Goods: Phonographs, silos, hospital supplies, beverages, foods, home pasteurizers | | | | | |

| Metro Area | Living Costs (U.S. Avg.=100) | Average Household Income and Taxes | Occupations (U.S. Avg.=100) | Five-Year Growth Income and Jobs | Places Rated Score | Places Rated Rank |
|---|---|---|---|---|---|---|
| Rochester, NY | Housing: 103<br>Food: 104*<br>Other: 97* | Income: $34,896<br>Taxes: $1,556<br>Bite: 4.46% | Blue-Collar Index: 103<br>White-Collar Index: 97<br>Unemployment Threat: Moderate | Income: 50.32%<br>Jobs: 9.74% | 6,304 | 69 |
| | Goods: Cameras, optical equipment, photographic film, enameled steel tanks, dental supplies, carburetors, thermometers, electrical components | | | | | |
| Rockford, IL | Housing: 91<br>Food: 99<br>Other: 104 | Income: $31,483<br>Taxes: $1,012<br>Bite: 3.21% | Blue-Collar Index: 115<br>White-Collar Index: 85<br>Unemployment Threat: Moderate | Income: 32.06%<br>Jobs: −2.41% | 4,592 | 269 |
| | Goods: Farm machinery, sports equipment, wire goods, pet food | | | | | |
| Sacramento, CA | Housing: 118<br>Food: 104<br>Other: 107 | Income: $31,292<br>Taxes: $920<br>Bite: 2.94% | Blue-Collar Index: 89<br>White-Collar Index: 111<br>Unemployment Threat: Low | Income: 35.40%<br>Jobs: 16.06% | 5,309 | 175 |
| | Goods: Rockets, guided missiles, olives, frozen foods, rice, polishers, mining equipment, lumber | | | | | |
| Saginaw–Bay City–Midland, MI | Housing: 88<br>Food: 100*<br>Other: 102* | Income: $29,181<br>Taxes: $1,357<br>Bite: 4.65% | Blue-Collar Index: 116<br>White-Collar Index: 84<br>Unemployment Threat: High | Income: 28.83%<br>Jobs: −12.62% | 3,709 | 319 |
| | Goods: Auto parts, power steering, chemicals, washtubs, aluminum, brass, iron | | | | | |
| St. Cloud, MN | Housing: 87<br>Food: 94<br>Other: 95 | Income: $23,954<br>Taxes: $930<br>Bite: 3.88% | Blue-Collar Index: 108<br>White-Collar Index: 92<br>Unemployment Threat: Moderate | Income: 41.85%<br>Jobs: 17.31% | 5,488 | 153 |
| | Goods: Dairy products, livestock, poultry, grain, floor sanders, truck bodies, sporting goods | | | | | |
| St. Joseph, MO | Housing: 67<br>Food: 96<br>Other: 97 | Income: $28,073<br>Taxes: $709<br>Bite: 2.53% | Blue-Collar Index: 113<br>White-Collar Index: 87<br>Unemployment Threat: Moderate | Income: 48.58%<br>Jobs: 6.09% | 5,991 | 101 |
| | Goods: Pet food, flour, paper, paper and wooden boxes, leather goods, clothing | | | | | |
| St. Louis, MO–IL | Housing: 91<br>Food: 95<br>Other: 101 | Income: $34,546<br>Taxes: $916<br>Bite: 2.65% | Blue-Collar Index: 100<br>White-Collar Index: 100<br>Unemployment Threat: Moderate | Income: 42.39%<br>Jobs: 3.55% | 5,800 | 119 |
| | Goods: Auto assembly, jet aircraft, railroad cars, space capsules, beer, hardware, shoes, pet food, clay, limestone, iron and steel | | | | | |
| Salem, OR | Housing: 100<br>Food: 109<br>Other: 103 | Income: $26,213<br>Taxes: $1,132<br>Bite: 4.32% | Blue-Collar Index: 98<br>White-Collar Index: 102<br>Unemployment Threat: Low | Income: 30.39%<br>Jobs: −2.39% | 3,835 | 314 |
| | Goods: Fruits and vegetables, juices, paper, wooden boxes, lumber, tin cans, woolens | | | | | |
| Salem–Gloucester, MA | Housing: 139<br>Food: 103<br>Other: 100 | Income: $36,643<br>Taxes: $1,695<br>Bite: 4.63% | Blue-Collar Index: 102<br>White-Collar Index: 98<br>Unemployment Threat: Moderate | Income: 53.86%<br>Jobs: 12.08% | 6,309 | 65 |
| | Goods: Fish packing, glue, ink, light bulbs, candy, cookware, mattresses | | | | | |
| Salinas–Seaside–Monterey, CA | Housing: 166<br>Food: 97*<br>Other: 101* | Income: $36,439<br>Taxes: $1,226<br>Bite: 3.36% | Blue-Collar Index: 96<br>White-Collar Index: 104<br>Unemployment Threat: Low | Income: 38.18%<br>Jobs: 19.49% | 5,656 | 135 |
| | Goods: Tires, pumps, electrical fixtures, chocolate milk, lettuce, beans, peas, strawberries | | | | | |
| Salt Lake City–Ogden, UT | Housing: 113<br>Food: 96<br>Other: 100 | Income: $27,076<br>Taxes: $1,305<br>Bite: 4.82% | Blue-Collar Index: 100<br>White-Collar Index: 100<br>Unemployment Threat: Moderate | Income: 37.01%<br>Jobs: 12.74% | 4,942 | 227 |
| | Goods: Surgical and medical supplies, mining, smelting, missiles, petroleum products | | | | | |
| ★ San Angelo, TX | Housing: 76<br>Food: 102*<br>Other: 97* | Income: $32,326<br>Taxes: $235<br>Bite: 0.73% | Blue-Collar Index: 106<br>White-Collar Index: 94<br>Unemployment Threat: Moderate | Income: 56.33%<br>Jobs: 25.96% | 7,720 | 10 |
| | Goods: Wool and mohair, meat, grain, cotton, leather goods, surgical sutures | | | | | |
| San Antonio, TX | Housing: 83<br>Food: 99<br>Other: 96 | Income: $28,367<br>Taxes: $214<br>Bite: 0.75% | Blue-Collar Index: 100<br>White-Collar Index: 100<br>Unemployment Threat: Moderate | Income: 52.94%<br>Jobs: 22.65% | 6,873 | 39 |
| | Goods: Beer, flour, soap, candy, batteries, metal containers, shortening, oil | | | | | |
| San Diego, CA | Housing: 173<br>Food: 97<br>Other: 101 | Income: $32,586<br>Taxes: $997<br>Bite: 3.06% | Blue-Collar Index: 93<br>White-Collar Index: 107<br>Unemployment Threat: Low | Income: 44.37%<br>Jobs: 16.82% | 5,489 | 152 |
| | Goods: Computers, golf carts, bamboo, wines, acoustical equipment, caskets, missiles, parachutes, ships | | | | | |
| San Francisco, CA | Housing: 206<br>Food: 108<br>Other: 120 | Income: $47,966<br>Taxes: $2,030<br>Bite: 4.23% | Blue-Collar Index: 81<br>White-Collar Index: 119<br>Unemployment Threat: Low | Income: 48.69%<br>Jobs: 12.53% | 6,063 | 88 |
| | Goods: Dehydrated fruits and vegetables, canning, sheet metal, sugarcane products, paper, pulp, printing and publishing, clothing, tools, electronic parts, ships | | | | | |

| Metro Area | Living Costs (U.S. Avg.=100) | Average Household Income and Taxes | Occupations (U.S. Avg.=100) | Five-Year Growth Income and Jobs | Places Rated Score | Places Rated Rank |
|---|---|---|---|---|---|---|
| ★ San Jose, CA | Housing: 192<br>Food: 101<br>Other: 104 | Income: $41,994<br>Taxes: $1,594<br>Bite: 3.80% | Blue-Collar Index: 93<br>White-Collar Index: 107<br>Unemployment Threat: Low | Income: 57.98%<br>Jobs: 29.70% | 7,270 | 24 |
| | Goods: Computers, electronic components, food canning, wine, beer, berries, atomic generating equipment | | | | | |
| Santa Barbara–Santa Maria–Lompoc, CA | Housing: 186<br>Food: 95*<br>Other: 105* | Income: $36,501<br>Taxes: $1,230<br>Bite: 3.37% | Blue-Collar Index: 91<br>White-Collar Index: 109<br>Unemployment Threat: Low | Income: 51.19%<br>Jobs: 13.37% | 5,821 | 116 |
| | Goods: Aircraft parts, electrical products, gimcracks, meat products, frozen foods, phonograph records, oil | | | | | |
| Santa Cruz, CA | Housing: 171<br>Food: 101*<br>Other: 104* | Income: $32,608<br>Taxes: $998<br>Bite: 3.06% | Blue-Collar Index: 95<br>White-Collar Index: 105<br>Unemployment Threat: Low | Income: 41.49%<br>Jobs: 16.95% | 5,335 | 170 |
| | Goods: Limes, chewing gum, wine, wire, lumber and wood products, electrical products | | | | | |
| Santa Rosa–Petaluma, CA | Housing: 155<br>Food: 108*<br>Other: 120* | Income: $31,743<br>Taxes: $941<br>Bite: 2.96% | Blue-Collar Index: 98<br>White-Collar Index: 102<br>Unemployment Threat: Low | Income: 44.77%<br>Jobs: 22.63% | 5,703 | 127 |
| | Goods: Wine, optical goods, macaroni, dairy products, fruits | | | | | |
| ★ Sarasota, FL | Housing: 115<br>Food: 97*<br>Other: 100* | Income: $39,474<br>Taxes: $378<br>Bite: 0.96% | Blue-Collar Index: 94<br>White-Collar Index: 106<br>Unemployment Threat: Low | Income: 51.56%<br>Jobs: 28.98% | 7,715 | 11 |
| | Goods: Boats, citrus fruits, celery, mobile homes, electrical equipment | | | | | |
| Savannah, GA | Housing: 83<br>Food: 97*<br>Other: 103* | Income: $27,359<br>Taxes: $989<br>Bite: 3.61% | Blue-Collar Index: 109<br>White-Collar Index: 91<br>Unemployment Threat: Moderate | Income: 44.73%<br>Jobs: 10.38% | 5,591 | 144 |
| | Goods: Ships, fish, timber, asphalt, airplanes, plywood, sugar, paper bags | | | | | |
| Scranton–Wilkes-Barre, PA | Housing: 80<br>Food: 101<br>Other: 102 | Income: $26,532<br>Taxes: $812<br>Bite: 3.06% | Blue-Collar Index: 119<br>White-Collar Index: 81<br>Unemployment Threat: High | Income: 43.19%<br>Jobs: −0.36% | 4,907 | 233 |
| | Goods: Shoes, artillery shells, swimming pools, wire rope, pencils, rayon, silk, chewing gum, television tubes | | | | | |
| Seattle, WA | Housing: 122<br>Food: 103*<br>Other: 112* | Income: $37,069<br>Taxes: $546<br>Bite: 1.47% | Blue-Collar Index: 95<br>White-Collar Index: 105<br>Unemployment Threat: Low | Income: 39.24%<br>Jobs: 14.71% | 5,901 | 106 |
| | Goods: Commercial and military jet aircraft, fisheries, electronic components, lumber | | | | | |
| Sharon, PA | Housing: 80<br>Food: 107*<br>Other: 106* | Income: $26,392<br>Taxes: $809<br>Bite: 3.07% | Blue-Collar Index: 123<br>White-Collar Index: 77<br>Unemployment Threat: High | Income: 35.00%<br>Jobs: −7.76% | 4,055 | 307 |
| | Goods: Railroad tank cars, chains, pipes and tubes | | | | | |
| Sheboygan, WI | Housing: 97<br>Food: 96*<br>Other: 95* | Income: $30,923<br>Taxes: $1,391<br>Bite: 4.50% | Blue-Collar Index: 124<br>White-Collar Index: 76<br>Unemployment Threat: High | Income: 39.22%<br>Jobs: −5.45% | 4,765 | 253 |
| | Goods: Bratwurst, sausage, enamelware, clothes, brooms, cheese | | | | | |
| Sherman–Denison, TX | Housing: 69<br>Food: 105<br>Other: 93 | Income: $29,386<br>Taxes: $214<br>Bite: 0.73% | Blue-Collar Index: 118<br>White-Collar Index: 82<br>Unemployment Threat: High | Income: 49.65%<br>Jobs: 6.77% | 6,213 | 75 |
| | Goods: Medical supplies, earth augers, cotton and wool clothing, flour, soybeans, margarine, meat | | | | | |
| Shreveport, LA | Housing: 78<br>Food: 104<br>Other: 105 | Income: $30,817<br>Taxes: $319<br>Bite: 1.04% | Blue-Collar Index: 109<br>White-Collar Index: 91<br>Unemployment Threat: Moderate | Income: 54.97%<br>Jobs: 11.84% | 6,585 | 50 |
| | Goods: Chain saws, cast metals, electrical equipment, sheet metal, feeds, lumber and wood products | | | | | |
| Sioux City, IA–NE | Housing: 78<br>Food: 92*<br>Other: 97* | Income: $29,565<br>Taxes: $961<br>Bite: 3.25% | Blue-Collar Index: 104<br>White-Collar Index: 96<br>Unemployment Threat: Moderate | Income: 32.60%<br>Jobs: −4.64% | 4,648 | 263 |
| | Goods: Autos, fishing tackle, forklifts, popcorn, radios, stock feeds | | | | | |
| Sioux Falls, SD | Housing: 96<br>Food: 96<br>Other: 105 | Income: $31,377<br>Taxes: $350<br>Bite: 1.12% | Blue-Collar Index: 98<br>White-Collar Index: 102<br>Unemployment Threat: Low | Income: 35.08%<br>Jobs: 6.31% | 5,204 | 192 |
| | Goods: Meat, bakery products, granite, sash weights, microwave appliances, dairy products | | | | | |

| Metro Area | Living Costs (U.S. Avg.=100) | Average Household Income and Taxes | Occupations (U.S. Avg.=100) | Five-Year Growth Income and Jobs | Places Rated Score | Places Rated Rank |
|---|---|---|---|---|---|---|
| South Bend–Mishawaka, IN | Housing: 71<br>Food: 97<br>Other: 92 | Income: $29,604<br>Taxes: $963<br>Bite: 3.25% | Blue-Collar Index: 106<br>White-Collar Index: 94<br>Unemployment Threat: Moderate | Income: 36.44%<br>Jobs: −3.51% | 5,056 | 216 |
| | Goods: Power transmission equipment, plastic-coated fabric, pajamas, varnish, auto equipment, machine tools | | | | | |
| Spokane, WA | Housing: 83<br>Food: 104*<br>Other: 99* | Income: $27,549<br>Taxes: $443<br>Bite: 1.61% | Blue-Collar Index: 96<br>White-Collar Index: 104<br>Unemployment Threat: Low | Income: 32.40%<br>Jobs: 3.75% | 4,722 | 259 |
| | Goods: Silver, lead, zinc, aluminum, magnesium, clay, cement products, flour, feeds, cereals | | | | | |
| Springfield, IL | Housing: 95<br>Food: 87<br>Other: 96 | Income: $32,790<br>Taxes: $1,056<br>Bite: 3.22% | Blue-Collar Index: 84<br>White-Collar Index: 116<br>Unemployment Threat: Low | Income: 34.95%<br>Jobs: 5.22% | 5,384 | 165 |
| | Goods: Road tractors, heavy machinery, radio parts, yeast, electrical meters, cereal products | | | | | |
| Springfield, MA | Housing: 96<br>Food: 94*<br>Other: 96* | Income: $29,327<br>Taxes: $1,290<br>Bite: 4.40% | Blue-Collar Index: 107<br>White-Collar Index: 93<br>Unemployment Threat: Moderate | Income: 45.15%<br>Jobs: 2.23% | 5,289 | 177 |
| | Goods: Women's underwear, plastic tile, surgical dressings, matches, firearms, envelopes | | | | | |
| Springfield, MO | Housing: 76<br>Food: 95<br>Other: 95 | Income: $27,266<br>Taxes: $677<br>Bite: 2.48% | Blue-Collar Index: 105<br>White-Collar Index: 95<br>Unemployment Threat: Moderate | Income: 45.56%<br>Jobs: 11.95% | 5,932 | 103 |
| | Goods: Typewriters, paper cups, furniture, eggs, milk, flour, meat | | | | | |
| Stamford, CT | Housing: 283<br>Food: 110*<br>Other: 103* | Income: $47,258<br>Taxes: $546<br>Bite: 1.16% | Blue-Collar Index: 79<br>White-Collar Index: 121<br>Unemployment Threat: Low | Income: 53.37%<br>Jobs: 17.60% | 6,158 | 79 |
| | Goods: Plastics, ball bearings, postage meters, electric shavers, X-ray tubes, ships | | | | | |
| State College, PA | Housing: 101<br>Food: 98*<br>Other: 100* | Income: $23,270<br>Taxes: $714<br>Bite: 3.07% | Blue-Collar Index: 96<br>White-Collar Index: 104<br>Unemployment Threat: Low | Income: 43.52%<br>Jobs: 4.91% | 4,677 | 262 |
| | Goods: Dairy, poultry, grain | | | | | |
| Steubenville–Weirton, OH–WV | Housing: 79<br>Food: 100*<br>Other: 92* | Income: $27,823<br>Taxes: $768<br>Bite: 2.76% | Blue-Collar Index: 132<br>White-Collar Index: 68<br>Unemployment Threat: High | Income: 26.67%<br>Jobs: −13.27% | 3,744 | 317 |
| | Goods: Iron, steel, ferrous alloys, fireclay, coke, tar, tinplate containers, petrochemicals | | | | | |
| Stockton, CA | Housing: 102<br>Food: 98*<br>Other: 99* | Income: $30,713<br>Taxes: $894<br>Bite: 2.91% | Blue-Collar Index: 107<br>White-Collar Index: 93<br>Unemployment Threat: Moderate | Income: 39.54%<br>Jobs: 14.27% | 5,672 | 131 |
| | Goods: Auto windshields, glass containers, plows, paving machinery, cereal products, ships | | | | | |
| Syracuse, NY | Housing: 92<br>Food: 100<br>Other: 94 | Income: $30,114<br>Taxes: $1,221<br>Bite: 4.05% | Blue-Collar Index: 100<br>White-Collar Index: 100<br>Unemployment Threat: Moderate | Income: 50.15%<br>Jobs: −22.15% | 4,474 | 282 |
| | Goods: Telephone equipment, roller bearings, soda ash, purses, china, wax candles, washing machines, electronic components | | | | | |
| Tacoma, WA | Housing: 93<br>Food: 103<br>Other: 112 | Income: $28,683<br>Taxes: $464<br>Bite: 1.62% | Blue-Collar Index: 104<br>White-Collar Index: 96<br>Unemployment Threat: Moderate | Income: 34.70%<br>Jobs: 7.71% | 4,887 | 238 |
| | Goods: Railroad-car wheels, meat, fish, flour, copper, gold, aluminum, ships | | | | | |
| Tallahassee, FL | Housing: 96<br>Food: 99<br>Other: 96 | Income: $24,144<br>Taxes: $280<br>Bite: 1.16% | Blue-Collar Index: 77<br>White-Collar Index: 123<br>Unemployment Threat: Low | Income: 45.36%<br>Jobs: 25.82% | 6,021 | 96 |
| | Goods: Crates, boxes, boats, pine extracts, feed, insecticides, sweet potatoes | | | | | |
| Tampa–St. Petersburg–Clearwater, FL | Housing: 89<br>Food: 96*<br>Other: 101* | Income: $29,890<br>Taxes: $310<br>Bite: 1.04% | Blue-Collar Index: 80<br>White-Collar Index: 120<br>Unemployment Threat: Low | Income: 52.61%<br>Jobs: 30.23% | 7,256 | 25 |
| | Goods: Cigars, cigar boxes, beer, macaroni, brooms, ceramics, phosphate | | | | | |
| Terre Haute, IN | Housing: 66<br>Food: 95*<br>Other: 102* | Income: $26,244<br>Taxes: $872<br>Bite: 3.32% | Blue-Collar Index: 111<br>White-Collar Index: 89<br>Unemployment Threat: Moderate | Income: 33.21%<br>Jobs: −5.16% | 4,353 | 291 |
| | Goods: Phonograph records, picnic boxes, coolers, baking powder, antibiotics, heavy road machinery | | | | | |
| Texarkana, TX–Texarkana, AR | Housing: 69<br>Food: 104<br>Other: 91 | Income: $25,947<br>Taxes: $192<br>Bite: 0.74% | Blue-Collar Index: 115<br>White-Collar Index: 85<br>Unemployment Threat: Moderate | Income: 26.39%<br>Jobs: 8.45% | 4,772 | 252 |
| | Goods: Mobile homes, tires, blue jeans, pulp, wood and paper, battery cases | | | | | |

| Metro Area | Living Costs (U.S. Avg.=100) | Average Household Income and Taxes | Occupations (U.S. Avg.=100) | Five-Year Growth Income and Jobs | Places Rated Score | Places Rated Rank |
|---|---|---|---|---|---|---|
| Toledo, OH | Housing: 93<br>Food: 100*<br>Other: 103* | Income: $30,497<br>Taxes: $873<br>Bite: 2.86% | Blue-Collar Index: 107<br>White-Collar Index: 93<br>Unemployment Threat: Moderate | Income: 33.53%<br>Jobs: −3.31% | 4,534 | 275 |
| | Goods: Auto axles, drive shafts, glass, spark plugs, die castings, gypsum, atomizers | | | | | |
| Topeka, KS | Housing: 85<br>Food: 102*<br>Other: 105* | Income: $33,199<br>Taxes: $864<br>Bite: 2.60% | Blue-Collar Index: 96<br>White-Collar Index: 104<br>Unemployment Threat: Low | Income: 40.97%<br>Jobs: 0.94% | 5,464 | 157 |
| | Goods: Serum, tires, cast metals, printing and publishing, flour mills, meat, poultry, egg packing | | | | | |
| Trenton, NJ | Housing: 127<br>Food: 108*<br>Other: 105* | Income: $36,520<br>Taxes: $999<br>Bite: 2.74% | Blue-Collar Index: 89<br>White-Collar Index: 111<br>Unemployment Threat: Low | Income: 49.08%<br>Jobs: 4.59% | 5,772 | 121 |
| | Goods: Refrigerated showcases, light bulbs, rubber goods, purses, auto-body hardware, pottery | | | | | |
| Tucson, AZ | Housing: 102<br>Food: 101<br>Other: 105 | Income: $27,913<br>Taxes: $834<br>Bite: 2.99% | Blue-Collar Index: 96<br>White-Collar Index: 104<br>Unemployment Threat: Low | Income: 47.46%<br>Jobs: 22.89% | 6,147 | 81 |
| | Goods: Air conditioners, missiles, airplane instruments, ammunition, dental tools, women's clothing, cotton, grain, cattle | | | | | |
| Tulsa, OK | Housing: 90<br>Food: 106<br>Other: 104 | Income: $35,700<br>Taxes: $891<br>Bite: 2.50% | Blue-Collar Index: 103<br>White-Collar Index: 97<br>Unemployment Threat: Moderate | Income: 50.98%<br>Jobs: 21.01% | 7,115 | 31 |
| | Goods: Oil, petroleum products, meats, feeds, fishing rods, natural gas, boilers, burners | | | | | |
| Tuscaloosa, AL | Housing: 78<br>Food: 105<br>Other: 102 | Income: $23,531<br>Taxes: $745<br>Bite: 3.17% | Blue-Collar Index: 105<br>White-Collar Index: 95<br>Unemployment Threat: Moderate | Income: 43.41%<br>Jobs: 5.59% | 4,900 | 235 |
| | Goods: Truck bodies, tires, monuments, fishing lures, fertilizer | | | | | |
| ★ Tyler, TX | Housing: 88<br>Food: 102<br>Other: 104 | Income: $32,930<br>Taxes: $235<br>Bite: 0.71% | Blue-Collar Index: 111<br>White-Collar Index: 89<br>Unemployment Threat: Moderate | Income: 56.23%<br>Jobs: 22.89% | 7,327 | 23 |
| | Goods: Battery cases, baskets, soil pipe, cast metals, water heaters | | | | | |
| Utica–Rome, NY | Housing: 81<br>Food: 100*<br>Other: 99* | Income: $27,305<br>Taxes: $1,035<br>Bite: 3.79% | Blue-Collar Index: 106<br>White-Collar Index: 94<br>Unemployment Threat: Moderate | Income: 47.11%<br>Jobs: 0.29% | 5,226 | 189 |
| | Goods: Golf clubs, fishing tackle, copper products, furnaces, magnesium castings, mufflers | | | | | |
| Vallejo–Fairfield–Napa, CA | Housing: 126<br>Food: 108*<br>Other: 100* | Income: $31,578<br>Taxes: $933<br>Bite: 2.95% | Blue-Collar Index: 104<br>White-Collar Index: 96<br>Unemployment Threat: Moderate | Income: 43.14%<br>Jobs: 18.53% | 5,819 | 117 |
| | Goods: Wine, flour, window screens, athletic equipment, sheet metal | | | | | |
| Vancouver, WA | Housing: 108<br>Food: 106*<br>Other: 112* | Income: $28,767<br>Taxes: $464<br>Bite: 1.61% | Blue-Collar Index: 111<br>White-Collar Index: 89<br>Unemployment Threat: Moderate | Income: 31.79%<br>Jobs: 7.70% | 4,571 | 272 |
| | Goods: Beer, pulp and paper, chemicals, brick, aluminum, lumber, paint, salmon, poultry | | | | | |
| ★ Victoria, TX | Housing: 86<br>Food: 103<br>Other: 104 | Income: $32,824<br>Taxes: $235<br>Bite: 0.72% | Blue-Collar Index: 117<br>White-Collar Index: 83<br>Unemployment Threat: High | Income: 55.17%<br>Jobs: 28.92% | 7,599 | 16 |
| | Goods: Boats, chemicals, concrete, cotton compresses | | | | | |
| Vineland–Millville–Bridgeton, NJ | Housing: 87<br>Food: 108*<br>Other: 105* | Income: $28,050<br>Taxes: $749<br>Bite: 2.67% | Blue-Collar Index: 123<br>White-Collar Index: 77<br>Unemployment Threat: High | Income: 46.93%<br>Jobs: −2.18% | 5,023 | 219 |
| | Goods: Fireworks, glassware, candy, fruit and dairy products | | | | | |
| Visalia–Tulare–Porterville, CA | Housing: 93<br>Food: 99<br>Other: 100 | Income: $25,804<br>Taxes: $730<br>Bite: 2.83% | Blue-Collar Index: 109<br>White-Collar Index: 91<br>Unemployment Threat: Moderate | Income: 36.90%<br>Jobs: 22.67% | 5,563 | 147 |
| | Goods: Wine, carpet, transformers, fruit canning, electronic equipment | | | | | |
| Waco, TX | Housing: 73<br>Food: 108*<br>Other: 100* | Income: $28,837<br>Taxes: $214<br>Bite: 0.74% | Blue-Collar Index: 108<br>White-Collar Index: 92<br>Unemployment Threat: Moderate | Income: 50.44%<br>Jobs: 11.83% | 6,259 | 71 |
| | Goods: Work clothes, brooms, patio furniture, venetian blinds, asbestos | | | | | |
| Washington, DC–MD–VA | Housing: 165<br>Food: 107<br>Other: 107 | Income: $41,888<br>Taxes: $2,371<br>Bite: 5.66% | Blue-Collar Index: 75<br>White-Collar Index: 125<br>Unemployment Threat: Low | Income: 47.67%<br>Jobs: 13.44% | 6,072 | 87 |
| | Goods: Printing and publishing, bakery goods, sausage, paper, paint, sewer pipe, textiles, railroad refrigerator cars | | | | | |

| Metro Area | Living Costs (U.S. Avg.=100) | Average Household Income and Taxes | Occupations (U.S. Avg.=100) | Five-Year Growth Income and Jobs | Places Rated Score | Places Rated Rank |
|---|---|---|---|---|---|---|
| Waterbury, CT | Housing: 120 Food: 110* Other: 103* | Income: $34,364 Taxes: $458 Bite: 1.33% | Blue-Collar Index: 113 White-Collar Index: 87 Unemployment Threat: Moderate | Income: 47.49% Jobs: 5.08% | 5,656 | 135 |
| | Goods: Brass and copper goods, clocks and watches, women's underwear, toys, tools, wire | | | | | |
| Waterloo–Cedar Falls, IA | Housing: 94 Food: 98* Other: 95* | Income: $30,881 Taxes: $1,025 Bite: 3.32% | Blue-Collar Index: 112 White-Collar Index: 88 Unemployment Threat: Moderate | Income: 33.91% Jobs: −8.63% | 4,407 | 287 |
| | Goods: Farm tractors, athletic uniforms, refrigerators, meat, cereal and grain | | | | | |
| Wausau, WI | Housing: 92 Food: 96 Other: 95 | Income: $26,168 Taxes: $1,086 Bite: 4.15% | Blue-Collar Index: 113 White-Collar Index: 87 Unemployment Threat: Moderate | Income: 35.14% Jobs: −2.51% | 4,300 | 295 |
| | Goods: Roofing granules, raincoats, snowplows, nameplates, sashes, granite monuments | | | | | |
| ★ West Palm Beach–Boca Raton–Delray Beach, FL | Housing: 126 Food: 106 Other: 108 | Income: $39,620 Taxes: $378 Bite: 0.95% | Blue-Collar Index: 96 White-Collar Index: 104 Unemployment Threat: Low | Income: 53.12% Jobs: 38.48% | 7,992 | 8 |
| | Goods: Aircraft equipment, transistors, tools and dies, fishing tackle | | | | | |
| Wheeling, WV–OH | Housing: 79 Food: 102* Other: 94* | Income: $27,594 Taxes: $859 Bite: 3.11% | Blue-Collar Index: 120 White-Collar Index: 80 Unemployment Threat: High | Income: 34.96% Jobs: 0.44% | 4,740 | 256 |
| | Goods: Metal stamping, garbage cans, washtubs, toys, brass, tinplate | | | | | |
| Wichita, KS | Housing: 85 Food: 101* Other: 103* | Income: $34,812 Taxes: $917 Bite: 2.63% | Blue-Collar Index: 107 White-Collar Index: 93 Unemployment Threat: Moderate | Income: 46.00% Jobs: 3.37% | 6,036 | 92 |
| | Goods: Airplanes, household appliances, oil, wheat, grain, meat | | | | | |
| Wichita Falls, TX | Housing: 77 Food: 108 Other: 101 | Income: $33,877 Taxes: $235 Bite: 0.69% | Blue-Collar Index: 112 White-Collar Index: 88 Unemployment Threat: Moderate | Income: 57.64% Jobs: 6.11% | 6,805 | 41 |
| | Goods: Float glass, cotton gins, oil-field machinery, surgical dressings, beef, electrical equipment | | | | | |
| Williamsport, PA | Housing: 87 Food: 101* Other: 102* | Income: $26,317 Taxes: $807 Bite: 3.07% | Blue-Collar Index: 122 White-Collar Index: 78 Unemployment Threat: High | Income: 20.24% Jobs: −7.62% | 3,288 | 327 |
| | Goods: Crepe paper, airplane and marine engines, stainless steel, wire rope, flashbulbs | | | | | |
| Wilmington, DE–NJ–MD | Housing: 95 Food: 103* Other: 103* | Income: $33,927 Taxes: $1,358 Bite: 4.00% | Blue-Collar Index: 100 White-Collar Index: 100 Unemployment Threat: Moderate | Income: 44.89% Jobs: 13.44% | 6,174 | 77 |
| | Goods: Chemicals, explosives, leather goods, cork, floor coverings, ships, iron, barges, yachts | | | | | |
| Wilmington, NC | Housing: 82 Food: 97 Other: 98 | Income: $26,633 Taxes: $1,005 Bite: 3.77% | Blue-Collar Index: 111 White-Collar Index: 89 Unemployment Threat: Moderate | Income: 41.38% Jobs: 10.09% | 5,390 | 164 |
| | Goods: Scrap iron, heavy machinery, paper, creosote, synthetic fibers, chemicals | | | | | |
| Worcester, MA | Housing: 104 Food: 94 Other: 97 | Income: $29,374 Taxes: $1,292 Bite: 4.40% | Blue-Collar Index: 103 White-Collar Index: 97 Unemployment Threat: Moderate | Income: 44.94% Jobs: −0.87% | 5,040 | 218 |
| | Goods: Abrasives and grinding wheels, woolens and worsteds, machine tools, knives, firearms, thread, brushes | | | | | |
| Yakima, WA | Housing: 77 Food: 104 Other: 99 | Income: $26,972 Taxes: $443 Bite: 1.64% | Blue-Collar Index: 109 White-Collar Index: 91 Unemployment Threat: Moderate | Income: 31.89% Jobs: 9.53% | 4,986 | 223 |
| | Goods: Wine, canvas goods, lumber, dried fruit, fruit sizers, sprayers, farm machinery | | | | | |
| York, PA | Housing: 100 Food: 98 Other: 102 | Income: $28,985 Taxes: $879 Bite: 3.03% | Blue-Collar Index: 125 White-Collar Index: 75 Unemployment Threat: High | Income: 40.01% Jobs: 2.69% | 4,946 | 226 |
| | Goods: Hydraulic turbines, pretzels, furniture, refrigerating and air-conditioning equipment | | | | | |
| Youngstown–Warren, OH | Housing: 84 Food: 100 Other: 93 | Income: $28,960 Taxes: $814 Bite: 2.81% | Blue-Collar Index: 122 White-Collar Index: 78 Unemployment Threat: High | Income: 30.30% Jobs: −14.27% | 3,894 | 313 |
| | Goods: Iron, steel, sheet metal and tubing, limestone, auto parts, fire extinguishers, ball bearings | | | | | |
| Yuba City, CA | Housing: 94 Food: 99* Other: 100* | Income: $27,501 Taxes: $724 Bite: 2.63% | Blue-Collar Index: 103 White-Collar Index: 97 Unemployment Threat: Moderate | Income: 30.46% Jobs: 8.21% | 4,694 | 261 |
| | Goods: Concrete pipe, seed cleaners, fruit canning | | | | | |

## WHERE THE MILLIONAIRES ARE

Figures compiled by the U.S. Trust Company in 1980 will make you think twice about the frowsy housewife in front of you in the supermarket checkout line: There are an estimated 574,300 millionaires in the United States, and not all of them live in Beverly Hills and Palm Beach.

The Gettys, Hunts, and Hearsts are where you would expect to find them, monitoring their empires from California, Texas, and New York. These states—along with Florida, Illinois, New Jersey, Ohio, Pennsylvania, Connecticut, and Michigan—have the greatest number of millionaires. But surprisingly, when the number of millionaires is related to the population of the state, the list looks quite different. Idaho, North Dakota, and Maine lead in terms of millionaires per 100,000 population, mainly because of the high land value and sparse population common in most agricultural states. California, Texas, and New York rank substantially lower because of their denser populations.

### Millionaires per 100,000: The States Ranked

| State | Millionaires per 100,000 Population | State | Millionaires per 100,000 Population |
|---|---|---|---|
| 1. Idaho | 2,621 | 26. Oklahoma | 205 |
| 2. North Dakota | 914 | 27. Mississippi | 194 |
| 3. Maine | 696 | 28. South Carolina | 189 |
| 4. Nebraska | 686 | 29. North Carolina | 187 |
| 5. Minnesota | 574 | 30. Michigan | 171 |
| 6. Iowa | 462 | 31. Washington | 169 |
| 7. Indiana | 453 | 32. California | 163 |
| 8. Wisconsin | 452 | 33. Texas | 162 |
| 9. Montana | 390 | 34. Alabama | 161 |
| 10. New Jersey | 389 | 34. Rhode Island | 161 |
| 11. Connecticut | 387 | 36. Virginia | 153 |
| 12. Delaware | 343 | 37. Pennsylvania | 148 |
| 13. New York | 319 | 38. Kentucky | 146 |
| 14. Massachusetts | 315 | 38. Louisiana | 146 |
| 15. Illinois | 311 | 40. South Dakota | 136 |
| 16. Florida | 303 | 41. Missouri | 123 |
| 17. Kansas | 293 | 42. Arizona | 115 |
| 18. Ohio | 289 | 43. Oregon | 102 |
| 19. Tennessee | 288 | 44. New Hampshire | 97 |
| 20. Hawaii | 269 | 45. Maryland/D.C. | 86 |
| 21. Colorado | 267 | 46. West Virginia | 65 |
| 22. Vermont | 239 | 47. Utah | 56 |
| 23. Alaska | 223 | 48. Arkansas | 44 |
| 23. New Mexico | 223 | 49. Nevada | 35 |
| 25. Georgia | 209 | 50. Wyoming | 29 |

*Source: U.S. Trust Company of New York, 1980 National Wealth Survey.*

## EXPENSIVE NEIGHBORHOODS: WHERE MONEY INCOME IS HIGHEST

Just as incomes are higher in metro areas than in the rural countryside, so are they higher in certain suburbs within a metro area. Among all the 7,749 incorporated cities, towns, boroughs, villages, and other places in the United States that have populations over 2,500, per capita money incomes in 75 metro area suburbs are at least two and a half times the national average of $7,298.

Where is the highest figure found? Not in tony Beverly Hills, Lake Forest, nor Chevy Chase. It's in Hunters Creek Village, out on Memorial Drive west of Houston, where average per capita income is a comfortable $32,859 a year.

### The 34 Metro Areas with the Most Affluent Suburbs

**Albany–Schenectady–Troy, NY**
Schaghticoke

**Anaheim–Santa Ana, CA**
Newport Beach

**Bergen–Passaic, NJ**
Saddle River

**Birmingham, AL**
Mountain Brook

**Chicago, IL**
Barrington Hills
Flossmoor
Glencoe
Inverness
Kenilworth
Oak Brook
Olympia Fields
Winnetka

**Cincinnati, OH–KY–IN**
Amberly
Village of Indian Hill

**Cleveland, OH**
Pepper Pike

**Dallas, TX**
Highland Park

**Denver, CO**
Cherry Hills

**Detroit, MI**
Bloomfield
Franklin
Grosse Pointe Farms
Grosse Pointe Shores

**Houston, TX**
Bunker Hill Village
Hunters Creek Village
Piney Point Village

**Kansas City, KS**
Mission Hills

**Lake County, IL**
Lake Forest
Lincolnshire
Riverwoods

**Los Angeles–Long Beach, CA**
Beverly Hills
Marina Del Rey
Palos Verdes Estates
Rolling Hills Estates
San Marino
Woodside

**Miami–Hialeah, FL**
Bal Harbour
Key Biscayne

**Milwaukee, WI**
Elm Grove
Fox Point

**Minneapolis–St. Paul, MN–WI**
North Oaks

**Nashville, TN**
Belle Meade
Forest Hills

**Nassau–Suffolk, NY**
East Hills
Flower Hill
Great Neck Estates
Kings Point
Lloyd Harbor
Muttontown
Old Westbury
Sands Point
Scarsdale

**New York, NY**
Bronxville

**Newark, NJ**
Harding
Millburn

**Oklahoma City, OK**
Nichols Hills

**Pittsburgh, PA**
Fox Chapel

**Riverside–San Bernardino, CA**
Rancho Mirage

**Saginaw–Bay City–Midland, MI**
Spaulding

**St. Louis, MO–IL**
Frontenac
Ladue
Town and Country

**San Diego, CA**
Rancho Santa Fe

**San Francisco, CA**
Atherton
Hillsborough
Portola Valley
Ross
Sausalito
Tiburon

**San Jose, CA**
Los Altos Hills

**Seattle, WA**
Clyde Hill
Medina

| Stamford, CT | Washington, DC–MD–VA |
|---|---|
| Darien | Chevy Chase Section Four |
| New Canaan | |
| | **West Palm Beach–Boca** |
| **Toledo, OH** | **Raton–Delray Beach, FL** |
| Ottawa Hills | Palm Beach |

Source: U.S. Bureau of the Census, 1980 Census of Population and Housing.

## THE TAXMAN COMETH

Question: Where in America can you find rock-bottom property taxes, no sales taxes, no taxes on any of your sources of income, no niggling nickel-and-dime fees for registering a car or taking out a license to catch largemouth bass, and no inheritance taxes for your heirs to pay?

Answer: Dream on. This ideal tax haven would have to combine the low property taxes of Louisiana, New Hampshire's absence of retail sales taxes, South Dakota's forgiveness of taxes on personal income, South Carolina's light licensing fees, and Nevada's lack of estate taxes. Unfortunately, you just can't find all these wonderful tax breaks in one state.

Most Americans don't object to governments raising money through taxes, according to 1983 polls conducted by the Advisory Commission on Intergovernmental Relations. What they do object to is the effect certain levies have on their lives. Although federal income taxes take the same bite whether you live in New Bedford, New Orleans, or New York, state taxes can differ dramatically around the country. Sales taxes, excise taxes, license taxes, income taxes, property taxes, death taxes, gift taxes, severance taxes, and head taxes are just some of the forms that state taxes take. Depending on where you live, you may encounter all of them or only a few.

*Property Taxes.* Taxes on land and the buildings on it—whether they are homes, farms, industrial plants, or commercial buildings—are the biggest source of cash for local governments. They are imposed not by states but by the 13,527 cities, townships, counties, school districts, sanitary districts, hospital districts, and other assessing jurisdictions in the nation. The states' role is to specify the maximum rate on the market value of the property, or a percentage of it, as the legal standard for local assessors to follow. The local assessor determines the value to be taxed. If you think the valuation is too high, you have a limited right of appeal.

You can't escape property taxes in any state except Alaska (where you must be over 65 to take advantage of that break), but you can find significantly low rates in certain parts of the country. Nationally, the average bills on homes amount to 1.25 percent of their market value, whereas the average bills in Alabama, Arizona, Hawaii, Louisiana, and West Virginia are based on less than half that rate.

*Sales Taxes.* If Americans had a choice of raising income taxes or raising sales taxes, they would overwhelmingly opt for the latter, according to recent polls. Sometimes called retail taxes or consumption taxes, sales taxes are collected at the retail level on the purchase of goods. After property taxes, they account for the second largest source of revenue for state and local governments.

Among the states, the average sales tax is 5 percent. If you're living in Connecticut, you're paying the nation's highest state rate: 7.5 percent. But the highest rate paid by anyone in the country is the 8.5 percent levied on retail purchases in New York City's five boroughs, a rate created in 1975 to help the city stay afloat.

Five states—Alaska, Delaware, Montana, New Hampshire, and Oregon—collect no sales taxes at all. To a four-person family, this could mean a savings of hundreds of dollars. But you can avoid paying almost that much in states where such basics as food, medicine, and clothing are excluded from any sales tax.

*Personal Income Taxes.* When the first federal income tax went into effect in 1913, two states—Mississippi and Wisconsin—were already collecting income taxes on their own. It was only during the 1920s and 1930s that the majority of states began to raise cash by tapping personal incomes. Today, 40 states impose the tax; two (New Hampshire and Tennessee) apply it only to income from interest and dividends; one (Connecticut) applies it only to income from capital gains and dividends; and seven (Alaska, Florida, Nevada, South Dakota, Texas, Washington, and Wyoming) don't tax incomes at all.

*License Taxes.* These usually are enacted as flat fees for regulating a certain kind of privilege. For example, you'll pay a license tax on the family car for the right to use it on public highways; you'll buy a fishing license for the privilege of trolling for trout at the lake main-

---

### Taxing the Necessities

**You'll pay sales tax on groceries in . . .**

| | | |
|---|---|---|
| Alabama | Mississippi | South Carolina |
| Arkansas | Missouri | South Dakota |
| Georgia | Nebraska | Tennessee |
| Hawaii | New Mexico | Utah |
| Idaho | North Carolina | Virginia |
| Kansas | Oklahoma | Wyoming |
| Michigan | | |

**And sales tax on medicine in . . .**

| | | |
|---|---|---|
| Arizona | Michigan | Utah |
| Arkansas | Mississippi | Vermont |
| Georgia | Missouri | Virginia |
| Hawaii | New Mexico | |

**But NO sales tax on clothes in . . .**

| | |
|---|---|
| Massachusetts | New Jersey |
| Minnesota | Rhode Island |

**And NO sales tax, period, in . . .**

| | |
|---|---|
| Alaska | New Hampshire |
| Delaware | Oregon |
| Montana | |

Source: Commerce Clearing House, State Tax Guide, 1984.

## Comparing Direct Tax Burdens: The States Ranked

| State | Per Capita Burden | Percent of U.S. Average | State | Per Capita Burden | Percent of U.S. Average |
|---|---|---|---|---|---|
| 1. New Hampshire | $ 77 | 15.12% | 26. North Carolina | $450 | 88.28% |
| 2. Alaska | 197 | 38.72 | 27. Kansas | 456 | 89.57 |
| 3. Montana | 285 | 55.97 | 28. Oregon | 457 | 89.63 |
| 4. Texas | 300 | 58.89 | 29. Louisiana | 459 | 90.21 |
| 5. Florida | 320 | 62.84 | 30. Oklahoma | 460 | 90.30 |
| 6. Nevada | 362 | 70.98 | 31. Georgia | 483 | 94.85 |
| 7. Vermont | 363 | 71.36 | 32. Pennsylvania | 505 | 99.17 |
| 8. Tennessee | 367 | 72.15 | 33. Michigan | 510 | 100.20 |
| 9. Connecticut | 371 | 72.87 | 34. Colorado | 511 | 100.31 |
| 10. South Dakota | 376 | 73.86 | 35. Iowa | 517 | 101.60 |
| 11. North Dakota | 380 | 74.56 | 36. Illinois | 523 | 102.82 |
| 12. Arkansas | 401 | 78.77 | 37. Washington | 528 | 103.82 |
| 12. New Jersey | 401 | 78.77 | 38. Utah | 535 | 105.20 |
| 14. Ohio | 421 | 82.70 | 39. Delaware | 545 | 107.15 |
| 15. Mississippi | 424 | 83.22 | 40. Arizona | 549 | 107.77 |
| 16. Alabama | 434 | 85.23 | 41. New Mexico | 556 | 109.19 |
| 17. Missouri | 436 | 85.57 | 42. Massachusetts | 565 | 110.88 |
| 18. Idaho | 438 | 86.09 | 43. Virginia | 575 | 112.81 |
| 19. Maine | 439 | 86.10 | 44. Minnesota | 605 | 118.78 |
| 20. Nebraska | 440 | 86.41 | 45. Wisconsin | 611 | 119.97 |
| 21. Indiana | 443 | 87.02 | 46. Wyoming | 622 | 122.23 |
| 22. South Carolina | 446 | 87.53 | 47. Maryland | 662 | 129.91 |
| 22. West Virginia | 446 | 87.53 | 48. California | 691 | 135.62 |
| 24. Kentucky | 447 | 87.67 | 49. New York | 788 | 154.65 |
| 25. Rhode Island | 449 | 88.20 | 50. Hawaii | 982 | 192.80 |

*Source:* Derived from the Advisory Commission on Intergovernmental Relations, *Tax Capacity of the Fifty States*, 1983.

Direct taxes include taxes on personal income, general sales, gasoline, driver's licenses, and automobile registration fees. The U.S. average per capita burden is $509.

tained by the state; you'll need a retail license to serve up beer and wine at the roadhouse you've just bought. Together, these license taxes and fees make up a small part of a state's revenues. Of all the states, Wyoming gets the most money per capita from the various taxes on driving a car, and New York—surprisingly—the least. Alaska's taxes on hunting and fishing privileges are the steepest in the country, Indiana's the lightest. If you're going to open a bar in Alaska or West Virginia, you can expect to shell out the highest license fees in the nation, whereas in Hawaii, Nevada, Wisconsin, and Wyoming, you'd pay nothing.

*Excise Taxes.* In most states, when you return from an errand having bought a tankful of gas for the family car, a bottle of gin, and a pack of cigarettes, you've also just paid excise taxes. Excise taxes are related to sales taxes but are different in that they are levied only on specific items. Gasoline at the pump, for example, is taxed in every state at a higher rate than the local sales tax rate (excise taxes on gasoline are heaviest in Wyoming, lightest in Texas). Tobacco and alcohol, too, are big targets for excise taxes, usually at rates that suggest social disapproval. In fact, taxes on cigarettes and liquor are popularly called sin taxes.

*Estate and Inheritance Taxes.* Death duties, as they are called sometimes, are taxes imposed when any kind of real property is transferred at death. They are imposed on the dead person's estate under the Federal Estate Tax, and in most states they take the form of inheritance taxes on the beneficiaries of the estate.

The philosophy underlying estate and inheritance taxes is that heirs should be required to pay a tax on additions to their wealth that they receive as an inheritance. To make the laws stick, however, gift taxes are also levied. Otherwise, property could be passed on tax-free by the owner in anticipation of death. Even though death and gift taxes are minor sources of revenue, several states—California, Connecticut, Iowa, New Jersey, and Pennsylvania—take greater pains to tap this source than the others.

## GOLDEN TRIANGLES, RESEARCH TRIANGLES

One of the few areas in the nation left untouched by the Great Depression was the humid East Texas oil fields, where the Lone Star State's most famous gusher, at Spindletop Hill, began pumping atop a salt-dome formation near Beaumont in 1901. Over the years, companies the likes of Gulf, Union, Texaco, and Mobil have put up sprawling tank farms and refineries to process a seemingly endless outpour of oil.

Bounded by three cities—Beaumont, Port Arthur, and Orange—the area is known as the Golden Triangle. Among Texas's 28 metro areas, it ranks second from the bottom in percentage of people who are college graduates, but seventh highest in personal income. In no other metro area in the state is there a greater portion of people with blue-collar jobs. Yet despite the Golden Triangle's history of prosperity, even during the flush times of 1983–84 the unemployment rate here didn't drop below 12 percent.

Northeast some 1,000 miles is an area bordered by North Carolina's capital, Raleigh, and two nearby cities, Chapel Hill and Durham. In their midst is Research Triangle Park, a 5,500-acre chunk of pine-lands tenanted by think tanks and white-smock research firms. The Research Triangle, as the three cities together have come to be called, is as different from East Texas as it is from nearby metro areas dominated by low-wage jobs in textile, furniture, and cigarette factories. Here you'll find North Carolina's highest portion of people with college degrees, white-collar jobs, and high personal incomes. You'll also find one of the nation's lowest unemployment rates.

Two rules on which labor economists agree are that a factory job producing durable and nondurable goods is anything but durable, and that a job in construction seldom rests on solid ground. In each of the seven business recessions that have hit the United States since the end of World War II, blue-collar workers have been the principal job losers.

During the 1974 recession, one of every three metro areas experienced sharp increases in unemployment because of large numbers of blue-collar workers who punched time clocks, whether in automobile plants in the Great Lakes states, in Pacific Northwest lumber mills, in factories that produced iron and steel in the Ohio Valley, or in petrochemical refineries in the Gulf South.

Nor was the Sun Belt immune. Orlando, Miami, and several other Florida metro areas experienced sharp increases in their numbers of jobless. So did Phoenix. A large number of building tradespeople were caught when the vacation- and retirement-home construction boom fizzled in mid-decade.

It hasn't been any different during the latest slumps of 1980 and 1981–82. Every section of the country had its share of hard times, but the stories that came out of muscle-bound metro areas—places with the largest numbers of blue-collar workers, who for the most part build the homes and make the goods that consumers buy in confident times—were the saddest.

Just as metro areas can be rated for features as diverse as their climates, the quality of their restaurants, and their supply of public golf courses, so can they be rated for how vulnerable they are to high unemployment during a business slump. It can be said that the cyclical threat of unemployment is:

- *High* if blue-collar workers represent 40 percent or more of the total of white-collar and blue-collar workers in the metro area

- *Moderate* if blue-collar workers represent from 34 percent to 39 percent of the total of white-collar and blue-collar workers in the metro area
- *Low* if blue-collar workers represent 33 percent or less of the total of white-collar and blue-collar workers in the metro area

In the 329 metropolitan areas, the unemployment threat is high in 64, moderate in 162, and low in 103. (See the Place Profiles earlier in this chapter for the unemployment threat in each metro area.)

### Unemployment Threat in the Metro Areas

| Highest | Blue-Collar Workers as Percent of Total Workforce |
|---|---|
| 1. Hickory, NC | 60.04% |
| 2. Danville, VA | 57.45 |
| 3. Anderson, SC | 56.41 |
| 4. Steubenville–Weirton, OH–WV | 54.97 |
| 5. Pawtucket–Woonsocket–Attleboro, RI–MA | 53.61 |
| 6. Burlington, NC | 51.90 |
| 7. Anderson, IN | 51.52 |
| 8. Gadsden, AL | 51.49 |
| 9. Beaver County, PA | 51.21 |
| 10. Fall River, MA–RI | 50.77 |

| Lowest | |
|---|---|
| 1. Lake County, IL | 17.42% |
| 2. Atlanta, GA | 17.86 |
| 3. Washington, DC–MD–VA | 17.90 |
| 4. Tallahassee, FL | 19.16 |
| 5. Stamford, CT | 20.06 |
| 6. Tampa–St. Petersburg–Clearwater, FL | 21.18 |
| 7. San Francisco, CA | 21.58 |
| 8. Columbia, MO | 21.70 |
| 9. Iowa City, IA | 22.62 |
| 10. Madison, WI | 22.65 |

*Source:* Derived from the U.S. Bureau of the Census, *1980 Census of Population and Housing.*

## COLLECTING UNEMPLOYMENT

If you are laid off or fired, or if you leave your job because of unusual circumstances such as your religious beliefs, the threat of sexual harassment, or illness, you are eligible for weekly cash benefits under local unemployment insurance programs. Unlike qualifying for food stamps or fuel assistance, to receive unemployment benefits you do not have to prove need; you must only show that you are involuntarily out of work. In Southern California, actors and aerospace workers queue up for weekly checks; in New York, so do longshoremen and advertising executives.

The unemployment insurance program, established in 1935 as part of the Social Security Act, is run jointly by the federal and state governments and covers nearly all nonfarm workers. The program was designed to provide both people and the local economy with partial replacement of wages and purchasing power during short periods of joblessness.

The amount of your unemployment check is related to how much you were earning before you became

## Unemployment Can Be Debilitating, Dangerous, and Deadly

Psychologists and physicians have long noted evidence of depression, anxiety, aggression, insomnia, loss of self-esteem, and marital problems among their patients who are out of work. The damage to the U.S. economy caused by the consecutive business slumps of 1980 and 1981–82 has been estimated at billions of dollars in lost output, but the costs to the jobless are still being totaled long after the start of the recovery.

According to M. Harvey Brenner, a Johns Hopkins University researcher who has studied the effects of business cycles on the nation's health, hard economic times are always followed by increases in the numbers of illnesses, crimes, and deaths. Based on the U.S. population in 1980, Dr. Brenner concludes that a 10 percent rise in unemployment (from 10 percent unemployment to 11 percent, for example) would result in:

5,885 *more admissions to mental institutions*
403,830 *more criminal arrests,* including
8,078 for fraud and embezzlement
4,919 for aggravated assault
24,450 *more deaths,* including
17,392 from heart disease and stroke
409 from cirrhosis
403 homicides
189 suicides

*Source:* U.S. Congress, Joint Economic Committee, Committee Prints 98–198 and 98–200, June 1984.

| State | Legal Range of Payments | Average Weekly Check | Average Duration |
|---|---|---|---|
| Hawaii | $5–$188 | $129.82 | 15 wks |
| Idaho | 45–173 | 116.45 | 15 |
| Illinois | 50–209 | 146.01 | 19 |
| Indiana | 40–141 | 94.24 | 14 |
| Iowa | 22–176 | 137.26 | 15 |
| Kansas | 43–175 | 128.05 | 15 |
| Kentucky | 22–140 | 116.01 | 16 |
| Louisiana | 10–205 | 144.75 | 17 |
| Maine | 22–208 | 101.40 | 15 |
| Maryland | 25–175 | 116.14 | 16 |
| Massachusetts | 14–278 | 115.36 | 16 |
| Michigan | 55–197 | 154.38 | 17 |
| Minnesota | 52–198 | 137.08 | 17 |
| Mississippi | 30–115 | 79.72 | 14 |
| Missouri | 14–105 | 93.72 | 14 |
| Montana | 42–171 | 122.11 | 14 |
| Nebraska | 12–120 | 96.73 | 13 |
| Nevada | 16–162 | 116.00 | 15 |
| New Hampshire | 26–141 | 95.37 | 9 |
| New Jersey | 20–170 | 120.09 | 17 |
| New Mexico | 29–145 | 105.49 | 17 |
| New York | 40–180 | 98.88 | 20 |
| North Carolina | 15–166 | 104.02 | 11 |
| North Dakota | 60–185 | 127.61 | 14 |
| Ohio | 10–233 | 143.59 | 18 |
| Oklahoma | 16–197 | 137.22 | 12 |
| Oregon | 47–204 | 117.48 | 18 |
| Pennsylvania | 35–222 | 146.38 | 18 |
| Rhode Island | 37–194 | 107.67 | 15 |
| South Carolina | 21–125 | 93.83 | 12 |
| South Dakota | 28–129 | 109.53 | 13 |
| Tennessee | 30–115 | 87.02 | 15 |
| Texas | 27–182 | 126.91 | 12 |
| Utah | 46–186 | 129.68 | 16 |
| Vermont | 18–146 | 107.42 | 15 |
| Virginia | 54–150 | 108.17 | 11 |
| Washington | 51–185 | 130.68 | 18 |
| West Virginia | 18–225 | 129.58 | 16 |
| Wisconsin | 37–196 | 136.62 | 16 |
| Wyoming | 20–183 | 136.56 | 13 |

*Source:* U.S. Department of Labor, Employment and Training Administration, 1984.

unemployed, subject to a ceiling. Of the possible payments allowed by law, those paid to workers with families in Alaska, Connecticut, Massachusetts, Ohio, and West Virginia are the highest in the country; those in Arizona, Missouri, Mississippi, and Tennessee are the lowest.

Most states limit eligibility to 26 weeks, although the limit is 30 weeks in Massachusetts and Washington and 28 weeks in West Virginia. Alaska, California, Connecticut, and Oregon continue benefits beyond 26 weeks if the state suffers high unemployment. Hawaii will pay benefits beyond 26 weeks if a man-made disaster creates high unemployment. During steep business slumps countrywide, the Federal-State Extended Compensation Program lengthens the time of eligibility another 13 weeks.

### Unemployment Insurance Benefits by State

| State | Legal Range of Payments | Average Weekly Check | Average Duration |
|---|---|---|---|
| Alabama | $22–$120 | $ 80.24 | 13 wks |
| Alaska | 34–228 | 130.25 | 15 |
| Arizona | 40–115 | 100.10 | 16 |
| Arkansas | 40–154 | 96.06 | 13 |
| California | 30–166 | 99.87 | 18 |
| Colorado | 25–206 | 140.83 | 12 |
| Connecticut | 15–252 | 122.47 | 13 |
| Delaware | 20–165 | 98.04 | 14 |
| Florida | 10–150 | 95.28 | 13 |
| Georgia | 27–125 | 96.39 | 11 |

## WHAT AND WHERE THE JOBS WILL BE BY 1995

Projections from the Bureau of Labor Statistics show the number of workers rising from 102 million in 1982, the base year for the projections, to between 125 million and 130 million in 1995. But technological and social changes mean that some jobs will go begging, others will be overcrowded, and still others will be obsolete.

Half of all the additional jobs will be found in only 40 of the thousands of possible occupations. Nearly all of these 40 jobs will require no extensive training, and only ten will require a college degree. The fastest-growing occupations, on the other hand, aren't found on the list that will add the most jobs over the period. These occupations are mainly in the health, data processing, or business services fields, and all of them will undoubtedly require extensive training.

Fewer people are expected to compete for many other jobs over the period, either because the occupations are becoming technologically obsolete (such as stenographers and telephone switchboard operators) or because they are found in dying industries (railroad conductors and brake operators).

### The Top 40 Job Gainers, 1982–1995

| Occupation | Growth in Thousands | Occupation | Growth in Thousands |
|---|---|---|---|
| 1. Janitors and sextons | 779 | 21. Licensed practical nurses | 220 |
| 2. Cashiers | 744 | 22. Computer-systems analysts | 217 |
| 3. Secretaries | 719 | 23. Electrical engineers | 209 |
| 4. General office clerks | 696 | 24. Computer programmers | 205 |
| 5. Salesclerks | 685 | 25. General maintenance repairers | 193 |
| 6. Registered nurses | 642 | | |
| 7. Waiters and waitresses | 562 | 26. Helpers in trades | 190 |
| 8. Kindergarten and elementary teachers | 511 | 27. Receptionists | 189 |
| 9. Truck drivers | 425 | 28. Electricians | 173 |
| 10. Nursing aides and orderlies | 423 | 29. Physicians | 163 |
| | | 30. Clerical supervisors | 162 |
| 11. Technical sales representatives | 386 | | |
| 12. Accountants and auditors | 344 | 31. Computer operators | 160 |
| 13. Automotive mechanics | 324 | 31. Nontechnical sales representatives | 160 |
| 14. Supervisors of blue-collar workers | 319 | 33. Lawyers | 159 |
| 15. Kitchen helpers | 305 | 34. Stockroom and warehouse clerks | 156 |
| | | 35. Typists | 155 |
| 16. Guards and doorkeepers | 300 | | |
| 17. Fast-food restaurant workers | 297 | 36. Delivery and route workers | 153 |
| | | 37. Bookkeepers | 152 |
| 18. Retail-store managers | 292 | 38. Restaurant cooks | 149 |
| 19. Carpenters | 247 | 39. Bank tellers | 142 |
| 20. Electrical and electronic technicians | 222 | 40. Short-order and fast-food cooks | 141 |

Source: U.S. Bureau of Labor Statistics, *Monthly Labor Review*, November 1983.

## WHAT IT TAKES TO JOIN THE *FORTUNE* CLUB

Imagine how long it would take to squander an inheritance of $1,686.7 billion. Even if you were to spend or give away $1 million of your endowment each day, it would take you 4,621 years—and 35 days. In 1983, the combined sales of the 500 industrial companies rated the nation's largest by *Fortune* magazine reached that figure, the largest annual total recorded by *Fortune* since it began compiling its list in 1955.

There are three basic requirements for admission to *Fortune*'s elite club of the top 500 corporations in the country:

- The firm must derive more than half its revenues from manufacturing or mining or both. Several large companies, most recently the Barnes Group (1982 rank: 484), have been dropped from the list because the portion of their sales coming from producer goods dropped below 50 percent.
- The firm's stock must be publicly traded rather than privately held, so that its financial records can be examined by anyone. Three companies, Cone Mills, Dan River, and Geosource, went private after a period of public ownership; consequently, they were ousted from the directory.
- The firm must ring up an annual sales total that places it among the top 500. For a quarter of a century, Detroit's General Motors reigned as the largest American industrial corporation. Since 1980, however, the first spot has been occupied by New York City's Exxon Corporation. In that year, Exxon also became the first company in *Fortune*'s directory to do more than 12 figures ($100 billion) in business. By 1983, Exxon's sales had declined to $88.6 billion.

Since 1970, there have been remarkable southerly and westerly shifts in the locations of corporate headquarters of the top 500. Atlanta, the home of Coca-Cola since the turn of the century, is now on the home office letterhead of six other firms on *Fortune*'s list. The number of high-tech members based in California's Silicon Valley (otherwise known as San Jose) has jumped from two to eight. Only 59 of the 500 had their headquarters in the Sun Belt in 1970; today, the number has more than doubled to 131.

Below are the 111 metro areas that were headquarters of one or more Fortune 500 firms as of 1983, along with the companies located there. (Twenty-three Fortune 500 companies are not included; their home offices aren't located within any metro area.) The companies are listed in order of their sales rank in the 500, which is given in parentheses. Exxon, in New York City, is ranked first; Tandem Computers, in Cupertino, California (the San Jose metro area), is number 500.

### Fortune 500 Metro Areas

**Akron, OH**
Goodyear Tire & Rubber (32)
Firestone Tire & Rubber (95)
B. F. Goodrich (125)
General Tire & Rubber (168)

**Albany–Schenectady–Troy, NY**
Mohasco (393)

**Allentown–Bethlehem, PA–NJ**
Bethlehem Steel (69)

Air Products & Chemicals (212)
Mack Trucks (259)

**Anaheim–Santa Ana, CA**
Baker International (192)
Smith International (375)

**Ann Arbor, MI**
Hoover Universal (351)

**Appleton–Oshkosh–Neenah, WI**
Kimberly-Clark (120)

**Atlanta, GA**
Coca-Cola (48)
Georgia-Pacific (51)
Gold Kist (238)
National Service Industries
   (311)
Fuqua Industries (367)
Oxford Industries (450)
Royal Crown Companies (459)

**Austin, TX**
Tracor (495)

**Baltimore, MD**
Crown Central Petroleum (208)
Black & Decker Manufacturing
   (265)
Easco (457)

**Battle Creek, MI**
Kellogg (158)

**Benton Harbor, MI**
Whirlpool (147)
Clark Equipment (327)

**Bergen–Passaic, NJ**
CPC International (90)
American Cyanamid (107)
Kidde (161)
Ingersoll-Rand (165)
Union Camp (204)
Becton Dickinson (273)
BOC (282)
Thomas J. Lipton (293)
Federal Paper Board (423)
Prentice-Hall (477)

**Birmingham, AL**
Vulcan Materials (339)

**Boise City, ID**
Boise Cascade (113)

**Boston, MA**
Raytheon (59)
Digital Equipment (84)
Gillette (169)
Cabot (224)
Polaroid (256)
General Cinema (312)
EG&G (318)
Data General (335)
M/A-Com (395)
Dennison Manufacturing
   (399)
Foxboro (442)
Prime Computer (451)

**Bridgeport–Milford, CT**
General Electric (10)
Warnaco (456)

**Buffalo, NY**
Agway (98)

**Canton, OH**
Timken (310)
Hoover (387)
Diebold (483)

**Charlotte–Gastonia–
Rock Hill, NC–SC**
Nucor (439)

**Chattanooga, TN–GA**
Dorsey (482)

**Chicago, IL**
Standard Oil of Indiana (8)
Dart & Kraft (33)
Beatrice Foods (36)
Consolidated Foods (49)
Motorola (81)
Esmark (88)
IC Industries (96)

International Harvester (104)
Borg-Warner (106)
FMC (110)
Inland Steel (127)
Abbott Laboratories (137)
Quaker Oats (146)
Swift Independent (152)
McGraw-Edison (175)
Northwest Industries (183)
Baxter Travenol Laboratories
   (191)
Gould (198)
National Can (210)
U.S. Gypsum (215)
Tribune (218)
R. R. Donnelley & Sons (226)
Morton Thiokol (231)
Marmon Group (235)
International Minerals &
   Chemical (237)
Zenith Radio (246)
Brunswick (260)
Square D (269)
G. D. Searle (296)
Hartmarx (304)
Interlake (332)
Dean Foods (333)
CBI Industries (337)
Household Manufacturing (340)
Lubrizol (343)
Outboard Marine (344)
Bell & Howell (379)
Nalco Chemical (389)
Stone Container (391)
Wm. Wrigley Jr. (414)
AM International (427)
Illinois Tool Works (455)
Amsted Industries (458)
Roper (462)
Ceco (469)
Pittway (491)
Masonite (499)

**Cincinnati, OH–KY–IN**
Procter & Gamble (22)
Cincinnati Milacron (433)
Eagle-Picher Industries (443)
Palm Beach (467)

**Cleveland, OH**
Standard Oil of Ohio (25)
TRW (63)
Eaton (138)
Republic Steel (145)
White Consolidated Industries
   (178)
Sherwin-Williams (184)
Parker Hannifin (289)
Midland-Ross (360)
American Greetings (369)
Scott & Fetzer (397)
Ferro (401)

**Columbus, OH**
Anchor Hocking (349)
Worthington Industries (475)

**Dallas, TX**
Texas Instruments (77)
LTV (78)
Diamond Shamrock (89)
Dresser Industries (112)
American Petrofina (176)
National Gypsum (270)
Mitchell Energy & Development
   (305)
Tyler (306)
Lafarge (324)
E-Systems (338)

## Business Climates: How the States Stack Up

Does it make a difference where in the country a company makes its products? According to Alexander Grant & Company, a national accounting firm, it may matter a great deal.

In 1983, the Chicago-based firm surveyed state manufacturing associations for their views on 22 local economic factors they deemed necessary for business success. These included labor cost, productivity, unionization, and energy costs, plus such considerations under local government control as taxes, debts, welfare expenditures, and environmental regulations.

States that had flexible environmental controls, laws that kept organized labor in check, and the lowest taxes, welfare aid, and debts received the highest scores and were judged the most favorable places to do business.

A comparison of the growth in manufacturing jobs in each of the states over the past five years shows that the Alexander Grant ratings have some validity. With the exception of South Dakota, all of the states ranked among the top ten for business climate experienced strong gains. All of the states in the bottom ten either held their own or lost ground.

### The States Ranked for Business Climate

| State | Score | State | Score |
|---|---|---|---|
| 1. Florida | 79.4 | 26. New Hampshire | 48.7 |
| 2. South Dakota | 76.5 | 27. Maryland | 48.6 |
| 3. North Dakota | 74.0 | 28. New Mexico | 48.1 |
| 4. Nebraska | 71.1 | 29. New Jersey | 47.2 |
| 5. Arizona | 70.8 | 30. California | 42.9 |
| 6. Texas | 68.8 | 31. Iowa | 42.6 |
| 7. Mississippi | 66.8 | 32. Wyoming | 41.8 |
| 8. Utah | 66.3 | 33. Massachusetts | 40.7 |
| 9. Arkansas | 65.9 | 34. Connecticut | 38.6 |
| 9. North Carolina | 65.9 | 35. Vermont | 37.8 |
| 11. Kansas | 65.6 | 36. Delaware | 37.7 |
| 12. Virginia | 65.1 | 37. Maine | 37.6 |
| 13. Georgia | 65.0 | 38. Washington | 34.5 |
| 14. Tennessee | 60.6 | 39. New York | 33.7 |
| 15. South Carolina | 60.5 | 40. West Virginia | 32.8 |
| 16. Louisiana | 59.0 | 41. Pennsylvania | 32.2 |
| 17. Idaho | 58.7 | 42. Wisconsin | 32.1 |
| 18. Colorado | 58.2 | 43. Minnesota | 29.4 |
| 19. Alabama | 57.4 | 44. Illinois | 29.3 |
| 20. Montana | 57.0 | 45. Rhode Island | 26.3 |
| 21. Oklahoma | 56.9 | 46. Ohio | 23.3 |
| 22. Missouri | 56.6 | 47. Oregon | 21.3 |
| 23. Nevada | 55.0 | 48. Michigan | 11.8 |
| 24. Kentucky | 50.1 | | |
| 25. Indiana | 49.8 | | |

*Source:* Alexander Grant & Company, *General Manufacturing Business Climates,* 1984.

Alaska and Hawaii are not included because their economies were considered too different from those of the other states for comparison.

Dr Pepper (432)
Trinity Industries (465)
Holly (484)

**Danbury, CT**
Union Carbide (37)
Lone Star Industries (313)
Bangor Punta (438)

**Davenport–Rock Island–Moline, IA–IL**
Deere (92)

**Dayton–Springfield, OH**
NCR (101)
Mead (149)
Dayco (371)

**Decatur, IL**
Archer-Daniels-Midland (83)
A. E. Staley Manufacturing (207)

**Denver, CO**
Manville (199)
Adolph Coors (278)
Storage Technology (322)

**Des Moines, IA**
Meredith (479)

**Detroit, MI**
General Motors (2)
Ford Motor (4)
Chrysler (21)
Burroughs (82)
American Motors (105)
Fruehauf (173)
Masco (286)
Ex-Cell-O (308)
Federal-Mogul (363)
Frederick & Herrud (377)
Michigan Milk Producers Association (430)
Guardian Industries (468)

**Elkhart–Goshen, IN**
Miles Laboratories (277)
Coachmen Industries (463)

**Erie, PA**
Hammermill Paper (214)

**Fayetteville–Springdale, AR**
Tyson Foods (407)

**Fort Wayne, IN**
Central Soya (200)

**Greeley, CO**
Monfort of Colorado (250)

**Green Bay, WI**
Fort Howard Paper (347)

**Greensboro–Winston-Salem–High Point, NC**
R. J. Reynolds Industries (23)
Burlington Industries (133)
Blue Bell (258)

**Greenville–Spartanburg, SC**
Riegel Textile (498)

**Hamilton–Middletown, OH**
Armco (87)

**Harrisburg–Lebanon–Carlisle, PA**
Hershey Foods (202)
AMP (228)
Harsco (331)

**Hartford, CT**
United Technologies (18)
Emhart (205)
Coleco Industries (410)
Dexter (431)

**Honolulu, HI**
Pacific Resources (225)

**Houston, TX**
Shell Oil (13)
Tenneco (19)
Coastal (58)
Pennzoil (163)
Cooper Industries (190)
Superior Oil (196)
Anderson Clayton (244)
Hughes Tool (267)
Cameron Iron Works (307)
Big Three Industries (385)

**Huntington–Ashland, WV–KY–OH**
Ashland Oil (45)

**Indianapolis, IN**
Eli Lilly (130)
Stokely–Van Camp (444)

**Jacksonville, FL**
Charter (61)

**Kalamazoo, MI**
Upjohn (182)

**Kankakee, IL**
Roper (462)

**Kansas City, MO**
Interstate Bakeries (388)

**Kenosha, WI**
Snap-on Tools (474)

**La Crosse, WI**
G. Heileman Brewing (268)
Trane (284)

**Lake County, IL**
CF Industries (328)

**Lancaster, PA**
Armstrong World Industries (240)

**Los Angeles–Long Beach, CA**
Atlantic Richfield (12)
Occidental Petroleum (14)
Getty Oil (24)
Unocal (31)
Lockheed (50)
Litton Industries (74)
Carnation (116)
Northrop (123)
Teledyne (135)
Tosco (153)
Times Mirror (154)
Lear Siegler (236)
Mattel (248)
Avery International (341)
NI Industries (368)
Smith International (375)

**Louisville, KY**
Brown-Forman Distillers (406)

**Lowell, MA–NH**
Wang Laboratories (227)

**Melbourne–Titusville–Palm Bay, FL**
Harris (201)

**Memphis, TN–AR–MS**
Federal Co. (275)

**Miami–Hialeah, FL**
Knight-Ridder Newspapers (234)

**Middlesex–Somerset–Hunterdon, NJ**
Johnson & Johnson (57)
American Hoechst (213)

**Milwaukee, WI**
Johnson Controls (251)
Allis-Chalmers (253)
Rexnord (342)
A. O. Smith (330)
Pabst Brewing (376)
Briggs & Stratton (403)
Bucyrus-Erie (434)
Universal Foods (448)

**Minneapolis–St. Paul, MN–WI**
Minnesota Mining & Manufacturing (47)
Honeywell (60)
General Mills (62)
Control Data (76)
Pillsbury (102)
Land O'Lakes (121)
Farmers' Union Central Exchange (243)
International Multifoods (274)
Bemis (373)
Economics Laboratory (384)
Deluxe Check Printers (400)
MEI (402)
H. B. Fuller (493)

**Muncie, IN**
Ball (315)

**Muskegon, MI**
Sealed Power (494)

**Nashua, NH**
Sanders Associates (415)
Nashua (426)

**Nashville, TN**
Genesco (394)

**Nassau–Suffolk, NY**
Grumman (167)

**New Britain, CT**
Stanley Works (298)

**New Haven–Meriden, CT**
Uniroyal (180)
Insilco (381)
Armstrong Rubber (411)
Echlin (428)
Harvey Hubbell (490)

**New Orleans, LA**
Louisiana Land & Exploration (257)

**New York, NY**
Exxon (1)
Mobil (3)
IBM (5)
Texaco (6)
ITT (20)
AT & T Technologies (26)
Philip Morris (35)
Amerada Hess (39)
Union Pacific (40)
General Foods (41)
PepsiCo (44)
W. R. Grace (53)
Sperry (66)
Gulf & Western Industries (67)
Colgate-Palmolive (72)
American Home Products (73)
American Brands (79)
International Paper (80)
Borden (85)
Time Inc. (91)
Bristol-Myers (93)
North American Philips (97)
Pfizer (99)
United Brands (109)
Warner Communications (114)

Celanese (122)
Avon Products (131)
Norton Simon (136)
St. Regis (141)
Penn Central (151)
Revlon (159)
National Distillers & Chemical (166)
American Standard (170)
J. P. Stevens (186)
Ogden (187)
Sterling Drug (188)
SCM (193)
Colt Industries (219)
Lever Brothers (223)
Asarco (229)
Westvaco (232)
Joseph E. Seagram & Sons (233)
NL Industries (239)
Witco Chemical (245)
McGraw-Hill (255)
Amstar (264)
New York Times (281)
Dover (292)
Crane (294)
Phelps Dodge (300)
General Instrument (302)
AMF (303)
Cluett Peabody (325)
Dow Jones (326)
Todd Shipyards (345)
Freeport-McMoRan (346)
Kane-Miller (353)
Capital Cities Communications (356)
Inspiration Resources (357)
Reichhold Chemicals (362)
Sun Chemical (364)
Newmont Mining (370)
GAF (374)
Collins & Aikman (378)
Harcourt Brace Jovanovich (392)
M. Lowenstein (412)
ACF Industries (416)
Handy & Harman (418)
Revere Copper & Brass (452)
American Bakeries (460)
United Merchants & Manufacturers (464)
International Flavors & Fragrances (470)
Phillips-Van Heusen (473)
Ametek (478)
Bairnco (486)
Macmillan (489)

**Newark, NJ**
Allied (29)
Nabisco Brands (56)
Merck (124)
Warner-Lambert (128)
Englehard (174)
Schering-Plough (194)
BASF Wyandotte (285)

**Norwalk, CT**
General Electric (10)
Richardson-Vicks (276)
Perkin-Elmer (291)

**Oakland, CA**
Kaiser Aluminum & Chemical (140)
Clorox (314)

**Oklahoma City, OK**
Kerr-McGee (108)
Wilson Foods (171)

**Omaha, NE–IA**
ConAgra (162)

**Peoria, IL**
Caterpillar Tractor (64)

**Philadelphia, PA–NJ**
Sun (17)
Campbell Soup (119)
SmithKline Beckman
 (126)
Scott Paper (156)
Rohm & Haas (189)
Crown Cork & Seal (254)
Pennwalt (301)
Westmoreland Coal (437)

**Phoenix, AZ**
Southwest Forest Industries
 (380)

**Pittsburgh, PA**
Gulf Oil (11)
U.S. Steel (15)
Westinghouse Electric (34)
Rockwell International (43)
Aluminum Co. of America (65)
H. J. Heinz (100)
PPG Industries (103)
National Intergroup (132)
Allegheny International (160)
Koppers (221)
Mobay Chemical (252)
Cyclops (290)
Wheeling-Pittsburgh Steel
 (352)
Joy Manufacturing (390)
H. H. Robertson (436)

**Portland, OR**
Tektronix (263)
Louisiana-Pacific (279)
Willamette Industries (287)
Hyster (497)

**Portsmouth–Dover–Rochester,
NH–ME**
Tyco Laboratories (419)

**Providence, RI**
Textron (134)

**Reading, PA**
VF (280)

**Richmond–Petersburg, VA**
Reynolds Metals (118)
Ethyl (197)
James River Corp. of Virginia
 (209)
A. H. Robins (429)
Media General (453)

**Riverside–San Bernardino,
CA**
Fleetwood Enterprises (329)
Kaiser Steel (396)

**Rochester, NY**
Eastman Kodak (30)
Gannett (203)
Sybron (404)
Bausch & Lomb (424)

**Rockford, IL**
Sunstrand (316)

**Saginaw–Bay City–
Midland, MI**
Dow Chemical (28)
Dow Corning (355)

**St. Louis, MO–IL**
McDonnell Douglas (42)
General Dynamics (46)
Monsanto (52)
Anheuser-Busch (55)
Ralston Purina (71)
Emerson Electric (111)
Interco (150)
Chromalloy American (297)
Kellwood (421)

**San Antonio, TX**
Datapoint (440)
Harte-Hanks Communications
 (485)

**San Diego, CA**
Signal Companies (54)
Rohr Industries (425)

**San Francisco, CA**
Standard Oil of California (9)

Kaiser Aluminum & Chemical
 (140)
Levi Strauss (143)
Crown Zellerbach (144)
Alumax (230)
Clorox (314)
Potlatch (317)
Kaiser Steel (396)
Raychem (413)
Shaklee (441)
Liquid Air (471)
Cooper Labs (476)

**San Jose, CA**
Hewlett-Packard (75)
National Semiconductor (261)
Intel (272)
Apple Computer (299)
Amdahl (350)
Varian Associates (358)
ROLM (454)
Tandem Computers (500)

**Savannah, GA**
Gulfstream Aerospace (417)
Savannah Foods & Industries
 (461)

**Seattle, WA**
Boeing (27)
PACCAR (242)

**Springfield, MO**
Mid-America Dairymen (247)

**Stamford, CT**
Xerox (38)
Continental Group (68)
Champion International (86)
American Can (117)
Combustion Engineering (129)
Singer (155)
AMAX (164)
Avco (179)
Olin (185)
Chesebrough-Pond's (206)
Pitney Bowes (211)
General Signal (220)
Great Northern Nekoosa (222)
Stauffer Chemical (249)

U.S. Industries (283)
Lone Star Industries (313)
Peabody International (481)
Moore McCormack Resources
 (496)

**Stockton, CA**
Sun-Diamond Growers of
 California (447)

**Syracuse, NY**
Agway (98)

**Tacoma, WA**
Weyerhaeuser (70)

**Tampa–St. Petersburg–
Clearwater, FL**
Jim Walter (181)

**Toledo, OH**
Owens-Illinois (115)
Dana (139)
Owens-Corning Fiberglas (142)
Libbey-Owens-Ford (266)
Champion Spark Plug (354)
Sheller-Globe (405)

**Tulsa, OK**
Phillips Petroleum (16)
Williams Companies (172)
Mapco (177)

**Washington, DC–MD–VA**
Martin Marietta (94)
Fairchild Industries (321)
Washington Post (323)

**Waterbury, CT**
Scovill (366)

**Wichita, KS**
Cessna Aircraft (445)

**Wilmington, DE–NJ–MD**
E. I. du Pont de Nemours (7)
Hercules (148)
NVF (295)

**Worcester, MA**
Norton (271)
Data General (335)
Idle Wild Foods (398)

Source: *Fortune*, "The 500: The Fortune Directory of the Largest U.S. Industrial Corporations," April 30, 1984, © 1984 Time Inc.

# Putting It All Together:

## Finding the Best Places to Live in America

When it comes to rating the livability of different places, there are three basic viewpoints: One says you can't do it; the second says you can but shouldn't; and the third says that you can, as long as you make it clear what your yardsticks are and go on to use them consistently.

Obviously, *Places Rated* subscribes to the third theory. Now comes the time when we summarize the findings of all the previous chapters and attempt to discern general patterns of desirability in America by ranking the metro areas for their overall showing in the nine categories.

In the first edition of *Places Rated Almanac*, this chapter aroused a great deal of controversy, and joy and ire as well. One major source of criticism stemmed from the erroneous impression that *Places Rated* knew (maybe even selected) beforehand which places would score well and which wouldn't. This was not the case. In each chapter, certain relevant data sets and source materials were chosen for being accurate, comprehensive, and important to metropolitan living. Most of the data were obtained from various agencies of the federal government; professional associations, nonprofit organizations, and a few specialized corporations were also tapped. *Places Rated* used no source with a particular bias for or against any region, state, or city. Next, the authors devised scoring systems, awarding points for factors that most people agree are desirable or beneficial, and occasionally subtracting points for factors generally agreed to be undesirable or harmful.

Throughout, we have concentrated as much as possible on what is good rather than bad about metropolitan living. All 329 metro areas are examined and run through the scoring systems in exactly the same manner, using exactly the same data sets. Due to the complexity of the information and the large size of our metropolitan universe, the outcome for any given chapter—and certainly the book as a whole—was virtually impossible to predict.

*Places Rated*'s nine categories for quality of life include some scored on facilities (health care, education, recreation, transportation, arts) and some scored on indicators (crime, housing, economics). Generally speaking, the smaller metro areas rank better on the indicators (usually having lower crime rates and less expensive housing, for example), while their larger cousins score higher on the facilities. Because of *Places Rated*'s strong emphasis on facilities, the larger metro areas are perhaps favored, but overall the scoring system seems to reflect the tastes and preferences of a great number of Americans.

In reviewing the findings of this or any other chapter, be sure to note the close groupings of scores. With such close results, ranking metro areas from first to 329th may give the impression of greater differences between them than actually exist. Any ranking of 50th or higher, for example, places a metro area in the top 15 percent of all American metro areas for that category, certainly an excellent showing.

## SOME GENERAL OBSERVATIONS

Before proceeding to the overall rankings, we would like to note a few broad patterns that we have seen emerge during our work on the almanac over the past eight years.

• Although there have been a few noteworthy changes in some ranking categories from one edition to the next, most places showed remarkably little change in all categories and in their final standing.

• Places that show dramatic recent population growth and economic promise also tend to have crime rates that are very high. This is particularly true of Sun Belt metro areas.

• Despite the gloom-and-doom predictions made in recent decades about the death of the older eastern cities, it is now clear that many of the oldest and largest metro areas in the East are among the most desirable places to live in America. Not only did our cities not die, they are undergoing a rejuvenation unparalleled in our history.

• In the previous edition of *Places Rated Almanac* we reported a new phenomenon of demographic migration in America from large metro areas to rural areas. But this trend has slowed almost to a halt in the intervening years, which perhaps is both cause and effect of the rebirth of many of our big cities.

• America's so-called cities of the future—found mostly in the Sun Belt regions of the Southeast, the Gulf, and the Southwest—have not as yet developed into metro areas with the most promising quality-of-life indicators. Some, such as Miami, Houston, and Los Angeles, are beset with severe social problems (many due to changes resulting from great influxes of immigrants) that will undoubtedly affect them adversely in the near future.

## FINDING THE BEST PLACES TO LIVE IN AMERICA

In 1970 the Urban Institute, located in Washington, D.C., rated 18 major American cities for livability according to such diverse factors as unemployment rates, crime rates, and per capita contributions to charity. Their method for determining the best all-around city (it was Minneapolis, by the way) was very

---

### For Those Who Read This Chapter First

Those of you who have skipped ahead to "see how it all comes out" may be surprised by many of the final results listed in the cumulative table on pages 420–429. If you are curious about why a metro area receives a rank in a particular category, consult the explanation of the scoring system in the appropriate chapter; each chapter uses different criteria and a somewhat different method of combining them.

Using San Diego as an example may help to review how all the rankings are arrived at. How does this popular Southern California vacation spot end up in 33rd place behind such metro areas as Buffalo, New York, and Providence, Rhode Island?

San Diego certainly beats out the northern metro areas when it comes to climate. Its coastal location and abundance of sunshine combine to give it one of the most mild, even climates in the country. Since *Places Rated* uses mildness as its chief criterion for ranking the metro areas for climate, San Diego finishes third best in this category, behind only Oakland and San Francisco.

In housing, however, it does very poorly, placing 321st, largely because of high property taxes, expensive utilities, and an average price tag for a single-family house that is the seventh highest among the metro areas. *Places Rated*'s standards for housing are strictly economic and do not take into account aesthetics or comfort.

San Diego's showing in health care facilities is excellent—it ranks 31st and has an impressive supply of teaching hospitals, medical schools, and other amenities. Offsetting this are fairly high rates of violent and property crime that place it 231st for personal safety.

In two other categories—education and economics—San Diego earns middling marks. For its effort to support schools at the K–12 level and provide a broad range of options at the college level, it ranks 165th. And the economic promise for the individual here—which is rated on the basis of household income and taxes, cost of living, and local job and income growth—is just above average, at 152nd place.

But in the remaining three categories, San Diego performs quite well. It ranks 68th in transportation, rated in terms of how well a variety of transit modes accommodates the metro area population. Such assets as zoos, a theme park, several professional and collegiate sports teams, and a huge national forest help boost the California metro area to a 22nd-place finish in recreation, which is scored for both manufactured and natural facilities. In the arts, San Diego finishes 20th due to its variety of museums, symphony orchestras, and dance companies, to name a few of *Places Rated*'s criteria for this category.

One final caveat: It should be remembered that throughout *Places Rated Almanac* the unit of comparison is the metro area rather than the city.

simple: The ranks for each city for each of the factors were added together for a cumulative score.

*Places Rated's* method, in this edition and the previous one, is similar to the Urban Institute's. Every metro area's ranks for each of the nine factors—climate, housing, health care and environment, crime, transportation, education, the arts, recreation, and economics—are totaled. Albuquerque, New Mexico, for example, ranks 30th in climate, 218th in housing, 60th in health care, 299th in safety from crime, 21st in transportation, 78th in education, 68th in the arts, 52nd in recreation, and 126th in economics. The total of these ranks— 30 + 218 + 60 + 299 + 21 + 78 + 68 + 52 + 126—equals 952. Because this system is based on ranks, the lower the cumulative score, the better the metro area is judged to be all-around. (Albuquerque places 22nd overall among the metro areas.) The list below highlights the metro areas that rise to the top as the best places to live in America.

### America's Top 50 Metro Areas

| Metro Area | Cumulative Score |
|---|---|
| 1. Pittsburgh, PA | 716 |
| 2. Boston, MA | 752 |
| 3. Raleigh–Durham, NC | 753 |
| 4. Philadelphia, PA–NJ | 774 |
| 4. San Francisco, CA | 774 |
| 6. Nassau–Suffolk, NY | 786 |
| 7. Louisville, KY–IN | 840 |
| 8. St. Louis, MO–IL | 845 |
| 9. Rochester, NY | 860 |
| 10. Norwalk, CT | 889 |
| 11. Dallas, TX | 898 |
| 12. Seattle, WA | 919 |
| 13. Atlanta, GA | 921 |
| 14. Knoxville, TN | 928 |
| 15. Buffalo, NY | 931 |
| 16. Baltimore, MD | 932 |
| 17. Washington, DC–MD–VA | 933 |
| 18. Cincinnati, OH–KY–IN | 938 |
| 19. Albany–Schenectady–Troy, NY | 941 |
| 19. Burlington, VT | 941 |
| 21. Syracuse, NY | 950 |
| 22. Albuquerque, NM | 952 |
| 23. Harrisburg–Lebanon–Carlisle, PA | 957 |
| 24. Richmond–Petersburg, VA | 960 |
| 25. New York, NY | 965 |
| 26. Providence, RI | 966 |
| 27. Chicago, IL | 968 |
| 28. Middlesex–Somerset–Hunterdon, NJ | 975 |
| 29. Denver, CO | 977 |
| 30. Cleveland, OH | 988 |
| 31. Charlottesville, VA | 999 |
| 32. New Haven–Meriden, CT | 1,009 |
| 33. San Diego, CA | 1,013 |
| 34. Wilmington, DE–NJ–MD | 1,014 |
| 35. Asheville, NC | 1,016 |
| 36. Los Angeles–Long Beach, CA | 1,021 |
| 37. Omaha, NE–IA | 1,022 |
| 38. Bridgeport–Milford, CT | 1,026 |

| Metro Area | Cumulative Score |
|---|---|
| 39. Norfolk–Virginia Beach–Newport News, VA | 1,028 |
| 40. Greensboro–Winston-Salem–High Point, NC | 1,030 |
| 41. Anaheim–Santa Ana, CA | 1,035 |
| 42. Bergen–Passaic, NJ | 1,060 |
| 43. San Jose, CA | 1,062 |
| 44. Nashville, TN | 1,066 |
| 45. Tampa–St. Petersburg–Clearwater, FL | 1,069 |
| 46. Johnson City–Kingsport–Bristol, TN–VA | 1,070 |
| 47. Oklahoma City, OK | 1,076 |
| 48. Monmouth–Ocean, NJ | 1,091 |
| 49. Jacksonville, FL | 1,092 |
| 50. Stamford, CT | 1,094 |

In many respects, the list of the top 50 metro areas in this second edition of *Places Rated Almanac* closely resembles that of the first edition. Although their rankings have changed somewhat, 33 of the metro areas were in the top 50 before. Seventeen places have dropped from the list this time around, but only two—Utica–Rome, New York, and Evansville, Indiana–Kentucky—dropped below 100th place.

Of the 17 newcomers to the top 50, five are metro areas that were not independently ranked in *Places Rated's* first edition: Bergen–Passaic, New Jersey; Burlington, Vermont; Charlottesville, Virginia; Middlesex–Somerset–Hunterdon, New Jersey; and Monmouth–Ocean, New Jersey. (Burlington and Charlottesville were non-metropolitan at that time; parts of the other three were in other metro areas.)

Four metro areas that ranked 109th or worse in the first edition of *Places Rated* improved their position dramatically by moving into the top 50: Johnson City–Kingsport–Bristol, Tennessee–Virginia; Norfolk–Virginia Beach–Newport News, Virginia; Norwalk, Connecticut; and Wilmington, Delaware–New Jersey–Maryland.

Why have the rankings changed? As mentioned in the introduction to the book, there are many possible reasons. A new set of boundaries is one, for only about half of the metro areas are exactly the same geographical entities that were rated in the first edition. The Norfolk–Virginia Beach–Newport News metro area, which moved up to 39th place, is a combination of parts of two former metro areas: Norfolk–Virginia Beach–Portsmouth, Virginia–North Carolina, and Newport News–Hampton, Virginia, which ranked 115th and 77th, respectively, in our earlier edition.

More recent data is of course another factor that could cause changes in ratings, but this in and of itself has generally not made any marked difference in the overall standing of a metro area. More meaningful have been new scoring criteria, either in the factors being considered or in the weightings given those factors, as discussed in detail in each chapter. Many metro areas, notably formerly top-ranked Atlanta, saw

## Consistency Counts

Many of *Places Rated*'s high-ranking metro areas are combinations of superior and dismal rankings in the individual categories. New York City is the classic example of an uneven performance. The Big Apple has no less than three first-place finishes: health care, transportation, and the arts. Anyone who knows New York can appreciate these rankings, too. But what of its miserable showings in housing (312th) and crime (329th)? High housing and real estate costs and dangerous streets could, for many people, cancel out the wonderful facilities that this supercity has to offer.

*Places Rated* decided to seek out those metro areas that show steady strength in *all* the categories, even though they might not have any dramatic first-place showings. We scanned, in vain, for places with no rankings below 150th. Since we struck out with this stringent standard, we looked for those with no ranks lower than 200th. Even with this more liberal guideline, we came up with just a handful of metro areas that showed consistent strength in all nine of the *Places Rated* categories.

### Super-Solid Metro Areas

| Metro Area (Overall Rank) | Highest Rank | Lowest Rank |
| --- | --- | --- |
| Asheville, NC (35) | Climate (25) | Arts (197) |
| Cincinnati, OH–KY–IN (18) | Arts (16) | Housing (191) |
| Greensboro–Winston-Salem–High Point, NC (40) | Climate (54) | Economics (192) |
| Harrisburg–Lebanon–Carlisle, PA (23) | Transportation (32) | Recreation (198) |
| Knoxville, TN (14) | Climate (26) | Education (179) |
| Louisville, KY–IN (7) | Health Care (48) | Economics (163) |
| Nashville, TN (44) | Health Care (61) | Crime (184) |
| Pittsburgh, PA (1) | Education (7) | Housing (186) |
| Raleigh–Durham, NC (3) | Health Care (13) | Housing (198) |

Interestingly, all these super-solid metro areas are found in roughly the same geographic area, stretching from the Ohio Valley in the north to the Piedmont and Appalachian regions of the Mid-South.

Somewhat disappointed at the small number of extremely solid metro areas, we went through the final grid again and selected those places with only one rank below 200th. The list of runners-up follows.

### Solid Metro Areas

| Metro Area (Overall Rank) | Highest Rank | Lowest Rank |
| --- | --- | --- |
| Albany–Schenectady–Troy, NY (19) | Transportation (15) | Climate (250) |
| Alton–Granite City, IL (75) | Housing (52) | Recreation (249) |
| Binghamton, NY (68) | Crime (16) | Housing (202) |
| Buffalo, NY (15) | Arts (23) | Economics (217) |
| Charlottesville, VA (31) | Education (12) | Housing (263) |
| Evansville, IN–KY (140) | Housing (78) | Transportation (214) |
| Middlesex–Somerset–Hunterdon, NJ (28) | Education (8) | Housing (306) |
| New Haven–Meriden, CT (32) | Education (11) | Housing (299) |
| Oklahoma City, OK (47) | Economics (5) | Crime (272) |
| Omaha, NE–IA (36) | Health Care (26) | Climate (276) |
| Portland, ME (55) | Recreation (20) | Climate (240) |
| Roanoke, VA (87) | Climate (33) | Arts (207) |
| Rochester, NY (9) | Education (5) | Housing (233) |
| St. Louis, MO–IL (8) | Education (9) | Crime (273) |
| Springfield, IL (93) | Transportation (31) | Crime (268) |
| Syracuse, NY (21) | Transportation (14) | Economics (282) |
| Wilmington, DE–NJ–MD (34) | Education (52) | Crime (234) |

Does this kind of consistency count? It certainly does: Of all these 26 solid and super-solid metro areas, only six fail to make it into *Places Rated*'s list of the 50 best places to live in America.

---

their rankings in the Recreation chapter change noticeably because of the many innovations made in that scoring system. Atlanta's recreation ranking fell from 28th to 239th, due in part to the addition of the major category Outdoor Recreation Assets to the chapter, improving the position of many other metro areas in relation to Atlanta, which receives few points in that category.

Also, the CMSA Access effect has been highly significant. For the first time, *Places Rated* has taken into account certain shared assets in health care, transportation, the arts, and recreation by crediting metro areas that are part of America's 22 Consolidated Metropolitan Statistical Areas with additional points. The CMSA Access effect is the major reason Nassau–Suffolk, New York, moved from 48th in *Places Rated*'s first edition to sixth place in this one. Norwalk, Connecticut, jumped from 148th place to tenth, and Wilmington, Delaware–New Jersey–Maryland, from 109th

to 34th. In all, 25 metro areas in our top 50 benefit to one degree or another from CMSA Access.

The majority of metro areas that perform best overall in this edition are located east of the Mississippi. Not only that, many are found in the northeastern quadrant of the country. The states of New York, New Jersey, and Connecticut are especially strong in highly ranked places, as is the multistate region of the Ohio Valley. The South and the West (excluding California), despite significant population growth in the last 20 years and generally favorable economic indicators, are still underrepresented in *Places Rated*'s list of top places.

As previously mentioned, the scoring systems used in some of the chapters—particularly those dealing with supply of various facilities—tend to favor bigger metro areas over smaller ones. Twenty-seven of the top 50 metro areas are therefore also among the 50 largest metro areas. There are, however, some note-

**Solid and Super-Solid Metro Areas**

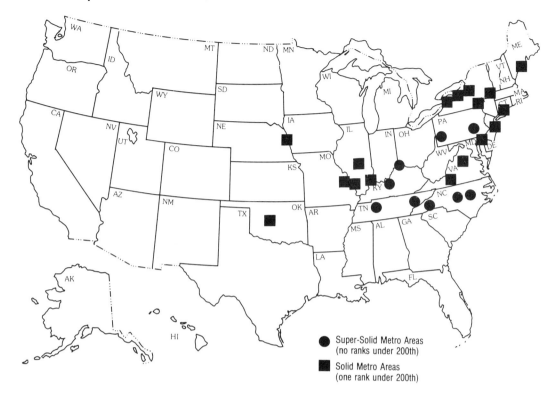

● Super-Solid Metro Areas
(no ranks under 200th)

■ Solid Metro Areas
(one rank under 200th)

worthy exceptions. Third-place Raleigh–Durham, for example, is 74th in size. Tiny Norwalk, which ranks tenth overall, is 258th in size, and Burlington, Vermont, a brand-new metro area in a state previously unrepresented in *Places Rated*, ranks 19th overall in desirability but only 274th in population.

These small and medium-sized metro areas tend to have consistently good rankings in every category (Raleigh–Durham ranks 58th or better in six categories and no worse than 198th in any), whereas the large metro areas can show considerable inconsistency. A good example is fourth-ranked San Francisco, which finishes tenth or better in five categories yet scrapes bottom in housing costs (327th) and safety from crime (318th). Seventeenth-place Washington earns four rankings of sixth or better, but it too falters in housing (314th) and crime (276th). And 27th-ranked Chicago achieves four ranks above 14th but finishes 295th in housing costs and 205th in safety from crime.

The prime example of across-the-board strength in a large metropolitan area is Pittsburgh, which emerges as the best place to live in *Places Rated*'s comprehensive survey of metropolitan America.

### AND THE WINNER IS . . .

Pittsburgh, Pennsylvania, which ranked fourth in the first edition of *Places Rated Almanac*, has climbed to the top of the list in this second edition. Many people who perhaps have a stereotyped and outdated image of a smoky, noisy, blast furnace of a city may be surprised

at this. But Pittsburgh shows great strength in the social indicators and is remarkably like a small town in many respects, despite its great size. Values are traditional and simple, neighborhoods tight yet friendly.

Pittsburgh's strengths lie as much in what it doesn't have as in what it does. Our number-one metro area heads an elite group of only nine places that have no rankings of 200th or worse in any of *Places Rated*'s nine major categories. Although its population of nearly 2.3 million people (about 450,000 in the city of Pittsburgh itself) places it tenth in population overall, the metro area ranks 78th in safety from crime, in the upper 24 percent of all metro areas as far as personal safety is concerned. Most comparably sized metro areas cannot even approach this level. Atlanta, the 12th largest metro area, ranks 274th in safety from crime, Baltimore (11th in population) 323rd, and Houston (eighth in population) 304th. Another odious fact of life in most large metro areas is the high cost of housing. A housing rank of 186th means Pittsburgh is in the 56th percentile, just under the midpoint. Several other large metro areas that also rank among the ten best overall have far higher housing prices: Boston ranks 300th, for example, and Nassau–Suffolk 298th.

Located at the confluence of the Allegheny and Monongahela rivers, which together form the Ohio River, Pittsburgh since the mid-1700s has provided a vital link between the interior waterways of the East and the Mississippi. These navigable waterways gave the city access to vast reserves of both coal and iron ore, which led to its growth as a foundry center.

Pittsburgh probably reached its zenith as the Steel City in the years during and immediately after World War II. Then, in the late 1940s, civic leaders grew increasingly distressed at the amount of dirt and smoke in their city. The problem of pollution was so severe, in fact, that architect Frank Lloyd Wright, when asked to suggest a solution for the city, gave his answer in two words: "Abandon it." But Pittsburgh's leaders were not dismayed. An urban redevelopment program was initiated that regulated industry and included strict measures for smoke control. The result, in the 1980s, is a smoke-free city of tall office buildings set in a stunning natural setting of rugged hills and river valleys, with plenty of recreational parks and a fine waterfront. The Golden Triangle, where the Allegheny joins the Monongahela, is the heart of the city's business district, with scores of handsome buildings and skyscrapers.

This manufacturing and commercial center in the southwest corner of the state still relies on primary metals as an important part of its economy, but in recent years there has been a dramatic shift away from heavy manufacturing to light assembly and commercial and service industries. A large number of major corporations have headquarters in Pittsburgh. As of 1984, Pittsburgh was home to 15 Fortune 500 corporations, which ranks it fifth among U.S. metro areas, after New York; Chicago; Stamford, Connecticut; and Los Angeles–Long Beach. Nonetheless, this metro area ranks only 184th in economic outlook. About a third of the work force is still blue collar, and the threat of unemployment is moderate. Although personal

income has increased by nearly 45 percent in recent years, the job market has declined slightly.

Despite its reputation as a workingman's town, Pittsburgh has big-city strength in many important facilities. The metro area ranks seventh in education; it is home to several fine universities, such as Carnegie-Mellon and the University of Pittsburgh, and claims two of the nation's top secondary schools, Mount Lebanon High School and Upper St. Clair High School. An array of cultural amenities including the Pittsburgh Symphony Orchestra, Pittsburgh Ballet Theatre, Pittsburgh Opera, and the Carnegie Museum of Natural History and Museum of Art helps the Steel City capture a 12th-place ranking in the arts. Pittsburgh's 14th-place finish in health care derives from its full range of medical facilities and an excellent hospitalization/insurance costs index.

There's more to the Pittsburgh metro area than the central city. Surrounding towns like Mount Lebanon (pop. 34,414) and Monroeville (pop. 30,977) offer suburban living styles. Bethel Park (pop. 34,755) remains an exclusive, and expensive, suburb catering to upper-echelon executives and their families. Beaver County, Pennsylvania, though officially a separate metro area, is included in the greater Pittsburgh CMSA. Here is an area for those who prefer country living within a reasonable commute of downtown.

*Pluses:* Across-the-board strength in nearly all categories; excellent rankings in education, health care, and the arts.

*Minuses:* Middling rankings for housing costs and economic indicators.

## Putting It All Together: Cumulative Scores and Overall Ranks of 329 Metro Areas

The following table shows the rank of every metro area for each of *Places Rated*'s nine categories. The sum of these—the cumulative score—is also shown, as is the overall rank. For example, Albuquerque's cumulative

score of 952 ranks it 22nd overall among the 329 metro areas. As in the game of golf, the lower the cumulative score, the better. The best possible score would be 9, meaning a first-place rank in all nine categories.

| Metro Area | Climate & Terrain | Housing | Health Care & Environment | Crime | Transportation | Education | The Arts | Recreation | Economics | Cumulative Score | Overall Rank |
|---|---|---|---|---|---|---|---|---|---|---|---|
| Abilene, TX | 200 | 33 | 320 | 156 | 167 | 180 | 231 | 232 | 15 | 1,534 | 168 |
| Akron, OH | 105 | 190 | 73 | 141 | 105 | 298 | 50 | 51 | 292 | 1,305 | 97 |
| Albany, GA | 257 | 129 | 226 | 175 | 290 | 261 | 302 | 304 | 188 | 2,132 | 325 |
| Albany–Schenectady–Troy, NY | 250 | 171 | 85 | 54 | 15 | 17 | 64 | 175 | 110 | 941 | 19 |

| Metro Area | Climate & Terrain | Housing | Health Care & Environment | Crime | Transportation | Education | The Arts | Recreation | Economics | Cumulative Score | Overall Rank |
|---|---|---|---|---|---|---|---|---|---|---|---|
| Albuquerque, NM | 30 | 218 | 60 | 299 | 21 | 78 | 68 | 52 | 126 | 952 | 22 |
| Alexandria, LA | 203 | 18 | 218 | 87 | 295 | 97 | 288 | 290 | 187 | 1,683 | 232 |
| Allentown–Bethlehem, PA–NJ | 129 | 205 | 224 | 34 | 269 | 44 | 132 | 278 | 212 | 1,527 | 162 |
| Alton–Granite City, IL | 173 | 52 | 143 | 82 | 96 | 103 | 189 | 249 | 120 | 1,207 | 75 |
| Altoona, PA | 124 | 32 | 288 | 9 | 151 | 170 | 301 | 261 | 301 | 1,637 | 210 |
| Amarillo, TX | 68 | 58 | 213 | 220 | 103 | 147 | 209 | 280 | 73 | 1,371 | 115 |
| Anaheim–Santa Ana, CA | 5 | 324 | 52 | 183 | 169 | 151 | 49 | 28 | 74 | 1,035 | 41 |
| Anchorage, AK | 324 | 307 | 235 | 267 | 90 | 302 | 131 | 33 | 14 | 1,703 | 242 |
| Anderson, IN | 185 | 9 | 248 | 139 | 271 | 290 | 276 | 309 | 325 | 2,052 | 320 |
| Anderson, SC | 85 | 14 | 168 | 178 | 280 | 173 | 307 | 327 | 298 | 1,830 | 283 |
| Ann Arbor, MI | 155 | 296 | 32 | 217 | 221 | 21 | 31 | 73 | 270 | 1,316 | 101 |
| Anniston, AL | 127 | 6 | 236 | 238 | 255 | 322 | 297 | 267 | 257 | 2,005 | 316 |
| Appleton–Oshkosh–Neenah, WI | 302 | 165 | 164 | 38 | 239 | 150 | 216 | 70 | 180 | 1,524 | 161 |
| Asheville, NC | 25 | 76 | 103 | 45 | 91 | 90 | 197 | 195 | 194 | 1,016 | 35 |
| Athens, GA | 76 | 71 | 233 | 159 | 319 | 231 | 92 | 291 | 195 | 1,667 | 224 |
| Atlanta, GA | 24 | 210 | 15 | 274 | 2 | 62 | 31 | 239 | 64 | 921 | 13 |
| Atlantic City, NJ | 61 | 297 | 221 | 325 | 204 | 110 | 262 | 46 | 6 | 1,532 | 166 |
| Augusta, GA–SC | 184 | 39 | 65 | 137 | 292 | 118 | 224 | 300 | 162 | 1,521 | 157 |
| Aurora–Elgin, IL | 253 | 286 | 104 | 119 | 171 | 321 | 82 | 145 | 212 | 1,693 | 238 |
| Austin, TX | 282 | 242 | 181 | 210 | 195 | 60 | 53 | 285 | 19 | 1,527 | 162 |
| Bakersfield, CA | 127 | 181 | 289 | 312 | 191 | 260 | 212 | 191 | 90 | 1,853 | 290 |
| Baltimore, MD | 119 | 250 | 12 | 323 | 8 | 15 | 15 | 39 | 151 | 932 | 16 |
| Bangor, ME | 272 | 124 | 182 | 69 | 58 | 109 | 155 | 89 | 200 | 1,258 | 85 |
| Baton Rouge, LA | 286 | 182 | 304 | 313 | 233 | 236 | 77 | 228 | 66 | 1,925 | 306 |
| Battle Creek, MI | 189 | 42 | 153 | 203 | 116 | 285 | 285 | 168 | 308 | 1,749 | 258 |
| Beaumont–Port Arthur, TX | 290 | 38 | 228 | 275 | 274 | 188 | 171 | 142 | 98 | 1,704 | 243 |
| Beaver County, PA | 88 | 163 | 159 | 2 | 262 | 270 | 204 | 212 | 328 | 1,688 | 235 |
| Bellingham, WA | 15 | 211 | 319 | 123 | 185 | 170 | 202 | 26 | 299 | 1,550 | 173 |
| Benton Harbor, MI | 120 | 84 | 250 | 260 | 258 | 265 | 325 | 213 | 322 | 2,097 | 324 |
| Bergen–Passaic, NJ | 129 | 322 | 22 | 132 | 211 | 2 | 18 | 124 | 100 | 1,060 | 42 |
| Billings, MT | 271 | 209 | 275 | 113 | 26 | 84 | 247 | 98 | 105 | 1,428 | 135 |
| Biloxi–Gulfport, MS | 93 | 48 | 286 | 113 | 293 | 255 | 258 | 93 | 118 | 1,557 | 178 |
| Binghamton, NY | 146 | 202 | 137 | 16 | 128 | 63 | 183 | 155 | 141 | 1,171 | 68 |
| Birmingham, AL | 66 | 86 | 72 | 237 | 87 | 149 | 81 | 256 | 246 | 1,280 | 90 |
| Bismarck, ND | 327 | 214 | 176 | 13 | 148 | 217 | 213 | 171 | 98 | 1,577 | 187 |
| Bloomington, IN | 134 | 104 | 193 | 72 | 323 | 136 | 145 | 107 | 248 | 1,462 | 144 |
| Bloomington–Normal, IL | 239 | 237 | 172 | 75 | 44 | 145 | 190 | 181 | 111 | 1,394 | 120 |
| Boise City, ID | 83 | 195 | 281 | 140 | 20 | 306 | 128 | 164 | 265 | 1,582 | 190 |
| Boston, MA | 56 | 300 | 3 | 266 | 16 | 14 | 5 | 32 | 60 | 752 | 2 |
| Boulder–Longmont, CO | 265 | 305 | 144 | 224 | 13 | 256 | 88 | 5 | 30 | 1,330 | 104 |

| Metro Area | Climate & Terrain | Housing | Health Care & Environment | Crime | Transportation | Education | The Arts | Recreation | Economics | Cumulative Score | Overall Rank |
|---|---|---|---|---|---|---|---|---|---|---|---|
| Bradenton, FL | 277 | 199 | 307 | 228 | 182 | 205 | 311 | 242 | 20 | 1,971 | 311 |
| Brazoria, TX | 290 | 219 | 287 | 100 | 298 | 204 | 188 | 203 | 97 | 1,886 | 298 |
| Bremerton, WA | 12 | 249 | 312 | 69 | 325 | 267 | 280 | 110 | 132 | 1,756 | 263 |
| Bridgeport–Milford, CT | 34 | 313 | 27 | 163 | 242 | 70 | 25 | 126 | 26 | 1,026 | 38 |
| Bristol, CT | 207 | 280 | 141 | 41 | 130 | 240 | 269 | 318 | 51 | 1,677 | 228 |
| Brockton, MA | 105 | 203 | 151 | 282 | 181 | 193 | 154 | 258 | 37 | 1,564 | 180 |
| Brownsville–Harlingen, TX | 277 | 3 | 328 | 177 | 249 | 303 | 309 | 33 | 225 | 1,904 | 300 |
| Bryan–College Station, TX | 305 | 197 | 218 | 197 | 291 | 95 | 153 | 228 | 7 | 1,691 | 237 |
| Buffalo, NY | 112 | 180 | 36 | 176 | 75 | 50 | 23 | 62 | 217 | 931 | 15 |
| Burlington, NC | 45 | 29 | 140 | 83 | 318 | 275 | 316 | 324 | 129 | 1,659 | 221 |
| Burlington, VT | 305 | 267 | 63 | 32 | 10 | 23 | 177 | 21 | 43 | 941 | 19 |
| Canton, OH | 105 | 128 | 285 | 68 | 149 | 181 | 233 | 268 | 245 | 1,662 | 222 |
| Casper, WY | 299 | 270 | 302 | 185 | 136 | 292 | 293 | 221 | 70 | 2,068 | 322 |
| Cedar Rapids, IA | 283 | 156 | 162 | 85 | 80 | 246 | 236 | 209 | 221 | 1,678 | 230 |
| Champaign–Urbana–Rantoul, IL | 195 | 234 | 211 | 200 | 7 | 42 | 139 | 160 | 154 | 1,342 | 107 |
| Charleston, SC | 115 | 134 | 81 | 303 | 152 | 40 | 106 | 53 | 207 | 1,191 | 70 |
| Charleston, WV | 53 | 160 | 201 | 86 | 70 | 129 | 121 | 306 | 185 | 1,311 | 100 |
| Charlotte–Gastonia–Rock Hill, NC–SC | 38 | 116 | 139 | 270 | 34 | 69 | 73 | 255 | 132 | 1,126 | 58 |
| Charlottesville, VA | 58 | 263 | 90 | 96 | 37 | 12 | 195 | 157 | 91 | 999 | 31 |
| Chattanooga, TN–GA | 103 | 30 | 251 | 164 | 226 | 301 | 127 | 253 | 280 | 1,735 | 254 |
| Chicago, IL | 211 | 295 | 2 | 205 | 6 | 13 | 2 | 43 | 191 | 968 | 27 |
| Chico, CA | 72 | 232 | 318 | 165 | 166 | 49 | 179 | 194 | 176 | 1,551 | 174 |
| Cincinnati, OH–KY–IN | 93 | 191 | 46 | 181 | 52 | 116 | 16 | 61 | 182 | 938 | 18 |
| Clarksville–Hopkinsville, TN–KY | 159 | 22 | 283 | 90 | 309 | 225 | 319 | 82 | 240 | 1,729 | 251 |
| Cleveland, OH | 101 | 251 | 16 | 241 | 9 | 97 | 9 | 23 | 241 | 988 | 30 |
| Colorado Springs, CO | 191 | 224 | 198 | 223 | 227 | 181 | 176 | 67 | 13 | 1,500 | 151 |
| Columbia, MO | 168 | 150 | 54 | 215 | 175 | 310 | 111 | 244 | 208 | 1,635 | 208 |
| Columbia, SC | 191 | 140 | 86 | 307 | 47 | 120 | 126 | 211 | 179 | 1,407 | 127 |
| Columbus, GA–AL | 206 | 17 | 164 | 118 | 257 | 224 | 166 | 260 | 250 | 1,662 | 222 |
| Columbus, OH | 134 | 185 | 62 | 226 | 143 | 111 | 41 | 103 | 202 | 1,207 | 75 |
| Corpus Christi, TX | 310 | 96 | 280 | 281 | 199 | 153 | 156 | 100 | 44 | 1,619 | 205 |
| Cumberland, MD–WV | 85 | 24 | 185 | 3 | 192 | 19 | 282 | 288 | 255 | 1,333 | 106 |
| Dallas, TX | 159 | 256 | 20 | 308 | 30 | 29 | 13 | 71 | 12 | 898 | 11 |
| Danbury, CT | 115 | 320 | 40 | 43 | 279 | 70 | 34 | 189 | 34 | 1,124 | 57 |
| Danville, VA | 157 | 11 | 241 | 7 | 245 | 105 | 323 | 328 | 278 | 1,695 | 239 |
| Davenport, Rock Island–Moline, IA–IL | 277 | 182 | 115 | 126 | 174 | 125 | 228 | 123 | 222 | 1,572 | 183 |
| Dayton–Springfield, OH | 159 | 145 | 43 | 244 | 109 | 173 | 40 | 276 | 276 | 1,465 | 146 |
| Daytona Beach, FL | 124 | 118 | 197 | 284 | 162 | 251 | 244 | 9 | 49 | 1,438 | 138 |

| Metro Area | Climate & Terrain | Housing | Health Care & Environment | Crime | Transportation | Education | The Arts | Recreation | Economics | Cumulative Score | Overall Rank |
|---|---|---|---|---|---|---|---|---|---|---|---|
| Decatur, IL | 246 | 133 | 191 | 149 | 177 | 219 | 294 | 257 | 297 | 1,963 | 310 |
| Denver, CO | 200 | 293 | 28 | 287 | 5 | 43 | 24 | 69 | 28 | 977 | 29 |
| Des Moines, IA | 274 | 177 | 96 | 209 | 67 | 250 | 167 | 144 | 167 | 1,551 | 174 |
| Detroit, MI | 176 | 227 | 7 | 314 | 106 | 59 | 14 | 58 | 312 | 1,273 | 89 |
| Dothan, AL | 314 | 10 | 241 | 158 | 308 | 320 | 318 | 321 | 159 | 2,149 | 326 |
| Dubuque, IA | 292 | 176 | 218 | 49 | 196 | 211 | 287 | 187 | 310 | 1,926 | 307 |
| Duluth, MN–WI | 326 | 23 | 109 | 29 | 83 | 246 | 129 | 30 | 311 | 1,286 | 92 |
| East St. Louis–Belleville, IL | 173 | 53 | 284 | 230 | 23 | 237 | 236 | 177 | 83 | 1,496 | 149 |
| Eau Claire, WI | 322 | 108 | 178 | 19 | 242 | 101 | 170 | 235 | 166 | 1,541 | 170 |
| El Paso, TX | 83 | 130 | 263 | 277 | 193 | 286 | 84 | 281 | 215 | 1,812 | 280 |
| Elkhart–Goshen, IN | 200 | 59 | 237 | 37 | 156 | 269 | 286 | 289 | 303 | 1,836 | 287 |
| Elmira, NY | 258 | 108 | 253 | 50 | 234 | 86 | 223 | 185 | 249 | 1,646 | 216 |
| Enid, OK | 263 | 88 | 222 | 130 | 302 | 177 | 304 | 264 | 4 | 1,754 | 261 |
| Erie, PA | 70 | 151 | 262 | 64 | 51 | 235 | 151 | 243 | 296 | 1,523 | 160 |
| Eugene–Springfield, OR | 18 | 259 | 258 | 138 | 79 | 51 | 120 | 19 | 329 | 1,271 | 88 |
| Evansville, IN–KY | 146 | 78 | 180 | 135 | 214 | 162 | 164 | 173 | 190 | 1,442 | 140 |
| Fall River, MA–RI | 40 | 248 | 153 | 134 | 120 | 295 | 252 | 105 | 239 | 1,586 | 191 |
| Fargo–Moorhead, ND–MN | 328 | 192 | 150 | 33 | 25 | 277 | 147 | 227 | 142 | 1,521 | 157 |
| Fayetteville, NC | 124 | 36 | 158 | 243 | 137 | 64 | 241 | 322 | 186 | 1,511 | 154 |
| Fayetteville–Springdale, AR | 148 | 69 | 240 | 41 | 201 | 314 | 163 | 161 | 266 | 1,603 | 198 |
| Fitchburg–Leominster, MA | 221 | 200 | 216 | 71 | 305 | 161 | 296 | 317 | 211 | 1,998 | 314 |
| Flint, MI | 170 | 119 | 196 | 320 | 101 | 276 | 143 | 241 | 318 | 1,884 | 296 |
| Florence, AL | 155 | 21 | 232 | 35 | 328 | 299 | 227 | 294 | 277 | 1,868 | 293 |
| Florence, SC | 144 | 54 | 169 | 280 | 97 | 53 | 261 | 314 | 247 | 1,619 | 205 |
| Fort Collins–Loveland, CO | 234 | 276 | 193 | 91 | 286 | 303 | 182 | 4 | 48 | 1,617 | 204 |
| Fort Lauderdale–Hollywood–Pompano Beach, FL | 111 | 294 | 97 | 310 | 154 | 191 | 152 | 60 | 29 | 1,398 | 123 |
| Fort Myers, FL | 313 | 255 | 257 | 107 | 123 | 193 | 281 | 6 | 27 | 1,562 | 179 |
| Fort Pierce, FL | 75 | 243 | 264 | 291 | 311 | 41 | 284 | 97 | 9 | 1,615 | 202 |
| Fort Smith, AR–OK | 244 | 15 | 278 | 73 | 253 | 112 | 315 | 152 | 243 | 1,685 | 233 |
| Fort Walton Beach, FL | 176 | 141 | 274 | 40 | 268 | 157 | 321 | 94 | 61 | 1,532 | 166 |
| Fort Wayne, IN | 217 | 77 | 126 | 84 | 73 | 173 | 112 | 156 | 304 | 1,322 | 102 |
| Fort Worth–Arlington, TX | 188 | 174 | 132 | 285 | 132 | 242 | 42 | 68 | 40 | 1,303 | 96 |
| Fresno, CA | 129 | 254 | 298 | 299 | 142 | 305 | 90 | 36 | 123 | 1,676 | 227 |
| Gadsden, AL | 191 | 4 | 223 | 93 | 310 | 317 | 312 | 329 | 302 | 2,081 | 323 |
| Gainesville, FL | 298 | 132 | 69 | 319 | 208 | 55 | 96 | 254 | 124 | 1,555 | 176 |
| Galveston–Texas City, TX | 20 | 153 | 84 | 265 | 223 | 157 | 175 | 33 | 95 | 1,205 | 74 |
| Gary–Hammond, IN | 240 | 146 | 89 | 187 | 48 | 273 | 80 | 118 | 315 | 1,496 | 149 |
| Glens Falls, NY | 250 | 112 | 329 | 47 | 306 | 221 | 263 | 130 | 201 | 1,859 | 291 |
| Grand Forks, ND | 329 | 169 | 117 | 12 | 62 | 201 | 161 | 248 | 139 | 1,438 | 138 |
| Grand Rapids, MI | 214 | 159 | 93 | 166 | 219 | 210 | 99 | 127 | 244 | 1,531 | 165 |

| Metro Area | Climate & Terrain | Housing | Health Care & Environment | Crime | Transportation | Education | The Arts | Recreation | Economics | Cumulative Score | Overall Rank |
|---|---|---|---|---|---|---|---|---|---|---|---|
| Great Falls, MT | 295 | 114 | 214 | 111 | 188 | 189 | 279 | 83 | 260 | 1,733 | 252 |
| Greeley, CO | 234 | 194 | 202 | 186 | 326 | 145 | 208 | 319 | 161 | 1,975 | 312 |
| Green Bay, WI | 308 | 220 | 151 | 51 | 184 | 245 | 124 | 121 | 137 | 1,541 | 170 |
| Greensboro–Winston-Salem–High Point, NC | 54 | 106 | 71 | 171 | 134 | 56 | 79 | 167 | 192 | 1,030 | 40 |
| Greenville–Spartanburg, SC | 32 | 41 | 94 | 259 | 170 | 32 | 122 | 230 | 220 | 1,200 | 72 |
| Hagerstown, MD | 118 | 152 | 169 | 57 | 222 | 90 | 242 | 210 | 281 | 1,541 | 170 |
| Hamilton–Middletown, OH | 164 | 196 | 113 | 143 | 232 | 185 | 133 | 182 | 268 | 1,616 | 203 |
| Harrisburg–Lebanon–Carlisle, PA | 140 | 168 | 49 | 59 | 32 | 35 | 103 | 198 | 173 | 957 | 23 |
| Hartford, CT | 207 | 302 | 30 | 271 | 11 | 4 | 89 | 146 | 67 | 1,127 | 59 |
| Hickory, NC | 56 | 82 | 138 | 99 | 281 | 198 | 306 | 315 | 258 | 1,733 | 252 |
| Honolulu, HI | 22 | 326 | 92 | 142 | 41 | 279 | 36 | 15 | 196 | 1,149 | 63 |
| Houma–Thibodaux, LA | 286 | 110 | 247 | 10 | 329 | 327 | 255 | 47 | 46 | 1,657 | 220 |
| Houston, TX | 288 | 269 | 34 | 304 | 119 | 28 | 11 | 138 | 18 | 1,209 | 77 |
| Huntington–Ashland, WV–KY–OH | 46 | 65 | 157 | 74 | 168 | 274 | 140 | 308 | 289 | 1,521 | 157 |
| Huntsville, AL | 79 | 37 | 208 | 157 | 285 | 318 | 161 | 284 | 57 | 1,586 | 191 |
| Indianapolis, IN | 138 | 101 | 44 | 192 | 50 | 216 | 44 | 128 | 214 | 1,127 | 59 |
| Iowa City, IA | 283 | 260 | 38 | 125 | 276 | 152 | 136 | 206 | 202 | 1,678 | 230 |
| Jackson, MI | 204 | 85 | 209 | 199 | 107 | 225 | 290 | 120 | 316 | 1,755 | 262 |
| Jackson, MS | 293 | 122 | 66 | 225 | 100 | 46 | 100 | 224 | 198 | 1,374 | 116 |
| Jacksonville, FL | 266 | 64 | 108 | 263 | 59 | 65 | 144 | 41 | 82 | 1,092 | 49 |
| Jacksonville, NC | 121 | 26 | 189 | 171 | 321 | 231 | 265 | 266 | 59 | 1,649 | 219 |
| Janesville–Beloit, WI | 260 | 136 | 203 | 133 | 253 | 271 | 220 | 176 | 290 | 1,942 | 308 |
| Jersey City, NJ | 76 | 241 | 67 | 293 | 95 | 259 | 33 | 291 | 237 | 1,592 | 195 |
| Johnson City–Kingsport–Bristol, TN–VA | 29 | 27 | 111 | 18 | 289 | 114 | 160 | 88 | 234 | 1,070 | 46 |
| Johnstown, PA | 154 | 55 | 193 | 5 | 145 | 215 | 259 | 302 | 305 | 1,633 | 207 |
| Joliet, IL | 248 | 258 | 127 | 129 | 117 | 139 | 101 | 170 | 266 | 1,555 | 176 |
| Joplin, MO | 99 | 1 | 271 | 58 | 300 | 137 | 324 | 313 | 172 | 1,675 | 226 |
| Kalamazoo, MI | 189 | 172 | 129 | 236 | 72 | 128 | 150 | 85 | 251 | 1,412 | 128 |
| Kankakee, IL | 240 | 120 | 231 | 179 | 220 | 144 | 326 | 277 | 146 | 1,883 | 295 |
| Kansas City, KS | 148 | 189 | 70 | 242 | 94 | 74 | 215 | 287 | 78 | 1,397 | 122 |
| Kansas City, MO | 148 | 107 | 55 | 296 | 46 | 102 | 51 | 99 | 242 | 1,146 | 62 |
| Kenosha, WI | 229 | 226 | 125 | 153 | 131 | 116 | 83 | 81 | 199 | 1,343 | 108 |
| Killeen–Temple, TX | 309 | 49 | 291 | 89 | 272 | 39 | 235 | 298 | 62 | 1,644 | 215 |
| Knoxville, TN | 26 | 72 | 145 | 55 | 150 | 179 | 97 | 56 | 148 | 928 | 14 |
| Kokomo, IN | 216 | 63 | 237 | 13 | 320 | 123 | 295 | 293 | 324 | 1,884 | 296 |
| La Crosse, WI | 311 | 207 | 207 | 76 | 35 | 77 | 191 | 113 | 138 | 1,355 | 111 |
| Lafayette, IN | 231 | 157 | 216 | 26 | 98 | 103 | 137 | 141 | 293 | 1,402 | 124 |
| Lafayette, LA | 285 | 230 | 256 | 202 | 81 | 316 | 173 | 153 | 2 | 1,698 | 240 |
| Lake Charles, LA | 255 | 94 | 311 | 228 | 206 | 313 | 192 | 135 | 107 | 1,841 | 288 |

| Metro Area | Climate & Terrain | Housing | Health Care & Environment | Crime | Transportation | Education | The Arts | Recreation | Economics | Cumulative Score | Overall Rank |
|---|---|---|---|---|---|---|---|---|---|---|---|
| Lake County, IL | 211 | 311 | 99 | 120 | 224 | 253 | 87 | 63 | 122 | 1,490 | 148 |
| Lakeland–Winter Haven, FL | 319 | 68 | 309 | 288 | 225 | 87 | 292 | 57 | 142 | 1,787 | 272 |
| Lancaster, PA | 129 | 236 | 116 | 13 | 173 | 54 | 229 | 270 | 209 | 1,429 | 136 |
| Lansing–East Lansing, MI | 246 | 170 | 88 | 147 | 64 | 130 | 78 | 178 | 254 | 1,355 | 111 |
| Laredo, TX | 288 | 28 | 279 | 211 | 235 | 154 | 313 | 323 | 183 | 2,014 | 318 |
| Las Cruces, NM | 144 | 98 | 246 | 294 | 258 | 190 | 114 | 178 | 168 | 1,690 | 236 |
| Las Vegas, NV | 140 | 274 | 290 | 326 | 43 | 319 | 184 | 8 | 93 | 1,677 | 228 |
| Lawrence, KS | 214 | 138 | 224 | 198 | 265 | 212 | 102 | 148 | 271 | 1,772 | 270 |
| Lawrence–Haverhill, MA–NH | 151 | 287 | 105 | 152 | 202 | 286 | 147 | 131 | 51 | 1,512 | 155 |
| Lawton, OK | 248 | 19 | 276 | 246 | 299 | 311 | 205 | 147 | 84 | 1,835 | 285 |
| Lewiston–Auburn, ME | 234 | 90 | 186 | 98 | 263 | 214 | 253 | 136 | 285 | 1,759 | 264 |
| Lexington–Fayette, KY | 48 | 212 | 59 | 212 | 165 | 142 | 90 | 233 | 72 | 1,233 | 81 |
| Lima, OH | 199 | 99 | 188 | 131 | 163 | 239 | 200 | 222 | 294 | 1,735 | 254 |
| Lincoln, NE | 300 | 201 | 183 | 108 | 56 | 133 | 67 | 143 | 232 | 1,423 | 133 |
| Little Rock–North Little Rock, AR | 227 | 123 | 58 | 279 | 154 | 258 | 142 | 216 | 181 | 1,638 | 212 |
| Longview–Marshall, TX | 223 | 62 | 268 | 179 | 284 | 155 | 288 | 311 | 38 | 1,808 | 278 |
| Lorain–Elyria, OH | 101 | 206 | 119 | 53 | 198 | 257 | 123 | 184 | 326 | 1,567 | 182 |
| Los Angeles–Long Beach, CA | 5 | 316 | 5 | 327 | 144 | 37 | 3 | 10 | 174 | 1,021 | 36 |
| Louisville, KY–IN | 60 | 87 | 48 | 160 | 71 | 74 | 60 | 117 | 163 | 840 | 7 |
| Lowell, MA–NH | 191 | 266 | 123 | 116 | 179 | 286 | 104 | 274 | 47 | 1,586 | 191 |
| Lubbock, TX | 71 | 100 | 153 | 316 | 159 | 265 | 95 | 159 | 104 | 1,422 | 132 |
| Lynchburg, VA | 42 | 97 | 191 | 66 | 102 | 160 | 221 | 220 | 229 | 1,328 | 103 |
| Macon–Warner Robins, GA | 273 | 34 | 241 | 104 | 246 | 229 | 193 | 262 | 134 | 1,716 | 248 |
| Madison, WI | 307 | 273 | 45 | 102 | 36 | 66 | 56 | 115 | 160 | 1,160 | 65 |
| Manchester, NH | 296 | 272 | 190 | 61 | 121 | 196 | 272 | 310 | 32 | 1,750 | 260 |
| Mansfield, OH | 134 | 91 | 313 | 219 | 270 | 137 | 266 | 273 | 288 | 1,991 | 313 |
| McAllen–Edinburg–Mission, TX | 323 | 2 | 296 | 128 | 313 | 234 | 210 | 286 | 124 | 1,916 | 304 |
| Medford, OR | 67 | 246 | 317 | 88 | 210 | 162 | 168 | 226 | 321 | 1,805 | 277 |
| Melbourne–Titusville–Palm Bay, FL | 98 | 240 | 266 | 208 | 287 | 156 | 275 | 12 | 33 | 1,575 | 185 |
| Memphis, TN–AR–MS | 211 | 102 | 51 | 301 | 28 | 159 | 69 | 106 | 204 | 1,231 | 80 |
| Miami–Hialeah, FL | 49 | 285 | 41 | 328 | 84 | 132 | 63 | 3 | 114 | 1,099 | 52 |
| Middlesex–Somerset–Hunterdon, NJ | 129 | 306 | 24 | 80 | 153 | 8 | 26 | 186 | 63 | 975 | 28 |
| Middletown, CT | 82 | 302 | 156 | 67 | 118 | 47 | 254 | 163 | 67 | 1,256 | 84 |
| Midland, TX | 72 | 238 | 327 | 251 | 78 | 300 | 274 | 208 | 1 | 1,749 | 258 |
| Milwaukee, WI | 264 | 282 | 17 | 124 | 99 | 67 | 21 | 40 | 224 | 1,138 | 61 |
| Minneapolis–St. Paul, MN–WI | 320 | 264 | 11 | 151 | 60 | 82 | 10 | 87 | 113 | 1,098 | 51 |
| Mobile, AL | 275 | 75 | 80 | 306 | 231 | 169 | 174 | 84 | 273 | 1,667 | 224 |

| Metro Area | Climate & Terrain | Housing | Health Care & Environment | Crime | Transportation | Education | The Arts | Recreation | Economics | Cumulative Score | Overall Rank |
|---|---|---|---|---|---|---|---|---|---|---|---|
| Modesto, CA | 43 | 235 | 301 | 245 | 315 | 249 | 260 | 312 | 210 | 2,170 | 327 |
| Monmouth–Ocean, NJ | 61 | 304 | 33 | 116 | 282 | 168 | 30 | 17 | 80 | 1,091 | 48 |
| Monroe, LA | 269 | 31 | 308 | 168 | 200 | 292 | 187 | 196 | 148 | 1,799 | 276 |
| Montgomery, AL | 240 | 81 | 166 | 115 | 212 | 308 | 198 | 279 | 236 | 1,835 | 285 |
| Muncie, IN | 185 | 16 | 147 | 104 | 146 | 100 | 125 | 222 | 309 | 1,354 | 110 |
| Muskegon, MI | 99 | 45 | 205 | 311 | 229 | 237 | 267 | 49 | 320 | 1,762 | 266 |
| Nashua, NH | 172 | 292 | 146 | 24 | 236 | 196 | 146 | 199 | 36 | 1,447 | 141 |
| Nashville, TN | 79 | 161 | 61 | 184 | 92 | 178 | 72 | 137 | 102 | 1,066 | 44 |
| Nassau–Suffolk, NY | 31 | 298 | 9 | 45 | 312 | 33 | 22 | 14 | 22 | 786 | 6 |
| New Bedford, MA | 40 | 184 | 265 | 194 | 240 | 295 | 249 | 219 | 228 | 1,914 | 303 |
| New Britain, CT | 207 | 289 | 98 | 150 | 104 | 47 | 199 | 258 | 53 | 1,405 | 126 |
| New Haven–Meriden, CT | 96 | 299 | 50 | 146 | 40 | 11 | 29 | 182 | 156 | 1,009 | 32 |
| New London–Norwich, CT–RI | 96 | 284 | 254 | 61 | 129 | 31 | 217 | 74 | 45 | 1,191 | 70 |
| New Orleans, LA | 226 | 225 | 25 | 315 | 124 | 88 | 27 | 18 | 54 | 1,102 | 53 |
| New York, NY | 44 | 312 | 1 | 329 | 1 | 92 | 1 | 16 | 169 | 965 | 25 |
| Newark, NJ | 76 | 318 | 8 | 295 | 209 | 20 | 8 | 140 | 128 | 1,202 | 73 |
| Niagara Falls, NY | 142 | 149 | 269 | 101 | 63 | 268 | 234 | 132 | 283 | 1,641 | 213 |
| Norfolk–Virginia Beach–Newport News, VA | 50 | 229 | 56 | 188 | 241 | 81 | 37 | 37 | 109 | 1,028 | 39 |
| Norwalk, CT | 34 | 328 | 29 | 56 | 207 | 70 | 35 | 75 | 55 | 889 | 10 |
| Oakland, CA | 1 | 310 | 39 | 309 | 24 | 231 | 45 | 65 | 158 | 1,182 | 69 |
| Ocala, FL | 316 | 80 | 273 | 278 | 183 | 141 | 299 | 31 | 34 | 1,635 | 208 |
| Odessa, TX | 72 | 70 | 294 | 322 | 316 | 201 | 300 | 303 | 17 | 1,895 | 299 |
| Oklahoma City, OK | 142 | 117 | 75 | 272 | 133 | 120 | 62 | 150 | 5 | 1,076 | 47 |
| Olympia, WA | 21 | 203 | 306 | 94 | 164 | 244 | 256 | 218 | 231 | 1,737 | 256 |
| Omaha, NE–IA | 277 | 113 | 26 | 193 | 49 | 58 | 85 | 109 | 112 | 1,022 | 37 |
| Orange County, NY | 217 | 281 | 79 | 112 | 238 | 181 | 38 | 134 | 115 | 1,395 | 121 |
| Orlando, FL | 266 | 193 | 184 | 320 | 45 | 94 | 118 | 42 | 21 | 1,283 | 91 |
| Owensboro, KY | 196 | 82 | 173 | 47 | 303 | 283 | 245 | 305 | 89 | 1,723 | 250 |
| Oxnard–Ventura, CA | 4 | 317 | 118 | 110 | 307 | 323 | 116 | 92 | 150 | 1,537 | 169 |
| Panama City, FL | 176 | 44 | 325 | 283 | 275 | 281 | 251 | 95 | 86 | 1,816 | 281 |
| Parkersburg–Marietta, WV–OH | 59 | 67 | 215 | 29 | 139 | 278 | 320 | 269 | 196 | 1,572 | 183 |
| Pascagoula, MS | 93 | 35 | 241 | 52 | 322 | 329 | 310 | 112 | 278 | 1,772 | 270 |
| Pawtucket–Woonsocket–Attleboro, RI–MA | 88 | 261 | 114 | 91 | 110 | 61 | 271 | 202 | 205 | 1,403 | 125 |
| Pensacola, FL | 176 | 51 | 252 | 297 | 266 | 119 | 159 | 86 | 94 | 1,500 | 151 |
| Peoria, IL | 233 | 217 | 107 | 155 | 261 | 294 | 134 | 162 | 306 | 1,869 | 294 |
| Philadelphia, PA–NJ | 52 | 207 | 4 | 214 | 42 | 1 | 6 | 108 | 140 | 774 | 4 |
| Phoenix, AZ | 176 | 244 | 77 | 269 | 113 | 106 | 65 | 59 | 56 | 1,165 | 67 |
| Pine Bluff, AR | 262 | 8 | 277 | 253 | 324 | 263 | 282 | 316 | 299 | 2,234 | 328 |

| Metro Area | Climate & Terrain | Housing | Health Care & Environment | Crime | Transportation | Education | The Arts | Recreation | Economics | Cumulative Score | Overall Rank |
|---|---|---|---|---|---|---|---|---|---|---|---|
| Pittsburgh, PA | 88 | 186 | 14 | 78 | 57 | 7 | 12 | 90 | 184 | 716 | 1 |
| Pittsfield, MA | 244 | 162 | 206 | 65 | 186 | 30 | 303 | 225 | 155 | 1,576 | 186 |
| Portland, ME | 240 | 187 | 163 | 122 | 86 | 95 | 130 | 20 | 76 | 1,119 | 55 |
| Portland, OR | 16 | 275 | 76 | 305 | 39 | 22 | 55 | 55 | 274 | 1,117 | 54 |
| Portsmouth–Dover–Rochester, NH–ME | 255 | 277 | 237 | 27 | 301 | 78 | 308 | 236 | 3 | 1,722 | 249 |
| Poughkeepsie, NY | 237 | 278 | 299 | 61 | 157 | 127 | 246 | 165 | 42 | 1,612 | 201 |
| Providence, RI | 88 | 253 | 34 | 189 | 69 | 6 | 46 | 76 | 205 | 966 | 26 |
| Provo–Orem, UT | 223 | 257 | 326 | 28 | 126 | 248 | 157 | 23 | 323 | 1,711 | 247 |
| Pueblo, CO | 227 | 66 | 277 | 257 | 213 | 227 | 201 | 174 | 264 | 1,906 | 301 |
| Racine, WI | 229 | 245 | 148 | 212 | 203 | 192 | 214 | 104 | 286 | 1,833 | 284 |
| Raleigh–Durham, NC | 37 | 198 | 13 | 182 | 22 | 16 | 47 | 180 | 58 | 753 | 3 |
| Reading, PA | 65 | 144 | 110 | 36 | 248 | 74 | 219 | 193 | 145 | 1,234 | 82 |
| Redding, CA | 27 | 231 | 315 | 143 | 53 | 289 | 240 | 64 | 284 | 1,646 | 216 |
| Reno, NV | 182 | 308 | 229 | 235 | 17 | 272 | 138 | 66 | 130 | 1,577 | 187 |
| Richland–Kennewick–Pasco, WA | 27 | 222 | 314 | 102 | 115 | 328 | 267 | 262 | 171 | 1,808 | 278 |
| Richmond–Petersburg, VA | 92 | 213 | 37 | 221 | 18 | 107 | 48 | 116 | 108 | 960 | 24 |
| Riverside–San Bernardino, CA | 61 | 268 | 42 | 298 | 247 | 254 | 54 | 124 | 230 | 1,578 | 189 |
| Roanoke, VA | 33 | 137 | 133 | 106 | 176 | 199 | 207 | 101 | 178 | 1,270 | 87 |
| Rochester, MN | 317 | 252 | 18 | 20 | 139 | 325 | 248 | 207 | 85 | 1,611 | 200 |
| Rochester, NY | 176 | 233 | 53 | 147 | 88 | 5 | 39 | 50 | 69 | 860 | 9 |
| Rockford, IL | 260 | 142 | 142 | 246 | 260 | 220 | 225 | 297 | 269 | 2,061 | 321 |
| Sacramento, CA | 103 | 271 | 135 | 286 | 89 | 166 | 70 | 72 | 175 | 1,367 | 113 |
| Saginaw–Bay City–Midland, MI | 210 | 131 | 136 | 218 | 244 | 173 | 178 | 96 | 319 | 1,705 | 244 |
| St. Cloud, MN | 324 | 121 | 234 | 4 | 125 | 279 | 165 | 189 | 153 | 1,594 | 196 |
| St. Joseph, MO | 252 | 7 | 322 | 173 | 283 | 112 | 238 | 251 | 101 | 1,739 | 257 |
| St. Louis, MO–IL | 173 | 143 | 19 | 273 | 12 | 9 | 19 | 78 | 119 | 845 | 8 |
| Salem, OR | 23 | 216 | 187 | 195 | 111 | 27 | 257 | 132 | 314 | 1,462 | 144 |
| Salem–Gloucester, MA | 38 | 301 | 100 | 31 | 217 | 193 | 98 | 80 | 65 | 1,123 | 56 |
| Salinas–Seaside–Monterey, CA | 9 | 315 | 300 | 233 | 158 | 295 | 230 | 27 | 135 | 1,702 | 241 |
| Salt Lake City–Ogden, UT | 168 | 262 | 74 | 173 | 29 | 312 | 52 | 11 | 227 | 1,308 | 99 |
| San Angelo, TX | 237 | 40 | 321 | 204 | 264 | 209 | 203 | 272 | 10 | 1,760 | 265 |
| San Antonio, TX | 300 | 93 | 91 | 261 | 74 | 108 | 75 | 204 | 39 | 1,245 | 83 |
| San Diego, CA | 3 | 321 | 31 | 231 | 68 | 165 | 20 | 22 | 152 | 1,013 | 33 |
| San Francisco, CA | 1 | 327 | 10 | 318 | 3 | 18 | 7 | 2 | 88 | 774 | 4 |
| San Jose, CA | 8 | 325 | 47 | 215 | 82 | 207 | 43 | 111 | 24 | 1,062 | 43 |
| Santa Barbara–Santa Maria–Lompoc, CA | 7 | 323 | 261 | 201 | 54 | 203 | 117 | 23 | 116 | 1,305 | 97 |
| Santa Cruz, CA | 9 | 319 | 134 | 169 | 93 | 252 | 86 | 158 | 170 | 1,390 | 119 |

| Metro Area | Climate & Terrain | Housing | Health Care & Environment | Crime | Transportation | Education | The Arts | Recreation | Economics | Cumulative Score | Overall Rank |
|---|---|---|---|---|---|---|---|---|---|---|---|
| Santa Rosa–Petaluma, CA | 19 | 309 | 128 | 154 | 237 | 200 | 94 | 77 | 127 | 1,345 | 109 |
| Sarasota, FL | 303 | 265 | 177 | 162 | 189 | 243 | 243 | 54 | 11 | 1,647 | 218 |
| Savannah, GA | 164 | 92 | 122 | 317 | 38 | 291 | 135 | 79 | 144 | 1,382 | 118 |
| Scranton–Wilkes–Barre, PA | 105 | 73 | 101 | 6 | 194 | 34 | 169 | 238 | 233 | 1,153 | 64 |
| Seattle, WA | 12 | 283 | 21 | 254 | 19 | 206 | 17 | 1 | 106 | 919 | 12 |
| Sharon, PA | 113 | 73 | 203 | 8 | 314 | 80 | 329 | 282 | 307 | 1,709 | 245 |
| Sheboygan, WI | 275 | 188 | 241 | 23 | 218 | 262 | 297 | 247 | 253 | 2,004 | 315 |
| Sherman–Denison, TX | 196 | 13 | 292 | 206 | 317 | 228 | 327 | 296 | 75 | 1,950 | 309 |
| Shreveport, LA | 220 | 57 | 82 | 261 | 138 | 143 | 113 | 237 | 50 | 1,301 | 95 |
| Sioux City, IA–NE | 304 | 56 | 161 | 97 | 147 | 222 | 196 | 240 | 263 | 1,686 | 234 |
| Sioux Falls, SD | 321 | 175 | 130 | 44 | 27 | 229 | 273 | 246 | 192 | 1,637 | 210 |
| South Bend–Mishawaka, IN | 157 | 20 | 167 | 207 | 55 | 135 | 119 | 139 | 216 | 1,215 | 78 |
| Spokane, WA | 110 | 95 | 272 | 136 | 65 | 172 | 107 | 200 | 259 | 1,416 | 130 |
| Springfield, IL | 196 | 167 | 57 | 268 | 31 | 57 | 158 | 197 | 165 | 1,296 | 93 |
| Springfield, MA | 270 | 179 | 200 | 264 | 33 | 10 | 93 | 201 | 177 | 1,427 | 134 |
| Springfield, MO | 159 | 43 | 249 | 143 | 178 | 207 | 180 | 151 | 103 | 1,413 | 129 |
| Stamford, CT | 34 | 329 | 23 | 127 | 250 | 70 | 28 | 154 | 79 | 1,094 | 50 |
| State College, PA | 105 | 221 | 230 | 39 | 278 | 38 | 206 | 264 | 262 | 1,643 | 214 |
| Steubenville–Weirton, OH–WV | 164 | 61 | 270 | 17 | 327 | 223 | 314 | 217 | 317 | 1,910 | 302 |
| Stockton, CA | 55 | 223 | 304 | 289 | 135 | 323 | 185 | 171 | 131 | 1,816 | 281 |
| Syracuse, NY | 151 | 148 | 131 | 79 | 14 | 44 | 57 | 44 | 282 | 950 | 21 |
| Tacoma, WA | 12 | 155 | 258 | 249 | 112 | 264 | 74 | 7 | 238 | 1,369 | 114 |
| Tallahassee, FL | 296 | 178 | 297 | 248 | 66 | 167 | 141 | 119 | 96 | 1,608 | 199 |
| Tampa–St. Petersburg–Clearwater, FL | 277 | 135 | 106 | 302 | 61 | 67 | 58 | 38 | 25 | 1,069 | 45 |
| Terre Haute, IN | 138 | 5 | 281 | 60 | 205 | 83 | 211 | 234 | 291 | 1,508 | 153 |
| Texarkana, TX–Texarkana, AR | 258 | 12 | 303 | 120 | 288 | 126 | 328 | 325 | 252 | 2,012 | 317 |
| Toledo, OH | 204 | 153 | 68 | 189 | 77 | 147 | 71 | 114 | 275 | 1,298 | 94 |
| Topeka, KS | 222 | 111 | 112 | 191 | 76 | 164 | 181 | 271 | 157 | 1,485 | 147 |
| Trenton, NJ | 46 | 291 | 87 | 257 | 108 | 24 | 59 | 169 | 121 | 1,162 | 66 |
| Tucson, AZ | 87 | 228 | 95 | 290 | 141 | 218 | 61 | 29 | 81 | 1,230 | 79 |
| Tulsa, OK | 185 | 139 | 78 | 222 | 187 | 240 | 76 | 102 | 31 | 1,260 | 86 |
| Tuscaloosa, AL | 254 | 50 | 210 | 195 | 114 | 307 | 194 | 283 | 235 | 1,842 | 289 |
| Tyler, TX | 223 | 127 | 211 | 167 | 216 | 26 | 278 | 326 | 23 | 1,597 | 197 |
| Utica–Rome, NY | 151 | 79 | 293 | 10 | 122 | 99 | 239 | 149 | 189 | 1,331 | 105 |
| Vallejo–Fairfield–Napa, CA | 11 | 288 | 124 | 169 | 160 | 282 | 109 | 192 | 117 | 1,452 | 142 |
| Vancouver, WA | 16 | 247 | 266 | 94 | 180 | 315 | 186 | 215 | 272 | 1,791 | 274 |
| Victoria, TX | 314 | 114 | 316 | 226 | 297 | 213 | 321 | 230 | 16 | 2,047 | 319 |
| Vineland–Millville–Bridgeton, NJ | 61 | 126 | 174 | 240 | 161 | 185 | 149 | 214 | 219 | 1,529 | 164 |

| Metro Area | Climate & Terrain | Housing | Health Care & Environment | Crime | Transportation | Education | The Arts | Recreation | Economics | Cumulative Score | Overall Rank |
|---|---|---|---|---|---|---|---|---|---|---|---|
| Visalia–Tulare–Porterville, CA | 163 | 157 | 324 | 239 | 252 | 326 | 270 | 45 | 147 | **1,923** | 305 |
| Waco, TX | 293 | 25 | 260 | 251 | 256 | 140 | 218 | 252 | 71 | **1,766** | 268 |
| Washington, DC–MD–VA | 51 | 314 | 6 | 276 | 4 | 3 | 4 | 188 | 87 | **933** | 17 |
| Waterbury, CT | 115 | 279 | 102 | 108 | 296 | 88 | 291 | 295 | 135 | **1,709** | 245 |
| Waterloo–Cedar Falls, IA | 312 | 166 | 149 | 81 | 230 | 131 | 105 | 129 | 287 | **1,590** | 194 |
| Wausau, WI | 317 | 147 | 169 | 22 | 214 | 184 | 250 | 166 | 295 | **1,764** | 267 |
| West Palm Beach–Boca Raton–Delray Beach, FL | 217 | 290 | 295 | 324 | 85 | 35 | 110 | 13 | 8 | **1,377** | 117 |
| Wheeling, WV–OH | 164 | 60 | 179 | 1 | 294 | 85 | 277 | 250 | 256 | **1,566** | 181 |
| Wichita, KS | 231 | 105 | 175 | 250 | 172 | 93 | 108 | 205 | 92 | **1,431** | 137 |
| Wichita Falls, TX | 268 | 46 | 255 | 255 | 273 | 185 | 264 | 275 | 41 | **1,862** | 292 |
| Williamsport, PA | 134 | 125 | 160 | 25 | 251 | 122 | 305 | 320 | 327 | **1,769** | 269 |
| Wilmington, DE–NJ–MD | 81 | 173 | 82 | 234 | 127 | 52 | 66 | 122 | 77 | **1,014** | 34 |
| Wilmington, NC | 121 | 89 | 120 | 292 | 267 | 134 | 222 | 48 | 164 | **1,457** | 143 |
| Worcester, MA | 123 | 239 | 64 | 77 | 197 | 25 | 172 | 301 | 218 | **1,416** | 130 |
| Yakima, WA | 182 | 47 | 310 | 232 | 190 | 283 | 231 | 91 | 223 | **1,789** | 273 |
| York, PA | 170 | 215 | 199 | 21 | 304 | 124 | 226 | 307 | 226 | **1,792** | 275 |
| Youngstown–Warren, OH | 113 | 103 | 121 | 161 | 228 | 115 | 115 | 245 | 313 | **1,514** | 156 |
| Yuba City, CA | 69 | 164 | 323 | 255 | 277 | 309 | 317 | 299 | 261 | **2,274** | 329 |

## Et Cetera

## AMERICA'S CHOICE METRO AREAS

After feeding stacks of data through nine different scoring systems and comparing the final rankings, *Places Rated* can now point to the very best of the 329 metro areas. But because statistics alone rarely tell the whole story, in this section of the chapter we offer brief prose sketches of the 20 metro areas that follow first-place Pittsburgh (Pittsburgh is described on pages 419–420). Even this small and select slice of *Places Rated*'s universe—which includes places in upstate New York, the South, and the California coast—will surprise you with its diversity.

★ **Boston, MA** (2)
Population: 2,805,911    Population Rank: 7

Boston, also known as the Hub and the Athens of America, takes second place in *Places Rated*'s overall ranking of American metro areas.

Boston's historic importance to the early days of the republic, unrivaled by any other city except Philadelphia, is known to every schoolchild. Here was the stage for the Boston Tea Party, Paul Revere's famous ride, and the battles of Lexington and Concord. What is usually surprising to the newcomer to New England is how compressed the distances are: From downtown Boston (pop. 562,994) out to Concord (pop. 6,400) is only 18 miles, and the perfect way to see the historic landmarks in the heart of the city is on foot, since most sites are within a brisk 20-minute walk.

As early as the mid-1600s, Boston's harbor contributed to making the city a center of trading for the New World. Many Yankee families who invested in shipping became wealthy early on, and some spent their fortunes not only on huge mansions on Beacon Hill and in Back Bay but on supporting the arts and letters as well. Soon Boston's reputation as a center of learning and culture was established—a reputation reflected today in its outstanding rankings in the arts (fifth) and education (14th).

Fine museums, symphony, opera, theatre, and dance—a wide array of these is available to residents and visitors alike. And no other metro area for its size has as many first-rate universities. Heading the list is of course Harvard, founded in 1636, when John Harvard donated his library to the new school that had been founded in Cambridge. Wellesley, M.I.T., Tufts, Northeastern, Boston College, and Boston University are also located here. The creativity and intellectual talent that issue continually from these fine schools are Boston's most precious resources. Polaroid, Digital Equipment Corporation, Wang, and a host of other high-tech electronic enterprises had their origins in Boston's prestigious universities. The ring of space-age corporations that encircles the city on Route 128 is at the heart of Boston's current economic boom and low unemployment rate. The many top-ranked medical schools help explain the metro area's tremendous health care facilities (ranked third among the metro areas) and New England's constant contributions to medical science.

Like many other major metro areas, Boston is a collection of diverse towns, each contributing to the general tone of the area but each with its own identity and charm. North of the city are places like Lynn (pop. 78,471), Revere (pop. 42,423), and Chelsea (pop. 25,431)—industrial towns with historical significance now primarily engaged in manufacturing. To the south are Braintree (pop. 36,337) and Quincy (pop. 84,743), the hometown of John Adams, John Quincy Adams, and John Hancock; and Plymouth (pop. 7,232), landing site of the *Mayflower*.

But what of the sections and neighborhoods within Boston? They, too, are diverse, each with their own ethnic composition and local economy. As the Industrial Revolution took hold in the New World, the earliest and most numerous immigrant group was the Irish, and they still play perhaps the most important role in the city. The Irish enclaves in Boston are South Boston and Charlestown. Both of these are predominantly working-class, blue-collar residential neighborhoods which are so tightly knit that they are sometimes cool, even hostile, to strangers and any outside interference.

The North End is home to many of Boston's Italian-Americans, the second most populous ethnic group. Here, on the northern tip of the stubby peninsula that is downtown Boston, the visitor can walk through the crowded, intimate streets lined with small shops selling pasta, meats, vegetables, wines, pastries, espresso, and cookware, and hear nothing but Italian spoken, sung, and shouted.

And then there is Beacon Hill, that stalwart monument to the old-time Yankee aristocracy. This rolling rise of ground behind the State House is where Boston's elite make their homes. The streets are still brick, and the houses are stately Georgian and Regency three- or four-story mansions, many of them converted into apartments or condominiums. Henry James once called Beacon Hill's Mount Vernon Street "the only respectable street in America."

Boston is where it all began for the United States. And perhaps, if the technological revolution continues unabated, Boston, ironically, will be the cradle of the second great revolution, 200 years after the first.

*Pluses:* Abundant historic and ethnic charm; outstanding health care facilities; top-notch educational and performing arts assets.

*Minuses:* Very high housing costs (300th) and high crime rate (266th).

### ★ Raleigh–Durham, NC (3)
Population: 561,222    Population Rank: 74

How did this midsize metro area with a total population of just over half a million wind up at the top of the list along with Pittsburgh (pop. 2,218,870) and Boston (pop. 2,805,911)?

Simple: Raleigh–Durham has a lot going for it. A center of learning, a capital of one of America's most varied and promising states, a research center, the southeastern mecca for high-tech industry and development, and a beautiful, genteel place to live—the more you find out about this Piedmont metro area, the less surprising it is that Raleigh–Durham is one of America's most livable metro areas.

About half its population is divided among Raleigh (pop. 150,255), Durham (pop. 100,538), and Chapel Hill (pop. 32,421). The remainder is scattered in small towns and suburbs in Durham, Wake, Orange, and Franklin counties. The metro area is multidimensional and spread out among many towns, giving it an open, relaxed, and rural feel. Each of the three main cities is home to a major university—Raleigh contains North Carolina State University; Durham is the site of Duke; and Chapel Hill is where the main campus of the University of North Carolina, the oldest state university in the nation, was established.

Raleigh, founded in 1792 and named for Sir Walter Raleigh, the British soldier and explorer, is encircled by a beltway studded with plants, shopping malls, and office buildings. The downtown section centers on Capitol Square. The capitol, which replaced the original (it burned in 1831), is Greek Revival in style and striking in its simplicity. Nearby are the Governor's Mansion and the Oakwood Historic District, a neighborhood of old frame houses that have been restored and that command handsome real estate prices. Besides the capitol area, perhaps the greatest attraction is North Carolina State University, NCAA Division I basketball champions in 1983. It's a large school (more than 21,000 students) that offers undergraduate and graduate courses in more than 90 fields of study. Still, what impresses many visitors to Raleigh is the manageable size, friendly spirit, and intimacy of this seat of government, business, and learning.

The city of Durham is tied inextricably to the Duke family, founders of the American Tobacco Company in the 1880s. Sensing that cigarettes might be more than just a passing fad, the Dukes began mass-producing and packaging them during the last part of the century. Almost overnight, the company and the family reaped a huge fortune. In 1924 James B. Duke contributed a considerable portion of that fortune to establish Duke University, which remains one of the most prestigious universities in the nation, with a renowned medical center.

In contrast to the Gothic stone of Duke are the many tobacco warehouses and textile mills that still form a cornerstone of the local economy. Residents can smell the pungent aroma of raw tobacco leaf all over the city, and trucks and freight cars filled with the raw material and finished product bustle in and out of town continually. In recent decades, Durham has diversified its economic base, relying increasingly on service industries and high-tech manufacturing.

The tone and charm of Chapel Hill, the smallest of the three major cities in the metro area, reflect the fact that it was founded not as a commercial or manufacturing site but as a home for a state university. And this university-town flavor is evident everywhere in Chapel Hill, from the tweedy campus clothing and tobacco shops to the snug eateries and boutiques, the raucous night spots, and the quiet splendor of the campus itself, which encompasses 3,900 acres and more than 200 buildings. The quads, walkways, and tree-covered knolls of the campus are famous for a dazzling variety of plants and trees.

One recent development that undoubtedly has had much to do with Raleigh–Durham's high ranking was the selection in the late 1950s of Durham County as the site of Research Triangle Park, a planned research center that is now sometimes referred to as a miniature version of Boston in the fields of scientific and medical research and high-tech entrepreneurship.

*Pluses:* A good showing in nearly every category; mild, temperate climate (37th), plus excellent rankings in health care facilities (13th), education (16th), and transportation (22nd).

*Minuses:* Mediocre rankings in housing costs (198th) and crime (182nd).

### ★ Philadelphia, PA–NJ (4)
Population: 4,716,818    Population Rank: 4

Philadelphia, a huge and historic metro area, has much to recommend it. Founded as a Quaker colony in 1682 by William Penn, the central city (pop. 1,688,210) retains Quaker ideals of public service and social progress. It is still headquarters of many artistic, philosophic, dramatic, musical, and scientific societies. Among these are the Pennsylvania Academy of the

Fine Arts, the Academy of Natural Sciences of Philadelphia, the American Philosophical Society, and the Franklin Institute of Science. Philadelphia's symphony orchestra is one of the elite performing ensembles in the world. It and the many area art and history museums, as well as 46 four-year colleges and universities (among them the University of Pennsylvania, Temple, Bryn Mawr, Drexel, Villanova, and St. Joseph's), all contribute to the metro area's rich cultural life. It's no surprise, then, that Philadelphia took first place in education and ranked sixth in the arts among *Places Rated*'s metro areas. The fine medical schools and hospitals that are a natural by-product of first-rate universities help establish Philadelphia's rank of fourth for health care options.

In addition to these impressive big-city blessings, however, is a more intimate side to the City of Brotherly Love. Philadelphia's neighborhoods, so well defined they act as mini-cities within the big one, are a key to understanding not only the physical place that is Philadelphia but its social and historical structure as well. Natives tend to tell you they're from Kingsessing, Northern Liberties, Strawberry Mansion, Brewerytown, Manayunk, or any one of the many Philadelphia neighborhoods. Urban renovation is currently and quickly transforming blighted sections of the city into resurgent neighborhoods while preserving the wonderful buildings and historic sections at their heart. In Manayunk, a textile center once referred to as the Manchester of America, countless solid-stone mill buildings became mostly vacant over the past 50 years with the decline of the textile industry in the Northeast. Now artists and designers are taking over the abandoned buildings and setting up studios. The old residents, primarily descendants of the Italian, Irish, Polish, and German immigrants who came over to run the looms, also remain in Manayunk, loyal to one another and to their neighborhood.

Another area that mirrors what's happening in Philadelphia is Society Hill. An old city quarter just south of Independence Hall, this once fashionable district had become a dismal island of poverty. Now its restored historic buildings attract top dollars. One of the driving forces behind this creative urban rehabbing is the Greater Philadelphia Partnership, which puts old homes and buildings back into use by practically giving them to prospective owners and residents along with grants for rehabilitating them. This style of urban renewal results in a high proportion of owner-occupied housing, which then leads to increased neighborhood pride, lower crime rates, and greater social stability.

Philadelphia is located in southeastern Pennsylvania between the Delaware and Schuylkill rivers, about 100 miles upstream from the mouth of the Delaware River at Delaware Bay. The land is low-lying and level, with a few rolling hills. The nearby Atlantic Coast to the east and the Appalachian Mountains to the west shield the area from temperature extremes both winter and summer, though summers can be muggy and hot.

Outlying parts of the metro area include places rich in history and scenic beauty, such as Swarthmore (pop. 5,950), home of Swarthmore College, founded in 1864 by the Society of Friends; Chester (pop. 45,794), settled in 1643 by the Swedish Trading Company; Valley Forge National Historical Park, a memorial to the trials of the Continental Army; and New Hope (pop. 1,473) in charming Bucks County, where Washington crossed the Delaware and where artists and writers have now settled, giving the area a reputation as an art center. These are all residential communities where one can enjoy the lushness and quaintness of the countryside while still being near the city.

*Pluses:* Top rankings in education, the arts, and health care; many landmarks of early American history; mild four-season climate (52nd).

*Minuses:* Below-average rankings for housing costs (207th) and crime (214th).

### ★ San Francisco, CA (4)
Population: 1,488,871    Population Rank: 26

San Francisco is probably America's most beautiful metro area. Its extremely high rankings in climate (first among the metro areas) and recreation (second) reflect its spectacular environment. Situated on the tip of a narrow peninsula that separates San Francisco Bay from the Pacific Ocean, the city of San Francisco (pop. 678,974) is surrounded by cool ocean waters. Many of the buildings in San Francisco are white or cream-colored, giving the impression that this city is Mediterranean. It isn't, of course, but the climate is. San Francisco's location in a temperate latitude in the path of Pacific winds provides the metro area with the mildest climate in America—and perhaps even in the world. The only aspect of the climate that could be considered a drawback is the fog. Rising currents of hot summer air from the San Joaquin Valley draw cold ocean air in through the bay, causing an almost daily intrusion of fog. Still, National Weather Service statistics show San Francisco getting 66 of every possible 100 hours of sunshine.

The Bay Area's environmental blessings don't end with the weather. San Francisco is a city of parks and gardens, including the magnificent Golden Gate Park, 1,017 acres stretching from the ocean to the center of the city. Golden Gate National Recreation Area, which includes most of the San Francisco shoreline, the Marin County coast, and the islands of Angel and Alcatraz, is evidence of San Francisco's resolve to keep thousands of acres of natural beauty intact for future generations. Quality restaurants and great spectator sports are among San Francisco's other top recreational amenities.

San Francisco ranks third among the metro areas in transportation, and some people consider its most famous mode of transit, the cable car, to be another form of recreation. The metro area garners high marks

in health care (tenth) and the arts (seventh) as well; in all, it has a rank of tenth or better in five of *Places Rated's* nine categories. Such elite performing arts groups as the San Francisco Symphony, the American Conservatory Theatre, San Francisco Opera, and San Francisco Ballet make this one of America's premier cultural centers. In contrast with its high marks in climate, health, arts, recreation, and transportation, however, San Francisco ranks very near the bottom of *Places Rated's* list in housing (327th) and crime (318th). These poor showings are due to a high population density, caused in turn by the city's other attractive features. Housing in nearly all segments of the metro area is expensive and hard to find.

Like most major metropolitan areas, San Francisco is not one homogeneous city but a collection of neighborhoods. Chinatown, the city's best-known ethnic neighborhood, is the largest Asian community outside the Orient. The North Beach section, now famous for its nightlife, remains a close-knit, traditional Italian neighborhood replete with religious festivals, a glorious Columbus Day celebration, and scores of first-rate Italian restaurants and coffeehouses. The Mission district, home of many Mexican-Americans, borders on the Castro and Polk Street neighborhoods, center of the city's influential gay population. The Sunset district, with the Pacific Ocean on the west and Golden Gate Park on the north, and Richmond, a somewhat cooler and foggier area, both provide more traditional, middle-class, single-family residential options. Two sections of the city itself cater almost exclusively to the establishment: the financial district, which houses the Bank of America (the world's biggest bank), many brokerage houses, and most of the city's law firms; and Nob Hill, the domain of the wealthy and upwardly mobile.

The San Francisco metro area includes San Francisco County itself, San Mateo County to the south, and Marin County to the north (just across the Golden Gate Bridge), one of the most coveted residential counties in the United States. Real estate prices there prove it. In Sausalito (pop. 7,338), a famous artists' colony with a distinct maritime flavor, many residents live in barge-type houseboats decorated with gingerbread woodwork, stained-glass windows, and innumerable flowerpots. Tiburon (pop. 6,685) features steep hills lined with homes that command spectacular views of the bay and the city across it.

*Pluses:* America's mildest climate; great natural beauty; outstanding cultural and recreational assets.

*Minuses:* Housing prices are out of sight; high crime rate.

### ★ Nassau–Suffolk, NY (6)
Population: 2,605,813    Population Rank: 9

East of the New York City boroughs of Brooklyn and Queens on Long Island lies a metro area that presents an interesting paradox. On one hand, Nassau–Suffolk serves New York, sending thousands of commuters daily into "the city" and providing weekend and vacation retreats for thousands of New Yorkers. Yet Nassau–Suffolk also exists for itself, deliberately determining its own facilities, industries, and way of life. The variety of activities, both commercial and recreational, is stunning.

Hardly a category of contemporary life is free of the contrasts that characterize the metro area. Residential Long Island includes apartment complexes, suburban single-family homes, estates, and summer cottages. Large urban industries like Grumman Aerospace Corporation (in Bethpage, pop. 29,900) and Brookhaven National Laboratory (in Upton) are countered by Long Island's agricultural and fishing industries. Recreational facilities range from the 17,000-seat Nassau Veterans Memorial Coliseum (in Hempstead, pop. 40,404) and Roosevelt Raceway (in Westbury, pop. 13,871) to the sand and surf of Jones Beach State Park and the unspoiled beauty of Fire Island National Seashore.

Part of this contrast is simply between the two counties. Nassau County, closer to New York City, is a bedroom county, with suburbs, stores, and recreational facilities responding to the pulse of a high-energy population eager to pay for goods and services while expecting the most for its money. Residential areas are tightly packed but maintained with the pride of those who have spent hard-earned money on choice real estate. Suffolk County, with its committed detachment from the frenzy of New York and the intensity of Nassau, lures many to its blend of rural farms, fishing villages, elegant mansions, art colonies, sedate old towns, and lazy, endless stretches of shoreline. The ultimate withdrawal is Montauk Point, 120 miles from New York City. Montauk Lighthouse, nearly 200 years old, marks the easternmost tip of Long Island. Suffolk County offers sanctuaries for the elite who want to get away from it all, with their own kind or alone, to visit such spots as the old whaling village of Sag Harbor (pop. 2,581) or to put down roots in places like the harbor town of Northport (pop. 7,651).

Because of its proximity to New York City (and because of its predominantly middle- and upper-class residents and visitors), Nassau–Suffolk's housing costs are quite high, giving it a very low housing rank (298th), but its ranks in health (ninth), arts (22nd), and education (33rd) all benefit for the same reason.

Both counties are changing from summer vacation spots to year-round residential communities. This trend is perhaps most notable in Long Beach, located just a short distance from Manhattan on Nassau County's south shore, where post–World War II deterioration, run-down housing, and high crime are being brought under control by new, carefully designed housing, stores, and public buildings.

*Pluses:* Proximity to New York City means good ranks in the arts, education, recreation, and health care facilities.

*Minuses:* Very high housing costs; very low ranking in transportation (312th).

★ **Louisville, KY–IN** (7)
Population: 956,756    Population Rank: 44

Mint juleps in frosted silver cups, paddle-wheel races on the Ohio, and Thoroughbreds steaming after a sunrise workout may all seem out of place in the hurry-up world of the eighties, but these are a way of life in Louisville, Kentucky (pop. 298,840), heart of the seventh-ranked metro area in the United States. One of the nine super-solid metro areas that earn no *Places Rated* ranking below 200th, Louisville (pronounced LOO-vull by natives) is a metro area in step with the present while preserving its past.

Ongoing maintenance of historic sites, such as Farmington and Locust Grove, is a poignant reminder of Louisville's gracious heritage. Other points of interest include Butchertown, which houses Bakery Square, antique shops, and the home of Thomas A. Edison; the restored downtown districts of Old Louisville and West Main Street; and Churchill Downs, first opened in May of 1875 and home of the annual Kentucky Derby.

Hand in hand with a reverence for history goes Louisville's commitment to the arts, evident in its ranking of 60th in this category. The Actor's Theatre of Louisville has received national recognition for its dedication to the promotion of new plays and rising playwrights and actors; the Louisville Children's Theatre is recognized for exemplary children's theatre in the Southeast; and Stage One was honored by an invitation to perform at the Kennedy Center. Louisville also supports two symphony orchestras, the Louisville Ballet, and the Kentucky Opera Association. In addition to many small historical museums, there are tours through the businesses that have made Louisville famous—Old Fitzgerald and Joseph E. Seagram Sons distilleries, Philip Morris, Louisville Stoneware Company, and Hillerich & Bradsby's Slugger Park.

Even though it produces the world's best baseball bats, bourbon, and racehorses, Louisville's economy is in a transitional phase. Some companies are closing their Louisville facilities. Still, Louisville's rank of 163rd in economic promise lands it precisely in the middle of the 329 metro areas. Also to the metro area's credit are the building and restoration efforts in the downtown area that are creating accommodations for business and pleasure.

Due to a recent focus on improving the quality of public schools and a good mix of degree options, Louisville ranks 74th in education. It does, however, face problems common to many school systems in the South and Southeast: overcrowded classroooms, low teacher salaries, and racial tension.

For a metro area with a population approaching the million mark, Louisville's ranks for housing costs (87th) and crime rate (160th) are surprisingly good. Its lack of inner-city congestion may help keep these two regrettable aspects of city living under control. This metro area, which spans seven counties in Kentucky and Indiana, is spread over farms, small towns, and cities where the people are friendly and hardworking. Out here in the towns of Shepherdsville (pop. 4,454), La Grange (pop. 2,971), and Shelbyville (pop. 5,329), and over the bridge in New Albany, Indiana (pop. 37,103), homes are available and affordable.

Louisville's high ranking of 48th for health care facilities goes deeper than its three teaching hospitals and the University of Louisville School of Medicine. November of 1984 saw the second successful implant of an artificial human heart, at the Humana Heart Institution International. The medical resources here are recognized as some of the best in the country.

On the first Saturday in May, just before the world's best Thoroughbreds run for the roses, the whole of Churchill Downs stands and sings "My Old Kentucky Home" while the rest of the world watches and listens. And for that moment the world understands the pride Louisvillians have in their city, their home, and their heritage.

*Pluses:* Good rankings in housing, health care facilities, the arts, and education; moderate climate, with four distinct seasons.

*Minuses:* Economy in a transitional phase; average crime rate; average recreation facilities.

### ★ St. Louis, MO–IL (8)
Population: 1,808,621    Population Rank: 19

Just the mention of St. Louis brings a myriad of responses: Gateway Arch, St. Louis Cardinals, Six Flags Over Mid-America, Anheuser-Busch, St. Louis Zoo, St. Louis *Post-Dispatch*. Names like T. S. Eliot, Stan Musial, Lewis and Clark, Eugene Field, Dred Scott, William Webster, and Yogi Berra are further reminders of the diversity of *Places Rated's* eighth-ranked metro area. Sports, entertainment, the arts, and industry all flourish here.

St. Louis (pop. 453,085) began as a center for trade on the mighty Mississippi and grew into a hub for national and international commerce. One of the world's largest markets for wool, lumber, and pharmaceuticals, St. Louis is also an important producer of shoes, beer, aircraft, and basic metals. Nine Fortune 500 companies including McDonnell Douglas, Monsanto, Anheuser-Busch, and Ralston Purina have headquarters in St. Louis.

Receiving a number-12 rank among the metro areas for its transit supply, St. Louis maintains its historic position as a major transportation center. River traffic still thrives as cargo-loaded barges drift from one end of the river to the other. Truck transport also abounds; a network of Interstate highways flows through St. Louis, connecting East with West and North with South. Lambert–St. Louis International Airport offers the same convenience for travelers and air freight.

An innovative voluntary desegregation program is improving the racial balance of area schools. The metro area ranks ninth for education, due mostly to its above-average effort in supporting public schools and its many options in higher learning: St. Louis proudly claims Washington University, St. Louis University, and the St. Louis campus of the University of Missouri among its numerous institutions. And six of its secondary schools were judged outstanding by the Department of Education's Secondary School Recognition Program.

St. Louis is often called the City of Neighborhoods, and rightly so. Descendants of the German immigrants who flocked to St. Louis in the mid-1800s populate many of the neighborhoods. The Central West End, with its grand turn-of-the-century brick and stucco homes, antique shops, boutiques, restaurants, sidewalk cafés, and lanterned streets, reflects St. Louis's rich heritage. Laclede's Landing, a renovation of old warehouses along the riverfront just north of Gateway Arch, provides an exciting array of activities day and night with its numerous restaurants, music-filled pubs, and specialty shops.

St. Louis County has its own blend of old (Webster Groves, pop. 23,097, and Kirkwood, pop. 27,987) and new (Westwood, pop. 319, and Chesterfield, pop. 800), offering a variety of housing from traditional neighborhoods to attractive subdivisions and conveniently located condominiums. The gracious homes of Clayton (pop. 14,273), the St. Louis county seat, vie in charm with the luxurious estate settings of Ladue (pop. 9,376). Homeowning costs are slightly lower than average in the St. Louis metro area, which ranks 143rd in this *Places Rated* category.

There is obviously a lot that is right about this high-ranking metro area, but what is wrong? First, the summers can be insufferably hot, with temperatures climbing above 90 degrees Fahrenheit more often than not. No wonder the ice-cream cone was introduced here! Second, as with nearly every major city, the crime rate is high, ranked 273rd among the 329 metro areas. But St. Louis is a city of determination and resilience: When parts of the city were declared blighted urban areas, it demolished and rebuilt; when business slumped and the economic outlook was poor, St. Louis created facilities to attract tourists and conventioneers. This city of grace, tradition, and charm is a testament to the words of one of its most colorful sons, Yogi Berra, who exclaimed, "The game isn't over till it's over."

*Pluses:* Ranks high in transportation, education, and health care; full spectrum of cultural facilities, for an arts rank of 19th.

*Minuses:* Often dangerously hot summers; high crime rate.

### ★ Rochester, NY (9)
Population: 971,230    Population Rank: 43

Rochester (pop. 241,741) is the namesake city of a five-county metro area encompassing rich fruit-orchard and truck-gardening country on the southern

## Large and Small Metro Areas

*Places Rated Almanac*'s top 50 metro areas include 24 with a population of more than one million, 21 between 250,000 and one million in size, and only five with a population of less than 250,000, despite the fact that there are more small metro areas (170) than medium-sized (119) or large (40).

The large metropolitan areas undoubtedly offer a number of advantages: economic diversity, the chance for personal achievement, a wide range of cultural and recreational facilities, and freedom for diverse life-styles. But the flip side of this is often high crime rates, high living costs, a sense of personal insignificance, and restricted access to the natural environment.

Many people who live in large metro areas actually prefer smaller places but feel compelled for economic reasons to stay near the big city. These people might do well to look at some of *Places Rated*'s high-ranking medium and small metro areas as the ideal compromise between big-city strengths and the more manageable, even intimate life-style associated with smaller places. To assist you in evaluating the relative merits of large, medium, and small metro areas, we present the top places in each category.

### America's Best Large Metro Areas
(Population 1,000,000 or more)

| Metro Area | Cumulative Score |
|---|---|
| 1. Pittsburgh, PA | 716 |
| 2. Boston, MA | 752 |
| 3. Philadelphia, PA–NJ | 774 |
| 3. San Francisco, CA | 774 |
| 5. Nassau–Suffolk, NY | 786 |
| 6. St. Louis, MO–IL | 845 |
| 7. Dallas, TX | 898 |
| 8. Seattle, WA | 919 |
| 9. Atlanta, GA | 921 |
| 10. Buffalo, NY | 931 |
| 11. Baltimore, MD | 932 |
| 12. Washington, DC–MD–VA | 933 |
| 13. Cincinnati, OH–KY–IN | 938 |
| 14. New York, NY | 965 |
| 15. Chicago, IL | 968 |
| 16. Denver, CO | 977 |
| 17. Cleveland, OH | 988 |
| 18. San Diego, CA | 1,013 |
| 19. Los Angeles–Long Beach, CA | 1,021 |
| 20. San Jose, CA | 1,062 |

### America's Best Medium-Sized Metro Areas
(Population 250,000 to 1,000,000)

| Metro Area | Cumulative Score |
|---|---|
| 1. Raleigh–Durham, NC | 753 |
| 2. Louisville, KY–IN | 840 |
| 3. Rochester, NY | 860 |
| 4. Knoxville, TN | 928 |
| 5. Albany–Schenectady–Troy, NY | 941 |
| 6. Syracuse, NY | 950 |
| 7. Albuquerque, NM | 952 |
| 8. Harrisburg–Lebanon–Carlisle, PA | 957 |
| 9. Richmond–Petersburg, VA | 960 |
| 10. Providence, RI | 966 |
| 11. Middlesex–Somerset–Hunterdon, NJ | 975 |
| 12. New Haven–Meriden, CT | 1,009 |
| 13. Wilmington, DE–NJ–MD | 1,014 |
| 14. Omaha, NE–IA | 1,022 |
| 15. Bridgeport–Milford, CT | 1,026 |
| 16. Greensboro–Winston-Salem–High Point, NC | 1,030 |
| 17. Nashville, TN | 1,066 |
| 18. Johnson City–Kingsport–Bristol, TN–VA | 1,070 |
| 19. Oklahoma City, OK | 1,076 |
| 20. Monmouth–Ocean, NJ | 1,091 |

### America's Best Small Metro Areas
(Population Less than 250,000)

| Metro Area | Cumulative Score |
|---|---|
| 1. Norwalk, CT | 889 |
| 2. Burlington, VT | 941 |
| 3. Charlottesville, VA | 999 |
| 4. Asheville, NC | 1,016 |
| 5. Stamford, CT | 1,094 |
| 6. Portland, ME | 1,119 |
| 7. Danbury, CT | 1,124 |
| 8. Galveston–Texas City, TX | 1,205 |
| 9. South Bend–Mishawaka, IN | 1,215 |
| 10. Middletown, CT | 1,256 |
| 11. Bangor, ME | 1,258 |
| 12. Roanoke, VA | 1,270 |
| 13. Springfield, IL | 1,296 |
| 14. Lynchburg, VA | 1,328 |
| 15. Boulder–Longmont, CO | 1,330 |
| 16. Cumberland, MD–WV | 1,333 |
| 17. Champaign–Urbana–Rantoul, IL | 1,342 |
| 18. Kenosha, WI | 1,343 |
| 19. Muncie, IN | 1,354 |
| 20. La Crosse, WI | 1,355 |

shore of Lake Ontario. One of its early nicknames was Flour City, an obvious if uninspired one for a town that dealt largely in milling wheat. As with many other New York State communities, Rochester's fortunes were closely tied to the opening of the Erie Canal in the early 1820s. With the Genesee River as an inland gateway, Rochester linked Lake Ontario ports with those on the canal, that famous east-west water route connecting the Great Lakes with the Hudson River and

Atlantic Ocean. Thus established as a commercial center, Rochester became the flour-milling capital of the nation, relying on the wheat grown in the Genesee Valley.

Flour milling dominated the town until just after the Civil War, when horticultural ventures in flowers, ornamental shrubbery, and other nursery items were introduced to the region. Accordingly, Flour City became known as Flower City, a name eclipsed when a new industry sprang up, started by a young inventor named George Eastman.

Few figures in American industry can rival George Eastman, the father of modern photography, in creative genius. In the 1880s, while still in his thirties, he discovered the dry-plate process for taking pictures, which vastly simplified the more cumbersome wet-plate process. Soon after, he developed the same chemicals on a transparent strip of celluloid, and so was born roll film. This, coupled with his introduction of the Kodak hand-held camera in 1888, made photography an inexpensive, convenient hobby within the reach of most Americans. The Eastman Kodak Company grew impressively over the years, with profound effects and benefits for the city of Rochester, for Eastman was a philanthropist and educator as well as an inventor. Thus, Rochester received an estimated $100 million from the Kodak corporation to support the University of Rochester, the Eastman School of Music, Rochester Institute of Technology, and a host of other charitable and educational institutions.

Today Rochester, which ranks a solid 69th in economics, is in the midst of a high-tech boom. In addition to Kodak (30th in *Fortune* magazine's 1984 list of leading industrial corporations), the city has become well known for the manufacture of office equipment, gear-grinding machinery, optical equipment, and dental tools. Other Fortune 500 companies headquartered in the metro area are Sybron and Bausch & Lomb.

The metro area's high ranking in recreation (50th) owes much to its natural setting. The city of Rochester is gateway to New York's Finger Lakes region, and the metro area is dotted with small cities such as Canandaigua (pop. 10,419), a resort located on the westernmost of the Finger Lakes; and Geneva (pop. 15,133), a fisherman's mecca on Seneca Lake. Recreational boating is popular both on Irondequoit Bay and the Genesee River. Beaches and parks line the river and lakeshore, providing additional outdoor recreation for Rochester's pleasant summertimes and falls.

Rochester ranks 39th in the arts and provides artistic and cultural variety for residents, including performances by the Rochester Philharmonic Orchestra, one of America's major symphonies, and the Opera Theatre of Rochester. Its fifth-place rank in education reflects an emphasis on quality nurtured by pioneers such as George Eastman.

*Pluses:* Nice mix of cultural, recreational, and educational facilities; pleasant summers.

*Minuses:* Rather long, snowy winters; cloudy; above-average housing costs (233rd).

★ **Norwalk, CT** (10)
Population: 126,692   Population Rank: 258

For many travelers, Norwalk, Connecticut, is an exit on the Connecticut Turnpike; to many commuters, Norwalk is a parking lot and a train station. But as its tenth-place ranking indicates, this dark-horse metro area is more than a stopover between Wall Street and home. Norwalk lies on Long Island Sound just an hour's drive from New York City and all it has to offer. A major factor contributing to Norwalk's leap from 148th place in the first edition of *Places Rated Almanac* to its present high status is its membership in the New York–Northern New Jersey–Long Island CMSA, which benefited its rankings in both the arts and recreational opportunities substantially.

The city of Norwalk (pop. 77,767) is surrounded by fashionable, affluent residential towns. Because of this, Norwalk's appeal might appear to be in its surroundings. In fact, Norwalk has its own history and identity. Founded in 1651, this pre–Revolutionary War settlement was an industrial center producing clocks, nails, and paper. Today Norwalk focuses on manufacturing astronomic instruments, aircraft radar equipment, electric components, chemicals, and plastics, and is also becoming a research and development center. Economic opportunities are good in the metro area, resulting in a solid 55th-place ranking.

A city of contrasts, Norwalk claims both the best and the worst in terms of available housing. Some of the area's finest residential sections are here, including comfortable Rowayton and Silvermine. On the other hand, South Norwalk is fighting a high crime rate and inadequate housing. It is heartening to note, however, that the late 1970s saw a trend toward the renovation of run-down Victorian homes in this section, and more recently a proposed waterfront revival.

Two neighboring communities that enhance the Norwalk metro area are Wilton (pop. 6,500) and Westport (pop. 25,290)—bedroom suburbs, like Norwalk, that send commuters daily into New York City. Wilton supports some of the finest public schools in the nation and has a two-acre residential zoning ordinance that keeps most of the old clapboard homes in wooded seclusion. Through landscaping and careful commercial architecture, great care is taken to preserve an "authentic" New England appearance.

Westport is best described as a strictly residential town. With its borders along Long Island Sound, it offers a full repertoire of real estate for those who can afford it: from posh estates and quiet retreats for harried New York executives to homes and cottages by the shore for seasonal vacationers and the yachting rich. Saugatuck, in south Westport, is rich in nautical flavor, sporting seaside homes, yacht clubs, and marinas. Downtown, the Boston Post Road is alive with restaurants, night spots, theatre, specialty and antique shops, and branches of the larger New York stores.

This combination of quietly elegant New England and the proximity of New York City gives Norwalk a desirability that leads to the second highest housing costs among the metro areas, behind only Stamford, Connecticut.

*Pluses:* Located near New York, it has access to all of that city's cultural, recreational, and medical facilities; rich in history and New England charm.

*Minuses:* Housing costs are extremely high (328th).

## ★ Dallas, TX (11)
Population: 1,957,378    Population Rank: 14

Dallas, rising out of the rolling plains of the cattle country of north-central Texas, has an aura about it that transcends guidebook descriptions or secondhand recounting. In the city proper (pop. 904,078), big skyscrapers—almost none more than 20 years old—soar from the gentle hills as a stark monument to the money, power, and growth of Texas. Dallas is big, growing, strong, rich, fast, tough, snazzy.

Not hundreds but thousands of millionaires live in the Dallas metro area, either on the Texas plains outside town, within walled estates in the affluent sections of the city or its suburbs, or in new high-rise condos. More than a third of all Texas bank deposits are made in Dallas or neighboring Fort Worth, and Dallas has the third largest number of million-dollar businesses in the nation. Beef and oil are still big industries, but Dallas is increasingly becoming a center of service industries and light manufacturing; it is also a world leader in the production of precision electronic equipment, aircraft, and defense hardware. All of this is indicative of Dallas's 12th-place ranking for economic growth and promise.

Despite the cowboy image projected by the city's history and by the popular TV show *Dallas*, a visitor walking one of the main streets in April might be hard-pressed to tell Dallas from Chicago. Smart shops, catering to every taste and income, reveal the city as one of the country's three leading fashion markets. Add to this the Dallas Symphony Orchestra, the Dallas Theatre Center (the only Frank Lloyd Wright public theatre), and the Dallas Museum of Natural History and you begin to see why this metro area scored so well in the arts (13th). The presence of several major universities helps Dallas achieve its rankings in health (20th) and education (29th).

Dallas has its weak spots, too. Housing is not reasonably priced, as it is in Austin and other Texas metro areas. The climate is enjoyable in every season except summer, which is long and very hot; air-conditioning in cars and homes is a must. Dallas's poorest showing is in safety from crime, where the fast-growing metro area ranks 308th.

*Pluses:* Vigorous, energetic atmosphere; outstanding rankings in economics, the arts, and health care.

*Minuses:* Very high crime rate; high housing costs (256th).

## ★ Seattle, WA (12)
Population: 1,607,469    Population Rank: 23

Imagine a city of a half million people nestled between a huge marine bay and a 20-mile-long freshwater lake.

To the east and the west of this city are two major mountain chains dominating the horizons and providing spectacular sunrises and sunsets. Forests of fir, cedar, and spruce cover the city's rolling hills. In the harbor, hundreds of fishing boats arrive and depart daily, depositing salmon and king crab onto the docks, while farther out are anchored ocean-going freighters bound for Anchorage, Honolulu, Yokohama, and Hong Kong.

Welcome to Seattle, center of one of America's youngest metro areas, which in recent years has placed near the top of every list that has ranked American cities or metro areas. Seattle has been recognized for its stable social situation, unrivaled recreational facilities, beautiful location, and very mild climate. True, Seattle is not as safe as it used to be, with crime rates on the rise. Also, its low housing score (283rd) reflects its high real estate costs—perhaps an indication of low supply and high demand for housing. An extensive bus system, ferryboats, and the first public monorail combine to give this metro area a transportation ranking of 19th.

Until gold was struck in the Yukon Territory at the turn of the century, Seattle was a sleepy little lumber and cannery town. Thousands of people poured northward into the Yukon and Alaska with the gold rush, and whether going by land or by sea, their point of embarkation was Seattle. In the years since, Seattle has remained the chief link between the mainland and Alaska, and now the Orient. The metro area is also a major manufacturing center for the aerospace industry, with facilities devoted not only to the construction of jet aircraft (Boeing is headquartered here), but to spacecraft and missiles. The metro area ranks 106th in terms of job opportunities and economic outlook.

Situated between the Cascade and Olympic mountain ranges and bounded by Puget Sound, Seattle is within easy reach of many wilderness areas. This, combined with its outstanding array of other assets—from fine restaurants to exciting professional sports—helps explain its emergence as *Places Rated's* premier recreational spot. Seattle also enjoys an international reputation in the arts (it ranks 17th among the metro areas), with the Seattle Symphony Orchestra, Pacific Northwest Ballet, and Seattle Repertory Theatre among the outstanding performing groups. The Seattle Opera's annual presentation of Wagner's *Ring* cycle draws performers and spectators from around the world.

Closely linked to a breathtaking natural setting is a climate that is best characterized as mild maritime. Directly in the path of the Pacific westerly winds, Seattle is constantly bathed by warm, moist ocean air. The cold air from the Arctic and interior regions is blocked by the eastern Cascades. The net effect of this airborne ocean bath is a mildness that has earned Seattle a 12th-place rank in climate.

To the north of Seattle is Everett (pop. 54,413), a major fishing port. Other surrounding towns like Bellevue (pop. 73,903), Renton (pop. 30,612), and Riverton Heights (pop. 33,500) offer suburban living for residents of the metro area who prefer the less crowded, country setting in the woods of the Pacific Northwest. And yet, even in downtown Seattle, amid the skyscrapers, the Kingdome, and the Space Needle, the impression a visitor gets is of mountains, forests, and water.

*Pluses:* Outstanding recreational assets in a beautiful natural setting; high rankings in the arts (17th) and health care facilities (21st).

*Minuses:* High housing costs; growing crime rate.

★ **Atlanta, GA** (13)
Population: 2,138,231    ^ Population Rank: 12

"If you want to go to heaven you'll have to go by way of Atlanta." This saying reflects the importance of Hartsfield International Airport, which is partly responsible for the Atlanta metro area's number-two ranking in transportation. The airport boasts a spanking-clean pedestrian tunnel in which travelers can hear taped directions to color-coded concourses leading to various airlines.

The theme of modern efficiency is prevalent throughout Atlanta. In many ways, it is no longer a traditional southern city. Many businesses have transplanted their corporate headquarters to the area over the past two decades, followed by multitudes of young professionals from the North and West. Because of its central location and urban opportunities, Atlanta also attracts many young people from the Southeast. This blend of new residents gives the city an unusual mix of rural and urban, down-home and uptown. Along with the business expansion have come new and varied facilities for housing, shopping, and entertainment. There are places to live and things to do for the most diversified tastes.

Adjacent to the central city is the upscale residential district of Buckhead. Miles of beautifully landscaped, elegant estates remind one of Atlanta's affluence. The Coca-Cola fortune is perhaps the best known made in Atlanta but certainly not the only one. Sandy Springs (pop. 20,300), a fairly new suburb, reflects the prosperity of a city on the move.

Many southerners are devoted to maintaining tradition, and Atlanta holds its own in the arts (31st) and education (62nd). Ample health care facilities are another benefit of big-city status, and Atlanta ranks 15th in this category. A high crime rate, perhaps a by-product of the city's sudden growth, is Atlanta's main problem, giving the metro area a crime rank of 274th.

*Pluses:* Exciting blend of old and new; mild climate (24th); excellent facilities for health care, arts, and transportation.

*Minuses:* High crime rate; below-average showing in recreation (239th) and housing costs (210th).

★ **Knoxville, TN** (14)
Population: 565,970    Population Rank: 73

What do dogwoods, power plants, symphonies, and funnel cakes have in common? Knoxville. These and other diverse entities have coexisted here, linking the pioneer past with an industrial present and a technological future. Located at the foothills of the scenic East Tennessee Appalachian Mountains, the city of Knoxville (pop. 175,045) was the last outpost for supplies needed by westward-bound pioneers from the Southeast. Currently, Knoxville reflects a continuing prosperity in farming, industry, and culture. Tobacco and produce markets are an active part of the local economy. Energy, a resounding theme of the recent Knoxville World's Fair, is more than a topic of conversation here: The headquarters of the Tennessee Valley Authority and Oak Ridge atomic energy complex are responsible for much of the area's growth.

Although not outstanding in any *Places Rated* category (its best rank is 26th, for its mild climate), this Mid-South metro area performs consistently well in all of them, joining the elite group of only nine metro areas with no rankings below 200th. Its good rankings in housing costs (72nd) and safety from crime (55th) set it apart from most of the other top-ranking places. Yet cultural, educational, and recreational amenities are readily available.

The University of Tennessee is a major asset, offering not only programs in the arts and sciences but also the Clarence Brown Theatre, whose season runs from January through June. "Shakespeare to the Schools" is a special outreach program designed to entertain and enlighten students unable to attend on-site theatre productions. The Knoxville area supports the Knoxville Symphony Orchestra and the Appalachian Ballet Company, along with its renowned Dogwood Arts Festival every spring.

Geographic location is a real plus for Knoxville. To the west is gently rolling fertile farmland; to the east are the mountains, with isolated hamlets, winding mountain roads, and breathtaking views. Nearby Gatlinburg (pop. 3,210) is the headquarters for Great Smoky Mountains National Park, where the seasons are reflected in the vibrant greens and pinks of spring and the reds, oranges, and yellows of fall, making it a major tourist attraction.

*Pluses:* Solid performance in nearly every category; splendid natural surroundings.

*Minuses:* Could do better in health care (145th), education (179th), and economics (148th).

★ **Buffalo, NY** (15)
Population: 1,015,472    Population Rank: 40

Probably the most widely known fact about Buffalo is that it gets a lot of snow, about 90 inches of it every year. Keeping highways, city streets, and airport runways clear during the winter is a major challenge; on at least one recent occasion, Buffalo had to borrow more sophisticated snow-removal equipment from Toronto to find the pavement at Greater Buffalo International Airport. In spite of the snow, this hearty city not only survives but continues to function in all its urban responsibilities. A solid metro area, it ranks below 200th in only one *Places Rated* category.

Buffalo is situated on gently rolling terrain at the southern end of the Niagara River, which separates the United States from Canada and joins Lake Erie and Lake Ontario. The river as a border affords both countries the benefits of tourism and electrical power from Niagara Falls. Buffalo has long been a manufacturing center. Steel and grain mills combine with farms and orchards to produce the freight for its impressive transport systems. These include one of the country's largest railroad centers: two passenger and 15 freight terminals process more than 25,000 trains per year. Buffalo has capitalized on its strategic location by developing ports on the Erie Canal, which opened in 1825, and on the St. Lawrence Seaway, which opened in 1959.

Two large institutions, the State University of New York at Buffalo and State University of New York College at Buffalo, which between them serve more than 35,000 students, provide higher education in Buffalo. Health care facilities are top-notch, and cultural opportunities abound. Studio Arena Theatre offers a full September-to-June season of dramatic performances, focusing on contemporary American productions. The Buffalo Philharmonic Orchestra provides notable symphonic and pops performances. Other assets include the Buffalo Museum of Science, the South Park Botanical Gardens, and the Buffalo Zoological Gardens; three professional sports teams and the Buffalo Raceway contribute to the metro area's creditable 62nd-place showing in recreation.

*Pluses:* Solid performance in almost every category, with strongest rankings in arts (23rd), health care (36th), and education (50th).

*Minuses:* Below-average economic picture (217th); snowy climate (not for the faint of heart).

### ★ Baltimore, MD (16)
Population: 2,199,531    Population Rank: 11

Baltimore—located on the world's largest estuary, city of the spice and crab trade, of endless seafood and German-American meals, home of Edgar Allan Poe, Babe Ruth, and H. L. Mencken—dominates this six-county metro area, which, not surprisingly, bumps nearby Washington from 16th place. In keeping with its past as a major port city and shipbuilding center, the metro area receives its highest category rank (eighth) in transportation. It is also the terminus of the Baltimore and Ohio Railroad, the nation's first.

Like many of the metro areas included in *Places Rated's* list of the best places to live, Baltimore is an old eastern city that's been through hard times but is now undergoing an urban renaissance. At Harborplace,

Baltimore's renovated inner harbor, the U.S.S. *Constellation* docks, and shoppers browse through stores and cafés while admiring the restored buildings of the area. In its first year open to the public, Harborplace had more visitors than Disney World; with the revenues collected, the restoration process was accelerated and broadened.

Baltimore (pop. 786,775) is renowned for its many sections of distinct ethnic and historic flavor. Parts of these neighborhoods are filled with Victorian brick row houses with scrubbed white steps. More affluent neighborhoods include Roland Park, Homeland, and Mount Washington. The metro area ranks relatively poorly for its homeownership costs (250th), partly because of the expensive housing in suburban neighborhoods like Green Spring Valley and nearby towns like Hill Farm and Hunt Valley. Maryland's capital, Annapolis (pop. 31,740), is also part of this historic metro area.

Baltimore excels in most big-city amenities, with such institutions as Johns Hopkins University (with its outstanding medical center), the U.S. Naval Academy, and the Baltimore Symphony Orchestra contributing to high rankings in health care (12th), education (15th), and the arts (15th). Baltimore enjoys a solid 39th-place ranking for recreation, despite the recent defection of the NFL Colts to Indianapolis.

*Pluses:* Interesting and historic blend of North and South; strong performance in almost every *Places Rated* category.

*Minuses:* Above-average housing costs; very poor ranking in safety from crime (323rd).

### ★ Washington, DC–MD–VA (17)
Population: 3,250,822    Population    Rank: 6

Home-away-from-hometown, U.S.A., is Washington, D.C. (pop. 638,432), center of this 17th-ranked metro area. Its highly transient population reflects the influences of government and tourism. Politicians are drawn to the District of Columbia by necessity and Yuppies by choice. For the young aggressive professional and the politician, Washington is the place to be; there is *everything* to do here. Not only does Washington exceed most cities in its amount of cultural, educational, and recreational resources but also in the quality of what it has to offer. This excellence is apparent in Washington's architecture. The lack of skyscrapers is immediately obvious and pleasing, and there are spectacular views in every direction, the Capitol and the Washington Monument commanding the most notice.

Washington is a city of culture and learning: Performing arts, libraries, and museums earn this metro area a fourth-place ranking in the arts. It also boasts outstanding ranks in education (third), transportation (fourth), and health care (sixth).

Overall, housing in Washington is expensive and scarce, giving the metro area a rank of 314th for housing. Housing for the city's native and predominantly black population is depressed and spread throughout the district. The large percentage of disadvantaged urban dwellers and a high crime rate are major problems for the city. Housing for middle-class and wealthy people is expensive and located in well-defined neighborhoods, some very exclusive. One such neighborhood is Georgetown, which has fine homes and diverse restaurants and nightlife.

Outside the District of Columbia but very much a part of the Washington metro area are numerous communities in Virginia and Maryland. To the west and south are Alexandria (pop. 103,217), Arlington (pop. 152,700), Fairfax (pop. 19,390), and Springfield (pop. 12,500). Many of the young adults who work in Washington make their homes in the Virginia suburbs. Farther out is Leesburg (pop. 8,357), representative of Virginia's horse country. To the north and east of Washington is Maryland, where exclusive Chevy Chase (pop. 12,232), Silver Spring (pop. 72,893), Gaithersburg (pop. 26,424), and College Park (pop. 23,614, home of the University of Maryland) provide other suburban living options.

*Pluses:* An area of international reputation; outstanding array of major cultural, educational, and medical facilities; mild climate (51st).

*Minuses:* Very high housing costs (314th) and crime rate (276th).

### ★ Cincinnati, OH–KY–IN (18)
Population: 1,401,491    Population Rank: 28

Like Pittsburgh, its sister river city to the east, and Louisville to the west, Cincinnati grew and prospered early because of its excellent location on the Ohio River. As river traffic declined in the period after the Civil War and more goods were moved by railroad, Cincinnati diversified, becoming a manufacturing and rail center. Today, the Queen City (pop. 385,457) is the bituminous coal center of the United States and the world's largest inland coal port. Manufacturing is the major industrial activity in Cincinnati; goods produced range from soap and playing cards to radar equipment, machine tools, and truck and car bodies.

Cincinnati's rolling hills and river valley provide lush surroundings for suburban communities like Covington, Kentucky (pop. 46,563), and they accent the city's handsome downtown buildings and active riverfront area. You can still tour the river on a sternwheeler: Cincinnati is the home port of the *Delta Queen* and many other steamboats. The center of town is Fountain Square, where each October the city celebrates Oktoberfest Zinzinnati, a festival handed down through several generations of German immigrants. The Cincinnati Zoo is another recreational asset; one of the world's finest, it has an excellent reputation for raising endangered species, such as the white Bengal tiger.

Cincinnati is home to major universities, a reperto-

ry theatre, a ballet, and an operatic company, as well as a renowned symphony orchestra. These, in addition to its fine museums, help explain the metro area's high rank (16th) in the arts. Cincinnati is one of the few metro areas with no *Places Rated* rankings lower than 200th in any category. It is gifted with a mild climate, a relatively low crime rate for a city its size, and good health care, transportation, and recreational facilities.

Will Rogers claimed he always judged a town by its chili. He would have liked Cincinnati very much. Not at all like its hot and spicy Texas counterpart, Cincinnati chili is sweet, made with beans, cheese, and even pasta. You can have your Cincinnati chili plain, or two-way, or three-way, or four-way. . . . It's just another of the pleasant surprises you'll find in this Heartland metro area.

*Pluses:* Solid all-around performer, with outstanding cultural assets; easy access to scenic bluegrass country.

*Minuses:* Below-average rankings for housing costs (191st) and economics (182nd).

### ★ Albany–Schenectady–Troy, NY (19)
Population: 835,880    Population Rank: 55

This three-city metro area in the Hudson River–Catskill Mountain region of New York State is not glamorous. But like other upstate New York metro areas, it is solid, safe, culturally sound, and has a plentiful supply of facilities and services in education, arts, and transportation.

Albany (pop. 101,727), as capital of the state, is fraught with political drama. The Empire State Plaza, a new and dramatic collection of handsome buildings on a hundred-acre tract of land, houses state offices as well as the New York State Museum and the New York State Modern Art Collection. Albany became important to U.S. trade beginning with the 1825 opening of the Erie Canal, linking the upper Midwest with the ocean ports of the East. Now the home of many manufacturers, Albany retains its historic feel as a capital city and trade center.

Some of General Electric's largest factories and research complexes are located in the active manufacturing center of Schenectady (pop. 67,972). Schenectady has one of the highest ratios of Ph.D.s per capita in the nation. A town of many two-family houses with walk-up front porches supporting roofs on round pillars, Schenectady also features the Historic Stockade Area with its elegant nineteenth-century homes. Union College, one of the finest private colleges in the state, forms part of the triad of major universities that gives the metro area its *Places Rated* rank of 17th in education (the other two are State University of New York at Albany and Rensselaer Polytechnic Institute in Troy, the nation's oldest private technical school).

Troy (pop. 56,638) is primarily a manufacturing town and has undergone a decline in recent years due to the general falling-off of the U.S. textile industry.

The three main cities of this metro area are complemented by some interesting smaller towns. In Amsterdam (pop. 21,872) one can see the only section of the Erie Canal that remains unchanged since the canal was built. Also on display is a building style that reflects an early Dutch heritage, a style common to the area. The Victorian resort city of Saratoga Springs (pop. 23,906), north of Albany, is home of the famous Saratoga Race Track, National Museum of Racing, Saratoga Performing Arts Center, and Yaddo (a 400-acre estate converted into a retreat for artists and writers).

*Pluses:* Strong showing in transportation (15th) and education (17th), with stable social indicators (ranks 54th in safety from crime).

*Minuses:* Harsh winters (mildness ranking 250th); mediocre ranking in recreation (175th); solid but unexciting.

### ★ Burlington, VT (19)
Population: 115,308    Population Rank: 274

Burlington is the sole metropolitan representative for Vermont, that upright state (in many ways) nestled between New England and the Adirondacks, where maple syrup, cheese, wood products, and ski resorts abound. Vermont in the last century was a veritable patchwork of dairy farms and orchards. But increasingly since 1900 the small farmers and fruit growers went broke and abandoned the countryside, allowing the dense northern forests to cover the fields and pastures. Thus, until this edition of *Places Rated Almanac,* the Green Mountain State had no metro areas at all. It is still America's most rural state; the greatest percentage of its population is outside urban areas.

The tiny Burlington metro area is located on the eastern shore of Lake Champlain. It is a scenic setting, and area residents take full advantage of the huge lake (430 square miles) for fishing and boating. The city of Burlington (pop. 37,712) has a large marina for private boats. There are docking facilities for oceangoing vessels, too, since Lake Champlain is connected to the St. Lawrence Seaway by the Richelieu River, which makes Burlington a seaport.

The Adirondack Mountains to the west and the Green Mountains to the east provide some shelter from severe storms, but Burlington is not without its rugged spells of weather. In winter, invading Arctic air from Hudson Bay causes intense cold snaps. The cold winters are primarily responsible for Burlington's lowest rank, a climate placing of 305th.

But in all other categories except housing (267th), Burlington shines. Ranks in health care (63rd) and the arts (177th) are surprisingly strong for a metro area as small and remote as this one. The low crime rate (32nd) simply reflects the general trend of the smaller New England metro areas, which have always been remarkably crime-free. Burlington's rankings in education (23rd), transportation (tenth), and recreation (21st) all help boost it toward the top. And finally, the economic outlook (43rd) for this city that manufactures missile components and data processing equipment as well as steel and wood products is as bright as the view at sunset across Lake Champlain from Battery Park in downtown Burlington.

*Pluses:* Small, unspoiled area with much to offer.

*Minuses:* Rigorous winters; somewhat remote; confirmed urbanites might be uncomfortable here.

### ★ Syracuse, NY (21)
Population: 642,971    Population Rank: 64

Syracuse is one of four upstate New York metro areas to make *Places Rated's* top 25, and like Buffalo, Albany–Schenectady–Troy, and Rochester, ranks 200th or below in only one category (economics, in which it places 282nd).

Syracuse (pop. 170,105) is truly an all-American city, founded in the eighteenth century and growing and prospering through the twentieth. Local companies produce pharmaceuticals and china as well as electronic, air-conditioning, missile, and radar equipment. It is also an active city: Hardy Syracusans, undaunted by the 109 inches of snow that fall annually, take advantage of year-round offerings in recreation. Home to the Burnet Park Zoo and the Syracuse University Orangemen and dotted with many beautiful lakes (including the Finger Lakes), the metro area ranks 44th in leisure amenities. The century-old New York State Fair also takes place here each year, drawing fairgoers from New England and the Midwest.

Culturally, this metro area has it all. Syracuse Stage is the only professional theatre in central New York State and works with the drama department at Syracuse University to provide a quality theatre experience. In addition, there are the Syracuse Symphony Orchestra, the Everson Museum of Art, and the Opera Theatre of Syracuse, all of which chip in toward Syracuse's 57th-place ranking in the arts.

Education is a high priority in the area, which has well-recognized public schools and an enviable selection of colleges and universities, among them Colgate University and the State University College of Forestry. The result is an impressive standing of 44th for Syracuse in education.

Syracuse also happens to be one of the nation's leading test markets for new products since the characteristics of its population so closely resemble the national norms. Perhaps this "average" population can be traced to the area's well-mixed heritage, evident in the names of towns, streets, and waterways: Chittenango, Oswego, Marcellus, Skaneateles, Oneida, Liverpool, Cicero, Euclid, and Syracuse itself.

*Pluses:* Seems to have many of the advantages and few of the disadvantages of a major metropolitan city; strongest showings in transportation (14th), education, recreation, and the arts.

*Minuses:* Poor standing in economics (282nd); snowy, rigorous climate (151st).

## MAKING THE RANKINGS WORK FOR YOU

At the spring 1984 meeting of the Association of American Geographers in Washington, D.C., a paper was read that drew more inquiries from the press and the public than any other in the association's 80-year history. "Rating America's Cities," by Prof. Robert M. Pierce of the State University of New York at Cortland, looked into what would happen if individual preferences were incorporated into the findings of the first edition of *Places Rated Almanac*. Pierce had asked 1,100 people in New York State to rank the almanac's nine dimensions of urban living according to their own preferences. Economics, climate, crime, and housing were thought most important by the people surveyed, whereas transportation and the arts were considered least important.

When Pierce reranked the 277 metro areas surveyed in the 1981 *Places Rated Almanac* according to these preferences, the list that emerged differed somewhat from *Places Rated*'s overall ranking. Atlanta, which came out first in *Places Rated*, ranked tenth in Pierce's study, while Greensboro–Winston-Salem–High Point, North Carolina (ranked third by *Places Rated*), finished first. Some rankings differed dramatically: The New York metro area, ranked 26th by *Places Rated*, fell to 156th in Pierce's list, and Kokomo, Indiana, leaped from 182nd to 75th.

Which ranking is "better"? It all depends—on who you are and what you're looking for. Although *Places Rated* can decide on diverse and comparable standards for metropolitan living and then suggest which of 329 metro areas come closest to these standards, finding the right spot is ultimately a matter of personal choice. (If you think you would prefer non-metropolitan living, for example, or are looking for a good place to retire, you might also want to consult *Places Rated Retirement Guide*, which rates and ranks 107 places for retirement living, most of them non-metropolitan.)

Using *Places Rated Almanac*, you can put together a custom-made list of metro areas that reflects your own personal preferences. There are two ways to make this job easy. One is to choose and consider only the metro areas that rank in the top 50 in the quality-of-life factor most important to you, be it climate, housing, crime, or whatever. Another way is to consider only the metro areas located in the region of the country you prefer. You may wish to add a certain category's rank to your total score twice if it is especially important to you; this will have the effect of further penalizing places that do poorly in that category.

What follows are three examples of how you can make *Places Rated*'s rankings work for you.

In 1982, Heidrick & Struggles, a national executive search firm, surveyed 2,000 senior managers whose names had appeared in the *Wall Street Journal*'s "Who's News" section over a 12-month period. The typical senior manager was forty-seven years old, white, and male; pulled down $173,000 a year; had one or more advanced degrees; worked 57 hours a week; was on the road 25 percent of the time; and was married to his first wife, who didn't work. If these senior managers were offered a job in another city, the survey showed, their prime considerations would be climate, cultural amenities, recreation opportunities, and economic outlook. The list below shows which of the 329 metro areas come to the fore when we add together the *Places Rated* rankings for these four categories.

### The Best Metro Areas for Mobile Managers
(Combined Rankings for Climate, Arts, Recreation, and Economics)

| Metro Area | Combined Ranking |
|---|---|
| 1. Nassau–Suffolk, NY | 89 |
| 2. San Francisco, CA | 98 |
| 3. Seattle, WA | 136 |
| 4. Boston, MA | 153 |
| 5. Anaheim–Santa Ana, CA | 156 |
| 6. San Jose, CA | 186 |
| 7. Monmouth–Ocean, NJ | 188 |
| 8. Los Angeles–Long Beach, CA | 192 |
| 9. San Diego, CA | 197 |
| 10. Norwalk, CT | 199 |
| 11. Bridgeport–Milford, CT | 211 |
| 12. Miami–Hialeah, FL | 229 |
| 13. New York, NY | 230 |
| 14. Norfolk–Virginia Beach–<br>Newport News, VA | 233 |
| 15. Dallas, TX | 255 |
| 16. Tucson, AZ | 258 |
| 17. Santa Barbara–Santa Maria–<br>Lompoc, CA | 263 |
| 18. Honolulu, HI | 269 |
| 18. Oakland, CA | 269 |
| 20. Salem–Gloucester, MA | 281 |

So much for the preferences of top managers. What about their subordinates with families—might they have different priorities? The same year that managers were surveyed, the Fantus Company, a site-location consultant to business clients, polled engineers who subscribed to *Industrial Research and Development* magazine for the standards they would use in judging a city as a place to live. Their concerns had more to do with family than those of mobile senior managers. The factor most often cited was housing cost (64 percent), followed by climate (51 percent), education (30 percent), and recreational opportunities (25 percent). Using their percent responses to weight the *Places Rated* ranks for housing, climate, education, and recreation, an interesting list emerges.

### The Best Metro Areas for Transferred Families
(Weighted Rankings for Housing, Climate, Education, and Recreation)

| Metro Area | Combined Ranking |
|---|---|
| 1. San Francisco, CA | 581 |
| 2. Los Angeles–Long Beach, CA | 667 |
| 3. Eugene–Springfield, OR | 686 |
| 4. Nassau–Suffolk, NY | 692 |
| 5. Boston, MA | 753 |
| 6. Portland, OR | 754 |
| 7. Charleston, SC | 780 |
| 8. Baltimore, MD | 829 |

| Metro Area | Combined Ranking |
|---|---|
| 9. Johnson City–Kingsport–Bristol, TN–VA | 831 |
| 10. Pittsburgh, PA | 846 |
| 11. Syracuse, NY | 850 |
| 12. Philadelphia, PA–NJ | 861 |
| 13. Albuquerque, NM | 867 |
| 14. Norfolk–Virginia Beach–Newport News, VA | 874 |
| 15. Providence, RI | 892 |
| 16. St. Louis, MO–IL | 905 |
| 17. Buffalo, NY | 915 |
| 18. Rochester, NY | 926 |
| 19. Louisville, KY–IN | 968 |
| 20. Miami–Hialeah, FL | 993 |

| Metro Area | Combined Ranking |
|---|---|
| 6. Boston, MA | 347 |
| 7. Middlesex–Somerset–Hunterdon, NJ | 352 |
| 8. Dallas, TX | 363 |
| 9. San Jose, CA | 364 |
| 10. Washington, DC–MD–VA | 371 |
| 10. Atlanta, GA | 371 |
| 12. Richmond–Petersburg, VA | 395 |
| 13. Seattle, WA | 396 |
| 14. Nassau–Suffolk, NY | 401 |
| 15. Philadelphia, PA–NJ | 402 |
| 16. Chicago, IL | 404 |
| 17. Honolulu, HI | 415 |
| 18. San Francisco, CA | 418 |
| 19. St. Louis, MO–IL | 423 |
| 20. Salt Lake City–Ogden, UT | 481 |

Now, what about a person who is just starting out? Suppose you are finishing college and are ready to launch a career in your chosen field, wherever the opportunity happens to be. You do have certain preferences, however. You don't want a place that's too small, and you're also interested in a low crime rate, good transportation facilities, a range of cultural activities, and promising economic opportunities. How will you narrow down the field to find which of the many metro areas might be best? Looking at the *Places Rated* rankings for crime, transportation, arts, and economics for places over a half million population could be a good way to start.

### The Best Metro Areas for Career Starters
(Combined Rankings for Crime, Transportation, Arts, and Economics)

| Metro Area | Combined Ranking |
|---|---|
| 1. Raleigh–Durham, NC | 309 |
| 2. Pittsburgh, PA | 331 |
| 3. Minneapolis–St. Paul, MN–WI | 334 |
| 4. Rochester, NY | 343 |
| 5. Denver, CO | 344 |

By now it should be apparent that the task of finding the best place for you can be as simple or as complicated as you wish. The person who enjoys numbers has been supplied with enough figures to turn the whole process into a never-ending parlor game in which various factors can be weighted, added, or deleted to fit individual needs. In fact, if you were to weight each of *Places Rated*'s nine factors differently on a scale of one to ten—rather than equally, as we have done in this book—you would come up with more than two and a half *billion* possible combinations.

Nonmathematicians may simply want to add up and compare the scores of the ten or 20 metro areas that sound most attractive to them. Remember, finding the ideal spot is a matter of personal choice. *Places Rated Almanac* does not pretend to be the final arbiter of the best and worst metro areas; rather, it is designed to serve as an instrument that you can fine-tune and adjust to help you find the kind of place where you want to live.

# Appendix

## Consolidated Metropolitan Statistical Areas (CMSAs) & Their Primary Metropolitan Statistical Area (PMSA) Components

**Boston–Lawrence–Salem, MA–NH**
Boston, MA
Brockton, MA
Lawrence–Haverhill, MA–NH
Lowell, MA–NH
Nashua, NH
Salem–Gloucester, MA

**Buffalo–Niagara Falls, NY**
Buffalo, NY
Niagara Falls, NY

**Chicago–Gary–Lake County, IL–IN–WI**
Aurora–Elgin, IL
Chicago, IL
Gary–Hammond, IN
Joliet, IL
Kenosha, WI
Lake County, IL

**Cincinnati–Hamilton, OH–KY–IN**
Cincinnati, OH–KY–IN
Hamilton–Middletown, OH

**Cleveland–Akron–Lorain, OH**
Akron, OH
Cleveland, OH
Lorain–Elyria, OH

**Dallas–Fort Worth, TX**
Dallas, TX
Fort Worth–Arlington, TX

**Denver–Boulder, CO**
Boulder–Longmont, CO
Denver, CO

**Detroit–Ann Arbor, MI**
Ann Arbor, MI
Detroit, MI

**Hartford–New Britain–Middletown, CT**
Bristol, CT
Hartford, CT
Middletown, CT
New Britain, CT

**Houston–Galveston–Brazoria, TX**
Brazoria, TX
Galveston–Texas City, TX
Houston, TX

**Kansas City, MO–Kansas City, KS**
Kansas City, KS
Kansas City, MO

**Los Angeles–Anaheim–Riverside, CA**
Anaheim–Santa Ana, CA
Los Angeles–Long Beach, CA
Oxnard–Ventura, CA
Riverside–San Bernardino, CA

**Miami–Fort Lauderdale, FL**
Fort Lauderdale–Hollywood–Pompano Beach, FL
Miami–Hialeah, FL

**Milwaukee–Racine, WI**
Milwaukee, WI
Racine, WI

**New York–Northern New Jersey–Long Island, NY–NJ–CT**
Bergen–Passaic, NJ
Bridgeport–Milford, CT
Danbury, CT
Jersey City, NJ
Middlesex–Somerset–Hunterdon, NJ
Monmouth–Ocean, NJ
Nassau–Suffolk, NY
New York, NY
Newark, NJ

Norwalk, CT
Orange County, NY
Stamford, CT

**Philadelphia–Wilmington–Trenton, PA–NJ–DE–MD**
Philadelphia, PA–NJ
Trenton, NJ
Vineland–Millville–Bridgeton, NJ
Wilmington, DE–NJ–MD

**Pittsburgh–Beaver Valley, PA**
Beaver County, PA
Pittsburgh, PA

**Portland–Vancouver, OR–WA**
Portland, OR
Vancouver, WA

**Providence–Pawtucket–Fall River, RI–MA**
Fall River, MA–RI
Pawtucket–Woonsocket–Attleboro, RI–MA
Providence, RI

**St. Louis–East St. Louis–Alton, MO–IL**
Alton–Granite City, IL
East St. Louis–Belleville, IL
St. Louis, MO–IL

**San Francisco–Oakland–San Jose, CA**
Oakland, CA
San Francisco, CA
San Jose, CA
Santa Cruz, CA
Santa Rosa–Petaluma, CA
Vallejo–Fairfield–Napa, CA

**Seattle–Tacoma, WA**
Seattle, WA
Tacoma, WA

# Metro Areas by State*

**Alabama**
Anniston
Birmingham
Columbus (GA–AL)
Dothan
Florence
Gadsden
Huntsville
Mobile
Montgomery
Tuscaloosa

**Alaska**
Anchorage

**Arizona**
Phoenix
Tucson

**Arkansas**
Fayetteville–Springdale
Fort Smith (AR–OK)
Little Rock–North Little Rock
Memphis (TN–AR–MS)
Pine Bluff
Texarkana (TX)–Texarkana
   (AR)

**California**
Anaheim–Santa Ana
Bakersfield
Chico
Fresno
Los Angeles–Long Beach
Modesto
Oakland
Oxnard–Ventura
Redding
Riverside–San Bernardino
Sacramento
Salinas–Seaside–Monterey
San Diego
San Francisco
San Jose
Santa Barbara–Santa
   Maria–Lompoc
Santa Cruz
Santa Rosa–Petaluma
Stockton
Vallejo–Fairfield–Napa
Visalia–Tulare–Porterville
Yuba City

**Colorado**
Boulder–Longmont
Colorado Springs
Denver
Fort Collins–Loveland
Greeley
Pueblo

**Connecticut**
Bridgeport–Milford
Bristol
Danbury
Hartford
Middletown
New Britain
New Haven–Meriden
New London–Norwich (CT–RI)
Norwalk
Stamford
Waterbury

**Delaware**
Wilmington (DE–NJ–MD)

**District of Columbia**
Washington (DC–MD–VA)

**Florida**
Bradenton
Daytona Beach
Fort Lauderdale–Hollywood–
   Pompano Beach
Fort Myers
Fort Pierce
Fort Walton Beach
Gainesville
Jacksonville
Lakeland–Winter Haven
Melbourne–Titusville–Palm Bay
Miami–Hialeah
Ocala
Orlando
Panama City
Pensacola
Sarasota
Tallahassee
Tampa–St. Petersburg–
   Clearwater
West Palm Beach–Boca
   Raton–Delray Beach

**Georgia**
Albany
Athens
Atlanta
Augusta (GA–SC)
Chattanooga (TN–GA)
Columbus (GA–AL)
Macon–Warner Robins
Savannah

**Hawaii**
Honolulu

**Idaho**
Boise City

**Illinois**
Alton–Granite City
Aurora–Elgin
Bloomington–Normal
Champaign–Urbana–Rantoul
Chicago
Davenport–Rock Island–Moline
   (IA–IL)
Decatur
East St. Louis–Belleville
Joliet
Kankakee
Lake County
Peoria
Rockford
St. Louis (MO–IL)
Springfield

**Indiana**
Anderson
Bloomington
Cincinnati (OH–KY–IN)
Elkhart–Goshen
Evansville (IN–KY)
Fort Wayne
Gary–Hammond
Indianapolis

Kokomo
Lafayette
Louisville (KY–IN)
Muncie
South Bend–Mishawaka
Terre Haute

**Iowa**
Cedar Rapids
Davenport–Rock Island–Moline
   (IA–IL)
Des Moines
Dubuque
Iowa City
Omaha (NE–IA)
Sioux City (IA–NE)
Waterloo–Cedar Falls

**Kansas**
Kansas City
Lawrence
Topeka
Wichita

**Kentucky**
Cincinnati (OH–KY–IN)
Clarksville–Hopkinsville
   (TN–KY)
Evansville (IN–KY)
Huntington–Ashland
   (WV–KY–OH)
Lexington–Fayette
Louisville (KY–IN)
Owensboro

**Louisiana**
Alexandria
Baton Rouge
Houma–Thibodaux
Lafayette
Lake Charles
Monroe
New Orleans
Shreveport

**Maine**
Bangor
Lewiston–Auburn
Portland
Portsmouth–Dover–Rochester
   (NH–ME)

**Maryland**
Baltimore
Cumberland (MD–WV)
Hagerstown
Washington (DC–MD–VA)
Wilmington (DE–NJ–MD)

**Massachusetts**
Boston
Brockton
Fall River (MA–RI)
Fitchburg–Leominster
Lawrence–Haverhill (MA–NH)
Lowell (MA–NH)
New Bedford
Pawtucket–Woonsocket–
   Attleboro (RI–MA)
Pittsfield
Salem–Gloucester
Springfield
Worcester

**Michigan**
Ann Arbor
Battle Creek
Benton Harbor
Detroit
Flint
Grand Rapids
Jackson
Kalamazoo
Lansing–East Lansing
Muskegon
Saginaw–Bay City–Midland

**Minnesota**
Duluth (MN–WI)
Fargo–Moorhead (ND–MN)
Minneapolis–St. Paul
   (MN–WI)
Rochester
St. Cloud

**Mississippi**
Biloxi–Gulfport
Jackson
Memphis (TN–AR–MS)
Pascagoula

**Missouri**
Columbia
Joplin
Kansas City
St. Joseph
St. Louis (MO–IL)
Springfield

**Montana**
Billings
Great Falls

**Nebraska**
Lincoln
Omaha (NE–IA)
Sioux City (IA–NE)

**Nevada**
Las Vegas
Reno

**New Hampshire**
Lawrence–Haverhill (MA–NH)
Lowell (MA–NH)
Manchester
Nashua
Portsmouth–Dover–Rochester
   (NH–ME)

**New Jersey**
Allentown–Bethlehem (PA–NJ)
Atlantic City
Bergen–Passaic
Jersey City
Middlesex–Somerset–
   Hunterdon
Monmouth–Ocean
Newark
Philadelphia (PA–NJ)
Trenton
Vineland–Millville–Bridgeton
Wilmington (DE–NJ–MD)

**New Mexico**
Albuquerque
Las Cruces

*Many metro areas include parts of two or more states; these are listed under every state in which they have a component county.

## New York
Albany–Schenectady–Troy
Binghamton
Buffalo
Elmira
Glens Falls
Nassau–Suffolk
New York
Niagara Falls
Orange County
Poughkeepsie
Rochester
Syracuse
Utica–Rome

## North Carolina
Asheville
Burlington
Charlotte–Gastonia–Rock Hill
    (NC–SC)
Fayetteville
Greensboro–Winston-Salem–
    High Point
Hickory
Jacksonville
Raleigh–Durham
Wilmington

## North Dakota
Bismarck
Fargo–Moorhead (ND–MN)
Grand Forks

## Ohio
Akron
Canton
Cincinnati (OH–KY–IN)
Cleveland
Columbus
Dayton–Springfield
Hamilton–Middletown
Huntington–Ashland
    (WV–KY–OH)
Lima
Lorain–Elyria
Mansfield
Parkersburg–Marietta (WV–OH)
Steubenville–Weirton (OH–WV)
Toledo

Wheeling (WV–OH)
Youngstown–Warren

## Oklahoma
Enid
Fort Smith (AR–OK)
Lawton
Oklahoma City
Tulsa

## Oregon
Eugene–Springfield
Medford
Portland
Salem

## Pennsylvania
Allentown–Bethlehem (PA–NJ)
Altoona
Beaver County
Erie
Harrisburg–Lebanon–Carlisle
Johnstown
Lancaster
Philadelphia (PA–NJ)
Pittsburgh
Reading
Scranton–Wilkes-Barre
Sharon
State College
Williamsport
York

## Rhode Island
Fall River (MA–RI)
New London–Norwich (CT–RI)
Pawtucket–Woonsocket–
    Attleboro (RI–MA)
Providence

## South Carolina
Anderson
Augusta (GA–SC)
Charleston
Charlotte–Gastonia–Rock Hill
    (NC–SC)
Columbia
Florence
Greenville–Spartanburg

## South Dakota
Sioux Falls

## Tennessee
Chattanooga (TN–GA)
Clarksville–Hopkinsville (TN–KY)
Johnson City–Kingsport–Bristol
    (TN–VA)
Knoxville
Memphis (TN–AR–MS)
Nashville

## Texas
Abilene
Amarillo
Austin
Beaumont–Port Arthur
Brazoria
Brownsville–Harlingen
Bryan–College Station
Corpus Christi
Dallas
El Paso
Fort Worth–Arlington
Galveston–Texas City
Houston
Killeen–Temple
Laredo
Longview–Marshall
Lubbock
McAllen–Edinburg–Mission
Midland
Odessa
San Angelo
San Antonio
Sherman–Denison
Texarkana (TX)–Texarkana
    (AR)
Tyler
Victoria
Waco
Wichita Falls

## Utah
Provo–Orem
Salt Lake City–Ogden

## Vermont
Burlington

## Virginia
Charlottesville
Danville
Johnson City–Kingsport–Bristol
    (TN–VA)
Lynchburg
Norfolk–Virginia Beach–
    Newport News
Richmond–Petersburg
Roanoke
Washington (DC–MD–VA)

## Washington
Bellingham
Bremerton
Olympia
Richland–Kennewick–Pasco
Seattle
Spokane
Tacoma
Vancouver
Yakima

## West Virginia
Charleston
Cumberland (MD–WV)
Huntington–Ashland
    (WV–KY–OH)
Parkersburg–Marietta (WV–OH)
Steubenville–Weirton (OH–WV)
Wheeling (WV–OH)

## Wisconsin
Appleton–Oshkosh–Neenah
Duluth (MN–WI)
Eau Claire
Green Bay
Janesville–Beloit
Kenosha
La Crosse
Madison
Milwaukee
Minneapolis–St. Paul (MN–WI)
Racine
Sheboygan
Wausau

## Wyoming
Casper

# List of Tables, Maps, & Diagrams

### The Arts

### Recreation

### Economics

### Putting It All Together

# ABOUT THE AUTHORS

The first appearance of *Places Rated Almanac,* in 1981, created much excitement and controversy. Authors Richard Boyer and David Savageau were featured on the *Today* show and appeared on the *David Susskind Show,* the *CBS Evening News,* and numerous local television and radio programs. In 1983 they collaborated on the highly successful *Places Rated Retirement Guide,* which rates and ranks 107 places, many of them non-metropolitan areas, for retirement living.

**Richard Boyer** writes both fiction and nonfiction. In addition to co-authoring *Places Rated Almanac* and *Places Rated Retirement Guide,* he is author of three novels, including *Billingsgate Shoal* (winner of the Mystery Writers of America's Edgar award for Best Mystery Novel of 1982) and *The Penny Ferry,* both published by Houghton Mifflin Company. Formerly of Chicago and Boston, Mr. Boyer, upon completion of the first edition of *Places Rated Almanac,* followed the book's advice for selecting good places to live and now resides in Asheville, North Carolina.

**David Savageau,** since the first publication of *Places Rated Almanac,* has made public appearances throughout the country discussing the inexhaustible topic of quality of life. Mr. Savageau is principal-in-charge of Pre-LOCATION, a personal relocation consulting firm. Over the previous 15 years, he and his wife, Karyl, have lived successively in Denver, St. Louis, Indianapolis, and Boston. They now make their home in Gloucester, Massachusetts.